RETHINKING THE COLOR LINE

RETHINKING THE COLOR LINE
Readings in Race and Ethnicity

Second Edition

Charles A. Gallagher
Georgia State University

Boston   Burr Ridge, IL   Dubuque, IA   Madison, WI   New York   San Francisco   St. Louis
Bangkok   Bogotá   Caracas   Kuala Lumpur   Lisbon   London   Madrid   Mexico City
Milan   Montreal   New Delhi   Santiago   Seoul   Singapore   Sydney   Taipei   Toronto

The McGraw-Hill Companies

McGraw Hill **Higher Education**

RETHINKING THE COLOR LINE

1 2 3 4 5 6 7 8 9 0 FGR / FGR 0 9 8 7 6 5 4 3

ISBN 0-7674-2091-8

Vice president and Editor-in-chief: Thalia Dorwick
Publisher: Phillip A. Butcher
Sponsoring editor: Sherith Pankratz
Developmental editor: Jill Gordon
Senior marketing manager: Daniel M. Loch
Media producer: Jessica Bodie
Production editor: Brett Coker
Production supervisor: Tandra Jorgensen
Design manager: Cassandra Chu
Interior designer: Linda Robertson
Cover designer: Bill Stanton
Art manager: Robin Mouat
Compositor: Thompson Type
Typeface: 10/12 Book Antiqua
Paper: 45# New Era Matte
Printer and binder: Fairfield Graphics, Quebecor World

Library of Congress Cataloging-in-Publication Data

Rethinking the color line: readings in race and ethnicity / [edited by] Charles A.
    Gallagher.—2nd ed.
        p. cm.
    Includes bibliographical references.
    ISBN 0-7674-2091-8
      1. United States—Race relations. 2. United States—Ethnic relations. 3. Minorities—Civil
    rights—United States. I. Gallagher, Charles A. (Charles Andrew), 1962–

    E184.A1R4485 2003
    305.8'00973—dc21

                                                                    2003048778

www.mhhe.com

Contents

Preface

It is difficult to think about life in America without directly confronting issues of race and ethnicity. Reflect for a moment on how recent events and trends both dominate and alter American social and cultural life: a black Texan is tied to the back of a pick-up truck and dragged to his death by racist whites while white rapper Eminem wins three Grammy awards; challenges to the University of Michigan's affirmative action program move up to the Supreme Court, creating a national dialogue on the extent to which the racial "playing field" is level while blacks are twice as likely to be unemployed than whites; after 9/11, tougher immigration laws are called for by politicians, while U.S. farmers and agra-business organizations discuss institution of a new *bracero* farm-labor program that would ease restrictions on seasonal immigrant farm workers; Oprah Winfrey has a net worth of over one billion dollars while almost a quarter of the total black population lives below the poverty line; racial profiling results in a new term, "DWB" (driving while black), while Colin Powell, Denzel Washington, Michael Jordan, and Tiger Woods are consistently voted among America's most celebrated and respected people; white suburban teenagers continue to be the largest consumers of rap and hip-hop, yet racially motivated hate crimes continue to happen on campuses throughout the country; Latinos now make up a larger part of the U.S. population than blacks, yet each group is significantly underrepresented in Congress and in corporate America. The readings in *Rethinking the Color Line* examine such contradictions of race and ethnicity and help prepare students to live in an increasingly racially and ethnically diverse society.

The media has seized on the implications of a U.S. Census Bureau figure that predicts that by the year 2060 whites will be outnumbered by Asians, blacks, Hispanics, and American Indians, but this rather simplistic demographic forecast misses the conflicts, contradictions, and cultural convergences that currently define race and ethnic relations in the United States. *Rethinking the Color Line* is designed to help make sense of how race and ethnicity influence aspects of social life in ways that are often made invisible by culture, politics, and economics. This theoretically informed, empirically grounded reader uses a social constructionist perspective to frame and define the concept of race and ethnicity in the United States. The selections should stimulate conversation in the classroom and allow students to think through solutions to what often seem to be intractable problems. As a pedagogical strategy, this text raises a number of questions in the part introductions that guide students through the readings by providing an overview of how each reading is conceptually linked to the others. Each chapter starts with a section called "Questions to Consider," which asks students to focus their attention on specific themes, issues, or questions raised in the reading.

It was important to me that my students be exposed to the classic paradigms in the study of race and ethnic relations in the United States. However, just as important was my desire that students be exposed to and explore new theories and paradigms that were challenging, supplanting, and redefining the classic race and ethnicity "canon," which itself changes over time. The biologically based, pseudoscientific assumptions that defined and guided race and ethnicity scholarship for much of the past century have been debunked, discredited, and discarded. What has emerged in the last thirty years are competing narratives of what race and ethnic identity mean and what the social pressures are that shape those meanings. Postcolonial, postmodern, postethnic, class-based, or primordialist perspectives each claim to elucidate how race and ethnicity shape identity construction, gender, political economy, and geopolitics. The modern idea of race and ethnicity has been and continues to be, thoroughly rethought.

The readings in the first part of this text provide students with the theoretical framework and analytical tools they will use throughout the book. Students come to understand what race and ethnicity as a social construction means. The news, situation comedies, MTV, the racial topography of neighborhoods—each become subjects for sociological scrutiny. *Rethinking the Color Line* allows students to learn how race and ethnicity influence life in ways that many students routinely take for granted. It has been my experience that a majority of students who read these articles internalize a version of the "sociological imagination" that forever changes how they understand race and ethnic relations. Raising consciousness about how each of us influence, and in turn are influenced by, race and ethnic relations is an explicit goal of this book.

Over the last decade, I have had the luxury of testing a large and varied number of readings on hundreds of students in dozens of race and ethnic relations classes at large public universities as well as at small, elite liberal arts colleges. The readings in this book represent the final outcome of classroom "hits and misses." I have used classroom experiences, the results of examinations, and how easily students were able to integrate the readings into research papers to gauge: (1) the extent to which the reading contributed to students' understanding of a particular theory or concept, (2) if the reading was intellectually engaging, and (3) if it lent itself to active learning in the classroom. If a reading could pass these hurdles in at least three of my classes, then it made it into this book. Teaching at both public universities and private colleges also provided me with the opportunity to observe how students from different regions, class backgrounds, and racial and ethnic identities reacted to the assigned readings. The articles speak to, challenge, and find common ground among students from racially, ethnically, culturally, and economically diverse backgrounds. *Rethinking the Color Line* is a response to my students' calls for a book that was user-friendly but did not sacrifice intellectual or theoretical rigor.

This book has been designed to be personally relevant for students while also helping them understand that race and ethnic relations are embedded in the institutions that structure their lives. The readings require students to constantly negotiate the tensions between individual agency and the often determining constraints of social structure. The common thread that links these readings is the ongoing debate about the relationship between agency and structure. It is this conceptual framework that will allow students to think about race and ethnicity in fluid rather than static terms.

Changes to the Second Edition

Race and ethnic relations are never static. The twenty-two new readings in this second edition reflect this fact. New articles such as Rebecca Blank's provide the most up-to-date information on the social and economic well-being of racial and ethnic groups in the

United States. Readings by George Lipsitz and Eduardo Bonilla-Silva on how racial privilege is reproduced, Herbert Gans's discussion of how social systems are racialized, and Robert Bullard's outline of recent developments in environmental justice, provide readers the most current perspectives on these important topics. In keeping with identifying those trends that are currently emerging as social issues, two new sections have been added to this edition. The first explores the interplay of race and the criminal justice system. The prison industrial complex as examined by Angela Davis, David Cole's explanation of racial disparities in sentencing, and the intersection of race, class, and social justice as told by Jeffrey Reiman, provide important sociological insight into how race and crime collide in the United States. The new section "Race and Romance" draws on research articles by Heather Dalmage, Maria Root, and Frank Wu to examine how trends in interracial marriage will challenge our thinking of race relations and the ways in which we currently define racial categories. Articles on the media, sports, immigration, and residential segregation have been updated to better reflect changes that have taken place since the first edition. The second edition ends with ten activities students can engage in as a way to address race relations and racism at the individual, interpersonal, and community level.

Instructor's Resource CD

My colleague Kristin Wilson has designed an instructor's resource CD to accompany the second edition. This resource provides instructors with relevant questions, theoretical overviews, interactive exercises, glossary terms, Internet resources, discussion points, multiple choice questions and essay questions about each reading.

Race, Class, and Gender Supersite

A Web site has been designed to accompany the second edition. The Web site contains flashcard exercises, Web and U.S. Census links, practice test questions, and other material which focus on race and ethnic relations in the United States. **Visit the Supersite at** *www.mhhe.com/raceclassgender*

Acknowledgments

The selections in this reader and the questions that frame each chapter reflect thousands of conversations I've had with friends and family about race in America. I have benefited greatly from the research and insights of the following people: Jim Ainsworth, Richard Alba, Robert Adelman, Eli Anderson, Maggie Anderson, Amy Ansell, Kathy Blee, Eduardo Bonilla-Silva, Sam and Linda Chororos, Francesca Coin, Heather Dalmage, Kevin Delaney, James Dievler, Woody Doane, Mitch Duneier, Abby Ferber, Joe Feagin, Tyrone Foreman, Ruth Frankenberg, Tommy Gallagher, Behrooz Ghamari, Charlie Jaret, Kathleen Odell Korgan, Jung Ha Kim, Karyn Lacy, Michael Landau, Ralph LaRossa, Magali Larson, Amanda Lewis, Bob Moore, Joane Nagel, Pam Perry, Dave Roediger, Mary Romero, Daniel and Marianne Siegal, Wendy Simonds, Steve Steinberg, Eric Stewart, Michele and Kenneth Taylor, France Winddance Twine, Sarah Willie, Frank Whittington, Howie Winant, Caroline Woods, and George Yancey.

This book is dedicated to my parents Tom and Marie Gallagher, my partner Alexia Chororos, and my daughters Sophia and Talia. Their sociological imagination and their love knows no bounds.

My thanks go to the following reviewers who provided suggestions about the form and content of the first edition reader: Richard

Alba, State University of New York at Albany; Marcia L. Bellas, University of Cincinnati; Eduardo Bonilla-Silva, Texas A&M; Ashley Doane, University of Hartford; Jennifer L. Eichstedt, Humboldt State University; Emily Noelle Ignacio, Loyola University of Chicago; Marcia Marx, California State University at San Bernardino; Samuel M. Richards, Pennsylvania State University; Garry L. Rolison, California State University at San Marcos; Deidre A. Royster, University of Massachusetts at Amherst; Gary Sandefur, University of Wisconsin at Madison; Anna M. Santiago, Wayne State University; and Scott Semau, Indiana University at South Bend. The second edition benefited from the insight of these reviewers: Paulina Ruf, St. Cloud State University; Daniel J. Monti, Boston University; Tri V. Nguyen, La Salle University; Wanda Rushing, University of Memphis; Edward D. Emerson, Rice University; Dorothy Graber, Washington State University; Michelle Harris-Reed, University of Michigan; Eileen O'Brien, SUNY Brockport; Ann Herda-Rapp, University of Wisconsin, Marathon.

Kristin Wilson took up the very difficult task of preparing the instructor's guide and supersite information.

Thanks also to the McGraw-Hill production team: project manager, Brett Coker; production supervisor, Tandra Jorgensen; designer, Cassandra Chu; supplement producer, Louis Swaim.

I welcome any comments, suggestions, or criticism concerning this reader. Please feel free to contact me about which readings work, or which do not, or to suggest readings I might include in future editions. Please send any comments directly to me. I look forward to your feedback.

Charles A. Gallagher
Department of Sociology
Georgia State University
University Plaza
Atlanta, GA 30303-3083
E-mail: cgallagher@gsu.edu

About the Contributors

Teresa Amott (Reading 23) is associate professor of economics at Bucknell University. She is committed to sharing economic analysis with unions, welfare rights and women's organizations, and other progressive groups. Amott is the co-author of *Race, Gender, and Work: A Multicultural Economic History of Women in the United States* (with Julie Matthaei) and is the author of *Caught in the Crisis: Women in U.S. Economic History,* as well as numerous articles. She is also an editorial associate with *Dollars and Sense* magazine.

Daniel R. Amundson (Reading 32) is research director of the Center for Media and Public Affairs. He is co-author (with S. Robert Lichter) of *Solid Waste Management: Comparing Expert Opinion, Media Coverage, and Public Opinion* (1992).

Elijah Anderson (Reading 30) is the Charles and William L. Day Professor of the Social Sciences, professor of sociology, and director of the Philadelphia Ethnography Project at the University of Pennsylvania. An expert on the sociology of black America, he is the author of *A Place on the Corner: A Study of Black Streetcorner Men* (1978), numerous articles on the black experience, and the forthcoming *The Code of the Streets.* For his ethnographic study *Streetwise: Race, Class, and Change in an Urban Community* (1990), he was honored with the Robert E. Park Award of the American Sociological Association. Anderson is also associate editor of *Qualitative Sociology* and a member of the board of directors of the American Academy of Political and Social Science.

Rebecca M. Blank (Reading 4) is dean of the Gerald R. Ford School of Public Policy, Henry Carter Adams Collegiate Professor of Public Policy, and professor of economics at the University of Michigan. Prior to going to Michigan, she served as a member of the President's Council of Economic Advisers from 1997–1999. Blank's research has focused on the interaction between the macro-economy, government antipoverty programs, and the behavior and well-being of low-income families. She is the author of *It Takes a Nation: A New Agenda for Fighting Poverty* (1997), *Finding Jobs: Work and Welfare Reform* (2000), and *The New World of Welfare* (2001).

Herbert Blumer (Reading 10) spent most of his professional career at the University of Chicago and the University of California, Berkeley. Blumer established symbolic interactionism as a major sociological perspective in American sociology.

Lawrence Bobo (Reading 12) is a professor of sociology and Afro-American studies and director of graduate studies at Harvard University. His research interests include social psychology, race and ethnic relations, and public opinion. He is the co-author of *Racial Attitudes in America: Trends and Interpretations.* Bobo is currently "conducting research in three areas: studies of prejudice and intergroup conflict with an emphasis on black–white relations, American Indian–white relations, and a general mapping of stereotyping and social distance feelings of whites toward African-Americans and Hispanic-Americans."

Frank Bonilla (Reading 38) is Thomas Hunter Professor of Sociology, emeritus, at Hunter College of the City University of New York. From 1973 to 1993, Bonilla was the director of C.U.N.Y's Centro de Estudios Puertorriquenos and Professor at C.U.N.Y's Ph.D. programs in sociology and political science. Bonilla's current research, writing, and advocacy efforts are focused on promoting a vitalization of Latino academic and policy research capabilities.

Eduardo Bonilla-Silva (Reading 14) is an associate professor of sociology at Texas A&M University. He is best known for his 1997 piece in the *American Sociological Review* entitled "Rethinking Racism: Toward a Structural Interpretation." He is also the author of three books: *White Supremacy and Racism in the Post–Civil Rights Era* (2001), *Racism Without Racism: Color Blind Racism and the Persistence of Racial Inequality in the USA* (2003), and *Whiteout: The Continuing Significance of Racism* (with Ashley Doane, 2003). He is currently working on a project examining the idea that race relations in the United States are becoming Latin America–like, and a book-length manuscript entitled *Anything but Racism: How Social Scientists Limit the Significance of Racism.*

Robert D. Bullard (Reading 19) is Ware Professor of Sociology and director of the Environmental Justice Resource Center at Clark Atlanta University. He is the author of numerous articles, monographs, and scholarly papers that address environmental justice and public participation concerns. His book, *Dumping in Dixie: Race, Class and Environmental Quality* (1990, 1994, 2000), has become a standard text in the environmental justice field. His most recent books are *People of Color Environmental Groups Directory 2000* (2000) and *Sprawl City: Race, Politics, and Planning in Atlanta* (2000).

Albert M. Camarillo (Reading 38) is a professor of American history and director of the Center for Comparative Studies in Race and Ethnicity at Stanford University. His first book, *Chicanos in a Changing Society: From Mexican Pueblos to American Barrios* (first published in 1979) is in its sixth printing and a new edition was issued in 1996. *Chicanos in California: A History of Mexican Americans* was first published in 1984 and is currently in its fourth printing. His most recent book comparing the history of various major ethnic and racial minority groups in American cities is entitled *Not White, Not Black: Mexicans and Racial/Ethnic Borderlands in American Cities.*

David Cole (Reading 20) was named one of the forty-five outstanding lawyers under the age of forty-five by *The American Lawyer*. He is a professor at Georgetown University Law Center, an attorney with the Center for Constitutional Rights, the chief litigator for *Karen Finley v. National Endowment for the Arts*, and a regular contributor to NPR's *All Things Considered, The Nation,* and op-ed pages in major newspapers nationwide. He is the author of *No Equal Justice* (1999).

Hector Cordero-Guzman (Reading 6) is an urban poverty fellow in the Department of Sociology at the University of Chicago and a researcher at the Center for Puerto Rican Studies.

Heather M. Dalmage (Reading 39) is an associate professor of sociology at the School of Policy Studies at Roosevelt University, Chicago. She is the author of *Tripping on the Color Line: Black–White Multiracial Families in a Racially Divided World* (2000) and a national expert on interracial relationships. She is editor of *The Multiracial Movement: The Politics of Color* (2003).

Angela Y. Davis (Reading 21) is professor of history of consciousness at the University of California, Santa Cruz. During the last twenty-five years, she has lectured in all fifty states, as well as in Africa, Europe, the Caribbean, and the former Soviet Union. Her articles and essays have appeared in numerous journals and anthologies, and she is the author of five books, including *Angela Davis: An Autobiography; Women, Race & Class;* and the recently published *Blues Legacies and Black Feminism: Gertrude "Ma" Rainey, Bessie Smith, and Billie Holiday. The Angela Y. Davis Reader,* a collection of Davis's writings that spans nearly three decades, was published in 1998.

Judith N. DeSena (Reading 29) teaches at St. John's University and is the author of *Protecting One's Turf: Social Strategies for Maintaining Urban Neighborhoods* (1990).

Catherine Ellis (Reading 24) is a visiting scholar at Radcliffe's Murray Center for the Study of Lives and is examining racial attitudes and memories of segregation among older whites and African Americans.

Yen Le Espiritu (Reading 8) teaches race and ethnic relations and Asian American studies in the ethnic studies department at the University of California, San Diego. She is the author of *Asian American Women and Men: Labor, Laws, and Love* (1997); *Filipino American Lives* (1995); and *Asian American Panethnicity: Bridging Institutions and Identities* (1992). She is also review editor of the *Journal of Asian-American Studies.*

Clairece Booher Feagin (Reading 3) is the author of *What Will School Be Like?* (1991) and co-author of *Stories for Parents* (1990) and *Discrimination American Style: Institutional Racism and Sexism* (1978).

Joe R. Feagin (Readings 3 and 15) is a professor of sociology at the University of Florida. He does research mainly on gender and racial discrimination. He has completed a major research project on the discrimination faced by successful black Americans, a major portion of which was published in 1994 as *Living with Racism: The Black Middle Class Experience.* He has also published a book, *White Racism: The Basics* (1995), with co-author and professor Hernan Vera and has served as scholar-in-residence at the U.S. Commission on Civil Rights. Feagin was nominated for a Pulitzer Prize for *Ghetto Revolts* (1973).

Charles Gallagher (Readings 42 and 45) is an assistant professor of sociology at Georgia State University. He has written extensively about race and ethnic relations in the United States. He has written on the changing nature of racial categories, specifically the ways in which whiteness can expand; the social functions of color-blind political narrative and the accounts individuals give for their misrepresentations of racial group size. He has been honored with four teaching awards, most recently the Michael Harrington Distinguished Teaching Award (2002) from the National Forum on Poverty and Inequality. He is currently finishing his manuscript based on interviews with whites from around the country.

Herbert J. Gans (Readings 17 and 43) is the Robert Lynd Professor of Sociology at Columbia University. He received his Ph.D. from the University of Pennsylvania. He has worked as a research planner for public and private agencies, and prior to coming to Columbia taught at the University of Pennsylvania, MIT, and Teachers College of Columbia University. He is the author of nine books and over 160 articles. His first book was *The Urban Villagers* (1962). Recent works include *War Against the Poor* (1995)

Making Sense of America (1999), and *Democracy and the News* (2003).

Marvin Harris (Reading 1) spent a portion of his life teaching in the anthropology department at Columbia University, where he served as department chair. He has published 16 books, including *Cannibals and Kings; Culture, People, and Nature;* and *Our Kind.*

Sut Jhally (Reading 31) is author of *The Codes of Advertising: Social Communication in Advertising* and *Enlightened Racism.* Co-editor of *Cultural Politics in Contemporary America* and the forthcoming *The Fantasy Factory.* He is founder and executive director of The Media Education Foundation. He is the producer of videotapes *Dreamworlds, Pack of Lies, The Killing Screens, The Date Rape Backlash, Slim Hopes, Tough Guise, Killing Us Softly III, Off the Straight and Narrow,* and *Advertising and the End of the World.*

Joleen Kirschenman (Reading 25) is an affiliate of the Center for the Study of Urban Equality at the University of Chicago.

Jonathan Kozol (Reading 16) taught in public schools for several years and is the award-winning author of many books, including *Death at an Early Age, Illiterate America, Free Schools,* and *Rachel and Her Children.*

Maria Krysan (Reading 12) is an assistant professor of sociology at Pennsylvania State University and a research affiliate in its Population Research Institute. She is the co-author of *Racial Attitudes in America: Trends and Interpretations.*

Richard E. Lapchick (Reading 33) is the DeVos Eminent Scholar Chair and director of the Business Sports Management graduate program in the College of Business Administration at the University of Central Florida. He founded both Northeastern University's Center for the Study of Sport in Society as well as the National Consortium for Academics and Sport and is now director emeritus of the center and director of the consortium. He is the son of Joe Lapchick, the former coach of the New York Knicks, who pioneered integrating the NBA. Among many honors, he was inducted into the Sports Hall of Fame of the Commonwealth Nations in the humanitarian category along with Nelson Mandela and Arthur Ashe. He has published eleven books and is a columnist for the *Sport Business Journal* and the *Sporting News.*

Justin Lewis (Reading 31) is professor of communication and deputy head of the School of Journalism, Media and Cultural Studies at Cardiff University. He has written many books and articles on media, politics and culture, and is currently series editor for the list in *Media and Culture* for Peter Lang Publishers.

S. Robert Lichter (Reading 32) is the founder of the Center for Media and Public Affairs, a nonpartisan, nonprofit research and educational organization that conducts scientific studies of news and entertainment media. He is the co-author (with Daniel Amundson) of *Solid Waste Management: Comparing Expert Opinion, Media Coverage, and Public Opinion* (1992).

George Lipsitz (Reading 13) researches racialization in U.S. society, including the racialization of space, urban culture, collective memory, and movements for social change. He is the author of *American Studies in a Moment of Danger* (2001), *The Possessive Investment in Whiteness: How White People Profit from Identity Politics* (1998), *Dangerous Crossroads: Postmodernism, Politics, and the Poetics of Place* (1994), *Rainbow at Midnight: Labor and Culture in the 1940s* (1991), *Time Passages: Collective Memory and American Pop*

Culture (1990), *A Life in the Struggle: Ivory Perry and the Culture of Opposition* (1988, 1995).

Douglas S. Massey (Reading 28) is chair and professor of sociology at the University of Pennsylvania. His book *American Apartheid* (co-authored with Nancy A. Denton) won the 1995 Distinguished Scholarly Publication Award from the American Sociological Association.

Julie Matthaei (Reading 23) is an associate professor of economics at Wellesley College and the author of *An Economic History of Women in America: Women's Work, the Sexual Division of Labor, and the Development of Capitalism.* She is a long-term feminist and has written widely on the political economy of gender and race.

Robert K. Merton (Reading 11) is an adjunct professor at Rockefeller University, a resident scholar at the Russell Sage Foundation, and a professor emeritus at Columbia University. He is an eminent sociological theorist and a well-known defender of sociology as a genuine science. His publications include *On the Shoulders of Giants: A Shandean Postscript* (1965) and *The Sociology of Science: Theoretical and Empirical Investigations* (1973).

Kathryn M. Neckerman (Reading 25) is an associate professor of sociology at Columbia University. She writes: "My research interests include education and race and ethnic relations and I am writing a book about minority education in Chicago, 1900–1960." For her latest project, she "interviewed African-American, Latino, and West Indian students who were enrolled in business college to prepare them for white-collar jobs, to see how these students reconciled identity with pressure to 'talk white.'"

Katherine S. Newman (Reading 24) is Malcolm Wiener Professor of Urban Studies, dean of Social Science at the Radcliffe Institute for Advanced Study, and chair of joint doctoral programs in sociology, government, and social policy. She is the author of several books on middle-class economic insecurity, including *Falling From Grace* (1988) and *Declining Fortunes* (1993). Her 1999 book, *No Shame in My Game: The Working Poor in the Inner City,* won both the Sidney Hillman Book Prize and the Robert F. Kennedy Book Award.

Michael Omi (Reading 2) is a professor in the Department of Ethnic Studies at the University of California, Berkeley, and the co-author of *Racial Formation in the United States from the 1960s to the 1980s* (1986). He has also written about racial theory and politics, right-wing political movements, Asian Americans and race relations, and race and popular culture. In 1990, he was the recipient of Berkeley's Distinguished Teaching Award.

Howard Pinderhughes (Reading 18) is an associate professor in the Department of Social and Behavioral Sciences at the University of California, San Francisco, and the author of *Race in the Hood: Conflict and Violence Among Urban Youth.*

Jeffrey Reiman (Reading 22) is the William Fraser McDowell Professor of Philosophy at American University in Washington D.C. He is the author of *In Defense of Political Philosophy* (1972), *The Rich Get Richer and the Poor Get Prison: Ideology, Class, and Criminal Justice* (1979), *Justice and Modern Moral Philosophy* (1990), *Critical Moral Liberalism: Theory and Practice* (1997), *The Death Penalty: For and Against* (with Louis P. Pojman, 1998), *Abortion and the Ways We Value Human Life* (1999), and more than 50 articles in philosophy and criminal justice journals and anthologies.

Clara E. Rodriguez (Reading 6) is a professor in the Division of Social Sciences at Fordham University. Her major areas of research and interest include race and ethnicity, Latino studies, media, labor markets, and migration.

Maria Root (Reading 41) is a clinical psychologist and president-elect of the Washington State Psychological Association. She is the leading published authority in the nation on the developmental and social issues raised by the "biracial baby boom." She has researched and published extensively on the topic of identity development and related topics such as minority mental health, gender, and trauma. Root has edited and authored six books. She has two award-winning books, *Racially Mixed People in America* (1992) and *The Multiracial Experience: Racial Borders As the New Frontier* (1996). Her last book is *Love's Revolution: Racial Intermarriage* (2001).

Howard Schuman (Reading 12) is a research scientist at the Institute for Social Research and a professor of sociology, both at the University of Michigan. Together with Charlotte Steeh and others, he is completing a revision of his book *Racial Attitudes in America: Trends and Interpretations*, first published in 1985 (Harvard University Press). He recently wrote a chapter on "Attitudes, Beliefs, and Behavior" for the edited volume *Sociological Perspectives on Social Psychology*, and he continues to write in two other areas: "generations and collective memory" and the "question–answer process in surveys."

Thomas M. Shapiro (Reading 44) is a professor of sociology and anthropology at Northeastern University. Shapiro and Melvin L. Oliver have been awarded the C. Wright Mills Award and the American Sociological Association's Distinguished Scholarly Publication Award for *Black Wealth/White Wealth*. Shapiro's books include *Population Control Politics: Women, Sterilization, and Re-productive Choice* and *Great Divides: Readings in Social Inequality in the United States*.

Charlotte Steeh (Reading 12) is an associate professor of public administration and urban studies at Georgia State University. She is co-author of *Racial Attitudes in America: Trends and Interpretations*.

Stephen Steinberg (Reading 35) teaches in the Department of Urban Studies at Queens College and the Ph.D. program in sociology at the CUNY Graduate Center. His recent book *Turning Back: The Retreat from Racial Justice in American Thought and Policy* received the Oliver Cromwell Cox Award for Distinguished Anti-Racist Scholarship. Other books include *The Ethnic Myth, The Academic Melting Pot,* and *The Tenacity of Prejudice*. In addition to his scholarly publications, he has published articles in *The Nation, New Politics, Reconstruction,* and *The UNESCO Courier.*

Michael W. Suleiman (Reading 36) is University Distinguished Professor in the Department of Political Science at Kansas State University. He has written and co-edited numerous works in the field of Arab American studies, including *U.S. Policy on Palestine from Wilson to Clinton* and *Arab Americans: Continuity and Change.*

Roger Waldinger (Reading 26) is a professor of race/ethnic/minority relations, urban sociology, and migration and immigration at the University of California, Los Angeles. He is the author of *Still the Promised City? New Immigrants and African-Americans in Post-Industrial New York* (1996) and *Ethnic Los Angeles,* co-edited with Medhi Bozorgmehr (1996).

Mary C. Waters (Readings 9 and 37) is a professor of sociology at Harvard University. She is the author of *Ethnic Options: Choosing*

Identities in America and the co-author of *From Many Strands: Ethnic and Racial Groups in Contemporary America.* She has consulted with the Census Bureau on issues of measurement of race and ethnicity, and was a member of the National Academy of Science's Study Panel on the Demographic and Economic Consequences of Immigration to the United States. She has been a Guggenheim Fellow and a visiting scholar at the Russell Sage Foundation, and is a member of the International Committee of the Social Science Research Council.

David E. Wilkins (Reading 7) is an associate professor of American Indian studies, political science, and law. He has authored several books and a number of articles dealing with the political/legal relationship between indigenous nations and the United States and state governments. His most recent book is *American Indian Politics and the American Political System* (2002).

William J. Wilson (Reading 27) is the Malcolm Wiener Professor of Social Policy and the director of the Joblessness and Urban Poverty Research Program at the John F. Kennedy School of Government, Harvard University. He is a MacArthur Prize fellow and the author of *The Declining Significance of Race* and *The Truly Disadvantaged,* among many other books and articles. Wilson's teaching interests include urban poverty, urban race and class relations, and social inequalities and cross-cultural perspective. His current projects include studies of race and the social organization of neighborhoods, the effects of high-risk neighborhoods on adolescent social outcomes, and the new social inequality and race-based social policy.

Howard Winant (Reading 2) is a professor of sociology at the University of California, Santa Barbara. He is the author of numerous books and articles, including *Racial Formation in the United States from the 1960s to the 1990s* (1994) (with Michael Omi), *Racial Conditions: Politics, Theory, Comparisons* (1994), and *Stalemate: Political Economic Origins of Supply-Side Policy* (1988). Winant states: "My abiding interests are in the sociology of race, particularly in the dynamics of racial politics and the theoretical logic of race. I have conducted research and taught in Brazil and Mexico. My current research focuses on the global dynamics of race at the end of the twentieth century."

Frank H. Wu (Reading 40) is the first Asian American to serve as a law professor at Howard University Law School. He has written for a range of publications, including the *Washington Post, L.A. Times, Chicago Tribune,* and *The Nation,* and writes a regular column for *Asian Week.* Wu participated in a major debate against Dinesh D'Souza on affirmative action that was televised by C-Span and was the host of the syndicated talk show *Asian America* on PBS. His most recent book is *Yellow: Race in America Beyond Black and White* (2002).

Min Zhou (Reading 34) is professor of sociology and chair of the Asian American Studies Interdepartmental Degree Program at the University of California, Los Angeles. Her main areas of research are immigration and immigrant adaptation, ethnic and racial studies, Asian Americans, entrepreneurship and ethnic economies, and the community and urban sociology. She is the author of *Chinatown: The Socioeconomic Potential of an Urban Enclave* (1992), co-author of *Growing Up American: How Vietnamese Children Adapt to Life in the United States* (1997), and co-editor of *Contemporary Asian American: A Multidisciplinary Reader* (2000).

Howard Zinn (Reading 5), professor, activist, and author, has dedicated his life to the notion that the knowledge of history is important to people's everyday lives and can be a powerful force for social change. Zinn is a champion of the idea that historical change occurs more through mass movements of ordinary people than through the wisdom and insight of so-called Great Men. His best-known book, *A People's History of the United States,* was one of the first major looks at American history from such a perspective.

RETHINKING THE COLOR LINE

INTRODUCTION
Rethinking the Color Line: Understanding How Boundaries Shift

The sociological promise implicit in the title *Rethinking the Color Line* is that this book will explore the contemporary meaning of race and ethnicity and will examine how social, political, economic, and cultural forces shape those meanings. This may seem like a straightforward task; however, it is not. Race and ethnicity are slippery concepts because they are always in a state of flux. Imagine for a moment the shape of the United States as analogous to a definition of race or ethnicity. It may appear that an outline or sketch of the U.S. border, like a definition of race or ethnicity, can be neatly described or mapped out. That is, just as we can imagine the borders of the United States, we can with reasonable certainty identify someone as black, white, Asian, or American Indian. We place people in these racial categories because we have been trained to focus on a combination of traits like skin color, hair texture, and eye shape. After we have placed individuals in racial categories, we typically use cultural markers, such as their ethnic background or ancestry, to further sort them. For instance, if a white person walks into a room, we *see* that individual's race. What happens when he or she starts talking and we hear an Irish brogue or a New York City dialect or a Southern dialect? What happens when the brown woman in front of us in the supermarket talks to the cashier and we recognize her accent as Jamaican or British? We tend to sort first by color and then by cultural background.

Consider again the shape of the United States. Since the founding of the country more than two hundred years ago, the lines that have defined the nation's borders have been redrawn dozens of times. The mental map we conjure up of the United States today is only about forty years old. The map was last redrawn in 1959 when Hawaii was admitted into the Union as the fiftieth state. Previously, the map had been redrawn after the Louisiana Purchase of 1803 and again after the Missouri Compromise of 1820, as well as after the admittance of every new state to the Union. And we will have to redraw our map yet again if the Commonwealth of Puerto Rico votes to enter the Union as the fifty-first state.

The problem with definitions of race and ethnicity, as with the shape of the United States, is that the borders or contours that give form and meaning to these concepts change over time. A person defined as white in the year 2005 might have been defined as black or Irish or Italian at various times in American history. For example, around the turn of the century Irish and Italian immigrants were *not* viewed as white when they first arrived in the United States. At that time, members of those groups did not easily fit into the existing racial hierarchy; they were in a racial limbo—not white, not black, not Asian. Their ethnic background—that is, the language, culture, and religious beliefs that distinguished them from the dominant group—was then used in various ways to define them as a racial group. Within a generation or two, these so-called Irish and Italian racial groups assimilated and were absorbed into the category we now know as white. The

1

journey from being considered not white to white was rather swift. It may seem odd, and may even shock our racial sensibilities, to think of Supreme Court Justice Antonin Scalia's or Senator Ted Kennedy's parents or grandparents as possibly being defined as nonwhite at different times in American history. But is a nonwhite Italian or nonwhite Irish any less curious an idea than a black Irish American or an Asian-Italian American? If one's ethnic identity is subsumed or taken over by a racial identity, the question we need to ask as sociologists is why?

Just as the shape of the United States has changed over time, so have the definitions of race and ethnicity. In fact, the idea of race as it is currently understood did not even exist until the Europeans colonized the Americas, Africa, and parts of Asia. Do you think your view of race and ethnicity is different from that of your parents or grandparents? How you understand race and ethnicity reflects a definition specific to this moment in time; one that in all likelihood will look quite different in three or four decades. *Rethinking the Color Line* will provide you with a theoretical framework for understanding how and why definitions of race and ethnicity change over time, what sociological forces bring about these changes, and what these categories might look like in the next century.

What these examples suggest, and what many of the readings in *Rethinking the Color Line* consciously explore, is how race and ethnicity are socially constructed. When we say that something is socially constructed, we mean that the characteristics deemed relevant to that definition are based on societal and cultural values. Race and ethnicity are social constructions because their meanings are derived from arbitrary characteristics that a given society deems important. In other words, race and ethnicity are social products based on cultural values, not scientific facts.

Think for a moment about gravity. If you push this book off your desk, do you expect it to fall to the ground? Obviously, you do. If you lived in Brazil or South Africa or Puerto Rico, would you expect the same thing to happen to your book? Of course you would because you know that gravity is a universal constant. However, someone defined as black in the United States could be defined as white in Brazil, Trigueno (intermediate) in Puerto Rico, and "coloured" in South Africa. Gravity is the same everywhere, but racial classifications vary across place and time because definitions of race and ethnicity are based on the physical traits a society chooses to value or devalue. Because each society's values are based on a different set of historical experiences, cultural circumstances, and political definitions, ideas about race and ethnicity can vary quite a bit, not only between countries but within them as well. For example, historically, it was not uncommon for someone to have been socially and legally defined as black in the southern part of the United States but to "pass" for white after migrating north. Thus, the beliefs and definitions that undergird the idea of race are very unstable and, as we will see in the readings, quite susceptible to political manipulation.

Racial and ethnic identity is culturally meaningful only because we define and understand it in that way. In other words, race exists because we say race exists. And because the characteristics that make up the idea of race and ethnicity reflect a social process, it is possible to imagine these concepts in a different way. For example, instead of looking at skin color, facial features, or hair texture as a way to sort individuals, we could create a racial category based on the size of people's feet. People with shoe sizes between 4 and 7 would be labeled the "petite race," those with sizes 8–11 would be designated the "bigger race," and the 12–15 shoe size crowd would be categorized as the "monster foot race." Those with feet smaller or larger than the existing categories would be the "other race." Likewise, we could use eye color, height, glove size, or nose length to create racial categories. Because the physical markers we use to define race are arbitrary and have no basis in genetics, biology, anthropology, or sociology, using shoe size as the criterion to fashion a new definition of race would be just as valid as the system currently in place. Similarly, we could redefine ethnicity by changing the focus from language, culture, religion, or nationality as a method of sorting people and instead create categories of people based on the amount of meat they eat or the way they style their hair.

What complicates our ability to accurately and easily map these definitions of race and ethnicity is that the definitions are constantly changing. Are the thirty million Latinos in the United States an ethnic group because they are defined by the U.S. Census Bureau as such, or are Latinos a racial group? If the current census categories of white, black, Asian, and American Indian do not adequately reflect what Latinos experience or how Latinos are viewed by non-Latinos, should a "brown" category be added to the census? Would a newly created brown category link Puerto Ricans in New York City with Cuban Americans in Miami and Mexican Americans in San Diego? Why or why not? How should we define the race of a child whose father was Mexican–African American and whose mother was Japanese–Irish American? What is this child's ethnicity?

For that matter, in what ways are race and ethnicity related?

In 1903, sociologist W. E. B. Du Bois wrote "the problem of the twentieth century is the problem of the color-line." It appears that a key problem of the twenty-first century, while different in degree and context from the one Du Bois chronicled, will still be the color line. A topic or issue may not initially seem to be linked to race or ethnicity, but on closer sociological scrutiny, patterns often emerge that make it clear that race and ethnicity matter quite a bit. How do you see race and ethnicity being connected to who gets a good education or adequate health care, who is likely to be poor, where toxic waste sites are built, who gets hired or promoted, or which racial or ethnic groups are more likely to have members sentenced to death and executed? Race and ethnicity are intertwined in every aspect of our lives.

Rethinking the Color Line will provide you with the tools necessary to navigate the complicated and often contradictory meaning of race and ethnicity in the United States. The readings will take you on a sociological journey and explore how you, your classmates, your family, and your friends fit into the racial and ethnic mosaic of the United States. The questions at the beginning of each reading are designed to direct your attention to key themes or ideas in the reading. If you focus carefully on the readings and discussion questions, your perspective on race and ethnic relations in the United States will likely be changed forever.

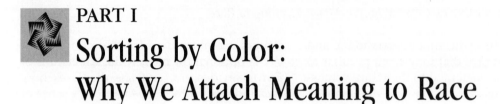

PART I
Sorting by Color:
Why We Attach Meaning to Race

How would you answer these questions?

Who taught you how to "be" black or American Indian or white or Asian? Did you learn about your race by watching sitcoms on television or by watching your peers in the schoolyard? Was it your parents or an older sibling or cousin who taught you how to act both your age and your race? In what social situations do you think about your racial identity? Is it only when you interact with an individual from a different racial background that you think about your racial identity? Do you think about your race, about other racial groups, or about race relations when you watch football games or MTV or the nightly news? Do you think about your race while you are in your neighborhood or only when you drive through an area with a different racial population? Were you ever in a social setting in which you were the only person of your color? How did that make you feel?

How did you learn to "be" Korean or Jamaican or German? In what situations do you think about your ancestry? Is it during the holidays or when you spend time with your family? Or has your family been in the United States for so many generations that the family tree linking you to the homeland is unimportant, nonexistent, or untraceable? Does that mean you have a racial identity but not an ethnic identity? Or does "American" best mirror your social identity?

The readings in Part I answer these questions by exposing you to the social theories used to define and understand the dynamics of race and ethnicity. The first three readings examine how the natural variation in human skin color has been used as a way to sort people into groups, create a racial hierarchy, and justify exploitation based on skin color. Marvin Harris explains why gradations of color, from black to white, are beautiful sociocultural responses to the environment. Michael Omi and Howard Winant explain the emergence of racial categories as a sociohistoric process they call racial formation; that is, the way we define ourselves racially reflects a process that has been hundreds of years in the making. Joe Feagin and Clairece Booher Feagin provide an overview of the theories central to ethnic and racial studies, theories that will reemerge throughout the book. As you will see, many of the articles in this reader draw on one or more of these theories to explain a particular aspect of racial inequality and race and ethnic relations.

The next six readings draw on the theories outlined in the first section but emphasize the extent to which racial and ethnic identity construction is shaped by politics and culture. Very real differences exist between these groups in terms of income, rates of poverty and incarceration, access to computers, and health status. Rebecca Blank provides descriptive statistics of the social and economic well-being of non-Hispanic whites, non-Hispanic blacks, Hispanics, Asian and Pacific Islanders, and American Indians and Alaska natives. Howard Zinn charts the evolution of the idea of race in early U.S. history. Clara Rodriguez and Hector Cordero-Guzman explain how the social and political organization of slavery in Puerto Rico differed from that in the United

States, resulting in an understanding and definition of race that may seem peculiar to those of us accustomed to the white-versus-black view of race relations so dominant in the United States. David Wilkins and Yen Le Espiritu demonstrate how, why, and in what situations racial and ethnic identities are used to organize politically. Finally, Mary Waters examines the idea that ethnic identity is optional for most white Americans of European descent, and she discusses how racial identity affects an American's sense of ethnicity. As these readings demonstrate, the creation of categories of racial and ethnic identity is as much a historical process as it is a political one.

Race and Ethnicity: Sociohistorical Constructions and . . .

1

HOW OUR SKINS GOT THEIR COLOR

Marvin Harris

Questions to Consider

Cultural anthropologist Marvin Harris links the variations in skin color one can observe around the world to the human body's ability to physically adapt to changes in exposure to solar radiation. How do you explain his assertion that "white was beautiful because white was healthy" and "black was beautiful because black was healthy"?

Most human beings are neither very fair nor very dark, but brown. The extremely fair skin of northern Europeans and their descendants, and the very black skins of central Africans and their descendants, are probably special adaptations. Brown-skinned ancestors may have been shared by modern-day blacks and whites as recently as 10,000 years ago. Human skin owes its color to the presence of particles known as melanin. The primary function of melanin is to protect the upper levels of the skin from being damaged by the sun's ultraviolet rays. This radiation poses a critical problem for our kind because we lack the dense coat of hair that acts as a sunscreen for most mammals. . . . Hairlessness exposes us to two kinds of radiation hazards: ordinary sunburn, with its blisters, rashes, and risk of infection; and skin cancers, including malignant melanoma, one of the deadliest diseases known. Melanin is the body's first line of defense against these afflictions. The more melanin particles, the darker the skin, and the lower the risk of sunburn and all forms of skin cancer. This explains why the highest rates for skin cancer are found in sun-drenched lands such as Australia, where light-skinned people of European descent spend a good part of their lives outdoors wearing scanty attire. Very dark-skinned people such as heavily pigmented Africans of Zaire seldom get skin cancer, but when they do, they get it on depigmented parts of their bodies—palms and lips.

If exposure to solar radiation had nothing but harmful effects, natural selection would have favored inky black as the color for all human populations. But the sun's rays do not present an unmitigated threat. As it falls on the skin, sunshine converts a fatty substance in the epidermis into vitamin D. The blood carries vitamin D from the skin to the intestines (technically making it a hormone rather than a vitamin), where it plays a vital role in the absorption of calcium. In turn, calcium is vital for strong bones. Without it, people fall victim to the crippling diseases rickets and osteomalacia. In women, calcium deficiencies can result in a deformed birth canal, which makes childbirth lethal for both mother and fetus.

Vitamin D can be obtained from a few foods, primarily the oils and livers of marine fish. But inland populations must rely on the sun's rays and their own skins for the supply of this crucial substance. The particular color of a human population's skin, therefore, represents in large degree a trade-off between the hazards of too much versus too little solar radiation: acute sunburn and skin cancer on the one hand, and rickets and osteomalacia on the other. It is this trade-off that largely accounts for the preponderance of brown people in the world and for the general tendency for skin color to be darkest among equatorial populations and lightest among populations dwelling at higher latitudes.

At middle latitudes, the skin follows a strategy of changing colors with the seasons. Around the Mediterranean basin, for example, exposure to the summer sun brings high risk of cancer but low risk for rickets; the body produces more melanin and people grow darker (i.e., they get suntans). Winter reduces the risk of sunburn and cancer; the body produces less melanin, and the tan wears off.

The correlation between skin color and latitude is not perfect because other factors—such as the availability of foods containing vitamin D and calcium, regional cloud cover during the winter, amount of clothing worn, and cultural preferences—may work

for or against the predicted relationship. Arctic-dwelling Eskimo, for example, are not as light-skinned as expected, but their habitat and economy afford them a diet that is exceptionally rich in both vitamin D and calcium.

Northern Europeans, obliged to wear heavy garments for protection against the long, cold, cloudy winters, were always at risk for rickets and osteomalacia from too little vitamin D and calcium. This risk increased sometime after 6000 B.C., when pioneer cattle herders who did not exploit marine resources began to appear in northern Europe. The risk would have been especially great for the brown-skinned Mediterranean peoples who migrated northward along with the crops and farm animals. Samples of Caucasian skin (infant penile foreskin obtained at the time of circumcision) exposed to sunlight on cloudless days in Boston (42°N) from November through February produced no vitamin D. In Edmonton (52°N) this period extended from October to March. But further south (34°N) sunlight was effective in producing vitamin D in the middle of the winter. Almost all of Europe lies north of 42°N. Fair-skinned, nontanning individuals who could utilize the weakest and briefest doses of sunlight to synthesize vitamin D were strongly favored by natural selection. During the frigid winters, only a small circle of a child's face could be left to peek out at the sun through the heavy clothing, thereby favoring the survival of individuals with translucent patches of pink on their cheeks characteristic of many northern Europeans. (People who could get calcium by drinking cow's milk would also be favored by natural selection.)

If light-skinned individuals on the average had only 2 percent more children survive per generation, the changeover in their skin color could have begun 5,000 years ago and reached present levels well before the beginning of the Christian era. But natural selection need not have acted alone. Cultural selection may also have played a role. It seems likely that whenever people consciously or unconsciously had to decide which infants to nourish and which to neglect, the advantage would go to those with lighter skin, experience having shown that such individuals tended to grow up to be taller, stronger, and healthier than their darker siblings. White was beautiful because white was healthy.

To account for the evolution of black skin in equatorial latitudes, one has merely to reverse the combined effects of natural and cultural selection. With the sun directly overhead most of the year, and clothing a hindrance to work and survival, vitamin D was never in short supply (and calcium was easily obtained from vegetables). Rickets and osteomalacia were rare. Skin cancer was the main problem, and what nature started, culture amplified. Darker infants were favored by parents because experience showed that they grew up to be freer of disfiguring and lethal malignancies. Black was beautiful because black was healthy.

2

RACIAL FORMATIONS

Michael Omi • Howard Winant

Questions to Consider

If race is not "real" in a scientific sense, why can I look around the classroom or campus and see that someone is black or Asian or white? What is the difference between something being "real," like the book in front of you, and something being a social construction, like race or gender? Use Omi and Winant's theory of racial formation to explain how and why we "see" race as we do.

In 1982–83, Susie Guillory Phipps unsuccessfully sued the Louisiana Bureau of Vital Records to change her racial classification from black to white. The descendant of an eighteenth-century white planter and a black slave, Phipps was designated "black" in her birth certificate in accordance with a 1970 state law which declared anyone with at least one-thirty-second "Negro blood" to be black. The legal battle raised intriguing questions about the concept of race, its meaning in contemporary society, and its use (and abuse) in public policy. Assistant Attorney General Ron Davis defended the law by pointing out that some type of racial classification was necessary to comply with

From *Racial Formation in the United States,* Second Edition, Michael Omi and Howard Winant, eds. Copyright © 1994 by Routledge, Inc. Reproduced by permission of Routledge, Inc., part of the Taylor & Francis Group.

federal record-keeping requirements and to facilitate programs for the prevention of genetic diseases. Phipps's attorney, Brian Begue, argued that the assignment of racial categories on birth certificates was unconstitutional and that the one-thirty-second designation was inaccurate. He called on a retired Tulane University professor who cited research indicating that most whites have one-twentieth "Negro" ancestry. In the end, Phipps lost. The court upheld a state law which quantified racial identity, and in so doing affirmed the legality of assigning individuals to specific racial groupings.[1]

The Phipps case illustrates the continuing dilemma of defining race and establishing its meaning in institutional life. Today, to assert that variations in human physiognomy are racially based is to enter a constant and intense debate. *Scientific* interpretations of race have not been alone in sparking heated controversy; *religious* perspectives have done so as well.[2] Most centrally, of course, race has been a matter of *political* contention. This has been particularly true in the United States, where the concept of race has varied enormously over time without ever leaving the center stage of US history.

What Is Race?

Race consciousness, and its articulation in theories of race, is largely a modern phenomenon. When European explorers in the New World "discovered" people who looked different than themselves, these "natives" challenged then existing conceptions of the origins of the human species, and raised disturbing questions as to whether *all* could be considered in the same "family of man."[3] Religious debates flared over the attempt to reconcile the Bible with the existence of "racially distinct" people. Arguments took place over creation itself, as

theories of polygenesis questioned whether God had made only one species of humanity ("monogenesis"). Europeans wondered if the natives of the New World were indeed human beings with redeemable souls. At stake were not only the prospects for conversion, but the types of treatment to be accorded them. The expropriation of property, the denial of political rights, the introduction of slavery and other forms of coercive labor, as well as outright extermination, all presupposed a worldview which distinguished Europeans—children of God, human beings, etc.—from "others." Such a worldview was needed to explain why some should be "free" and others enslaved, why some had rights to land and property while others did not. Race, and the interpretation of racial differences, was a central factor in that worldview.

In the colonial epoch science was no less a field of controversy than religion in attempts to comprehend the concept of race and its meaning. Spurred on by the classificatory scheme of living organisms devised by Linnaeus in *Systema Naturae,* many scholars in the eighteenth and nineteenth centuries dedicated themselves to the identification and ranking of variations in humankind. Race was thought of as a *biological* concept, yet its precise definition was the subject of debates which, as we have noted, continue to rage today. Despite efforts ranging from Dr. Samuel Morton's studies of cranial capacity[4] to contemporary attempts to base racial classification on shared gene pools,[5] the concept of race has defied biological definition. . . .

Attempts to discern the *scientific meaning* of race continue to the present day. Although most physical anthropologists and biologists have abandoned the quest for a scientific basis to determine racial categories, controversies have recently flared in the area of genetics and educational psychology. For instance, an essay by Arthur Jensen argued that hereditary factors shape intelligence not only revived the "nature or nurture" controversy, but raised highly volatile questions about racial equality itself.[6] Clearly the attempt to establish a *biological* basis of race has not been swept into the dustbin of history, but is being resurrected in various scientific arenas. All such attempts seek to remove the concept of race from fundamental social, political, or economic determination. They suggest instead that the truth of race lies in the terrain of innate characteristics, of which skin color and other physical attributes provide only the most obvious, and in some respects most superficial, indicators.

Race as a Social Concept

The social sciences have come to reject biologistic notions of race in favor of an approach which regards race as a *social* concept. Beginning in the eighteenth century, this trend has been slow and uneven, but its direction clear. In the nineteenth century Max Weber discounted biological explanations for racial conflict and instead highlighted the social and political factors which engendered such conflict.[7] The work of pioneering cultural anthropologist Franz Boas was crucial in refuting the scientific racism of the early twentieth century by rejecting the connection between race and culture, and the assumption of a continuum of "higher" and "lower" cultural groups. Within the contemporary social science literature, race is assumed to be a variable which is shaped by broader societal forces.

Race is indeed a pre-eminently *socio-historical* concept. Racial categories and the meaning of race are given concrete expression by the specific social relations and historical context in which they are embedded. Racial meanings have varied tremen-

dously over time and between different societies.

In the United States, the black/white color line has historically been rigidly defined and enforced. White is seen as a "pure" category. Any racial intermixture makes one "nonwhite." In the movie *Raintree County*, Elizabeth Taylor describes the worst of fates to befall whites as "havin' a little Negra blood in ya'—just one little teeny drop and a person's all Negra."[8] This thinking flows from what Marvin Harris has characterized as the principle of *hypo-descent*:

> By what ingenious computation is the genetic tracery of a million years of evolution unraveled and each man [sic] assigned his proper social box? In the United States, the mechanism employed is the rule of hypo-descent. This descent rule requires Americans to believe that anyone who is known to have had a Negro ancestor is a Negro. We admit nothing in between. . . . "Hypo-descent" means affiliation with the subordinate rather than the superordinate group in order to avoid the ambiguity of intermediate identity. . . . The rule of hypo-descent is, therefore, an invention, which we in the United States have made in order to keep biological facts from intruding into our collective racist fantasies.[9]

The Susie Guillory Phipps case merely represents the contemporary expression of this racial logic.

By contrast, a striking feature of race relations in the lowland areas of Latin America since the abolition of slavery has been the relative absence of sharply defined racial groupings. No such rigid descent rule characterizes racial identity in many Latin American societies. Brazil, for example, has historically had less rigid conceptions of race, and thus a variety of "intermediate" racial categories exist. Indeed, as Harris notes, "One of the most striking consequences of the Brazilian system of racial identification is that parents and children and even brothers and sisters are frequently accepted as representatives of quite opposite racial types."[10] Such a possibility is incomprehensible within the logic of racial categories in the US.

To suggest another example: the notion of "passing" takes on new meaning if we compare various American cultures' means of assigning racial identity. In the United States, individuals who are actually "black" by the logic of hypo-descent have attempted to skirt the discriminatory barriers imposed by law and custom by attempting to "pass" for white.[11] Ironically, these same individuals would not be able to pass for "black" in many Latin American societies.

Consideration of the term "black" illustrates the diversity of racial meanings which can be found among different societies and historically within a given society. In contemporary British politics the term "black" is used to refer to all nonwhites. Interestingly this designation has not arisen through the racist discourse of groups such as the National Front. Rather, in political and cultural movements, Asian as well as Afro-Caribbean youth are adopting the term as an expression of self-identity.[12] The wide-ranging meanings of "black" illustrate the manner in which racial categories are shaped politically.[13]

The meaning of race is defined and contested throughout society, in both collective action and personal practice. In the process, racial categories themselves are formed, transformed, destroyed and reformed. We use the term *racial formation* to refer to the process by which social, economic and political forces determine the content and importance of racial categories, and by which they are in turn shaped by racial meanings. Crucial to this formulation is the treatment of race as a *central axis* of social relations which cannot be subsumed under or reduced to some broader category or conception.

Racial Ideology and Racial Identity

The seemingly obvious, "natural" and "common sense" qualities which the existing racial order exhibits themselves testify to the effectiveness of the racial formation process in constructing racial meanings and racial identities.

One of the first things we notice about people when we meet them (along with their sex) is their race. We utilize race to provide clues abut *who* a person is. This fact is made painfully obvious when we encounter someone whom we cannot conveniently racially categorize—someone who is, for example, racially "mixed" or of an ethnic/racial group with which we are not familiar. Such an encounter becomes a source of discomfort and momentarily a crisis of racial meaning. Without a racial identity, one is in danger of having no identity.

Our compass for navigating race relations depends on preconceived notions of what each specific racial group looks like. Comments such as, "Funny, you don't look black," betray an underlying image of what black should be. We also become disoriented when people do not act "black," "Latino," or indeed "white." The content of such stereotypes reveals a series of unsubstantiated beliefs about who these groups are and what "they" are like.[14]

In US society, then, a kind of "racial etiquette" exists, a set of interpretative codes and racial meanings which operate in the interactions of daily life. Rules shaped by our perception of race in a comprehensively racial society determine the "presentation of self,"[15] distinctions of status, and appropriate modes of conduct. "Etiquette" is not mere universal adherence to the dominant group's rules, but a more dynamic combination of these rules with the values and beliefs of subordinated groupings. This racial "subjection" is quintessentially ideological. Everybody learns some combination, some version, of the rules of racial classification, and of their own racial identity, often without obvious teaching or conscious inculcation. Race becomes "common sense"—a way of comprehending, explaining and acting in the world.

Racial beliefs operate as an "amateur biology," a way of explaining the variations in "human nature."[16] Differences in skin color and other obvious physical characteristics supposedly provide visible clues to differences lurking underneath. Temperament, sexuality, intelligence, athletic ability, aesthetic preferences and so on are presumed to be fixed and discernible from the palpable mark of race. Such diverse questions as our confidence and trust in others (for example, clerks or salespeople, media figures, neighbors), our sexual preferences and romantic images, our tastes in music, films, dance, or sports, and our very ways of talking, walking, eating and dreaming are ineluctably shaped by notions of race. Skin color "differences" are thought to explain perceived differences in intellectual, physical and artistic temperaments, and to justify distinct treatment of racially identified individuals and groups.

The continuing persistence of racial ideology suggests that these racial myths and stereotypes cannot be exposed as such in the popular imagination. They are, we think, too essential, too integral, to the maintenance of the US social order. Of course, particular meanings, stereotypes and myths can change, but the presence of a *system* of racial meanings and stereotypes, of racial ideology, seems to be a permanent feature of US culture.

Film and television, for example, have been notorious in disseminating images of racial minorities which establish for audiences what people from these groups look like, how they behave, and "who they are."[17] The power of the media lies not only in their ability to reflect the dominant racial ideology, but in their capacity to shape that ideology in the first place. D.W. Griffith's epic *Birth of a Nation*, a sympathetic treatment of the rise of the Ku Klux Klan during Reconstruction, helped to generate, consolidate and "nationalize" images of blacks which had been more disparate (more regionally specific, for example) prior to the film's appearance.[18] In US television, the necessity to define characters in the briefest and most condensed manner has led to the perpetuation of racial caricatures, as racial stereotypes serve as shorthand for scriptwriters, directors and actors, in commercials, etc. Television's tendency to address the "lowest common denominator" in order to render programs "familiar" to an enormous and diverse audience leads it regularly to assign and reassign racial characteristics to particular groups, both minority and majority.

These and innumerable other examples show that we tend to view race as something fixed and immutable—something rooted in "nature." Thus we mask the historical construction of racial categories, the shifting meaning of race, and the crucial role of politics and ideology in shaping race relations. Races do not emerge full-blown. They are the results of diverse historical practices and are continually subject to challenge over their definition and meaning.

Racialization: The Historical Development of Race

In the United States, the racial category of "black" evolved with the consolidation of racial slavery. By the end of the seventeenth century, Africans whose specific identity was Ibo, Yoruba, Fulani, etc., were rendered "black" by an ideology of exploitation based on racial logic—the establishment and maintenance of a "color line." This of course did not occur overnight. A period of indentured servitude which was not rooted in racial logic preceded the consolidation of racial slavery. With slavery, however, a racially based understanding of society was set in motion which resulted in the shaping of a specific *racial* identity not only for the slaves but for the European settlers as well. Winthrop Jordan has observed: "From the initially common term *Christian,* at mid-century there was a marked shift toward the terms *English* and *free.* After about 1680, taking the colonies as a whole, a new term of self-identification appeared—*white.*"[19]

We employ the term *racialization* to signify the extension of racial meaning to a previously racially unclassified relationship, social practice or group. Racialization is an ideological process, an historically specific one. Racial ideology is constructed from pre-existing conceptual (or, if one prefers, "discursive") elements and emerges from the struggles of competing political projects and ideas seeking to articulate similar elements differently. An account of racialization processes that avoids the pitfalls of US ethnic history[20] remains to be written.

Particularly during the nineteenth century, the category of "white" was subject to challenges brought about by the influx of diverse groups who were not of the same Anglo-Saxon stock as the founding immigrants. In the nineteenth century, political and ideological struggles emerged over the classification of Southern Europeans, the Irish and Jews, among other "nonwhite" categories.[21] Nativism was only effectively curbed by the institutionalization of a racial order that drew the color line *around,* rather than *within,* Europe.

By stopping short of racializing immigrants from Europe after the Civil War, and by subsequently allowing their assimilation, the American racial order was reconsolidated in the wake of the tremendous challenge placed before it by the abolition of racial slavery.[22] With the end of Reconstruction in 1877, an effective program for limiting the emergent class struggles of the later nineteenth century was forged: the definition of the working class *in racial terms*—as "white." This was not accomplished by any legislative decree or capitalist maneuvering to divide the working class, but rather by white workers themselves. Many of them were recent immigrants, who organized on racial lines as much as on traditionally defined class lines.[23] The Irish on the West Coast, for example, engaged in vicious anti-Chinese race-baiting and committed many pogrom-type assaults on Chinese in the course of consolidating the trade union movement in California.

Thus the very political organization of the working class was in important ways a racial project. The legacy of racial conflicts and arrangements shaped the definition of interests and in turn led to the consolidation of institutional patterns (e.g., segregated unions, dual labor markets, exclusionary legislation) which perpetuated the color line *within* the working class. Selig Perlman, whose study of the development of the labor movement is fairly sympathetic to this process, notes that:

> The political issue after 1877 was racial, not financial, and the weapon was not merely the ballot, but also "direct action"—violence. The anti-Chinese agitation in California, culminating as it did in the Exclusion Law passed by Congress in 1882, was doubtless the most important single factor in the history of American labor, for without it the entire country might have been overrun by Mongolian [sic] labor and *the labor movement*

might have become a conflict of races instead of one of classes.[24]

More recent economic transformations in the US have also altered interpretations of racial identities and meanings. The automation of southern agriculture and the augmented labor demand of the postwar boom transformed blacks from a largely rural, impoverished labor force to a largely urban, working-class group by 1970.[25] When boom became bust and liberal welfare statism moved rightwards, the majority of blacks came to be seen, increasingly, as part of the "underclass," as state "dependents." Thus the particularly deleterious effects on blacks of global and national economic shifts (generally rising unemployment rates, changes in the employment structure away from reliance on labor intensive work, etc.) were explained once again in the late 1970s and 1980s (as they had been in the 1940s and mid-1960s) as the result of defective black cultural norms, of familial disorganization, etc.[26] In this way new racial attributions, new racial myths, are affixed to "blacks."[27] Similar changes in racial identity are presently affecting Asians and Latinos, as such economic forces as increasing Third World impoverishment and indebtedness fuel immigration and high interest rates, Japanese competition spurs resentments, and US jobs seem to fly away to Korea and Singapore.[28] . . .

Once we understand that race overflows the boundaries of skin color, super-exploitation, social stratification, discrimination and prejudice, cultural domination and cultural resistance, state policy (or of any other particular social relationship we list), once we recognize the racial dimension present to some degree in *every* identity, institution and social practice in the United States—once we have done this, it becomes possible to speak of *racial formation*. This recognition is hard-won; there is a continuous temptation to think of race as an *essence*, as something fixed, concrete and objective, as (for example) one of the categories just enumerated. And there is also an opposite temptation: to see it as a mere illusion, which an ideal social order would eliminate.

In our view it is crucial to break with these habits of thought. The effort must be made to understand race as *an unstable and "decentered" complex of social meanings constantly being transformed by political struggle.*

NOTES

1. *San Francisco Chronicle,* 14 September 1982, 19 May 1983. Ironically, the 1970 Louisiana law was enacted to supersede an old Jim Crow statute which relied on the idea of "common report" in determining an infant's race. Following Phipps's unsuccessful attempt to change her classification and have the law declared unconstitutional, a legislative effort arose which culminated in the repeal of the law. See *San Francisco Chronicle,* 23 June 1983.
2. The Mormon church, for example, has been heavily criticized for its doctrine of black inferiority.
3. Thomas F. Gossett notes:
   Race theory . . . had up until fairly modern times no firm hold on European thought. On the other hand, race theory and race prejudice were by no means unknown at the time when the English colonists came to North America. Undoubtedly, the age of exploration led many to speculate on race differences at a period when neither Europeans nor Englishmen were prepared to make allowances for vast cultural diversities. Even though race theories had not then secured wide acceptance or even sophisticated formulation, the first contacts of the Spanish with the Indians in the Americas can now be recognized as the beginning of a struggle between conceptions of the nature of primitive peoples which has not yet been wholly settled. (Thomas F. Gossett, *Race: The History of an Idea in America* [New York: Schocken Books, 1965], p. 16.)

Winthrop Jordan provides a detailed account of early European colonialists' attitudes about color and race in *White over Black: American Attitudes Toward the Negro, 1550–1812* (New York: Norton, 1977 [1968]), pp. 3–43.

4. Pro-slavery physician Samuel George Morton (1799–1851) compiled a collection of 800 crania from all parts of the world which formed the sample for his studies of race. Assuming that the larger the size of the cranium translated into greater intelligence, Morton established a relationship between race and skull capacity. Gossett reports that:

> In 1849, one of his studies included the following results: The English skulls in his collection proved to be the largest, with an average cranial capacity of 96 cubic inches. The Americans and Germans were rather poor seconds, both with cranial capacities of 90 cubic inches. At the bottom of the list were the Negroes with 83 cubic inches, the Chinese with 82, and the Indians with 79. (Ibid., p. 74.)

On Morton's methods, see Stephen J. Gould, "The Finagle Factor," *Human Nature* (July 1978).

5. Definitions of race founded upon a common pool of genes have not held up when confronted by scientific research which suggests that the differences *within* a given human population are greater than those between populations. See L.L. Cavalli-Sforza, "The Genetics of Human Populations," *Scientific American,* September 1974, pp. 81–89.

6. Arthur Jensen, "How Much Can We Boost IQ and Scholastic Achievement?" *Harvard Educational Review* 39 (1969):1–123.

7. Ernst Moritz Manasse, "Max Weber on Race," *Social Research* 14 (1947):191–221.

8. Quoted in Edward D. C. Campbell, Jr., *The Celluloid South: Hollywood and the Southern Myth* (Knoxville: University of Tennessee Press, 1981), pp. 168–70.

9. Marvin Harris, *Patterns of Race in the Americas* (New York: Norton, 1964), p. 56.

10. Ibid., p. 57.

11. After James Meredith had been admitted as the first black student at the University of Mississippi, Harry S. Murphy announced that he, and not Meredith, was the first black student to attend "Ole Miss." Murphy described himself as black but was able to pass for white and spent nine months at the institution without attracting any notice (ibid., p. 56).

12. A. Sivanandan, "From Resistance to Rebellion: Asian and Afro-Caribbean Struggles in Britain," *Race and Class* 23(2–3) (Autumn–Winter 1981).

13. Consider the contradictions in racial status which abound in the country with the most rigidly defined racial categories—South Africa. There a race classification agency is employed to adjudicate claims for upgrading of official racial identity. This is particularly necessary for the "coloured" category. The apartheid system considers Chinese as "Asians" while the Japanese are accorded the status of "honorary whites." This logic nearly detaches race from any grounding in skin color and other physical attributes and nakedly exposes race as a juridical category subject to economic, social and political influences. (We are indebted to Steve Talbot for clarification of some of these points.)

14. Gordon W. Allport, *The Nature of Prejudice* (Garden City, NY: Doubleday, 1958), pp. 184–200.

15. We wish to use this phrase loosely, without committing ourselves to a particular position on such social psychological approaches as symbolic interactionism, which are outside the scope of this study. An interesting study on this subject is S.M. Lyman and W.A. Douglass, "Ethnicity: Strategies of Individual and Collective Impression Management," *Social Research* 40(2) (1973).

16. Michael Billig, "Patterns of Racism: Interviews with National Front Members," *Race and Class* 20(2) (Autumn 1978):161–79.

17. "Miss San Antonio USA Lisa Fernandez and other Hispanics auditioning for a role in a television soap-opera did not fit the Hollywood image of real Mexicans and had to darken their faces before filming." Model Aurora Garza said that their faces were bronzed with powder because they looked too white. "'I'm a real Mexican [Garza said] and very dark anyway. I'm even darker right now because I have a tan. But they kept wanting me to make my face darker and darker'" (*San Francisco Chronicle,* 21 September 1984). A similar dilemma faces Asian American actors who feel that Asian character lead roles inevitably go to white actors who make themselves up to be Asian. Scores of Charlie Chan films, for example, have been made with white leads (the last one was the 1981 *Charlie Chan and the Curse of the Dragon Queen*). Roland Winters, who played in six Chan features, was

asked by playwright Frank Chin to explain the logic of casting a white man in the role of Charlie Chan: "'The only thing I can think of is, if you want to cast a homosexual in a show, and get a homosexual, it'll be awful. It won't be funny . . . and maybe there's something there . . .' " (Frank Chin, "Confessions of the Chinatown Cowboy," *Bulletin of Concerned Asian Scholars* 4(3) (Fall 1972)).

18. Melanie Martindale-Sikes, "Nationalizing 'Nigger' Imagery Through 'Birth of a Nation'," paper prepared for the 73rd Annual Meeting of the American Sociological Association, 4–8 September 1978, San Francisco.

19. Jordan, *White over Black,* p. 95; emphasis added.

20. Historical focus has been placed either on particular racially defined groups or on immigration and the "incorporation" of ethnic groups. In the former case the characteristic ethnicity theory pitfalls and apologetics such as functionalism and cultural pluralism may be avoided, but only by sacrificing much of the focus on race. In the latter case, race is considered a manifestation of ethnicity.

21. The degree of antipathy for these groups should not be minimized. A northern commentator observed in the 1850s: "An Irish Catholic seldom attempts to rise to a higher condition than that in which he is placed, while the Negro often makes the attempt with success." Quoted in Gossett, op. cit., p. 288.

22. This analysis, as will perhaps be obvious, is essentially DuBoisian. Its main source will be found in the monumental (and still largely unappreciated) *Black Reconstruction in the United States, 1860–1880* (New York: Atheneum, 1977 [1935]).

23. Alexander Saxton argues that:

    North Americans of European background have experienced three great racial confrontations: with the Indian, with the African, and with the Oriental. Central to each transaction has been a totally one-sided preponderance of power, exerted for the exploitation of nonwhites by the dominant white society. In each case (but especially in the two that began with systems of enforced labor), white workingmen have played a crucial, yet ambivalent, role. They have been both exploited and exploiters. On the one hand, thrown into competition with nonwhites as enslaved or "cheap" labor they suffered economically; on the other hand, being white, they benefited by that very exploitation which was compelling the nonwhites to work for low wages or for nothing. Ideologically they were drawn in opposite directions. *Racial identification cut at right angles to class consciousness.* (Alexander Saxton, *The Indispensable Enemy: Labor and the Anti-Chinese Movement in California* [Berkeley and Los Angeles: University of California Press, 1971], p. 1; emphasis added.)

24. Selig Perlman, *The History of Trade Unionism in the United States* (New York: Augustus Kelley, 1950), p. 52; emphasis added.

25. Whether southern blacks were "peasants" or rural workers is unimportant in this context. Some time during the 1960s blacks attained a higher degree of urbanization than whites. Before World War II most blacks had been rural dwellers and nearly 80 percent lived in the South.

26. See George Gilder, *Wealth and Poverty* (New York: Basic Books, 1981); Charles Murray, *Losing Ground* (New York: Basic Books, 1984).

27. A brilliant study of the racialization process in Britain, focused on the rise of "mugging" as a popular fear in the 1970s, is Stuart Hall et al., *Policing the Crisis* (London: Macmillan, 1978).

28. The case of Vincent Chin, a Chinese American man beaten to death in 1982 by a laid-off Detroit auto worker and his stepson who mistook him for Japanese and blamed him for the loss of their jobs, has been widely publicized in Asian American communities. On immigration conflicts and pressures, see Michael Omi, "New Wave Dread: Immigration and Intra-Third World Conflict," *Socialist Review* 60 (November–December 1981).

3
_____

THEORETICAL PERSPECTIVES IN RACE AND ETHNIC RELATIONS

Joe R. Feagin • Clairece Booher Feagin

Questions to Consider

Which theories outlined by Feagin and Feagin do you believe best explain contemporary race relations in the United States? Do you need to pull together many theories in this reading to best explain the experiences of different racial and ethnic groups in the United States? Can one theory explain or fully capture the dynamics of race and ethnic relations in the United States? Why or why not?

Assimilation and Other Order Perspectives

In the United States much social theorizing has emphasized assimilation, the more or less orderly adaptation of a migrating group to the ways and institutions of an established group. Hirschman has noted that "the assimilation perspective, broadly defined, continues to be the primary theoretical framework for sociological research on racial and ethnic inequality." The reason for this dominance, he suggests, is the "lack of convincing alternatives."[1] The English word *assimilate* comes from the Latin *assimulare*, "to make similar."

Robert E. Park

Robert E. Park, a major sociological theorist, argued that European out-migration was a

major catalyst for societal reorganization around the globe. In his view intergroup contacts regularly go through stages of a *race relations cycle*. Fundamental social forces such as out-migration lead to recurring cycles in intergroup history: "The race relations cycle which takes the form, to state it abstractly, of *contacts, competition, accommodation* and eventual *assimilation,* is apparently progressive and irreversible."[2] In the contact stage migration and exploration bring people together, which in turn leads to economic competition and thus to new social organization. Competition and conflict flow from the contacts between host peoples and the migrating groups. Accommodation, an unstable condition in the race relations cycle, often takes place rapidly. It involves a forced adjustment by a migrating group to a new social situation. . . . Nonetheless, Park and most scholars working in this tradition have argued that there is a long-term trend toward assimilation of racial and ethnic minorities in modern societies. "Assimilation is a process of interpenetration and fusion in which persons and groups acquire the memories, sentiments, and attitudes of other persons or groups, and, by sharing their experience and history, are incorporated with them in a common cultural life."[3] Even racially subordinate groups are expected to assimilate.[4]

Stages of Assimilation: Milton Gordon

Since Park's pioneering analysis in the 1920s, many U.S. theorists of racial and ethnic relations and numerous textbook writers have adopted an assimilationist perspective, although most have departed from Park's framework in a number of important ways. Milton Gordon, author of the influential *Assimilation in American Life*, distinguishes a variety of initial encounters between race and ethnic groups and an array of possible assimilation outcomes. While Gordon presents three competing images of assimilation—the melting pot, cultural pluralism, and Anglo-conformity—he focuses on Anglo-conformity as the descriptive reality. That is, immigrant groups in the United States, in Gordon's view, have typically tended to give up much of their heritage for the dominant, preexisting Anglo-Saxon core culture and society. The touchstone of adjustment is viewed thus: "If there is anything in American life which can be described as an overall American culture which serves as a reference point for immigrants and their children, it can best be described, it seems to us, as the middle-class cultural patterns of, largely, white Protestant, Anglo-Saxon origins, leaving aside for the moment the question of minor reciprocal influences on this culture exercised by the cultures of later entry into the United States."[5]

Gordon notes that Anglo-conformity has been substantially achieved for most immigrant groups in the United States, especially in regard to cultural assimilation. Most groups following the English have adapted to the Anglo core culture. Gordon distinguishes seven dimensions of adaptation:

1. *cultural assimilation:* change of cultural patterns to those of the core society;
2. *structural assimilation:* penetration of cliques and associations of the core society at the primary-group level;
3. *marital assimilation:* significant intermarriage;
4. *identification assimilation:* development of a sense of identity linked to the core society;
5. *attitude-receptional assimilation:* absence of prejudice and stereotyping;
6. *behavior-receptional assimilation:* absence of intentional discrimination;
7. *civic assimilation:* absence of value and power conflict.[6]

Whereas Park believed structural assimilation, including primary-group ties such as intergroup friendships, flowed from cultural assimilation, Gordon stresses that these are separate stages of assimilation and may take place at different rates.

Gordon conceptualizes structural assimilation as relating to primary-group cliques and relations. Significantly, he does not highlight as a separate type of structural assimilation the movement of a new immigrant group into the *secondary groups* of the host society—that is, into the employing organizations, such as corporations or public bureaucracies, and the critical educational and political institutions. The omission of secondary-structural assimilation is a major flaw in Gordon's theory. Looking at U.S. history, one would conclude that assimilating into the core society's secondary groups does *not necessarily* mean entering the dominant group's friendship cliques. In addition, the dimension Gordon calls *civic assimilation* is confusing since he includes in it "values," which are really part of cultural assimilation, and "power," which is a central aspect of structural assimilation at the secondary-group level.

Gordon's assimilation theory has influenced a generation of researchers. . . . In a recent examination of Gordon's seven dimensions of assimilation, J. Allen Williams and Suzanne Ortega drew on interviews with a midwestern sample to substantiate that cultural assimilation was not necessarily the first type of assimilation to occur. For example, the Mexican Americans in the sample were found to be less culturally assimilated than African Americans, yet were more assimilated structurally. Those of Swiss and Swedish backgrounds ranked about the same on the study's measure of cultural assimilation, but the Swedish Americans were less assimilated structurally. Williams and Ortega conclude that assimilation varies considerably from one group to another and that Gordon's seven types can be grouped into three more general categories of structural, cultural, and receptional assimilation.[7]

In a later book, *Human Nature, Class, and Ethnicity* (1978), Gordon has recognized that his assimilation theory neglects power issues and proposed bringing these into his model, but so far he has provided only a brief and inadequate analysis. Gordon mentions in passing the different resources available to competing racial groups and refers briefly to black-white conflict, but gives little attention to the impact of economic power, inequalities in material resources, or capitalistic economic history on U.S. racial and ethnic relations.[8]

Focused on the millions of white European immigrants and their adjustments, Gordon's model emphasizes *generational* changes within immigrant groups over time. Substantial acculturation to the Anglo-Protestant core culture has often been completed by the second or third generation for many European immigrant groups. The par-

tially acculturated first generation formed protective communities and associations, but the children of those immigrants were considerably more exposed to Anglo-conformity pressures in the mass media and in schools.[9] Gordon also suggests that substantial assimilation along certain other dimensions, such as the civic, behavior-receptional, and attitude-receptional ones, has occurred for numerous European groups. Most white groups have also made considerable progress toward equality at the secondary-structural levels of employment and politics, although the dimensions of this assimilation are neither named nor discussed in any detail by Gordon.

For many white groups, particularly non-Protestant ones, structural assimilation at the primary-group level is underway, yet far from complete. Gordon suggests that substantially complete cultural assimilation (for example, adoption of the English language) along with structural (primary-group) pluralism form a characteristic pattern of adaptation for many white ethnic groups. Even these relatively acculturated groups tend to limit their informal friendships and marriage ties either to their immediate ethnic groups or to *similar* groups that are part of their general religious community. Following Will Herberg, who argued that there are three great community "melting pots" in the United States—Jews, Protestants, and Catholics—Gordon suggests that primary-group ties beyond one's own group are often developed with one's broad socioreligious community, whether that be Protestant, Catholic, or Jewish.[10]

In his influential books and articles Gordon recognizes that structural assimilation has been retarded by racial prejudice and discrimination, but he seems to suggest that non-European Americans, including African Americans, will eventually be absorbed into the core culture and society. He gives the most attention to the gradual assimilation of middle-class non-Europeans. In regard to blacks he argues, optimistically, that the United States has "moved decisively down the road toward implementing the implications of the American credo of [equality and justice] for race relations"—as in employment and housing. This perceived tremendous progress for black Americans has created a policy dilemma for the government: should it adopt a traditional political liberalism that ignores race, or a "corporate liberalism" that recognizes group rights along racial lines? Gordon includes under corporate liberalism government programs of affirmative action, which he rejects.[11] . . .

Some assimilation-oriented analysts such as Gordon and Alba have argued that the once prominent ethnic identities, especially of European American groups, are fading over time. Alba suggests that there is still an ethnic identity of consequence for non-Latino whites, but declares that "a new ethnic group is forming—one based on a vague *ancestry* from anywhere on the European continent."[12] In other words, such distinct ethnic identities as English American and Irish American are gradually becoming only a vague identification as "European American," although Alba emphasizes this as a trend, not a fact. Interestingly, research on intermarriages between members of different white ethnic groups has revealed that large proportions of the children of such marriages see themselves as having multiple ethnic identities, while others choose one of their heritages, or simply "American," as their ethnic identity.[13]

Ethnogenesis and Ethnic Pluralism

Some theorists working in the assimilation tradition reject the argument that most European American groups have become substantially assimilated to a generic Anglo-Protestant or Euro-American identity and

way of life. A few have explored models of adjustment that depart from Anglo-conformity in the direction of ethnic or cultural pluralism. Most analysts of pluralism accept some Anglo-conformity as inevitable, if not desirable. In *Beyond the Melting Pot*, Glazer and Moynihan agree that the original customs and home-country ways of European immigrants were mostly lost by the third generation. But this did not mean the decline of ethnicity. The European immigrant groups usually remained distinct in terms of name, identity, and, for the most part, primary-group ties.[14]

Andrew Greeley has developed the interesting concept of *ethnogenesis* and applied it to white immigrant groups, those set off by nationality and religion. Greeley is critical of the traditional assimilation perspective because it assumes "that the strain toward homogenization in a modern industrial society is so great as to be virtually irresistible."[15] Traditionally, the direction of this assimilation in the United States is assumed to be toward the Anglo-Protestant core culture. But from the ethnogenesis perspective, adaptation has meant more than this one-way conformity. The traditional assimilation model does not explain the persistence of ethnicity in the United States— the emphasis among immigrants on ethnicity as a way of becoming American and, in recent decades, the self-conscious attempts to create ethnic identity and manipulate ethnic symbols.[16]

. . . Greeley suggests that in many cases host and immigrant groups had a somewhat similar *cultural* inheritance. For example, some later European immigrant groups had a cultural background initially similar to that of earlier English settlers. As a result of interaction in schools and the influence of the media over several generations the number of cultural traits common to the host and immigrant groups often grew. Yet late in the adaptive process certain aspects of the heritage of the home country remained very important to the character of the immigrant-ethnic group. From this perspective, ethnic groups share traits with the host group *and* retain major nationality characteristics as well. A modern ethnic group is one part home-country heritage and one part common culture, mixed together in a distinctive way because of a unique history of development within the North American crucible.[17]

A number of research studies have documented the persistence of distinctive white ethnic groups such as Italian Americans and Jewish Americans in U.S. cities, not just in New York and Chicago but in San Francisco, New Orleans, and Tucson as well. Yancey and his associates have suggested that ethnicity is an "emergent phenomenon"—that its importance varies in cities and that its character and strength depend on the specific historical conditions in which it emerges and grows.[18]

Some Problems with Assimilation Theories

Most assimilation theorists take as their examples of ethnic adaptation white European groups migrating more or less voluntarily to the United States. But what of the adaptation and assimilation of non-European groups beyond the stage of initial contact? Some analysts of assimilation include non-white groups in their theories, despite the problems that arise from such an inclusion. Some analysts have argued that assimilation, cultural and structural, is the necessary, if long-term, answer to the racial problem in the United States. . . .

More optimistic analysts have emphasized progressive inclusion, which will eventually provide black Americans and other minority groups with full citizenship, in fact as well as principle. For that reason, they expect ethnic and racial conflict to disappear as various groups become fully as-

similated into the core culture and society. Nathan Glazer, Milton Gordon, and Talcott Parsons have stressed the egalitarianism of U.S. institutions and what they view as the progressive emancipation of non-European groups. Gordon and others have underscored the gradual assimilation of middle-class black Americans over the last several decades. Full membership for black Americans seems inevitable, notes Parsons, for "the only tolerable solution to the enormous [racial] tensions lies in constituting a single societal community with full membership for all."[19] The importance of racial, as well as ethnic, stratification is expected to decline as powerful, universalistic societal forces wipe out the vestiges of earlier ethnocentric value systems. White immigrants have desired substantial assimilation, and most have been absorbed. The same is expected to happen eventually for non-European groups.

Assimilation theories have been criticized as having an "establishment" bias, as not distinguishing carefully enough between what *has* happened to a given group and what the establishment at some point felt *should have* happened. For example, a number of Asian American scholars and leaders have reacted vigorously to the application of the concept of assimilation to Asian Americans, arguing that the very concept originated in a period (1870–1925) of intense attacks by white Americans on Asian Americans. The term was thus tainted from the beginning by its association with the dominant European American group's ideology that the only "good groups" were those that assimilated (or could assimilate) in Anglo-conformity fashion.

Unlike Park, who paid substantial attention to the historical and world-economy context of migration, many of today's assimilation theorists do not analyze sufficiently the historical background and development of a particular racial or ethnic group within a national or world context. In addition, assimilation analysts such as Gordon tend to neglect the power imbalance and inequality in racial and ethnic relations, which are seen most clearly in the cases of non-European Americans. As Geschwender has noted, "they seem to have forgotten that exploitation is the driving force that gives meaning to the study of racial and ethnic relations."[20]

Biosocial Perspectives

Some U.S. theorists, including assimilationists, now accent a biosocial perspective on racial and ethnic relations. The idea of race and ethnicity being deeply rooted in the biological makeup of human beings is an old European and American notion that has received renewed attention from a few social scientists and biologists in the United States since the 1970s. In *Human Nature, Class, and Ethnicity,* for example, Gordon suggests that ethnic ties are rooted in the "biological organism of man." Ethnicity is a fundamental part of the physiological as well as the psychological self. Ethnicity "cannot be shed by social mobility, as for instance social class background can, since society insists on its inalienable ascription from cradle to grave." What Gordon seems to have in mind is not the old racist notion of the unchanging biological character and separateness of racial groups, but rather the rootedness of intergroup relation, including racial and ethnic relations, in the everyday realities of kinship and other socially constructed group boundaries. Gordon goes further, however, emphasizing that human beings tend to be "selfish, narcissistic and perpetually poised on the edge of aggression." And it is these selfish tendencies that lie behind racial and ethnic tensions.[21] Gordon is here adopting a Hobbesian (dog-eat-dog) view of human nature. . . .

Although decidedly different from the earlier biological theories, the modern biosocial analysis remains problematical. The exact linkages between the deep genetic underpinnings of human nature and concrete racial or ethnic behavior are not spelled out beyond some vague analysis of kin selection and selfish behavior. . . .

Another difficulty with the biosocial approach is that in the everyday world, racial and ethnic relations are *immediately social* rather than biological. As Edna Bonacich has pointed out, many racial and ethnic groups have mixed biological ancestry. Jewish Americans, for example, have a very mixed ancestry: as a group, they share no distinct biological characteristics. Biologically diverse Italian immigrants from different regions of Italy gained a sense of being Italian American (even Italian) in the United States. The bonds holding Jewish Americans together and Italian Americans together were not genetically based or biologically primordial, but rather the result of real *historical* experiences as these groups settled into the United States. Moreover, if ethnicity is primordial in a biological sense, it should always be a prominent force in human affairs. Sometimes ethnicity leads to recurring conflict, as in the case of Jews and Gentiles in the United States; in other cases, as with Scottish and English Americans, it quietly disappears in the assimilation process. Sentiments based on common ancestry are important, but they are activated primarily in the concrete experiences and histories of specific migrating and host groups.[22]

Emphasizing Migration: Competition Theory

. . . The *human ecology* tradition in sociological thought draws on the ideas of Park and other ecologists and emphasizes the "struggle of human groups for survival" within their physical environments. This tradition, which highlights demographic trends such as the migration of groups and population concentration in cities, has been adopted by competition analysts researching racial and ethnic groups.[23]

Competition theorists such as Susan Olzak and Joane Nagel view ethnicity as a social phenomenon distinguished by boundaries of language, skin color, and culture. They consider the tradition of human ecology valuable because it emphasizes the stability of ethnic population boundaries over time, as well as the impact of shifts in these boundaries resulting from migration; ethnic group membership often coincides with the creation of a distinctive group niche in the labor force. Competition occurs when two or more ethnic groups attempt to secure the same resources, such as jobs or housing. Competition theorists have accented the ways in which ethnic group competition and the accompanying ethnic solidarity lead to collective action, mobilization, and protest.[24]

According to competition theorists, collective action is fostered by immigration across borders and by the expansion of once-segregated minorities into the same labor and housing markets to which other ethnic groups have access. A central argument of these theorists is that collective attacks on a subordinate ethnic group—immigrant and black workers, for instance—increase at the local city level when the group moves up and out of segregated jobs and challenges other groups and not, as one might expect, in cities where ethnic groups are locked into residential segregation and poverty. . . .

Competition theorists explicitly contrast their analyses with the power-conflict views we will discuss in the next section, perspectives that emphasize the role of capitalism, economic subordination, and institutionalized discrimination. Competition theorists write about urban ethnic worlds as though institutionalized racism and capitalism-generated exploitation of workers are not major forces in recurring ethnic and racial

competition in cities. As we have seen, they emphasize migration and population concentration, as well as other demographic factors. . . .

Power-Conflict Theories

The last few decades have witnessed the development of power-conflict frameworks explaining U.S. racial and ethnic relations, perspectives that place much greater emphasis on economic stratification and power issues than one finds in assimilation and competition theories. Within this broad category of power-conflict theories are a number of subcategories, including the internal colonialism viewpoint, and a variety of class-based and neo-Marxist theories. . . .

Internal Colonialism

Analysts of internal colonialism prefer to see the racial stratification and the class stratification of U.S. capitalism as *separate but related* systems of oppression. Neither should be reduced in social science theories to the other. An emphasis on power and resource inequalities, particularly white-minority inequalities, is at the heart of the internal colonialism model.

The framework of internal colonialism is built in part upon the work of analysts of *external colonialism*—the worldwide imperialism of certain capitalist nations, including the United States and European nations.[25] For example, Balandier has noted that capitalist expansion has affected non-European peoples since the fifteenth century: "Until very recently the greater part of the world population, not belonging to the white race (if we exclude China and Japan), knew only a status of dependency on one or another of the European colonial powers."[26] External colonialism involves the running of a country's economy and politics by an outside colonial power. Many colonies eventually became independent of their colonizers, such as Britain or France, but continued to have their economies directed by the capitalists and corporations of the colonial powers. This system of continuing dependency has been called *neocolonialism*. Neocolonialism is common today where there are few white settlers in the colonized country. Colonies experiencing a large in-migration of white settlers often show a different pattern. In such cases external colonialism becomes *internal colonialism* when the control and exploitation of non-European groups in the colonized country passes from whites in the home country to white immigrant groups within the newly independent country.[27]

Non-European groups entering later, such as African slaves and Mexican farm workers in the United States, can also be viewed in terms of internal colonialism. Internal colonialism here emerged out of classical European colonialism and imperialism and took on a life of its own. The origin and initial stabilization of internal colonialism in North America predate the Revolutionary War. The systematic subordination of non-Europeans began with "genocidal attempts by colonizing settlers to uproot native populations and force them into other regions."[28] Native Americans were killed or driven off desirable lands. Slaves from Africa were a cheap source of labor for capital accumulation before and after the Revolution. Later, Asians and Pacific peoples were imported as contract workers or annexed in an expansionist period of U.S. development. Robert Blauner, a colonialism theorist, notes that agriculture in the South depended on black labor; in the Southwest, Mexican agricultural development was forcibly taken over by European settlers, and later agricultural development was based substantially on cheap Mexican labor coming into what was once northern Mexico.[29]

In exploiting the labor of non-European peoples, who were made slaves or were paid low wages, white agricultural and industrial capitalists reaped enormous profits. From the internal colonialism perspective, contemporary racial and ethnic inequality is grounded in the economic *interests* of whites in low-wage labor—the underpinning of capitalistic economic exploitation. Non-European groups were subordinated to European American desires for *labor* and *land*. Internal colonialism theorists have recognized the central role of *government* support of the exploitation of minorities. The colonial and U.S. governments played an important role in legitimating slavery in the sixteenth through the nineteenth centuries and in providing the government soldiers who subordinated Native Americans across the nation and Mexicans in the Southwest.

Most internal colonialism theorists are not concerned primarily with white immigrant groups, many of which entered the United States after non-European groups were subordinated. Instead, they wish to analyze the establishment of racial stratification and the control processes that maintain persisting white dominance and ideological racism. Stokely Carmichael and Charles Hamilton, who in their writings in the 1960s were among the first to use the term *internal colonialism,* accented institutional racism—discrimination by the white community against blacks as a group.[30] From this perspective African Americans are still a "colony" in the United States in regard to education, economics, and politics. . . .

A Neo-Marxist Emphasis on Class

Analysts of racial and ethnic relations have combined an internal colonialism perspective with an emphasis on class stratification that draws on the Marxist research pioneered by [black sociologists W. E. B.] Du Bois and [Oliver] Cox. Mario Barrera, for example, has suggested that the heart of current internal

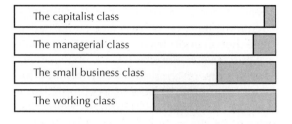

The capitalist class	
The managerial class	
The small business class	
The working class	

FIGURE 1 The Class and Race Structure of Internal Colonialism. *Note:* Shaded area represents nonwhite segment.

colonialism is an interactive structure of class *and* race stratification that divides our society. Class, in the economic-exploitation sense of that term, needs to be central to a colonialism perspective. Basic to the U.S. system of internal colonialism are four classes that have developed in U.S. capitalism:

1. *capitalists:* that small group of people who control capital investments and the means of production and who buy the labor of many others;

2. *managers:* that modest-sized group of people who work as administrators for the capitalists and have been granted control over the work of others;

3. *petit bourgeoisie:* that small group of merchants who control their own businesses and do most of their work themselves, buying little labor power from others;

4. *working class:* that huge group of blue-collar and white-collar workers who sell their labor to employers in return for wages and salaries.

The dominant class in the U.S. political-economic system is the capitalist class, which in the workplace subordinates working people, both nonwhite and white, to its profit and investment needs. And it is the capitalists who decide whether and where to create jobs. They are responsible for the flight of capital and jobs from many central cities to the suburbs and overseas.

Barrera argues that each of these classes contains important segments that are set off in terms of race and ethnicity. Figure 1 suggests how this works. Each of

the major classes is crosscut by a line of racial segmentation that separates those suffering institutionalized discrimination, such as black Americans and Mexican Americans, from those who do not. Take the example of the working class. Although black, Latino, and other minority workers share a similar *class* position with white workers, in that they are struggling against capitalist employers for better wages and working conditions, they are *also* in a subordinate position because of structural discrimination along racial lines within that working class. Barrera notes that the dimensions of this discrimination often include lower wages for many minority workers, as well as their concentration in lower-status occupations. Many Americans suffer from both class exploitation (as wage workers) and racial exploitation (as workers of color).

Ideology and Oppositional Culture

Internal colonialism theorists have studied the role of cultural stereotyping and ideology in limiting the opportunities of subordinate groups of color. A racist ideology dominates an internal colonialist society, intellectually dehumanizing the colonized. Stereotyping and prejudice, seen in many traditional assimilation theories as more or less temporary problems, are viewed by colonialism analysts as a way of rationalizing exploitation over a very long period, if not permanently. Discrimination is a question not of individual bigots but rather of a system of racial exploitation rationalized by prejudice.[31]

In his book on the English colonization of Ireland, Michael Hechter has developed a theory of internal colonialism that emphasizes how the subordinate group utilizes its own culture to *resist* subordination. Hechter argues that in a system of internal colonialism, cultural as well as racial markers are used to set off subordinate groups such as African Americans in the United States and the Irish in the United Kingdom. Resistance to the dominant group by the subordinate group often takes the form of cultural solidarity in opposition to the dominant culture. This solidarity can become the basis for protest movements by the subordinated group.[32]

Beginning in the 1960s, a number of power-conflict scholars and activists have further developed this idea of *oppositional culture* as a basis for understanding the resistance of non-European groups to the Euro-American core culture. Bonnie Mitchell and Joe Feagin have built on the idea of oppositional culture suggested in the work of Hechter and Blauner.[33] They note that in the centuries of contact before the creation of the United States, Mexico, and Canada, North America was populated by a diverse mixture of European, African, and Native American cultures. The U.S. nation created in the late 1700s encompassed African enslavement and the genocide of Native Americans. Faced with oppression, these and other victims of internal colonialism have long drawn on their own cultural resources, as well as their distinctive knowledge of Euro-American culture and society, to resist oppression in every way possible.

The cultures of those oppressed by European Americans have not only provided a source of individual, family, and community resistance to racial oppression and colonialism but have also infused, albeit often in unheralded ways, some significant elements into the evolving cultural mix that consti-

tutes the core culture of the United States. The oppositional cultures of colonized groups such as African Americans, Latino Americans, and Native Americans have helped preserve several key elements of U.S. society, including its tradition of civil rights and social justice. Another key element, ironically enough given the usual white image of minority families, is the value of extended kinship relations. The tendency toward extended kin networks is both culturally encouraged and economically beneficial for oppressed minority groups. For example, research on black and Latino communities has found extensive kinship networks to be the basis of social and economic support in difficult times. Native American groups have also been known for their communalism and extended family networks.[34]

. . . This reality contrasts with the exaggerated stereotypes of endemic family pathology in these groups. Internal colonialism theories accent both the oppression of minority Americans and the oppositional cultures that enable minority groups not only to survive but also to resist oppression, passively and actively.

Criticism of Internal Colonialism Theories

. . . Joan Moore has criticized the term *neocolonialism*. As we have noted, a neocolonial situation is one in which a Third World country (for example, an African country) has separated itself politically from a European colonial power but continues to be dependent on that country. The former colony needs "foreign experts." It has a class of indigenous leaders who help the former colonial power exploit the local population. It has a distinct territorial boundary. Moore suggests that this neocolonialism model does not apply very well to subordinate nonwhite groups in the United States, in that these groups are not generally confined to a specific bounded territory, nor do they contain the exploitative intermediary elite of Third World neocolonialism. This space-centered critique has been repeated by Omi and Winant, who argue that the social and spatial intermixing of white and nonwhite groups in the United States casts serious doubt on the internal colonialism argument about territorially bounded colonization.[35]

However, most internal colonialism researchers have recognized the differences between internal colonial and neocolonial oppression. These theorists note that the situations of minority groups in the United States are different from those of, for instance, Africans in a newly independent nation still dependent on a European country. In response to Moore's critique, internal colonialism analysts might argue that there are many aspects of colonialism evident in U.S. racial and ethnic relations; they might emphasize that non-European groups in the United States (1) are usually residentially segregated, (2) are typically "super-exploited" in employment and deficient in other material conditions when compared with white immigrants, (3) are culturally stigmatized, and (4) have had some of their leaders co-opted by whites. While these conditions in the United States are not defined as precisely as they are in the case of Third World neocolonialism, they are similar enough to allow the use of the idea of colonialism to assess racial and ethnic relations in the United States.

The Split Labor Market View: Another Class-Based Theory

Colonialism analysts such as Blauner are sometimes unclear about whether all classes of whites benefit from the colonization of nonwhites, or just the dominant class of capitalist employers. A power-conflict perspective that helps in assessing this question is the *split labor market* view, which treats class

in the sense of position in the "means of production." This viewpoint has been defended by Edna Bonacich. She argues that in U.S. society the majority-group (white) workers do not share the interests of the dominant political and economic class, the capitalists. Yet both the dominant employer class and the white part of the working class discriminate against the nonwhite part of the working class.[36]

. . . Bonacich emphasizes that discrimination against minority workers by ordinary white workers seeking to protect their own privileges, however limited these may be, is important. Capitalists bring in nonwhite laborers to decrease labor costs, but white workers resist because they fear job displacement or lower wages. For example, over the last century white workers' unions have restricted the access of black workers to many job ladders, thus splitting the labor market and reducing black incomes. . . . White workers gain and lose from this structural racism. They gain in the short run, because there is less competition for privileged job categories from the nonwhites they have excluded. But they lose in the long run because employers can use this cordoned-off sector of nonwhites to undercut them.[37]

"Middleman" Minorities and Ethnic Enclaves

Drawing on insights of earlier scholars, Bonacich has explored the in-between position, in terms of power and resources, that certain racial and ethnic groups have occupied in stratified societies. These groups find their economic niche serving elites and workers as small-business people positioned between producers and consumers. Some ethnic and racial groups become small-scale traders and merchants doing jobs that dominant groups are not eager to do. For example, many first-generation Jewish and Japanese Americans, excluded from mainstream employment by white Protestants, became small-scale merchants, tailors, restaurant operators, or gardeners. These groups have held "a distinctive class position that is of special use to the ruling class." They "act as a go-between to this society's more subordinate groups."[38]

Bonacich and Modell have found that Japanese Americans fit the middleman minority model. Before World War II Japanese Americans resided in highly organized communities. Their local economies were based on self-employment, including gardening and truck farming, and on other nonindustrial family businesses. The group solidarity of the first generation of Japanese Americans helped them establish successful small businesses. However, they faced hostility from the surrounding society, and in fact were driven into the businesses they developed because they were denied other employment opportunities. By the second generation there was some breakdown in the middleman position of Japanese Americans, for many of that generation moved into professional occupations outside the niche economy.[39]

Some middleman minorities, such as Jewish and Korean American merchants in central cities, have become targets of hostility from less well off groups, such as poor African Americans. In addition, strong ethnic bonds can make the middleman group an effective competitor, and even Anglo-Protestant capitalists may become hostile toward an immigrant middleman minority that competes too effectively. Thus Jewish Americans have been viewed negatively by better-off Anglo-Protestant merchants, who have the power to discriminate against them, as well as by poor black renters and customers with whom Jews deal as middleman landlords and merchants. . . .

A somewhat similar perspective, *enclave theory*, examines secondary-structural incorporation into the economy, especially the ways in which certain non-European immigrant groups have created social and economic enclaves in cities. Both the middleman and the enclave perspectives give more emphasis to economic inequality and discrimination than assimilation perspectives, and they stress the incorporation of certain groups, such as Asians and Cubans, into the United States through the means of small businesses and specialized ethnic economies. The major differences between the two viewpoints seem to stem from the examples emphasized. Groups accented by enclave theorists, such as Cuban Americans, have created ethnic enclaves that are more than merchant or trading economies—they often include manufacturing enterprises, for example. In addition, ethnic enclaves usually compete with established Anglo-Protestant business elites. In contrast, the middleman minorities and those described as enclave minorities develop trading economies and are likely to fill an economic niche that *complements* that of established white elites. However, the aforementioned research of Bonacich on Jewish Americans suggests that there is little difference between the real-world experiences of those described as middleman minorities. . . .

Women and Gendered Racism: New Perspectives

Most theories of racial and ethnic relations have neglected gender stratification, the hierarchy in which men as a group dominate women as a group in terms of power and resources. In recent years a number of scholars have researched the situations of women within racial and ethnic groups in the United States. Their analyses assess the ways in which male supremacy, or a patriarchal system, interacts with and operates within a system of racial and ethnic stratification. Discussing racial and ethnic cultures

around the globe, Adrienne Rich has defined a *patriarchal system* as "a familial-
social, ideological, political system in which
men—by force, direct pressure, or through
ritual, tradition, law and language, customs,
etiquette, education, and the division of
labor—determine what part women shall or
shall not play, and in which the female is
everywhere subsumed under the male."[40]

Asking whether racism or patriarchy
has been the primary source of oppression,
social psychologist Philomena Essed examined black women in the United States and
the Netherlands.[41] She found racism and sexism interacting regularly. The oppression of
black women can be seen as *gendered racism.*
For example, under slavery African American women were exploited not only for labor
but also as sex objects for white men. And after slavery they were excluded from most
job categories available to white men and
white women; major employment changes
came only with the civil rights movement of
the 1960s. Today racism has many gendered
forms. In the U.S. mass media the white female is the standard for female beauty. Minority women are often stereotyped as
matriarchs in female-headed families and
are found disproportionately in lower-status
"female jobs," such as typists. Some women
of color are closely bound in their social relations with those who oppress them in such
areas as domestic employment ("maids")
and other low-paid service work.[42]

In her book *Black Feminist Thought*
Patricia Hill Collins argues that a black feminist theoretical framework can help highlight and analyze the negative stereotypes of
black women in white society—the stereotypes of the docile mammy, the domineering matriarch, the promiscuous whore, and
the irresponsible welfare mother. These severely negative images persist among many
whites because they undergird white discrimination against black women in the
United States.[43]

Scholars assessing the situations of
other women of color, including Native
American, Asian, and Latino women, have
similarly emphasized the cumulative and
interactive character of racial and gender
oppression and the necessity of liberating
these women from white stereotypes and
discrimination. For example, Denise Segura
has examined labor-force data on Mexican
American women and developed the concept
of "triple oppression," the mutually reinforcing and interactive set of race, class, and gender forces whose cumulative effects "place
women of color in a subordinate social and
economic position relative to men of color
and the majority white population."[44]

Class, the State, and Racial Formation

Looking at the important role of governments in creating racial and ethnic designations and institutionalizing discrimination,
Michael Omi and Howard Winant have developed a theory of *racial formation.* Racial
tensions and oppression, in their view, cannot be explained solely in terms of class or
nationalism. Racial and ethnic relations are
substantially defined by the actions of governments, ranging from the passing of legislation, such as restrictive immigration laws,
to the imprisonment of groups defined as a
threat (for example, Japanese Americans in
World War II). Although the internal colonialism viewpoint gives some emphasis to
the state's role in the exploitation of nonwhite minorities, it has not developed this
argument sufficiently.

Omi and Winant note that the U.S. government has shaped the politics of race: the
U.S. Constitution and a lengthy series of laws
openly defined racial groups and interracial
relationships (for example, slavery) in racist
terms. The U.S. Constitution counted each
African American slave as three-fifths of a
person, and the Naturalization Law of 1790

explicitly declared that only *white* immigrants could qualify for naturalization. Many non-Europeans, including Africans and Asians, were prevented from becoming citizens. Japanese and other Asian immigrants, for example, were until the 1950s banned by law from becoming citizens. In 1854 the California Supreme Court ruled that Chinese immigrants should be classified as "Indians" (!), therefore denying them the political rights available to white Americans.[45]

For centuries, the U.S. government officially favored northern European immigrant groups over non-European and southern European groups such as Italians. For example, the Immigration Act of 1924 was used to exclude Asian immigrants and most immigrants from southern and eastern Europe, whom political leaders in Congress saw as racially inferior and as a threat to their control of the society. North European Americans working through the government thereby shaped the subsequent racial and ethnic mix that is the United States.

Another idea accented by Omi and Winant is that of *social rearticulation,* the recurring historical process of rupturing and reconstructing the understandings of race in this country. The social protest movements of various racial and ethnic groups periodically challenge the governments' definition of racial realities, as well as individual definitions of those realities. The 1960s civil rights movement, for instance, rearticulated traditional cultural and political ideas about race in the United States, and in the process changed the U.S. government and broadened the involvement of minority Americans in the politics of that government. New social movements regularly emerge, sometimes bringing new identities and political norms.[46]

Resistance to the Dominant Group

Recent research has highlighted the many ways in which powerless groups fight back against the powerful. One power-conflict theorist who has made an important contribution to our understanding of how the oppressed react to oppression is James Scott. Influenced by the work of scholars such as John Gaventa on the many "faces of power" Scott has shown that at the heart of much interaction between the powerless and the powerful is intentional deception.[47] For example, the African American slaves were not free to speak their minds to their white masters, but they did create a crucial discourse among themselves that was critical of their white oppressors. Scott cites a proverb of African slaves on the Caribbean island of Jamaica: "Play fool, to catch wise." Looking closely at the lives of slaves and the poor everywhere, Scott has developed the idea of a backstage discourse by the oppressed that includes views that cannot be discussed in public for fear of retaliation. In addition to secret ideological resistance on the part of slaves and other poor people, a variety of other resistance tactics are used, including foot-dragging, pilfering, dissimulation, and flight. Scott cites Afro-Christianity as an example of how African American slaves resisted the "ideological hegemony" (attempts to brainwash) of white slavemasters. In public religious services African American slaves controlled their gestures and facial expressions and pretended to accept Christian preaching about meekness and obedience. Backstage, where no whites were present, Afro-Christianity emphasized "themes of deliverance and redemption, Moses and the Promised Land, the Egyptian captivity, and emancipation."[48] For slaves the Promised Land meant the North and freedom, and the afterlife was often viewed as a place where the slaves' enemies would be severely punished.

Historian Sterling Stuckey has noted that slave spirituals, although obviously affected by Christianity, "take on an altogether new coloration when one looks at slave religion on the plantations where most slaves were found and where African religion, contrary to the accepted scholarly wisdom, was practiced." The religion of African Americans mixed African and European elements from the beginning. Yet at its core the expressive, often protest-inclined African values prevailed over the European values.[49] Stuckey has shown that African culture and religion were major sources of the slaves' inclination to rebellion. The work of Scott and Stuckey can be linked to the analyses of Hechter and Mitchell and Feagin that we cited previously, for they too have accented the role of an oppositional culture in providing the foundation of resistance to racial oppression.

We can conclude this discussion of the most important critical power-conflict theories by underscoring certain recurring themes:

1. a central concern for racial and ethnic inequalities in economic position, power, and resources;

2. an emphasis on the links of racial inequalities to the economic institutions of capitalism and to the subordination of women under patriarchal systems;

3. an emphasis on the role of the government in legalizing exploitation and segregation and in defining racial and ethnic relations;

4. an emphasis on resistance to domination and oppression by those oppressed.

NOTES

1. Charles Hirschman, "America's Melting Pot Reconsidered," *Annual Review of Sociology* 9 (1983): 397–423.

2. Robert E. Park, *Race and Culture* (Glencoe, IL: Free Press, 1950), p. 150 (italics added).

3. Robert E. Park and Ernest W. Burgess, *Introduction to the Science of Society* (Chicago: University of Chicago Press, 1924), p. 735.

4. Janice R. Hullum, "Robert E. Park's Theory of Race Relations" (M.A. thesis, University of Texas, 1973), pp. 81–88; Park and Burgess, *Introduction to the Science of Society*, p. 760.

5. Milton M. Gordon, *Assimilation in American Life* (New York: Oxford University Press, 1964), pp. 72–73.

6. Ibid., p. 71.

7. Silvia Pedraza, *Political and Economic Migrants in America: Cubans and Mexicans* (Austin: University of Texas Press, 1985), pp. 5–7; Richard Alba, *Ethnic Identity: The Transformation of White America* (New Haven, CT: Yale University Press, 1990), p. 311; J. Allen Williams and Suzanne T. Ortega, "Dimensions of Assimilation," *Social Science Quarterly* 71 (1990):697–709.

8. Milton M. Gordon, *Human Nature, Class, and Ethnicity* (New York: Oxford University Press, 1978), pp. 67–89.

9. Gordon, *Assimilation in American Life*, pp. 78–108.

10. See Will Herberg, *Protestant—Catholic—Jew*, rev. ed. (Garden City, NY: Doubleday, Anchor Books, 1960).

11. Milton M. Gordon, "Models of Pluralism: The New American Dilemma," *Annals of the American Academy of Political and Social Science* 454 (1981):178–88.

12. Alba, *Ethnic Identity*, p. 3.

13. Stanley Lieberson and Mary Waters, "Ethnic Mixtures in the United States," *Sociology and Social Research* 70 (1985):43–53: Cookie White Stephan and Walter Stephan, "After Intermarriage," *Journal of Marriage and the Family* 51 (May 1989):507–19.

14. Nathan Glazer and Daniel P. Moynihan, *Beyond the Melting Pot* (Cambridge, MA: M.I.T. Press and Harvard University Press, 1963).

15. Andrew M. Greeley, *Ethnicity in the United States* (New York: Wiley, 1974), p. 293.

16. Ibid., pp. 295–301.

17. Ibid., p. 309.

18. William L. Yancey, D. P. Ericksen, and R. N. Juliani, "Emergent Ethnicity: A Review and Reformulation," *American Sociological Review* 41 (June 1976):391–93. See also Greeley, *Ethnicity in the United States*, pp. 290–317.

19. Talcott Parsons, "Full Citizenship for the Negro American? A Sociological Problem," in *The Negro American*, edited by Talcott Parsons and Kenneth B. Clark (Boston: Houghton Mifflin, 1965–66), p. 740.

20. James Geschwender, *Racial Stratification in America* (Dubuque, IA: Brown, 1978), p. 58.

21. Gordon, *Human Nature, Class, and Ethnicity*, pp. 73–78. See also Clifford Geertz, "The Integrative Revolution," in *Old Societies and New States*, edited by Clifford Geertz (New York: Free Press, 1963), p. 109.

22. Edna Bonacich, "Class Approaches to Ethnicity and Race," *Insurgent Sociologist* 10 (Fall 1980):11.

23. Frederik Barth, "Introduction," in *Ethnic Groups and Boundaries: The Social Organization of Culture Difference* (Oslo: Universitets Forlaget, 1969), pp. 10–17.

24. Susan Olzak, "A Competition Model of Collective Action in American Cities," in *Competitive Ethnic Relations*, edited by Susan Olzak and Joane Nagel (Orlando, FL: Academic Press, 1986), pp. 17–46.

25. Ronald Bailey and Guillermo Flores, "Internal Colonialism and Racial Minorities in the U.S.: An Overview," in *Structures of Dependency*, edited by Frank Bonilla and Robert Girling (Stanford, CA: privately published by a Stanford faculty–student seminar, 1973), pp. 151–53.

26. G. Balandier, "The Colonial Situation: A Theoretical Approach," in *Social Change*, ed. Immanuel Wallerstein (New York: Wiley, 1966), p. 35.

27. Pablo Gonzalez-Cassanova, "Internal Colonialism and National Development," in *Latin American Radicalism*, edited by Irving L. Horowitz et al. (New York: Random House, 1969), p. 130; Bailey and Flores, "Internal Colonialism," p. 156.

28. Bailey and Flores, "Internal Colonialism," p. 156.

29. Blauner, *Racial Oppression in America*, p. 55. Our analysis of internal colonialism draws throughout on Blauner's provocative discussion.

30. Stokely Carmichael and Charles Hamilton, *Black Power* (New York: Random House, Vintage Books, 1967), pp. 2–7.

31. Guillermo B. Flores, "Race and Culture in the Internal Colony: Keeping the Chicano in His Place," in *Structures of Dependency*, edited by Bonilla and Girling, p. 192.

32. Michael Hechter, *Internal Colonialism* (Berkeley: University of California Press, 1975), pp. 9–12; Michael Hechter, "Group Formation and the Cultural Division of Labor," *American Journal of Sociology* 84 (1978): 293–318; Michael Hechter, Debra Friedman, and Malka Applebaum, "A Theory of Ethnic Collective Action," *International Migration Re-*

view 16 (1982):412–34. See also Geschwender, *Racial Stratification in America*, p. 87.

33. Joe Feagin and Bonnie Mitchell, "America's Non-European Cultures: The Myth of the Melting Pot," in *The Inclusive University: Multicultural Perspectives in Higher Education*, edited by Benjamin Bowser, Gale Auletta, and Terry Jones (forthcoming).

34. Carol B. Stack, "Sex Roles and Survival Strategies in an Urban Black Community," in *Women, Culture and Society*, edited by Michelle Zimbalist Rosaldo and Louise Lamphere (Stanford, CA: Stanford University Press, 1974), p. 128; Ronald Angel and Marta Tienda, "Determinants of Extended Household Structure: Cultural Pattern or Economic Need?" *American Journal of Sociology* 87 (1981–82):1360–83.

35. Joan W. Moore, "American Minorities and 'New Nation' Perspectives," *Pacific Sociological Review* 19 (October 1976):448–55; Michael Omi and Howard Winant, *Racial Formation in the United States* (New York: Routledge & Kegan Paul, 1986), pp. 47–49.

36. Bonacich, "Class Approaches to Ethnicity and Race," p. 14.

37. Barrera, *Race and Class in the Southwest*, pp. 201–203; Bonacich, "Class Approaches to Ethnicity and Race," p. 14.

38. Bonacich, "Class Approaches to Ethnicity and Race," pp. 14–15.

39. Edna Bonacich and John Modell, *The Economic Basis of Ethnic Solidarity* (Berkeley: University of California Press, 1980), pp. 1–37. For a critique, see Eugene Wong, "Asian American Middleman Minority Theory: The Framework of an American Myth," *Journal of Ethnic Studies* 13 (Spring 1985): 51–87.

40. Quoted in Michael Albert et al., *Liberating Theory* (Boston: South End Press, 1986), p. 35.

41. Philomena Essed, *Understanding Everyday Racism* (Newbury Park, CA: Sage, 1991), pp. 30–32.

42. Ibid., p. 32.

43. Patricia Hill Collins, *Black Feminist Thought: Knowledge, Consciousness, and the Politics of Empowerment* (Boston: Unwin Hyman, 1990), pp. 40–48.

44. Denise A. Segura, "Chicanas and Triple Oppression in the Labor Force," in *Chicana Voices: Intersections of Class, Race and Gender*, edited by Teresa Cordova et al. (Austin, TX: Center for Mexican American Studies, 1986), p. 48.

45. Omi and Winant, *Racial Formation in the United States*, pp. 75–76.
46. Howard Winant, "Racial Formation Theory and Contemporary U.S. Politics," in *Exploitation and Exclusion*, edited by Abebe Zegeye, Leonard Harris, and Julia Maxted (London: Hans Zell, 1991), pp. 130–40.
47. James C. Scott, *Domination and the Arts of Resistance* (New Haven, CT: Yale University Press, 1990); John Gaventa, *Power and Powerlessness* (Urbana: University of Illinois Press, 1980).
48. Scott, *Domination and the Arts of Resistance*, p. 116.
49. Sterling Stuckey, *Slave Culture* (New York: Oxford University Press, 1987), pp. 27, 42–46.

. . . Contemporary Trends

4

AN OVERVIEW OF TRENDS IN SOCIAL AND ECONOMIC WELL-BEING, BY RACE

Rebecca M. Blank

Questions to Consider

In this reading, Rebecca Blank discusses seven indicators of well-being for various racial and ethnic groups in the United States. List her seven indicators on the side of a piece of paper and write white, black, Hispanic, Asian and American Indian across the top of the page. For each group and quality of life indicator, place a plus sign (+), an equal sign (=), or a minus sign (–) to indicate how well or poorly a group is doing relative to one another. A plus sign (+) would mean that group is doing well compared to other groups, an equal sign (=) would mean that group is holding its own, and a minus sign (–) would mean that group is faring poorly compared to other groups. Which group or groups received the greatest number of pluses, minuses, or equal signs? How do you explain group-level disparities in these quality of life indicators?

Introduction

In general, there are many signs of improvement across all racial and ethnic groups in a wide variety of measures of measures of well-being, such as educational achievement, health status, and housing quality. In some cases, disparities between different racial groups have narrowed, as all groups have experienced improvements. But in too many cases, overall improvement in well-being among all groups has brought about no lessening of racial or ethnic disparities. In a few key measures, disparities have actually widened. The primary conclusion of this paper is that race and ethnicity continue to be salient predictors of well-being in American society. To understand what is happening in America today and what will be happening in America tomorrow, one must understand the role of race.

Indicators of Well-Being

This chapter discusses trends in seven areas:

1. population/demographic change,
2. education,
3. labor markets,
4. economic status,
5. health status,
6. crime and criminal justice, and
7. housing and neighborhoods.

Wherever possible, trends over time are presented for key variables, focusing on five major population groups: non-Hispanic Whites, non-Hispanic Blacks, Hispanics,

Rebecca M. Blank, "An Overview of Trends in Social and Economic Well-Being, by Race" from *America Becoming: Racial Trends and Their Consequences*, Vol. 1, National Academies Press, 2001, pp. 21–39. Reprinted with permission from *America Becoming*.

Asian and Pacific Islanders, and American Indians and Alaska Natives. These data are taken almost entirely from U.S. government sources. In many cases, however, data for all groups are not available, or not available for the entire time period. Data available for as many groups as possible are presented in the 14 figures. The term "minority" is used to refer to a group that composes a minority of the total population. Although these five groups are currently minorities in the population, current trends project they will, together, constitute more than half the U.S. population by 2050.

This brief introduction does not attempt to provide anything like a comprehensive discussion of the available data.[1] Provided here is an overview of some of the more interesting trends, particularly focusing on issues that introduce key topics that will be addressed in this book. One particular limitation of these data is that they present averages across very large aggregate categories pf racial and ethnic classification. This hides much of the rather important information about subgroups. For instance, although data for Dominican and Cuban Americans might show very different trends, they are both combined within the Hispanic category. Similarly, Japanese and Laotian Americans are grouped together in the Asian and Pacific Islander category; Italian and Norwegian Americans are grouped together as non-Hispanic Whites.

An Increasingly Diverse Population

The U.S. population is becoming increasingly diverse. Hispanics, non-Hispanic Blacks, Asian and Pacific Islanders, and American Indians and Alaska Natives currently constitute 27 percent of the population. By 2005, Hispanics will be the largest of these groups in the United States, surpassing non-Hispanic Blacks. These changes will present this nation with a variety of social and economic opportunities and challenges.

Recent high levels of immigration are also increasing diversity within these groups. At present, 38 percent of Hispanics are foreign-born; 61 percent of Asian and Pacific Islanders are foreign-born. This raises questions of assimilation and generational change. Will the second generation among these groups show a narrowing of the disparities that distinguish their foreign-born parents from the U.S.-born population?

Where people live and who they live next to is important in determining how individuals experience racial and ethnic diversity. The population in the West is the most diverse, with more than one-third of the population composed of racial and ethnic minorities. The West is also the region where a higher percentage of Hispanics, Asian and Pacific Islanders, and American Indians and Alaska Natives reside. The South is the second most diverse region and has the largest percentage of non-Hispanic Blacks. The Midwest is the region with the least population diversity; 85 percent of its population is non-Hispanic Whites.

The household structure of these different groups varies greatly. Household structure, based on data for 1970 and 1996, correlates with a variety of other variables, particularly variables relating to economic well-being. More adults in a family means more potential earnings as well as more available adults to care for children. Single-parent households are among the poorest groups in the country. Individuals who live alone are also often more economically vulnerable than are persons who live with other family members.

All groups show significant increases in the number of people living alone or in single-parent families between 1970 and 1996, but the percentage living in single-parent families is much larger among Blacks, Hispanics, and American Indians and Alaska Natives. In fact, the biggest recent percentage of all families are in single-father families, rather than single-mother families, although single-father families continue to be a small percentage of all families. The reasons for these trends—and why some groups have much larger percentages of single-parent families in particular—are much debated.

Household structure is closely related to age distribution as well. Minority populations have a significantly larger percentage of children under the age of 17 than do non-Hispanic Whites, whereas Whites have a much larger percentage of elderly persons. The result is that the school-aged population—persons aged 5 to 17—is more racially and ethnically diverse than the population as a whole, so that today's schools reflect tomorrow's more diverse adult population—and also mirror some of the conflicts and the benefits that accompany growing diversity.

Educational Attainment

In a society growing increasingly complex, educational skills are key to future life opportunities. Disparities in education are fundamental because they can determine lifetime earning opportunities and influence an individual's ability to participate in civic activities as well.

The labor market of the twenty-first century will rely increasingly on computers; thus, obtaining computer skills is fundamental. Figure 1 shows how children's access to computers has changed over time, both in their schools and in their homes. Clearly, more and more children have access to computers, particularly in their schools; but there is an ongoing gap in computer use between White children versus Black and Hispanic children. Between 1984 and 1993, the years for which these data are available,

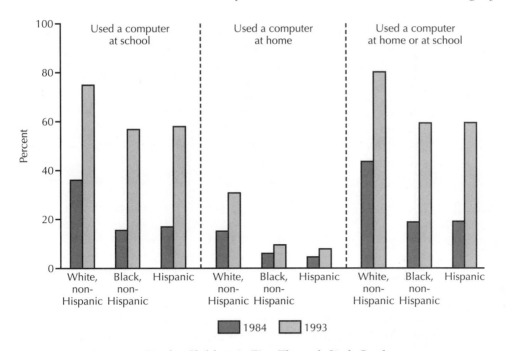

FIGURE 1   Computer Use by Children in First Through Sixth Grades. *Source:* Council of Economic Advisers (1998).

this gap increased for computer use at home, leaving children in minority groups further behind.

Other more conventional measures of achievement in elementary and secondary schooling have generally shown narrowing gaps across racial groups. Mathematics proficiency scores, as measured among children of different ages by the National Assessment of Educational Progress, have shown ongoing gains, particularly by Black children. High school completion continues to inch up among both Whites and Blacks, with substantially greater progress among Blacks; so that the White-Black high school dropout rates are slowly converging over time. Among Hispanics, high school completion has been stagnant at approximately 60 percent since the early 1980s. Hence, the gap between Hispanics and other groups in terms of educational achievement is widening.

Figure 2 shows trends in attainment of college degrees, through 1997, among Whites, Blacks, and Hispanics. Economic returns to a college education have increased dramatically in recent years, and college degrees continue to be an important credential for entry into many white-collar jobs. Although college completion has increased steeply among Whites, it has increased only modestly among Blacks, leading to a widening gap since the early 1990s. Among Hispanics, college completion rates are not much higher now than they were in the mid-1980s.

The more stagnant educational trends among Hispanics reflect, in part, the growing immigrant percentage of that population. Immigrants are less likely to hold high school or college degrees. U.S.-born Hispanics are making progress in increasing both their high school and college completion levels, but this progress is being diluted by

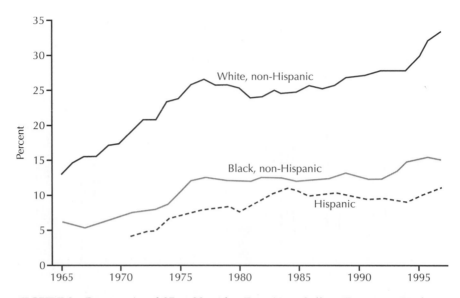

FIGURE 2   Persons Aged 25 to 29 with a Four-Year College Degree or Higher. Prior to 1971, data for Whites include Hispanic Whites, and data for Blacks include Hispanic Blacks. Data for non-Hispanic Blacks and Hispanics are three-year centered averages. Prior to 1991, data are for persons having completed four or more years of college. *Source:* Council of Economic Advisers (1998).

the growing pool of less-educated immigrants. This re-emphasizes the question of how second-generation Hispanic children will fare. If they follow the trends of other U.S.-born populations, Hispanic educational attainment will start to increase over time.

Labor-Market Involvement

Involvement in the labor force means integration with the mainstream U.S. economy. Earnings are the primary source of income for most persons. Although job-holding may create some stress, it also produces economic rewards. Access to jobs is key for economic progress.

Figure 3 plots the labor-force participation rates from the 1950s to 1997 for Whites, Blacks, and Hispanics, by gender. The chart shows rapidly increasing convergence in labor-force participation rates, as men's rates have slowly decreased while women's rates

have increased steadily. White women, who used to be much less likely to work than Black women, are now just as likely to be in the labor force. In fact, both White women's and Black women's labor-force participation rates are rapidly converging with those of Black men, who have experienced steady decreases in work involvement.

Hispanic women also have shown increases in labor-force participation, but remain much less likely to work than other women. A major question for the Hispanic population is whether adult women will show rapid increases in labor-force participation, to the level of women from other groups. Such changes in women's labor-market involvement not only mean changes in the economic base of families—and probably in the economic security and decision-making power of husbands versus wives—but may also mean substantial changes in family functioning and in child-rearing practices.

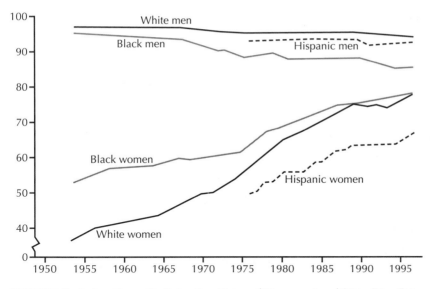

FIGURE 3 Labor Force Participation Rates of Persons Aged 25 to 54.   Prior to 1972, data for Blacks include all non-Whites. *Source:* Council of Economic Advisers (1998).

Along with labor-force participation, unemployment is another measure of access (or lack of access) to jobs. After two decades of higher unemployment rates, unemployment in the late 1990s was at 25-to-30-year lows among all groups. The differentials between groups, however, remained quite large. For instance, unemployment rates among Blacks have consistently been at least twice as high as those of Whites.

The labor-market issue that has received the most attention in recent years is wage opportunities. Figure 4 plots median weekly earnings among male and female full-time workers from 1965 through the first two quarters of 1998. Among all groups, men's wages decreased steadily from 1980 until 1995, when there was evidence of an upturn. The pay gap between White and Black men changed little, however, with no sign of relative progress in wages for Black men. Hispanic men have actually seen decreases in both absolute and relative wages, compared with White and Black men. Again, this pattern is at least partially the result of the

growing percentage of less-educated immigrants in the Hispanic population.

In contrast, women have not experienced wage decreases. In fact, White women's wages have grown slowly since the 1980s, so that they now earn more than both Hispanic and Black men. Black women's wages have been largely stagnant, although they show a recent upturn; and Hispanic women's wages have decreased slightly. Thus, the wage gap between White women and both Black and Hispanic women has increased.

Economic Status

Continued and even growing gaps in earnings imply that the economic situation is not improving for minority populations relative to the White population. Other measures of family economic well-being reinforce this conclusion. Figure 5 shows median family income for Asian and Pacific Islanders, non-Hispanics Whites, Hispanics, and Blacks

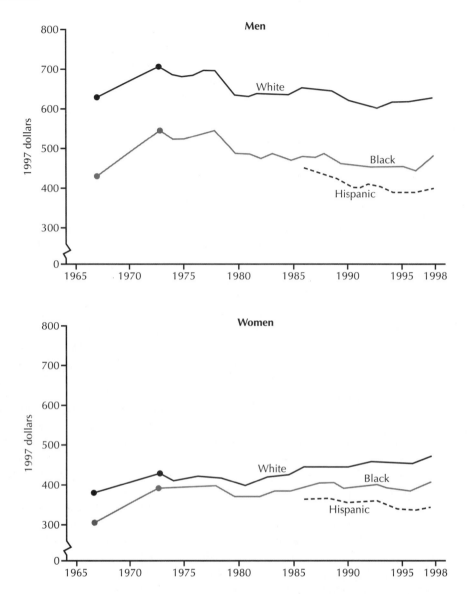

FIGURE 4   Median Weekly Earnings of Male and Female Full-Time Workers. Straight line between dots indicates data are not available for intervening years. Prior to 1979, data for Blacks include all non-Whites. Data for 1998 are from the first two quarters. *Source:* Council of Economic Advisers (1998).

through 1996. Family income is probably the most widely used measure of overall economic well-being. Among non-Hispanic Whites, family income has been rising steadily. Essentially, the growth in female labor-force participation and increases in

White women's wages have resulted in more family income, even though men's earnings have deteriorated somewhat. Asian families earn even more than Whites. Black family income has been relatively stagnant since the 1970s, although there

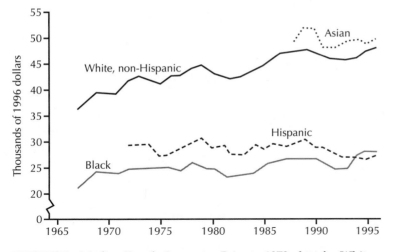

FIGURE 5   Median Family Income.   Prior to 1972, data for Whites include Hispanic Whites. *Source:* Council of Economic Advisers (1998).

were signs of increase after 1993. Hispanic family income decreased in the 1990s.

This means that income differentials have widened between Whites and Asian and Pacific Islanders on the upper end of the income brackets and Blacks and Hispanics on the lower end. American Indians and Alaska Natives, for whom we only have data from the 1990 Census, show lower income than Blacks in that year.

These median family income numbers hide very different experiences at different points in the income distribution. Households headed by less skilled workers—particularly those headed by single parents—have generally experienced income decreases over the past several decades. Households headed by a person with a college degree have generally experienced income increases.

One might be particularly concerned with the number of families at very low income levels. Figure 6 shows poverty rates among individuals by racial group, indicating the percentage of the population in each group living in families with incomes below the official U.S. poverty line, which was less than $8,000 per year in the late 1990s. In general, poverty rates have been relatively flat

since the early 1970s. About 10 percent of the White population has been poor over this period. Asian and Pacific Islanders show a slightly higher poverty rate, underscoring the diversity within the Asian and Pacific Islander populations—they have both higher median incomes than Whites as well as higher poverty rates, reflecting the fact that at least some Asian groups are experiencing economic difficulties.

Black poverty has also been relatively constant, but at nearly 30 percent—three times the White poverty rate. Hispanic poverty rates are now higher than Black poverty rates. Poverty rates among subgroups, such as children or the elderly, show similar differentials between racial and ethnic groups.

Health Status

Economic well-being is often closely linked to other aspects of well-being, such as health status. Interestingly, health differences do not necessarily show the same patterns as economic differences. Infant-mortality rates provide a primary indicator of both health status and access to health care in a

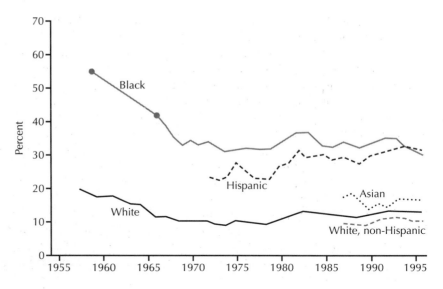

FIGURE 6   Poverty Rates for Individuals.   Straight line between dots indicates data not available for intervening years. *Source:* Council of Economic Advisers (1998).

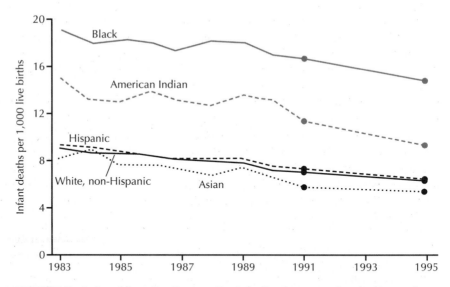

FIGURE 7   Infant Mortality Rates.   Straight line between dots indicates data not available for intervening years. *Source:* Council of Economic Advisers (1998).

population. Figure 7 plots infant-mortality rates by race from the early 1980s through 1995. Infant mortality has been steadily decreasing among all groups, indicating major health improvements within all populations. The disparities between groups, how-ever, have remained largely constant. Black infant-mortality rates are about two-and-a-half times White rates. American Indian and Alaska Native rates have fallen a bit faster than other groups, but remain well above White rates.

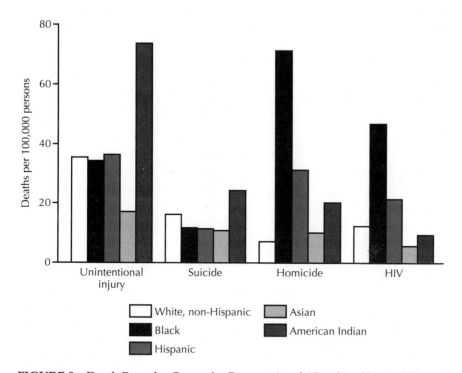

FIGURE 8 Death Rates by Cause, for Persons Aged 15 to 34, 1996 to 1995. Data for 1994 and 1995 are averaged to provide more reliable estimates. HIV data for American Indians are for 1993–1995. *Source:* Council of Economic Advisers (1998).

Figure 7 also shows a pattern visible in much health data—namely, although Hispanics show substantial educational and economic differentials, they show far fewer health differentials. Hispanic infant-mortality rates are almost identical to White and Asian and Pacific Islander infant mortality rates.

Clearly, smoking is a health issue that emerges in adolescence. Smoking is correlated with a shorter life expectancy and greater health risks. In general, smoking rates have fallen for both young women and men over the past 30 years; and this is one of the few indicators where Blacks and Hispanics do better than Whites. Black smoking rates have fallen faster than White rates, so that young Blacks, who used to be more likely to smoke than Whites, are now less likely to smoke.

In contrast, Figure 8 shows death rates among 15- to 34-year-olds in the mid-1990s. There are very large differences in death rates by cause among different racial groups. American Indians and Alaska Natives are far more likely to die as a result of unintentional injuries—typically automobile accidents—and suicide. Blacks are far more likely to die as a result of homicide and HIV infection. These differences emphasize that living conditions and health-risk factors are quite different among different populations.

Crime and Criminal Justice

There is no single aggregate measure of the likelihood of being a victim of crime. Figure 9 plots homicide rates, which constitute a small percentage of all crimes but are among

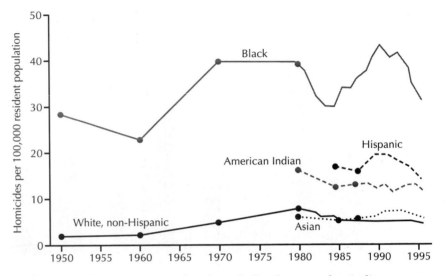

FIGURE 9   Victims of Homicide.   Straight line between dots indicates data not available for intervening years. Data include deaths from "legal intervention" (use of police force). Prior to 1985, data for Whites include Hispanic Whites. Prior to 1970, data include nonresidents. *Source:* Council of Economic Advisers (1998).

the best measured crime statistics (few homicides go unnoticed or unreported). Figure 9 shows that Blacks are far more likely to be homicide victims than is any other group. The homicide victimization rate of Blacks is more than twice that of Hispanics and six times that of non-Hispanic Whites and Asian and Pacific Islanders. American Indian and Alaska Native homicide rates are about twice those of Whites and Asian and Pacific Islanders, and slightly below those of Hispanics. Although public discussion often focuses on the higher likelihood that Blacks will be arrested for crimes, there is little discussion of the fact that Blacks are also much more likely to be victims. There are large disparities by race in both the likelihood of being a victim of a crime, as well as in the likelihood of being arrested and incarcerated by the criminal justice system. Although other crime statistics, such as property crimes, show smaller racial disparities, they also show higher victimization among minority groups.

Data on experience within the criminal justice system are largely tabulated only for Whites and Blacks, and hence provide less comprehensive measures across racial groups. Blacks are far more likely to be arrested and incarcerated than are Whites. Some of these differences reflect differences in the crimes for which Blacks are disproportionately arrested, and some may reflect discriminatory behavior on the part of the police and other persons within the criminal justice system. In 1995, more than 9 percent of the Black population was under correctional supervision, either on probation or parole, or in jail or prison, compared to 2 percent of the White population. Among young Black men 20 to 29 years old, more than 25 percent are under correctional supervision. Because arrests and prison stays often fracture families and reduce future labor-market opportunities, these high rates of involvement with the criminal justice system are correlated with the reduced economic opportunities of Black families.

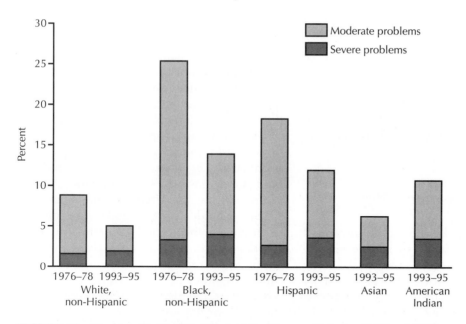

FIGURE 10   Housing Units with Physical Problems.   Data for 1976 and 1978, or 1993 and 1995, are averaged to provide more reliable estimates. Data for Asians exclude Hispanic Asians, and data for American Indians exclude Hispanic American Indians. *Source:* Council of Economic Advisers (1998).

Housing and Neighborhoods

Where people live, and the housing they live in, is correlated with their health and economic status. Increasing concern among social scientists about "neighborhood effects"—the influence of peers and of neighborhood characteristics on individual health and behavior—has raised interest in housing and neighborhood issues. Figure 10 shows the percentage of populations living in housing units with physical problems, such as substandard plumbing or heating as well as electrical and other serious upkeep problems. All groups for which we have data, from the mid-1970s to the mid-1990s, show substantial improvement in housing quality; but, as in other areas, large disparities remain across groups. Non-Hispanic Blacks, Hispanics, and American Indians and Alaska Natives are far more likely to live in substandard housing than are Whites

or Asian and Pacific Islanders. Other measures of housing adequacy, such as crowding, show similar trends, with overall improvement among all groups, butcontinuing large disparities between groups.

Information about neighborhoods raises again the question of where people live and who they live next to. The diversity of a person's neighborhood can affect his or her overall sense of national diversity and knowledge of members of other races or ethnicities.

Whites are by far the most segregated population, even more than their larger population percentage would justify. The average White person lives in a neighborhood that is more than 80 percent White. Blacks are the next most segregated, living in neighborhoods that are, on average, about 60 percent Black and 30 percent White.

Hispanics live in neighborhoods that have close to equal amounts (about 40 percent each) of Whites and Hispanics. Asian and Pacific Islanders live in the most diverse neighborhoods, composed of a mix of Whites, Blacks, Hispanics, and other Asian and Pacific Islanders. This suggests that these two population groups are experiencing and living in the midst of diversity in this country to a much greater degree than Whites or Blacks.

What Do These Disparities Mean?

This very quick and quite limited review of some of the key indicators of economic and social well-being underscores the ongoing importance of disparities by race and by Hispanic origin in U.S. society. Of course, there are multiple reasons behind these disparities. Many of the other chapters in this book summarize what the research literature indicates about the causes and effects of racial disparities in key areas of society. Three over-arching conclusions, based on the data, are presented here.

First, race and Hispanic origin continue to be defining characteristics for many Americans. They are correlated with educational and economic opportunities, with health status, and with where people live and who they live next to. The magnitude of these differences, especially for Blacks and Hispanics, is extremely significant on average, suggesting that these disparities are widely experienced. Relative to the White and Asian populations, the Black population on average has only two-fifths as many college graduates, three-fourths as much earnings, and only slightly more than one-half as much income. The Hispanic population fares even worse. Although we do not have as much comparable information for American Indians and Alaska Natives, their data tend to be closer to those of Blacks and Hispanics than to those of Whites. Whatever their causes, these are substantial differentials; they shape our life opportunities and they shape our

opinions about behavior toward each other. To repeat the point I started with at the beginning of this chapter, race continues to be a salient predictor of well-being in America.

Second, the growing presence of Hispanic and Asian and Pacific Islander populations is fundamentally changing the face of America. The displacement of Blacks as the largest minority group in the population in the early 2000s may cause some political and social tension. High numbers of immigrants within the Hispanic and Asian and Pacific Islander groups make questions of assimilation and second-generation progress particularly important in the years ahead. If second-generation Hispanic women behave more like other U.S.-born women, there will be many more Hispanic families with wives in the labor market two decades from now. If second-generation Hispanics acquire education at the rate of other U.S.-born populations, the education levels within the Hispanic community will rise substantially.

Third, Whites may be less aware of the changes and the challenges of growing population diversity than any other group. In part, there is often a "blindness" among the majority to the situation of other groups, because their own situation is typically taken as the norm. This "blindness" is reinforced by locational patterns and neighborhood choice. Whites are much more likely to live in the Midwest than other groups, the least diverse part of the nation; and they tend to live in the most segregated neighborhoods in the other regions. In contrast, Asian and Pacific Islanders—who do as well as Whites on many measures of well-being—live in much more diverse neighborhoods and are almost surely more aware of issues relating to diversity and difference, even when these issues do not translate into personal economic differentials. In short, the growing population of Hispanics and Asian and Pacific Islanders, as well as many Blacks, may be better prepared to address the challenges, and to take the advantage of the benefits, of an increasingly diverse population than are Whites.

This introduction has provided a set of data-based "snapshots" of diversity and differentials by race and Hispanic origin in some key areas. The rest of this book provides in-depth examinations of these same key areas. The chapters that follow look beneath the averages and the aggregate snapshots and disclose a nuanced sense of how and why racial differentials continue to exist, and how they have been influenced by policy choices.

Acknowledgments

The opinions expressed in this paper reflect the personal views of the author and not the official position of the Council of Economic Advisers. I thank all my staff at the CEA who worked on putting together the information summarized here.

REFERENCE

COUNCIL OF ECONOMIC ADVISERS. 1998. *Changing America: Indicators of Social and Economic Well-Being by Race and Hispanic Origin*. Washington, D.C.: U.S. Government Printing Office.

NOTES

1. See Council of Economic Advisers (1998) for a more comprehensive discussion of all data presented here, as well as other related data. Data and trends discussed in this paper are all documented and discussed in greater detail in this publication.

Race as Chameleon: How the Idea of Race Changes over Time

5

DRAWING THE COLOR LINE

Howard Zinn

Questions to Consider

In this article, Howard Zinn chronicles the beginning of slavery in North America. How did law, custom, and culture reconcile the emergence of chattel slavery with Christian precepts, which reject the idea that one human could own or forcibly control another human being? What arguments were used to justify slavery? List which groups profited from the slave trade.

A black American writer, J. Saunders Redding, describes the arrival of a ship in North America in the year 1619:

Sails furled, flag drooping at her rounded stern, she rode the tide in from the sea. She was a strange ship, indeed, by all accounts, a frightening ship, a ship of mystery. Whether she was trader, privateer, or man-of-war no one knows. Through her bulwarks black-mouthed cannon yawned. The flag she flew was Dutch; her crew a motley. Her port of call, an English settlement, Jamestown, in the colony of Virginia. She came, she traded, and shortly afterwards was gone. Probably no ship in modern history has carried a more portentous freight. Her cargo? Twenty slaves.

There is not a country in world history in which racism has been more important, for so long a time, as the United States. And the problem of "the color line," as W. E. B. Du Bois put it, is still with us. So it is more than a purely historical question to ask: How does it start?—and an even more urgent question: How might it end? Or, to put it differently: Is it possible for whites and blacks to live together without hatred?

If history can help answer these questions, then the beginnings of slavery in North America—a continent where we can trace the coming of the first whites and the first blacks—might supply at least a few clues.

Some historians think those first blacks in Virginia were considered as servants, like the white indentured servants brought from Europe. But the strong probability is that, even if they were listed as "servants" (a more familiar category to the English), they were viewed as being different from white

From *A People's History of the United States,* pp. 23–38, by Howard Zinn. Copyright © 1980 by Howard Zinn. Reprinted by permission of HarperCollins Publishers, Inc.

servants, were treated differently, and in fact were slaves. In any case, slavery developed quickly into a regular institution, into the normal labor relation of blacks to whites in the New World. With it developed that special racial feeling—whether hatred, or contempt, or pity, or patronization—that accompanied the inferior position of blacks in America for the next 350 years—that combination of inferior status and derogatory thought we call racism.

Everything in the experience of the first white settlers acted as a pressure for the enslavement of blacks.

The Virginians of 1619 were desperate for labor, to grow enough food to stay alive. Among them were survivors from the winter of 1609–1610, the "starving time," when, crazed for want of food, they roamed the woods for nuts and berries, dug up graves to eat the corpses, and died in batches until five hundred colonists were reduced to sixty.

In the *Journals* of the House of Burgesses of Virginia is a document of 1619 which tells of the first twelve years of the Jamestown colony. The first settlement had a hundred persons, who had one small ladle of barley per meal. When more people arrived, there was even less food. Many of the people lived in cavelike holes dug into the ground, and in the winter of 1609–1610, they were

. . . driven thru insufferable hunger to eat those things which nature most abhorred, the flesh and excrements of man as well of our own nation as of an Indian, digged by some out of his grave after he had lain buried three days and wholly devoured him; others, envying the better state of body of any whom hunger has not yet so much wasted as their own, lay wait and threatened to kill and eat them; one among them slew his wife as she slept in his bosom, cut her in pieces, salted her and fed upon her till he had clean devoured all parts saving her head. . . .

A petition by thirty colonists to the House of Burgesses, complaining against the twelve-year governorship of Sir Thomas Smith, said:

> In those 12 years of Sir Thomas Smith, his government, we aver that the colony for the most part remained in great want and misery under most severe and cruel laws. . . . The allowance in those times for a man was only eight ounces of meale and half a pint of peas for a day . . . mouldy, rotten, full of cobwebs and maggots, loathsome to man and not fit for beasts, which forced many to flee for relief to the savage enemy, who being taken again were put to sundry deaths as by hanging, shooting and breaking upon the wheel . . . of whom one for stealing two or three pints of oatmeal had a bodkin thrust through his tongue and was tied with a chain to a tree until he starved. . . .

The Virginians needed labor, to grow corn for subsistence, to grow tobacco for export. They had just figured out how to grow tobacco, and in 1617 they sent off the first cargo to England. Finding that, like all pleasurable drugs tainted with moral disapproval, it brought a high price, the planters, despite their high religious talk, were not going to ask questions about something so profitable.

They couldn't force Indians to work for them, as Columbus had done. They were outnumbered, and while, with superior firearms, they could massacre Indians, they would face massacre in return. They could not capture them and keep them enslaved; the Indians were tough, resourceful, defiant, and at home in these woods, as the transplanted Englishmen were not.

White servants had not yet been brought over in sufficient quantity. Besides, they did not come out of slavery, and did not have to do more than contract their labor for a few years to get their passage and a start in the New World. As for the free white settlers, many of them were skilled craftsmen, or even men of leisure back in England, who were so little inclined to work the land that John Smith, in those early years, had to declare a kind of martial law, organize them into work gangs, and force them into the fields for survival.

There may have been a kind of frustrated rage at their own ineptitude, at the Indian superiority at taking care of themselves, that made the Virginians especially ready to become the masters of slaves. Edmund Morgan imagines their mood as he writes in his book *American Slavery, American Freedom:*

> If you were a colonist, you knew that your technology was superior to the Indians'. You knew that you were civilized, and they were savages. . . . But your superior technology had proved insufficient to extract anything. The Indians, keeping to themselves, laughed at your superior methods and lived from the land more abundantly and with less labor than you did. . . . And when your own people started deserting in order to live with them, it was too much. . . . So you killed the Indians, tortured them, burned their villages, burned their cornfields. It proved your superiority, in spite of your failures. And you gave similar treatment to any of your own people who succumbed to their savage ways of life. But you still did not grow much corn. . . .

Black slaves were the answer. And it was natural to consider imported blacks as slaves, even if the institution of slavery would not be regularized and legalized for several decades. Because, by 1619, a million blacks had already been brought from Africa to South America and the Caribbean, to the Portuguese and Spanish colonies, to work as slaves. Fifty years before Columbus, the Portuguese took ten African blacks to Lisbon—this was the start of a regular trade in slaves. African blacks had been stamped as slave labor for a hundred years. So it would have been strange if those twenty blacks, forcibly transported to Jamestown, and sold as objects to settlers anxious for a steadfast source of labor, were considered as anything but slaves.

Their helplessness made enslavement easier. The Indians were on their own land. The whites were in their own European culture. The blacks had been torn from their land and culture, forced into a situation where the heritage of language, dress, custom, family relations, was bit by bit obliterated except for the remnants that blacks could hold on to by sheer, extraordinary persistence.

Was their culture inferior—and so subject to easy destruction? Inferior in military capability, yes—vulnerable to whites with guns and ships. But in no other way—except that cultures that are different are often taken as inferior, especially when such a judgment is practical and profitable. Even militarily, while the Westerners could secure forts on the African coast, they were unable to subdue the interior and had to come to terms with its chiefs.

The African civilization was as advanced in its own way as that of Europe. In certain ways, it was more admirable; but it also included cruelties, hierarchical privilege, and the readiness to sacrifice human lives for religion or profit. It was a civilization of 100 million people, using iron implements and skilled in farming. It had large urban centers and remarkable achievements in weaving, ceramics, sculpture.

European travelers in the sixteenth century were impressed with the African kingdoms of Timbuktu and Mali, already stable and organized at a time when European states were just beginning to develop into the modern nation. In 1563, Ramusio, secretary to the rulers in Venice, wrote to the Ital-

ian merchants: "Let them go and do business with the King of Timbuktu and Mali and there is no doubt that they will be well-received there with their ships and their goods and treated well, and granted the favours that they ask. . . ."

A Dutch report, around 1602, on the West African kingdom of Benin, said: "The Towne seemeth to be very great, when you enter it. You go into a great broad street, not paved, which seemeth to be seven or eight times broader than the Warmoes Street in Amsterdam. . . . The Houses in this Towne stand in good order, one close and even with the other, as the Houses in Holland stand."

The inhabitants of the Guinea Coast were described by one traveler around 1680 as "very civil and good-natured people, easy to be dealt with, condescending to what Europeans require of them in a civil way, and very ready to return double the presents we make them."

Africa had a kind of feudalism, like Europe based on agriculture, and with hierarchies of lords and vassals. But African feudalism did not come, as did Europe's, out of the slave societies of Greece and Rome, which had destroyed ancient tribal life. In Africa, tribal life was still powerful, and some of its better features—a communal spirit, more kindness in law and punishment—still existed. And because the lords did not have the weapons that European lords had, they could not command obedience as easily.

In his book *The African Slave Trade*, Basil Davidson contrasts law in the Congo in the early sixteenth century with law in Portugal and England. In those European countries, where the idea of private property was becoming powerful, theft was punished brutally. In England, even as late as 1740, a child could be hanged for stealing a rag of cotton. But in the Congo, communal life persisted, the idea of private property was a strange one, and thefts were punished with fines or various degrees of servitude. A Congolese leader, told of the Portuguese legal codes, asked a Portuguese once, teasingly: "What is the penalty in Portugal for anyone who puts his feet on the ground?"

Slavery existed in the African states, and it was sometimes used by Europeans to justify their own slave trade. But, as Davidson points out, the "slaves" of Africa were more like the serfs of Europe—in other words, like most of the population of Europe. It was a harsh servitude, but they had rights which slaves brought to America did not have, and they were "altogether different from the human cattle of the slave ships and the American plantations." In the Ashanti Kingdom of West Africa, one observer noted that "a slave might marry; own property; himself own a slave; swear an oath; be a competent witness and ultimately become heir to his master. . . . An Ashanti slave, nine cases out of ten, possibly became an adopted member of the family, and in time his descendants so merged and intermarried with the owner's kinsmen that only a few would know their origin."

One slave trader, John Newton (who later became an antislavery leader), wrote about the people of what is now Sierra Leone:

> The state of slavery, among these wild barbarous people, as we esteem them, is much milder than in our colonies. For as, on the one hand, they have no land in high cultivation, like our West India plantations, and therefore no call for that excessive, unintermitted labour, which exhausts our slaves: so, on the other hand, no man is permitted to draw blood even from a slave.

African slavery is hardly to be praised. But it was far different from plantation or mining slavery in the Americas, which was lifelong, morally crippling, destructive of family ties, without hope of any future. African slavery lacked two elements that made American slavery the most cruel form of slavery in history: the frenzy for limitless profit that comes from capitalistic agriculture; the reduction of the slave to less than human status by the use of racial hatred, with that relentless clarity based on color, where white was master, black was slave.

In fact, it was because they came from a settled culture, of tribal customs and family ties, of communal life and traditional ritual, that African blacks found themselves especially helpless when removed from this. They were captured in the interior (frequently by blacks caught up in the slave trade themselves), sold on the coast, then shoved into pens with blacks of other tribes, often speaking different languages.

The conditions of capture and sale were crushing affirmations to the black African of his helplessness in the face of superior force. The marches to the coast, sometimes for 1,000 miles, with people shackled around the neck, under whip and gun, were death marches, in which two of every five blacks died. On the coast, they were kept in cages until they were picked and sold. One John Barbot, at the end of the seventeenth century, described these cages on the Gold Coast:

> As the slaves come down to Fida from the inland country, they are put into a booth or prison . . . near the beach, and when the Europeans are to receive them, they are brought out onto a large plain, where the ship's surgeons examine every part of everyone of them, to the smallest member, men and women being stark naked. . . . Such as are allowed good and sound are set on one side . . . marked on the breast with a red-hot iron, imprinting the mark of the French, English, or Dutch companies. . . . The branded slaves after this are returned to their former booths where they await shipment, sometimes 10–15 days. . . .

Then they were packed aboard the slave ships, in spaces not much bigger than coffins, chained together in the dark, wet slime of the ship's bottom, choking in the stench of their own excrement. Documents of the time describe the conditions:

The height, sometimes, between decks, was only eighteen inches; so that the unfortunate human beings could not turn around, or even on their sides, the elevation being less than the breadth of their shoulders; and here they are usually chained to the decks by the neck and legs. In such a place the sense of misery and suffocation is so great, that the Negroes . . . are driven to frenzy.

On one occasion, hearing a great noise from belowdecks where the blacks were chained together, the sailors opened the hatches and found the slaves in different stages of suffocation, many dead, some having killed others in desperate attempts to breathe. Slaves often jumped overboard to drown rather than continue their suffering. To one observer a slave-deck was "so covered with blood and mucus that it resembled a slaughter house."

Under these conditions, perhaps one of every three blacks transported overseas died, but the huge profits (often double the investment on one trip) made it worthwhile for the slave trader, and so the blacks were packed into the holds like fish.

First the Dutch, then the English, dominated the slave trade. (By 1795 Liverpool had more than a hundred ships carrying slaves and accounted for half of all the European slave trade.) Some Americans in New England entered the business, and in 1637 the first American slave ship, the *Desire*, sailed from Marblehead. Its holds were partitioned into racks, 2 feet by 6 feet, with leg irons and bars.

By 1800, 10 to 15 million blacks had been transported as slaves to the Americas, representing perhaps one-third of those originally seized in Africa. It is roughly estimated that Africa lost 50 million human beings to death and slavery in those centuries we call the beginnings of modern Western civilization, at the hands of slave traders and plantation owners in Western Europe and America, the countries deemed the most advanced in the world.

In the year 1610, a Catholic priest in the Americas named Father Sandoval wrote back to a church functionary in Europe to ask if the capture, transport, and enslavement of African blacks was legal by church doctrine. A letter dated March 12, 1610, from Brother Luis Brandaon to Father Sandoval gives the answer:

Your Reverence writes me that you would like to know whether the Negroes who are sent to your parts have been legally captured. To this I reply that I think your Reverence should have no scruples on this point, because this is a matter which has been questioned by the Board of Conscience in Lisbon, and all its members are learned and conscientious men. Nor did the bishops who were in Sao Thome, Cape Verde, and here in Loando—all learned and virtuous men—find fault with it. We have been here ourselves for forty years and there have been among us very learned Fathers . . . never did they consider the trade as illicit. Therefore we and the Fathers of Brazil buy these slaves for our service without any scruple. . . .

With all of this—the desperation of the Jamestown settlers for labor, the impossibility of using Indians and the difficulty of using whites, the availability of blacks offered in greater and greater numbers by profit-seeking dealers in human flesh, and with such blacks possible to control because they had just gone through an ordeal which if it did not kill them must have left them in a state of psychic and physical helplessness— is it any wonder that such blacks were ripe for enslavement?

And under these conditions, even if some blacks might have been considered servants, would blacks be treated the same as white servants?

The evidence, from the court records of colonial Virginia, shows that in 1630 a white man named Hugh Davis was ordered "to be soundly whipt . . . for abusing himself . . . by defiling his body in lying with a Negro." Ten years later, six servants and "a negro of Mr. Reynolds" started to run away. While the whites received lighter sentences, "Emanuel the Negro to receive thirty stripes and to be burnt in the cheek with the letter R, and to work in shackle one year or more as his master shall see cause."

Although slavery was not yet regularized or legalized in those first years, the lists of servants show blacks listed separately. A law passed in 1639 decreed that "all persons except Negroes" were to get arms and ammunition—probably to fight off Indians. When in 1640 three servants tried to run away, the two whites were punished with a lengthening of their service. But, as the court put it, "the third being a negro named John Punch shall serve his master or his assigns for the time of his natural life." Also in 1640, we have the case of a Negro woman servant who begot a child by Robert Sweat, a white man. The court ruled "that the said negro woman shall be whipt at the whipping post and the said Sweat shall tomorrow in the forenoon do public penance for his offense at James citychurch. . . ."

This unequal treatment, this developing combination of contempt and oppression, feeling and action, which we call "racism"— was this the result of a "natural" antipathy of white against black? The question is important, not just as a matter of historical accuracy, but because any emphasis on "natural" racism lightens the responsibility of the social system. If racism can't be shown to be natural, then it is the result of certain conditions, and we are impelled to eliminate those conditions.

We have no way of testing the behavior of whites and blacks toward one another under favorable conditions—with no history of subordination, no money incentive for exploitation and enslavement, no desperation for survival requiring forced labor. All the conditions for black and white in seventeenth-century America were the opposite of that, all powerfully directed toward antagonism and mistreatment. Under such conditions even the slightest display of humanity between the races might be considered evidence of a basic human drive toward community.

Sometimes it is noted that, even before 1600, when the slave trade had just begun, before Africans were stamped by it—literally and symbolically—the color black was distasteful. In England, before 1600, it meant, according to the *Oxford English Dictionary*: "Deeply stained with dirt; soiled, dirty, foul. Having dark or deadly purposes, malignant; pertaining to or involving death, deadly; baneful, disastrous, sinister. Foul, iniquitous, atrocious, horribly wicked. Indicating disgrace, censure, liability to punishment, etc." And Elizabethan poetry often used the color white in connection with beauty.

It may be that, in the absence of any other overriding factor, darkness and blackness, associated with night and unknown, would take on those meanings. But the presence of another human being is a powerful fact, and the conditions of that presence are crucial in determining whether an initial prejudice, against a mere color, divorced from humankind, is turned into brutality and hatred.

In spite of such preconceptions about blackness, in spite of special subordination of blacks in the Americas in the seventeenth century, there is evidence that where whites and blacks found themselves with common problems, common work, common enemy in their master, they behaved toward one another as equals. As one scholar of slavery, Kenneth Stampp, has put it, Negro and white servants of the seventeenth century were "remarkably unconcerned about the visible physical differences."

Black and white worked together, fraternized together. The very fact that laws had to be passed after a while to forbid such relations indicates the strength of that tendency. In 1661 a law was passed in Virginia that "in case any English servant shall run away in company of any Negroes" he would have to give special service for extra years to the master of the runaway Negro. In 1691, Virginia provided for the banishment of any "white man or woman being free who shall intermarry with a negro, mulatoo, or Indian man or woman bond or free."

There is an enormous difference between a feeling of racial strangeness, perhaps fear, and the mass enslavement of millions of black people that took place in the Americas. The transition from one to the other cannot be explained easily by "natural" tendencies. It is not hard to understand as the outcome of historical conditions.

Slavery grew as the plantation system grew. The reason is easily traceable to something other than natural racial repugnance: the number of arriving whites, whether free or indentured servants (under four to seven years contract), was not enough to meet the need of the plantations. By 1700, in Virginia, there were 6,000 slaves, one-twelfth of the population. By 1763, there were 170,000 slaves, about half the population.

Blacks were easier to enslave than whites or Indians. But they were still not easy to enslave. From the beginning, the imported black men and women resisted their enslavement. Ultimately their resistance was controlled, and slavery was established for 3 million blacks in the South. Still, under the most difficult conditions, under pain of mutilation and death, throughout their two hundred years of enslavement in North America, these Afro-Americans continued to rebel. Only occasionally was there an organized insurrection. More often they showed their refusal to submit by running away. Even more often, they engaged in sabotage, slowdowns, and subtle forms of resistance which asserted, if only to themselves and their brothers and sisters, their dignity as human beings.

The refusal began in Africa. One slave trader reported that Negroes were "so wilful and loth to leave their own country, that they have often leap'd out of the canoes, boat and ship into the sea, and kept under water till they were drowned."

When the very first black slaves were brought into Hispaniola in 1503, the Spanish governor of Hispaniola complained to the Spanish court that fugitive Negro slaves were teaching disobedience to the Indians. In the 1520s and 1530s, there were slave revolts in Hispaniola, Puerto Rico, Santa Marta, and what is now Panama. Shortly after those rebellions, the Spanish established a special police for chasing fugitive slaves.

A Virginia statute of 1669 referred to "the obstinacy of many of them," and in 1680 the Assembly took note of slave meetings "under the pretense of feasts and brawls" which they considered of "dangerous consequence." In 1687, in the colony's Northern Neck, a plot was discovered in which slaves planned to kill all the whites in the area and escape during a mass funeral.

Gerald Mullin, who studied slave resistance in eighteenth-century Virginia in his work *Flight and Rebellion,* reports:

> The available sources on slavery in 18th-century Virginia—plantation and county records, the newspaper advertisements for runaways—describe rebellious slaves and few others. The slaves described were lazy and thieving; they feigned illnesses, destroyed crops, stores, tools, and sometimes

attacked or killed overseers. They operated blackmarkets in stolen goods. Runaways were defined as various types, they were truants (who usually returned voluntarily), "outlaws" . . . and slaves who were actually fugitives: men who visited relatives, went to town to pass as free, or tried to escape slavery completely, either by boarding ships and leaving the colony, or banding together in cooperative efforts to establish villages or hide-outs in the frontier. The commitment of another type of rebellious slave was total; these men became killers, arsonists, and insurrectionists.

Slaves recently from Africa, still holding on to the heritage of their communal society, would run away in groups and try to establish villages of runaways out in the wilderness, on the frontier. Slaves born in America, on the other hand, were more likely to run off alone, and, with the skills they had learned on the plantation, try to pass as free men.

In the colonial papers of England, a 1729 report from the lieutenant governor of Virginia to the British Board of Trade tells how "a number of Negroes, about fifteen . . . formed a design to withdraw from their Master and to fix themselves in the fastnesses of the neighboring Mountains. They had found means to get into their possession some Arms and Ammunition, and they took along with them some Provisions, their Cloths, bedding and working Tools. . . . Tho' this attempt has happily been defeated, it ought nevertheless to awaken us into some effectual measures. . . ."

Slavery was immensely profitable to some masters. James Madison told a British visitor shortly after the American Revolution that he could make $257 on every Negro in a year, and spend only $12 or $13 on his keep. Another viewpoint was of slaveowner Landon Carter, writing about fifty years earlier,

complaining that his slaves so neglected their work and were so uncooperative ("either cannot or will not work") that he began to wonder if keeping them was worthwhile.

Some historians have painted a picture—based on the infrequency of organized rebellions and the ability of the South to maintain slavery for two hundred years—of a slave population made submissive by their condition; with their African heritage destroyed, they were, as Stanley Elkins said, made into "Sambos," "a society of helpless dependents." Or as another historian, Ulrich Phillips, said, "by racial quality submissive." But looking at the totality of slave behavior, at the resistance of everyday life, from quiet noncooperation in work to running away, the picture becomes different.

In 1710, warning the Virginia Assembly, Governor Alexander Spotswood said:

> . . . freedom wears a cap which can without a tongue, call together all those who long to shake off the fetters of slavery and as such an Insurrection would surely be attended with most dreadful consequences so I think we cannot be too early in providing against it, both by putting our selves in a better posture of defence and by making a law to prevent the consultations of those Negroes.

Indeed, considering the harshness of punishment for running away, that so many blacks did run away must be a sign of a powerful rebelliousness. All through the 1700s, the Virginia slave code read:

> Whereas many times slaves run away and lie hid and lurking in swamps, woods, and other obscure places, killing hogs, and commiting other injuries to the inhabitants . . . if the slave does not immediately return, anyone whatsoever may kill or destroy such slaves by such ways

and means as he . . . shall think fit . . . . If the slave is apprehended . . . it shall . . . be lawful for the county court, to order such punishment for the said slave, either by dismembering, or in any other way . . . as they in their discretion shall think fit, for the reclaiming any such incorrigible slave, and terrifying others from the like practices. . . .

Mullin found newspaper advertisements between 1736 and 1801 for 1,138 men runaways, and 141 women. One consistent reason for running away was to find members of one's family—showing that despite the attempts of the slave system to destroy family ties by not allowing marriages and by separating families, slaves would face death and mutilation to get together.

In Maryland, where slaves were about one-third of the population in 1750, slavery had been written into law since the 1660s, and statutes for controlling rebellious slaves were passed. There were cases where slave women killed their masters, sometimes by poisoning them, sometimes by burning tobacco houses and homes. Punishments ranged from whipping and branding to execution, but the trouble continued. In 1742, seven slaves were put to death for murdering their master.

Fear of slave revolt seems to have been a permanent fact of plantation life. William Byrd, a wealthy Virginia slaveowner, wrote in 1736:

We have already at least 10,000 men of these descendants of Ham, fit to bear arms, and these numbers increase every day, as well by birth as by importation. And in case there should arise a man of desperate fortune, he might with more advantage than Cataline kindle a servile war . . . and tinge our rivers wide as they are with blood.

It was an intricate and powerful system of control that the slaveowners developed to maintain their labor supply and their way of life, a system both subtle and crude, involving every device that social orders employ for keeping power and wealth where it is. As Kenneth Stampp puts it:

A wise master did not take seriously the belief that Negroes were natural-born slaves. He knew better. He knew that Negroes freshly imported from Africa had to be broken into bondage; that each succeeding generation had to be carefully trained. This was no easy task, for the bondsman rarely submitted willingly. Moreover, he rarely submitted completely. In most cases there was no end to the need for control—at least not until old age reduced the slave to a condition of helplessness.

The system was psychological and physical at the same time. The slaves were taught discipline, were impressed again and again with the idea of their own inferiority to "know their place," to see blackness as a sign of subordination, to be awed by the power of the master, to merge their interest with the master's, destroying their own individual needs. To accomplish this there was the discipline of hard labor, the breakup of the slave family, the lulling effects of religion (which sometimes led to "great mischief," as one slaveholder reported), the creation of disunity among slaves by separating them into field slaves and more privileged house slaves, and finally the power of law and the immediate power of the overseer to invoke whipping, burning, mutilation, and death. Dismemberment was provided for in the Virginia Code of 1705. Maryland passed a law in 1723 providing for cutting off the ears of blacks who struck whites, and that for certain serious crimes, slaves should be hanged and the body quartered and exposed.

Still, rebellions took place—not many, but enough to create constant fear among white planters. The first large-scale revolt in the North American colonies took place in New York in 1712. In New York, slaves were 10 percent of the population, the highest proportion in the northern states, where economic conditions usually did not require large numbers of field slaves. About twenty-five blacks and two Indians set fire to a building, then killed nine whites who came on the scene. They were captured by soldiers, put on trial, and twenty-one were executed. The governor's report to England said: "Some were burnt, others were hanged, one broke on the wheel, and one hung alive in chains in the town. . . ." One had been burned over a slow fire for eight to ten hours—all this to serve notice to other slaves.

A letter to London from South Carolina in 1720 reports:

> I am now to acquaint you that very lately we have had a very wicked and barbarous plot of the designe of the negroes rising with a designe to destroy all the white people in the country and then to take Charles Town in full body but it pleased God it was discovered and many of them taken prisoners and some burnt and some hang'd and some banish'd.

Around this time there were a number of fires in Boston and New Haven, suspected to be the work of Negro slaves. As a result, one Negro was executed in Boston, and the Boston Council ruled that any slaves who on their own gathered in groups of two or more were to be punished by whipping.

At Stono, South Carolina, in 1739, about twenty slaves rebelled, killed two warehouse guards, stole guns and gunpowder, and headed south, killing people in their way, and burning buildings. They were joined by others, until there were perhaps eighty slaves in all and, according to one account of the time, "they called out Liberty, marched on with Colours displayed, and two Drums beating." The militia found and attacked them. In the ensuing battle perhaps fifty slaves and twenty-five whites were killed before the uprising was crushed.

Herbert Aptheker, who did detailed research on slave resistance in North America for his book *American Negro Slave Revolts*, found about 250 instances where a minimum of ten slaves joined in a revolt or conspiracy.

From time to time, whites were involved in the slave resistance. As early as 1663, indentured white servants and black slaves in Gloucester County, Virginia, formed a conspiracy to rebel and gain their freedom. The plot was betrayed, and ended with executions. Mullin reports that the newspaper notices of runaways in Virginia often warned "ill-disposed" whites about harboring fugitives. Sometimes slaves and free men ran off together, or cooperated in crimes together. Sometimes, black male slaves ran off and joined white women. From time to time, white ship captains and watermen dealt with runaways, perhaps making the slave a part of the crew.

In New York in 1741, there were ten thousand whites in the city and two thousand black slaves. It had been a hard winter and the poor—slave and free—had suffered greatly. When mysterious fires broke out, blacks and whites were accused of conspiring together. Mass hysteria developed against the accused. After a trial full of lurid accusations by informers, and forced confessions, two white men and two white women were executed, eighteen slaves were hanged, and thirteen slaves were burned alive.

Only one fear was greater than the fear of black rebellion in the new American colonies. That was the fear that discontented whites would join black slaves to overthrow the existing order. In the early years of slavery, especially, before racism as a way of thinking was firmly ingrained, while white indentured servants were often treated as badly as black slaves, there was a possibility of cooperation. As Edmund Morgan sees it:

> There are hints that the two despised groups initially saw each other as sharing the same predicament. It was common, for example, for servants and slaves to run away together, steal hogs together, get drunk together. It was not uncommon for them to make love together. In Bacon's Rebellion, one of the last groups to surrender was a mixed band of eighty negroes and twenty English servants.

As Morgan says, masters, "initially at least, perceived slaves in much the same way they had always perceived servants . . . shiftless, irresponsible, unfaithful, ungrateful, dishonest. . . ." And "if freemen with disappointed hopes should make common cause with slaves of desperate hope, the results might be worse than anything Bacon had done."

And so, measures were taken. About the same time that slave codes, involving discipline and punishment, were passed by the Virginia Assembly,

> Virginia's ruling class, having proclaimed that all white men were superior to black, went on to offer their social (but white) inferiors a number of benefits previously denied them. In 1705 a law was passed requiring masters to provide white servants whose indenture time was up with ten bushels of corn, thirty shillings, and a gun, while women servants were to get 15 bushels of corn and forty shillings. Also, the newly freed servants were to get 50 acres of land.

Morgan concludes: "Once the small planter felt less exploited by taxation and began to prosper a little, he became less turbulent, less dangerous, more respectable. He could begin to see his big neighbor not as an extortionist but as a powerful protector of their common interests."

We see now a complex web of historical threads to ensnare blacks for slavery in America: the desperation of starving settlers, the special helplessness of the displaced African, the powerful incentive of profit for slave trader and planter, the temptation of superior status for poor whites, the elaborate controls against escape and rebellion, the legal and social punishment of black and white collaboration.

The point is that the elements of this web are historical, not "natural." This does not mean that they are easily disentangled, dismantled. It means only that there is a possibility for something else, under historical conditions not yet realized. And one of these conditions would be the elimination of that class exploitation which has made poor whites desperate for small gifts of status, and has prevented that unity of black and white necessary for joint rebellion and reconstruction.

Around 1700, the Virginia House of Burgesses declared:

> The Christian Servants in this country for the most part consists of the Worser Sort of the people of Europe. And since . . . such numbers of Irish and other Nations have been brought in of which a great many have been soldiers in the late warrs that according to our present Circumstances we can hardly governe them and if they were fitted with Armes and had the Opertunity of meeting together by Musters we have just reason to fears they may rise upon us.

It was a kind of class consciousness, a class fear. There were things happening in early Virginia, and in the other colonies, to warrant it.

REFERENCES

APTHEKER, HERBERT, ed. 1974. *A Documentary History of the Negro People in the United States.* Secaucus, NJ: Citadel.

BOSKIN, JOSEPH. 1966. *Into Slavery: Radical Decisions in the Virginia Colony.* Philadelphia: Lippincott.

CATTERALL, HELEN. 1937. *Judicial Cases Concerning American Slavery and the Negro.* 5 vols. Washington, DC: Negro University Press.

DAVIDSON, BASIL. 1961. *The African Slave Trade.* Boston: Little, Brown.

DONNAN, ELIZABETH, ed. 1965. *Documents Illustrative of the History of the Slave Trade to America.* 4 vols. New York: Octagon.

ELKINS, STANLEY. 1976. *Slavery: A Problem in American Institutional and Intellectual Life.* Chicago: University of Chicago Press.

FEDERAL WRITERS PROJECT. 1969. *The Negro in Virginia.* New York: Arno.

FRANKLIN, JOHN HOPE. 1974. *From Slavery to Freedom: A History of American Negroes.* New York: Knopf.

JORDAN, WINTHROP. 1968. *White over Black: American Attitudes toward the Negro, 1550–1812.* Chapel Hill: University of North Carolina Press.

MORGAN, EDMUND S. 1975. *American Slavery, American Freedom: The Ordeal of Colonial Virginia.* New York: Norton.

MULLIN, GERALD. 1974. *Flight and Rebellion: Slave Resistance in Eighteenth-Century Virginia.* New York: Oxford University Press.

MULLIN, MICHAEL, ed. 1975. *American Negro Slavery: A Documentary History.* New York: Harper & Row.

PHILLIPS, ULRICH B. 1966. *American Negro Slavery: A Survey of the Supply, Employment and Control of Negro Labor as Determined by the Plantation Regime.* Baton Rouge: Louisiana State University Press.

REDDING, J. SAUNDERS. 1973. *They Came in Chains.* Philadelphia: Lippincott.

STAMPP, KENNETH M. 1956. *The Peculiar Institution.* New York: Knopf.

TANNENBAUM, FRANK. 1963. *Slave and Citizen: The Negro in the Americas.* New York: Random House.

6

PLACING RACE IN CONTEXT

Clara E. Rodriguez • Hector Cordero-Guzman

Questions to Consider

How and in what specific ways have definitions of race and ethnicity changed over time and place? How is it possible to be defined as belonging to one race in one country and to a different race in another country? What insight into this question do Rodriguez and Cordero-Guzman provide in their description of how and why the definition of race is different in the United States and Puerto Rico? If there is a "social context" to race, as Rodriguez and Cordero-Guzman suggest, what are the sociological factors that make that "context" vary from country to country?

Introduction

By the 1960s a consensus had been reached that race as a biological concept was useless (Alland 1971; Harris 1968; Mead et al. 1968; Montagu 1964). There was only one human race and it had infinite variation and some population clusters. Yet, race, as people experience it, is a cultural construct (Sanjek 1990). Thus, how "races" or racial paradigms are determined also varies from culture to culture, as does the meaning of the term "race."

For example, in the United States of America race is conceived as being biologically or genetically based. The White race was defined by the absence of any non-White blood, and the Black race was defined by the presence of any Black blood. This cultural conception of race differed from that which evolved in Latin America. In Latin America, race may have had blood lines as a referent, but there were also other dimensions brought into "racial classification": for example, class, physical type, and ethnic background. Thus, in the US and in Latin America, two different cultural definitions of "race" arose, each of which took different referents. Each system of racial classification was seen, by those who utilized it, to be the only correct way of viewing individuals.

The fact that popular definitions of "race" vary from culture to culture suggests the importance of historical events, developments or context in determining "race." That there are different systems of racial classification in different countries (and sometimes within countries) is quite counter to the usual perception that most White Americans hold of race in the United States. This is because of the particular way in which race is

popularly viewed in the US where race is seen to be genetically based and therefore unchanging. In the words of American sociologists, it is an ascribed characteristic.

An example of how race changes from context to context is the description of the man who, in travelling from Puerto Rico to Mexico to the United States, changes his race from "White to Mulatto to Black" (Mintz 1971). Then there is the case of the Japanese who were accorded the status of honorary Whites in South Africa because of the changing business context. Again, there is the example of the Jews in Europe, who were classified by the Germans as a race apart from other Europeans, despite the fact that they were a group with highly varied phenotypes and quite diverse genetic strains. In nineteenth-century US and in the early twentieth-century immigration laws, race was used to describe not only Blacks and Whites, but also Slavs, Italians, Anglo-Saxons, etc. A basic white-non-white dichotomous categorization was present, but many European groups were also viewed as sub-races, different from Anglo-Saxon stock.

Given the significance of context in determining popular conceptions of race, it is also important to understand what happens to the conceptions of race and racial self-identity of individuals when they move from a country with one racial paradigm to a country with another. Are dual racial paradigms maintained? Do individuals adhere to their own perceptions of race? What determines whether they adopt or maintain their own perceptions of race? Are responses to questions of racial identity altered depending on how respondents interpret the question and its context?

These issues are brought into sharp relief when studying Puerto Ricans, a group with a history of contact with the US but with a different racial paradigm. In this article we study the way in which Puerto Ricans, who have been exposed to both cultures, identify themselves racially, how they are identified

Clara Rodriguez and Hector Cordero-Guzman, "Placing Race in Context" from *Ethnic and Racial Studies,* 1992, Vol. 14, 4, October, pp. 523–529, 539–541. Copyright © 1992. Reprinted with permission of Routledge, Inc., part of the Taylor & Francis Group. Journal's Web site: http://www. tandf.co.uk/journals.

by interviewers and how they think that they would be viewed by North Americans. This research sheds light on these two racial paradigms—that of the US and Puerto Rico—and what happens when they come into contact with each other.

Race in Historical Perspective

Although both the United States and Latin America relied on the importation of African slaves to meet labour needs, the conception and incorporation of peoples of African-descent as a "race" took different directions in the two areas (Denton and Massey 1989; Pitt-Rivers 1975; Wagley 1965). Of special interest is the case of the Spanish Caribbean and, in particular, Puerto Rico. In Puerto Rico race came to be seen as a continuum of categories, with different gradations and shades of colour as the norm. In the US race was conceived as a dichotomous concept in which individuals were envisaged, and legally defined, as being either White or Black. Although both areas had instituted slavery and both had clear demarcations between free whites and slaves, the category "White" included more people in Puerto Rico than it would have done in the United States. In addition, there was a variety of race categories in Puerto Rico and many were fluid.[1]

The population of Puerto Rico is mostly descended from the original Taino Indian settlers, white Spanish colonizers, black slaves brought from Africa, and countless other immigrants. The variety of phenotypes in Puerto Rico, then, is mostly the result of a relatively unexamined history of racial mixing and diverse migratory flows. A number of works have touched on the issue of racial mixing in the island, but there is no real consensus on its extent. Puerto Rican and American researchers at different times have discussed or found Puerto Rico to be everything from a mulatto country to a predominantly white country with small subgroups of blacks and mulattos. Compare, for example, the accounts of Seda Bonilla (1961) with those of Gordon (1949), Mills, Senior and Goldsen (1950), and Senior (1965).

The historical formation of race relations in Puerto Rico was accompanied by the development of a distinct nomenclature to describe the different groups. This nomenclature and the racial discourse in Puerto Rico reflected the fact that race was seen to be multidimensional. This was quite distinct from the conception of race that developed in the United States, where new "racial" categories and terms were not developed. On some occasions the US census did separately count mulattos and other mixtures of European and African peoples, but this practice fluctuated and by 1930 the census used only the "Negro" category to describe those with any trait of African descent (Martin et al. 1990). Thus, the offspring of Native American Indians, Asians or Europeans who intermarried with Blacks would simply be counted as Negro.

The 1896 decision of the US Supreme Court in the *Plessy v Ferguson* case legitimated the more dichotomous black/white view of "race." In this case, the petitioner averred that since he was ". . . seven eighths Caucasian and one eighth African blood; and that the mixture of colored blood was not discernible in him . . . ," he was entitled to the rights and privileges of citizens of the white race. The Supreme Court, however, decided against the plaintiff, thus further legitimating the genetic or blood quantum definition of race and sanctioning Jim Crow legislation (Blaustein and Zangrando 1968). The "separate but equal" doctrine elaborated in *Plessy v Ferguson* regulated the level of contact between White and Black Americans and went so far as to define as "Black" any individual who had even a small fraction of "Black" ancestry (Chang 1985, p. 52).

In Puerto Rico and in other parts of Latin America, race was based more on phenotypic and socio-economic definitions of the person rather than on genotypic definitions. Thus, in the US race is generally seen as a fact of biology, while in many parts of Latin America—particularly in the Spanish Caribbean—a more socio-economic conception of race has been the norm. This more socio-economic conception of race has emphasized dimensions that are freely varying, such as physical appearance (as opposed to genetic make-up), social class, and cultural modes of behaviour. For example, Sanjek (1971, p. 1128) notes that in Brazil classification is affected by contextual variables, that is, by situational and sociological variables that would include

> economic class, the dress, personality, education, and relation of the referent to the speaker; the presence of other actors and their relations to the speaker and referent; and contexts of speech, such as gossip, insult, joking, showing affection, maintenance of equality or of differential social status, or pointing out the referent in a group.

This perspective of race is opposed to the US conception, which relies mainly on genetic inheritance. In the United States race is an ascribed characteristic that does not change after birth, or from country to country. It is more dependent on a person's supposed genetic make-up and physical appearance than on socio-economic characteristics. The US conception of race with its emphasis on genetic or biological inheritance privileges a static conception of race. One is and always will be the race into which one was born, one is one's blood. This conception also disallows or ignores more contextual definitions.

In many Latin American countries, race is not a meta-concept based on biological categories, but rather a classification dependent on time and context. According to this

more fluid view of race, the determination and relative salience of race categories depend not on their "inherent" nature as physical characteristics but on the historical development of the contexts in which these categories are valued. Within this framework, the points of social reference in which a given individual operates are important determinants of racial identity.

A number of arguments seek to account for the different racial conceptions that evolved in the United States and in Puerto Rico. For example, Denton and Massey (1989) cite three elements of the Spanish colonial system that contributed to a greater blending of the peoples in the Spanish Caribbean. First, they argue that the Spanish history of contact with northern African populations made them more tolerant of different colour groups than were northeastern Europeans. Hence, groups of Mediterranean origin, in contrast to northeastern Europeans, tend to see darker people as white. Second, they maintain that the Spanish conceived of slaves and Indians as being subjects or vassals of the crown and as having certain rights. This differed from the North American conception of slaves as being property. (That is not to say, however, that the Spanish treatment of slaves was necessarily more benevolent, merely that it was sanctioned and conceived of differently.) The third factor that Denton and Massey (1989) discuss is the Spanish Catholic Church. They argue that the Church had a central role in the conquest and promoted the conversion, baptism, and attendance of slaves at integrated religious services. Thus, the role of the Church was analogous to that of the Spanish legal code. It promoted ". . . a positive cultural attitude towards persons of color in theory" but failed "to implement the idea in practice."

The history of a country's economic development has also been seen as an important determinant of race relations and racial conceptions. Duany (1985), for example, has argued that Puerto Rico's economy was less dependent on slaves than was that of other countries in the Caribbean. Thus, there was less commitment to slavery as an institution and there were fewer slaves in Puerto Rico, both absolutely and proportionately. This, together with substantial immigration into the island of Europeans and former slaves in the nineteenth century, made for a conception of race that was rather fluid as opposed to strictly dichotomous. Lastly, the greater migration of European women and families to North America as compared with Latin America—where men predominated and European women were scarce—may also have influenced the relations between races and the consequent conceptions of race that evolved.

The differences between these two conceptions of race have been accentuated and made more apparent with the increasing number of Latinos in the United States. In this article, we explore responses by Puerto Ricans to questions about racial identity. We contend that these responses reflect a conception of race that is different from that generally found in the classical social science literature and from that conventionally held in the US. We also argue that racial identity is contextually influenced, determined and defined.

Race and the United States Census

In the 1980 decennial census results the Puerto Rican conception of race appears to have been manifested. In response to the race item, which asked respondents to identify themselves as White, Black, or Other, 48 per cent of Puerto Ricans living in New York City replied that they were "Other" and wrote in a Spanish descriptor. Another 4 per cent replied that they were "Other" but did not write in any additional comment, 44 per cent said they were "White,"

and 3.9 per cent said they were "Black." This unique distribution of responses to the race item ran parallel with the national level where a full 40 per cent of all Hispanics (or 7.5 million) replied that they were "Other."

On the national level, where over 60 per cent of the nation's Hispanics are of Mexican origin and Puerto Ricans constitute about 12 per cent, there were similar results. The distribution of Latinos on the race item is particularly surprising in the light of the fact that in no state, including Hawaii, did more than 2 per cent of the general population indicate that they were of "other race" (Rodriguez 1991). See also Denton and Massey (1989) for a detailed discussion of racial identity among Mexican-Americans and Telles and Murguia (1990) for an interesting discussion of the effects of phenotype on the incomes of Mexicans in the United States.

It has been well documented (Denton and Massey 1989; Martin et al. 1990; Tienda and Ortiz 1986) that the Hispanic responses to the race item differed considerably from those of the general population. It is less clear why this is so. One interpretation stresses that the format of the race question may have led to misinterpretation. The question did not include the word race, but rather asked, "Is this person . . . ?" and provided tick-off categories. Included as possible answers were various Asian groups. This may have induced some Latino respondents to respond culturally, namely, to say that they were "Other" and write in "Mexican," "Dominican," etc. (Tienda and Ortiz 1986). In addition, the fact that the race question preceded the Hispanic identifier may have caused a cultural response to the race item. However, Martin et al. (1990) altered the sequence of the race and Hispanic identifier items and found that this affected the responses only of those Hispanics born in the US; it did not affect the tendency of foreign-born Hispanics to report that they were "Other."

Other research also suggests that there are contextual factors that affect the way in which Latinos respond to questions about race. A Content Reinterview Study by census personnel found that of those who reported that they were "Other" in the census, only 10 per cent were similarly classified in the reinterviewing (McKenney, Fernandez and Masamura 1985). Martin et al. (1990) conclude: "[I]t appears that many Hispanic people will report themselves as 'Other race' on a self-administered questionnaire, but will be classified as 'White' by enumerators." Chevan (1990) reports on a Current Population Survey in March 1980 in which Hispanics identified themselves overwhelmingly as "White." Thus, in the presence of an interviewer who presented them with four non-Hispanic choices, 97 per cent of Hispanics identified themselves as "White," while "one month later in filling out the Census form in the privacy of their home, almost 40 per cent of Hispanics chose 'Other' and were prompted to write in the meaning of 'Other' on the form." Of those who specified a meaning 90 per cent wrote in a Hispanic identifier (Chevan 1990, p. 8). . . .

Our results also provide insight into the racial responses by Hispanics reported in the 1980 Census. The findings indicate that, regardless of how the "race" question was asked, many Puerto Ricans chose *not* to use the conventional racial categories of White and Black. The "Other" response did not represent a misunderstanding. Nor did it represent self-classification as a racially intermediate person in all cases. These results suggest a more complex reality than that which assumes that this "Other" response simply represented a misunderstanding of the question, or that it represented a homogeneous middle category of mestizos or mulattos.

The findings indicate that we cannot automatically assume that because Puerto Ricans choose to identify as "Other" they are placing themselves in a racially intermediate situation. For some Puerto Ricans a cultural response also carries a racial implication, that is, they see race and culture as being fused. They emphasize the greater validity of ethnic or cultural identity. Culture is race, regardless of the physical types within the culture.

Others see their culture as representing a "mixed" people. Still others view these concepts as independent, and a cultural response does not imply a racial designation for them. In this latter case, a respondent may identify as "Other-Puerto Rican" because he or she is not culturally or politically like White Americans or Black Americans, regardless of his or her particular race. In essence, the United States of America may choose to divide its culture into White and Black races, but a Puerto Rican will not (Rodriguez et al. 1991).

The findings suggest that race can be viewed in more than one way. For many of our respondents, race was something more than phenotype and genotype and was influenced by contextual factors such as class, education, language, and birthplace. These findings challenge the hegemonic and more static biological view of race prevalent in the US and its data-collection agencies. They challenge the arrogance behind the biological view of race implying, as it does, that there is no other view of race. These findings also raise questions about the extent to which culture, class and race are inextricably tied together even within a classification system that purports to be "biologically" anchored. Thus, "race" in the US may also, in practice, be more of a social construction than is generally admitted.

Acknowledgments

Dr. Clara Rodriguez would like to acknowledge the financial assistance of the Rockefeller Foundation and the Inter-University Program for Latino Research/Social Science Research Council.

NOTES

1. Clearly, the fact that there are different conceptions of race in Puerto Rico and in the US is not meant to imply that there is no racism in Puerto Rico.

REFERENCES

ALLAND, ALEXANDER. 1971. *Human Diversity*. New York: Columbia University Press.

BLAUSTEIN, ALBERT P., and ROBERT L. ZANGRANDO. 1968. *Civil Rights and the American Negro: A Documentary History*. New York: Washington Square Press.

CHANG, HARRY. 1985. "Toward a Marxist Theory of Racism: Two Essays by Harry Chang." *Review of Radical Political Economics,"* 17(3):34–45.

CHEVAN, ALBERT. 1990. "Hispanic Racial Identity: Beyond Social Class." Paper presented at the American Sociological Association meetings, Washington, DC, 14 August 1990.

DENTON, NANCY, and DOUGLAS S. MASSEY. 1989. "Racial Identity Among Caribbean Hispanics: The Effect of Double Minority Status on Residential Segregation." *American Sociological Review* 54:790–808.

DUANY, JORGE. 1985. "Ethnicity in the Spanish Caribbean: Notes on the Consolidation of Creole Identity in Cuba and Puerto Rico, 1762–1868." *Ethnic Groups* 6:99–123.

GORDON, MAXINE W. 1949. "Race Patterns and Prejudice in Puerto Rico," *American Sociological Review* 14:294–301.

HARRIS, MARVIN. 1968. *Patterns of Race in the Americas*. New York: Walker.

MARTIN, ELIZABETH, THERESA J. DEMAIO, and PAMELA C. CAMPANELLI. 1990. "Context Effects for Census Measures of Race and Hispanic Origin." *Public Opinion Quarterly* 54(4):551–66.

MCKENNEY, NAMPEO R., EDWARD W. FERNANDEZ, and WILFRED T. MASAMURA. 1985. "The Quality of the Race and Hispanic Origin Information Reported in the 1980 Census," Proceedings of the Survey Research Methods Section (American Statistical Association), pp. 46–50.

MEAD, MARGARET, THEODOSIUS DOBZHANSKY, ETHEL TOBACH, and ROBERT LIGHT, eds. 1968. *Science and the Concept of Race*. New York: Columbia University Press.

MILLS, C. WRIGHT, CLARENCE SENIOR, and ROSE GOLDSEN. 1950. *The Puerto Rican Journey: New York's Newest Migrants*. New York: Harper & Row.

MINTZ, SIDNEY W. 1971. "Groups, Group Boundaries and the Perception of Race." *Comparative Studies in Society and History* 13(4):437–50.

MONTAGU, ASHLEY, ed. 1964. *The Concept of Race*. New York: Free Press.

PITT-RIVERS, JULIAN. 1975. "Race, Color and Class in Central America and the Andes." In *Majority and Minority*, edited by Norman Yetman and C. Hoy Steele. Boston: Allyn & Bacon.

RODRIGUEZ, CLARA E. 1974. "Puerto Ricans: Between Black and White." *New York Affairs* I(4):92–101.

———. 1991. *Puerto Ricans: Born in the USA*. Boulder, CO: Westview Press.

RODRIGUEZ, CLARA E., AIDA CASTRO, OSCAR GARCIA, and ANALISA TORRES. 1991. "Latino Racial Identity: In the Eye of the Beholder?" *Latino Studies Journal* 2(3):33–48.

SANJEK, ROGER. 1971. "Brazilian Racial Terms: Some Aspects of Meaning and Learning." *American Anthropology* 73(5):1126–43.

———. 1990. "Conceptualizing Caribbean Asians: Race, Acculturation, Creolization." Asian/American Center Working Papers, Queens College/City University of New York.

SEDA BONILLA, E. 1961. "Social Structure and Race Relation." *Social Forces* 40:141–48.

SENIOR, CLARENCE. 1965. *Strangers, Then Neighbors: From Pilgrims to Puerto Ricans*. Chicago: Quadrangle.

TELLES, EDWARD, and EDWARD MURGUIA. 1990. "Phenotypic Discrimination and Income Differences Among Mexican Americans." *Social Science Quarterly* 71(4):682–96.

TIENDA, MARTA, and VILMA ORTIZ. 1986. " 'Hispanicity' and the 1980 Census." *Social Science Quarterly* 67:3–20.

WAGLEY, CHARLES. 1965. "On the Concept of Social Race in the Americas." In *Contemporary Cultures and Societies of Latin America: A Reader in the Social Anthropology of Middle and South America and the Caribbean*, edited by Dwight B. Heath and Richard N. Adams. New York: Random House.

7

A TOUR OF INDIAN PEOPLES
AND INDIAN LANDS

David E. Wilkins

Questions to Consider

Why has it been so difficult to find a political and cultural definition of who is an American Indian, what constitutes a tribe, and what criteria need to be met to claim tribal membership? How are race, culture, identity, and politics linked in David Wilkins's discussion of American Indians?

One of the greatest obstacles faced by the Indian today in his desire for self-determination . . . is the American public's ignorance of the historical relationship of the United States with Indian tribes and the lack of general awareness of the status of the American Indian in our society today.
American Indian Policy Review
Commission, 1977[1]

This chapter provides descriptions, definitions, and analysis of the most important concepts necessary for a solid foundation for the study of Indian politics. I will attempt to clarify how indigenous peoples, variously grouped, are defined, and discuss why such definitions are necessary. I will then analyze how the term Indian is defined and discuss what constitutes a reservation or Indian Country. Finally, I will conclude the chapter with a description of the basic demographic facts and socioeconomic data that applies throughout Indian lands.

David E. Wilkins, "A Tour of Indian Peoples and Indian Lands" from *American Indian Politics and the American Political System*, pp. 11–40. Copyright © 2002. Reprinted by permission of Rowman & Littlefield Publishers, Inc.

What Is an Indian Tribe?

American Indians, tribal nations, Indian tribes, indigenous nations, Fourth World Peoples, Native American Peoples, Aboriginal Peoples First Nations, and Native peoples—these are just a sample of current terms that are used to refer to indigenous peoples in the continental United States in a collective sense. Alaska Natives, including Aleuts, Inuit, and Indians, and Native Hawaiians are the indigenous people of those respective territories. While I will provide some descriptive details about Alaska Natives, I will have less to say about Native Hawaiians because their legal status is unique among aboriginal peoples of the United States.[2]

This was brought to light in the Supreme Court's 2000 ruling in *Rice v. Cayetano*.[3] In that case, the Court struck down restrictions that had allowed only persons with Native Hawaiian blood to vote for the trustees of the Office of Hawaiian Affairs, a state agency created to better the lives of Hawaii's aboriginal people. While *Cayetano* did not specifically address the political relationship of the Native Hawaiians to the federal government, it called into question the status of the more than 150 federal statutes that recognize that Hawaii's native peoples do, in fact, have a unique legal status.

The departments of the Interior and Justice issued a preliminary report of August 23, 2000, that recommended that Congress "enact further legislation to clarify Native Hawaiians' political status and to create a framework for recognizing a government-to-government relationship with a representative Native Hawaiian governing body."[4] If Congress acts to create such a framework, and a bill was introduced on July 20, 2000 (S. 2898), by Senator Daniel K. Akaka (D-HI), then Hawaii's Natives would have a political relationship with the federal government similar to that of federally recognized tribes. The sovereignty movement in Hawaii is very complex, however, and some segments of the population desire more than mere federal recognition of their status because of their nation's preexisting sovereign status.[5]

Indigenous communities expect to be referred to by their own names—Navajo or Diné, Ojibwe or Anishinabe, Sioux or Lakota, Suquamish, or Tohono O'odham—since they constitute separate political, legal, and cultural entities. In fact, before Europeans arrived in the Americas, it is highly doubtful whether any tribes held a "conception of that racial character which today we categorize as 'Indian.' People recognized their neighbors as co-owners of the lands given to them by the Great Spirit and saw themselves sharing a basic status within creation as a life form."[6] However, when discussing Indian people generically, *American Indian tribes* and *Native Americans* remain the most widely used terms despite the inherent problems with both. For instance, America's indigenous people are not *from* India, and the term *Native American* was "used during the nativist (anti-immigration, anti-foreign) movement (1860s–1925) and the anti-black, anti-Catholic, and anti-Jewish Ku Klux Klan resurgence during the early 1900s."[7]

There is no universally agreed upon definition of what constitutes an Indian tribe, in part because each tribal community defines itself differently and because the U.S. government in its relations with tribes has operated from conflicting sets of cultural and political premises across time. Although no universal definition exists, many statutes give definitions for purposes of particular laws, federal agencies like the Bureau of Indian Affairs generate their own definitions, numerous courts have crafted definitions, and the term *tribe* is found—though not defined—in the Constitution's commerce clause.

For example, the Indian Self-Determination Act of 1975 (as amended) defines an Indian tribe as "any Indian tribe, band, nation, or other organized group or community . . . which is recognized as eligible for the special programs and services provided by the United States to Indians because of their status as Indians." By contrast, the Supreme Court in *Montoya v. United States* (1901) even more ambiguously said that "by a 'tribe' we understand a body of Indians of the same or a similar race united in a community under one leadership or government, and inhabiting a particular though sometimes ill-defined territory."[8]

Broadly, the term *tribe* can be defined from two perspectives—*ethnological* and *political-legal.*[9] From an ethnological perspective, a tribe may be defined as a group of indigenous people connected by biology or blood; kinship, cultural, and spiritual values; language; political authority; and a territorial land base. But for our purposes, it is the political-legal definition (since there is no single definitive legal definition) of tribe, especially by the federal government, which is crucial since whether or not a tribal group is *recognized* as a tribe by the federal government has important political, cultural, and economic consequences, as we shall see shortly.

Federally Recognized Tribal and Alaska Native Entities

The extension of federal recognition by the United States to a tribal nation is the formal diplomatic acknowledgment by the federal government of a tribe's legal status as a sovereign. This is comparable to when the United States extended "recognition" to the former republics of the Soviet Union after that state's political disintegration. It is the beginning point of a government-to-government relationship between an indigenous people and the U.S. government.[10] The reality is that an American Indian tribe is not a legally recognized entity in the eyes of the federal government unless some explicit action by an arm of the government (i.e., congressional statute, administrative ruling by the BIA, presidential executive order, or a judicial opinion) decides that it exists in a formal manner.

Federal recognition has historically had two distinctive meanings. Before the 1870s, "recognize" or "recognition" was used in the cognitive sense. In other words, federal officials simply acknowledged that a tribe existed, usually by negotiating treaties with them or enacting specific laws to fulfill specific treaty pledges.[11] During the 1870s, however, "recognition," or more accurately, "acknowledgment," began to be used in a formal jurisdictional sense. It is this later usage that the federal government most often employs to describe its relationship to tribes. In short, federal acknowledgment is a formal act that establishes a political relationship between a tribe and the United States. It affirms a tribe's sovereign status. Simultaneously, it outlines the federal government's responsibilities to the tribe.

More specifically, federal acknowledgment means that a tribe is not only entitled to the immunities and privileges available to other tribes, but is also subject to the same federal powers, limitations, and other obligations of recognized tribes. What this means, particularly the "limitations" term, is that "acknowledgment shall subject the Indian tribe to the same authority of Congress and the United States to which other federally acknowledged tribes are subjected."[12] In other words, tribes are informed that they are now subject to federal plenary power and may, ironically, benefit from the virtually unlimited and still largely unreviewable authority of the federal government. For example, recognized tribes have exemptions from most state tax laws, enjoy sovereign immunity, and are not subject to the same constitutional constraints as are the federal and state governments.

Until 1978, federal recognition or acknowledgment was usually bestowed by congressional act or presidential action. But in 1978 the BIA, the Department of the Interior agency primarily responsible for carrying out the federal government's treaty and trust obligations to tribal nations, published regulations which contained specific criteria that unacknowledged or nonrecognized tribal groups had to meet in order to be formally recognized by the United States. The set of guidelines was based mainly on confirmation by individuals and groups outside the petitioning tribe that members of the group were Indians. The mandatory criteria were the following: the identification of the petitioners "from historical times until the present on a substantially continuous basis, as 'American Indian' or 'Aboriginal'" by the federal government, state or local governments, scholars, or other Indian tribes; the habitation of the tribe on land identified as Indian; a functioning government that had authority over its members; a constitution; a roll of members based on criteria acceptable to the secretary of the interior; not being a terminated tribe, and members not belonging to other tribes.[13]

These criteria largely were designed to fit the "aboriginal" or "mythic" image of the western and already recognized tribes. They were problematic for many eastern tribes who sought recognition, since they paid little heed to the massive historical, cultural, economic, and legal barriers those tribes had to endure merely to survive as tribes into the late twentieth century, lacking any semblance of federal support or protection.

Since the late 1970s there has been tension between those who support BIA or administrative recognition versus those who believe that only the Congress has authority to recognize tribes. The debate over administrative versus legislative recognition rages on, with some advocates from each camp asserting their exclusive right to extend or withhold recognition. This raises an important question: Is there a qualitative difference between the two types of recognition? There are two important differences. First, tribes that opt for administrative variety must meet the formalized set of criteria mentioned earlier. Tribes that pursue congressional recognition, provided they can muster enough proof that they are a legitimate group composed of people of Indian ancestry, have only to make a compelling case to the congressional representative(s) of the state they reside in. The congressional sponsor(s) then make(s) the case for the tribe via legislation.

The second major difference involves the administrative law component known as "subordinate delegation." The major grant of authority the Congress has delegated to the secretary of the interior is located in title 25—*Indians*—of the *U.S. Code.* Section 1 states that the head of Indian affairs, formerly the commissioner of Indian Affairs, today the assistant secretary of Indian Affairs, is "appointed by the President, by and with the advice and consent of the Senate."[14] In section 2, the head is authorized to "have the management of all Indian affairs and of all matters arising out of Indian relations."[15] As William Quinn states, this law "would arguably not authorize the Secretary or Commissioner to establish a

perpetual government-to-government relationship via federal acknowledgment with an Indian group not already under the Department's aegis."[16] Nevertheless, Quinn asserts that the secretary of the interior, with the U.S. Supreme Court's approval, has historically exercised the authority to "recognize" tribes "when a vacuum of responsibility existed over decades, resulting in a gradual and unchallenged accretion of this authority."[17]

The problem, however, is not that the secretary is usurping unused congressional authority; instead, it is the manner and degree to which secretarial discretion and interpretation of federal laws have been discharged by BIA officials. As Felix Cohen said more than forty years ago, "Indians for some decades have had neither armies nor lawyers to oppose increasingly broad interpretations of the power of the Commissioner of Indian Affairs, and so little by little 'the management of all Indian affairs' has come to be read as 'the management of all the affairs of Indians.'"[18] This statement has relevance today, notwithstanding the federal government's policy of Indian self-determination and the more recent policy of tribal self-governance.

The Congress's track record is problematic as well. Generally speaking, however, tribes with explicit congressional acknowledgment have found their status less subject to the whims of BIA officials, though even that is no guarantee of smooth affairs, because BIA oversees and administers most of the government's political relationship with tribes.

A prime example involves the Pascua Yaqui tribe of southern Arizona. The Yaqui were legislatively recognized in 1978. However, in the late 1980s, when they solicited the approval of the BIA on some changes in their constitution, they were informed by bureau officials that they were limited in what governmental powers they could exercise because they were not a "historic tribe," but were instead merely a "created adult Indian community":

> A historic tribe has existed since time immemorial. Its powers derive from its unextinguished, inherent sovereignty. Such a tribe has the full range of governmental powers except where it has been removed by Federal law in favor of either the United States or the state in which the tribe is located. By contrast, a community of adult Indians is composed simply of Indian people who reside together on trust land. A community of adult Indians may have a certain status which entitles it to certain privileges and immunities. . . . However, that status is derived as a necessary scheme to benefit Indians, not from some historical inherent sovereignty.[19]

The bureau's attempt to create two categories of recognized tribes, a novel and disturbing approach to determining tribal identity, was halted by Congress, which declared that no department or agency of the government could develop regulations that negated or diminished the privileges and immunities of any federally recognized tribes.[20] The Congress has, moreover, in recent years tried to reassert its constitutional authority in the field by introducing legislation that would transfer administrative and congressional consideration of applications for federal recognition to an independent commission.[21]

Congress's actions, along with the increasing politicization of the administrative recognition process because of Indian gaming operations and state concerns, compelled Kevin Gover, the assistant secretary of Indian Affairs (head of the BIA), in May 2000 to testify before Congress that his agency was no longer able to do the job of recognizing tribes. Gover admitted that he had been unable to streamline the recognition process, which in some cases had taken

years to resolve, but he placed larger blame on the fact that Indian gaming revenues had enabled some groups to wage protracted legal battles that often involved nonrecognized tribes, non-Indian citizens and towns, and recognized tribes.[22]

As of 2001, the Department of the Interior officially recognizes 561 indigenous entities—332 are Indian nations, tribes, bands, organized communities, or Pueblos in the lower forty-eight states; 229 are Alaska Native villages or corporations—on a list annually prepared by the BIA (see appendix A for a list of recognized native entities). These constitute the indigenous people eligible for special programs and services provided by the United States to indigenous communities because of their status as Indians or Alaska Natives.

The situation of Alaska Native villages and corporations is complicated not only by distinctive ethnological differences but also by their unique political and legal status. Although Alaska Natives are eligible to receive services from the BIA, their political sovereignty as self-governing bodies has been questioned and at times constrained by the federal government. A recent Supreme Court case, *Alaska v. Native Village of Venetie Tribal Government* (1998),[23] cast some doubts on the sovereign status of Alaskan villages. *Venetie* dealt with the jurisdictional status of Alaska Native villages and whether or not lands owned in fee simple by these communities—a type of ownership defined by the Alaska Native Claims Settlement Act of 1971—constituted "Indian Country."

In a major victory for Alaskan state authorities and a blow to the sovereignty of the village of Venetie, an Athabaskan community of some 350 people, Justice Clarence Thomas for a unanimous court held that Venetie's 1.8 million acres of fee-simple lands did not qualify as "Indian Country" because they had not been set aside by the federal government for tribal use and were not "under federal supervision." Thus, the tribal government lacked the inherent authority to impose a 5 percent business tax on a contractor building a state-funded school in the village. In denying Venetie, and by extension every other Alaskan village, the power to tax, this ruling called into question what the actual political status of these villages was.

In addition, the indigenous people of Hawaii, who prefer to be called Hawaiians, Hawaiian Natives, or Native Hawaiians, although they are treated as Native Americans for some legal purposes, are not on the Department of the Interior's list of federally recognized tribal entities and have a unique status under federal law.[24]

But there are other indigenous people in the United States who are *not federally recognized,* who had their recognized status *terminated* by the federal government, or who have *state recognition* only. I will discuss these three categories briefly.

Nonrecognized or Unacknowledged Groups

These are groups exhibiting a tremendous degree of racial, ethnic, and cultural diversity. In some cases, they are descendants of tribes who never fought the United States, had no resources desired by the federal government, or lived in geographic isolation and were simply ignored, and hence may never have participated in a treaty or benefited from the trust relationship which forms the basis of most contemporary recognized tribes' status. Despite these circumstances, some of these groups retain their aboriginal language, hold some lands in common, and in some cases have retained some degree of traditional structures of governance. These groups feel entitled to recognition status and have petitioned the United States to be so recognized.[25]

In other cases, groups have questionable genealogical connections to legitimate historical tribes but, for varying reasons, have chosen to self-identify as particular tribes and desire to be recognized by the federal government.[26] As of 2000, the BIA had received a total of 237 letters of intent and petitions for federal recognition. The acknowledgment process, established in 1978 and administered by the Branch of Acknowledgment and Research (BAR) in the BIA, proved to be an extremely slow, expensive, and politicized process that required excessive historical documentation and was greatly influenced by already recognized tribes who were reluctant to let other groups, regardless of their historical legitimacy, gain politically recognized status.[27] Because of these and other problems, the bureau surrendered its power to administratively recognize tribal groups in the fall of 2000. Between 1978 and 2000, the BIA officially recognized only fifteen tribes (e.g., Grand Traverse Band of Ottawa & Chippewa and Jamestown S'Klallam) and denied the petitions of fifteen groups (e.g., Lower Muscogee Creek Tribe east of Mississippi, Kaweah Indian Nation, Southeastern Cherokee Confederacy).[28]

Terminated Tribes

From 1953 to the mid-1960s, the federal government's Indian policy was called "termination" because the United States wanted to sever the trust relationship and end federal benefits and support services to as many tribes, bands, and California rancherias as was feasible in an effort to expedite Indian assimilation and to lift discriminatory practices and policies that negatively affected indigenous peoples.[29] This policy was exemplified by House Concurrent Resolution No. 108, passed in 1953. This measure declared that,

> Whereas it is the policy of Congress, as rapidly as possible, to make the Indians within the territorial limits of the United States subject to the same laws and entitled to the same privileges and

responsibilities as are applicable to other citizens of the United States, to end their status as wards of the United States, and to grant them all the rights and prerogatives pertaining to American citizenship; and Whereas the Indians within the territorial limits of the United States should assume their full responsibilities as American citizens: Now, therefore, be it resolved . . . that it is declared to be the sense of Congress that, at the earliest possible time, all of the Indian tribes and the individual members thereof located within the States of California, Florida, New York . . . should be freed from Federal supervision and control and from all disabilities and limitations specially applicable to Indians.[30]

Over one hundred tribes, bands, and California rancherias—totaling a little more than eleven thousand Indians—were "terminated" and lost their status as "recognized" and sovereign Indian communities. Termination thus subjected the tribes and their members to state law, their trust assets were usually individualized and either sold or held by the banks, and they were no longer eligible for the other benefits and exemptions recognized tribes enjoy.

The terminated tribes, other tribes faced with termination, and Indian and non-Indian interest groups began to lobby Congress to end this disastrous policy, because of the economic and political hardships it was causing. By the mid-1960s, the policy was stifled. Gradually, terminated tribes began to push for "restoration" of their recognized status. The first tribe terminated, the Menominee of Wisconsin (terminated in 1954), was also the first tribe to be legislatively "restored," in 1973.

Although discredited as policy by the mid-1960s, and rejected by presidents Nixon and Reagan in their Indian policy statements, termination was not officially rejected by

Congress until 1988 in a largely symbolic gesture that declared that "the Congress hereby repudiates and rejects HCR 108 of the 83rd Congress and any policy of unilateral termination of federal relations with any Indian nation."[31]

State-Recognized Tribes

Some Indian tribes have been recognized by their host states since the colonial era (e.g., Pamunkey Tribe of Virginia), although others have been recognized by state decrees (governor's action or state statute) in contemporary times. There are currently over fifty state-recognized tribes in Alabama, Connecticut, Georgia, Louisiana, Massachusetts, Michigan, Montana, New Jersey, North Carolina, New York, Oklahoma, Virginia, Washington, and West Virginia. See Table 1 for a list of these tribes. Depending on the policy established by the individual state, state recognition may or may not depend on prior federal recognition. Importantly, state recognition is not a prerequisite for federal recognition, although a long-standing relationship with a state is one factor in the federal recognition criteria that the BIA weighs in its determination of whether a group has historical longevity in a particular place.

For example, the Lumbee Tribe of North Carolina was legislatively recognized by the state in 1953.[32] Confident, the Lumbee leadership two years later asked Representative Frank Carlyle (D-NC) to introduce a bill before Congress that would extend federal recognition to the Lumbee. On June 7, 1956, the Congress passed an act which provided a measure of recognition to the Lumbee Nation,[33] without giving them the full range of benefits and services other federally recognized tribes received because federal policy at the time was focused on terminating the unique trust relationship between tribes and the United States. To date, the Lumbee Tribe is still not considered a federally recognized

TABLE 1   State Recognized Tribes

Alabama
Echota Cherokee
Northeast Alabama Cherokee
MaChis Lower Creek
Southeast Alabama Cherokee
Star Muscogee Creek
Mowa Band of Choctaw

Georgia
Georgia Eastern Cherokee
Cherokee of Georgia
Lower Muskogee Creek
Tama Tribal Town

New Jersey
Nanticoke Lenni-Lanape
Powhatan Renape
Ramapough Mountain

Michigan
Burt Lake Band of Ottawa & Chippewa Indians
Gun Lake Band of Grand River Ottawa Indians
Grand River Band of Ottawa Indians
Swan Creek Black River Confederated Tribes

North Carolina
Coharie Intra-Tribal Council
Haliwa-Saponi Tribe
Lumbee
Meherrin Tribe
Person County Indians
Waccamaw-Siouan Tribe

Virginia
Chickahominy Indian Tribe
Eastern Chickahominy Indian Tribe
Mattaponi Indian Tribe
Monacan Indian Tribe

Nansemond Indian Tribe
Pamunkey Indian Tribe
United Rappahannock Tribe
Upper Mattaponi Indian Tribe

West Virginia
Appalachian American Indians of West Virginia

Connecticut
Golden Hill Paugussett
Paucatuck Eastern Pequot
Schagticoke

Louisiana
Choctaw-Apache of Ebarb
Caddo Tribe
Clifton Choctaw
Four Winds Cherokee
United Houma Nation

New York
Shinnecock
Poospatuk

Montana
Little Shell Tribe of Chippewa

Oklahoma
Delaware Tribe of East Oklahoma
Loyal Shawnee Tribe
Yuchi Tribe

Washington
Chinook Indian Tribe
Duwamish Tribe
Kikiallus Indian Nation
Marietta Band of Nooksack Indians
Steilacoom Indian Tribe
Snohomish Tribe of Indians.

Source: http://www.thespike.com/tablest.htm

tribe by the BIA or the Indian Health Service, though they qualify for and receive other federal services as a recognized tribe.[34]

Who Is an American Indian?

Having established the complexity of determining what an Indian tribe is from a legal-political perspective, we now turn to a brief but necessary examination of the equally if not more cumbersome question of "Who is an Indian?" This is important, as McClain and Stewart note, because "the question of who is an Indian is central to any discussion of American Indian politics."[35] The political relationship that exists between tribes and the federal government, bloated with issues of disparate power, cultural biases, and race and ethnicity, makes this so. Of course, like the concept of "Indian tribe," before Columbus arrived in 1492 there were no peoples in the Americas known as "Indians" or "Native Americans." Each indigenous community had its own name relating to the character of its people and the lands they inhabited.

With the political status of Indian nations defined, the question of deciding just "who is an Indian" would not appear to be a difficult one to answer. The decision rests with the tribal nations who retain, as one of their inherent sovereign powers, the power to decide who belongs in their nation. Unless this right has been expressly ceded in a treaty, it remains probably the most essential component of self-government. If tribes were to lose the right to decide who their citizens/members were, then it would logically follow that any government could dictate or influence what the tribe's membership should entail.

Since the identification of individuals as Indians depends upon or coincides with their association in a unique body politic and distinctive cultural and linguistic systems, historically, at least, "allegiance rather than ancestry per se [was] the deciding factor" in determining who was an Indian.[36] In other words, historically, to be considered an Indian one had to meet certain basic tribally defined criteria, including the social, cultural, linguistic, territorial, sociopsychological, and ceremonial. These criteria, of course, varied from tribal nation to tribal nation. However, as the federal government's power waxed by the late nineteenth century, with the corresponding waning of tribal power, indigenous cultural-social-territorial–based definitions of tribal identity were sometimes ignored and replaced by purely legal and frequently race-based definitions often arbitrarily articulated in congressional laws, administrative regulations, or court cases.

Congress, in particular, began to employ and still uses ethnological data, including varying fractions of blood quantum. In fact, blood quantum remains one of the most important criteria used by the federal government and tribal governments to determine Indian status, despite the fact that its continued use "poses enormous conceptual and practical problems" since blood is not the carrier of genetic material and cultural traits as was thought in the nineteenth century.[37]

When blood quantum was first used in the Indian context in the early part of the twentieth century as a mechanism to reduce federal expenditures for Indian education, it "was meant to measure the amount of Indian blood possessed by an individual. Because racial blood types could not be observed directly, Indian blood quantum was inferred from the racial backgrounds of parents. If both parents were reputed to have 'unadulterated' Indian blood, then the blood quantum of their children was fixed at 100 percent. For children of racially mixed parents, their Indian blood quantum might be some fractional amount such as $3/4$, $1/2$, or $1/8$."[38]

The federal government's principal function in formulating definitions of "Indian," since like the concept "tribe" there is no single constitutional or universally accepted definition, is to "establish a test whereby it may be determined whether a given individual is to be excluded from the scope of legislation dealing with Indians."[39] The most widely accepted "legal" definition of "Indian" is from Felix Cohen, who wrote in 1943 that:

> The term "Indian" may be used in an ethnological or in a legal sense. Ethnologically, the Indian race may be distinguished from the Caucasian, Negro, Mongolian, and other races. If a person is three-fourths Caucasian and one-fourth Indian, it is absurd, from the ethnological standpoint, to assign him to the Indian race. Yet legally such a person may be an Indian. From a legal standpoint, then, the biological question of race is generally pertinent, but not conclusive. Legal status depends not only upon biological, but also upon social factors, such as the relation of the individual concerned to a white or Indian community. . . . Recognizing the possible diversity of definitions of

"Indianhood," we may nevertheless find some practical value in a definition of "Indian" as a person meeting two qualifications: (a) That some of his ancestors lived in America before its discovery by the white race, and (b) That the individual is considered an "Indian" by the community in which he lives.[40]

Because of the Constitution's silence on the issue of who is an Indian, Congress, the BIA, and the federal courts have had great latitude in developing specific meanings for specific situations which only sometimes reflect the definitions of particular tribes. But because of the plenary power doctrine and the trust doctrine, these federal actors, but especially the Congress, have vested themselves with the right to define "who an Indian is" for purposes relating to legislation and have sometimes established base rolls which actually identify who a tribe's members are. This was done in the case of the so-called Five Civilized Tribes of present-day Oklahoma. Congress, in 1893, enacted a law that all but secured to the federal government the right to determine membership of these tribes.[41]

Over thirty "legal" definitions have been promulgated by various agencies, departments, and congressional committees and subcommittees that explain who is and is not an Indian eligible for federal services.[42] These definitions can be grouped into six categories. First, and most common, are those definitions that require a specific blood quantum, with one-fourth being the most widely accepted fraction. Second, there is a set of definitions clustered under the requirement that the individual be a member of a federally recognized indigenous community.

A third category includes definitions that mandate residence "on or near" a federal Indian reservation. A fourth class includes definitions grouped under descendancy. These entail definitions that extend eligibility not only to tribal members but

also to their descendants up to a specified degree. For example, the definition of Indian found in a 1998 bill, Indian Trust-Estate Planning and Land Title Management Improvement Act, declares that "the term 'Indian' means any individual who is a member, or a descendant of a member, of a North American tribe, band, pueblo, or other organized group of natives who are indigenous to the continental U.S., or who otherwise has a special relationship with the U.S. through a treaty, agreement, or other form of recognition." The bill's sponsors described an "Alaska Native" as "an individual who is an Alaskan Indian, Eskimo, Aleut, or any combination thereof, who are indigenous to Alaska."

Under the fifth grouping are several definitions that rely on self-identification. The U.S. Census Bureau, for example, allows individuals to simply declare that they are Indian. Finally, the sixth class is a miscellaneous category that includes definitions which do not easily fit in the other categories.[43]

Defining "Indian" and "tribe" are not simple tasks in part because of the political and economic resources involved and because of the number and power of the respective actors: tribal governments, individual Indians, Congress, the president, the Department of the Interior, the BIA, federal courts and, increasingly, state governments and the various agencies and individuals who constitute those sovereigns. But who does the defining and how these emotionally laden terms are defined are crucial in expanding our understanding of the politics of individual tribes, intertribal relations, and intergovernmental relations.

For example, in terms of identity, high outmarriage rates, steadily decreasing federal dollars, and an intensified tribal-state relationship have prompted questions about "whether the rules defining Indianness and tribal membership should be relaxed or tightened—that is, made more inclusionary or more exclusionary."[44] For instance, some tribes are eliminating blood quantum and adopting descent criteria, while others are pursuing an "ethnic purification strategy" by adopting a stricter set of blood quantum rules concerning tribal enrollment. These decisions impact tribes and their political relationship with the federal government.

While tribes retain the right to establish their own membership criteria, the BIA in August 2000 published proposed regulations on the documentation requirements and standards necessary for Indians to receive a "certificate of degree of Indian blood" (CDIB), which is the federal government's way of determining whether individuals possess sufficient Indian blood to be eligible for certain federal programs and services provided exclusively to American Indians or Alaska Natives.[45]

But a number of Indian leaders, like W. Ron Allen, chairman of the Jamestown S'Klallam Tribe of Washington, charged that the federal government should not be in the business of determining who is Indian. The proposed regulations, he argued, by requiring applicants to show a relationship to an enrolled member of a federally recognized tribe, would potentially exclude members of descendants of terminated tribes, state-recognized tribes, and nonrecognized tribes.

Since the BIA's standard blood quantum is one-fourth, and with the high rates of outmarriage, Russell Thornton, an anthropologist, suggests that sometime in this century the proportion of the Indian population with less than one-fourth blood quantum will rise to 60 percent. If this trend is correct, from the federal government's standpoint "decreasing blood quanta of the total Native American population may be perceived as meaning that the numbers of Native Americans to whom it is obligated have declined."[46] This will not mean the extinction of Indian tribes, but it will mean a new form of federal termination of Indians who are eligible for federal aid and services.

Questions around whether a tribe is federally recognized, state-recognized, nonrecognized, or terminated have direct bearing on the internal and external political dynamics of tribes, and directly affect intergovernmental relations, since only recognized tribes may engage in gaming operations that are not directly subject to state law, may exercise criminal jurisdiction over their members and a measure of civil jurisdiction over nonmembers, and are exempt from a variety of state and federal taxes.

What Are Indian Lands?

The first and most obvious difference between Indian peoples and all other groups in the United States is that Indians were here before anyone else. All the land in the continental United States, Alaska, and Hawaii was inhabited and revered by the over six hundred distinctive indigenous peoples who dwelt here. Gradually, however, from 1492 forward, various foreign nations—Russia, Holland, Spain, Great Britain, France, Sweden, and later the United States—competed for an economic foothold in North America. For the three most dominant European states, France, Spain, and Great Britain (and later the United States, as Britain's successor), this usually included efforts to secure title to indigenous lands through formal treaties, which were sometimes coercive and occasionally fraudulent, while some were fairly negotiated.[47]

When the United States declared independence in 1776, it wisely opted to continue the policy of negotiating treaties with tribes, which it continued to do until 1871, when Congress unilaterally declared that "hereafter no Indian nation or tribe within the territory of the United States shall be acknowledged or recognized as an independent nation, tribe, or power with whom the United States may contract by treaty."[48] However, this stance proved unworkable and within a short period the United States was again negotiating *agreements* with tribal nations that were often referred to and accorded the legal status of treaties. The negotiation of agreements continued until 1912.

Many of these documents were primarily viewed as land cession arrangements by the federal government, in which the United States purchased varying amounts of tribal lands in exchange for monies, goods, and services. In addition, tribes "reserved" their remaining lands, or agreed to relocate to new lands, which were usually designated as reservations. These reserved lands were to be held "in trust" by the United States on behalf of the tribe(s), who were deemed the beneficiaries. As the tribes' "trustee," the federal government theoretically exercised the responsibility to assist the tribes in the protection of their lands, resources, and cultural heritage and pledged that it would hold itself to the highest standards of good faith and honesty in all its dealings with the tribes.

For example, article 1 of a treaty the Kickapoo signed on October 24, 1832 , contained a cession of land:

> The Kickapoo tribe of Indians, in consideration of the stipulations hereinafter made, do hereby cede to the United States, the lands assigned to them by the treaty of Edwardsville, and concluded at St. Louis . . . and all other claims to lands within the State of Missouri.[49]

The second article, however, described the lands the tribe had secured for their land cessions:

> The United States will provide for the Kickapoo tribe, a country to reside in, southwest of the Missouri river, as their permanent place of residence as long as they remain a tribe . . . [and] it is hereby agreed that the country within the following boundaries shall be assigned, conveyed, and forever secured . . . to the said Kickapoo tribe.[50]

In this case the Kickapoo agreed to relocate to a little over 700,000 acres of new lands in Kansas that were to serve as their permanent "reservation."

In short, a reservation is an area of land—whether aboriginal or new—that has been reserved for an Indian tribe, band, village, or nation. Generally, the United States holds, in trust for the tribe, legal title to the reserved territory. The tribe in these instances holds a beneficial title to the lands, or, in other words, an exclusive right of occupancy. Of course, reservations were not all created by treaty. Congress established a number of reservations by statute.

The president, through the use of executive order power, established many other reservations. For instance, the state of Arizona has twenty-one reservations—twenty of which were created by presidents. The core foundation of the Navajo Reservation (the largest in the country), was treaty-established in 1868, though the many additions to it were mostly by executive orders. In 1919, Congress forbade the president from establishing any more reservations via executive order. Finally, the secretary of the interior is empowered under the 1934 Indian Reorganization Act to establish, expand, or restore reservations.

As of 1998, there were 314 reservations and other restricted and trust lands in the United States. These reserved lands are located in thirty-one states, mostly in the West. There are also twelve state-established reservations in Connecticut, Massachusetts, Michigan, New York, New Jersey, South Carolina, Georgia, and Virginia. Despite the large number of federally recognized Alaska Native groups, there is only one reservation, the Annette Island Indian Reserve.[51]

At present, the indigenous land base in the United States, including Alaska, is approximately 100 million acres—fifty-six million in the continental United States, forty-four million in Alaska. This represents approximately 4 percent of all lands in the

United States. Map 1 graphically shows the rapid and enormous loss of aboriginal territory to the United States from the birth of the American republic to the present day.

The roughly one hundred million acres constitutes territory over which tribal governments and Alaska Native villages and corporations exercise varying amounts of governmental jurisdiction, and where state laws are generally inapplicable, with exceptions.

In 1999, 1,397,931 Indians were identified in a BIA report out of the total U.S. Indian population in 2000 of 2,475,956 (individuals self-identifying as single race American Indian or Alaska Native).

What Is Indian Country?

For an indigenous government to be able to exercise criminal or civil jurisdiction over their territory, their own members, and, in some limited cases, non-Indians, the land in question must be designated as *Indian Country*. In the colonial era, Indian Country encompassed all the lands beyond the frontier lands "populated by tribes and bands of Indians who rejected contact with 'civilized' populations."[52] Today, however, the concept "has been elevated by federal law above other ideas because it transcends mere geographical limitations and represents that sphere of influence in which Indian traditions and federal laws passed specifically to deal with the political relationship of the United States to American Indians have primacy."[53]

Indian Country: Beyond the Reservation

Broadly, the term "Indian Country" means land within which Indian laws and customs and federal laws relating to Indians are generally applicable. But it is also defined as all the land under the supervision and protection of the federal government that has been set aside primarily for the use of Indians. Federal law defines it, first, as all land within the boundaries of an Indian reservation, whether owned by Indians or non-Indians. Second, it includes all "dependent Indian communities" in the United States. These are lands—pueblos of New Mexico, Oklahoma Indian tribal lands, and California rancherias—previously recognized by European nations and now by the successor government, the United States, as belonging to the tribes or as set aside by the federal government for use and benefit of the Indians.

Pueblo lands, because they were previously recognized as belonging to the pueblos under Spanish, Mexican, and later U.S. law, are not, strictly speaking, reservations, but are considered Indian lands and are held in trust by the federal government because they are held in communal ownership with fee-simple title residing in each pueblo. Some Pueblo Indian lands are held in equitable ownership by various pueblos, with the United States holding legal title. These lands include reservations created by congressional statute and executive order reservations established by the president.

Oklahoma's numerous Indian tribes also have a distinctive history, though their lands also constitute Indian Country. It is important to note that the tribes in the eastern part of the state, what was called "Indian Territory," home of the Five Civilized Tribes, have a somewhat different history from tribes in the western part of the state, or what was called "Oklahoma Territory, home of the Cheyenne, Arapaho, Kiowa, Comanche, etc. Although the BIA and the Bureau of the Census have asserted that there are no Indian reservations in Oklahoma, except for the Osage, John Moore argues that the reservation status of Oklahoma tribes persists, notwithstanding allotment and other policies designed to terminate Indian communal land holdings.[54]

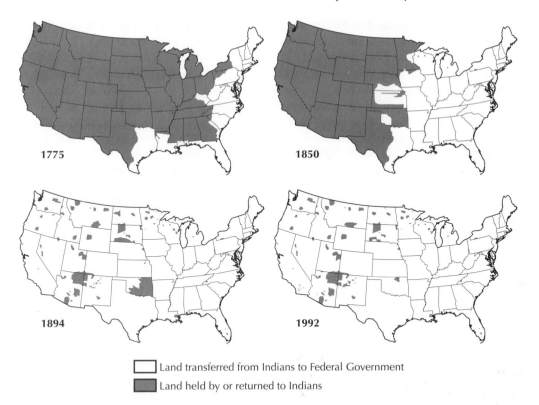

1775   1850   1894   1992

☐ Land transferred from Indians to Federal Government

■ Land held by or returned to Indians

MAP 1   American Indian Land Losses. *Source: Encyclopedia of North American Indians,* edited by Frederick E. Hoxie. Copyright © 1996 by Houghton Mifflin Company. All rights reserved.

Some California tribes, because of heavy Spanish influence dating from 1769, live on rancherias, a Spanish term meaning "small reservation" and originally applied to Indians who had not been settled in Christian mission communities. The history of death and dispossession visited upon California's indigenous population may well be the worst of any aboriginal peoples in the United States. From a population of well over 300,000 at the time of contact, California Indians experienced a staggering rate of decline from diseases, outright genocide, and displacement.[55] That they have retained any lands at all is a remarkable testimony to their fortitude.

Finally, the Indian Country designation includes all individual Indian allotments (I will discuss the allotment policy shortly) that are still held in trust or restricted status by the federal government—whether inside or outside an Indian reservation.[56]

For political and legal purposes, the designation of Indian Country is crucial because the reach of a tribal nation's jurisdiction is generally restricted to lands so designated. And it is Indian Country where most jurisdictional disputes arise between tribes and their members, tribes and non-Indians, and tribes and the local, county, state, or federal governments.

For example, this was the central question in the recent U.S. Supreme Court case involving indigenous people, *Alaska v. Native Village of Venetie Tribal Government* (1998). In this case, the court had to decide whether the village of Venetie constituted Indian Country. If so, then the tribal government had the right to impose a tax on a construction company; if not, then it lacked such taxing power. In a harmful ruling for Alaska Native sovereignty, the Supreme Court held that the village's fee-simple lands did not constitute Indian Country, thus depriving Alaska villages and corporations of the power to exercise a number of governmental powers that tribal nations in the lower forty-eight states exercise routinely. The Supreme Court, however, need not have relied so exclusively on the question of whether or not Venetia constituted "Indian Country" since the statutes articulating this concept clearly did not encompass Alaska at the time they were enacted.

Demography and Indian Country

According to a report, *Changing America,* prepared by the Council of Economic Advisers for President Clinton's Race Initiative in 1998, the population of the United States is increasingly diverse. In recent years the four major racial/ethnic minority groups—Latinos, Asian Americans, African Americans, and American Indians—have each grown faster than the population as a whole. Whereas in 1970 the combination of these four groups represented only 16 percent of the entire population, by 1998 this had increased to 27 percent.[57] The Bureau of the Census, the report noted, projects that by 2050, these groups will account for "almost half of the U.S. Population." Early data from the 2000 U.S. census, which shows a total population of 281,421,906, indicate the continuing transformation of race and ethnicity in America. While the categories of white (211,460,626), Hispanic or Latino (35,305,818), black or African American (34,658,190), American Indian or Alaska Native (2,475,956), Asian (10,242,998), and Native Hawaiian or other Pacific Islander (398,835) were familiar, for the first time in history individuals could choose self-identify as having more than one race. Some 6,826,228 people, 2.4 percent of the total population, claimed affiliation with two or more races.[58]

While this projected growth has potentially staggering political and economic implications, the fact is that the total indigenous population, despite the large number of indigenous nations—561 and counting—is comparatively quite small (see figures 1–5). In 2000, there were a reported 2,475,956 self-identified Indians and Alaska Natives, a 26 percent increase since 1990. This is a drastic decline from pre-European figures of over seven million, but it is far more than the nadir of perhaps only 250,000 around 1900.[59] The 2000 figure represents only 0.9 percent of the total U.S. population of 281,421,906.

Although the overall population of self-identified American Indians and Alaska Natives is still quite small, because of the new category allowing individuals to identify as belonging to more than one race (sixty-three racial options were possible), the 2000 census data are not directly comparable with data from the 1990 census or previous censuses. Thus, while approximately 2.5 million individuals identified themselves as American Indian and Alaska Native alone, an additional 1.6 million people reported themselves as being indigenous and belonging to "at least one other race." Within this group, the most common combinations were "American Indian and Alaska Native *and* White" (66 percent of the population reported this); "American Indian and Alaska Native *and* Black or African American" (11 percent of the population); and "American Indian and Alaska Native *and* White *and* Black or African American" (7 percent). In sum, approximately 4.1 million people reported themselves as being American Indian and Alaska Native "alone or in combination with one or more other races."[60] The wide diversity within this population will be discussed in greater detail in forthcoming Census reports not yet available.

Suffice it to say, the amount of racial mixing acknowledged in the American Indian context is extreme when compared to that of other racial/ethnic groups. As Russell Thor-

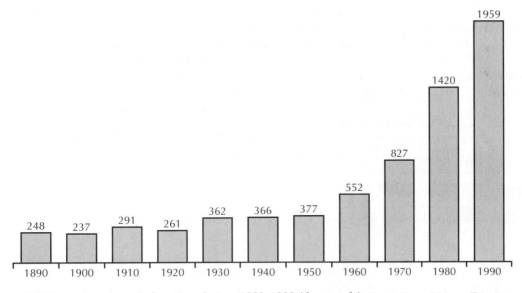

FIGURE 1   American Indian Population, 1890–1990 (thousands). *Source:* Larry Hajime Shinagawa and Michael Jang, *Atlas of American Diversity* (Walnut Creek, Calif.: AltaMira, 1998), 107–8. *Notes:* 1900, partially estimated: 1930 Eskimo and Aleut populations are based on 1939 counts.

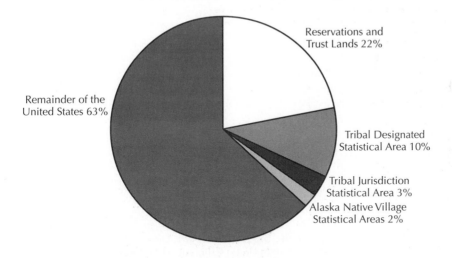

FIGURE 2   American Indian Population by Type of Area, 1990 (percent). *Source:* Larry Hajime Shinagawa and Michael Jang, *Atlas of American Diversity* (Walnut Creek, Calif.: AltaMira, 1998), 107–8.

ton, a Cherokee anthropologist, noted in his analysis of the 2000 census data, American Indians have a racial mixture of 37 percent, which "far exceeds percentages for other groups." Thornton noted that only about 5 percent of African Americans reported mixed ancestry.[61]

In Alaska, there is only one small reservation, Annette Island Reserve, though for census purposes lands are designated as "Alaska Native Village Statistical areas" that are inhabited and recognized as indigenous areas. Approximately 47,244 Alaska Natives live on these lands. In sum, more than

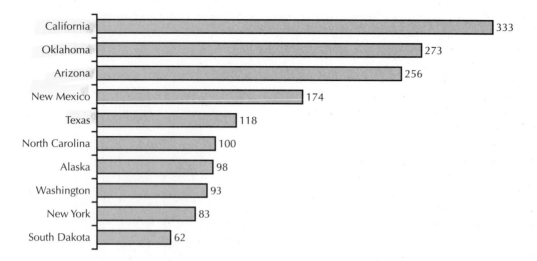

FIGURE 3   States with the Ten Largest American Indian Populations, 2000 (thousands).
Source: www.census.gov/clo/www/redistricting.html

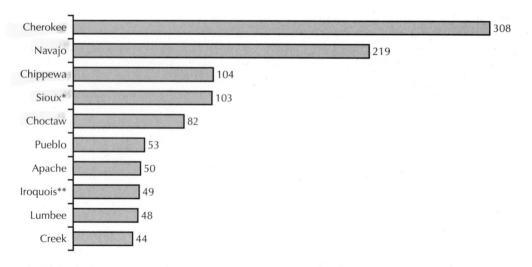

FIGURE 4   Ten Largest American Indian Tribes, 1990 (thousands). *Source:* Larry Hajime Shinagawa and Michael Jang, *Atlas of American Diversity* (Walnut Creek, Calif.: AltaMira, 1998), 107–8.
*Any entry with the spelling "Siouan" was miscoded to Sioux in North Carolina.
**Reporting and/or processing problems have affected the data for this tribe.

60 percent, over one million, of all Indian people do not live on Indian reservations.[62] A majority of indigenous peoples, in fact some 56.2 percent, live in metropolitan or suburban areas. And roughly half of all urban Indians can be found in as few as sixteen cities, largely as a result of the 1950s and 1960s termination, relocation, and educational programs of the federal government.

In the early days of relocation, the BIA generally helped send Indians to Chicago, Los Angeles, Denver, or Salt Lake City. By 1990, Indians had migrated to a number of other metropolitan areas. Cities with the

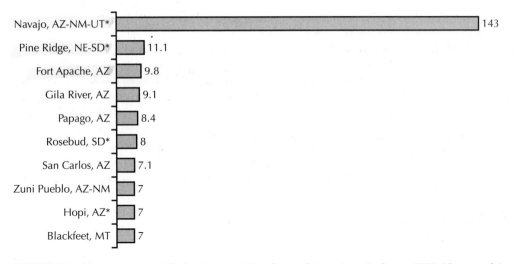

FIGURE 5 Reservations with the Largest Numbers of American Indians, 1990 (thousands). *Source: Larry Hajime Shinagawa and Michael Jang, Atlas of American Diversity (Walnut Creek, Calif.: AltaMira, 1998), 107–8.*
*Includes trust lands

largest Indian populations in 1990 were Tulsa, Oklahoma (48,348); Oklahoma City, Oklahoma (46,111); Los Angeles-Long Beach, California (43,689); Phoenix, Arizona (38,309); and Seattle-Tacoma, Washington (32,980).[63] The vast majority of Indians still live in the western half of the United States.

The states with the ten largest indigenous populations are shown in figure 4. The District of Columbia had the fewest Indians, 1,466.

There is also great variation in the population of individual tribes (see figure 5). The largest tribe is the Cherokee Nation of Oklahoma, with 369,035 members. The smallest tribes have fewer than one hundred members. The indigenous population is also a young population, with more than 35 percent younger than age seventeen. In fact, the median age for reservation Indians is more than ten years younger than that of the general U.S. population. The Indian population, like that of the Jews and the Japanese Americans in Hawaii, is also one that experiences an extremely high level of intergroup marriage (marriage between persons of dif-

ferent races). Although intergroup marriage couples accounted for only 4 percent of all married couples in the United States in 1990, American Indians had a 53 percent intergroup marriage rate. Potentially, this figure could have severe cultural and political implications for indigenous nations.[64]

As Snipp mused:

The extraordinarily high level of racial intermarriage for American Indians provides a good reason to expect that growing numbers of American Indians and their descendants will choose non-Indians for spouses and to a greater or lesser degree become absorbed into the dominant culture. Some of these Indians will abandon their cultural heritage altogether, while others may make only minor accommodations as a result of having a non-Indian spouse. This raises a question that is extremely controversial within many quarters of the American Indian community: Are American Indians assimilating so quickly through racial intermarriage that they will eventually, in the not to distant future, marry themselves out of existence?[65]

Predicting the future is an impossible task and I will not hazard a guess as to whether this intermarriage rate will continue. Suffice it to say, this is viewed as a serious predicament by some tribes and raises some important questions. For instance, will Indians, like many intermarried Jews, be able to show a propensity for combining extensive intermarriage with a surge in ethnic and religious pride? For while the rate of Jewish intermarriage is higher today than at any other point, American Jewish culture and community life appear to be flourishing, including a resurgent interest in Yiddish.[66]

Other questions confront tribes as well. Will they continue to use blood quantum as their primary definitional criteria? Will the federal government claim that its legal and moral obligations to Indians dissipate if a tribal nation's blood quantum falls below a certain percentage? Will tribes be able to exercise jurisdiction over a multiracial citizenry? These are questions some tribes are beginning to address as we begin the new millennium.

Conclusion

The power to define—what is a tribe, who is an Indian, what constitutes Indian Country, which group gets recognized—along with the power to decide whether or not to act in a colonial capacity in relation to indigenous nations are important means by which the federal government has gained and retains a dominant position vis-à-vis tribal groups. While on one hand supporting the right of indigenous polities to exercise self-determination, the United States on the other still insists that it has the power and the right to trump important tribal governmental decisions regarding identity and has

shown throughout its history that it will so act if it deems it necessary to further its own economic, political, and cultural interests.

The demographic data presented glaringly show that diversity and uncertainty are hallmarks of Indian Country, with more than half the indigenous population living off reservations and Indians outmarrying at increasing rates. What the impact of such movement and marriage rates will be on tribal national identity, federal Indian policy, and the government-to-government relationship is, however, impossible to predict.

NOTES

1. U.S. Congress, *American Indian Policy Review Commission: Final Report,* vol. 1 (Washington, D.C.: Government Printing Office, 1977), 3.
2. See, e.g., Haunani-Kay Trask, *From a Native Daughter: Colonialism and Sovereignty in Hawai'i* (Monroe, Maine: Common Courage, 1993) and Roger MacPherson Furrer, ed., *He Alo á He Alo (Face to Face): Hawaiian Voices on Sovereignty* (Honolulu, Hawaii: American Friends Service Committee-Hawai'i, 1993).
3. 3528 U.S. 495 (2000).
4. Http://www.doi.gov/nativehawaiians/.
5. See, S. James Anaya, "The Native Hawaiian People and International Human Rights Law: Toward a Remedy for Past and Continuing Wrongs," *Georgia Law Review* 28 (1994), 309–64.
6. Vine Deloria Jr. "The American Indian Image in North America," *Encyclopedia of Indians of the Americas,* vol. 1 (St. Clair Shores, Mich.: Scholarly Press, 1974), 43.
7. Paula D. McClain and Joseph Stewart Jr., *"Can We All Get Along?" Racial and Ethnic Minorities in American Politics* (Boulder, Colo.: Westview, 1998), 6, citing John Higham, *Strangers in the Land: Patterns of American Nativism, 1860–1925* (Westport, Conn.: Greenwood, 1963).
8. 180 U.S. 261 (1901).
9. Felix S. Cohen, *Handbook of Federal Indian Law,* reprint ed. (Albuquerque: University of New Mexico Press, 1972), 268.
10. Jack Utter, *American Indians: Answers to Today's Questions* (Lake Ann, Mich.: National Woodlands, 1993), 1972), 30–31.
11. William Quinn Jr., "Federal Acnowledgment of American Indian Tribes? The Historical

Development of a Legal Concept," *American Journal of Legal History* 34 (October 1990): 331–63.

12. 56 *Federal Register* 47, 325 (1991).

13. 25 Code of Federal Regulations 83.7 (a)–(g) (1991).

14. 25 *U.S.C.* chapter 1, section 1, 961.

15. 25 *U.S.C.* chapter 1, 962.

16. William W. Quinn Jr., "Federal Acknowledgment of American Indian Tribes: Authority, Judicial Interposition, and 25 C.F.R. Sec. 83," *American Indian Law Review* 17 (fall 1992): 48.

17. Quinn, "Federal Acknowledgment of American Indian Tribes," 52.

18. Felix Cohen, "The Erosion of Indian Rights, 1950–1953: A Case Study in Bureaucracy," *Yale Law Journal* 62 (February 1953): 352.

19. Letter from Carol A. Bacon, acting director of the Office of Tribal Services, Bureau of Indian Affairs, 3 December 1991. The author has copy of the letter.

20. 108 Stat., 709.

21. See U.S. Congress, House, "A Bill to Provide for Administrative Procedures to Extend Federal Recognition to Certain Indian Groups, and for Other Purposes," 105th Cong., 2d sess., 1998, H. Rept. 1154. As of this writing—May 1999—none of these bills has become law.

22. Ellen Barry, "Agency Willing to Relinquish Power to Recognize Tribes," *Boston Globe,* 26 May 2000, B1.

23. 118 U.S. 948 (1998).

24. See, e.g., Trask, *From a Native Daughter,* and Anaya, "The Native Hawaiian People," 309.

25. Allogan Slagle, "Unfinished Justice: Completing the Resoration and Acknowledgment of California Indian Tribes," *American Indian Journal* 13, no. 4 (fall 1989): 325–45.

26. William W. Quinn Jr., "The Southeast Syndrome: Notes on Indian Descendant Recruitment Organizations and Their Perceptions of Native American Culture," *American Indian Quarterly* 14, no. 2 (spring 1990): 147–54.

27. Jackie J. Kim, "The Indian Federal Recognition Procedures Act of 1995: A Congressional Solution to an Administrative Morass," *Thw Administrativwe Law Journal of the American University* 9, no. 3 (Fall 1995): 899–932.

28. See http://www.doi.gov/bia/bar/indexq.htm for statistical details of the acknowledgment project's efforts.

29. Donald Fixico, *Termination and Relocation: Federal Indian Policy, 1945–1960* (Albuquerque, N. Mex.: University of New Mexico Press, 1986).

30. 67 Stat., B132.

31. 110 Stat., 130.

32. N.C. Public Laws, 1953, chapter 874, p. 747.

33. 70 Stat., 254.

34. David E. Wilkins, "Breaking into the Intergovernmental Matrix: The Lumbee Tribe's Efforts to Secure Federal Acknowledgment," *Publius: The Journal of Federalism* 23 (Fall 1993): 123–42.

35. McClain and Stewart, "Can We All Get Along?" 6.

36. Bart Vogel, "Who Is an Indian in Federal Indian Law?" in *Studies in American Indian Law,* ed. Ralph Johnson (Pullman, Wash.: Washington State University, 1970), 53.

37. C. Matthew Snipp, *American Indians: The First of This Land* (New York: Russell Sage Foundation, 1989), 34.

38. Snipp, *First of This Land,* 33.

39. Cohen, *Handbook,* 2.

41. 29 Stat., 321.

42. Abdul G. Kahn, *Report on the Indian Definition Study* (Washington, D.C.: Department of Education, 1980).

43. Kahn, *Indian Definition Study,* 56.

44. Joane Nagel, *American Indian Ethnic Renewal: Red Power and the Resurgence of Identity and Culture* (New York: Oxford University Press, 1996), 243.

45. Brian Stackes, "Planned Bureau of Indian Affairs Regulations Stir Concerns Among Tribal Leaders," *Indian Country Today,* 18 August 2000, 1.

46. Russell Thornton, "Tribal Membership Requirements and the Demography of 'Old' and 'New' Native Americans," in *Changing Numbers, Changing Needs: American Indian Demogrphy and Public Health,* ed. Gary D. Sandefur, Ronald R. Rindfuss, and Barney Cohen (Washington, D.C.: National Academy Press, 1996), 110–11.

47. See, e.g., Francis Paul Prucha, *American Indian Treaties: The History of a Political Anomaly* (Berkeley, Calif.: University of California Press, 1994) and Robert A. Williams Jr. *Linking Arms Together: American Indian Treaty Visions of Law and Peace, 1600–1800* (New York: Oxford University Press, 1997).

48. 16 Stat., 566.

49. 7 Stat., 391.

50. 7 Stat., 391.

51. Cesare Marino, "Reservations," in *Native America in the Twentieth Century: An Encyclopedia,* ed. Mary B. Davis (New York: Garland Publishing, Inc., 1996), 544–56.

52. Vine Deloria Jr. and Clifford M. Lytle, *American Indians, American Justice* (Austin: University of Texas Press, 1983), 58.
53. Deloria and Lytle, *American Indians,* 58.
54. John H. Moore, "The Enduring Reservations of Oklahoma," in *State & Reservation: New Perspectives on Federal Indian Policy,* ed. George Pierre Castile and Robert L. Bee (Tucson: University of Arizona Press, 1992), 92–109.
55. See, Robert F. Heizer, *The Destruction of California Indians* (Lincoln: University of Nebvraska Press, 1993) for a first rate account of what these ntions experienced from 1847 to 1865.
56. Title 18, *U.S. Code,* section 1151.
57. Council of Economic Advisers, *Changing America: Indicators of Social and Economic Well-Being by Race and Hispanic Origin* (Washington, D.C.: Government Printing Office, 1998), 4.
58. www.census.gov/prod/2001 pubs.

59. Russell Thornton, *American Indian Holocauwst and Survival: A Population History Since 1492* (Norman: University of Oklahoma Press, 1987).
60. www.census.gov/prod/2001 pubs.
61. Russell Thornton, "What the Census Doesn't Count," *New York Times,* 23 March 2001, A21.
62. C. Matthew Snipp, "The Size and Distribution of the American Indian Population: Fertility, Mortality, Migration, and Residence," in *Changing Numbers, Changing Needs: American Indian Demography and Public Health,* ed. Gary D. Sandefur, Ronald R. Rindfuss, and Barney Cohen (Washington, D.C.: National Academy Press, 1996), 42–43.
63. Snipp, "The Size and Distribution," 39.
64. Snipp, *The First of This Land,* 171.
65. Snipp, *The First of This Land,* 165.
66. Lawrence H. Fuchs, *The American Kaleidoscope* (Hanover, N.H.: Wesleyan University Press, 1990), 329.

8

ASIAN AMERICAN PANETHNICITY
Bridging Institutions and Identities

Yen Le Espiritu

Questions to Consider

Korean, Chinese, Japanese, and Philippine Americans share very different cultural histories. Each group has their own language, culture, religious beliefs, and immigration experiences yet they get "lumped" under the category Asian. What political function does panethnic identity serve, according to Yen Le Espiritu, for these ethnic groups?

Goals, Definitions, and Scope

Pan-Asian American ethnicity is the development of bridging organizations and solidarities among several ethnic and immigrant groups of Asian ancestry. Although subject to the same general prejudice and similar discriminatory laws, Asians in the United States have rarely conceived of themselves as a single people and many still do not. "Asiatic," "Oriental," and "Mongolian" were merely convenient labels used by outsiders to refer to all Asians. The development of panethnicity among Asian Americans has a short history. While examples of white oppression of Asian Americans stretch back over a century, a meaningful pan-Asian movement was not constructed until the late 1960s (Daniels 1988, p. 113). This [reading] tells the story of this construction—of the resultant unity and division, and corresponding benefits and costs. The emphasis here is on the *political* nature of panethnicity, that is, on the distribution and exercise of, and the struggle for, power and resources inside and outside the community. Panethnicity is political not only because it serves as a basis for interest group mobilization but also because it is linked with the expansion of the role of the polity (Enloe 1980, p. 5).

Panethnicity has not been well studied. Moreover, the few existing works on panethnicity have dealt primarily with Native American and Latino American panethnicities (Cornell 1988; Nagel 1982; Padilla 1985). Except for several essays from the proponents of the 1960s Asian American movement (Uyematsu 1971; P. Wong 1972), the process of pan-Asianization has not been well documented. While social scientists have devoted substantial attention to individual Asian groups (Bonacich and Modell 1980; Kim 1981; Montero 1979), few have focused on Asian Americans as a collectivity. Yet a host of pan-Asian organizations testify to the salience of pan-Asian consciousness, as do the numerous cooperative efforts by Asian American groups and organizations on behalf of both subgroup and pan-Asian interests.

There are two dimensions of groupness: the conceptual and the organizational. The conceptual refers to individual behavior and attitude—the ways group members view

themselves; the organizational refers to political structures—the ways groups are organized as collective actors. The boundaries of these two dimensions usually but do not necessarily coincide (Cornell 1988, p. 72). Some key indicators of pan-Asian consciousness include self-identification, pan-Asian residential, friendship, and marriage patterns, and membership in pan-Asian organizations. Given the multiple levels of Asian American ethnicity, a study of individual ethnicity can also document "ethnic switching"—the relabeling of individuals' ethnic affiliation to meet situational needs. That is, a person is a Japanese American or an Asian American depending on the ethnic identities available to him or her in a particular situation. Sometimes the individual has a choice, and sometimes not (see Nagel 1986, pp. 95–96). While recognizing the importance of the conceptual dimension of panethnicity, this work is primarily a study of the organizational dimension: the institutionalization of Asian American consciousness, and not the state of panethnic consciousness itself. Thus, most of the evidence is drawn from the level of formal organizations. The research methods are basically those of the historically grounded community study, combining organization archives, public records, interviews with the leaders of organizations, participant observation, and library research.

Naturally, the rank and file's level of Asian American consciousness influences its institutionalization. On the other hand, grass-roots consciousness does not necessarily precede the process of organizational consolidation. As this study documents, panethnic organizations need not merely reflect existing panethnic consciousness but can also generate and augment it. In building themselves, pan-Asian organizations also build pan-Asian consciousness. Thus, the organizational level is intrinsically worthy of examination because it tells us about

From *Asian American Panethnicity: Bridging Institutions and Identities*, pp. 14–52, by Yen Le Espiritu. Reprinted by permission of Temple University Press. Copyright © 1992 by Temple University. All rights reserved.

the directions of the populations supposedly represented.

Moreover, pan-Asian institutions cannot survive without support; their very existence presupposes some amount of consensus. One research strategy would be to quantify this consensus. Another would be to identify the individuals who may have vested interests in promoting pan-Asian ethnicity, and in so doing name the dominant groups and sectors in the pan-Asian coalitions. The research question then becomes not who identifies with pan-Asian ethnicity, but who benefits the most from it—and at whose expense? Such an approach allows us to look beyond numbers to the power struggles and the resultant intergroup conflicts and competition.

The influx of the post-1965 Asian immigrants and refugees—who are distinct in ethnic and class composition from the more "established" Asian Americans—has exacerbated intergroup conflicts. The determination of what and whose interests will be defended often factionalizes the pan-Asian collectivity, as newcomers and old-timers pursue their separate goals (Lopez and Espiritu 1990, p. 206). On the other hand, the pan-Asian concept is now so well institutionalized that new Asian immigrants and refugees often encounter extensive pressure to consider themselves Asian Americans, regardless of whether or not they see themselves in such terms. For example, Southeast Asian refugees have had to adopt the Asian American designation because this category resonates in the larger society (Hein 1989; Skinner and Hendricks 1979). Accordingly, this study examines the benefits as well as the limitations of pan-Asian coalitions.

Scholars and laypersons alike have argued that Asian Americans are not a panethnic group because they do not share a common culture (Ignacio 1976; Trottier 1981). While Native Americans can trace their common descent to their unique relationship to the land, and Latino Americans to their common language, Asian Americans have no readily identifiable symbols of ethnicity. This view involves the implicit assumption that ethnic boundaries are unproblematic. However, as Frederick Barth (1969) suggested, when ethnic boundaries are strong and persistent, cultural solidarity will result. But ethnic groups that are merging need not exhibit such solidarity. Discussing the ongoing efforts to build an Asian American culture, John Liu (1988 pp. 123–24) stated, "The admonition that we can no longer assume that Asian Americans share a common identity and culture is not a setback in our efforts, but rather a reminder that the goals we set for ourselves need to be constantly struggled for."

The construction of pan-Asian ethnicity involves the creation of a common Asian American heritage out of diverse histories. Part of the heritage being created hinges on what Asian Americans share: a history of exploitation, oppression, and discrimination. However, individuals' being treated alike does not automatically produce new groups. "Only when people become aware of being treated alike on the basis of some arbitrary criterion do they begin to establish identity on that basis" (Shibutani and Kwan 1965, p. 210). For Asian Americans, this "arbitrary criterion" is their socially defined racial distinctiveness, or their imposed identity as "Asians." As such, an important task for pan-Asian leaders is to define racist activities against one Asian American subgroup as hostilities against all Asian Americans. In her call for pan-Asian organization, Amy Uyematsu (1971, pp. 10–11) referred to the internment of Japanese Americans as a "racist treatment of *'yellows,'*" and the mistreatment of Chinese immigrants in 1885 as mistreatment of *Asians* in America (emphasis mine). More recently, Asian American leaders characterized the 1982 fatal beating of Chinese American Vincent Chin as a racial attack against all Asian Americans (Zia 1984). Thus, following Barth (1969), the task at hand is to document the process of culture building and its function in the construction and maintenance of panethnic boundaries—not to define and inventory cultural symbols. . . .

Social and Demographic Changes: Setting the Context

Although Asians in the United States have long been engaged in political action, their efforts never drew public attention until the 1960s (Chan 1991, p. 171). Prompted by broader political struggles and internal demographic changes, college students of Asian ancestry spearheaded the Asian American movement. Critical to its development was the mobilization of American blacks. Besides offering tactical lessons, the civil rights and the Black Power movements had a profound impact on the consciousness of Asian Americans, sensitizing them to racial issues (Uyematsu 1971). The anticolonial nationalist movements in Asia also stirred racial and cultural pride and provided a context for the emergence of the Yellow Power movement (P. Wong 1972). Influenced by these broader political struggles, Americans of Asian ancestry united to denounce racist institutional structures, demand new or unattended rights, and assert their cultural and racial distinctiveness. Normal urban issues such as housing, education, and social welfare began to take on ethnic coloration.

While important, these broader societal developments alone do not explain why the Asian American movement became panethnic. To understand this development, we first need to understand the underlying social and demographic factors that allowed pan-Asianism to take root in the 1960s but not earlier. Before World War II, pan-Asian unity was not feasible because the predominantly foreign-born Asian population did not share a common language. During the postwar years, increasing intergroup communication and contact facilitated the emergence of a pan-Asian consciousness. The breakdown of economic and residential barriers during the postwar period provided the first opportunity for an unprecedented number of Asian Americans to come into intimate, sustained contact with the larger society—and with one another.

From an Immigrant to a Native Population

Before 1940, the Asian population in the United States was primarily an immigrant population. Immigrant Asians faced practical barriers to pan-Asian unity. Foremost was their lack of a common language. Old national rivalries were another obstacle, as many early Asian immigrants carried the political memories and outlook of their homelands. For example, Japan's occupation of Korea resulted in pervasive anti-Japanese sentiments among Koreans in the United States. According to Brett Melendy (1977, p. 155), "Fear and hatred of the Japanese appeared to be the only unifying force among the various Korean groups through the years." Moreover, these historical enmities and linguistic and cultural differences reinforced one another as divisive agents.

During the postwar period, due to immigration restrictions and the growing dominance of the second and third generations, American-born Asians outnumbered immigrants. The demographic changes of the 1940s were pronounced. During this decade, nearly twenty thousand Chinese American babies were born. For the first time, the largest five-year cohort of Chinese Americans was under five years of age (Kitano and Daniels 1988, p. 37). By 1960, approximately two-thirds of the Asian population in California had been born in the United States (Ong 1989, pp. 5–8). As the

Asian population became a native-born community, linguistic and cultural differences began to blur. Although they had attended Asian-language schools, most American-born Asians possessed only a limited knowledge of their ethnic language (Chan 1991, p. 115). By 1960, with English as the common language, persons from different Asian backgrounds were able to communicate with one another (Ling 1984, p. 73), and in so doing create a common identity associated with the United States.

Moreover, unlike their immigrant parents, native-born and American-educated Asians could muster only scant loyalties to old world ties. Historical antagonisms between their mother countries thus receded in importance (P. Wong 1972, p. 34). For example, growing up in America, second-generation Koreans "had difficulty feeling the painful loss of the homeland and understanding the indignity of Japanese domination" (Takaki 1989, p. 292). Thus, while the older generation of Koreans hated all Japanese, "their children were much less hostile or had no concern at all" (Melendy 1977, p. 156). As a native-born Japanese American community advocate explained, "By 1968, we had a second generation. We could speak English; so there was no language problem. And we had little feelings of historical animosity" (Kokubun interview).

As national differences receded in subjective importance, generational differences widened. For the most part, American-born Asians considered themselves to have more in common with other American-born Asians than they did with foreign-born compatriots. According to a third-generation Japanese American who is married to a Chinese American, "As far as our experiences in America, I have more things in common than differences with a Chinese American. Being born and raised here gives us something in common. We have more in common with each other than with a Japanese from

Japan, or a Chinese from China" (Ichioka interview). Much to their parents' dismay, young Asian Americans began to choose their friends and spouses from other Asian groups. Eui-Young Yu (1983, p. 47) related that second- and third-generation Koreans "identify and intermingle as much with other Asian minorities as with fellow Koreans, especially with the Japanese and Chinese." Similarly, Stephen Fugita and David O'Brien (1991, p. 146) reported that the Sansei (third-generation) were much more likely than the Nisei (second-generation) to see themselves as Asian Americans. This muting of cultural and historical divisions distressed their parents, who, more often than not, had supported these divisions for most of their lives. As a young Chinese American asserted:

> My parents mean well and I try to respect them, but they do not understand what it's all about. We have buried the old hatreds between Chinese and Japanese, and my friends and I must go beyond our parents' "hang-ups." My mother is upset because I'm engaged to a Japanese girl but she knows she can do nothing about it. (Cited in Weiss 1974, p. 235)

The Watershed of World War II

Before World War II, Asian immigrant communities were quite distinct entities, isolated from one another and from the larger society. Because of language difficulties, prejudice, and lack of business opportunities elsewhere, there was little chance for Asians in the United States to live outside their ethnic enclaves (Yuan 1966, p. 331). Shut out of the mainstream of American society, the various immigrant groups struggled separately in their respective Chinatowns, Little Tokyos, or Manilatowns. Stanford Lyman (1970, pp. 57–63) reported that the early Chinese and Japanese communities in the western states had little to do with one another—either socially or politically. Although statistical data do not exist, ethnographic accounts confirm the ethnic homogeneity of each early Asian immigrant community. For example, according to a study of New York's Chinatown in the 1890s, "The entire triangular space bounded by Mott, Pell, and Doyers Streets and Chatham Square is given to the exclusive occupancy of these Orientals" (cited in Yuan 1966, p. 323). Within these enclaves, diversity among Asian nationalities was more salient than commonality.

Economic and residential barriers began to crumble after World War II. The war against Nazism called attention to racism at home and discredited the notions of white superiority. The fifteen years after the war was a period of largely positive change as civil rights statutes outlawed racial discrimination in employment as well as housing (Daniels 1988, ch. 7). Popular attitudes were also changing. Polls taken during World War II showed a distinct hostility toward Japan: 74 percent of the respondents favored either killing off all Japanese, destroying Japan as a political entity, or supervising it. On the West Coast, 97 percent of the people polled approved of the relocation of Japanese Americans. In contrast, by 1949, 64 percent of those polled were either friendly or neutral toward Japan (Feraru 1950).

During the postwar years, Asian American residential patterns changed significantly. Because of the lack of statistical data, a longitudinal study of the changing residential patterns of Asian Americans cannot be made. However, descriptive accounts of Asian American communities indicate that these enclaves declined in the postwar years. Edwin Hoyt (1974, p. 94) reported that in the 1940s, second-generation Chinese Americans moved out of the Chinatowns. Although they still came back to shop or to see friends, they lived elsewhere. In 1940,

Rose Hum Lee found twenty-eight cities with an area called Chinatown in the United States. By 1955, Peter Sih found only sixteen (Sung 1967, pp. 143–44). New York's Chinatown exemplifies the declining significance of Asian ethnic enclaves. In 1940, 50 percent of the Chinese in New York City lived in its Chinatown; by 1960, less than one-third lived there (Yuan 1966, p. 331). Similarly, many returning Japanese Americans abandoned their prewar settlement in old central cities and joined the migration to suburbia (Daniels 1988, p. 294). In the early 1970s, Little Tokyo in Los Angeles remained a bustling Japanese American center, "but at night the shop owners [went] home to the houses in the suburbs" (Hoyt 1974, p. 84).

Although single-ethnic communities were still the norm, residential segregation between Asian nationalities declined in the postwar years. Formerly homogeneous, the ethnic enclaves started to house other Asian groups—as well as non-Asian groups. In 1957, driving past 7th and H streets in Washington, D.C., Betty Lee Sung (1967, pp. 142–43) reported, "I passed the length of Chinatown before I suddenly realized that the place was almost deserted. The faces that I did see on the street were not Chinese but Filipinos." In 1970, due to the influx of Japanese and Filipinos, there was a proposal to rename Oakland Chinatown "Asiantown" (Sano 1970). Multigroup urban centers also emerged. Paul Wong (1972, p. 34) reported that since the early 1960s, Asian Americans of diverse national origins have moved into the suburbs outside the major Asian communities such as Berkeley or San Mateo, California. Although a small proportion of the local population, these Asian Americans tended to congregate in pockets; consequently, in some residential blocks a majority of the residents were Asian Americans.

Moreover, recent research on suburban segregation indicates that the level of segregation between certain Asian American groups is often less than that between them and non-Asians. Using Standard Metropolitan Statistical Area (SMSA) data for 1960, 1970, and 1980, Frankie Lam (1986) computed indices of dissimilarity (ID) among Chinese, Japanese, black, and white Americans in 822 suburbs. As indicated in Table 1, from 1960 to 1980 the level of segregation between Chinese and Japanese Americans was much less than that between these two groups and blacks and, in one case, less than that between these groups and whites. But the actual level of segregation is only one issue. The decline of segregation over time is another. From 1960 to 1980, Chinese segregation from the Japanese shows a more pronounced decline (–14.14) than that of Chinese or Japanese from whites (–10.61 and –7.23 respectively) and from blacks (–4.59 and –2.65 respectively). Though not comprehensive, these studies together suggest that Asian residential segregation declined in the postwar years.

As various Asian groups in the United States interacted, they became aware of common problems and goals that transcended parochial interests and historical antagonisms. One recurrent problem was employment discrimination. According to a 1965 report published by the California Fair Employment Practices Commission, for every $51 earned by a white male Californian, Japanese males earned $43 and Chinese males $38—even though Chinese and Japanese American men had become slightly

better educated than the white majority (Daniels 1988, p. 315). Moreover, although the postwar period marked the first time that well-trained Chinese and Japanese Americans could find suitable employment with relative ease, they continued to be passed over for promotion to administrative and supervisory positions (Kitano and Daniels 1988, p. 47). Asians in the United States began to see themselves as a group that shared important common experiences: exploitation, oppression, and discrimination (Uyematsu 1971).

Because inter-Asian contact and communication were greatest on college campuses, pan-Asianism was strongest there (P. Wong 1972, pp. 33–34). Exposure to one another and to the mainstream society led some young Asian Americans to feel that they were fundamentally different from whites. Disillusioned with the white society and alienated from their traditional communities, many Asian American student activists turned to the alternative strategy of pan-Asian unification (Weiss 1974, pp. 69–70).

The Construction of Pan-Asian Ethnicity

Although broader social struggles and internal demographic changes provided the impetus for the Asian American movement, it was the group's politics—confrontational

TABLE 1 Mean Segregation Indices for Chinese and Japanese Americans in 822 U.S. Suburbs, 1960, 1970, and 1980

Ethnic Groups	1960	1970	1980	Change, 1960–80
Chinese–White	38.83	31.45	28.22	–10.61
Chinese–Black	54.02	50.42	49.43	–4.59
Japanese–White	34.00	22.16	26.77	–7.23
Japanese–Black	48.62	48.46	45.97	–2.65
Chinese–Japanese	39.11	27.70	24.97	–14.14

Source: Lam (1986: tables 1, 2, and 3).

and explicitly pan-Asian—that shaped the movement's content. Influenced by the internal colonial model, which stresses the commonalities among "colonized groups," college students of Asian ancestry declared solidarity with fellow Asian Americans— and with other Third World minorities (Blauner 1972, ch. 2). Rejecting the label "Oriental," they proclaimed themselves "Asian American." Through pan-Asian organizations, publications, and Asian American studies programs, Asian American activists built pan-Asian solidarity by pointing out their common fate in American society. The pan-Asian concept enabled diverse Asian American groups to understand their "unequal circumstances and histories as being related" (Lowe 1991, p. 30).

From "Yellow" to "Asian American"

Following the example of the Black Power movement, Asian American activists spearheaded their own Yellow Power movement to seek "freedom from racial oppression through the power of a consolidated yellow people" (Uyematsu 1971, p. 12). In the summer of 1968, more than one hundred students of diverse Asian backgrounds attended an "Are You Yellow?" conference at UCLA to discuss issues of Yellow Power, identity, and the war in Vietnam. In 1970, a new pan-Asian organization in northern California called itself the "Yellow Seed" because "Yellow [is] the common bond between Asian-Americans and Seed symboliz[es] growth as an individual and as an alliance" (Masada 1970). This "yellow" reference was dropped when Filipino Americans rejected the term, claiming that they were brown, not yellow (Ignacio 1976, p. 84; Rabaya 1971, p. 110). At the first Asian American national conference in 1972, Filipino Americans "made it clear to the conferees that we were 'Brown Asians'" by forming a Brown Asian Caucus (Ignacio 1976,

pp. 139–41). It is important to note, however, that Filipino American activists did not reject the term "yellow" because they objected to the pan-Asian framework. Quite the contrary, they rejected it because it allegedly excluded them from that grouping (Rabaya 1971, p. 110).

Other community organizers used the term "Oriental" to define their organizations and service centers. In Southern California, the Council of Oriental Organizations (COO) became the political base for the diverse Asian American communities. In 1968, COO lobbied for federal funding to establish the Oriental Service Center in Los Angeles County, serving Chinese, Japanese, Filipinos, and Koreans. But Asian American activists also rejected *Oriental* because the term conjures up images of "the sexy Susie Wong, the wily Charlie Chan, and the evil Fu Manchu" (Weiss 1974, p. 234). It is also a term that smacks of European colonialism and imperialism: *Oriental* means "East"; Asia is "east" only in relationship to Europe, which was taken as the point of reference (Browne 1985). To define their own image and to claim an *American* identity, college students of Asian ancestry coined the term *Asian American* to "stand for all of us Americans of Asian descent" (Ichioka interview). While *Oriental* suggests passivity and acquiescence, *Asian Americans* connotes political activism because an Asian American "gives a damn about his life, his work, his beliefs, and is willing to do almost anything to help Orientals become Asian Americans" (cited in Weiss 1974, p. 234).

The account above suggests that the creation of a new name is a significant symbolic move in constructing an ethnic identity. In their attempt to forge a pan-Asian identity, Asian American activists first had to coin a composite term that would unify and encompass the constituent groups. Filipino Americans' rejection of the term "yellow" and the activists' objection to the cliché-ridden

Oriental forced the group to change its name to Asian American. . . . It is noteworthy that while *Yellow, Oriental,* and *Asian American* connote different ideologies, all three terms signify panethnicity. . . .

Conclusion

The development of a pan-Asian consciousness and constituency reflected broader societal developments and demographic changes, as well as the group's political agenda. By the late 1960s, pan-Asianism was possible because of the more amicable relationships among the Asian countries, the declining residential segregation among diverse Asian groups in America, and the large number of native-born, American-educated political actors. Disillusioned with the larger society and estranged from their traditional communities, third- and fourth-generation Asian Americans turned to the alternative strategy of pan-Asian unification. Through pan-Asian organizations, media, and Asian American Studies programs, these political activists assumed the role of "cultural entrepreneurs" consciously creating a community of culture out of diverse Asian peoples. This process of pan-Asian consolidation did not proceed smoothly nor did it encompass all Asian Americans. Ethnic chauvinism, competition for scarce resources, and class cleavages continued to divide the subgroups. However, once established, the pan-Asian structure not only reinforced the cohesiveness of already existing networks but also expanded these networks. Although first conceived by young Asian American activists, the pan-Asian concept was subsequently institutionalized by professionals and community groups, as well as government agencies. The confrontational politics of the activists eventually gave way to the conventional and electoral politics of the politicians, lobbyists, and professionals, as Asian Americans continued to rely on the pan-Asian framework to enlarge their political capacities.

REFERENCES

BARTH, FREDERICK. 1969. *Ethnic Groups and Boundaries.* Boston: Little, Brown.

BLAUNER, ROBERT. 1972. *Racial Oppression in America.* New York: Harper & Row.

BONACICH, EDNA, and JOHN MODELL. 1980. *The Economic Basis of Ethnic Solidarity: A Study of Japanese Americans.* Berkeley: University of California Press.

BROWNE, BLAIN T. 1985. "A Common Thread: American Images of the Chinese and Japanese, 1930–1960." Ph.D. dissertation, University of Oklahoma.

CHAN, SUCHENG. 1991. *Asian Americans: An Interpretive History.* Boston: Twayne.

CORNELL, STEPHEN. 1988. *The Return of the Native: Native American Political Resurgence.* New York: Oxford University Press.

DANIELS, ROGER. 1988. *Asian America: Chinese and Japanese in the United States Since 1850.* Seattle: University of Washington Press.

ENLOE, CYNTHIA H. 1980. *Police, Military, and Ethnicity: Foundations of State Power.* New Brunswick, NJ: Transaction Books.

FERARU, ARTHUR N. 1950. "Public Opinion Polls on Japan." *Far Eastern Survey* 19(10):101–103.

FUGITA, STEPHEN S., and DAVID J. O'BRIEN. 1991. *Japanese American Ethnicity: The Persistence of Community.* Seattle: University of Washington Press.

HEIN, JEREMY. 1989. "States and Political Migrants: The Incorporation of Indochinese Refugees in France and the United States." Ph.D. dissertation, Northwestern University.

HOYT, EDWIN P. 1974. *Asians in the West.* New York: Thomas Nelson.

IGNACIO, LEMUEL F. 1976. *Asian Americans and Pacific Islanders (Is There Such an Ethnic Group?)* San Jose, CA: Filipino Development Associates.

KIM, ILLSOO. 1981. *New Urban Immigrants: The Korean Community in New York.* Princeton, NJ: Princeton University Press.

KITANO, HARRY H. L., and ROGER DANIELS. 1988. *Asian Americans: Emerging Minorities.* Englewood Cliffs, NJ: Prentice-Hall.

LAM, FRANKIE. 1986. "Suburban Residential Segregation of Chinese and Japanese Americans, 1960, 1970, and 1980." *Sociology and Social Research* 70(4):263–65.

LING, SUSIE HSIUHAN. 1984. "The Mountain Movers: Asian American Women's Movement in Los Angeles." *Amerasia Journal* 15(1):51–67.

LIU, JOHN. 1988. "The Relationship of Migration Research to Asian American Studies: Unity and Diversity Within the Curriculum." Pp. 117–25 in *Reflections on Shattered Windows,* edited by Gary Okihiro, Shirley Hune, Arthur Hansen, and John Liu. Pullman: Washington State University Press.

LOPEZ, DAVID, and YEN ESPIRITU. 1990. "Panethnicity in the United States: A Theoretical Framework." *Ethnic and Racial Studies* 13(2): 198–224.

LOWE, LISA. 1991. "Heterogeneity, Hybridity, Multiplicity: Marking Asian American Differences." *Diaspora* 1:24–44.

LYMAN, STANFORD M. 1970. *The Asian in the West.* Reno and Las Vegas: Desert Research Institute, University of Nevada.

MASADA, SABURO. 1970. "Stockton's Yellow Seed." *Pacific Citizen,* 9 October.

MELENDY, H. BRETT. 1977. *Asians in America: Filipinos, Koreans, and East Indians.* Boston: Twayne.

MONTERO, DARRELL. 1979. *Vietnamese Americans: Patterns of Resettlement and Socioeconomic Adaptations in the United States.* Boulder, CO: Westview Press.

NAGEL, JOANE. 1982. "The Political Mobilization of Native Americans." *Social Science Journal* 19:37–45.

———. 1986. "The Political Construction of Ethnicity." Pp. 93–112 in *Competitive Ethnic Relations,* edited by Susan Olzal and Joane Nagel. San Diego: Academic Press.

ONG, PAUL. 1989. "California's Asian Population: Past Trends and Projections for the Year 2000." Los Angeles: Graduate School of Architecture and Urban Planning.

PADILLA, FELIX M. 1985. *Latino Ethnic Consciousness: The Case of Mexican Americans and Puerto Ricans in Chicago.* Notre Dame, IN: Notre Dame University Press.

RABAYA, VIOLET. 1971. "I Am Curious (Yellow?)." Pp. 110–11 in *Roots: An Asian American Reader,* edited by Amy Tachiki, Eddie Wong, and Franklin Odo. Los Angeles: UCLA Asian American Studies Center.

SANO, ROY. 1970. "Asiantown in Oakland." *Pacific Citizen,* 4 August.

SHIBUTANI, TAMOTSU, and KIAN M. KWAN. 1965. *Ethnic Stratification.* New York: Macmillan.

SKINNER, KENNETH, and GLEN HENDRICKS. 1979. "The Shaping of Self-Identity Among Indochinese Refugees." *Journal of Ethnic Studies* 7:25–41.

SUNG, BETTY LEE. 1967. *Mountain of Gold: The Story of the Chinese in America.* New York: Macmillan.

TAKAKI, RONALD. 1989. *Strangers from a Different Shore: A History of Asian Americans.* Boston: Little, Brown.

TROTTIER, RICHARD. 1981. "Charters of Panethnic Identity: Indigenous American Indians and Immigrant Asian Americans." Pp. 271–305 in *Ethnic Change,* edited by Charles F. Keyes. Seattle: University of Washington Press.

UYEMATSU, AMY. 1971. "The Emergence of Yellow Power in America." Pp. 9–13 in *Roots: An Asian American Reader,* edited by Amy Tachiki, Eddie Wong, and Franklin Odo. Los Angeles: UCLA Asian American Studies Center.

WEISS, MELFORD S. 1974. *Valley City: A Chinese Community in America.* Cambridge, MA: Schenkman.

WONG, PAUL. 1972. "The Emergence of the Asian American Movement." *Bridge* 2(1):33–39.

YU, EUI-YOUNG. 1983. "Korean Communities in America: Past, Present, and Future." *Amerasia Journal* 10(2):23–51.

YUAN, D. Y. 1966. "Chinatown and Beyond: The Chinese Population in Metropolitan New York." *Phylon* 23(4):321–32.

ZIA, HELEN. 1984. "The Real Violence." *Bridge* 9(2):18–23.

9

OPTIONAL ETHNICITIES
For Whites Only?

Mary C. Waters

Questions to Consider

Is it possible to be Italian or Irish in one situation but not in another? Are older members of your extended family (great-grandparents or grandparents) "more ethnic" than younger family members? Why? Do you agree with Mary Waters's assertion that racial identity shapes when and to what extent ethnicity matters? How and why does this happen? How is ethnic identity more fluid than racial identity?

This paper reviews the current meaning of ethnicity for the descendants of nineteenth- and early twentieth-century European immigrants to the United States and contrasts that experience with the identities of people with non-European origins—the descendants of earlier forced immigrants and conquered peoples and the growing number of voluntary immigrants from non-European countries. The paper proceeds as follows. First the proposition that ethnic identity is optional for most Americans of European background is put forth. Empirical evidence that this is the case is reviewed. The social and historical forces that allow ethnicity to be an option are described.

The experience of non-Whites in the United States is then contrasted. Non-Whites have much more limited options with regard to their ethnicity because of particular historical and social circumstances in the United States. Using the example of current relations on college campuses between Blacks and Whites, I trace the influence that different degrees of options have on everyday encounters between people and the everyday social psychological consequences of failing to recognize this key difference between race and ethnicity.

Ethnic Identity for Whites in the 1990s

What does it mean to talk about ethnicity as an option for an individual? To argue that an individual has some degree of choice in their ethnic identity flies in the face of the common sense notion of ethnicity many of us believe in—that one's ethnic identity is a fixed characteristic, reflective of blood ties and given at birth. However, social scientists who study ethnicity have long concluded that while ethnicity is based in a *belief* in a common ancestry, ethnicity is primarily a *social* phenomenon, not a biological one (Alba 1985, 1990; Barth 1969; Weber [1921] 1968, p. 389). The belief that members of an ethnic group have that they share a common ancestry may not be a fact. There is a great deal of change in ethnic identities across generations through intermarriage, changing allegiances, and changing social categories. There is also a much larger amount of change in the identities of individuals over their life than is commonly believed. While most people are aware of the phenomenon known as "passing"—people raised as one race who change at some point and claim a different race as their identity—there are similar life course changes in ethnicity that happen all the time and are not given the same degree of attention as "racial passing."

White Americans of European ancestry can be described as having a great deal of choice in terms of their ethnic identities. The two major types of options White Americans can exercise are (1) the option of whether to claim any specific ancestry, or to just be "White" or American (Lieberson [1985] called these people "unhyphenated Whites"), and (2) the choice of which of their European ancestries to choose to include in their description of their own identities. In both cases, the option of choosing how to present yourself on surveys and in everyday social interactions exists for Whites because of social changes and societal conditions that have created a great deal of social mobility, immigrant assimilation, and political and economic power for Whites in the United States. Specifically, the option of being able to not claim any ethnic identity exists for Whites of European background in the United States because they are the majority group—in terms of holding political

and social power, as well as being a numerical majority. The option of choosing among different ethnicities in their family backgrounds exists because the degree of discrimination and social distance attached to specific European backgrounds has diminished over time.

The Ethnic Miracle

When European immigration to the United States was sharply curtailed in the late 1920s, a process was set in motion whereby the European ethnic groups already in the United States were for all intents and purposes cut off from any new arrivals. As a result, the composition of the ethnic groups began to age generationally. The proportion of each ethnic group made up of immigrants or the first generation began to gradually decline, and the proportion made up of the children, grandchildren, and eventually great-grandchildren began to increase. Consequently, by 1990 most European-origin ethnic groups in the United States were composed of a very small number of immigrants, and a very large proportion of people whose link to their ethnic origins in Europe was increasingly remote.

This generational change was accompanied by unprecedented social and economic changes. The very success of the assimilation process these groups experienced makes it difficult to imagine how much the question of the immigrants' eventual assimilation was an open one at the turn of the century. At the peak of immigration from southern and central Europe there was widespread discrimination and hostility against the newcomers by established Americans. Italians, Poles, Greeks, and Jews were called derogatory names, attacked by nativist mobs, and derided in the press. Intermarriage across ethnic lines was very uncommon—castelike in the words of some sociologists. The immigrants and their children were residentially segregated, occupationally specialized, and generally poor.

After several generations in the United States, the situation has changed a great deal. The success and social mobility of the grandchildren and great-grandchildren of that massive wave of immigrants from Europe has been called "The Ethnic Miracle" (Greeley 1976). These Whites have moved away from the inner-city ethnic ghettos to White middle-class suburban homes. They are doctors, lawyers, entertainers, academics, governors, and Supreme Court justices. But contrary to what some social science theorists and some politicians predicted or hoped for, these middle-class Americans have not completely given up ethnic identity. Instead, they have maintained some connection with their immigrant ancestors' identities—becoming Irish American doctors, Italian American Supreme Court justices, and Greek American presidential candidates. In the tradition of cultural pluralism, successful middle-class Americans in the late twentieth century maintain some degree of identity with their ethnic backgrounds. They have remained "hyphenated Americans." So while social mobility and declining discrimination have created the option of not identifying with any European ancestry, most White Americans continue to report some ethnic background.

With the growth in intermarriage among people of European ethnic origins, increasingly these people are of mixed ethnic ancestry. This gives them the option of which ethnicity to identify with. The U.S. census has asked a question on ethnic ancestry in the 1980 and 1990 censuses. In 1980, 52 percent of the American public responded with a single ethnic ancestry, 31 percent gave multiple ethnic origins (up to three were coded, but some individuals wrote in more than three), and only 6 per-

cent said they were American only, while the remaining 11 percent gave no response. In 1990 about 90 percent of the population gave some response to the ancestry question, with only 5 percent giving American as a response and only 1.4 percent reporting an uncodeable response such as "don't know" (McKenney and Cresce 1992; U.S. Bureau of the Census 1992).

Several researchers have examined the pattern of responses of people to the census ancestry question. These analyses have shown a pattern of flux and inconsistency in ethnic ancestry reporting. For instance, Lieberson and Waters (1986, 1988, p. 93) have found that parents simplify children's ancestries when reporting them to the census. For instance, among the offspring in situations where one parent reports a specific single White ethnic origin and the other parent reports a different single White origin, about 40 percent of the children are not described as the logical combination of the parents' ancestries. For example, only about 60 percent of the children of English-German marriages are labeled as English-German or German-English. About 15 percent of the children of these parents are simplified to just English, and another 15 percent are reported as just German. The remainder of the children are either not given an ancestry or are described as American (Lieberson and Waters 1986, 1993).

In addition to these intergenerational changes, researchers have found changes in reporting ancestry that occur at the time of marriage or upon leaving home. At the ages of eighteen to twenty-two, when many young Americans leave home for the first time, the number of people reporting a single as opposed to a multiple ancestry goes up. Thus while parents simplify children's ancestries when they leave home, children themselves tend to report less complexity in their ancestries when they leave their parents' homes and begin reporting their ancestries themselves (Lieberson and Waters 1986, 1988; Waters 1990).

These individual changes are reflected in variability over time in the aggregate numbers of groups determined by the census and surveys. Farley (1991) compared the consistency of the overall counts of different ancestry groups in the 1979 Current Population Survey, the 1980 census, and the 1986 National Content Test (a pretest for the 1990 census). He found much less consistency in the numbers for northern European ancestry groups whose immigration peaks were early in the nineteenth century—the English, Dutch, Germans, and other northern European groups. In other words each of these different surveys and the census yielded a different estimate of the number of people having this ancestry. The 1990 census also showed a great deal of flux and inconsistency in some ancestry groups. The number of people reporting English as an ancestry went down considerably from 1980, while the number reporting German ancestry went up. The number of Cajuns grew dramatically. This has led officials at the Census Bureau to assume that the examples used in the instructions strongly influence the responses people give. (Cajun was one of the examples of an ancestry given in 1990 but not in 1980, and German was the first example given. English was an example in the 1980 instructions, but not in 1990.)

All of these studies point to the socially variable nature of ethnic identity—and the lack of equivalence between ethnic ancestry and identity. If merely adding a category to the instructions to the question increases the number of people claiming that ancestry, what does that mean about the level of importance of that identity for people answering the census? Clearly identity and ancestry for Whites in the United States, who increasingly are from mixed backgrounds, involve some change and choice.

Symbolic Ethnicities for White Americans

What do these ethnic identities mean to people and why do they cling to them rather than just abandoning the tie and calling themselves American? My own field research with suburban Whites in California and Pennsylvania found that later-generation descendants of European origin maintain what are called "symbolic ethnicities." Symbolic ethnicity is a term coined by Herbert Gans (1979) to refer to ethnicity that is individualistic in nature and without real social cost for the individual. These symbolic identifications are essentially leisure time activities, rooted in nuclear family traditions and reinforced by the voluntary enjoyable aspects of being ethnic (Waters 1990). Richard Alba (1990) also found later-generation Whites in Albany, New York, who chose to keep a tie with an ethnic identity because of the enjoyable and voluntary aspects to those identities, along with the feelings of specialness they entailed. An example of symbolic ethnicity is individuals who identify as Irish, for example, on occasions such as Saint Patrick's Day, on family holidays, or for vacations. They do not usually belong to Irish American organizations, live in Irish neighborhoods, work in Irish jobs, or marry other Irish people. The symbolic meaning of being Irish American can be constructed by individuals from mass media images, family traditions, or other intermittent social activities. In other words, for later-generation White ethnics, ethnicity is not something that influences their lives unless they want it to. In the world of work and school and neighborhood, individuals do not have to admit to being ethnic unless they choose to. And for an increasing number of European-origin individuals whose parents and grandparents have intermarried, the ethnicity they claim is largely a matter of personal choice as they sort through all of the possible combinations of groups in their genealogies.

Individuals can choose those aspects of being Italian, for instance, that appeal to them, and discard those that do not. Or a person whose father is Italian, and mother part Polish and part French, might choose among the three ethnicities and present herself as a Polish American. For instance, a nineteen-year-old college student, interviewed in California in 1986, told me he would have answered Irish on the 1980 census form that asked about ethnic ancestry. These are his reasons:

Q: Why would you have answered that?
A: Well my Dad's name is Kerrigan and my mom's name is O'Leary, and I do have some German in me, but if you figure it out, I am about 75% Irish, so I usually say I am Irish.
Q: You usually don't say German when people ask?
A: No, no, I never say I am German. My dad just likes being Irish. . . . I don't know I just never think of myself as being German.
Q: So your dad's father is the one who immigrated?
A: Yes. On his side is Irish for generations. And then my grandmother's name is Dubois, which is French, partly German, partly French, and then the rest of the family is all Irish. So it is only the maternal grandmother who messes up the line. (Waters 1990, p. 10)

Thus in the course of a few questions, this man labeled himself Irish, admitted to being part German but not identifying with it, and then as an afterthought added that he was also part French. This is not an unusual case. With just a little probing, many people will describe a variety of ancestries in their family background, but do not consider these ancestries to be a salient part of their own identities. Thus the 1990 census ances-

try question, which estimated that 30 percent of the population is of mixed ancestry, most surely underestimates the degree of mixing among the population. My research, and the research of Richard Alba (1990), shows that many people have already sorted through what they know of their ethnic ancestries and simplified their responses before they ever answer a census or survey question (Waters 1990).

But note that this freedom to include or exclude ancestries in your identification to yourself and others would not be the same for those defined racially in our society. They are constrained to identify with the part of their ancestry that has been socially defined as the "essential" part. African Americans, for example, have been highly socially constrained to identify as Blacks, without other options available to them, even when they know that their forebears included many people of American Indian or European background. Up until the mid-twentieth century, many state governments had specific laws defining one as Black if as little as one-thirty-second of one's ancestors were defined as Black (Dominguez 1986; Spickard 1989). Even now when the one drop rule has been dropped from our legal codes, there are still strong societal pressures on African Americans to identify in a particular way. Certain ancestries take precedence over others in the societal rules on descent and ancestry reckoning. If one believes one is part English and part German and identifies in a survey as German, one is not in danger of being accused of trying to "pass" as non-English and of being "redefined" English by the interviewer. But if one were part African and part German, one's self identification as German would be highly suspect and probably not accepted if one "looked" Black according to the prevailing social norms.

This is reflected in the ways the census collects race and ethnic identity. While the ethnic ancestry question used in 1980 and 1990 is given to all Americans in the sample regardless of race and allows multiple responses that combine races, the primary source of information on people defined racially in the United States is the census race question or the Hispanic question. Both of these questions require a person to make a choice about an identity. Individuals are not allowed to respond that they are both Black and White, or Japanese and Asian Indian on the race question even if they know that is their background. In fact, people who disobey the instructions to the census race question and check off two races are assigned to the first checked race in the list by the Census Bureau.

In responding to the ancestry question, the comparative latitude that White respondents have does not mean that Whites pick and choose ethnicities out of thin air. For the most part people choose an identity that corresponds with some element of their family tree. However, there are many anecdotal instances of people adopting ethnicities when they marry or move to a strongly identified neighborhood or community. For instance Micaela di Leonardo (1984) reported instances of non-Italian women who married into Italian American families and "became Italian." Karen Leonard (1992) describes a community of Mexican American women who married Punjabi immigrants in California. Some of the Punjabi immigrants and their descendants were said to have "become Mexican" when they joined their wives' kin group and social worlds. Alternatively she describes the community acknowledging that Mexican women made the best curry, as they adapted to life with Indian-origin men.

But what do these identities mean to individuals? Surely an identity that is optional in a number of ways—not legally defined on a passport or birth certificate, not socially consequential in terms of societal discrimination in terms of housing or job access, and not economically limiting in terms of blocking opportunities for social mobility—cannot be the same as an identity that results from and is nurtured by societal exclusion and rejection. The choice to have a symbolic ethnicity is an attractive and widespread one despite its lack of demonstrable content, because having a symbolic ethnicity combines individuality with feelings of community. People reported to me that they liked having an ethnic identity because it gave them a uniqueness and a feeling of being special. They often contrasted their own specialness by virtue of their ethnic identities with "bland" Americanness. Being ethnic makes people feel unique and special and not just "vanilla" as one of my respondents put it. For instance, one woman describes the benefits she feels from being Czech American:

> I work in an office and a lot of people in there always talk about their background. It's weird because it is a big office and people are of all different backgrounds. People are this or that. It is interesting I think to find out. Especially when it is something you do not hear a lot about. Something that is not common like Lithuania or something. That's the good part about being Czech. People think it is something different. (Waters 1990, p. 154)

Because "American" is largely understood by Americans to be a political identity and allegiance and not an ethnic one, the idea of being "American" does not give people the same sense of belonging that their hyphenated American identity does. When I asked people about their dual identities—American and Irish or Italian or whatever—they usually responded in a way that showed how they conceived of the relationship between the two identities. Being an American was their primary identity; but it was so primary that they rarely, if ever, thought about it—most commonly only when they left the country. Being Irish American, on the other hand, was a way they had of differentiating themselves from others whom they interacted with from day to day—in many cases from spouses or in-laws. Certain of their traits—being emotional, having a sense of humor, talking with their hands—were understood as stemming from their ethnicity. Yet when asked about their identity as Americans, that identity was both removed from their day-to-day consciousness and understood in terms of loyalty and patriotism. Although they may not think they behave or think in a certain way because they are American, being American is something they are both proud of and committed to.

Symbolic ethnicity is the best of all worlds for these respondents. These White ethnics can claim to be unique and special, while simultaneously finding the community and conformity with others that they also crave. But that "community" is of a type that will not interfere with a person's individuality. It is not as if these people belong to ethnic voluntary organizations or gather as a group in churches or neighborhoods or union halls. They work and reside within the mainstream of American middle-class life, yet they retain the interesting benefits— the "specialness"—of ethnic allegiance, without any of its drawbacks.

It has been suggested by several researchers that this positive value attached to ethnic ancestry, which became popular in the ethnic revival of the 1970s, is the result of assimilation having proceeded to an advanced stage for descendants of White Europeans (Alba 1985; Crispino 1980; Steinberg 1981). Ironically, people celebrate and embrace their ethnic backgrounds precisely because assimilation has proceeded to the point where such identification does not have that much influence on their day-to-

day life. Rather than choosing the "least ethnic" and most bland ethnicities, Whites desire the "most ethnic" ones, like the once-stigmatized "Italian," because it is perceived as bringing the most psychic benefits. For instance, when an Italian father is married to an English or a Scottish or a German mother, the likelihood is that the child will be reported to the census with the father's Italian ancestry, rather than the northern European ancestries, which would have been predicted to have a higher social status. Italian is a good ancestry to have, people told me, because they have good food and a warm family life. This change in the social meaning of being Italian American is quite dramatic, given that Italians were subject to discrimination, exclusion, and extreme negative stereotyping in the early part of the twentieth century.

Race Relations and Symbolic Ethnicity

However much symbolic ethnicity is without cost for the individual, there is a cost associated with symbolic ethnicity for the society. That is because symbolic ethnicities of the type described here are confined to White Americans of European origin. Black Americans, Hispanic Americans, Asian Americans, and American Indians do not have the option of a symbolic ethnicity at present in the United States. For all of the ways in which ethnicity does not matter for White Americans, it does matter for non-Whites. Who your ancestors are does affect your choice of spouse, where you live, what job you have, who your friends are, and what your chances are for success in American society, if those ancestors happen not to be from Europe. The reality is that White ethnics have a lot more choice and room to maneuver than they themselves think they do. The situation is very different for members of racial minorities, whose lives are strongly influenced by their race or national origin regardless of how much they may choose not to identify themselves in terms of their ancestries.

When White Americans learn the stories of how their grandparents and great-grandparents triumphed in the United States over adversity, they are usually told in terms of their individual efforts and triumphs. The important role of labor unions and other organized political and economic actors in their social and economic successes are left out of the story in favor of a generational story of individual Americans rising up against communitarian, Old World intolerance and New World resistance. As a result, the "individualized" voluntary, cultural view of ethnicity for Whites is what is remembered.

One important implication of these identities is that they tend to be very individualistic. There is a tendency to view valuing diversity in a pluralist environment as equating all groups. The symbolic ethnic tends to think that all groups are equal; everyone has a background that is their right to celebrate and pass on to their children. This leads to the conclusion that all identities are equal and all identities in some sense are interchangeable—"I'm Italian American, you're Polish American. I'm Irish American, you're African American." The important thing is to treat people as individuals and all equally. However, this assumption ignores the very big difference between an individualistic symbolic ethnic identity and a socially enforced and imposed racial identity.

My favorite example of how this type of thinking can lead to some severe misunderstandings between people of different backgrounds is from the *Dear Abby* advice column. A few years back a person wrote in who had asked an acquaintance of Asian background where his family was from. His acquaintance answered that this was a rude question and he would not reply. The bewildered White asked Abby why it was rude, since he thought it was a sign of respect to wonder where people were from, and he certainly would not mind anyone asking HIM about where his family was from. Abby asked her readers to write in to say whether it was rude to ask about a person's ethnic background. She reported that she got a large response, that most non-Whites thought it was a sign of disrespect, and Whites thought it was flattering:

> Dear Abby,
> I am 100 percent American and because I am of Asian ancestry I am often asked "What are you?" It's not the personal nature of this question that bothers me, it's the question itself. This query seems to question my very humanity. "What am I? Why I am a person like everyone else!"
>
> Signed, A REAL AMERICAN

> Dear Abby,
> Why do people resent being asked what they are? The Irish are so proud of being Irish, they tell you before you even ask. Tip O'Neill has never tried to hide his Irish ancestry.
>
> Signed, JIMMY

In this exchange JIMMY cannot understand why Asians are not as happy to be asked about their ethnicity as he is, because he understands his ethnicity and theirs to be separate but equal. Everyone has to come from somewhere—his family from Ireland, another's family from Asia—each has a history and each should be proud of it. But the reason he cannot understand the perspective of the Asian American is that all ethnicities are not equal; all are not symbolic, costless, and voluntary. When White Americans equate their own symbolic ethnicities with the socially enforced identities of non-White Americans, they obscure the fact that the experiences of Whites and non-Whites have been qualitatively different in the United States and that the current identities of individuals partly reflect that unequal history.

In the next section I describe how relations between Black and White students on college campuses reflect some of these asymmetries in the understanding of what a racial or ethnic identity means. While I focus on Black and White students in the following discussion, you should be aware that the myriad other groups in the United States—Mexican Americans, American Indians, Japanese Americans—all have some degree of social and individual influences on their identities, which reflect the group's social and economic history and present circumstance.

Relations on College Campuses

Both Black and White students face the task of developing their race and ethnic identities. Sociologists and psychologists note that at the time people leave home and begin to live independently from their parents, often ages eighteen to twenty-two, they report a heightened sense of racial and ethnic identity as they sort through how much of their beliefs and behaviors are idiosyncratic to their families and how much are shared with other people. It is not until one comes in close contact with many people who are different from oneself that individuals realize the ways in which their backgrounds may influence their individual personality. This involves coming into contact with people who are different in terms of their ethnicity, class, religion, region, and race. For White students, the ethnicity they claim is more often than not a symbolic one—with all of the voluntary, enjoyable, and intermittent characteristics I have described above.

Black students at the university are also developing identities through interactions with others who are different from them. Their identity development is more compli-

cated than that of Whites because of the added element of racial discrimination and racism, along with the "ethnic" developments of finding others who share their background. Thus Black students have the positive attraction of being around other Black students who share some cultural elements, as well as the need to band together with other students in a reactive and oppositional way in the face of racist incidents on campus.

Colleges and universities across the country have been increasing diversity among their student bodies in the last few decades. This has led in many cases to strained relations among students from different racial and ethnic backgrounds. The 1980s and 1990s produced a great number of racial incidents and high racial tensions on campuses. While there were a number of racial incidents that were due to bigotry, unlawful behavior, and violent or vicious attacks, much of what happens among students on campuses involves a low level of tension and awkwardness in social interactions.

Many Black students experience racism personally for the first time on campus. The upper-middle-class students from White suburbs were often isolated enough that their presence was not threatening to racists in their high schools. Also, their class background was known by their residence and this may have prevented attacks being directed at them. Often Black students at the university who begin talking with other students and recognizing racial slights will remember incidents that happened to them earlier that they might not have thought were related to race.

Black college students across the country experience a sizeable number of incidents that are clearly the result of racism. Many of the most blatant ones that occur between students are the result of drinking. Sometimes late at night, drunken groups of White students coming home from parties will yell slurs at single Black students on the street. The other types of incidents that happen include being singled out for special treatment by employees, such as being followed when shopping at the campus bookstore, or going to the art museum with your class and the guard stops you and asks for your I.D. Others involve impersonal encounters on the street—being called a nigger by a truck driver while crossing the street, or seeing old ladies clutch their pocketbooks and shake in terror as you pass them on the street. For the most part these incidents are not specific to the university environment, they are the types of incidents middle-class Blacks face every day throughout American society, and they have been documented by sociologists (Feagin 1991).

In such a climate, however, with students experiencing these types of incidents and talking with each other about them, Black students do experience a tension and a feeling of being singled out. It is unfair that this is part of their college experience and not that of White students. Dealing with incidents like this, or the ever-present threat of such incidents, is an ongoing developmental task for Black students that takes energy, attention, and strength of character. It should be clearly understood that this is an asymmetry in the "college experience" for Black and White students. It is one of the unfair aspects of life that results from living in a society with ongoing racial prejudice and discrimination. It is also very understandable that it makes some students angry at the unfairness of it all, even if there is no one to blame specifically. It is also very troubling because, while most Whites do not create these incidents, some do, and it is never clear until you know someone well whether they are the type of person who could do something like this. So one of the reactions of Black students to these incidents is to band together.

In some sense then, as Blauner (1992) has argued, you can see Black students coming together on campus as both an "ethnic" pull of wanting to be together to share common experiences and community, and a "racial" push of banding together defensively because of perceived rejection and tension from Whites. In this way the ethnic identities of Black students are in some sense similar to, say, Korean students wanting to be together to share experiences. And it is an ethnicity that is generally much stronger than, say, Italian Americans. But for Koreans who come together there is generally a definition of themselves as "different from" Whites. For Blacks reacting to exclusion, there is a tendency for the coming together to involve both being "different from" but also "opposed to" Whites.

The anthropologist John Ogbu has documented the tendency of minorities in a variety of societies around the world, who have experienced severe blocked mobility for long periods of time, to develop such oppositional identities. An important component of having such an identity is to describe others of your group who do not join in the group solidarity as devaluing and denying their very core identity. This is why it is not common for successful Asians to be accused by others of "acting White" in the United States, but it is quite common for such a term to be used by Blacks and Latinos. The oppositional component of a Black identity also explains how Black people can question whether others are acting "Black enough." On campus, it explains some of the intense pressures felt by Black students who do not make their racial identity central and who choose to hang out primarily with non-Blacks. This pressure from the group, which is partly defining itself by not being White, is exacerbated by the fact that race is a physical marker in American society. No one immediately notices the Jewish students sitting together in the dining hall, or the one Jewish student sitting surrounded by non-Jews, or the Texan sitting with the Californians, but everyone notices the Black student who is or is not at the "Black table" in the cafeteria.

An example of the kinds of misunderstandings that can arise because of different understandings of the meanings and implications of symbolic versus oppositional identities concerns questions students ask one another in the dorms about personal appearances and customs. A very common type of interaction in the dorm concerns questions Whites ask Blacks about their hair. Because Whites tend to know little about Blacks, and Blacks know a lot about Whites, there is a general asymmetry in the level of curiosity people have about one another. Whites, as the numerical majority, have had little contact with Black culture; Blacks, especially those who are in college, have had to develop bicultural skills—knowledge about the social worlds of both Whites and Blacks. Miscommunication and hurt feelings about White students' questions about Black students' hair illustrate this point. One of the things that happens freshman year is that White students are around Black students as they fix their hair. White students are generally quite curious about Black students' hair—they have basic questions such as how often Blacks wash their hair, how they get it straightened or curled, what products they use on their hair, how they comb it, etc. Whites often wonder to themselves whether they should ask these questions. One thought experiment Whites perform is to ask themselves whether a particular question would upset them. Adopting the "do unto others" rule, they ask themselves, "If a Black person was curious about my hair would I get upset?" The answer usually is "No, I would be happy to tell them." Another example is an Italian American student wondering to herself, "Would I be upset if someone asked me about calamari?" The answer is no, so she asks her Black roommate about collard greens, and the roommate explodes with an angry response such as, "Do you think all Black people eat watermelon too?" Note that if this Italian American knew her friend was Trinidadian American and asked about peas and rice the situation would be more similar and would not necessarily ignite underlying tensions.

Like the debate in *Dear Abby,* these innocent questions are likely to lead to resentment. The issue of stereotypes about Black Americans and the assumption that all Blacks are alike and have the same stereotypical cultural traits has more power to hurt or offend a Black person than vice versa. The innocent questions about Black hair also bring up a number of asymmetries between the Black and White experience. Because Blacks tend to have more knowledge about Whites than vice versa, there is not an even exchange going on; the Black freshman is likely to have fewer basic questions about his White roommate than his White roommate has about him. Because of the differences historically in the group experiences of Blacks and Whites there are some connotations to Black hair that don't exist about White hair. (For instance, is straightening your hair a form of assimilation, do some people distinguish between women having "good hair" and "bad hair" in terms of beauty and how is that related to looking "White"?) Finally, even a Black freshman who cheerfully disregards or is unaware that there are these asymmetries will soon slam into another asymmetry if she willingly answers every innocent question asked of her. In a situation where Blacks make up only 10 percent of the student body, if every non-Black needs to be educated about hair, she will have to explain it to nine other students. As one Black student explained to me, after you've been asked a couple of times about something so personal you begin to feel like you are an attraction in a zoo, that you are at the university for the education of the White students.

Institutional Responses

Our society asks a lot of young people. We ask young people to do something that no one else does as successfully on such a wide scale—that is to live together with people from very different backgrounds, to respect one another, to appreciate one another, and to enjoy and learn from one another. The successes that occur every day in this endeavor are many, and they are too often overlooked. However, the problems and tensions are also real, and they will not vanish on their own. We tend to see pluralism working in the United States in much the same way some people expect capitalism to work. If you put together people with various interests and abilities and resources, the "invisible hand" of capitalism is supposed to make all the parts work together in an economy for the common good.

There is much to be said for such a model—the invisible hand of the market can solve complicated problems of production and distribution better than any "visible hand" of a state plan. However, we have learned that unequal power relations among the actors in the capitalist marketplace, as well as "externalities" that the market cannot account for, such as long-term pollution, or collusion between corporations, or the exploitation of child labor, means that state regulation is often needed. Pluralism and the relations between groups are very similar. There is a lot to be said for the idea that bringing people who belong to different ethnic or racial groups together in institutions with no interference will have good consequences. Students from different backgrounds will make friends if they share a dorm room or corridor, and there is no need for the institution to do any more than provide the locale. But like capitalism, the in-

visible hand of pluralism does not do well when power relations and externalities are ignored. When you bring together individuals from groups that are differentially valued in the wider society and provide no guidance, there will be problems. In these cases the "invisible hand" of pluralist relations does not work, and tensions and disagreements can arise without any particular individual or group of individuals being "to blame." On college campuses in the 1990s some of the tensions between students are of this sort. They arise from honest misunderstandings, lack of a common background, and very different experiences of what race and ethnicity mean to the individual.

The implications of symbolic ethnicities for thinking about race relations are subtle but consequential. If your understanding of your own ethnicity and its relationship to society and politics is one of individual choice, it becomes harder to understand the need for programs like affirmative action, which recognize the ongoing need for group struggle and group recognition, in order to bring about social change. It also is hard for a White college student to understand the need that minority students feel to band together against discrimination. It also is easy, on the individual level, to expect everyone else to be able to turn their ethnicity on and off at will, the way you are able to, without understanding that ongoing discrimination and societal attention to minority status makes that impossible for individuals from minority groups to do. The paradox of symbolic ethnicity is that it depends upon the ultimate goal of a pluralist society, and at the same time makes it more difficult to achieve that ultimate goal. It is dependent upon the concept that all ethnicities mean the same thing, that enjoying the traditions of one's heritage is an option available to a group or an individual, but that such a heritage should not have any social costs associated with it.

As the Asian Americans who wrote to *Dear Abby* make clear, there are many societal issues and involuntary ascriptions associated with non-White identities. The developments necessary for this to change are not individual but societal in nature. Social mobility and declining racial and ethnic sensitivity are closely associated. The legacy and the present reality of discrimination on the basis of race or ethnicity must be overcome before the ideal of the pluralist society, where all heritages are treated equally and are equally available for individuals to choose or discard at will, is realized.

REFERENCES

ALBA, RICHARD D. 1985. *Italian Americans: Into the Twilight of Ethnicity.* Edgewood Cliffs, NJ: Prentice-Hall.

_____. 1990. *Ethnic Identity: The Transformation of White America.* New Haven, CT: Yale University Press.

BARTH, FREDERIK. 1969. *Ethnic Groups and Boundaries.* Boston: Little, Brown.

BLAUNER, ROBERT. 1992. "Talking Past Each Other: Black and White Languages of Race." *American Prospect* (Summer):55–64.

CRISPINO, JAMES. 1980. *The Assimilation of Ethnic Groups: The Italian Case.* Staten Island, NY: Center for Migration Studies.

DI LEONARDO, MICAELA. 1984. *The Varieties of Ethnic Experience: Kinship, Class and Gender Among Italian Americans.* Ithaca, NY: Cornell University Press.

DOMINGUEZ, VIRGINIA. 1986. *White by Definition: Social Classification in Creole Louisiana.* New Brunswick, NJ: Rutgers University Press.

FARLEY, REYNOLDS. 1991. "The New Census Question About Ancestry: What Did It Tell Us?" *Demography* 28:411–29.

FEAGIN, JOE R. 1991. "The Continuing Significance of Race: Antiblack Discrimination in Public Places." *American Sociological Review* 56:101–117.

GANS, HERBERT. 1979. "Symbolic Ethnicity: The Future of Ethnic Groups and Cultures in America." *Ethnic and Racial Studies* 2:1–20.

GREELEY, ANDREW M. 1976. "The Ethnic Miracle." *Public Interest* 45 (Fall):20–36.

LEONARD, KAREN. 1992. *Making Ethnic Choices: California's Punjabi Mexican Americans.* Philadelphia: Temple University Press.

LIEBERSON, STANLEY. 1985. "Unhyphenated Whites in the United States." *Ethnic and Racial Studies* 8:159–80.

LIEBERSON, STANLEY, and MARY WATERS. 1986. "Ethnic Groups in Flux: The Changing Ethnic Responses of American Whites." *Annals of the American Academy of Political and Social Science* 487:79–91.

_____. 1988. *From Many Strands: Ethnic and Racial Groups in Contemporary America.* New York: Russell Sage.

_____. 1993. "The Ethnic Responses of Whites: What Causes Their Instability, Simplification, and Inconsistency?" *Social Forces* 72(2):421–50.

MCKENNEY, NAMPEO R., and ARTHUR R. CRESCE. 1992. "Measurement of Ethnicity in the United States: Experiences of the U.S. Census Bureau." Paper presented at the Joint Canada–United States Conference on the Measurement of Ethnicity, Ottawa, Canada, April 1–3.

SPICKARD, PAUL R. 1989. *Mixed Blood.* Madison: University of Wisconsin Press.

STEINBERG, STEPHEN. 1981. *The Ethnic Myth: Race, Ethnicity, and Class in America.* Boston: Beacon Press.

U.S. BUREAU OF THE CENSUS. 1992. *Census of Population and Housing, 1990: Detailed Ancestry Groups for States.* Supplementary Reports CP-S-1–2. Washington, DC: U.S. Government Printing Office.

WATERS, MARY C. 1990. *Ethnic Options: Choosing Identities in America.* Berkeley and Los Angeles: University of California Press.

WEBER, MAX. 1921. *Economy and Society: An Outline of Interpretive Sociology,* edited by Guenther Roth and Claus Wittich, translated by Ephraim Fischoff. New York: Bedminster Press.

PART II
Prejudice and Discrimination

Imagine you are a 57-year-old white vice president with Friendly Bank. You earn a considerable amount of money, have a large mortgage and car payments, and support four kids, two of whom are in college. You are the primary breadwinner in your family. At lunch, your boss asks you about the new manager you will be hiring. He hints to you in a subtle way, a way you could never prove in court, that he has had bad experiences working with Asian Americans and would be extremely upset if one was hired. You are not racist toward Asians. In fact, one of your best friends is an Asian American. You do, however, need this job, your family needs to eat, two of your children are in college, and you are at an age at which moving from one job to another would be very difficult and extremely costly. Of the three hundred people who apply for this position, several Asian American candidates appear to be highly qualified, and one unquestionably would make an excellent bank manager. Would you turn a blind eye to the resumes of the Asian Americans or would you hire the most qualified person, even if that meant hiring an Asian American and being marginalized or conveniently downsized by your boss?

How do feelings of antipathy toward or dislike of a group of people because of their skin color, ethnicity, or religion culminate in actions against members of that group? As the preceding example indicates, individuals may act in discriminatory ways and not be prejudiced or racist. Conversely, someone may be prejudiced and racist toward a group and not discriminate. The Asian or black shoe salesperson who does not like whites may still sell a white customer a pair of shoes in order to earn a commission.

Prejudice and discrimination are linked in complicated ways. In "The Complexity of Race Relations" (Reading 12), Howard Schuman and associates use longitudinal, or decade-by-decade, survey data to chart how the racial attitudes of whites toward blacks and Asians have improved in the United States. Their findings are quite impressive. Since World War II, whites' views on integration, interracial marriage, voting for non-white politicians, and sharing social space with blacks and Asians suggest that whites are gradually embracing the idea of a color-blind society. However, such findings are encouraging only if you believe that respondents' answers are an accurate reflection of what they really think or feel. Perhaps these trends reflect pressure to conform to what respondents believe is a socially desirable attitude. Typically, individuals want to present themselves to others in a positive way. This pressure to conform may lead respondents to conveniently forget or tightly monitor racist or prejudiced beliefs. Are answers to questions about racial attitudes merely a reflection of what takes place in the abstract, unnatural interview setting, or are these responses a valid and reliable window into Americans' racial attitudes? Frankly, social scientists are not always sure. To further complicate matters, it's not clear what connection, if any, exists between attitudes and actions or between prejudice and discrimination. Demonstrating a strong, consistent causal link between attitudes and actions has proved elusive in the social sciences. The proposition that actions flow from attitudes may seem straightforward, but as we will see in the readings, it is not. It seems logical that individuals would behave in a manner consistent with their attitudes, opinions, or beliefs about a particular topic. If, for example, you define yourself as not being racist, you would not engage in racial discrimination. But as the example about the vice president of Friendly Bank suggests, various social and economic pressures mediate what we would like to do, what we should do, and what we actually do.

Prejudice and discrimination take many forms. The first five readings in Part II examine those forms and the way certain social and structural conditions can create an environment in which prejudice and discrimination are likely to emerge. In an insightful and classic piece of sociology, Herbert Blumer explains race prejudice (racism) as a reflection of how individuals place themselves in a racial hierarchy relative to other racial groups they encounter. That is, individuals attempt to maintain privilege and status by reserving the "prerogatives" of their racial group, even if they are not consciously aware of it. Robert Merton provides examples of the social context in which a nonprejudiced individual like our vice president at Friendly Bank might act in a discriminatory fashion. Like Blumer, Merton outlines how prejudice and discrimination are often rooted in efforts to maintain privileges or advantages that accrue to individuals because of their skin color. As mentioned previously, Howard Schuman and colleagues use survey research findings to trace shifts in the racial attitudes of whites. George Lipsitz chronicles how racism by the federal government in housing, bank lending, and huge subsidies to spur suburbanization—and white flight from the cities—after World War II should be understood as institutional practices that resulted in substantial long-term, intergenerational "investments" in the white population. Eduardo Bonilla-Silva suggests that racism becomes an organizing principle of social relations and affects how different races develop different interests

The next five articles in Part II focus on how a particular social environment shapes both our behavior and attitudes and the way others see us. Joe Feagin explores how racism directed at middle and upper-middle class blacks plays out in ways that nonblacks do not, cannot, or will not see. Jonathan Kozol and Herbert Gans each examine how structural inequality disproportionately affects racial minorities in the United States. Not only does institutional racism result in a two-tiered educational system, but poverty can provide various social functions to the nonpoor—not the least of which is a sense of superiority. Howard Pinderhughes describes how acting in a racist fashion provides status for poor white youths in a working class neighborhood in Brooklyn. Finally, Robert Bullard details how poor and nonwhite neighborhoods are disproportionately exposed to toxic waste—perhaps the most obvious way in which social space gets colored.

"Some of My Best Friends Are . . .":
Linking Group Position to Attitudes and Action

10

RACE PREJUDICE AS A SENSE OF GROUP POSITION

Herbert Blumer

Questions to Consider

Herbert Blumer writes "to characterize another racial group is, by opposition, to define one's own group." How does a "sense of group position" shape how we see other racial and ethnic groups? Have you ever defined your racial group membership in such a way as to heighten your group's status at the expense of another? What was the context?

In this paper I am proposing an approach to the study of race prejudice different from that which dominates contemporary scholarly thought on this topic. My thesis is that race prejudice exists basically in a sense of group position rather than in a set of feelings which members of one racial group have toward the members of another racial group. This different way of viewing race prejudice shifts study and analysis from a preoccupation with feelings as lodged in individuals to a concern with the relationship of racial groups. It also shifts scholarly treatment away from

individual lines of experience and focuses interest on the collective process by which a racial group comes to define and redefine another racial group. Such shifts, I believe, will yield a more realistic and penetrating understanding of race prejudice.

There can be little question that the rather vast literature on race prejudice is dominated by the idea that such prejudice exists fundamentally as a feeling or set of feelings lodged in the individual. It is usually depicted as consisting of feelings such as antipathy, hostility, hatred, intolerance, and aggressiveness. Accordingly, the task of scientific inquiry becomes two-fold. On one hand, there is a need to identify the feelings which make up race prejudice—to see how they fit together and how they are supported by other psychological elements, such as

Herbert Blumer, "Race Prejudice as a Sense of Group Position" from *The Pacific Sociological Review*, Vol. 1, No. 1, Spring 1958, pp. 3–7. Reprinted by permission of Dean S. Dorn for the Pacific Sociological Association.

mythical beliefs. On the other hand, there is need of showing how the feeling complex has come into being. Thus, some scholars trace the complex feelings back chiefly to innate dispositions; some trace it to personality composition, such as authoritarian personality; and others regard the feelings of prejudice as being formed through social experience. However different may be the contentions regarding the make-up of racial prejudice and the way in which it may come into existence, these contentions are alike in locating prejudice in the realm of individual feeling. This is clearly true of the work of psychologists, psychiatrists, and social psychologists, and tends to be predominantly the case in the work of sociologists.

Unfortunately, this customary way of viewing race prejudice overlooks and obscures the fact that race prejudice is fundamentally a matter of relationship between racial groups. A little reflective thought should make this very clear. Race prejudice presupposes, necessarily, that racially prejudiced individuals think of themselves as belonging to a given racial group. It means, also, that they assign to other racial groups those against whom they are prejudiced. Thus, logically and actually, a scheme of racial identification is necessary as a framework for racial prejudice. Moreover, such identification involves the formation of an image or a conception of one's own racial group and of another racial group, inevitably in terms of the relationship of such groups. To fail to see that racial prejudice is a matter (a) of the racial identification made of oneself and of others, and (b) of the way in which the identified groups are conceived in relation to each other, is to miss what is logically and actually basic. One should keep clearly in mind that people necessarily come to identify themselves as belonging to a racial group; such identification is not spontaneous or inevitable but a result of experience. Further, one must realize that the

kind of picture which a racial group forms of itself and the kind of picture which it may form of others are similarly products of experience. Hence, such pictures are variable, just as the lines of experience which produce them are variable.

The body of feelings which scholars, today, are so inclined to regard as constituting the substance of race prejudice is actually a resultant of the way in which given racial groups conceive of themselves and of others. A basic understanding of race prejudice must be sought in the process by which racial groups form images of themselves and of others. This process, as I hope to show, is fundamentally *a collective process*. It operates chiefly through the public media in which individuals who are accepted as the spokesmen of a racial group characterize publicly another racial group. To characterize another racial group is, by opposition, to define one's own group. This is equivalent to placing the two groups in relation to each other, or defining their positions *vis-à-vis* each other. It is the *sense of social position* emerging from this collective process of characterization which provides the basis of race prejudice. The following discussion will consider important facets of this matter.

I would like to begin by discussing several of the important feelings that enter into race prejudice. This discussion will reveal how fundamentally racial feelings point to and depend on a positional arrangement of the racial groups. In this discussion I will confine myself to such feelings in the case of a dominant racial group.

There are four basic types of feeling that seem to be always present in race prejudice in the dominant group. They are (1) a feeling of superiority, (2) a feeling that the subordinate race is intrinsically different and alien, (3) a feeling of proprietary claim to certain areas of privilege and advantage, and (4) a fear and suspicion that the subordinate race harbors designs on the prerogatives of the dominant race. A few words about each of these four feelings will suffice.

In race prejudice there is a self-assured feeling on the part of the dominant racial group of being naturally superior or better. This is commonly shown in a disparagement of the qualities of the subordinate racial group. Condemnatory or debasing traits, such as laziness, dishonesty, greediness, unreliability, stupidity, deceit and immorality, are usually imputed to it. The second feeling, that the subordinate race is an alien and fundamentally different stock, is likewise always present. "They are not of our kind" is a common way in which this is likely to be expressed. It is this feeling that reflects, justifies, and promotes the social exclusion of the subordinate racial group. The combination of these two feelings of superiority and of distinctiveness can easily give rise to feelings of aversion and even antipathy. But in themselves they do not form prejudice. We have to introduce the third and fourth types of feeling.

The third feeling, the sense of proprietary claim, is of crucial importance. It is the feeling on the part of the dominant group of being entitled to either exclusive or prior rights in many important areas of life. The range of such exclusive or prior claims may be wide, covering the ownership of property such as choice lands and sites; the right to certain jobs, occupations or professions; the claim to certain kinds of industry or lines of business; the claim to certain positions of control and decision-making as in government and law; the right to exclusive membership in given institutions such as schools, churches and recreational institutions; the claim to certain positions of social prestige and to the display of the symbols and accoutrements of these positions; and the claim to certain areas of intimacy and privacy. The feeling of such proprietary claims is exceedingly strong in race prejudice. Again, however,

this feeling even in combination with the feeling of superiority and the feeling of distinctiveness does not explain race prejudice. These three feelings are present frequently in societies showing no prejudice, as in certain forms of feudalism, in caste relations, in societies of chiefs and commoners, and under many settled relations of conquerors and conquered. Where claims are solidified into a structure which is accepted or respected by all, there seems to be no group prejudice.

The remaining feeling essential to race prejudice is a fear or apprehension that the subordinate racial group is threatening, or will threaten, the position of the dominant group. Thus, acts or suspected acts that are interpreted as an attack on the natural superiority of the dominant group, or an intrusion into their sphere of group exclusiveness, or an encroachment on their area of proprietary claim are crucial in arousing and fashioning race prejudice. These acts mean "getting out of place."

It should be clear that these four basic feelings of race prejudice definitely refer to a positional arrangement of the racial groups. The feeling of superiority places the subordinate people *below*; the feeling of alienation places them *beyond*; the feeling of proprietary claim excludes them from the prerogatives of position; and the fear of encroachment is an emotional recoil from the endangering of group position. As these features suggest, the positional relation of the two racial groups is crucial in race prejudice. The dominant group is not concerned with the subordinate group as such but it is deeply concerned with its position *vis-à-vis* the subordinate group. This is epitomized in the key and universal expression that a given race is all right in "its place." The sense of group position is the very heart of the relation of the dominant to the subordinate group. It supplies the dominant group with its framework of perception, its standard of judgment, its patterns of sensitivity, and its emotional proclivities.

It is important to recognize that this sense of group position transcends the feelings of the individual members of the dominant group, giving such members a common orientation that is not otherwise to be found in separate feelings and views. There is likely to be considerable difference between the ways in which the individual members of the dominant group think and feel about the subordinate group. Some may feel bitter and hostile, with strong antipathies, with an exalted sense of superiority and with a lot of spite; others may have charitable and protective feelings, marked by a sense of piety and tinctured by benevolence; others may be condescending and reflect mild contempt; and others may be disposed to politeness and considerateness with no feelings of truculence. These are only a few of many different patterns of feeling to be found among members of the dominant racial group. What gives a common dimension to them is a sense of the social position of their group. Whether the members be humane, or callous, cultured or unlettered, liberal or reactionary, powerful or impotent, arrogant or humble, rich or poor, honorable or dishonorable—all are led, by virtue of sharing the sense of group position, to similar individual positions.

The sense of group position is a general kind of orientation. It is a general feeling without being reducible to specific feelings like hatred, hostility or antipathy. It is also a general understanding without being composed of any set of specific beliefs. On the social psychological side it cannot be equated to a sense of social status as ordinarily conceived, for it refers not merely to vertical positioning but to many other lines of position independent of the vertical dimension. Sociologically it is not a mere reflection of the objective relations between racial groups. Rather, it stands for "what ought to be" rather than for "what is." It is a sense of where the two racial groups *belong*.

In its own way, the sense of group position is a norm and imperative—indeed a very powerful one. It guides, incites, cows, and coerces. It should be borne in mind that this sense of group position stands for and involves a fundamental kind of group affiliation for the members of the dominant racial group. To the extent they recognize or feel themselves as belonging to that group they will automatically come under the influence of the sense of position held by that group. Thus, even though given individual members may have personal views and feelings different from the sense of group position, they will have to conjure with the sense of group position held by their racial group. If the sense of position is strong, to act contrary to it is to risk a feeling of self-alienation and to face the possibility of ostracism. I am trying to suggest, accordingly, that the locus of race prejudice is not in the area of individual feeling but in the definition of the respective positions of the racial groups.

The source of race prejudice lies in a felt challenge to this sense of group position. The challenge, one must recognize, may come in many different ways. It may be in the form of an affront to feelings of group superiority; it may be in the form of attempts at familiarity or transgressing the boundary line of group exclusiveness; it may be in the form of encroachment at countless points of proprietary claim; it may be a challenge to power and privilege; it may take the form of economic competition. Race prejudice is a defensive reaction to such challenging of the sense of group position. It consists of the disturbed feelings, usually of marked hostility, that are thereby aroused. As such, race prejudice is a protective device. It functions, however shortsightedly, to preserve the integrity and the position of the dominant group.

It is crucially important to recognize that the sense of group position is not a mere summation of the feelings of position such as might be developed independently by separate individuals as they come to compare themselves with given individuals of the subordinate race. The sense of group position refers to the position of group to group, not to that of individual to individual. Thus, *vis-à-vis* the subordinate racial group the unlettered individual with low status in the dominant racial group has a sense of group position common to that of the elite of his group. By virtue of sharing this sense of position such an individual, despite his low status, feels that members of the subordinate group, however distinguished and accomplished, are somehow inferior, alien, and properly restricted in the area of claims. He forms his conception as a representative of the dominant group; he treats individual members of the subordinate group as representative of that group.

An analysis of how the sense of group position is formed should start with a clear recognition that it is an historical product. It is set originally by conditions of initial contact. Prestige, power, possession of skill, numbers, original self-conceptions, aims, designs and opportunities are a few of the factors that may fashion the original sense of group position. Subsequent experience in the relation of the two racial groups, especially in the area of claims, opportunities and advantages, may mould the sense of group position in many diverse ways. Further, the sense of group position may be intensified or weakened, brought to sharp focus or dulled. It may be deeply entrenched and tenaciously resist change for long periods of time. Or it may never take root. It may undergo quick growth and vigorous expansion, or it may dwindle away through slow-moving erosion. It may be firm or soft, acute or dull, continuous or intermittent. In short, viewed compara-

tively, the sense of group position is very variable.

However variable its particular career, the sense of group position is clearly formed by a running process in which the dominant racial group is led to define and redefine the subordinate racial group and the relations between them. There are two important aspects of this process of definition that I wish to single out for consideration.

First, the process of definition occurs obviously through complex interaction and communication between the members of the dominant group. Leaders, prestige bearers, officials, group agents, dominant individuals and ordinary laymen present to one another characterizations of the subordinate group and express their feelings and ideas on the relations. Through talk, tales, stories, gossip, anecdotes, messages, pronouncements, news accounts, orations, sermons, preachments and the like definitions are presented and feelings are expressed. In this usually vast and complex interaction separate views run against one another, influence one another, modify each other, incite one another and fuse together in new forms. Correspondingly, feelings which are expressed meet, stimulate each other, feed on each other, intensify each other and emerge in new patterns. Currents of view and currents of feeling come into being; sweeping along to positions of dominance and serving as polar points for the organization of thought and sentiment. If the interaction becomes increasingly circular and reinforcing, devoid of serious inner opposition, such currents grow, fuse and become strengthened. It is through such a process that a collective image of the subordinate group is formed and a sense of group position is set. The evidence of such a process is glaring when one reviews the history of any racial arrangement marked by prejudice.

Such a complex process of mutual interaction with its different lines and degrees of formation gives the lie to the many schemes which would lodge the cause of race prejudice in the make-up of the individual—whether in the form of innate disposition, constitutional make-up, personality structure, or direct personal experience with members of the other race. The collective image and feelings in race prejudice are forged out of a complicated social process in which the individual is himself shaped and organized. The scheme, so popular today, which would trace race prejudice to a so-called authoritarian personality shows a grievous misunderstanding of the simple essentials of the collective process that leads to a sense of group position.

The second important aspect of the process of group definition is that it is necessarily concerned with *an abstract image* of the subordinate racial group. The subordinate racial group is defined as if it were an entity or whole. This entity or whole—like the Negro race, or the Japanese, or the Jews—is necessarily an abstraction, never coming within the perception of any of the senses. While actual encounters are with individuals, the picture formed of the racial group is necessarily of a vast entity which spreads out far beyond such individuals and transcends experience with such individuals. The implications of the fact that the collective image is of an abstract group are of crucial significance. I would like to note four of these implications.

First, the building of the image of the abstract group takes place in the area of the remote and not of the near. It is not the experience with concrete individuals in daily association that gives rise to the definitions of the extended, abstract group. Such immediate experience is usually regulated and orderly. Even where such immediate experience is disrupted the new definitions which are formed are limited to the individuals involved. The collective image of the abstract group grows up not by generalizing from experiences gained in close, first-hand contacts but through the transcending characterizations that are made of the group as an entity. Thus, one must seek the central stream of definition in those areas where the dominant group as such is characterizing the subordinate group as such. This occurs in the "public arena" wherein the spokesmen appear as representatives and agents of the dominant group. The extended public arena is constituted by such things as legislative assemblies, public meetings, conventions, the press, and the printed word. What goes on in this public arena attracts the attention of large numbers of the dominant group and is felt as the voice and action of the group as such.

Second, the definitions that are forged in the public arena center, obviously, about matters that are felt to be of major importance. Thus, we are led to recognize the crucial role of the "big event" in developing a conception of the subordinate racial group. The happening that seems momentous, that touches deep sentiments, that seems to raise fundamental questions about relations, and that awakens strong feelings of identification with one's racial group is the kind of event that is central in the formation of the racial image. Here, again, we note the relative unimportance of the huge bulk of experiences coming from daily contact with individuals of the subordinate group. It is the events seemingly loaded with great collective significance that are the focal points of the public discussion. The definition of these events is chiefly responsible for the development of a racial image and of the sense of group position. When this public discussion takes the form of a denunciation of the subordinate racial group, signifying that it is unfit and a threat, the discussion becomes particularly potent in shaping the sense of social position.

Third, the major influence in public discussion is exercised by individuals and groups who have the public ear and who are felt to have standing, prestige, authority and power. Intellectual and social elites, public figures of prominence, and leaders of powerful organizations are likely to be the key figures in the formation of the sense of group position and in the characterization of the subordinate group. It is well to note this in view of the not infrequent tendency of students to regard race prejudice as growing out of the multiplicity of experiences and attitudes of the bulk of the people.

Fourth, we also need to perceive the appreciable opportunity that is given to strong interest groups in directing the lines of discussion and setting the interpretations that arise in such discussion. Their self-interests may dictate the kind of position they wish the dominant racial group to enjoy. It may be a position which enables them to retain certain advantages, or even more to gain still greater advantages. Hence, they may be vigorous in seeking to manufacture events to attract public attention and to set lines of issue in such a way as to predetermine interpretations favorable to their interests. The role of strongly organized groups seeking to further special interest is usually central in the formation of collective images of abstract groups. Historical records of major instances of race relations, as in our South, or in South Africa, or in Europe in the case of the Jew, or on the West Coast in the case of the Japanese, show the formidable part played by interest groups in defining the subordinate racial group.

I conclude this highly condensed paper with two further observations that may throw additional light on the relation of the sense of group position to race prejudice. Race prejudice becomes entrenched and tenacious to the extent the prevailing social order is rooted in the sense of social posi-

tion. This has been true of the historic South in our country. In such a social order race prejudice tends to become chronic and impermeable to change. In other places the social order may be affected only to a limited extent by the sense of group position held by the dominant racial group. This I think has been true usually in the case of anti-Semitism in Europe and this country. Under these conditions the sense of group position tends to be weaker and more vulnerable. In turn, race prejudice has a much more variable and intermittent career, usually becoming pronounced only as a consequence of grave disorganizing events that allow for the formation of a scapegoat.

This leads me to my final observation which in a measure is an indirect summary. The sense of group position dissolves and race prejudice declines when the process of running definition does not keep abreast of major shifts in the social order. When events touching on relations are not treated as "big events" and hence do not set crucial issues in the arena of public discussion; or when the elite leaders or spokesmen do not define such big events vehemently or adversely; or where they define them in the direction of racial harmony; or when there is a paucity of strong interest groups seeking to build up a strong adverse image for special advantage—under such conditions the sense of group position recedes and race prejudice declines.

The clear implication of my discussion is that the proper and fruitful area in which race prejudice should be studied is the collective process through which a sense of group position is formed. To seek, instead, to understand it or to handle it in the arena of individual feeling and of individual experience seems to me to be clearly misdirected.

11

DISCRIMINATION AND
THE AMERICAN CREED

Robert K. Merton

Questions to Consider

Have you ever been in a situation in which social, economic, or peer pressure forced you to treat someone from a different racial group in an inappropriate way? Robert Merton suggests that individuals who are not prejudiced often act in bigoted and discriminatory ways. How and why does this happen? Is it possible to live our lives in the category Merton calls the "unprejudiced non-discriminator"?

The primary function of the sociologist is to search out the determinants and consequences of diverse forms of social behavior. To the extent that he succeeds in fulfilling this role, he clarifies the alternatives of organized social action in a given situation and of the probable outcome of each. To this extent, there is no sharp distinction between pure research and applied research. Rather, the difference is one between research with direct implications for particular problems of social action and research which is remote from these problems. Not infrequently, basic research which has succeeded only in clearing up previously confused concepts may have an immediate bearing upon the problems of men in society to a degree not approximated by applied research oriented exclusively to these problems. At least, this is the assumption underlying the present paper: clarification of apparently unclear and confused concepts in the sphere of race and ethnic relations is a step necessarily prior to the devising of effective programs for reducing intergroup conflict and for promoting equitable access to economic and social opportunities. . . .

The American Creed: As Cultural Ideal, Personal Belief and Practice

The American creed as set forth in the Declaration of Independence, the preamble of the Constitution and the Bill of Rights has often been misstated. This part of the cultural heritage does *not* include the patently false assertion that all men are created equal in capacity or endowment. It does *not* imply that an Einstein and a moron are equal in intellectual capacity or that Joe Louis and a small, frail Columbia professor (or a Mississippian Congressman) are equally endowed with brawny arms harboring muscles as strong as iron bands. It does *not* proclaim universal equality of innate intellectual or physical endowment.

Instead, the creed asserts the indefeasible principle of the human right to full equity—the right of equitable access to justice, freedom and opportunity, irrespective of race or religion or ethnic origin. It proclaims further the universalist doctrine of the dignity of the individual, irrespective of the groups of which he is a part. It is a creed announcing full moral equities for all, not an absurd myth affirming the equality of intellectual and physical capacity of all men everywhere. And it goes on to say that though men differ in innate endowment, they do so as individuals, not by virtue of their group memberships.

Viewed sociologically, the creed is a set of values and precepts embedded in American culture, to which Americans are expected to conform. It is a complex of affirmations, rooted in the historical past and ceremonially celebrated in the present, partly enacted in the laws of the land and partly not. Like all creeds, it is a profession of faith, a part of cultural tradition sanctified by the larger traditions of which it is a part.

It would be a mistaken sociological assertion, however, to suggest that the creed is a fixed and static cultural constant, unmodified in the course of time, just as it would be an error to imply that as an integral part of culture, it evenly blankets all subcultures of the national society. It is indeed dynamic, subject to change and in turn promoting change in other spheres of culture and society. It is, moreover, unevenly distributed throughout the society, being institutionalized as an integral part of local culture in some regions of the society and rejected in others.

. . . Learned men and men in high public positions have repeatedly observed and deplored the disparity between ethos and behavior in the sphere of race and ethnic relations. In his magisterial volumes on the American Negro, for example, Gunnar Myrdal called this gulf between creed and conduct "an American dilemma," and centered his attention on the prospect of narrowing or closing the gap. The President's Committee on Civil Rights, in their report to the nation, and . . . President [Truman] himself, in a message to Congress, have called public attention to this "serious gap between our ideals and some of our practices."

But as valid as these observations may be, they tend so to simplify the relations between creed and conduct as to be seriously misleading both for social policy and for social science. All these high authorities notwithstanding, the problems of racial and ethnic inequities are not expressible as a discrepancy between high cultural principles and low social conduct. It is a relation not between two variables, official creed and private practice, but between three: first, the cultural creed honored in cultural tradition and partly enacted into law; second, the beliefs and attitudes of individuals regarding the principles of the creed; and third, the actual practices of individuals with reference to it.

Once we substitute these three variables of cultural ideal, belief and actual practice for the customary distinction between the two variables of cultural ideals and actual practices, the entire formulation of the problem becomes changed. We escape from the virtuous but ineffectual impasse of deploring the alleged hypocrisy of many Americans into the more difficult but potentially effectual realm of analyzing the problem in hand.

To describe the problem and to proceed to its analysis, it is necessary to consider the official creed, individuals' beliefs and attitudes concerning the creed, and their actual behavior. Once stated, the distinctions are readily applicable. Individuals may *recognize* the creed as part of a cultural tradition, *without having any private conviction of its moral validity or its binding quality.* Thus, so far as the beliefs of individuals are concerned, we can identify two types: those who genuinely believe in the creed and those who do not (although some of these may, on public or ceremonial occasions, profess adherence to its principles). Similarly, with respect to actual practices: conduct may or may not conform to the creed. But, and this is the salient consideration: *conduct may or may not conform with individuals' own beliefs concerning the moral claims of all men to equal opportunity.*

Stated in formal sociological terms, this asserts that attitudes and overt behavior vary independently. *Prejudicial attitudes need not coincide with discriminatory behavior.* The implications of this statement can be drawn out in terms of a logical syntax whereby the variables are diversely combined, as can be seen in the following typology.

By exploring the interrelations between prejudice and discrimination, we can identify four major types in terms of their attitudes toward the creed and their behavior with respect to it. Each type is found in every region and social class, though in varying numbers. By examining each type, we shall be better prepared to understand their interdependence and the appropriate types of action for curbing ethnic discrimination. The folklabels for each type are intended to aid in their prompt recognition.

Type I: The Unprejudiced Non-Discriminator or All-Weather Liberal

These are the racial and ethnic liberals who adhere to the creed in both belief and practice. They are neither prejudiced nor given to discrimination. Their orientation toward the creed is fixed and stable. Whatever the environing situation, they are likely to abide by their beliefs: hence, the *all-weather* liberal.

This is, of course, the strategic group which *can* act as the spearhead for the progressive extension of the creed into effective practice. They represent the solid foundation both for the measure of ethnic equities which now exist and for the future enlargement of these equities. Integrated with the creed in both belief and practice, they would seem most motivated to influence others toward the same democratic outlook. They represent a reservoir of culturally legitimatized goodwill which can be channeled into an active program for extending belief in the creed and conformity with it in practice.

Most important, as we shall see presently, the all-weather liberals comprise the group which can so reward others for conforming with the creed, as to transform deviants into conformists. They alone can provide the positive social environment for the other types who will no longer find it expedient or rewarding to retain their prejudices or discriminatory practices.

But though the ethnic liberal is a *potential* force for the successive extension of the American creed, he does not fully realize this potentiality in actual fact, for a variety of reasons. Among the limitations on effective action are several fallacies to which the ethnic liberal seems peculiarly subject. First among these is the *fallacy of group soliloquies.* Ethnic liberals are busily engaged in talking to themselves. Repeatedly, the same groups of like-minded liberals seek each other out, hold periodic meetings in which they engage in mutual exhortation and thus lend social and psychological support to one another. But however much these unwittingly self-selected audiences may reinforce the creed among themselves, they do not thus appreciably diffuse the creed in belief or practice to groups which depart from it in one respect or the other.

More, these group soliloquies in which there is typically wholehearted agreement among fellow-liberals tend to promote another fallacy limiting effective action. This is the *fallacy of unanimity.* Continued association with like-minded individuals tends to produce the illusion that a large measure of consensus has been achieved in the community at large. The unanimity regarding essential cultural axioms which obtains in these small groups provokes an overestimation of the strength of the movement and of its effective inroads upon the larger population which does not necessarily share these creedal axioms. Many also mistake participation in the groups of like-minded individuals for effective action. Discussion accordingly takes the place of action. The reinforcement of the creed for oneself is mistaken for the extension of the creed among those outside the limited circle of ethnic liberals.

Arising from adherence to the creed is a third limitation upon effective action, the *fallacy of privatized solutions* to the problem. The ethnic liberal, precisely because he is at one with the American creed, may rest content with his own individual behavior and thus see no need to do anything about the problem at large. Since his own spiritual house is in order, he is not motivated by guilt or shame to work on a collective problem. The very freedom of the liberal from guilt thus prompts him to secede from any *collective* effort to set the national house in order. He essays a *private* solution to a *social* problem. He assumes that numerous individual adjustments will serve in place of a collective adjustment. His outlook, compounded of good moral philosophy but poor sociology, holds that each individual must put his own house in order and fails to recognize that privatized solutions cannot be effected for problems which are essentially social in nature. For clearly, if each person *were* motivated to abide by the American creed, the problem would not be likely to exist in the first place. It is only when a social environment is established by conformists to the creed that deviants can in due course be brought to modify their behavior in the direction of con-

formity. But this "environment" can be constituted only through collective effort and not through private adherence to a public creed. Thus we have the paradox that the clear conscience of many ethnic liberals may promote the very social situation which permits deviations from the creed to continue unchecked. Privatized liberalism invites social inaction. Accordingly, there appears the phenomenon of the inactive or passive liberal, himself at spiritual ease, neither prejudiced nor discriminatory, but in a measure tending to contribute to the persistence of prejudice and discrimination through his very inaction.

The fallacies of group soliloquy, unanimity and privatized solutions thus operate to make the potential strength of the ethnic liberals unrealized in practice.

It is only by first recognizing these limitations that the liberal can hope to overcome them. With some hesitancy, one may suggest initial policies for curbing the scope of the three fallacies. The fallacy of group soliloquies can be removed only by having ethnic liberals enter into organized groups not comprised merely by fellow-liberals. This exacts a heavy price on the liberal. It means that he faces initial opposition and resistance rather than prompt consensus. It entails giving up the gratifications of consistent group support.

The fallacy of unanimity can in turn be reduced by coming to see that American society often provides large rewards for those who express their ethnic prejudice in discrimination. Only if the balance of rewards, material and psychological, is modified will behavior be modified. Sheer exhortation and propaganda are not enough. Exhortation verges on a belief in magic if it is not supported by appropriate changes in the social environment to make conformity with the exhortation rewarding.

Finally, the fallacy of privatized solutions requires the militant liberal to motivate the passive liberal to collective effort, possibly by inducing in him a sense of guilt for his unwitting contribution to the problems of ethnic inequities through his own systematic inaction.

One may suggest a unifying theme for the ethnic liberal: goodwill is not enough to modify social reality. It is only when this goodwill is harnessed to social-psychological realism that it can be used to reach cultural objectives.

Type II: The Unprejudiced Discriminator or Fair-Weather Liberal

The fair-weather liberal is the man of expediency who, despite his own freedom from prejudice, supports discriminatory practices when it is the easier or more profitable course. His expediency may take the form of holding his silence and thus implicitly acquiescing in expressions of ethnic prejudice by others or in the practice of discrimination by others. This is the expediency of the timid: the liberal who hesitates to speak up against discrimination for fear he might lose status or be otherwise penalized by his prejudiced associates. Or his expediency may take the form of grasping at advantages in social and economic competition deriving solely from the ethnic status of competitors. This is the expediency of the self-assertive: the employer, himself not an anti-Semite or Negrophobe, who refuses to hire Jewish or Negro workers because "it might hurt business"; the trade union leader who expediently advocates racial discrimination in order not to lose the support of powerful Negrophobes in his union.

In varying degrees, the fair-weather liberal suffers from guilt and shame for departing from his own effective beliefs in the American creed. Each deviation through which he derives a limited reward from passively acquiescing in or actively supporting discrimination contributes cumulatively to this fund of guilt. He is, therefore, peculiarly vulnerable to the efforts of the all-weather liberal who would help him bring his conduct into accord with his beliefs, thus removing this source of guilt. He is the most amenable to cure, because basically he wants to be cured. His is a split conscience which motivates him to cooperate actively with those who will help remove the source of internal conflict. He thus represents the strategic group promising the largest returns for the least effort. Persistent re-affirmation of the creed will only intensify his conflict; but a long regimen in a favorable social climate can be expected to transform the fair-weather liberal into an all-weather liberal.

Type III: The Prejudiced Non-Discriminator or Fair-Weather Illiberal

The fair-weather illiberal is the reluctant conformist to the creed, the man of prejudice who does not believe in the creed but conforms to it in practice through fear of sanctions which might otherwise be visited upon him. You know him well: the prejudiced employer who discriminates against racial or ethnic groups until a Fair Employment Practice Commission, able and willing to enforce the law, puts the fear of punishment into him; the trade union leader, himself deeply prejudiced, who does away with Jim Crow in his union because the rank-and-file demands that it be done away with; the businessman who forgoes his own prejudices when he finds a profitable market among the very people he hates, fears or despises; the timid bigot who will not express his prejudices when he is in the presence of powerful men who vigorously and effectively affirm their belief in the American creed.

It should be clear that the fair-weather illiberal is the precise counterpart of the fair-weather liberal. Both are men of expediency, to be sure, but expediency dictates different courses of behavior in the two cases. The timid bigot conforms to the creed only when there is danger or loss in deviations, just as the timid liberal deviates from the creed when there is danger or loss in conforming. *Superficial similarity in behavior of the two in the same situation should not be permitted to cloak a basic difference in the meaning of this outwardly similar behavior,* a difference which is as important for social policy as it is for social science. Whereas the timid bigot is under strain when he conforms to the creed, the timid liberal is under strain when he deviates. For ethnic prejudice has deep roots in the character structure of the fair-weather bigot, and this will find overt expression unless there are powerful countervailing forces, institutional, legal and interpersonal. He does not accept the moral legitimacy of the creed; he conforms because he must, and will cease to conform when the pressure is removed. The fair-weather liberal, on the other hand, is effectively committed to the creed and does not require strong institutional pressure to conform; continuing interpersonal relations with all-weather liberals may be sufficient.

This is the one critical point at which the traditional formulation of the problem of ethnic discrimination as a departure from the creed can lead to serious errors of theory and practice. Overt behavioral deviation (or conformity) may signify importantly different situations, depending upon the underlying motivations. Knowing simply that ethnic discrimination is rife in a community does not, therefore, point to appropriate lines of social policy. It is necessary to know also the distribution of ethnic prejudices and basic motivations for these prejudices as well. Communities with the same amount of overt discrimination may represent vastly different types of problems, dependent on whether the population is comprised by a large nucleus of fair-weather liberals ready to abandon their discriminatory practices under slight interpersonal pressure or a large nucleus of fair-weather illiberals who will abandon discrimination only if major changes in the local institutional setting can be effected. Any statement of the problem as a gulf between creedal ideals and prevailing practice is thus seen to be overly-simplified in the precise sense of masking this decisive difference between the type of discrimination exhibited by the fair-weather liberal and by the fair-weather illiberal. That the gulf-between-ideal-and-practice does not adequately describe the nature of the ethnic problem will become more apparent as we turn to the fourth type in our inventory of prejudice and discrimination.

Type IV: The Prejudiced Discriminator or the All-Weather Illiberal

This type, too, is not unknown to you. He is the confirmed illiberal, the bigot pure and unashamed, the man of prejudice consistent in his departure from the American creed. In some measure, he is found everywhere in the land, though in varying numbers. He derives large social and psychological gains from his conviction that "any white man (including the village idiot) is 'better' than any nigger (including George Washington Carver)." He considers differential treatment of Negro and white not as "discrimination," in the sense of unfair treatment, but as "discriminating," in the sense of showing acute discernment. For him, it is as clear that one "ought" to accord a Negro and a white different treatment in a wide diversity of situations, as it is clear to the population at large that one "ought" to accord a child and an adult different treatment in many situations.

This illustrates anew my reason for questioning the applicability of the unusual formula of the American dilemma as a gap between lofty creed and low conduct. For the confirmed illiberal, ethnic discrimination does *not* represent a discrepancy between *his* ideals and *his* behavior. His ideals proclaim the right, even the duty, of discrimination. Accordingly, his behavior does not entail a sense of social deviation, with the resultant strains which this would involve. The ethnic illiberal is as much a conformist as the ethnic liberal. He is merely conforming to a different cultural and institutional pattern which is centered, not about the creed, but about a doctrine of essential inequality of status ascribed to those of diverse ethnic and racial origins. To overlook this is to overlook the well-known *fact* that our national culture is divided into a number of local subcultures which are not consistent among themselves in all respects. And again, to fail to take this fact of different subcultures into account is to open the door for all manner of errors of social policy in attempting to control the problems of racial and ethnic discrimination.

This view of the all-weather illiberal has one immediate implication with wide bearing upon social policies and sociological theory oriented toward the problem of discrimination. The extreme importance of the social surroundings of the confirmed illiberal at once becomes apparent. For as these surroundings vary, so, in some measure, does the problem of the consistent illiberal. The illiberal, living in those cultural regions where the American creed is widely repudiated and is no effective part of the subculture, has his private ethnic attitudes and practices supported by the local mores, the local institutions and the local power-structure. The illiberal in cultural areas dominated by a large measure of adherence to the American creed is in a social environment where he is isolated and receives small social support for his beliefs and practices. In both instances, the *individual* is an illiberal, to be sure, but he represents two significantly different *sociological types*. In the first instance, he is a *social*

conformist, with strong moral and institutional reinforcement, whereas in the second, he is a *social deviant,* lacking strong social corroboration. In the one case, his discrimination involves him in further integration with his network of social relations; in the other, it threatens to cut him off from sustaining interpersonal ties. In the first cultural context, personal change in his ethnic behavior involves alienating himself from people significant to him; in the second context, this change of personal outlook may mean fuller incorporation in groups meaningful to him. In the first situation, modification of his ethnic views requires him to take the path of greatest resistance whereas in the second, it may mean the path of least resistance. From all this, we may surmise that any social policy aimed at changing the behavior and perhaps the attitudes of the all-weather illiberal will have to take into account the cultural and social structure of the area in which he lives. . . .

Implications of the Typology for Social Policy

. . . In approaching problems of policy, two things are plain. First, these should be considered from the standpoint of the militant ethnic liberal, for he alone is sufficiently motivated to engage in positive action for the reduction of ethnic discrimination. And second, the fair-weather liberal, the fair-weather illiberal and the all-weather illiberal represent types differing sufficiently to require diverse kinds of treatment.

Treatment of the Fair-Weather Liberal

The fair-weather liberal, it will be remembered, discriminates only when it appears expedient to do so, and experiences some measure of guilt for deviating from his own belief in the American creed. He suffers from this conflict between conscience and conduct. Accordingly, he is a relatively easy target for the all-weather liberal. He represents the strategic group promising the largest immediate returns for the least effort. Recognition of this type defines the first task for the militant liberal who would enter into a collective effort to make the creed a viable and effective set of social norms rather than a ceremonial myth. . . .

Since the fair-weather liberal discriminates only when it seems rewarding to do so, the crucial need is so to change social situations that there are few occasions in which discrimination proves rewarding and many in which it does not. This would suggest that ethnic liberals self-consciously and deliberately seek to draw into the social groups where they constitute a comfortable majority a number of the "expedient discriminators." This would serve to counteract the dangers of self-selection through which liberals come to associate primarily with like-minded individuals. It would, further, provide an interpersonal and social environment for the fair-weather liberal in which he would find substantial social and psychological gains from abiding by his own beliefs, gains which would more than offset the rewards attendant upon occasional discrimination. It appears that men do not long persist in behavior which lacks social corroboration.

We have much to learn about the role of numbers and proportions in determining the behavior of members of a group. But it seems that individuals generally act differently when they are numbered among a minority rather than the majority. This is not to say that minorities abdicate their practices in the face of a contrary-acting majority, but only that the same people are subjected to different strains and pressures according to whether they are included in the majority or the minority. And the fair-weather liberal who finds himself associated with militant ethnic liberals may be expected to forgo his occasional deviations into discrimination; he may move from category II into category I. . . .

Treatment of the Fair-Weather Illiberal

Because his *beliefs* correspond to those of the full-fledged liberal, the fair-weather liberal can rather readily be drawn into an interpersonal environment constituted by those of a comparable turn of mind. This would be more difficult for the fair-weather illiberal, whose beliefs are so fully at odds with those of ethnic liberals that he may, at first, only be alienated by association with them. If the initial tactic for the fair-weather liberal, therefore, is a change in interpersonal environment, the seemingly most appropriate tactic for the fair-weather illiberal is a change in the institutional and legal environment. It is, indeed, probably this type which liberals implicitly have in mind when they expect significant changes in behavior to result from the introduction of controls on ethnic discrimination into the legal machinery of our society.

For this type—and it is a major limitation for planning policies of control that we do not know his numbers or his distribution in the country—it would seem that the most effective tactic is the institution of legal controls administered with strict efficiency. This would presumably reduce the amount of *discrimination* practiced by the fair-weather illiberal, though it might *initially* enhance rather than reduce his *prejudices*. . . .

A second prevalent tactic for modifying the prejudice of the fair-weather illiberal is that of seeking to draw him into interethnic groups explicitly formed for the promotion of tolerance. This, too, seems largely ineffectual, since the deeply prejudiced individual will not enter into such groups of his own volition. As a consequence of this process of self-selection, these tolerance groups soon come to be comprised by the very ethnic liberals who initiated the enterprise.

This barrier of self-selection can be partially hurdled only if the ethnic illiberals are brought into continued association with militant liberals in groups devoted to significant common values, quite remote from objectives of ethnic equity as such. Thus, as our Columbia-Lavanburg researches have found, many fair-weather illiberals *will* live in interracial housing projects in order to enjoy the rewards of superior housing at a given rental. And some of the illiberals thus brought into personal contact with various ethnic groups under the auspices of prestigeful militant liberals come to modify their prejudices. It is, apparently, only through interethnic collaboration, initially enforced by pressures of the situation, for immediate and significant objectives (other than tolerance) that the self-insulation of the fair-weather illiberal from rewarding interethnic contacts can be removed.

But however difficult it may presently be to affect the *prejudicial sentiments* of the fair-weather illiberal, his *discriminatory practices* can be lessened by the uniform, prompt and prestigeful use of legal and institutional sanctions. The critical problem is to ascertain the proportions of fair-weather and all-weather illiberals in a given local population in order to have some clue to the probable effectiveness or ineffectiveness of anti-discrimination legislation.

Treatment of the All-Weather Illiberal

It is, of course, the hitherto confirmed illiberal, persistently translating his prejudices into active discrimination, who represents the most difficult problem. But though he requires longer and more careful treatment, it is possible that he is not beyond change.

In every instance, his social surroundings must be assiduously taken into account. It makes a peculiarly large difference whether he is in a cultural region of bigotry or in a predominantly "liberal" area, given over to verbal adherence to the American creed, at the very least. As this cultural climate varies, so must the prescription for his cure and the prognosis for a relatively quick or long delayed recovery.

In an unfavorable cultural climate—and this does not necessarily exclude the benign regions of the Far South—the immediate resort will probably have to be that of working through legal and administrative federal controls over extreme discrimination, with full recognition that, in all probability, these regulations will be systematically evaded for some time to come. In such cultural regions, we may expect nullification of the law as the common practice, perhaps as common as was the case in the nation at large with respect to the Eighteenth Amendment, often with the connivance of local officers of the law. The large gap between the new law and local mores will not *at once* produce significant change of prevailing practices; token punishments of violations will probably be more common than effective control. At best, one may assume that significant change will be fitful, and excruciatingly slow. But secular changes in the economy may in due course lend support to the new legal framework of control over discrimination. As the economic shoe pinches because the illiberals do not fully mobilize the resources of industrial manpower nor extend their local markets through equitable wage-payments, they may slowly abandon some discriminatory practices as they come to find that these do not always pay—even the discriminator. So far as discrimination is concerned, organized counteraction is possible and some small results may be expected. But it would seem that wishes father thoughts, when one expects basic changes in the immediate future in these regions of institutionalized discrimination.

The situation is somewhat different with regard to the scattered, rather than aggregated, ethnic illiberals found here and there throughout the country. Here the mores and a social organization oriented toward the American creed still have some measure of prestige and the resources of a majority of liberals can be mobilized to isolate the illiberal. In these surroundings, it is possible to move the all-weather illiberal toward Type III—he can be brought to conform with institutional regulations, even though he does not surrender his prejudices. And once he has entered upon this role of the dissident but conforming individual, the remedial program designed for the fair-weather illiberal would be in order.

12

THE COMPLEXITY OF RACE RELATIONS

Howard Schuman • Charlotte Steeh • Lawrence Bobo • Maria Krysan

Questions to Consider

Schuman and associates raise a question about individuals who endorse principles of equality but reject social programs that would help level socioeconomic differences. How is it possible that someone could both strongly support the idea of equal opportunity but not endorse race-based programs designed to promote equal opportunity?

Seek simplicity and distrust it.
—A. N. WHITEHEAD

Color and other racial identifications are such powerful ascriptive markers that nobody can fully escape them, regardless of

their pursuits or achievements in life. The late Secretary of Commerce Ronald Brown kept in his desk a news photograph from a Midwestern paper that had been sent to him by Colin Powell. The picture was of Mr. Brown, but the caption identified him as General Powell. Attached to the clipping was a handwritten note from Powell: "Ron, they *still* can't tell us apart" (*New York Times*, April 4, 1996, p. A10). Such perceived similarities in appearance, and the complementary distinction between whites and blacks, are fundamental in the United States, as they are to varying degrees in other parts of the world.[1]

There is no evidence that this virtually absolute differentiation of the American population has been reduced by the changes of the last half century, though it has no doubt been further complicated by the increase in several Asian, Hispanic, and other minorities. Indeed, the black-white division may even have deepened in some respects as a result of the growth of black consciousness and the use of racial enumeration as a way of monitoring progress in civil rights. Americans are not much more color-blind today than they ever were, and despite some growth in the rate of racial intermarriage (Harrison and Bennett 1995), a melting-pot solution to racial differences in the United States is not likely to occur in the foreseeable future.

What *has* changed over the past half century is the normative definition of appropriate relations between blacks and whites. Whereas discrimination against, and enforced segregation of, black Americans were taken for granted by most white Americans as recently as the World War II years, today the norm holds that black Americans deserve the same treatment and respect as whites, and in addition that racial integration in all public spheres of life is a desirable goal. . . . How far back in time the development of the new norm goes, and what led to both the initial and the continuing movement of whites toward acceptance of the principle of equal treatment are interesting questions, but available survey data do not allow us to answer them very well.[2] In any case, the more pressing problem here is the meaning for the present of this great normative shift and its implications for the future.

Do the changes in individual attitudes that flow from the larger normative shift mean anything outside the survey interview? It is difficult to believe that they do not, for the evidence is all around us of important and pervasive changes in the relations between blacks and whites in the United States. Beyond the total elimination of a vast structure of legal segregation throughout the South and Southwest and within the U.S. armed forces, there is an abundance of *non*survey evidence of genuine change in white actions toward blacks. Black Americans today hold a wide range of high elected and appointed political positions, and not by any means only in areas with black majorities. African Americans are also prominent in television and film, in major universities and colleges, and to a greater or lesser degree in many other public spheres of life.[3] In most of these spheres they are still greatly underrepresented in proportion to their numbers in the total population, and the large black lower class is almost totally excluded from participation in this change. But these crucial qualifications do not alter the fact that actual change in public life over the past half century has been very substantial. Only because so much of the population of the United States—both black and white—is now too young to have any memory of race relations circa 1940 or even 1960 can there be any doubt about the magnitude of the change.

The tendency to look for exact consistency between attitudes and behavior also misses a useful distinction that can be made between literal consistency and correlational consistency (Schuman and Johnson 1976). The former asks whether people do what they say they will do; the latter asks whether people are ordered or ranked in the same way along both attitude and behavioral dimensions. . . .

In other words, attitude measures can be seen as tapping broad currents of social change, though of course imperfectly, and if they show correlational consistency we should be able at the same time to see similar trends in directly relevant behaviors. . . .

Yet even where behavior is consistent correlationally with attitudes, one can still ask whether changes in either survey responses *or* public behavior represent a true inner transformation by white Americans. Or are the changes a kind of veneer that conceals continued profound racism on the part of most or all white Americans? This is a complex question: in the language of social science, it asks whether the new norm has been internalized. One legitimate response is to insist that the change in public norms is important in itself, especially as it is reflected in white actions. If a white president appoints a black general to the position of chief of staff of the armed forces, or if a substantial part of a white electorate votes for a black gubernatorial or congressional candidate, we may never know whether they do so because in their hearts they are genuinely nondiscriminatory, or because they have temporarily put aside their deep racism to make that particular decision. But all of us conform to norms that we may or may not have internalized deeply, yet that guide our actions in ways that are of considerable consequence for our relations with others. Myrdal spoke of the American Dilemma as being "in the heart of the American," but what he surely meant was that it was located in the values and norms of our society, and that most Americans are capable of feeling pressure from these values and norms—if not out of personal guilt, then from social shaming when they are blatantly violated. We should not overpsychologize the problem of conformity to social norms, as though each of us has either internalized a norm completely or chosen to ignore it completely.

Another approach to the same issue is to acknowledge that white persons who respond to a survey question on the principle of school integration by saying "blacks and whites should go to the same schools" doubtless run the full gamut from those deeply committed to that idea to those who feel quite otherwise but are embarrassed to admit it to an interviewer. However, most Americans, black as well as white, probably fall some-

where in the middle: they feel some genuine belief in the norm but also have other beliefs and preferences that put them in conflict on the issue. It is clear from the combination of questions we have examined that many white respondents do feel conflict about school integration and similar issues, and that their responses in support of integration in principle are unlikely to be translated directly and completely into action. It is therefore important to try to understand—and to measure—the sources of these conflicts.

One such source is the fact that questions like the one about blacks and whites going to the same schools are too simple, asking in dichotomous form about "segregation" versus "integration," without defining these abstractions or allowing consideration of either the amount or the form of integration. The questions we reviewed on white willingness to be personally involved in integration, as well as other survey data (Farley et al. 1994; Levine 1971; Rothbart 1976; Smith 1981), make it quite clear that whites are much more positive toward a situation with a white majority and a black minority than toward one defined as fifty-fifty or certainly one with a black majority. Given the history of white dominance in this country and the persistence of color as a significant dividing line, this is not a surprising finding; nor is it out of keeping with the way majority ethnic groups behave in other countries, including black African countries. These propensities are at least as much a matter of power and control and of fear of being controlled by others as they are of "prejudice" as a separate and self-contained psychological state.

One sign of this fact of political life about intergroup relations in America is the ability of a black candidate frequently to obtain more white votes when blacks are clearly in the minority than when blacks approach a majority (Hacker 1995). White voting in the latter instances tends to be determined not so much by attitudes toward the race of the candidate as by the perceived balance of power between blacks and whites as groups. For a similar reason, Colin Powell has appeared attractive as a presidential candidate to many white Americans in part because he did not ever suggest that he represented or would represent blacks as a collective political force.

Resistance to government intervention in support of black employment, school integration, or open housing is probably at least partly due to the same perceived conflict between blacks and whites as competing groups, which in turn is based on the way in which physical appearance shapes personal identification of individuals with one group or the other and its political positions. The identification can range from a relatively innocuous form, much like boosting one's hometown sports team, all the way to the most extreme forms of ethnocentrism. Thus many questions about government intervention can be understood as implying large-scale group change, and they suggest a degree of integration that many whites are reluctant to accept, at least at this point in time.

Norms, Preferences, and Personal Conflicts

As we consider the implications of attitudes based on norms, it is useful to get some sense of their generality and of the distinction that many people make between larger societal norms and those attitudes that reflect personal preferences or more local norms. As Myrdal (1944) clearly recognized, a great deal of social behavior is a compromise between the two. We summarize below a series of experimental investigations that show both the power and limitations of norms of equal treatment and the importance of distinguishing them from personal preferences. The experiments focused on

issues of residential discrimination, but would apply in other spheres as well.[4]

Individual vs. Group Rights

The first experiment was developed to test the intuitively attractive notion that there would be more support for the right of a single black family to move into an all-white neighborhood than there is for a broad open housing law, which at that point in time (1986) showed an approximately 50-50 division of opinion by whites. First, the focus on a single black family points up forcefully the implications of the norm of equal treatment for real individuals. Second, by keeping the focus on a single family, there should be somewhat less concern about rapid transformation of a neighborhood from entirely or largely white to majority black, as might be implied by an open housing law. However, the initial results of the experiment were unexpected and led to surprising directions.

Half of a national telephone sample was randomly assigned to answer the Open Housing question, and half was assigned to answer a specially written question about a single black family. Moreover, unlike the typical survey interview, we explicitly instructed interviewers to allow and immediately record any volunteered answer that did not fit the alternatives offered to respondents. This change in procedure proved instructive.

There is, as predicted, a great deal more support for government enforcement of the rights of a single black family than for a general open housing law. Of those making a clear choice, 80 percent express support for government enforcement of the rights of a single black family, as against only 61 percent who support a general open housing law, a difference that is highly significant statistically. Taken by itself, this finding indicates that when the focus is on an individual or an individual family, the norm of equal treatment has greater efficacy than when a more general racial transformation is proposed.

A large proportion of respondents (35 percent) who were asked the question about the single black family avoided choosing either of the alternatives offered, whereas only a tiny fraction (7 percent) failed to give a direct answer to the question about open housing laws. Most of those who volunteered their own response to the single family question claimed to favor the right of a black family to live wherever it wished *but* also opposed any use of government power to enforce that right. Such answers, quite overt rather than concealed, show respondents who are trying to conform to the norm of equal treatment yet avoid committing themselves to government enforcement of that norm. The responses emphasize the conflict in the minds of about a quarter of the white population between support of a principle and support of its implementation through government action. . . .

Our results thus far indicate that when blacks are involved, a substantial portion of the white population either opposes residential integration or tries to have it both ways by supporting the goal but not the means to equal treatment. Is this a sign of the special barriers erected against African Americans? A series of further experiments indicates that the implications are different than they initially appeared. We first considered the possibility that white American "racism" applies to *all* nonwhite groups. We repeated the previous experiment with a new variation: half of a national sample was asked the question about a single black family; the other half was asked the same question about another nonwhite group, a single Japanese-American family, on the assumption that white resistance would be somewhat less in this case. To our surprise, there was no difference approaching statistical significance between the two distributions (enforcement vs. all nonenforcement re-

sponses combined), and the trend is in the direction of greater support for enforcement in the case of the black family.

Next, in order to allow for the possibility that white opposition to enforcement of equal rights may have roots in a still broader ethnocentrism (Adorno et al. 1950), a further experiment was carried out. A "Jewish family" was substituted for a "Japanese-American family" and a "Christian neighborhood" was substituted for a "white neighborhood." The comparison was again with the parallel question about a single black family and a white neighborhood.[5] And again we discovered that there was no significant difference between the two questions: no greater willingness to enforce equal treatment for the Jewish family than for the black family.

Finally, we carried out a still more extreme experiment that reversed the issue posed between Jews and non-Jews. This time the question about the single black family was compared with a parallel question about enforcing the right of a single Christian family to move into a previously all-Jewish neighborhood. The basic finding remained the same: the distribution of answers to the two questions does not differ significantly, and in fact the trend is toward more support for the black family than for the presumably white, Christian family.

In sum, there is little evidence from this series of experiments that opposition to enforcement of a single black family's right to move into a white neighborhood represents simply a form of antiblack sentiment. On the contrary, there is evidence that it reflects a more general resistance to government enforcement of equal treatment in residential integration, though not necessarily rejection of the desirability of equal treatment. This conclusion fits our impressions based on occasional monitoring of the actual interviews and also the impressions of the interviewers themselves. Opposition to government enforcement in this area of life takes on the force of a principle for many respondents, regardless of the group involved and regardless of what may seem a contradiction inherent in statements by many of these same people that all individuals should be allowed to live where they wish.[6]

Norms vs. Preferences

Given the patterns of actual segregation in the United States, it is difficult to believe that there is the same resistance on the part of whites to Japanese-American or Jewish families moving into a previously white, non-Jewish neighborhood as there is to blacks (Thomas Wilson 1996). How can we explain that fact if the same degree of adherence to the norm of equal treatment is found regardless of the ethnic group involved? A further experiment casts some light on this question.

The new experiment shifted attention from "rights" to "preferences." This time half the respondents were asked if they would "mind a lot, a little, or not at all" if a black family moved next door, and the other half was asked a parallel question about a Japanese-American family's moving next door. (The word "mind" was intended to emphasize personal preference rather than a general norm.) Moreover, the experiment was carried out twice, once with the addition of a phrase stating that the family moving next door would have "the same income and education" as the respondent, and a second time without that phrase.

There is noticeably (and significantly) less personal objection to a Japanese-American family's moving next door than to a black family's, and this is true regardless of whether or not the income and education of the new neighbors are equated to the respondent's income and education. Thus our earlier finding that acceptance of equal treatment and support for government en-

forcement do not vary by racial or ethnic group is indeed restricted to these normative issues, since personal preferences *do* vary by the race of the group mentioned. The distinction here is reminiscent of one made [previously] between attitudes based on norms and attitudes based on personal preferences, though that is not meant to be an absolute distinction: insofar as attitudes based on norms are deeply internalized, they become personal, while at the same time even the most personal attitudes are almost always shaped by the larger culture (that is, by norms). . . .

This series of experiments indicates something of the complexity of the forces that are likely to operate in real situations when neighborhood integration becomes a concrete issue. The norm of equal treatment is one such force and we believe that it has some efficacy, but obviously it is not the only factor influencing the outcome. Perceptions of social class differences clearly play a role, so that the potential similarity of a new black (or Japanese American or any other) neighbor in these terms is likely to influence concrete behavior on the part of those already making up the neighborhood. Still an additional element derives from the level of personal preference, and it is important to recognize that some whites who do not seem to distinguish among different groups when considering government enforcement of the norm of equal treatment do make such distinctions when answering in terms of their own preferences.[7] Thus it is not, or not only, a matter of respondents' concealing preferences, but of their overtly making a distinction between their preferences and what they think they ought to do in a situation. Finally, we should add a further important complication that we deliberately eliminated in these experiments: the proportion of blacks likely to move into a previously white neighborhood makes a considerable difference to white respondents (Farley et al. 1978; Farley et al. 1994).

In real life, all the above elements come into play. Moreover, the balance among them is likely to be greatly affected by the positions taken by community leaders, as well as by external laws and government actions, whether wanted or not. Our survey data can help identify the elements that enter the picture, as they have done in these experiments, but they cannot lead to simple predictions about outcomes. If the experiments are repeated over time, however, it should be possible to measure changes in the balance of the forces.

Of course, neighborhood integration, or indeed an even broader perspective on racial integration, omits other major issues of race in America. Not even mentioned in the evidence just reviewed are the social and economic obstacles faced by a substantial proportion of the black population, obstacles that may have little to do directly with issues of integration. Most relevant here from our earlier chapters and from writings by other social scientists are findings about white explanations for black disadvantage. It is particularly important to recall that racial discrimination is not seen by whites as the major factor in racial inequalities, despite the evidence of continuing discrimination. Furthermore, there are signs that whites increasingly believe that discrimination has virtually disappeared in the United States, or has now been reversed and favors African Americans. This leads to even more emphasis on the attribution of all problems to failures of black motivation and effort. Only with regard to making greater investment in education does there seem to be much white support for further intervention to improve the standard of living and op-

portunities for blacks at the bottom of the socioeconomic ladder. Since the majority of blacks do believe that discrimination is still a major factor in American racial relations, both the causes and the solutions for racial problems in the United States are perceived from quite different perspectives by most members of the two racial groups.

Epilogue: History and Social Psychology

. . . The data and interpretations we have discussed are efforts to view from one vantage point the complex and changing meaning of race in America.

When President Truman's Committee on Civil Rights reported in 1947, Jim Crow laws were still alive and constituted in many places an unchallenged set of social rules. Black Americans were second-class citizens, mostly impoverished, poorly educated, and widely disdained by the white majority. The prosperity and social dislocation brought about by World War II, the importance of the black labor force to the war effort, the growing influence of black urban voters within the Democratic coalition, the heightened impatience of black leaders (driven in part by their increasingly urban, educated, and politicized constituencies), and the need of the United States as the self-proclaimed leader of the Free World to rid itself of racial bigotry, were some of the factors that placed a challenge to Jim Crow high on the national agenda. Other evidence suggests that this was also part of a larger ideological transformation that affected attitudes toward other minorities as well (for example, toward Jews, and eventually toward women and other disadvantaged groups).

Many of those who tried to understand America's glaring racial discrimination in the postwar era emphasized prejudice as the core of the problem. Prejudice, in turn, was regarded primarily as the product of ignorance. From this standpoint, prejudice could be attacked by teaching tolerance and by facilitating contact between blacks and whites in ways not structured by Jim Crow. The emotional roots of white contempt for blacks depended upon the regular symbolic humbling of blacks through petty exclusions, separate and starkly unequal facilities, a demand for traditional deference, and even lynchings in parts of the country. If the government could intervene in these practices, both the symbolic and the concrete social relations required by Jim Crow would be weakened. Contact on new terms would gradually reduce the level of prejudice and set us on the path toward becoming a color-blind society.

In many ways, this analysis of the American racial dilemma bore fruit in the 1940s, 1950s, and early 1960s. The slow, steady decline of norms supporting prejudice is consistent with, for example, the strong educational differentials in response to racial principle items, the liberalizing impact of the cohort-replacement process, the positive changes in the attitudes of individuals, the nearly complete rejection of biological arguments for white racial superiority, and an increasing recognition of the importance of black-white relations to U.S. world leadership. It is understandable that one of the most forceful governmental statements opposing segregation came from nine white male Supreme Court justices in 1954—individuals likely to be sensitive to changes in both social norms and national needs insofar as they can be construed as relevant to law.

These shifts in public opinion seemed to support Myrdal's view that, at core, Americans maintained a value for equality (surely equality before the law). This value would break through more plainly as soon as the intellectual and emotional underpinnings of prejudice began to dissipate. Government played its role through court decisions (like the *Brown* ruling) and executive actions (like Truman's order to desegregate the armed forces). Prejudice seemed an enemy that could be overcome. Categorical inequalities overtly premised upon notions of innate inferiority fell as the government intervened, backed by public attitudes that not only increasingly rejected such views but were moving toward full endorsement of the principle of racial equality. This process was fueled by insistent and often integrated civil rights demonstrations, which not only focused national attention upon black grievances but served an educational purpose and pressed the government to act more urgently in racial matters.

There was a growing consensus to all of this, and in the late 1960s the government began to move beyond the paradigm of reducing prejudice through ending discrimination—though this goal had by no means been achieved—to the often implicit paradigm of increasing the economic and political standing of blacks; that is, to treating the race problem as a matter of social inequality as well as of prejudice. But during these same years, the civil rights movement was becoming not only more visible but also more variegated. In many of its important branches, it was no longer itself integrated. The thrust of the demand for change was decreasingly toward integration and increasingly toward redistribution. The sudden outburst and then decline of the riots and the Black Power Movement; the assassination of Martin Luther King, which silenced the most widely listened to voice for nonviolent racial change; and Richard Nixon's victory over Hubert Humphrey, the national white political figure most closely associated with civil rights legislation, were both symbols and partial causes of a halt, or at least a pause, in government action in favor of racial equality. The later election of more conservative presidents and legislatures placed further brakes on change.

Moreover, the issues shifted from removing an absolute color bar to eliminating the pervasive inequalities that the bar had furthered. There were no longer struggles over allowing *one* or *two* black students to enroll at a public university; instead, there were struggles over city-wide desegregation plans. Our data indicate that survey researchers were attentive, though not always quickly so, to these changing issues and social contexts. Questions on the implementation of racial principles were asked beginning around 1964. The results showed that enthusiasm for large-scale policy change was less strong than the support of broad principles of equal treatment. Still later, questions concerning the causes of black disadvantage and questions about strong forms of affirmative action issues were added, in both cases producing evidence that a large part of the white population was reluctant to go beyond supporting more general principles of equal treatment, and indeed was coming to think that those principles were already in effect throughout much of the society.

The changes of the past half century are seldom of transparent meaning for students of racial attitudes. Nonetheless, our examination of the attitudinal record—this venture in historical social psychology—points to some important considerations for those grappling with racial inequality today. To the extent that public attitudes are important, it is possible to bring societal pressure, indeed public shame, on any white American who clearly discriminates against blacks, provided that the discrimination can be brought to light, as in videotapes of police beatings, audiotapes of corporate obstruction of equal opportunity laws, or public remarks that impugn African Americans. The application of the term "racist" to a person or an organization is itself a severe sanction in most

parts of the country. Such pressures will not always be successful, but they often are and they are not a trivial force. Moreover, there is willingness to go further and to elect black leaders, provided they offer assurance that their concern clearly includes whites equally with blacks.[8]

But beyond the enforcement of norms of equal treatment, there seems to be little public support for any but remedial forms of special training to help disadvantaged African Americans, or perhaps for broader programs that can be described in ways that do not emphasize race. It is not likely that affirmative action plans that call for clear forms of preferential treatment of blacks will survive for long outside a few insulated places (for example, academic departments in liberal universities), except where clear and recent discrimination has been documented. Exactly how the black underclass can escape from its present cycle of poverty, crime, and hopelessness is unclear, and this in turn adds to the alienation of the black middle class from white society.[9] There is no real sign that the larger white public is prepared to see norms of equal treatment reconceptualized to support substantial steps toward drastically reducing economic and social inequality in this country. It would be worth trying to present questions to the white population that succinctly point to the basic problem of disappearing employment opportunities for lower-class blacks in central cities: perhaps then there would be greater support for government efforts to create substitute training and jobs.

A final word about our own research. In terms of the data on which this book is based, we must recognize that not only do our attitude questions measure changes over time, but the changes themselves affect our surveys. We pointed out earlier that a question first asked in 1964 about federal intervention in the area of employment may have shifted somewhat in meaning over the years. It asked: "Should the government in Washington see to it that black people get fair treatment in jobs, or is this not the federal government's business?" When the question was first posed in the mid-1960s, "fair treatment" could be assumed to refer to "equal treatment," but by the 1990s "fair treatment" could be taken by some proportion of the population—both black and white—to mean affirmative action in the sense of compensatory preferential treatment. In this case, and in some others as well, surveys reflect change not only in terms of the movement of percentages across tables and graphs, but by the new meanings that questions take on for those who are asked to answer them.[10]

NOTES

1. Rigid categorization can be enforced even where the physical signs of race lead in an opposite direction, as in the occasional case of someone who seems white in appearance but either elects or is forced to be viewed as black. One striking account can be found in an autobiography by Williams (1995) with the subtitle *The True Story of a White Boy Who Discovered He Was Black.* The clear contrast of racial identity with the "symbolic ethnicity" of many white Americans is discussed by Waters (1990).

2. The normative change was clearly a broad one that extended to other minorities besides blacks (see, for example, Stember et al. 1966).

3. Ironically, one recent commentator considers the success of some blacks and the portrayal of friendly black-white relations in the media to be dangerous, since they allow the white population to ignore the tremendous obstacles faced by the larger black lower class (DeMott 1995).

4. The experiments were first reported in Schuman and Bobo (1988), which includes some additional analysis.

5. All Jewish respondents were omitted from this comparison and from the one described below.

6. Despite these results, which are important in themselves, we suspect that our hypothesis

about the difference between application of the norm of equal treatment to a single person and application to a large group is likely to prove correct, and that our original way of operationalizing that distinction was not adequate, perhaps because the Open Housing question itself is already written with something of a focus on individuals.

7. We do not actually ask the same white individuals both types of questions, but since the two samples were drawn to represent the same population of individuals, one can reasonably draw this inference.

8. Of course, there are individuals and groups, mostly well outside the American mainstream, that continue to be openly racist in words and actions. But despite the individual tragedies that such virulent racism can produce—as in the random assassination of a black couple in 1995 by two army paratroopers—one should not give extreme deviance a larger social significance than it deserves. One can see this even more clearly in the case of another group: Jews represent a minority that has been highly successful and highly assimilated in almost all respects, yet one that is still the target of hostility and occasional violence from scattered extremist groups. Sometimes such hostility occurs because of progress toward incorporating a racial or ethnic minority into the larger society, which becomes a threat to those who feel themselves estranged from what they see the society becoming (Green et al. 1996).

9. A short but sensitive description of this complex of problems is found in Anderson's (1990) ethnographic account of one such area in Philadelphia, and of course there are other large-scale research efforts such as Thomas Wilson (1996).

10. We also increasingly feel that questions asked on racial issues have lacked useful variation in format. More scales like that for the NORC Residential Choice question would be of value, and more attention should be paid experimentally to what happens when middle alternative and no opinion options are offered. Scattered throughout this book are hints that a good deal can be learned about the *strength* of racial attitudes by such variations, as distinct from simple dichotomous questions and also from the multi-item indexes sometimes made up of such questions.

REFERENCES

ADORNO, T. W., E. FRENKEL-BRUNSWIK, D. J. LEVINSON, and R. N. SANFORD. 1950. *The Authoritarian Personality.* New York: Harper.

ANDERSON, ELIJAH. 1990. *Streetwise: Race, Class, and Change in an Urban Community.* Chicago: University of Chicago Press.

DEMOTT, BENJAMIN. 1995. *The Trouble with Friendship: Why Americans Can't Think Straight About Race.* New York: Atlantic Monthly Press.

FARLEY, REYNOLDS, HOWARD SCHUMAN, SUZANNE BIANCHI, DIANE COLASANTO, and SHIRLEY HATCHETT. 1978. "Chocolate City, Vanilla Suburbs: Will the Trend Toward Racially Separate Communities Continue?" *Social Science Research* 7:319–44.

FARLEY, REYNOLDS, CHARLOTTE STEEH, MARIA KRYSAN, TARA JACKSON, and KEITH REEVES. 1994. "Stereotypes and Segregation: Neighborhoods in the Detroit Area." *American Journal of Sociology* 100:750–80.

GREEN, DONALD P., ROBERT P. ABELSON, MARGARET GARNER, JOHN GLASER, ANDREW RICH, and AMY RICHMOND. 1996. "Cultural Encroachment and Hate Crime: An Ecological Analysis of Cross-burnings in North Carolina." Paper presented at the Annual Meeting of the American Criminal Justice Society, Boston.

HACKER, ANDREW. 1995. *Two Nations: Black and White, Separate, Hostile, Unequal.* New York: Ballantine Books.

HARRISON, RODERICK J., and CLAUDETTE E. BENNETT. 1995. "Racial and Ethnic Diversity." In *State of the Union: America in the 1990s,* Vol. 2: *Social Trends,* edited by Reynolds Farley. New York: Russell Sage Foundation.

LEVINE, ROBERT E. 1971. "The Silent Majority: Neither Simple nor Simple Minded." *Public Opinion Quarterly* 33:571–77.

MYRDAL, GUNNAR. 1994. *An American Dilemma: The Negro Problem and Modern Democracy.* 2 vols. New York: Harper & Brothers.

ROTHBART, MYRON. 1976. "Achieving Racial Equality: An Analysis of Resistance to Social Reform." In *Towards the Elimination of Racism.* New York: Pergamon Press.

SCHUMAN, HOWARD, and LAWRENCE BOBO. 1988. "Survey-Based Experiments on White Racial Attitudes Toward Residential Integration." *American Journal of Sociology* 94:273–99.

SCHUMAN, HOWARD, and MICHAEL P. JOHNSON. 1976. "Attitudes and Behavior." *Annual Review of Sociology* 6:161–207.

SMITH, A. WADE. 1981. "Racial Tolerance as a Function of Group Position." *American Sociological Review* 46:558–73.

STEMBER, CHARLES HERBERT, et al. 1996. *Jews in the Mind of America.* Boston: Beacon Press.

WATERS, MARY C. 1990. *Ethnic Options: Choosing Identities in America.* Berkeley: University of California Press.

WILLIAMS, GREGORY HOWARD. 1995. *Life in the Color Line: The True Story of a Boy Who Discovered That He Was Black.* New York: Dutton.

WILSON, THOMAS. 1996. "Cohort and Prejudice: Whites' Attitudes Toward Blacks, Hispanics, Jews, and Asians." *Public Opinion Quarterly* 60:253–74.

13

_____

THE POSSESSIVE INVESTMENT
IN WHITENESS: RACIALIZED
SOCIAL DEMOCRACY

George Lipsitz

Questions to Consider

What does George Lipsitz mean by a "possessive investment in whiteness"? How is it possible that being a member of a particular racial group could confer social and economic privileges (or disadvantages) that are both institutional and intergenerational? How many specific programs does Lipsitz identify as being party to institutional racism?

Shortly after World War II, a French reporter asked expatriate Richard Wright his opinion about the "Negro problem" in the United States. The author replied "There isn't any Negro problem; there is only a white problem."[1] By inverting the reporter's question, Wright called attention to its hidden assumptions—that racial polarization comes from the existence of blacks rather than from the behavior of whites, that black people are a "problem" for whites rather than fellow citizens entitled to justice, and that unless otherwise specified "American" means whites.[2] But Wright's formulation also placed political mobilization by African Americans in context, attributing it to the systemic practices of aversion, exploitation, denigration, and discrimination practiced by people who think of themselves as white."

Whiteness is everywhere in American culture, but it is very hard to see. As Richard Dyer argues, "white power secures its dominance by seeming not to be anything in particular."[3] As the unmarked category against which difference is constructed, whiteness never has to speak its name, never has to acknowledge its role as an organizing principle in social and cultural relations.[4]

To identify, analyze, and oppose the destructive consequences of whiteness, we need what Walter Benjamin called "presence of mind." Benjamin wrote that people visit fortune-tellers not so much out of a desire to know the future but rather out of a fear of not noticing some important aspect of the present. "Presence of mind," he argued, "is

George Lipsitz, "The Possessive Investment in Whiteness: Racialized Social Democracy and the 'White' Problem in American Studies." *American Quarterly* 47:3 (1995), 369–387. Copyright © The American Studies Association. Reprinted with permission of The John Hopkins University Press.

an abstract of the future, and precise awareness of the present moment more decisive than foreknowledge of the most distant events."[5] In our society at this time, precise awareness of the present moment requires an understanding of the existence and the destructive consequences of "white" identity.

In recent years, an important body of American studies scholarship has started to explore the role played by cultural practices in creating "whiteness" in the United States. More than the product of private prejudices, whiteness emerged as a relevant category in American life largely because of realities created by slavery and segregation, by immigration restriction and Indian policy, by conquest and colonialism. A fictive identity of "whiteness" appeared in law as an abstraction, and it became actualized in everyday life in many ways. American economic and political life gave different racial groups unequal access to citizenship and property, while cultural practices including Wild West shows, minstrel shows, racist images in advertising, and Hollywood films institutionalized racism by uniting ethnically diverse European-American audiences into an imagined community—one called into being through inscribed appeals to the solidarity of white supremacy.[6] Although cross-ethnic identification and pan-ethnic antiracism in culture, politics, and economics have often interrupted and resisted racialized white supremacist notions of American identity, from colonial days to the present, successful political coalitions serving dominant interests have often relied on exclusionary concepts of whiteness to fuse unity among otherwise antagonistic individuals and groups.[7]

In these accounts by American studies scholars, cultural practices have often played crucial roles in prefiguring, presenting, and preserving political coalitions based on identification with the fiction of "whiteness." Andrew Jackson's coalition of the "common man," Woodrow Wilson's "New Freedom," and Franklin D. Roosevelt's New Deal all echoed in politics the alliances announced on stage and screen by the nineteenth-century minstrel show, by D. W. Griffith's cinema, and by Al Jolson's ethnic and racial imagery.[8] This impressive body of scholarship helps us understand how people who left Europe as Calabrians or Bohemians became something called "whites" when they got to America and how that designation made all the difference in the world.

Yet, while cultural expressions have played an important role in the construction of white supremacist political alliances, the reverse is also true (i.e., political activity has also played a constitutive role in racializing U.S. culture). Race is a cultural construct, but one with sinister structural causes and consequences. Conscious and deliberate actions have institutionalized group identity in the United States, not just through the dissemination of cultural stories but also through systematic efforts from colonial times to the present to create a possessive investment in whiteness for European Americans. Studies of culture too far removed from studies of social structure leave us with inadequate explanations for understanding racism and inadequate remedies for combatting it.

From the start, European settlers in North America established structures encouraging possessive investment in whiteness. The colonial and early-national legal systems authorized attacks on Native Americans and encouraged the appropriation of their lands. They legitimated racialized chattel slavery, restricted naturalized citizenship to "white" immigrants, and provided pretexts for exploiting labor, seizing property, and denying the franchise to Asian Americans, Mexican Americans, Native Americans, and African Americans. Slavery and "Jim Crow" segregation institutionalized possessive identification with whiteness visibly and openly, but an elaborate interaction of largely *covert* public and private decisions during and after the days of slavery and segregation also produced a powerful legacy with enduring effects on the racialization of experience, opportunities, and rewards in the United States. Possessive investment in whiteness pervades public policy in the United States past and present—not just long ago during slavery and segregation but in the recent past and present as well—through the covert but no less systematic racism inscribed within U.S. social democracy.

Even though there has always been racism in American history, it has not always been the same racism. Political and cultural struggles over power shape the contours and dimensions of racism in any era. Mass mobilizations against racism during the Civil War and civil rights eras meaningfully curtailed the reach and scope of white supremacy, but in each case reactionary forces then engineered a renewal of racism, albeit in new forms, during successive decades. Racism changes over time, taking on different forms and serving different social purposes in different eras.

Contemporary racism is not just a residual consequence of slavery and *de jure* segregation but rather something that has been created anew in our own time by many factors including the putatively race-neutral liberal social democratic reforms of the past five decades. Despite hard-fought battles for change that secured important concessions during the 1960s in the form of civil rights legislation, the racialized nature of social democratic policies in the United States since the Great Depression has, in my judgment, actually increased the possessive investment in whiteness among European Americans over the past half-century.

The possessive investment in whiteness is not a simple matter of black and white; all racialized minority groups have suffered from it, albeit to different degrees and in different ways. Most of my argument here addresses relations between European Americans and African Americans because they contain many of the most vivid oppositions and contrasts, but the possessive investment in whiteness always emerges from a fused sensibility drawing on many sources at once—on antiblack racism to be sure, but also on the legacies of racialization left by federal, state, and local policies toward Native Americans, Asian Americans, Mexican Americans, and other groups designated by whites as "racially other."

During the New Deal, both the Wagner Act and the Social Security Act excluded farm workers and domestics from coverage, effectively denying those disproportionately minority sectors of the work force protections and benefits routinely channeled to whites. The Federal Housing Act of 1934 brought home ownership within reach of millions of citizens by placing the credit of the federal government behind private lending to home buyers, but overtly racist categories in the Federal Housing Administration's (FHA's) "confidential" city surveys and appraisers' manuals channeled almost all of the loan money toward whites and away from communities of color.[9] In the post–World War II era, trade unions negotiated contract provisions giving private medical insurance, pensions, and job security largely to the mostly white workers in unionized mass-production industries rather than fighting for full employment, universal medical care, and old age pensions for all or for an end to discriminatory hiring and promotion practices by employers.[10]

Each of these policies widened the gap between the resources available to whites and those available to aggrieved racial communities, but the most damaging long-term effects may well have come from the impact of the racial discrimination codified by the policies of the FHA. By channeling loans away from older inner-city neighborhoods and toward white home buyers moving into segregated suburbs, the FHA and private lenders after World War II aided and abetted the growth and development of increased segregation in U.S. residential neighborhoods. For example, FHA appraisers denied federally supported loans to prospective home buyers in the racially mixed Boyle Heights neighborhood of Los Angeles because it was a "'melting pot' area literally honeycombed with diverse and subversive racial elements."[11] Similarly, mostly white St. Louis County secured five times as many FHA mortgages as the more racially mixed city of St. Louis between 1943 and 1960. Home buyers in the county received six times as much loan money and enjoyed per capita mortgage spending 6.3 times greater than those in the city.[12]

In concert with FHA support for segregation in the suburbs, federal and state tax monies routinely provided water supplies and sewage facilities for racially exclusive suburban communities in the 1940s and 1950s. By the 1960s, these areas often incorporated themselves as independent municipalities in order to gain greater access to federal funds allocated for "urban aid."[13] At the same time that FHA loans and federal highway building projects subsidized the growth of segregated suburbs, urban renewal programs in cities throughout the country devastated minority neighborhoods.

During the 1950s and 1960s, federally assisted urban renewal projects destroyed 20 percent of the central city housing units occupied by blacks, as opposed to only 10 percent of those inhabited by whites.[14] Even after most major urban renewal programs had been completed in the 1970s, black central city residents continued to lose housing units at a rate equal to 80 percent of what had been lost in the 1960s. Yet white displacement declined back to the relatively low levels of the 1950s.[15] In addition, the refusal first to pass, then to enforce, fair housing laws, has enabled realtors, buyers, and sellers to profit from racist collusion against minorities without fear of legal retribution.

During the decades following World War II, urban renewal helped construct a new "white" identity in the suburbs by helping destroy ethnically specific European-American urban inner-city neighborhoods. Wrecking balls and bulldozers eliminated some of these sites, while others became transformed by an influx of minority residents desperately competing for a declining number of affordable housing units. As increasing numbers of racial minorities moved into cities, increasing numbers of European-American ethnics moved out. Consequently, ethnic differences among whites became a less important dividing line in American culture, while race became more important. The suburbs helped turn European Americans into "whites" who could live near each other and intermarry with relatively little difficulty. But this "white" unity rested on residential segregation and on shared access to housing and life chances largely unavailable to communities of color.[16]

During the 1950s and 1960s, local "pro-growth" coalitions led by liberal mayors often justified urban renewal as a program designed to build more housing for poor people, but it actually destroyed more housing than it created. Ninety percent of the low-income units removed for urban renewal were never replaced. Commercial, industrial, and municipal projects occupied more than 80 percent of the land cleared for these projects, with less than 20 percent allocated for replacement housing. In addition, the loss of taxable properties and tax abatements granted to new enterprises in urban renewal zones often meant serious tax increases for poor, working-class, and middle-class home owners and renters.[17] Although the percentage of black suburban dwellers also increased during this period, no significant desegregation of the suburbs took place. From 1960 to 1977, four million whites moved out of central cities, while the number of whites living in suburbs increased by twenty-two million.[18] During the same years, the inner-city black population grew by six million, but the number of blacks living in suburbs increased by only 500,000 people.[19] By 1993, 86 percent of suburban whites still lived in places with a black population below 1 percent. At the same time, cities with large numbers of minority residents found themselves cut off from loans by the FHA; in 1966, because of their growing black and Puerto Rican populations, Camden and Paterson, New Jersey, received no FHA-sponsored mortgages between them.[20]

Federally funded highways designed to connect suburban commuters with downtown places of employment destroyed already scarce housing in minority communities and often disrupted neighborhood life as well. Construction of the Harbor Freeway in Los Angeles, the Gulf Freeway in Houston, and the Mark Twain Freeway in St. Louis displaced thousands of residents and bisected previously connected neighborhoods, shopping districts, and political precincts. The process of urban renewal and highway construction set in motion a vicious cycle: population loss led to decreased political power, which made minority neighborhoods more likely to be victimized by further urban renewal and freeway construction, not to mention more susceptible to the placement of prisons, waste dumps, and other projects that further depopulated these areas.

In Houston, Texas—where blacks make up slightly more than one-quarter of the local population—more than 75 percent of municipal garbage incinerators and 100 percent of the city-owned garbage dumps are located in black neighborhoods.[21] A 1992 study by staff writers for the *National Law Journal* examined the Environmental Protection Agency's response to 1,177 toxic waste cases and found that polluters of sites near the greatest white population received penalties 500 percent higher than penalties imposed on polluters in minority areas—an average of $335,566 for white areas contrasted with $55,318 for minority areas. Income did not account for these differences—penalties for low-income areas on average actually exceeded those for areas with the highest median incomes by about 3 percent. The penalties for violating all federal environmental laws about air, water, and waste pollution in minority communities were 46 percent lower than in white communities. In addition, Superfund remedies left minority communities with longer waiting times for being placed on the national priority list, cleanups that begin from 12 to 42 percent later than at white sites, and a 7 percent greater likelihood of "containment" (walling off a hazardous site) than cleanup, while white sites experienced treatment and cleanup 22 percent more often than containment.[22]

Urban renewal failed as a program for providing new housing for the poor, but it played an important role in transforming the U.S. urban economy away from factory production and toward producer services. Urban renewal projects subsidized the development of downtown office centers on land previously used for residences, and they frequently created buffer zones of empty blocks dividing poor neighborhoods from new shopping centers designed for affluent commuters. In order to help cities compete for corporate investment by making them appealing to high-level executives, federal urban aid favored construction of luxury housing units and cultural centers, such as symphony halls and art museums, over affordable housing for workers. Tax abatements granted to these producer-services centers further aggravated the fiscal crisis that cities faced, leading to tax increases on existing industries, businesses, and residences.

Workers from aggrieved racial minorities bore the brunt of this transformation. Because the 1964 Civil Rights Act came so late, minority workers who received jobs because of it found themselves more vulnerable to seniority-based layoffs when businesses automated or transferred operations overseas. Although the act initially made real progress in reducing employment discrimination, lessened the gaps between rich and poor and black and white, and helped bring minority poverty to its lowest level in history in 1973, that year's recession initiated a reversal of minority progress and a reassertion of white privilege.[23] In 1977, the U.S. Civil Rights Commission reported on the disproportionate impact of layoffs on minority workers. In cases where minority workers made up only 10 to 12 percent of the work force in their area, they accounted for from 60 to 70 percent of those laid off in 1974. The principle of seniority, a social democratic triumph, in this case worked to guarantee that minority workers would suffer most from technological changes because the legacy of past discrimination by their employers left them with less seniority than white workers.[24]

When housing prices doubled during the 1970s, white homeowners who had been able to take advantage of discriminatory FHA financing policies received increased equity in their homes, while those excluded from the housing market by earlier policies found themselves facing higher costs of entry into the market in addition to the traditional obstacles presented by the discriminatory practices of sellers, realtors, and lenders. The contrast between European Americans and African Americans is instructive in this regard. Because whites have access to broader housing choices than blacks, whites pay 15 percent less than blacks for similar housing in the same neighborhood. White neighborhoods typically experience housing costs 25 percent less expensive than would be the case if the residents were black.[25]

A recent Federal Reserve Bank of Boston study showed that minority applicants had a 60 percent greater chance of being denied home loans than white applicants with the same credit-worthiness. Boston bankers made 2.9 times as many mortgage loans per one thousand housing units in neighborhoods inhabited by low-income whites than they did to neighborhoods populated by low-income blacks.[26] In addition, loan officers were far more likely to overlook flaws in the credit records of white applicants or to arrange creative financing for them than they were with black applicants.[27]

A Los Angeles study found that loan officers more frequently used dividend income and underlying assets criteria for judging black applicants than they did for whites.[28] In Houston, the NCNB Bank of Texas disqualified 13 percent of middle-income white loan applicants but disqualified 36 percent of middle-income black applicants.[29] Atlanta's home loan institutions gave five times as many home loans to whites as to blacks in the late 1980s. An analysis of sixteen Atlanta neighborhoods found that home buyers in white neighborhoods received conventional financing four times as often as those in black sections of the city.[30] Nationwide, financial institutions get more money in deposits from black neighborhoods than they invest in them in the form of home mortgage loans, making home lending a vehicle for the transfer of capital away from black savers and toward white investors.[31] In many locations, high-income blacks were denied loans more often than low-income whites.[32]

Federal home loan policies have placed the power of the federal government behind private discrimination. Urban renewal and highway construction programs have enhanced the possessive investment in whiteness directly through government initiatives. In addition, decisions about the location of federal jobs have also systematically supported the subsidy for whiteness. Federal civilian employment dropped by 41,419 in central cities between 1966 and 1973, but total federal employment in metropolitan areas grew by 26,558.[33] While one might naturally expect the location of government buildings that serve the public to follow population trends, the federal government's policies in locating offices and records centers in suburbs helped aggravate the flight of jobs to suburban locations less accessible to inner-city residents. Since racial discrimination in the private sector forces minority workers to seek government positions disproportionate to their numbers, these moves exact particular hardships on them. In addition, minorities who follow their jobs to the suburbs generally encounter increased commuter costs because housing discrimination makes it harder and more expensive for them to relocate than for whites.

The racialized aspects of fifty years of these social democratic policies became greatly exacerbated by the anti–social democratic policies of neoconservatives in the Reagan and Bush administrations during the 1980s and 1990s. They clearly contributed to the reinforcement of possessive investments in whiteness through their regressive policies in respect to federal aid to education and their refusal to challenge segregated education, housing, and hiring, as well as their cynical cultivation of an antiblack, counter-subversive consensus through attacks on affirmative action and voting rights legislation. In the U.S. economy, where 86 percent of available jobs do not appear in classified advertisements and where personal connections provide the most important factor in securing employ-

ment, attacks on affirmative action guarantee that whites will be rewarded for their historical advantages in the labor market rather than for their individual abilities or efforts.[34]

Yet even seemingly race-neutral policies supported by both neoconservatives and social democrats in the 1980s and 1990s have also increased the absolute value of being white. In the 1980s, changes in federal tax laws decreased the value of wage income and increased the value of investment income—a move harmful to minorities who suffer from an even greater gap between their total wealth and that of whites than in the disparity between their income and white income. Failure to raise the minimum wage between 1981 and 1989 and the more than one-third decline in value of Aid for Families with Dependent Children payments hurt all poor people, but they exacted special costs on nonwhites facing even more constricted markets for employment, housing, and education than poor whites.[35]

Similarly, the "tax reforms" of the 1980s made the effective rate of taxation higher on investment in actual goods and services than it was on profits from speculative enterprises. This encouraged the flight of capital away from industrial production with its many employment opportunities and toward investments that can be turned over quickly to allow the greatest possible tax write-offs. Consequently, government policies actually discouraged investments that might produce high-paying jobs and encouraged investors to strip companies of their assets in order to make rapid short-term profits. These policies hurt almost all workers, but they exacted particularly high costs from minority workers who, because of employment discrimination in the retail and small business sectors, were overrepresented in blue-collar industrial jobs.

On the other hand, while neoconservative tax policies created incentives for employers to move their enterprises elsewhere, they created disincentives for home owners to move. Measures such as California's Proposition 13 granting tax relief to property owners badly misallocate housing resources because they make it financially unwise for the elderly to move out of large houses, further reducing the supply of housing available to young families. While one can well understand the necessity for protecting senior citizens on fixed incomes from tax increases that would make them lose their homes, the rewards and punishments provided by Proposition 13 are so extreme that they prevent the kinds of generational succession that have routinely opened up housing to young families in the past. This reduction works particular hardships on those who also face discrimination by sellers, realtors, and lending institutions.

Subsidies to the private sector by government agencies also tend to reward the results of past discrimination. Throughout the country, tax increment redevelopment programs give tax-free, low-interest loans to developers whose projects use public services, often without having to pay taxes to local school boards or county governments. Industrial development bonds resulted in a $7.4 billion tax loss in 1983, a loss that ordinary tax payers had to make up through increased payroll taxes. Compared to white Americans, people of color, who are more likely to be poor or working class, suffer disproportionately from these changes as tax payers, as workers, and as tenants. A study by the Citizens for Tax Justice found that wealthy Californians spend less than eleven cents in taxes for every dollar earned, while poor residents of the state paid fourteen cents out of every dollar in taxes. As groups overrepresented among the poor, minorities have been forced to shoulder this burden in order to subsidize the tax breaks given to the wealthy.[36] While holding property tax assessments for businesses and some home

owners to about half of their market value, California's Proposition 13 deprived cities and counties of $13 billion a year in taxes. Businesses alone avoided $3.3 billion to $8.6 billion in taxes per year under this statute.[37]

Because they are ignorant of even the recent history of the possessive investment in whiteness—generated by slavery and segregation but augmented by social democratic reform—Americans produce largely cultural explanations for structural social problems. The increased possessive investment in whiteness generated by dis-investment in America's cities, factories, and schools since the 1970s disguises the general problems posed to our society by de-industrialization, economic restructuring, and neoconservative attacks on the welfare state as *racial* problems. It fuels a discourse that demonizes people of color for being victimized by these changes, while hiding the privileges of whiteness by attributing them to family values, fatherhood, and foresight—rather than to favoritism.

The demonization of black families in public discourse since the 1970s is particularly instructive in this regard. During the 1970s, the share of low-income households headed by blacks increased by one-third, while black family income fell from 60 percent of white family income in 1971 to 58 percent in 1980. Even when adjusting for unemployment and for African-American disadvantages in life-cycle employment (more injuries, more frequently interrupted work histories, confinement to jobs most susceptible to layoffs), the wages of full-time year-round black workers fell from 77 percent of white workers' income to 73 percent by 1986. In 1986, white workers with high school diplomas earned three thousand dollars per year more than African Americans with the same education.[38] Even when they had the same family structure as white workers, blacks found themselves more likely to be poor.

Among black workers between the ages of twenty and twenty-four, 46 percent held blue-collar jobs in 1976, but that percentage fell to only 20 percent by 1984. Earnings by young black families had reached 60 percent of the amount secured by white families in 1973, but by 1986 they fell back to 46 percent. Younger African-American families experienced a 50 percent drop in real earnings between 1973 and 1986, with the decline in black male wages particularly steep.[39]

Many recent popular and scholarly studies have explained clearly the causes for black economic decline over the past two decades.[40] Deindustrialization has decimated the industrial infrastructure that formerly provided high-wage jobs and chances for upward mobility to black workers. Neoconservative attacks on government spending for public housing, health, education, and transportation have deprived African Americans of needed services and opportunities for jobs in the public sector. A massive retreat from responsibility to enforce antidiscrimination laws at the highest levels of government has sanctioned pervasive overt and covert racial discrimination by bankers, realtors, and employers.

Yet public opinion polls conducted among white Americans display little recognition of these devastating changes. Seventy percent of whites in one poll said that African Americans "have the same opportunities to live a middle-class life as whites."[41] Nearly three-fourths of white respondents to a 1989 poll believed that opportunities for blacks had improved during the Reagan presidency.[42]

Optimism about the opportunities available to African Americans does not necessarily demonstrate ignorance of the dire conditions facing black communities, but, if not, it then indicates that many whites believe that blacks suffer deservedly, that they do not take advantage of the opportunities offered them. In the opinion polls, favorable assessments of black chances for success often accompanied extremely negative judgments about the abilities, work habits, and character of black people. A National Opinion Research Report in 1990 disclosed that more than 50 percent of American whites viewed blacks as innately lazy and less intelligent and less patriotic than whites.[43] Furthermore, more than 60 percent of whites questioned in that survey said that they believed that blacks suffer from poor housing and employment opportunities because of their own lack of willpower. Some 56.3 percent of whites said that blacks preferred welfare to employment, while 44.6 percent contended that blacks tended toward laziness.[44] Even more important, research by Mary and Thomas Byrne Edsall indicates that many whites structure nearly all of their decisions about housing, education, and politics in response to their aversions to black people.[45]

The present political culture in this country gives broad sanction for viewing white supremacy and antiblack racism as forces from the past, as demons finally put to rest by the passage of the 1964 Civil Rights Act and the 1965 Voting Rights Act. [46] Jurists, journalists, and politicians have generally been more vocal in their opposition to "quotas" and to "reverse discrimination" mandating race-specific remedies for discrimination than to the thousands of well-documented incidents every year of routine, systematic, and unyielding discrimination against blacks.

It is my contention that the stark contrast between black experiences and white opinions during the past two decades cannot be attributed solely to ignorance or intolerance on the part of individuals but stems instead from the overdetermined inadequacy of the language of liberal individualism to describe collective experience.[47] As long as we define social life as the sum total of conscious and deliberate individual activities, then only *individual* manifestations of personal prejudice and hostility will be seen as racist. Systemic, collective, and coordinated behavior disappears from sight. Collective exercises of group power relentlessly channeling rewards, resources, and opportunities from one group to another will not appear to be "racist" from this perspective because they rarely announce their intention to discriminate against individuals. But they work to construct racial indentities by giving people of different races vastly different life chances.

The gap between white perceptions and minority experiences can have explosive consequences. Little more than a year after the 1992 Los Angeles rebellion, a sixteen-year-old high school junior shared her opinions with a reporter from the *Los Angeles Times*. "I don't think white people owe anything to black people," she explained. "We didn't sell them into slavery, it was our ancestors. What they did was wrong, but we've done our best to make up for it."[48] A seventeen-year-old senior echoed those comments, telling the reporter:

> I feel we spend more time in my history class talking about what whites owe blacks than just about anything else when the issue of slavery comes up. I often received dirty looks. This seems strange given that I wasn't even alive then. And the few members of my family from that time didn't have the luxury of owning much, let alone slaves. So why, I ask you, am I constantly made to feel guilty?[49]

More ominously, after pleading guilty to bombing two homes and one car, to vandalizing a synagogue, and attempting to start a race war by murdering Rodney King and bombing Los Angeles's First African Methodist Episcopal Church, twenty-year-old Christopher David Fisher explained that "sometimes whites were picked on because of the color of their skin. . . . Maybe we're blamed for slavery."[50] Fisher's actions were certainly extreme, but his justification of them drew knowingly and precisely on a broadly shared narrative about the victimization of innocent whites by irrational and ungrateful minorities.

The comments and questions raised about the legacy of slavery by these young whites illumine broader currents in our culture that have enormous implications for understanding the enduring significance of race in our country. These young people associate black grievances solely with slavery, and they express irritation at what they perceive as efforts to make them feel guilty or unduly privileged in the present because of things that happened in the distant past. Because their own ancestors may not have been slave owners or because "we've done our best to make up for it," they feel that it is unreasonable for anyone to view them as people who owe "anything" to blacks. On the contrary, Fisher felt that his discomfort with being "picked on" and "blamed" for slavery gave him good reason to bomb homes, deface synagogues, and plot to kill black people.

Unfortunately for our society, these young whites accurately reflect the logic of the language of liberal individualism and its ideological predispositions in discussions of race. They seem to have no knowledge of the disciplined, systemic, and collective *group* activity that has structured white identities in American history. They are not alone in their ignorance; in a 1979 law journal article, future Supreme Court Justice Antonin Scalia argued that affirmative action "is based upon concepts of racial indebtedness and racial entitlement rather than individual worth and individual need" and is thus "racist."[51]

Yet liberal individualism is not completely color blind on this issue. As Cheryl I. Harris demonstrates, the legacy of liberal individualism has not prevented the Supreme Court from recognizing and protecting the group interests of *whites* in the Bakke, Croson, and Wygant cases.[52] In each case, the Court nullified affirmative action programs because they judged efforts to help blacks as harmful to whites: to white expectations of entitlement, expectations based on the possessive investment in whiteness they held as members of a group. In the Bakke case, for instance, neither Bakke nor the court contested the legitimacy of medical school admissions standards that reserved five seats in each class for children of wealthy donors to the university or that penalized Bakke for being older than most of the other applicants. The group rights of not-wealthy people or of people older than their classmates did not compel the Court or Bakke to make any claim of harm. But they did challenge and reject a policy designed to offset the effects of past and present discrimination when they could construe the medical school admission policies as detrimental to the interests of whites as a group—and as a consequence they applied the "strict scrutiny" standard to protect whites while denying that protection to people of color. In this case, as in so many others, the language of liberal individualism serves as a cover for coordinated collective group interests.

Group interests are not monolithic, and aggregate figures can obscure serious differences within racial groups. All whites do not benefit from the possessive investment in whiteness in precisely the same way; the experiences of members of minority groups are not interchangeable. But the possessive investment in whiteness always affects individual and group life chances and opportunities. Even in cases where minority groups secure political and economic power through collective mobilization, the terms and conditions of their collectivity and the logic of group solidarity are always influenced and intensified by the absolute value

of whiteness in American politics, economics, and culture.[53]

In the 1960s, members of the Black Panther Party used to say that "if you're not part of the solution, you're part of the problem." But those of us who are "white" can only become part of the solution if we recognize the degree to which we are already part of the problem—not because of our race, but because of our possessive investment in it. Neither conservative "free market" policies nor liberal social democratic reforms can solve the "white problem" in America because both of them reinforce the possessive investment in whiteness. But an explicitly antiracist pan-ethnic movement that acknowledges the existence and power of whiteness might make some important changes. Pan-ethnic, antiracist coalitions have a long history in the United States—in the political activism of John Brown, Sojourner Truth, and the Magon brothers, among others—but we also have a rich cultural tradition of pan-ethnic antiracism connected to civil rights activism of the kind detailed so brilliantly in rhythm and blues musician Johnny Otis's recent book, *Upside Your Head! Rhythm and Blues on Central Avenue*.[54] These efforts by whites to fight racism, not out of sympathy for someone else but out of a sense of self-respect and simple justice, have never completely disappeared; they remain available as models for the present.[55]

Walter Benjamin's praise for "presence of mind" came from his understanding of how difficult it may be to see the present. But more important, he called for presence of mind as the means for implementing what he called "the only true telepathic miracle"—turning the forbidding future into the fulfilled present.[56] Failure to acknowledge our society's possessive investment in whiteness prevents us from facing the present openly and honestly. It hides from us the devastating costs of disinvestment in

America's infrastructure over the past two decades and keeps us from facing our responsibilities to reinvest in human capital by channeling resources toward education, health, and housing—and away from subsidies for speculation and luxury. After two decades of disinvestment, the only further disinvestment we need is to disinvest in the ruinous pathology of whiteness that has always undermined our own best instincts and interests. In a society suffering so badly from an absence of mutuality, an absence of responsibility, and an absence of simple justice, presence of mind might be just what we need.

NOTES

1. Raphael Tardon, "Richard Wright Tells Us: The White Problem in the United States," *Action,* 24 Oct. 1946. Reprinted in Kenneth Kinnamon and Michel Fabre, *Conversations with Richard Wright* (Jackson, Miss., 1993), 99. Malcolm X and others used this same formulation in the 1960s, but I believe that it originated with Wright, or at least that is the earliest citation I have found so far.
2. This is also Toni Morrison's point in *Playing in the Dark: Whiteness in the Literary Imagination* (Cambridge, Mass., 1992).
3. Richard Dyer, "White," *Screen* 29 (fall 1988): 44.
4. I thank Michael Schudson for pointing out to me that since the passage of civil rights legislation in the 1960s whiteness dares not speak its name, cannot speak in its own behalf, but rather advances through a color-blind language radically at odds with the distinctly racialized distribution of resources and life chances in American society.
5. Walter Benjamin, "Madame Ariane: Second Courtyard on the Left," from *One-Way Street* (London, 1969), 98–99.
6. Richard Slotkin, *Gunfighter Nation: The Myth of the Frontier in Twentieth Century America* (New York, 1992); Eric Lott, *Love and Theft* (New York, 1993); David Roediger, *Wages of Whiteness* (New York, 1992); Michael Rogin, "Blackface White Noise: The Jewish Jazz Singer Finds His Voice," *Critical Inquiry* 18 (spring 1992).
7. Robin Kelley, *Hammer and Hoe* (Chapel Hill, N.C., 1990); Lizabeth Cohen, *Making A New*

Deal (Cambridge, 1991); George Sanchez, *Becoming Mexican American* (New York, 1993); Edmund Morgan, *American Slavery, American Freedom* (New York, 1975); John Hope Franklin, *The Color Line: Legacy for the Twenty-first Century* (Columbia, Mo., 1993).
8. Alexander Saxton, *The Rise and Fall of the White Republic* (New York, 1992); Roediger, *Wages;* Michael Rogin, *Ronald Reagan, the Movie: and Other Episodes in Political Demonology* (Berkeley, 1987); Michael Rogin, "Blackface"; Michael Rogin, "'Democracy and Burnt Cork': The End of Blackface, the Beginning of Civil Rights," presented at the University of California Humanities Research Institute Film Genres Study Group, November 1992.
9. See Kenneth Jackson, *Crabgrass Frontier: The Suburbanization of the United States* (New York, 1985); and Douglas S. Massey and Nancy A. Denton, *American Apartheid: Segregation and the Making of the Underclass* (Cambridge, Mass., 1993).
10. I thank Phil Ethington for pointing out to me that these aspects of New Deal policies emerged out of political negotiations between the segregationist Dixiecrats and liberals from the North and West. My perspective is that white supremacy was not a gnawing aberration within the New Deal coalition but rather an essential point of unity between southern whites and northern white ethnics.
11. Records of the Federal Home Loan Bank Board of the Home Owners Loan Corporation. City Survey File, Los Angeles, 1939, Neighborhood D-53, National Archives, Washington, D.C., box 74, records group 195.
12. Massey and Denton, *American Apartheid,* 54.
13. John R. Logan and Harvey Molotch, *Urban Fortunes: The Political Economy of Place* (Berkeley, 1987), 182.
14. Ibid., 114.
15. Ibid., 130.
16. See Gary Gerstle, "Working-Class Racism: Broaden the Focus," *International Labor and Working Class History* 44 (fall 1993): 36.
17. Logan and Molotch, *Urban Fortunes,* 168–69.
18. Troy Duster, "Crime, Youth Unemployment, and the Black Urban Underclass," *Crime and Delinquency* 33 (Apr. 1987): 308.
19. Ibid., 309.
20. Massey and Denton, *American Apartheid,* 55.
21. Logan and Molotch, *Urban Forunes,* 113.
22. Robert D. Bullard, "Environmental Justice for All," in *Unequal Protection: Environmental*

Justice and Communities of Color, ed. Robert Bullard (San Francisco, 1994), 9–10.

23. Massey and Denton, *American Apartheid,* 61.

24. Gertrude Ezorsky, *Racism and Justice: The Case for Affirmative Action* (Ithaca, N.Y., 1991), 25.

25. Logan and Molotch, *Urban Fortunes,* 116.

26. Jim Campen, "Lending Insights: Hard Proof That Banks Discriminate," *Dollars and Sense* 191 (Jan.–Feb. 1991): 17.

27. Mitchell Zuckoff, "Study Shows Racial Bias in Lending," *The Boston Globe,* 9 October 1992, 1, 77, 78.

28. Paul Ong and J. Eugene Grigsby III, "Race and Life-Cycle Effects on Home Ownership in Los Angeles, 1970 to 1980," *Urban Affairs Quarterly* 23 (June 1988): 605.

29. Massey and Denton, *American Apartheid,* 108.

30. Gary Orfield and Carol Ashkinaze, *The Closing Door: Conservative Policy and Black Opportunity* (Chicago, 1991), 58, 78.

31. Logan and Molotch, *Urban Fortunes.*

32. Campen, "Lending Insights," 18.

33. Gregory Squires, "'Runaway Plants,' Capital Mobility, and Black Economic Rights," in *Community and Capital in Conflict: Plant Closings and Job Loss,* ed. John C. Raines, Lenora E. Berson, and David McI. Gracie (Philadelphia, 1982), 70.

34. Gertrude Ezorsky, *Racism and Justice: The Case for Affirmative Action* (Ithaca, N.Y., 1991), 15.

35. Orfield and Ashkinaze, *The Closing Door,* 225–26.

36. McClatchy News Service, "State Taxes Gouge the Poor, Study Says," *Long Beach Press-Telegram,* 23 April 1991, A1.

37. "Proposition 13," *UC Focus* (June–July 1993): 2.

38. William Chafe, *The Unfinished Journey* (New York, 1986), 442; Noel J. Kent, "A Stacked Deck: Racial Minorities and the New American Political Economy," *Explorations in Ethnic Studies* 14 (Jan. 1991): 11.

39. Kent, "Stacked Deck," 13.

40. Melvin Oliver and James Johnson, "Economic Restructuring and Black Male Joblessness in United States Metropolitan Areas," *Urban Geography* 12 (Nov.–Dec. 1991); Gerald David Jaynes and Robin M. Williams, Jr., eds., *A Common Destiny: Blacks and American Society* (Washington, D.C., 1989); Reynolds Farley and Walter R. Allen, *The Color Line and the Quality of Life in America* (New York, 1987); Melvin Oliver and Tom Shapiro, "Wealth of a Nation: A Reassessment of Asset Inequality in America Shows at Least ¹/₃ of Households Are Asset Poor," *Journal of Eco-nomics and Sociology* 49 (Apr. 1990); Jonathan Kozol, *Savage Inequalities: Children in America's Schools* (New York, 1991); Cornell West, *Race Matters* (Boston, 1993).

41. Orfield and Ashkinaze, *Closing Door,* 46.

42. Ibid., 206.

43. Bart Landry, "The Enduring Dilemma of Race in America," in Alan H. Wolfe, *America at Century's End* (Berkeley, 1991), 206; Franklin, *Color Line,* 36–37.

44. Kathleen Hall Jamieson, *Dirty Politics: Deception, Distraction, and Democracy* (New York, 1992), 100.

45. Mary Edsall and Thomas Byrne Edsall, *Chain Reaction* (New York, 1991).

46. Nathan Glazer makes this argument in *Affirmative Discrimination* (New York, 1975).

47. I borrow the term "overdetermination" here from Louis Althusser, who uses it to show how dominant ideologies become credible to people in part because various institutions and agencies independently replicate them and reinforce their social power.

48. Rogena Schuyler, "Youth: We Didn't Sell Them into Slavery," *Los Angeles Times,* 21 June 1993, B4.

49. Ibid.

50. Jim Newton, "Skinhead Leader Pleads Guilty to Violence, Plot," *Los Angeles Times,* 20 Oct. 1993 A1, A15.

51. Antonin Scalia, quoted in Cheryl I. Harris, "Whiteness as Property," *Harvard Law Review,* 106 (June 1993): 1767.

52. Ibid.

53. The rise of a black middle class and the setbacks suffered by white workers during deindustrialization may seem to subvert the analysis presented here. Yet the black middle class remains fragile, far less able than other middle-class groups to translate advances in income into advances in wealth and power. Similarly, the success of neoconservatism since the 1970s has rested on securing support from white workers for economic policies that do them objective harm by mobilizing counter-subversive electoral coalitions against busing and affirmative action, while carrying out attacks on public institutions and resources by representing "public" space and black space. See Oliver and Shapiro, "Wealth of a Nation." See also Logan and Harvey, *Urban Fortunes.*

54. Johnny Otis, *Upside Your Head! Rhythm and Blues on Central Avenue* (Hanover, N.H., 1993).

55. Mobilizations against plant shutdowns, for environmental protection, against cutbacks in education spending, and for reproductive rights all contain the potential for pan-ethnic antiracist organizing, but, too often, neglect of race as a central modality for how issues of employment, pollution, education, or repro- ductive rights are experienced isolates these social movements from their broadest possible base.

56. Walter Benjamin, "Madame Ariane: Second Courtyard on the Left," from *One-Way Street* (London, 1969), 98, 99.

14

RACIALIZED SOCIAL SYSTEM APPROACH TO RACISM

Eduardo Bonilla-Silva

Questions to Consider

Eduardo Bonilla-Silva argues that "after a society becomes racialized, racialization develops a life of its own." What does this mean? How does society become "racialized" and how is it possible that the idea of race can develop a "life" of its own? How, according to the author, is the United States characterized by racialized social systems?

In order to capture the society-wide, organized, and institutional character of racism I build my alternative theory around the notion of *racialized social systems.*[1] This term refers to societies in which economic, political, social, and ideological levels are partially structured by the placement of actors in racial categories or races. Races typically are identified by their phenotype, but (as we see later) the selection of some human traits to designate a racial group is always socially rather than biologically based.

These systems are structured partially by race because modern social systems incorporate two or more forms of hierarchical patterns. Although processes of racialization are always embedded in other forms of hierarchy, they acquire autonomy and have independent social effects. This implies that the phenomenon that has been conceived as a free-floating ideology in fact has its own structural foundation.

In all racialized social systems the placement of actors in racial categories involves some form of hierarchy[2] that produces definite social relations among the races. The race placed in the superior position tends to receive greater economic remuneration and access to better occupations and prospects in the labor market, occupies a primary position in the political system, is granted higher social estimation (e.g., is viewed as "smarter" or "better looking"), often has the license to draw physical (segregation) as well as social (racial etiquette) boundaries between itself and other races, and receives what W.E.B. Du Bois called a "psychological wage."[3] The totality of these racialized social relations and practices constitutes the racial structure of a society.

Although all racialized social systems are hierarchical, the particular character of the hierarchy, and, thus, of the racial structure, is variable. For example, the domination of blacks in the United States was achieved through dictatorial means during slavery, but in the post–civil rights period this domination has been *hegemonic,* that is in the Gramscian sense of the term, achieved through consent rather than coercion.[4] Similarly, the form of securing domination and white privilege is variable too. For instance, the racial practices and mechanisms that kept blacks subordinated changed from overt and eminently racist in the Jim Crow era to covert and indirectly racist in the contemporary period. The unchanging element of these systems is racial inequality—that the subordinated races' life chances are significantly lower than those of the dominant race. This is the feature that ultimately distinguishes this form of hierarchical social organization. Generally, the higher the level of racial inequality, the more racialized the social system, and vice versa.

Because the races receive different social rewards at all levels, they develop different interests, which can be detected in their struggles to either transform or maintain a particular racial order. These interests are collective rather than individual, are based on relations among races rather than on particular group needs, and are practical; that is, they are related to concrete struggles. Although one race's general interest may ultimately lie in the complete elimination of a society's racial structure, its array of alternatives may not include that possibility. For instance, the historical struggle against chattel slavery led not to the development of race-free societies but to the establishment of social systems with a different kind of racialization. Race-free societies were not among the available alternatives because the non-slave populations had the capacity to preserve some type of racial privilege. The historical "exceptions" occurred in racialized societies in which the nonslaves' power was almost completely superseded by that of the slave population.[5]

A simple criticism of the argument I have advanced so far is that it ignores the internal divisions of the races along class and gender lines. Such criticism, however, does not deal squarely with the issue at hand. The fact that not all members of the dominant race receive the same level of rewards and (conversely) that not all members of the subordinate race or races are at the bottom of the social order does not negate the fact that races, as social groups, are in either a superordinate or a subordinate position in a social system. Historically the racialization of social systems did not imply the exclusion of other forms of oppression. In fact, racialization occurred in social formations also structured by class and gender. Hence, in these societies, the racialization of subjects is fragmented along class and gender lines. The important question—Which interests move actors to struggle?—is historically contingent and cannot be ascertained a priori.[6] Depending on the character of racialization in a social order, class interests may take precedence over racial interests as in contemporary Brazil, Cuba, and Puerto Rico. In other situations, racial interests may take precedence over class interests as in the case of blacks throughout most of U.S. history.

In general, the systemic salience of class in relation to race increases when the economic, political, and social inequality among the races decreases substantially. Yet this broad argument generates at least one warning: The narrowing of within-class differences among racial actors usually causes *more* rather than *less* racial conflict, at least in the short run, as the competition for resources increases.[7] More significantly, even when class-based conflict becomes more salient in a social order, this cannot be interpreted as prima facie evidence that race has subsided as a social factor. For instance, because of the way in which Latin American racial formations rearticulated race and racial discourse in the nineteenth-century–post-emancipation era,[8] these societies silenced from above the political space for public racial contestation. Yet more than 100 years after these societies developed the myth of racial democracy, they have more rather than less racial inequality than countries such as the United States.[9]

Because racial actors are also classed and gendered (that is, they belong to class and gender groups), analysts must control for class and gender to ascertain the material advantages enjoyed by a dominant race. In a racialized society such as the United States, the independent effects of race are assessed by analysts who (1) compare data between whites and nonwhites in the *same* class and gender positions, (2) evaluate the proportion as well as the general character of the races' participation in some domain of life, and (3) examine racial data at all levels—social, political, economic, and ideological—to ascertain the general position of racial groups in a social system.

The first of these procedures has become standard practice in sociology. No serious sociologist would present racial statistics without controlling for gender and class (or at least the class of persons' socioeconomic status). By doing this, analysts assume they can measure the unadulterated effects of "discrimination" manifested in unexplained "residuals." Despite its usefulness, however, this technique provides only a partial account of the "race effect" because (1) a significant amount of racial data cannot be retrieved through surveys and (2) the technique of "controlling for" a variable neglects the obvious—why a group is over- or underrepresented in certain categories of the control variables in the first place.[10] Moreover, these analysts presume that it is possible to analyze the amount of discrimination in one domain (e.g, income, occupational status) "without analyzing the extent to which discrimination also affects the factors they hold constant."[11] Hence to evaluate "race effects" in any domain, analysts must attempt to make sense of their findings in relation to a race's standing in other domains.

But what is the nature of races or, more properly, of racialized social groups? Omi and Winant state that races are the outcome of the racialization process, which they define as "the extension of racial meaning to a previously racially unclassified relationship, social practice, or group."[12] Historically the classification of a people in racial terms has been a highly political act associated with practices such as conquest and colonization, enslavement, peonage, indentured servitude, and, more recently, colonial and neocolonial labor immigration. Categories such as "Indians" and "Negroes" were invented in the sixteenth and seventeenth centuries to justify the conquest and exploitation of various peoples.[13] The invention of such categories entails a dialectical process of construction; that is, the creation of the category "Other" involves the creation of a category "Same." If "Indians" are depicted as "savages," Europeans are characterized as "civilized"; if "blacks" are defined as natural candidates for slavery, "whites" are defined as free subjects.[14] Yet although the racialization of peoples was socially invented and did not override previous forms of social distinction based on class or gender, it did not lead to imaginary relations but generated new forms of human association with definite status differences. After the process of attaching meaning to a "people" is instituted, race becomes a real category of group association and identity.[15]

Because racial classifications partially organize and limit actors' life chances, racial practices of opposition emerge. Regardless of the form of racial interaction (overt, covert, or inert), races can be recognized in the realm of racial relations and positions. Viewed in this light, races are the effect of racial practices of opposition ("we" versus "them") at the economic, political, social, and ideological levels.[16]

Races, as most social scientists acknowledge, are not biologically but socially determined categories of identity and group association. In this regard, they are analogous to class and gender.[17] Actors in racial positions do not occupy those positions because they are of X or Y race, but because X or Y has been socially defined as a race. Actors' phenotypic (i.e., biologically inherited) characteristics, such as skin tone and hair color and texture, are usually, although not always, used to denote racial distinctions.[18] For example, Jews in many European nations and the Irish in England have been treated as racial groups.[19] Also, Indians in the United States have been viewed as one race despite the tremendous phenotypic and cultural variation among nations. Because races are socially constructed, both the meaning and the position assigned to races in the racial structure are always contested. Who is to be black or white or Indian reflects and affects the social, political, ideological, and economic struggles among the races. The global effects of these struggles can change the meaning of the racial categories as well as the position of a racialized group in a social formation.

This latter point is illustrated clearly by the historical struggles of several "white ethnic" groups in the United States in their efforts to become accepted as legitimate whites or "Americans."[20] Neither light-skinned nor, for that matter, dark-skinned immigrants necessarily came to this country as members of X or Y race. Light-skinned Europeans, after brief periods of "not-yet white," became "white" but did not lose their "ethnic character.[21] Their struggle for inclusion had specific implications: racial inclusion as members of the white community allowed Americanization and class mobility. On the other hand, among dark-skinned immigrants from Africa, Latin America, and the Caribbean, the struggle was to avoid classification as "black." These immigrants challenged the reclassification of their identity for a single reason: In the United States "black" signified a subordinate status in society. Hence many of these groups struggled to keep their own ethnic or cultural identity, as denoted in expressions such as "I am not black; I am Jamaican," or "I am not black; I am Senegalese."[22] Yet eventually many of these groups resolved this contradictory situation by accepting the duality of their situation: In the United States, they were classified socially as black yet they retained and nourished their own cultural or ethnic heritage—a heritage deeply influenced by African traditions.

Although the content of racial categories changes over time through manifold processes and struggles, race is not a secondary category of group association. The meaning of black and white, the "racial formation," changes within the larger racial structure. This does not mean that the racial structure is immutable and completely independent of the action of racialized actors. It means only that the social relations among the races become institutionalized (form a structure as well as a culture) and affect social life whether or not individual members of the races want it to. In Frederick Barth's words, "Ethnic identity implies a series of constraints on the kinds of roles an individual is allowed to play [and] is similar to sex and rank, in that it constrains the incumbent in all his activities."[23] For instance, free blacks during the slavery period struggled to change the meaning of "blackness," specifically to dissociate it from slavery. Yet they could not escape the larger racial structure that restricted their life chances and their freedom.[24]

The placement of a group of people in a racial category stemmed initially[25] from the interests of powerful actors in the social system (e.g., the capitalist class, the planter class, and colonizers). After racial categories were employed to organize social relations in societies, however, race became an independent element of the operation of the social system.

What are the dynamics of racial issues in racialized systems? Most important, after a social formation is racialized, its "normal" dynamics always include a racial component. Societal struggles based on class or gender contain a racial component because both of these social categories are also racialized; that is, both class and gender are constructed along racial lines. In 1922, for example, white South African workers in the middle of a strike inspired by the Russian revolution rallied under the slogan "Workers of the world unite for a white South Africa." One of the state's "concessions" to this "class" struggle was the passage of the Apprenticeship Act of 1922, "which prevented Black workers acquiring apprenticeships."[26] In another example, the struggle of women in the United States to attain their civil and human rights has always been plagued by deep racial tensions.[27]

Nonetheless, some of the strife that exists in a racialized social formation has a distinct racial character; I call such strife *racial contestation*—the struggle of racial groups for systemic changes regarding their position at one or more levels. Such a struggle may be social (Who can be here? Who belongs here?), political (Who can vote? How much power should they have? Should they be citizens?), economic (Who should work, and what should they do? They are taking our jobs!), or ideological (Black is beautiful!).

Although much of this contestation is expressed at the individual level and is disjointed, sometimes it becomes collective and general and can effect meaningful systemic changes in a society's racial organization. The form of contestation may be relatively passive and subtle (e.g., in situations of fundamental overt racial domination such as slavery and apartheid) or more active and overt (e.g., in quasi-democratic situations such as the contemporary United States). As a rule, however, fundamental changes in racialized social systems are accompanied by struggles that reach the point of overt protest.[28] This does not mean that a violent racially based revolution is the only way of accomplishing effective changes in the relative position of racial groups. It is simply an extension of the argument that social systems and their supporters must be "shaken" if fundamental transformations are to take place.[29] On this structural foundation rests the phenomenon labeled racism by social scientists.

I reserve the term *racial ideology* for the segment of the ideological structure of a social system that crystallizes racial notions and stereotypes. Racial ideology provides the rationalization for social, political, and economic interactions among the races. Depending on the particular character of a racialized social system and on the struggles of the subordinated races, racial ideology may be developed highly (as in apartheid) or loosely (as in slavery) and its content expressed in overt or covert terms.

Although racial ideology originates in race relations, it acquires relative autonomy in the social system and performs practical functions.[30] In Paul Gilroy's words, racial ideology "mediates the world of agents and the structures which are created by their social praxis."[31] Racism crystallizes the changing "dogma" on which actors in the social system operate and becomes "common sense"; it provides the rules for perceiving and dealing with the Other in a racialized society. In the United States, for instance, because racial notions about what blacks and whites are or ought to be pervade their encounters, whites still have difficulty in dealing with black bankers, lawyers, professors, and doctors.[32] Thus, although racist ideology is ultimately false, it fulfills a practical role in racialized societies.

At this point it is possible to sketch the framework of the racialized social system. First, racialized social systems are societies that allocate differential economic, political, social, and even psychological rewards to groups along racial lines, lines that are socially constructed. After a society becomes racialized, a set of social relations and practices based on racial distinctions develops at all societal levels. I designate the aggregate of those relations and practices as the racial structure of a society. Second, races historically are constituted according to the process of racialization; they become the effect of relations of opposition among racialized groups at all levels of a social formation. Third, on the basis of this structure, a racial ideology develops. This ideology is not simply a "superstructural" phenomenon (a mere reflection of the racialized system) but becomes the organizational map that guides actions of racial actors in society. It becomes as real as the racial relations it organizes. Fourth, most struggles in a racialized social system contain a racial component, but sometimes they acquire or exhibit a distinct racial character. Racial contestation is the logical outcome of a society with a racial hierarchy. A social formation that includes some form of racial contestation. Finally, the process of racial contestation reveals the different objective interests of the races in a racialized social system.

Conclusion

My central argument in this chapter is that the commonsense understanding of racism, which is not much different than the definition developed by mainstream social scientists or even by many critical analysts, does not provide an adequate theoretical foundation for understanding racial phenomena. With notable exceptions,[33] analysts in academia are still entangled in ungrounded ideological interpretations of racism. Lacking a structural view, they tend to reduce racial phenomena to a derivation of the class structure (as Marxist interpreters do) or the result of an irrational ideology (as mainstream social scientists do).

In the racialized social system framework, I suggest, as do Omi and Winant, that racism should be studied from the viewpoint of racialization. I contend that after a society becomes racialized, racialization develops a life of its own.[34] Although racism interacts with class and gender structurations in society, it becomes an organizing principle of social relations in itself. Race, as most analysts suggest, is a social construct, but that construct, like class and gender, has independent effects in social life. After racial stratification is established, race becomes an independent criterion for vertical hierarchy in society. Therefore different races experience positions of subordination and superordination in society and develop different interests. This framework has the following advantages over traditional views of racism:

Racial phenomena are regarded as the "normal" outcome of the racial structure of a society Thus we can account for all racial manifestations. Instead of explaining racial phenomena as deriving from other structures or from racism (conceived of as a free-floating ideology), we can trace cultural, political, economic, social, and even psychological racial phenomena to the racial organization of that society.

The changing nature of what analysts label "racism" is explained as the normal outcome of racial contestation in a racialized social system. In this framework, changes in racism are explained rather than described. Changes are due to specific struggles at different levels among the races, resulting from differences in interests. Such changes may transform the nature of racialization and the global character of racial relations in the system (the racial structure). Therefore, change is viewed as a normal component of the racialized system.

The racialized social system framework allows analysts to explain overt as well as covert racial behavior. The covert or overt nature of racial contacts depends on how the process of racialization is manifested; this in turns depends on how race originally was articulated in a social formation and on the process of racial contestation. This point implies that rather than conceiving of racism as a universal and uniformly orchestrated phenomenon, analysts should study "historically-specific racisms."[35] This insight is not new: Robert Park, Oliver Cox, Pierre van den Bergue, and Marvin Harris described varieties of "situations of race relations" with distinct forms of racial interaction.

Racially motivated behavior, whether or not the actors are conscious of it, is regarded as "rational"—that is, based on the given race's individual interests.[36] This framework accounts for Archie Bunker–type racial behavior as well as for more "sophisticated" varieties of racial conduct. Racial phenomena are viewed as systemic; therefore all actors in the system participate in racial affairs. Some members of the dominant racial group tend to exhibit less virulence toward members of the subordinated races because they have greater control over the form and outcome of their racial interactions. When they can-

not control that interaction—as in the case of revolts or blacks moving into "their" neighborhood—they behave much like other members of the dominant race.

The reproduction of racial phenomena in contemporary societies is explained in this framework not by reference to a long-distant past but in relation to its contemporary structure. Because racism is viewed as systemic (possessing a racial structure) and as organized around the races' different interests, racial aspects of social systems today are viewed as fundamentally related to hierarchical relations among the races in those systems. Elimination of the racialized character of a social system entails the end of racialization, and hence of races altogether. This argument clashes with social scientists' most popular policy prescription for "curing" racism, namely education. This "solution" is the logical outcome of defining racism as a belief. Most analysts regard racism as a matter of individuals subscribing to an irrational view, thus the cure is educating them to realize that racism is wrong. Education is also the choice pill prescribed by Marxists for healing workers from racism. The alternative theory offered here implies that because the phenomenon has structural consequences for the races, the only way to cure society of racism is by eliminating its systemic roots. Whether this can be accomplished democratically or only through revolutionary means is an open question, and one that depends on the particular racial structure of the society in question.

A racialization framework accounts for the ways in which racial and ethnic stereotypes emerge, are transformed, and disappear. Racial stereotypes are crystallized at the ideological level of a social system. These images ultimately indicate—although in distorted ways—and justify the stereotyped group's position in a society. Stereotypes may originate out of (1) material realities or conditions endured by the group, (2) genuine ignorance about the group, or (3) rigid, distorted views on the group's physical, cultural, or moral nature. Once they emerge, however, stereotypes must relate—although not necessarily fit perfectly—to the group's true social position in the racialized system if they are to perform their ideological function. Stereotypes that do not tend to reflect a group's situation do not work and are bound to disappear. For example, notions of the Irish as stupid or of Jews as athletically talented have all but vanished since the 1940s, as the Irish moved up the educational ladder and Jews gained access to multiple routes of social mobility. Generally, then, stereotypes are reproduced because they reflect a group's distinct position and status in society. As a corollary, racial or ethnic notions about a group disappear only when the group's status mirrors that of the dominant racial or ethnic group in the society.

The framework of the racialized social system is not a universal theory explaining racial phenomena in societies. It is intended to trigger a serious discussion of how race shapes social systems. Moreover, the important question of how race interacts and intersects with class and gender has not yet been addressed satisfactorily. Provisionally I maintain that a nonfunctionalist reading of the concept of social system may give us clues for comprehending societies *structured in dominance*, to use Stuart Hall's term. If societies are viewed as systems that articulate different structures (organizing principles on which sets of social relations are systematically patterned), it is possible to claim that race—as well as gender—has both individual and combined (interactive) effects in society.

To test the usefulness of the racialized social system framework as a theoretical basis for research, we must perform comparative work on racialization in various societies. One of the main objectives of this comparative work should be to determine the specific mechanisms, practices, and so-cial relations that produce and reproduce racial inequality at all levels—that is, uncover the society's racial structure. Unlike analysts who believe that "racism" has withered away, I argue that the persistent inequality experienced by blacks and other racial minorities in the United States today is due to the *continued* albeit *changed* existence of a racial structure. In contrast to race relations in the Jim Crow period, however, racial practices that reproduce racial inequality in contemporary America are (1) increasingly covert, (2) embedded in normal operations of institutions, (3) void of direct racial terminology, and (4) invisible to most whites.

NOTES

1. All racialized social systems operate along white supremacist lines. See Mills, *Blackness Visible* (Ithaca, NY: Cornell University Press, 1998).
2. I make a distinction between race and ethnicity. Ethnicity has a primarily sociocultural foundation, and ethnic groups have exhibited tremendous malleability in terms of who belongs. In contrast, racial ascriptions (initially) are imposed externally to justify the collective exploitation of a people and are maintained to preserve status differences. The distinction I make was part of a debate that appeared recently in the *American Sociological Review*. For specialists interested in this matter, see Bonilla-Silva, "The Essential Social Fact of Race," *American Sociological Review* 64, no. 6 (1999): 899–906.
3. Herbert Blumer was one of the first analysts to make this argument about systemic rewards received by the races ascribed the primary position in a racial order. See Herbert Blumer, "Reflections on Theory of Race Relations," pp. 3–21 in *Race Relations in World Perspective*, edited by A. W. Lind (Honolulu, HI: University of Hawaii Press, 1955). Du Bois's argument about the psychological wages of whiteness has been used recently by Manning Marable, *How Capitalism Underdeveloped Black America*; and by David Roediger, *The Wages of Whiteness*.
4. This point has been made by Omi and Winant, *Racial Formation in the United States*; Winant, *Racial Conditions*.

5. I am referring to cases such as Haiti. Nonetheless, recent research has suggested that even in such places, the abolition of slavery did not end the racialized character of the social formation. See Michel-Rolph Troillot, *Haiti, State Agency Nation: Origins and Legacy of Duvalierism* (New York: Monthly Review Press, 1990).

6. For a similar argument, see Floya Anthias and Nira Yuval-Davis, *Racialized Boundaries: Race, Nation, Gender, Colour, and the Anti-Racist Struggle* (London, England: Tavistock, 1992).

7. For an early statement on this matter, see Hubert M. Blalock, Jr., *Toward a Theory of Minority-Majority Group Relations* (New York: John Wiley and Sons, 1967). For a more recent statement, see Susan Olzack, *The Dynamics of Ethnic Competition and Conflict* (Stanford, CA: Stanford University Press, 1992).

8. Nineteenth century nation-building processes throughout Latin America included the myth of racial democracy and color- or race-blindness. This facilitated the struggles for independence and the maintenance of white supremacy in societies wherein white elites were demographically insignificant. For discussions pertinent to this argument see the excellent collection edited by Michael Hanchard, *Racial Politics in Contemporary Brazil* (Durham and London: Duke University Press, 1999).

9. See my "The Essential Social Fact of Race," *American Sociological Review* 64, no. 6 (December 1999): 899–906.

10. On this point, see Warren Whatley and Gavin Wright, *Race, Human Capital, and Labor Markets in American History,* Working Paper #7 (Ann Arbor, MI: Center for Afroamerican and Africa Studies, University of Michigan, 1994). For an incisive discussion, see Samuel L. Meyers, Jr., "Measuring and Detecting Discrimination in the Post–Civil Rights Era," pp. 172–197 in *Race and Ethnicity in Research Methods,* edited by John H. Stanfield II and Rutledge M. Dennis (London: Sage Publications, 1993).

11. Michael Reich, "The Economics of Racism," in *Racial Conflict, Discrimination, and Power: Historical and Contemporary Studies,* edited by William Barclay, Krishma Kumar, and Ruth P. Simms (New York: AMS Press, 1976), p. 224.

12. Omi and Winant, *Racial Formation in the United States,* 64.

13. On the invention of the white race, see Theodore W. Allen *The Invention of the White Race,* Vol. I (London: Verso, 1994). On the invention of the "Indian" race, see Robert E. Berkhofer, *The White Man's Indian* (New York: Vintage, 1978). On the invention of the black and white races, see Winthrop Jordan, *White over Black.*

14. A classic book on the ideological binary construction of the races in the United States is Thomas Gossett, *Race: The History of an Idea in America* (Dallas, TX: Southern Methodist University Press, 1963). For an analysis of an earlier period in the Americas, see Tzevetan Todorov, *The Conquest of America: The Question of the Other* (New York: Harper Colophon, 1984).

15. On this matter, I stated in my recent debate in the pages of the *American Sociological Review* with Mara Loveman that "'race,' like 'class' or 'gender,' is *always contingent* but is also *socially real*. Race operates 'as a shuttle between socially constructed meanings and practices, between subjective and lived, material reality' (Hanchard 1994:4)." (901). Michael G. Hanchard, *Orpheus and Power* (Princeton, NJ: Princeton University Press, 1994).

16. This last point is an extension of Poulantza's view on class. Races—as classes—are not an "empirical thing"; they denote racialized social relations or racial practices at all levels. Poulantzas, *Political Power and Social Classes* (London: Verso, 1982), p. 67.

17. For a full discussion, see my "The Essential Social Fact of Race." For a similar argument, see Teresa Amott and Julie Matthaei, *Race, Gender, and Work: A Multicultural Economic History of Women in the United States* (Boston, MA: South End Press, 1996).

18. Frederick Barth, "Introduction," pp. 9–38 in *Ethnic Groups and Boundaries: The Social Organization of Culture Difference,* edited by F. Barth (Bergen, Norway: Universitetsforlaget, 1969).

19. For the case of the Jews, see Miles, *Racism After "Race Relations"* (London: Routledge, 1993). For the case of the Irish, see Allen, *The Invention of the White Race.*

20. For a recent excellent discussion on ethnicity with many examples from the United States, see Stephen Cornell and Douglas Hartmann, *Ethnicity and Race: Making Identities in a Changing World* (London: Pine Forge Press, 1998).

21. Roediger, *The Wages of Whiteness.* See also Noel Ignatiev, *How the Irish Became White* (New York: Routledge, 1995).

22. For identity issues among Caribbean immigrants, see the excellent edited collection by Constance R. Sutton and E. M. Chaney,

Caribbean Life in New York City: Sociocultural Dimensions (New York: Center for Migration Studies of New York, 1987).

23. Barth, "Introduction," 17.

24. A few notable discussions on this matter are Ira Berlin, *Slaves Without Masters: The Free Negro in Antebellum South* (New York: Pantheon, 1975); John Hope Franklin, *From Slavery to Freedom: A History of the Negro Americans* (New York: Alfred Knopf, 1974); August Meir and Elliot Rudwick, *From Plantation to Ghetto* (New York: Hill and Wang, 1970).

25. The motivation for racializing human relations may have originated in the interests of powerful actors, but after social systems are racialized, all members of the dominant race participate in defending and reproducing the racial structure. This is the crucial reason why Marxist analysts (e.g., Cox, Reich) have not succeeded in successfully analyzing racism. They have not been able to accept the fact that after the phenomenon originated with the expansion of European capitalism into the New World, it acquired a life of its own. The subjects who were racialized as belonging to the superior race, whether or not they were members of the dominant class, became zealous defenders of the racial order. For an interesting Marxist-inspired treatment, see Bush, *We Are Not What We Seem.*

26. Hillel Ticktin, *The Politics of Race: Discrimination in South Africa* (London: Pluto, 1991), p. 26.

27. The classic book on this is Paula Giddings, *When and Where I Enter: The Impact of Black Women on Race and Sex in America* (New York: Bantam, 1984). See also Nancy Caraway, *Segregated Sisterhood: Racism and the Politics of American Feminism* (Knoxville, TN: University of Tennessee Press, 1991).

28. This argument is not new. Analysts of the racial history of the United States have always pointed out that most of the significant historical changes in this country's race relations were accompanied by some degree of overt violence. See Harold Cruse, *Rebellion or Revolution* (New York: William Morrow, 1968); Franklin, *From Slavery to Freedom;* and James W. Button, *Blacks and Social Change: Impact of the Civil Rights Movement in Southern Communities* (Princeton, NJ: Princeton University Press, 1989).

29. This point is important in literature on revolutions and democracy. On the role of violence in the establishment of bourgeois democracies, see Barrington Moore, Jr., *Social Origins of Dictatorship and Democracy* (Boston, MA: Beacon Press, 1966). On the pivotal role of violence in social movements, see Frances Fox Piven and Richard A. Cloward, *Poor People's Movements: Why They Succeed, How They Fail* (New York: Vintage, 1979).

30. The notion of relative autonomy comes from the work of Poulantzas (*Power and Social Classes*) and implies that the ideological and political levels in a society are partially autonomous in relation to the economic level; that is, they are not merely expressions of the economic level.

31. Paul Gilroy, *"There Ain't No Black in the Union Jack": The Cultural Politics of Race and Nation* (Chicago, IL: University of Chicago Press, 1991), p. 17.

32. See Ellis Cose, *The Rage of a Privileged Class: Why Are Black Middle Class Angry? Why Should America Care?* (New York: HarperCollins, 1993); Lawrence Otis-Graham, *Member of the Club: Reflections on Life in a Racially Polarized World* (New York: HarperCollins, 1995).

33. In addition to the work by Joe R. Feagin and Hernán Vera already cited, see Lawrence Bobo, J. Kluegel, and R. Smith, "Laissez Faire Racism: The Crystallization of a Kinder, Gentler, Antiblack Ideology," and, particularly, Mary R. Jackman, *Velvet Glove: Paternalism and Conflict in Gender, Class and Race Relations* (Berkeley, CA: University of California Press, 1994).

34. Curiously, historian Eugene Genovese made a similar argument in his book *Red and Black*. Although he still regarded racism as an ideology, he stated that once it "arises it alters profoundly the material reality and in fact becomes a partially autonomous feature of that reality." *Red and Black: Marxian Explorations in Southern and Afroamerican History* (New York: Pantheon, 1971), p. 340.

35. Hall, "Race Articulation and Societies Structured in Dominance," in *Sociological Theories: Race and Colonialism,* edited by UNESCO (Paris: UNESCO, 1980), p. 336.

36. Actions by the Ku Klux Klan have an unmistakably racial tone, but many other actions (choosing to live in a suburban neighborhood, sending one's children to a private school, and opposing government intervention in hiring policies) also have racial undertones.

The Color of Space

15

THE CONTINUING SIGNIFICANCE OF RACE
Antiblack Discrimination in Public Places

Joe R. Feagin

Questions to Consider

Joe Feagin suggests that being middle or upper-middle class does not neces-sarily insulate blacks from being the target of discriminatory behavior in public settings. How does racism manifest itself for this part of the African-American population? What social resources or responses do some members of the black middle class use to minimize discrimination in public places?

Title II of the 1964 Civil Rights Act stipulates that "all persons shall be entitled to the full and equal enjoy-ment of the goods, services, facilities, privi-leges, advantages, and accommodations of any place of public accommodation . . . without discrimination or segregation on the ground of race, color, religion, or na-tional origin." The public places empha-sized in the act are restaurants, hotels, and motels, although racial discrimination oc-curs in many other public places. Those black Americans who would make the greatest use of these public accommoda-tions and certain other public places would

be middle-class, i.e., those with the requisite resources. . . .

Discrimination can be defined in social-contextual terms as "actions or practices carried out by members of dominant racial or ethnic groups that have a differential and negative impact on members of subordinate racial and ethnic groups" (Feagin and Eck-berg 1980, pp. 1–2). This differential treat-ment ranges from the blatant to the subtle (Feagin and Feagin 1986). Here I focus pri-marily on blatant discrimination by white Americans targeting middle-class blacks. Historically, discrimination against blacks has been one of the most serious forms of racial/ethnic discrimination in the United States and one of the most difficult to overcome, in part because of the institutionalized charac-ter of color coding. I focus on three important aspects of discrimination: (1) the variation in sites of discrimination; (2) the range of discriminatory actions; and (3) the range of responses by blacks to discrimination.

Sites of Discrimination

There is a spatial dimension to discrimination. The probability of experiencing racial hostility varies from the most private to the most public sites. If a black person is in a relatively protected site, such as with friends at home, the probability of experiencing hostility and discrimination is low. The probability increases as one moves from friendship settings to such outside sites as the workplace, where a black person typically has contacts with both acquaintances and strangers, providing an interactive context with greater potential for discrimination.

In most workplaces, middle-class status and its organizational resources provide some protection against certain categories of discrimination. This protection probably weakens as a black person moves from those work and school settings where he or she is well-known into public accommodations such as large stores and city restaurants where contacts are mainly with white strangers. On public streets blacks have the greatest public exposure to strangers and the least protection against overt discriminatory behavior, including violence. A key feature of these more public settings is that they often involve contacts with white strangers who react primarily on the basis of one ascribed characteristic. The study of the micro-life of interaction between strangers in public was pioneered by Goffman and his students, but few of their analyses have treated hostile discriminatory interaction in public places. A rare exception is the research by Gardner (1980; see also Gardner 1988), who documented the character and danger of passing remarks by men directed against women in unprotected public places. Gardner writes of women (and blacks) as "open persons," i.e. particularly vulnerable targets for harassment that violates the rules of public courtesy.

The Range of Discriminatory Actions

In his classic study, *The Nature of Prejudice,* Allport (1958, pp. 14–5) noted that prejudice can be expressed in a series of progressively more serious actions, ranging from antilocution to avoidance, exclusion, physical attack, and extermination. Allport's work suggests a continuum of actions from avoidance, to exclusion or rejection, to attack. In his travels in the South in the 1950s a white journalist who changed his skin color to black encountered discrimination in each of these categories (Griffin 1961). In my data, discrimination against middle-class blacks still ranges across this continuum: (1) avoidance actions, such as a white couple crossing the street when a black male approaches; (2) rejection actions, such as poor service in public accommodations; (3) verbal attacks, such as shouting racial epithets in the street; (4) physical threats and harassment by white police officers; and (5) physical threats and attacks by other whites, such as attacks by white supremacists in the street. Changing relations between blacks and whites in recent decades have expanded the repertoire of discrimination to include more subtle forms and to encompass discrimination in arenas from which blacks were formerly excluded such as formerly all-white public accommodations.

Black Responses to Discrimination

Prior to societal desegregation in the 1960s much traditional discrimination, especially in the South, took the form of an asymmetrical "deference ritual" in which blacks were typically expected to respond to discriminating whites with great deference. . . .

Such rituals can be seen in the obsequious words and gestures—the etiquette of race relations—that many blacks, including middle-class blacks, were forced to utilize to survive the rigors of segregation (Doyle 1937). However, not all responses in this period were deferential. From the late 1800s to the 1950s, numerous lynchings and other violence targeted blacks whose behavior was defined as too aggressive (Raper 1933). Blauner's (1989) respondents reported acquaintances reacting aggressively to discrimination prior to the 1960s.

Deference rituals can still be found today between some lower-income blacks and their white employers. In her northeastern study Rollins (1985, p. 157) found black maids regularly deferring to white employers. Today, most discriminatory interaction no longer involves much asymmetrical deference, at least for middle-class blacks. Even where whites expect substantial deference, most middle-class blacks do not oblige. For middle-class blacks contemporary discrimination has evolved beyond the asymmetrical deference rituals and "No Negroes served" type of exclusion to patterns of black-contested discrimination. . . .

Some white observers have suggested that many middle-class blacks are paranoid about white discrimination and rush too quickly to charges of racism (Wieseltier 1989, June 5; for male views of female "paranoia" see Gardner 1988). But the daily reality may be just the opposite, as middle-class black Americans often evaluate a situation carefully before judging it discriminatory and taking additional action. This careful evaluation, based on past experiences (real or vicarious), not only prevents jumping to conclusions, but also reflects the hope that white behavior is not based on race, because an act not based on race is easier to endure. After evaluation one strategy is to leave the site of discrimination rather than to create a disturbance.

Another is to ignore the discrimination and continue with the interaction, a "blocking" strategy similar to that Gardner (1980, p. 345) reported for women dealing with street remarks. In many situations resigned acceptance is the only realistic response. More confrontational responses to white actions include verbal reprimands and sarcasm, physical counterattacks, and filing lawsuits. Several strategies may be tried in any given discriminatory situation. In crafting these strategies middle-class blacks, in comparison with less privileged blacks, may draw on middle-class resources to fight discrimination.

The Research Study

To examine discrimination, I draw primarily on 37 in-depth interviews from a larger study of 135 middle-class black Americans in Boston, Buffalo, Baltimore, Washington, D.C., Detroit, Houston, Dallas, Austin, San Antonio, Marshall, Las Vegas, and Los Angeles. . . .

Although all types of mistreatment are reported, there is a strong relationship between type of discrimination and site, with rejection/poor-service discrimination being most common in public accommodations and verbal or physical threat discrimination by white citizens or police officers most likely in the street. [Table 1] . . .

The most common black responses to racial hostility in the street are withdrawal or a verbal reply [Table 2]. In many avoidance situations (e.g., a white couple crossing a street to avoid walking past a black college student) or attack situations (e.g., whites throwing beer cans from a passing car), a verbal response is difficult because of the danger or the fleeting character of the hostility. A black victim often withdraws, endures this treatment with resigned acceptance, or replies with a quick verbal retort. In the case

TABLE 1   Percentage Distribution of Discriminatory Actions by Type and Site: Middle-Class Blacks in Selected Cities, 1988–1990

Type of Discriminatory Action	Site of Discriminatory Action	
	Public Accommodations	*Street*
Avoidance	3	7
Rejection/poor service	79	4
Verbal epithets	12	25
Police threats/harassment	3	46
Other threats/harassment	3	18
Total	100	100
Number of actions	34	28

TABLE 2   Percentage Distribution of Primary Responses to Discriminatory Incidents by Type and Site: Middle-Class Blacks in Selected Cities, 1988–1990

Response to Discriminatory Incident	Site of Discriminatory Incident	
	Public Accommodations	*Street*
Withdrawal/exit	4	22
Resigned acceptance	23	7
Verbal response	69	59
Physical counterattack	4	7
Response unclear	—	4
Total	100	99
Number of responses	26	27

of police harassment, the response is limited by the danger, and resigned acceptance or mild verbal protests are likely responses. Rejection (poor service) in public accommodations provides an opportunity to fight back verbally—the most common responses to public accommodations discrimination are verbal counterattacks or resigned acceptance. Some black victims correct whites quietly, while others respond aggressively and lecture the assailant about the discrimination or threaten court action. A few retaliate physically. Examining materials in these 37 interviews . . . we will see that the depth and complexity of contemporary black middle-class responses to white discrimination accents the changing character

of white-black interaction and the necessity of continual negotiation of the terms of that interaction.

Responses to Discrimination: Public Accommodations

Two Fundamental Strategies: Verbal Confrontation and Withdrawal

In the following account, a black news director at a major television station shows the interwoven character of discriminatory action and black response. The discrimination took the form of poor restaurant service, and the responses included both suggested withdrawal and verbal counterattack.

> He [her boyfriend] was waiting to be seated. . . . He said, "You go to the bathroom and I'll get the table. . . ." He was standing there when I came back; he continued to stand there. The restaurant was almost empty. There were waiters, waitresses, and no one seated. And when I got back to him, he was ready to leave, and said, "Let's go." I said, "What happened to our table?" He wasn't seated. So I said, "No, we're not leaving, please." And he said, "No, I'm leaving." So we went outside and we talked about it. And what I said to him was, you have to be aware of the possibilities that this is not the first time that this has happened at this restaurant or at other restaurants, but this is the first time it has happened to a black news director here or someone who could make an issue of it, or someone who is prepared to make an issue of it.
>
> So we went back inside after I talked him into it and, to make a long story short, I had the manager come. I made most of the people who were there (while conducting myself professionally the whole time) aware that I was incensed at being treated this way. . . . I said, "Why do you think we weren't seated?" And the manager said, "Well, I don't really know." And I said, "Guess." He said, "Well I don't know, because you're black?" I said, "Bingo. Now isn't it funny that you didn't guess that I didn't have any money" (and I opened up my purse) and I said, "because I certainly have money. And isn't it odd that you didn't guess that it's because I couldn't pay for it because I've got two American Express cards and a Master Card right here. I think it's just funny that you would have assumed that it's because I'm black." . . . And then I took out my card and gave it to him and said, "If this happens again, or if I hear of this happening again, I will bring the full wrath of an entire news department down on this restaurant." And he just kind of looked at me. "Not [just] because I am personally offended. I am. But because you have no right to do what you did, and as a people we have lived a long time with having our rights abridged. . . ." There were probably three or four sets of diners in the restaurant and maybe five waiters/ waitresses. They watched him standing there waiting to be seated. His reaction to it was that he wanted to leave. I understood why he would have reacted that way, because he felt that he was in no condition to be civil. He was ready to take the place apart and . . . sometimes it's appropriate to behave that way. We hadn't gone the first step before going on to the next step. He didn't feel that he could comfortably and calmly take the first step, and I did. So I just asked him to please get back in the restaurant with me, and then you don't have to say a word, and let me handle it from there. It took some convincing, but I had to appeal to his sense of, this is not just you, this is not just for you. We are finally in a position as black people where there are some of us who can genuinely get their attention. And if they don't want to do this because it's right for them to do it, then they'd better do it because they're afraid to do otherwise. If it's fear, then fine, instill the fear.

This example provides insight into the character of modern discrimination. The discrimination was not the "No Negroes" exclusion of the recent past, but rejection in the form of poor service by restaurant personnel. The black response indicates the change in black-white interaction since the 1950s and 1960s, for discrimination is handled with vigorous confrontation rather than deference. The aggressive black response and the white backtracking underscore Brittan and Maynard's (1984, p. 7) point that black-white interaction today is being renegotiated. It is possible that the white personnel defined the couple as "poor blacks" because of their jeans, although the jeans were fashionable and white patrons wear jeans. In comments not quoted here the news director rejects such an explanation. She forcefully articulates a theory of rights—a response that signals the critical impact of civil rights laws on the thinking of middle-class blacks. The news director articulates the American dream: she has worked hard, earned the money and credit cards, developed the appropriate middle-class behavior, and thus has under the law a *right* to be served. There is defensiveness in her actions too, for she feels a need to legitimate her status by showing her purse and credit cards. One important factor that enabled her to take such assertive action was her power to bring a TV news team to the restaurant. This power marks a change from a few decades ago when very few black Americans had the social or economic resources to fight back successfully. . . .

The confrontation response is generally so costly in terms of time and energy that acquiescence or withdrawal are common options. An example of the exit response was provided by a utility company executive in an East Coast city:

I can remember one time my husband had picked up our son . . . from camp; and he'd stopped at a little store in the neighborhood near the camp. It was hot, and he was going to buy him a snowball. And the proprietor of the

store—this was a very old, white neighborhood, and it was just a little sundry store. But the proprietor said he had the little window where people could come up and order things. Well, my husband and son had gone into the store. And he told them, "Well, I can't give it to you here, but if you go outside to the window, I'll give it to you." And there were other [white] people in the store who'd been served [inside]. So, they just left and didn't buy anything.

. . . This site differed from the previous example in that the service was probably not of long-term importance to the black family passing through the area. In the previous site the possibility of returning to the restaurant for business or pleasure may have contributed to the choice of a confrontational response. The importance of the service is a likely variable affecting black responses to discrimination in public accommodations. . . .

The complex process of evaluation and response is described by a college dean, who commented generally on hotel and restaurant discrimination encountered as he travels across the United States:

When you're in a restaurant and . . . you notice that blacks get seated near the kitchen. You notice that if it's a hotel, your room is near the elevator, or your room is always way down in a corner somewhere. You find that you are getting the undesirable rooms. And you come there early in the day and you don't see very many cars on the lot and they'll tell you that this is all we've got. Or you get the room that's got a bad television set. You know that you're being discriminated against. And of course you have to act accordingly. You have to tell them, "Okay, the room is fine, [but] this television set has got to go. Bring me another television set." So in my personal experience, I simply cannot sit and let them get away with it [discrimination] and not let them know that I know that that's what they are doing. . . .

When I face discrimination, first I take a long look at myself and try to determine whether or not I am seeing what I think I'm seeing in 1989, and if it's something that I have an option [about]. In other words, if I'm at a store making a purchase, I'll simply walk away from it. If it's at a restaurant where I'm not getting good service, I first of all let the people know that I'm not getting good service, then I [may] walk away from it. But the thing that I have to do is to let people know that I know that I'm being singled out for a separate treatment. And then I might react in any number of ways—depending on where I am and how badly I want whatever it is that I'm there for.

This commentary adds another dimension to our understanding of public discrimination, its cumulative aspect. Blacks confront not just isolated incidents—such as a bad room in a luxury hotel once every few years—but a lifelong series of such incidents. Here again the omnipresence of careful assessments is underscored. The dean's interview highlights a major difficulty in being black—one must be constantly prepared to assess accurately and then decide on the appropriate response. This long-look approach may indicate that some middle-class blacks are so sensitive to white charges of hypersensitivity and paranoia that they err in the opposite direction and fail to see discrimination when it occurs. In addition, as one black graduate student at a leading white university in the

Southeast put it: "I think that sometimes timely and appropriate responses to racially motivated acts and comments are lost due to the processing of the input." The "long look" can result in missed opportunities to respond to discrimination.

Using Middle-Class Resources for Protection

One advantage that middle-class blacks have over poorer blacks is the use of the resources of middle-class occupations. A professor at a major white university commented on the varying protection her middle-class status gives her at certain sites:

If I'm in those areas that are fairly protected, within gatherings of my own group, other African Americans, or if I'm in the university where my status as a professor mediates against the way I might be perceived, mediates against the hostile perception, then it's fairly comfortable. . . . When I divide my life into encounters with the outside world, and of course that's ninety percent of my life, it's fairly consistently unpleasant at those sites where there's nothing that mediates between my race and what I have to do. For example, if I'm in a grocery store, if I'm in my car, which is a 1970 Chevrolet, a real old ugly car, all those things—being in a grocery store in casual clothes, or being in the car—sort of advertises something that doesn't have anything to do with my status as far as people I run into are concerned.

Because I'm a large black woman, and I don't wear whatever class status I have, or whatever professional status [I have] in my appearance when I'm in the grocery store, I'm part of the mass of large black women shopping. For most whites, and even for some blacks, that translates into negative status. That means that they are free to treat me the way they treat most poor black people, because they can't tell by looking at me that I differ from that.

This professor notes the variation in discrimination in the sites through which she travels, from the most private to the most public. At home with friends she faces no problems, and at the university her professional status gives her some protection from discrimination. The increase in unpleasant encounters as she moves into public accommodations sites such as grocery stores is attributed to the absence of mediating factors such as clear symbols of middle-class status—displaying the middle-class symbols may provide some protection against discrimination in public places. . . .

Responses to Discrimination: The Street

Reacting to White Strangers

As we move away from public accommodations settings to the usually less protected street sites, racial hostility can become more fleeting and severer, and thus black responses are often restricted. The most serious form of street discrimination is violence. Often the reasonable black response to street discrimination is withdrawal, resigned acceptance, or a quick verbal retort. The difficulty of responding to violence is seen in this report by a man working for a media surveying firm in a southern industrial city:

> I was parked in front of this guy's house. . . . This guy puts his hands on the window and says, "Get out of the car, nigger." . . . So, I got out, and I thought, "Oh, this is what's going to happen here." And I'm talking fast. And they're, "What are you doing

here?" And I'm, "This is who I am. I work with these people. This is the man we want to put in the survey." And I pointed to the house. And the guy said, "Well you have an out-of-state license tag, right?" "Yea." And he said, "If something happened to you, your people at home wouldn't know for a long time, would they?" . . . I said, "Look, I deal with a company that deals with television. [If] something happens to me, it's going to be a national thing." . . . So, they grab me by the lapel of my coat, and put me in front of my car. They put the blade on my zipper. And now I'm thinking about this guy that's in the truck [behind me], because now I'm thinking that I'm going to have to run somewhere. Where am I going to run? Go to the police? [laughs] So, after a while they bash up my headlight. And I drove [away].

Stigmatized and physically attacked solely because of his color, this man faced verbal hostility and threats of death with courage. Cautiously drawing on his middle-class resources, he told the attackers his death would bring television crews to the town. This resource utilization is similar to that of the news director in the restaurant incident. Beyond this verbal threat his response had to be one of caution. For most whites threatened on the street, the police are a sought-after source of protection; this is often not the case. . . .

Responses to Discrimination by White Police Officers

Most middle-class blacks do not have such governmental authority as their personal protection. In fact, white police officers are a major problem. Encounters with the police can be life-threatening and thus limit the range of responses. A television commentator recounted two cases of police harassment when he was working for a survey firm in the mid-1980s. In one of the incidents, which took place in a southern metropolis, he was stopped by several white officers:

"What are you doing here?" I tell them what I'm doing here. . . . And so me spread on top of my car. [What had you done?] Because I was in the neighborhood, I left this note on these peoples' house: "Here's who I am. You weren't here, and I will come back in thirty minutes." [Why were they searching you?] They don't know. To me, they're searching, I remember at that particular moment when this all was going down, there was a lot of reports about police crime on civilians. . . . It took four cops to shake me down, two police cars, so they had me up there spread out. I had a friend of mine with me who was making the call with me, because we were going to have dinner together, and he was black, and they had me up, and they had him outside. . . . They said, "Well, let's check you out." . . . And I'm talking to myself, and I'm not thinking about being at attention, with my arms spread on my Ford [a company car], and I'm sitting there talking to myself, "Man, this is crazy, this is crazy."

[How are you feeling inside?] Scared. I mean real scared. [What did you think was going to happen to you?] I was going to go to jail. . . . Just because they picked me. Why would they stop me? It's like, if they can stop me, why wouldn't I go to jail, and I could sit there for ten days before the judge sees me. I'm thinking all this crazy stuff. . . . Again, I'm talking to myself. And the guy takes his stick. And he doesn't whack me hard, but he does

it with enough authority to let me know they mean business. "I told you stand still; now put your arms back out." And I've got this suit on, and the car's wet. And my friend's hysterical. He's outside the car. And they're checking him out. And he's like, "Man, just be cool, man." And he had tears in his eyes. And I'm like, oh, man, this is a nightmare. This is not supposed to happen to me. This is not my style! And so finally, this other cop comes up and says, "What have we got here Charlie?" "Oh, we've got a guy here. He's running through the neighborhood, and he doesn't want to do what we tell him. We might have to run him in." [You're "running through" the neighborhood?] Yeah, exactly, in a suit in the rain?! After they got through doing their thing and harassing me, I just said, "Man, this has been a hell of a week."

And I had tears in my eyes, but it wasn't tears of upset. It was tears of anger; it was tears of wanting to lash back. . . . What I thought to myself was, man, blacks have it real hard down here. I don't care if they're a broadcaster; I don't care if they're a businessman or a banker. . . . They don't have it any easier than the persons on skid row who get harassed by the police on a Friday or Saturday night.

It seems likely that most black men—including middle-class black men—see white police officers as a major source of danger and death. (See "Mood of Ghetto America" 1980, June 2, pp. 32–34; Roddy 1990, August 26.) Scattered evidence suggests that by the time they are in their twenties, most black males, regardless of socioeconomic status, have been stopped by the police because "blackness" is considered a sign of possible criminality by police officers (Moss 1990; Roddy 1990, August 26). This treatment probably marks a dramatic contrast with the experiences of young white middle-class males. In the incident above the respondent and a friend experienced severe police mal-treatment— detention for a lengthy period, threat of arrest, and the reality of physical violence. The coping response of the respondent was resigned acceptance somewhat similar to the deference rituals highlighted by Goffman. The middle-class suits and obvious corporate credentials (for example, survey questionnaires and company car) did not protect the two black men. The final comment suggests a disappointment that middle-class status brought no reprieve from police stigmatization and harassment. . . .

Conclusion

I have examined the sites of discrimination, the types of discriminatory acts, and the responses of the victims and have found the color stigma still to be very important in the public lives of affluent black Americans. The sites of racial discrimination range from relatively protected home sites, to less protected workplace and educational sites, to the even less protected public places. The 1964 Civil Rights Act guarantees that black Americans are "entitled to the full and equal enjoyment of the goods, services, facilities, privileges, advantages, and accommodations" in public accommodations. Yet the interviews indicate that deprivation of full enjoyment of public facilities is not a relic of the past: deprivation and discrimination in public accommodations persist. Middle-class black Americans remain vulnerable targets in public places. Prejudice-generated aggression in public places is, of course, not limited to black men and women—gay men and white women are also targets of street harassment (Benokraitis and Feagin 1986). Nonetheless, black women and men face an unusually broad range of discrimination on the street and in public accommodations.

The interviews highlight two significant aspects of the additive discrimination faced by black Americans in public places and elsewhere: (1) the cumulative character of an *individual's* experiences with discrimination; and (2) the *group's* accumulated historical experiences as perceived by the individual. A retired psychology professor who has worked in the Midwest and Southwest commented on the pyramiding of incidents:

> I don't think white people, generally, understand the full meaning of racist discriminatory behaviors directed toward Americans of African descent. They seem to see each act of discrimination or any act of violence as an "isolated" event. As a result, most white Americans cannot understand the strong reaction manifested by blacks when such events occur. They feel that blacks tend to "over-react." They forget that in most cases, we live lives of quiet desperation generated by a litany of *daily* large and small events that whether or not by design, remind us of our "place" in American society.

Particular instances of discrimination may seem minor to outside white observers when considered in isolation. But when blatant acts of avoidance, verbal harassment, and physical attack combine with subtle and covert slights, and these accumulate over months, years, and lifetimes, the impact on a black person is far more than the sum of the individual instances.

The historical context of contemporary discrimination was described by the retired psychologist, who argued that average white Americans

> . . . ignore the personal context of stimulus. That is, they deny the historical impact that a negative act may have

on an individual. "Nigger" to a white may simply be an epithet that should be ignored. To most blacks, the term brings into sharp and current focus all kinds of acts of racism—murder, rape, torture, denial of constitutional rights, insults, limited opportunity structure, economic problems, unequal justice under the law and a myriad of . . . other racist and discriminatory acts that occur daily in the lives of *most* Americans of African descent— including professional blacks.

Particular acts, even antilocution that might seem minor to white observers, are freighted not only with one's past experience of discrimination but also with centuries of racial discrimination directed at the entire group, vicarious oppression that still includes racially translated violence and denial of access to the American dream. Anti-black discrimination is a matter of racial-power inequality institutionalized in a variety of economic and social institutions over a long period of time. The microlevel events of public accommodations and public streets are not just rare and isolated encounters by individuals; they are recurring events reflecting an invasion of the microworld by the macroworld of historical racial subordination.

REFERENCES

ALLPORT, GORDON. 1958. *The Nature of Prejudice.* Abridged. New York: Doubleday Anchor Books.

BENOKRAITIS, NIJOLE, and JOE R. FEAGIN. 1986. *Modern Sexism: Blatant, Subtle and Covert Discrimination.* Englewood Cliffs, NJ: Prentice-Hall.

BLAUNER, BOB. 1989. *Black Lives, White Lives.* Berkeley: University of California Press.

BRITTAN, ARTHUR, and MARY MAYNARD. 1984. *Sexism, Racism and Oppression.* Oxford: Basil Blackwell.

DOYLE, BERTRAM W. 1937. *The Etiquette of Race Relations in the South.* Port Washington, NY: Kennikat Press.

FEAGIN, JOE R., and DOUGLAS ECKBERG. 1980. "Prejudice and Discrimination." *Annual Review of Sociology* 6:1–20.

FEAGIN, JOE R., and CLAIRECE BOOHER FEAGIN. 1986. *Discrimination American Style,* rev. ed. Melbourne, FL: Krieger.

GARDNER, CAROL BROOKS. 1980. "Passing By: Street Remarks, Address Rights, and the Urban Female." *Sociological Inquiry* 50:328–56.

———. 1988. "Access Information: Public Lies and Private Peril." *Social Problems* 35:384–97.

GOFFMAN, ERVING. 1956. "The Nature of Deference and Demeanor." *American Anthropologist* 58:473–502.

GRIFFIN, JOHN HOWARD. 1961. *Black Like Me.* Boston: Houghton Mifflin.

"The Mood of Ghetto America." 1980. *Newsweek,* 2 June, pp. 32–4.

MOSS, E. YVONNE. 1990. "African Americans and the Administration of Justice." Pp. 79–86 in *Assessment of the Status of African-Americans,* edited by Wornie L. Reed. Boston: University of Massachusetts, William Monroe Trotter Institute.

RAPER, ARTHUR F. 1933. *The Tragedy of Lynching.* Chapel Hill: University of North Carolina Press.

RODDY, DENNIS B. 1990. "Perceptions Still Segregate Police, Black Community." *The Pittsburgh Press,* 26 August, p. B1.

ROLLINS, JUDITH. 1985. *Between Women.* Philadelphia: Temple University Press.

WIESELTIER, LEON. 1989. "Scar Tissue." *New Republic,* 5 June, pp. 19–20.

16

SAVAGE INEQUALITIES

Jonathan Kozol

Questions to Consider

It is a core belief in the United States that every child has the right to a quality education. We also subscribe to the belief that education is the path to, intergenerational, upward mobility. In this reading, Jonathan Kozol compares schools in poor, overwhelmingly nonwhite communities and those in middle class, primarily white communities and finds that they are grossly and "savagely" unequal. Schools in poor neighborhoods lack basic supplies and are dirty and overcrowded, while schools located in affluent suburbs have the newest textbooks, up-to-date libraries, advanced placement classes, and small student-to-teacher ratios. How do race, class, schooling, and the potential for upward socioeconomic mobility intersect in Kozol's study?

"In a country where there is no distinction of class," Lord Acton wrote of the United States 130 years ago, "a child is not born to the station of its parents, but with an indefinite claim to all the prizes that can be won by thought and labor. It is in conformity with the theory of equality . . . to give as near as possible to every youth an equal stake in life."[1] Americans, he said, "are unwilling that any should be deprived in childhood of the means of competition."

It is hard to read these words today without a sense of irony and sadness. Denial of "the means of competition" is perhaps the single most consistent outcome of the education offered to poor children in the schools of our large cities; and nowhere is this pattern of denial more explicit or more absolute than in the public schools of New York City.

Average expenditures per pupil in the city of New York in 1987 were some $5,500. In the highest spending suburbs of New York (Great Neck or Manhasset, for example, on Long Island) funding levels rose above $11,000, with the highest districts in the state at $15,000.[2] "Why . . .", asks the city's Board of Education, "should our students receive less" than do "similar students" who live elsewhere? "The inequity is clear."[3]

But the inequality to which these words refer goes even further than the school board may be eager to reveal. "It is perhaps the supreme irony," says the nonprofit Community Service Society of New York, that "the same Board of Education which perceives so clearly the inequities" of funding between separate towns and cities "is perpetuating similar inequities" right in New

York. And, in comment on the Board of Education's final statement—"the inequity is clear"—the CSS observes, "New York City's poorest . . . districts could adopt that eloquent statement with few changes."

New York City's public schools are subdivided into 32 school districts. District 10 encompasses a large part of the Bronx but is, effectively, two separate districts. One of these districts, Riverdale, is in the northwest section of the Bronx. Home to many of the city's most sophisticated and well-educated families, its elementary schools have relatively few low-income students. The other section, to the south and east, is poor and heavily nonwhite.

The contrast between public schools in each of these two neighborhoods is obvious to any visitor. At Public School 24 in Riverdale, the principal speaks enthusiastically of his teaching staff. At Public School 79, serving poorer children to the south, the principal says that he is forced to take the "tenth-best" teachers. "I thank God they're still breathing," he remarks of those from whom he must select his teachers.

Some years ago, District 10 received an allocation for computers. The local board decided to give each elementary school an equal number of computers, even though the schools in Riverdale had smaller classes and far fewer students. When it was pointed out that schools in Riverdale, as a result, had twice the number of computers in proportion to their student populations as the schools in the poor neighborhoods, the chairman of the local board replied, "What is fair is what is determined . . . to be fair."

The superintendent of District 10, Fred Goldberg, tells *The New York Times* that "every effort" is made "to distribute resources equitably." He speculates that some gap might exist because some of the poorer schools need to use funds earmarked for computers to buy basic supplies like pens and paper. Asked about the differences in

teachers noted by the principals, he says there are no differences, then adds that next year he'll begin a program to improve the quality of teachers in the poorer schools. Questioned about differences in physical appearances between the richer and the poorer schools, he says, "I think it's demographics."[4]

Sometimes a school principal, whatever his background or his politics, looks into the faces of the children in his school and offers a disarming statement that cuts through official ambiguity. "These are the kids most in need," says Edward Flanery, the principal of one of the low-income schools, "and they get the worst teachers." For children of diverse needs in his overcrowded rooms, he says, "you need an outstanding teacher. And what do you get? You get the worst."

In order to find Public School 261 in District 10, a visitor is told to look for a mortician's office. The funeral home, which faces Jerome Avenue in the North Bronx, is easy to identify by its green awning. The school is next door, in a former roller-skating rink. No sign identifies the building as a school. A metal awning frame without an awning supports a flagpole, but there is no flag.

In the street in front of the school there is an elevated public transit line. Heavy traffic fills the street. The existence of the school is virtually concealed within this crowded city block.

In a vestibule between the outer and inner glass doors of the school there is a sign with these words: "All children are capable of learning."

Beyond the inner doors a guard is seated. The lobby is long and narrow. The ceiling is low. There are no windows. All the teachers that I see at first are middle-aged white women. The principal, who is also a white woman, tells me that the school's "capacity" is 900 but that there are 1,300 children here. The size of classes for fifth and sixth grade children in New York, she says, is "capped" at 32, but she says that class size in the school goes "up to 34." (I later see classes, however, as large as 37.) Classes for younger children, she goes on, are "capped at 25," but a school can go above this limit if it puts an extra adult in the room. Lack of space, she says, prevents the school from operating a pre-kindergarten program.

I ask the principal where her children go to school. They are enrolled in private school, she says.

"Lunchtime is a challenge for us," she explains. "Limited space obliges us to do it in three shifts, 450 children at a time."

Textbooks are scarce and children have to share their social studies books. The principal says there is one full-time pupil counselor and another who is here two days a week: a ratio of 930 children to one counselor. The carpets are patched and sometimes taped together to conceal an open space. "I could use some new rugs," she observes.

To make up for the building's lack of windows and the crowded feeling that results, the staff puts plants and fish tanks in the corridors. Some of the plants are flourishing. Two boys, released from class, are in a corridor beside a tank, their noses pressed against the glass. A school of pinkish fish inside the tank are darting back and forth. Farther down the corridor a small Hispanic girl is watering the plants.

Two first grade classes share a single room without a window, divided only by a blackboard. Four kindergartens and a sixth grade class of Spanish-speaking children have been packed into a single room in which, again, there is no window. A second grade bilingual class of 37 children has its own room but again there is no window.

By eleven o'clock, the lunchroom is already packed with appetite and life. The kids line up to get their meals, then eat them in ten minutes. After that, with no place they

can go to play, they sit and wait until it's time to line up and go back to class.

On the second floor I visit four classes taking place within another undivided space. The room has a low ceiling. File cabinets and movable blackboards give a small degree of isolation to each class. Again, there are no windows.

The library is a tiny, windowless and claustrophobic room. I count approximately 700 books. Seeing no reference books, I ask a teacher if encyclopedias and other reference books are kept in classrooms.

"We don't have encyclopedias in classrooms," she replies. "That is for the suburbs."

The school, I am told, has 26 computers for its 1,300 children. There is one small gym and children get one period, and sometimes two, each week. Recess, however, is not possible because there is no playground. "Head Start," the principal says, "scarcely exists in District 10. We have no space."

The school, I am told, is 90 percent black and Hispanic; the other 10 percent are Asian, white or Middle Eastern.

In a sixth grade social studies class the walls are bare of words or decorations. There seems to be no ventilation system, or, if one exists, it isn't working.

The class discusses the Nile River and the Fertile Crescent.

The teacher, in a droning voice: "How is it useful that these civilizations developed close to rivers?"

A child, in a good loud voice: "What kind of question is that?"

In my notes I find these words: "An uncomfortable feeling—being in a building with no windows. There are metal ducts across the room. Do they give air? I feel asphyxiated. . . ."

On the top floor of the school, a sixth grade of 30 children shares a room with 29 bilingual second graders. Because of the high class size there is an assistant with each teacher. This means that 59 children and four grown-ups—63 in all—must share a room that, in a suburban school, would hold no more than 20 children and one teacher. There are, at least, some outside windows in this room—it is the only room with windows in the school—and the room has a high ceiling. It is a relief to see some daylight.

I return to see the kindergarten classes on the ground floor and feel stifled once again by lack of air and the low ceiling. Nearly 120 children and adults are doing what they can to make the best of things: 80 children in four kindergarten classes, 30 children in the sixth grade class, and about eight grown-ups who are aides and teachers. The kindergarten children sitting on the worn rug, which is patched with tape, look up at me and turn their heads to follow me as I walk past them.

As I leave the school, a sixth grade teacher stops to talk. I ask her, "Is there air conditioning in warmer weather?"

Teachers, while inside the building, are reluctant to give answers to this kind of question. Outside, on the sidewalk, she is less constrained: "I had an awful room last year. In the winter it was 56 degrees. In the summer it was up to 90. It was sweltering."

I ask her, "Do the children ever comment on the building?"

"They don't say," she answers, "but they know."

I ask her if they see it as a racial message.

"All these children see TV," she says. "They know what suburban schools are like. Then they look around them at their school. This was a roller-rink, you know. . . . They don't comment on it but you see it in their eyes. They understand."

On the following morning I visit P.S. 79, another elementary school in the same district. "We work under difficult circumstances," says the principal, James Carter, who is black. "The school was built to hold one thousand students. We have 1,550. We are badly overcrowded. We need smaller classes but, to do this, we would need more space. I can't add five teachers. I would have no place to put them."

Some experts, I observe, believe that class size isn't a real issue. He dismisses this abruptly. "It doesn't take a genius to discover that you learn more in a smaller class. I have to bus some 60 kindergarten children elsewhere, since I have no space for them. When they return next year, where do I put them?

"I can't set up a computer lab. I have no room. I had to put a class into the library. I have no librarian. There are two gymnasiums upstairs but they cannot be used for sports. We hold more classes there. It's unfair to measure us against the suburbs. They have 17 to 20 children in a class. Average class size in this school is 30.

"The school is 29 percent black, 70 percent Hispanic. Few of these kids get Head Start. There is no space in the district. Of 200 kindergarten children, 50 maybe get some kind of preschool."

I ask him how much difference preschool makes.

"Those who get it do appreciably better. I can't overestimate its impact but, as I have said, we have no space."

The school tracks children by ability, he says. "There are five to seven levels in each grade. The highest level is equivalent to 'gifted' but it's not a full-scale gifted program. We don't have the funds. We have no science room. The science teachers carry their equipment with them."

We sit and talk within the nurse's room. The window is broken. There are two holes in the ceiling. About a quarter of the ceiling has been patched and covered with a plastic garbage bag.

"Ideal class size for these kids would be 15 to 20. Will these children ever get what white kids in the suburbs take for granted?

I don't think so. If you ask me why, I'd have to speak of race and social class. I don't think the powers that be in New York City understand, or want to understand, that if they do not give these children a sufficient education to lead healthy and productive lives, we will be their victims later on. We'll pay the price someday—in violence, in economic costs. I despair of making this appeal in any terms but these. You cannot issue an appeal to conscience in New York today. The fair-play argument won't be accepted. So you speak of violence and hope that it will scare the city into action."

While we talk, three children who look six or seven years old come to the door and ask to see the nurse, who isn't in the school today. One of the children, a Puerto Rican girl, looks haggard. "I have a pain in my tooth," she says. The principal says, "The nurse is out. Why don't you call your mother?" The child says, "My mother doesn't have a phone." The principal sighs. "Then go back to your class." When she leaves, the principal is angry. "It's amazing to me that these children ever make it with the obstacles they face. Many *do* care and they *do* try, but there's a feeling of despair. The parents of these children want the same things for their children that the parents in the suburbs want. Drugs are not the cause of this. They are the symptom. Nonetheless, they're used by people in the suburbs and rich people in Manhattan as another reason to keep children of poor people at a distance."

I ask him, "Will white children and black children ever go to school together in New York?"

"I don't see it," he replies. "I just don't think it's going to happen. It's a dream. I simply do not see white folks in Riverdale agreeing to cross-bus with kids like these. A few, maybe. Very few. I don't think I'll live to see it happen."

I ask him whether race is the decisive factor. Many experts, I observe, believe that wealth is more important in determining these inequalities.

"This," he says—and sweeps his hand around him at the room, the garbage bag, the ceiling—"would not happen to white children."

In a kindergarten class the children sit cross-legged on a carpet in a space between two walls of books. Their 26 faces are turned up to watch their teacher, an elderly black woman. A little boy who sits beside me is involved in trying to tie bows in his shoelaces. The children sing a song: "Lift Every Voice." On the wall are these handwritten words: "Beautiful, also, are the souls of my people."

In a very small room on the fourth floor, 52 people in two classes do their best to teach and learn. Both are first grade classes. One, I am informed, is "low ability." The other is bilingual.

"The room is barely large enough for one class," says the principal.

The room is 25 by 50 feet. There are 26 first graders and two adults on the left, 22 others and two adults on the right. On the wall there is the picture of a small white child, circled by a Valentine, and a Gainsborough painting of a child in a formal dress.

"We are handicapped by scarcity," one of the teachers says. "One fifth of these children may be at grade level by the year's end."

A boy who may be seven years old climbs on my lap without an invitation and removes my glasses. He studies my face and runs his fingers through my hair. "You have nice hair," he says. I ask him where he lives and he replies, "Times Square Hotel," which is a homeless shelter in Manhattan.

I ask him how he gets here.

"With my father. On the train," he says.

"How long does it take?"

"It takes an hour and a half."

I ask him when he leaves his home.

"My mother wakes me up at five o'clock."

"When do you leave?"

"Six-thirty."

I ask him how he gets back to Times Square.

"My father comes to get me after school."

From my notes: "He rides the train three hours every day in order to attend this segregated school. It would be a shorter ride to Riverdale. There are rapid shuttle-vans that make that trip in only 20 minutes. Why not let him go to school right in Manhattan, for that matter?"

At three o'clock the nurse arrives to do her recordkeeping. She tells me she is here three days a week. "The public hospital we use for an emergency is called North Central. It's not a hospital that I will use if I am given any choice. Clinics in the private hospitals are far more likely to be staffed by an experienced physician."

She hesitates a bit as I take out my pen, but then goes on: "I'll give you an example. A little girl I saw last week in school was trembling and shaking and could not control the motions of her arms. I was concerned and called her home. Her mother came right up to school and took her to North Central. The intern concluded that the child was upset by 'family matters'—nothing more—that there was nothing wrong with her. The mother was offended by the diagnosis. She did not appreciate his words or his assumptions. The truth is, there was nothing wrong at home. She brought the child back to school. I thought that she was ill. I told her mother, 'Go to Montefiore.' It's a private hospital, and well respected. She took my advice, thank God. It turned out that the child had a neurological disorder. She is now in treatment.

"This is the kind of thing our children face. Am I saying that the city underserves this population? You can draw your own conclusions."

Out on the street, it takes a full half hour to flag down a cab. Taxi drivers in New York are sometimes disconcertingly direct in what they say. When they are contemptuous of poor black people, their contempt is unadorned. When they're sympathetic and compassionate, their observations often go right to the heart of things. "Oh . . . they neglect these children," says the driver. "They leave them in the streets and slums to live and die." We stop at a light. Outside the window of the taxi, aimless men are standing in a semicircle while another man is working on his car. Old four-story buildings with their windows boarded, cracked or missing are on every side.

I ask the driver where he's from. He says Afghanistan. Turning in his seat, he gestures at the street and shrugs. "If you don't, as an American, begin to give these kids the kind of education that you give the kids of Donald Trump, you're asking for disaster."

Two months later, on a day in May, I visit an elementary school in Riverdale. The dogwoods and magnolias on the lawn in front of P.S. 24 are in full blossom on the day I visit. There is a well-tended park across the street, another larger park three blocks away. To the left of the school is a playground for small children, with an innovative jungle gym, a slide and several climbing toys. Behind the school there are two playing fields for older kids. The grass around the school is neatly trimmed.

The neighborhood around the school, by no means the richest part of Riverdale, is nonetheless expensive and quite beautiful. Residences in the area—some of which are large, free-standing houses, others condominiums in solid red-brick buildings—sell for prices in the region of $400,000; but some of the larger Tudor houses on the winding and tree-shaded streets close to the school can cost up to $1 million. The excellence of P.S. 24, according to the principal, adds to the value of these homes. Advertisements in *The New York Times* will frequently inform prospective buyers that a house is "in the neighborhood of P.S. 24."

The school serves 825 children in the kindergarten through sixth grade. This is approximately half the student population crowded into P.S. 79, where 1,550 children fill a space intended for 1,000, and a great deal smaller than the 1,300 children packed into the former skating rink; but the principal of P.S. 24, a capable and energetic man named David Rothstein, still regards it as excessive for an elementary school.

The school is integrated in the strict sense that the middle- and upper-middle-class white children here do occupy a building that contains some Asian and Hispanic and black children; but there is little integration in the classrooms since the vast majority of the Hispanic and black children are assigned to "special" classes on the basis of evaluations that have classified them "EMR"—"educable mentally retarded"—or else, in the worst of cases, "TMR"—"trainable mentally retarded."

I ask the principal if any of his students qualify for free-lunch programs. "About 130 do," he says. "Perhaps another 35 receive their lunches at reduced price. Most of these kids are in the special classes. They do not come from this neighborhood."

The very few nonwhite children that one sees in mainstream classes tend to be Japanese or else of other Asian origins. Riverdale, I learn, has been the residence of choice for many years to members of the diplomatic corps.

The school therefore contains effectively two separate schools: one of about 130 children, most of whom are poor, Hispanic, black, assigned to one of the 12 special classes; the other of some 700 mainstream students, almost all of whom are white or Asian.

There is a third track also—this one for the students who are labeled "talented" or "gifted." This is termed a "pull-out" program since the children who are so identified remain in mainstream classrooms but are taken out for certain periods each week to be provided with intensive and, in my opinion, excellent instruction in some areas of reasoning and logic often known as "higher-order skills" in the contemporary jargon of the public schools. Children identified as "gifted" are admitted to this program in first grade and, in most cases, will remain there for six years. Even here, however, there are two tracks of the gifted. The regular gifted classes are provided with only one semester of this specialized instruction yearly. Those very few children, on the other hand, who are identified as showing the most promise are assigned, beginning in the third grade, to a program that receives a full-year regimen.

In one such class, containing ten intensely verbal and impressive fourth grade children, nine are white and one is Asian. The "special" class I enter first, by way of contrast, has twelve children of whom only one is white and none is Asian. These racial breakdowns prove to be predictive of the schoolwide pattern.

In a classroom for the gifted on the first floor of the school, I ask a child what the class is doing. "Logic and syllogisms," she replies. The room is fitted with a planetarium. The principal says that all the elementary schools in District 10 were given the same planetarium ten years ago but that certain schools, because of overcrowding, have been forced to give them up. At P.S. 261, according to my notes, there was a domelike space that had been built to hold a planetarium, but the planetarium had been removed to free up space for the small library collection. P.S. 24, in contrast, has a spacious library that holds almost 8,000 books. The windows are decorated with attractive, brightly colored curtains and look out on flowering trees. The principal says that it's inadequate, but it appears spectacular to me after the cubicle that holds a meager 700 books within the former skating rink.

The district can't afford librarians, the principal says, but P.S. 24, unlike the poorer schools of District 10, can draw on educated parent volunteers who staff the room in shifts three days a week. A parent organization also raises independent funds to buy materials, including books, and will soon be running a fund-raiser to enhance the library's collection.

In a large and sunny first grade classroom that I enter next, I see 23 children, all of whom are white or Asian. In another first grade, there are 22 white children and two others who are Japanese. There is a computer in each class. Every classroom also has a modern fitted sink.

In a second grade class of 22 children, there are two black children and three Asian children. Again, there is a sink and a computer. A sixth grade social studies class has only one black child. The children have an in-class research area that holds some up-to-date resources. A set of encyclopedias (World Book, 1985) is in a rack beside a window. The children are doing a Spanish language lesson when I enter. Foreign languages begin in sixth grade at the school, but Spanish is offered also to the kindergarten children. As in every room at P.S. 24, the window shades are clean and new, the floor is neatly tiled in gray and green, and there is not a single light bulb missing.

Walking next into a special class, I see twelve children. One is white. Eleven are black. There are no Asian children. The room is half the size of mainstream classrooms. "Because of overcrowding," says the principal, "we have had to split these rooms in half." There is no computer and no sink.

I enter another special class. Of seven children, five are black, one is Hispanic, one is white. A little black boy with a large head sits in the far corner and is gazing at the ceiling.

"Placement of these kids," the principal explains, "can usually be traced to neurological damage."

In my notes: "How could so many of these children be brain-damaged?"

Next door to the special class is a woodworking shop. "This shop is only for the special classes," says the principal. The children learn to punch in time cards at the door, he says, in order to prepare them for employment.

The fourth grade gifted class, in which I spend the last part of the day, is humming with excitement. "I start with these children in the first grade," says the teacher. "We pull them out of mainstream classes on the basis of their test results and other factors such as the opinion of their teachers. Out of this group, beginning in third grade, I pull out the ones who show the most potential and they enter classes such as this one."

The curriculum they follow, she explains, "emphasizes critical thinking, reasoning and logic." The planetarium, for instance, is employed not simply for the study of the universe as it exists. "Children also are designing their own galaxies," the teacher says.

A little girl sitting around a table with her classmates speaks with perfect poise: "My name is Susan. We are in the fourth grade gifted program."

I ask them what they're doing and a child says, "My name is Laurie and we're doing problem-solving."

A rather tall, good-natured boy who is half-standing at the table tells me that his name is David. "One thing that we do," he says, "is logical thinking. Some problems, we find, have more than one good answer. We need to learn not simply to be logical in our own thinking but to show respect for someone else's logic even when an answer may be technically incorrect."

When I ask him to explain this, he goes on, "A person who gives an answer that is not 'correct' may nonetheless have done some interesting thinking that we should examine. 'Wrong' answers may be more useful to examine than correct ones."

I ask the children if reasoning and logic are innate or if they're things that you can learn.

"You know some things to start with when you enter school," Susan says. "But we also learn some things that other children don't."

I ask her to explain this.

"We know certain things that other kids don't know because we're *taught* them."

She has braces on her teeth. Her long brown hair falls almost to her waist. Her loose white T-shirt has the word TRI-LOGIC on the front. She tells me that Tri-Logic is her father's firm.

Laurie elaborates on the same point: "Some things you know. Some kinds of logic are inside of you to start with. There are other things that someone needs to teach you."

David expands on what the other two have said: "Everyone can think and speak in logical ways unless they have a mental problem. What this program does is bring us to a higher form of logic."

The class is writing a new "Bill of Rights." The children already know the U.S. Bill of Rights and they explain its first four items to me with precision. What they are examining today, they tell me, is the very *concept* of a "right." Then they will create their own compendium of rights according to their own analysis and definition. Along one wall of the classroom, opposite the planetarium, are seven Apple II computers on which children have developed rather subtle color animations that express the themes—of greed and domination, for example—that they also have described in writing.

"This is an upwardly mobile group," the teacher later says. "They have exposure to whatever New York City has available.

Their parents may take them to the theater, to museums. . . ."

In my notes: "Six girls, four boys. Nine white, one Chinese. I am glad they have this class. But what about the others? Aren't there ten black children in the school who could enjoy this also?"

The teacher gives me a newspaper written, edited and computer-printed by her sixth grade gifted class. The children, she tells me, are provided with a link to kids in Europe for transmission of news stories.

A science story by one student asks if scientists have ever falsified their research. "Gregor Mendel," the sixth grader writes, "the Austrian monk who founded the science of genetics, published papers on his work with peas that some experts say were statistically too good to be true. Isaac Newton, who formulated the law of gravitation, relied on unseemly mathematical sleight of hand in his calculations. . . . Galileo Galilei, founder of modern scientific method, wrote about experiments that were so difficult to duplicate that colleagues doubted he had done them."

Another item in the paper, also by a sixth grade student, is less esoteric: "The Don Cossacks dance company, from Russia, is visiting the United States. The last time it toured America was 1976. . . . The Don Cossacks will be in New York City for two weeks at the Neil Simon Theater. Don't miss it!"

The tone is breezy—and so confident! That phrase—"Don't miss it!"—speaks a volume about life in Riverdale.

"What makes a good school?" asks the principal when we are talking later on. "The building and teachers are part of it, of course. But it isn't just the building and the teachers. Our kids come from good families and the neighborhood is good. In a three-block area we have a public library, a park, a junior high. . . . Our typical sixth grader reads at eighth grade level." In a quieter voice he says, "I see how hard my colleagues work in schools like P.S. 79. You have children in those neighborhoods who live in virtual hell. They enter school five years behind. What do they get?" Then, as he spreads his hands out on his desk, he says: "I have to ask myself why there should be an elementary school in District 10 with fifteen hundred children. Why should there be an elementary school within a skating rink? Why should the Board of Ed allow this? This is not the way that things should be."

Stark as the inequities in District 10 appear, educators say that they are "mild" in comparison to other situations in the city. Some of the most stunning inequality, according to a report by the Community Service Society, derives from allocations granted by state legislators to school districts where they have political allies. The poorest districts in the city get approximately 90 cents per pupil from these legislative grants, while the richest districts have been given $14 for each pupil.

Newspapers in New York City have reported other instances of the misallocation of resources. "The Board of Education," wrote the *New York Post* during July of 1987, "was hit with bombshell charges yesterday that money earmarked for fighting drug abuse and illiteracy in ghetto schools was funneled instead to schools in wealthy areas."

In receipt of extra legislative funds, according to the *Post,* affluent districts were funded "at a rate 14 times greater than low-income districts." The paper said the city's poorest areas were underfunded "with stunning consistency."

The report by the Community Service Society cites an official of the New York City Board of Education who remarks that there is "no point" in putting further money "into some poor districts" because, in his belief, "new teachers would not stay

there." But the report observes that, in an instance where beginning teacher salaries were raised by nearly half, "that problem largely disappeared"—another interesting reminder of the difference money makes when we are willing to invest it. Nonetheless, says the report, "the perception that the poorest districts are beyond help still remains. . . ." Perhaps the worst result of such beliefs, says the report, is the message that resources would be "wasted on poor children." This message "trickles down to districts, schools, and classrooms." Children hear and understand this theme—they are poor investments—and behave accordingly. If society's resources would be wasted on their destinies, perhaps their own determination would be wasted too. "Expectations are a powerful force . . . ," the CSS observes.

Despite the evidence, the CSS report leans over backwards not to fuel the flames of racial indignation. "In the present climate," the report says, "suggestions of racism must be made with caution. However, it is inescapable that these inequities are being perpetrated on [school] districts which are virtually all black and Hispanic. . . ." While the report says, very carefully, that there is no "evidence" of "deliberate individual discrimination," it nonetheless concludes that "those who allocate resources make decisions over and over again which penalize the poorest districts." Analysis of city policy, the study says, "speaks to systemic bias which constitutes a conspiracy of effect. . . . Whether consciously or not, the system writes off its poorest students." [5]

NOTES

1. Lord Acton cited: George Alan Hickrod, "Reply to the 'Forbes' Article," *Journal of School Finance* 12 (1987).
2. Per-pupil spending, New York City and suburbs: Office for Policy Analysis and Program

Accountability, New York State Board of Education, "Statistical Profiles of School Districts" (Albany: 1 January 1989). Numbers cited are for 1986–1987 school year.

3. Question asked by New York City Board of Education and response of Community Service Society: Community Service Society of New York, "Promoting Poverty: The Shift of Resources Away from Low-Income New York City School Districts" (New York: 1987).

4. Contrasts between Schools in District 10, statements of principals and superintendent: *The New York Times,* January 2, 1987. District 10 Superintendent Fred Goldberg resigned under pressure in 1991. A highly respected veteran of the New York City public schools, he struck me, in the course of an April 1990 interview, as an enlightened educator caught up in a compromising situation that was not of his own making. Educators in New York believe that he was made to pay an unfair price for the profound racism rooted in the city's public schools.

5. Inequities in New York City Schools: *The New York Times,* 2 July 1987; *New York Post,* 2 July 1987; *The* (New York) *City Sun,* 15–21 July 1987; "Promoting Poverty" (Community Service Society of New York), cited above.

17

POSITIVE FUNCTIONS OF THE UNDESERVING POOR
Uses of the Underclass in America

Herbert J. Gans

Questions to Consider

Herbert Gans asks us to think about poverty in a unique and troubling way. All of us benefit in one way or another by having a large, disposable population that does society's dirty work. After reading Gans's article, ask yourself how you benefit, both economically and emotionally, from having a large poor population in the United States. How are poverty and which racial groups are more likely to do society's onerous tasks linked? Take an inventory of the race and ethnicity of individuals who do most of America's dirty, dangerous, and demeaning work. What is their racial background?

I. Introduction

Poverty, like any other social phenomenon, can be analyzed in terms of the *causes* which initiate and perpetuate it, but once it exists, it can also be studied in terms of the consequences or *functions* which follow. These functions can be both *positive* and *negative*, adaptive and destructive, depending on their nature and the people and interests affected.

Poverty has many negative functions (or dysfunctions), most for the poor themselves, but also for the nonpoor. Among those of most concern to both populations, perhaps the major one is that a small but visible proportion of poor people is involved in activities which threaten their physical safety, for example street crime, or which deviate from important norms claimed to be "mainstream," such as failing to work, bearing children in adolescence and out of wedlock, and being "dependent" on welfare. In times of high unemployment, illegal and even legal immigrants are added to this list for endangering the job opportunities of native-born Americans.

Furthermore, many better-off Americans believe that the number of poor people who behave in these ways is far larger than it actually is. More important, many think that poor people act as they do because of moral shortcomings that express themselves in lawlessness or in the rejection of mainstream norms. Like many other sociologists, however, I argue that the behavior patterns which concern the more fortunate classes are *poverty-related*, because they are, and have historically been, associated with poverty. After all, mugging is only practiced by the poor. They are in fact caused by poverty, although a variety of other causes must also be at work since most poor people are not involved in any of these activities, including mugging.

Because their criminal or disapproved behavior is ascribed to moral shortcomings, the poor people who resort to it are often classified as unworthy or *undeserving*. For example, even though the failure of poor young men (or women) to work may be the effect of a lack of jobs, they are frequently accused of laziness, and then judged undeserving. Likewise, even though poor young mothers may decide not to marry the fathers of their chil-

Herbert Gans, "Positive Functions of the Undeserving Poor" from *Politics & Society,* Vol. 22, No. 3, September 1994, pp. 269–283. Copyright © 1994 by Sage Publications, Inc. Reprinted by permission of Sage Publications, Inc.

dren, because they, being jobless, cannot support them, the women are still accused of violating conventional familial norms, and also judged undeserving. Moreover, once judged to be undeserving, poor people are then no longer thought to be deserving of public aid that is financially sufficient and secure enough to help them escape poverty.

Judgments of the poor as undeserving are not based on evidence, but derive from a stereotype, even if, like most others, it is a stereotype with a "kernel of truth" (e.g., the monopolization of street crime by the poor). Furthermore, it is a very old stereotype; Cicero already described the needy of Rome as criminals.[1] By the middle of the sixteenth century, complicated laws to distinguish between the deserving and undeserving were in existence.[2] However, the term *undeserving poor* was first used regularly in England in the 1830s, at the time of the institution of the Poor Law.[3]

In America, a series of other, more specific, terms were borrowed or invented, with new ones replacing old ones as conditions and fashions changed.[4] Such terms have included *beggar, pauper,* the *dangerous class, rabble, vagabond* and *vagrant,* and so on, which the United States borrowed from Europe. America also invented its own terms, including *shiftless, tramp,* and *feeble-minded,* and in the late twentieth century, terms like *hardcore, drifter, culturally deprived*—and most recently, *underclass.*[5] Nonetheless, in terms of its popular uses and the people to whom it is applied, the term *underclass* differs little from its predecessors.[6]

It is not difficult to understand why people, poor and more fortunate, are fearful of street crime committed by poor people, and even why the jobless poor and welfare recipients, like paupers before them, may be perceived as economic threats for not working and drawing on public funds, at least in bad economic times. Also, one can understand why other forms of poverty-related behavior, such as the early sexual activity of poor youngsters and the dramatic number of poor single-parent families, are viewed as moral threats, since they violate norms thought to uphold the two-parent nuclear family and related normative bases of the social order. However, there would seem to be no inherent reason for exaggerating these threats, for example, in the case of welfare recipients who obtain only a tiny proportion of governmental expenditures, or more generally, by stereotyping poor people as undeserving without evidence of what they have and have not done, and why.

One reason, if not the only one, for the exaggeration and the stereotyping, and for the continued attractiveness of the concept of the undeserving poor itself, is that undeservingness has a number of *positive* functions for the better-off population. Some of these functions, or uses, are positive for everyone who is not poor, but most are positive only for some people, interest groups, and institutions, ranging from moderate income to wealthy ones. Needless to say, that undeservingness has uses for some people does not justify it; the existence of functions just helps to explain why it persists.

My notion of function, or empirically observable adaptive consequence, is adapted from the classic conceptual scheme of Robert K. Merton.[7] My analysis will concentrate on those positive functions which Merton conceptualized as *latent*, which are unrecognized and/or unintended, but with the proviso that the functions which are identified as latent would probably not be abolished once they were widely recognized. Positive functions are, after all, also benefits, and people are not necessarily ready to give up benefits, including unintended ones, even if they become aware of them.[8]

The rest of this article deals only with the functions of the poor labeled undeserving. It can also be read as a sequel to an earlier article, in which I analyzed the positive functions

of poverty without distinguishing between the deserving and undeserving poor.[9]

II. Functions of the Undeserving Poor[10]

I will discuss five sets of positive functions: microsocial, economic, normative-cultural, political, and macrosocial, which I divide into 13 specific functions, although the sets are arbitrarily chosen and interrelated, and I could add many more functions. The funtions are not listed in order of importance, for such a listing is not possible without empirical research on the various beneficiaries of undeservingness.

Two Microsocial Functions

1. *Risk reduction.* Perhaps the primary use of the idea of the undeserving poor, primary because it takes place at the microsocial scale of everyday life, is that it distances the labeled from those who label them. By stigmatizing people as undeserving, labelers protect themselves from the responsibility of having to associate with them, or even to treat them like moral equals, which reduces the risk of being hurt or angered by them. Risk reduction is a way of dealing with actual or imagined threats to physical safety, for example from people who might be muggers, or cultural threats attributed to poor youngsters or normative ones imagined to come from welfare recipients. All pejorative labels and stereotypes serve this function, which may help to explain why there are so many such labels.

2. *Scapegoating and displacement.* By being thought undeserving, the stigmatized poor can be blamed for virtually any shortcoming of everyday life which can be credibly ascribed to them—violations of the laws of logic or social causation notwithstanding. Faulting the undeserving poor can also sup-

port the desire for revenge and punishment. In a society in which punishment is reserved for legislative, judicial, and penal institutions, *feelings* of revenge and punitiveness toward the undeserving poor supply at least some emotional satisfaction.

Since labeling poor people undeserving opens the door for nearly unlimited scapegoating, the labeled are also available to serve what I call the displacement function. Being too weak to object, the stigmatized poor can be accused of having caused social problems which they did not actually cause and can serve as cathartic objects on which better-off people can unload their own problems, as well as those of the economy, the polity, or of any other institution, for the shortcomings of which the poor can be blamed.

Whether societywide changes in the work ethic are displaced on to "shiftlessness," or economic stagnation on to "welfare dependency," the poor can be declared undeserving for what ails the more affluent. This may also help to explain why the national concern with poor Black unmarried mothers, although usually ascribed to the data presented in the 1965 Moynihan Report, did not gather steam until the beginning of the decline of the economy in the mid-1970s. Similarly, the furor about poor "babies having babies" waited for the awareness of rising adolescent sexual activity among the better-off classes in the 1980s—at which point rates of adolescent pregnancy among the poor had already declined. But when the country became ambivalent about the desirability of abortions, the issue was displaced on the poor by making it almost impossible for them to obtain abortions.

Many years ago, James Baldwin, writing in *The Fire Next Time,* illustrated the displacement function in racial terms, arguing that, as Andrew Hacker put it, Whites "need the 'nigger' because it is the 'nigger' within themselves that they cannot tolerate. Whatever it is that Whites feel 'nigger' sig-

nifies about Blacks—lust and laziness, stupidity or squalor—in fact exists within themselves. . . . By creating such a creature, Whites are able to say that because only members of the Black race can carry that taint, it follows that none of its attributes will be found in White people."[11]

Three Economic Functions

3. *Economic banishment and the reserve army of labor.* People who have successfully been labeled as undeserving can be banished from the formal labor market. If young people are designated "school dropouts," for example, they can also be thought to lack the needed work habits, such as proper adherence to the work ethic, and may not be offered jobs to begin with. Often, they are effectively banished from the labor market before entering it because employers imagine them to be poor workers simply because they are young, male, and Black.[12] Many ex-convicts are declared unemployable in similar fashion, and some become recidivists because they have no other choice but to go back to their criminal occupations.

Banishing the undeserving also makes room for immigrant workers, who may work for lower wages, are more deferential, and are more easily exploitable by being threatened with deportation. In addition, banishment helps to reduce the official jobless rate, a sometimes useful political function, especially if the banished drop so completely out of the labor force that they are not even available to be counted as "discouraged workers."

The economic banishment function is in many ways a replacement for the old reserve army of labor function, which played itself out when the undeserving poor could be hired as strikebreakers, as defense workers in the case of sudden wartime economic mobilization, as "hypothetical workers," who by their very presence could be used to depress the wages of other workers, or to put pressure on the unions not to make wage and other demands. Today, however, with a plentiful supply of immigrants, as well as of a constantly growing number of banished workers who are becoming surplus labor, a reserve army is less rarely needed—and when needed, can be recruited from sources other than the undeserving poor.[13]

Welfare recipients may, however, turn out to continue to be a part of the reserve army. Currently, they are encouraged to stay out of the labor market by remaining eligible for the Medicaid benefits they need for their children only if they remain on welfare.[14] Should the Clinton administration welfare reform program become reality, however, welfare recipients, who will be required to work for the minimum wage or less, could exert pressure on the wages of the employed, thus bringing them right back into the reserve army.

4. *Supplying illegal goods.* The undeserving poor who are banished from other jobs remain eligible for work in the manufacture and sale of illegal goods, including drugs. Although it is estimated that 80 percent of all illegal drugs are sold to Whites who are not poor, the sellers are often people banished from the formal labor market.[15] Other suppliers of illegal goods include the illegal immigrants, considered undeserving in many American communities, who work for garment industry sweatshops manufacturing clothing under illegal conditions.

5. *Job creation.* Perhaps the most important economic function of the undeserving poor today is that their mere presence creates jobs for the better-off population, including professional ones. Since the undeserving poor are thought to be dangerous or improperly socialized, their behavior either has to be modified so that they act in socially approved ways, or they have to be isolated from the deserving sectors of society. The larger the number of people who are declared undeserving, the larger also the number of people needed to modify and isolate as well as control, guard, and care for them. Among these are the social workers, teachers, trainers, mentors, psychiatrists, doctors and their support staffs in juvenile training centers, "special" schools, drug treatment centers, and penal behavior modification institutions, as well as the police, prosecutors, defense attorneys, judges, court officers, probation personnel and others who constitute the criminal courts, and the guards and others who run the prisons.

Jobs created by the presence of undeserving poor also include the massive bureaucracy of professionals, investigators, and clerks who administer welfare. Other jobs go to the officials who seek out poor fathers for child support monies they may or may not have, as well as the welfare office personnel needed to take recipients in violation of welfare rules off the rolls, and those needed to put them back on the rolls when they reapply. In fact, one can argue that some of the rules for supervising, controlling, and punishing the undeserving poor are more effective at performing the latent function of creating clerical and professional jobs for the better-off population than the manifest function of achieving their official goals.

More jobs are created in the social sciences and in journalism for conducting research about the undeserving poor and producing popular books, articles, and TV documentaries for the more fortunate who want to learn about them. The "job chain" should also be extended to the teachers and others who train those who serve, control, and study the undeserving poor.

In addition, the undeserving poor make jobs for what I call the salvation industries, religious, civil, or medical, which also try to modify the behavior of those stigmatized as undeserving. Not all such jobs are paid, for the undeserving poor also provide occasional targets for charity and thus offer volunteer jobs for those providing it—and paid jobs for the professional fundraisers who obtain most of the charitable funds these days. Among the most visible volunteers are the members of "cafe" and "high" society who organize and contribute to these benefits.[16]

Three Normative Functions

6. *Moral legitimation.* Undeservingness justifies the category of deservingness and thus supplies moral and political legitimacy, almost by definition, to the institutions and social structures that include the deserving and exclude the undeserving.[17] Of these structures, the most important is undoubtedly the class hierarchy, for the existence of an undeserving class or stratum legitimates the deserving classes, if not necessarily all of their class-related behavior.[18] The alleged immorality of the undeserving also gives a moral flavor to, and justification for, the class hierarchy, which may help to explain why upward mobility itself is so praiseworthy.[19]

7. *Norm reinforcement.* By violating, or being imagined as violating, a number of mainstream behavioral patterns and values, the undeserving poor help to reaffirm and reinforce the virtues of these patterns—and to do so visibly, since the violations by the undeserving are highly publicized. As Emile Durkheim pointed out nearly a century ago, norm violations and their punishments also provide an opportunity for preserving and reaffirming the norms. This is not insignificant, for norms sometimes disparaged as "motherhood" values gain new moral power when they are violated, and their violators are stigmatized.

If the undeserving poor can be imagined to be lazy, they help to reaffirm the Protestant work ethic; if poor single-parent families are publicly condemned, the two-parent family is once more legitimated as ideal. In the 1960s, middle-class morality was sometimes criticized as culturally parochial and therefore inappropriate for the poor, but since the 1980s, mainstream values have once more been regarded as vital sources of behavioral guidance for them.[20]

Enforcing the norms also contributes further to preserving them in another way, for one of the standard punishments of the undeserving poor for misbehaving—as well as a standard obligation in exchange for help—is practicing the mainstream norms, including those that the members of the mainstream may only be preaching, and that might die out if the poor were not required to incorporate them in their behavior. Old work rules that can no longer be enforced in the rest of the economy can be maintained in the regulations for workfare; old-fashioned austerity and thrift are built into the consumption patterns expected of welfare recipients. Economists like to argue that if the poor want to be deserving, they should take any kind of job, regardless of its low pay or demeaning character, reflecting the work ethic which economists themselves have never practiced.

Similarly, welfare recipients may be removed from the rolls if they are found to be living with a man—but the social worker who removes them has every right to cohabit and not lose his or her job. In most states, welfare recipients must observe rules of housecleaning and child care that middle-class people are free to ignore without being punished. While there are many norms and laws governing child care, only the poor are monitored to see if they obey these. Should they use more physical punishment on their children than social workers consider desirable, they can be charged with child neglect or abuse and can lose their children to foster care.[21]

The fact is that the defenders of such widely preached norms as hard work, thrift, monogamy, and moderation need people who can be accused, accurately or not, of being lazy, spendthrift, promiscuous, and immoderate. One reason that welfare recipients are a ready target for punitive legislation is that politicians, and most likely some of their constituents, imagine them to be enjoying leisure and an active sex life at public expense. Whether or not very many poor people actually behave in the ways that are judged undeserving is irrelevant if they can be imagined as doing so. Once imagining and stereotyping are allowed to take over, then judgments of undeservingness can be made without much concern for empirical accuracy. For example, in the 1990s, the idea that young men from poor single-parent families were highly likely to commit street crimes became so universal that the news media no longer needed to quote experts to affirm the accuracy of the charge.

Actually, most of the time most of the poor are as law abiding and observant of mainstream norms as are other Americans. Sometimes they are even more observant; thus the proportion of welfare recipients who cheat is always far below the percentage of taxpayers who do so.[22] Moreover, survey after survey has shown that the poor, including many street criminals and drug sellers, want to hold respectable jobs like everyone else, hope someday to live in the suburbs, and generally aspire to the same American dream as most moderate and middle-income Americans.[23]

8. *Supplying popular culture villains.* The undeserving poor have played a long-term role in supplying American popular culture with villains, allowing the producers of the culture both to reinforce further mainstream norms and to satisfy audience demands for revenge, notably by showing that crime and other norm violations do not pay. Street criminals are shown dead or alive in the hands of the police on local television news virtually every day, and more dramatically so in the crime and action movies and television series.

For many years before and after World War II, the criminal characters in Hollywood movies were often poor immigrants, frequently of Sicilian origin. Then they were complemented for some decades by communist spies and other Cold War enemies who were not poor, but even before the end of the Cold War, they were being replaced by Black and Hispanic drug dealers and gang leaders.

At the same time, however, the popular culture industry has also supplied music and other materials offering marketable cultural and political protest which does not reinforce mainstream norms, or at least not directly. Some of the creators and performers come from poor neighborhoods, however, and it may be that some rap music becomes commercially successful by displacing on ghetto musicians the cultural and political protest of record buyers from more affluent classes.[24]

Three Political Functions

9. *Institutional scapegoating.* The scapegoating of the undeserving poor mentioned in Function 2 above also extends to institutions which mistreat them. As a result, some of the responsibility for the existence of poverty, slums, unemployment, poor schools, and the like is taken off the shoulders of elected and appointed officials who are supposed to deal with these problems. For example, to the extent that educational experts decide that the children of the poor are learning disabled or that they are culturally or genetically inferior in intelligence, attempts to improve the schools can be put off or watered down.

To put it another way, the availability of institutional scapegoats both personalizes and exonerates social systems. The alleged laziness of the jobless and the anger aimed at beggars take the heat off the failure of the economy, and the imagined derelictions of slum dwellers and the homeless, off the housing industry. In effect, the undeserving poor are blamed both for their poverty and also for the absence of "political will" among the citizenry to do anything about it.

10. *Conservative power shifting.* Once poor people are declared undeserving, they also lose their political legitimacy and whatever little political influence they had before they were stigmatized. Some cannot vote, and many do not choose to vote or mobilize because they know politicians do not listen to their demands. Elected officials might ignore them even if they voted or mobilized, because these officials and the larger polity cannot easily satisfy their demands for economic and other kinds of justice.[25] As a result, the political system is able to pay additional attention to the demands of more affluent constituents. It can therefore shift to the "right."

The same shift to the right also takes place ideologically. Although injustices of poverty help justify the existence of liberals and the more radical left, the undeserving poor themselves provide justification and opportunities for conservatives to attack their ideological enemies on their left. When liberals can be accused of favoring criminals over victims, their accusers can launch and legitimate incursions on the civil liberties and rights of the undeserving poor, and concurrently on the liberties and rights of defenders of the poor. Moreover, the undeservingness of the poor can be used to justify attacks on the welfare state. Charles Murray understood the essence of this ideological function when he argued that welfare and other welfare state legislation for the poor only increased the number of poor people.[26]

11. *Spatial purification.* Stigmatized populations are often used, deliberately or not, to stigmatize the areas in which they live, making such areas eligible for various kinds of purification. As a result, "underclass areas" can be torn down and their inhabitants moved to make room for more affluent residents or higher taxpayers.

However, such areas can also be used to isolate stigmatized poor people and facilities by selecting them as locations for homeless shelters, halfway houses for the mentally ill or for ex-convicts, drug treatment facilities, and even garbage dumps, which have been forced out of middle- and working-class areas following NIMBY (not in my backyard) protests. Drug dealers and other sellers of illegal goods also find a haven in areas stigmatized as underclass areas, partly because these supply some customers, but also because police protection in such areas is usually minimal enough to allow illegal activities without significant interference from the law.[27] In fact, municipalities would face major economic and political obstacles to their operations without stigmatized areas in which stigmatized people and activities can be located.

Two Macrosocial Functions

12. *Reproduction of stigma and the stigmatized.* For centuries now, undeservingness has given rise to policies and agencies which are manifestly set up to help the poor economically and otherwise to become deserving, but which actually prevent the undeserving poor from being freed of their stigma, and which also manage, unwittingly, to see to it that their children face the same obstacles.[28] In some instances, this process works so speedily that the children of the stigmatized face "anticipatory stigmatization," among them the children of welfare recipients who are frequently predicted to be unable to learn, to work, and to remain on the right side of the law even before they have been weaned.

If this outcome were planned deliberately, one could argue that politically and culturally dominant groups are reluctant to give up an easily accessible and always available scapegoat. In actuality, however, the reproduction function results unwittingly from other intended and seemingly popular practices. For example, the so-called War on Drugs, which has unsuccessfully sought to keep hard drugs out of the United States, but has meanwhile done little to provide drug treatment to addicts who want it, thereby aids the continuation of addiction, street crime, and a guaranteed prison population, not to mention the various disasters that visit the families of addicts and help to keep them poor.

The other major source of reproducing stigma and the stigmatized is the routine activities of the organizations which service welfare recipients, the homeless, and other stigmatized poor, and end up mistreating them.[29] For one thing, such agencies, whether they exist to supply employment to the poor or to help the homeless, are almost certain to be underfunded because of the powerlessness of their clientele. No organization has ever had the funds or power to buy, build, or rehabilitate housing for the homeless in sufficient number. Typically, they have been able to fund or carry out small demonstration projects.

In addition, organizations which serve stigmatized people often attract less well-trained and qualified staff than those with high-status clients, and if the clients are deemed undeserving, competence may become even less important in choosing staff.[30] Then too, helping organizations generally reflect the societal stratification hierarchy, which means that organizations with poor, low-status clients frequently treat them as undeserving. If they also fear some of their clients, they may not only withhold help, but attack the clients on a preemptive strike basis. Last but not least, the agencies that serve the undeserving poor are bureaucracies which operate by rules and regulations that routinize the work, encourage the stability and growth of the organizations, and serve the needs of their staffs before those of their clients.

When these factors are combined, as they often are, and become cumulative, as they often do, it should not be surprising that the organizations cut off escape routes from poverty not only for the clients, but in doing so, also make sure that some of their children remain poor as well.

13. *Extermination of the surplus.* In earlier times, when the living standards of all poor people were at or below subsistence, many died at an earlier age than the better off, thus performing the set of functions for the latter forever associated with Thomas Malthus. Standards of living, even for the very poor, have risen considerably in the last century, but even today, morbidity and mortality rates remain much higher among the poor than among moderate-income people. To put it another way, various social forces combine to do away with some of the people who have become surplus labor and are no longer needed by the economy.

Several of the killing illnesses and pathologies of the poor change over time; currently, they include AIDS, tuberculosis, hypertension, heart attacks, and cancer, as well as psychosis, substance abuse, street crime, injury and death during participation in the drug trade and other underworld activities, and intraclass homicide resulting from neighborhood conflicts over turf and "respect." Whether the poor people whose only problem is being unfairly stereotyped and stigmatized as undeserving die earlier than other poor people is not known.[31]

Moreover, these rates can be expected to remain high or even to rise as rates of unemployment—and of banishment from the labor force—rise, especially for the least skilled. Even the better-off jobless created by the downsizing of the 1990s blame themselves for their unemployment if they cannot eventually find new jobs, become depressed, and in some instances begin the same process of being extruded permanently from the labor market experienced by the least skilled of the jobless.

In effect, contemporary advanced capitalism may well have created the conditions for a new Malthusian hypothesis. In any case, the early departure of poor people from an economy and society which do not need them is useful for those who remain. Since the more fortunate classes have already developed a purposive blindness to the structural causes of unemployment and to the poverty-related causes of pathology and crime that follow, those who benefit from the current job erosion and the possible extermination of the surplus labor may not admit it consciously either. Nonetheless, those left over to compete for scarce jobs and other resources will have a somewhat easier time in the competition, thus assigning undeservingness a final positive function for the more fortunate members of society.[32]

III. Conclusion

I have described thirteen of the more important functions of the undeserving poor, enough to support my argument that both the idea of the undeserving poor and the stigmas with which some poor people are thus labeled may persist in part because they are useful in a variety of ways to the people who are not poor.

This analysis does not imply that undeservingness will or should persist. Whether it *will* persist is going to be determined by what happens to poverty in America. If it declines, poverty-related crime should also decline, and then fewer poor people will probably be described as undeserving. If poverty worsens, so will poverty-related crime, as well as the stereotyping and stigmatization of the poor, and any worsening of the country's economy is likely to add to the kinds and numbers of undeserving poor, if only because they make convenient and powerless scapegoats.

The functions that the undeserving poor play cannot, by themselves, perpetuate either poverty or undeservingness, for as I noted earlier, functions are not causes. For example, if huge numbers of additional unskilled workers should be needed, as they were for the World War II war effort, the undeserving poor will be welcomed back into the labor force, at least temporarily. Of course, institutions often try to survive once they have lost both their reasons for existence and their functions. Since the end of the Cold War, parts of the military-industrial establishment both in the United States and Russia have been campaigning for the maintenance of some Cold War forces and weapons to guarantee their own futures, but these establishments also supply jobs to their national economies, and in the United States, for the constituents of elected officials. Likewise, some of the institutions and interest groups that benefit from the existence of undeservingness, or from controlling the undeserving poor, may try to maintain undeservingness and its stigma. They may not even need to, for if Emile Durkheim was right, the decline of undeservingness would lead to the criminalization, or at least stigmatization, of new behavior patterns.

Whether applying the label of undeservingness to the poor *should* persist is a normative question which ought to be answered in the negative. Although people have a right to judge each other, that right does not extend to judging large numbers of people as a single group, with one common moral fault, or to stereotyping them without evidence either about their behavior or their values. Even if a case could be made for judging large cohorts of people as undeserving, these judgments should be distributed up and down the socioeconomic hierarchy, requiring Americans also to consider whether and how people in the working, middle, and upper classes are undeserving.

The same equality should extend to the punishment of crimes. Today, many Americans and courts still treat white-collar and upper-class criminals more leniently than poor ones. The public excuse given is that the street crime of the undeserving poor involves violence and thus injury or death, but as many students of white-collar and corporate crime have pointed out, these also hurt and kill people, and often in large numbers, even if they do so less directly and perhaps less violently.

Changes also need to be made in the American conception of deviance, which like that of other countries, conflates people whose behavior is *different* with those whose behavior is socially *harmful*. Bearing children without marriage is a long-standing tradition among the poor. Born of necessity rather than preference, it is a poverty-related practice, but it is not, by itself, harmful, or at least not until it can be shown that either the children—or the moral sensibilities of the people who oppose illegitimacy— are significantly hurt. Poor single-parent families are hardly desirable, but as the lack of condemnation of more affluent single-parent families should suggest, the major problem of such families is not the number of parents, actual or surrogate, in the family, but its poverty.

Finally, because many of the poor are stereotyped unjustly as undeserving, scholars, writers, journalists, and others should launch a systematic and public effort to deconstruct and delegitimate the notion of the undeserving poor. This effort, which is necessary to help make effective antipoverty programs politically acceptable again, should place the following five ideas on the public agenda and encourage discussion as well as dissemination of available research.

The five ideas, all discussed earlier in this article, are that (1) the criminal and deviant behavior among the poor is largely poverty related rather than the product of free choice based on distinctive values; (2) the undeservingness of the poor is an ancient stereotype, and like all stereotypes, it vastly exaggerates the actual dangers that stem from the poor; (3) poverty-related deviance is not necessarily harmful just because it does not accord with mainstream norms; (4) the notion of undeservingness survives in part because of the positive functions it has for the better-off population; and (5) the only certain way to eliminate both this notion and the functions is to eliminate poverty.[33]

NOTES

1. However, Cicero had a distinctive perspective; in today's terminology, he was a slumlord. See R. A. Brunt, *Social Conflicts in the Roman Republic* (New York: Norton), pp. 128–29.
2. Sidney Webb and Beatrice Webb, *English Poor Law History, Part I: The Old Poor Law* (Hamden, CT: Shoestring Press, 1963 [1927]), pp. 20–50.
3. However, the *Oxford English Dictionary*, compiled by J. A. Simpson and E. S. Weiner (New York: Oxford University Press, 1989), 19:996, already has a 1647 reference to beggars as undeserving, and the adjective itself was earlier used to refer to nonpoor people, for example, by Shakespeare.
4. David Matza, "Poverty and Disrepute," in *Contemporary Social Problems,* 2nd ed., edited by Robert K. Merton and Robert A. Nisbet (New York: Harcourt Brace & World, 1966), pp. 619–66.
5. These terms were often, but not exclusively, applied to the poor "races" who arrived in the nineteenth and early twentieth century from Ireland, Germany and later, Eastern and Southern Europe. They have also been applied, during and after slavery, to Blacks. Nonetheless, the functions to be discussed in this article are consequences of poverty, not of race, even though a disproportionate rate of those "selected" to be poor have always

been darker-skinned than the more fortunate classes.

6. See Michael B. Katz, *The Undeserving Poor: From the War on Poverty to the War on Welfare* (New York: Pantheon Books, 1989), chap. 5; Herbert J. Gans, "The Dangers of the Underclass," in my *People, Plans and Policies* (New York: Columbia University Press and Russell Sage Foundation), chap. 21. The popular definition of underclass must be distinguished from Gunnar Myrdal's initial, scholarly one, which viewed the underclass as a stratum driven to the margins or out of the labor force by what are today called the postindustrial and global economies. Gunnar Myrdal, *Challenge to Affluence* (New York: Pantheon Books, 1963), p. 10 and passim. Myrdal's definition viewed the underclass as victims of economic change, and said nothing about its moral state.

7. Robert K. Merton, "Manifest and Latent Functions," in his *Social Theory and Social Structure: Toward the Codification of Social Research* (Glencoe, IL, 1949), chap. 1.

8. Actually, some of the functions that follow may in fact have been intended by some interest groups in society, but neither intended nor recognized by others, adding an interesting conceptual variation—and empirical question—to Merton's dichotomy.

9. Herbert J. Gans, "The Positive Functions of Poverty," *American Journal of Sociology* 78(2) (1972):275–89. That article also had another purpose, to show that functional analysis could come to liberal or radical conclusions, to counter the charge commonly launched against functional analysis that it is inherently conservative or supportive of the status quo. That article, like its present complement, was a straightforward analysis, written sans irony, even though the analysis of latent functions often becomes a debunking exercise that can take on an unintentionally ironic tone.

10. For brevity's sake, I will hereafter refer to the undeserving poor instead of the poor labeled undeserving, but I always mean the latter.

11. Hacker is paraphrasing Baldwin. Andrew Hacker, *Two Nations: Black and White, Separate, Hostile, Unequal* (New York: Scribner, 1992), p. 61. Mark Stern applies the displacement function to the economy of the 1990s, writing that "if economic dislocation . . . and urban restructuring were taking their toll on all of us, perhaps it was reas-

suring to imagine that there was a class at the bottom . . . whose vices made us look virtuous." Mark Stern, "Poverty and Family Composition Since 1940," in *The 'Underclass' Debate: Views from History*, edited by Michael B. Katz (Princeton, NJ: Princeton University Press, 1993), p. 253.

12. Kathryn M. Neckerman and Joleen Kirschenman, "Hiring Strategies, Racial Bias and Inner-City Workers," *Social Problems* 38(4) (1991):433–47.

13. Dahrendorf has suggested, surely with Marx's *Lumpenproletariat* in mind, that when the very poor are excluded from full citizenship, they can become "a reserve army for demonstrations . . . including soccer violence, race riots, and running battles with the police." Ralf Dahrendorf, *Law and Order* (London: Stevens, 1985), p. 107. He is writing with Europe in mind, however.

14. Consequently, they are part of the reserve army only if and when they also work off-the-books in the informal economy. For the argument that recipients are permanently part of the reserve army, see Frances F. Piven and Richard A. Cloward, *Regulating the Poor: The Functions of Public Welfare*, 2nd ed. (New York: Pantheon Books, 1993).

15. Ron Harris, "Blacks Feel Brunt of Drug War," *Los Angeles Times*, 22 April 1990, p. 1.

16. While most charity benefits target the deserving poor, they are also held for poor AIDS victims and the homeless, who are considered undeserving, at least by some members of the better-off classes. The undeserving poor who are served by these charities thus help to justify the continued existence of these upper-class "societies."

17. Since political legitimacy is involved here, these functions could also be listed among the political ones below.

18. That many of the undeserving poor, and literally those of the underclass, are also thought to be *declasse*, adds to the moral and political legitimacy of the rest of the class system.

19. Although Marxists might have been expected to complain that the notion of the undeserving poor enables the higher classes to create a split in the lower ones, instead Marxist theory creates a mirror image of the capitalist pattern. In declaring undeserving the owners of the means of production, and sometimes the entire bourgeoisie,

the theorists ennobled the working class and the poor together with it. Nonetheless, Marx found it necessary to make room for the *Lumpenproletariat,* although for him if not all of his successors, its moral failures were largely determined by the needs of Marxist ideology, just as those of the undeserving poor were shaped by capitalist ideology.

20. See Isabel Sawhill, "The Underclass: An Overview," *The Public Interest* 96 (1989): 3–15. For a contrary analysis, which finds and criticizes the acceptance of poverty-related deviance as normal, see Daniel P. Moynihan, "Defining Deviancy Down," *American Scholar* 62(1) (1993):17–30.

21. Poor immigrants who still practice old-country discipline norms are particularly vulnerable to being accused of child abuse.

22. Teresa Funiciello, *Tyranny of Kindness: Dismantling the Welfare System to End Poverty in America* (New York: Atlantic Monthly Press, 1993), p. 60.

23. See Mark R. Rank, *Living on the Edge: The Realities of Welfare in America* (New York: Columbia University Press, 1994), p. 93.

24. A sizable proportion of the blues, country music, cowboy songs, and jazz of earlier eras was originally composed and played in prisons, brothels, and slum area taverns. It is probably not coincidental that as far back as the eighteenth century, at least, English "actors, fencers, jugglers, minstrels, and in fact all purveyors of amusements to common folk," were thought undeserving by the higher classes. Webb and Webb, *English Poor Law History,* p. 354.

25. In addition, the undeserving poor make a dangerous constituency. Politicians who say kind words about them or who act to represent their interests are likely to be attacked for their words and actions. Jesse Jackson was hardly the first national politician to be criticized for being too favorable to the poor.

26. Charles Murray, *Losing Ground: American Social Policy, 1950–1980* (New York: Basic Books, 1984). Myron Magnet went him one step better, blaming the increase in undeserv-

ingness also on various unnamed radicals associated with the conservative image of the 1960s. Myron Magnet, *The Dream and the Nightmare: The Sixties' Legacy to the Underclass* (New York: Morrow, 1993).

27. Since even middle-class drug buyers are willing to travel to underclass areas for drugs, neighborhoods convenient to expressways and bridges that serve the suburbs often become major shopping centers for hard drugs.

28. It is well known that many policies and agencies reproduce the positions and statuses of the people they are asked to raise, notably the public schools.

29. For some examples of the literature on client mistreatment, see Michael B. Katz, *In the Shadow of the Poor House: A Social History of Welfare in America* (New York: Basic Books, 1986); Michael Lipsky, *Street Level Bureaucracy: Dilemmas of the Individual in Public Services* (New York: Russell Sage Foundation, 1980); Piven and Cloward, *Regulating the Poor,* chaps. 4 and 5; and for mistreatment of the homeless, Elliot Liebow, *Tell Them Who I Am: The Lives of Homeless Women* (New York: Free Press, 1993), chap. 4.

30. They may also attract young professionals with reforming or missionary impulses, but many of them either burn out or leave for financial reasons when they begin to raise families.

31. Poor Blacks and members of some other racial minorities pay additional "health penalties" for being non-White.

32. Killing off the undeserving poor may conflict with the prior function (see Function 12) of reproducing them, but functional analysis describes consequences which do not have to be logically consistent. Moreover, since turning poor people into undeserving ones can be a first step toward eliminating them, Functions 12 and 13 may even be logically consistent.

33. A fuller discussion of policy proposals will appear in my forthcoming book, *Ending the War against the Poor.*

18

THE ANATOMY OF RACIALLY MOTIVATED VIOLENCE IN NEW YORK CITY
A Case Study of Youth in Southern Brooklyn

Howard Pinderhughes

Questions to Consider

Howard Pinderhughes suggests that some people benefit from engaging in racist behavior. Who are these people? In what ways have people benefited from such behavior? What role do individuals at the social and economic margins play in terms of race relations in their community? How were the young men in Pinderhughes's case study rewarded for engaging in racial violence? What structural changes could you suggest that would shift the energies of these youths from something negative to something positive?

Ethnic diversity in New York City has been described in many ways, from a "melting pot" to a "gorgeous mosaic." But in the spring of 1990, the melting pot seemed on the verge of boiling over; the mosaic ripped apart by racial tension. Three news stories filled the pages of the city's major newspapers: the Bensonhurst murder trial, the rape case of the Central Park jogger, and the boycott of two Korean grocery stores in Flatbush. Each of these events symbolized a growing problem in New York City and the nation as a whole—racial tension, conflict, and confrontation had increased and hate violence was on the rise.

Howard Pinderhughes, "The Anatomy of Racially Motivated Violence in New York City" from *Social Problems*, pp. 478–492, Vol. 40, No. 4, November 1993. Copyright © 1993 by The Society for the Study of Social Problems. Reprinted by permission of the University of California Press Journals: www.ucpress.edu.

As a result of the public perception that the racial situation in the city was spiralling out of control, David Dinkins, the first African-American mayor in the city's history, made a public plea for ethnic and racial harmony. In his speech, the mayor called for calm and cooperation. His appeal assumed that the rise in racial conflict resulted from prejudice—which could be resolved if people would simply try to get along and be more tolerant of other groups.

The mayor's speech, and reports which followed analyzing the city's racial climate, made no attempt to explain the causes of deteriorating race relations in the city. There was no analysis of the complex network of interrelated factors which combined to produce an alarming increase in bias related violence. The fact that young people perpetrate the majority of racially motivated attacks was not discussed. Nor were the content and substance of racial attitudes among youth in the city examined. There was no discussion of the structural factors which created fertile soil for racial animosity—a prominent concern more than three years earlier when, on 20 December 1986, a group of over twenty white youths attacked three black men in the Howard Beach section of New York City.

In the wake of the death of one of the Howard Beach victims, Michael Griffith, the eyes of the entire nation focused on race relations in New York. The incident shocked the city and the rest of the country. Racial murders were supposed to be a thing of the past—part of the dark days of segregation in the South, perpetrated by small town whites in anonymous sheets. Yet, this was the North, the nation's largest city, the lap of liberalism.

In hindsight, the Howard Beach incident should have been a warning signal. Howard Beach was the first high profile incident in an alarming increase in bias related crimes in New York and throughout the country. It was one of 235 racially motivated crimes investigated by the New York City Human Rights Commission in 1986.

This study uses statistics collected by the New York City Police Department Bias Unit and the Human Rights Commission which establish a dramatic increase in the number of verified bias incidents. It is virtually impossible to determine unconditionally that this increase in verified cases is the result of an actual increase in the number of bias crimes perpetrated. The increase in verified incidents could be the result of increased reporting. However, the evidence strongly suggests a rise in racially motivated violence. Interviews with representatives of the New York City Police Department, the Human Rights Commission, youth program coordinators, school teachers, administrators, and officials yielded different interpretations of the meaning of the increase. Human Rights Commission officials argue that there was an increase. Further, most of the individuals interviewed for the present

study who worked with youth agreed that there had been an increase in racial tension, conflict, and violence; New York City youths confirmed this conclusion. In 1987, the number of racially motivated crimes shot up to 463, and reached 550 in 1988.

Two differences in the character of bias motivated crimes of the last five years, as compared to the three previous years, are the racial and ethnic backgrounds of the victims and the types of attacks. In 1982, 50 percent of the confirmed bias motivated crimes were characterized as anti-Semitic and the vast majority were directed against property. This trend continued through 1985; after that point, blacks became the number one target of bias related crimes and the percentage of physical assaults increased significantly. Of the 500 reported ethnically or racially motivated attacks in 1987, 118 victims were white, 220 were black, 82 were Jewish, and 33 were Latino.

The present pattern reveals a rise in physical bias related attacks, with people of color and gays and lesbians as the primary targets. Attacks occurred in many different neighborhoods and in all five boroughs of the city. Victims and assailants came from many different backgrounds. The one common feature of the assailants was their age. Over 70 percent of those arrested for perpetrating bias crimes in 1987 and 1988 were under the age of 20.

One of the most infamous bias incidents was the racial murder of Yusuf Hawkins which took place in Bensonhurst, Brooklyn. On 23 August 1989, Yusuf Hawkins and two companions were in Bensonhurst looking for a used car when they were attacked by a mob of over 20 white youths. In the trial which followed, the incident was presented in the courtroom and media as a tragic one-night occurrence which happened almost accidentally. The incident was presented as the result of a confluence of factors which included Hawkins and his companions being "in the wrong place at the wrong time"—walking down a street in Bensonhurst where the mob of young whites mistook them for another group of blacks they believed were coming into the neighborhood to cause trouble.

In this article, I argue that such racial violence in New York City is the result of a combination of factors shaping the behavior of youth in the city. These factors include (1) structural conditions, (2) ethnic and racial attitudes, and (3) peer group participation and community sentiment. I argue that bleak structural economic conditions have laid the foundation for racial conflict by leaving some young people with extremely uncertain futures. The anxieties and fears of these youth about their futures are directed at other racial groups they view as threats. Peer groups reinforce negative attitudes towards other ethnic and racial groups and facilitate violence. White youths who live in close-knit ethnic communities which fear blacks and other minorities are supported in keeping unwanted minorities out of their neighborhoods. The article challenges the popular view of the Bensonhurst incident as an aberration. Data from interviews with white youth from southern Brooklyn reveal a consistent pattern of racially motivated violence linked to specific factors.

Scholars have reported a strong and steady change in the attitudes of U.S. whites towards the principle of racial equality in the last thirty years (Kinder and Sears 1981; Schuman, Steeh, and Bobo 1985; Sheatsley 1966; Taylor, Sheatsley, and Greeley 1978). Schuman, Steeh, and Bobo (1985) point to an important finding in their study of racial attitudes in the United States: positive trends in attitudes of whites towards blacks have largely been the result of cohort replacement rather than individual attitude change. They predict that this trend will not continue, which is consistent with the pattern of increased racial conflict among youth in New York City.

Traditionally, social scientific examinations of race relations and racial attitudes have focused either on adults or young children. Little has been written about adolescence, although this is obviously a crucial period for identity development and attitude formation. In contrast, this study focuses directly on adolescents. It combines elements of Blumer's (1958) theory of racism as a sense of group position, Omi and Winant's (1986) theory of ideology's role in producing racial meanings, and competition theory which analyzes racial violence as the result of ethnic competition activated by the rising supply of low wage labor due to immigration and the migration of blacks into tight labor markets. I argue that racial conflict and violence result from a combination of structural conditions of intense competition, racialized ideologies, and racial and ethnic identities which incorporate negative attitudes towards other groups.

Methodology

The data analyzed in this article were drawn from a larger study conducted in 1990 of ethnic and racial attitudes among youth and the rise in racial conflict in New York City. That study examined the attitudes of 270 youths between the ages of 14 and 21, from 37 different neighborhoods in New York City, in a purposive sample. The sample came from a wide range of ethnic and racial backgrounds, including significant numbers of Italians, African Americans, Puerto Ricans, Jews, Albanians, and Irish.

This article focuses on a subsample of 88 participants in a youth program in southern Brooklyn. The program works primarily with white delinquents in an educational setting, offering an alternative high school program for at-risk youth and a GED program. Participants generally resided in the surrounding communities of Gravesend,

Bensonhurst, Sheepshead Bay, and Canarsie. The sample limitations make it difficult to generalize beyond the groups represented and impossible to generalize about all youth in the city of New York. The sample *is,* however, representative of a small universe of neighborhood youth who have had trouble in school, have dropped out, and/or who spend significant time "hanging out" on the streets.

Two methods were used to collect data on ethnic and racial attitudes. First, a survey questionnaire to gather general demographic data (socioeconomic background, ethnic and racial identity, age) and a short survey of attitudes towards other groups were developed. The survey instrument used a combination of questions from "The Study of High School Students and Educational Staff on Prejudice and Race Relations" (Martin Luther King, Jr. Institute for Nonviolence 1990), and questions developed specifically for this study. The questionnaire was field tested and revised accordingly.

Second, focus group interviews were conducted, using open-ended questions designed to elicit information about the youths' views of race relations. Interviews were structured and data were analyzed in accordance with established methodological guidelines for focus groups (Krueger 1988; Morgan 1988). Eleven focus groups were conducted, ranging in size from five to seventeen participants.[1] The interviews were conducted immediately after the administration of the survey, lasted between 45 and 90 minutes, and were tape-recorded. Tapes of the interviews were transcribed and analyzed systematically for patterns and trends of responses. The patterns were established through a content analysis of the data which entailed systematic coding.

---

[1] Twenty-three focus groups were conducted in the larger study.

The interviews followed a set guideline of open-ended questions structured around four themes: (1) the state of race relations in New York City; (2) relations among youths of different ethnic and racial backgrounds; (3) relations among different ethnic and racial groups in respondents' neighborhoods; and (4) the future of race relations in the city. Data from the focus group interviews provided detailed information about the substance and content of ethnic and racial attitudes among youth in New York City. Finally, data from the focus group interviews were compared to survey data to confirm patterns of attitudes about race and ethnicity.

A Brief History of Structural Conditions in New York City

In the past 20 years, significant demographic changes have taken place in the composition of New York City's population. As a result of the massive outmigration of New Yorkers to the suburbs and other parts of the state and nation, between 1970 and 1980 the population per square mile declined between 5 and 20 percent in four of the five boroughs, with an overall reduction of 800,000, or 10.4 percent. Much of this decline was the result of "white flight," the movement from the city of middle- and upper-income families to escape the rapidly increasing numbers of African Americans and Latinos and the social problems whites associated with this demographic change. During that same period, the population of people of color grew by one million. From 1965 to 1980, the foreign-born population increased by almost one million. Most of these immigrants arrived from Third World nations; of the 772,040 immigrants who are classified by their country of origin, close to 80 percent (598,500) were from Third World countries (New York City Department of Planning

1985).[2] Meanwhile, working- and lower-class families in New York City found it increasingly difficult to locate or maintain affordable housing. Beginning in the 1980s, neighborhoods in all five boroughs were gradually, but steadily converted from lower- and working-class tracts to middle- and upper-income tracts. Wealthier people, whose resources allowed them to move out of the city when threatened with the encroachment of "undesirable" groups, returned to the urban areas from which they fled in the 1950s and 1960s as these areas became "gentrified." As a result of the conversion of existing rental units to co-ops and condominiums, the proportion of households that owned their homes increased by 2.5 percent from 1981 to 1987 (Harris 1991). By 1987, vacancy rates for inexpensive apartments throughout the city were low: less than 1 percent for apartments asking below $300; below 2.5 percent for those asking between $300 and $500; and 4.28 percent for apartments asking more than $500 (Stegman 1988). The result was an intensification of the housing shortage for lower- and working-class people and a dramatic increase in the number of homeless people. By the end of the 1980s, the stage had been set for intensified competition for housing and employment among New York City's diverse working- and lower-class communities.

Beginning in the late 1960s, the city's economy underwent a profound restructuring, which has been analyzed as a simultaneous process of decay and growth (Drennan 1991). Although the manufacturing sector was in serious decline during the

last two decades, during the same period, the finance and service industries experienced rapid expansion. Between 1969 and 1977, New York City lost over 600,000 jobs, primarily in the manufacturing sector (Drennan 1991); the largest decline was in manufacturing jobs in Brooklyn and the Bronx (Harris 1991). As a result, after a decade of expansion in the 1960s, employment decreased steadily from 1969 to 1977. Although the number of workers increased from 1978 to 1984, this increase was almost exclusively in the service sector. The highest percentage of these jobs was in business and related professional services. Jobs in business, professional, social and religious services, education, media, and health care accounted for 76 percent of the increase. Even though some of these were clerical, janitorial, and support jobs, the prospects for working-class youth remained severely restricted. Although some sectors of New York's population benefited from this decade of economic expansion, poverty increased from 15 percent in 1975, about 20 percent over the national average, to 23 percent in 1987, almost twice the national average (Mollenkopf and Castells 1991). Unemployment rates have been consistently higher in New York City than the rest of the state and the nation. While the city's unemployment rate dropped from 11.2 percent in 1976 to 8.9 percent in 1984, New York City has remained among the top ten cities in the United States in unemployment. Among youth under 20, unemployment rates are as high as 22.2 percent for whites and 47.5 percent for blacks. The employment to population ratio, a more reliable indicator of actual employment, decreased steadily from 1967 to 1984. In 1984, the ratio in New York City was below the U.S. average in all categories. Thus, only 49.1 percent of whites, 47 percent of blacks, and 42 percent of Latinos were working. Among those below the age of 20, less than 20 percent were working, compared

---

[2]The U.S. Bureau of the Census estimated a slight increase in the city's overall population between 1980 and 1990. This recent increase is attributed to a reversal of the trend of urban flight by the white middle class, combined with a continued influx of new immigrants to the city. Nevertheless, the demographic changes in the last 30 years have made non-Hispanic whites a minority of the city's population (Mollenkopf and Castells 1991).

to the national average of almost 44 percent (U.S. Department of Labor 1986).

At the time when competition for employment intensified, the dropout rate among the city's youth increased from 13.5 percent in 1983 to 25 percent in 1987. The situation was worst for black and Puerto Rican youth, with official dropout rates of 24.3 and 31.3 percent respectively (*New York Times* 21 June 1988). Italian Americans are now the third most likely group to drop out of high school. The percentage of white students in the New York City public schools decreased steadily, from 62.7 percent in 1960 to 23.7 percent in 1980. In addition, the percentage of white students in the New York City public schools steadily decreased from 63 percent in 1960 to 23 percent in 1980 (New York City Board of Education 1984). Whereas whites were the majority in 1960, and remained the single largest group in 1970, by 1980 they were a distinct minority in the city's public schools. By the late 1980s, though the racial composition differed from school to school, schools in Brooklyn were 25 percent white (Sullivan 1989).

For youth living in southern Brooklyn's white working-class neighborhoods, these structural changes were ominous developments which reinforced fears, already widespread in their communities, of other racial groups.

Community Sentiment in Southern Brooklyn

Bensonhurst, Sheepshead Bay, Gravesend, and Canarsie are adjacent communities; they are part of a strip of white ethnic, primarily working-class, predominantly Italian-American and Jewish neighborhoods stretching across the southern section of Brooklyn. Bensonhurst is 89.2 percent white, second only to neighboring Bay Ridge among the 18 community board districts in Brook-

lyn in its percentage of whites. The Sheepshead Bay and Gravesend areas are 86.1 percent white and Canarsie is 76.8 percent white (Stegman 1988). Bensonhurst is one of only three areas in the entire city with no appreciable black population; Sheepshead Bay and Gravesend are 3.0 percent black and Canarsie is 14.3 percent black.

For the most part, these four neighborhoods are stable working-class communities, which have some of the lowest inmigration (influx of new residents) rates of any of the predominantly white communities in New York City (Stegman 1988). Yet, in 1986, the median household income in Bensonhurst was $16,000, as contrasted with the citywide median of $20,000, well below the median household income of $25,000 for whites in New York City. The median household income in Sheepshead Bay and Gravesend was $20,000, and in Canarsie it was $24,000.

Many of the residents in these four neighborhoods used to live in other parts of New York City, especially central Brooklyn and Queens. In a classic case of neighborhood racial succession, many of these families moved out of their previous neighborhoods 30 to 40 years ago when African Americans, Puerto Ricans, and West Indians began to move in. This historical experience profoundly affected the attitudes and sentiments of these whites towards other groups. All minority groups, but particularly African Americans, were perceived as a direct threat to the quality of neighborhood life, as intruders who had the potential to ruin the stable, safe, close-knit ethnic niche the white community had taken years to establish.

These attitudes and sentiments have been well documented by Rieder (1985) in *Canarsie: The Jews and Italians of Brooklyn Against Liberalism*, which focuses on the Canarsie community which has a similar history and demographic composition to Gravesend, Sheepshead Bay, and Bensonhurst. Rieder found that Italian and Jewish residents in Canarsie viewed maintaining the ethnic and racial composition of their neighborhood as the most important factor for community harmony. Canarsie residents viewed African Americans and Puerto Ricans with mistrust, fear, and loathing as the harbingers of neighborhood deterioration, crime, decay and chaos. A July 1988 article in the *Wall Street Journal* painted a similar portrait of Bensonhurst.

Both Bensonhurst and Canarsie include housing projects, whose residents are primarily African American, located on the northeast fringes of the neighborhoods. In both communities these housing projects have become the focal points of racial animosity and conflict. White residents view the projects as the first foothold gained by poor African Americans encroaching on their communities. For their part, African-American residents in the projects describe their situation as reminiscent of the European Jewish ghettos where residents could not venture outside after dark for fear of being attacked. The Marlboro housing project, located on the border between Gravesend and Bensonhurst, has been at the center of much of the racial conflict in these two predominantly white communities. White youths interviewed in this study revealed a deep distrust and antagonism toward racial minorities in their community generally, and in these projects specifically.

The Attitudes of Community Youth

Analysis of the data revealed that the attitudes of the white youths in Bensonhurst and Gravesend were influenced by their neighborhoods' histories of racial tension and neighborhood defense. They had grown up in close-knit, exclusively white communities which distrusted strangers and feared blacks. Consequently, these youths dis-

played a distrust of all outsiders, and of blacks particularly.

The youths interviewed in the study were surprisingly open in discussing and describing their feelings about racial tension in New York City. All of the young people had strong opinions about race relations and believed that they had worsened in the past decade and that racial tensions in the city were high.

The youths listed five factors which they perceived were the cause of heightened racial tensions in New York City: (1) the deteriorating economic situation, (2) blacks starting trouble, (3) a media which favors blacks, (4) racial prejudice, and (5) black political and economic power in the city.

One important finding of the study is that these young people felt they were the victims of favoritism towards blacks, reverse discrimination, double standards, and increasing black power in the city.

> Everybody is leaning over backwards to give the blacks everything. They get all the jobs. They get all the attention from the mayor. These days white people don't have a chance. Because blacks are controlling the city. You got your black mayor. The main police chief is black. They never do nothin' for us.

> You know I been lookin' for work for awhile, but I can't get a job 'cause they're givin' them all to the black people.

The sense of victimization was heightened by the youths' fear that blacks were "taking over the city."

> You know, Italians used to run this city. We didn't have any problems 'cause we had political juice [power]. Now the blacks have taken over and we don't get nothin' from the politicians.

The election of a black mayor, David Dinkins, was viewed as strengthening the political and economic power of blacks in New York City. The youths believed the mayor was working only to help black people and that the city government was being run by black people, for black people. The mayor's victory fueled preexisting prejudices and fears among whites that blacks were gaining control of New York City, which would make it more difficult for working-class whites like them to maintain the ethnic composition of their neighborhoods, and as importantly to achieve economic and job security.

> My father told me that [as a result of the new black mayor] they are going to fire all the white construction workers in the city and hire all black guys.
>
> Dinkins, he's all for the blacks, 100 percent. Not like Ed Koch who used to care about people in white neighborhoods.
>
> Youth 1: Koch, he was for everybody. He went out into the neighborhoods and talked to people one on one.
>
> Youth 2: When Dinkins was elected I wanted to move out of the city.
>
> Youth 3: The black people will get more attention than they already receive— they get power.
>
> Youth 2: That's right, the black people really think they got it now.

The youths consistently described economic constraints and problems as the primary reasons for racial problems in the city.

> The situation is more racial because the economy has changed. Some people are out of work and they want to have some fun.
>
> People in my neighborhood don't like how things are going. There aren't enough jobs. You got all these homeless people. When things get bad, it gets tense. Especially when the blacks get all of the attention. Except when some

black guy gets beat up or somethin'. Then everybody's lookin' at us and callin' us racist.

Although they lacked a developed analysis or ideology, these teens felt they were in unfair competition with other groups, particularly blacks, whom they saw as benefiting from "special" treatment.

The attitudes of the youth towards blacks were clearly linked to their sense of the position of whites vis-a-vis blacks in the city. Blumer states that "it is the sense of social position emerging from this collective process of characterization which provides the basis of racial prejudice" (Blumer 1958:4). This held true for these white youths; their attitudes towards blacks were significantly influenced by their perception that blacks were achieving success at the expense of whites. The following quotes from several interviews illustrate this perception.

> The situation is much worse for white people than it used to be. There is more competition. They are going to give blacks more jobs because people will be afraid of calling it racial.
>
> Companies have to give certain jobs to blacks even though they don't qualify as much as the whites, and I don't think that's fair.
>
> If there is a white and a black going after the same job, and they don't hire the black, the black might make something out of it. The white person might let it pass.
>
> Why is it that black people think we owe them something?
>
> Youth 1: How come when somebody white gets shot, we don't make a big deal about it?
>
> Youth 2: We don't do nothing, we all sit on our asses.
>
> Youth 3: We should be fighting for our rights.

Youth 4: That's right, fight back.

Youth 3: Instead of fighting among ourselves, we need to get together and fight back.

The interviews also revealed that the youths perceived blacks as benefiting from preferential treatment in the media. They consistently described the media as distorting the image of white youth and white communities, unfairly portraying young whites, and misrepresenting young black males. They had a strong perception that the media only showed the bad things that happened in their neighborhoods and reported events as racially motivated which they felt were not. They strongly believed there should be "more equal and fair media coverage."

> The media is more worried about what white people are doing to blacks than what black people are doing to whites.

> If a white person attacks a black person, they throw the book at him. Meanwhile black kids are getting away with murder and nobody says anything about it, not the media, not the police, nobody.

> There's a double standard in the media. If a black kid gets jumped by a bunch of white kids, they say it's racial. Friends of mine get jumped by black kids all the time and no one describes it as racial.

> The media is pushing the black people's case and it's pissing off white people.

> The media makes a little issue into a big racial shit.

Many of the young people described crimes committed by blacks as the main reason for racial tension in the city. There was a widespread feeling that blacks were violent troublemakers who were especially dangerous and bold in large groups. Many told stories and anecdotes about blacks committing crimes which went unpunished by the police or school administrators. The youths uniformly described blacks who ventured into their neighborhoods as "looking for trouble." According to them, everybody in their community believed that the only reason for blacks to come into their neighborhoods was to commit crimes. Consequently, they felt they had the right and obligation to defend their territory against blacks; that it was up to them to "stop the blacks"; that if they attacked these outsiders, they would send a message to all blacks from outside the neighborhood to stay out of their communities.

> A group of black kids come into your neighborhood—they are looking for trouble. Why else are they there?

> The police know the blacks don't belong in our neighborhoods—everybody knows if they are here they must be looking for trouble. It's up to us to make sure they stay out of our neighborhood.

> What is a 16 year old kid [Yusuf Hawkins] without a driver's license doing walking into an all white neighborhood at 9:30 at night looking for a used car? He was out looking for trouble and he found it. Those guys did what they had to do.

> If they are stupid enough to walk, one person, at night—they're not looking for a fight but they are stupid and crazy. They should know that they don't belong there.

> If a white guy walks on my block, nobody will say anything to him. But if a black guy walks on my block everybody puts their heads out the window to make sure he leaves the block.

> Yeah, if a black guy comes around, they are usually trying to rob or beat up on

people. They would call the cops on a black guy if they see him. The black guy is probably better off if the cops show up than if the Avenue X boys find him first.

Blacks just keep stealing everybody's sneakers. They will kill you for your sneakers. They start a lot of trouble. If they want trouble, they're going to get trouble.

These statements illustrate the youths' desire to maintain their neighborhoods' ethnic and racial composition. Their statements were consistent with the survey data. While the overwhelming majority (80 percent) agreed that people have the right to live wherever they choose, 51 percent agreed that it is better to have people of the same race living in the same neighborhoods and disagreed that it is better to have mixed neighborhoods with people of different racial and ethnic backgrounds. Thirty-eight percent of the youths agreed that whites, blacks, Asians, and Hispanics should stay in their own neighborhoods. Fifteen percent agreed that people have a right to physically prevent people who are different from them from coming into their neighborhoods.

The Importance of Peer Groups

Like young people everywhere, the youths from these neighborhoods hung out together. Analysis of the interviews reveals that negative attitudes towards blacks served a social cohesion function within peer groups. The youths explained that the expression of negative attitudes towards blacks and other people of color provided status and respect and "proof positive that they are down with the program."

The link between these attitudes and the individual and group identities of the white youths is very strong. Many of the youths

interviewed had dropped out of high school and many had behavioral problems in school and on the streets. Consequently, they often were viewed by adult members of their community as "hoodlums" or "outcasts"; many were also alienated from their families. These young white men repeatedly stated that other community residents held such opinions of them.

With my friends I get respect. I can't talk to my mother, that's why I moved out when I was fifteen. The rest of the people in my neighborhood think I'm crazy. They think we are bums who hang out on the street and cause trouble. In some ways they're right.

In this context, their primary positive reinforcement was on the street, hanging out with other neighborhood teens. As a result, they were constantly trying to prove themselves worthy to their peers. In the context of the street, that proof lay in their ability to express the peer group's collective ideology and a willingness to back up those ideas with brute force ranging from harassment to mayhem, and sometimes even murder.

In the focus group interviews, several youths revealed that they were "going on missions." When asked to explain what "missions" were, one young Bensonhurst man described how informal groups of neighborhood teens would get together at night to hang out. After several hours of drinking or taking drugs, the group would look for people to harass and beat up.

We'll just be hanging out, partying. And somebody will say "hey, let's go on a mission." That's when you go look for people who don't belong in the neighborhood and you beat 'em up. Sometimes, they go out lookin' for blacks to jump. Sometimes they look for anybody who ain't supposed to be there.

The rest of the group responded with noticeable enthusiasm to discussing missions. They seemed excited by descriptions of late night searches for individuals who "did not belong in the neighborhood." They talked openly and excitedly about going on missions, and the entire ambience of the interview changed as they began to describe them in detail.

At first, the youths steadfastly proclaimed that there was nothing "racial" about the missions. They argued the media was responsible for making things "look racial"; they were simply "defending their neighborhood" and would attack whites as well as blacks since their main objective was to "take care of outsiders." However, analysis of the interview data revealed that the perception that missions were not racially motivated was contradicted by the youths' descriptions of nightly group activities, which included regular searches for people of color, particularly blacks.

> If we fight against Bay Parkway, that's because we don't like each other. When we fight the blacks, it's because we don't like their color. All of Bensonhurst unites against them.

> Youth 1: Every weekend, me and him and a group of others would go out and get racial with—against Mexicans.

> Youth 2: It wasn't really racial . . .

> Youth 1: Oh, yeah, we were racial. Alright, would you call this racial? Every Mexican we see, no matter what they were doing, if they weren't doing nothing, we'd still beat 'em up.

> You go out and you're lookin for people. The best is if you catch a couple of black guys. Or if you can't find no blacks, maybe you find an Indian or an Arab or a Dominican.

The youth described a hierarchy of desirable targets for assault. Blacks were their primary targets. If they could not find a black person, then a Dominican, a Pakistani, or an Indian would do. The list varied in its order of preference, with the exception that blacks were always at the top of the list. The youth said they would attack other whites as well, but only if they were from a rival neighborhood that had started trouble in their neighborhood.

> Blacks, Pakistanis, everybody gets a little bit, racial slurs—like that. And if you're really hyped, you fuck them up good. Especially Dominicans.

> We go after a lot of people. But, it's the blacks, mostly, who you want to take care of.

> Youth 1: The problem is mostly with blacks. There is not as much problem between whites and Asians or whites and Hispanics.

> Youth 2: We don't have no problem with Asians.

Their language reflected how central race was to their outlook towards other groups. It provides an illustration of what Omi and Winant call "racialization," defined as "the extension of racial meaning to a previously unclassified relationship, social practice or group" (1986:64). These youths described their actions towards other groups as "getting racial"—an indication of missions' racially motivated character and of the perceived meaning of racial differences with the people of color they attacked. Racial differences were the critical motivating factor. Italian, Jewish, and a few light-skinned Puerto Rican youths all engaged in these activities, some in mixed ethnic groups.

The youths seemed to get a sense of self-worth and individual power from going on missions which was lacking in their lives. A sense of group cohesion and solidarity was heightened if the victim was from a racial or ethnic group high on the list of desirable targets. Recall that these young people consistently expressed feelings of economic and political powerlessness and frustration. Feelings of powerlessness, stemming from their economic positions and prospects and from their social positions within their own communities, appear to contribute to the visceral nature of their racial attitudes.

Analysis of the interviews shows that the missions gave these teens a sense of power. They seemed to describe themselves as itching to feel the elation of the power, control, and status which would result from administering a beating to a neighborhood intruder, usually while primed with alcohol and/or drugs.

What emerges from an analysis of white youths in South Brooklyn, is a picture of the relationship between their (1) negative attitudes and actions towards other groups, (2) individual identities, (3) developing ethnic identities, and (4) perceptions of themselves in their communities and in society more generally. Racism and racial violence are essentially group activities rarely perpetrated by a single individual. For these young people, establishing a strong, cohesive individual and group identity required showing the rest of the group that they were "down with the program." In this case, the program includes concrete proof of being tough, hating the appropriate enemies, and a readiness to take those enemies on to defend principles and turf.

> You go on missions to impress your friends. You get a name as a tough guy who is down with the neighborhood and down with his people.

> You prove you're a real Bensonhurst Italian who don't take no shit, who don't let the wrong kind of people into the neighborhood.

> You do it to feel powerful, to feel like you're somebody. So people will respect you.

> Youth 1: You do it cause you want to be cool.

> Youth 2: To get out their frustrations.

> Youth 3: Because there is nothing else to do.

The Importance of Community Support

The study subjects claimed they fought to "protect the neighborhood" and for "unity in their community." Delinquent behavior had been translated into acts of neighborhood defense. The language the youths used reflected a feeling of responsibility for protecting their community, defending their turf, and keeping undesirable outsiders (i.e., people of color) out of their neighborhood. Numerous statements about how they "did what they had to do," reveal this rationalization.

> I did what I had to do. I have a reputation as a tough guy who defends the neighborhood and I want to keep it. People know when you've taken care of people who don't belong in the neighborhood. You get respect. Especially if it is some of the blacks from Marlboro projects.

> When you're hanging out with your partners and you see somebody who don't belong on your block, like a black guy or a Dominican, and you do him [beat him up], you feel real together. Everybody's together doing what we have to do.

> Everybody in the neighborhood knows what the deal is. The police don't care about it unless somebody gets killed. Everybody else figures we're just doing them a favor. As long as we don't bother neighborhood folks, it's no problem.

The youths clearly see themselves as defending the community from individuals and groups they believe do not belong in their neighborhoods. Consequently, they can explain and justify their actions as "helpful" to the community and in sync with its sentiments and values.

Like many teens, these youths engage in behaviors which are aimed at proving themselves worthy to their peers. In this context, they demonstrate their toughness and hatred of certain groups by beating them up.

By interpreting racially motivated behavior as beneficial to the community, the youths gain a sense of self-worth. This is reinforced by positive feedback from their peers and from some members of the community. I encountered evidence of support in discussions with various community residents. These discussions included one shopowner who was disgusted with the activities of the youths and complained that the problem was neighborhoodwide.

> The problem is that some of the people around here like what they are doing. People don't want blacks around here and these kids keep them out. These kids even get rewards from some of the shopowners for taking care of blacks who look suspicious. A fellah up the street gives away free pizza, if you can believe it.

Conclusion

The white youths from southern Brooklyn interviewed for this study provide important insights into racially motivated attacks and partly explain the increase in bias related violence in New York City. The analysis reveals four major factors contributing to involvement in racially motivated attacks: (1) structural economic conditions; (2) the societal racial climate and ideology; (3) the history of neighborhood race relations and the community's racial ideology; (4) participation in neighborhood-based peer groups.

Economic conditions are an important factor. These young people face extremely uncertain futures. In the last 15 to 20 years, industrial jobs have disappeared from the city's economy at an alarming rate and the employment prospects for working-class youth, particularly males, are constricted. Competition for employment in New York City was accompanied by an increase in the dropout rate from 13 percent in 1983 to 25 percent in 1987. These conditions laid the foundation for rising ethnic and racial violence by increasing anxiety and competition between groups. Most of the youths in this study had done poorly in school or had dropped out completely, placing them in a precarious position in a labor market which places a high value on education. As a result of changes in the labor market, jobs like those of their parents and older brothers or sisters are no longer available. These young people believe jobs are scarce for whites because of special treatment towards blacks. In their view, affirmative action functions as reverse discrimination against whites, and Third World immigrants take away additional jobs and invade their neighborhoods. They perceive *themselves* as disadvantaged, while people of color gain political and economic power by getting special treatment.

In addition, the attitudes of these white youths reflect the neoconservative ideas and principles which have achieved prominence on a national level in debates over civil rights, affirmative action, and racial inequality. In the last ten years, neoconservative ideology has emerged as a strong current in public policy, academia, and politics (Omi and Winant 1986). The public positions taken by the Reagan and Bush administrations on these issues; the emerging theories of neoconservative scholars such as Sowell (1990), Murray (1984), and Glazer (1975);

and the imagery and language of the 1988 Bush campaign and of politicians such as Jesse Helms and David Duke all lend credence to a sense of victimization and provide a target for anger, frustration, and economic anxiety. While these teens were not well informed about the specifics of neoconservative analysis, they related to its images and symbols; for example, a black person getting a job that a white person was more qualified for; blacks getting preferential treatment; young black males as criminals; black and Puerto Rican families as welfare dependent, single-parent households with a violent culture and unclean habits. Several young whites referred to Professor Michael Levin in discussing the violent, criminal danger blacks posed to their neighborhood.[3] These ideologies fuel the perception that African Americans have power. In this context, the youths view their violent actions as "fighting back," though the tragic reality is that African Americans and other people of color lack the power to deter racially motivated attacks and therefore are vulnerable targets.

Another contributing factor is the close-knit ethnic communities with histories of "flight" from neighborhoods where African Americans and other minorities have moved in. Though community members frown on delinquent activities, there is evidence of tacit support for the role these young people play in keeping unwanted minorities out of their neighborhoods. There is no doubt that the youths believe neighborhood residents either look the other way or directly support

their attacks on "unwanted" nonwhite outsiders.

For example, much of the Bensonhurst community rallied to the defense of the white youths involved in the attack on Yusuf Hawkins, staunchly proclaiming that the incident was not racially motivated. A cloak of silence was placed over the events of 23 August 1989, based on an implicit understanding that the participants were not to be criticized openly. In one focus group interview, a young woman inadvertently broke this code of silence and was immediately rebuked with angry stares and verbal reminders of the code.

Other evidence of tacit community support for the youths' activities can be drawn from an analysis of previous incidents. All four communities have a history of racial tensions marked in the 1970s and 1980s by frequent racial violence at their high schools (*Wall Street Journal* 1988). In 1982, an African-American transit worker was attacked and killed by a mob of whites. In 1988, on three separate occasions, flyers asserting that "Orientals" were trying to take over the neighborhood and encouraging residents to boycott Asian businesses and to refuse to sell their homes to Asians were distributed throughout the neighborhood (Mayor's Advisory Council on Community Relations 1989). There was little coordinated neighborhood response to these incidents. In the absence of community control over racial violence, the youth of Bensonhurst and Gravesend felt encouraged and supported in their racially motivated actions.

Since the murder of Yusuf Hawkins in August 1989, Bensonhurst has been the focus of nationwide attention. As a result, the people of Bensonhurst, as well as the surrounding white working-class communities, are extremely sensitive to the issue of race. Many residents complain that their neighborhood has been unfairly labeled as a "racist community." One of the difficulties

---

[3] Michael Levin is a professor of philosophy at the City University of New York. In the spring of 1990, he became the center of controversy when he gave several lectures and interviews in which he stated that whites have justifiable fear of young black males because they have a higher propensity to be violent. Among other measures, Levin advocated specific subway cars for young black males—a position which resonated deeply with the youths involved in this study.

in discussing community collusion is that it treats the neighborhood as an exception; it appears more racist than other neighborhoods in South Brooklyn or in other parts of New York City.

In fact, labeling Bensonhurst as a "racist community" shifts the analysis from wider conditions and factors to an analysis of the people of Bensonhurst—from a systematic and generalizable examination of the problem to a more microscopic, individual analysis. What sets Bensonhurst apart is simply that Yusuf Hawkins died there. The statements of youths elsewhere in southern Brooklyn reveal that racially motivated attacks occur regularly in other white ethnic communities.

As in all communities, the number of youths involved in violent activity is small. However, in white ethnic communities in South Brooklyn, they serve a function; in the case of Bensonhurst and Howard Beach they have a profound effect on how the communities are viewed by outsiders. The actions of the youths are well known in other parts of the city. As a result, these communities have a reputation throughout New York City for being inhospitable to African Americans. This reputation helps to deter African Americans and other minorities from settling in or even visiting these communities.

Finally, the peer groups of these white youths reinforce negative attitudes and thereby facilitate violence against other ethnic and racial groups. The youths gain a positive sense of themselves, a more cohesive group solidarity, and a heightened sense of identity from participating in group attacks against people or groups from different ethnic and racial backgrounds. Through peer group membership and activity these youths develop a racialized perspective concretized through group action.

The most powerful motivations for white youths to participate in acts of racial violence were turf defense, personal power, self-worth, and the need to belong to a group. Ethnic and racial attitudes were directly linked to these issues and were imparted by family, friends, the community, and the wider society; attitudes were internalized through participation in peer groups. Maintenance of these attitudes was clearly linked to developing a racialized self-identity and ethnic identity; internalizing and exhibiting the image of a tough, important, powerful member of the neighborhood who defended the community and received its tacit support was part of the identification process.

Processes of affiliation are often linked to processes of differentiation (Pinderhughes 1982). In this case, the process of differentiation from African Americans and other groups by white youths is linked to the process of affiliation with the neighborhood and ethnic group. Thus, these Italian and Jewish working-class youths from Gravesend and Bensonhurst believe that disliking blacks is part of what it means to be a "good" Italian or Jew within the context of their community place and role. For many, the street has replaced the home and the school as the context in which identity is developed; neighborhood peers supply values and models.

However, the behavior of these young people is an extension of neighborhood and societal attitudes and ideologies which have been translated to the street. Messages from parents, community residents, and political representatives at many different levels have been incorporated into a street ideology which provides justifications for racial violence.

The research findings support the hypothesis that a combination of structural factors, neighborhood influences, and peer group dynamics produce ethnic and racial conflict among youth. Deteriorating economic prospects for teens have raised anxieties and fears and have fueled competition with other youth. Community sentiments and peer group participation direct these anxieties and fears against other ethnic and racial groups by encouraging an oppositional sense of group position and linking group membership to particular racial attitudes. The peer group provides a mechanism for expressing negative attitudes towards other groups in the form of ethnic and racial violence, which is seen by the youth as a defense of turf and neighborhood.

In conclusion, the process of racial conflict can only be understood by examining how a number of factors *combine* to produce ethnic and racial conflict. None of the factors alone can plausibly explain the presence or absence of conflict. For example, not all Italian or Jewish youth have negative attitudes towards blacks. Only when ethnicity is combined with neighborhood support and participation in peer groups which encourage and facilitate these attitudes is there the potential for ethnic and racial violence. All working-class white youths from Bensonhurst do not have negative attitudes towards blacks. Nor do all white youths who do poorly in school or who drop out have negative attitudes towards blacks. However, an Italian or Jewish youth who is from a neighborhood with a history of conflict with blacks, does poorly in school or has dropped out, spends time on the street with a neighborhood-based peer group with an established oppositional sense of ethnic group position and that sees itself as threatened by members of another group is more likely to have negative attitudes towards blacks and to engage in acts of racial violence.

Finally, the problem of racially motivated violence is not isolated to the white communities of southern Brooklyn. The same factors which result in racial conflict and violence in southern Brooklyn are present or developing in many communities with different ethnic and racial compositions. Until the factors discussed in this paper are

addressed comprehensively, they will continue to provide the foundation for persistent racial violence in communities across the country.

REFERENCES

BLUMER, HERBERT. 1958. "Race Prejudice as a Sense of Group Position." *Pacific Sociological Review* 1:3–7.

DRENNAN, MATTHEW. 1991. "The Decline and Rise of the New York Economy." Pp. 25–42 in *Dual City: Restructuring New York,* edited by John Mollenkopf and Manuel Castells. New York: Russell Sage Foundation.

GLAZER, NATHAN. 1975. *Affirmative Discrimination.* New York: Basic Books.

HARRIS, RICHARD. 1991. "The Geography of Employment and Residence in New York Since 1950." Pp. 129–52 in *Dual City,* edited by Mollenkopf and Castells.

KINDER, D., and D. SEARS. 1981. "Prejudice and Politics: Symbolic Racism Versus Racial Threats to the Good Life." *Journal of Personality and Social Psychology* 40:414–31.

KRUEGER, RICHARD. 1988. *Focus Groups: A Practical Guide for Applied Research.* Newbury Park, CA: Sage.

Martin Luther King, Jr., Institute for Nonviolence. 1990. "A Study of New York City High School Students and Educational Staff on Prejudice and Race Relations." Unpublished document.

The Mayor's Advisory Council on Community Relations. 1989. *Final Report.* New York: Office of the Mayor of the City of New York.

MOLLENKOPF, JOHN, and MANUEL CASTELLS, eds. 1991. Introduction to *Dual City: Restructuring New York.* New York: Russell Sage Foundation.

MORGAN, DAVID. 1988. *Focus Groups as Qualitative Research.* Newbury Park, CA: Sage.

MURRAY, CHARLES. 1984. *Losing Ground: American Social Policy 1950–1980.* New York: Basic Books.

New York City Board of Education, Office of Student Information Services. 1984. *Annual Pupil Ethnic Census,* 1960–1983. New York: New York City Board of Education.

New York City Department of Planning, Population Division and Office of Immigrant Affairs. 1985. Unpublished Report.

New York Times. 1988. "Dropout Rate for Hispanic Teenagers Is Highest in New York." 21 June.

OMI, M., and H. WINANT. 1986. *Racial Formation in the United States: From the 1960s to the 1980s.* New York: Routledge & Kegan Paul.

PINDERHUGHES, CHARLES. 1982. "Paired Differential Bonding in Biological, Psychological, and Social Systems." *The American Journal of Social Psychiatry* 2:5–14.

RIEDER, JONATHAN. 1985. *Canarsie: The Jews and Italians of Brooklyn Against Liberalism.* Cambridge, MA: Harvard University Press.

SCHUMAN, HOWARD, CHARLOTTE STEEH, and LAWRENCE BOBO. 1985. *Racial Attitudes in America.* Cambridge, MA: Harvard University Press.

SHEATSLEY, PAUL. 1966. "White Attitudes Toward the Negro. *Daedalus* 95:217–38.

SOWELL, THOMAS. 1990. *Preferential Policies.* New York: Morrow.

STEGMAN, MICHAEL. 1988. *Housing and Vacancy Report: New York City, 1987.* New York: City of New York Department of Housing Preservation and Development.

STEINBERG, STEPHEN. 1981. *The Ethnic Myth.* New York: Atheneum.

SULLIVAN, MERCER. 1989. *Getting Paid: Youth Crime and Work in the Inner City.* Ithaca, NY: Cornell University Press.

TAYLOR, D., P. SHEATSLEY, and A. GREELEY. 1978. "Attitudes Toward Racial Integration." *Scientific American* 238:42–49.

U.S. Department of Labor, Bureau of Labor Statistics. 1986. *Current Population Survey.* Washington, DC: U.S. Government Printing Office.

Wall Street Journal. 1988. "Turf Defenders: The Mood Gets Nasty in City Neighborhoods as Racial Tension Rises—Working-Class Bensonhurst, Next to New York Ghetto, Fears Drugs and Crime." 25 July.

19

ENVIRONMENTAL JUSTICE IN THE 21st CENTURY: RACE STILL MATTERS

Robert D. Bullard

Questions to Consider

Where is the trash dump, the water treatment plant, or the power plant in your community? Is there one? In this reading, Robert Bullard argues that in all likelihood these environmental dangers are in low income, black, and brown neighborhoods. Why do some communities get "dumped on" while others remain free of toxic waste sites?

Hardly a day passes without the media discovering some community or neighborhood fighting a landfill, incinerator, chemical plant, or some other polluting industry. This was not always the case. Just three decades ago, the concept of environmental justice had not registered on the radar screens of environmental, civil rights, or social justice groups.[1] Nevertheless, it should not be forgotten that Dr. Martin Luther King, Jr., went to Memphis in 1968 on an environmental and economic justice mission for the striking black garbage workers. The strikers were demanding equal pay and better work conditions. Of course, Dr. King was assassinated before he could complete his mission.

Another landmark garbage dispute took place a decade later in Houston, when African-American homeowners in 1979 began a bitter fight to keep a sanitary landfill out of their suburban middle-income neighborhood.[2] Residents formed the Northeast Community Action Group or NECAG. NECAG and their attorney, Linda McKeever Bullard, filed a class-action lawsuit to block the facility from being built. The 1979 lawsuit, *Bean v. Southwestern Waste Management, Inc.,* was the first of its kind to challenge the siting of a waste facility under civil rights law.

The landmark Houston case occurred three years before the environmental justice movement was catapulted into the national limelight in the rural and mostly African-American Warren County, North Carolina. The environmental justice movement has come a long way since its humble beginning in Warren County, North Carolina, where a PCB landfill ignited protests and over 500 arrests. The Warren County protests provided the impetus for a U.S. General Accounting Office study, *Siting of Hazardous Waste Landfills and Their Correlation with Racial and Economic Status of Surrounding Communities.*[3] That study revealed that three out of four of the off-site, commercial hazardous waste landfills in Region 4 (which comprises eight states in the South) happen to be located in predominantly African-American communities, although African-Americans made up only 20% of the region's population. More important, the protesters

put "environmental racism" on the map. Fifteen years later, the state of North Carolina is required to spend over $25 million to clean up and detoxify the Warren County PCB landfill.

The Warren County protests also led the Commission for Racial Justice to produce *Toxic Waste and Race,*[4] the first national study to correlate waste facility sites and demographic characteristics. Race was found to be the most potent variable in predicting where these facilities were located—more powerful than poverty, land values, and home ownership. In 1990, *Dumping in Dixie: Race, Class, and Environmental Quality* chronicled the convergence of two social movements—social justice and environmental movements—into the environmental justice movement. This book highlighted African-Americans, environmental activism in the South, the same region that gave birth to the modern civil rights movement. What started out as local and often isolated community-based struggles against toxics and facility siting blossomed into a multiissue, multi-ethnic, and multiregional movement.

The 1991 First National People of Color Environmental Leadership Summit was probably the most important single event in the movement's history. The Summit broadened the environmental justice movement beyond its early antitoxics focus to include issues of public health, worker safety, land use, transportation, housing, resource allocation, and community empowerment.[5]

The meeting also demonstrated that it is possible to build a multiracial grassroots movement around environmental and economic justice.[6]

Held in Washington, DC, the four-day Summit was attended by over 650 grassroots and national leaders from around the world. Delegates came from all fifty states including Alaska and Hawaii, Puerto Rico, Chile, Mexico, and as far away as the Marshall Islands. People attended the summit to

Robert D. Bullard, "Environmental Justice in the 21st Century: Race Still Matters" from *Phylon,* 2001, Vol. 49, No. 3–4, pp. 151–171. Copyright © 2001 *Phylon.* Reprinted by permission.

share their action strategies, redefine the environmental movement, and develop common plans for addressing environmental problems affecting people of color in the United States and around the world.

On September 27, 1991, Summit delegates adopted 17 "Principles of Environmental Justice." These principles were developed as a guide for organizing, networking, and relating to government and nongovernmental organizations (NGOs). By June 1992, Spanish and Portuguese translations of the Principles were being used and circulated by NGOs and environmental justice groups at the Earth Summit in Rio de Janeiro.

In response to growing public concern and mounting scientific evidence, President Clinton on February 11, 1994 (the second day of the national health symposium), issued Executive Order 12898, "Federal Actions to Address Environmental Justice in Minority Populations and Low-Income Populations." This Order attempts to address environmental injustice within existing federal laws and regulations.

Executive Order 12898 reinforces the 35-year-old Civil Rights Act of 1964, Title VI, which prohibits discriminatory practices in programs receiving federal funds. The Order also focuses the spotlight back on the National Environmental Policy Act (NEPA), a twenty-five-year-old law that set policy goals for the protection, maintenance, and enhancement of the environment. NEPA's goal is to ensure for all Americans a safe, healthful, productive, and aesthetically and culturally pleasing environment. NEPA requires federal agencies to prepare a detailed statement on the environmental effects of proposed federal actions that significantly affect the quality of human health.

The Executive Order calls for improved methodologies for assessing and mitigating impacts, health effects from multiple and cumulative exposure, collection of data on low-income and minority populations who may be disproportionately at risk, and impacts on subsistence fishers and wildlife consumers. It also encourages participation of the impacted populations in the various phases of assessing impacts—including scoping, data gathering, alternatives, analysis, mitigation, and monitoring.

The Executive Order focuses on "subsistence" fishers and wildlife consumers. Everybody does not buy fish at the supermarket. There are many people who are subsistence fishers, who fish for protein, who basically subsidize their budgets, and their diets by fishing from rivers, streams, and lakes that happen to be polluted. These subpopulations may be underprotected when basic assumptions are made using the dominant risk paradigm.

Many grassroots activists are convinced that waiting for the government to act has endangered the health and welfare of their communities. Unlike the federal EPA, communities of color did not first discover environmental inequities in 1990. The federal EPA only took action on environmental justice concerns in 1990 after extensive prodding from grassroots environmental justice activists, educators, and academics.[7]

People of color have known about and have been living with inequitable environmental quality for decades—most without the protection of the federal, state, and local governmental agencies. Environmental justice advocates continue to challenge the current environmental protection apparatus and offer their own framework for addressing environmental inequities, disparate impact, and unequal protection.

An Environmental Justice Framework

The question of environmental justice is not anchored in a debate about whether or not decision makers should tinker with risk management. The framework seeks to prevent environmental threats before they occur.[8] The environmental justice framework incorporates other social movements that seek to eliminate harmful practices (discrimination harms the victim) in housing, land use, industrial planning, health care, and sanitation services. The impact of redlining, economic disinvestments, infrastructure decline, deteriorating housing, lead poisoning, industrial pollution, poverty, and unemployment are not unrelated problems if one lives in an urban ghetto or barrio, rural hamlet, or reservation.

The environmental justice framework attempts to uncover the underlying assumptions that may contribute to and produce unequal protection. This framework brings to the surface the ethical and political questions of "who gets what, why, and how much." Some general characteristics of the framework include:

1. *The environmental justice framework incorporates the principle of the "right" of all individuals to be protected from environmental degradation.* The precedents for this framework are the Civil Rights Act of 1964, Fair Housing Act of 1968 and as amended in 1988, and Voting Rights Act of 1965.

2. *The environmental justice framework adopts a public health model of prevention (elimination of the threat before harm occurs) as the preferred strategy.* Impacted communities should not have to wait until causation or conclusive "proof" is established before preventive action is taken. For example, the framework offers a solution to the lead problem by shifting the primary focus from treatment (after children have been poisoned) to prevention (elimination of the threat via abating lead in houses).

Overwhelming scientific evidence exists on the ill effects of lead on the human body. However, very little action has been taken to rid the nation of childhood lead poisoning in urban areas. Former Health and Human Secretary Louis Sullivan tagged this among the "number one environmental health threats to children."[9]

The Natural Resources Defense Council, NAACP Legal Defense and Educational Fund, ACLU, and Legal Aid Society of Alameda County joined forces in 1991 and won an out-of-court settlement worth $15–20 million for a blood-lead testing program in California. The *Matthews v. Coye* lawsuit involved the State of California not living up to the federally mandated testing of some 557,000 poor children for lead who receive Medicaid. This historic agreement triggered similar actions in other states that failed to live up to federally mandated screening.[10]

Lead screening is an important element in this problem. However, screening is not the solution. Prevention is the solution. Surely, if termite inspections can be mandated to protect individual home investment, a lead-free home can be mandated to protect public health. Ultimately, the lead abatement debate, public health (who is affected) vs. property rights (who pays for cleanup), is a value conflict that will not be resolved by the scientific community.

3. *The environmental justice framework shifts the burden of proof to polluter/dischargers who do harm, discriminate, or who do not give equal protection to racial and ethnic minorities, and other "protected" classes.* Under the current system, individuals who challenge polluters must "prove" that they have been harmed, discriminated against, or disproportionately impacted. Few impacted communities have the resources to hire lawyers, expert witnesses, and doctors needed to sustain such a challenge.

The environmental justice framework would require the parties that are applying for operating permits (landfills, incinerators, smelters, refineries, chemical plants, etc.) to "prove" that their operations are not harmful to human health, will not disproportionately impact racial and ethnic minorities and other protected groups, and are nondiscriminatory.

4. *The environmental justice framework would allow disparate impact and statistical weight, as opposed to "intent," to infer discrimination.* Proving intentional or purposeful discrimination in a court of law is next to impossible, as demonstrated in *Bean v. Southwestern Waste.* It took nearly a decade after *Bean v. Southwestern Waste* for environmental discrimination to resurface in the courts.

5. *The environmental justice framework redresses disproportionate impact through "targeted" action and resources.* This strategy would target resources where environmental and health problems are greatest (as determined by some ranking scheme but not limited to risk assessment). Reliance solely on "objective" science disguises the exploitative way the polluting industries have operated in some communities and condones a passive acceptance of the status quo.

Human <u>values</u> are involved in determining <u>which</u> geographic areas are worth public investments. In the 1992 EPA report, *Securing Our Legacy,* the agency describes geographic initiatives as "protecting what we love."[11]

The strategy emphasizes "pollution prevention, multimedia enforcement, research into causes and cures of environmental stress, stopping habitat loss, education, and constituency building."[12] Geographic initiatives are underway in the Chesapeake Bay, Great Lakes, Gulf of Mexico programs, and the U.S.-Mexican Border program. Environmental justice targeting would channel resources to "hot spots," communities that are overburdened with more than their "fair" share of environmental and health problems.

The dominant environmental protection paradigm reinforces instead of challenges the stratification of people (race, ethnicity, status, power, etc.), place (central cities, suburbs, rural areas, unincorporated areas,

Native American reservations, etc.), and work (i.e., office workers are afforded greater protection than farm workers). The dominant paradigm exists to manage, regulate, and distribute risks. As a result, the current system has (1) institutionalized unequal enforcement, (2) traded human health for profit, (3) placed the burden of proof on the "victims" and not the polluting industry, (4) legitimated human exposure to harmful chemicals, pesticides, and hazardous substances, (5) promoted "risky" technologies such as incinerators, (6) exploited the vulnerability of economically and politically disenfranchised communities, (7) subsidized ecological destruction, (8) created an industry around risk assessment, (9) delayed cleanup actions, and (10) failed to develop pollution prevention as the overarching and dominant strategy.[13]

The mission of the federal EPA was never designed to address environmental policies and practices that result in unfair, unjust, and inequitable outcome. EPA and other government officials are not likely to ask the questions that go to the heart of environmental injustice: What groups are most affected? Why are they affected? Who did it? What can be done to remedy the problem? How can the problem be prevented? Vulnerable communities, populations, and individuals often fall between the regulatory cracks.

Impetus for a Paradigm Shift

The environmental justice movement has changed the way scientists, researchers, policy makers, and educators go about their daily work. This bottom-up movement has redefined environment to include where people live, work, play, go to school, as well as how these things interact with the physical and natural world. The impetus for changing the dominant environmental protection paradigm did <u>not</u> come from within regulatory agencies, the polluting industry, academia, or the "industry" that has been built around risk management. The environmental justice movement is led by a loose alliance of grassroots and national environmental and civil rights leaders who question the foundation of the current environmental protection paradigm.

Despite significant improvements in environmental protection over the past several decades, millions of Americans continue to live, work, play, and go to school in unsafe and unhealthy physical environments.[14] During its 30-year history, the U.S. EPA has not always recognized that many of our government and industry practices (whether intended or unintended) have adverse impact on poor people and people of color. Growing grass roots community resistance emerged in response to practices, policies, and conditions that residents judged to be just, unfair, and illegal. Discrimination is a fact of life in America. Racial discrimination is also illegal.

The EPA is mandated to enforce the nations environmental laws and regulations equally across the board. It is also required to protect all Americans—not just individuals or groups who can afford lawyers, lobbyists, and experts. Environmental protection is a right, not a privilege reserved for a few who can vote with their feet and escape or fend off environmental stressors that address environmental inequities.

Equity may mean different things to different people. Equity is distilled into three broad categories: procedural, geographic, and social equity.

Procedural equity refers to the "fairness" question: the extent that governing rules, regulations, evaluation criteria, and enforcement are applied uniformly across the board and in a nondiscriminatory way. Unequal protection might result from non-scientific and undemocratic decisions, ex-clusionary practices, public hearing held in remote locations and at inconvenient times, and use of English-only material as the language to communicate and conduct hearings for non-English speaking publics.

Geographic equity refers to location and spatial configuration of communities and their proximity to environmental hazards, noxious facilities, and locally unwanted land uses (LULUs) such as landfills, incinerators, sewer treatment plants, lead smelters, refineries, and other noxious facilities. For example, unequal protection may result from land-use decisions that determine the location of residential amenities and disamenities. Unincorporated, poor, and communities of color often suffer a "triple" vulnerability of noxious facility siting.

Social Equity assesses the role of sociological factors (race, ethnicity, class, culture, life styles, political power, etc.) on environmental decision making. Poor people and people of color often work in the most dangerous jobs, live in the most polluted neighborhoods, and their children are exposed to all kinds of environmental toxins on the playgrounds and in their homes.

The nation's environmental laws, regulations, and policies are not applied uniformly–resulting in some individuals, neighborhoods, and communities being exposed to the elevated health risks. A 1992 study by staff writers from the *National Law Journal* uncovered glaring inequities in the way the federal EPA enforces its laws. The authors write:

> There is a racial divide in the way the U.S. Government cleans up toxic waste sites and punishes polluters. White communities see faster action, better results and stiffer penalities than communities where blacks, Hispanics and other minorities live. This unequal protection often occurs whether the community is wealthy or poor.[15] These

findings suggest that unequal protection is placing communities of color at special risk.

The *National Law Journal* study supplements the findings of earlier studies and reinforces what many grassroots leaders have been saying all along: not only are people of color differentially impacted by industrial pollution they can expect different treatment from the government. Environmental decision-making operates at the juncture of science, economics, politics, special interests, and ethics. This current environmental model places communities of color at special risk.

The Impact of Racial Apartheid

Apartheid-type housing, development, and environmental policies limit mobility, reduce neighborhood options, diminish job opportunities, and decrease choices for millions of Americans.[16] The infrastructure conditions in urban areas are a result of a host of factors including the distribution of wealth, patterns of racial and economic discrimination, redlining, housing and real estate practices, location decisions of industry, and differential enforcement of land use and environmental choices, and diminished job communities for African Americans.

Race still plays a significant part in distributing public "benefits" and public "burdens" associated with economic growth. The roots of discrimination are deep and have been difficult to eliminate. Housing discrimination contributes to the physical decay of inner-city neighborhoods and denies a substantial segment of the African-American community a basic form of wealth accumulation and investment through home ownership.[17] The number of African-American homeowners would probably be higher in the absence of discrimination by lending institutions.[18] Only about 59 percent of the nation's middle-class African Americans own their homes, compared with 74 percent of whites.

Eight out of every ten African Americans live in neighborhoods where they are in majority. Residential segregation decreases for most racial and ethnic groups with additional education, income, and occupational status. However, this scenario does not hold true for African Americans. African Americans, no matter what their educational or occupational achievement or income level, are exposed to higher crime rates, less effective educational systems, high mortality risks, more dilapidated surroundings, and greater environmental threats because of their race. For example, in the heavily populated South Coast air basin of the Los Angeles area, it is estimated that over 71 percent of African Americans and 50 percent of whites live in highly polluted areas.[19]

It has been difficult for millions of Americans in segregated neighborhoods to say "not in my backyard" (NIMBY) if they do not have a backyard.[20] Nationally, only about 44 percent of African Americans own their homes compared to over two-thirds of the nation as a whole. Homeowners are the strongest advocates of the NIMBY positions taken against locally unwanted uses or LULUs such as the construction of garbage dumps, landfills, incinerators, sewer treatment plants, recycling centers, prisons, drug treatment units, and public housing projects. Generally, white communities have greater access than people-of-color communities when it comes to influencing land use and environmental decision making.

The ability of an individual to escape a health-threatening physical environment is usually related to affluence. However, racial barriers complicate this process for many Americans.[21] The imbalance between residential amenities and land uses assigned to central cities and suburbs cannot be explained by class factors alone. People of color and whites do not have the same opportunities to "vote with their feet" and escape undesirable physical environments.

Institutional racism continues to influence housing and mobility options available to African Americans of all income levels—and is a major factor that influences quality of neighborhoods they have available to them. The "web of discrimination" in the housing market is a result of action and inaction of local and federal government officials, financial institutions, insurance companies, real estate marketing firms, and zoning boards. More stringent enforcement mechanisms and penalties are needed to combat all forms of discrimination.

Uneven development between central cities and suburbs combined with the systematic avoidance of inner-city areas by many businesses have heightened social and economic inequalities. For the past two decades, manufacturing plants have been fleeing central cities and taking their jobs with them. Many have moved offshore to Third-World countries where labor is cheap and environmental regulations are lax or nonexistent.

Industry flight from central cities had left behind a deteriorating urban infrastructure, poverty, and pollution. What kind of replacement industry can these communities attract? Economically depressed communities do not have a lot of choices available to them. Some workers have become so desperate that they see even a low-paying hazardous job as better than no job at all. These workers are forced to choose between unemployment and a job that may result in risks to their health, their family's health, and the health of their community. This practice amounts to "economic blackmail." Economic conditions in many people-of-color communities make them especially vulnerable to this practice.

Some polluting industries have been eager to exploit this vulnerability. Some have even used the assistance of elected officials in obtaining special tax breaks and government operating permits. Clearly, economic development and environmental policies flow from forces of production and are often dominated and subsidized by state actors. Numerous examples abound where state actors have targeted cities and regions for infrastructure improvements and amenities such as water irrigation systems, ship channels, road and bridge projects, and mass transit systems. On the other hand, state actors have done a miserable job in protecting central city residents from the ravages of industrial pollution and nonresidential activities valued as having a negative impact on quality of life.[22]

Racial and ethnic inequality is perpetuated and reinforced by local governments in conjunction with urban-based corporations. Race continues to be a potent variable in explaining urban land use, streets and highway configuration, commercial and industrial development, and industrial facility siting. Moreover, the question of "who gets what, where, and why" often pits one community against another.[23]

Zoning and Land Use

Some residential areas and their inhabitants are at a greater risk than the larger society from unregulated growth, ineffective regulation of industrial toxins, and public policy decisions authorizing industrial facilities that favor those with political and economic clout.[24] African Americans and other communities of color are often victims of land-use decision making that mirrors the power arrangements of the dominant society. Historically, exclusionary zoning (and rezoning) has been a subtle form of using government authority and power to foster and perpetuate discriminatory practices.

Zoning is probably the most widely applied mechanism to regulate urban land use in the United States. Zoning laws broadly define land for residential, commercial, or industrial uses, and may impose narrower land-use restrictions (e.g., minimum and maximum lot size, number of dwellings per acre, square feet and height of buildings, etc.). Zoning ordinances, deed restrictions, and other land-use mechanisms have been widely used as a "NIMBY" tool, operating through exclusionary practices. Thus, exclusionary zoning has been used to zone against something rather than for something. With or without zoning, deed restrictions or other devices, various groups are unequally able to protect their environmental interests. More often than not, people-of-color communities get shortchanged in the neighborhood protection game.

In Houston, Texas, a city that does not have zoning, NIMBY was replaced with the policy of PIBBY (place in black's back yard).[25] The city government and private industry targeted landfills, incinerators, and garbage dumps for Houston's black neighborhoods for more than five decades. These practices lowered resident's property values, accelerated physical deterioration, and increased disinvestment in the communities. Moreover, the discriminatory siting of landfills and incinerators stigmatized the neighborhoods as "dumping grounds" for a host of other unwanted facilities, including salvage yards, recycling operations, and automobile "chop shops."[26]

The Commission for Racial Justice's landmark *Toxic Wastes and Race* study found race to be the single most important factor (i.e., more important than income, home ownership rate, and property values) in the location of abandoned toxic waste sites.[27] The study also found that (1) three out of five African Americans live in communities with abandoned toxic waste sites; (2) sixty percent (15 million) African Americans live

in communities with one or more abandoned toxic waste sites; (3) three of the five largest commercial hazardous waste landfills are located in predominately African American or Latino communities and accounts for 40 percent of the nation's total estimated landfill capacity; and (4) African Americans are heavily overrepresented in the population of cities with the largest number of abandoned toxic waste sites, which include Memphis, St. Louis, Houston, Cleveland, Chicago, and Atlanta.

Waste facility siting imbalances that were uncovered by the U.S. General Accounting Office (GAO) in 1983 have not disappeared.[28] The GAO discovered three out of four of the offsite commercial hazardous waste landfills in Region IV (Alabama, Florida, Georgia, Kentucky, Mississippi, North Carolina South Carolina, and Tennessee) were located in predominately African American communities. African Americans still made up about one-fifth of the population in EPA Region IV. In 2000, 100 percent of the off-site commercial hazardous wastes landfills in the region is dumped in two mostly African-Americans communities.

Environmental Racism

Many of the differences in environmental quality between black and white communities result from institutional racism influences local land use, enforcement of environmental regulations, industrial facility siting, and where people of color live, work and play. The roots of institutional racism are deep and have been difficult to eliminate. Discrimination is a manifestation of institutional racism and causes life to be very different for whites and blacks. Historically, racism has been and continues to be a major part of the American sociological system, and as a result, people of color find themselves at a disadvantage in contemporary society.

Environmental racism is real. It is just as real as the racism found in the housing industry, educational institutions, employment arena, and judicial system. What is environmental racism and how does one recognize it? *Environmental racism refers to any policy, practice, or directive that differentially affects or disadvantages (whether intended or unintended) individuals, groups, or communities based on race or color.* Environmental racism combines with public policies and industry practices to provide benefits for whites while shifting costs to people of color.[29] Environmental racism is reinforced by government, legal, economic, political, and military institutions.

Environmental decision making and policies often mirror the power arrangements of the dominant society and its institutions. Environmental racism disadvantages people of color while providing advantages or privileges for whites. A form of illegal "exaction" forces people of color to pay costs of environmental benefits for the public at large. The question of who pays and who benefits from the current environmental and industrial policies is central to this analysis of environmental racism and other systems of domination and exploitation.

Racism influences the likelihood of exposure to environmental and health risks as well as accessibility to health care.[30] Many of the nation's environmental policies distribute the costs in a regressive pattern while providing disproportionate benefits for whites and individuals who fall at the upper end of the education and income scale. Numerous studies, dating back to the seventies, reveal that people of color have borne greater health and environmental risk burdens than the society at large.[31]

Elevated public health risks are found in some populations even when social class is held constant. For example, race has been found to be independent of class in the distribution of air pollution,[32] contaminated fish consumption,[33] location of municipal landfills and incinerators,[34] toxic waste dumps,[35] cleanup of superfund sites,[36] and lead poisoning in children.[37]

Lead poisoning is a classic example of an environmental health problem that disproportionately impacts children of color at every class level. Lead affects between 3 to 4 million children in the United States—most of whom are African-American and Latinos who live in urban areas. Among children 5 years old and younger, the percentage of African-American children who have excessive levels of lead in their blood far exceeds the percentage of whites at all income levels.

In 1988, the federal Agency for Toxic Substances Disease Registry (ATSDR) found that for families earning less than $6,000, 68 percent of African-American children had lead poisoning, compared with 36 percent for white children. In families with income exceeding $15,000, more than 38 percent of African-American children suffer from lead poisoning compared with 12 percent of whites. The average blood-lead level has dropped for all children with the phasing out of leaded gasoline. Today, the average blood-lead level for all children in the U.S. is under 6 ug/dl.[38] However, these efforts have not had the same positive benefits on all populations. There is still work to be done to address the remaining problem. The lead problem is not randomly distributed across the nation. The most vulnerable populations are low-income African-American and Hispanic-American children who live in older urban housing.[39]

Figures reported in the July 1994 *Journal of American Medical Association* on the Third National Health and Nutrition Examination Survey (NHANES III) revealed that 1.7 million children (8.9 percent of children aged 1 to 5) are lead poisoned, defined as blood-lead levels equal to or above 10 ug/dl.[40] Lead-based paint (chips and dust) is the most common source of lead exposure for children. Children may also be exposed through soil and dust contamination built up from vehicle exhaust, lead concentration in soils in urban areas, lead dust brought into the home on parents work clothes, lead used in ceramics and pottery, folk medicines, and lead in plumbing.

The Right to Breathe Clean Air

Urban air pollution problems have been with us for some time now. Before the federal government stepped in, issues related to air pollution were handled primarily by states and local government. Because states and local governments did such a poor job, the federal government set out to establish national clean air standards. Congress enacted the Clean Air Act (CAA) in 1970 and mandated the U.S. Environmental Protection Agency (EPA) to carry out this law. Subsequent amendments (1977 and 1990) were made to the CAA that form the current federal program. The CAA was a response to states, unwillingness to protect air quality. May states used their lax enforcement of environmental laws as lures for business and economic development.[41]

Central cities and suburbs do not operate on a level playing field. They often compete for scarce resources. One need not be a rocket scientist to predict the outcome between affluent suburbs and their less affluent central city competitors.[42] Freeways are the lifeline for suburban commuters, while millions of central-city residents are dependent on public transportation as their primary mode of travel. But recent cuts in mass transit subsidies and fare hikes have reduced access to essential social services and economic activities. Nevertheless, road construction programs are booming—even in areas choked with automobiles and air pollution.[43]

The air quality impacts of transportation are especially significant to people of color who are more likely than whites to live in urban areas with reduced air quality. National Argonne Laboratory researchers discovered that 437 of the 3,109 counties and independent cities failed to meet at least one of the EPA ambient air quality standards.[44] Specifically, 57 percent of whites, 65 percent of African Americans, and 80 percent of Hispanics live in 437 counties with substandard air quality. Nationwide, 33 percent of whites, 50 percent of African Americans, and 60 percent of Hispanics live in the 136 counties in which two or more air pollutants exceed standards. Similar patterns were found for the 29 counties designated as nonattainment areas for three or more pollutants. Again, 12 percent of whites, 20 percent of African Americans, and 31 percent of Hispanics resided in the worse nonattainment areas.

Asthma is an emerging epidemic in the United States. The annual age-adjusted death rate from asthma increased by 40% between 1982 through 1991, from 1.34 to 1.88 per 100,000 population,[45] with the highest rates being consistently reported among blacks aged 15–24 years of age during the period 1980–1993.[46] Poverty and minority status are important risk factors for asthma mortality.

Children are at special risk from ozone.[47] Children also represent a considerable share of the asthma burden. It is the most common chronic disease of childhood. Asthma affects almost 5 million children under 18 years. Although the overall annual age-adjusted hospital discharge rate for asthma among children under 15 years old decreased slightly from 184 to 179 per 100,000 between 1982 and 1992, the decrease was slower compared to other childhood diseases[48] resulting in a 70% increase in the proportion of hospital admissions related to asthma during the 1980s.[49] Inner-city children have the highest rates for asthma prevalence, hospitalization, and mortality.[50] In the United States, asthma is the fourth leading cause of disability among children aged less than 18 years.[51]

The public health community has insufficient information to explain the magnitude of some of the air pollution-related health problems. However, they do know that persons suffering from asthma are particularly sensitive to the effects of carbon monoxide, sulfur dioxides particulate matter, ozone, and nitrogen oxides. Ground-level ozone may exacerbate health problems such as asthma, nasal congestions, throat irritation, respiratory tract inflammation, reduced resistance to infection, changes in cell function, loss of lung elasticity, chest pains, lung scarring, formation of lesions within the lungs, and premature aging of lung tissues.[52]

Nationally, African Americans and Latino Americans have significantly higher prevalence of asthma than the general population. A 1996 report from the federal Centers for Disease Control shows hospitalization and deaths rates from asthma increasing for persons twenty-five years or less.[53] The greatest increases occurred among African Americans. African Americans are two to six times more likely than whites to die from asthma.[54] Similarly, the hospitalization rate for African Americans is 3 to 4 times the rate for whites.

A 1994 CDC-sponsored study showed that pediatric emergency department visits at Atlanta Grady Memorial Hospital increased by one-third following peak ozone levels. The study also found that asthma rate among African-American children is 26 percent higher than the asthma rate among whites.[55] Since children with asthma in Atlanta may not have visited the emergency department for their care, the true prevalence of asthma in the community is likely to be higher.

Exploitation of Land, Environment, and People

Environmental decision-making and local land-use planning operate at the juncture of science, economics, politics, and special interests that place communities of color at special risk.[56] This is especially true in America's Deep South. The Deep South has always been thought of as a backward land based on its social, economic, political, and environmental policies. By default, the region became a "sacrifice zone," a sump for the rest of the nation's toxic waste.[57] A colonial mentality exists in the South where local government and big business take advantage of people who are politically and economically powerless. Many of these attitudes emerged from the region's marriage to slavery and the plantation system—a brutal system that exploited humans and the land.[58] The Deep South is stuck with this unique legacy—the legacy of slavery, Jim Crow, and white resistance to equal justice for all. This legacy has also affected race relations and the region's ecology. Southerners, black and white, have less education, lower incomes, higher infant mortality, and lower life expectancy than Americans elsewhere. It should be no surprise that the environmental quality that Southerners enjoy is markedly different from that of other regions of the country.

The South is characterized by "look-the-other-way environmental policies and give-away tax breaks."[59] It is our nation's Third World where "political bosses encourage outsiders to buy the region's human and natural resources at bargain prices."[60] Lax enforcement of environmental regulations have left the region's air, water, and land the most industry-befouled in the United States.

Toxic waste discharge and industrial pollution are correlated with poorer economic conditions. Louisiana typifies this pattern. Nearly three-fourths of Louisiana's population—more that 3 million people—get their drinking water from underground aquifers. Dozens of the aquifers are threatened by contamination from polluting industries.[61] The Lower Mississippi River Industrial Corridor has over 125 companies that manufacture a range of products including fertilizers, gasoline, paints, and plastics. This corridor has been dubbed "Cancer Alley" by environmentalists and local residents.[62] Ascension Parish typifies what many people refer to as a toxic "sacrifice zone." In two parish towns of Geismer and St. Gabriel, 18 petrochemical plants are crammed into a nine-and-a-half-square-mile area. Petrochemical plants discharge millions of pounds of pollutants annually into the water and air.

Louisiana citizens subsidize this corporate welfare with their health and the environment. Tax breaks given to polluting industries have created a few jobs at high cost. Nowhere is the polluter-welfare scenario more prevalent than in Louisiana. The state is a leader in doling out corporate welfare to polluters. A 1998 *Time Magazine* article reported that in the 1990s, Louisiana wiped off the books $3.1 billion in property taxes to polluting companies.[63] The state's top five worse polluters received $111 million dollars over the past decade.

Global Dumping Grounds

There is a direct correlation between exploitation of land and exploitation of people. It should not be a surprise to anyone to discover that Native Americans have to contend with some of the worst pollution in the United States.[64] Native American nations have become prime targets for waste trading.[65] More than three dozen Indian reservations have been targeted for landfills, incinerators, and other waste facilities.[66] The

vast majority of these waste proposals were defeated by grassroots groups on the reservations. However, "radioactive colonialism" is alive and well.[67] The legacy of institutional racism has left many sovereign Indian nations without an economic infrastructure to address poverty, unemployment, inadequate education and health care, and a host of other social problems. In 1999, Eastern Navajo reservation residents filed suit against the Nuclear Regulatory Commission to block uranium mining in Church Rock and Crown Point communities.

Hazardous waste generation and international movement of hazardous waste pose some important health, environmental, legal, and ethical dilemmas. It is unlikely that many of the global hazardous waste proposals can be effectuated without first addressing the social, economic, and political context in which hazardous wastes are produced (industrial processes), controlled (regulations, notification and consent documentation), and managed (minimization, treatment, storage, recycled, transboundary shipment, pollution prevention, etc.). The "unwritten" policy of targeting Third-World nations for waste trade received international media attention in 1991. Lawrence Summers, at the time he was chief economists of the World Bank, shocked the world and touched off an international scandal when his confidential memorandum on waste trade was leaked. Summers writes:" 'Dirty' Industries: Just between you and me, shouldn't the World Bank be encouraging MORE migration of the dirty industries to the LDCs?[68]

Consumption and production patterns, especially in nations with wasteful "throwaway" life styles as the United States, and the interests of transnational corporations create and maintain unequal and unjust waste burdens within and between affluent and poor communities, states, and regions of the world. Shipping hazardous wastes from rich communities to poor communities is not a solution to the growing global waste problem. Not only is it immoral, but it should be illegal. Moreover, making hazardous waste transactions legal does not address the ethical issues imbedded in such transactions.[69] The practice is a manifestation of power arrangements and a larger stratification system where some people and some places are assigned greater value than others.

In the real world, all people, communities, and nations are not created equal. Some populations and interests are more equal than others. Unequal interests and power arrangements have allowed poisons of the rich to be offered as short term remedies for poverty of the poor. This scenario plays out domestically (as in the United States where low-income and people-of-color communities are disproportionately impacted by waste facilities and "dirty" industries) and internationally (where hazardous wastes move from OECD states flow to non-OECD states).

The conditions surrounding the more than 1,900 maquiladoras, assembly plants operated by American, Japanese, and other foreign countries, located along the 2,000-mile U.S.-Mexico border may further exacerbate the waste trade.[70] The industrial plants use cheap Mexican labor to assemble imported components and raw material and then ship finished products back to the United States. Nearly a half million Mexican workers are employed in the maquiladoras.

A 1983 agreement between the United States and Mexico required American companies in Mexico to return waste products to the United States. Plants were required to notify the federal EPA when returning wastes. Results from a 1986 survey of 20 of the plants informed the U.S. EPA that they were returning waste to the United States, even though 86 percent of the plants used toxic chemicals

in their manufacturing process. Much of the waste ends up being illegally dumped in sewers, ditches, and the desert. All along the Lower Rio Grande River Valley maquiladoras dump their toxic wastes into the river, from which 95 percent of the region's residents get their drinking water.[71]

The disregard for the environment and public safety has placed border residents' health at risk. In the border cities of Brownsville, Texas, and Matamoras, Mexico, the rate of anecephaly—babies born without brains—is four times the national average. Affected families have filed lawsuits against 88 of the area's 100 maquiladoras for exposing the community to xylene, a cleaning solvent that can cause brain hemorrhages, and lung and kidney damage.

Contaminated well and drinking water looms as major health threats. Air pollution has contributed to a raging asthma and respiratory epidemic. The Mexican environmental regulatory agency is understaffed and ill-equipped to adequately enforce its environmental laws.[72] Only time will tell if the North American Free Trade Agreement (NAFTA) will "fix" or exacerbate the public health, economic, and environmental problems along the U.S.-Mexico border.

Setting the Record Straight

The environmental protection apparatus is broken and needs to be fixed. The environmental justice movement has set out clear goals of eliminating unequal enforcement of environmental, civil rights, and public health laws. Environmental justice leaders have made a difference in the lives of people and the physical environment. They have assisted public decision makers in identifying "at risk" populations, toxic "hot spots," research gaps, and action models to correct existing imbalances and prevent future threats. However, impacted communities are not waiting for the government or industry to get their acts together. Grassroots groups have taken the offensive to ensure that government and industry do the right thing,

Communities have begun to organize their own networks and force their inclusion into the mainstream of public decision making. They have also developed communication channels among environmental justice leaders, grassroots groups, professional associations (i.e., legal, public health, education, etc.), scientific groups, public policy makers to assist them in identifying "at-risk" populations, toxic "hot spots," research gaps, and work to correct imbalances.

In response to growing public concern and mounting scientific evidence, President Clinton signed Executive Order 12898. The Executive Order is not a new law. It only reinforces what has been the law of the land for over three decades. Environmental justice advocates are calling for vigorous enforcement of civil rights laws and environmental laws.

The number of environmental justice complaints is expected to escalate against industry, government, and institutions that receive funds. Citizens have a right to challenge discrimination—including environmental discrimination, It is a smokescreen for anyone to link Title VI or other civil rights enforcement to economic disinvestment in low-income and people-of-color communities. There is absolutely no empirical evidence to support the contention that environmental justice hurts Brownfields redevelopment efforts.

The ERA has awarded over 200 Brownfield grants. In 1998, the agency had received some five dozen Title VI complaints. It is worth noting that not a single Title VI complaint involves a Brownfields site. On the other hand, two decades of solid empirical evidence documents the impact of racial redlining by banks, savings and loans, insurance companies, grocery chains, and even pizza delivery companies thwarts economic vitality in black communities–not enforcement of civil rights laws. Racial redlining was such a real problem that Congress passed the Community Reinvestment Act in 1977.

States have had three decades to implement Title VI of the Civil Rights Act of 1964. Most states have chosen to ignore the law. States need to do a better job assuring nondiscrimination in the application and the implementation of permitting decisions, enforcement, and investment decisions. Environmental justice also means sharing in the benefits. Governments must live up to their mandate of protecting all people and the environment. Anything less is unacceptable. The solution to environmental injustice lies in the realm of equal protection of all individuals, groups, and communities. No community, rich or poor, urban or suburban, black or white, should be allowed to become a "sacrifice zone" or the dumping ground.

Hazardous wastes and "dirty" industries have followed the "path of least resistance." Poor people and poor communities are given a false choice of "no jobs and no development" versus "risky low-paying jobs and pollution." Industries and governments (including the military) have often exploited the economic vulnerability of poor communities, poor states, poor regions, and poor nations for their "risky" operations. The environmental racism, and the international toxics trade at home and abroad.

NOTES

1. Robert D. Bullard, 1994, *Dumping in Dixie: Race, Class and Environmental Quality.* Boulder, CO: Westview Press.
2. Robert D. Bullard, "Solid Waste Sites and the Black Houston Community," *Sociological Inquiry* 53 (Spring 1983): 273–288.
3. U.S. General Accounting Office (1983), *Siting of Hazardous Waste Landfills and Their Correlation with Racial and Economic Status of*

Surrounding Communities, Washington, DC: Government Printing Office.

4. Commission for Racial Justice (1987), *Toxic Wastes and Race in the United States,* New York: United Church of Christ.

5. Charles Lee, 1992, *Proceedings: The First National People of Color Environmental Leadership Summit.* New York: United Church of Christ Commission for Racial Justice.

6. Dana Alston, "Transforming a Movement: People of Color Unite at Summit against Environmental Racism," *Sojourner* 21 (1992), pp. 30–31.

7. William K. Reilly, "Environmental Equity: EPA's Position," *EPA Journal* 18 (March/April 1992): 18–19.

8. R. D. Bullard and B. H. Wright, "The Politics of Pollution: Implications for the Black Community," *Phylon* 47 (March 1986): 71–78.

9. Robert D. Bullard, "Race and Environmental Justice in the United States," *Yale Journal of International Law* 18 (Winter 1993): 319–335; Robert D. Bullard, "The Threat of Environmental Racism," *Natural Resources & Environment* 7 (Winter 1993): 23–26, 55–56.

10. Louis Sullivan, "Remarks at the First Annual Conference on Childhood Lead Poisoning," in Alliance to End Childhood Lead Poisoning: Final Report. Washington DC: Alliance to End Childhood Lead Poisoning, October, 1991, p. A-2.

11. Bill Lann Lee, "Environmental Litigation on Behalf of Poor, Minority Children, *Matthews v. Coye:* A Case Study." Paper presented at the Annual Meeting of the American Association for the Advancement of Science, Chicago (February 9, 1992).

12. Ibid., p. 32.

13. Ibid.

14. Robert D. Bullard, "The Environmental Justice Framework: A Strategy for Addressing Unequal Protection." Paper presented at Resources for the Future Conference on Risk Management, Annapolis, MD (November 1992).

15. Paul Mohai and Bunyan Bryant, "Race, Poverty, and the Environment," *EPA Journal* 18 (March/April 1993): 1–8; R. D. Bullard, "In Our Backyards," *EPA Journal* 18 (March/April 1992): 11–12; D. R. Wernette and L. A. Nieves;, "Breathing Polluted Air," *EPA Journal* 18 (March/April 1992): 16–17; Patrick C. West, "Health Concerns for Fish-Eating Tribes?" *EPA Journal* 18 (March/April 1992): 15–16.

16. Marianne Lavelle and Marcia Coyle, "Unequal Protection," *National Law Journal* (September 21, 1992): S1–S2.

17. Robert D. Bullard, ed., *Confronting Environmental Racism: Voices from the Grassroots.* Boston: South End Press. 1993, chapter 1; Robert D. Bullard, "Waste and Racism: A Stacked Deck?" *Forum for Applied Research and Public Policy* 8 (Spring 1993): 29–35; Robert D. Bullard (ed.), *In Search of the New South—The Black Urban Experience in the 1970s and 1980s* (Tuscaloosa, AL: University of Alabama Press, 1991).

18. Florence Wagman Roisman, "The Lessons of American Apartheid: The Necessity and Means of Promoting Residential Racial Integration," *Iowa Law Review* 81 (December 1995): 479–525.

19. Joe R. Feagin, "A House Is Not A Home: White Racism and U.S. Housing Practices," in R. D. Bullard, J. E. Grigsby, and Charles Lee, eds., *Residential Apartheid: The American Legacy.* Los Angeles: UCLA Center for Afro-American Studies Publication, 1994, pp. 17–48.

20. Eric Mann, *L.A.'s Lethal Air: New Strategies for Policy, Organizing, and Action.* Los Angeles: Labor/Community Strategy Center, 1991, p. 31.

21. Jim Motavalli, "Toxic Targets: Polluters that Dump on Communities of Color are Finally Being Brought to Justice," *E Magazine,* 4 (July/August 1997): 29–41.

22. Joe Bandy, "Reterritorializing Borders: Transnational Environmental Justice on the U.S./Mexico Border," *Race, Gender, and Class* 5 (1997): 80–103.

23. Bunyan Bryant and Paul Mohai, *Race and the Incidence of Environmental Hazards* (Boulder, CO: Westview Press, 1992); Bunyan Bryant, ed., *Environmental Justice,* pp. 8–34.

24. R. Pinderhughes, "Who Decides What Constitutes a Pollution Problem?" *Race, Gender, and Class* 5 (1997): 130–152.

25. Diane Takvorian, "Toxics and Neighborhoods Don't Mix," *Land Use Forum: A Journal of Law, Policy and Practice* 2 (Winter 1993): 28–31; R. D. Bullard, "Examining the Evidence of Environmental Racism," *Land Use Forum: A Journal of Law, Policy, and Practice* 2 (Winter 1993): 6–11.

26. For an in-depth examination of the Houston case study, see R. D. Bullard, 1987, *Invisible Houston: The Black Experience in Boom and*

Bust. College Station, TX: Texas A&M University Press, pp. 60–75.

27. Ruth Rosen, "Who Gets Polluted: The Movement for Environmental Justice," *Dissent* (Spring 1994): 223–230; R. D. Bullard, "Environmental Justice: It's More than Waste Facility Siting," *Social Science Quarterly* 77 (September 1996): 493–499.

28. Commission for Racial Justice, *Toxic Wastes and Race in the United States*, pp. xiii–xiv.

29. U.S. General Accounting Office, *Siting of Hazardous Waste Landfills and Their Correlation with Racial and Economic Status of Surrounding Communities*. Washington, DC: U.S. General Accounting Office, 1983, p.1.

30. Robert D. Bullard, ed., *Confusing Environmental Racism: Voices from the Grassroots* Boston: South End, 1993; Robert D. Bullard, "The Threat of Environmental Racism," *Natural Resources & Environment* 7 (Winter 1993): 23–26; Bunyan Bryant and Paul Mohai, eds., *Race and the Incidence of Environmental Hazards*. Boulder, CO: Westview Press, 1992; Regina Austin and Michael Schill, "Black, Brown, Poor and Poisoned: Minority Grassroots Environmentalism and the Quest for Eco-Justice." *The Kansas Journal of Law and Public Policy* 1 (1991): 69–82; Kelly C. Colquette and Elizabeth A. Henry Robertson, "Environmental Racism: The Causes, Consequences, and Commendations." *Tulane Environmental Law Journal* 5 (1991); 153–207; Rachel D. Godsil, "Remedying Environmental Racism." *Michigan Law Review* 90 (1991): 394–427.

31. Bullard and Feagin, "Racism and the City," pp. 55–76; Robert D. Bullard, "Dismantling Environmental Racism in the USA," *Local Environment* 4 (1999): 5–19.

32. W. J. Kruvant, "People, Energy, and Pollution." Pp. 125–167 in D. K. Newman and Dawn Day, eds., *The American Energy Consumer*. Cambridge, Mass.: Ballinger, 1975; Robert D. Bullard, "Solid Waste Sites and the Black Houston Community." *Sociological Inquiry* 53 (Spring 1983): 273–288; United Church of Christ Commission for Racial Justice, *Toxic Wastes and Race in the United States*. New York: Commission for Racial Justice, 1987; Dick Russell, "Environmental Racism," *The Amicus Journal* 11 (Spring 1989): 22–32; Eric Mann, *L.A.'s Lethal Air: New Strategies for Policy, Organizing, and Action*. Los Angeles: Labor/Community Strategy Center, 1991; D. R. Wernette and L. A. Nieves, "Breathing Polluted Air: Minorities are Disproportionately Exposed." *EPA Journal* 18 (March/April 1992): 16–17; Bryant and Mohai, Race and the Incidence of Environmental Hazards; Benjamin Goldman and Laura J. Fitton, *Toxic Wastes and Race Revisited*. Washington, DC: Center for Policy Alternatives; NAACP, and United Church of Christ, 1994.

33. Myrick A. Freedman, "The Distribution of Environmental Quality." In Allen V. Kneese and Blair T. Bower (eds.), *Environmental Quality Analysis*. Baltimore: Johns Hopkins University Press for Resources for the Future, 1971; Michael Gelobter, "The Distribution of Air Pollution by Income and Race." Paper presented at the Second Symposium on Social Science in Resource Management, Urbana, Illinois (June 1988); Gianessi et al., "The Distributional Effects of Uniform Air Pollution Policy in the U.S." *Quarterly Journal of Economics* (May 1979): 281–301.

34. Patrick C. West, J. Mark Fly, and Robert Marans, "Minority Anglers and Toxic Fish Consumption: Evidence from a State-Wide Survey in Michigan." In Bryant and Mohai, *Race and the Incidence of Environmental Hazards*, pp. 100–113.

35. Robert D. Bullard, "Solid Waste Sites and the Black Houston Community." *Sociological Inquiry* 53 (Spring 1983): 273–288; Robert D. Bullard, *Invisible Houston: The Black Experience in Boom and Bust*. College Station, TX: Texas A&M University Press, 1987, chapter 6; Robert D. Bullard, "Environmental Racism and Land Use." *Land Use Forum: A Journal of Law, Policy & Practice* 2 (Spring 1993): 6–11.

36. United Church of Christ Commission for Racial Justice, *Toxic Wastes and Race*; Paul Mohai and Bunyan Bryant, "Environmental Racism: Reviewing the Evidence." In Bryant and Mohai, *Race and the Incidence of Environmental Hazards*; Paul Stretesky and Michael J. Hogan, "Environmental Justice: An Analysis of Superfund Sites in Florida," *Social Problems* 45 (May 1998): 268–287.

37. Marianne Lavelle and Marcia Coyle, "Unequal Protection: The Racial Divide in Environmental Law." *National Law Journal*, September 21, 1992.

38. Agency for Toxic Substances Disease Registry, *The Nature and Extent of Lead Poisoning in Children in the United States: A Report to Congress*. Atlanta: U.S. Department of Health and Human Resources, 1988, pp. 1–12.

39. J. Schwartz and R. Levine, "Lead: An Example of the Job Ahead," *EPA Journal* 18 (March/April 1992): 32–44.

40. Centers for Disease Control and Prevention, "Update: Blood Lead Levels—United States, 1991–1994," *Mortality and Morbidity Weekly Report* 46, no. 7 (February 21, 1997): 141–146.

41. James L. Pinkle, D. J. Brody, E. W. Gunter, R. A. Kramer, D. C. Paschal, K. M. Glegal, and T. D. Matte, "The Decline in Blood Lead Levels in the United States: The National Health and Nutrition Examination Survey (NHANES)," *Journal of the American Medical Association* 272 (1994): 284–291.

42. Arnold W. Reitze, Jr., "A Century of Air Pollution Control Law: What Worked; What Failed; What Might Work," *Environmental Law* 21 (1991): 1549.

43. For an in-depth discussion of transportation investments and social equity issues, see R.D. Bullard and G. S. Johnson, eds., *Just Transportation: Dismantling Race and Class Barriers to Mobility*. Gabriola Island, BC: New Society Publishers, 1997.

44. Sid Davis, "Race and the Politics of Transportation in Atlanta," in R. D. Bullard and G. S. Johnson, Just Transportation, pp. 84–96; Environmental Justice Resource Center, *Sprawl Atlanta: Social Equity Dimensions of Uneven Growth and Development*. A Report prepared for the Turner Foundation, Atlanta: Clark Atlanta University (January 1999).

45. D. R. Wernette and L. A. Nieves, "Breathing Polluted Air: Minorities Are Disproportionately Exposed," *EPA Journal* 18 (March 1992): 16–17.

46. CDC, "Asthma—United States, 1982–1992." *MMWR* 43 (1995): 952–955.

47. CDC, "Asthma morality and hospitalization among children and young adults—United States, 1980–1993." *MMWR* 45 (1996): 350–353.

48. Anna E. Pribitkin, "The Need for Revision of Ozone Standards: Why Has the EPA Failed to Respond?" *Temple Environmental Law & Technology Journal* 13 (1994): 104.

49. CDC/NCHS, *Health United States* 1994. DHHS Pub. No. (PHS) 95-1232; Tables 83, 84, 86 & 87.

50. CDC, "Asthma—United States, 1982–1992." *MMWR* 43 (1995): 952–955.

51. CDC, "Disabilities among children aged less than or equal to 17 years—United States, 1991-1992." *MMWR* 44 (1995): 609–613.

52. U.S. EPA, "Review of National Ambient Air Quality Standards for Ozone, Assessment of Scientific and Technical Information," OAQPS Staff Paper. Research Triangle Park, NC: EPA, 1996; Haluk Ozkaynk, John D. Spengler, Marie O'Neil, Jianping Xue, Hui Zhou, Kathy Gilbert, and Sonja Ramstrom, "Ambient Ozone Exposure and Emergency Hospital Admissions and Emergency Room Visits for Respiratory Problems in Thirteen U.S. Cities," in American Lung Association, *Breathless: Air Pollution and Hospital Admissions/Emergency Room Visits in 13 Cities*. Washington, DC: American Lung Association, 1996; American Lung Association, *Out of Breath: Populations-at-Risk to Alternative Ozone Levels*. Washington, DC: American Lung Association, 1995.

53. Centers for Disease Control and Prevention, National Center for Environmental Health, Division of Environmental Hazards and Health Effects, Air Pollution and Respiratory Branch, "Asthma Mortality and Hospitalization Among Children and Young Adults—United States, 1980–1993," *Morbidity and Mortality Weekly Report*, 45 (1996).

54. Centers for Disease Control, "Asthma: United States, 1980–1990," *MMWR* 39 (1992): 733–735.

55. Mary C. White, Ruth Etzel, Wallace D. Wilcox, and Christine Lloyd, "Exacerbations of Childhood Asthma and Ozone Pollution in Atlanta," *Environmental Research* 65 (1994), p. 56.

56. R. D. Bullard, "The Legacy of Apartheid and Environmental Racism," *St. John's Journal of Legal Commentary* 9 (Spring, 1994): 445–474.

57. Donald Schueler, "Southern Exposure," *Sierra* 77 (November/December 1992): 45.

58. Robert D. Bullard, "Ecological Inequities and the New South: Black Communities Under Siege." *Journal of Ethnic Studies* 17 (Winter 1990): 101–115; Donald L. Bartlett and James B. Steele, "Paying a Price for Polluters," *Time* (November 23, 1998), pp. 72–80.

59. Schueler, "Southern Exposure," p. 46.

60. Ibid., pp. 46–47.

61. James O'Byrne and Mark Schleifstein, "Drinking Water in Danger," *The Times Picayune*, February 19, 1991, p. A5.

62. Conger Beasley, "Of Poverty and Pollution: Keeping Watch in Cancer Alley," pp. 39–45.

63. Bartlett and Steele, "Paying a Price for Polluters," p. 77.

64. Conger Beasley, "Of Pollutions and Poverty: Deadly Threat on Native Lands," *Buzzworm,*

2 (5) (1990): 39–45; Robert Tomsho, "Dumping Grounds: Indian Tribes Contend with Some of the Worst of America's Pollution," *The Wall Street Journal* (November 29, 1990); Jane Kay, "Indian Lands Targeted for Waste Disposal Sites," *San Francisco Examiner* (April 10, 1991); Valerie Taliman, "Stuck Holding the Nation's Nuclear Waste," *Race, Poverty & Environment Newsletter* (Fall 1992): 6–9.

65. Bradley Angel, *The Toxic Threat to Indian Lands: A Greenpeace Report.* San Francisco: Greenpeace, 1992; Al Geddicks, *The New Resource Wars: Native and Environmental Struggles Against Multinational Corporations.* Boston: South End Press, 1993.

66. Jane Kay, "Indian Lands Targeted for Waste Disposal Sites," *San Francisco Examiner* (April 10, 1991).

67. Ward Churchill and Winona la Duke, "Native America: The Political Economy of Radioactive Colonialism," *Insurgent Sociologist* 13 (1) (1983): 61–63.

68. Greenpeace, "The Logic Behind Hazardous Waste Export," *Greenpeace Waste Trade Update* First Quarter 1992): 1–2.

69. Dana Alston and Nicole Brown, "Global Threats to People of Color," pp. 179–194 in R. D. Bullard, ed., *Confronting Environmental Racism: Voices from the Grassroots.* Boston: Southend Press, 1993.

70. Roberto Sanchez, "Health and Environmental Risks of the Maquiladora in Mexicali," *Natural Resources Journal* 30 (1) (1990): 163–186.

71. Beatriz Johnston Hernandez, "Dirty Growth," *The New Environmentalist* (August 1993).

72. T. Barry and B. Simms, *The Challenge of Cross Border Environmentalism: The U.S.-Mexico Case,* Albuquerque, NM: The Inter-Hemispheric Education Resource Center, 1994.

PART III
Race and Ethnicity in Social Institutions

Answer the questions that follow.

1. As of 2003, what percentage of the United States do you think was:
   a. black _____%
   b. white _____%
   c. Asian _____%
   d. American Indian _____%
   e. Latino _____%
2. Who are your three best friends?
   1)_____ 2)_____ 3)_____
3. Does the unemployment rate in the United States vary by color or ethnicity? _____

Each of your answers, whether you realize it or not, reflects how you have been shaped by social institutions. Compare your answers on question 1 to the percentages reported by the U.S. Bureau of the Census for 2003: 12.1% black, 75% white, 3.6% Asian/Pacific Islander, 0.9% American Indian, and 12.5% Latino. (These numbers add up to more than 100% because Latinos can be any race.)

Did your estimates of the size of these groups differ from the actual numbers? If you said that the black population was around 30% or that the Asian population was 10%, your answer was similar to the average American response. How do you explain the fact that most people in the United States almost triple the actual size of the black and Asian population? From a sociological perspective, what does the overcounting of the nonwhite population mean?

Question 2 asked you to list your three best friends. How many of the people you listed are from a different race? How many are the same sex as you? If you don't have any best friends who are from a racial background different from your own, why not? Is it that you do not like people from other races? Does this mean you are a racist? Do you only have friends of the same sex? Why?

With regard to question 3, the unemployment rate in the United States does vary by color or ethnicity, with blacks and Latinos twice as likely as whites to be unemployed. How is the unemployment rate linked to how close people live to areas of high job growth, and how are both of these factors linked to race and ethnicity?

The answers to these questions reflect the ways in which institutions shape how we view the world. Your beliefs, opinions, attitudes, and the "commonsense" knowledge that guides your moment-to-moment understanding of the world may all seem to be highly individualistic. Upon closer sociological inspection, however, we see that it is institutions and other social arrangements that influence, mediate, and structure how we think about and come to understand the world in which we live. Think for a moment about your answers to the preceding questions. People of all colors typically overestimate the nonwhite population and underestimate the white population. Perhaps you overestimated the nonwhite population because you live in an all black or all Latino neighborhood. When you look out the window or walk down the street, you see that everyone in your neighborhood is like you. That local information is then used to make a judgment about the rest of the United States. But what if you are white and you overestimated the nonwhite population? How do you explain doubling or tripling the black or Asian population? Do you get your information about other racial groups secondhand, from watching television? Might there be a difference between the media's portrayal of race and ethnic relations and what is actually taking place in society? Do you watch professional sports, music videos, or the local television news? Might your estimates reflect something about your television viewing habits? If you do live in a racially segregated neighborhood, might that explain why your best friends are all the same color as you? Do you think you might have close friends from different racial backgrounds if your high school or neighborhood was racially integrated? Why is it that jobs in black or Latino neighborhoods are often not as plentiful or as well paying as they are in white areas or suburbs?

In Part III, we focus on how race and ethnic identity intersect with the criminal justice system, the labor market, where and why individuals live where they do, and how the media shapes our views on race and ethnic relations. The first theme in this section examines the influence of race and class in the American justice system. In reading 20, law professor David Cole examines racial disparities in capital punishment sentencing. His research found that courts are more likely to sentence someone to death if a black person kills someone who is white than if a white person kills someone who is black, suggesting that the value society places on who lives and dies varies by race. In reading 21, scholar-activist Angela Davis links the "war on drugs" and the skyrocketing number of incarcerated young black and brown men to the growth of the extremely profitable "prison industrial com-

plex." Finally in the section on criminal justice, Jeffrey Reiman examines a very obvious but often unstated fact: that people in prison tend to be quite poor. It is not, he argues, that poor people are more prone to criminal behavior. He asserts instead that the criminal justice system is rife with racial and economic bias.

The next five readings in the race and work section examine the extent to which and sociological reasons why economic and occupational outcomes vary by race and ethnicity. Julie Matthaei and Teresa Amott detail how Asian women were exploited economically, socially, and sexually by all those who could profit from their immigration to the United States in the early 1900s. Their research demonstrates how racism and sexism constrained every aspect of these women's lives. In reading 24, Katherine Newman and Catherine Ellis document the work strategies used by fast food workers in Harlem. The "McJob" experiences of two hundred black and brown respondents in their study challenge a number of common sense assumptions about work at a fast food restaurant and workers' attitudes about upward mobility. Kathryn Neckerman and Joleen Kirschenman focus on hiring practices in Chicago to reveal the extent to which employers use stereotypes as a way to exclude blacks, particularly black men. Roger Waldinger and William J. Wilson provide historical and contemporary examples of how employment opportunities have changed over time. Waldinger examines the different occupational niches that ethnic and racial groups occupied in New York City, while Wilson demonstrates that the poorest, most isolated, and disproportionately black parts of the nation's inner cities face a crisis of joblessness.

The next three readings reveal a nation highly segregated by race and ethnicity. Douglas Massey argues that residential segregation results in a loss of occupational and educational mobility for racial minorities and cuts off communities from so-called mainstream America. Judith DeSena traces the informal mechanisms individuals and organizations use to keep certain people out of their neighborhoods. Elijah Anderson explains how many poor, young African Americans use fear and intimidation as a way to gain respect among their peers.

The final three readings in Part III explore how the media shape our views on race and ethnicity. Justin Lewis and Sut Jhally use a research project conducted on exposure to *The Cosby Show* as a window into the ways in which racial attitudes and perceptions of mobility are influenced by the television shows people watch. The reading by S. Robert Lichter and Daniel R. Amundson focuses on the invidious ways in which blacks in the nightly news and Latinos in television programming are reduced to a series of degrading stereotypes. Each of these last three readings asks us to consider how representations of race and ethnicity on the nightly news or on situation comedies shape our worldview. Finally, Richard Lapchick reports on one unintended consequence of America's romance with professional sports: the cementing of racial stereotypes. He also explores how athletes, particularly college athletes, are often subjected to a double standard because their lives are so closely scrutinized by the media.

Race and Crime

20

THE COLOR OF PUNISHMENT

David Cole

Questions to Consider

In the McClesky v. Kemp *case, the Supreme Court found that even though sentencing disparities were found to be significantly correlated with the race of the defendant, those findings did not necessarily mean there was racist intent. However, David Cole's research challenges the deeply held belief that the rule of law is applied to all citizens without regard to race, creed, status or lineage. How do you explain differences in the length of sentencing according to race? What would happen if there were a "war on drugs" and the suburbs, rather than the city, were the target? What would white America's response be if millions of young, white, middle-class suburbanites were arrested, sentenced, and put in jail for an extended period of time for recreational marijuana or ecstasy use?*

Tonya Drake, a twenty-five-year-old mother of four on welfare, needed the money. So when a man she hardly knew gave her a $100 bill and told her she could keep the change if she mailed a package for him, she agreed, even though she suspected it might contain drugs. The change amounted to $47.40. The package contained crack cocaine. And for that, Tonya Drake, whose only prior offenses were traffic violations, received a ten-year manda-

tory minimum prison sentence. When federal judge Richard A. Gadbois, Jr., sentenced her, he said, "This woman doesn't belong in prison for 10 years for what I understand she did. That's just crazy, but there's nothing I can do about it." Had the cocaine in the package been in powder rather than crack form, she would have faced a prison sentence of less than three years, with no mandatory minimum.[1]

Tonya Drake is joined by thousands of prisoners serving lengthy mandatory prison terms for federal crack cocaine violations.[2] What unites them is skin color. About 90 percent of federal crack cocaine defendants are black. Indeed, a 1992 U.S. Sentencing Com-

David Cole, *No Equal Justice: Race and Class in the American Criminal Justice System.* Copyright © 1998 by David Cole. Reprinted by permission of The New Press, (800) 233-4830.

mission study found that in seventeen states, not a single white had been prosecuted on federal crack cocaine charges.[3]

Crack cocaine is nothing more than powder cocaine cooked up with baking soda. Wholesalers deal in powder; retailers deal in crack. But under the federal sentencing guidelines, a small-time crack "retailer" caught selling 5 grams of crack receives the same prison sentence as a large-scale powder cocaine dealer convicted of distributing 500 grams of powder cocaine. The U.S. Sentencing Commission has estimated that 65 percent of crack users are white.[4] In 1992, however, 92.6 percent of those convicted for crimes involving crack cocaine were black, while only 4.7 percent were white; at the same time, 45.2 percent of defendants convicted for powder cocaine crimes were white, and only 20.7 percent were black.[5] In Minnesota, where state sentencing guidelines drew a similar distinction between crack and powder cocaine, African Americans made up 96.6 percent of those charged with possession of crack cocaine in 1988, while almost 80 percent of those charged with possession of powder cocaine were white.[6] Sentencing guidelines were ostensibly adopted to eliminate disparity in sentencing, yet the crack/powder distinction has ensured that significant racial inequities remain.

Black defendants have challenged the crack/powder disparity on constitutional grounds, but every federal challenge has failed.[7] The courts, echoing the Supreme Court in *McCleskey,* have held that "mere" statistical disparities do not prove that congress or the Sentencing Commission adopted the disparities for the purpose of harming African Americans. And it is not wholly irrational to treat crack as more harmful than powder cocaine, because crack is more often associated with violence, is more potent as typically ingested, and is more accessible to low-income people. Accordingly, even though black cocaine offenders in the federal system serve sentences on average five years longer than white cocaine offenders, the courts see no constitutional problem.

In 1995, however, the U.S. Sentencing Commission, which administers the federal sentencing guidelines, concluded that the disparities could not be justified by qualitative differences between the two drugs, particularly as powder cocaine distributors provide the raw material for crack. It proposed to reduce the differential, noting the racial disparities and their corrosive effect on criminal justice generally.[8] Congress and President Clinton responded like politicians; they reframed the issue as whether we should be "tough on crime," and opposed any change. For the first time since the sentencing guidelines were created in 1984, Congress passed a law overriding a Sentencing Commission recommendation to alter the guidelines.[9]

In 1995, the Georgia Supreme Court very briefly took a different approach. Georgia has a "two strikes and you're out" sentencing scheme that imposes life imprisonment for a second drug offense. As of 1995, Georgia's district attorneys, who have unfettered discretion to decide whether to seek this penalty, had invoked it against only 1 percent of white defendants facing a second drug conviction, but against more than 16 percent of eligible black defendants. The result: 98.4 percent of those serving life sentences under the provision were black. On March 17, 1995, the Georgia Supreme Court ruled, by a 4-3 vote, that these figures presented a threshold case of discrimination, and required prosecutors to explain the disparity.[10]

Instead of offering an explanation, however, Georgia Attorney General Michael Bowers took the unusual step of filing a petition for rehearing signed by every one of the state's forty-six district attorneys, all of whom were white. The petition warned that the Court's approach was a "substantial step toward invalidating" the death penalty, and would "paralyze the criminal justice system," presumably because racial disparities in other areas might also have to be explained. Thirteen days later, the Georgia Supreme Court took the highly unusual step of reversing itself, and held that the figures established no discrimination and required no justification. The court's new decision relied almost exclusively on the U.S. Supreme Court's decision in *McCleskey*.[11]

The crack/powder differential and the Georgia experience with "two strikes and you're out" life sentences are but two examples of the widespread racial disparities caused by the war on drugs. Between 1986 and 1991, arrests of members of racial and ethnic minorities for all crimes increased by twice as much as nonminority arrests.[12] Yet when that figure is broken down by type of crime, drug offenses were the *only* area in which minority arrests actually increased more than nonminority arrests. The five-year increase in arrests of minorities for drug offenses was *almost ten times* the increase in arrests of white drug offenders.[13]

In 1992, the United States Public Health Service estimated, based on self-report surveys, that 76 percent of illicit drug users were white, 14 percent black, and 8 percent Hispanic—figures which roughly match each group's share of the general population[14] Yet African Americans make up 35 percent of all drug arrests, 55 percent of all drug convictions, and 74 percent of all sentences for drug offenses.[15] In Baltimore, blacks are five times more likely than whites to be arrested for drug offenses.[16] In Columbus, Ohio, black males are less than 11 percent of the population, but account for 90 percent of drug arrests; they are arrested at a rate eighteen times greater than white males.[17] In Jacksonville, Florida, black males are 12 percent of the population, but 87 percent of drug arrests.[18] And in Minneapolis, black

males are arrested for drugs at a rate twenty times that for white males.[19]

Similar racial disparities are found in incarceration rates for drug offenses. From 1986 to 1991, the number of white drug offenders incarcerated in state prisons increased by 110 percent, but the number of black drug offenders increased by 465 percent.[20] In New York, which has some of the most draconian drug laws in the country—selling two ounces of cocaine receives the same sentence as murder—90 percent of those incarcerated for drugs each year are black or Hispanic.[21] The "war on drugs" is also responsible for much of the growth in incarceration since 1980. Federal prisoners incarcerated for drug offenses increased nearly tenfold from 1980 to 1993, and that increase accounted for nearly three-quarters of the total increase in federal prisoners.[22] The number of state prisoners incarcerated for drug offenses during the same period increased at a similar rate.[23]

The same pattern emerges in the treatment of juveniles. Between 1986 and 1991, arrests of minority juveniles (under age eighteen) for drug offenses increased by 78 percent, while arrests of nonminority juveniles for drugs actually *decreased* by 34 percent.[24] As with adults, black youth are also treated progressively more severely than whites at each successive stage of the juvenile justice process. In 1991, white youth were involved in 50 percent of all drug-related cases, while black youth accounted for 48 percent.[25] Yet blacks were detained for drug violations at nearly twice the rate of whites.[26] Four times as many black juvenile drug cases were transferred to criminal courts for adult prosecution as white cases.[27] And black youth involved in drug-related cases were placed outside the home almost twice as often as white youth. These disparities are only getting worse: from 1987 to 1991, such placement for black juveniles in drug cases increased 28.5 percent, while placement for whites *decreased* 30 percent.[28] The situation in Baltimore is illustrative. In 1980, eighteen white juveniles and eighty-six black juveniles were arrested for selling drugs—already a fairly stark five-to-one disparity. In 1990, the number of white juveniles arrested on drug charges fell to thirteen, while the number of black juveniles arrested grew to 1,304—a disparity of more than one hundred to one.[29]

Thus, the victims of the war on drugs have been disproportionately black. Some argue that this is neither surprising nor problematic, but simply reflects the unfortunate fact that the drug problem itself disproportionately burdens the black community.[30] If more blacks are using and selling drugs, equal enforcement of the drug laws will lead to disproportionate arrests and incarceration of African Americans. Even if that were the case, the fact that the disparities increase at each successive stage of both the criminal and juvenile justice processes suggests that greater drug use by blacks is not the whole story. In addition, as noted earlier, official estimates of drug use by race do not reflect the disparities evident in the criminal justice system, and in fact suggest very little racial disparity in drug use.

The effects of the drug war are difficult to measure. Critics contend that drugs are just as prevalent and cheap today as they were before the crackdown began in the mid-1980s. Proponents point to signs that crack use has declined, and that teen use of drugs generally has also fallen. But it is extremely difficult to say whether these trends are a result of the war on drugs. Scholars find that drug use goes in cycles, but they have never been able to find a correlation between fluctuations in drug use and criminal-law enforcement. One thing is certain, however: the stigmatization and incarceration of such a high proportion of young African-American males for drug crimes will have significant adverse long-term effects on the black community. A criminal record makes it much more difficult to find a legitimate job. We are disabling tens of thousands of young black men at the outset of their careers. The short-term "benefits" of removing offenders from the community may well come back to haunt us in the long term.

Three Strikes

Not so long ago, "three strikes and you're out" was just a baseball slogan. Today, it passes for a correctional philosophy. And here again, African Americans are disproportionately the losers. Between 1993 and 1995, twenty-four states and the federal government adopted some form of "three strikes and you're out" legislation, under which repeat offenders face life sentences for a third felony conviction.[31] (Georgia and South Carolina went even further, adopting "two strikes and you're out" laws). California's three-strikes law, one of the first, was sparked by a repeat offender's abduction and murder of twelve-year-old Polly Klaas in Petaluma in 1993.[32] Under California's version, a second felony conviction doubles the sentence otherwise authorized, and a third felony conviction receives a mandatory twenty-five-year-to-life term, no matter how insubstantial the third conviction, so long as the prior convictions were for "violent" or "serious" crimes. The "three strikes" idea has been wildly popular; 72 percent of California's voters approved it in a popular referendum, and President Clinton himself jumped on the three-strikes bandwagon during the 1994 mid-term election campaign.[33] But the implementation of the laws has led to many problems.

First, the laws lead to draconian results. Jerry Dewayne Williams, for example, received a twenty-five-year sentence for stealing a slice of pizza from four young men at a Los Angeles beach.[34] Another defendant's third strike consisted of stealing five bottles of liquor from a supermarket.[35] In its first two years, California's law led to life sentences for twice as many marijuana users as murderers, rapists, and kidnappers combined.[36] A California Department of Corrections study reported that 85 percent of those sentenced under the law were convicted most recently of a nonviolent crime.[37] Some have argued that focusing on the third strike is an unfair basis for criticism, because most offenders sentenced under the law have long criminal histories.[38] But the law is triggered even where a defendant's prior offenses are in the distant past, the third conviction is for a minor offense, and there is little likelihood that public safety required anything like a life sentence. Robert Wayne Washington, for example, received twenty-five years to life for a minor cocaine possession charge; his prior offenses were two eight-year-old burglaries and an intervening conviction for possession of contraband.[39]

Second, if the purpose of the law is to incapacitate those who would otherwise repeatedly prey on society, it is overinclusive. Most violent criminals have a relatively limited "criminal career," tailing off after ten years or so.[40] An individual's third strike often will not occur until his criminal career is on the wane. Thus, the three-strikes laws will impose life sentences on many offenders who pose little future danger to the community.

Third, such laws increase the costs of administering the criminal justice system. They make police work more dangerous, because a repeat offender facing a life sentence, in the words of Los Angeles Police Department spokesman Anthony Alba, is like "a cornered animal. If he knows he is going to get life in jail, he is definitely going to up the ante in eluding his captors."[41] Once apprehended, many defendants facing a third strike are unwilling to plead guilty, leading to a marked increase in criminal tri-

als. Michael Judge, the chief public defender for Los Angeles County, said, "The law has created the single greatest increase in workload in the thirty years since I've been associated with the criminal justice system."[42] Two years into the California law's existence, an auditor estimated that it had cost Los Angeles County alone an extra $169 million.[43] The increase in criminal trials causes backlogs in the civil justice system, as the courts must increasingly devote themselves to criminal trials; as of 1996, 47 of California's 125 civil courts had to be diverted to hearing criminal cases.[44]

Three-strikes and other mandatory minimum laws have contributed to startling growth in our prison population. From 1980 to 1994, the national prison and jail population increased 195.6 percent.[45] By comparison, the general population increased from 1980 to 1990 by only 9.8 percent.[46] If the prison population continues to grow at the rate of increase from 1995–96, it would top 3.2 million in 2009. California alone has built seventeen new jails in the last fifteen years. Its prison spending has increased over that period from 2 percent to almost 10 percent of its state budget, and it now spends more on corrections than on higher education.[47]

Despite these problems, the three-strikes approach remains extraordinarily popular. Why? One possibility is that, as with many other "get tough" policies, its direct burdens fall disproportionately on minorities. The Georgia case discussed above involving racially disparate application of a two-strikes law is not unique. In California, for example, blacks make up only 7 percent of the general population, yet as of 1996 they accounted for 43 percent of the third-strike defendants sent to state prison. Whites, by contrast, make up 53 percent of the general population in California, but only 24.6 percent of third-strike prisoners. This means that blacks are being imprisoned under California's three-strikes law at a rate 13.3 times that of the rate for whites. And because three-strikes convicts serve such long sentences, their proportion of the prison population will steadily increase; third-strikers comprised 8 percent of the total prison population in 1996, but the California Department of Corrections estimates that by 2024 they will amount to 49 percent.[48] Without a change in direction, the already stark racial disparities in our nation's prisons will only get worse. Yet it is precisely for that reason that there is unlikely to be a change in direction. As long as the effects of this get-tough measure are felt principally in minority communities, there is not likely to be sufficient political pressure for change.

When Is Disparity Discrimination?

As the figures above illustrate, it is beyond dispute that criminal sentencing is marked by stark racial *disparities*. But does this amount to *discrimination*? Everyone agrees that black defendants should not receive harsher penalties simply because they are black, and that criminals who attack white victims should not be punished more severely because the victims were white. But the disparities identified above may be attributable to factors other than race discrimination. Perhaps blacks commit more serious crimes per capita than whites. Social scientists and criminologists have long sought to determine through statistical analysis whether criminal sentencing is impermissibly affected by race, and have reached contradictory conclusions.

In the death penalty setting, as we have seen, most studies conclude that there is discrimination based on the race of the victim, even after controlling for other possible factors. In non-death penalty cases, however, the results are more mixed. In a 1993 study of the racial impact of the federal sentencing

guidelines, for example, the U.S. Justice Department's Bureau of Justice Statistics found that although blacks on average received sentences that were almost two years longer than whites, the bulk of this disparity was due to the crack/cocaine sentencing disparity.[49] The study concluded that other racial differences in sentencing for drug trafficking, fraud, and embezzlement could be explained by nonracial factors such as prior prison records, guilty pleas, and severity of offense.[50] But the study also found that even after controlling for such factors, black offenders were 50 to 60 percent more likely to be sentenced for larceny than white offenders, and twice as likely as whites to be sentenced for weapons offenses.[51] Several other studies have concluded that racial disparities in sentencing are largely attributable to race-neutral factors, such as offense severity or prior criminal record.[52] Most criminologists agree that a substantial part—but not all—of sentencing disparity is attributable to blacks committing more serious crimes than whites.[53] However, all of these findings—both those that find discrimination and those that do not—are plagued by several inescapable problems.

First, in order to determine whether a racial *disparity* is the result of racial *discrimination*, one must compare similar cases. Where defendants similar in all respects but race are treated differently, one may reasonably conclude that discrimination has occurred. The rub lies in defining "similar." As Barbara Meierhoefer has argued,

> There is no disagreement that similar offenders should be sentenced similarly. The problem . . . is that there is no consensus as to what defines "similar offenders." Even outwardly empirical assessments of whether unwarranted disparity has been reduced will be strongly influenced by which offense and offender

characteristics are selected to define "similarly situated" offenders.[54]

Thus, for example, critics of the Baldus study used in *McCleskey* have argued that it did not sufficiently identify "similar" cases, and that therefore its conclusion that the remaining disparities were racial in nature was flawed.[55]

Second, even if we could identify and agree on all relevant race-neutral factors that might conceivably explain a disparity, no study can possibly measure all such factors.[56] Some of the most important factors, such as strength of evidence, credibility of witnesses, or the effectiveness of a lawyer's representation, are simply not susceptible to quantification. Quantifiable factors may be missing from available data. No study can absolutely eliminate the possibility that some unaccounted-for race-neutral variable that correlates with race has caused the apparent racial disparity.

Third, statistical studies may also err in the opposite direction, by concealing racial discrimination. A study of sentencing decisions that found that all racial disparities could be explained by offense severity and prior criminal records, for example, might conceal racial discrimination in police or prosecutorial practices. If police officers observe, stop, and arrest blacks at a higher rate than whites because of their race, blacks are more likely to develop criminal records, all other things being equal. Similarly, if prosecutors offer more generous plea bargains to white than black defendants because of their race, black defendants' sentencing reports will reflect higher "offense severity" and more serious criminal records. By focusing only on one stage of the criminal justice system, a statistician may miss discrimination occurring at another stage. At the same time, statistical studies may miss discrimination if, in the aggregate, two forms of discrimination can-

cel each other out. For example, some biased sentencers might assign a longer sentence for a black-on-black crime because the *defendant* is black; others might impose a shorter sentence because the *victim* is black. If these biases cancel each other out in the aggregate, statistics may conceal actual discrimination.

For these reasons, statistical studies can rarely prove intentional discrimination. But even if none of the sentencing disparities outlined above is attributable to discrimination as the Supreme Court has defined it, they nonetheless raise serious questions about the racial fairness of our criminal justice policy. To see that this is so, one need only imagine the public response if the current racial disparities in criminal justice were reversed. Imagine what kind of pressure legislatures would feel, for example, if one in three young *white* men were in prison or on probation or parole. Imagine what the politics of the death penalty would look like if prosecutors sought the death penalty 70 percent of the time when whites killed blacks, but only 19 percent of the time when blacks killed whites. Or imagine what our juvenile justice policies would be like if white youth charged with drug offenses were four times as likely as black youth to be tried as adults, and twice as likely to be placed outside the home. One thing is certain: the nation would not accept such a situation as "inevitable."

Indeed, turning the tables on some of these statistics is almost beyond comprehension. If the per capita incarceration rate for whites were equal to that for blacks, more than 3.5 million white people would be incarcerated today, instead of 570,000, and we would need more than three times the prison capacity (and prosecution and court capacity) that we currently have. And because white people comprise about 80 percent of the general population, it would be literally impossible for whites to be overrepresented in the prison population to the same degree that black people currently are—four times their representation in the general population.

To see what happens when the criminal law begins to affect large numbers of white middle- and upper-class people, one need only look at the history of marijuana laws. The country's first marijuana users were largely nonwhite, mostly Mexicans.[57] By 1937, every state had criminalized marijuana. In the 1950s, federal penalties for the sale of marijuana ranged from two to five years imprisonment; a second offense brought a sentence of five to ten years; and a third brought ten to twenty years. State penalties followed suit. In 1956, Congress imposed mandatory minimum sentences for marijuana possession and sale.

In the 1960s, however, marijuana spread to the white middle and upper classes. By 1970, some college campuses reported that at least 70 percent of their student population had tried marijuana. As one author wrote in 1970, "Vast numbers of people have recently adopted the drug as their principal euphoriant; however, by all estimates, the new users are the sons and daughters of the middle class, not the ethnic minorities and ghetto residents formerly associated with marijuana,"[58] The harsh penalties imposed when their effect was primarily felt by minorities were no longer acceptable, and marijuana laws were liberalized. As Dr. Stanley Yolles explained in 1970,

> Nobody cared when it was a ghetto problem. Marijuana—well, it was used by jazz musicians or the lower class, so you didn't care if they got 20 years. But when a nice, middle-class girl or boy in college gets busted for the same thing, then the whole community sits up and takes notice. And that's the name of the game today. The problem has begun to come home to roost—in all strata of

society, in suburbia, in middle-class homes, in the colleges. Suddenly, the punitive, the vindictive approach was touching all classes of society. And now the most exciting thing that's really happening is the change in attitude by the people. Now we have a willingness to examine the problem, as to whether it's an experimentation, or an illness rather than an "evil."[59]

Police and prosecutors began to leave users alone, and instead targeted dealers and sellers. The courts limited enforcement, using their discretion to invalidate convictions on a variety of grounds. And the legislatures amended the laws, eliminating strict penalties for possession. As one commentator described the development, "In response to the extraordinary explosion in marijuana consumption and the penetration of its use into the mainstream of American life, every state amended its penalties in some fashion between 1969 and 1972, the overall result being a massive downward shift in penalties for consumption-related offenses. Simple possession of less than one ounce was classified as a misdemeanor in all but eight states by the end of 1972."[60] In 1973, Oregon went further and actually decriminalized possession of small amounts of marijuana, and by 1981 ten other states had followed suit.[61]

When the effects of a criminal law reach the sons and daughters of the white majority, our response is not to get tough, but rather to get lenient. Americans have been able to sustain an unremittingly harsh tough-on-crime attitude precisely because the burden of punishment falls disproportionately on minority populations. The white majority could not possibly maintain its current attitude toward crime and punishment were the burden of punishment felt by the same white majority that prescribes it.

NOTES

1. Jim Newton, "Judges Voice Anger Over Mandatory U.S. Sentences," *L.A. Times,* 21 August 1993, A1.
2. As of 1995, there were 14,000 people in prison for federal crack convictions, 80 percent of whom were black. Ronald Smothers, "Wave of Prison Uprisings Provokes Debate on Crack," *N.Y. Times,* 24 October 1995, A18.
3. H. R. Rep. No. 104-272 at 20 (1995), reprinted in 1995 U.S.C.C.A.N. 335,353 (citing U.S. Sentencing Commission study).
4. *United States v. Armstrong,* 517 U.S. 456 (1996) (Stevens, J., dissenting) (citing United States Sentencing Commission, Special Report to Congress: *Cocaine and Federal Sentencing Policy,* 39, 161 (1995).
5. *United States v. Clary,* 846 F. Supp. 768, 787 (E.D. Mo. 1994); see also *United States v. Walls,* 841 F. Supp. 24, 28 (D.D.C. 1994).
6. *State v. Russell,* 477 N.W.2d 886, 887 n.1 (Minn. 1991). In the Eastern District of Missouri, 98.2 percent of defendants convicted of crack cocaine charges from 1988 to 1992 were black. *United States v. Clary,* 846 F. Supp. at 786.
7. See, e.g., *United States v. Richardson,* 130 F.3d 765 (7th Cir. 1997); *United States v. Andrade,* 94 F.3d 9 (1st Cir. 1996); *United States v. Teague,* 93 F.3d 81 (2d Cir. 1996), *cert. denied,* 117 S. Ct. 708 (1997); *United States v. Lloyd,* 10 F.3d 1197 (6th Cir. 1993), *cert. denied,* 513 U.S. 883 (1994); *United States v. Jackson,* 67 F.3d 1359 (8th Cir. 1995), *cert. denied,* 517 U.S. 1192 (1996).
8. United States Sentencing Comm., Special Report to the Congress, *supra* note 4.
9. In 1997, the Sentencing Commission recommended reducing rather than eliminating the disparity, and the Clinton Administration supported the proposal. As of this writing, Congress has not acted on the recommendation.
10. *Stephens v. State,* 1995 WL 116292 (Ga. S. Ct. Mar. 17, 1995).
11. *Stephens v. State,* 456 S.E.2d 560 (Ga. 1995).
12. American Bar Association, *The State of Criminal Justice,* 9 (February 1993) (23 percent minority increase, 10 percent nonminority).
13. Id.
14. Jerome G. Miller, *Search and Destroy: African American Males in the Criminal Justice System,* 81 (New York: Cambridge Univ. Press, 1996).
15. Marc Mauer & Tracy Juling, The Sentencing Project, *Young Black Americans and the Criminal Justice System: Five Years Later,* 12 (1995).
16. David J. Rothman, "The Crime of Punishment," *New York Rev. of Books,* 17 February 1994, 34, 37.
17. Jerome G. Miller, *Search and Destroy, supra* note 14.
18. Id.
19. Id.
20. Marc Mauer, *Intended and Unintended Consequences: State Racial Disparities in Imprisonment,* 10 (Sentencing Project, Jan. 1997).
21. Human Rights Watch, *Cruel and Unusual: Disproportionate Sentences for New York Drug Offenders,* 2 (March 1997).
22. Dep't of Justice, Bureau of Justice Statistics Bulletin, *Prisoners in 1994,* 10, Table 13 (1995).
23. Id. at 11, Table 14 (state prisoners incarcerated on drug offenses increased from 19,000 in 1980 to 186,000 in 1993).
24. American Bar Association, *State of Criminal Justice, supra* note 12.
25. Office of Juvenile Justice and Delinquency Programs, *Juvenile Court Statistics 1991,* 25, Table 35, 71, Table 114 (May 1994). In this source, Hispanic youth were included in the "white" racial category.
26. 13,800 black juveniles were detained for drug violations, as compared to 7,400 white juveniles. Id. at 74, Table 118, 28, Table 39.
27. Id. at 29, Table 40.
28. Id. at 25, Table 37.
29. National Center on Institutions and Alternatives, *Hobbling a Generation: Young African American Males in the Criminal Justice System of America's Cities: Baltimore, Maryland* (September 1992).
30. See, e.g., Randall Kennedy, "The State, Criminal Law, and Racial Discrimination: A Comment, 107 Harv. L. Rev. 1255 (1994). For a detailed response, see David Cole, "The Paradox of Race and Crime: A Comment on Randall Kennedy's 'Politics of Distinction,'" 83 Geo. L.J. 2547 (1995); see also Randall Kennedy, "A Response to Professor Cole's 'Paradox of Race and Crime,'" 83 *Geo. L.J.* 2573 (1995).
31. National Institute of Justice, Department of Justice, *Three Strikes and You're Out: A Review of State Legislation,* 1 (September 1997); Tom Rhodes, "Third Strike and Pizza Thief Is Out for 25 Years," *The Times,* 4 April 1996 (available on NEXIS).

32. Maura Dolan & Tony Perry, "Justices Deal Blow to '3 Strikes,'" *L.A. Times,* 31 June 1996, A1.

33. Id.; see also The President's Radio Address, Weekly Comp. Pres. Doc. 1493 (July 16, 1994) (supporting "three strikes and you're out" provision in federal crime bill).

34. Rhodes, *supra* note 31.

35. Daniel B. Wood, "Softer Three-Strikes Law Brings Wave of Appeals," *Christian Science Monitor,* 24 June 1996, 3.

36. Christopher Davis, Richard Estes, and Vincent Schiraldi, *"Three Strikes:" The New Apartheid* (Report of the Center on Juvenile and Criminal Justice, San Francisco, March 1996).

37. Fox Butterfield, "Tough Law on Sentences is Criticized," *N.Y. Times,* 8 March 1996, A14.

38. See, e.g., Andy Furillo, "Most Offenders Have Long Criminal Histories," *Sacramento Bee,* 31 March 1996, A1.

39. Id.

40. William Spelman, *Criminal Incapacitation,* 15 (New York: Plenum Press, 1994) ("the typical criminal career lasts only 5 to 10 years"); 1 *Criminal Careers and Career Criminals,* 94 (Alfred Blumstein et al., eds.) (Washington, D.C.: National Academy Press, 1986) (same).

41. Daniel B. Wood, "LA Police Lash Out Against Three Strikes," *Christian Science Monitor,* 29 March 1996, 3.

42. Fox Butterfield, *supra* note 37.

43. Id.

44. Ian Katz, "Bull Market in Prisons and Knee-Jerk Politics," *The Guardian,* 25 May 1996 (available on NEXIS).

45. Bureau of Justice Statistics, *Sourcebook of Criminal Justice Statistics—1995,* Table 6.11 (1996).

46. Ann Golenpaul, ed., *Information Please Almanac,* 829 (Boston: Houghton Mifflin, 1997).

47. Ian Katz, *supra* note 44.

48. Christopher Davis, et al., *supra* note 36.

49. Douglas C. McDonald & Kenneth E. Carlson, *Sentencing in the Federal Courts: Does Race Matter? The Transition to Sentencing Guidelines, 1986–90: Summary,* 1–2 (Washington, D.C.: Bureau of Justice Statistics, 1993).

50. Id. at 13–17.

51. Id. at 16–17.

52. See, e.g. Stephen Klein, Joan Petersilia, and Susan Turner, "Race and Imprisonment Decisions in California," 247 *Science* 812–16 (Feb. 16, 1990) (studying California sentences and concluding that race did not improve the accuracy of predicting what type of punishment offenders would receive); Alfred Blumstein, "On the Racial Disproportionality of United States Prison Populations," 73 J. of Crim. L. & Crim. 1259 (1983) (finding little evidence of racial bias in incarceration for serious crimes); but see Jerome Miller, *Search and Destroy, supra* note 14 (reviewing studies finding evidence of racial discrimination); Crutchfield, et. al, "Analytical and Aggregation Biases in Analysis of Imprisonment: Reconciling Discrepancies in Studies of Racial Disparity," 31 J. of Res. In Crime & Delinquency 178 (1994) (critiquing prior studies for aggregating information in a way that might conceal discrimination; finding evidence of discrimination).

53. Michael H. Tonry, *Malign Neglect: Race, Crime, and Punishment in America,* 29 (New York: Oxford Univ. Press, 1995).

54. Barbara S. Meierhoefer, "Individualized and Systemic Justice in the Federal Sentencing Process," 29 Am. Crim. L. Rev. 889, 891 (1992).

55. William Wilbanks, *The Myth of a Racist Criminal Justice System* (Monterey, CA: Brooks/ Cole, 1986).

56. Stephen P. Klein, *Racial Disparities in Sentencing Decisions,* 5 (Santa Monica, CA: Rand, 1991).

57. Unless otherwise indicated, the information in the next two paragraphs is drawn from Bonnie Whitebread, "Marijuana Prohibition," 56 U.Va. L. Rev. 983 (1970).

58. Whitebread, 56 Va. L. Rev. at 1096.

59. Gertrude Samuels, "Pot, Hard Drugs, and the Law," *N.Y. Times Magazine,* 15 February 1970, 14.

60. Richard J. Bonnie, "The Meaning of 'Decriminalization': A Review of the Law," Contemporary Drug Problems 277, 278 (Fall 1981).

61. Id. at 279; see also Bureau of Justice Statistics, U.S. Dept of Justice, *Drugs, Crime and the Justice System,* 84–85 (1992) (reporting that when large numbers of white middle-class youth were arrested for marijuana possession in the late 1960s and early 1970s, public complaints led Congress and eleven states to decriminalize or reduce substantially the penalties for that crime).

21

RACE AND CRIMINALIZATION
Black Americans and the Punishment Industry

Angela Y. Davis

Questions to Consider

Angela Davis links the growth of the prison system to the "war on drugs" and to institutional racism. How do race and racism figure into her analysis of who gets targeted for America's "war on drugs"? How might racial stereotypes and the huge profits generated by the prison system shape the ways in which legislation is written by corporate lobbyists and lawmakers?

In this post–civil rights era, as racial barriers in high economic and political realms are apparently shattered with predictable regularity, race itself becomes an increasingly proscribed subject. In the dominant political discourse it is no longer acknowledged as a pervasive structural phenomenon, requiring the continuation of such strategies as affirmative action, but rather is represented primarily as a complex of prejudicial attitudes, which carry equal weight across all racial boundaries. Black leadership is thus often discredited and the identification of race as a public, political issue itself called into question through the invocation of, and application of the epithet "black racist" to, such figures as Louis Farrakhan and Khalid Abdul Muhammad. Public debates about the role of the state that once

focused very sharply and openly on issues of "race" and racism are now expected to unfold in the absence of any direct acknowledgment of the persistence—and indeed further entrenchment—of racially structured power relationships. Because race is ostracized from some of the most impassioned political debates of this period, their racialized character becomes increasingly difficult to identify, especially by those who are unable—or do not want—to decipher the encoded language. This means that hidden racist arguments can be mobilized readily across racial boundaries and political alignments. Political positions once easily defined as conservative, liberal, and sometimes even radical therefore have a tendency to lose their distinctiveness in the face of the seductions of this camouflaged racism.

President Clinton chose the date of the Million Man March, convened by Minister Louis Farrakhan of the Nation of Islam, to issue a call for a "national conversation on race," borrowing ironically the exact words of Lani Guinier (whose nomination for assistant attorney general in charge of civil rights he had previously withdrawn because her writings focused too sharply on issues of race).[1] Guinier's ideas had been so easily dismissed because of the prevailing ideological equation of the "end of racism" with the removal of all allusions to race. If conservative positions argue that race consciousness itself impedes the process of solving the problem of race—i.e., achieving race blindness—then Clinton's speech indicated an attempt to reconcile the two, positing race consciousness as a means of moving toward race blindness. "There are too many today, white and black, on the left and the right, on the street corners and radio waves, who seek to sow division for their own purposes. To them I say: 'No more. We must be one.'"

While Clinton did acknowledge "the awful history and the stubborn persistence of racism," his remarks foregrounded those reasons for the "racial divide" that "are rooted in the fact that we still haven't learned to talk frankly, to listen carefully and to work together across racial lines." Race, he insisted, is not about government, but about the hearts of people. Of course, it would be absurd to deny the degree to which racism infects in deep and multiple ways the national psyche. However, the relegation of race to matters of the heart tends to render it increasingly difficult to identify the deep structural entrenchment of contemporary racism.

When the structural character of racism is ignored in discussions about crime and the rising population of incarcerated people, the racial imbalance in jails and prisons is treated as a contingency, at best as a product of the "culture of poverty," and at worst as proof of an assumed black monopoly on criminality. The high proportion of black people in the criminal justice system is thus normalized and neither the state nor the general public is required to talk about and act on the meaning of that racial imbalance.

Thus Republican and Democratic elected officials alike have successfully called for laws mandating life sentences for three-time "criminals," without having to answer for the racial implications of these laws. By relying on the alleged "race-blindness" of such laws, black people are surreptitiously constructed as racial subjects, thus manipulated, exploited, and abused, while the structural persistence of racism—albeit in changed forms—in social and economic institutions, and in the national culture as a whole, is adamantly denied.

Crime is thus one of the masquerades behind which "race," with all its menacing ideological complexity, mobilizes old public fears *and* creates new ones. The current anti-crime debate takes place within a reified mathematical realm—a strategy reminiscent of Malthus's notion of the geometrical increase in population and the arithmetical increase in food sources, thus the inevitability of poverty and the means of suppressing it: war, disease, famine, and natural disasters. As a matter of fact, the persisting neo-Malthusian approach to population control, which, instead of seeking to solve those pressing social problems that result in real pain and suffering in people's lives, calls for the elimination of those suffering lives—finds strong resonances in the public discussion about expurgating the "nation" of crime. These discussions include arguments deployed by those who are leading the call for more prisons and employ statistics in the same fetishistic and misleading way as Malthus did more than two centuries ago. Take for example James Wooten's comments in the *Heritage Foundation State Backgrounder*:

> If the 55% of the 800,000 current state and federal prisoners who are violent offenders were subject to serving 85% of their sentence, and assuming that those violent offenders would have committed 10 violent crimes a year

while on the street, then the number of crimes prevented each year by truth in sentencing would be 4,000,000. That would be over ⅔ of the 6,000,000 violent crimes reported.[2]

In *Reader's Digest,* Senior Editor Eugene H. Methvin writes:

> If we again double the present federal and state prison population—to somewhere between 1 million and 1.5 million and leave our city and county jail population at the present 400,000, we will break the back of America's 30 year crime wave.[3]

The real human beings—a vastly disproportionate number of whom are black and Latino/a men and women—designated by these numbers in a seemingly race-neutral way are deemed fetishistically exchangeable with the crimes they have or will allegedly commit. The real impact of imprisonment on their lives never need be examined. The inevitable part played by the punishment industry in the reproduction of crime never need be discussed. The dangerous and indeed fascistic trend toward progressively greater numbers of hidden, incarcerated human populations is itself rendered invisible. All that matters is the elimination of crime—and you get rid of crime by getting rid of people who, according to the prevailing racial common sense, are the most likely people to whom criminal acts will be attributed. Never mind that if this strategy is seriously and consistently pursued, the majority of young black women spend a good portion of their lives behind walls and bars in order to serve as a reminder that the state is aggressively confronting its enemy.[4]

While I do not want to locate a response to these arguments on the same level of mathematical abstraction and fetishism I have been problematizing, it is helpful, I think, to consider how many people are presently incarcerated or whose lives are subject to the direct surveillance of the criminal justice system. There are already approximately 1 million people in state and federal prisons in the United States, not counting the 500,000 in city and county jails or the 600,000 on parole or the 3 million people on probation or the 60,000 young people in juvenile facilities. Which is to say that there are presently over 5.1 million people either incarcerated, on parole, or on probation. Many of those presently on probation or parole would be behind bars under the conditions of the recently passed crime bill. According to the Sentencing Project, even before the passage of the crime bill, black people were 7.8 times more likely to be imprisoned than whites.[5] The Sentencing Project's most recent report[6] indicates that 32.2 percent of young black men and 12.3 percent of young Latino men between the ages of twenty and twenty-nine are either in prison, in jail, or on probation or parole. This is in comparison with 6.7 percent of young white men. A total of 827,440 young African-American males are under the supervision of the criminal justice system, at a cost of $6 billion per year. A major strength of the 1995 report, as compared to its predecessor, is its acknowledgment that the racialized impact of the criminal justice system is also gendered and that the relatively smaller number of African-American women drawn into the system should not relieve us of the responsibility of understanding the encounter of gender and race in arrest and incarceration practices. Moreover, the increases in women's contact with the criminal justice system have been even more dramatic than those of men.

> The 78% increase in criminal justice control rates for black women was more than double the increase for black men and for white women, and more than nine times the increase for white

men. . . . Although research on women of color in the criminal justice system is limited, existing data and research suggest that it is the combination of race and sex effects that is at the root of the trends which appear in our data. For example, while the number of blacks and Hispanics in prison is growing at an alarming rate, the rate of increase for women is even greater. Between 1980 and 1992 the female prison population increased 276% compared to 163% for men. Unlike men of color, women of color thus belong to two groups that are experiencing particular dramatic growth in their contact with the criminal justice system.[7]

It has been estimated that by the year 2000 the number of people imprisoned will surpass 4 million, a grossly disproportionate number of whom will be black people, and that the cost will be over $40 billion a year,[8] a figure that is reminiscent of the way the military budget devoured—and continues to devour—the country's resources. This out-of-control punishment industry is an extremely effective criminalization industry, for the racial imbalance in incarcerated populations is not recognized as evidence of structural racism, but rather is invoked as a consequence of the assumed criminality of black people. In other words, the criminalization process works so well precisely because of the hidden logic of racism. Racist logic is deeply entrenched in the nation's material and psychic structures. It is something with which we are all very familiar. The logic, in fact, can persist, even when direct allusions to "race" are removed.

Even those communities that are most deeply injured by this racist logic have learned how to rely upon it, particularly when open allusions to race are not necessary. Thus, in the absence of broad, radical grassroots movements in poor black communities so devastated by new forms of youth-perpetuated violence, the ideological options are extremely sparse. Often there are no other ways to express collective rage and despair but to demand that police sweep the community clean of crack and Uzis, and of the people who use and sell drugs and wield weapons. Ironically, Carol Moseley-Braun, the first black woman senator in our nation's history, was an enthusiastic sponsor of the Senate Anticrime Bill, whose passage in November 1993 paved the way for the August 25, 1994, passage of the bill by the House. Or perhaps there is little irony here. It may be precisely because there is a Carol Moseley-Braun in the Senate and a Clarence Thomas in the Supreme Court— and concomitant class differentiations and other factors responsible for far more heterogeneity in black communities than at any other time in this country's history—that implicit consent to antiblack racist logic (not to speak of racism toward other groups) becomes far more widespread among black people. Wahneema Lubiano's explorations of the complexities of state domination as it operates within and through the subjectivities of those who are the targets of this domination facilitates an understanding of this dilemma.[9]

Borrowing the title of Cornel West's recent work, race *matters*. Moreover, it matters in ways that are far more threatening and simultaneously less discernible than those to which we have grown accustomed. Race matters inform, more than ever, the ideological and material structures of U.S. society. And, as the current discourses on crime, welfare, and immigration reveal, race, gender, and class matter enormously in the continuing elaboration of public policy and its impact on the real lives of human beings.

And how does race matter? Fear has always been an integral component of racism. The ideological reproduction of a fear of black people, whether economically or sexually grounded, is rapidly gravitating toward and being grounded in a fear of crime. A question to be raised in this context is whether and how the increasing fear of crime—this ideologically produced fear of crime—serves to render racism simultaneously more invisible and more virulent. Perhaps one way to approach an answer to this question is to consider how this fear of crime effectively summons black people to imagine black people as the enemy. How many black people present at this conference have successfully extricated ourselves from the ideological power of the figure of the young black male as criminal—or at least seriously confronted it? The lack of a significant black presence in the rather feeble opposition to the "three strikes, you're out" bills, which have been proposed and/or passed in forty states already, evidences the disarming effect of this ideology.

California is one of the states that has passed the "three strikes, you're out" bill. Immediately after the passage of that bill, Governor Pete Wilson began to argue for a "two strikes, you're out" bill. Three, he said, is too many. Soon we will hear calls for "one strike, you're out." Following this mathematical regression, we can imagine that at some point the hardcore anticrime advocates will be arguing that to stop the crime wave, we can't wait until even one crime is committed. Their slogan will be: "Get them before the first strike!" And because certain populations have already been criminalized, there will be those who say, "We know who the real criminals are—let's get them before they have a chance to act out their criminality."

The fear of crime has attained a status that bears a sinister similarity to the fear of communism as it came to restructure social perceptions during the fifties and sixties. The figure of the "criminal"—the racialized figure of the criminal—has come to repre-

sent the most menacing enemy of "American society." Virtually anything is acceptable—torture, brutality, vast expenditures of public funds—as long as it is done in the name of public safety. Racism has always found an easy route from its embeddedness in social structures to the psyches of collectives and individuals precisely because it mobilizes deep fears. While explicit, old-style racism may be increasingly socially unacceptable—precisely as a result of antiracist movements over the last forty years—this does not mean that U.S. society has been purged of racism. In fact, racism is more deeply embedded in socioeconomic structures, and the vast populations of incarcerated people of color is dramatic evidence of the way racism systematically structures economic relations. At the same time, this structural racism is rarely recognized as "racism." What we have come to recognize as open, explicit racism has in many ways begun to be replaced by a secluded, camouflaged kind of racism, whose influence on people's daily lives is as pervasive and systematic as the explicit forms of racism associated with the era of the struggle for civil rights.

The ideological space for the proliferations of this racialized fear of crime has been opened by the transformations in international politics created by the fall of the European socialist countries. Communism is no longer the quintessential enemy against which the nation imagines its identity. This space is now inhabited by ideological constructions of crime, drugs, immigration, and welfare. Of course, the enemy within is far more dangerous than the enemy without, and a black enemy within is the most dangerous of all.

Because of the tendency to view it as an abstract site into which all manner of undesirables are deposited, the prison is the perfect site for the simultaneous production and concealment of racism. The abstract character of the public perception of prisons militates against an engagement with the real issues afflicting the communities from which prisoners are drawn in such disproportionate numbers. This is the ideological work that the prison performs—it relieves us of the responsibility of seriously engaging with the problems of late capitalism, of transnational capitalism. The naturalization of black people as criminals thus also erects ideological barriers to an understanding of the connections between late-twentieth-century structural racism and the globalization of capital.

The vast expansion of the power of capitalist corporations over the lives of people of color and poor people in general has been accompanied by a waning anticapitalist consciousness. As capital moves with ease across national borders, legitimized by recent trade agreements such as NAFTA and GATT, corporations are allowed to close shop in the United States and transfer manufacturing operations to nations providing cheap labor pools. In fleeing organized labor in the U.S. to avoid paying higher wages and benefits, they leave entire communities in shambles, consigning huge numbers of people to joblessness, leaving them prey to the drug trade, destroying the economic base of these communities, thus affecting the education system, social welfare—and turning the people who live in those communities into perfect candidates for prison. At the same time, they create an economic demand for prisons, which stimulates the economy, providing jobs in the correctional industry for people who often come from the very populations that are criminalized by this process. It is a horrifying and self-reproducing cycle.

Ironically, prisons themselves are becoming a source of cheap labor that attracts corporate capitalism—as yet on a relatively small scale—in a way that parallels the attraction unorganized labor in Third World coun-

tries exerts. A statement by Michael Lamar Powell, a prisoner in Capshaw, Alabama, dramatically reveals this new development:

> I cannot go on strike, nor can I unionize. I am not covered by workers' compensation or the Fair Standards Act. I agree to work late-night and weekend shifts. I do just what I am told, no matter what it is. I am hired and fired at will, and I am not even paid minimum wage: I earn one dollar a month. I cannot even voice grievances or complaints, except at the risk of incurring arbitrary discipline or some covert retaliation.
>
> You need not worry about NAFTA and your jobs going to Mexico and other Third World countries. I will have at least five percent of your jobs by the end of this decade.
>
> I am called prison labor. I am The New American Worker.[10]

This "new American worker" will be drawn from the ranks of a racialized population whose historical superexploitation—from the era of slavery to the present—has been legitimized by racism. At the same time, the expansion of convict labor is accompanied in some states by the old paraphernalia of ankle chains that symbolically links convict labor with slave labor. At least three states—Alabama, Florida, and Arizona—have reinstituted the chain gang. Moreover, as Michael Powell so inclusively reveals, there is a new dimension to the racism inherent in this process, which structurally links the superexploitation of prison labor to the globalization of capital.

In California, whose prison system is the largest in the country and one of the largest in the world, the passage of an inmate initiative in 1990 has presented businesses seeking cheap labor with opportunities uncannily similar to those in Third World countries. As of June 1994, a range of companies were employing prison labor in nine California prisons. Under the auspices of the Joint Venture Program, work now being performed on prison grounds includes computerized telephone messaging, dental apparatus assembly, computer data entry, plastic parts fabrication, electronic component manufacturing at the Central California Women's facility at Chowchilla, security glass manufacturing, swine production, oak furniture manufacturing, and the production of stainless steel tanks and equipment. In a California Corrections Department brochure designed to promote the program, it is described as "an innovative public-private partnership that makes good business sense."[11] According to the owner of Tower Communications, whom the brochure quotes,

> The operation is cost effective, dependable and trouble free. . . . Tower Communications has successfully operated a message center utilizing inmates on the grounds of California state prison. If you're a business leader planning expansion, considering relocation because of a deficient labor pool, starting a new enterprise, look into the benefits of using inmate labor.

The employer benefits listed by the brochure include

> federal and state tax incentives; no benefit package (retirement pay, vacation pay, sick leave, medical benefits); long term lease agreements at far below market value costs; discount rates on Workers Compensation; build a consistent, qualified work force; on call labor pool (no car breakdowns, no babysitting problems); option of hiring job-ready ex-offenders and minimizing costs; becoming a partner in public safety.

There is a major, yet invisible, racial supposition in such claims about the profitability of a convict labor force. The acceptability of the superexploitation of convict labor is largely based on the historical conjuncture of racism and incarceration practices. The already disproportionately black convict labor force will become increasingly black if the racially imbalanced incarceration practices continue.

The complicated yet unacknowledged structural presence of racism in the U.S. punishment industry also includes the fact that the punishment industry which sequesters ever-larger sectors of the black population attracts vast amounts of capital. Ideologically, as I have argued, the racialized fear of crime has begun to succeed the fear of communism. This corresponds to a structural tendency for capital that previously flowed toward the military industry to now move toward the punishment industry. The ease with which suggestions are made for prison construction costing in the multibillions of dollars is reminiscent of the military buildup: economic mobilization to defeat communism has turned into economic mobilization to defeat crime. The ideological construction of crime is thus complemented and bolstered by the material construction of jails and prisons. The more jails and prisons are constructed, the greater the fear of crime, and the greater the fear of crime, the stronger the cry for more jails and prisons, ad infinitum.

The law enforcement industry bears remarkable parallels to the military industry (just as there are anti-Communist resonances in the anti-crime campaign). This connection between the military industry and the punishment industry is revealed in a *Wall Street Journal* article entitled "Making Crime Pay: The Cold War of the '90s":

> Parts of the defense establishment are cashing in, too, scenting a logical new

line of business to help them offset military cutbacks. Westinghouse Electric Corp., Minnesota Mining and Manufacturing Co., GDE Systems (a division of the old General Dynamics) and Alliant Techsystems Inc., for instance, are pushing crime-fighting equipment and have created special divisions to retool their defense technology for America's streets.

According to the article, a conference sponsored by the National Institute of Justice, the research arm of the Justice Department, was organized around the theme "Law Enforcement Technology in the 21st Century." The secretary of defense was a major presenter at this conference, which explored topics like "the role of the defense industry, particularly for dual use and conversion":

> Hot topics: defense-industry technology that could lower the level of violence involved in crime fighting. Sandia National Laboratories, for instance, is experimenting with a dense foam that can be sprayed at suspects, temporarily blinding and deafening them under breathable bubbles. Stinger Corporation is working on "smart guns," which will fire only for the owner, and retractable spiked barrier strips to unfurl in front of fleeing vehicles. Westinghouse is promoting the "smart car," in which mini-computers could be linked up with big mainframes at the police department, allowing for speedy booking of prisoners, as well as quick exchanges of information.[12]

Again, race provides a silent justification for the technological expansion of law enforcement, which, in turn, intensifies racist arrest and incarceration practices. This skyrocketing punishment industry, whose growth is silently but powerfully sustained by the persistence of racism, creates an economic demand for more jails and prisons and thus for similarly spiraling criminalization practices, which, in turn fuels the fear of crime.

Most debates addressing the crisis resulting from overcrowding in prisons and jails focus on male institutions. Meanwhile, women's institutions and jail space for women are proportionately proliferating at an even more astounding rate than men's. If race is largely an absent factor in the discussions about crime and punishment, gender seems not even to merit a place carved out by its absence. Historically, the imprisonment of women has served to criminalize women in a way that is more complicated than is the case with men. This female criminalization process has had more to do with the marking of certain groups of women as undomesticated and hypersexual, as women who refuse to embrace the nuclear family as paradigm. The current liberal-conservative discourse around welfare criminalizes black single mothers, who are represented as deficient, manless, drug-using breeders of children, and as reproducers of an attendant culture of poverty. The woman who does drugs is criminalized both because she is a drug user and because as a consequence, she cannot be a good mother. In some states, pregnant women are being imprisoned for using crack because of possible damage to the fetus.

According to the U.S. Department of Justice, women are far more likely than men to be imprisoned for a drug conviction.[13] However, if women wish to receive treatment for their drug problems, often their only option, if they cannot pay for a drug program, is to be arrested and sentenced to a drug program via the criminal justice system. Yet when U.S. Surgeon General Jocelyn Elders alluded to the importance of opening discussion on the decriminalization of drugs, the Clinton administration immediately disassociated itself from her remarks.

Decriminalization of drugs would greatly reduce the numbers of incarcerated women, for the 278 percent increase in the numbers of black women in state and federal prisons (as compared to the 186 percent increase in the numbers of black men) can be largely attributed to the phenomenal rise in drug-related and specifically crack-related imprisonment. According to the Sentencing Project's 1995 report, the increase amounted to 828 percent.[14]

Official refusals to even consider decriminalization of drugs as a possible strategy that might begin to reverse present incarceration practices further bolsters the ideological staying power of the prison. In his well-known study of the history of the prison and its related technologies of discipline, Michel Foucault pointed out that an evolving contradiction is at the very heart of the historical project of imprisonment.

> For a century and a half, the prison has always been offered as its own remedy: . . . the realization of the corrective project as the only method of overcoming the impossibility of implementing it.[15]

As I have attempted to argue, within the U.S. historical context, racism plays a pivotal role in sustaining this contradiction. In fact, Foucault's theory regarding the prison's tendency to serve as its own enduring justification becomes even more compelling if the role of race is also acknowledged. Moreover, moving beyond the parameters of what I consider the double impasse implied by his theory—the discursive impasse his theory discovers and that of the theory itself—I want to conclude by suggesting the possibility of radical race-conscious strategies designed to disrupt the stranglehold of criminalization and incarceration practices.

In the course of a recent collaborative research project with U.C. Santa Barbara sociologist Kum-Kum Bhavnani, in which we interviewed thirty-five women at the San Francisco County Jail, the complex ways in which race and gender help to produce a punishment industry that reproduces the very problems it purports to solve become dramatically apparent. Our interviews focused on the women's ideas about imprisonment and how they themselves imagine alternatives to incarceration. Their various critiques of the prison system and of the existing "alternatives," all of which are tied to reimprisonment as a last resort, led us to reflect more deeply about the importance of retrieving, retheorizing, and reactivating the radical abolitionist strategy first proposed in connection with the prison-reform movements of the sixties and seventies.

We are presently attempting to theorize women's imprisonment in ways that allow us to formulate a radical abolitionist strategy departing from, but not restricted in its conclusions to, women's jails and prisons. Our goal is to formulate alternatives to incarceration that substantively reflect the voices and agency of a variety of imprisoned women. We wish to open up channels for their involvement in the current debates around alternatives to incarceration, while not denying our own role as mediators and interpreters and our own political positioning in these debates. We also want to distinguish our explorations of alternatives from the spate of "alternative punishments" or what are now called "intermediate sanctions" presently being proposed and/or implemented by and through state and local correctional systems.

This is a long-range project that has three dimensions: academic research, public policy, and community organizing. In other words, for this project to be successful, it must build bridges between academic work, legislative and other policy interventions, and grassroots campaigns calling, for example, for the decriminalization of drugs and prostitution—and for the reversal of the present proliferation of jails and prisons.

Raising the possibility of abolishing jails and prisons as the institutionalized and normalized means of addressing social problems in an era of migrating corporations, unemployment and homelessness, and collapsing public services, from health care to education, can hopefully help to interrupt the current law-and-order discourse that has such a grip on the collective imagination, facilitated as it is by deep and hidden influences of racism. This late-twentieth-century "abolitionism," with its nineteenth-century resonances, may also lead to a historical recontextualization of the practice of imprisonment. With the passage of the Thirteenth Amendment, slavery was abolished for all except convicts—and in a sense the exclusion from citizenship accomplished by the slave system has persisted within the U.S. prison system. Only three states allow prisoners to vote, and approximately 4 million people are denied the right to vote because of their present or past incarceration. A radical strategy to abolish jails and prisons as the normal way of dealing with the social problems of late capitalism is not a strategy for abstract abolition. It is designed to force a rethinking of the increasingly repressive role of the state during this era of late capitalism and to carve out a space for resistance.

NOTES

1. See, for instance, the *Austin-American States-man*, October 17, 1995.
2. Charles S. Clark, "Prison Overcrowding," *Congressional Quarterly Researcher* 4, no. 5 (Feb. 4, 1994): 97–119.
3. Ibid.
4. Marc Mauer, "Young Black Men and the Criminal Justice System: A Growing National Problem," Washington, D.C.: The Sentencing Project, February 1990.
5. Alexander Cockburn, *Philadelphia Inquirer*, August 29, 1994.
6. Marc Mauer and Tracy Huling, "Young Black Americans and the Criminal Justice System: Five Years Later," Washington, D.C.: The Sentencing Project, October 1995.
7. Ibid., 18.
8. *See* Cockburn.
9. *See* Lubiano's essay in this volume, as well as "Black Ladies, Welfare Queens, and State Minstrels: Ideological War by Narrative Means," in *Race-ing Justice, En-gendering Power: Essays on Anita Hill, Clarence Thomas, and the Construction of Social Reality*, ed. Toni Morrison (New York: Pantheon, 1992), 323–63.
10. Unpublished essay, "Modern Slavery American Style," 1995.
11. I wish to acknowledge Julie Brown, who acquired this brochure from the California Department of Correction in the course of researching the role of convict labor.
12. *Wall Street Journal*, May 12, 1994.
13. Lawrence Rence, A. Greenfield, Stephanie Minor-Harper, *Women in Prison* (Washington, D.C.: U.S. Dept. of Justice, Office of Justice Programs, Bureau of Statistics, 1991).
14. Mauer and Huling, "Young Black Americans," 19.
15. Michel Foucault, *Discipline and Punish: The Birth of the Prison,* trans. Alan Sheridan (New York: Vintage, 1979), 395.

22
_____

. . . AND THE POOR GET PRISON

Jeffrey Reiman

Questions to Consider

It is unlikely that many CEOs or white-collar administrators from companies such as Enron, Global Crossing, and Tyco will go to jail in the wake of the corporate scandals that have rocked Wall Street. A corporate CEO who has raided his company's pension fund and destroyed the future of thousands of workers typically receives a fine and/or community service for his crime, while low-level, nonviolent drug dealers are often sentenced to long and hard time in a federal penitentiary. Wealthy lawbreakers, argues Jeffrey Reiman, rarely see the inside of a prison. Why? How is this pattern linked to race?

Weeding Out the Wealthy

The offender at the end of the road in prison is likely to be a member of the lowest social and economic groups in the country.[1]

This statement in the *Report of the President's Commission on Law Enforcement and Administration of Justice* is as true today as it was over three decades ago when it was written. Our prisons are indeed, as Ronald Goldfarb has called them, the "national poorhouse."[2] To most citizens this comes as no surprise—recall the Typical Criminal and the Typical Crime. Dangerous crimes, they think, are committed mainly by poor people. Seeing that prison populations are made up pri-

marily of the poor only makes them surer of this. They think, in other words, that the criminal justice system gives a true reflection of the dangers that threaten them.

In my view, it also comes as no surprise that our prisons and jails predominantly confine the poor. This is not because these are the individuals who most threaten us. It is because the criminal justice system effectively weeds out the well-to-do, so that at *the end of the road in prison,* the vast majority of those we find there come from the lower classes. This weeding-out process starts before the agents of law enforcement go into action. [I argue] that our very definition of crime *excludes* a wide variety of actions at least as dangerous as those included and often worse. Is it any accident that the kinds of dangerous actions excluded are the kinds most likely to be performed by the affluent in America? Even before we mobilize our troops in the war on crime, we have already guaranteed that large numbers of upper-class individuals will never come within their sights.

This process does not stop at the definition of crime. It continues throughout each level of the criminal justice system. At each step, from arresting to sentencing, the likelihood of being ignored or released or treated lightly by the system is greater the better off one is economically. As the late U.S. Senator Philip Hart wrote:

> Justice has two transmission belts, one for the rich and one for the poor. The low-income transmission belt is easier to ride without falling off and it gets to prison in shorter order.
>
> The transmission belt for the affluent is a little slower and it passes innumerable stations where exits are temptingly convenient.[3]

This means that the criminal justice system functions from start to finish in a way that makes certain that "the offender at the end of the road in prison is likely to be a member of the lowest social and economic groups in the country."

For the same criminal behavior, the poor are more likely to be arrested; if arrested, they are more likely to be charged; if charged, more likely to be convicted; if convicted, more likely to be sentenced to prison; and if sentenced, more likely to be given longer prison terms than members of the middle and upper classes.[4] In other words, the image of the criminal population one sees in our nation's jails and prisons is distorted by the shape of the criminal justice system itself. It is the face of evil reflected in a carnival mirror, but it is no laughing matter.

The face in the criminal justice carnival mirror is also, as we have already noted, very frequently a black face. Although blacks do not make up the majority of the inmates in our jails and prisons, they make up a proportion that far outstrips their proportion in the population.[5] Here, too, the image we see is distorted by the processes of the criminal justice system itself. Edwin Sutherland and Donald Cressey write in their widely used textbook *Criminology* that

> . . . numerous studies have shown that African-Americans are more likely to be arrested, indicted, convicted, and committed to an institution than are whites who commit the same offenses, and many other studies have shown that blacks have a poorer chance than whites to receive probation, a suspended sentence, parole, commutation of a death sentence, or pardon.[6]

William Wilbanks has attacked this conclusion in *The Myth of a Racist Criminal Justice System.*[7] He uses as "perhaps the most important criticism" of the charge that there is discrimination against blacks in arrests the work of Michael Hindelang, which compares the rate at which respondents to the National Crime Survey report being victimized by assailants perceived to be black with the rate at which blacks are arrested for the relevant crimes according to the *UCR,* and finds "that the racial gap in *offending* for robbery, assault, and rape (whether or not an arrest occurred) was almost equal to that found for *arrest* statistics. Wilbanks concludes, "these results indicate that police select black and white arrestees in approximately the same proportion as they are found in the pool of offenders," and thus "argue against police bias in the arrest process."[8] Recent statistics, however, suggest quite the opposite. Consider the following.

In 1998, respondents to the *National Criminal Victimization Survey* reported that approximately 22 percent of their assailants in violent victimizations (rape, robbery, simple and aggravated assault) were perceived to be black. That same year, the *UCR* indicates that 42 percent of the individuals arrested for these crimes were black. If we drop simple assault on the assumption that it is less often reported to the police than the other violent crimes, the figures change only slightly: 25 percent of violent victimizers are perceived to be black, whereas 44 percent of those arrested for rape, robbery, and aggravated assault are black. These figures indicate that police are arresting blacks almost two times more frequently than the occurrence of their perceived offenses.[9] Because arrest determines the pool from which charged, convicted, and imprisoned individuals are selected, this suggests that deep bias persists throughout the criminal justice system.

I am aware that there are various problems with comparing *UCR* and *NCVS* statistics and various possible explanations for the divergence of black-white arrest rates from the rate at which blacks and whites are perceived offenders. Thus I do not claim that the results just presented prove definitively the presence of racism. Nonetheless, because they come from the statistics that Wilbanks uses as "the most important criticism" of the discrimination thesis, I think they suffice to cast significant doubt on Wilbanks's claim. Thus, I shall treat his thesis as currently unsubstantiated and continue to follow the majority of researchers in holding that the criminal justice system is widely marked by racial discrimination as well as by economic bias.[10] Moreover, I shall shortly present the results of numerous studies that demonstrate this point.

Curiously enough, statistics on differential treatment of races are available in greater abundance than our statistics on differential treatment of economic classes. For instance, although the FBI tabulates arrest rates by race (as well as by sex, age, and geographic area), it omits class or income. Similarly, both the President's Crime Commission report and Sutherland and Cressey's *Criminology* have index entries for race or racial discrimination but none for class or income

of offenders. It would seem that both independent and government data gatherers are more willing to own up to America's racism than to its class bias. Nevertheless, it does not pay to look at these as two independent forms of bias. It is my view that, at least as far as criminal justice is concerned, racism is simply one powerful form of economic bias. I use evidence on differential treatment of blacks as evidence of differential treatment of members of the lower classes. There are five reasons for this.

1. First and foremost, black Americans are disproportionately poor. In 1996, while slightly more than one of every ten white Americans received income below the poverty line, nearly three of every ten black Americans did.[11] The picture is even worse when we shift from income to wealth (property such as a home, land, stocks). Blacks in America own one-fifth of the wealth that whites do.[12] Moreover, "the homeownership rate among non-Hispanic whites is more than 50 percent higher than that of blacks." Among homeowners, in 1993, the median equity "was about $50,000 for whites (in 1993 dollars) [and] $29,000 for blacks." Only about 5 percent of black households owned stocks. Compared to 25 percent of white households.[13] Unemployment figures give a similarly dismal picture: In 1997, 2.8 percent of white workers were unemployed and 6.5 percent of blacks were. Among those in the crime-prone ages of 16 to 24, 12.7 percent of white youngsters (with no college) and 31.6 percent of black youngsters (with no college)—nearly one of every three—were jobless.[14]

2. The factors most likely to keep one out of trouble with the law and out of prison, such as a suburban living room instead of a tenement alley to gamble in or legal

counsel able to devote time to one's case instead of an overburdened public defender, are the kinds of things that money can buy regardless of one's race, creed, or national origin. For example, as we shall see, arrests of blacks for illicit drug possession or dealing have skyrocketed in recent years, rising way out of proportion to drug arrests for whites—though research shows no greater drug use among blacks than among whites. However, drug arrests are most easily made in "disorganized inner-city" areas, where drug sales are more likely to take place out of doors, and dealers are more willing to sell to strangers. Blacks are (proportionately) more likely than whites to live in such inner-city areas and thus more likely than whites to be arrested on drug charges.[15] And one very important reason that blacks are more likely than whites to live in disorganized inner-city areas is that a greater percentage of blacks than whites are poor and unemployed. What might at first look like a straightforward racial disparity turns out to reflect economic status.

3. Blacks who travel the full route of the criminal justice system and end up in jail or prison are close in economic condition to whites who do. In 1978, 53 percent of black jail inmates had pre-arrest incomes below $3,000, compared with 44 percent of whites.[16] In 1983, the median pre-arrest income of black jail inmates was $4,067 and that of white jail inmates was $6,312. About half of blacks in jail were unemployed before arrest, and 44 percent of whites were.[17] In 1991, 30 percent of whites in the prison population and 38 percent of blacks reported no full- or part-time employment during the month before their arrest.[18]

4. Some studies suggest that race works to heighten the effects of economic condition on criminal justice outcomes, so that "being unemployed *and* black substantially increase[s] the chances of incarceration over those associated with being either unemployed or black."[19] This means that racism will produce a kind of selective economic bias, making a certain segment of the unemployed even more likely to end up behind bars.

5. Finally, it is my belief that the economic powers that be in America have sufficient power to end or drastically reduce racist bias in the criminal justice system. To the extent that they allow it to exist, it is not unreasonable to assume that it furthers their economic interests.

For all these reasons, racism will be treated here as either a form of economic bias or a tool that achieves the same end.

In the remainder of this chapter, I show how the criminal justice system functions to *weed out the wealthy* (meaning both middle- and upper-class offenders) at each stage of the process and thus produces a distorted image of the crime problem. Before entering into this discussion, however three points are worth noting.

First, it is not my view that the poor are all innocent victims persecuted by the evil rich. The poor do commit crimes, and my own assumption is that the vast majority of the poor who are confined in our prisons are guilty of the crimes for which they were sentenced. In addition, there is good evidence that the poor do commit a greater portion of the crimes against person and property listed in the FBI Index than the middle and upper classes do, relative to their numbers in the national population. What I have already tried to prove is that the crimes in the FBI Index are not the only acts that threaten us nor are they the acts that threaten us the most. What I will try to prove in what follows is that the poor are arrested and punished by the criminal justice system much more frequently than their contribution to the crime problem would warrant—thus the criminals who populate our prisons as well as the public's imagination are disproportionately poor.

Second, the following discussion has been divided into three sections that correspond to the major criminal-justice decision points. As always, such classifications are a bit neater than reality, and so they should not be taken as rigid compartments. Many of the distorting processes operate at all criminal-justice decision points. So, for example, while I will primarily discuss the light-handed treatment of white-collar criminals in the section on charging and sentencing, it is also true that white-collar criminals are less likely to be arrested or convicted than are blue-collar criminals. The section in which a given issue is treated is a reflection of the point in the criminal justice process at which the disparities are the most striking. Suffice it to say, however, that the disparities between the treatment of the poor and the nonpoor are to be found at all points of the process.

Third, it must be borne in mind that the movement from arrest to sentencing is a funneling process, so that discrimination that occurs at any early stage shapes the population that reaches later stages. Thus, for example, some recent studies find little economic bias in sentence length for people convicted of similar crimes.[20] When reading such studies, however, one should remember that the population that reaches the point of sentencing has already been subject to whatever discrimination exists at earlier stages. If, for example, among people with similar offenses and records, poor people are more likely to be charged and more likely to be convicted, then even if the sentencing of convicted criminals is even-handed, it will reproduce the discrimination that occurred before.

Arrest and Charging

The problem with most official records of who commits crime is that they are really statistics on who gets arrested and convicted. If, as I will show, the police are more likely to arrest some people than others, these official statistics may tell us more about the police than about criminals. In any event, they give us little reliable data about those who commit crimes and do not get caught. Some social scientists, suspicious of the bias built into official records, have tried to devise other methods of determining who has committed a crime. Most often, these methods involve an interview or questionnaire in which the respondent is assured of anonymity and asked to reveal whether he or she has committed any offenses for which he or she could be arrested and convicted. Techniques to check reliability of these self-reports also have been devised; however, if their reliability is still in doubt, common sense dictates that they would understate rather than overstate the number of individuals who have committed crimes and never come to official notice. In light of this, the conclusions of these studies are rather astounding. It seems that crime is the national pastime. The President's Crime Commission conducted a survey of 10,000 households and discovered that "91 percent of all Americans have violated laws that could have subjected them to a term of imprisonment at one time in their lives."[21]

A number of other studies support the conclusion that serious criminal behavior is widespread among middle- and upper-class individuals, although these individuals are rarely, if ever arrested. Some of the studies show that there are no significant differences between economic classes in the incidence of criminal behavior.[22] The authors of a recent review of literature on class and delinquency conclude that "Research published since 1978, using both official and self-reported data suggests . . . that there is no pervasive relationship between SES [socioeconomic status] and delinquency."[23] This conclusion is echoed by Jensen and Thompson, who argue that

> The safest conclusion concerning class structure and delinquency is the same one that has been proposed for several decades: class, no matter how defined, contributes little to explaining variation in self-reports of common delinquency.[24]

Others conclude that while lower-class individuals do commit more than their share of crimes, arrest records overstate their share and understate that of the middle and upper classes.[25] Still other studies suggest that some forms of serious crime—forms usually associated with lower-class youth—show up *more frequently* among higher-class persons than among lower.[26] For instance, Empey and Erikson interviewed 180 white males aged 15 to 17 who were drawn from different economic strata. They found that "virtually all respondents reported having committed not one but a variety of different offenses," Although youngsters from the middle classes constituted 55 percent of the group interviewed, they admitted to 67 percent of the instances of breaking and entering, 70 percent of the instances of property destruction, and an astounding 87 percent of all the armed robberies admitted to by the entire sample.[27] Williams and Gold studied a national sample of 847 males and females between the ages of 13 and 16.[28] Of these, 88 percent admitted to at least one delinquent offense.

Even those who conclude "that more lower status youngsters commit delinquent acts more frequently than do higher status youngsters"[29] also recognize that lower-class youth are significantly overrepresented in official records. Gold writes that "about five times more lowest than highest status boys appear in the official records; if

records were complete and unselective, we estimate that the ratio would be closer to 1.5:1."[30] The simple fact is that for the same offense, *a poor person is more likely to be arrested and, if arrested charged, than a middle- or upper-class person.*[31]

This means, first of all, that poor people are more likely to come to the attention of the police. Furthermore, even when apprehended, the police are more likely to formally charge a poor person and release a higher-class person *for the same offense.* Gold writes that

> . . . boys who live in poorer parts of town and are apprehended by police for delinquency are four to five times more likely to appear in some official record than boys from wealthier sections who commit the same kinds of offenses. These same data show that, at each stage in the legal process from charging a boy with an offense to some sort of disposition in court, boys from different socioeconomic backgrounds are treated differently, so that those eventually incarcerated in public institutions, that site of most of the research on delinquency, are selectively poorer boys.[32]

From a study of self-reported delinquent behavior, Gold finds that when individuals were apprehended, "if the offender came from a higher status family, police were more likely to handle the matter themselves without referring it to the court."[33]

Many writers have commented on the extent and seriousness of "white-collar crime," so I will keep my remarks to a minimum. Nevertheless, for those of us trying to understand how the image of crime is created, four points should be noted.

1. White-collar crime is costly; it takes far more dollars from our pockets than all the FBI Index crimes combined.

2. White-collar crime is widespread, probably much more so than the crimes of the poor.

3. White-collar criminals are rarely arrested or charged; the system has developed kindlier ways of dealing with the more delicate sensibilities of its higher-class clientele.

4. When white-collar criminals are prosecuted and convicted, their sentences are either suspended or very light when judged by the cost their crimes have imposed on society.

The first three points will be discussed here, and the fourth will be presented in the section on sentencing below.

Everyone agrees that the cost of white-collar crime is enormous. In 1985, *U.S. News & World Report Report* reported that "Experts estimate that white-collar criminals rake in a minimum of $200 billion annually."[34] Marshall Clinard also cites the $200 billion estimate in his recent book, *Corporate Corruption: The Abuse of Corporate Power.*[35] Nonetheless, $200 billion probably understates the actual cost. Some experts place the cost of white-collar crime for firms doing business in the government sector alone at $500 billion a year.[36] Tax evasion alone has been estimated to cost from 5 to 7 percent of the gross national product. For 1997, that would be between $403 and $564 billion.[37]

Let me close with one final example that typifies this particular distortion of justice policy. Embezzlement is the crime of misappropriating money or property entrusted to one's care, custody, or control. Because the poor are rarely entrusted with tempting sums of money or valuable property, this is predominantly a crime of the middle and upper classes. The U.S. Chamber of Commerce estimate of the annual economic cost of embezzlement, adjusted for inflation and population growth, is $12.42 billion—more than four-fifths the total value of all property and money stolen in all FBI Index property crimes in 1997. (Don't be fooled into thinking that this cost is imposed only on the rich or on big companies with lots of resources. They pass on their losses—and their increased insurance costs—to consumers in the form of higher prices. Embezzlers take money out of the very same pockets that muggers do: yours!) Nevertheless, the FBI reports that in 1997, when there were 1,805,600 arrests for property crimes, there were 17,100 arrests for embezzlement nationwide.[38] Although their cost to society is comparable, the number of arrests for property crimes was *more than 100 times greater* than the number of arrests for embezzlement. Roughly, this means there was one property crime arrest for every $8,000 stolen, and even the language becomes more delicate as we deal with a "better" class of crook.

The clientele of the criminal justice system forms an exclusive club. Entry is largely a privilege of the poor. The crimes they commit are the crimes that qualify one for admission—and they are admitted in greater proportion than their share of those crimes. Curiously enough, the crimes the affluent commit are not the kind that easily qualify one for membership in the club.

And as we have seen, the reluctance to use the full force of the criminal justice system in pursuit of white-collar criminals is matched by a striking reluctance to use the full force of current public and private research organizations to provide up-to-date estimates of its cost. This coincidence is worth pondering by anyone interested in how criminal justice policy gets made and how research and statistics function in the process.

Conviction

Between arrest and imprisonment lies the crucial process that determines guilt or innocence. Studies of individuals accused of similar offenses and with similar prior records show that the poor defendant is more likely to be adjudicated guilty than is the wealthier defendant.[39] In the adjudication process the only thing that *should* count is whether the accused is guilty and whether the prosecution can prove it beyond a reasonable doubt. Unfortunately, at least two other factors that are irrelevant to the question of guilt or innocence significantly affect the outcome: One is the ability of the accused to be free on bail prior to trial, and the second is access to legal counsel able to devote adequate time and energy to the case. Because both bail and high-quality legal counsel cost money, it should come as no surprise that here as elsewhere the poor do poorly.

The advantages of access to adequate legal counsel during the adjudicative process are obvious but still worthy of mention. In 1963, the U.S. Supreme Court handed down the landmark *Gideon v. Wainwright* decision, holding that the states must provide legal counsel to the indigent in all felony cases. As a result, no person accused of a serious crime need face his or her accuser without a lawyer. However, the Supreme Court has not held that the Constitution entitles individuals to lawyers able to devote equal time and resources to their cases. Even though *Gideon* represents significant progress in making good on the constitutional promise of equal treatment before the law, we still are left with two transmission belts of justice: one for the poor and one for the affluent. There is an emerging body of case law on the right to effective assistance of counsel[40]; however, this is yet to have any serious impact on the assembly-line legal aid handed out to the poor.

Needless to say, the distinct legal advantages that money can buy become even more salient when we enter the realm of corporate and other white-collar crime. Indeed, it is often precisely the time and cost involved in bringing to court a large corporation with its army of legal eagles that is offered as an excuse for the less formal and more genteel treatment accorded to corporate crooks. This excuse is, of course, not equitably distributed to all economic classes, any more than quality legal service is. This means that, regardless of actual innocence or guilt, one's chances of beating the rap increase as one's income increases. Regardless of what fraction of crimes are committed by the poor, the criminal justice system is distorted so that an even greater fraction of those convicted will be poor. And with conviction comes sentencing.

Sentencing

The simple fact is that the criminal justice system reserves its harshest penalties for its lower-class clients and puts on kid gloves when confronted with a better class of crook. We will come back to the soft treatment of S&L crooks shortly. For the moment, note that the tendency to treat higher-class criminals more leniently than lower-class criminals has been with us for a long time. In 1972, *The New York Times* did a study on sentencing in state and federal courts. The *Times* stated that "crimes that tend to be committed by the poor get tougher sentences than those committed by the well-to-do," that federal "defendants who could not afford private counsel were sentenced nearly twice as severely as defendants with private counsel," and that a "study by the Vera Institute of Justice of the courts in the Bronx indicates a similar pattern in the state courts."[41]

More recently, D'Alessio and Stoltzenberg studied a random sample of 2,760 offenders committed to the custody of Florida Department of Corrections during fiscal year 1985. Although they found no greater sentence severity for poor offenders found guilty of property crimes, they found that poor offenders did receive longer sentences for violent crimes, such as manslaughter, and for moral offenses, such as narcotics possession. Nor, by the way, did sentencing guidelines reduce this disparity.[42] A study of individuals convicted of drunk driving found that increased education (taken as an indicator of higher occupational status) "increase[d] the rate of movement from case filing to probation and decrease[d] the rate of movement to prison." And though, when probation was given, more-educated offenders got longer probation, they also got shorter prison sentences, if sentenced to prison at all.[43]

Chiricos and Bales found that, for individuals guilty of similar offenses and with similar prior records, unemployed defendants were more likely to be incarcerated while awaiting trial, and for longer periods, than employed defendants. They were more than twice as likely as their employed counterparts to be incarcerated upon a finding of guilt. And defendants with public defenders experienced longer periods of jail time than those who could afford private attorneys.[44] McCarthy noted a similar link between unemployment and greater likelihood of incarceration.[45] In his study of 28,315 felony defendants in Tennessee, Virginia, and Kentucky, Champion also found that offenders who could afford private counsel had a greater likelihood of probation, and received shorter sentences when incarceration was imposed.[46] A study of the effects of implementing Minnesota's determinate sentencing program shows that socio-economic bias is "more subtle, but no less real" than before the new program.[47]

Tillman and Pontell examined the sentences received by individuals convicted of Medicaid provider fraud in California. Because such offenders normally have no prior arrests and are charged with grand theft, their sentences were compared with the sentences of other offenders convicted of grand theft and who also had no prior records.

While 37.7 percent of the Medicaid defrauders were sentenced to jail or prison time, 79.2 percent of the others convicted of grand theft were sentenced to jail or prison. This was so even though the median dollar loss due to the Medicaid frauds was $13,000, more than ten times the median loss due to the other grand thefts ($1,149). Tillman and Pontell point out that most of the Medicaid defrauders were health professionals, while most of the others convicted of grand theft had low-level jobs or were unemployed. They conclude that "differences in the sentences imposed on the two samples are indeed the result of the different social statuses of their members."[48]

As usual, data on racial discrimination in sentencing tell the same story of the treatment of those who cannot afford the going price of justice. A study of offender processing in New York State counties found that, for offenders with the same arrest charge and the same prior criminal records, minorities were incarcerated more often than comparably situated whites.[49] A study of sentencing in Miami concludes that when case-related attributes do not clearly point to a given sentence, sentencing disparities are more likely to be based on race.[50] A study of 9,690 males who entered Florida prisons in 1992 and 1993, and who were legally eligible for stricter sentencing under the habitual offender statute, shows that, for similar prior records and seriousness of crime, race had a "significant and substantial" effect: Black defendants were particularly disadvantaged "for drug offenses and for property crimes."[51]

Most striking perhaps is that, in 1993, 51 percent of inmates in state and federal prisons were black and 44 percent of inmates of jails were black, whereas blacks make up only 36.5 percent of those arrested for serious (FBI Index) crimes.[52] Furthermore, when we look only at federal prisons, where there is reason to believe that racial and economic discrimination is less prevalent than in state institutions, we find that in 1986, nonwhite inmates were sentenced, on average, to 33 more months for burglary than white inmates and 22 more months for income tax evasion. In 1989, the average federal sentence for blacks found guilty of violent offenses was 10 months longer than that for whites. [53]

Here must be mentioned the notorious "100-to-1" disparity between sentences for possession of cocaine in powder form (popular in the affluent suburbs) and in crack form (popular in poor inner-city neighborhoods). Federal laws require a mandatory five-year sentence for crimes involving 500 grams of powder cocaine or 5 grams of crack cocaine. This yields a sentence for the first-time offenders (with no aggravating factors, such as possession of a weapon) that is longer than the sentence for kidnapping, and only slightly shorter than the sentence for attempted murder![54] About 90 percent of those convicted of federal crack offenses are black; about 4 percent are white. "As a result, the average prison sentence served by Black federal prisoners is 40 percent longer than the average sentence for Whites."[55] In 1995, the United States Sentencing commission recommended ending the 100-to-1 disparity between powder and crack penalties, and, in an unusual display of bipartisanship, both the Republican Congress and the Democratic President rejected their recommendation.[56]

Sentencing disparities between the races are, of course, not new. An extensive study by the *Boston Globe* of 4,500 cases of armed robbery, aggravated assault, and rape found that "blacks convicted in the superior courts of Massachusetts receive harsher penalties than whites for the same crimes."[57] The authors of a study of almost 1,200 males sentenced to prison for armed robbery in a southwestern state found that "in 1977 whites incarcerated for armed robbery had a greater than average chance of receiving

the least severe sentence, while nonwhites had a greater than average chance of receiving a moderately severe sentence."[58] A study of 229 adjudicated cases in a Florida judicial district yielded the finding that "whites have an 18 percent greater chance in the predicated probability of receiving probation than blacks when all other things are equal."[59] A recent study of criminal justice systems in California, Michigan, and Texas by Petersillia confirms the continuation of this trend. "Controlling for the factors most likely to influence sentencing and parole decisions," she writes, "the analysis still found that blacks and Hispanics are less likely to be given probation, more likely to receive *prison* sentences, more likely to receive longer sentences, and more likely to serve a greater portion of their original time."[60] Myers found that "harsher treatment of persons with fewer resources (e.g., female, unemployed, unmarried, black) is . . . pronounced in highly unequal counties."[61]

The federal government has introduced sentencing guidelines and mandatory minimum sentences that might be expected to eliminate discrimination, and many states have followed suit. The effect of this however, has been not to eliminate discretion but to transfer it from those who sentence to those who decide what to charge—that is, from judges to prosecutors. Prosecutors can charge in a way that makes it likely that the offender will get less than the mandatory minimum sentence. Says U.S. District Judge J. Lawrence Irving of San Diego, "the system is run by the U.S. attorneys. When they decide how to indict, they fix the sentence."[62] And discrimination persists. To examine the effects of mandatory minimum sentences, Barbara Meierhoefer studied 267,178 offenders sentenced in federal courts from January 1984 to June 1990. She found that whites were consistently more likely than blacks to be sentenced to less than the minimum sentence. The disparity varied from year to year, reaching a high point in 1988, when blacks were 30 percent more likely than whites to receive at least the minimum. Hispanics fared even worse than blacks. Concludes Meierhoefer,

> . . . despite the laws' emphasis on offense behavior, sentences still vary by offender characteristics. . . . Further, both black and Hispanic offenders now receive notably more severe sentences than their white counterparts.
>
> The latter trend suggests that there may be questions to be considered concerning the impact of shifting discretion affecting sentencing from the court to the prosecutor's office.[63]

A growing number of judges are speaking out against the system of sentencing guidelines and mandatory minimum sentences. According to U.S. District Judge Terry Hatter of Los Angeles, "the toughest sentences are now strictly 'applied to basically one group of people: poor minority people.'" Appellate Judge Gerald W. Heaney of Duluth, Minnesota, conducted his own study "and found that young black men got longer sentences than their white counterparts for similar crimes. Using 1989 data, he compared sentences under the new system with those under the old. The average sentence for black males was 40 months longer, he found, while the average sentence for white males was 19 months longer."[64]

There is considerable evidence that *double discrimination*—by race of the victim and of the offender—affects death penalty sentencing. In Florida, for example, blacks "who kill whites are nearly forty times more likely to be sentenced to death than those who kill blacks." Moreover, among "killers of whites, blacks are five times more likely than whites to be sentenced to death." This pattern of double discrimination was also evidenced, though less pronouncedly, in Texas, Ohio and Georgia, the other states surveyed.

Together, these four states "accounted for approximately 70 percent of the nation's death sentences" between 1972 and 1977.[65]

More recent studies have shown the same pattern. It was on the basis of such research that what may have been the last constitutional challenge to the death penalty was raised and rejected. In the 1987 case of *McCleskey v. Kemp*, evidence of discrimination on the basis of the victim's race was provided by a study by Professor David Baldus, of the University of Iowa, who examined 2,484 Georgia homicide cases that occurred between 1973 (when the current capital murder law was enacted) and 1979 (a year after McCleskey received his death sentence).[66] After controlling for all legitimate nonracial factors—such as severity of crime and the presence of aggravating factors—Baldus found that "murderers of white victims are still being sentenced to death 4.3 times more often than murderers of black victims."[67] The justices of the Supreme Court acknowledged the systemic disparities, but a majority held that the disparities would not invalidate death penalty convictions unless discrimination could be shown in the individual case at hand.

A 1990 report of the General Accounting Office to the Senate and House Committees on the Judiciary reviewed 28 studies on racial disparities in death penalty sentencing and concluded that the race of the victim strongly influenced the likelihood of a death penalty: "[T]hose who murdered whites were found to be more likely to be sentenced to death than those who murdered blacks."[68] Note that all these discriminatory sentences were rendered under statutes that had passed constitutional muster and were therefore presumed free of the biases that led the Supreme Court to invalidate all American death penalty statutes in *Furman v. Georgia* in 1972.

Another study has shown that among blacks and whites on death row, whites are more likely to have their sentences commuted. Also, blacks or whites who have private counsel are more likely to have their execution commuted than condemned persons defended by court-appointed attorneys.[69]

As I have already pointed out, justice is increasingly tempered with mercy as we deal with a better class of crime. The Sherman Antitrust Act is a criminal law. It was passed in recognition of the fact that one virtue of a free enterprise economy is that competition tends to drive consumer prices down, so agreements by competing firms to refrain from price competition is the equivalent of stealing money from the consumer's pocket. Nevertheless, although such conspiracies cost consumers far more than lower-class theft, price fixing was a misdemeanor until 1974.[70] In practice, few conspirators end up in prison, and when they do, the sentence is a mere token, well below the maximum provided in the law.

In the historical *Electrical Equipment* cases in the early 1960s, executives of several major firms met secretly to fix prices on electrical equipment to a degree that is estimated to have cost the buying public well over $1 billion. The executives involved knew they were violating the law. They used plain envelopes for their communications, called their meetings "choir practice," and referred to the list of executives in attendance as the "Christmas card list." This case is rare and famous because it was one in which the criminal sanction was actually imposed. Seven executives received and served jail sentences. In light of the amount of money they had stolen from the American public, however, their sentences were more an indictment of the government than of themselves: *thirty days in jail!*

Speaking about the record of federal antitrust prosecution, Clinard and Yeager write that

. . . even in the most widespread and flagrant price conspiracy cases, few corporate executives are ever imprisoned; of the total 231 cases with individual defendants from 1955 to 1975, prison sentences were given in only 19 cases. Of a total of 1,027 individual defendants, only 49 were sentenced to prison.[71]

There is some (slight) indication of a toughening in the sentences since antitrust violations were made a felony in 1974 and penalties were increased. "In felony cases prosecuted under the new penalties through March 1978, 15 of 21 sentenced individuals (71 percent) were given terms averaging 192 days each."[72] Nevertheless, when the cost to society is reckoned, even such penalties as these are hardly severe.

After the "anything goes" attitude of the Reagan era, which brought us such highly publicized white collar skullduggery as the multibillion dollar savings and loan scandal, the 1990s have seen a kind a backlash, with the government under pressure to up the penalties for corporate offenders. Here too, however, progress follows a slow and zigzagging course. Consider, for example, the following series of titles of articles from *The Washington Post:* March 2, 1990. "Criminal Indictments: Training Bigger Guns on Corporations"; April 1, 1990, "Going Soft on Corporate Crime"; April 28, 1990, "Justice Dept. Shifts on Corporate Sentencing" ("Attorney General Dick Thornburgh last month withdrew the Justice Department's longstanding support for tough mandatory sentences for corporate criminals following an intense lobbying campaign by defense contractors, oil companies and other *Fortune* 500 firms."); April 27, 1991, "Corporate Lawbreakers May Face Tougher Penalties."[73] Lest this last one be taken as truly reversing the trend to leniency, note that it reports new sentencing guidelines approved by the U.S.

Sentencing Commission, and it points out: "The only penalties set forth by the guidelines are fines and probation because the defendants in such cases are not individuals." Compare this with a statement from Ira Reiner, Los Angeles district attorney, quoted in the first of the articles just listed: "A fine, no matter how substantial, is simply a cost of doing business for a corporation. But a jail term for executives is different. What we are trying to do is to change the corporate culture." Good luck, Ira.

Studies have shown that even though corporate and white-collar lawbreakers are being more frequently brought to justice and more frequently being sanctioned, they still receive more lenient sentences than do those who are sentenced for common property crimes.[74] A study by Hagan and Palloni, which focuses particularly on the differences between pre- and post-Watergate treatments of white-collar offenders, concludes that likelihood of prosecution after Watergate was increased, but that the effect of this was canceled out by the leniency of the sentences meted out:

> . . . the new incarcerated white-collar
> offenders received relatively light sen-
> tences that counterbalanced the
> increased use of imprisonment. Relative
> to less-educated common criminals,
> white-collar offenders were more likely
> to be imprisoned after Watergate than
> before, but for shorter periods.[75]

Even after the heightened public awareness of white-collar crime that came in the wake of Watergate and the S&L scandals, it remains the case that crimes of the poor lead to stiffer sentences than the crimes of the well-to-do (see Table 1). Keep in mind while looking at these figures that *each* of the "crimes of the affluent" costs the public more than *all* of the "crimes of the poor" put together.

I do not deny that there has been some toughening of the treatment of white-collar offenders in recent years. Nonetheless, this toughening has been relatively mild, especially when compared with the treatment dealt out to lower-class offenders. Before turning to the "great" scandals of Watergate and the savings and loan industry, here are two "small" cases that illustrate the new developments.

In September 1991, a fire destroyed a chicken-processing plant in Hamlet, North Carolina. When the 100 employees in the plant tried to escape, they found that the company executives had ordered the doors locked "to keep out insects and to keep employees from going outside for coffee breaks, or stealing chickens." Twenty-five workers died in the fire; some were found burned to death at the doors they couldn't open. Another 50 people were injured. The owner of the company and two plant managers were charged with involuntary manslaughter. The outcome: The owner pleaded guilty and was sentenced to 19 years and 6 months in prison. You may or may not think this is severe as a punishment for someone responsible for 25 very painful deaths, but note three revealing facts. First, as part of the plea agreement, the involuntary manslaughter cases against the two plant managers were dismissed, though they surely knew the doors were locked and what the risks were. Second, the owner is eligible for parole after $2^{1}/_{2}$ years. And third, the sentence is "believed to be the harshest judgment ever handed out for a workplace safety violation."[76]

We have seen in this chapter and the one before that the criminal justice system is triply biased against the poor. First, there is the economic class bias *among harmful acts* as to which get labeled crimes and which are treated as regulatory matters, as we saw in the previous chapter. Second, there is economic class bias *among crimes* that we have

TABLE 1   Sentences Served for Different Classes of Crime, 1996–97

	Percent Sentenced to Prison	Average Time Served (in months)
Crimes of the poor		
Robbery	99	60
Burglary	89	28
Auto Theft	63	24
Crime of the affluent		
Fraud	63	16
Tax Law Violation	42	15
Embezzlement	58	9

Source: Sourcebook—1998 (compiled from Tables 5.28 and 6.54, and rounded off).

already seen in this chapter. The crimes that poor people are likely to commit carry harsher sentences than the "crimes in the suites" committed by well-to-do people. Third, *among defendants convicted of the same crimes,* the poor receive less probation and more years of confinement than well-off defendants, assuring us once again that the vast majority of those put behind bars are from the lowest social and economic classes in the nation. On either side of the law, the rich get richer. . .

. . . and the Poor Get Prison

At 9:05 A.M. on the morning of Thursday, September 9, 1971, a group of inmates forced their way through a gate at the center of the prison, fatally injured a guard named William Quinn, and took 50 hostages. The Attica uprising had begun. It lasted four days, until 9:43 A.M. on the morning of Monday, September 13, when corrections officers and state troopers stormed the prison and killed 29 inmates and 10 hostages.[77] During those four days the nation saw the faces of its captives on television—the hard black faces of young men who had grown up on the streets of Harlem and other urban ghettos. Theirs were the faces of crime in America. The television viewers who saw them were not surprised. Here were faces of dangerous men who should be locked up. Nor were people outraged when the state launched its murderous attack on the prison, killing many more inmates and guards than did the prisoners themselves. Maybe they were shocked—but not outraged. Neither were they outraged when two grand juries refused to indict any of the attackers, nor when the mastermind of the attack, New York Governor Nelson Rockefeller, was named vice president of the United States three years after the uprising and massacre.[78]

They were not outraged because the faces they saw on the TV screens fit and confirmed their beliefs about who is a deadly threat to American society—and a deadly threat must be met with deadly force. How did those men get to Attica? How did Americans get their beliefs about who is a dangerous person? These questions are interwoven. People get their notions about who is a criminal at least in part from the occasional television or newspaper picture of who is inside our prisons. The individuals they see there have been put in prison because people believe certain kinds of individuals are dangerous and should be locked up.

I have agued in this chapter that this is not a simple process of selecting the dangerous and the criminal from among the peace-loving and the law-abiding. It is also a process of *weeding out the wealthy* at every stage, so that the final picture—a picture like that that appeared on the TV screen on September 9, 1971—is not a true reflection of the real dangers in our society but a distorted image, the kind reflected in a carnival mirror.

It is not my view that the inmates in Attica were innocent of the crimes that sent them there. I assume they and just about all the individuals in prisons in America are probably guilty of the crime for which they were sentenced and maybe more. My point is that people who are equally or more dangerous, equally or more criminal, are not there; that the criminal justice system works systematically not to punish and confine the dangerous and the criminal, *but to punish and confine the poor who are dangerous and criminal.*

It is successful at all levels. In 1973, there were 204,211 individuals in state and federal prisons, or 96 prisoners for every 100,000 individuals (of all ages) in the general population. By 1979, state and federal inmates numbered 301,470, or 133 per 100,000 Americans. By 1998, there were a total of 1,825,400 persons in state and federal prisons and in the local jails, a staggering 672 for every 100,000 in the population. One in 149 U.S. residents (of all ages and both sexes) was behind bars in 1998. However, of the 1,825,400 inmates in federal and state prisons and in jails, some 1,715,000 are men, virtually all above the age of 18. Because the adult male population in the United States is about 94 million, *this means that roughly one out of every 55 American adult men is behind bars.*[79] This enormous number of prisoners is, of course, predominantly from the bottom of society.

Of the estimated 1.2 million people in state prisons in 1998, one-third were not employed at all (full or part time) prior to their arrests. Just over half were employed at all, thus nearly half were without full-time employment prior to arrest. These statistics are comparable to those in 1986, when 31 percent of state inmates had no pre-arrest employment at all, and 43 percent had no full-time pre-arrest employment.[80] Among jail inmates in 1996, 36 percent were not employed prior to arrest—20 percent were looking for work and 16 percent were not. Approximately half of jail inmates reported pre-arrest incomes below $7,200 a year.[81]

To get an idea of what part of society is in prison, we should compare these figures with comparable figures for the general population. Because more than 90 percent of inmates are male, we can look at employment and income figures for males in the general population in the mid-1990s.

In 1994, 5.4 percent of males, 16 years old and above, in the labor force were unemployed and looking for work. Since it is normally thought that the number of unemployed people who are not looking for work is something less than equal to the number looking, doubling this rate will give us a conservative estimate of the percentage of males above age 16 who are unemployed, looking and not looking. Then, whereas one-third of state prison inmates and 36 percent of jail inmates were unemployed (looking and not looking for work) in the year prior to their arrest, the rate for unincarcerated males above the age of 16, was approximately 11 percent. Prisoners were unemployed at a rate more than three times that of their counterparts in the general population.[82] In 1994, the median income for males, 15 years old and above, with any income at all, was $22,995.[83] This means that half of these males in the general population with any income at all were earning this amount or less. Compare this to jail inmates, about half of whom earned $7,200 a year or less in the year before they were arrested.

Our prisoners are not a cross section of America. They are considerably poorer and considerably less likely to be employed than the rest of Americans. Moreover, they are also less educated, which is to say less in possession of the means to improve their sorry situations. Of all U.S. prison inmates, 41 percent did not graduate from high school, compared to 20 percent of the U.S. adult population.[84]

The criminal justice system is sometimes thought of as a kind of sieve in which the innocent are progressively sifted out from the guilty, who end up behind bars. I have tried to show that the sieve works another way as well. It sifts the affluent out from the poor, so it is not merely the guilty who end up behind bars, but the *guilty poor.*

. . . The criminal justice system does not simply weed the peace-loving from the dangerous, the law-abiding from the criminal. At every stage, starting with the very definitions of crime and progressing through the stages of investigation, arrest, charging, conviction, and sentencing, the system *weeds out the wealthy.* It refuses to define as "crimes" or as serious crimes the dangerous and predatory acts of the well-to-do—acts that, as we have seen, result in the loss of thousands of lives and billions of dollars. Instead, the system focuses its attention on those crimes likely to be committed by members of the lower classes. Thus, it is no surprise to find that so many of the people behind bars are from the lower classes. The people we see in our jails and prisons are no doubt dangerous to society, but they are not *the danger* to society, not the gravest danger to society. Individuals who pose equal or greater threats to our well-being walk the streets with impunity.

. . . In the present chapter I have argued that the criminal justice system works to make crime appear to be the monopoly of the poor by . . . more actively pursuing and prosecuting the poor rather than the well off for the acts that are labeled crime. *The . . . effect . . . is to maintain a real threat of crime that the vast majority of Americans believes is a threat from the poor.* The criminal justice system is a carnival mirror that throws back a distorted image of the dangers that lurk in our midst—and conveys the impression that those dangers are the work of the poor.

REFERENCES

ANDERSON, DAVID. *Crime and the Politics of Hysteria: How the Willie Horton Story Changed American Justice.* New York: Times Books, 1995.

CLINARD, MARSHALL. *Corporate Corruption: The Abuse of Power.* New York: Praeger, 1990.

DAY, KATHLEEN. *S & L Hell: The People and the Politics Behind the $1 Trillion Savings and Loan Scandal.* New York: Norton, 1993.

LUSANE, CLARENCE. *Pipe Dream Blues: Racism and the War on Drugs.* Boston: South End Press, 1991.

LYNCH, MICHAEL, and E. BRITT PATTERSON. *Race and Criminal Justice.* New York: Harrow & Heston, 1991.

MILLER, JEROME. *Search and Destroy: African-American Males in the Criminal Justice System.* New York: Cambridge University Press, 1996.

PEARCE, FRANK, and LAUREN SNIDER. *Corporate Crime.* Toronto: University of Toronto Press, 1995.

PIZZO, STEPHEN ET AL. *Inside Job: The Looting of America's Savings and Loans.* New York: McGraw-Hill, 1989.

SIMON, DAVID, and STANLEY EITZEN. *Elite Deviance,* 6th ed. Boston: Allyn & Bacon, 1999.

TIMMER, DOUG, and STANLEY EITZEN. *Crimes in the Streets and Crimes in the Suites.* Boston: Allyn & Bacon, 1989.

NOTES

1. *Challenge,* p. 44.
2. Ronald Goldfarb, "Prisons: The National Poorhouse," *New Republic,* November 1, 1969, pp. 15–17.
3. Philip Hart, "Swindling and Knavery, Inc.," *Playboy,* August 1972, p. 158.
4. Compare the statement, written more than half a century ago, by Professor Edwin H. Sutherland, one of the major luminaries of twentieth-century criminology:

   First, the administrative processes are more favorable to persons in economic comfort than to those in poverty, so that if two persons on different economic levels are equally guilty of the same offense, the one on the lower level is more likely to be arrested, convicted, and committed to an institution. Second, the laws are written, administered, and implemented primarily with reference to the types of crimes committed by people of lower economic levels [E. H. Sutherland, Principles of Criminology *(Philadelphia: Lippincott, 1939), p. 179].*

5. For example, in 1991, when blacks made up 12 percent of the national population, they accounted for 46 percent of the U.S. state prison population. BJS, *Survey of State Prison Inmates,* 1991, p. 3.

6. Edwin H. Sutherland and Donald R. Cressey, *Criminology,* 9th ed. (Philadelphia: Lippincott, 1974), p. 133. The following studies are cited in support of this point (p. 133, note 4): Edwin M. Lemert and Judy Roseberg, "The Administration of Justice to Minority Groups in Los Angeles County," University of California Publications in Culture and Society 2, no. 1 (1948), pp. 1–28; Thorsten Sellin, "Race Prejudice in the Administration of Justice," *American Journal of Sociology* 41 (September 1935), pp. 212–217; Sidney Alexrad, "Negro and White Male Institutionalized Delinquents," *American Journal of Sociology* 57 (May 1952). Pp. 569–74; Marvin E. Wolfgang, Arlene Kelly and Hans C. Nolde, "Comparisons of the Executed and the Commuted among Admissions to Death Row," *Journal of Criminal Law, Criminology, and Police Science 53* (September 1962), pp. 301–11; Nathan Goldman, *The Differential Selection of Juvenile Offenders for Court Appearance* (New York: National Council on Crime and Delinquency, 1963); Irving Piliavin and Scott Briar, "Police Encounters with Juveniles," *American Journal of Sociology* 70 (September 1964), pp. 206–14; Robert M. Terry, "The Screening of Juvenile Offenders," *Journal of Criminal Law, Criminology, and Police Science* 58 (June 1967), pp. 173–81. See also Ramsey Clark, *Crime in America* (New York: Simon & Schuster, 1970), p. 51: "Negoes are arrested more frequently and on less evidence than whites and are more often victims of mass or sweep arrests"; and Donald Taft, *Criminology,* 3rd ed. (New York: Macmillan, 1956), p. 134:

Negroes are more likely to be suspected of crime than are whites. They are also more likely to be arrested. If the perpetrator of a crime is known

to be a Negro the police may arrest all Negroes who were near the scene–a procedure they would rarely dare to follow with whites. After arrest Negroes are less likely to secure bail, and so are more liable to be counted in jail statistics. They are more liable than whites to be indicted and less likely to have their case nol prossed or otherwise dismissed. If tried, Negroes are more likely to be convicted. If convicted they are less likely to be given probation. For this reason they are more likely to be included in the count of prisoners. Negroes are also more likely than whites to be kept in prison for the full terms of their commitments and correspondingly less likely to be paroled.

7. William Wilbanks, *The Myth of a Racist Criminal Justice System* (Monterey, Calif.: Brooks/Cole, 1987).

8. Ibid., pp. 64–65.

9. *Sourcebook—1998,* p. 186, Table 3.26; p. 342, Table 4.10, *UCR—1998;* pp. 228.

10. For an overview of this double distortion, see Thomas J. Dolan, "The Case for Double Jeopardy: Black and Poor," *International Journal of Criminology and Penology* 1 (1973), pp. 129–50.

11. *StatAbst—1998,* p. 480, Table 762. See also Karen Pennar, "The Rich Are Richer—And America May Be the Poorer," *Business Week,* November 18, 1991, pp. 85–88.

12. Francine Blau and John Graham, "Black-White Differences in Wealth and Asset Composition," *Quarterly Journal of Economics* (May 1990), p. 323; David Swinton, "The Economic Status of African Americans during the Reagan-Bush Era: Withered Opportunities, Limited Outcomes, and Uncertain Outlook," in *The State of Black America* (New York: National Urban League, 1993), p. 138.

13. *Economic Report of the President,* February 1998, pp. 130–31.

14. *StatAbst—1998,* p. 407, Table 651.

15. Michael Tonry, "Racial Politics, Racial Disparities, and the War on Crime," *Crime & Delinquency* 40, no. 4 (October 1994), pp. 483, 485–86.

16. *Sourcebook—1981,* p. 463.

17. *StatAbst—1988,* p. 175, Table 304.

18. BJS, *Profile of Inmates in the United States and England and Wales, 1991* (October 1994, NCJ-145863), p. 13.

19. Theodore Chiricos and William Bales, "Unemployment and Punishment: An Empirical Assessment," *Criminology* 29, no. 4 (1991), p. 718.

20. "An offender's socioeconomic status . . . did not impact sentence length for any of the property offenses." Stewart J. D'Alession and Lisa Stolzenberg, "Socioeconomic Status and the Sentencing of the Traditional Offender," *Journal of Criminal Justice* 21 (1993), p. 73. The same study did find that lower-socioeconomic status offenders received harsher sentences for violent and moral-order crimes. Another study that finds no greater likelihood of incarceration based on socioeconomic status is Michael Benson and Esteban Walker, "Sentencing the White-Collar Offender," *American Sociological Review* 53 (April 1988), pp. 294–302. And yet another found higher-status offenders to be more likely to be incarcerated: David Weisburd, Elin Waring, Stanton Wheeler, "Class, Status, and the Punishment of White Collar Criminals," *Law and Social Inquiry* 15 (1990), pp. 223–41. These last two studies are limited to offenders convicted of white-collar crimes, and so they deal with a sample that has already been subject to whatever discrimination exists in the arrest, charging, and conviction of white-collar offenders.

21. Isidore Silver, "Introduction to the Avon edition of *The Challenge of Crime in a Free Society* (New York: Avon, 1968), p. 31.

22. This is the conclusion of Austin L. Porterfield, *Youth in Trouble* (Fort Worth, Tex.: Leo Potishman Foundation, 1946); Fred J. Murphy, M. Shirley, and H. L. Witmer, "The Incidence of Hidden Delinquency," *American Journal of Orthopsychiatry* 16 (October 1946), pp. 686–96; James F. Short, Jr., "A Report on the Incidence of Criminal Behavior, Arrests, and Convictions in Selected Groups," *Proceedings of the Pacific Sociology Society, 1954,* pp. 110–18, published as vol. 22, no. 2 of *Research Studies of the State College of Washington* (Pullman: State College of Washington, 1954); F. Ivan Nye, James F. Short, Jr., and Virgil J. Olson, "Socioeconomic Status and Delinquent Behavior," *American Journal of Sociology* 63 (January 1958), pp. 381–89; Maynard L. Erikson and Lamar T. Empey, "Class Position, Peers and Delinquency," *Sociology and Social Research* 49 (April 1965), pp. 268–82; William J. Chambliss and Richard H. Nagasawa, "On the Validity of Official Statistics; A Comparative Study of White, Black, and Japanese High-School Boys," *Journal of Research in Crime and Delinquency* 6 (January 1969), pp. 71–77; Eugene Dolescal, "Hidden Crime," *Crime and Delinquency Literature 2,* no. 5 (October 1970), pp. 546–72; Nanci Koser Wilson, *Risk Ratios in Juvenile Delinquency* (Ann Arbor, Mich.: University Microfilms, 1972); and Maynard L. Erikson, "Group Violations, Socioeconomic Status, and Official Delinquency," *Social Forces* 52, no. 1 (September 1973), pp. 41–52.

23. Charles R. Tittle and Robert F. Meier, "Specifying the SES/Delinquency Relationship," *Criminology* 28, no. 2 (1990), p. 292.

24. Gary F. Jensen and Kevin Thompson, "What's Class Got to Do With It? A Further Examination of Power-Control Theory," *American Journal of Sociology* 95, no. 4 (January 1990), p. 1021.

25. This is the conclusion of Martin Gold, "Undetected Delinquent Behavior," *Journal of Research in Crime and Delinquency* 3, no. 1 (1966), pp. 27–46; and of Sutherland and Cressey, *Criminology,* pp. 137, 220.

26. Cf. Larry Karacki and Jackson Toby, "The Uncommitted Adolescent: Candidate for Gang Socialization," *Sociological Inquiry* 32 (1962), pp. 203–15; William R. Arnold, "Continuities in Research—Scaling Delinquent Behavior," *Social Problems* 13, no. 1 (1965), pp. 59–66; Harwin L. Voss, "Socio-economic Status and Reported Delinquent Behavior," *Social Problems,* 13, no. 3 (1966), pp. 314–24; LaMar Empey and Maynard L. Erikson, "Hidden Delinquency and Social Status," *Social Forces* 44, no. 4 (1966), pp. 546–54; Fred J. Shanley, "Middle-Class Delinquency As a Social Problem," *Sociology and Social Research* 51 (1967), pp. 185–98; Jay R. Williams and Martin Gold, "From Delinquent Behavior to Official Delinquency," *Social Problems* 20, no. 2 (1972), pp. 209–29.

27. Empey and Erikson, "Hidden Delinquency and Social Status," pp. 549, 551. Nye, Short, and Olson also found destruction of property to be committed most frequently by upper-class boys and girls, "Socioeconomic Status and Delinquent Behavior," p. 385.

28. Williams and Gold, "From Delinquent Behavior to Official Delinquency."

29. Gold, "Undetected Delinquent Behavior," p. 37.

30. Ibid., p. 44.

31. Comparing socioeconomic status categories, "scant evidence is found that would support the contention that group delinquency is more characteristic of the lower-status levels than other socioeconomic status levels. In fact, only

arrests seem to be more characteristic of the low-status category than the other categories." Erikson, "Group Violations, Socioeconomic Status and Official Delinquency," p. 15.

32. Gold, "Undetected Delinquent Behavior," p. 28 (emphasis added).

33. Ibid., p. 38.

34. "Stealing $200 Billion the Respectable Way," *U.S. News & World Report,* May 20, 1985, p. 83.

35. Marshall B. Clinard, *Corporate Corruption: The Abuse of Corporate Power* (New York: Praeger, 1990), p. 15.

36. August Bequai, "High-Tech Security and the Failings of President Clinton's Commission on Critical Infrastructure Protection," *Computer and Security* 17 (1998), pp. 19–21.

37. Michael Levi, *Regulating Fraud: White-Collar Crime and the Criminal Process* (London: Tavistock, 1987), p. 33; *StatAbst—1998,* p. 456, Table 721.

38. *UCR—1998,* p. 210, Table 29.

39. See, for example, Theodore G. Chiricos, Philip D. Jackson, and Gordon P. Waldo, "Inequality in the Imposition of a Criminal Label," *Social Problems* 19, no. 4 (Spring 1972), pp. 553–72.

40. A good summary of these developments can be found in Joel Jay Finer, "Ineffective Assistance of Counsel," *Cornell Law Review* 58, no. 6 (July 1973), pp. 1077–1120.

41. Lesely Oelsner, "Wide Disparities Mark Sentences Here," *The New York Times,* September 27, 1972, p. 1.

42. Stewart J. D'Alession and Lisa Stolzenberg, "Socioeconomic Status and the Sentencing of the Traditional Offender," *Journal of Criminal Justice* 21 (1993), pp. 71–74.

43. Barbara C. Nienstedt, Marjorie Zatz, and Thomas Epperlein, "Court Processing and Sentencing of Drinking Drivers," *Journal of Quantitative Criminology* 4, no. 1 (1988), pp. 39–59.

44. Theodore Chiricos and William Bales, "Unemployment and Punishment: An Empirical Assessment," *Criminology* 29, no. 4 (1991), pp. 701–24.

45. Belinda R. McCarthy, "A Micro-Level Analysis of Social Control: Intrastate Use of Jail and Prison Confinement," *Justice Quarterly* 7, no. 2 (June 1990), pp. 334–35.

46. Dean J. Champion, "Private Counsels and Public Defenders: A Look at Weak Cases, Prior Records, and Leniency in Plea Bargaining," p. 143.

47. T. Miethe and C. Moore, "Socioeconomic Disparities under Determinate Sentencing Systems: A Comparison of Preguideline and Postguideline Practices in Minnesota," *Criminology* 23, no. 2 (1985), p. 358.

48. Robert Tillman and Henry Pontell, "Is Justice 'Collar-Blind'?: Punishing Medical Provider Fraud," *Criminology* 30, no. 4 (1992), pp. 547–73, quote from p. 560.

49. James F. Nelson, "Hidden Disparities in Case Processing: New York State, 1985–1986," *Journal of Criminal Justice* 20 (1992), pp. 181–200.

50. J. D. Unnever and L.A. Hembroff, "The Prediction of Racial/Ethnic Sentencing Disparities," *Journal of Research in Crime and Delinquency* 25 (1988), p. 53.

51. C. Crawford, T. Chiricos, and G. Kleck, "Race, Racial Threat, and Sentencing of Habitual Offenders," *Criminology* 36, no. 3 (1998), pp. 481–511.

52. BJS, *Prisoners in 1994,* August 1995 (NCJ-151654), p. 9; BJS, *Prison and Jail Inmates, 1995,* p. 10; *Sourcebook—1994,* Table 4.11, p. 388.

53. *Sourcebook—1987,* pp. 376, 491, 518; *Sourcebook—1992,* p. 492, Table 5.21.

54. *Criminal Justice Newsletter,* March 1, 1995, p. 3; *Criminal Justice Newsletter,* April 17, 1995, p. 5.

55. McDonald, Douglas, and Ken Carlson, *Sentencing in the Federal Courts: Does Race Matter?* (Washington, D.C.: BJS, 1993), cited in Michael Tonry, "Racial Politics, Racial Disparities, and the War on Crime," *Crime & Delinquency* 40, no. 4 (October 1994), p. 487.

56. Ronald Smothers, "Wave of Prison Uprisings Provokes Debate on Crack," *The New York Times,* October 24, 1995, p. A12.

57. "Blacks Receive Stiffer Sentences," *Boston Globe,* April 4, 1979, pp. 1, 50f.

58. Randall Thomson and Matthew Zingraff, "Detecting Sentencing Disparity: Some Problems and Evidence," *American Journal of Sociology* 86, no. 4 (1981), pp. 869–80, especially p. 875.

59. J. Unnever, C. Frazier, and J. Henretta, "Race Differences in Criminal Sentencing," *Sociological Quarterly* 21 (Spring 1980), pp. 197–205, especially p. 204.

60. J. Petersillia, "Racial Disparities in the Criminal Justice System: A Summary," *Crime & Delinquency* 31, no. 1 (1985), p. 28. See also G. Bridges and R. Crutchfield, "Law, Social Standing and Racial Disparities in Imprisonment," *Social Forces* 66, no. 3 (1988), pp. 699–724.

61. M. Myers, "Economic Inequality and Discrimination in Sentencing," *Social Forces* 65, no. 3 (1987), p. 761.

62. Mary Pat Flaherty and Joan Biskupic, "Rules Often Impose Toughest Penalties on Poor, Minorities," *The Washington Post,* October 9, 1996, p. A26.

63. Barbara S. Meierhoefer, *The General Effect of Mandatory Minimum Prison Terms: A Longitudinal Study of Federal Sentences Imposed* (Washington, D.C.: Federal Judicial Center, 1992), especially pp. 1, 20, 25. Between October 1989 and 1990, 46 percent of whites received federal sentences below the mandatory minimum, but 32 percent of blacks did. *Sourcebook—1991,* p. 542, Table 5.43.

64. Mary Pat Flaherty and Joan Biskupic, "Rules Often Impose Toughest Penalties on Poor, Minorities."

65. William J. Bowers and Glenn L. Pierce, "Racial Discrimination and Criminal Homicide under Post-Furman Capital Statutes," in H. A. Bedau, ed., *The Death Penalty in America* (New York: Oxford University Press, 1982), pp. 206–24.

66. *McCleskey v. Kemp,* 107 S. Ct. 1756 (1987). The research central to this case was that of David Baldus, reported in D. Baldus, C. Pulaski, and G. Woodworth, "Comparative Review of Death Sentences: An Empirical Study of the Georgia Experience," *Journal of Criminal Law and Criminology* 74 (1983), pp. 661–725. Other studies that support the notion of discrimination in capital sentencing based on race of victim are R. Paternoster, "Race of Victim and Location of Crime: The Decision to Seek the Death Penalty in South Carolina," *Journal of Criminal Law and Criminology* 74, no. 3 (1983), pp. 754–88; R. Paternoster, "Prosecutorial Discretion in Requesting the Death Penalty: A Case of Victim Based Racial Discrimination," *Law and Society Review* 18 (1984), pp. 437–78; S. Gross and R. Mauro, "Patterns of Death: An Analysis of Racial Disparities in Capital Sentencing and Homicide Victimization," *Stanford Law Review* 37 (1984), pp. 27–120; Radelet and Pierce, "Race and Prosecutorial Discretion in Homicide Cases," *Law and Society Review* 19 (1985), pp. 587, 615–19.

67. Anthony G. Amsterdam, "Race and the Death Penalty," in S. Gold, ed., *Moral Controversies* (Belmont, Calif.: Wadsworth, 1993), pp. 268–69.

68. U.S. General Accounting Office, Report to the Senate and House Committees on the Judiciary, *Death Penalty Sentencing: Research Indicates Pattern of Racial Disparities* (February 1990), especially p. 5.

69. Marvin E. Wolfgang, Arlene Kelly, and Hans C. Nolde, "Comparison of the Executed and the Commuted among Admissions to Death Row," in *Crime and Justice in Society,* ed. Quinney. Pp. 508, 513.

70. "Antitrust: Kauper's Last Stand," *Newsweek,* June 21, 1976, p. 70. On December 21, 1974, the Antitrust Procedures and Penalty Act was passed, striking out the language of the Sherman Antitrust Act, which made price fixing a misdemeanor punishable by a maximum sentence of one year in prison. According to the new law, price fixing is a felony punishable by up to three years in prison. Because prison sentences were a rarity under the old law and usually involved only 30 days in jail when actually imposed, there is little reason to believe the new law will strike fear in the hearts of corporate crooks.

71. Marshall Clinard and Peter Yeager, *Corporate Crime* (New York: Free Press, 1980), pp. 291–92.

72. Ibid., p. 153.

73. *The Washington Post,* March 2, 1990, pp. A1, A20; April 1, 1990, p. C3; April 28, 1990, pp. A1, A14; April 27, 1991, p. A6.

74. K. Johnson, "Federal Court Processing of Corporate, White Collar, and Common Crime Economic Offenders over the Past Three Decades," *Mid-American Review of Sociology* 11, no. 1 (1986), pp. 25–44.

75. J. Hagan and P. Palloni, "'Club Fed' and the Sentencing of White-Collar Offenders Before and After Watergate," *Criminology* 24, no. 4 (1986), pp. 616–17. See also J. Hagan and P. Parker, "White-Collar Crime and Punishment: The Class Structure and Legal Sanctioning of Securities Violations," *American Sociological Review* 50 (1985), pp. 302–16.

76. John P. Wright, Francis T. Cullen, and Michael B. Blankenship, "The Social Construction of Corporate Violence: Media Coverage of the Imperial Food Products Fire," *Crime & Delinquency* 41, no. 1 (January 1995), pp. 23–24; Laurie Grossman, "Owner Sentenced to Nearly 20 Years over Plant Fire," *The Wall Street Journal,* September 15, 1992, p. A10.

77. Tom Wicker, *A Time to Die* (New York: Quadrangle, 1975), pp. 311, 314.

78. Ibid., p. 310.

79. *Sourcebook—1987*, p. 486, BJS, *Correctional Populations in the United States, 1985*, p. 10, Table 2.6; *StatAbst—1988*, p. 13, Table 13; BJS, *Prisoners in 1998* (NCJ175687); BJS, Prison and Jail Inmates at Midyear 1998 (NCJ173414); U.S. Bureau of the Census, Current Population Reports, Series PPL-57, U.S. Population Estimates by Age, Sex, Race, and Hispanic Origin: 1990–1996.

80. BJS, *Survey of State Prison Inmates*, 1991, p. 3.

81. BJS, *Criminal Offender Statistics,* at *http://www.ojp.usdoj.gov/bjs/crimoff.htm* (last revised December 5, 1999); and BJS, *Profile of Jail Inmates 1996* (April 1998, NCJ164620).

82. *Economic Report of the President*, February 1998, p. 331, Table B-43.

83. *Economic Report of the President*, February 1998, p. 320, Table B-33.

84. BJS, *Criminal Offender Statistics*, "Comparing Federal and State Prison Inmates."

Race and Work

23

RACE, GENDER, WORK
The History of Asian and Asian-American Women

Julie Matthaei • Teresa Amott

Questions to Consider

Julie Matthaei and Teresa Amott describe the horrible experiences of Asian and Asian American women who entered this country at the start of the twentieth century. Why was the treatment of this particular group—Asian females—so brutal? How did animosity toward Asians and women by the dominant group shape the experiences of these immigrants?

From 1840 until the Second World War, Asian immigrants—first Chinese, then Japanese, and finally Filipinos—were

recruited into the western United States (US) and Hawaii as a low-wage, second-class labour force. Unlike white immigrants, they were not seen as permanent settlers and laws specially restricted their rights. Only Asian Americans born in the US were accepted as citizens; the immigrants were permanent "aliens," and whites were able to pass numerous laws to discriminate against them (for example, preventing them from purchasing lands) simply by referring to their alien status. They faced vicious discrimination from white workers (who resented their low-wage competition and their use as strike-breakers), from white employers (who found them less attractive as they began to form effective labour organisations) and from self-employed whites (who resented Asian successes in small businesses). From the late nineteenth century until the Depression, there were broad-based white movements to try and restrict Asian immigration and even to send migrants back to Asia. In response to these pressures, between 1850 and 1950, federal and state governments passed about fifty laws aimed at restricting and subordinating Asian immigrants. Anti-Asian sentiment culminated in laws excluding further immigration: Chinese immigration was cut off in 1882 and 1892; Japanese in 1907, 1908 and 1924; Indian in 1917, and Filipino in 1934.

Initially, the numbers of women relative to men were low—one to nineteen among the Chinese in 1860, for example. Employers sought out single male workers, most of whom came as "sojourners," planning to return home after they had made their fortunes. Although laws and experiences with women's immigration varied between the groups, all faced the difficulty of forming families across the ocean—miscegenation laws prevented marriage with white women—especially when further immigration was cut off. For all groups, it took decades before a sizeable second generation of Asians was born.*

---

*There is some difficulty in characterizing Asians in the US as Asians or Asian Americans. Generally, we will describe immigrants as Asians and second generation and on (i.e., those born in the US of Asian parentage) Asian-American.

Chinese-American Women

In the mid-nineteenth century, the needs of US capitalists for cheap labour coincided with economic crisis and massive dislocation in China, compounded of internal rebellion, loss of peasant lands to large landowners and the Opium wars, in which China was forced to cede territory, including Hong Kong, to the British. To take advantage of the situation, western firms set up a lucrative "coolie" trade (literally "bitter labour"), aided by highly-paid Chinese middlemen who recruited workers and contracted them out. While physical coercion was not unknown, most Chinese men came to the US voluntarily, if forced by desperate economic straits, expecting to strike it rich on "Gold Mountain" (as they called San Francisco) and return.

Chinese workers were especially attractive to US and Hawaiian employers who could contract mainly young, able-bodied men whose children and wives were prevented from joining them. By 1852, 11,787 Cantonese Chinese had come to the United States, only seven of whom were women.[1] Since the costs of producing another generation of workers and caring for the dependants were borne in China, employers could keep wages low, and the men were ideal for migrant farm work, mining and railroad construction, where a mobile work-force was needed. Finally, Chinese men were desirable because of their experience in China, working in "excavation work in hilly terrain" and in sugar cultivation.

Early Chinese Male Employment

Chinese men first came to the US in large numbers in the late 1840s, during the Gold Rush; by 1860, they comprised 10 per cent of California's population and almost 25 percent of its labour force. In the next twenty years, another 105,000 immigrated.

Independent white miners had exhausted most lands, and mining companies used the Chinese as contract labourers to search for the dregs, primarily in California but also in other northwest states. A second wave of Chinese workers came to work on the most dangerous segment of the transcontinental railroad, through the Rockies—thousands lost their lives in this work. Chinese men were also employed in San Francisco's woollen mills as a cheap substitute for white workers: "Stop paying American workmen three dollars a day and substitute Chinamen at a dollar and a quarter, and then you will make money," urged businessman Louis McLane.[2] They were also concentrated in citrus- and celery-harvesting, fishery work and cigar-making, and urban Chinese men could be found in the cigar, slipper, sewing and shoe-making industries.

Although most Chinese immigrants worked as low-paid wage workers, some were able to work for themselves. Some miners, especially the early migrants, laboured independently, even if under debt. In response to the shortage of domestic servants, Chinese men set up hundreds of small laundry businesses in San Francisco. Many were successful in truck gardening and large-scale tenant farming, and others accumulated large amounts of land to farm and ranch. Chinese fishermen in southern California villages successfully exported millions of dollars worth of abalone and shrimp annually in the 1870s and 1880s. In urban Chinatowns, too, there were many small Chinese businesses: 1878 San Francisco boasted grocers, restaurants, apothecaries, fancy goods and jewelry stores, for example. Although women were fewer in number, their unpaid labour as wives was crucial for the success of many of these small businesses.

Wealthy Chinese import-export merchants from the scholar-gentry class formed the elite of nineteenth-century communities in the US. Although they differed from the mass of Chinese immigrants in class, culture and language, they dominated the Chinese political organisations, including the patriarchal clan organisations and the secret societies. Some merchants were also capitalist producers, hiring poor Chinese at meagre wages to produce goods such as cigars and garments. Others became rich by contracting out Chinese workers to white capitalists, or by profiting from prostitution. Merchants' wives lived sheltered lives, cared for by servants and filling their time with decorative needlework and socialising with others of their class.

On the plantations of the Hawaiian sugar industry, Chinese, and later Japanese and Filipinos, were used in large numbers. From the 1850s to 1870s, Chinese men (an estimated 93 per cent of immigrants were men)[3] were the largest group of workers. Many married Hawaiian women, but a few immigration companies did encourage men to bring their wives, with an eye both to using female labour in the fields and to encouraging stability among the workers.

The majority of women immigrants in Hawaii were Cantonese, many of whose feet had been bound. "Lily feet," as they were called, were desirable among brides, even though they made walking unassisted very difficult and painful, so women with bound feet performed light work such as cane cutting and stripping. Southern Chinese women, however, did not practise footbinding, and they worked in the fields alongside their husbands.

The Split-Household Family, the Gum-Shan-Poo and Prostitution

In nineteenth century China, marriages were arranged between parents: the couple met on the day of their marriage, and then moved to the husband's town to live with his parents. Village leaders pressured the male emigrant to marry and attempt to conceive a male descendant before he left. The emigrant had to promise to send money for his family and village, and his wife and children remained in his parents' home to guarantee his cooperation with the arrangement.

The migration of Chinese women into the US was kept to a trickle by a combination of factors: the economic motives of family patriarchs in China, the view that it was indecent for a woman to travel abroad, reports of sexual molestation by sailors and anti-Chinese violence in the US, and contractors' and employers' insistence on single men. What Evelyn Nakano Glenn has called a "split-household family system" was created,[4] and some families remained split through many generations. Thousands of Chinese women led the life of a Gum-Shan-Poo, a "Golden Mountain lady," married to a man who lived and worked in the US and who returned seldom, if ever.

Most immigrant men were able to send enough money home to keep their families alive, supplementing whatever a wife and children could provide for themselves through subsistence farming or other means. Emigrants who could afford to returned for visits and to father children—boy children often joined their fathers in the US when of age. However, when the flow of money stopped during times of war or natural disaster, families in China were left in dire straits, and "became refugees or were compelled to sell their belongings, homes, children, or even themselves to stay alive."[5]

Prostitution of Chinese women in the US developed and thrived within this split-family situation, and it was encouraged by white capitalists, who wanted to keep wives and children from immigrating and increasing labour costs, and by racist whites, who wanted to keep the Chinese from reproducing in the US.[6] In the early years, a few Chinese women came to the US of their own accord and worked independently. Ah Toy arrived in San Francisco in 1849 to "better her condition," worked as a prostitute, and then became the madam of a brothel of Chinese women.[7] Soon, however, the Chinese secret societies or tongs took over and organised the lucrative trade—between 1852 and 1873, the Hip Yee Tong imported an estimated 6,000 women (87 per cent of all Chinese women arrivals).[8]

Male Chinese purchasing agents for the tongs went to Canton and Hong Kong to recruit young girls into prostitution. Sometimes the exchange was open: agents bought girls from poor families as outright slaves or under contract for an average of four and a half years. When the contract expired, a prostitute was theoretically free, but other rules, which lengthened the years of contract if she was ill or had a child, made such freedom difficult to achieve. When they arrived in California, the girls were sold to wealthy Chinese as concubines, to higher-class brothels reserved only for Chinese men, or to "inferior dens of prostitution which served a racially mixed clientele."[9] Not only the Hip Yee Tong made money on the trade: white policemen were paid off (at $10 a head), white lawyers and customs officials grew rich as increasingly restrictive immigration codes were passed, and Chinatown landlords (over 90 per cent of land was owned by whites) were able to charge brothel owners exorbitant rents.

Chinese prostitutes worked in conditions far inferior to those of white prostitutes. No wages were paid, although gifts could be kept, and in the daytime they were forced to do sewing work subcontracted out to their employers. Those in low-grade brothels lived locked in tiny rooms, often facing dim alleyways, and some were shipped into mining camps, where their treatment was especially harsh.

While many Chinese prostitutes were never able to free themselves, almost all found ways to keep their daughters out of prostitution. White society, however, saw it as natural for Chinese women—"the Chinese are lustful and sensual in their dispositions; every female is a prostitute of the basest order," said the New York *Tribune* in 1856.[10] Indeed, the immorality of Chinese prostitution was cited as one of the reasons to stop Chinese immigration in 1882, although white prostitution was equally prevalent.

Organised Chinese prostitution began to decline in the 1870s as whites passed laws against it and then ended Chinese immigration in 1882, and as a result of raids by Chinese missionaries. More and more Chinese women were married and worked as homemakers. In cities, they also worked for pay at home, doing laundry or sewing, rolling cigars, making slippers or taking in boarders; in rural areas, they earned income from gardening, fishing or raising livestock. Chinese women were also servants, cooks and farm labourers, and a few fished, mined, ran lodging houses or worked on the railroads.

The Anti-Chinese Movement

By the 1870s, US whites began a movement against the Chinese. Town after town passed laws which pushed them out of mining. Although the essential motive seems to have been economic self-interest, it was combined with virulent racism. An Arizona editorial called Chinese "filthy," "heathens," "disgusting" and "barbarous"; a Montana journalist wrote: "We don't mind hearing of a Chinaman being killed now and then. . . . Don't kill them unless they deserve it, but when they do—why kill 'em lots."[11] All over the West they were expelled from small towns and rural areas in what the Chinese called "the Great Driving Out."

Sinophobia was also strong among urban whites in California, fuelled by the use of Asian workers as strike-breakers or low-wage competition. The white Working-men's Party of California led the assault, with "The Chinese Must Go" as its slogan; it called the Chinese "the most debased order of humanity known to the civilised world."[12] Political and labour leaders incited violence—in one of the worst episodes, a white mob attacked the Los Angeles Chinatown in 1871, lynching nineteen people and stealing $40,000 in cash.[13]

White activism resulted in numerous anti-Chinese laws in states and localities, especially in California. Taking advantage of the alien status of Asians, California state laws levied special taxes on them, preventing them from testifying against whites (by declaring them American Indians) and buying land (from 1913 to the 1950s), and legalised their exclusion from public schools, among other things. And Chinese immigration itself was terminated in 1882 by the Chinese Exclusion Act. As a result of such laws and of anti-Chinese sentiment, the Chinese-American community actually contracted from 124,000 in 1890 to a low of 85,000 in 1920, rising again only very gradually, to 106,000 in 1940.[14] West Coast and Hawaiian employers turned to Japan for their cheap labour.

The 1882 Exclusion Act prevented single Chinese women as well as the wives of US residents (except those of merchants) from immigrating, solidifying the sex imbalance. Those sojourners who now wished to send for their wives could not do so. Further, miscegenation laws (in operation until 1967) prevented Chinese men from marrying white women—only a few married Indian, African-American or Mexican women. Most Chinese men who had migrated to the US single could only start a family by going to China, marrying and returning, leaving their wives and future children there. Thus, the split-household family system continued over generations, well into the twentieth century. In one typical family history, a 21-year-old college student in the 1980s was the first in four generations of split families to be born in the US.

During the "Great Driving Out" of the late nineteenth century, many Chinese lost their land and businesses and moved into the urban ghettos, "Chinatowns." The proportion of Chinese farm labourers fell, as did the number of Chinese wage-workers in urban areas, as white workers prevented white capitalists from hiring them. Chinese capitalists could not offer many jobs because white consumers boycotted Chinese-made products. Many Chinese women, however, continued to work as seamstresses, in canning or as domestics—garment work was especially common, some girls beginning to work as young as 7 years of age. In 1938, in the middle of the Depression, Chinese women garment workers employed by the National Dollar Stores organised their own union chapter, went on strike for thirteen weeks and won a contract and better wages and working conditions.

Many Chinese were able to circumvent the restricted labour market by forming small businesses, despite white hostility—in 1937, in San Antonio, Texas, the Chinese community stopped a drive to push Chinese out of the grocery business. Most Chinese businesses were in Chinatowns, but not all—for instance, some Chinese set up small shops in the South to serve blacks, who were refused by whites.

Once Chinese men registered as merchants, they could send for their wives and children. "Small-producer" families were formed, much like the white family businesses in colonial times. Super-self-exploitation of the whole family was necessary to turn a profit. One Chinese woman from Boston's Chinatown described her family's laundry business in the 1930s and 1940s: it employed all four children and both parents, and the work day was 7 A.M. to midnight, six days a week; the children worked the same hours, except for school

and a short nap, and did their homework from midnight to 2 A.M.

The Second World War Watershed and the New Immigrants

The Second World War proved to be a watershed. Since Japan had invaded China in 1931, Chinese Americans, for once, felt a common interest with the US when war was declared on Japan after the bombing of Pearl Harbour in 1941, and both women and men served in the armed forces. The labour shortage created by the war forced the US government to prohibit discrimination against Chinese and Chinese-American workers in defence industries. Chinese-American women workers were finally allowed into office work outside Chinatowns. Jobs in the civil service, professional fields and factories also opened up—and the new stereotype of Chinese-American women as obedient "office wives" was formed.

Political alliance with China and Madame Chiang Kai-shek's visit to the US further eased anti-Chinese-American sentiment. In 1943, the Chinese Exclusion Act was repealed: Chinese were put under the racial quota system for immigration (allowing 105 Chinese immigrants a year) and Chinese immigrants became eligible for citizenship if they could prove they had entered before 1924, or had come in under the new laws as permanent residents. A later amendment to the "War Brides Act" also allowed Chinese servicemen, once they had become citizens, to bring their wives and children to the US. Many rushed to China to marry before the Act expired in 1949.

For five years, almost all the immigrants from China were women and children. Upon arrival, they were interrogated to prove their right to immigrate and some were detained or harassed. In 1948, Leong Bick Ha hanged herself in an immigration detention centre after being held three months there. One hundred Chinese women detainees protested her death with a day-long hunger strike. Finally, in response to adverse publicity and public pressure, the Immigration and Naturalisation Service ended its policy of detaining Chinese immigrants, after over 100 years of the inhuman practice. Subsequent immigration acts—in 1952 and 1965—eased the sex imbalance in the Chinese American community.

The Chinese immigration of the 1940s and 1950s, however, was small compared to that after the 1965 Immigration Act. The Chinese-American population quadrupled between 1960 and 1985, from 236,084 to 1,079,400.[15] But the specific provisions of the laws created two very different communities: the "Uptown" and the "Downtown" Chinese. On the one hand, elite professionals, particularly scientists and engineers, have been actively encouraged by the US government. On the other, a substantial proportion of the immigration quota is allocated to relatives of Chinese already settled in the US—mostly poor, rural Cantonese who had resettled in Hong Kong.

The "Uptown" Chinese, many of them women, come with considerable resources, and their experiences have raised average income statistics for Chinese Americans, giving the false impression of upward mobility in the US. Actually, the "Uptown" Chinese were already educationally and socially elevated in Taiwan and China, and have simply transferred that status. And, indeed, discrimination has ensured the downward mobility even of such model immigrants.

The "Downtown" Chinese, on the other hand, live and work in Chinatowns—where they need not know English—and have revitalised these areas, which had been declining as second-generation Chinese moved out. But garment sweatshops and other Chinatown employment, in restaurants and laundries, are often part of the "underground economy," unprotected by labour laws. While the garment workers have become increasingly militant, Chinese women have taken the lead in struggles over community control and education in Chinatowns across the US. In Los Angeles, in the 1970s, the Chinatown Education Project won improved education for Chinatown children, and in Boston, Chinese women led the fight for local input into "urban renewal" plans that threatened Chinatown. Chinese immigrant women organised "It's Time," a New York City group serving tenants, mostly from the Chinese community, facing evictions, harassment and deteriorating buildings.

Japanese-American Women

Japanese workers were not sought until Chinese immigration was stopped in 1882. Although similarities existed between Japanese and Chinese immigration—contract work in Hawaii and on the West Coast, limitations on immigration as a result of US racism, initial unbalanced sex ratios—there were also profound differences. Japanese women were key to these differences, since they came in greater numbers than Chinese women and came earlier in the immigration period.

For the Japanese government, which first permitted and later encouraged emigration to the US, it was seen as a solution to the growing problem of landlessness, while the remittances of the emigrants were looked upon as an important source of income to impoverished families.[16] In contrast to Chinese emigrants, most of those who left Japan were literate, including the women—an education was deemed to make them good wives and wise mothers. Such education had much in common with the nineteenth-century cult of domesticity. As among whites, however, not all women were able to live their lives according to such precepts; for the vast majority of peasants and tenant farmers, backbreaking work for economic survival took precedence over notions of womanhood.

By 1910, there were over 72,000 Japanese in the continental US, mostly educated young, single males who worked as unskilled labourers on the railroads and in the mines, as gardeners or laundrymen, as "houseboys" in domestic service or as field hands. Conditions for the field hands were harsh, and many workers died from the heat, beriberi and tuberculosis. According to one account from the 1890s: During those days around Fresno, labourers did not even carry blankets. They slept in the field with what they had on. They drank river water brought in by irrigation ditches. . . . If they ate supper, it consisted of flour dumplings in a soup seasoned with salt."[17] Nearly all these agricultural workers were recruited by Japanese labour contractors who earned high incomes by charging the workers not only a daily commission, withheld from their wages, but also medical fees and service fees for sending money back to families in Japan.

Some "Issei" (first-generation immigrants) were able to set up small businesses, including laundries, hotels and stores, catering primarily for Japanese clients who faced discrimination by white-owned businesses. And by 1900, there was a sizeable number of Japanese sharecroppers and tenant farmers.

Issei Women, Prostitution and "Picture Brides"

During the early years, most Japanese migrants were men—in 1900, there were twenty-five Japanese men for every woman. Most women immigrants came as part of families and worked in agriculture, as domestic servants and alongside their husbands in small family businesses. The most common form of non-agricultural employment for Japanese women was domestic service.

However, as with the Chinese, the unbalanced sex ratio made prostitution a thriving business. The first reports of the presence of Japanese prostitutes date back to the 1880s.[18] Many of the women were abducted or tricked into coming; others were sold into prostitution by their impoverished families. Once they arrived in the US the women were often held in bondage by *amegoro,* pimps who used physical intimidation and lived off their prostitutes' earnings. Prostitution was fairly strictly segregated by race: *Hakujin-tori* catered to whites, *Shinajin-tori* to Chinese and *Nihonjin-tori* to Japanese.

In the 1890s, San Francisco and Seattle newspapers began to publish a series of sensationalist articles about the presence of Japanese prostitutes. The Japanese government adopted a number of measures to stem their immigration to the US, fearing that exclusionary measures would be imposed on the mass of Japanese immigrants, as they had on the Chinese. Japanese student leaders in San Francisco petitioned the Japanese Foreign Ministry, claiming the women were "a blot on our national image and national morality" and that "if this notorious vice spreads, America will adopt measures against us in the same manner as she did formerly against the Chinese."[19] However, Japanese leaders' attempts to protect their communities by dissociating themselves from Chinese immigrants failed and Japanese workers and farmers became the targets of racist violence and agitation. In 1907, the Japanese government was finally forced by the US to limit the emigration of Japanese men, and entry was closed to the unskilled. But the entry of wives and relatives was still permitted. With the exclusive immigration of Japanese women, the ratio of men to women began to fall, and by 1920, 34 per cent of the Japanese immigrant community was female.[20]

Of the women who entered the US between 1909 and 1920, over half—an estimated 23,000 [21]—were "picture brides" who had never seen their husbands. The picture-bride practice was a variation on the traditional Japanese marriage form, in which families selected marriage partners for their children using go-betweens. The picture brides tended to come from the same backgrounds as the men they married, who, typically, were approximately ten years their senior and had lived in the US for a while. The Japanese government regulated the practise of photo marriage in a number of ways: men were required to show evidence of stable employment and have savings of anywhere from $800 to $1,000— labourers were ineligible until 1915. The brides had to pass physical examinations and be no more than thirteen years younger than their husbands.

Women became picture brides for a number of reasons. Most obeyed their parents, since "to refuse would have been an act of filial disobedience, a grave moral offence;"[22] others came to help their families by remitting money back to Japan. One traveller described her thoughts:

> gazing upon the rising majestic Mount Fuji in a cloudless sky aboard the ship, I made a resolve. For a woman who was going to a strange society and relying upon an unknown husband whom she had married through photographs, my heart had to be as beautiful as Mount Fuji. I resolved that the heart of a Japanese woman had to be sublime, like that soaring majestic figure, eternally constant through wind and rain, heat and cold. Thereafter, I never forgot that resolve on the ship, enabling me to overcome sadness and suffering.[23]

When they arrived, picture brides, having been subjected to degrading inspections, saw their husbands for the first time at the station. Until 1917, the US government did not recognise photo marriages as legal, so group marriages were conducted on arrival. Once outfitted in uncomfortable western clothing, picture brides followed their husbands to their new homes. According to Evelyn Nakano Glenn:

> Some went to remote labour camps that were built for railroad workers in the Mountain states, coal miners in Wyoming, sugar beet field hands in Utah and Idaho, labourers in lumbering camps and sawmills in Washington, and fish cannery workers in Alaska. Others, particularly those who stayed in California, went into the fields where their husbands tilled the soil as tenant farmers. In addition to working alongside their husbands, women in labour camps and farms often drew their own water, gathered wood to cook and heat the house, and fought to keep dirt out of houses that were little more than shacks. . . . Women whose husbands resided in urban areas were more fortunate. They too worked long hours and kept house in crowded quarters, but conditions were less primitive, and the presence of an ethnic community eased their adjustment.[24]

Although most marriages were stable, some women deserted their husbands, often for another man. Accurate figures are impossible to obtain, but such desertion was common enough to feature frequently in the Japanese press. The close network of Japanese associations (local and business associations, language schools, temples, churches) which regulated and controlled community life were often involved in apprehending such couples, eager to uphold the strict moral tone of the community and concerned that such incidents reflected badly on the Japanese in general.

Then, in 1920, the picture-bride practice was ended, in response to a new wave of anti-Japanese sentiment—the brides, it was claimed by one Californian senator, were breeding a new generation of US citizens who would take over agricultural land.[25] The Japanese associations and the Japanese government stopped issuing passports to picture brides—and over 24,000 single male Issei were left stranded in the US without possibility of marriage, since the vast majority of them could not afford to return to Japan to find a wife.[26]

Agriculture and Economic Advance

Women played a key role in shaping the economic status of Japanese America, since their presence made it possible for Japanese Americans to enter agriculture. The unpaid family labour of women and children "allowed Issei truck farmers to compete effectively with white farmers, enabling them to gain a dominant share of the produce market."[27] The Japanese success in agriculture was impressive: from thirty-seven Japanese farms in California in 1900, the number grew to over 1800 by 1910. By 1920, Japanese farms produced one-third of the truck crops in California. This success was the result of a labour-intensive, high-yield style of farming, very different from most of California agriculture, which tended to use more machinery and larger plots of land, and generated low yields.

This success was threatened in 1913 when California and other western states passed a series of laws banning aliens "ineligible for citizenship" from purchasing land or leasing it for more than three years. But Japanese agriculture continued to expand between 1914 and 1920, largely because Japanese bought land in the names of "Nisei" (the second generation, born on US soil and, hence, US citizens) or through land companies set up to circumvent the ban. The passage of yet another law, in 1920, aimed at plugging these loopholes, led Japanese farmers to develop a variety of new strate-gies to stay in agriculture. Besides forming land companies and issuing stock to Nisei or other US citizens, some Japanese farmers found Nisei middlemen to lease land and then hire them as managers or foremen. Others entered into oral agreements with landowners, who publicly hired the Japanese farmer as an employee, but privately permitted them to sharecrop or tenant farm. Whites entered these arrangements for economic reasons: Japanese farmers were so skilled at intensive cultivation that they were able to pay higher rents and achieve higher yields—in essence, they paid a "racial rent premium."

The Second World War and the Aftermath

Japanese Americans had achieved great economic success by 1940, but bitter times were ahead. The bombing of Pearl Harbour in 1941 set in motion a war not only between Japan and the US but also against Japanese Americans in the US. Immediately, their economic assets were frozen and hundreds of community leaders were rounded up and detained. Then, in February 1942, the "evacuation" of 110,000 Issei and Nisei from the coastal areas of Washington, Oregon and California was authorised on the grounds of potential sabotage and espionage. (During the course of the war, not one such incident was ever reported.) In one week families had to dispose of possessions, close up businesses and report to a temporary assembly centre. Farmers who had invested years of painstaking effort in raising orchards from seedlings had to sell them quickly, at low prices. Once they arrived at the assembly centre, Japanese Americans were tagged like luggage and transported to ten "permanent relocation camps" in Utah, Arizona, Colorado, California, Wyoming, Idaho and Arkansas.

The camps, which held an average of 10,000 people each and were situated in desert or swamp areas where temperatures fluctuated between freezing and boiling, were surrounded by barbed wire and patrolled by armed guards. Camp life was extraordinarily difficult. Families lived in tar-paper barracks divided into rooms housing an average of eight people. Walls did not reach the ceiling, latrines and showers had few or no partitions, and all meals were eaten in large communal mess halls. Adult internees were expected to work, for very low wages, at jobs such as cooking, farming, teaching and providing medical care.

Despite these conditions, Matsumoto suggests that camp life produced some aspects of equality for Issei and Nisei women.[28] And since they were now able to meet young men on their own, Nisei women moved further away from traditional Japanese practices of arranged marriages. Also, the war had generated such a severe labour shortage that the War Relocation Authority, which oversaw the camps, soon began to let internees leave to do domestic, agricultural or factory labour. Issei parents were reluctant to let their daughters go, but their hopes for the future rested on the Nisei generation, and so women were able to leave for schooling and on work releases. Although most work release requests were for domestic servants, Nisei women also found clerical and factory jobs. Some internees left to join the armed forces. Nearly 3,000 Nisei men from the camps joined other Hawaii and US Nisei in the segregated 442nd Combat Team, which became the most highly decorated combat unit of the war,[29] while 100 Nisei women joined the Women's Army Corps.[30] White newspapers refused to print the names of the Nisei war dead.

In 1945, the War Relocation Authority ended the West Coast exclusion and began closing the camps. By then, over a third of adult internees had already left. Japanese Americans returned to a dramatically altered way of life. Much agricultural land

had been lost, along with businesses and homes, and whites in many of their former home towns greeted them with signs warning "No Japanese Welcome." Thus, the end of internment also saw the end of the highly segregated Japanese America, concentrated in the Pacific Northwest and in Japanese-owned or -operated businesses. Although many remained on the West Coast, others dispersed across the US: some of those who had been relocated to the Midwest or the East remained there; others found that their small farms had been displaced by competition from huge corporate farms; still others left the Japanese ghetto in cities like San Francisco and Oakland to disperse throughout the city.

The ban on Japanese immigration was lifted in 1952 with the McCarran-Walter Act (the Japanese quota, however, was only 100 persons); this act also struck down racial barriers to naturalisation, making those born in Japan but living in the US finally eligible for US citizenship. The 1965 Immigration Act further opened up immigration to Asians by eliminating the quota system, but, in contrast to the Chinese-American and Filipino-American communities, the Japanese-American community has not experienced a huge second wave of immigration in response to the act.

The Japanese America of the 1970s and 1980s is dramatically different from that of the prewar period. Most Japanese Americans do not live in ethnic ghettos, and although they continue to experience discrimination and racist violence, they rank in the upper middle class economically.

Filipina-American Women

A major cause of Filipino migration to the US prior to the Second World War has been the US colonisation of the Philippines from 1898 onwards, which followed centuries of

Spanish colonisation. The US used the islands for agricultural export crops, as Spain had done before, and also as a growing market for US manufactured goods. Already, by the early years of the twentieth century the Filipino economy was in a shambles, following years of fighting and epidemics of cholera. Land ownership became increasingly concentrated and poverty, landlessness and tenancy grew in the rural areas. Along with the English-language public schools set up by the US, the stage was set for the first wave of Filipino migration. But whereas Chinese and Japanese immigrants were "aliens," their colonial status made Filipinos US nationals, with the right to immigrate freely to the US. At the same time, they could be kept at the very bottom of the economic hierarchy because they were not allowed to naturalise unless they had served in the US Navy.

Apart from recruitment to the Hawaiian sugar plantations after first Chinese and then Japanese immigration had been halted, Filipinos sought an education in the US. In the early 1900s, an estimated 14,000 Filipino young men, backed by the immense financial sacrifices of their families, came to study, most working as domestic servants to pay their way. This group of young Filipino men was joined, in the 1920s, by 16,000 from Hawaii and 9,000 from Asia. Of the 24,000 Filipinos who entered California between 1925 and 1929, only 1,300 were women. Most Filipinos found jobs at the bottom of the economic hierarchy: in agriculture, as servants, in hotels or restaurants, or in the Alaskan canneries.

Women, Family and Work

There were very few Filipinas in the US until the Second World War: in 1930, the male/female ratio was 14 to 1.[31] Perhaps the most important reason was that employers preferred single men (although, in response

to worker unrest and strikes in 1920 and 1924, planters—supposedly to calm the workers—shipped in about 3,000 Filipinas). Also, Filipinos planned to return home; indeed, many did. Another factor was the different family structure in the Philippines, compared to China and Japan. When a Filipina marries, her ties with her blood family remain equal in importance to those with her husband's families. Hence, Filipinas may have been unwilling to migrate as part of a nuclear family—many waited for their husbands in the Philippines, similar to the Chinese Gum-Shan-Poo. Most Filipinos and Filipinas were Catholic as a result of Spanish colonisation, and divorce was unacceptable. Men who were successful financially tended to return home to their wives and families or to marry; those who stayed in Hawaii or in the continental US tended to remain single, often forming stable households together and paying prostitutes or "taxi-dance girls" for their company.

White racism against Filipinos was organised by the anti-Asian movement. At a 1930 House Committee on immigration hearing, Fred Hart of Salinas claimed: "The Filipinos are poor labour and a social menace as they will not leave our white girls alone and frequently intermarry."[32] Whites verbally harassed Filipinos on the streets, calling them "go-go" and "monkey," and refused to allow them in their restaurants, barbershops, cinemas, swimming pools and tennis courts.

In the Second World War, young Filipino Americans were drafted and others found work in war-related industry. In Hawaii, planters contracted them out to war industries, but paid them their former wages and pocketed the difference. One tangible result of the war was an act in 1946 which finally allowed Filipinos who had entered the US before 1934 to naturalise, thus giving them the right to vote for the first time and freeing them from the restrictions of the Alien Land Laws.

Some new immigration, especially of women, accompanied these changes. During the war, many men in the Philippines had enlisted in the US navy, even though they were confined to stewards' jobs. Many of these veterans applied for citizenship when a 1942 Act of Congress permitted foreign veterans to naturalise. Then the 1947-amended War Brides Act allowed Filipino-American citizens who had served in the war to bring wives in as citizens. Filipinos, often in their 50s and 60s, returned to the Philippines to find wives.

Many Filipinas were, by this time, eager to come, convinced by colonial ideology that "all Americans were beautiful and rich and that America must be like heaven." Most wives ended up working in agriculture or in canneries with their husbands on the West Coast, as domestic servants in cities, or in family businesses. Large numbers of Filipinas came to the US after the Second World War, some as the wives of white servicemen who were stationed in the Philippines: over 63,000 arrived between 1950 and 1980.[33]

The third wave of Filipinos, following the 1965 Immigration Act with its provisions for Filipino immigration—for family reunification, or for professional workers—has created a bipolar income and job distribution among new immigrants, similar to that experienced by the Chinese. Family reunification provisions have allowed the relatives of present Filipino Americans to join their families. Most of these are poor, although many have basic education in English from their Philippine schools. The other, highly visible group of Filipino immigrants, however, is made up of well-trained scientific professionals for whom demand had grown sharply in the US during the 1960s, particularly medical personnel, many of whom are women. However, severe institutional dis-crimination ensures that they earn far less than their white counterparts, so that the economic situation of these professional Filipino immigrants is far from rosy.

War Brides and the Sexploitation of Asian Women

Apart from the institutionalised racism and high levels of racist violence meted out to Asian communities generally, Asian-American women have faced a special kind of discrimination. The US involvement in wars in Asia—the Second World War in Japan and the Philippines, the Korean War and the Vietnam War—and US bases in those countries have placed generations of US non-Asian servicemen in contact with Asian women, mostly as prostitutes or teahouse girls. Amerasian children abound in Korea and Vietnam, ostracised by the local communities. Many of the 200,000 Japanese, Korean, Vietnamese, Thai and Filipino women who married white US servicemen and came to live in the US, many on military bases, lead difficult lives, due to language difficulties, lack of familiarity with US ways and psycho-social isolation. Many husbands, far from assisting their wives' efforts to adapt, become abusive or disenchanted; unaware of their legal rights, wives have been divorced without their knowledge, lost financial support and custody of their children and even faced deportation.

Thousands more difficult relationships between new immigrant Asian women and white men have been produced by the recent growth of the mail-order bride industry, which supplies Asian women as wives to non-Asian US and European men. Unlike long-distance arranged marriages or wife-sales of the past, which located wives of the same racial/ethnic background as the men, the mail-order marriage business is centred on the presumed difference of Asian women from US women. One survey of the men involved found that they "see the women's liberation movement as the cause of their problems. They start with certain negative stereotypes of American women as aggressive, selfish, not family oriented. Then they add positive stereotypes of Asian women—family centred, undemanding, untouched by women's liberation."[34]

The women involved, mostly extremely poor Filipinas, respond to advertisements placed by agencies in local newspapers which offer prospective husbands in the US (and in Europe). The agencies compile catalogues with the women's pictures, descriptions and addresses, which they sell to US men for about $150; the men write to the women who interest them, "fall in love by mail," and marry. An estimated 2,000–3,000 US men find wives in this way each year. Many mail-order brides complain of beatings by their husbands, but fear deportation if they ask for help. Siriporn Skrobanek, a founder of the Women's Information Center in Bangkok, Thailand, views these marriages as "another form of economic exploitation of the periphery by the centre, one which is so intensive that women in the peripheral countries have to sell their labour and sexuality to men on a commercial marriage market."

The sexual stereotypes of Asian women affect Asian-American women in the economic and legal arenas. As Germaine Wong points out:

> The men who used Asian-Pacific women as prostitutes very likely feel today, consciously or not, that Asian-Pacific-American women are beneath their dignity; that we do not value ourselves because we are "willing" to sell ourselves so cheaply; that we are only good for meeting their base needs; etc., etc.
>
> The men who saw Asian-Pacific women in places like tea houses may have come to expect us to be good, faithful, uncomplaining, totally compliant, self-effacing, gracious servants who will do anything and everything to please, entertain, and make them feel comfortable and carefree. All of this they had for "free" when buying drinks or a meal; in present-day circumstances they expect this behaviour to come "free" for the salary paid in exchange for work performed. They expect Asian-Pacific women to be like this "by nature"; it is part of the charm of the Oriental culture.[35]

These stereotypes reinforce Asian women's segregation in office work. Assuming Asian-American women to be particularly pleasing and unaggressive, employers deny them pay rises and claim they lack the leadership qualities needed for executive jobs. These stereotypes have also led to sexual harassment of Asian-American women by police, and women reporting such incidents do not receive justice from the courts because of "the prostitute stereotype."[36]

. . .

Asian patriarchal practices, white society's racism, and the special sexploitation of Asian women have led increasing numbers of Asian-American women to become active in Asian civil rights organising, in Asian women's movements, and in Asian lesbian and gay groups. They face many impediments: hostility from Asian men (who criticise Asian feminists and lesbians for destroying Asian community solidarity), the racism of white women (few of whom have any knowledge of the history or present status of Asian-American women), vast differences among them (from ethnicity and language to class and sexuality), and the needs of many Asian-American women, still, to focus on economic survival. Nevertheless, Asian-American women have started Asian women's studies courses and study groups; writers' groups, such as the Pacific Asian American Women's Writers West; health and mental health projects and advocacy groups, such as the Pacific Asian Shelter for Battered Women in Los Angeles and the Asian Pacific Outreach Center in Long Beach; and regional feminist organisations, such as the National Organisation of Pan Asian Women, the National Network of Asian and Pacific Women, and Asian American Women United. Asian lesbians have formed political networks such as ALOEC (Asian Lesbians of the East Coast), which has created a slide-show of Asian lesbian history in India, China and Japan. Further, Asian feminists have begun to join in coalitions with other feminists of colour, in spite of historical differences and antagonisms.

In her "Letter to Ma," Merle Woo tells her:

> Do you realise, Ma, that I could never have reacted the way I have if you had not provided for me the opportunity to be free of the binds that have held you down . . . ? Because of your life, because of the physical security you have given me . . I saw myself as having worth: now I . . . see our potential, and fight for just that kind of social change that will reaffirm me, my race, my sex, my heritage. And while I affirm myself, Ma, I affirm you.[37]

NOTES

For this excerpt most of the references have been eliminated for reasons of space. In addition to the works cited below, see also Jayjia Hsia, *Asian Americans in higher education and at work* (New Jersey, 1988); H. B. Melendy, *Asians in America: Filipinos, Koreans and East Indians* (Boston, 1977); A. T. Moriyama, *Imingaisha: Japanese emigration companies and Hawaii 1894–1908* (Honolulu, 1985); A. J. A. Pido, *The Filipinos in America: macro/micro dimensions of immigration and integration* (New York, 1986); A. Saxton, *The indispensable enemy: labor and the anti-Chinese movement* (Berkeley, 1971); B. L. Sung, *A survey of Chinese-American manpower and employment* (New York, 1977); R. V. Vallangca, *Pinoy: the first wave (1898–1941)* (San Francisco, 1977). For more information, see the complete work.

1. Paul C.P. Siu, *The Chinese Laundryman: A Study of Social Isolation* (New York, 1987), pp. 44–45.
2. Ibid., p. 49.
3. John Liu, "Race, Ethnicity, and the Sugar Plantation System: Asian Labor in Hawaii, 1850–1900," in *Labor Immigration Under Capitalism: Asian Workers in the United States before World War II*, edited by Lucie Cheng and Edna Bonacich (Berkeley, 1984), p. 195.
4. Evelyn Nakano Glenn, "Split Household, Small Producer and Dual Wage Earner: An Analysis of Chinese-American Family Strategies," *Journal of Marriage and the Family* (February 1983).
5. June Mei, "Socioeconomic Origins of Emigration: Guangdong to California, 1850–1882," in *Labor Immigration Under Capitalism*, ed. Cheng and Bonacich, p. 240.
6. Lucie Cheng, "Free, Indentured, Enslaved: Chinese Prostitutes in Nineteenth-Century America," in *Labor Immigration Under Capitalism*, ed. Cheng and Bonacich.
7. Judy Yung, *Chinese Women of America: A Pictorial History* (Seattle, 1986), pp. 14–15.
8. Cheng, "Free, Indentured, Enslaved," in *Labor Immigrants Under Capitalism*, ed. Cheng and Bonacich.
9. Ibid., p. 411.
10. June Mei, "Socioeconomic Developments Among the Chinese in San Francisco, 1848–1906," in *Labor Immigration Under Capitalism*, ed. Cheng and Bonacich. Diane Mei, Lin Mark and Ginger Chih, *A Place Called Chinese America* (Organization of Chinese Americas, 1982), pp. 54–56; Roger Daniels, *The Politics of Prejudice: The Anti-Japanese Movement in California and the Struggle for Japanese Exclusion* (New York, 1969), pp. 81–83.
11. Stanford Lyman, "Strangers in the City: The Chinese in the Urban Frontier," in *Roots: An Asian American Reader*, edited by Amy Tachiki, Eddie Wong and Franklin Odo with Buck Wong (UCLA Asian American Studies Center, 1971), pp. 159–87.
12. Ibid., p. 173.
13. Ibid., p. 174 and Siu, *The Chinese Laundryman*, p. 50.
14. Calculated from tables 2.1 and 2.5 in Bonacich; numbers include Hawaii.

15. Peter Kwong, *The New Chinatown* (New York, 1987), p. 22.
16. Alan Moriyama, "The Causes of Emigration," in *Labor Immigration Under Capitalism,* ed. Cheng and Bonacich.
17. Yuji Ichioka, *The Issei: The World of the First Generation Japanese Immigrants 1885–1924* (New York, 1988), p. 83.
18. The following material on prostitutes comes from Yuji Ichioka, "Ameyuki-san: Japanese Prostitutes in Nineteenth Century America," *Amerasia* 4(1), (1977).
19. Ichioka, *The Issei,* p. 39.
20. Yukiko Hanawa, *The Several Worlds of Issei Women* (dissertation, Dept. of Asian Studies, California State University, 1982), p. 51.
21. Evelyn Nakano Glenn, "The Dialectics of Wage Work: Japanese American Women and Domestic Service, 1905–40," and Alan Moriyama, "The Causes of Emigration: The Background of Japanese Emigration to Hawaii 1885–94," pp. 268–70, both in *Labor Immigration Under Capitalism,* ed. Cheng and Bonacich.
22. Ichioka, *The Issei,* p. 345.
23. Emma Gee, "Issei Women," in *Counterpoint: Perspectives on Asian America,* edited by Emma Gee (Los Angeles, Asian American Studies Center, 1976), p. 11.
24. Evelyn Nakano Glenn, *Issei, Nisei, War Bride: Three Generations of Japanese Women in Domestic Service* (Philadelphia, 1986), pp. 47–48.
25. Ichioka, *The Issei,* p. 173.
26. Ibid., p. 175.
27. Victor Nee, and Herbert Y. Wong, "Asian American Socioeconomic Achievement: The Strength of the Family Bond," *Sociological Perspectives* 28(3), (July 1985), p. 294.
28. Valerie Matsumoto, "Japanese American Women During World War II," *Frontiers* 8(1), (1984).
29. Roger Daniels, *Asian America: Chinese and Japanese in the United States Since 1850* (Seattle, 1988), pp. 252–54.
30. Ibid., p. 285.
31. Violet Rabaya, "Filipino Immigration: The Creation of a New Social Problem," in *Roots,* ed. Tachiki et al., pp. 188–200.
32. Brett Melendy, *Asians in America: Filipinos, Koreans and East Indians* (Boston, 1977), p. 67.
33. Elaine Kim, *With Silk Wings* (San Francisco, 1983), pp. 120–30.
34. Lisa Belkin, "The Mail-Order Marriage Business," *New York Times Magazine,* 11 May 1986, p. 51.
35. Germaine Wong, "Impediments to Asian-Pacific-American Women Organizing," in *Conference on the Educational and Occupational Needs of Asian-Pacific-American Women* (National Institute of Education, October 1980), p. 93.
36. Diane Yen-Mei Wong, "Asian/Pacific American Women: Legal Issues," in U.S. Commission on Civil Rights, *Civil Rights Issues of Asian and Pacific Americans,* pp. 142, 146.
37. Merle Woo, "Letter to Ma," in *This Bridge Called My Back,* edited by Gloria Anzaldua and Cherie Moraga (Watertown, MA, 1981).

24

"THERE'S NO SHAME IN MY GAME": STATUS AND STIGMA AMONG HARLEM'S WORKING POOR

Katherine S. Newman and Catherine Ellis

Questions to Consider

Katherine Newman and Catherine Ellis ask us to imagine what life is like working a "McJob." How do individuals maintain self-respect working at a job that provides little in the way of social status? Is it possible that these workers could find employment that pays a living wage (about $16/hour in New York City)? What does "No Shame in My Game" mean, and what does this phrase suggest about our attitude toward work?

In the early 1990s, the McDonald's Corporation launched a television ad campaign featuring a young black man named Calvin, who was portrayed sitting atop a Brooklyn stoop in his golden-arches uniform while his friends passed by to hard-time him about holding down a "McJob." After brushing off their teasing with good humor, Calvin is approached furtively by one young black man who asks, sotto voce, whether Calvin might help him get a job. He allows that he too could use some earnings and that, despite the ragging he has just given Calvin, he thinks the uniform is really pretty cool—or at least that having a job is pretty cool.

Every fast-food worker we interviewed for this study knew the Calvin series by heart: Calvin on the job; Calvin in the street; Calvin helping an elderly woman cross the street on his way to work; Calvin getting promoted to management. They knew what McDonald's was trying to communicate to young people by producing the series in the first place. Fast-food jobs are burdened by a lasting stigma, but one that can be overcome in time. Eventually, so the commercial suggests, the public "dissing" will give way to private admiration as the value of sticking with a job eclipses the stain of a burger flipper's lowly reputation.

One of the moral maxims of American culture is that work defines the person. We carry around in our heads a rough tally that tells us what kinds of jobs are worthy of respect or of disdain, a pyramid organized by the income attached to a particular job, the educational credentials it demands, and the social characteristics of an occupation's incumbents. We use this system of stratification (ruthlessly at times) to boost the status of some and humiliate others.[1]

Given our tradition of equating moral value with employment, it stands to reason that the most profound dividing line in our culture is that which separates the working person from the unemployed.[2] Only after this line has been crossed do we begin to make the finer gradations that distinguish a white-collar worker from his blue-collar counterpart, a CEO from a secretary. A whole host of moral virtues—discipline, personal responsibility, pragmatism—are ascribed to those who have found and kept a job, almost any job, while those who have not are dismissed in public discourse as slothful and irresponsible.[3]

We inhabit an unforgiving culture that fails to acknowledge the many reasons some people cross that employment barrier and others are left behind. We may remember, for a time, that unemployment rates are high; that particular industries have downsized millions of workers right out of their jobs; or that racial barriers or negative attitudes toward teenagers make it harder for some people to get jobs than others. Yet in the end American culture wipes out these background truths in favor of a simpler dichotomy: the worthy and the unworthy, the working folk and the lazy deadbeats.

For those on the positive side of the divide, those who work for a living, the rewards are far greater than a paycheck. The employed enter a social world in which their identities as mainstream Americans are shaped, structured, and reinforced. The workplace is the main institutional setting—and virtually the only one after one's school career is over—in which individuals become part of the collective American enterprise that lies at the heart of our culture: the market. We are so divided in other domains—race, geography, family organization, gender roles, and the like—that common ground along almost any other lines is difficult to

achieve. For our diverse and divided society, participation in the world of work is the most powerful source of social integration.

It is in the workplace that we are most likely to mix with those who come from different backgrounds, are under the greatest pressure to subordinate individual idiosyncrasy to the requirements of an organization, and are called upon to contribute to goals that eclipse the personal. All workers have these experiences in common, even as segregation constrains the real mix of workers, conformity is imposed on some occupations more than others, and he goals to which we must subscribe are often elusive, unreachable, or at odds with personal desire.

The creation of a workplace identity is rarely the task of the self-directed individualist, moving along some preordained path. It is a miracle worked by organizations, firms, supervisors, fellow workers, and by the whole long search that leads from the desire to find a job to the endpoint of landing one. This transformation is particularly fraught for ghetto youth and adults, for they face a difficult job market, high hurdles in convincing employers to take a chance on them, and relatively poor rewards—from a financial point of view—for their successes. But the crafting of an identity is an important developmental process for them, just as it is for their more privileged counterparts.

Powerful forces work to exclude African-Americans, Latinos, and other minorities from full participation in American society. From the schools that provide a substandard education for millions of inner-city kids, to an employment system rife with discrimination, to a housing market that segregates minority families, there is almost no meaning to the notion that Americans all begin from the same starting line.[4] Precisely because this is the case, blasting one's way through the job barrier and starting down that road of acquiring a common identity as mainstream worker is of the greatest importance for black and brown youth in segregated communities. It may be one of the few accessible pipelines into the core of American society and the one with the greatest payoff, symbolic and material.

This paper draws upon a two-year study of fast-food workers and job seekers in central and northern Harlem. Two hundred African-American and Latino workers participated in this study by participating in face-to-face interviews. Sixty of them completed extensive life histories, and a smaller group contributed yearlong personal diaries and permitted the members of our research group to spend extensive periods of time with them, their family members, and their friends. We draw upon all of these data here to explore the nature of values among the working poor in the inner city.

The Social Costs of Accepting Low-Wage Work

While the gainfully employed may be honored over those who stand outside the labor force, all jobs are not created equal. Fast-food jobs, in particular, are notoriously stigmatized and denigrated. "McJob" has become a common epithet meant to designate work without redeeming value. The reasons for this heavy valence are numerous and worthy of deconstruction, for the minority workers who figure in this study have a mountain of stigma to overcome if they are to maintain their self-respect. Indeed, this is one of the main goals of the organizational culture they join when they finally land a job in the restaurant chain we will call "Burger Barn."

Fast-food jobs epitomize the assembly line structure of deskilled service jobs: they are highly routinized, and appear to the untutored observer to be entirely lacking in discretion—almost military in their scripted nature. The symbolic capital of these routinized jobs can be measured in negative numbers. They represent the opposite of the autonomous entrepreneur who is lionized in popular culture (from *Business Week* to hip-hop).

Burger Barn workers are told that they must, at all cost to their own dignity, defer to the public. Customers can be unreasonably demanding, rude, and demeaning, and workers must count backwards from one hundred in an effort to stifle their outrage. Servicing the customer with a smile is music to management's ears because making money depends on keeping the clientele happy, but it can be an exercise in humiliation for inner-city teenagers. It is hard for them to refrain from reading this public nastiness as another instance of society's low estimation of their worth. But if they want to hold on to these minimum-wage jobs, they soon realize that they have to tolerate comments that would almost certainly provoke a fistfight outside the workplace.

It is well known among ghetto consumers that fast-food crew members have to put up with whatever verbiage comes across the counter. That knowledge occasionally prompts nasty exchanges designed explicitly to anger workers, to push them to retaliate verbally. Testing those limits is an outlet for customers down on their luck, and a favorite pastime of teenagers in particular. This may be the one opportunity they have to put someone else down in public, knowing there is little the worker can do in return.

It is bad enough to be on the receiving end of this kind of abuse from adults, especially white adults, for that has its own reading along race lines. It is, in some respects, even worse to have to contend with it from minority peers, for there is much more personal honor at stake, more pride to be lost, and an audience whose opinion matters more. This no doubt is why harassment is a continuous problem for fast-food workers. It hurts. Their peers, with plenty of anger bottled up for all kinds of reasons extraneous to the restaurant experience, find counterparts working the cash register convenient targets for venting.

Roberta Sampson[5] is a five-year veteran of Burger Barn who has worked her way up to management. A formidable African-American woman, Roberta has always prided herself on her ability to make it on her own. Most of Roberta's customers have been perfectly pleasant people; many have been long-time repeat visitors to her restaurant. But she has also encountered many who radiate disrespect.

> Well, I had alcoholics, derelicts. People that are aggravated with life. I've had people that don't even have jobs curse me out. I've dealt with all kinds.
>
> Sometimes it would get to me. If a person yelled out [in front of] a lobby full of people, "Bitch, that's why you work at Burger Barn," I would say [to myself], "I'm probably making more than you and your mother." It hurts when people don't even know what you're making and they say those things. Especially in Harlem, they do that to you. They call you all types of names and everything.

Natasha Robins is younger than Roberta and less practiced at these confrontations. But she has had to contend with them nevertheless, especially from age-mates who are (or at least claim to be) higher up the status hierarchy than she is. Hard as she tries, Natasha cannot always control her temper and respond the way the firm wants her to:

> It's hard dealing with the public. There are good things, like old people. They sweet. But the younger people around my age are always snotty. Think they better than you because they not

working at Burger Barn. They probably work at something better than you.

How do you deal with rude or unfriendly customers? They told us that we just suppose to walk to the back and ignore it, but when they in your face like that, you get so upset that you have to say something. . . . I got threatened with a gun one time. 'Cause this customer had threw a piece of straw paper in the back and told me to pick it up like I'm a dog. I said, "No." And he cursed at me. I cursed at him back and he was like, "Yeah, next time you won't have nothing to say when I come back with my gun and shoot your ass." Oh, *excuse* me.

Ianna Bates, who had just turned sixteen the summer she found her first job at Burger Barn, has had many of the same kinds of problems Natasha Robins complains of. The customers who hard-time her are just looking for a place to vent their anger about things that have nothing to do with buying lunch. Ianna recognizes that this kind of thing could happen in any restaurant, but believes it is a special problem in Harlem, for ghetto residents have more to be angry about and fewer accessible targets for one-upmanship. Cashiers in fast-food shops catch the results:

> What I hate about Burger Barn is the customers, well, some of them that I can't stand. . . . I don't want to stereotype Harlem . . . , but since I only worked in Harlem that's all I can speak for. Some people have a chip on their shoulders. . . . Most of the people that come into the restaurant are black. Most of them have a lot of kids. It's in the ghetto. Maybe, you know, they are depressed about their lifestyles or whatever else that is going on in their lives and they just. . . . I don't know. They just are like *urff!*

And no matter what you do you cannot please them. I'm not supposed to say anything to the customer, but that's not like me. I have a mouth and I don't take no short from nobody. I don't care who it is, don't take anybody's crap.

Despite this bravado, Ianna well knows that to use her mouth is to risk her job. She has had to work hard to find ways to cope with this frustration that do not get her into trouble with management:

I don't say stuff to people most of the time. Mostly I just look at them like they stupid. Because my mother always told me that as long as you don't say nothin' to nobody, you can't never get in trouble. If you look at them stupid, what are they going to do? If you roll your eyes at somebody like that, I mean, that's really nothing [compared to] . . . cursing at them. Most of the time I try to walk away.

As Ianna observes, there is enough free-floating fury in Harlem to keep a steady supply of customer antagonism coming the way of service workers every day of their work lives. The problem is constant enough to warrant official company policies on how Burger Barn's crew members should respond to insults, what managers should do to help, and the evasive tactics that work best to quell an incendiary situation without losing business.[6] Management tries to minimize the likelihood of such incidents by placing girls on the registers rather than boys, in the apparent belief that young men will attract more abuse and find it harder to quash their reactions than their female counterparts.

Burger Barn does what it can to contend with these problems on the shop floor. But the neighborhood is beyond its reach and there too fast-food workers are often met with ridicule from the people they grew up with. They have to learn to defend themselves against the criticism that they have lowered themselves in taking these jobs coming from people they have known all their lives. Stephanie Harmon, who has worked at Burger Barn for over a year, explains that here too she leans on the divide between the worker and the do-nothing:

People I hang out with, they know me since I was little. We all grew up together. When they see me comin', they laugh and say, "Here come Calvin, here come Calvin sister." I just laugh and keep on going. I say, "You're crazy. But that's OK cause I got a job and you all standing out here on the corner." Or I say, "This is my job, it's legal." Something like that. That Calvin commercial show you that even though his friends tease him and he just brushed them off, then he got a higher position. Then you see how they change toward him.

As Stephanie indicates, the snide remarks of peers and neighbors when a worker first dons a Burger Barn uniform are often replaced with requests for help in getting hired and a show of respect when that worker sticks with the job, shows up with money in her pockets and, best of all, moves into management. Still, the scorn is a burden to endure.

Tiffany Wilson, also a teen worker in a central Harlem Burger Barn, thinks she knows why kids in her community who don't work give her such a hard time. They don't want her to succeed because if no one is making it, then no one needs to feel bad about failing. But if someone claws their way up and looks like they have a chance to escape the syndrome of failure, it must mean everyone could, in theory, do so as well. The teasing, a thinly veiled attempt to enforce conformity, is designed to push would-be success stories back into the fold:

What you will find in any situation, more so in the black community, is that if you are in the community and you try to excel, you will get ridicule from your own peers. It's like the "crab down" syndrome. . . . If you put a bunch of crabs in a big bucket and one crab tries to get out, what do you think the other crabs would do now? According to my thinking, they should pull him up or push him or help him get out. But the crabs pull him back in the barrel. That's just an analogy for what happens in the community a lot.

Keeping everyone down prevents any particular person from feeling that creeping sense of despair that comes from believing things could be otherwise but aren't.

Swallowing ridicule would be a hardship for almost anyone in this culture, but it is particularly hard on minority youth in the inner city. They have already logged several years' worth of interracial and cross-class friction by the time they climb behind a Burger Barn cash register. More likely than not, they have also learned from peers that no self-respecting person allows themselves to be "dissed" without striking back. Yet this is precisely what they must do if they are going to survive on the shop floor.

This is one of the main reasons why these jobs carry such a powerful stigma in American popular culture: they fly in the face of a national attraction to autonomy, independence, and the individualist's right to respond in kind when their dignity is threatened. In ghetto communities, this stigma is even more powerful because—ironically—it is in these enclaves that this mainstream value of independence is elaborated and embellished. Film characters—from the Superfly variety to the political version (e.g., Malcolm X)—rap stars, and local idols base their claims to notoriety on standing above the crowd, going their own way, being be-

yond the ties that bind ordinary mortals. There are white parallels, to be sure, but this is a powerful genre of icons in the black community, not because it is a disconnected subculture, but because it is an intensified version of a perfectly recognizable American middle- and working-class fixation.

It is therefore noteworthy that thousands upon thousands of minority teens, young adults, and even middle-aged adults line up for jobs that will subject them, at least potentially, to a kind of character assassination. They do so not because they start the job-hunting process with a different set of values, one that can withstand society's contempt for fast-food workers. They take these jobs because in so many inner-city communities, there is nothing better in the offing. In general, they have already tried to get better jobs and have failed, landing instead at the door of Burger Barn as a last resort.

The stigma of these jobs has other sources beyond the constraints of enforced deference. Low pay and poor prospects for mobility matter as well. Fast-food jobs are invariably minimum-wage positions.[7] Salaries rise very little over time, even for first-line management. In ghetto areas, where jobs are scarce and the supply of would-be workers chasing them is relatively large, downward pressure keeps these jobs right down at the bottom of the wage scale.[8]

The public perception (fueled by knowledge of wage conditions) is that there is very little potential for improvement in status or responsibility either. Even though there are Horatio Algers in this industry, there are no myths to prop up a more glorified image. As a result, the epithet "McJob" develops out of the perception that a fast-food worker is not likely to end up in a prestigious position as a general manager or restaurant owner; she is going to spend her whole life flipping burgers.

As it happens, this is only half true. The fast-food industry is actually very good about internal promotion. Shop floor management is nearly always recruited from the ranks of entry-level workers. Carefully planned training programs make it possible for people to move up, to acquire transferable skills, and to at least take a shot at entrepreneurial ownership. Industry leaders, like McDonald's, are proud of the fact that half of their present board of directors started out on the shop floor as crew members. One couldn't say as much for most other Fortune 500 firms.

Nevertheless, the vast majority of workers never even get close to management. The typical entry-level worker cycles through the job in short order, producing an industry average job tenure of less than six months. Since this is just an average, it suggests that a large number of employees are there and gone in a matter of weeks. It is this pattern, a planned operation built around low skills and high turnover, that has given fast-food jobs such a bad name. Although it is quite possible to rise above the fray and make a very respectable living in fast-food management, most crew members remain at the entry level and leave too soon to see much upward movement. Observing this pattern on such a large scale—in practically every town and city in the country—Americans naturally conclude that there is no real future in a job of this kind and anyone with more on the ball wouldn't be caught dead working behind the counter.

The stigma also stems from the low socioeconomic status of the people who hold these jobs. This includes teenagers, immigrants who often speak halting English, those with little education, and (increasingly in affluent communities afflicted with labor shortages) the elderly. To the extent that the prestige of a job refracts the social characteristics of its average incumbents, fast-food jobs are hobbled by the perception that people with better choices would never purposively opt for a McJob. We argue that

entry-level jobs of this kind don't merit this scorn: a lot more skill, discretion, and responsibility are locked up in a fast-food job than meets the public eye. But this truth hardly matters where public perception is concerned. There is no faster way to indicate that a person is barely deserving of notice than to point out that they hold a "chump change" job in Kentucky Fried Chicken or Burger King. We "know" this is the case just by looking at the age, skin color, or educational credentials of the people already on the job: the tautology has a staying power that even the most expensive public relations campaign cannot shake.

It is hard to know the extent to which this stigma discourages young people in places like central Harlem from knocking on the doors of fast-food restaurants in search of employment. It is clear that the other choices aren't much better and that necessity drives thousands, if not millions, of teens and older job seekers to repudiate the stigma associated with fast-food work or learn to live with it.[9] But no one comes into the central Harlem job market without having to contend with the social risks to their identity that come with approaching stigmatized ground.

Tiffany Wilson started working in the underground economy bagging groceries when she was little more than ten years old because her mother was having trouble supporting the family, "checks weren't coming in," and there was "really a need for food" in the family. She graduated to summer youth by the time she was fourteen and landed a job answering phones in a center that dealt with domestic violence cases, referring terrified women to shelters. By the time she was sixteen, Tiffany needed a real job that would last beyond the summertime, so she set about looking—everywhere. As a black teenager, she quickly discovered there wasn't a great deal open to her. Tiffany ended up at Burger Barn in the Bronx, a restaurant two blocks from her house and close enough to her high school to make after-school hours feasible.

> The first Burger Barn I worked at was because nobody else would take me. It was a last resort. I didn't want to go to Burger Barn. You flip burgers. People would laugh at you. In high school, I didn't wanna be in that kind of environment. But lo and behold, after everything else failed, Martin Paints, other jobs, Burger Barn was welcoming me with open arms. So I started working there.

Tiffany moved to Harlem when she finished high school and found she couldn't commute back to the Bronx. Reluctant to return to the fast-food business, Tiffany tried her luck at moving up, into a service job with more of a white-collar flavor. She looked everywhere for a position in stores where the jobs are free of hamburger grease and hot oil for French fries, stores where clerks don't wear aprons or hair nets. Nothing panned out, despite her best efforts:

> I'm looking at Lerners and Plymouth [clothing stores] and going to all these stores and lo and behold Burger Barn is there with open arms because I had two years of experience by then.

The new Burger Barn franchise was right in the middle of Harlem, not far from the room she rents over a storefront church. It had the additional appeal of being a black-owned business, something that mattered to Tiffany in terms of the "more cultural reasons why [she] decided to work there." But she confesses to a degree of disappointment that she was not able to break free of entry-level fast-food jobs. With a high-school diploma in hand, Tiffany was hoping for something better.

William Johnson followed a similar pathway to Burger Barn, graduating from summer youth jobs in the middle of high school and looking for something that would help pay for his books and carfare. The Department of Labor gave him a referral to Burger Barn, but he was reluctant at first to pursue it:

> To go there and work for Burger Barn, that was one of those real cloak-and-dagger kind of things. You'll be coming out [and your friends say], "Yo, where you going?" You be, "I'm going, don't worry about where I'm going." And you see your friends coming [to the restaurant] and see you working there and now you be [thinking], "No, the whole [housing] project gonna know I work in Burger Barn." It's not something I personally proclaim or pride and stuff. . . . If you are a crew member, you really aren't shit there. . . . You got nothing there, no benefits, nothing. It was like that [when I was younger] and it's like that now.

William tried every subterfuge he could think of to conceal his job from the kids he knew. He kept his uniform in a bag and put it on in the back of the restaurant so that it would never be visible on the street. He made up fake jobs to explain to his friends where his spending money was coming from. He took circuitous routes to the Barn and hid back by the gigantic freezer when he spotted a friend coming into the store. The last thing William wanted was to be publicly identified as a shift worker at Burger Barn.

In this, William was much like the other teen and young adult workers we encountered. They are very sensitive to stigma, to challenges to their status, and by taking low-wage jobs of this kind they have positioned themselves to receive exactly the kind of insults they most fear. But the fact is that they do take these risks and, in time, latch onto other "narratives" that undergird their legitimacy.

Breaking the Stigma

One of the chief challenges of an organization like Burger Barn is how to take people who have come to them on the defensive and turn them into workers who at least appear on the surface, if not deep in their souls, to enjoy their work. Customers have choices; they can vote with their feet. If ordering french fries at Burger Barn requires them to run a gauntlet of annoyance, rudeness, or diffidence from the person who takes their order, they can easily cross the street to a competitor the next time. It is clearly in the company's interest to find ways to turn the situation around. Ideally, from the industry's viewpoint, it would be best if the whole reputation of these jobs could be reversed. This is what McDonald's had in mind when it launched the Calvin series. But for all the reasons outlined earlier in this chapter, that is not likely to happen, for the conditions that give rise to the stigma in the first place—low wages, high turnover, enforced deference—are not likely to change. Beyond publicizing the opportunities that are within reach, much of which falls on deaf ears, there is little the industry can do to rehabilitate its workers in the eyes of the public and thereby dampen the tension across the counter.

Yet behind the scenes, managers and workers, and peers working together in restaurant crews, do build a moral defense of their work. They call upon timeless American values, values familiar to many, including conservatives, to undergird their respectability. Pointing to the essential virtues of the gainfully employed, Burger Barn workers align themselves with the great mass of men and women who work for a living. "We are like them," they declare, and in so doing separate themselves from the people in their midst who are not employed.

They have plenty of experience with individuals who don't work, often including members of their own families: beggars who come around the restaurants looking for handouts every day; fast-talkers who come into Burger Barn hoping for free food; and age-mates who prefer to deal drugs. In general, these low-wage workers are far less forgiving, and far less tolerant, of these people than are the liberals who champion the cause of the working poor. Since they hold hard, exhausting, poorly paid jobs, they see little reason why anyone ought to get a free ride. What the indigent should do, on this account, is to follow their example: get a job, any job.

Ianna Bates is an articulate case in point. She has had to confront the social degradation that comes from holding a "low job" and has developed a tough hide in response. Her dignity is underwritten by the critique she has absorbed about the "welfare dependent":

> I'm not ashamed because I have a job. Most people don't and I'm proud of myself that I decided to get up and do something at an early age. So as I look at it, I'm not on welfare. I'm doing something.
>
> I'm not knocking welfare, but I know people that are on it that can get up and work. There's nothing wrong with them. And they just choose not to. . . . They don't really need to be on [welfare]. They just want it because they can get away with it. I don't think it's right because that's my tax dollars going for somebody who is lazy, who don't wanna get up. I can see if a woman had three children, her husband left her and she don't have no job cause she was a housewife. OK. But after a while, you know, welfare will send you to school. Be a nurse assistant, a home attendant, something!
>
> Even if you were on welfare, it should be like, you see all these dirty streets we have? Why can't they go out

and sweep the streets, clean up the parks. I mean, there is so much stuff that needs to be done in this city. They can do that and give them their money. Not just sit home and not do anything.

Patricia Hull, a mother of five children in her late thirties, couldn't agree more. Patty has worked at Burger Barn for five years now, having pulled herself off of welfare by the sheer determination to be a decent role model for her children. One might imagine that she would be more tolerant of AFDC recipients, since she has been there. She moved up to the Big Apple from Tennessee after her husband walked out on her, hoping to find more job opportunities than the few that were available in the rural south. It took a long time for her to get on her feet and even Patty would agree that without "aid" she would not have made it this far. Still, having finally taken the hard road to a real job, she sees no reason why anyone else should have an easier ride:

> There's so much in this city; it's always hiring. It may not be what you want. It may not be the pay you want. But you will always get a job. If I can work at Burger Barn all week and come home tired and then have to deal with the kids and all of that, and be happy with $125 a week, so can you. Why would I give quarters [to bums on the street]? My quarter is tax-free money for you! No way.

Or, in a variation on the same theme, Larry Peterson reminds us that any job is better than no job. The kids who would dare to hard-time Larry get nothing but a cold shoulder in return because Larry knows in his soul that he has something they don't have: work for which he gets paid.

> I don't care what other people think. You know, I just do not care. I have a job, you know. It's my job. You ain't

puttin' *no* food on my table; you ain't puttin' *no* clothes on my back. I will walk tall with my Burger Barn uniform on. Be proud of it, you know.

These views could have come straight from the most conservative Republicans in the country, bent on justifying draconian cuts in the welfare budget. For they trade on a view held by many of the ghetto-based working poor: that work equals dignity and no one deserves a free ride. The difference between them is simply that the working poor know whereof they speak: they have toiled behind the hot grease pits of french-fry vats, they have stood on their feet for eight or nine hours at a stretch, all for the magnificent sum of $4.25 an hour. Virtually all they have to show for their trouble is the self-respect that comes from being on the right side of that gaping cavern that separates the deserving (read working) and the undeserving (read nonworking) poor (Katz 1989).

Other retorts to status insults emerge as well. Flaunting financial independence often provides a way of lashing back at acquaintances who dis young workers for taking Burger Barn jobs. Brian Gray, born in Jamaica but raised in one of Harlem's tougher neighborhoods, knows that his peers don't really think much of his job. "They just make fun," he says. "Ah, you flipping burgers. You gettin' paid $4.25. They'd go snickering down the street." But it wasn't long after Brian started working that he picked up some serious money, serious at least for a teenager in his neighborhood.

> What I did was made Sam [the general manager] save my money for me. Then I got the best of clothes and the best sneakers with my own money. Then I added two chains. Then [my friends] were like, "Where you selling drugs at?" And I'm like, "the same place you said making fun of me, flipping burgers.

That's where I'm getting my money from. Now, where are you getting yours from?" They couldn't answer.

Contrary to public perception, most teenagers in Harlem are afraid of the drug trade and won't go near it. They know too many people who are six feet under, in jail, or permanently disabled by the ravages of drugs. If you aren't willing to join the underground economy, where are you going to get the money to dress yourself, go out on the town, and do the other things teens throughout the middle class do on Mom and Dad's sufferance? Most of Harlem's youth cannot rely on their parents' financial support to meet these needs. Indeed, this is one of the primary pressures that pushes young people out into the labor market in the first place, and at an early age. Most workers we interviewed had their first job by the age of fourteen.

What Brian does, then, is to best his mates at their own game by showing them that he has the wherewithal to be a consumer, based on his own earnings. He derives no small amount of pleasure from turning these tables, upending the status system by outdoing his friends on style grounds they value as much as he does.

It might be comforting to suggest that these hard-working low-wage workers were, from the very beginning, different from their nonworking counterparts, equipped somehow to withstand the gauntlet of criticism that comes their way when they start out on the bottom of the labor market. It would be comforting because we would then be able to sort the deserving, admirable poor (who recognize the fundamental value of work and are willing to ignore stigma) from the undeserving (who collapse in the face of peer pressure and therefore prefer to go on the dole). This is too simplistic. Burger Barn workers of all ages and colors fully admit that their employment is the butt of jokes

and that it has subjected them to ridicule. Some, like Larry Peterson, argue that they don't care what other people think, but even these brave souls admit that it took a long time for them to build up this confidence.

Where, then, does the confidence come from? How do ghetto residents develop the rejoinders that make it possible to recapture their dignity in the face of peer disapproval? To some degree, they can call on widely accepted American values that honor working people, values that float in the culture at large.[10] But this is not enough to construct a positive identity when the reminders of low status—coming from customers, friends, and the media—are abundant. Something stronger is required: a workplace culture that actively works to overcome the negatives by reinforcing the value of the work ethic. Managers and veteran employees on the shop floor play a critical role in the reinforcement process by counseling new workers distressed by bad-mouthing.

Kimberly Sampson, a twenty-year-old African-American woman, began working at Burger Barn when she was sixteen and discovered firsthand how her "friends" would turn on her for taking a low-wage job. Fortunately, she found a good friend at work who steadied her with a piece of advice:

> Say it's a job. You are making money. Right? Don't care what nobody say. You know? If they don't like it, too bad. They sitting on the corner doing what they are doing. You got to work making money. You know? Don't bother with what anybody has to say about it.

Kim's advisor, a workplace veteran who had long since come to terms with the insults of his peers, called upon a general status hierarchy that places the working above the nonworking as a bulwark against the slights. His point was later echoed by Kim's manager in the course of a similar episode, as she explained:

> Kids come in here . . . they don't have enough money. I'll be like, "You don't have enough money; you can't get [the food you ordered]." One night this little boy came in there and cursed me out. He [said], "That's why you are working at Burger Barn. You can't get a better job. . . ."
>
> I was upset and everything. I started crying. [My manager] was like, "Kim, don't bother with him. I'm saying, *you got a job*. You know. It is a *job*."

Absorbing this defensive culture is particularly important for immigrant workers in Harlem who often find fast-food jobs the first venue where they have sustained interaction with African-Americans who resent the fact that they have jobs at all, much less jobs in their community. Marisa Gonzalez, a native of Ecuador, had a very difficult time when she first began working as a hostess at Burger Barn. A pretty, petite nineteen-year-old, she was selected for the job because she has the kind of sparkle and vivaciousness that any restaurant would want customers to see. But some of her more antagonistic black customers saw her as an archetype: the immigrant who barely speaks a word of English who snaps up a job some native-born English speaker ought to have. Without the support of her bilingual, Latino manager, she would not have been able to pull herself together and get on with the work:

> I wasn't sent to the grill or the fries [where you don't need to communicate with customers]. I was sent to the cash register, even though the managers knew I couldn't speak English. That was only one week after my arrival in the United States! So I wasn't feeling very well at all. Three weeks later I met

a manager who was Puerto Rican. He was my salvation. He told me, "Marisa, it's not that bad." He'd speak to me in English, even though he knows Spanish. He'd tell me, "Don't cry. Dry off those tears. You'll be all right, you'll make it." So he encouraged me like no other person in that Burger Barn, especially when the customers would curse at me for not knowing English. He gave me courage and after that it went much better.

Among the things this manager taught Marisa was that she should never listen to people who give her a hard time about holding a job at Burger Barn. Having been a white-collar clerical worker in her native country, it did bother Marisa that she had slipped down the status hierarchy—and it still does. She was grateful, nevertheless, to have a way to earn money and her family was desperate for her contribution. When customers would insult her, insinuating that someone who speaks limited English was of lowly status, she turned to management for help. And she found it in the form of fellow Latino bosses who told her to hold her head up because she was, after all, working, while her critics on the whole were not.

Once these general moral values are in place, many Burger Barn workers take the process one step further: they argue their jobs have hidden virtues that make them more valuable than most people credit. Tiffany Wilson, the young black woman who reluctantly settled for a Burger Barn job when none of the clothing stores she wanted to work for would take her, decided in the end that there was more substance to her job than she credited initially:

> When I got in there, I realized it's not what people think. It's a lot more to it than flipping burgers. It's a real system of business. That's when I really got to

see a big corporation at play. I mean, one part of it, the foundation of it: cashiers, the store, how it's run. Production of food, crew workers, service. Things of that nature. That's when I really got into it and understood a lot more.

Americans tend to think of values as embedded in individuals, transmitted through families, and occasionally reinforced by media images or role models. We tend not to focus on the powerful contribution that institutions and organizations make to the creation and sustenance of beliefs. Yet it is clear that the workplace itself is a major force in the creation of a rebuttal culture among these workers. Without this line of defense it would be very hard for Burger Barn employees to retain their dignity. With the support of fellow workers, however, they are able to hold their heads up, not by defining themselves as separate from society, but by calling upon the values they hold in common with the rest of the working world.

This is but one of the reasons why exclusion from the society of the employed is such a devastating source of social isolation. We could hand people money, as various guaranteed income plans of the past thirty years have suggested. But we can't hand out honor. For a majority of Americans, honor comes from participation in this central setting in our culture and from the positive identity it confers.

Franklin Roosevelt understood this during the Great Depression and responded with the creation of thousands of publicly funded jobs designed to put people to work building the national parks, the railway stations, the great highways that criss-cross the country, and the murals that decorate public walls from San Francisco to New York. Social scientists studying the unemployed in the 1930s showed convincingly that people who held WPA jobs were far happier and healthier than those who were on the dole, even when their incomes did not differ significantly. WPA workers had their dignity in the midst of poverty; those on the dole were vilified and could not justify their existence or find an effective cultural rationale for the support they received.

This historical example has its powerful parallels in the present. Joining the workforce is a fundamental, transforming experience that moves people across barriers of subculture, race, gender, and class. It never completely eradicates these differences and in some divisive settings it may even reinforce consciousness of them—through glass ceilings, discriminatory promotion policies, and the like. But even in places where pernicious distinctions are maintained, there is another, overarching identity competing with forms that stress difference: a common bond within the organization and across the nation of fellow workers. This is what makes getting a job so much more than a means to a financial end. It becomes a crucial developmental hurdle, especially for people who have experienced exclusion before, including minorities, women, the elderly, and teenagers. Any experience that can speak back to the stigma that condemns burger flippers as the dregs, resurrecting them as exemplars of the American work ethic, has extraordinary power.

Those who choose to earn a living in the legitimate job market receive few material rewards for their effort, but they can claim moral legitimacy from the traditional American work ethic. They can't flash large rolls of cash before the eyes of their neighbors, but they can pride themselves on "doing the right thing," avoiding the dangers of the drug trade and the sloth of welfare recipients. While they understand that some people have a legitimate need to receive government assistance, they don't see the payoff of dealing drugs, and this in not an opinion they keep to themselves. Workers with friends or family in the drug trade often implore them to get out, warning them of the dangers, and reasoning that they each make about the same amount of money in a week, while the one involved with drugs has to work longer hours.

Nadine Stevens has worked at Burger Barn since graduating from high school five years ago. By all accounts she lives in one of the most dangerous neighborhoods in Harlem. Her apartment building is the home of an active drug trade and, indeed, the mailboxes were recently removed from the building by police because they were being used for drug transactions. She knows most of the drug dealers who sit on her stoop every day and night, having grown up with them. She and her mother and sister, whose ground-floor apartment faces the street, have seen many young women they know wasted by drugs, and young men killed in their hallway.

Nadine tries to convince the dealers she knows to get out of the trade, and to shoot for getting into management at Burger Barn. She and her sister, Rachael, with whom she works at Burger Barn, recently accosted a young teen they knew on the street whom they suspected of drug running. They told her that if she was desperate for money they'd get her a job at Burger Barn. Sensing the girl's reluctance, Nadine cried, "There's no shame in my game! Come work with me."

The dealers they know argue that the Burger Barn employee is working in a poorly paid, demeaning job and that, furthermore, they couldn't get hired there if they tried. Although their work is dangerous, illegal, and despised by neighbors, they brandish the accoutrements of success glorified in the United States: expensive cars, stylish clothes, and lots of cash. Their honor is measured in dollars, a common American standard that competes for the attention of people otherwise destined to earn little more than the minimum wage.

Anthony Vallo has had to choose on which side of the law to work and, once he secured his Burger Barn job, had to decide what to do about his friends and acquaintances who chose the wrong side. Two of his best friends are in jail. Another friend is dealing drugs and probably isn't far from a jail term himself. What Anthony does is try to maintain a cordial relationship with these guys, but to put as much distance between himself and them as he can without giving offense:

> This friend of mine is selling and stuff like that, but he's my friend. We used to go to school back then. He was like, "Damn, you still doin' that Burger Barn shit? I can get you a real job!" I think he respects me; at least he don't criticize me behind my back. But I try to avoid him, you know.

Drug dealers are not the only problem cases with which Harlem workers must contend. At least until welfare reform began to force women on AFDC back into the labor force, many young mothers working low-wage jobs were faced with the fork in the road that led either to a job at a place like Burger Barn or public assistance. Since most know a fair number of women who have elected, or had no choice but to opt for, the latter, it takes no small amount of fortitude to go for a minimum-wage job.[11] Indeed, given that AFDC offered greater financial benefits—when health coverage, food stamps, and subsidized housing are part of the package—than these jobs provide, it takes a strong attachment to the work ethic and a willingness to sacrifice elements of one's financial well-being in favor of the dignity that goes with holding a real job.

The Importance of Going to Work

Although having a well-paid, respected career is prized above all else in the United States, our culture confers honor on those who hold down jobs of any kind over those who are outside of the labor force. Independence and self-sufficiency—these are virtues that have no equal in this society. But there are other reasons why we value workers besides the fact that their earnings keep them above water and therefore less in need of help from government, communities, or charities. We also value workers because they share certain common views, experiences, and expectations. The work ethic is more than an attitude toward earning money—it is a disciplined existence, a social life woven around the workplace.

For all the talk of "family values," we know that in the contemporary period, family often takes a backseat to the requirements of a job, even when the job involves flipping burgers. What we are supposed to orient toward primarily is the workplace and its demands. This point could not be made more forcefully than it is in the context of the welfare reform bills of 1996. Public policy in the late 1990s makes clear that poor women are now supposed to be employed even if they have young children.[12] With a majority of women with children, even those under a year of age, in the labor force, we are not prepared to cut much slack to those who have been on welfare. They can and should work like the rest of us, or so the policy mantra goes. This represents no small change in the space of a few decades in our views of what honorable women and mothers should do. But it also reflects the growing dominance of work in our understanding of adult priorities.

We could think of this increasingly work-centered view of life as a reflection of America's waning economic position, a pragmatic response to wage stagnation, downsizing, and international competition: we must work harder. And this it may be. But it is also part of a secular transformation that has been ongoing for decades as we've moved away from home-centered work lives in the agricultural world to employment-centered lives outside the domestic sphere altogether. The more work departs from home, the more it becomes a social system of its own, a primary form of integration that rivals the family as a source of identity, belonging, and friendship. Women like Antonia Piento are not content only to take care of children at home. They want a life that is adult centered, where they have peers they can talk to. Where they might once have found that company in the neighborhood, now they are more likely to find it on the shop floor. Those primary social ties are grounded in workplace relations, hence to be a worker is also to be integrated into a meaningful community of fellow workers, the community that increasingly becomes the source of personal friends, intimate relations and the world view that comes with them.

Work is therefore much more than a means to a financial end. This is particularly the case when the work holds little intrinsic satisfaction. No one who gets paid for boiling french fries in hot oil thinks they are playing a world-shattering role. They know their jobs are poorly valued; they can see that in their paychecks, in the demeanor of the people whom they serve across the counter, even among some managers. But what they have that their nonworking counterparts lack is both the dignity of being employed and the opportunity to participate in a social life that increasingly defines their adult lives. This community gives their lives structure and purpose, humor and pleasure, support and understanding in hard times, and a backstop that extends beyond the instrumental purposes of a fast-food restaurant. It is the crucible of their values, values that we have argued here are decidedly mainstream.

The working poor sit at the bottom of the occupational structure and feel the weight of disapproval coming down upon their shoulders from better paid, more respectable employees. Yet they stand at the top of another pyramid and can look down the slope toward people they know well who have taken another pathway in the world.

NOTES

The research for this chapter was made possible by generous grants from the Russell Sage, Ford, Rockefeller, Spencer, and William T. Grant Foundations. A revised version of this chapter appears in Newman 1999.

1. See Michèle Lamont's chapter in this volume for an analysis of the way working-class men bolster their self-worth by evaluating individuals according to moral criteria such as honesty and self-reliance rather than by socioeconomic characteristics like income and education. They may sit below the elite in this country based on standards of wealth, power, and education, but they see themselves as sitting atop another hierarchy, a moral one, which they consider most important.
2. There are further shades of gray below the line of the employed that distinguish those who are searching for work and those who have accepted their fate as nonworkers, with the latter suffering the greatest stigma of all.
3. For more on the moral structure associated with work and achievement of the American dream, see Hochschild 1995.
4. See Wilson 1996, Massey and Denton 1993, Hacker 1992, and Urban Institute 1991.
5. All names and identifying information have been changed to protect confidentiality.
6. Hochschild 1983 documents similar attempts in the airline industry. One airline holds a mandatory seminar for flight attendants to teach them "anger-desensitization" when dealing with rude and demeaning customers.

7. In areas experiencing exceptionally tight labor markets—including much of the Midwest in the late 1990s—wages for these jobs are climbing above the minimum-wage line.
8. This is one of the many reasons why increasing the minimum wage is so important. Ghettos have such impoverished job bases to begin with that they are almost always characterized by slack labor markets. Only when the labor supply outside ghetto walls has tightened down to almost impossible levels do we begin to see this tide lift inner-city boats. Eventually employers do turn to the workers who are low on their preference queues (as we learned in the 1980s during the Massachusetts miracle), but these conditions are, sadly, rare and generally short-lived.
9. Indeed, over a five-month period in 1993 there were fourteen job applicants for every job opening at two different Burger Barns in Harlem (Newman and Lennon 1995).
10. The fact that Harlem residents rejected for these jobs hold these values is some evidence for the preexisting nature of this mind-set—although these rejects had already piled up work experience that may have contributed to the sharpening of this alternative critique.
11. It should be noted that women on welfare and women in low-wage jobs are not necessarily two distinct groups. Many women find it necessary to go back and forth between holding a low-wage job and relying solely on welfare, and many supplement one form of income with the other (not to mention other income from friends, family, and unreported work), since neither source alone provides enough money to support a family (see Edin 1994).
12. As Jane Mansbridge mentions in her chapter discussing race, activism, and the evolution of feminist ideas in this volume, this expectation is nothing new for many black women. Julia Wrigley indicates the same thing in her discussion of the historic relationship between black domestic workers and white employers in this volume.

REFERENCES

ANDERSON, ELIJAH. 1990. *Streetwise*. Chicago: University of Chicago Press.

EDIN, KATHRYN. 1994. "The Myths of Dependency and Self-Sufficiency: Women, Welfare, and

Low-Wage Work." Unpublished paper. Department of Sociology and Center for Urban Policy Research, Rutgers University.

HACKER, ANDREW. 1992. *Two Nations.* New York: Ballantine.

HOCHSCHILD, ARLIE. 1983. *The Managed Heart.* Berkeley: University of California Press.

HOCHSCHILD, JENNIFER L. 1995. *Facing Up to the American Dream.* Princeton: Princeton University Press.

KATZ, MICHAEL. 1989. *The Undeserving Poor.* New York: Pantheon.

MASSEY, DOUGLAS S., and NANCY A. DENTON. 1993. *American Apartheid.* Cambridge: Harvard University Press.

NEWMAN, KATHERINE S. 1999. *No Shame in My Game: The Working Poor in the Inner City.* New York: Knopf/Russell Sage Foundation.

NEWMAN, KATHERINE S., and CHAUNCY LENNON. 1995. "The Job Ghetto." *American Prospect,* summer, 66–67.

URBAN INSTITUTE. 1991. *Opportunities Denied, Opportunities Diminished.* Report 91–9. Washington: Urban Institute Press.

WALLER, MAUREEN. 1996. "Redefining Fatherhood: Paternal Involvement, Masculinity, and Responsibility in the 'Other America.'" Ph.D. diss., Princeton University.

WILSON, WILLIAM JULIUS. 1996. *When Work Disappears.* New York: Knopf.

25

"WE'D LOVE TO HIRE THEM BUT . . ."
The Meaning of Race for Employers

Kathryn M. Neckerman • Joleen Kirschenman

Questions to Consider

Like the reading before it, this article examines the dynamics of race and class in the labor market. How do employers use cultural and social markers to exclude certain racial groups from employment? Why is it that written skill tests, rather than employers just using interviews, result in more blacks being hired at the firms investigated by Neckerman and Kirschenman?

Employers and black job applicants encounter one another in a specific context of race and class relations. Widespread publicity, emphasizing poor schools, drug use, crime, and welfare dependency, shapes the way city residents view the inner city and whom they associate with it. These perceptions shade the relations between black and white, middle class and poor, sometimes engendering suspicion, resentment, and misunderstanding (Anderson 1990).

Given the uncertainty that characterizes most hiring decisions, it is likely that these perceptions and strained relations influence employers' hiring practices. For instance, employers might recruit selectively in order to avoid inner-city residents because of expectations that they would be poor employees. Race and class misunderstanding or tension might be manifest in the job interview itself. If hiring practices are largely subjective, the influence of these perceptions about the inner city may be even more influential than would otherwise be the case.

Using data from interviews with Chicago employers, we examine employers' hiring strategies and consider their potential for racial bias. We focus on three hiring practices: selective recruitment, job interviews, and employment tests. We examine employers' views of different categories of workers and the way these preconceptions guide their recruitment strategies, and then discuss employers' accounts of job interviews with inner-city blacks. Finally, we examine the relationship between employment testing and black representation in entry-level jobs. The research is exploratory. We cannot provide rigorous evidence about the extent of racial bias. However, our interview data lend themselves to a fine-grained description of patterns of racial bias in hiring strategies. The description can serve as the basis for future empirical work on the employment problems of disadvantaged minorities.

Kathryn Neckerman and Joleen Kirschenman, "Hiring Strategies, Racial Bias, and Inner-City Workers" from *Social Problems*, Vol. 38, No. 4, Nov. 1991, pp. 433–447. Copyright © 1991 by The Regents of the University of California. Reprinted by the permission of University of California Press Journals: www.ucpress.edu.

While there has been sustained interest in the high joblessness of blacks in the United States, most research considers skill deficiencies or spatial mismatches in labor supply and demand rather than barriers to employment that exist in the hiring process. To the extent that research examines access to jobs, most studies focus on the use of networks in filling lower-skilled positions and on inner-city blacks' lack of access to job networks (Braddock and McPartland 1987, Wilson 1987). The following survey of the literature examines the hiring process in more detail and explores how racial bias might occur at different points, from recruitment of the applicant pool to screening and interviewing.

Selective Recruitment and Racial Bias

Employers' recruitment practices are influenced by many considerations, including cost and time. For instance, employers use personal networks to recruit because they are inexpensive and fast. Small firms, lacking elaborate personnel offices, are especially likely to use informal networks, while larger firms are more likely to supplement networks with recruitment through classified ads and other formal sources.

Because screening applicants is costly, employers have an incentive to recruit selectively, excluding potential applicants they view as unpromising. Selective recruitment might be based on "statistical discrimination" or the use of nonproductive characteristics such as race to predict productive characteristics that are more difficult to observe (Aigner and Cain 1977, Bielby and Baron 1986, Phelps 1972, Thurow 1975). Employers' expectations about the productivity of different groups may be influenced by past experience, prejudice, or the mass media. Selective recruitment might also, of course, be motivated by a "taste" for discrimination or a reluctance to hire, work with, or be served by members of a particular group (Becker 1957).

Previous research suggests that employers recruit selectively based on race, ethnicity, class, and neighborhood. Of these categories, race and ethnicity have received the most attention, and empirical research has documented less favorable treatment of black and Hispanic job applicants (e.g., Braddock and McPartland 1987, Cross et al. 1990, Culp and Dunson 1986). But employers also share the larger society's perceptions of the "underclass," associating crime, illiteracy, drug use, and poor work ethic with the inner-city black population. Thus, they may look for indicators of class and "space," or neighborhood of reference, among black workers (Kirschenman and Neckerman 1991). Studies find that employers evaluate the educational credentials and references of blacks differently depending on whether applicants are from the central city or the suburbs (Crain n.d.; see also Braddock et al. 1986). Other employers confound race, class, and "space," generalizing their negative perceptions of lower-class or inner-city workers to all black applicants (Kirschenman and Neckerman 1991).

Race Bias in the Job Interview

Almost all employers select new employees by using job interviews, usually in combination with other bases for screening such as test scores, work experience, references, and credentials. Job interviews are widely used despite psychological research showing little correlation between interviewer ratings of job applicants and measured skills or job performance.

Research on white-black interaction suggests that prejudice or cultural misunderstanding create difficulties for blacks, especially lower-class blacks who interview with white employers. While classic racism—the view of people of color as undifferentiated—has declined, race relations between strangers are often tense and shaded with fear, suspicion, and moral contempt (Blauner 1989; see also Anderson 1990). Those from different racial or ethnic groups lack the common experiences and conversation patterns that ease interaction in impersonal settings (Erickson 1975). Blacks and whites often misread each others' verbal and nonverbal cues (Kochman 1983). These misunderstandings are exacerbated when class as well as race separates people (Berg forthcoming, Glasgow 1981).

In research on employment interviews, race itself typically has little or no effect on interviewers' ratings, but race is significantly associated with interviewer ratings of nonverbal cues such as facial expression, posture, and certain aspects of voice that are known to influence employers (Arvey 1979, Parsons and Liden 1984). In one field study, for instance, black job applicants were rated significantly less favorably than whites on posture, voice articulation, voice intensity, and eye contact (Parsons and Liden 1984). Behavior or language seen as inappropriate also lowered interviewer ratings of objective characteristics such as education and experience (Hollenbeck 1984).

Race Bias in Employment Testing

Employment tests have been used for decades to measure general aptitude and specific job skills. Testing is used in hiring for perhaps one out of four high-school-level positions, with tests more common in the public sector and less common in unionized firms (Braddock and McPartland 1987, Cohen and Pfeffer 1986, Hamilton and Roessner 1972). Estimates of test validity vary. A recent meta-analysis of studies of the General Aptitude Test Battery (GATB), a widely used test of cognitive and psychomotor skills, estimated a .19 correlation between test scores and job performance (Hartigan and Wigdor 1989).

Racial bias in hiring stemming from the use of employment tests has been a long-standing concern. In 1971, the *Griggs v. Duke Power* decision required that if employment tests or other apparently neutral means of screening were shown to have an adverse impact on the hiring of protected groups, the firm must demonstrate that the test is job-related. Employers have found it difficult to validate general aptitude tests to the courts' satisfaction and have lost most testing cases since 1971 (Burstein and Pitchford 1990). However, this litigation stimulated the research on test validation. The meta-analysis cited above found that the correlation between test scores and job performance ratings was lower for minority employees than for nonminority employees but that on average test scores did not underpredict minority job performance (Hartigan and Wigdor 1989). Tests of skills such as typing are more easily validated and have not been open to the same legal challenges.

Most research on employment testing simply compares test scores to job performance rather than comparing testing to other means of employee selection. Yet if employers do not test applicants, they may rely more heavily on selective recruitment or on subjective impressions in the job interview. Thus, even if tests introduced some racial bias, subjective means of screening might disadvantage minority applicants more. For instance, if employers base hiring decisions on their preconceptions about inner-city schools rather than on tests of individual job applicants, then *all* graduates of those schools might be screened out. This hypothesis is consistent with other research suggesting that formal job search methods work better for blacks than informal methods because the formal methods provide more objective criteria by which employers can evaluate job applicants (Holzer 1987).

The Chicago Employer Survey

Our research is based on face-to-face interviews with 185 employers in Chicago and the surrounding Cook County. The sample was stratified by location, industry, and size, and firms were sampled in proportion to the distribution of employment in Cook County.[1] Inner-city firms were oversampled. Unless otherwise specified, all descriptive statistics presented here are weighted to adjust for oversampling in the inner city. As no comprehensive list exists of Chicago-area employers, the sampling frame was assembled from two directories of Illinois businesses, supplemented with the telephone book for categories of firms underrepresented in the business directories. The field period lasted from July 1988 to March 1989, and yielded a completion rate of 46 percent. In terms of industry and size, the completed sample's weighted distribution roughly matches the distribution of employment in Cook County.[2]

Our initial contacts and the majority of interviews themselves were conducted with the highest ranking official at the sampled establishment. The interviewers and respondents were not matched by race with the

---

[1] Given our focus on employment opportunities, the purpose of the design was to yield a sample that approximately matched the distribution of employment in Cook County. For instance, if 5 percent of Cook County jobs were in large, inner-city manufacturing firms, then 5 percent of the interviews should be in large, inner-city manufacturing firms. The sample necessarily underrepresents small *firms,* but does so in order to gain a more representative picture of employment opportunities.

[2] About 22 percent of employers we contacted refused to take part. We did not have the resources to pursue all potential respondents who were willing to be interviewed. Halfway through the field period, we set a minimum 40 percent completion rate in all industry-by-location categories and stopped pursuing unresolved cases in categories with completion rates higher than 40 percent. Response rates by industry, firm size, and location were monitored, and special efforts were made to pursue cases in categories with low completion rates.

respondents. All of the interviewers were non-Hispanic white; 8.5 percent of the respondents were black, 1.5 percent were Hispanic, and the remainder were non-Hispanic white.

The interview schedule included both closed- and open-ended questions about employers' hiring and recruitment practices and about their perceptions of Chicago's labor force and business climate. Because of the many open-ended questions, we taped the interviews. Item nonresponse varied depending on the sensitivity and factual difficulty of the question, with most nonresponse due to lack of knowledge rather than refusal to answer. In addition, the length and detail of responses to open-ended questions varied widely. Some employers volunteered additional information in response to closed-ended questions, which provided useful context for interpretation of the survey results.

Most closed-ended questions focused on the "sample job," defined as the most typical entry-level position in the firm's modal category—sales, clerical, skilled, semi-skilled, unskilled, or service. Entry-level jobs were selected for study in order to focus on the employment of disadvantaged workers, many of whom are first-time job seekers with limited skills. Because we sampled firms by industry and size, we do not have a random sample of entry-level jobs. However, when we compared the occupational distribution of our sample jobs to that of Cook County (excluding professional, managerial, and technical categories), we found that the two distributions were quite similar. The sample job serves as the unit of analysis for the quantitative part of this research. In the text, employers are categorized based on these sample jobs.

The interview schedule included several questions that bear on issues of hiring strategies and racial bias. We asked closed-ended questions about the race and ethnicity of employees in the sample job, as well as about

use of various recruitment sources, the importance of specific hiring criteria, and any credentials or skills required for the sample job. Additionally, in the context of a general discussion of the quality of the work force and of inner-city problems, we asked employers to comment on the high unemployment rates of inner-city black men and women and on any differences they saw between immigrant and native-born workers and among black, white, and Hispanic workers. . . .

Hiring Strategies and Racial Bias

During the time of the survey, the main problem most employers faced was not quantity of job applicants, but "quality." Employers complained that Chicago's work force lacked both basic skills and job skills. They were also dissatisfied with work attitudes, with many saying that employees were not as loyal and hard-working as they once were. Also, employers' traditional ways of getting information about job applicants had become less useful. For example, respondents told us that a high school diploma was no longer a reliable indicator of good basic skills. In addition, the threat of lawsuits has made it increasingly difficult to get information from an applicant's previous employers.

In this context, careful screening has become both more important to employers and more difficult to do. To identify good workers, some employers screened applicants using skills tests, "integrity interviews," psychological profiles, and drug tests. Others tried to recruit selectively or used informal networks. Almost half of our respondents said that employee referrals were their best source of qualified applicants, and it has become more common for employers to pay recruitment bonuses to employees whose referrals are hired. One respondent estimated that he hired 80 percent of all employee referrals, compared to only 5 percent of all applicants attracted by a newspaper ad.

In the following sections, we examine the implications of these hiring strategies for black employment. We consider three ways of screening potential workers: selective recruitment, job interviews, and employment testing.

Selective Recruitment

More often than not, employers recruited selectively, limiting their search for job candidates rather than casting a wide net. Employers sometimes explained their recruitment strategies in terms of practicality, for instance the ease or low cost of using personal networks or the difficulty of screening the large numbers of applications yielded by newspaper ads. But far more often they said their recruitment strategies were intended to bring them better applicants. The criteria of applicant quality they expressed were formally race- and class-neutral, but the recruitment strategies designed to attract high-quality applicants were not. When employers targeted their recruitment efforts at neighborhoods or institutions, they avoided inner-city populations. In addition, selective recruiting was more widespread among employers in poor, black neighborhoods than among those located elsewhere. The perceptions that employers expressed of inner-city black workers are consistent with the interpretation that they avoid these applicants because on average they expect them to be lower-quality workers.

One way of screening the applicant pool is by not advertising job openings in the newspapers. More than 40 percent of our respondents did not use newspaper advertising for their entry-level jobs, and those who did place ads often did so as a last resort after employee networks had been unsuccessful. Moreover, about two-thirds of all city employers who advertised used neighborhood, suburban, or ethnic papers in addition to or instead of the metropolitan papers. Using neighborhood or ethnic papers (here, "local" papers) allowed employers to target particular populations, usually white, ethnic, or Hispanic. For instance, one downtown law firm advertised in white ethnic neighborhoods because its residents were believed to have a better work ethic. On the other hand, a few white-collar employers told us they advertised jobs in the *Defender*, a black newspaper, because of a commitment to minority hiring or simply to "keep the numbers in balance." In most cases we cannot identify the specific neighborhoods which employers targeted because respondents were not asked for this detailed information. But the effect of recruiting from local papers is evident from the survey. City employers who advertised only in local papers averaged 16 percent black in the sample job, compared to 32 percent black for those who advertised in the metropolitan papers.

Recruiting based on the quality or location of schools also provided employers with a way of screening. A downtown employer, for instance, believed that youth from suburban schools had better writing skills. Although the firm advertised over the entire metropolitan area, suburban resumes received more attention. When employers volunteered which schools they recruited from, it was usually Catholic schools and those from the city's white northwest side neighborhoods. One manufacturer posted ads at a Catholic school as well as at two of the city's magnet technical schools. A downtown bank recruited from three northwest side Catholic schools. Recruitment from Catholic schools selects white students disproportionately, but this form of recruitment was not necessarily seen in racial terms. Black Catholic school students were also viewed as more desirable employees than black public school students.

On the other hand, the state employment service and welfare programs which disproportionately refer inner-city blacks were associated with low-quality applicants, or in one respondent's words, "the dregs of the year." Neither agency screened adequately, most employers felt, and as a result tended to send inappropriate or unqualified applicants. A manufacturer who had hired white workers through Job Corps criticized the program, saying that none of them had worked out: "As a group I would be prejudiced against them." Another said:

Any time I've taken any recommendations from state agencies, city agencies, or welfare agencies I get really people who are not prepared to come to work on time, not prepared to see that a new job is carried through, that it's completed. I mean there just doesn't seem to be a work ethic involved in these people.

Most employers did not recruit through these agencies; only a third of all employers used the state employment agency, and 16 percent used welfare programs.

Employers in inner-city areas of the city were more likely than other employers to recruit selectively. For instance, they were less likely to recruit from schools or local newspapers. They tried to recruit the best of the local labor force by using labor market intermediaries such as informal networks or formal agencies to screen workers. As other research has shown, because blacks were seen as higher-risk employees, the recommendations and information provided by these intermediaries could be especially important for them (Coverdill 1990). One respondent attributed her firm's success with black workers to their heavy use of employee referrals. Another said employers were likely to be wary of a black man "unless he's got an 'in.'" A large southside

employer recruited local high school or college students and added, "It gets them in the door if they're children of university people we know."

Large inner-city employers were especially likely to use formal labor market intermediaries. An inner-city day labor agency was able to place many black workers although many clients preferred "carloads of Mexicans"; its manager attributed this success partly to a computerized record-keeping system:

Having so much detail on each individual employee allows us to record in their files good performance and bad performance, and we're therefore much more able to discriminate between good workers and bad, much more so than our competitors, who would just take anybody off the street, and because they can't really monitor somebody's performance, why take a risk? Whereas we're in a position to take a risk, because if the person doesn't pan out, either he goes to a different job, or we tell him good-bye. . . . It's after they're on the payroll that you really do your screening.

An inner-city hospital developed a "feeder network" into nearby elementary and high schools, funding tutors, child care for teen mothers, and other educational assistance, and providing information about health care careers for those who went on to college. The hospital used its feeder system to "draw the best talent on the top to us. . . . They've already got the work ethic down, they've been dealing with both school and work, we also know what's going on with the schooling, the grades and all." The hospital also recruited staff through community jobs programs and employee networks, but not newspapers. "If you are just a cold applicant," the hospital's representative said, "chances of you getting in are almost nil."

Inner-city employers not large enough to develop these extensive screening mechanisms were at a disadvantage. One inner-city retailer said that young workers were disrespectful and prone to steal; she added, "I think I'm getting the best of what I've got to select from, and they're still no good. And other people in the same line of business say the same thing. I know the guy at the gas station, the guy who runs the Burger King, and all of us say the same thing." Even these smaller employers tried less elaborate means of screening. The retailer just cited recruited some employees through a youth mentoring program. A fast food manager sent prospective workers to a distant suburb for training as a way of selecting the most motivated.

The interviews suggest that selective recruitment designed to attract higher-quality applicants disproportionately screens out inner-city blacks. Employers' perceptions of inner-city black workers are consistent with the interpretation that at least some do this deliberately. "The blacks that are employed are just not as good, not that there aren't good blacks, but it's a smaller percent than it would be of whites, for whatever reasons, cultural things, or family background, whatever," said one respondent. . . . Employers were especially likely to say that inner-city blacks lacked the work ethic, had a bad attitude toward work, and were unreliable; they also expected them to lack skills, especially basic skills. About half said that these workers had a poor work ethic. In the words of employers: "they don't want to work," "they don't know how to work," "they cannot handle the simplest of tasks," and "they come late and leave early." About 40 percent said inner-city black workers had attitude problems, including a bad attitude toward work as well as apathy and arrogance: "They've got an attitude problem. They want to be catered to . . . they want it handed to them, they don't want to do anything." Another respondent said that black

men have a "chip on their shoulder; [they] resent being told what to do." One third of all employers said black workers tended to be undependable, "here today, gone tomorrow."

These perceptions of inner-city black workers are likely to underlie much of the selective recruitment discussed earlier. It is impossible for us to say whether employers avoid these applicants because of their race or their class, or for some other reason; race and class are so confounded in a setting like Chicago. But the effect of selective recruitment is to screen out disadvantaged black workers.

Social Interaction in the Job Interview

Virtually all employers interviewed job applicants, using these interviews to assess a wide range of qualities including literacy, values, common sense, integrity, dependability, intelligence, and character. Although they acknowledged the subjectivity of selection through interviews, they were confident their real world experience gave them the ability to spot good workers. The interview may take on particular importance for inner-city black applicants. Potentially, it is an arena in which they might overcome the negative images associated with their race or other markers such as neighborhood or school. One respondent described his bad experiences with black employees, but added that not all blacks were bad workers: "Well, you know when you talk to somebody you can tell a certain amount of something." Another noted that if she interviewed someone from the projects, "I would really spend a lot of time on prior work history and the types of things, the tasks that their job [requires]." These employers, and perhaps others, gave greater weight to the interview when applicants were poor or black.

Discussion of past work experience is generally an important aspect of the job interview. Searching for indications of dependability and willingness to work, employers said they probed reasons for gaps in applicants' work records. Unemployment itself did not disqualify an applicant with an acceptable excuse, such as illness or family responsibilities, and the interview provided a chance for an applicant to justify his or her work history.

In addition to relatively straightforward questions about work experience, employers often developed their own subjective "tests" of productivity and character. For instance, a manufacturer of transportation equipment asked if applicants had a "personal philosophy about work, a personal work ethic." Another manufacturer used the interview to judge "how the person looks at life, you know, is it what's in it for me or . . . is it a positive attitude." Much depended on the "gut reaction" of the employer. When one respondent was hired, she described how she and the recruiter "just clicked. I had the stuff, but also we just, just clicked. It's real important." Many paid attention to how expressive or open an applicant was. A law firm supervisor scorned the textbook job interview methods, saying what mattered to her was how "casual, frank, and honest" people were. A real estate developer looked for "someone that appears to sit up straight, talk expressively . . . [who] appears to be intelligent, articulate, forthcoming with their answers—you don't have to drag every word out of them." A hotelier, looking for desk clerks who could handle stress, said "I think you can determine that from how forthright they are in the interview."

Complicating interaction during the job interview is many employers' distrust of job applicants in general, and perhaps minority applicants in particular. Employers complained that some applicants lied about their work record and skills. Lying on applications was one common reason for rejecting applicants at a security firm: "Well, you know, you lied about your driver's license. They have previously been suspended or a couple of your references said they don't even know you or you said you went to a certain school, you didn't go to this particular school." A clerical employer complained, "They'll come in, say they type 50, 60 words a minute, and you put them on a typewriter and they type 20. Or they'll say they have computer experience, and then it turns out they don't know what a cursor is." Another said, "They've gotten to be so good at conning people that it's just frightening." Such falsification was mentioned more often by employers who saw many minority applicants, and one respondent said that black men were more likely to falsify their applications.

Other research suggests that inner-city black applicants experience difficulty in job interview interactions, and indeed, we heard some explicit criticisms of how inner-city blacks interview. Most common were complaints about applicants dressed in shabby or inappropriate clothing or coming late to interviews. But some respondents said more generally that inner-city blacks, especially men, did not know how to interview: they "aren't prepared; they don't have the enthusiasm"; they were belligerent or had "a chip on their shoulder"; they didn't know dates of employment or provided inconsistent information. One respondent commented that black men were not willing to "play the game" and to "follow the rules."

Our question about whether employers might be wary of poor people or those from the projects drew similar responses: applicants from a poor neighborhood did not know how to present themselves. A manufacturer said that project residents would be favorably evaluated if they had a positive attitude, but that they were not well equipped to "come in and really sell themselves." A clerical employer commented. "You don't need to look at the address to know where they're from; it's how people come across; they don't know how to behave in an office." A number of respondents remarked on cultural differences between inner-city blacks and the middle-class whites who dominate in business settings. Inner-city residents come from "a different world," said one manufacturer; "we don't realize that their rules are very different than ours."

It is obvious that job interviews are biased in favor of people who are friendly and articulate. But we find evidence that interviewing well goes beyond interpersonal skills to common understandings of appropriate interaction and conversational style—in short, shared culture. Job applicants must be sensitive to verbal and non-verbal cues and to the hidden agenda underlying interviewers' questions. They may be called upon to talk about abstract matters such as philosophy of work. And in discussing their past work experience, potentially an awkward subject for inner-city applicants with few previous jobs, they must be forthcoming and honest. Because inner-city blacks have trouble with this interaction, heavy reliance on the interview to assess qualities such as honesty, intelligence, reliability, and so on is likely to disadvantage them.

Skills Tests and Black Representation

About 40 percent of the Chicago employers used formal skills tests to screen for the sample job. It is likely that this high incidence of testing is associated with city employers' distrust of the Chicago public school system and the quality of the city labor force. Only 30 percent of suburban firms in our survey used skills tests. Use of formal skills tests was much more common among clerical employers than among anyone else. More than half of all white-collar employers used conventional tests, measuring skills such as

language, spelling, composition, math, typing, and filing speed. The clerical tests ranged from standard typing tests to "matching words in columns and seeing whether they know their ABCs" for filing.

Blue-collar employers also gave tests, most often informally. Skilled and craft employers often asked prospective employees to name tools or perform a given task. A precision tool manufacturer thought certification was helpful, "But most everything's going to come out on the test anyway; no matter what kind of paper people bring in, when he sets them up out there and they make the piece, it'll show." Employers of semi-skilled or unskilled blue-collar workers often screened for basic skills informally, observing how well employees filled out job applications; a few required a high school diploma as a proxy for literacy. Some had simple tests embedded in job application forms. A transportation employer described his firm's hiring process: "They fill out an application, which includes a little test—see whether they can read, write, and add." Another employer "sit[s] them down at a machine, [to] see how well they can do."

When employers have relatively objective means of getting information about job candidates, we would expect them to place less weight on more subjective and presumably more racially-biased hiring strategies. . . .

Chicago employers who test for skills, either formally or informally, tend to have higher proportions of blacks in the sample job than employers who do not test. These findings must be interpreted cautiously because there are alternative explanations for which we could not adequately test. For instance, it is possible that these employers test for skills because they attract more black applicants. It might also be that their hiring criteria differ from those of employers who do not test. However, our results suggest the need for future research to address these issues.

. . .

Our evidence suggests that negative preconceptions and strained race relations both hamper inner-city black workers in the labor market. Many respondents perceived inner-city black workers to be deficient in work ethic and work attitudes, as well as in skills. Employers commonly directed their recruitment to white neighborhoods and Catholic or magnet schools and avoided recruiting from city-wide newspapers and public agencies because they believed these recruiting strategies brought them better workers. By design or not, these practices excluded blacks disproportionately from their applicant pool.

The job interview could be an opportunity for inner-city black job applicants to counter these negative stereotypes. But inner-city black job seekers with limited work experience and little familiarity with the white, middle-class world are also likely to have difficulty in the typical job interview. A spotty work record will have to be justified; misunderstanding and suspicion may undermine rapport and hamper communication. However qualified they are for the job, inner-city black applicants are more likely to fail subjective "tests" of productivity given during the interview.

Finally, employers who use skills tests have on average a higher proportion of black workers in the sample job than employers who do not test. Again, our results do not indicate that skills tests involve no racial bias but simply that skills tests are less biased than more subjective means of assessing job applicants. It should be emphasized that the survey on which these results were based took place in the context of legal restrictions on the use of employment tests and in a particular social context. The findings may not be generalizable to the time before these legal restrictions were enacted, nor do they indicate the likely effects of lifting these restrictions.

Our study was restricted to entry-level jobs and excluded professional, managerial, and technical positions; therefore, our results cannot be generalized to higher-level positions or to promotion rather than hiring. It is possible that promotion decisions are less prone to racial bias because employers have more information about individual job performance and need not guess about productivity based on markers such as race or class. Consistent with this, one study shows that educational credentials are more influential in hiring than in promotion (Bills 1988). On the other hand, to the extent that higher-level positions require contact with clients, supervision of staff, or interaction with executive or professional personnel, then the hiring criteria are likely to emphasize social skills and cultural compatibility, and promotion decisions may be more subjective. More research will be needed to distinguish these two effects.

The ways some employers have adapted to increasing skill demands and declining labor force quality are not race- or class-neutral. By directing recruitment away from inner-city neighborhoods, employers may provide themselves with a higher-skilled applicant pool but at the expense of qualified inner-city applicants. Attention should be given to ways that inner-city residents can demonstrate their competence, whether through certification by schools, screening by labor market intermediaries, or more extensive testing by employers. If rewards are not forthcoming for those who do improve their educational and work skills, inner-city residents' motivation to get education and training is likely to diminish.

Although we have emphasized the role of racial bias in the hiring process, the findings of this study are consistent with other interpretations of inner-city residents' employment problems. Problems of skills mismatch are evident in employers' concern with "quality" not "quantity" of applicants.

Researchers' criticisms of the quality of ghetto schools are certainly echoed by employers. Finally, this work supports the emphasis others have given to job networks, suggesting that personal and institutional "connections" may be even more important in the inner city than they are elsewhere.

REFERENCES

AIGNER, DENNIS J., and GLEN C. CAIN. 1977. "Statistical Theories of Discrimination in the Labor Market." *Industrial and Labor Relations Review* 30:175–87.

ANDERSON, ELIJAH. 1990. *Streetwise: Race, Class, and Change in an Urban Community*. Chicago: University of Chicago Press.

ARVEY, RICHARD D. 1979. "Unfair Discrimination in the Employment Interview: Legal and Psychological Aspects." *Psychological Bulletin* 86:736–65.

BECKER, GARY S. 1957. *The Economics of Discrimination*. Chicago: University of Chicago Press.

BERG, LINNEA. Forthcoming. Ph.D. dissertation. Evanston, IL: Northwestern University.

BIELBY, WILLIAM T., and JAMES N. BARON. 1986. "Men and Women at Work: Sex Segregation and Statistical Discrimination." *American Journal of Sociology* 91:759–99.

BILLS, DAVID B. 1988. "Educational Credentials and Promotions: Does Schooling Do More Than Get You in the Door?" *Sociology of Education* 61:52–60.

BLAUNER, BOB. 1989. *Black Lives, White Lives: Three Decades of Race Relations in America*. Berkeley: University of California Press.

BRADDOCK, JOMILLS HENRY, II, and JAMES M. MCPARTLAND. 1987. "How Minorities Continue to Be Excluded from Equal Employment Opportunities: Research on Labor Market and Institutional Barriers." *Journal of Social Issues* 43:5–39.

BRADDOCK, JOMILLS HENRY, II, ROBERT L. CRAIN, JAMES M. MCPARTLAND, and R. L. DAWKINS. 1986. "Applicant Race and Job Placement Decisions: A National Survey Experiment." *International Journal of Sociology and Social Policy* 6:3–24.

BURSTEIN, PAUL, and SUSAN PITCHFORD. 1990. "Social-Scientific and Legal Challenges to Education and Test Requirements in Employment." *Social Problems* 37:243–57.

COHEN, YINON, and JEFFREY PFEFFER. 1986. "Organizational Hiring Standards." *Administrative Science Quarterly* 31:1–24.

COVERDILL, JAMES E. 1990. "Personal Contacts and Youth Employment." Unpublished manuscript. Evanston, IL: Northwestern University.

CRAIN, ROBERT L. n.d. "The Quality of American High School Graduates: What Personnel Officers Say and Do About It." Baltimore: Johns Hopkins University, Center for the Social Organization of Schools.

CROSS, HARRY, G. KEWNNEY, J. MELL, and W. ZIMMERMANN. 1990. *Employer Hiring Practices: The Differential Treatment of Hispanic and Anglo Job Seekers*. Washington, DC: Urban Institute Press, Report 90-4.

CULP, JEROME and BRUCE H. DUNSON. 1986. "Brothers of a Different Color: A Preliminary Look at Employer Treatment of White and Black Youth." Pp. 233–59 in *The Black Youth Employment Crisis*, edited by Richard B. Freeman and Harry J. Holzer. Chicago: University of Chicago Press.

ERICKSON, FREDERICK. 1975. "Gatekeeping and the Melting Pot: Interaction in Counseling Encounters." *Harvard Educational Review* 45:44–70.

GLASGOW, DOUGLAS G. 1981. *The Black Underclass: Poverty, Unemployment and Entrapment of Ghetto Youth*. New York: Vintage Press.

HAMILTON, GLORIA SHAW, and J. DAVID ROESSNER. 1972. "How Employers Screen Disadvantaged Job Applicants." *Monthly Labor Review* 95:14–21.

HARTIGAN, JOHN A., and ALEXANDRA K. WIGDOR, eds. 1989. *Fairness in Employment Testing: Validity Generalization, Minority Issues and the General Aptitude Test Battery*. Washington, DC: National Academy Press.

HOLLENBECK, KEVIN. 1984. *Hiring Decisions: An Analysis of Columbus Employer Assessments of Youthful Job Applicants*. Columbus: Ohio State University, National Center for Research on Vocational Education.

HOLZER, HARRY. 1987. "Informal Job Search and Black Youth Unemployment." *American Economic Review* 77:446–52.

KIRSCHENMAN, JOLEEN, and KATHRYN M. NECKERMAN. 1991. "We'd Love to Hire Them But . . .": The Meaning of Race to Employers." Pp. 203–32 in *The Urban Underclass*, edited by Christopher Jencks and Paul Peterson. Washington, DC: Brookings Institution.

KOCHMAN, THOMAS. 1983. *Black and White Styles of Conflict*. Chicago: University of Chicago Press.

Parsons, Charles, and Robert C. Liden. 1984. "Interviewer Perceptions of Applicant Qualifications: A Multivariate Field Study of Demographic Characteristics and Nonverbal Cues." *Journal of Applied Psychology* 69:557–68.

Phelps, Edmund. 1972. "The Statistical Theory of Racism and Sexism." *American Economic Review* 62:659–61.

Thurow, Lester. 1975. *Generating Inequality.* New York: Basic Books.

Turner, Margery Austin, Michael Fix, and Raymond J. Struyk. 1991. "Opportunities Denied, Opportunities Diminished: Discrimination in Hiring." Project report. Washington, DC: Urban Institute.

Wilson, William Julius. 1987. *The Truly Disadvantaged: The Inner City, the Underclass, and Public Policy.* Chicago: University of Chicago Press.

26

WHEN THE MELTING POT BOILS OVER
The Irish, Jews, Blacks, and Koreans of New York

Roger Waldinger

Questions to Consider

Roger Waldinger makes a number of astute observations about how racial and ethnic groups get sorted into certain occupations. How and in what ways does the historical timing of a group's entry into the United States— for example, the Irish, Jews, Italians, and Afro-Caribbeans—affect its economic and social mobility? How is it that one group will come to monopolize one trade or occupation? How are race, ethnicity, and control of local politics linked to upward mobility?

Assimilation is the grand theme of American immigration research. The classic sociological position provided an optimistic counter to the dim assessments of the new immigrants prevalent at the early part of the century. Notwithstanding the marked differences that impressed contemporaries, Robert Park, Ernest Burgess, W. I. Thomas, and others contended that the new immigrant groups would lose their cultural distinctiveness and move up the occupational hierarchy. Milton Gordon's now classic volume distilled the essence of the sociological view: immigrant-ethnic groups start at the bottom and gradually move up; their mobility takes place through individual advancement, not group collective action; in the process of moving up, ethnic groups lose their distinctive social structure; and as ethnics become like members of the core group, they become part of the core group, joining it in neighborhoods, in friendship, and eventually in marriage.

But the image of immigrants moving onward and upward is hard to reconcile with the darker, conflictual side of American ethnic life. Conflict, often of the fiercest kind, runs like a red thread through the history of American ethnic groups. Certainly New Yorkers evince an extraordinary propensity to come to blows over racial and ethnic differences. The latest conflicts pitting blacks against Hasidim and Koreans in Brooklyn or Chinese against Puerto Ricans in Manhattan are but the latest episodes in a longer saga, extending from the anti-Catholic crusades of the 1850s to the school conflicts of the 1890s, to the controversies engendered by the Coughlinites and the German Bund of the 1930s, to the school integration struggles of the 1960s, right up to this day.

The contradiction between ethnic assimilation and ethnic conflict is more apparent than real. Where the classic sociological model goes wrong is not in its depiction of an upward trajectory, but rather in its individualistic assumptions about the process of ethnic change. The story of ethnic progress in America can be better thought of as a collective search for mobility, in which the succession of one migrant wave after another ensures a continuous competitive conflict over resources. Groups move up from the bottom by specializing in and dominating a particular branch of economic life; that specialization goes unchallenged as long as the newest arrivals are content to work in the bottom-level jobs for which they were initially recruited. This [reading] develops the story in the form of brief episodes from the New York experience of four ethnic groups—Irish, Jews, African Americans, and Koreans. Each group is associated with the four successive waves of migration that have swept over New York in the past two hundred years.

The Irish

Nearly one and a half million Irish flocked to the United States between 1846 and 1855 in flight from famine; they converged on the eastern port cities of Boston, Philadelphia, and New York, where, lacking resources, about a quarter stayed. Low levels of education, lack of exposure to industrial or craft work, and lack of capital led the Irish into the lower ranges of manual work, with women taking domestic work and men engaging in insecure, low-paid itinerant employment, especially in construction. Irish progress from the bottom proceeded at a slow pace.

By 1900, however, the Irish had already established themselves in public employment. At the time, the public sector provided relatively few jobs, but this was soon to change. Irish employment in New York City government almost quadrupled between 1900 and 1930, increasing from just under 20,000 to 77,000, while the total number of city workers climbed from 54,000 to 148,000, less than a factor of three.[1]

Irish penetration into the public sector reflected the growing political power of the Democratic machine, which remained Irish dominated. But the machine's hold on local government was met by opposition from WASP reformers. Seeking to break the machine's power by severing the link between political activity and government employment, the reformers installed a civil service system—to little avail. The Irish encountered few effective competitors for city jobs. There was never any serious threat that WASPs would dislodge the Irish. Moreover, the increasingly numerous Poles, Jews, Italians, and others who were just off the boat had little chance of doing well in essay-type exams against the Irish, who were, after all, native English speakers.

The liabilities of the new immigrants lasted hardly a generation; with the Jews' rapid educational and occupational advancement, another competitor entered the scene. But as long as the Irish, through Tammany Hall's grip over city government, could control municipal hiring, interethnic competition posed little threat. Competition was structured in such a way as to minimize the value of Jews' educational advantages. The patronage system functioned unencumbered throughout Tammany's dominance between 1917 and 1933.

The depression severely challenged Irish control over public jobs; LaGuardia's election in 1933 delivered the coup de grace. Keeping control of City Hall required LaGuardia to undermine the material base of Tammany's power and consolidate his support among groups not firmly under Tammany's tow—the most important of which were the Jews, who had split between LaGuardia and his Tammany opponent in 1933. Both goals could be accomplished in the same way, namely pursuing the administrative changes long championed by the reformers.[2]

The depression and LaGuardia's reforms made city jobs more attractive to highly educated workers, which, under the circumstances, mainly meant Jews. One door at which Jewish competitors knocked was teaching, previously an Irish reserve (as the 1900 statistics show). If Jewish entrance into teaching produced antagonism, far more explosive was the situation in the police force. Twenty-nine thousand men sat for the exam held in April 1939, from whom three hundred were selected to enter the department in 1940. Of these, over one-third were Jews. Not surprisingly, this class of 1940 constituted the first significant proportion of Jews to enter the police.[3]

Jewish-Irish competition produced some other episodes, but conflict between them abated, thanks to the prosperity of the postwar era and the new opportunities it provided. Outmigration to the suburbs and the Sun Belt and mobility into the middle class depleted the ranks of the city's Irish population. By the late 1950s, as Nathan Glazer and Daniel Moynihan noted, so profound was the sense of displacement that the remaining Irish New Yorkers reminded themselves, "There are still some of us left."[4]

Those who are left have kept up the long-established Irish occupational ways. Although the commissioners of the police and fire departments are black and Puerto Rican, respectively, the top brass retains a strongly Irish cast, as does the rank and file. Indeed, the fire department presents a glimpse of New York gone by, with a workforce that is 93 percent white and 80 percent Catholic. Some unions still have a distinctly Irish makeup.[5]

In the 1980s, some of the old niches at last gained new blood, as an influx of new, illegal Irish immigrants fled unemployment in the Republic of Ireland for better times in New York. Whereas black Americans still found the doors of construction unions closed, the new arrivals, dubbed "JFK carpenters," were warmly welcomed by their aging compatriots. Women also retraced the steps of the past, as could be seen from the classified pages of the *Irish Echo*, with its columns of ads for nannies, babysitters, and housekeepers.

The Jews

Although the Jewish presence in New York extends far back, almost to the city's founding, Jews did not become an important, visible element in the city's economic life until the 1880s. Rising anti-Semitism, combined with the pressures of modernization, led to a huge outflow of Jews from Eastern Europe.

By 1920, New York, with two million Jews, had become the world's largest Jewish city.

The new arrivals came just when the demand for factory-made clothing began to surge. Many had been tailors in the old country, and although most had worked with needle and thread, they quickly adapted themselves to machine production. As the various components of the clothing industry grew in synergistic fashion, the opportunities for mobility through the ethnic economy multiplied. Through rags, some immigrants found riches; the sweatshop workers who moved to contracting and then to manufacturing, or possibly careers in retailing, filled the newly formed ranks of New York's *alrightniks*.[6]

The Jewish concentration in commerce and clothing manufacture defined their initial place in the ethnic division of labor. Jewish specializations seldom overlapped with the Irish: domestic service and general labor were rarities among the Russians but were common Irish pursuits; by the same token, tailoring and retailing, whether by merchant or peddler, were far more likely to engage Russians than Irish.

As Jews sought to move beyond the ethnic economy, interethnic competition and antagonism grew more intense. The relatively rapid educational progress of younger immigrants and of the second generation prepared them to work outside the ethnic economy, but gentile employers were rarely eager to hire Jews. One study, completed just before the Great Depression, found that the doors of New York's large, corporate organizations— "railroads, banks, insurance companies, lawyers' offices, brokerage houses, the New York Stock Exchange, hotels . . . and the home offices of large corporations of the first rank"—were infrequently opened to Jews.[7] The surge into the schools, and through the schools into the professions, met with resistance from the older, largely Protestant population that dominated these institutions.

In the 1930s, depression and discrimination outside the ethnic economy led many second-generation Jews to seek an alternative in public employment. Although the quest for government jobs, and in particular teaching positions, had started earlier, the straitened circumstances of the 1930s accelerated this search. The quality and quantity of Jews vying for government employment increased, heightening the competitive pressure on the Irish and yielding the antagonism we've already observed.

Jewish-Irish conflict reached its height in the late 1930s; it gradually subsided, replaced by a more explosive, deeply antagonistic relationship with blacks. Although black occupations were more similar to those of the Irish than they were to the Jews', the economic pursuits of Jews put them at odds with blacks on various counts. The Jews dominated small retail activity throughout the city and were particularly prominent in Harlem. The Jewish storeowners in Harlem sold to blacks but preferred not to employ them until protests in the mid-1930s finally forced them to relent. Antagonism toward Jewish shopkeepers in Harlem rose during the 1930s, fueled by the depression and by Jews' broader role as middlemen in the Harlem economy. Frustration boiled over in the riot of 1943, when black Harlemites burned down the stores of Jews in a fury that presaged events to come.[8] Hostility simmered thereafter, reaching the boiling point during the 1960s.

The transformation of the ethnic economy also engendered black-Jewish conflict, Rapid Jewish social mobility meant a dwindling Jewish working class; the diminishing supply of Jewish workers had a particularly notable effect on the garment industry, where Jewish factory owners were forced to hire outsiders in growing numbers—first Italians, then blacks. In World War II, desperate for workers, Jewish employers hired blacks in great numbers. By 1950, there were

25,000 African American garment workers, 20,000 more than were working in clothing factories ten years before.[9]

But relations between blacks and Jews proved uneasy. Blacks moved into less-skilled, poorer-paying positions, from which mobility into better-remunerated positions proved difficult. Although the garment unions made explicit efforts to organize black workers and integrate them into union structures, few blacks moved up to elected offices, and none high up in the union hierarchy. To protect jobs from southern competitors, the unions adopted a policy of wage restraint, which inevitably meant a softened stance on union employers at home—much to the dismay of black New York garment workers.[10]

The garment business was the Jewish enclave of the past; Jewish mobility into the middle class had made teaching the Jewish niche of the mid-1960s. As the schools came to serve a growing black population, their role was increasingly contested by black students, parents, and protest organizations. The complaints were various, and not all directly linked to the Jews' prominent role in the school system; but the situation in which so many Jews were teachers and so many schools in black neighborhoods were staffed by Jews inevitably led to conflict. In 1968, a black-dominated school board in Brooklyn dismissed a group of white, largely Jewish teachers and replaced them with a mainly black staff; these actions set off a three-month-long strike by the Jewish-led teachers' union. Although the union eventually won, its victory was pyrrhic, at least concerning black-Jewish relations. Memory of the strike and the resentments it fueled have not significantly changed, even a generation later.[11]

What has altered, however, is the economic position of the Jews. The ethnic economy of the immigrant days remains, but in vestigial form. Although Jews are still active in the garment industry, they mainly con-

centrate in the designing and merchandising ends. "Goldberg" no longer runs clothing factories; his place has been taken by "Kim" and "Wong," who only employ compatriots, not blacks. The same transformations have changed the face of petty retailing and small landlording—the older flash points of black-Jewish conflict. The Jewish presence in the public sector is also fading fast: working as a city engineer or accountant used to be a Jewish occupation; now these careers engage far many more Patels than Cohens.[12] Only in teaching and in higher education do the Jewish concentrations of the past remain in full force.[13]

A distinctive Jewish role in New York's economy still lives on. It is to be found in the professions, in the persistently high rate of Jewish self-employment, in the prominence of Jews in law, real estate, finance, and the media. But the current Jewish pursuits differ crucially from the older ethnic economy in that they are detached from the dynamics of interethnic competition that characterized earlier periods. In a sense, the material basis that underlay anti-Semitic currents in New York for most of the twentieth century is gone. But its legacy and the many other resources around which groups can compete—status, politics, and territory—ensure continued conflict between Jews and their ethnic neighbors.

The Blacks

In 1890, the black share of the New York population was 1.6 percent—just about what it had been on the eve of the Civil War. But in the 1890s the South started losing blacks due to outmigration, and that loss quickly translated into New York's gain. By 1920, New York housed 150,000 black residents—who, although only 3 percent of the city's population, made New York the country's largest black urban concentration. In the next twenty years, as European immigration faltered and then stopped, and bad conditions in the rural South provided additional reasons to leave, the number of black New Yorkers tripled. Postwar prosperity and a new wave of mechanization down South launched a final, massive flow northward: by 1960, the African American population of New York numbered 1,088,000, of whom approximately 320,000 had moved to the city from other areas (mainly the South) in the previous ten years.[14]

It was not until 1940 that black New Yorkers moved out of the peripheries of the New York economy. At the turn of the century, blacks mainly found work in domestic labor, with 90 percent of black women and 55 percent of black men working in some type of domestic service occupation. Blacks' confinement to domestic service reflected, in part, the unfavorable terms of competition with immigrants, who had evicted them from trades where they had previously been accepted. The continued expansion of New York's economy slowly opened doors in a few manufacturing industries; the shutoff of immigration during World War I and its permanent demise after 1924 further accelerated dispersion into other fields.[15]

But the depression largely put an end to these gains. By 1940, 40 percent of blacks still worked in personal service—a far greater proportion than among the workforce overall.[16] With the advent of World War II doors to other jobs were finally unlocked; manufacturing, in particular, saw very large black employment gains. Yet unlike the case in Chicago or Detroit, the black sojourn in New York's manufacturing sector proved short-lived. Lacking auto factories or steel mills, New York's goods-producing sector was a concentration of low-wage jobs; white workers remained ensconced in the better-paying, more skilled positions. Opportunities for blacks were more easily found in the burgeoning service sector—for example, health

care—and in government; hence, blacks quickly dispersed into other fields.

Government, where 35 percent of native-born black New Yorkers worked in 1990,[17] has become the black niche par excellence. The history of black employment in the public sector provides yet another example of the continuing, interethnic competitive conflicts over jobs and economic resources in which New York's ethnic groups have been engaged.

In the early years of the twentieth century, local government, like most other New York employers, closed its doors to blacks: in 1911, the city only employed 511 blacks, almost all of whom were laborers. In the early 1920s, Tammany installed the leader of its black client organization, the United Colored Democracy, as a member of the three-person Civil Service Commission, but black access to public jobs changed marginally. By the late 1920s, the city counted 2,275 black workers on its payroll, of whom 900 were in laboring jobs and an additional 700 were in other noncompetitive or per diem positions.[18] The reform regime did more for blacks, pushing black employment above parity by 1940.[19] But these effects occurred as a result of the government's burgeoning payrolls, and they were mainly felt in the black concentrations of hospitals, sanitation, and public works, where more than 80 percent of the city's black job holders worked in 1935.[20] Moreover, blacks remained vulnerable to discriminatory practices, as in the city-owned subway system, where blacks only worked as porters, with the exception of a few stations in Harlem. Most important, the employment system that emerged during the depression put blacks at a structural disadvantage in competition with whites. Lacking the educational skills and credentials needed to qualify for most city jobs, blacks and Puerto Ricans found themselves channeled into noncompetitive positions, of which the single largest concentration was found in the municipal hospital system. From here there were few routes of movement upward, as these bottom-level positions were disconnected from the competitive system, which promoted from within.

Race didn't reach the top of the government's agenda until 1965, when John Lindsay arrived in office, the first reformer elected mayor since LaGuardia.[21] Elected with the votes of liberals and minorities, Lindsay lacked his predecessors' commitments to the interests of the largely white, civil service workforce and pledged to increase black and Puerto Rican employment in city agencies. But the new mayor quickly discovered that the civil service structure was not easily amenable to change. Lindsay gradually made progress in reducing the inflated eligibility requirements inherited from the depression, but resistance proved severe when his reforms threatened established white ethnic workers in the better-paid ranks.

Lindsay's main focus, in contrast to earlier reform administrations, was to evade the civil service system and its unionized defenders. The Lindsay administration created new, less-skilled positions for which minority residents could be more easily hired. But this approach never involved large numbers and, more important, left existing eligibility requirements unchallenged, shunting minority recruits into dead-end jobs, where they were marooned.

Lindsay backed off from his confrontations with the civil service system and its defenders in the aftermath of the disastrous 1968 teachers' strike. Where the mayor could both accommodate the unions and pursue his earlier goals of increasing minority employment, he did—mainly by tripling the number of exempt workers and shifting them from agency to agency to avoid the requirement of taking an examination. But in other instances, pressure from civil service interests proved overwhelming. With

Abraham Beame's accession to City Hall in 1973, followed in 1977 by Edward Koch, mayoral support for black employment gains vanished for the next sixteen years.

The 1970s and 1980s nevertheless saw dramatic gains in black government employment. Like earlier white ethnic groups that had developed a concentration in public jobs, blacks benefited from simultaneous shifts in the structure of employment and in the relative availability of competing groups.

Changes in the structure of employment came from a variety of sources. The Equal Employment Opportunity (EEO) Act of 1972 prohibited discrimination in local government. By requiring local governments to maintain records on all employees by race and gender and to submit them to the Equal Employment Opportunity Commission, with the clear expectation that governments would show improvement over time, the act also led to institutional changes. As EEO functions were established in each city agency, recruitment and personnel practices changed in ways that benefited previously excluded groups, as recruitment became focused on minority and immigrant communities.

Moreover, the 1972 act provided minority employees with levers to act on more recalcitrant agencies, which they used with greatest effectiveness in the uniformed services. For example, in 1973 the Vulcan Society (the organization of black firefighters) successfully challenged the results of a 1971 exam, leading to an imposition of a 1:3 quota for the duration of that list (1973–79). In 1979, the Guardians and the Hispanic Society challenged the 1979 police officer's exam; court findings of disparate impact led to the imposition of a 33.3 percent minority quota for the duration of the list.

While the advent of affirmative action helped increase access for blacks and other minorities, other changes on the supply side hastened the growth of black employment. Although the city's attraction to its traditional white ethnic labor force had begun to diminish by the 1960s, the fiscal crisis of the mid-1970s decisively exacerbated and extended the city's recruitment difficulties among its traditional workforce. By the time large-scale hiring resumed in the early 1980s, public employment had become a less attractive option than before. Moreover, municipal salaries and benefits took a severe beating during the fiscal crisis; although compensation edged back upward during the 1980s, real gains never recaptured the losses endured during the 1970s. The strength enjoyed by New York's private sector during the 1980s pulled native white workers up the hiring queue and out of the effective labor supply for many city agencies.[22]

In a situation where "the City was hiring a great deal and not turning away anyone who was qualified," as one deputy commissioner told me in an interview, the disparity in the availability of minority and white workers led to rapid recruitment of minority workers. Minorities had constituted only 40 percent of the new workers hired in 1977, making up the majority in only two low-paid occupational categories. By 1987, minorities made up 56 percent of all hires, dominating the ranks of new recruits in five out of eight occupational categories.[23]

Thus, the Koch years of 1977 to 1989 saw the ethnic composition of the municipal workforce completely transformed, notwithstanding the mayor's opposition to affirmative action and the disfavor with which minority leaders greeted his hiring policies. By 1990, whites constituted 48 percent of the 375,000 people working for the city and just slightly more—50 percent—of the 150,000 people working in the agencies that the mayor directly controlled.[24] The declining white presence in municipal employment chiefly benefited blacks. Blacks constituted 25 percent of the city's population and a still smaller proportion of residents who were older than eighteen and

thus potentially employable, but made up 36 percent of the city's total workforce and 38 percent of those who worked in the mayoral agencies. Although blacks were still underrepresented in some of the city's most desirable jobs, the earlier pattern of concentration at the bottom was overcome. The municipal hospital system, which employed two-thirds of the city's black employees in the early 1960s, in 1990 employed less than one-fifth, reflecting the dispersion of blacks throughout the municipal sector. And higher-level jobs showed clusters of considerable black overrepresentation as well, with blacks accounting for 40 percent of the administrators and 36 percent of the professionals employed in the direct mayoral agencies.

By 1990, when David Dinkins became New York's first black mayor, the phase of black-for-white succession in municipal employment was nearly complete. Blacks held just over 35 percent of all city jobs; although unevenly represented among the city's many agencies, they were often a dominant presence, accounting for more than 40 percent of employment in six of the ten largest agencies, and more than 50 percent of employment in three of the largest ten.

The comparison with Latinos underlines blacks' advantage in the new ethnic division that has emerged in city government. Whereas the city's Latinos and black populations are equal in number, Latinos hold one-third as many municipal jobs as do blacks. The discrepancies are even greater as one moves up the occupational hierarchy into the ranks of managers and professionals. And blacks have been far more successful than Latinos in gaining new permanent civil service jobs, rather than the provisional appointments on which Latinos have mainly relied. The disparity has not gone unnoticed, as the Commission on Hispanic Concerns pointed out in a 1986 report.[25] Of course, other answers might be invoked to explain Latinos' municipal jobs deficit relative to blacks'. But whatever the precise explanation, Mayor Dinkins's continuing conflicts with the Hispanic community suggest that earlier patterns of interethnic competition over municipal jobs remain alive and well.

The Koreans

In the mid-1960s, just when New York could no longer retain its native population, it reverted back to its role as an immigrant mecca. Immigrants began flocking to New York immediately after the liberalization of U.S. immigration laws in 1965. Their arrival has been the principal driving force of demographic and ethnic change in New York ever since—and will continue to be for the foreseeable future.

In 1965, what no one expected was the burgeoning of Asian immigration. The reforms tilted the new system toward immigrants with kinship ties to permanent residents or citizens. Since there had been so little Asian immigration in the previous fifty years, how could Asian newcomers find settlers with whom to seek reunification? The answer is that kinship connections were helpful, but not essential. The 1965 reforms also created opportunities for immigrants whose skills—as engineers, doctors, nurses, pharmacists—were in short supply. Along with students already living in the United States and enjoying easy access to American employers, these professionals made up the first wave of new Asian immigrants, creating the basis for the kinship migration of less well educated relatives.

Thus, well-educated, highly skilled immigrants have dominated the Korean influx to the United States and to New York in particular. Although Koreans constitute a small portion of New York's new immigrants—rarely more than 3 percent of the eighty thousand to ninety thousand legal immigrants who come to New York each year—they play an important and very visible role. As middle-aged newcomers with poor English-language skills and often lacking professional licenses, relatively few Koreans have managed to steer a route back into the fields for which they trained. Instead they have turned to small business, setting up new businesses at a rate that few other groups can rival.

Koreans started in fruit and vegetable stores, taking over shops in all areas of the city, regardless of neighborhood composition or customer clientele. From there, Koreans moved on to other retail specialties—dry cleaning, fish stores, novelty shops, and nail salons. By 1980, a third of New York Korean males were already self-employed. The *1991 Korean Business Directory* provides a ready indicator of commercial growth over the 1980s, listing over 120 commercial specialties in which Korean firms are to be found.[26]

The roots of the Korean ethnic economy are found in several sources. The competitive field was open. By the middle to late 1960s, the sons and daughters of Jewish and Italian storekeepers had better things to do than mind a store, and their parents, old, tired, and scared of crime, were ready to sell out to the newcomers from Korea. By the 1980s, the supply of new, native-born white entrepreneurs had virtually dried up. One survey of neighborhood businesses in Queens and Brooklyn found that almost half of the white-owned shops were run by immigrants and that most white businesses were long-established entities, in contrast to the newly founded Korean shops with which they competed.[27]

Another spur to growth came from within the ethnic community. Koreans, like every other immigrant group, have special tastes and needs that are best served by an insider: the growth of the Korean population has created business for Korean accountants, doctors, brokers, hair stylists, and restaurant owners. Although the Korean community is too small to support a huge commercial infrastructure oriented to ethnic needs, the community has utilized its ethnic connections to Korea to develop commercial activities oriented toward non-Korean markets. Active trade relations between South Korea and the United States have provided a springboard for many Korean-owned import-export businesses, of which 119 are listed in the *1991 Korean Business Directory*.

Finally, the social structure of the Korean community itself generates advantages for business success that few other immigrant groups share. Many Koreans emigrate with capital, and those who are cash poor can raise money through rotating credit associations known as *gae*. Because Koreans migrate in complete family units, family members provide a supply of cheap and trusted labor. The prevalence of self-employment means that many Koreans have close ties to other business owners, who in turn are a source of information and support, and the high organizational density of the Korean community—which is characterized by an incredible proliferation of alumni clubs, churches, businessman's associations—provides additional conduits for the flow of business information and the making of needed contacts. These community resources distinguish the Koreans from their competitors, who are less likely to be embedded in ethnic or family ties that can be drawn upon for help with business information, capital assistance, or staffing problems.

The Koreans have discovered that conflict *need not* be interethnic; there are other sources of threat, and in the 1980s they mobilized Korean merchants on a considerable scale. Like other small business owners, Koreans were unhappy with local government, usually with something that government was doing or was threatening to do. Fruit and vegetable store owners felt that sanitation officials were too conscien-

tious about sidewalk cleanliness, especially since the result of the officials' demands was often a fine that the Korean store owner had to pay. Pressuring the city to relax inspections became a high priority for Korean organizations. In the late 1980s, as the city's fiscal crisis led it to search for new sources of revenue, fiscal planners thought of placing a special tax on dry cleaners. So Korean dry cleaners entered an unusual coalition with the white owners of commercial laundries, and the union that represented the laundryworkers, to roll back the planned tax. Like other small business owners, Korean merchants could also become dissatisfied with government's *failure* to act. The prosperity of the 1980s gave commercial landlords license to raise rents to the maximum, much to the distress of small business owners throughout the city. Koreans joined with their non-Korean counterparts to push for commercial rent control—to no avail.

Although Italians and Jews have largely deserted petty retail trade, they have remained in wholesaling, where the businesses are larger and profits more sizable. Thus Jewish and Italian fruit and vegetable or fish wholesalers have acquired a substantial Korean trade. The encounter has not always been a happy one, as Illsoo Kim recounted in his pathbreaking book: "Especially in their first years of emergence into the fruit and vegetable business, Koreans reported many incidents at the Hunts Point [wholesale] Market. The incidents ranged from unfair pricing and sale of poor-quality produce by the Italian and Jewish wholesalers, to physical threats and beatings administered by competing white retailers."[28] Such conflicts sparked the first mass demonstration by Koreans ever in New York. Although Kim reports that Koreans were subsequently accepted by the wholesaling community, there have been continued incidents and protests, including a recent boycott by Koreans of one of the city's largest fish wholesalers.[29]

In New York, as in almost every other major American city, black neighborhoods have provided new immigrants from Asia and the Middle East with an important economic outlet. To some extent, Koreans and other immigrants have simply replaced older white groups that had long sold to blacks and were now eager to bail out of an increasingly difficult and tense situation. By opening stores in black neighborhoods Koreans were also filling the gap left by the departure of large, nonethnic chain stores, which were steadily eliminating the low-margin, high-cost operations involved in serving a ghetto clientele. Selling to black customers proved fraught with conflict. Small protests erupted in the late 1970s. In 1981 a boycott erupted along 125th Street, Harlem's main commercial thoroughfare, with black leaders calling Korean shop owners "vampires" who came to Harlem to "suck black consumers dry."[30]

Repeated security problems as well as more organized clashes led Korean store owners to establish neighborhood prosperity associations, in addition to those organizations that grouped merchants in a particular retail branch. Thus, alongside groups like the Korean Produce Association or the Korean Apparel Contractors Associations, one finds neighborhood groups like the Korean Merchant Association of the Bronx or the Uptown Korean Merchants Association, which seek "to improve Korean merchants' relations with local residents or communities" while lobbying local police for more effective support.[31]

In 1990 antagonism between black shoppers and Korean merchants erupted in picket lines set up in front of two Korean stores in the Flatbush section of Brooklyn. The clash started with a dispute between a Korean store owner and a black Haitian customer who charged assault; that claim then provoked black activist groups—of fairly dubious repute[32]—to establish a boycott that targeted not only the offending owner, but a neighboring Korean merchant against whom no injury was ever charged.

The boycott lasted for months, choking off business at both stores. Although customers disappeared, the two stores were kept alive by contributions from the organized Korean community, which perceived a broader danger to its economic viability should the boycott succeed. As time went on, government officials were inevitably involved. The boycott became a crisis for Mayor Dinkins, who was widely criticized for not actively seeking an end to the dispute.

The boycott ground to a halt, and a court threw out the legal suit brought by the aggrieved Haitian shopper. Other, fortunately short-lived boycotts were started in New York even while the Flatbush dispute lingered on. A clash in a nearby Brooklyn area between blacks and a small group of Vietnamese refugees—possibly mistaken for Koreans—showed how quickly tensions generated in one arena could move to another.

Conclusion

The story of New York's Irish, Jews, blacks, and Koreans is richer and more complicated than the occupational histories I've recounted in the preceding pages. But if the [reading's] deliberately one-sided focus provides only a partial account, it reminds us of ethnicity's continuing importance, and not simply because of feelings for one's own kind or animosities toward outsiders. Rather, ethnicity's centrality stems from its role as the mechanism whereby groups of categorically different workers have been sorted into an identifiably distinct set of jobs. In this sense, the ethnic division of labor has been the central division of labor in modern New York. Now, as in the past, distinctive roles in the ethnic division of labor impart a sense of "we-ness" and group interest—ensuring the persistence of ethnic fragmentation and conflict.

NOTES

1. Stephen Erie, *Rainbow's End* (Berkeley: University of California Press, 1988), 88–89.

2. Thomas Kessner, *Fiorella H. LaGuardia* (New York: McGraw-Hill, 1989); Charles Garrett, *The LaGuardia Years* (New Brunswick, NJ: Rutgers University Press, 1961).

3. A survey of the surviving members of the class indicates that 38 percent were Catholic and 36 percent Jewish, with Russia and Ireland the leading countries of origin of the respondents' grandparents (Richard Herrnstein et al., "New York City Police Department Class of 1940: A Preliminary Report" [unpublished manuscript, Department of Psychology, Harvard University, n.d.]).

4. Nathan Glazer and Daniel P. Moynihan, *Beyond the Melting Pot* (Cambridge, MA: MIT Press, 1969).

5. Data on the ethnic composition of the fire department are from *Equal Employment Opportunity Statistics: Agency Full Report* (New York: New York City Department of Personnel, 1990); data on the religious composition are from Center for Social Policy and Practice in the Workplace, *Gender Integration in the Fire Department of the City of New York* (New York: Columbia University School of Social Work, 1988), p. 41.

6. Roger Waldinger, *Through the Eye of the Needle* (New York: New York University Press, 1986).

7. Heywood Broun and George Britt, *Christians Only* (New York: Vantage Press, 1931), 244.

8. Dominic Capeci, *The Harlem Riot of 1943* (Philadelphia: Temple University Press, 1977), 172.

9. Waldinger, *Through the Eye of the Needle*, 109–10. Employment data calculated from the census apply to employed persons twenty-five to sixty-four years old only. "Blacks" refers to native-born African Americans only. Data calculated from the Public Use Microdata Samples (U.S. Bureau of the Census, *Census of Population, 1940*, Public Use Microdata Samples [Computer file] [Washington, DC: U.S. Dept. of Commerce, Bureau of the Census, producer, 1983; Ann Arbor, MI: Inter-university Consortium for Political and Social Research, distributor, 1984]; U.S. Bureau of the Census, Census of Population, 1950, Public Use Microdata Samples [computer file] [Washington, DC: U.S. Dept. of Commerce, Bureau of the Census, and Madison: University of Wisconsin, Center for Demography and Ecology, producers, 1984; Ann Arbor, MI: Inter-university Consortium for Political and Social Research, distributor, 1984]).

10. Hasia Diner, *In the Almost Promised Land* (Westport, CT: Greenwood Press, 1977), presents a favorable account of the response among the Jewish trade union elite to the black influx into the garment industry; see chap. 6. Herbert Hill has offered a far more critical account in numerous writings, most important, "The Racial Practices of Organized Labor: The Contemporary Record," in *Organized Labor and the Negro,* edited by Julius Jacobson (New York: Doubleday, 1968), 286–337. For a judicious balancing of the issues, see Nancy Green, "Juifs et noirs aux etats-unis: La rupture d'une 'alliance naturelle,'" *Annales, E.S.C.,* 2 (March–April 1987):445–64.

11. Diane Ravitch, *The Great School Wars* (New York: Basic Books, 1974).

12. Roger Waldinger, "The Making of an Immigrant Niche," *International Migration Review* 28(1)(1994).

13. "The Debate Goes On," *Alumnus: The City College of New York* 87(1)(Winter 1992):8–11.

14. Emmanuel Tobier, "Population," in *Setting Municipal Priorities,* edited by Charles Brecher and Raymond Horton (New York: New York University Press, 1981), 24.

15. Data are from U.S. Bureau of the Census, *Occupations at the 1900 Census* (Washington, DC: GPO, 1904). See also Herman Bloch, *The Circle of Discrimination* (New York: New York University Press, 1969).

16. Data are from the U.S. Bureau of the Census, *Census of Population, 1940.*

17. Calculated from the U.S. Bureau of the Census, *Census of Population and Housing, 1990,* Public Use Microdata Sample (a Sample): 5-Percent Sample (computer file) (Washington, DC: U.S. Dept. of Commerce, producer, 1993; Ann Arbor, MI: Inter-university Consortium for Political and Social Research, distributor, 1993).

18. Colored Citizens' Non-Partisan Committee for the Re-election of Mayor Walker, *New York City and the Colored Citizen* (n.d. [1930?]),

LaGuardia Papers, Box 3530, New York Municipal Archives.

19. Calculated from U.S. Bureau of the Census, *Census of Population, 1940,* Public Use Microdata Samples. Also see Edwin Levinson, *Black Politics in New York City* (New York: Twayne, 1974).

20. Ira Katznelson, *Black Men, White Cities* (New York: Oxford University Press, 1973), 82.

21. For a more detailed discussion of the Lindsay period, see Roger Waldinger, "The Ethnic Politics of Municipal Jobs," working paper no. 248, UCLA Institute of Industrial Relations, Los Angeles, 1993.

22. Raymond Horton, "Human Resources," in *Setting Municipal Priorities,* edited by Charles Brecher and Raymond Horton (New York: New York University Press, 1986). See also Roger Waldinger, "Changing Ladders and Musical Chairs," *Politics and Society* 15(4) (1986–87): 369–402, and "Making of an Immigrant Niche."

23. City of New York, Citywide Equal Employment Opportunity Committee, *Equal Employment Opportunity in New York City Government, 1977–1987* (New York: Citywide Equal Employment Opportunity Committee, 1988), 6.

24. Data are from unpublished EEOC reports from the New York City Department of Personnel, New York Board of Education, New York City Transit Authority, and New York City Health and Hospitals Corporation.

25. City of New York, Mayor's Commission on Hispanic Concerns, *Report* (New York: Mayor's Commission on Hispanic Concerns, 1986), 109.

26. *1991 Korean Business Directory* (Long Island City, NY: Korean News, 1991).

27. Roger Waldinger, "Structural Opportunity or Ethnic Advantage: Immigrant Business Development in New York," *International Migration Review* 23(1)(1989):61.

28. Illsoo Kim, *The New Urban Immigrants* (Princeton, NJ: Princeton University Press, 1981), 51.

29. Pyong Gap Min, "Cultural and Economic Boundaries of Korean Ethnicity: A Comparative Analysis," *Ethnic and Racial Studies* 14(2)(1991):235.

30. Lucie Cheng and Yen Espiritu, "Korean Businesses in Black and Hispanic Neighborhoods," *Sociological Perspectives* 32(4)(1989): 521.

31. Illsoo Kim, "The Koreans: Small Business in an Urban Frontier," in *New Immigrants in New York,* edited by Nancy Foner (New York: Columbia University Press, 1987), 238.

32. Tamar Jacoby, "Sonny Carson and the Politics of Protest," *NY: The City Journal* 1(4)(1991): 29–40.

27

WHEN WORK DISAPPEARS

William Julius Wilson

Questions to Consider

According to William J. Wilson, why is it that even during times of low unemployment, blacks and Latinos are twice as likely to be unemployed as whites? How do structural changes in the economy often more harshly impact poor and nonwhite communities? Are Wilson's public policy suggestions for creating job opportunities in blighted neighborhoods realistic given federal, state, and city budget cutbacks that are taking place across the nation?

For the first time in the twentieth century most adults in many inner-city ghetto neighborhoods are not working in a typical week. The disappearance of work has adversely affected not only individuals, families, and neighborhoods, but the social life of the city at large as well. Inner-city joblessness is a severe problem that is often overlooked or obscured when the focus is placed mainly on poverty and its consequences. Despite increases in the concentration of poverty since 1970, inner cities have always featured high levels of poverty, but the current levels of joblessness in some neighborhoods are unprecedented.

The consequences of high neighborhood joblessness are more devastating than those of high neighborhood poverty. A neighborhood in which people are poor but employed is different from a neighborhood in which people are poor and jobless. Many of today's problems in the inner-city ghetto neighborhoods—crime, family dissolution, welfare, low levels of social organization, and so on—are fundamentally a consequence of the disappearance of work.

The disappearance of work and the growth of related problems in the ghetto have aggravated an already tense racial situation in urban areas. Our nation's response to racial discord in the central city and to the growing racial divide between the city and the suburbs has been disappointing. In discussing these problems we have a tendency to engage in the kind of rhetoric that exacerbates, rather than alleviates, urban and metropolitan racial

tensions. Ever since the 1992 Los Angeles riot, the media have focused heavily on the factors that divide rather than those that unite racial groups. Emphasis on racial division peaked in 1995 following the jury's verdict in the O. J. Simpson murder trial. Before the verdict was announced, opinion polls revealed that whites overwhelmingly thought Mr. Simpson was guilty, while a substantial majority of blacks felt he was innocent. The media clips showing public reaction to the verdict dramatized the racial division—blacks appeared elated and jubilant; whites appeared stunned, angry, and somber. Blacks believed that O. J. Simpson had been framed by a racist police conspiracy; whites were convinced that he was guilty of the murder of two people and was being allowed to walk free. The racial divide, as depicted in the media, seemed as wide as ever.

The implications of these developments for the future of race relations and for programs perceived to benefit blacks remain to be seen. As one observer, on the eve of the Simpson verdict, put it: "When O. J. gets off, the whites will riot the way we whites do: leave the cities, go to Idaho or Oregon or Arizona, vote for Gingrich . . . and punish the blacks by closing the day-care programs and cutting off their Medicaid."[1]

The extent of the racial divisions in this country should not be minimized. The different reactions to the Simpson trial and the verdict reflect in part the fundamentally dissimilar racial experiences of blacks and whites in America—the former burdened by racial injustice, the latter largely free of the effects of bigotry and hatred. Nonetheless,

[1] Frank Rich, "The L.A. Shock Treatment," *New York Times,* 4 October 1995.

the emphasis on racial differences has obscured the fact that African-Americans, whites, and other ethnic groups share many common concerns, are beset by many common problems, and have many common values, aspirations, and hopes.

Job Shrinkage in the Global Economy

Changes in the global economy are placing strains on the welfare state in both the United States and Europe and are contributing to growing social dislocations, including racial conflicts. The question that Secretary of Labor Robert Reich raised at a 1994 conference of finance and labor ministers from seven industrial democracies is central and timely: "Are we condemned to choose between more jobs but greater inequality and insecurity, as we have in this country, or better jobs but higher unemployment and a thicker social safety net, as in Europe?"[2] This question implicitly asks whether Europeans and Americans can learn from one another in the creation of programs that simultaneously address the problems of economic growth, joblessness, and wage inequality.

There is a growing recognition that proposed solutions to the problems of jobs and wages in any of the major industrial democracies cannot ignore developments in the highly integrated global market place. Indeed, because of concerns about the problem of creating good jobs in the global economy, the finance and labor ministers from the major industrial democracies (Britain, Canada, France, Germany, Italy, Japan, and the United States, or the Group of Seven, commonly called G7) held a jobs conference in Detroit in March 1994. In previous years, only heads of state and finance ministers

met "to discuss high diplomacy and the high finance exchange rates and interest rate management."[3] However, that exalted approach was considered insufficient to address the concrete issue of jobs that now confronts all of these nations.

In addition to the more familiar themes, such as the importance of stimulating economic growth and of avoiding protectionist policies to safeguard shrinking job markets, the officials at the conference also agreed "that the only way to create more jobs in the face of rapid technological change was to upgrade education, particularly for those who are least skilled."[4] It was the first time the G7 policy makers had addressed, as a global problem, the widening gap in wages between skilled and unskilled workers and the strong association between low levels of education, joblessness, and poorly paid work.[5]

Although the conference did more to highlight than to solve these problems, the main hope of the ministers was that the discussions could "teach them something about what each of them has done right, and wrong, in confronting the jobs question."[6] As I examine possible policy prescriptions in cross-national perspective, a framework for discussing the appropriateness of long-term solutions to the jobs problem in the United States (solutions that take several years before the desired ends are achieved or realized) and one for discussing more immediate solutions come to mind.

My framework for long-term solutions outlines two types of relationships in an effort to address the issues of generating good jobs and combating the growing wage inequality among workers—namely, the

---

[2] Thomas L. Friedman, "World's Big Economies Turn to the Jobs Issue," *New York Times,* 14 March 1994.

[3] Ibid.
[4] Thomas L. Friedman, "Accent on Education as Talks on Jobs End," *New York Times,* 16 March 1994.
[5] Ibid.
[6] Ibid.

relationship between employment and education and family support systems and, in the metropolitan context, the relationship between the cities and the suburbs. My framework for immediate solutions delineates ways in which to either revise current programs or create new programs to decrease joblessness among disadvantaged adults. Each framework involves the integration of programs that involve both the public sector and the private sector.

I hasten to point out that the following presentation and discussion of policy frameworks is not constrained by an awareness of the current political climate in the United States. The dramatic retreat from using public policy as a means to fight social inequality has effectively discouraged calls for bold new social programs. Indeed, at the time of this writing, the trend is toward slicing or reducing social programs and the spending for such programs. The emphasis is on personal responsibility, not inequities in the larger society, and therefore the assumption is that people should help themselves and not turn to the government for handouts. It is said that the growth of joblessness and welfare receipt mainly reflects a declining commitment to the core values of society and therefore that the incentives for idleness or the factors that lead to a lack of personal and family responsibilities ought to be removed.

These arguments have been advanced with such force and consistency in public discussions since the 1994 congressional elections that even some of the most dedicated liberals feel intimidated and powerless. Accordingly, traditional programs benefiting the poor, such as Aid to Families with Dependent Children (AFDC), Medicaid, and the earned income tax credit, have either been eliminated or are being threatened with severe reductions.

This retreat from public policy as a way to alleviate problems of social inequality will have profound negative consequences for the future of disadvantaged groups such as the ghetto poor. High levels of joblessness, growing wage inequality, and the related social problems are complex and have their source in fundamental economic, social, and cultural changes. They therefore require bold, comprehensive, and thoughtful solutions, not simplistic and pious statements about the need for greater personal responsibility. Progressives who are concerned about the current social conditions of the have-nots and the future generation of have-nots not only have to fight against the current public policy strategies; they are morally obligated to offer alternative strategies designed to alleviate, not exacerbate, the plight of the poor, the jobless, and other disadvantaged citizens of America.

My aim, therefore, is to galvanize and rally concerned Americans to fight back with the same degree of force and dedication displayed by those who have moved us backward, rather than forward, in combating social inequality. I therefore do not advance proposals that seem acceptable or "realistic" given the current political climate. Rather, I have chosen to talk about what *ought to be done to address the problems of social inequality,* including record levels of joblessness in the inner-city ghetto that threaten the very fabric of our society.

Some who acknowledge the need to confront the growing social inequality also feel that new social programs should be put on hold until the huge budget deficit has been significantly reduced. In the final analysis, however, we must recognize that spending is directly related to political priorities. Decisions about budget cuts for federal programs now indisputably favor the advantaged segments of the population at the expense of the disadvantaged.

I believe that steps must be taken to galvanize Americans from all walks of life who are concerned about human suffering and the public policy direction in which we are now moving. I therefore present policy frameworks that call for the integration and mobilization of resources from both the public and the private sectors. We need to generate a public/private partnership to fight social inequality. In the final analysis, I hope to stimulate thought about what ought to be done and how we should do it among those who support positive social reforms and see the need for action now. The following policy frameworks, therefore, are suggestive and provide a basis for further discussion and debate. Let me begin by first focusing on the part of my framework for long-term solutions that involves relationships between employment and education, and family support systems.

Creating National Performance Standards for Schools

The United States can learn from industrial democracies like Japan and Germany. These countries have developed policies designed to increase the number of workers with "higher-order thinking skills," including policies that require young people to meet high performance standards before they can graduate from secondary schools and that hold each school responsible for meeting these national standards. As Ray Marshall points out, "Standards are important because they provide incentives for students, teachers and other school personnel; information to employers and postsecondary institutions; and a means for policy makers and the public to evaluate schools. Indeed, by strengthening linkages, standards have helped fashion systems out of disjointed activities."[7]

Students who meet high standards are not only prepared for work, they are ready for technical training and other kinds of postsecondary education.[8] Currently, there are no national standards for secondary students or schools in the United States. Accordingly, students who are not in college preparatory courses have severely limited options with respect to pursuing work or secondary technical training after high school. A commitment to a system of national performance standards for every public school in the United States would be an important first step in addressing the huge gap in educational performance between the schools in advantaged and disadvantaged neighborhoods.

But because the quality of local public schools in the United States is in large measure related to the resources of local governments, national standards may not be attractive to taxpayers and local officials in some areas. Also, some schools will encounter greater difficulties in meeting a national performance standard because of fewer resources and a greater concentration of students from disadvantaged backgrounds and neighborhoods. . . .

Recent research on the nationwide distribution of science and mathematics opportunities indicates that low-income, minority, and inner-city students are in school environments that are not as conducive to learning because of less qualified teachers, fewer material resources, less engaging activities for learning in the classroom, and considerably less exposure to good training and knowledge in mathematics and science.[9] The problem of finding qualified teachers is particularly acute. Teacher shortages in

---

[7] Ray Marshall, "School-to-Work Processes in the United States" (paper presented at the Carnegie Corporation/Johann Jacobs Foundation, Marbach Castle, Germany, 3–5 November 1994).

[8] Ibid.

[9] Jeannie Oakes, *Multiplying Inequalities: The Effects of Race, Social Class and Ability Grouping on Access to Science and Mathematics Education* (Santa Monica, CA: Rand Corporation, 1990).

many central-city and poor rural schools have resulted in a disproportionate number of underprepared and inexperienced teachers, many of whom provide instruction in fields outside their areas of preparation, and a continuous flow of short-term and long-term substitutes.[10]

A system of national performance standards should include the kind of support that would enable schools in disadvantaged neighborhoods to meet the standards that are set. State government, with federal support, not only would have to create equity in local school funding and give birth to programs that would foster teacher development (through scholarships and forgivable loans for teacher education to attract more high-quality teachers, through increased supports for teacher training in schools of education, and through reforms in teacher certification and licensing) but would also have to ensure that highly qualified teachers are distributed in local school districts in ways that provide all students with access to excellent instruction. In some cases this would require greater flexibility in the public school system, not only to attract and hire qualified teachers, but also to displace those who perform poorly in the classroom and lack a dedication to teaching. Local education agencies and state education departments should be helped to identify schools that need support in curriculum development and assessment, teacher development, educational and material resources, and so on.". . ."[11]

Targeting education would be part of a national effort to raise the performance stan-

dards of all public schools in the United States to a desirable level, including schools in the inner city. Every effort should be made to enlist the support and involvement of the private sector in this national effort. Corporations, local businesses, civic clubs, community centers, churches, and community-based organizations should be encouraged to work with the schools to enhance computer-competency training. Some examples of private-sector involvement in such endeavors should be touted to spur others on. For example, Frank C. Weaver, director of the Office of Commercial Space Transportation at the U.S. Department of Transportation, reported:

> Bell Atlantic and Tele-Communications, Inc. announced in 1994 that they would provide free linkage to the information superhighways for 26,000 elementary and secondary schools in areas served by the two companies. Under the plan, known as the Basic Education Connection (BEC), the school would receive free educational cable television programming and free access to certain data and online services, such as access to the Internet.
>
> Another project, the Hughes Galaxy Classroom, is enabling 51,000 elementary school children around the country to access more of the educational resources on television available via satellite. Under the auspices of the Galaxy Classroom Foundation, which provides antenna dishes and related equipment to schools, the project offers a science and English curriculum beamed into classrooms through satellite transmissions. Student feedback and questions are faxed to the producers of the program for inclusion in subsequent shows. Particular attention is paid to inner-city and minority schools. There are 480 schools participating this

---

[10] Linda Darling-Hammond, "Teacher Quality and Equality," in *Access to Knowledge: An Agenda for Our Nation's Schools,* edited by John Goodlad and Pamela Keating (New York: College Entrance Examination Board, 1990); Darling-Hammond, "National Standards and Assessments."

[11] Darling-Hammond, "National Standards and Assessments."

year, and the goal for next year is 1,500 schools with 150,000 to 200,000 students.[12]

Since the creation of national performance standards would provide a clear means for the public to evaluate the different schools, data on school performances could be widely disseminated. This would enable parents of all backgrounds, including those in disadvantaged neighborhoods, to compare nearby schools and make appropriate decisions about which ones their children should attend. . . .

Improving Family Support Programs

The learning system in other industrial democracies has also been strengthened by family policies to support children. Among industrialized countries, the United States is alone in having no universal preschool, child-support, or parental leave programs. "The absence of such policies makes many of our families, particularly low-income families, very poor learning systems," states Ray Marshall. "Many of our children therefore start school far behind their more advantaged counterparts, and subsequently receive inadequate learning opportunities at home as well as in school."[13] The family structure has undergone fundamental changes in the last several decades. There has been a sharp increase in single-parent families, and many of them are trapped in persistent poverty. Also, in many "intact" families both the husband and wife must work outside the home to make ends meet.

The absence of widely available high-quality preschool and child-support assurance programs places additional stress on these families and hampers their ability to provide a learning environment that prepares children for school and reinforces the learning process.

The French system of child welfare stands in sharp contrast to the American system. In France, children are supported by three interrelated government programs—child care, income support, and medical care.[14] The child care program includes establishments for infant care, high-quality nursery schools (*écoles maternelles*), and paid leave for parents of newborns. The income support program includes child-support enforcement (so that the absent parent continues to contribute financially to his or her child's welfare), children allowances, and welfare payments for low-income single mothers. Finally, medical care is provided through a universal system of national health care financed by social security, a preventive care system for children, and a group of public health nurses who specialize in child welfare.

The *école maternelle* is perhaps the most distinctive institution in the French system. Children who are no longer in diapers may enter the nursery school and attend until they are enrolled in the first grade. Because parents view participation in the *école maternelle* as highly beneficial to their children, even those mothers who are not working send their children.

As the economist Barbara Bergmann points out:

> The *école maternelle* serves the integration of all children, minority children included, to full participation in regular

---

[12] Frank C. Weaver, "Preparing Our Youth for the Information Age," *Focus,* Joint Center for Political and Economic Studies, May 1995, 7. See also Richard M. Krieg, "Information Technology and Low Income Inner-City Communities," *Journal of Urban Technology* (forthcoming).

[13] Marshall, "School-to-Work Processes in the United States," 21.

[14] Barbara Bergmann, "The French Child Welfare System: An Excellent System We Could Adapt and Afford" in *Sociology and the Public Agenda,* edited by William Julius Wilson (Newbury Park, CA: Sage, 1993), 341–50.

school and as future citizens. One of its most important functions, especially for the 4- and 5-year-olds, is getting the children ready for the regular school. Each year a child spends at an *école maternelle* reduces considerably the likelihood that the child will fail the rigorous first grade and have to repeat it. Of children from poorer backgrounds who have not attended an *école maternelle,* more than half fail the first grade. Four years of preschool attendance for such poorer children cuts their first grade failure rate in half. Children from more affluent backgrounds are also materially helped to pass.[15]

. . .

City-Suburban Economic Integration?

If the other industrial democracies offer lessons for a long-term solution to the jobs problem involving relationships between employment, education, and family support systems, they also offer lessons on the importance of another solution from a metropolitan perspective—namely, city-suburban integration and cooperation. None of the other industrialized democracies has allowed its city centers to deteriorate as has the United States. In European countries, suburbanization has not been associated with the abandonment of cities as residential areas. "The central governments continued to treat cities as a national resource to be protected and nurtured."[16] Indeed, the city centers in Europe remain very desirable

places to reside because of better public transportation, more effective urban renewal programs, and good public education that is more widely available to disadvantaged students. Moreover, unlike in the United States, cheap public transportation makes suburbanized employment sites more accessible.

It will be difficult to address growing racial tensions in U.S. cities unless we tackle the problems of shrinking revenue and inadequate social services and the gradual disappearance of work in certain neighborhoods. The city has become a less desirable place in which to live, and the economic and social gap between the cities and suburbs is growing. The groups left behind compete, often along racial lines, for declining resources, including the remaining decent schools, housing, and neighborhoods. The rise of the new urban poverty neighborhoods has exacerbated these problems. Their high rates of joblessness and social disorganization have created problems that often spill over into other parts of the city at large. All of these factors aggravate race relations and elevate racial tensions.

Ideally, we need to restore the federal contribution to the city budget that existed in 1980 and to increase sharply the employment base. Regardless of changes in federal urban policy, however, the fiscal crisis in the cities would be significantly eased if the employment base could be substantially increased. Indeed, the social dislocations caused by the steady disappearance of work have led to a wide range of urban social problems, including racial tensions. Increased employment would help stabilize the new poverty neighborhoods, halt the precipitous decline in density, and ultimately enhance the quality of race relations in urban areas.

Perhaps at no other time in the nation's history has it been more important to talk about the need to promote city and suburban

---

[15] Ibid., 343–44.
[16] Margaret Weir, "Race and Urban Poverty: Comparing Europe and America" (occasional paper no. 93–9, Center for American Political Studies, Harvard University, March 1993), 26.

cooperation, not separation. The political fragmentation of many metropolitan areas in the United States has contributed to the problems of joblessness and related social dislocations of the inner-city poor. As David Rusk, the former mayor of Albuquerque, New Mexico, has pointed out, because the older cities of the East and the Midwest were unable to expand territorially through city-county consolidation or annexation, they failed to reap such benefits of suburban growth as the rise of shopping malls, offices, and industrial parks in new residential subdivisions. As areas in which poor minorities live in higher and higher concentration, these cities face an inevitable downward spiral because they are not benefitting from suburban growth. Rusk argues, therefore, that neighborhood revitalization programs, such as community development banks, nonprofit inner-city housing developments, and enterprise zones, will not be able "to reverse the downward slide of inner cities" if they are not carried out within "a framework of actions to bring down the walls between city and suburb."[17]

Efforts to promote city and suburban cooperation will not benefit cities alone. There is mounting evidence that cities and suburbs are economically interdependent. The more central cities are plagued by joblessness, dysfunctional schools, and crime, the more the surrounding suburbs undergo a decline in their own social and economic fortunes. Suburbs that experienced increases in income during the 1980s tended to be linked to a thriving urban center.[18] In the global economy, metropolitan regions continue to compete for jobs. Suburbs that will remain or become competitive are those with a well-trained workforce, good schools, a concentration of professional services, first-class hospitals, a major university and research center, and an efficient transportation network to link executives with other parts of the United States and with countries around the world. However, many of these elements cannot come solely from suburbs. They require a viable central city. It is important for Americans to realize that city-suburban *integration* is the key to the health of metropolitan regions and to the nation as a whole.

Reforms put forward to achieve the objective of city-suburban cooperation range from proposals to create metropolitan governments to proposals for metropolitan tax base sharing (currently in effect in Minneapolis/St. Paul), collaborative metropolitan planning, and the creation of regional authorities to develop solutions to common problems if communities fail to reach agreement.[19] Among the problems shared by many metropolises is a weak public transit system. A commitment to address this problem through a form of city-suburban collaboration would benefit residents of both the city and the suburbs. Theoretically, everyone would benefit from mobility within the metropolitan areas, and inner-city residents would have greater means to prevent high joblessness.

Solutions to the Jobs Problem

The problems of joblessness and social dislocation in the inner city are, in part, related to the processes in the global economy that have contributed to greater inequality and insecurity among American workers in gen-

---

[17] David Rusk, *Cities Without Suburbs* (Washington, DC: Woodrow Wilson Center Press, 1993), 121.
[18] Derek Bok, "Cities and Suburbs" (paper presented for the Aspen Institute Domestic Strategy Group, Aspen Institute, Washington, DC, 1994).

[19] Ibid., 13. See also Margaret Weir, "Urban Policy and Persistent Urban Poverty" (background memorandum prepared for the Social Science Research Council Policy Conference on Persistent Urban Poverty, Washington, DC, 9–10 November 1993).

eral, and to the failure of U.S. social policies to adjust to these processes. It is therefore myopic to view the problems of jobless ghettos as if they were separate from those that plague the larger society.

In using this cross-cultural perspective I am not suggesting that we can or even should simply import the social policies of the Japanese, Germans, or other West Europeans. As Ray Marshall has appropriately pointed out, the approaches in these other countries are embedded in their own cultures and have their "own flaws and deficiencies, as well as strengths." We should instead "learn from the approaches used in other countries and adapt the best aspects into our own homegrown solutions."[20]

The strengths of some of the approaches in other countries are apparent. For example, in Japan and Germany most high school and college graduates leave school with skills in keeping with the demands of the highly technological marketplace in the global economy.[21] In the United States, by contrast, only college graduates and those few with extra-specialized post–high school training acquire such skills. Those with only high school diplomas or less do not.

The flaws and deficiencies of some of the approaches in the other countries are also apparent. Except for Germany, European countries have the same gap in worker skills.[22] Because of the generous unemployment benefits, however, the low-skilled European workers tend to be less willing to accept the lower-paying jobs that their counterparts in the United States are often forced to take. Therefore, the problems of unskilled European workers are not only restricted to low wages, they also include

high levels of unemployment. The growing problem of unemployment among low-skilled European workers is placing a strain on the welfare state. Immigrant minorities are disproportionately represented among the jobless population, and therefore tend to be publicly identified with the problem of maintaining welfare costs. These perceptions contribute to growing intergroup tensions. Accordingly, the problems of race, unemployment, and concentration of urban poverty that have traditionally plagued the United States are now surfacing in various countries in Europe.

Just as the United States can learn from some of the approaches in the other countries, the Europeans could learn from the United States how to make their workforces more flexible instead of paying them to stay unemployed indefinitely. In particular, they could learn how to get unskilled workers into low-wage jobs that would be buttressed by maintaining certain desirable aspects of the safety net, such as universal health insurance, that prevent workers from slipping into the depths of poverty, as so often happens to their American counterparts.

Expand the Earned Income Tax Credit

It is important to discuss immediate solutions to the jobs problem in the United States. Because of their level of training and education, the inner-city poor and other disadvantaged workers mainly have access only to jobs that pay the minimum wage or less and are not covered by health insurance. However, recent policies of the federal government could make such jobs more attractive. The United States Congress enacted an expansion of the earned income tax credit (EITC) in 1993. By 1996, the expanded EITC will increase the earnings from a minimum-wage job to $7 an hour. Families with incomes from $8,400 to

---

[20] Marshall, "School-to-Work Processes in the United States," 26.
[21] Ibid.
[22] Friedman, "Accent on Education as Talks on Jobs End."

$11,000 will receive cash payments of up to $3,370.[23] This expansion, and the previous expansions of the EITC in 1986 and 1990 under the Reagan and Bush administrations, reflected a recognition that wages for low-paying work have eroded and that other policies to aid the working poor—for example, the minimum wage—have become weaker.[24]

However, even when the most recent expansion of the EITC is fully in effect in 1996, it will still fall notably short of compensating for the sharp drop in the value of the minimum wage and the marked reductions in AFDC benefits to low-income working families since the early 1970s. Nonetheless, "the 1993 law set the EITC for a family with two or more children at the level that would bring a family of four with a full-time minimum wage worker to the poverty line if the family also received food stamps and the minimum wage was modestly raised.[25]

If this benefit is paid on a monthly basis and is combined with universal health care, the condition of workers in the low-wage sector would improve significantly and would approach that of comparable workers in Europe. The passage of universal health care is crucial in removing from the welfare rolls single mothers who are trapped in a public-assistance nightmare by the health care needs of their children. It would also make low-paying jobs more attractive for all low-skilled workers and therefore improve the rate of employment.

However, at the time of this writing, not only has legislation for universal health care been shelved, but the traditional bipartisan support for the EITC is beginning to erode in the Republican-controlled Congress. In May 1995, the Senate passed a budget resolution that includes an assumption that the EITC would be cut by roughly $13 billion over five years and $21 billion over seven years. . . .

Improving Accessibility to Suburban Jobs

The mismatch between residence and the location of jobs is a special problem for some workers in America because, unlike in Europe, the public transportation system is weak and expensive. This presents a special problem for inner-city blacks because they have less access to private automobiles and, unlike Mexicans, do not have a network system that supports organized car pools. Accordingly, they depend heavily on public transportation and therefore have difficulty getting to the suburbs, where jobs are more plentiful and employment growth is greater.[26] Until public transit systems are improved in metropolitan areas, the creation of privately subsidized car-pool and van-pool networks to carry inner-city residents to the areas of employment, particularly suburban areas, would be a relatively inexpensive way to increase work opportunities.[27]

---

[23] "Clinton Wages a Quiet but Energetic War Against Poverty," *New York Times,* 30 March 1994.

[24] Center on Budget and Policy Priorities, "Is the EITC Growing at a Rate That Is 'Out of Control'?" Washington, DC, 9 May 1995; and "The Earned Income Tax Credit Reductions in the Senate Budget Resolution," 5 June 1995.

[25] Center on Budget and Policy Priorities, "The Earned Income Tax Credit Reductions in the Senate Budget Resolution," 2.

[26] Mark Alan Hughes, "Over the Horizon: Jobs in the Suburbs of Major Metropolitan Areas" (report to Public/Private Ventures, December 1993).

[27] Based on several local transportation programs in Chicago (especially the "JobExpress" program created by the Suburban Job Link Corporation), Public/Private Ventures, a nonprofit research organization, "has designed a research demonstration to test a transportation strategy that links inner-city residents to job opportunities outside city centers. The elements of Bridges to Work are transportation (public or private), a mechanism *(continued)*

In the inner-city ghettos, the problems of spatial mismatch have been aggravated by the breakdown in the informal job information network. In neighborhoods in which a substantial number of adults are working, people are more likely to learn about job openings or be recommended for jobs by working kin, relatives, friends, and acquaintances. Job referrals from current employees are important in the American labor market. Individuals in jobless ghettos are less likely to gain employment through this process. But the creation of for-profit or not-for-profit job information and placement centers in various parts of the inner city not only could significantly improve awareness of the availability of employment in the metropolitan area but could also serve to refer workers to employers.[28] . . .

Increasing Public Sector Employment

If firms in the private sector cannot use or refuse to hire low-skilled adults who are willing to take minimum-wage or subminimum-wage jobs, then the jobs problem for inner-city workers cannot be adequately addressed without considering a policy of public-sector employment of last resort. Indeed, until current changes in the labor market are reversed or until the skills of the next generation can be upgraded before it enters the labor market, many workers, especially those who are not in the official labor force, will not be able to find jobs unless the government becomes an employer of last resort.[29] This argument applies especially to low-skilled inner-city black workers. It is bad enough that they face the problem of shifts in labor market demand shared by all low-skilled workers; it is even worse that they confront negative employer perceptions about their work-related skills and attitudes.

If jobs are plentiful even for less skilled workers during periods of economic expansion, then labor shortages reduce the likelihood that hiring decisions will be determined by subjective negative judgments concerning a group's job-related traits. Prior to the late 1970s, there was less need for the creation of public-sector jobs.[30] Not only was economic growth fairly rapid during periods of expansion, but "the gains from growth were widely shared." Before the late 1970s, public jobs of last resort were thought of in terms of "a counter-cyclical policy to be put in place during recessions and retired during recoveries. It is only since the late 1970s that the disadvantaged have been left behind during recoveries. The labor market changes . . . seem to have been permanently reduced private sector demand for less-skilled workers.[31]

Given the current need for public jobs to enhance the employment opportunities of low-skilled workers, what should be the nature of these jobs and how should they be implemented? Three thoughtful recent proposals for the creation of public jobs deserve serious consideration. One calls for the creation of public-sector infrastructure maintenance jobs, the second for public service jobs for less-skilled workers, and the third, which combines aspects of the first two, for WPA-style jobs of the kind created during the Franklin D. Roosevelt administration.

---

for connecting trained workers with available suburban jobs (a regional alliance of providers of employment services), and special support services (provided by a community agency). A four-year demonstration of the model is planned to begin in up to nine sites in Fall 1995." Annual Report, Public/Private Ventures (Philadelphia, 1994).

[28] For this short-term policy recommendation I am indebted to James S. Tobin.

[29] Sheldon Danziger and Peter Gottschalk, *America Unequal* (Cambridge, MA: Harvard University Press, 1995), 156.

[30] Ibid.

[31] Ibid., 174.

Edward V. Regan has advanced a proposal for a public-investment infrastructure maintenance program. He points out that "infrastructure maintenance and upgrading can . . . benefit the economy by creating jobs, particularly for the relatively unskilled, and by raising productivity, thereby contributing to long-term economic growth."[32] According to one estimate, $1 billion spent on road maintenance will directly generate 25,000 jobs and indirectly put 15,000 people to work.[33] On the other hand, new construction creates fewer jobs at higher wages. Another study reports that new building projects or major construction employs 40 percent fewer workers than do maintenance projects.[34] Just as other low-skill jobs are made more attractive by programs of health care, child care, and earned income tax credits, so would low-skill jobs in infrastructure maintenance.

Aside from creating jobs, infrastructure maintenance could lead to higher productivity. On this point, Regan states:

> Intuitively, fixing roads and bridges means less axle damage to trucks, fewer road mishaps and congestion, lowered costs of goods, and increased transportation productivity. Congested and deteriorated highways, broken water mains, inadequate sewage treatment, reduced transit services—all of these infrastructure deficiencies reduce productivity, drive up costs of goods and services, and inhibit people's access to employment. Any state or local government official who has tried to attract business facilities to a particu-

lar area and has watched business decision makers turn up their noses at cracked concrete and rusting bridges knows the practical meaning of those statements.[35]

Regan also points out that there are many other benefits stemming from an improved infrastructure that are not accounted for in standard economic measures, including shortened commuting times and reduced traffic congestion. If well selected, public investment in infrastructure maintenance could contribute to economic growth. According to the Congressional Budget Office, the national real rate of return for investments to maintain the current quality of the highway system would be 30 to 40 percent; those involving selected expansion in congested urban areas would be 10 to 20 percent.[36]

Although the creation of infrastructure maintenance jobs will provide some employment opportunities for low-skilled workers, the condition of today's labor market makes it unlikely that many of these jobs will actually go to high school dropouts or even to high school graduates with little or no work experience. To address this problem, the economists Sheldon Danziger and Peter Gottschalk, in a recently published book, have advocated the creation of a labor-intensive, minimum-wage public service jobs program of last resort for today's low-skilled and jobless workers.[37] They have in mind jobs such as daycare aides and playground assistants who can supervise in school gyms and public parks during after-school hours. These would be jobs for poor workers who cannot find a place in the private sector, jobs providing services that the fiscally strapped cities can no longer afford to supply through local resources.

[32] Edward V. Regan, "Infrastructure Investment for Tomorrow" (Public Policy Brief no. 141, Jerome Levy Economics Institute, Bard College), 43.

[33] Michael Montgomery and David Wyes, "The Impact of Infrastructure," *DRI/McGraw-Hill U.S. Review* (October 1992).

[34] Clark Wieman, "Road Work Ahead," *Technology Review* 96 (January 1993):42–48.

[35] Regan, "Infrastructure Investment," 44.

[36] Ibid.

[37] Danziger and Gottschalk, America Unequal.

Their plan for public service jobs differs in two important respects from recent proposals aimed at increasing work requirements and work incentives for recipients of welfare. First, their proposal is directed not just at welfare recipients but at *all poor workers* adversely affected by current economic shifts, including those who have been ineligible for, or who have chosen not to participate in, welfare. Only a small proportion of those whose labor-market prospects have diminished since the early 1970s have been welfare recipients. Second, their proposal addresses changes in the demand side of the labor market by emphasizing work opportunities and earnings supplements rather than work requirements or incentives. . . .

The final proposal under consideration here was advanced by the perceptive journalist Mickey Kaus of *The New Republic*. Kaus's proposal is modeled on the Works Progress Administration (WPA), a large public works program announced in 1935 by Franklin D. Roosevelt in his State of the Union address. The public works jobs that Roosevelt had in mind included highway construction, slum clearance, housing construction, rural electrification, and so on. As Kaus points out:

> In its eight-year existence, according to official records, the WPA built or improved 651,000 miles of roads, 953 airports, 124,000 bridges and viaducts, 1,178,000 culverts, 8,000 parks, 18,000 playgrounds and athletic fields, and 2,000 swimming pools. It constructed 40,000 buildings (including 8,000 schools) and repaired 85,000 more. Much of New York City—including LaGuardia Airport, FDR Drive, plus hundreds of parks and libraries—was built by the WPA. . . . Lester Thurow has suggested that New York's infrastructure is now decaying because no

WPA has existed to replace these public works in the half-century since.[38]

Kaus advances what he calls a neo-WPA program of employment for every American citizen over 18 who wants it. The program would provide useful public jobs at wages slightly below the minimum wage. Kaus's proposed program would not only eliminate the need to provide public assistance or "workfare" for able-bodied workers but, unlike welfare, the WPA-style jobs would be

> available to everybody, men as well as women, single or married, mothers and fathers alike. No perverse "anti-family" incentives. It wouldn't even be necessary to limit the public jobs to the poor. If Donald Trump showed up, he could work too. But he wouldn't. Most Americans wouldn't. There'd be no need to "target" the program to the needy. The low wage itself would guarantee that those who took the jobs would be those who needed them, while preserving the incentive to look for better work in the private sector.[39]

Kaus maintains that the work relief under his proposal, like the work relief under Roosevelt's WPA, would not carry the stigma of a cash dole. People would be earning their money. Although some workers in the WPA-style jobs "could be promoted to higher-paying public service positions," most of them would advance occupationally by moving to the private sector. "If you have to work anyway," asks Kaus, "why do it for $4 an hour?"

Kaus's proposal would also place a time limit on welfare for able-bodied recipients. After a certain date they would no longer be eligible for cash payments. However, unlike

---

[38] Mickey Kaus, *The End of Equality* (New York: Basic Books), 259.
[39] Ibid., 125.

the welfare program proposed in 1995 by the Republican-controlled Congress, public jobs would be available to those who move off welfare. Kaus argues that to allow poor mothers to work, government-funded day care most be provided for their children if needed. But this service has to be integrated into the larger system of child care for other families in the United States to avoid creating a "day-care ghetto" for low-income children.

In Kaus's proposal the WPA-style jobs would be supplemented with the earned income tax credit, which could be expanded at reasonable cost to lift all poor working families who work full-time throughout the year out of poverty. Because this subsidy would augment the income of all low-wage workers, those in low-level private-sector jobs would not be treated unfairly and their wages on average would be slightly higher than those in the guaranteed subminimum-wage public jobs.

Kaus maintains that there will be enough worthwhile WPA-style jobs for anyone who wants one. The crumbling infrastructure in American cities has to be repaired. Services cut back by the government for financial reasons, such as picking up trash two times a week and opening libraries every evening and on Saturdays, could be reinstated. Jobs for men and women could range from filling potholes and painting bridges to serving as nurse's aides, clerks, and cooks. "With a neo-WPA maintaining highways, schools, playgrounds, and subways, with libraries open every evening and city streets cleaned twice a day, we would have a common life more people would find worth reclaiming.[40] . . .

Prospects

Programs proposed to increase employment opportunities, such as the creation of WPA-

style jobs, should be aimed at broad segments of the U.S. population, not just inner-city workers, in order to provide the needed solid political base of support. In the new, highly integrated global economy, an increasing number of Americans across racial, ethnic, and income groups are experiencing declining real incomes, increasing job displacement, and growing economic insecurity. The unprecedented level of inner-city joblessness represents one important aspect of the broader economic dislocations that cut across racial and ethnic groups in the United States. Accordingly, when promoting economic and social reforms, it hardly seems politically wise to focus mainly on the most disadvantaged groups while ignoring other segments of the population that have also been adversely affected by global economic changes.

Yet, just when bold new comprehensive initiatives are urgently needed to address these problems, the U.S. Congress has retreated from using public policy as an instrument with which to fight social inequality. Failure to deal with this growing social inequality, including the rise of joblessness in U.S. inner cities, could seriously worsen the economic life of urban families and neighborhoods.

Groups ranging from the inner-city poor to those working- and middle-class Americans who are struggling to make ends meet will have to be effectively mobilized in order to change the current course and direction taken by policy makers. Perhaps the best way to accomplish this is through coalition politics that promote race-neutral programs such as jobs creation, further expansion of the earned income tax credit, public school reform, child care programs, and universal health insurance. A broad-based political coalition is needed to successfully push such programs through the political process.

Because an effective political coalition in part depends upon how the issues to be

---

[40]Ibid., 137.

addressed are defined, it is imperative that the political message underscore the need for economic and social reform that benefits all groups, not just America's minority poor.[41] The framers of this message should be cognizant of the fact that changes in the global economy are creating growing social inequality and situations which intensify antagonisms between different racial and ethnic groups, and that these groups, although often seen as adversaries, are potential allies in a reform coalition because they suffer from a common problem—economic distress caused by forces outside their own control.

In the absence of an effective political coalition, priorities will be established that do not represent the interests of disadvantaged groups. For example, in the House of Representatives, 67 percent of proposed spending cuts from the federal budget for the year 2000 would come from low-income programs, even though these programs represent only 21 percent of the current federal budget. Without an effective political coalition it is unlikely that Congress would be willing to finance the kinds of reforms that are needed to combat the new social inequality. At the time of this writing, the momentum is away from, not toward, social programs. Instead of recognizing and dealing with the complex and changing realities that have led to economic distress for many Americans, policy makers seek to assign blame and associate the economic problems of families and individuals with personal shortcomings such as lack of initiative, work ethic, or motivation. Consequently, there is very little support in favor of financing any social programs—even the creation of public service jobs for the limited number of welfare recipients who reach a time limit for receipt of welfare checks. Considering the deleterious consequences this shortsighted retreat from public policy will have for so many Americans, it is distressing that progressive groups, far from being energized to reverse the public policy direction in which the country is now moving, seem to be almost intimidated and paralyzed by the rhetoric of the Republican "Contract with America."

Accordingly, the kinds of long-term and immediate-term solutions that I have proposed stand little chance of being adopted, not to mention seriously considered, in the absence of a new political coalition of groups pressing for economic and social reform. Political leaders concerned about the current shift in public policy will have to develop a unifying rhetoric, a progressive message that resonates with broad segments of the American population, a message that enables groups to recognize that it is in their interest to join a reform coalition dedicated to moving America forward.

The solutions I have outlined were developed with the idea of providing a policy framework that would be suitable for and could be easily adopted by a reform coalition. The long-term solutions, which include the development of a system of national performance standards in public schools, family policies to reinforce the learning system in the schools, a national system of school-to-work transition, and ways to promote city-suburban integration and cooperation, would be beneficial to and could draw the support of a broad range of groups in America. The short-term solutions, which range from the development of job information and placement centers and subsidized car pools in the ghetto to the creation of WPA-style jobs, are more relevant to low-income Americans, but they are the kinds of opportunity-enhancing programs that Americans of all racial and class backgrounds tend to support.

Although my policy framework is designed to appeal to broad segments of the

---

[41] William Julius Wilson, *The Truly Disadvantaged: The Inner City, The Underclass, and Public Policy,* 2nd ed. (Chicago: University of Chicago Press, 1980).

population, I firmly believe that if adopted, it would alleviate a good deal of the economic and social distress currently plaguing the inner cities. The immediate problem of the disappearance of work in many inner-city neighborhoods would be confronted. The employment base in these neighborhoods would be increased immediately by the creation of WPA-style jobs, and income levels would rise because of the expansion of the earned income tax credit. Programs such as universal health care and day care would increase the attractiveness of low-wage jobs and "make work pay."

Increasing the employment base would have an enormous positive impact on the social organization of ghetto neighborhoods. As more people become employed, crime, including violent crime, and drug use will subside; families will be strengthened and welfare receipt will decline significantly; ghetto-related culture and behavior, no longer sustained and nourished by persistent joblessness, will gradually fade. As more people become employed and gain work experience, they will have a better chance of finding jobs in the private sector when they become available. The attitudes of employers toward inner-city workers will undergo change, in part because they would be dealing with job applicants who have steady work experience and would furnish references from their previous supervisors.

This is not to suggest that all the jobless individuals from the inner-city ghetto would take advantage of these employment opportunities. Some have responded to persistent joblessness by abusing alcohol and drugs, and these handicaps will affect their overall job performance, including showing up for work on time or on a consistent basis. But they represent only a small segment of the worker population in the inner city. Most workers in the inner city are ready, willing, able, and anxious to hold a steady job.

The long-term solutions that I have advanced would reduce the likelihood that a new generation of jobless workers would be produced from the youngsters now in school and preschool. We must break the cycle of joblessness and improve the youngsters' preparation for the new labor market in the global economy.

My framework for long-term and immediate solutions is based on the notion that the problems of jobless ghettos cannot be separated from those of the rest of the nation. Although these solutions have wide-ranging application and would alleviate the economic distress of many Americans, their impact on jobless ghettos would be profound. Their most important contribution would be their effect on the children of the ghetto, who would be able to anticipate a future of economic mobility and share the hopes and aspirations that so many of their fellow citizens experience as part of the American way of life.

Race and Residence

28

RESIDENTIAL SEGREGATION AND NEIGHBORHOOD CONDITIONS IN U.S. METROPOLITAN AREAS

Douglas S. Massey

Questions to Consider

Douglas Massey points out that almost all racial and ethnic groups are highly segregated in the United States. Racially integrated neighborhoods are an anomaly. Why is this the case? Why are blacks subject to the most severe discrimination in the housing market?

Social scientists have long studied patterns of racial and ethnic segregation because of the close connection between a group's spatial position in society and its socioeconomic well-being. Opportunities and resources are unevenly distributed in space; some neighborhoods have safer streets, higher home values, better services, more effective schools, and more supportive peer environments than others. As people and families improve their socioeconomic circumstances, they generally move to gain access to these benefits. In doing so,

they seek to convert past socioeconomic achievements into improved residential circumstances, yielding tangible immediate benefits and enhancing future prospects for social mobility by providing greater access to residentially determined resources.

Throughout U.S. history, racial and ethnic groups arriving in the United States for the first time have settled in enclaves located close to an urban core, in areas of mixed land use, old housing, poor services, and low or decreasing socioeconomic status. As group members build up time in the city, however, and as their socioeconomic status rises, they have tended to move out of these enclaves into areas that offer more amenities and improved conditions—areas in which majority members are more prevalent— leading to their progressive spatial assimilation into society.

The twin processes of immigrant settlement, on the one hand, and spatial assimilation, on the other, combine to yield a diversity of segregation patterns across groups and times, depending on the particular histories of in-migration and socioeconomic mobility involved (Massey, 1985). Groups experiencing recent rapid in-migration and slow socioeconomic mobility tend to display relatively high levels of segregation, whereas those with rapid rates of economic mobility and slow rates of in-migration tend to be more integrated.

When avenues of spatial assimilation are systematically blocked by prejudice and discrimination, however, residential segregation increases and persists over time. New minorities arrive in the city and settle within enclaves, but their subsequent spatial mobility is stymied, and ethnic concentrations increase until the enclaves are filled, whereupon group members are forced into adjacent areas, thus expanding the boundaries of the enclave (Duncan and Duncan, 1957). In the United States, most immigrant groups experienced relatively few residential barriers, so levels of ethnic segregation historically were not very high. Using a standard segregation index (the index of dissimilarity), which varies from 0 to 100, European ethnic groups rarely had indexes of more than 60 (Massey, 1985; Massey and Denton, 1992).

Blacks, in contrast, traditionally experienced severe prejudice and discrimination in urban housing markets. As they moved into urban areas from 1900 to 1960, therefore, their segregation indices rose to unprecedented heights, compared with earlier times and groups. By mid-century, segregation indices exceeded 60 virtually everywhere; and in the largest Black communities they often reached 80 or more (Massey and Denton, 1989b, 1993).

Such high indices of residential segregation imply a restriction of opportunity for Blacks compared with other groups. Discriminatory barriers in urban housing markets mean individual Black citizens are less able to capitalize on their hard-won attainments and achieve desirable residential locations. Compared with Whites of similar social status, Blacks tend to live in systematically disadvantaged neighborhoods, even within suburbs (Schneider and Logan, 1982; Massey et al., 1987; Massey and Fong, 1990; Massey and Denton, 1992).

In a very real way, barriers to spatial mobility are barriers to social mobility; and a racially segregated society cannot logically claim to be "color blind." The way a group is spatially incorporated into society is as important to its socioeconomic well-being as the manner in which it is incorporated into the labor force. It is important, therefore, that levels and trends in residential segregation be documented so that this variable can be incorporated fully into research and theorizing about the causes of urban poverty. To accomplish this, presented here is an overview and interpretation of historical trends in the residential segregation of Blacks, Hispanics, and Asians.

Long-Term Trends in Black Segregation

Massey and Hajnal (1995) examined historical trends in Black segregation at the state, county, municipal, and neighborhood levels. Their interpretation focused on two specific time periods—pre-World War II; 1900 to 1940; and postwar, from 1950 to 1990. Table 1 presents their data[1] on the geographic

---

[1] Residential segregation was measured using the index of dissimilarity, and racial isolation was measured using the P* index (Massey and Denton, 1988). The index of dissimilarity is the relative number of Blacks who would have to change geographic units so that an even Black-White spatial distribution could be achieved. The P* index is the percentage of Blacks residing in the geographic unit of the average Black person.

TABLE 1   Indices of Black-White Segregation Computed at Three
Geographic Levels, 1900 to 1940

	Years				
	1900	*1910*	*120*	*1930*	*1940*
Between states					
Dissimilarity	64	65	61	54	52
Isolation	36	34	30	25	24
Between counties					
Dissimilarity	69	70	66	60	59
Isolation	45	43	38	33	32
Between wards					
Dissimilarity					
Boston	—	64	65	78	79
Buffalo	—	63	72	81	82
Chicago	—	67	76	85	83
Cincinnati	—	47	57	73	77
Cleveland	—	61	70	85	86
Philadelphia	—	46	48	63	68
Pittsburgh	—	44	43	61	65
St. Louis	—	54	62	82	84
Average	—	56	62	76	78
Isolation					
Boston	06	11	15	19	—
Buffalo	04	06	10	24	—
Chicago	10	15	38	70	—
Cincinnati	10	13	27	45	—
Cleveland	08	08	24	51	—
Philadelphia	16	16	21	27	—
Pittsburgh	12	12	17	27	—
St. Louis	13	17	30	47	—
Average	10	13	23	39	—

Source: Massey and Hajnal (1995).

structure of Black segregation and racial isolation during the earlier period. Because of data limitations, segregation or isolation at the municipal level during this early period could not be measured.

As Table 1 shows, Blacks and Whites were distinctly segregated from one another across state boundaries early in the twentieth century. In 1900, for example, 64 percent of all Blacks would have had to move to a different state to achieve an even distribution across state lines, and most Blacks lived in a state that was 36 percent Black. These figures simply state the obvious, that in 1900,

some 90 percent of Blacks lived in a handful of southern states, which contained only 25 percent of all Whites (U.S. Bureau of the Census, 1979).

The isolation index shows that in the South, most Blacks lived in rural counties that were approximately 45 percent Black, yielding a high degree of segregation and racial isolation at the county level as well. The dissimilarity index for 1900 reveals that nearly 70 percent of all Blacks would have had to shift their county of residence to achieve an even racial distribution across county lines.

At the beginning of this century, for Blacks, the typical residential setting was southern and rural; for Whites it was northern and urban. Under conditions of high state- and county-level segregation, race relations remained largely a regional problem centered in the South. Successive waves of Black migration out of the rural South into the urban North transformed the geographic structure of Black segregation during the twentieth century, however, ending the regional isolation and rural confinement of Blacks. From 1900 to 1940, the index of Black-White dissimilarity fell from 64 to 52 at the state level and from 69 to 59 at the county level. Black isolation likewise dropped from 36 to 24 within states, and from 45 to 32 within counties.

The movement of Blacks out of rural areas, however, was accompanied by their progressive segregation within cities. Although we lack indices of Black-White dissimilarity for 1900, research has demonstrated that blacks were not particularly segregated in northern cities during the nineteenth century. Ward-level dissimilarity for Blacks in 11 northern cities circa 1860 had average indices of approximately 46 (Massey and Denton, 1993).

By 1910, however, the eight cities listed in Table 1 had an average index of 56, and the level of Black-White dissimilarity increased sharply during each decade after 1910, suggesting the progressive formation of black ghettos in cities throughout the nation. As Lieberson (1980) has shown, the growth of Black populations in urban areas triggered the imposition of higher levels of racial levels of racial segregation within cities. Before the U.S. Supreme Court declared them unconstitutional in 1916, many U.S. cities actually passed apartheid laws establishing separate Black and White districts. Thereafter, however, segregation was achieved by less formal means (see Massey and Denton, 1993:26–42). Whatever the

mechanism, the end result was a rapid increase in Black residential segregation, with the neighborhood segregation index rising from 56 to 78 between 1910 and 1940, a remarkable increase of 39 percent in just three decades.

The combination of growing urban Black populations and higher levels of segregation could only produce one possible outcome—higher levels of Black isolation. In 1900, the relatively small number of urban Blacks and the rather low level of Black-White segregation resulted in a low degree of racial isolation within neighborhoods. Among the eight cities shown in Table 1, the average isolation index was just 10; the typical urban Black resident lived in a ward that was 90 percent non-Black. Moreover, the index of isolation did not vary substantially from city to city. Urban Blacks early in the century were quite likely to know and interact socially with Whites (Massey and Denton, 1993:19–26). Indeed, on average they were more likely to share a neighborhood with a White person than with a Black person.

By 1930, however, the geographic structure of segregation had changed dramatically, shifting from state and county levels to the neighborhood level. The average isolation index was now 39 in neighborhoods, indicating that most Black residents in the cities under study lived in a ward that was almost 40 percent Black. In some cities, the degree of racial isolation reached truly extreme levels. The transformation was most dramatic in Chicago, where the isolation index went from 10 in 1900 to 70 in 1930, by which time, moreover, the dissimilarity index had reached 85. Similar conditions of intense Black segregation occurred in Cleveland, which by 1930 displayed a dissimilarity index of 85 and an isolation index of 51.

During the first half of the twentieth century, therefore, Black segregation was characterized by countervailing trends at opposite ends of the American geographic hierarchy. As Blacks and Whites became more integrated across states and counties, and as the regional isolation of Blacks declined, progressively higher levels of segregation were imposed on Blacks within cities. The regional integration of Blacks was accompanied by neighborhood segregation in the creation of urban ghettos that caused higher indices of segregation at the neighborhood level. In the course of this shift, however, one outcome remained constant: White exposure to Blacks was minimized. The only thing that changed was the geographic level at which the most extreme indices of segregation occurred.

Table 2 shows trends in Black segregation and racial isolation during the decades following World War II. In addition to indices computed at the state, county, and neighborhood levels, data permit a series of measures to be computed at the city level. These computations are based on cities with more than 25,000 inhabitants and measure the degree to which Blacks and Whites reside in separate municipalities.

From 1950 to 1970, the move toward integration at the state and county levels continued as Black out-migration from the South accelerated after World War II. At the state level, the Black-White segregation index dropped from 42 in 1950 to 28 in 1970, and at the county level from 52 to 47. Over the same period, the degree of Black isolation decreased from 20 to 16 at the state level, and from 27 to 23 in counties. As a result, from 1900 to 1970, macro-level segregation largely disappeared from the United States. Indices of Black segregation and racial isolation at the state level were cut in half, with segregation going from 64 to 28 and isolation from 36 to 16. Through a process of out-migration and regional redistribution, Blacks and Whites came to live together in states and counties throughout the nation. By 1970, race relations were no longer a regional problem peculiar to the South; race relations became a salient issue of national scope and importance.

The integration of Blacks at the state and county levels culminated around 1970, when Black migration from the South waned and then reversed, causing state-level indices to stabilize. After 1970, the index of Black-White dissimilarity at state levels remained fixed at 28, while Black isolation held virtually constant at 16 or 17. At the county level, indices of Black-White dissimilarity varied narrowly from 46 to 48, while the degree of black isolation increased slightly from 23 to 26.

At the neighborhood level, however, Black segregation continued to increase from 1950 to 1970, although at a decelerating pace that reflected the high level of racial segregation already achieved. The average dissimilarity index for the 12 metropolitan areas shown in Table 2 stood at 77 in 1950, rising to 81 in 1960, and 83 in 1970. Throughout this period, the average index of Black isolation stood at 67, indicating that most Black urban dwellers lived in a census tract[2] that was two-thirds Black. Thus the geographic structure of segregation that emerged early in the century was fully formed and stable by 1970. Whites and Blacks were integrated at the state and county levels, but segregated at the neighborhood level. Of the 12 metropolitan areas shown in the table, 9 had tract-level dissimilarity indices in excess of 80 in 1970, and 8 had isolation indices of 66 or more. By the end of the Civil Rights era, the geographic

---

[2] Tracts are relatively small, homogenous spatial units of 3,000 to 6,000 people defined by the U.S. Bureau of the Census to appropriate urban "neighborhoods" (White, 1987). Although the Census Bureau endeavors to maintain constant boundaries between censuses, population shifts and physical changes invariable require reclassifications that yield small inconsistencies over time. These changes, however, are unlikely to affect broad trends and patterns.

TABLE 2 Indices of Black-White Segregation Computed at Four Geographic Levels, 1950 to 1990

	Years				
	1950	*1960*	*1970*	*1980*	*1990*
Between states					
Dissimilarity	42	34	28	28	28
Isolation	20	18	16	17	17
Between Counties					
Dissimilarity	52	49	47	48	46
Isolation	27	24	23	26	26
Between cities (>25,000)					
Dissimilarity	35	35	40	49	49
Isolation	19	24	29	35	35
Between tracts					
Dissimilarity					
Chicago	88	90	92	88	86
Cleveland	87	90	91	88	85
Dayton	87	90	87	78	75
Detroit	83	87	88	87	88
Greensboro	59	67	65	56	60
Houston	71	79	78	70	67
Indianapolis	77	80	82	76	74
Milwaukee	86	86	91	84	83
Philadelphia	71	76	80	79	77
Pittsburgh	69	75	75	73	71
San Diego	65	69	83	64	58
Average	77	81	83	77	75
Isolation					
Chicago	—	84	86	83	84
Cleveland	—	80	82	80	81
Dayton	—	78	73	65	62
Detroit	—	—	76	77	82
Greensboro	—	64	56	50	56
Houston	—	73	66	59	64
Indianapolis	—	—	65	62	61
Milwaukee	—	—	74	70	72
Philadelphia	—	—	68	70	72
Pittsburgh	—	47	54	54	53
San Diego	—	42	42	26	36
Average	—	67	67	63	66

Source: Massey and Hajnal (1995).

isolation of urban Blacks, on the neighborhood level, was nearly complete. Although the number of cases examined here is small, the trends are consistent with those established by Massey and Denton (1987), based on a larger sample of metropolitan areas.

The Fair Housing Act of 1968 theoretically put an end to housing discrimination; however, residential segregation proved to be remarkably persistent (Massey and Denton, 1993:186–216). Among the 12 cities shown in Table 2, the average segregation index fell lightly from 1970 to 1990, going from 83 to 75, but Black isolation indices hardly changed. Scanning trends among individual metropolitan areas, it is difficult to detect a consistent pattern toward residential integration between 1970 and 1990, although Frey and Farley (1994) report some movement toward integration in smaller metropolitan areas, particularly those containing small Black population, military bases, universities, or large stocks of post-1970 housing.

Despite the relative stability of segregation achieved by 1970 at the state, county, and neighborhood levels, a remarkable change was occurring at the city level. From 1950 onward, Blacks and Whites were becoming more and more segregated across *municipal* boundaries. After 1950, Blacks and Whites not only tended to live in different neighborhoods; increasingly they lived in different municipalities as well. After 1950, in other words, Blacks and Whites came to reside in wholly different towns and cities. From 1950 to 1980, the index of Black-White dissimilarity increased from 35 to 49 at the municipal level, a change of 40 percent in just 30 years, a shift that was remarkably similar to the rapid change observed in neighborhood-level segregation during the early period of ghetto formation. Black isolation went from an index of 19 to 35 at the municipal level, an increase of 84 percent. By the end of the 1970s, the average Black urban dweller lived in a municipality that was 35 percent Black; and one-half of all urban Blacks would have had to exchange places with Whites to achieve an even municipal distribution.

The emergence of significant municipal-level segregation in the United States reflects demographic trends that occurred in all parts of the urban hierarchy—in non-metropolitan areas as well as central cities and suburbs. In 1950, there were no pre-dominantly Black central cities in the United States. Among cities with more than 100,000

inhabitants, none had a Black percentage in excess of 50 percent. By 1990, however, 14 cities were at least 50 percent Black, including Atlanta, Baltimore, Detroit, Gary, Newark, New Orleans, and Washington; together they were home to 11 percent of all Blacks in the United States. In addition, another 11 cities were approaching Black majorities by 1990, with percentages ranging from 40 percent to 50 percent, including Cleveland, St. Louis, and Oakland. Among cities with populations of 25,000 or more, only two municipalities in the entire United States were more than 50 percent Black in 1950, both in the South; but by 1990 the number had increased to 40. Some of these cities—such Prichard, Alabama, Kinston, North Carolina; and Vicksburg, Mississippi—were located in nonmetropolitan areas of the South. Others—such as Maywood, Illinois; Highland Park, Michigan; and Inglewood, California—were suburbs of large central cities in the North and West.

Recent Trends in Black Segregation

Table 3 shows indicators of Black residential segregation for the 30 U.S. metropolitan areas with the largest Black populations. As in Tables 1 and 2, these data are used to evaluate racial segregation from two vantage points. The first three columns show trends in the indices of spatial separation between Blacks and Whites using the index of dissimilarity, and the next three columns show trends in indices of Black residential isolation. The indices for 1970 and 1980, from Massey and Denton (1987), are metropolitan areas base on 1970 boundaries. Indices for 1990, from Harrison and Weinberg (1992), are based on 1990 geographic definitions. White and Black Hispanics were excluded, by both sets of researchers, from their subject sets of Whites and Blacks, and both sets

TABLE 3   Trends in Black Segregation and Isolation in the 30 Metropolitan Areas
with the Largest Black Populations, 1970 to 1990

Metropolitan	Dissimilarity Indices			Isolation Indices		
	1970[a]	1980[a]	1990[b]	1970[a]	1980[a]	1990[b]
Northern						
Boston, MA	81.2	77.6	68.2	56.7	55.1	51.2
Buffalo, NY	87.0	79.4	81.8	71.2	63.5	68.1
Chicago, IL	91.9	87.8	85.8	85.8	82.8	83.9
Cincinnati, OH	76.8	72.3	75.8	59.1	54.3	61.0
Cleveland, OH	90.8	87.5	85.1	81.9	90.4	80.8
Columbus, OH	81.8	71.4	67.3	63.5	57.5	52.5
Detroit, MI	88.4	86.7	87.6	75.9	77.3	82.3
Gary-Hammond- E. Chicago, IL	91.4	90.6	89.9	80.4	77.3	84.2
Indianapolis, IN	81.7	76.2	74.3	64.5	62.3	61.0
Kansas City, MO	87.4	78.9	72.6	74.2	69.0	61.6
Los Angeles- Long Beach, CA	91.0	81.1	73.1	70.3	60.4	69.3
Milwaukee, WI	90.5	83.9	82.8	73.9	69.5	72.4
New York, NY	81.0	82.0	82.2	58.8	62.7	81.9
Newark, NJ	81.4	81.6	82.5	67.0	69.2	78.6
Philadelphia, PA	79.5	78.8	77.2	68.2	69.6	72.2
Pittsburgh, PA	75.0	72.7	71.0	53.5	54.1	53.1
St. Louis, MO	84.7	81.3	77.0	76.5	72.9	69.5
San Francisco- Oakland, CA	80.1	71.7	66.8	56.0	51.1	56.1
Average	84.5	80.1	77.8	68.7	66.1	68.9
Southern						
Atlanta, GA	82.1	78.5	67.8	78.0	74.8	66.5
Baltimore, MD	81.9	74.7	71.4	77.2	72.3	70.6
Birmingham, AL	37.8	40.8	71.7	45.1	50.2	69.6
Dallas-Ft. Worth, TX	86.9	77.1	63.1	76.0	64.0	58.0
Greensboro- Winston Salem, NC	65.4	56.0	60.9	56.1	50.1	55.5
Houston, TX	78.1	69.5	66.8	66.4	59.3	63.6
Memphis, TN	75.9	71.6	69.3	78.0	75.9	75.0
Miami, FL	85.1	77.8	71.8	75.2	64.2	47.1
New Orleans, LA	73.1	68.3	68.8	71.3	68.8	71.9
Norfolk- Virginia Beach, VA	75.7	63.1	50.3	73.5	62.8	55.9
Tampa-St. Petersburg, FL	79.9	72.6	69.7	58.0	51.5	51.0
Washington, DC	81.1	70.1	66.1	77.2	68.0	66.7
Average	75.3	68.3	66.5	69.3	63.5	64.9

[a]Indices are from Massey and Denton (1987).
[b]Indices are from Harrison and Weinberg (1992).

of researchers computed indices using tracts as units of analysis.

Among the northern metropolitan areas shown, there is little evidence of any trend toward Black residential integration. Black segregation indices averaged about 85 in 1970, 80 in 1980, and 78 in 1990, a decline of only 8 percent in 20 years. Dissimilarity indices more than 60 are generally considered high, whereas those between 30 and 60 are considered moderate (Kantrowitz, 1973). At the rate of change observed between 1970 and 1990, the average level of Black-White segregation in northern areas would not reach the lower limits of the high range until the year 2043. At the slower rate of change prevailing from 1970 to 1980, it would take until 2067. As of 1990, no large northern Black community approached even a moderate level of residential segregation.

Indeed, in most metropolitan areas, racial segregation remained very high throughout the 20-year period. Dissimilarity indices were essentially constant in seven metropolitan areas—Cincinnati, Detroit, Gary, New York, Newark, and Philadelphia; in seven others—Buffalo, Chicago, Cleveland, Indianapolis, Milwaukee, Pittsburgh, and St. Louis—small declines still left Blacks extremely segregated. All the latter metropolitan areas had dissimilarity indices exceeding 70 in 1990, and in four cases, the index was more than 80. No other ethnic or racial group in the history of the United States has ever, even briefly, experienced such high levels of residential segregation (Massey and Denton, 1993).

A few metropolitan areas experienced significant declines in the level of Black-White segregation between 1970 and 1990, although the pace of change slowed considerably during the 1980s, compared with the 1970s. In Columbus, Ohio, for example, Black-White dissimilarity fell by more than 10 index points from 1970 to 1880 (from 82 to 71), but then dropped by only 4 points

through 1990. Likewise, San Francisco dropped from 80 to 72 during the 1970s, but went to just 68 by 1990.

The only areas that experienced a sustained decline in Black-White segregation across both decades were Los Angeles and Boston; but in each case, the overall index of segregation remained well within the high range. The drop in Los Angeles probably reflects the displacement of Blacks by the arrival of large numbers of Asian and, particularly, Hispanic immigrants (Massey and Denton, 1987). By 1990, for example, Watts, the core of the 1960s Black ghetto, had become predominantly Hispanic (Turner and Allen, 1991). The arrival of more than a million new immigrants in Los Angeles County between 1970 and 1980 put substantial pressure on the housing stock, and increased intergroup competition for residential units, especially at the low end of the market, leading to considerable neighborhood flux and residential mixing (Frey and Farley, 1996).

When large Black communities are subject to high levels of segregation, intense racial isolation is inevitable. In 1990, six metropolitan areas—Chicago, Cleveland, Detroit, Gary, New York, and Newark—had isolation indices of 80 or more, meaning that most Black people lived in neighborhoods that were more than 80 percent Black. Detailed analyses of neighborhoods show, however, that this overall average is misleading, because it represents a balance between a small minority of Blacks who reside in highly integrated neighborhoods and a large majority of Blacks who live in all-Black neighborhoods (Denton and Massey, 1991). Moreover, in four of the six metropolitan areas, the level of Black isolation actually increased between 1970 and 1990.

In other northern areas, the prevailing pattern of change in racial isolation was one of stability, with shifts of less than 5 percent from 1970 to 1990. The average isolation index of 68.9 in 1990 was virtually identical to the index of 68.7 observed two decades earlier; in other words, 20 years after the Fair Housing Act, Blacks were still unlikely to come into residential contact with members of other groups. The large ghettos of the North have remained substantially intact and were largely unaffected by Civil Right legislation of the 1960s.

Trends in Black segregation and isolation are somewhat different in the South, where segregation levels traditionally have been lower because of the distinctive history and character of southern cities. With social segregation enforced by Jim Crow legislation, Blacks and Whites before 1960 often lived in close physical proximity, with Black-inhabited alleys being interspersed between larger, White-occupied avenues (Demerath and Gilmore, 1954). During the postwar housing boom, moreover, rural Black settlements were often overtaken by expanding White suburbs, thereby creating the appearance of racial integration. For these and other reasons, Black-White segregation scores in the South traditionally have averaged about 10 points lower than in the North (Massey and Denton, 1993).

This regional differential is roughly maintained, as shown in Table 1, but southern areas display considerably greater diversity, despite the regional averages, than in the North. In some metropolitan areas, such as Baltimore, Houston, and Tampa, significant declines in segregation occurred during the 1970s, but declines slowed during the 1980s. In others, such as Dallas, Miami, and Norfolk, steady declines occurred throughout both decades. In Memphis and New Orleans, relatively small changes occurred, no matter which decade one considers. Two southern areas displayed increasing levels of Black-White segregation—Birmingham, where the increase was very sharp after 1970, and Greensboro, where an initial decline during the 1970s was reversed during the 1980s.

In general, then, Black-White segregation scores in the South appear to be converging on indices from 60 to 70, yielding an average of 67 and maintaining the traditional differential compared with the North. Metropolitan areas with segregation indices higher than the 60 to 70 range in 1970 experienced decreasing segregation, whereas those with indices less than 60 to 70 displayed increasing segregation; and those with indices within that range did not change much.

Only Norfolk differed from this pattern, with a significant and sustained decline in segregation during both decades, producing by 1990 a level of Black-White dissimilarity well within the moderate range. Many Norfolk residents are in the military, which has been more successfully integrated than other institutions in American life (Moskos and Butler, 1996: see also Volume II, Chapter 8). Frey and Farley (1994) demonstrated that areas dominated, economically, by military bases have significantly lower levels of Black-White segregation than others, controlling for a variety of other factors.

Although indices of Black-White dissimilarity may be lower in the South, the relative number of Blacks in urban areas is greater; so the average level of racial isolation within neighborhoods is not much different than in the North. From 1970 to 1990, there was relatively little change in the overall degree of Black isolation, with the average index decreasing from 69 in 1970 to 65 in 1990. In four southern areas—Baltimore, Memphis, Miami, and New Orleans—the Black isolation index was more than 70 in both decades; and in Birmingham, the index of Black isolation rose from 45 to 70 between 1970 and 1990. Only in Norfolk, which was rapidly desegregating, and in Tampa, which had relatively few Blacks, did isolation scores fall below 60. In most cities in the South, as in the North, Blacks were relatively unlikely to share neighborhoods with members of other racial or ethnic groups.

Thus, despite evidence of change in the South, Blacks living within the nation's largest urban Black communities are still highly segregated and spatially isolated from the rest of American society. Of the 30 northern and southern areas examined here, 19 still had Black-White dissimilarity indices in excess of 70 in 1990, and 12 had isolation indices in excess of 70. Either in absolute terms or in comparison to other groups, Blacks remain a very residentially segregated and spatially isolated people.

Recent Trends in Hispanic Segregation

Based on the historical experience of Blacks, recent demographic trends of Hispanics would be expected to have produced increasing levels of segregation during the 1970s and 1980s. In this period, there has been a remarkable resurgence of Hispanic immigration, yielding rapidly growing Hispanic populations in many metropolitan areas. In the Los Angeles metropolitan area, for example, the Hispanic population increased by 1.3 million between 1970 and 1990; Hispanics went from being 28 percent of the population to 38 percent. Because migrant networks channel new arrivals to neighborhoods where immigrants have already settled, such rapid in-migration could be expected to increase the concentration of Hispanics within enclaves and raise overall levels of isolation and segregation (Massey, 1985).

Although spatial assimilation may occur as income rises and the generations succeed one another, these socioeconomic mechanisms occur at a much slower pace than immigration and settlement. During periods of rapid immigration, therefore, segregation levels tend to rise; and the greater and more rapid the immigration, the more pronounced the increase in segregation.

Table 4 presents indicators of Hispanic-White dissimilarity and Hispanic residential isolation for the 30 metropolitan areas containing the largest Hispanic communities in the United States. In a significant subset of these metropolitan areas, Hispanics constitute an absolute majority of the total population, a condition that does not hold for any of the Black communities listed in Table 3. Because large minority populations increase the demographic potential for isolation, and because theorists hypothesize that high minority percentages foment greater discrimination on the part of majority members (Allport, 1958; Blalock, 1967), indices are tabulated separately for areas where Hispanics comprise a majority or near-majority (48 to 49 percent) of the population.

Despite the fact that demographic conditions in these metropolitan areas operate to maximize the potential for segregation, the degree of Hispanic-White residential dissimilarity proved to be quite moderate, and actually decreases over the two decades, going from an average of 55 in 1970 to 47 in 1990. Indices of Hispanic-White segregation were essentially constant in El Paso and Miami, and changed little in San Antonio and Corpus Christi. In Brownsville and McAllen, there were pronounced declines in segregation; but in no case was there an increase in Hispanic segregation from Whites within Hispanic-majority areas.

Indices of isolation, in contrast, were high and rose somewhat from 1970 to 1990. The increases did not stem from an increasing tendency for Whites and Hispanics to live apart, however, but from the large size and rapid growth of the Hispanic population. Isolation indices of 85 and 87 in Brownsville and McAllen mainly reflect the fact that Hispanics represent 82 and 85 percent of the metropolitan populations, respectively. Even if Hispanics were evenly

TABLE 4   Trends in Hispanic Segregation and Isolation in the 30 Metropolitan Areas with the Largest Hispanic Populations, 1970 to 1990

Metropolitan Area	Dissimilarity Indices			Isolation Indices		
	1970[a]	1980[a]	1990[b]	1970[a]	1980[b]	1990[b]
Hispanic majority						
Brownsville-Harlingen, TX	54.0[c]	42.0[d]	39.8	NA	NA	85.2
Corpus Christi, TX	55.9	51.6	47.5	63.5	63.6	67.8
El Paso, TX	49.6	51.2	49.7	71.5	74.1	80.0
McAllen-Pharr, TX	62.0[c]	48.0[d]	37.9	NA	NA	87.4
Miami, FL	50.4	51.9	50.3	46.5	58.3	73.4
San Antonio, TX	59.1	57.2	53.7	67.5	67.5	69.1
Other metropolitan						
Albuquerque, NM	45.7	42.5	41.9	54.4	50.6	53.4
Anaheim-Santa Ana, CA	32.0	41.6	49.9	19.4	31.0	50.1
Bakersfield, CA	5.8	54.5	55.4	34.9	42.1	55.7
Chicago, IL	58.4	63.5	63.2	25.1	38.0	51.3
Dallas-Ft. Worth, TX	42.5	47.8	49.5	18.6	24.0	41.1
Denver-Boulder, CO	47.4	47.4	46.5	27.4	27.5	33.8
Fresno, CA	40.8	45.4	47.8	37.6	44.6	58.7
Houston, TX	45.3	46.4	49.3	26.9	32.8	49.3
Jersey City, NJ	54.8	48.8	42.9	34.5	46.5	56.0
Los Angeles, CA	46.8	57.0	61.0	37.8	50.1	71.5
Nassau-Suffolk, NY	29.1	36.2	42.3	6.0	9.6	22.1
New York, NY	64.9	65.6	65.8	36.1	40.0	66.6
Newark, NJ	60.4	65.6	66.7	16.7	26.3	48.5
Oxnard-Simi Valley, CA	NA	NA	52.3	NA	NA	51.2
Philadelphia, PA	54.0	62.9	62.6	10.6	21.6	42.9
Phoenix, AZ	48.4	49.4	48.1	32.1	32.1	39.8
Riverside- San Bernardino, CA	37.3	36.4	35.8	30.2	31.6	42.7
Sacramento, CA	34.7	36.4	37.0	16.3	16.5	23.9
San Diego, CA	33.1	42.1	45.3	19.8	26.9	43.6
San Francisco-Oakland, CA	34.7	40.2	43.9	19.2	19.3	41.1
San Jose, CA	40.2	44.5	47.8	29.6	31.7	47.1
Tampa, FL	56.0	48.4	45.3	25.0	18.2	21.5
Tucson, AZ	52.6	51.9	49.7	46.7	43.1	48.8
Washington, DC	31.8	30.5	40.9	4.3	5.4	22.5
Average	45.3	48.0	49.6	26.5	30.8	45.1

Note: The Massey-Denton computations did not include several metropolitan areas that housed large Hispanic populations in 1990; therefore, additional indices have been taken from Lopez (1981) and Hwang and Murdock (1982). These figures, however, were computed for central cities rather than metropolitan areas and are therefore somewhat higher thus underestimating increases and overestimating declines in the level of Hispanic-White segregation.

[a] Indices are from Massey and Denton (1987).
[b] Indices from Harrison and Weinberg (1992).
[c] Indices are from Lopez (1981).
[c] Indices are from Hwang and Murdock (1982).

distributed, high levels of Hispanic-White contact are impossible to achieve in areas that are so predominantly Hispanic.

Among Blacks, however, isolation indices in the 80s, as in Chicago and Detroit, generally reflect the intense segregation of Blacks, rather than high Black population percentages; in both these metropolitan areas, Blacks constitute about 22 percent of the population. The contrast in the indices between Hispanics and Blacks is put into perspective by comparing indices for Hispanics in San Antonio with indices for Blacks in northern areas (see Table 1). Although Hispanic constitute 48 percent of San Antonio's population, its Hispanic-White dissimilarity index of 54 is less than that for Black-White indices in any northern area; and San Antonio's Hispanic isolation index of 69 is less than it is for 7 of the 18 black isolation indices.

A better indication of what happens to Hispanics in U.S. cities can be seen by examining segregation measures computed for metropolitan areas where Hispanics do not constitute such a large percentage of the population. On average, indices of Hispanic-White dissimilarity changed little in these areas, moving upward slightly from 45 in 1970 to 50 in 1990. In about one-third of these metropolitan areas—Chicago, Denver, Houston, New York, Phoenix, Riverside, Sacramento, and Tucson—Hispanic segregation remained nearly constant from 1970 to 1990; and in three cases—Albuquerque, Jersey City, and Tampa—indices of Hispanic-White dissimilarity decreased somewhat over the decades. In the remainder of the areas, indices of Hispanic segregation increased. In most cases, the increases were modest; but in several instances, segregation increased substantially over the two decades. In Los Angeles, for example, indices of Hispanic-White segregation increased from 47 to 61; in Anaheim the increase was from 32 to 50. Large increases

were also recorded in Nassau-Suffolk, San Diego, San Francisco, and Washington, D.C. In all these metropolitan areas there were rapid rates of Hispanic population growth and immigration from 1970 to 1990.

Despite these increases, indices of Hispanic-White segregation still remained moderate in 1990. Only 5 of the 24 metropolitan areas displayed indices in excess of 60. In 3 of these—New York, Newark, and Philadelphia—Puerto Ricans predominated; and since 1970, this group has stood apart from other Hispanic populations in displaying uniquely high levels of segregation (Jackson, 1981; Massey, 1981), a pattern largely attributable to the fact that many Puerto Ricans are of African ancestry (Massey and Bitterman, 1985; Massey and Denton, 1989a). The two remaining areas are Los Angeles, which experienced more Hispanic immigration than any other metropolitan area in the country, and Chicago, which contained a large population of Puerto Ricans in addition to a rapidly growing Mexican immigrant community.

Reflecting the increase in the proportion of Hispanics in most metropolitan areas, Hispanic isolation indices rose markedly throughout the nation. In those few areas where rates of Hispanic population increase were relatively slow—Albuquerque, Denver, Phoenix, and Tucson—the level of Hispanic isolation hardly changed; but as the rate of Hispanic immigration increased, so did the extent of spatial isolation. Given its popularity as a destination for Hispanic immigration, Hispanic isolation rose most strongly in Southern California cities, going from 19 to 50 in Anaheim, 38 to 72 in Los Angeles, and 20 to 40 in San Diego.

By the 1990, isolation indices equaled or exceeded 50 in about half of the metropolitan areas under consideration, but in only two cases—New York and Los Angeles, the two metropolitan areas with the largest Hispanic communities—did the index exceed 60. By way of contrast, only eight of the 30 Black communities examined earlier had Black isolation indices less than 60. Although contemporary demographic conditions suggest trends toward high segregation and rising isolation among Hispanics, they still do not display the high index ratings characteristic for Blacks in large urban areas.

Recent Trends in Asian Segregation

Although Asian immigration into U.S. urban areas accelerated rapidly after 1970, Asian populations are still quite small compared with either Black or Hispanic populations. Moreover, Asians are more highly concentrated regionally and found in a relatively small number of metropolitan areas. Table 5, therefore, presents indices of Asian segregation and isolation only for the 20 largest Asian communities, rather than the 30 largest.

Again demographic conditions for Asians favor substantial increases in segregation and isolation. In most metropolitan areas, immigration led to the rapid expansion of a rather small 1970 population base. In some areas, the number of post-1970 migrants actually exceeds the size of the original Asian community severalfold. Only 25,000 Asians lived in the Anaheim-Santa Ana metropolitan area in 1970, for example, but by 1990, their number had multiplied ten times, to 249,000. Over the same period, the Asian community of Los Angeles quadrupled, going from 243,000 to 943,000; and Chicago's Asian population grew from 62,000 to 230,000. In such cases where a sudden massive in-migration overwhelms a small, established community, indices of segregation often decrease initially as new arrivals distribute themselves widely, and then increase as these pioneers attract sub-sequent settlers to the same residential areas.

Such a patter of decreasing and then increasing Asian segregation is the most common pattern of change among the metropolitan areas shown in Table 5. The Asian-White dissimilarity index averaged 44 in 1970, decreased to 36 in 1980, and then increased to 41 in 1990. This basic trend occurred in 12 of the 20 metropolitan areas. In three more areas, an initial decline was followed by no change from 1980 to 1990. Only one area—San Jose—experienced a sustained increase in Asian segregation; but it began from a very low level of segregation in 1970. Four areas displayed uninterrupted declines in segregation across both decades—Boston, Nassau-Suffolk, Newark, and Paterson.

Despite rapid immigration and population growth, Asian segregation indices remained quite moderate in 1990. Increases observed between 1980 and 1990 simply restored the indices to their 1970 levels, yielding little net change over the two decades. Thus, Asian-White dissimilarity indices ranged from the low 30s in Anaheim, Nassau-Suffolk, Newark, Riverside, and Washington to 50 in San Francisco-Oakland. In no metropolitan area did the index of Asian segregation approach the high levels characteristic of Blacks in the nation's largest metropolitan areas.

Rapid Asian immigration into moderately segregated communities did produce rather sharp increases in the extent of Asian isolation, however, consistent with a process of enclave consolidation. The most pronounced increases occurred in areas where southeast-Asian refugees settled in large numbers—Anaheim, where the isolation index rose from 3 in 1970 to 22 in 1990; Fresno, where the increase was from 6 to 33; and San Diego, where the increase was from 6 to 29. Despite these increases, however, Asians still are not very isolated anywhere,

TABLE 5   Trends in Asian Segregation and Isolation in the 20 Metropolitan Areas with the Largest Asian Populations, 1970 to 1990

Metropolitan Area	Dissimilarity Indices			Isolation Indices		
	1970[a]	1980[a]	1990[b]	1970[a]	1980[a]	1990[b]
Anaheim, CA	27.4	24.9	33.3	2.6	7.7	22.4
Boston, MA	49.9	47.4	44.8	8.0	10.5	12.9
Chicago, IL	55.8	43.9	43.2	7.6	8.7	15.9
Dallas, TX	43.9	29.1	40.5	1.7	2.6	9.6
Fresno, CA	35.1	22.9	43.4	5.7	5.3	33.1
Houston, TX	42.7	34.6	45.7	1.5	4.5	15.7
Los Angeles, CA	53.1	43.1	46.3	12.3	15.2	40.5
Minneapolis, MN	45.2	36.9	41.2	3.0	6.2	15.1
Nassau-Suffolk, NY	42.2	34.5	32.4	1.0	2.2	5.9
New York, NY	56.1	48.1	48.4	11.6	14.3	32.8
Newark, NJ	50.2	34.4	29.6	1.5	2.9	7.5
Paterson-Clifton-Passaic, NJ	46.6	40.4	34.4	1.3	3.1	12.1
Philadelphia, PA	49.1	43.7	43.2	2.4	4.0	11.0
Riverside-San Bernardino, CA	31.9	21.5	32.8	2.5	4.1	10.2
Sacramento, CA	47.6	35.5	47.7	11.8	11.6	23.6
San Diego, CA	41.3	40.5	48.1	5.9	11.1	29.1
San Francisco-Oakland, CA	48.6	44.4	50.1	21.0	23.2	46.0
San Jose, CA	25.4	29.5	38.5	5.3	11.6	36.6
Seattle, WA	46.6	33.3	36.5	11.7	12.4	20.0
Washington, DC	36.5	26.8	32.3	2.2	5.7	12.6
Average	43.8	35.8	40.6	6.0	8.3	20.6

[a] Indices are from Massey and Denton (1987).
[b] Indices are from Harrison and Weinberg (1992).

including San Francisco-Oakland, where they constitute a higher percentage of the population (21 percent) than in any other metropolitan area. The isolation index of 46 means that Asians in the Bay Area are more likely to share a neighborhood with non-Asians than with each other; and in Los Angeles, which received the highest number of Asian immigrants between 1970 and 1990, the isolation index rose to just under 41. Thus, the largest and most segregated Asian communities in the United States are much less isolated than the most integrated Black communities.

Black Hypersegregation

Despite their apparent clarity, the above data actually understate the extent of Black isolation in U.S. society, because the data only incorporate two dimensions of segregation: evenness, as measured by the dissimilarity index, and isolation, as measured by the P* index. Massey and Denton (1988, 1989b), however, conceptualize segregation as a multidimensional construct. They contend there are five dimensions of spatial variation; in addition to evenness and isolation, residential segregation should be conceptualized in terms of clustering, concentration, and centralization. This five-dimensional conceptualization of segregation recently has been updated and revalidated with 1990 data (Massey et al., 1996).

Clustering is the extent to which minority areas adjoin one another spatially. It is maximized when Black neighborhoods form one large, contiguous ghetto; and it is minimized when they are scattered, as in a checkerboard pattern. *Centralization* is the degree to which Blacks are distributed in and around the center of an urban area, usually defined as the central-business district. *Concentration* is the relative amount of physical space occupied by Blacks; as segregation increases, Blacks are increasingly confined to smaller, geographically compacted areas.

A high level of segregation on any single dimension is problematic because it isolates a minority group from amenities, opportunities, and resources that affect socioeconomic well-being. As high levels of segregation accumulate across dimensions, however, the deleterious effects of segregation multiply. Indices of evenness and isolation (i.e., dissimilarity and P*), by themselves, cannot capture this multidimensional layering of segregation; therefore, there is a misrepresentation of the nature of Black segregation and an understatement of its severity. Blacks are not only more segregated than other groups on any single dimension of segregation; they are more segregated across all dimensions simultaneously.

Massey and Denton (1993) identified a set of 16 metropolitan areas that were highly segregated—i.e., had an index higher than 60—on at least four of the five dimensions of segregation, a pattern they called "hypersegregation." These metropolitan areas included Atlanta, Baltimore, Buffalo, Chicago, Cleveland, Dallas, Detroit, Gary, Indianapolis, Kansas City, Los Angeles, Milwaukee,

New York, Newark, and St. Louis. Within this set of areas, the Black-White dissimilarity index averaged 82, the average isolation index was 71, the mean clustering index was 58, the mean centralization index was 88, and the average concentration index was 83. By way of contrast, neither Hispanics nor Asians were hypersegregated within *any* metropolitan area.

These 16 metropolitan areas are among the most important in the country, incorporating 6 of the 10 largest urban areas in the United States. Blacks in these areas live within large, contiguous settlements of densely inhabited neighborhoods packed tightly around the urban core. Inhabitants typically would be unlikely to come into contact with non-Blacks in the neighborhood where they live. If they were to travel to an adjacent neighborhood, they would still be unlikely to see a White face. If they went to the next neighborhood beyond that, no Whites would be there either. People growing up in such an environment would have little direct experience with the culture, norms, and behaviors of the rest of American society, and have few social contacts with members of other racial groups.

Denton (1994) reexamined the issue of hypersegregation using data from the 1990 Census. According to her analysis, not only has Black hypersegregation continued, in many ways it has grown worse. Of the 16 metropolitan areas defined as hypersegregated in 1980, 14 remained so in 1990. In Atlanta the index of spatial concentration decreased to 59, just missing the criteria for hypersegregation, and in Dallas the isolation index decreased to 58. But both these figures are *just* below the threshold index of 60. All other metropolitan areas that were hypersegrated in 1980 showed an increase on at least one dimension by 1990. In 10 areas, isolation increased; concentration grew more acute in 9 areas; and clustering increased in 8. In Newark and Buffalo, segregation increased in all five dimensions simultaneously; and in Detroit, segregation increased on all dimensions but one.

In short, area that were hypersegregated in 1980 generally remained so in 1990, and there was little evidence of movement away from this extreme pattern. On the contrary, hypersegregation appears to have spread to several new urban areas during the 1980s. Of the 44 nonhypersegregated metropolitan areas studied by Massey and Denton in 1980, Denton (1994) found that 6 had come to satisfy the criteria by 1990—Birmingham, Cincinnati, Miami, New Orleans, Oakland, and Washington, D.C.—bringing the total number of hypersegregated metropolitan areas to 20. Taken together, these 20 contain roughly 11 million Blacks and constitute 36 percent of the entire U.S. Black population. As already pointed out, the percentage of Hispanics and Asians who are hypersegregated is zero.

Explaining the Persistence of Racial Segregation

A variety of explanations have been posited to account for the unusual depth and persistence of Black segregation in American cities. One hypothesis is that racial segregation reflects class differences between Blacks and Whites—i.e., because Blacks, on average, have lower incomes and fewer socioeconomic resources than Whites, they cannot afford to move into White neighborhoods in significant numbers. According to this hypothesis, Back-White segregation, to some extent, reflects segregation on the basis of income, with poor households, which happen to be predominantly Black, living in different neighborhoods than affluent households, which happen to be disproportionately White.

This explanation has not been sustained empirically, however. When indices of racial

segregation are computed within categories of income, occupation, or education, researchers have found that levels of Black-White segregation do not vary by social class (Farley, 1977; Simkus, 1978; Massey, 1979, 1981; Massey and Fischer, 1999). According to Denton and Massey (1988), Black families annually earning at least $50,000 were just as segregated as those earning less than $2,500. Indeed, Black families annually earning more than $50,000 were more segregated than Hispanic or Asian families earning less than $2,500. In other words, the most affluent Blacks appear to be more segregated than the poorest Hispanics or Asians; and in contrast to the case of Blacks, Hispanic and Asian segregation levels fall steadily as income rises, reaching low or moderate levels at incomes of $50,000 or more (Denton and Massey, 1988).

Another explanation for racial segregation is that Blacks prefer to live in predominantly Black neighborhoods, and that segregated housing simply reflects these preferences. This line of reasoning does not square well with survey evidence on Black attitudes, however. Most Blacks continue to express strong support for the ideal of integration. When asked on opinion polls whether they favor "desegregation, strict segregation, or something in-between," Blacks answer "desegregation" in large numbers (Schuman et al., 1985). Blacks are virtually unanimous in agreeing that "Black people have a right to live wherever they can afford to," and 71 percent would vote for a community-wide law to enforce this right (Bobo et al., 1986).

Black respondents are not only committed to integration as an ideal, survey results suggest they also strongly prefer it in practice. When asked about specific neighborhood racial compositions, Blacks consistently select racially mixed areas as most desirable (Farley et al., 1978, 1979, 1994; Clark, 1991). Although the most popular choice is a neighborhood that is half-black and half-White, as late as 1992, nearly 90 percent of Blacks in Detroit would be willing to live in virtually any racially mixed area (Farley et al., 1994).

Although Blacks express a reluctance about moving into all-White neighborhoods, this apprehension does not indicate a rejection of White neighbors per se, but stems from well-founded fears of hostility and rejection. Among Black respondents to a 1976 Detroit survey who expressed a reluctance to moving into all-White areas, 34 percent thought that White neighbors would be unfriendly and make them feel unwelcome, 37 percent felt they could be made to feel uncomfortable, and 17 percent expressed a fear of outright violence (Farley et al., 1979). Moreover, 80 percent of all Black respondents rejected the view that moving into a White neighborhood constituted a desertion of the Black community. More recently, Jackson (1994) linked the reluctance of Blacks to "pioneer" White areas not only to fears of rejection by White neighbors, but also to an *expectation* of discrimination by real estate agents and lenders.

Thus evidence suggests that racial segregation in urban America is not a voluntary reflection of Black preferences. If it were up to them, Blacks would live in racially mixed neighborhoods. But it is not up to them only, of course; their preferences interact with those of Whites and, thus, produce the residential configurations actually observed. Even though Blacks may prefer neighborhoods with an even racial balance, integration will not occur if most Whites find this level of racial mixing unacceptable.

On the surface, Whites seem to share Blacks' ideological commitment to open housing. The percentage of Whites on national surveys who agree that "Black people have a right to live wherever they can afford to" approached 90 percent in the late 1970s; and the percentage who disagreed with the view that "White people have a right to keep Blacks out of their [Whites'] neighborhoods," reached 67 percent in 1980. At present, few Whites openly call for the strict segregation of American society (Schuman et al., 1985, 1998; Sniderman and Piazza, 1993; Hochschild, 1995).

However, Whites remain quite uncomfortable with the implications of open housing in practice; only 40 percent, in 1980, said they would be willing to vote for a community-wide law stating that "a homeowner cannot refuse to sell to someone because of their race or skin color" (Schuman and Bobo, 1988). In other words, 60 percent of Whites would vote *against* an open housing law, which, in fact, has been federal law for 25 years.

White support for open housing generally declines as the hypothetical number of Blacks in their neighborhood increases. Whereas 86 percent of Whites in 1978 said they would not move if "a Black person came to live next door," only 46 percent stated they would not move if "Black people came to live in large numbers," and only 28 percent of Whites would be willing to live in a neighborhood that was half-Black and half-White (Schuman et al., 1985). Likewise, the severity of White prejudice toward Blacks increases as the percentage of Blacks in the area increases, a relationship that is *not* observed for Hispanics or Asians (Taylor, 1998).

When questions are posed about specific neighborhood compositions, moreover, it becomes clear that White tolerance for racial mixing is quite limited. According to Farley et al. (1994), 16 percent of Whites responding to a 1992 Detroit survey said they would feel uncomfortable in a neighborhood where only 7 percent of the residents were Black; 13 percent would be unwilling to enter such an area. When the Black percentage reaches 20 percent, one-third of all Whites say they would be unwilling to enter, 30 percent would feel uncomfortable, and 15 percent would seek to leave. A neighborhood about 30 percent Black exceeds the limits of racial tolerance for most Whites; 59 percent would be unwilling to move in, 44 percent would feel uncomfortable, and 29 percent would try to leave. Beyond a 50:50 balance, a neighborhood becomes unacceptable to all except a small minority of Whites; 73 percent said they would not wish to move into such a neighborhood, 53 percent would try to leave, and 65 percent would feel uncomfortable. As was stated, most Blacks feel a 50:50 racial mixture is desirable. This fundamental disparity between the two races has been confirmed by surveys conducted in Milwaukee, Omaha, Cincinnati, Kansas City, and Los Angeles (Clark, 1991).

The discrepancy between Whites' acceptance of open housing in principal and their reluctance to live among Blacks in practice yields a rather specific hypothesis about the nature of trends in Black-White segregation over the past 20 years. Hypothetically, declines in Black-White segregation should be confined primarily to metropolitan areas with relatively small Black populations, because in these places, desegregation can occur without Whites having to share their neighborhoods with too many Black people (Massey and Gross, 1991). If Black people make up 3 percent of the metropolitan population, for example, then complete desegregation yields an average of 3 percent Black within every neighborhood, which is well within most Whites' tolerance limits. If, however, Black people make up 20 percent of the metropolitan population, desegregation would produce neighborhoods that are 20 percent Black, on average, which exceeds the tolerance limits of many Whites, creates instability, and fuels a process of neighborhood turnover. In keeping with this hypothesis, Krivo and Kaufman (1999) show that desegregation between 1980 and 1990 was quite likely

where the Black population was small but very unlikely where it was large. As a result, observed declines in segregation during the 1980s were confined largely to metropolitan areas that contained very few Blacks.

Over the last three decades, U.S. metropolitan areas have been transformed by immigration and many have moved well beyond the simple Black-White dichotomy of earlier years, necessitating new approaches to the measurement of racial attitudes. A recent survey in Los Angeles sought to replicate the Detroit survey within an ethnically diverse metropolis. Analysis of these data by Zubrinsky and Bobo (1996) showed that all non-Black groups—Whites, Asians, and Hispanics—attribute a variety of negative traits to Blacks and consider Blacks to be the least desirable neighbors (see, also, Bobo and Zubrinsky, 1996). Blacks experience by far the greatest likelihood of hostility from other groups, and are universally acknowledged to face the most severe housing discrimination. The end result is a clear hierarchy of neighborhood racial preferences in Los Angeles, with Whites at the top, followed by Asians and Hispanics, and Blacks at the bottom. Segregation does not result from Black ethnocentrism so much as from avoidance behavior by other groups, all of whom seek to circumvent potential coresidence with Blacks.

These contrasting racial attitudes create large intergroup disparities in the demand for housing in racially mixed neighborhoods. Given the violence, intimidation, and harrassment that historically have followed their entry into White areas, Blacks express reluctance at being first across the color line. After one or two Black families have moved into a neighborhood, however, Black demand grows rapidly, given the high value placed on integrated housing. This demand escalates as the Black percentage rises toward 50 percent, the most preferred neighborhood configuration; beyond this point,

Black demand stabilizes and then falls off as the Black percentage rises toward 100 percent.

The pattern of white, Asian, and Hispanic demand for housing in racially mixed areas follows precisely the opposite trajectory. Demand is strong for homes in all-White areas, but once one or two Black families enter a neighborhood, demand begins to falter as some non-Black families leave and others refuse to move in. The acceleration in residential turnover coincides with the expansion of Black demand, making it likely that outgoing White, Hispanic, or Asian households are replaced by Black families. As the Black percentage rises, overall demand drops ever more steeply, and Black demand rises at an increasing rate. By the time Black demand peaks at the 50 percent mark, practically no other groups are willing to enter and most are trying to leave. Thus, racial segregation appears to be created by a process of racial turnover fueled by the persistence of significant anti-Black prejudice on the part of virtually every other group.

This model of racial change was proposed two decades ago by Schelling (1971), who argued that integration is an unstable outcome because Whites prefer lower minority proportions than Blacks—even though Whites might accept some Black neighbors. Yet by itself, Schelling's explanation is incomplete. Whites can only avoid coresidence with Blacks if mechanisms exist to keep Blacks out of neighborhoods to which they might otherwise be attracted. Whites can only flee a neighborhood where Blacks have entered if there are other all-White neighborhoods to go to, and this escape will only be successful if Blacks are unlikely or unable to follow.

Racial discrimination was institutionalized in the real estate industry during the 1920s and well established in private practice by the 1940s (Massey and Denton, 1993). Evidence shows that discriminatory behavior was widespread among realtors at least until 1968, when the Fair Housing Act was passed (Helper, 1969; Saltman, 1979). After that, outright refusals to rent or sell to Blacks became rare, given that overt discrimination could lead to prosecution under the law.

Black home seekers now face a more subtle process of exclusion. Rather than encountering "White only" signs, they encounter a covert series of barriers. Blacks who inquire about an advertised unit may be told that it has just been sold or rented; they may be shown only the advertised unit and told that no others are available; they may only be shown houses in Black or racially mixed areas and led away from White neighborhoods; they may be quoted a higher rent or selling price than Whites; they may be told that the selling agents are too busy and to come back later; their phone number may be taken but a return call never made; they may be shown units but offered no assistance in arranging financing; or they simply may be treated brusquely and discourteously in hopes that they will leave.

Although individual acts of discrimination are small and subtle, they have a powerful cumulative effect in lowering the probability of Black entry into White neighborhoods. Because the discrimination is latent, however, it is not easily observable, and the only way to confirm whether or not it has occurred is to compare the treatment of both Black and White clients that have similar social and economic characteristics. If White clients receive systematically more favorable treatment, then one can safely conclude that discrimination has taken place (Fix et al., 1993).

Differences in the treatment of White and Black home seekers are measured by means of a housing audit. Teams of White and Black auditors are paired and sent to randomly selected realtors to pose as clients seeking a home or apartment. The auditors are trained to present comparable housing needs and family characteristics, and to express similar tastes; they are assigned equivalent social and economic traits by the investigator. After each encounter, the auditors fill out a detailed report of their experiences and the results are tabulated and compared to determine the nature and level of discrimination (Yinger, 1986, 1989).

Local fair-housing organizations began to conduct such studies at the end of the 1960s. These efforts revealed that discrimination was continuing despite the Fair Housing Act. A 1969 audit of realtors in St. Louis, for example, documented a pattern and practice of discrimination sufficient to force four realty firms to sign a consent decree with the U.S. Department of Justice wherein they agreed to desist from certain biased practices (Saltman, 1979). Likewise, a 1971 audit study carried out in Palo Alto, California, found that Blacks were treated in a discriminatory fashion by 50 percent of the area's apartment complexes; and a 1972 audit of apartments in suburban Baltimore uncovered discrimination in more than 45 percent of the cases (Saltman, 1979).

Racial discrimination clearly persisted through the 1980s. In one 1983 Chicago study, suburban realtors showed homes to 67 percent of White auditors but only 47 percent of Black auditors (Hintzen, 1983). Another Chicago study done in 1985 revealed that Whites were offered financial information at nearly twice the rate it was offered to Blacks (Schroeder, 1985). One developer working in Chicago's south suburbs refused to deal with Blacks at all; Blacks were always told that no properties were available, even though 80 percent of Whites were shown real estate (Bertram, 1988). In the same study, realtors told 92 percent of Whites that apartments were available but

gave this information to only 46 percent of Blacks.

Audit studies of other metropolitan areas reveal similar levels of racial discrimination. According to Yinger's (1986) review of studies conducted in metropolitan Boston and Denver during the early 1980s, Black home seekers had between a 38 and a 59 percent chance of receiving unfavorable treatment, compared to whites, on any given real estate transaction. Through various lies and deceptions, Blacks were informed of only 65 of every 100 units presented to Whites, and they inspected fewer than 54 of every 100 shown to Whites.

In 1987, Galster (1990a) wrote to more than 200 local fair-housing organizations and obtained written reports of 71 different audit studies carried out during the 1980s— 21 in the home sales market and 50 in the rental market. Despite differences in measures and methods, he concluded that "racial discrimination continues to be a dominant feature of metropolitan housing markets in the 1980s" (p. 172). Using a conservative measure of racial bias, he found that Blacks averaged a 20 percent chance of experiencing discrimination in the sales market and a 50 percent chance in the rental market.

Studies have also examined the prevalence of "steering" by real estate agents. Steering occurs when White and Black clients are guided to neighborhoods that differ systematically with respect to social and economic characteristics, especially racial composition. A study carried out in Cleveland during the early 1970s found that 70 percent of companies engaged in some form of steering (Saltman, 1979); and an examination of realtors in metropolitan Detroit during the mid-1970s revealed that, compared to Whites, Blacks were shown homes in less-expensive areas that were located closer to Black population centers (Pearce, 1979).

Galster (1990b) studied six real estate firms located in Cincinnati and Memphis and found that racial steering occurred in roughly 50 percent of the transactions sampled during the mid-1980s. As in the Detroit study, homes shown to Blacks tended to be in racially mixed areas and were more likely to be adjacent to neighborhoods with a high percentage of Black residents. White auditors were rarely shown homes in integrated neighborhoods, unless they specifically requested them, and even after the request was honored, they continued to be guided primarily to homes in White areas. Sales agents also made numerous positive comments about White neighborhoods to White clients but said little to Black home buyers. In a broader review of 36 different audit studies, Galster (1990c) discovered that such selective commentary by agents is probably more common than overt steering.

These local studies, however suggestive, do not provide a comprehensive national assessment of housing discrimination in contemporary American cities. The first such effort was mounted by the U.S. Department of Housing and Urban Development (HUD) in 1977. The study covered 40 metropolitan areas with significant Black populations and confirmed the results of earlier local audits. Discrimination clearly was not confined to a few isolated cases. Nationwide, Whites were favored on 48 percent of transactions in the sales market and on 39 percent of those in the rental market (Wienk et al., 1979).

The 1977 HUD audit survey was replicated in 1988: the Housing Discrimination Study (HDS) covered both the rental and sales markets, and the auditors were given incomes and family characteristics appropriate to the housing unit advertised (Yinger, 1995). Twenty audit sites were randomly selected from among metropolitan areas having a central city population exceeding 100,000 with Blacks constituting more than 12 percent of the population. Real estate ads in major metropolitan newspapers were randomly sampled.

The typical advertised unit was located in a White, middle-to-upper-class area, as were most of the real estate offices; remarkably few homes were in Black or racially mixed neighborhoods. Even after controlling for the social and economic composition of its neighborhood, the percentage of Black residents was strong predictor of whether a unit was advertised at all (Turner et al., 1991). Galster and his colleagues found a similar bias in real estate advertising in Milwaukee from 1981 to 1984 (Galster et al., 1987). Compared to homes in White areas, those in racially mixed or Black areas were much less likely to be advertised, much more likely to be represented by one-line ads when they were advertised, and much less likely to be favorably described. Real estate companies apparently do a poor job of marketing homes in racially mixed neighborhoods, thereby restricting White demand for integrated housing and promoting segregation.

Realtors were approached by auditors who inquired about the availability of the advertised unit; they also asked about other units that might be on the market. Based on the results, HDS provided evidence that discrimination against Blacks had declined little since 1977. Indeed, it appears the 1977 HUD study may have understated both the incidence and severity of housing discrimination in American cities (Yinger, 1995). According to HDS data, housing was made more available to Whites in 45 percent of the transactions in the rental market and in 34 percent of those in the sales market. Whites received more favorable credit assistance in 46 percent of sales encounters, and were offered more favorable terms in 17 percent of rental transactions. When housing availability and financial assistance were considered together, the likelihood of experiencing racial discrimination was 53 percent in both the rental and sales markets.

The sales audits also assessed the frequency of racial steering; when this form of discrimination was also considered, the likelihood of discrimination rose to 60 percent (Yinger, 1995). Because these figures refer to the odds on any single visit to a realtor, over a series of visits, they accumulate to extremely high probabilities—well over 90 percent in three visits. In the course of even the briefest search for housing, therefore, Blacks are almost certain to encounter discrimination.

In addition to measuring the incidence of discrimination—i.e., the percentage of encounters during which discrimination occurs—HDS also measured its severity—i.e., the number of units made available to Whites but not to Blacks. In stark terms, Backs were systematically shown, offered, and invited to inspect far fewer homes than comparably qualified Whites. As a result, Blacks' access to urban housing is substantially reduced.

The likelihood that an additional unit was shown to Whites but not Blacks was 65 percent, and the probability that an additional unit was recommended to Whites but not Blacks was 91 percent. The HDS auditors encountered equally severe bias in the marketing of nonadvertised units; the likelihood that an additional unit was inspected by Whites only was 62 percent, and the probability that Whites only were invited to see another unit was 90 percent. Comparable results were found in urban sales markets, where the severity of discrimination varied from 66 percent to 89 percent. Thus, no matter what index one considers, between 60 percent and 90 percent of the housing units made available to Whites were not brought to the attention of Blacks (Yinger, 1995).

The 1988 HDS audit found equally severe discrimination in the provision of credit assistance to home buyers. Of every 100 times that agents discussed a fixed-rate mortgage, 89 of the discussions were with Whites only, and of 100 times that adjustable-rate loans were brought up, 91 percent of the discussions excluded Blacks (Yinger, 1995).

Although these audit results are compelling, they do not directly link discrimination to segregation. They show only that discrimination and segregation exist and persist simultaneously across time. Fortunately, several studies have been conducted to document and quantify the links among discrimination, prejudice, and segregation.

Using data from the 1977 HUD audit study, Galster (1986) related cross-metropolitan variation in housing discrimination to the degree of racial segregation in different urban areas. He not only confirmed the empirical linkage, he also discovered that segregation itself has important feedback effects on socioeconomic status (see also Galster and Keeney, 1988). Discrimination not only leads to segregation; segregation, by restricting economic opportunities for Blacks, produces interracial economic disparities that incite further discrimination and more segregation.

In a detailed study of census tracts in the Cleveland area, Galster found that neighborhoods that were all-White or racially changing evinced much higher rates of discrimination than areas that were stably integrated or predominantly Black (Galster, 1987, 1990d). Moreover, the pace of racial change was strongly predicted by the percentage of Whites who agreed that "White people have a right to keep Blacks out of their neighborhoods." Areas where such sentiment was documented experienced systematic White population loss after only a few Blacks had moved in, and the speed of transition accelerated rapidly beyond a point of 3 percent Black. Tracts where Whites expressed a low degree of racist sentiment, however, showed little tendency for White flight up to a composition of around 40 percent Black. Rather than declining in significance, race remains the dominant organizing principal of U.S. urban housing markets. When it comes to determining where, and with whom, Americans live, race appears to overwhelm other considerations.

Compared with Blacks, relatively few studies of prejudice and discrimination against Hispanics have been conducted, and there are no national studies that examine attitudes and behaviors concerning Asians. Hakken (1979) found that discrimination against Hispanics in the rental housing market of Dallas was as likely as that against Blacks, and similar results were reported by Feins and colleagues for Boston (Feins et al., 1981). James and Tynan (1986) replicated these results in a study of Denver's sales market, but they found a substantially lower probability of discrimination against Hispanics in the rental market; and despite the relatively high likelihood of discrimination in home sales, in reality, severity of discrimination against Hispanics was not great; the average number of housing units offered to Hispanics was not significantly different than the number offered to non-Hispanic whites (James and Tynan, 1986).

As with Blacks, however, discrimination against Hispanics appears to have a racial basis. Hakken (1979) found that dark-skinned Chicanos were more likely to experience discriminatory treatment than Blacks, whereas light-skinned Hispanics were less likely to experience such treatment. Consistent with this finding, Massey and Denton (1992) found that Mexicans who identified themselves as mestizos (people of mixed European and Indian origin) were less likely to achieve suburban residence than those who identified themselves as White.

The extent of the racial effect is greater among Caribbean Hispanics, particularly Puerto Ricans, among whom the racial continuum runs from European to African. Denton and Massey (1989) showed that for Puerto Ricans who identified themselves as Black, housing was as segregated as for U.S. Blacks, whereas those who identified themselves as White experienced low-to-moderate levels of separation. Discrimination was mixed for Caribbean Hispanics who said they were of mixed Black-White origins, but were much closer to the high level of Black segregation. The degree of segregation experienced by racially mixed Caribbean Hispanics was generally greater than that experienced by racially mixed Mexicans, suggesting greater White antipathy toward Africans than Amerindians.

The most complete and systematic data on the treatment of Hispanics in urban real estate markets comes from HUD's 1988 HDS (Yinger, 1995). Results from this study indicate that the overall incidence of housing discrimination was greater for Hispanics than Blacks in the sale market (42 versus 34 percent), but less for Hispanics than Blacks in the rental market (32 versus 45 percent), replicating the earlier results of James and Tynan (1986) in Denver. Also in keeping with the findings of James and Tynan was the fact that the severity of discrimination in the sales market was considerable lower for Hispanics than for Blacks; whereas the marginal probability that an additional housing unit was denied to Blacks was 88 percent, it was only 66 percent for Hispanics. As in earlier research, in the 1988 HDS, race figured prominently in the treatment of Hispanics— dark-skinned Hispanics were much more likely to experience discrimination in the sales market than light-skinned Hispanics (Yinger, 1995). Paradoxically, therefore, recent research on discrimination involving Hispanics reaffirms the conclusion that race remains the dominant organizing principle in U.S. urban housing markets.

Segregation and the Concentration of Poverty

The past two decades have been hard on the socioeconomic well-being of many Americans. The structural transformation of the U.S. economy from goods production to service provision generated a strong demand for workers with high and low levels of schooling, but offered few opportunities for those with modest education and training. In the postindustrial economy that emerged after 1973, labor unions withered, the middle class bifurcated, income inequality grew, and poverty spread; and this new stratification between people was accompanied by a growing spatial separation between them. The stagnation of income proved to be remarkably widespread, and inequality rose not only for minorities—Blacks, Hispanics, and Asians—but also for non-Hispanic Whites (Danziger and Gottschalk, 1995; Levy, 1995; Morris et al., 1994). As a result of their continued racial segregation, however, the spatial concentration of poverty was especially severe for Blacks (Massey and Eggers, 1990; Massey et al., 1991; Krivo et al., 1998). High levels of income inequality paired with high levels of racial or ethnic segregation result in geographically concentrated poverty, because the poverty is localized in a small number of densely settled, racially homogenous, tightly clustered areas, often in an older, urban core abandoned by industry. Had segregation not been in place, the heightened poverty would be distributed widely throughout the metropolitan area (Massey, 1990; Massey and Denton, 1993). By 1990, 83 percent of poor inner-city Blacks lived in neighborhoods that were at least 20 percent poor (Kasarda, 1993).

In a recent paper, Massey and Fischer (2000) broadened this theoretical perspective by arguing that racial segregation interacts with any structural shift that affects the distribution of income, or the spatial configuration of the classes, to concentrate poverty spatially. Specifically, they hypothesize that as racial segregation increases, decreasing incomes, increasing inequality, increasing class segregation, and increasing immigration are more strongly translated into geographic isolation of the poor. Thus, these structural trends produce high and increasing concentrations of poverty for highly segregated groups, but low and falling concentrations of poverty among nonsegregated groups.

Because more than 70 percent of urban Blacks are highly segregated, but 90 percent of all other groups are not, the population of poor experiencing high concentrations of poverty is overwhelmingly Black (Massey and Fischer, 2000). Given the interaction between racial segregation and the changing socioeconomic structure of American society, the issue of race cannot be set aside to focus on the politics of race versus class. Although the implementation of policies that raise average incomes, lower income inequality, and reduce class segregation would lower the spatial isolation of the urban poor, policies to promote the desegregation of urban society would probably have an even greater effect, given segregation's critical role in determining how these factors generate concentrated poverty.

The Consequences of Concentrated Poverty

The argument that the prevalence of concentrated poverty among Blacks decisively undermines the life chances of the Black poor was first made forcefully by Wilson (1987). He argued that class isolation, through a variety of mechanisms, reduced employment, lowered incomes, depressed marriage, and increased unwed childbearing *over and above any effects of individual or family deprivation.* At the time Wilson made this argument, relatively little evidence existed to support it (Jencks and Mayer, 1990), but over the past decade a growing number of studies have accumulated to sustain the basic thrust of Wilson's hypothesis.

In 1988, the Rockefeller and Russell Sage Foundations funded the Social Science Research Council (SSRC) to establish a program of research into the causes and consequences of persistent urban poverty. One SSRC subcommittee—the Working Group on Communities and Neighborhoods, Family Processes, and Individual Development—met regularly over the next eight years to conceptualize and then implement a program of research to determine how concentrated poverty affected social and cognitive development. The ultimate product was a recently published series of studies (Brooks-Gunn et al., 1997) examining the effect of neighborhood conditions on cognitive and social development at three points in the life cycle—early childhood (ages 3–7), late childhood/early adolescence (ages 11–15), and late adolescence (ages 16–19).

The empirical analyses clearly show that socioeconomic inequality is perpetuated by mechanisms operating at the neighborhood level, although the specific pathways are perhaps more complex than Wilson or others imagined. Not only do neighborhood effects vary in their nature and intensity at different stages of the life cycle, they are often conditioned by gender, mediated by family processes, and possibly interactive in how they combine with individual factors to determine social outcomes. Despite these complexities, however, research permits three broad generalizations.

- First, neighborhoods seem to influence individual development most powerfully in early childhood and late adolescence.
- Second, the spatial concentration of affluence appears to be more important in determining cognitive development and

academic achievement than the concentration of poverty.
- Third, the concentration of male joblessness affects social behavior more than cognitive development, particularly among Blacks.

These effects persist even after controlling for unobserved heterogeneity. Thus, Wilson's (1987) theory is basically correct—there is something to the hypothesis of neighborhood effects.

One of the most important disadvantages transmitted through prolonged exposure to the ghetto is educational failure. Datcher (1982) estimates that moving a poor Black male from his typical neighborhood (66 percent Black with an average annual income of $8,500) to a typical White neighborhood (86 percent White with a mean income of $11,500) would raise his educational attainment by nearly a year. Corcoran and colleagues (1989) found similar results. Crane (1991) likewise shows that the dropout probability for Black teenage males increases dramatically as the percentage of low-status workers in the neighborhood increases. Residence in a poor neighborhood also decreases the odds of success in the labor market. Datcher (1982) found that growing up in a poor Black area lowered male earnings by at least 27 percent, although Corcoran and colleagues (1989) put the percentage at about 18 percent.

Exposure to conditions typical of the ghetto also dramatically increases the odds of pregnancy and childbirth among teenage girls. According to estimates by Crane (1991), the probability of a teenage birth increases dramatically as the percentage of low-status workers in the neighborhood increases. Similarly, Hogan and Kitagawa (1985) found that living in a very poor neighborhood raised the monthly pregnancy rate among Black adolescents by 20 percent and lowered the age at which they became sexually active. Furstenburg et al. (1987) have shown that attending school in integrated, rather than segregated, classrooms substantially lowers the odds that 15- to 16-year-old Black girls will experience sexual intercourse. Brooks-Gunn et al. (1993) found that the probability of giving birth before age 29 rose markedly as the percentage of high-income families fell.

In a dynamic longitudinal analysis that followed young Black men and women from ages 15 to 30, Massey and Shibuya (1995) found that young men who live in neighborhoods of concentrated male joblessness are more likely to be jobless themselves, controlling for individual and family characteristics, and that Black women in such neighborhoods were significantly less likely to get married.

Massey and Shibuya (1995) also linked concentrated disadvantage to higher probabilities of criminality, a link well-documented by Krivo and Peterson (1996) using aggregate data. The concentration of criminal activity that accompanies the concentration of deprivation accelerates the process of neighborhood transition and, for Blacks, resegregation (Morenoff and Sampson, 1997); it also helps drive up rates of Black-on-Black mortality, which have reached heights unparalled for any other group (Almgren et al., 1998; Guest et al., 1998). The spatial concentration of crime presents special problems for the Black middle class, who must adopt extreme strategies to insulate their children from the temptations and risks of the street (Anderson, 1990; Patillo, 1998).

The quantitative evidence thus suggests that any process that concentrates poverty within racially isolated neighborhoods will simultaneously increase the odds of socioeconomic failure within the segregated group. People who grow up and live in environments of concentrated poverty and social isolation are more likely to become teenage parents, drop out of school, achieve

low educations, earn lower adult incomes, and become involved with crime—either as perpetrator or victim.

One study has directly linked the socioeconomic disadvantages suffered by individual minority members to the degree of segregation they experience in society. Using individual, community, and metropolitan data from the 50 largest U.S. metropolitan areas in 1980, Massey et al. (1991) showed that group segregation and poverty rates interacted to concentrate poverty geographically within neighborhoods, and that exposure to neighborhood poverty subsequently increased the probability of male joblessness and single motherhood among group members. In this fashion, they linked the structural condition of segregation to individual behaviors widely associated with the underclass through the intervening factor of neighborhood poverty, holding individual and family characteristics constant. As the structural factor controlling poverty concentration, segregation is directly responsible for the perpetuation of socioeconomic disadvantage among Blacks.

The Road Ahead

This review yields several well-supported conclusions about residential segregation in the United States at the end of the twentieth century.

- First, the extreme segregation of Blacks continues unabated in the nation's largest metropolitan areas, and is far more severe than anything experienced by Hispanics or Asians.

- Second, this unique segregation can in no way be attributed to class.

- Third, although Whites now accept open housing in principle, they have yet to come to terms with its implications in practice. Whites still harbor strong anti-Black sentiments and are unwilling to live with more than a small percentage of Blacks in the neighborhood. As a result, declines in Black-White segregation have been confined almost entirely to metropolitan areas where few Blacks live.

- Fourth, color prejudice apparently extends to dark-skinned Hispanics, and discrimination against both Blacks and Afro-Hispanics is remarkably widespread in U.S. housing markets. Through a variety of deceptions and exclusionary actions, Black access to housing in White neighborhoods is systematically reduced.

- Fifth, White biases and discrimination apparently do not extend to Asians or light-skinned Hispanics, at least to the same degree. In no metropolitan area are Asians or Hispanics hypersegregated; and despite the recent arrival of large numbers of immigrants and rapid rates of population growth, they display levels of segregation and isolation that are far below those of Blacks.

- Sixth, as a result of segregation, poor Blacks are forced to live in conditions of intensely concentrated poverty. Recent shifts in U.S. socio-economic structure and patterns of class segregation have interacted with Black segregation to produce unusual concentrations of poverty among Blacks. Poor Blacks are far more likely to grow up and live in neighborhoods surrounded by other poor people than poor Whites, Hispanics, or Asians.

- Finally, as a result of their prolonged exposure to high rates of neighborhood poverty, Blacks experience much higher risks of educational failure, joblessness, unwed childbearing, crime, and premature death compared with other groups.

Given the central role that residence plays in determining one's life chances, these results suggest the need to incorporate the effects of racial segregation more fully into theories about the perpetuation of poverty and the origins of the urban underclass. These results also suggest the need to incorporate desegregation efforts more directly into public policies developed to ameliorate urban poverty. All too often, U.S. policy debates have devolved into arguments about the relative importance of race versus class. The issue, however, is not whether race *or* class perpetuates the urban underclass, but how race *and* class *interact* to undermine the social and economic well-being of Black Americans.

Public policies must address both race and class issues if they are to be successful. Race-conscious steps need to be taken to dismantle the institutional apparatus of segregation, and class-specific policies must be implemented to improve the socioeconomic status of Blacks. By themselves, programs targeting low-income Blacks will fail because they will be swamped by powerful environmental influences arising from the disastrous neighborhood conditions that Blacks experience because of segregation. Likewise, efforts to reduce segregation will falter unless Blacks acquire the socioeconomic resources that enable them to take full advantage of urban housing markets and the benefits they provide.

Eliminating residential segregation will require the direct involvement of the federal government to an unprecedented degree, and two departments—Housing and Urban Development, and Justice—must throw their institutional weight behind fair-housing enforcement if residential desegregation is to occur. If the ghetto is to be dismantled, HUD, in particular must intervene forcefully in *eight* ways.

1. HUD must increase its financial assistance to local fair-housing organizations to enhance their ability to investigate and prosecute individual complaints of

housing discrimination. Grants made to local agencies dedicated to fair-housing enforcement will enable them to expand their efforts by hiring more legal staff, implementing more extensive testing programs, and making their services more widely available.

2. HUD should establish a permanent testing program capable of identifying realtors who engage in a pattern and practice of discrimination. A special unit dedicated to the regular administration of housing audits should be created in HUD under the Assistant Secretary for Fair Housing and Equal Opportunity. Audits of randomly selected realtors should be conducted annually within metropolitan areas that have large Black communities, and when evidence of systematic discrimination is uncovered, the department should compile additional evidence and turn it over to the Attorney General for vigorous prosecution. Initially these audits should be targeted to hypersegregated cities.

3. A staff should be created at HUD under the Assistant Secretary for Fair Housing and Equal Opportunity to scrutinize lending data for unusually high rates of rejection among minority applicants and Black neighborhoods. When the rejection rates cannot be explained statistically by social, demographic, economic, credit histories, or other background factors, a systematic case study of the lending institution's practices should be initiated. If clear evidence of discrimination is uncovered, the case should be referred to the Attorney General for prosecution, and/or an equal-opportunity lending plan should be conciliated, implemented, and monitored.

4. Funding for housing-certificate programs, authorized under Section 8 of the 1974 Housing and Community Development Act, should be expanded, and programs modeled on the Gautreaux Demonstration Project or the Move to Opportunity Program should be more widely implemented. Black public-housing residents in Chicago who moved into integrated settings through this demonstration project have been shown to have had greater success in education and employment than a comparable group who remained behind in the ghetto (see Rosenbaum et al., 1988; Rosenbaum and Popkin, 1991; Rosenbaum, 1991).

5. Given the overriding importance of residential mobility to individual well-being, hate crimes directed against Blacks moving into White neighborhoods must be considered more severe than ordinary acts of vandalism or assault. Rather than being left only to local authorities, they should be prosecuted at the federal level as violations of the victim's civil right. Stiff financial penalties and jail terms should be imposed, not in recognition of the severity of the vandalism or violence itself, but to acknowledge the serious damage that segregation does to our national well-being.

6. HUD should work to strengthen the Voluntary Affirmative Marketing Agreement, a pact between HUD and the National Association of Realtors, instituted during the Ford Administration. The agreement originally established a network of housing resource boards to enforce the Fair Housing Act with support from HUD; during the Reagan Administration, funds were cut and the agreement was modified to relieve realtors of responsibility for fair-housing enforcement. New regulations also prohibited the use of testers by local resource boards and made secret the list of real estate boards that had signed the agreement. In strengthening this agreement, this list should once again be made public, the use of testers should be encouraged, and the responsibilities of realtors to enforce the Fair Housing Act should be spelled out explicitly.

7. HUD should establish new programs and expand existing programs to train realtors in fair-housing marketing procedures, especially those serving Black neighborhoods. Agents serving primarily White clients should be instructed about advertising and marketing methods to ensure that Blacks in segregated communities gain access to information about housing opportunities outside the ghetto, whereas agents serving primarily Black clients should be trained to market homes throughout the metropolitan area, and instructed especially in how to use multiple-listing services. HUD officials and local fair-housing groups should carefully monitor whether realtors serving Blacks are given access to multiple-listing services.

8. The Assistant Secretary for Fair Housing and Equal Opportunity at HUD must take a more active role in overseeing real estate advertising and marketing practices, two areas that have received insufficient federal attention in the past. Realtors in selected metropolitan areas should be sampled and their advertising and marketing practices regularly examined for conformity with federal fair-housing regulations. HUD should play a larger role in ensuring that Black home seekers are not systematically and deliberately overlooked by prevailing marketing practices.

For the most part, these policies do not require major changes in legislation. What they require is political will. Given the will to end segregation, the necessary funds and legislative measures will follow. For America, failure to end segregation will perpetuate a bitter dilemma that has long divided the nation. If segregation is permitted to continue, poverty inevitably will deepen and become more persistent within a large share of the Black community, crime and drugs will become more firmly rooted, and social institutions will fragment further under the weight of deteriorating conditions. As racial inequality sharpens, White fears will grow, racial prejudices will be reinforced, and hostility toward Blacks will increase, making the problems of racial justice and equal opportunity even more insoluble. Until we decide to end the long reign of American apartheid, we cannot hope to move forward as a people and a nation.

REFERENCES

ALLPORT, G. 1958. *The Nature of Prejudice*. Garden City, N.Y.: Doubleday Anchor.

ALMGREN, G., A. GUEST, G. IMERWAHR, and M. SPITTEL. 1998. Joblessness, family disruption, and violent death in Chicago: 1970–1990. *Social Forces* 76:1465–1494.

ANDERSON, E. 1990. *Streetwise: Race, Class, and Change in an Urban Community*. Chicago: University of Chicago Press.

BERTRAM, S. 1988. *An Audit of the Real Estate Sales and Rental Markets of Selected Southern Suburbs*. Homewood, Ill.: South Suburban Housing Center.

BLALOCK, H.M., JR. 1967. *Toward a Theory of Minority-Group Relations*. New York: Wiley.

BOBO, L., H. SCHUMAN, and C. STEEH. 1986. Changing racial attitudes toward residential integration. Pp. 152–169 in *Housing Desegregation and Federal Policy*, ed. Chapel Hill; University of North Carolina Press.

BOBO, L., and C. ZUBRINSKY. 1996. Attitudes on residential integration: Perceived status differences, mere in-group preference, or racial prejudice? *Social Forces* 74:883–909.

BROOKS-GUNN, J., G. DUNCAN, and J. ABER, eds. 1997. *Neighborhood Poverty: Context and Consequences for Children*. New York: Russell Sage.

BROOKS-GUNN, J., G. DUNCAN, P. KLEBANOV, and N. SEALAND. 1993. Do neighborhoods influence child and adolescent development? *American Journal of Sociology* 99:353–395.

CLARK, W. 1991. Residential preferences and neighborhood racial segregation: A test of the Schelling segregation model. *Demography* 28:1–19.

CORCORAN, M., R. GORDON, D. LAREN, and G. SOLON. 1989. Effects of family and community background on men's economic status. Working Paper 2896, National Bureau of Economic Research, Cambridge, Mass.

CRANE, J. 1991. The epidemic theory of ghettos and neighborhood effects on dropping out and teenage childbearing. *American Journal of Sociology* 96:1226-1259.

DANZIGER, S., and P. GOTTSCHALK. 1995. *America Unequal.* Cambridge: Harvard University Press and the Russell Sage Foundation.

DATCHER, L. 1982. Effects of community and family background on achievement. *The Review of Economics and Statistics* 64:32–41.

DEMERATH, N., and H. GILMORE. 1954. The ecology of southern cities. Pp. 120–125 in *The Urban South,* R. Vance and N. Demerath, eds. Chapel Hill; University of North Carolina Press.

DENTON, N. 1994. Are African Americans still hypersegregated? Pp. 49–81 in *Residential Apartheid: The American Legacy,* R. Bullard, J. Grigsby III, and C. Lee, eds. Los Angeles: CAAS Publications, University of California.

DENTON, N., and D. MASSEY. 1988. Residential segregation of Blacks, Hispanics, and Asians by socioeconomic status and generation. *Social Science Quarterly* 69:797–817. 1989. Racial identity among Caribbean Hispanics: The effect of double minority status on residential segregation. *American Sociological Review* 54:790–808. 1991. Patterns of neighborhood transition in a multiethnic world. *Demography* 28:41–64.

DUNCAN, O., and B. DUNCAN. 1957. *The Negro Population of Chicago: A Study of Residential Succession.* Chicago: University of Chicago Press.

FARLEY, R. 1977. Residential segregation in urbanized areas of the United States in 1970: An analysis of social class and racial differences. *Demography* 14:497–518.

FARLEY, R., S. BIANCHI, and D. COLASANTO. 1979. Barriers to the racial integration of neighborhoods: The Detroit case. *Annals of the American Academy of Political and Social Science* 441:97–113.

FARLEY, R., H. SCHUMAN, S. BIANCHI, D. COLASANTO, and S. HATCHETT. 1978. "Chocolate city, vanilla suburbs": Will the trend toward racially separate communities continue? *Social Science Research* 7:319–344.

FARLEY, R., C. STEEH, M. KRYSAN, T. JACKSON, and K. REEVES. 1994. Stereotypes and segregation: Neighborhoods in the Detroit area. *American Journal of Sociology* 100:750–780.

FEINS, J., R. BRATT, and R. HOLLISTER. 1981. *Final Report of a Study of Racial Discrimination in the Boston Housing Market.* Cambridge: Abt Associates.

FIX, M., G. GALSTER, and R. STRUYK. 1993. An overview of auditing for discrimination. Pp. 1–68 in *Clear and Convincing Evidence: Measurement of Discrimination in America,* M. Fix and R. Struyk, eds. Washington, D.C.: The Urban Institute Press.

FREY, W., and R. FARLEY. 1994. Changes in the segregation of Whites from Blacks during the 1980s; Small steps toward a more integrated society. *American Sociological Review* 59:23–45. 1996. Latino, Asian, and Black segregation in U.S. metropolitan areas: Are multiethnic metros different? *Demography* 33:35–50.

FURSTENBURG, F. JR., S. MORGAN, K. MOORE, and J. PETERSON. 1987. Race differences in the timing of adolescent intercourse. *American Sociological Review* 52:511–518.

GALSTER, G. 1986. More than skin deep: The effect of housing discrimination on the extent and pattern of racial residential segregation in the United States. Pp. 119–138 in *Housing Discrimination and Federal Policy,* J. Goering, ed. Chapel Hill: University of North Carolina Press. 1987. The ecology of racial discrimination in housing: An exploratory model. *Urban Affairs Quarterly* 23:84–107. 1990a. Racial discrimination in housing markets during the 1980s: A review of the audit evidence. *Journal of Planning Education and Research* 9:165–175. 1990b. Racial steering by real estate agents: Mechanisms and motives. *The review of Black Political Economy* 19:39–63. 1990c. White flight from racially integrated neighborhoods in the 1970s: The Cleveland experience. *Urban Studies* 27:385–399. 1990d. Neighborhood racial change, segregationist sentiments, and affirmative marketing policies. *Journal of Urban Economics* 27:244–361.

GALSTER, G., F. FREIBERG, and D. HOUK. 1987. Racial differentials in real estate advertising practices: An exploratory case study. *Journal of Urban Affairs* 9:199-215.

GALSTER, G., and W. KEENEY. 1988. Race, residence, discrimination, and economic opportunity: Modeling the nexus of urban racial phenomena. *Urban Affairs Quarterly* 24:87–117.

GUEST, A., G. ALMGREN, and J. HUSSEY. 1998. The ecology of race and socioeconomic distress: Infant and working age mortality in Chicago. *Demography* 35:23–34.

HAKKEN, J. 1979. *Discrimination Against Chicanos in the Dallas Rental Housing Market: An Experimental Extension of the Housing Market Practices Survey.* Washington, D.C.: Office of Policy Development and Research, U.S. Department of Housing and Urban Development.

HARRISON, R., and D. WEINBERG. 1992. Racial and ethnic residential segregation in 1990. Paper presented at the annual meeting of the Population Association of America, Denver, April 13.

HELPER, R. 1969. *Racial Policies and Practices of Real Estate Brokers.* Minneapolis: University of Minnesota Press.

HINTZEN, H. 1983. *Report of an Audit of Real Estate Sales Practices of 15 Northwest Chicago Real Estate Sales Offices.* Chicago: Leadership Council for Metropolitan Open Communities.

HOCHSCHILD, J. 1995. *Facing up to the American Dream: Race, Class, and the Soul of the Nation.* Princeton: Princeton University Press.

HOGAN, D., and E. KITAGAWA. 1985. The impact of social status, family structure, and neighborhood on the fertility of Black adolescents. *American Journal of Sociology* 90:825–855.

HWANG, S., and S. MURDOCK. 1982. Residential segregation in Texas in 1980. *Social Science Quarterly* 63(1982):737–748.

JACKSON, P. 1981. Paradoxes of Puerto Rican segregation in New York. Pp. 109–126 in *Ethnic Segregation in Cities,* C. Peach, V. Robinson, and S. Smith, eds. London: Croom Helm.

JACKSON, T. 1994. The other side of the residential segregation equation: Why Detroit area Blacks are reluctant to pioneer integration. Paper presented at the Russell Sage Foundation Multi-City conference.

JAMES, F., and E. TYNAN. 1986. Segregation and discrimination against Hispanic Americans. Pp. 83-98 in *Housing Discrimination and Federal Policy,* J. Goering, ed. Chapel Hill: University of North Carolina Press.

JENCKS, C., and S. MAYER. 1990. The social consequences of growing up in a poor neighborhood. Pp. 111–186 in *Inner City Poverty in the United States,* L. Lynn, Jr., and M. McGeary, eds. Washington, D.C.: National Academy of Sciences.

KANTROWITZ, N. 1973. *Ethnic and Racial Segregation in the New York Metropolis.* New York: Praeger.

KASARDA, J. 1993. Inner city concentrated poverty and neighborhood distress; 1970–1990. *Housing Policy Debate* 4(3):253–302.

KRIVO, L., and R. KAUFMAN. 1999. How low can it go? Declining Black-White segregation in a multi-ethnic context. *Demography* 36:93–110.

KRIVO, L., and R. PETERSON. 1996. Extremely disadvantaged neighborhoods and urban crime. *Social Forces* 75:619–648.

KRIVO, L., R. PETERSON, H. RIZZO, and J. REYNOLDS. 1998. Race segregation, and the concentration of disadvantage: 1980–1990. *Social Problems* 45:61–80.

LEVY, F. 1995. Incomes and income inequality. Pp 1–58 in *State of the Union: America in the 1990s,* Farley, ed. New York: Russell Sage.

LIEBERSON, S. 1980. *A Piece of the Pie: Blacks and White Immigrants Since 1880.* Berkeley: University of California Press.

LOPEZ, M. 1981. Patterns of interethnic residential segregation in the urban Southwest, 1960 and 1970. *Social Science Quarterly* 62:50–63.

MASSEY, D. 1979. Effects of socioeconomic factors on the residential segregation of Blacks and Spanish Americans in United States urbanized areas. *American Sociological Review* 44:1015–1022. 1981. Hispanic residential segregation: A comparison of Mexicans, Cubans, and Puerto Ricans. *Sociology and Social Research* 65:311–322. 1985. Ethnic residential segregation: A theoretical synthesis and empirical review. *Sociology and Social Research* 69:315–350. 1990. American apartheid: Segregation and the making of the underclass. *American Journal of Sociology* 96:329–358.

MASSEY, D., and B. BITTERMAN. 1985. Explaining the paradox of Puerto Rican segregation. *Social Forces* 64:306–331.

MASSEY, D., G. CONDRAN, and N. DENTON. 1987. The effect of residential segregation on Black social and economic well-being. *Social Forces* 66:29–57.

MASSEY, D., and N. DENTON. 1987. Trends in the residential segregation of Blacks, Hispanics, and Asians. *American Sociological Review* 52:802–825. 1988. The dimensions of residential segregation. *Social Forces* 67:281–315. 1989a. Residential segregation of Mexicans, Puerto Ricans, and Cubans in U.S. metropolitan areas. *Sociology and Social Research* 73:73–83. 1989b. Hypersegregation in U.S. metropolitan areas: Black and Hispanic segregation along five dimensions. *Demography* 26:373–393. 1992. Racial identity and the spatial assimilation of Mexicans in the the United States. *Social Science Research* 21:235–260. 1993. *American Apartheid: Segregation and the Making of the Underclass.* Cambridge: Harvard University Press.

MASSEY, D., and M. EGGERS. 1990. The ecology of inequality: Minorities and the concentration of poverty, 1970–1980. *American Journal of Sociology* 95:1153–1189.

MASSEY, D., and M. FISCHER. 1999. Does rising income bring integration? New results for Blacks, Hispanics, and Asians in 1990. *Social*

Science Research 28:316–326. 2000. How segregation concentrates poverty. *Ethnic and Racial Studies* 23:670–691.

MASSEY, D., and E. FONG. 1990. Segregation and neighborhood quality: Blacks, Hispanics, and Asians in the San Francisco metropolitan area. *Social Forces* 69:15–32.

MASSEY, D., and A. GROSS. 1991. Explaining trends in residential segregation 1970–1980. *Urban Affairs Quarterly* 27:13–35.

MASSEY, D., A. GROSS, and M. EGGERS. 1991. Segregation, the concentration of poverty, and the life chances of individuals. *Social Science Research* 20:397–420.

MASSEY, D., and Z. HAJNAL. 1995. The changing geographic structure of Black-White segregation in the United States. *Social Science Quarterly* 76:527–542.

MASSEY, D., K. SHIBUYA. 1995. Unraveling the tangle of pathology: The effect of spatially concentrated joblessness on the well-being of African Americans. *Social Science Research* 24:252–366.

MASSEY, D., M. WHITE, and V. PHUA. 1996. The dimensions of segregation revisited. *Sociological Methods and Research.* 25:172–206.

MORENOFF, J., and R. SAMPSON. 1997. Violent crime and the spatial dynamics of neighborhood transition: Chicago, 1970–1990. *Social Forces* 76:31–64.

MORRIS, M., A. BERNHARDT, and M. HANCOCK. 1994. Economic inequality: New methods for new trends. *American Sociological Review* 59:205–219.

MOSKOS, C., and J. BUTLER. 1996. *All That We Can Be: Black Leadership and Racial Integration the Army Way.* New York: Basic Books.

PATILLO, M. 1998. Sweet mothers and gang-bangers: Managing crime in a Black middle-class neighborhood. *Social Forces* 76:747–774.

PEARCE, D. 1979. Gatekeepers and homeseekers: Institutional patterns in racial steering. *Social Problems* 26:325–342.

ROSENBAUM, J. 1991. Black pioneers: Do their moves to suburbs increase economic opportunity for mothers and children? *Housing Policy Debate* 2:1179–1214.

ROSENBAUM, J., M. KULIEKE, and L. RUBINOWITZ. 1988. White suburban schools' responses to low-income Black children: Sources of success and problems. *The Urban Review* 20:28–41.

ROSENBAUM, J., and S. POPKIN. 1991. Employment and earnings of low-income Blacks who move to middle class suburbs. Pp. 342–56 in *The Urban Underclass,* C. Jencks and P. Peterson, eds. Washington, D.C.: The Brookings Institution.

SALTMAN, J. 1979. Housing discrimination: Policy research, methods, and results. *Annals of the American Academy of Political and Social Science.* 441:186–196.

SCHELLING, T. 1971. Dynamic models of segregation. *Journal of Mathematical Sociology* 1:143–186.

SCHNEIDER, M., and J. LOGAN. 1982. Suburban racial segregation and Black access to local public resources. *Social Science Quarterly* 63:762–770.

SCHROEDER, A. 1985. *Report on an Audit of Real Estate Sales Practices of Eight Northwest Suburban Offices.* Chicago: Leadership Council for Metropolitan Open Communities.

SCHUMAN, H., and L. BOBO. 1988. Survey-based experiments on White racial attitudes toward residential integration. *American Journal of Sociology* 2:273–299.

SCHUMAN, H., C. STEEH, and L. BOBO. 1985. *Racial Attitudes in America: Trends and Interpretations.* Cambridge: Harvard University Press.

SCHUMAN, H., C. STEEH, L. BOBO, and M. KRYSAN. 1998. *Racial Attitudes in America: Trends and Interpretations.* Cambridge: Harvard University Press.

SIMKUS, A. 1978. Residential segregation by occupation and race in ten urbanized areas, 1950–1970. *American Sociological Review* 43:81–93.

SNIDERMAN, P., and T. PIAZZA. 1993. *The Scar of Race.* Cambridge: Harvard University Press.

TAYLOR, M. 1998. The effect of racial composition on racial attitudes of Whites. *American Sociological Review* 63:512–535.

TURNER, E. and J. ALLEN. 1991. *An Atlas of Population Patterns in Metropolitan, Los Angeles and Orange Counties.* Occasional Publication in Geography No. 8. Northridge, Calif.: Center for Geographical Studies, California State University at Northridge.

TURNER, M., J. EDWARDS, and M. MIKELSONS. 1991. *Housing Discrimination Study: Analyzing Racial and Ethnic Steering.* Washington, D.C.: U.S. Department of Housing and Urban Development, Office of Policy Development and Research.

U.S. BUREAU OF THE CENSUS. 1979. The Social and Economic Status of the Black Population in the

United States: An Historical View, 1790–1978. Current Population Reports, Special Studies Series P–23, No. 80. Washington, D.C.: U.S. Government Printing Office.

WHITE, M. 1987. *American Neighborhoods and Residential Differentiation*. New York: Russell Sage Foundation.

WIENK, R., C. REID, J. SIMONSON, and F. EGGERS. 1979. *Measuring Racial Discrimination in American Housing Markets: The Housing Market Practices Survey*. Washington, D.C.: U.S. Department of Housing and Urban Development.

WILSON, W. 1987. *Truly Disadvantaged: The Inner City, the Underclass, and Public Policy*. Chicago: University of Chicago Press.

YINGER, J. 1986. Measuring racial discrimination with fair housing audits: Caught in the act.

American Economic Review 76:991–993. 1985. The racial dimension of urban housing markets in the 1980s. Pp. 43–67 in *Divided Neighborhoods: Changing Patterns of Racial Segregation*, G.A. Tobin, ed. Newbury Park, Calif.: Sage Publications. 1989. Measuring discrimination in housing availability. Final Research Report No. 2 to the U.S. Department of Housing and Urban Development. Washington, D.C.: The Urban Institute. 1995. *Closed Doors, Opportunities Lost: The Continuing Costs of Housing Discrimination*. New York: Russell Sage.

ZUBRINSKY, C., and L. BOBO. 1996. Prismatic metropolis: Race and residential segregation in the City of Angels. *Social Science Research* 25:335–374.

29

LOCAL GATEKEEPING PRACTICES AND RESIDENTIAL SEGREGATION

Judith N. DeSena

Questions to Consider

Judith DeSena describes the informal mechanisms used to keep the neighborhood of Greenpoint in Brooklyn segregated. What are they? How are individual actions linked to patterns of residential segregation and institutional racism? How are a few well-placed individuals able to perform the role of racial gatekeeper in a neighborhood?

Research on the causes of residential segregation has focused on the "institutional web" created by redlining, racial steering, and market forces to explain the dual housing market in the United States (Farley 1987; Foley 1973; Kain 1968; Kain and Quigley 1975; Pearce 1979). This article examines the informal practices of local residents in perpetuating residential segregation. It is a study of the strategies used by white non-Hispanic residents in Greenpoint, Brooklyn, to maintain the segregation of Hispanics and to discourage people of color from moving into the neighborhood. An informal housing network in which available rental apartments and houses for sale are advertised by word of mouth is reinforced by the functioning of local institutions, namely, the Roman Catholic church and electoral politics. I propose that such actions reflect an invisible link between the micro-level analyses of discrimination documented by studies of real estate steering (Pearce 1979; Wienk et al. 1979) and macro-level analyses of patterns of residential segregation (Farley and Allen 1987; Lieberson 1980).

Studies on segregation in the United States have focused primarily on black-white separation. Taeuber and Taeuber (1965) analyzed census data for over two hundred cities in the United States between 1940 and 1960 and used an index of dissimilarity to measure segregation. They found segregation to be quite high, with an average index of 86.2. This analysis was followed up for 1970 (Sorenson, Taeuber, and Hollingsworth 1975) and showed a decline in segregation throughout the United States. Although there has been a slight decline in racial segregation over time, the level remained high in 1980 (Farley 1987; Farley and Allen 1987). In addition, suburbanization by blacks has continued to increase. Some blacks have settled in predominantly white communities (Spain and Long 1981). However, it is believed that "suburban ghettos" will form (Farley 1987, p. 108) as blacks who move to the suburbs locate themselves in established black areas.

Residential segregation of Hispanics has not received the same level of investigation as that of blacks. In general, Hispanics are less separated than blacks from non-Hispanic whites (Farley 1987; Massey and Denton 1987). Among Hispanic groups, Puerto Ricans experience the most segregation from non-Hispanic whites (Farley 1987; Massey and Bitterman 1985; Woolbright and Hartmann 1987), possibly because Puerto Ricans are disproportionately poor and tend to be darker in complexion than other Hispanics (Massey and Bitterman 1985, p. 326; Woolbright and Hartmann 1987). Some studies find that Puerto Ricans are segregated at rates similar to and greater than that of blacks (Guest and Weed 1976; Hershberg et al. 1978; Kantrowitz 1978). More recently, research conducted by the federal government, which examined the contribution of housing discrimination to residential segregation, concluded that "the problem is more prevalent in New York City and its suburbs than in any of 24 other major metropolitan areas across the United States, particularly for the Spanish-speaking minority" (Lueck 1991, p. R1). This finding is especially relevant to the case of Greenpoint. White non-Hispanic residents of Greenpoint attempt to relegate Hispanic residents to the northern section of the neighborhood and seclude them there. Non-Hispanic whites accomplish residential segregation by a series of informal strategies.

On a neighborhood level, segregation has been conceptualized as ordered segmentation (Suttles 1968) and the defended neighborhood (Suttles 1972). In actual practice, attempts to maintain separation among people of different ethnic and racial groups have taken the form of restrictive covenants or zones (Krase 1982), acts of violence (Rieder 1985), and the use of local networks (DeSena 1990). This study connects the national and statistical data on segregation with the informal practices of ordinary people. It offers an additional dimension to research on segregation. The analysis presents how white non-Hispanic residents of Greenpoint, in their everyday life, contribute to the maintenance of residential segregation. This

Judith N. DeSena, "Local Gatekeeping Practices and Residential Segregation" from *Sociological Inquiry,* Vol. 64, No. 3, August 1994, pp. 307–321. Reprinted by permission of Blackwell Publishing.

research indicates that to a large extent the "work" of segregation on a neighborhood level is done by women who serve as "gatekeepers and homeseekers" (Pearce 1979). The article begins with a description of Greenpoint followed by a discussion of the study's research design. The strategies used to accomplish residential segregation in Greenpoint will be presented, with a focus on an informal housing network and local institutional arrangements.

Description of Greenpoint

Geography

Greenpoint is a peninsula at the northernmost tip of Brooklyn bounded on the north and east by Newtown Creek and on the west by the East River. The Brooklyn-Queens Expressway (Meeker Avenue) and North 7th Street serve as Greenpoint's southern boundary (New York City Planning Commission 1969). The Brooklyn-Queens Expressway is an elevated structure as it extends through Greenpoint and breaks up the continuity of residential areas.

Population

Greenpoint is a working-class neighborhood. Since the early 1900s Greenpoint's population has been largely white ethnic, composed mostly of Irish, Italian, and Polish families. The Irish were the largest group through the 1920s. A significant influx of Polish immigration occurred in Greenpoint after World War II (Susser 1982). More recently there has been an additional wave of Polish refugees who fled martial law in Poland. The relocation efforts of these immigrants are aided by local Polish organizations and churches. Greenpoint is currently viewed as the largest Polish community in New York City.

In 1990, the population of Greenpoint was approximately 39,365.[1] Of these, 73 percent were members of white non-Hispanic ethnic groups. Since 1950 northern Greenpoint has seen an influx of Hispanic residents. In 1990 Hispanics constituted 22 percent of the neighborhood's population;[2] and Asian and Pacific Islanders totaled 4 percent and blacks 1 percent of the population. The average across ethnic groupings for median household income in 1989 was $29,121, approximately the median household income of New York City in 1989, which amounted to $29,823. In 1990, a majority of Greenpoint's residents 25 years and older had between an elementary and a high school education. Moreover, in 1990 Greenpoint's employed persons 16 years and older worked mostly in technical, sales, and administrative support occupations, as professionals and managers, and in service jobs.

Housing

A majority of Greenpoint's housing was built before 1939 and many structures were built before 1900. More than 60 percent of the residential buildings are frame dwellings (New York City Planning Commission 1974). There are a few blocks in Greenpoint that consist of brownstones and brick townhouses—remnants of Dutch settlement from the nineteenth century. These particular streets are presently part of a seven-block historic district bordered by Franklin Street, Manhattan Avenue, Calyer, and Kent Streets.

Residential structures in Greenpoint are six stories or less, and 71 percent contain four or fewer dwelling units (New York City Planning Commission 1974). In addition, "the percentage of owner-occupied buildings with rental units is usually high" (Wellisz 1982, p. R9). Most homeowners share their building with renters. In 1990 the average median rent in Greenpoint was

$450, compared with $496 for New York City. Long-term residents may pay less than the median rent because of tenure and rent control laws. However, rents in Greenpoint have been escalating. Some residents report monthly rents as high as $750 to $1,000.

Religion

There are approximately twelve churches in Greenpoint. Those with the largest congregations are Roman Catholic; Catholic churches in Greenpoint are recognized by residents as the center of ethnic life. There are two types of Roman Catholic churches in Greenpoint: Diocesan churches lie within small territorial boundaries, or parishes, which in turn form, with other parishes, a larger territory, or diocese (the parishes of diocesan churches do not overlap). National churches are those that serve a particular ethnic group; they are usually located within the boundaries of a diocesan church. There are three national churches in Greenpoint: two Polish and one Italian. There is also one diocesan church that is reportedly dominated by Irish residents.

Research Methods

The findings reported here are part of a larger qualitative study in which I conducted fifty-five open-ended interviews with residents of Greenpoint for the purpose of ascertaining the strategies employed to maintain residential segregation. A technique in interviewing was used by which I asked residents to tell me about the practices of their neighbors. The respondents seemed comfortable with this approach, since the focus of discussion was not on their behavior, but on the habits of locals and the customs of the neighborhood. The respondents talked freely. Interviews lasted anywhere from 1 hour to 2.5 hours. They were recorded on tape.

The interviews were obtained by a snowball sampling technique. The sample was stratified for sex, ethnicity, and age. Since ethnicity was an important variable in this study, I began by identifying ethnic clusters through block, and block group, data from the 1980 Census. Clusters were identified for four major ethnic groups in Greenpoint: Hispanics, Irish, Italians, and Polish. Once the boundaries of these ethnic enclaves were apparent, I contacted individuals residing in each of these clusters. These individuals became key informants, directing me to others of the same ethnic background. At the end of each interview I asked respondents to refer me to others.

I also used content analysis and reviewed written accounts of the events described in the interviews. In particular, I examined local newspapers, church bulletins, and various flyers advertising meetings in the community. This approach enabled me to use the information in subsequent interviews, to probe these matters more effectively, and to keep abreast of current issues and concerns. Data were collected between 1983 and 1990. The data collection focusing on the neighborhood dynamics presented here is ongoing.

Greenpoint: A Segregated Neighborhood

According to its residents, Greenpoint is divided into two areas: the north and the south. Northern Greenpoint is composed mainly of Poles and Hispanics. Southern Greenpoint is made up of Polish, Irish, Italian, and Hispanic groups. Because of the existence of an Hispanic community in northern Greenpoint, residents point to Greenpoint Avenue as the symbolic boundary that separates the north from the south. One northern Greenpoint resident commented: "Like I said, I've been here twenty-nine years and after Greenpoint Avenue, to me, that's the white neighborhood, and this side is more Puerto Rican."

"The boundary," Greenpoint Avenue, is a major thoroughfare and includes a bus route, truck route, and subway station. However, in many ways and for many residents, particularly those who live in southern Greenpoint, it marks the end of the area's commercial strip and the end of the neighborhood. A couple of residents from southern Greenpoint reported the following:

> We never really went down that end, we had St. Anthony [Church] and we never really associated with St. Alphonsus [Church], that was like the other territory or something.

> I always remember, once you cross Greenpoint Avenue, except for a few white blocks, that wasn't the good section of Greenpoint.

The urban landscape reinforces residents' differential perceptions of north and south. No banks are located north of Greenpoint Avenue and the annual street fair, and outdoor Christmas lights provided by local merchants to the south stop there. As one crosses Greenpoint Avenue going north, the ground slopes downhill. Bodegas are numerous on street corners. During the summer salsa music plays in the streets. Buildings are larger and show signs of deterioration to a greater extent than those in the south; some have been condemned and only their shells remain. Houses in the north have a lower market value than those in the south, and it is more difficult to obtain mortgages and home improvement loans for housing in the north. As one resident noted "as long as I remember, that was the poorer end of the neighborhood."

Southern Greenpoint is different. It tends to be better-maintained. Homes are renovated and building deterioration is less visible than in northern Greenpoint. Ethnic specialty stores are typically Polish, and butcher shops, bakeries, and grocery stores dot each corner. All kinds of retail stores can be found in the southern area.

White non-Hispanic respondents see a causal relationship between people of color and deteriorated living conditions. One resident reported:

> Most of the Spanish people that I've seen move into homes and let them deteriorate. Maybe because most of them rent, I really don't know. . . . But to me, it's just the way that everything is let to fall apart. They really don't care if the windows are hanging open. It's not a good feeling when you go through the blocks where the Spanish people live, and then the streets where white people live. There's no pride whatsoever.

Northern Greenpoint came to be viewed by long-term white non-Hispanic residents as the undesirable part of the community because of the clustering of Hispanic residents, and their perception that people of color create urban decay. Because of this view, non-Hispanic whites resist residence by people of color.

How Greenpoint's symbolic boundary and its attendant segregation are maintained is the focus of this study. I propose that it is through the process of an informal housing network.

Greenpoint's Informal Housing Network

It is difficult for an outsider to rent an apartment or purchase a house in southern Greenpoint. Local realtors have said that "there isn't one-, two- or three-family houses available." The local newspaper lists only a few apartments and houses for sale, while the lengths of its "Apts. Wanted" and "Houses

Wanted" columns increase. Residents of southern Greenpoint are particularly cautious about renting their vacant apartments. Not only do they want to control rigidly the type of tenants they may get, but they also want to determine who will be informed about the availability of an apartment. All respondents in southern Greenpoint, regardless of ethnicity, claimed that available apartments are rented "by word of mouth."

> There are some ads in the local paper, but I think most of the time it's by word of mouth. I think they mostly don't put ads in the paper, because when you put an ad in the paper, you don't know who is gonna come.

> Yeh, definitely . . . when there's an apartment vacant, no one knows about it. They're very hush, or word of mouth. Even if they're not Hispanic, they still watch who they rent to.

Resident homeowners go about finding a tenant by an informal network through which they tell family, friends, and neighbors that an apartment is available. Consequently, a person who knows someone is "in the market" for an apartment will recommend the individual to the owner. In other words, individuals seeking apartments are "sponsored" by local informants to homeowners. According to residents:

> Recommendations, absolutely. You want rooms, I know that Mary has rooms. I'll say "Mary, I know so and so, she seems to be a nice person, why don't you give her the rooms?"

> You keep it to yourself and rent it word of mouth. If you're a friend of mine [and] you hear of an apartment, you say, "Here I got a good friend," you guarantee him.

Those who are selected as informants are assumed to have similar social characteristics as the homeowner and to possess the same values. They are the gatekeepers of the community. Most informants are local women. It is therefore presumed by both parties that an informant would sponsor only a potential tenant who is the "type" of person the homeowner is seeking. Thus, it is expected that an informant would sponsor only an individual whom the homeowner would find acceptable. As one resident stated:

> What they do is, they don't want strangers that they don't know in their house. They want people to come who are recommended, or people who may be friends of people that they know. They're cautious because they're not necessarily anxious for the dollars that would be coming in. They want to have a family type of residence, people that they can get along with. They do that for their own security and for their own happiness, because sometimes you can rent to somebody and not know who they are. And, you know, they may be flamingo [sic] dancers and you're subject to this sort of stuff all the time.

The practice of sponsoring an individual as a potential tenant to a homeowner places the reputation of the sponsor "on the line." Their standing in the community could be spoiled if a tenant they sponsored turned out not to be the kind of person initially expected. One presumption is that people who are selected as informants will sponsor only white non-Hispanic ethnics, not people of color. When a neighbor is chosen as an informant by a homeowner, the homeowner does not need to list specific requirements. Informants know what homeowners expect. Likewise, homeowners select informants who they presume will know the characteristics expected in a tenant. Given this relationship between homeowners and their selected informants, most people of color are unable to gain access to apartments or houses in southern Greenpoint. One resident summed up this practice of sponsorship by saying, "They tell you because they know you're not gonna tell Spanish or black."

Intimidation is used within the informal housing network. According to respondents, neighbors sometimes pressure one another about potential tenants and homeowners. The major focus is for people of color to be unable to gain access to available apartments or houses.

> This house was almost bought by a Cuban gentleman, and the lady on this side of us told our landlord that they are not welcome here, in very choice words she used; and they almost threatened him, Don't sell, and the sale did not go through.

> When the guy across the street was selling his house, somebody came out and said, "I hope you're not selling to blacks."

Other respondents indicated that applying pressure is unnecessary because there is an "unwritten agreement," analogous to a "pact" among neighbors. They agree that they will not rent or sell to minority individuals.

> It's a, how can I put it, it's an unwritten law. In other words, you know your family's gonna hear it if you rent to a black. . . . I know what they would go through; that's why I wouldn't really do it.

This response suggests that the "pact" operates without any overt coercion. It further suggests that residents who violate the pact will be confronted by their neighbors.

One respondent spoke about a friend who rehabilitates abandoned housing in southern Greenpoint. This developer was thinking about renting to blacks, but was advised by his friend and Greenpoint resident:

> I think it will hurt you tremendously and I don't see that you should do that . . . because of their color. . . . It seems that the power brokers don't want any more minorities than they have already.

The developer was advised not to violate the pact in order to avoid unfavorable repercussions which might have caused his business to suffer.

Neighborhood Women

To a large extent, local women control who obtains housing in Greenpoint by serving as the primary gatekeepers of the community. They "pass along the word" regarding the availability of housing to family, friends, and neighbors. In this way, they have replaced local realtors. Their "work" is carried out through the maintenance of a local network in which they serve as informal brokers in the local housing market, and are involved in renting available apartments and recruiting potential tenants. Information about available housing and "homeseekers" is conveyed orally through a network of women who interact in the street, at social and religious functions, and at civic meetings. Women's activities, to a large extent, are informal. As part of their daily routine, women will meet as they shop, walk children to and from school, go to and from work, and attend community meetings at night, or play bingo. It is during these informal occasions that matters concerning housing are discussed. A local woman's anecdote illustrates this point:

> I was in a butcher shop one day, and we were talking. I just happen to mention that my niece was looking for rooms. And this woman says, "Hello"; she told me who she was, and that she had rooms. So there right in the butcher

shop, not that I ever got the rooms. But [if I wanted] rooms for a friend of mine or for anybody, I would spread the word around in the Society [a women's religious organization]. That would be the first place. I'd say, "Girls, anybody hears of rooms let me know." They would tell someone.

Although this research documents a housing network, the local women's network involves other aspects of neighborhood life as well. Women exchange local news. They discuss who is moving, what the implications are for friends and family seeking housing, where the best sales are, what the new priest is like, who has recently been robbed. Women's networks in communities have been trivialized as gossip and mistakenly viewed as having no purpose. Greenpoint's informal housing network is an example of the importance of women's networks in shaping communities.

In summary, by controlling accessibility to housing, residents of southern Greenpoint resist minority growth and maintain segregation. To a large extent, local women control who obtains housing. Most apartments are rented through an informal housing network by which residents sponsor individuals as tenants. Some houses are also sold this way, while others are sold through realtors who are trusted not to "blockbust" because many of the realtors are also residents. In most cases available housing never reaches the open market, but remains part of the neighborhood's "underlife" (Suttles 1972). Moreover, by keeping news of the availability of housing out of the open market, southern Greenpoint residents are not discriminating in the traditional sense (they are not turning people away). Instead, residents take an offensive position and prevent people of color from applying for housing.

Local Institutions

Local institutions also participate in making Greenpoint a segregated neighborhood. This section will focus particularly on the contributions of the Roman Catholic church and local politics.

The Church

As stated earlier, there are a number of Roman Catholic churches in Greenpoint, which are of two types: Some are national churches, while others are diocesan churches. In northern Greenpoint there is a national, Polish church called Sts. Cyril and Methodius, which is located in the heart of the Hispanic community. This church holds masses and other services in Polish and English. It does not accommodate the Spanish-speaking community. St. Anthony–St. Alphonsus, a diocesan church located near the boundary that divides Greenpoint's northern and southern areas, offers masses in English and Spanish, thereby ministering to the Spanish-speaking community. Hispanics are not assisted by any other church. However, the Spanish-speaking and English-speaking congregations are segregated.[3] Hispanics and other ethnic groups are physically separated, not only by a different mass, but also because Spanish masses take place in the lower church (basement) of St. Anthony's church building.

In addition, parish activities are also segregated.

> Whenever it is social, for example, they don't allow it. [The parish] is going to have a dance for St. Valentine's Day but we are all going to be Spanish there, not one English speaker is going to go. They don't cross lines. I am trying to do something in that respect. Not only to bring the Hispanics into the English community, but I want to do the

opposite too, take the English speakers and invite them over to our activities. Otherwise you're going to continue on and on with this problem of segregation because it's real. You have two parishes in one and I don't like that. I would like for all the people to be one.

Moreover, it was reported that parish committees are dominated by white non-Hispanics, mostly Irish parishioners.

Hence, local churches reinforce neighborhood segregation in two ways. They either block the participation of some ethnic groups, as in the case of national churches, or attend to ethnic groups separately. In northern Greenpoint, Sts. Cyril and Methodius is a Polish island in the midst of a Hispanic population. Even when all ethnic groups are aided by the local diocesan church, the Hispanic and non-Hispanic white congregations are spatially segregated in church services and activities.

Local Politics

Greenpoint has long been a stronghold for the regular Democratic party. Control of the countywide party through the years reflects the successive waves of immigrants and their assimilation. During the 1920s and 1930s, the Irish controlled the countywide party. This was also reflected in Greenpoint, where a man named Peter J. McGuinness was district leader (McGuinness had replaced Patrick McCarren). At that time in the history of New York politics, the district leader's position was a powerful one. It was a party position that carried a number of patronage "goodies" (such as jobs and dismissed traffic violations). On Thursday nights residents would line up at the clubhouse to ask for favors. The district leader, through his network of influence, would deliver these favors. McGuinness contributed to defending Greenpoint by speak-

ing against the development of public housing in Greenpoint. McGuinness stated to the City Planning Commission, "It's nothing personal. We just don't want any of them things in Greenpoint. We're a community by ourselves."[4] Public housing was not built in Greenpoint, but it was constructed in adjacent neighborhoods such as Williamsburg, in Brooklyn, and Long Island City, in Queens.

The use of scare tactics in local political campaigns is another way that the local party resists population growth and representation of people of color. In 1980 there was a primary election held for state senator. The candidates were Thomas Bartosiewicz, the incumbent and a Greenpoint resident (who indicates ethnic succession in politics), and Lucille Rose, a black woman from Bedford-Stuyvesant. At this time, the boundaries of the district for state senator included Greenpoint, Bedford-Stuyvesant, and other areas. In an attempt to increase voter turnout in Greenpoint (the idea being that these were Bartosiewicz supporters), the local newspaper ran a front page story, "Remember: Vote on Tuesday, Sept. 9th." This article began:

> The future of Greenpoint–Williamsburg is at stake on Tuesday, September 9 as Democrats must turn out to vote in all time record numbers to support our Senator in the Primary Election. Senator Bartosiewicz is fighting against all odds in a fierce election campaign battle against boss-backed Bedford-Stuyvesant candidate Lucille Rose. (*Greenpoint Gazette*, 2 September 1980, 1)

Also on the front page were pictures of Bartosiewicz and Rose, with a caption that stated, "The Choice Is Clear." The use of pictures along with the article attempted to encourage residents to "get out and vote" for Bartosiewicz out of fear that someone black would be elected to represent Greenpoint. Moreover, on the day of the election, flyers were left on the windshields of cars in Greenpoint that had a picture of Lucille Rose with the caption, "Our New State Senator?" This was a last attempt to encourage people to vote through the use of racial overtones. Bartosiewicz won this primary and also won the general election.

These two examples demonstrate how the local political system is involved in promoting segregation. Political tactics play on residents' fears that the neighborhood will be overtaken by people of color. In this way, the red flags of public housing or public officials who are people of color enable local party leaders to easily organize residents against change.

Since 1990, Greenpoint has also been subjected to legislative reapportionment plans (mandated after every census) that have aligned Greenpoint with other, white non-Hispanic areas of Brooklyn. Rather than draw district lines that might place the community with areas like Bushwick and Bedford–Stuyvesant, which are composed largely of people of color, recent reapportionment plans have placed the neighborhood in districts with white non-Hispanic communities such as Brooklyn Heights, Park Slope, and Bay Ridge (reflecting a desire on the part of the state legislature that "safe" seats for people of color are created and to insure that Greenpoint and other white non-Hispanic communities in Brooklyn continue to be represented by European American officials).

A complication that Greenpoint faces in political defense is that as a political entity it is absorbed into larger geographic districts. In recent years, Greenpoint has remained a Democratic bastion, and has done so by joining forces with other residents in adjoining communities. For example, the dominant political club, the Seneca Club, is headed by a Jewish district leader who has managed to bridge the diverse communities

of Greenpoint and Williamsburg in an electoral coalition (Orthodox Jews in Williamsburg being the other key constituency) to defeat efforts by Hispanics and blacks seeking to gain political dominance.

Local institutions of religion and politics have contributed to Greenpoint's success in remaining a defended neighborhood. Families and individual persons of color face difficulties in finding housing and running for public office, as well as in being accepted as residents in the community and as participants of local institutions. In both informal and formal areas of neighborhood life, people of color have been blocked from full integration.

Conclusions

This article illustrates how residential segregation is perpetuated in the United States through the everyday activities of individuals. In conjunction with the formal practices of institutions, the informal actions of people attempting to preserve the local culture of their neighborhoods play a major part. Casual conversations among neighbors on the streets, in church, and around political events are the medium by which the preferences of individuals are translated into macro-level patterns of residential segregation.

The basic question raised by this study is the extent to which the actions of individuals perpetuate residential segregation. Some neighborhoods, like Greenpoint, wish to maintain their local culture and therefore attempt to exclude people of color. Although the working class is sometimes accused of being racist, they in fact share this characteristic with other social classes. Affluent groups do not need to resist population growth of people of color and defend their neighborhoods in the same way as the working class. Affluent groups use their economic position to exclude others from their neighborhoods. Zoning laws and local covenants also work to the advantage of the affluent. If neighborhood change should occur, affluent groups have the economic wherewithal to move. Working-class people cannot use economics as a resource. They actively resist minority growth through the strategies described here and therefore may be more quickly accused of racism than other social classes. However, their activism is felt to be their only means of expressing control and power. They are reactive because of their limited economic position; to defend what they have, they answer most community events by actively organizing against population influx of people of color, city policy decisions, or public housing locations. When social scientists try to explain the persistence of residential segregation, the importance of everyday social exchange as a mechanism of information control should not be underestimated. Combined with the actions of institutional players such as the Roman Catholic church and political parties, what people say and don't say has the power to shape metropolitan-wide patterns of residential segregation.

NOTES

1. This information was obtained from tract data from the *1990 Census of Population and Housing,* Summary Tape File 3A.
2. Hispanics can be of any race.
3. See Molotch (1972) for a discussion of the exclusionary practices of churches.
4. "McGuinness Puts the Crimp in Any Greenpoint Rehousing," *Brooklyn Eagle,* 13 December 1939.

REFERENCES

DeSena, Judith N. 1990. *Protecting One's Turf: Social Strategies for Maintaining Urban Neighborhoods.* Lanham, MD: University Press of America.

Farley, John E. 1987. "Segregation in 1980: How Segregated Are America's Metropolitan Areas?" Pp. 95–114 in *Divided Neighborhoods,* edited by Gary A. Tobin. Newbury Park, CA: Sage.

Farley, Reynolds, and Walter R. Allen. 1987. *The Color Line and the Quality of Life in America.* New York: Russell Sage Foundation.

Foley, Donald L. 1973. "Institutional and Contextual Factors Affecting the Housing Choices of Minority Residents." Pp. 85–147 in *Segregation in Residential Areas,* edited by Amos H. Hawley and Vincent P. Rock. Washington, DC: National Academy of Sciences.

Guest, Avery M., and James A. Weed. 1976. "Ethnic Residential Segregation: Patterns of Change." *American Journal of Sociology* 81:1088–1111.

Hershberg, Theodore, Hans Burstein, Eugene P. Ericksen, Stephanie Greenberg, and William L. Yancey. 1978. "A Tale of Three Cities: Blacks and Immigrants in Philadelphia, 1850–1880, 1930, and 1970." *Annals of the American Academy of Political and Social Science* 441:55–81.

Kain, John F. 1968. "Housing Segregation, Negro Employment and Metropolitan Decentralization." *Quarterly Journal of Economics* 82:175–97.

Kain, John F., and J. M. Quigley. 1975. *Housing Markets and Racial Discrimination: A Micro-Economic Analysis.* New York: National Bureau of Economic Research.

Kantrowitz, Nathan. 1978. "Racial and Ethnic Segregation in Boston 1930–1970." *Annals of the American Academy of Political and Social Science* 441:41–54.

Krase, Jerome. 1982. *Self and Community in the City.* Washington, DC: University Press of America.

Lieberson, Stanley. 1980. *A Piece of the Pie: Black and White Immigrants Since 1880.* Berkeley: University of California Press.

Lueck, Thomas J. 1991. "New York Ranks High in Housing Bias." *New York Times,* November 3, real estate section.

Massey, Douglas S., and Brooks Bitterman. 1985. "Explaining the Paradox of Puerto Rican Segregation." *Social Forces* 64(2):306–331.

Massey, Douglas S., and Nancy A. Denton. 1987. "Trends in the Residential Segregation of Blacks, Hispanics, and Asians: 1970–1980." *American Sociological Review* 52:802–825.

Molotch, Harvey L. 1972. *Managed Integration.* Berkeley: University of California Press.

New York City Planning Commission. 1969. *Plan for New York City: A Proposal.* Part 3, *Brooklyn.* New York: Author.

———. 1974. *Greenpoint: Striking a Balance Between Industry and Housing.* New York: Author.

PEARCE, DIANA M. 1979. "Gatekeepers and Homeseekers." *Social Problems* 26:325–42.

RIEDER, JONATHAN. 1985. *Canarsie: The Jews and Italians of Brooklyn Against Liberalism.* Cambridge, MA: Harvard University Press.

SORENSON, ANNEMETTE, KARL E. TAEUBER, and LESLIE J. HOLLINGSWORTH. 1975. "Indexes of Racial Residential Segregation for 109 Cities in the United States, 1940 to 1970." *Sociological Focus* 8 (April):125–42.

SPAIN, DAPHNE, and LARRY LONG. 1981. "Black Movers to the Suburbs: Are They Moving to Predominantly White Neighborhoods?" *Special Demographic Analysis.* Washington, DC: U.S. Bureau of the Census.

SUSSER, IDA. 1982. *Norman Street.* New York: Oxford University Press.

SUTTLES, GERALD D. 1968. *The Social Order of the Slum.* Chicago: University of Chicago Press.

———. 1972. *The Social Construction of Communities.* Chicago: University of Chicago Press.

TAEUBER, KARL E., and ALMA F. TAEUBER. 1965. *Negroes in Cities: Residential Segregation and Neighborhood Change.* Chicago: Aldine.

WELLISZ, CHRISTOPHER. 1982. "If You're Thinking of Living in Greenpoint." *New York Times,* December 12, R9.

WIENK, RONALD E., CLIFFORD E. REID, JOHN C. SIMONSON, and FREDERICK J. EGGERS. 1979. *Measuring Racial Discrimination in American Housing Markets: The Housing Market Practices Survey.* Washington, DC: Department of Housing and Urban Development, Office of Policy Development and Research.

WOOLBRIGHT, LOUIE ALBERT, and DAVID J. HARTMANN. 1987. "The New Segregation: Asians and Hispanics." Pp. 138–157 in *Divided Neighborhoods: Changing Patterns of Racial Segregation,* edited by Gary A. Tobin. Newbury Park, CA: Sage.

30

THE CODE OF THE STREETS

Elijah Anderson

Questions to Consider

In "The Code of the Streets," Elijah Anderson chronicles how an individual's environment can create a set of expectations that are at odds with the dominant culture. How is oppositional culture often detrimental to children and young adults in these communities? How is oppositional culture linked to Anderson's discussion of "street" and "decent" families?

Of all the problems besetting the poor inner-city black community, none is more pressing than that of interpersonal violence and aggression. It wreaks havoc daily with the lives of community residents and increasingly spills over into downtown and residential middle-class areas. Muggings, burglaries, carjackings, and drug-related shootings, all of which may leave their victims or innocent bystanders dead, are now common enough to concern all urban and many suburban residents. The inclination to violence springs from the circumstances of life among the ghetto poor— the lack of jobs that pay a living wage, the stigma of race, the fallout from rampant drug use and drug trafficking, and the resulting alienation and lack of hope for the future.

Simply living in such an environment places young people at special risk of falling victim to aggressive behavior. Although there are often forces in the community which can counteract the negative influences, by far the most powerful being a strong, loving, "decent" (as inner-city residents put it) family committed to middle-class values, the despair is pervasive enough to have spawned an oppositional culture, that of "the streets," whose norms are often consciously opposed to those of mainstream society. These two orientations— decent and street—socially organize the community, and their coexistence has important consequences for residents, particularly children growing up in the inner city. Above all, this environment means that even youngsters whose home lives reflect mainstream values—and the majority of homes in the community do—must be able to handle themselves in a street-oriented environment.

This is because the street culture has evolved what may be called a code of the streets, which amounts to a set of informal rules governing interpersonal public behavior, including violence. The rules prescribe both a proper comportment and a proper way to respond if challenged. They regulate the use of violence and so allow those who are inclined to aggression to precipitate violent encounters in an approved way. The rules have been established and are enforced mainly by the street-oriented, but on the streets the distinction between street and decent is often irrelevant; everybody knows that if the rules are violated, there are penalties. Knowledge of the code is thus largely defensive; it is literally necessary for operating in public. Therefore, even though families with a decency orientation are usually opposed to the values of the code, they often reluctantly encourage their children's familiarity with it to enable them to negotiate the inner-city environment.

At the heart of the code is the issue of respect—loosely defined as being treated "right," or granted the deference one deserves. However, in the troublesome public environment of the inner city, as people increasingly feel buffeted by forces beyond their control, what one deserves in the way of respect becomes more and more problematic and uncertain. This in turn further opens the issue of respect to sometimes intense interpersonal negotiation. In the street culture, especially among young people, respect is viewed as almost an external entity that is hard-won but easily lost, and so must constantly be guarded. The rules of the code in fact provide a framework for negotiating respect. The person whose very appearance—including his clothing, demeanor, and way of moving—deters transgressions feels that he possesses, and may be considered by others to possess, a measure of respect. With the right amount of respect, for instance, he can avoid "being bothered" in public. If he is bothered, not only may he be in physical danger but he has been disgraced or "dissed" (disrespected). Many of the forms that dissing can take might seem petty to middle-class people (maintaining eye contact for too long, for example), but to those invested in the street code, these actions become serious indications of the other person's intentions. Consequently, such people become very sensitive to advances and slights, which could well serve as warnings of imminent physical confrontation.

This hard reality can be traced to the profound sense of alienation from mainstream society and its institutions felt by many poor inner-city black people, particularly the young. The code of the streets is actually a cultural adaptation to a profound lack of faith in the police and the judicial system. The police are most often seen as representing the dominant white society and not caring to protect inner-city residents. When called, they may not respond, which is one reason many residents feel they must be prepared to take extraordinary measures to defend themselves and their loved ones against those who are inclined to aggression. Lack of police accountability has in fact been incorporated into the status system: the person who is believed capable of "taking care of himself" is accorded a certain deference, which translates into a sense of physical and psychological control. Thus the street code emerges where the influence of the police ends and personal responsibility for one's safety is felt to begin. Exacerbated by the proliferation of drugs and easy access to guns, this volatile situation results in the ability of the street-oriented minority (or those who effectively "go for bad") to dominate the public spaces.

Decent and Street Families

Although almost everyone in poor inner-city neighborhoods is struggling financially and therefore feels a certain distance from the rest of America, the decent and the street family in a real sense represent two poles of value orientation, two contrasting conceptual categories. The labels "decent" and "street," which the residents themselves use, amount to evaluative judgments that confer status on local residents. The labeling is often the result of a social contest among individuals and families of the neighborhood. Individuals of the two orientations often coexist in the same extended family. Decent residents judge themselves to be so while judging others to be of the street, and street individuals often present themselves as decent, drawing distinctions between themselves and other people. In addition, there is quite a bit of circumstantial behavior—that is, one person may at different times exhibit both decent and street orientations, depending on the circumstances. Although these designations result from so much social jockeying, there do exist concrete features that define each conceptual category.

Generally, so-called decent families tend to accept mainstream values more fully and attempt to instill them in their children. Whether married couples with children or single-parent (usually female) households, they are generally "working poor" and so tend to be better off financially than their street-oriented neighbors. They value hard work and self-reliance and are willing to sacrifice for their children. Because they have a certain amount of faith in mainstream society, they harbor hopes for a better future for their children, if not for themselves. Many of them go to church and take a strong interest in their children's schooling. Rather than dwelling on the real hardships and inequities facing them, many such decent people, particularly the increasing number of grandmothers raising grandchildren, see their difficult situation as a test from God and derive great support from their faith and from the church community.

Extremely aware of the problematic and often dangerous environment in which they reside, decent parents tend to be strict in their child-rearing practices, encouraging children to respect authority and walk a straight moral line. They have an almost obsessive concern about trouble of any kind and remind their children to be on the lookout for people and situations that might lead to it. At the same time, they are themselves polite and considerate of others, and teach their children to be the same way. At home, at work, and in church, they strive hard to maintain a positive mental attitude and a spirit of cooperation.

So-called street parents, in contrast, often show a lack of consideration for other people and have a rather superficial sense of family and community. Though they may love their children, many of them are unable to cope with the physical and emotional demands of parenthood, and find it difficult to reconcile their needs with those of their children. These families, who are more fully invested in the code of the streets than the decent people are, may aggressively socialize their children into it in a normative way. They believe in the code and judge themselves and others according to its values.

In fact the overwhelming majority of families in the inner-city community try to approximate the decent-family model, but there are many others who clearly represent the worst fears of the decent family. Not only are their financial resources extremely limited, but what little they have may easily be misused. The lives of the street-oriented are often marked by disorganization. In the most desperate circumstances people frequently have a limited understanding of priorities and consequences, and so frustrations mount over bills, food, and, at times, drink, cigarettes, and drugs. Some tend toward self-destructive behavior; many street-oriented women are crack-addicted ("on the pipe"), alcoholic, or involved in complicated relationships with men who abuse them. In addition, the seeming intractability of their situation, caused in large part by the lack of well-paying jobs and the persistence of racial discrimination, has engendered deep-seated bitterness and

anger in many of the most desperate and poorest blacks, especially young people. The need both to exercise a measure of control and to lash out at somebody is often reflected in the adults' relations with their children. At the least, the frustrations of persistent poverty shorten the fuse in such people—contributing to a lack of patience with anyone, child or adult, who irritates them.

In these circumstances a woman—or a man, although men are less consistently present in children's lives—can be quite aggressive with children, yelling at and striking them for the least little infraction of the rules she has set down. Often little if any serious explanation follows the verbal and physical punishment. This response teaches children a particular lesson. They learn that to solve any kind of interpersonal problem one must quickly resort to hitting or other violent behavior. Actual peace and quiet, and also the appearance of calm, respectful children conveyed to her neighbors and friends, are often what the young mother most desires, but at times she will be very aggressive in trying to get them. Thus she may be quick to beat her children, especially if they defy her law, not because she hates them but because this is the way she knows to control them. In fact, many street-oriented women love their children dearly. Many mothers in the community subscribe to the notion that there is a "devil in the boy" that must be beaten out of him or that socially "fast girls need to be whupped." Thus much of what borders on child abuse in the view of social authorities is acceptable parental punishment in the view of these mothers.

Many street-oriented women are sporadic mothers whose children learn to fend for themselves when necessary, foraging for food and money any way they can get it. The children are sometimes employed by drug dealers or become addicted themselves. These children of the street, growing up with little supervision, are said to "come up hard."

They often learn to fight at an early age, sometimes using short-tempered adults around them as role models. The street-oriented home may be fraught with anger, verbal disputes, physical aggression, and even mayhem. The children observe these goings-on, learning the lesson that might makes right. They quickly learn to hit those who cross them, and the dog-eat-dog mentality prevails. In order to survive, to protect oneself, it is necessary to marshal inner resources and be ready to deal with adversity in a hands-on way. In these circumstances physical prowess takes on great significance.

In some of the most desperate cases, a street-oriented mother may simply leave her young children alone and unattended while she goes out. The most irresponsible women can be found at local bars and crack houses, getting high and socializing with other adults. Sometimes a troubled woman will leave very young children alone for days at a time. Reports of crack addicts abandoning their children have become common in drug-infested inner-city communities. Neighbors or relatives discover the abandoned children, often hungry and distraught over the absence of their mother. After repeated absences, a friend or relative, particularly a grandmother, will often step in to care for the young children, sometimes petitioning the authorities to send her, as guardian of the children, the mother's welfare check, if the mother gets one. By this time, however, the children may well have learned the first lesson of the streets: survival itself, let alone respect, cannot be taken for granted; you have to fight for your place in the world.

Campaigning for Respect

These realities of inner-city life are largely absorbed on the streets. At an early age, often even before they start school, children from street-oriented homes gravitate to the streets, where they "hang"—socialize with their peers. Children from these generally permissive homes have a great deal of latitude and are allowed to "rip and run" up and down the street. They often come home from school, put their books down, and go right back out the door. On school nights eight- and nine-year-olds remain out until nine or ten o'clock (and teenagers typically come in whenever they want to). On the streets they play in groups that often become the source of their primary social bonds. Children from decent homes tend to be more carefully supervised and are thus likely to have curfews and to be taught how to stay out of trouble.

When decent and street kids come together, a kind of social shuffle occurs in which children have a chance to go either way. Tension builds as a child comes to realize that he must choose an orientation. The kind of home he comes from influences but does not determine the way he will ultimately turn out—although it is unlikely that a child from a thoroughly street-oriented family will easily absorb decent values on the streets. Youths who emerge from street-oriented families but develop a decency orientation almost always learn those values in another setting—in school, in a youth group, in church. Often it is the result of their involvement with a caring "old head" (adult role model).

In the street, through their play, children pour their individual life experiences into a common knowledge pool, affirming, confirming, and elaborating on what they have observed in the home and matching their skills against those of others. And they learn to fight. Even small children test one another, pushing and shoving, and are ready to hit other children over circumstances not to their liking. In turn, they are readily hit by other children, and the child who is toughest prevails. Thus the violent resolution of disputes, the hitting and cursing, gains social reinforcement. The child in effect is initiated into a system that is really a way of campaigning for respect.

In addition, younger children witness the disputes of older children, which are often resolved through cursing and abusive talk, if not aggression or outright violence. They see that one child succumbs to the greater physical and mental abilities of the other. They are also alert and attentive witnesses to the verbal and physical fights of adults, after which they compare notes and share their interpretations of the event. In almost every case the victor is the person who physically won the altercation, and this person often enjoys the esteem and respect of onlookers. These experiences reinforce the lessons the children have learned at home: might makes right, and toughness is a virtue, while humility is not. In effect they learn the social meaning of fighting. When it is left virtually unchallenged, this understanding becomes an ever more important part of the child's working conception of the world. Over time the code of the streets becomes refined.

Those street-oriented adults with whom children come in contact—including mothers, fathers, brothers, sisters, boyfriends, cousins, neighbors, and friends—help them along in forming this understanding by verbalizing the messages they are getting through experience: "Watch your back." "Protect yourself." "Don't punk out." "If somebody messes with you, you got to pay them back." "If someone disses you, you got to straighten them out." Many parents actually impose sanctions if a child is not sufficiently aggressive. For example, if a child loses a fight and comes home upset, the parent might respond, "Don't you come in here crying that somebody beat you up; you better get back out there and whup his ass. I didn't raise no punks! Get back out there and whup his ass. If you don't whup his ass, I'll whup your ass when you come home." Thus the child obtains reinforcement for being tough and showing nerve.

While fighting, some children cry as though they are doing something they are ambivalent about. The fight may be against their wishes, yet they may feel constrained to fight or face the consequences—not just from peers but also from caretakers or parents, who may administer another beating if they back down. Some adults recall receiving such lessons from their own parents and justify repeating them to their children as a way to toughen them up. Looking capable of taking care of oneself as a form of self-defense is a dominant theme among both street-oriented and decent adults who worry about the safety of their children. There is thus at times a convergence in their child-rearing practices, although the rationales behind them may differ.

Self-Image Based on "Juice"

By the time they are teenagers, most youths have either internalized the code of the streets or at least learned the need to comport themselves in accordance with its rules, which chiefly have to do with interpersonal communication. The code revolves around the presentation of self. Its basic requirement is the display of a certain predisposition to violence. Accordingly, one's bearing must send the unmistakable if sometimes subtle message to "the next person" in public that one is capable of violence and mayhem when the situation requires it, that one can take care of oneself. The nature of this communication is largely determined by the demands of the circumstances but can include facial expressions, gait, and verbal expressions—all of which are geared mainly to deterring aggression. Physical appearance, including clothes, jewelry, and grooming, also plays an important part in how a person is viewed; to be respected, it is important to have the right look.

Even so, there are no guarantees against challenges, because there are always people around looking for a fight to increase their share of respect—or "juice," as it is sometimes called on the street. Moreover, if a person is assaulted, it is important, not only in the eyes of his opponent but also in the eyes of his "running buddies," for him to avenge himself. Otherwise he risks being "tried" (challenged) or "moved on" by any number of others. To maintain his honor he must show he is not someone to be "messed with" or "dissed." In general, the person must "keep himself straight" by managing his position of respect among others; this involves in part his self-image, which is shaped by what he thinks others are thinking of him in relation to his peers.

Objects play an important and complicated role in establishing self-image. Jackets, sneakers, gold jewelry, reflect not just a person's taste, which tends to be tightly regulated among adolescents of all social classes, but also a willingness to possess things that may require defending. A boy wearing a fashionable, expensive jacket, for example, is vulnerable to attack by another who covets the jacket and either cannot afford to buy one or wants the added satisfaction of depriving someone else of his. However, if the boy forgoes the desirable jacket and wears one that isn't "hip," he runs the risk of being teased and possibly even assaulted as an unworthy person. To be allowed to hang with certain prestigious crowds, a boy must wear a different set of expensive clothes—sneakers and athletic suit—every day. Not to be able to do so might make him appear socially deficient. The youth comes to covet such items—especially when he sees easy prey wearing them.

In acquiring valued things, therefore, a person shores up his identity—but since it is an identity based on having things, it is highly precarious. This very precariousness gives a heightened sense of urgency to staying even with peers, with whom the person is actually competing. Young men and women who are able to command respect through their presentation of self—by allowing their possessions and their body language to speak for them—may not have to campaign for regard but may, rather, gain it by the force of their manner. Those who are unable to command respect in this way must actively campaign for it—and are thus particularly alive to slights.

One way of campaigning for status is by taking the possessions of others. In this context, seemingly ordinary objects can become trophies imbued with symbolic value that far exceeds their monetary worth. Possession of the trophy can symbolize the ability to violate somebody—to "get in his face," to take something of value from him, to "dis" him, and thus to enhance one's own worth by stealing someone else's. The trophy does not have to be something material. It can be another person's sense of honor, snatched away with a derogatory remark. It can be the outcome of a fight. It can be the imposition of a certain standard, such as a girl's getting herself recognized as the most beautiful. Material things, however, fit easily into the pattern. Sneakers, a pistol, even somebody else's girlfriend, can become a trophy. When a person can take something from another and then flaunt it, he gains a certain regard by being the owner, or the controller, of that thing. But this display of ownership can then provoke other people to challenge him. This game of who controls what is thus constantly being played out on inner-city streets, and the trophy—extrinsic or intrinsic, tangible or intangible—identifies the current winner.

An important aspect of this often violent give-and-take is its zero-sum quality. That is, the extent to which one person can raise himself up depends on his ability to put another person down. This underscores the alienation that permeates the inner-city ghetto community. There is a generalized sense that very little respect is to be had, and therefore everyone competes to get what affirmation he can of the little that is available. The craving for respect that results gives people thin skins. Shows of deference by others can be highly soothing, contributing to a sense of security, comfort, self-confidence, and self-respect. Transgressions by others which go unanswered diminish these feelings and are believed to encourage further transgressions. Hence one must be ever vigilant against the transgressions of others or even *appearing* as if transgressions will be tolerated. Among young people, whose sense of self-esteem is particularly vulnerable, there is an especially heightened concern with being disrespected. Many inner-city young men in particular crave respect to such a degree that they will risk their lives to attain and maintain it.

The issue of respect is thus closely tied to whether a person has an inclination to be violent, even as a victim. In the wider society people may not feel required to retaliate physically after an attack, even though they are aware that they have been degraded or taken advantage of. They may feel a great need to defend themselves *during* an attack, or to behave in such a way as to deter aggression (middle-class people certainly can and do become victims of street-oriented youths), but they are much more likely than street-oriented people to feel that they can walk away from a possible altercation with their self-esteem intact. Some people may even have the strength of character to flee, without any thought that their self-respect or esteem will be diminished.

In impoverished inner-city black communities, however, particularly among young males and perhaps increasingly among females, such flight would be extremely difficult. To run away would likely leave one's self-esteem in tatters.

Hence people often feel constrained not only to stand up and at least attempt to resist during an assault but also to "pay back"—to seek revenge—after a successful assault on their person. This may include going to get a weapon or even getting relatives involved. Their very identity and self-respect, their honor, is often intricately tied up with the way they perform on the streets during and after such encounters. This outlook reflects the circumscribed opportunities of the inner-city poor. Generally people outside the ghetto have other ways of gaining status and regard, and thus do not feel so dependent on such physical displays.

By Trial of Manhood

On the street, among males these concerns about things and identity have come to be expressed in the concept of "manhood." Manhood in the inner city means taking the prerogatives of men with respect to strangers, other men, and women—being distinguished as a man. It implies physicality and a certain ruthlessness. Regard and respect are associated with this concept in large part because of its practical application: if others have little or no regard for a person's manhood, his very life and those of his loved ones could be in jeopardy. But there is a chicken-and-egg aspect to this situation: one's physical safety is more likely to be jeopardized in public *because* manhood is associated with respect. In other words, an existential link has been created between the idea of manhood and one's self-esteem, so that it has become hard to say which is primary. For many inner-city youths, manhood and respect are flip sides of the same coin; physical and psychological well-being are inseparable, and both require a sense of control, of being in charge.

The operating assumption is that a man, especially a real man, knows what other men know—the code of the streets. And if one is not a real man, one is somehow diminished as a person, and there are certain valued things one simply does not deserve. There is thus believed to be a certain justice to the code, since it is considered that everyone has the opportunity to know it. Implicit in this is that everybody is held responsible for being familiar with the code. If the victim of a mugging, for example, does not know the code and so responds "wrong," the perpetrator may feel justified even in killing him and may feel no remorse. He may think, "Too bad, but it's his fault. He should have known better."

So when a person ventures outside, he must adopt the code—a kind of shield, really—to prevent others from "messing with" him. In these circumstances it is easy for people to think they are being tried or tested by others even when this is not the case. For it is sensed that something extremely valuable is at stake in every interaction, and people are encouraged to rise to the occasion, particularly with strangers. For people who are unfamiliar with the code— generally people who live outside the inner city—the concern with respect in the most ordinary interactions can be frightening and incomprehensible. But for those who are invested in the code, the clear object of their demeanor is to discourage strangers from even thinking about testing their manhood. And the sense of power that attends the ability to deter others can be alluring even to those who know the code without being heavily invested in it—the decent inner-city youths. Thus a boy who has been leading a basically decent life can, in trying circumstances, suddenly resort to deadly force.

Central to the issue of manhood is the widespread belief that one of the most effective ways of gaining respect is to manifest "nerve." Nerve is shown when one takes another person's possessions (the more valuable the better), "messes with" someone's woman, throws the first punch, "gets in someone's face," or pulls a trigger. Its proper display helps on the spot to check others who would violate one's person and also helps to build a reputation that works to prevent future challenges. But since such a show of nerve is a forceful expression of disrespect toward the person on the receiving end, the victim may be greatly offended and seek to retaliate with equal or greater force. A display of nerve, therefore, can easily provoke a life-threatening response, and the background knowledge of that possibility has often been incorporated into the concept of nerve.

True nerve exposes a lack of fear of dying. Many feel that it is acceptable to risk dying over the principle of respect. In fact, among the hard-core street-oriented, the clear risk of violent death may be preferable to being "dissed" by another. The youths who have internalized this attitude and convincingly display it in their public bearing are among the most threatening people of all, for it is commonly assumed that they fear no man. As the people of the community say, "They are the baddest dudes on the street." They often lead an existential life that may acquire meaning only when they are faced with the possibility of imminent death. Not to be afraid to die is by implication to have few compunctions about taking another's life. Not to be afraid to die is the quid pro quo of being able to take somebody else's life—for the right reasons, if the situation demands it. When others believe this is one's position, it gives one a real sense of power on the streets. Such credibility is what many inner-city youths strive to achieve, whether they are decent or street-oriented, both because of its practical defensive value and because of the positive way it makes them feel about themselves. The difference between the decent and the street-oriented youth is often that the decent youth makes a conscious decision to appear tough and manly; in another setting—with teachers, say, or at his part-time job—he can be polite and deferential. The street-oriented youth, on the other hand, has made the concept of manhood a part of his very identity; he has difficulty manipulating it—it often controls him.

Girls and Boys

Increasingly, teenage girls are mimicking the boys and trying to have their own version of "manhood." Their goal is the same—to get respect, to be recognized as capable of setting or maintaining a certain standard. They try to achieve this end in the ways that have been established by the boys, including posturing, abusive language, and the use of violence to resolve disputes, but the issues for the girls are different. Although conflicts over turf and status exist among the girls, the majority of disputes seem rooted in assessments of beauty (which girl in a group is "the cutest"), competition over boyfriends, and attempts to regulate other people's knowledge of and opinions about a girl's behavior or that of someone close to her, especially her mother.

A major cause of conflicts among girls is "he say, she say." This practice begins in the early school years and continues through high school. It occurs when "people," particularly girls, talk about others, thus putting their "business in the streets." Usually one girl will say something negative about another in the group, most often behind the person's back. The remark will then get back to the person talked about. She may retaliate or her friends may feel required to "take up for" her. In essence this is a form of group gossiping in which individuals are negatively assessed and evaluated. As with much gossip, the things said may or may

not be true, but the point is that such imputations can cast aspersions on a person's good name. The accused is required to defend herself against the slander, which can result in arguments and fights, often over little of real substance. Here again is the problem of low self-esteem, which encourages youngsters to be highly sensitive to slights and to be vulnerable to feeling easily "dissed." To avenge the dissing, a fight is usually necessary.

Because boys are believed to control violence, girls tend to defer to them in situations of conflict. Often if a girl is attacked or feels slighted, she will get a brother, uncle, or cousin to do her fighting for her. Increasingly, however, girls are doing their own fighting and are even asking their male relatives to teach them how to fight. Some girls form groups that attack other girls or take things from them. A hard-core segment of inner-city girls inclined toward violence seems to be developing. As one thirteen-year-old girl in a detention center for youths who have committed violent acts told me, "To get people to leave you alone, you gotta fight. Talking don't always get you out of stuff." One major difference between girls and boys: girls rarely use guns. Their fights are therefore not life-or-death struggles. Girls are not often willing to put their lives on the line for "manhood." The ultimate form of respect on the male-dominated inner-city street is thus reserved for men.

"Going for Bad"

In the most fearsome youths such a cavalier attitude toward death grows out of a very limited view of life. Many are uncertain about how long they are going to live and believe they could die violently at any time. They accept this fate; they live on the edge. Their manner conveys the message that nothing intimidates them; whatever turn the encounter takes, they maintain their attack—rather like a pit bull, whose spirit many such boys admire. The demonstration of such tenacity "shows heart" and earns their respect.

This fearlessness has implications for law enforcement. Many street-oriented boys are much more concerned about the threat of "justice" at the hands of a peer than at the hands of the police. Moreover, many feel not only that they have little to lose by going to prison but that they have something to gain. The toughening-up one experiences in prison can actually enhance one's reputation on the streets. Hence the system loses influence over the hard core who are without jobs, with little perceptible stake in the system. If mainstream society has done nothing *for* them, they counter by making sure it can do nothing *to* them.

At the same time, however, a competing view maintains that true nerve consists in backing down, walking away from a fight, and going on with one's business. One fights only in self-defense. This view emerges from the decent philosophy that life is precious, and it is an important part of the socialization process common in decent homes. It discourages violence as the primary means of resolving disputes and encourages youngsters to accept nonviolence and talk as confrontational strategies. But "if the deal goes down," self-defense is greatly encouraged. When there is enough positive support for this orientation, either in the home or among one's peers, then nonviolence has a chance to prevail. But it prevails at the cost of relinquishing a claim to being bad and tough, and therefore sets a young person up as at the very least alienated from street-oriented peers and quite possibly a target of derision or even violence.

Although the nonviolent orientation rarely overcomes the impulse to strike back in an encounter, it does introduce a certain confusion and so can prompt a measure of soul-searching, or even profound ambiva-lence. Did the person back down with his respect intact or did he back down only to be judged a "punk"—a person lacking manhood? Should he or she have acted? Should he or she have hit the other person in the mouth? These questions beset many young men and women during public confrontations. What is the "right" thing to do? In the quest for honor, respect, and local status—which few young people are uninterested in—common sense most often prevails, which leads many to opt for the tough approach, enacting their own particular versions of the display of nerve. The presentation of oneself as rough and tough is very often quite acceptable until one is tested. And then that presentation may help the person pass the test, because it will cause fewer questions to be asked about what he did and why. It is hard for a person to explain why he lost the fight or why he backed down. Hence many will strive to appear to "go for bad," while hoping they will never be tested. But when they are tested, the outcome of the situation may quickly be out of their hands, as they become wrapped up in the circumstances of the moment.

An Oppositional Culture

The attitudes of the wider society are deeply implicated in the code of the streets. Most people in inner-city communities are not totally invested in the code, but the significant minority of hard-core street youths who are have to maintain the code in order to establish reputations, because they have—or feel they have—few other ways to assert themselves. For these young people the standards of the street code are the only game in town. The extent to which some children—particularly those who through upbringing have become most alienated and those lacking in strong and conventional social support—experience, feel, and internalize racist rejection and contempt from mainstream society may strongly encourage them to express contempt for the more conventional society in turn. In dealing with this contempt and rejection, some youngsters will consciously invest themselves and their considerable mental resources in what amounts to an oppositional culture to preserve themselves and their self-respect. Once they do, any respect they might be able to garner in the wider system pales in comparison with the respect available in the local system; thus they often lose interest in even attempting to negotiate the mainstream system.

At the same time, many less alienated young blacks have assumed a street-oriented demeanor as a way of expressing their blackness while really embracing a much more moderate way of life; they, too, want a nonviolent setting in which to live and raise a family. These decent people are trying hard to be part of the mainstream culture, but the racism, real and perceived, that they encounter helps to legitimate the oppositional culture. And so on occasion they adopt street behavior. In fact, depending on the demands of the situation, many people in the community slip back and forth between decent and street behavior.

A vicious cycle has thus been formed. The hopelessness and alienation many young inner-city black men and women feel, largely as a result of endemic joblessness and persistent racism, fuels the violence they engage in. This violence serves to confirm the negative feelings many whites and some middle-class blacks harbor toward the ghetto poor, further legitimating the oppositional culture and the code of the streets in the eyes of many poor young blacks. Unless this cycle is broken, attitudes on both sides will become increasingly entrenched, and the violence, which claims victims black and white, poor and affluent, will only escalate.

Race and the Media

31

TELEVISION AND THE POLITICS OF RACIAL REPRESENTATION

Justin Lewis and Sut Jhally

Questions to Consider

Justin Lewis and Sut Jhally use The Cosby Show *as a way to deconstruct the meaning of race, racial representations, and the role of social class on television. They argue that far from being just a well-written and successful situation comedy, the show sent a number of messages that were both positive and negative. What were they?*

One of the abiding concerns in contemporary North American culture has been the many attempts to deal with race and racial inequality. Because racism is often understood as a perception dependent on negative or stereotypical images, debates about race often have centered on the issue of representation, with analytical glances increasingly cast toward television, as the main image-maker in our culture.

To make sense of the many competing claims about the way black people are represented on television, we carried out an extensive study based on a content analysis of prime time television together with a series of 52 focus group interviews (made up of 26 white, 23 black, and 3 Latino groups) from a range of class backgrounds. The interviews were designed to probe attitudes about race and the media representation thereof. To facilitate these discussions, each interview began with the viewing of an episode of *The Cosby Show.*

The Cosby Show was chosen because it has, in many ways, changed the way television thinks about the portrayal of African Americans. During the time it took for *The Cosby Show* to go from being innovative to institutional, African Americans became a fairly common sight on network television in the United States. And not just any African Americans: Our content analysis confirmed that we now see a plethora of middle- and upper-middle-class black characters populating our screens. Major black characters—from *ER* to *Sportsnight*—are now much more likely to be well-heeled professionals than blue-collar workers. In this sense, Bill Cosby can be credited with spurring a move toward racial equality on television. Fictional characters on U.S. television always have tended to be middle or upper-middle class—and since the late 1980s, black people have become an equal and everyday part of this upwardly mobile world.

The Cosby Show was, in this sense, more than just another sitcom. It represents a turning point in television culture, to a new era in which black actors have possibilities beyond the indignities of playing a crude and limited array of black stereotypes, an era in which white audiences can accept TV programs with more than just an occasional "token" black character. There is, it seems, much to thank Bill Cosby for. He has, quite literally, changed the face of network television.

At first reading, our study suggested that the upward mobility of black representation precipitated by *The Cosby Show* was an unambiguously positive phenomenon. It appeared, from our focus groups, to promote an attitude of racial tolerance among white viewers, for whom black television characters have become ordinary and routine, and to generate a feeling of pride and relief among black viewers. But *The Cosby Show* and the new generation of black professionals on U.S. television are caught up in a set of cultural assumptions about race and class that complicates the political ramifications of such a trend.

It is true that, in recent decades, the size of the black middle class in the U.S. has grown. This much said, the social success of black TV characters in the wake of *The Cosby Show* does not reflect any overall trend to-

ward black prosperity in the world beyond television. On the contrary, the period in which *The Cosby Show* dominated television ratings—1984 to 1990—witnessed a comparative decline in the fortunes of most African Americans in the United States. The racial inequalities that scarred the United States before the civil rights movement could only be rectified by instituting major structural changes in the nation's social, political, and economic life—an idea informing Great Society interventions in the 1960s and 1970s. Since the election of Ronald Reagan in 1980, both Republican and Democratic administrations generally have withdrawn from any notion of large-scale public intervention in an iniquitous system, committing themselves instead to promoting a global free enterprise economy. This laissez-faire approach has resulted in the stagnation or gradual erosion of advances made by black people during the 1960s. For all the gains made in the fictional world of TV, by almost all demographic measures (such as education, health, levels of incarceration, income, and wealth), the United States remains a racially divided society.

As William Julius Wilson (1987) has documented, maintaining these divisions are a set of socioeconomic conditions that keep most people in their place. The "American Dream" of significant upward mobility is an aspiration that few can or will ever realize. It is an idea sustained by fictions and by anecdotes that focus on the exceptions rather than the rule of class division. If we are to begin any kind of serious analysis of racial inequality in the United States, we must acknowledge the existence of the systematic disadvantages that exclude most people on low incomes in poor neighborhoods—a condition in which black people in the United States have disproportionately been placed—from serious economic advancement.

Left unchecked, it is the laws of free market capitalism—rather than more overt, individual forms of racial discrimination—that reproduce a racially skewed class structure. Most major institutions in the United States have officially declared themselves nonracist and invited black citizens to compete alongside everyone else. This is important but insufficient. If three white people begin a game of Monopoly, a black player who is invited to join the game halfway through enters at a serious disadvantage. Unless blessed by a disproportionate degree of good luck, the black player will be unable to overcome these economic disadvantages and compete on equal terms. This is, in effect if not in intention, how the United States has treated most of its black citizens: It offers the promise of equal opportunity without providing the means—good housing, good education, good local job opportunities—to fulfill it.

There is a wealth of evidence about the operation of these structural inequalities (see, e.g., Wilson 1987; Hacker 1992). What is remarkable about our culture is that it refuses to acknowledge the existence of class structures, let alone understand how they influence racial inequalities. And yet, at certain moments, we do accept these things as obvious. We expect rich white children to do better than poor black children. We expect it, because we know that they will go to better schools, be brought up in more comfortable surroundings, and be offered more opportunities to succeed. And our expectations would, most often, be proved quite right. The child who succeeds in spite of these odds is a glamorous figure in our culture precisely because he or she has defied these expectations. Unfortunately, our culture teaches us to ignore these social structures and offers us instead a naive obsession with individual endeavor. Instead of a *collective* war on poverty, we have welfare reforms that increase poverty and homelessness in the name of *individual* responsibility.

We would argue that U.S. television—and popular culture generally—is directly culpable for providing an endless slew of apocryphal stories that sustain a cultural refusal to deal with class inequalities and the racial character of those inequalities.

The Upscale World of Television Fiction

Televison in the United States is notable for creating a world that shifts the class boundaries upward. If the path to heaven is more arduous for the rich than the poor, the opposite can be said of entry to the ersatz world of television. Data from the University of Pennsylvania's Cultural Indicators project suggest that, in recent decades, television gives the overwhelming majority of its main parts to characters from middle- and professional class backgrounds, whereas significant working class roles are few and far between (Jhally and Lewis 1992). This is in notable contrast to the norms of other English-speaking television programs from countries like Britain and Australia, where working-class characters are much more commonplace. In the United States, the TV world is skewed to such an extent that the definition of what looks normal on television no longer includes the working class. The bias is neither obvious nor clearly stated. On the contrary, television's professionals are generally universalized so that the class barriers that divide working class viewers from upper-middle TV characters melt away. As some of our working class viewers said of Cliff Huxtable, he may be a doctor, but he's not as aloof as some of the real doctors they encounter in the non-TV world. This is seen in the words of two respondents:

I guess he doesn't really seem professional, you know, not the way a doctor would be. The ones I meet are very uppity and they really look down on the lower class.

They don't play the status they are in the show. You expect them to be living a much higher class, flashing the money, but they're very down to earth.

Television's characters are thus well-off but accessible. These are pictures of the American Dream, and they are paraded in front of us in sitcoms and drama series night after night. On television, most people, or most people with an ounce of merit, are making it.

But surely, it is only television, isn't it? Most people realize that the real world is different, don't they? Well, yes and no. Our study suggested that the line between the TV world and the world beyond the screen has become, for most people, exceedingly hazy. Many of the respondents in our study would shift from immersion in television's world to critical distance in the same interview, praising *The Cosby Show* at one moment for its realism and criticizing it at another for its lack of realism. Thus, for example, one respondent began with an endorsement of the show's realism: "I think that Cosby is much more true to life; you can put yourself right into the picture. Just about everything they do has happened to you, or you've seen it happen."

Later in the interview, the same respondent criticized the show:

It's totally a fantasy to me, a fairy tale. . . . I think if you bring the real humdrum of what really life is all about, it would be a total bore. I would much prefer to see a little bit of fairy tale and make-believe.

It seems we watch at one moment with credulity and at another with disbelief. We mix skepticism with an extraordinary faith in television's capacity to tell us the truth. We know that the succession of doctors, lawyers, and other professionals that dominate television's stories is not real, yet we continually think about them as if they were. We have thereby learned to live in the dreams of network executives.

Exceptions to this—perhaps the most notable in recent television history being *Roseanne*—become conspicuous because (at least until the last show in the series when the family wins the lottery) they defy this norm. Simply by being sympathetic and assertively working class, the characters in *Roseanne* stood out from the sea of upscale images that surrounded them. In the United States, there are nearly twice as many janitors as all the lawyers and doctors put together, and yet, on television, the legal or medical professions are run of the mill, whereas to portray a major character as a janitor seems "ostentatiously" class-conscious. The negative response to *thirtysomething* in the 1980s was, in this context, extremely revealing. Here was a show that dealt, fairly intimately, with the lives of a group of middle- and upper-middle-class people. In demographic terms, these characters were the standard fare offered by network television, where most characters of any importance are middle or upper-middle class. Why, then, was this show in particular invariably described, often pejoratively, as a yuppie drama?

The answer tells us a great deal about the way class is represented on television. The show *thirtysomething* was unusual not because it was about young professionals but because it was self-consciously about young professionals. It was difficult to watch an episode without being aware that this was a group of people who were, in class terms, fairly privileged. Here was a show that was conspicuously and unapologetically class-conscious. When most TV characters display a liberal concern for the poor or the homeless, we are invited to applaud their altruism. When characters on *thirtysomething* did so, we were more likely to cringe with embarrassment at the class contradictions thrown up by such philanthropic gestures. Thus, *thirtysomething's* principal sin was not that it showed us yuppies, but that it made them appear part of an exclusive world that many people will never inhabit. With its coy realism, *thirtysomething* was killjoy television, puncturing the myth of the American Dream.

Although we see echoes of this class consciousness on shows like *Frasier*, they are represented in ways that tend to elide rather than confirm class distinctions. It is not just that Frasier and Niles Crane's high cultural, upper-middle-class affectations are often parodied, but the constant presence of their working-class father reminds us that class background is unimportant.

The prosperous, comfortable world in which most television characters live is generally welcoming, and it is into this world that upscale black characters—from the Huxtables onward—fit like the proverbial glove. It is, we would argue, hard to underestimate the significance of this in the politics of representation. Thus, we can say that to be "normal" on television—the prerequisite for a "positive image"—black characters are necessarily presented as middle or upper-middle class. Indeed, *The Cosby Show* itself used two of television's favorite professions—what, after all, could be more routine than a household headed by a lawyer and a doctor? But unlike *thirtysomething*, it also had to look normal, to portray these wealthy professionals as a regular, "everyday" family. The respondents in our study suggested that the show was particularly skillful and adroit in absorbing this contradiction; indeed, its popularity depends on this combination of accessibility and affluence. Professionals and blue-collar workers can both watch the show and see themselves reflected in it. Social barriers, like class or race are absent from this world. They have

to be. To acknowledge the presence of such things would make too many viewers uncomfortable. Television has thereby imposed a set of cultural rules on us that give us certain expectations about the way the TV world should be.

The bombardment from this image world makes it difficult for people schooled in the evasive language of North American television to comprehend the world around them seriously. If a serious analysis of class structures is generally absent from our popular vocabulary, then that absence is confirmed by a television environment that makes upward mobility desirable but class barriers irrelevant. As a consequence, when our respondents tried to make sense of class issues thrown up by a discussion of *The Cosby Show*, many were forced to displace the idea of class onto a set of racial categories. This was often the case for our black respondents, who often became enmeshed in the debate about whether the show was "too white" (an idea that, incidentally, the great majority repudiated). Yet, we would argue, the very terms of such a debate involve a misleading syllogism, one that declares that because black people are disproportionately less likely to be upper-middle class, if they become so they have not entered a class category (upper-middle class) but a racial one (white). One of our black middle-class respondents revealed the confusion involved in this way of thinking when he said, "What's wrong with showing a black family who has those kind of values? I almost said *white* values but *that's not the word I want*" (italics added). The context of a portrayal like *The Cosby Show* is not so much "white culture" (whatever that may be), but "upper-middle-class culture." It is partly by echoing the stilted discourse of U.S. television that many of our respondents found it difficult to make such a distinction.

In creating *The Cosby Show* Bill Cosby can hardly be blamed for playing by the rules of network television. Indeed, what our study makes clear is that it was only by conforming to these cultural limitations that he was able to make a black family so widely acceptable to white TV viewers. This discomfort or distance that most of the white viewers in our study expressed about black television characters was articulated not only in racial terms, but also—albeit indirectly—in class terms. What many white viewers found off-putting about other black sitcoms was not blackness per se but working-class blackness:

> I mean it's not a jive show, like *Good Times*. I think those other shows are more jive, more soul shows, say as far as the way the characters are with making you aware that they are more separate. Where Cosby is more of American down the line thing, which makes everybody feel accepted.

> I remember that it (*The Jeffersons*) was a little bit more slapstick, a little bit more stereotypical. They were concerned with racial issues. And it was much more interested in class, and the difference between class, middle-class versus working class.

> They talk with the slick black accent, and they work on the mannerisms, and I think they make a conscious effort to act that way like they are catering to the black race in that show. Whereas Cosby, you know, definitely doesn't do that. He's upper middle class and he's not black stereotypical. There's a difference in the tone of those shows, completely.

The Price of Admission and Its Political Consequences

Although there may be dimensions to this race/class inflection that go beyond television, the difficulty some white viewers have in inviting black working-class characters into their living rooms is partly a function of television's class premise, in which normalcy is middle and upper-middle class and where working-class characters are, to some extent, outsiders. In terms of the politics of representation, our study raises a difficult question: If black characters must be upscale to be accepted into this image world, is such an acceptance worth the price of admission? To answer this question, we must consider the broader consequences of this representational move.

Among white people, the repeated appearance of black characters in TV's upwardly mobile world gives credence to the idea that racial divisions, whether perpetuated by class barriers or by racism, do not exist. Most white people are extremely receptive to such a message. It allows them to feel good about themselves and about the society of which they are a part. The many black professionals who easily inhabit the TV world suggest to people that, as one of our respondents put it, "There really is room in the Untied States for minorities to get ahead, without affirmative action."

If affirmative action has become a hot issue in contemporary politics, it is because the tide has turned against it, with states and universities (including our own) buckling under to pressure to abandon the policy. As Gray (1996) suggested in his analysis of the Reagan years, conservatives are able to use their opposition to such policies as a way of mobilizing white votes. Indeed, our study reveals that the opposition to affirmative action among white people is overwhelming. What was particularly notable was that although most white people are prepared to acknowledge that such a policy was once necessary, the prevailing feeling was that this was no longer so.

> I think I've become less enamored of it. I think that when the whole idea was

first discussed, it was a very good idea. . . . In recent years, I don't think it's necessarily getting anybody anywhere.

I think in a lot of respects it's carried too far and that it results in reverse discrimination because you have quotas to meet for different job positions and that kind of stuff, it's like, a white person no longer has equal opportunity towards a job because you have to fill a quota.

Well, I think it has gone too far, where the white people don't have the opportunities. I think it has come to a point where people should be hired now, not because of their color or their race, but because of what they're able to do. I mean there are people who are much better qualified but can't get hired because they are white, and I don't think that's right. Maybe in the beginning, they needed this. . . but it has gone too far.

There are, of course, circumstances in which a qualified black person will receive a warm reception from employees concerned to promote an "equal opportunities" image. Any cursory glance at social statistics, however, demonstrates that this is because employers are sheepish or embarrassed by current levels of inequality in the workplace. Almost any social index suggests that we live in a society in which black and white people are not equal, whether in terms of education, health, housing, employment, or wealth. So why is affirmative action suddenly no longer necessary? Partly, we would suggest, because our popular culture tells us so.

During our content analysis of the three main networks, we came across only one program that offered a glimpse of these racial divisions. What was significant about this program, however, was that it did not take place in the present, but in the past, during the early days of the civil rights

movement. TV was only able to show us racial divisions in the United States by traveling back in time to the "bad old days." Most of the black characters in television's here-and-now seemed blissfully free of such things. Attempts by Hollywood to deal with racial inequality adopt the same strategy. Racism, whether in *Driving Miss Daisy, The Long Walk Home,* or *Amistad,* is confined to the safe distance of history. There are some notable exceptions—such as Spike Lee's work—but the general impression is clear: The social causes of racial inequality are behind us.

Television, despite—and in some ways because of—the liberal intentions of many who write its stories, has pushed our culture backward. White people are not prepared to deal with the problem of racial inequality because they are no longer sure if or why there is a problem. James Patterson and Peter Kim (1992) conducted a survey of contemporary American belief systems:

> In the 1990s, white Americans hold blacks, and blacks alone, to blame for their current position in American society. "We tried to help," whites say over and over, "but blacks wouldn't help themselves." This is the basis for what we've called the new racism. Everything flows from it. It is a change from the hardcore racism that existed in our country's earlier years. It is also a dramatic contrast to the attitude of the 1960s, when many whites, from the President on down, publicly stated that black people were owed compensation for centuries of oppression. (P. 183)

The use of upscale black television characters, our study made increasingly clear, is an intrinsic part of this process. Television becomes Dr. Feelgood, indulging its white audience so that their response to racial inequality becomes a guilt-free, self-righteous inactivity.

This has saddled us, as Patterson and Kim (1992) suggest, with a new, repressed form of racism. For although television now portrays a world of equal opportunity, most white people know enough about the world to see that black people achieve less, on the whole, than do white people—a discourse emphasized by television news (Entman 1990). They know that black people are disproportionately likely to live in poor neighborhoods, drop out of school, or be involved in crime. Indeed, overall, television's representation of black people is bifurcated —a Jekyll-and-Hyde portrayal in which the bulk of ordinary working-class black Americans have few images of themselves outside of those connected with crime, violence, and drugs.

Media Images: Accentuating the Positive and the Negative

The most striking aspect of the interviews with black Americans in our study was the ubiquity of comments about the role that media images play in how white America looks at them—of how stereotypical images of blacks as criminals affected their own everyday interaction with white society and institutions, as one person put it:

> Nobody can believe that you can actually have the intelligence, the fortitude, the dedication and the determination to go out and earn a decent living to afford you some nice things. The mentality today is that if you're black and you get something, you either got it through drugs or through prostitution.

The role that the media played in the cultivation of this perception was clearly understood. As another of our respondents stated, "We seem to be the only people in the world that TV tries to pick out the negative to portray as characteristic of us. What television is doing to us, I think, is working a hell of a job on us."

For minority groups, then, living in the kind of residential and social apartheid that characterizes much of contemporary America, media images are vital, as they are the primary way that the broader society views them. Black America, after all, is well aware of what white perception of black males in particular can lead to. In the Rodney King case, an all-white suburban jury acquitted four LAPD officers for a brutal beating on the basis that the person receiving the beating was, in the words of one of the jurors, "controlling the action." When your image of black people is as subhuman criminals, muggers drug addicts, gang members, and welfare cheats, then even when a black man is lying hog-tied on the ground, he is still dangerous, and any action to subdue him becomes justified.

It is not surprising, in this framework, that Bill Cosby's self-conscious attempt to promote a series of very different black images was so well received by the black respondents in our study. But if it is a kind of representational rescue mission, it is one with an almost fairy-tale script. Thus, we can move away from news images of black criminals to fictional images of black lawyers and judges in a matter of network minutes.

In this way, the media images turn real and complex human beings into crude one-dimensional caricatures, which then come to define minority populations for the majority. Perhaps the apotheosis of this bifurcated imagery was the figure of O.J. Simpson. If many white Americans were bemused by the degree to which black Americans felt they had a stake in the innocence of a rich TV celebrity, it was because they did not understand the representational issues at stake. The rush to a judgment of innocence was a mechanism of self-defense against a popular culture that offers a limited and bifurcated view of black life, one that can be symbolized by two characters in the recent history of black representation: Bill Cosby and Willie Horton.

The Cosby Show epitomized and inspired a move in network television toward the routine presentation of black professionals in drama and situation comedy. The flip side to this is the world of the news or so-called reality programming (like *Cops*), in which it is blacks as violent criminals, drug dealers, crackheads, and welfare mothers that dominate the screen. Perhaps the embodiment of this side of the story is Willie Horton, the image used by the Bush presidential campaign in 1988 to scare white America away from voting for Mike Dukakis. (In a now infamous TV campaign ad that is credited with turning the election around, Horton was represented as a crazed murderer, whom the Dukakis prison furlough program, in a moment of foolish liberal do-goodery, allowed out of prison.)

These are the two predominant images of black Americans with which the majority of white people are familiar. The O.J. case was pivotal, as Simpson came to be located precisely at the conjuncture between the two. He *was* Bill Cosby (affluent, friendly, smiling, cultured). If he was guilty of brutal double murder, he would *become* Willie Horton. The representational identity of black America as a whole, given the incredible visibility of the case, was the prize at stake.

Writer Anthony Walton (1989) commented on what is at stake in these battles over representation:

I am recognizing my veil of double consciousness, my American self and my black self. I must battle, like all humans, to see myself. I must also battle, because I am black, to see myself as others see me; increasingly my life, literally, depends upon it. I might meet Bernard Goetz in the subway. . . . The armed security guard might mistake me for a burglar in the lobby of my building. And they won't see a mild-mannered English major trying to get home. They will see Willie Horton. (p. 77)

In this context, it is little wonder that black Americans took the Simpson case so personally. His innocence would, in some ways, maintain the representational progress forged by Bill Cosby, whereas his guilt would tilt it back to Willie Horton. He *had* to be innocent because African Americans, like all people, want the world to recognize their humanity and their dignity. In a context in which their identity is at stake, the "evidence" had little relevance. Any story—however implausible—of conspiracy and racism would eradicate the forensics, the DNA tests, and so forth. That is precisely what Johnny Cochran offered the jury and black America, and it was accepted with thanks.

But for white viewers, how can sense be made of this bifurcated world? How can black failure in reality programming be reconciled with television's fictions, so replete with images of black success? How to explain racial inequalities in the context of the racial equality of television's upscale world? Without some acknowledgment that the roots of racial inequality are embedded in our society's class structure, there is only one way to reconcile this paradoxical state of affairs. If black people are disproportionately unsuccessful, then they must be disproportionately less deserving. Although few of our respondents were prepared to be this explicit (although a number came very close), their failure to acknowledge class or racial barriers means that this is the only explanation available. The consequence, in the apparently enlightened welcome white viewers extend to television's black professionals, is a new, sophisticated form of racism. Their success casts a shadow across the majority of black people who, by these standards, have failed. Television, which tells us very little about the structures behind success or failure (Iyengar 1991), leaves white viewers to assume that the black people who do not match up to their television counterparts have only themselves to blame.

In a rather different way, the effect of *The Cosby Show* on its black audience is also one of flattering to deceive. The dominant reaction of our black viewers to the show was "for this relief, much thanks." After suffering years of negative media stereotyping, most black viewers were delighted by a show that portrayed African Americans as intelligent, sensitive, and successful:

> I admire him. I like his show because it depicts black people in a positive way. It's good to see that black people can be professionals.
>
> Thank you Dr. Cosby for giving us back ourselves.

The problem with this response is that it embraces the assumption that, on television, a positive image is a prosperous image. This dubious equation means that African Americans are trapped in a position in which any reflection of more typical black experience—which is certainly not upper-middle class—is "stereotypical." As one of our respondents said, even though he was painfully aware that *The Cosby Show* presented a misleading picture of what life was like for most black Americans, "There's part of me that says, in a way, I don't want white America to see us, you know, struggling or whatever." On TV, there is no dignity in struggling unless you win

This analysis of stereotyping dominates contemporary thought. It is the consequence of a television world that has told us that to be working class is to be marginal. Thus, it is that viewers in our study were able to see

the Huxtable family on *The Cosby Show* as both "regular" and "everyday" *and* as successful, well-heeled professionals.

For black viewers, this deceit amounts to a form of cultural blackmail. It leaves two choices, either to be complicit partners in an image system that masks the deep racial divisions in the United States or forced to buy into the fiction that, as one respondent put it, "there are black millionaires all over the place," thereby justifying *The Cosby Show* as a legitimate portrayal of average African American life.

The Structural Confines of Network Television

If our story tells us anything, it is that we need to be more attentive to the attitudes cultivated by "normal" everyday television. In the case of representations of race, these attitudes can affect the way we think about "issues" like race and class and, in so doing, even influence the results of elections.

As we have suggested, it does not have to be this way. There is no reason why TV characters cannot be working class and dignified, admirable—or even just plain normal. Bill Cosby's more recent sitcom—*Cosby*—is one attempt to do this, although his enormous popularity as a performer gives him a license that other shows, such as the short-lived *Frank's Place*, do not have. Other television cultures have managed to avoid distorting and suppressing the class structure of their societies; why can't we manage it in the United States?

The American Dream is much more than a gentle fantasy; it is the dominant discourse in the United States for understanding (or misunderstanding) class. It is a cultural doctrine that encompasses vast tracts of American life. No politician would dare question our belief in it, any more than they would publicly question the existence of God. Even though politicians of many different persuasions pay lip service to the dream (it is, in conventional wisdom, "what's great about America"), it is not a politically neutral idea. It favors those on the political right to say that anyone, regardless of circumstance, can make it if they try. In such an egalitarian world, the free market delivers a kind of equity, making public intervention and regulation an unnecessary encumbrance. For government to act to eradicate the enormous social problems in the United States is to defy the logic of the dream. Intervention implies, after all, that the system is not naturally fair, and opportunity is not universal.

The American Dream is, in this context, insidious rather than innocent. It is part of a belief system that allows people in the United States to disregard the inequalities that generate its appalling record on poverty, crime, health, homelessness, and education. It is not surprising that the more fortunate cling to the self-justifying individualism the dream promotes. One of the saddest things about the United States is that sometimes, the less fortunate do too.

The ideological dominance of the American Dream is sustained by its massive presence in popular culture. The television and film industries churn out fable after fable, thereby reducing us to a state of spellbound passivity in which decades of stagnating incomes for many Americans have been accepted with little protest. The success we are encouraged to strive for is always linked to the acquisition of goods, a notion fueled by the ubiquitous language of advertising, in which consumers do not usually see themselves in commercials; rather, they see a vision of a glamorous and affluent world to which they aspire. Underlying the preponderance of middle- and upper-middle class characters on display is the relentless mes-

sage that this is what the world of happiness and contentment looks like. In this context, ordinary settings seem humdrum or even depressing. Not only do we expect television to be more dramatic than everyday life, but, in the United States, we also expect it to be more affluent. We do not want a good story; we want a "classy" setting.

> I liked the background. I like to look at the background on a TV program, I enjoy that. The setting, the clothes, that type of thing. I don't enjoy dismal backgrounds.

> "This is nice, it looks good and it's kind of, you accept it; they have a beautiful home and everything is okay.

This is the language of advertising. It is also, now, the discourse of the American Dream. This language is now so much a part of our culture that these attitudes seem perfectly natural. It is only when we look at other television cultures that we can see that they are not.

Few other industrial nations leave their cultural industries to be as dependent on advertising revenue as they are in the United States. In the United States, very little happens in our popular culture without a commercial sponsor. This takes place in a lightly regulated free market economy in which cultural industries are not accountable to a notion of public service but to the bottom line of profitability.

Apart from tiny grants to public broadcasting, the survival of radio and television stations depends almost entirely on their ability to sell consumers (viewers or listeners) to advertisers. Moreover, broadcasters in the United States are required to do little in the way of public service. There are no regulations that encourage quality, diversity, innovation, or educational value in programming. This means that the influence of advertising is twofold. Not only does it create a cultural climate that influences the form and style of programs that fill the spaces between commercials; it also commits television to the production of formulaic programming. Once cultural patterns are established, it is difficult to deviate from them without losing the ratings that bring in the station's revenue.

This is not merely a tyranny of the majority and the logic of the lowest common denominator. A ratings system driven by advertising does not so much favor popularity as the quest for the largest pockets of disposable income. The 1999 season of *Dr. Quinn, Medicine Woman* was cancelled by CBS even though it was regularly the most popular show during its Saturday night time slot. The problem was simply that its viewers were generally not wealthy enough to be of interest to advertisers. The ad-driven chase for well-heeled demographics thereby gives network television an in-built class bias, creating a climate in which portrayals of working-class black characters may make good television but are an unlikely way to attract television's most sought-after demographic group.

Which brings us back to the many representational offshoots of *The Cosby Show*. To be successful and to stay on the air, *The Cosby Show* had to meet certain viewers' expectations. This, as we have seen meant seducing viewers with the vision of comfortable affluence the Huxtables epitomized. Once television has succumbed to the discourse of the American Dream, where a positive image is a prosperous one, it cannot afford the drop in ratings that will accompany a redefinition of viewers' expectations. TV programs that do so are necessarily short-lived. Programs like *Frank's Place*, *Cop Rock*, or *Twin Peaks* all deviated from a norm, and, although still watched by millions of viewers, they did not attain the mass audience required to keep them on the air. This puts us on a treadmill of cultural stagnation. It is a system in which the bland repetition of fantasies tailored to the interests of wealthier viewers makes sound business sense.

In such a system, *The Cosby Show*'s survival depended on meeting the demands of a formula that pleases as many people as possible and especially its more upscale audience. Our study suggests that it did so with consummate success, pleasing black and white people, blue-collar workers and professionals, all in slightly different ways. The more blue-collar *Cosby* has been less universally embraced, and in this context we should applaud Bill Cosby's attempt to use his popularity to offer audiences a less upscale image.

When our book *Enlightened Racism: The Cosby Show, Audiences, and the Myth of the American Dream* was first published in 1992, we were widely credited with holding *The Cosby Show* responsible for promoting the routine fiction of effortless black success. But this was not the thrust of our argument. *The Cosby Show* and many black professionals portrayed in its wake are genuine attempts to make television's upscale world more racially diverse. The problem is not with individual instances of black success but with a television environment whose structural conditions make a wider array of images less profitable.

REFERENCES

ENTMAN, R. 1990. "Modern Racism and the Images of Blacks in Local Television News." *Critical Studies in Mass Communication* 7 (4, December): 332–345.

GRAY, H. 1996. *Watching Race: Television and the Struggle for Blackness.* Minneapolis: University of Minnesota Press.

HACKER, A. 1992. *Two Nations: Black and White, Separate, Hostile, Unequal.* New York: Scribner.

IYENGAR, S. 1991, *Is Anyone Responsible?* Chicago: University of Chicago Press.

JHALLY, S. and J. LEWIS. 1992. *Enlightened Racism: The Cosby Show, Audiences, and the Myth of the American Dream.* Boulder, CO: Westview.

PATTERSON, J. and P. KIM. 1992. *The Day America Told the Truth.* New York: Dutton.

WALTON, A. 1989. "Willie Horton and Me." *The New York Times Magazine,* August 20, section 6, p. 77.

WILSON, W. J. 1987. *The Truly Disadvantaged.* Chicago: University of Chicago Press.

32
_____

DISTORTED REALITY
Hispanic Characters in TV Entertainment

S. Robert Lichter • Daniel R. Amundson

Questions to Consider

Latinos are now larger than the black population in the United States but they are mostly invisible on prime-time television. Robert Lichter and Daniel Amundson provide a historical overview of the ways Latinos have been characterized by the media. Have stereotypical depictions of Latinos changed in recent years? Are you able to name five main characters who appear on prime-time television (8 p.m. to 11 p.m.) who are Latino? Are these representations favorable? What are the occupations of these Latino characters?

The Past as Prologue

It takes diff'rent strokes to move the world.
—"Diff'rent Strokes" Theme Song

When Kingfish uttered his last "Holy Mackerel, Andy!" in 1953, it marked the end of television's most controversial depiction of

blacks. Ironically, the departure of "Amos 'n' Andy" also signaled the end of a brief period of ethnic diversity that would not reappear in prime time for two decades. Several of the earliest family sitcoms were transplanted radio shows set in America's black or white ethnic subcultures. "The Goldbergs" followed the lives of a Jewish immigrant family in New York for twenty years on radio before switching to the new medium in 1949. It featured Gertrude Berg as Molly Goldberg, everyone's favorite Jewish mother. An even more successful series that premiered the same year was "Mama," which chronicled a Norwegian immigrant family in turn-of-the-century San Francisco. Theme music by Grieg added to the "ethnic" atmosphere, as did accents that made Aunt "Yenny" into a popular character. These white ethnic shows were soon joined by the all-black "Amos 'n' Andy" as well as "Beulah," which starred the black maid of a white middle-class family.

All these shows relied on stereotypical dialogue and behavior for much of their humor. But social standards were changing, and the new medium created its own demands and perceptions. For example, not only Amos and Andy but even Beulah had been portrayed on radio by white males. When the popular radio show "Life with Luigi" made the switch to TV in 1952, Italian American groups protested its stereotyped portrayal of Italian immigrants. Black groups were equally outraged over "Amos 'n' Andy," which had been an institution on radio since 1929. As the program evolved, it centered on the schemes of George "Kingfish" Stevens, who combined the soul of Sgt. Bilko with the fate of Ralph Kramden. A small-time con man with big plans that never panned out, he became an immensely popular, lovable loser. His schemes usually pulled in the ingenuous cabbie Andy and the slow-moving janitor Lightnin'.

From Kingfish's fractured syntax ("I'se regusted") to Lightnin's shuffle and falsetto "yazzuh," the series drew on overtly racial stereotypes. The NAACP blasted the portrayal of blacks as "inferior, lazy, dumb, and dishonest," and urged a boycott of Blatz beer, the sponsor. The pressure from civil rights groups probably helped bring the series to a premature end, since it attracted sizeable audiences throughout its two year run.

. . .

While controversy surrounded "Amos and Andy," little debate attended television's earliest and most high profile Latino portrayal. From 1950 through 1956, Ziv pro-

ductions sold 156 episodes of "The Cisco Kid" in syndication to individual stations across the country. Resplendent in his heavily embroidered black costume, Cisco rode across the southwest righting wrongs and rescuing damsels in distress. He was accompanied by his portly sidekick, Pancho, who served as a comic foil. Pancho was loyal and brave, but his English was every bit as fractured as the Kingfish's. Further, although Cisco and Pancho were positive and even heroic characters, they were often outnumbered by evil and frequently criminal Latino adversaries. In its simplistic presentation that combined positive and negative ethnic stereotypes, "Cisco" set the tone for the "Zorro" series that would follow it on ABC from 1957 through 1959. Thus, these early high-profile representations of Latinos proved a mixed bag, as television's conventions of the day were applied to both network and syndicated fare.

The All-White World

"Cisco" and "Zorro," which were aimed at children, outlasted the first generation of ethnic sitcoms for general audiences. By the 1954 season "Mama" was the only survivor of this once-thriving genre. Thus, by the time our study period began, TV's first era of ethnic humor had already come and gone. The urban ethnic sitcoms were replaced by homogeneous suburban settings. There was nothing Irish about the life of Chester Riley, nothing Scandinavian about Jim and Margaret Anderson. The new family shows were all-American, which meant vaguely northern European and carefully noncontroversial. The few remaining ethnics were mostly relegated to minor roles or single episodes.

Just how homogeneous was this electronic neighborhood? From 1955 through 1964, our coders could identify only one character in ten as anything other than northern European on the basis of name, language, or appearance. Such a small slice of the pie got cut up very quickly, and many groups got only crumbs. Just one character in fifty was Hispanic, fewer than one in a hundred was Asian, and only one in two hundred was black.

. . .

Hispanics had virtually no starring roles. For most Hispanic characters, life consisted of lounging in the dusty square of a sleepy Latin town, waiting for the stars to come on stage. Occasionally Hispanics would show up as outlaws in the Old West, but even then mostly as members of someone else's gang. Their comic roles were epitomized by Pepino Garcia, a farmhand for "The Real McCoys," who functioned mainly as a target of Grandpa Amos McCoy's tirades. Pepino and "The Real McCoys" were replaced in 1963 by Jose Jimenez in the "Bill Dana Show."

Like their black colleagues, a few stars stood out in a sea of marginal and insignificant roles. A notable exception was Cuban band leader Ricky Ricardo in "I Love Lucy," played by Desi Arnaz. As the co-star of one of the most popular shows on TV (and co-owner of Desilu Productions, along with wife Lucille Ball), Arnaz was a prominent figure in Hollywood. When exasperated by Lucy's schemes and misadventures, Ricky added a comic touch with displays of "Latin" temper and lapses into Spanish. "I Love Lucy" made its mark on television comedy and TV production in general, but it did little for Hispanic characters. The same could be said of another early show with a Hispanic setting, which nonetheless cast Anglos in the major roles. Guy Williams played Don Diego, alias Zorro, the masked champion of the poor and oppressed in old Los Angeles. Their oppressors were evil, greedy Spanish governors and landowners. In one episode Annette Funicello, fresh from

the Mickey Mouse Club, showed up as the singing senorita Anita Cabrillo. Despite its "Hispanic" characters, the show was not a generous portrayal of either the people or the culture.

The departure of "Amos and Andy" and "Beulah" all but eliminated black stars. Jack Benny's valet Rochester was one of the few major roles still held by a black in the late 1950s. Black characters didn't even show up in the backgrounds of early shows. Urban settings might feature a black delivery man, porter, or waiter, but black professionals and businessmen were virtually nonexistent. Some westerns like "Rawhide" and "Have Gun, Will Travel" presented a few black cowboys riding the range with their white counterparts. Aside from such occasional and insignificant roles, black characters were simply not a part of the early prime time world.

The Return of Race

In the mid-1960s, the portrayal of ethnic and racial minorities underwent major changes. The proportion of non–northern European roles doubled over the next decade. Before 1965, all racial and ethnic groups to the south or east of England, France, and Germany had scrambled for the one role in ten available to them. Now nonwhite characters alone could count on better than one role in ten. From the first to the second decade in our study [1955–1975], the proportion of English characters was cut in half, while Hispanics became half again as numerous and the proportion of Asians doubled. Blacks were the biggest winners, gaining a dramatic fourteen-fold increase in what had been virtually an all-white landscape.

The invisibility of Hispanics during this period remained more than metaphorical. They were simply not part of television's new ethnic "relevance." Latinos had few continuing prime time roles of any sort during the late 1960s, and certainly no major star parts like Bill Cosby's Alexander Scott. In fact, most Latinos who were cast during this period showed up in episodes of international espionage series that used Central and South American locales. "I Spy" had many episodes set in Mexico, bringing the agents into contact with some positive and many more negative Hispanic characters. In other espionage shows, such as "Mission Impossible," the action often centered on a fictitious Central American country, which was inevitably run by a jack-booted junta that could only be stopped by the enlightened Anglo-led team from north of the border.

One of the few exceptions to this pattern was the western "High Chaparral." Rancher John Cannon had settled in the Arizona territory to found a cattle empire. When his first wife was killed by Apaches, John married Victoria Montoya, the daughter of a wealthy Mexican rancher. The marriage was as much a business move as a romance, since it united the two families. Once tied by marriage, Don Montoya helped John build his herds and produce good breeding stock. Together the two families fought off Apaches and other marauders. Culture clashes between the two families occurred, but usually as a minor part of the plot. Unlike most Mexicans shown in previous westerns, the Montoyas were rich, powerful, sophisticated, and benevolent. In most episodes, Victoria attempted to civilize her more rustic husband and establish a proper home on the range. To be sure, this series still presented semiliterate Hispanic ranchhands, but these portrayals were overshadowed by the Montoyas.

The other exception was the short-lived social relevancy series "Man and the City." This series presented more contemporary problems of Latinos in an unnamed southwestern city. The show was notable for frequently asserting the dignity and rights of Latinos. For example, in a 1971 segment, a cop is killed in the city's barrio. The police department pulls out all the stops to catch the killers, imposing a curfew and holding suspects incommunicado without legal counsel. All the suspects are Hispanics from the barrio who have little connection to the case. The mayor is forced to intervene and remind the police chief that the city has laws. He demands that all suspects, including minority groups, be given their full rights. The police are reluctant, believing this will impede their investigation. The mayor insists and the police obey his order. They eventually capture a key suspect who helps them catch the killers. There is no indication that racial tensions in the city have ended, merely that one violent episode is over. The groups involved have not learned to like each other; nor are they presented as peacefully coexisting. The point here is that all people have rights and deserve to be treated with dignity and equality. This seems to be the only series that attempted to derive socially relevant plotlines from the barrio.

Not only did the proportion of black characters jump to 7 percent between 1965 and 1975, but the range and quality of roles expanded even more dramatically. In adventure series like "I Spy" and "Mission: Impossible," blacks moved into their first starring roles in over a decade. Not only were these roles more prominent, they offered a new style of character. Alexander Scott of "I Spy" and Barney Collier of "Mission: Impossible" were competent, educated professionals. These men were highly successful agents whose racial backgrounds were clearly secondary to their bravery and skill. They opened the way for blacks to appear in roles that did not require the actor to be black. There was no more use of poor English, servile shuffling, or popeyed double takes for comic effect. Instead, Collier was presented as an electronics expert and Scott as a multilingual Rhodes Scholar.

The new visibility of blacks quickly moved beyond the secret agent genre. In 1968 the first of television's relevance series managed to convert a negative stereotype into a positive one by casting a young black rebel as a member of "The Mod Squad." Linc Hayes' militant credentials included an afro haircut, aviator sunglasses, and an arrest during the Watts riots. Not to worry, though. This brooding black rebel was working with the good guys on the L.A.P.D.'s undercover "youth squad," where the dirty dozen met the counterculture every Tuesday at 7:30.

While ABC was coopting the Black Panthers into the establishment, NBC looked to the black middle class for "Julia," the first black-oriented sitcom in fifteen years. As a dedicated nurse and loving mother in an integrated world, the Julia Baker character looked ahead to "The Cosby Show" rather than backward to "Amos 'n' Andy." She certainly had more in common with Claire Huxtable than with Kingfish's nagging wife, Sapphire. Unfortunately, she also lacked the vitality and wit of either Sapphire or future mother figures who would be more firmly rooted in black culture, like "Good Times" Florida Evans.

"Julia" suffered from the dullness of being a prestige series, just as "The Mod Squad" labored under the hype that attended the relevance series. What they had in common with better-written shows like "I Spy" and "Mission Impossible" was a tendency to replace the old negative black stereotypes with new positive ones. The authors of *Watching TV* wrote with a touch of hyperbole, "They were no longer bumbling, easygoing, po' folk like Beulah, but rather articulate neo-philosophers just descended from Olympus, though still spouting streetwise jargon."[1] Having discovered that blacks didn't have to be cast as valets and janitors, white writers turned them into James Bonds and Mary Tyler Moores. Thus, as blacks suddenly began to appear on the tube after a decade's absence, they remained invisible in Ralph Ellison's sense. The frantic search for positive characters smothered individuality with good intentions.

Let a Hundred Flowers Bloom

In the early 1970s TV began to broadcast a different message about minorities. The unlikely agent of change was an equal opportunity bigot named Archie Bunker, who excoriated "spics," "jungle bunnies," "chinks," "yids," and every other minority that ever commanded an epithet. When "All in the Family" became the top-rated show within five months of its 1971 premiere, it attracted a barrage of criticism for making the tube safe for ethnic slurs. The producer of public television's "Black Journal" found it "shocking and racist."[2] Laura Hobson, who wrote "Gentlemen's Agreement," an attack on anti-Semitism, decried its attempt to sanitize bigotry, "to clean it up, deodorize it, make millions of people more comfy about indulging in it."[3] Of course, the point of the show was to poke fun at Archie and all he stood for, as the script and laugh track tried to make clear.

Norman Lear's strategy was to educate audiences by entertaining them instead of preaching at them. So he created a kind of politicized Ralph Kramden, whom audiences could like in spite of his reactionary views, not because of them. He intended that the contrast between Archie's basic decency and his unattractive rantings would prod viewers to reexamine the retrograde ideas they permitted themselves. As Lear put it, the show "holds up a mirror to our prejudices. . . . We laugh now, swallowing just the littlest bit of truth about ourselves, and it sits there for the unconscious to toss about later."[4] As a tool for improving race relations, this approach may have been too subtle for its own good. Several studies suggest that liberals watched the show to confirm their disdain for Archie's views, while conservatives identified with him despite his creator's best intentions.[5] But another legacy of the program was to pioneer a more topical and (by television's standards) realistic portrayal of ethnic relations.

An immediate consequence of "All in the Family" was to introduce the first sitcoms populated by black families since "Amos 'n' Andy." A year after demonstrating the audience appeal of a white working class milieu not portrayed successfully since "The Honeymooners," Lear and his partner Bud Yorkin transferred the setting to a black ghetto in "Sanford and Son." Unlike the integrated middle class world of TV blacks in the late 1960s, "Sanford and Son" revolved around the foibles of a junk dealer in a poor black section of Los Angeles. "Sanford" proved so popular that it soon trailed only "All in the Family" in the Nielsen ratings.

Meanwhile, in an irony Archie would not have appreciated, "All in the Family" spawned not one but two additional black family sitcoms. "The Jeffersons" featured Archie's one-time neighbor George Jefferson as an upwardly mobile businessman whose snobbishness and inverted racism made him almost a black Archie Bunker. "Good Times" was actually a second-generation spinoff. When Archie's liberal nemesis Maude got her own show in 1972, the scriptwriters gave her a quick-witted and tart-tongued black maid named Florida Evans. Two years later the popular Florida got her own show as the matriarch of a family living in a Chicago housing project. This series developed the "Sanford" technique of finding sometimes bitter humor among lower status characters trying to cope with life in the ghetto while looking for a way out of it. Scripts featured ward heelers, loan

sharks, abused children, and other facets of life on the edge, in sharp contrast to the comfortable middle class world of "Julia" or the glamorous and exotic locales of "I Spy."

By this time, other producers, stimulated by Norman Lear's enormous success, were providing sitcoms that drew their characters from minority settings. "What's Happening!!" followed the adventures of three big city high school kids. "Diff'rent Strokes" created an unlikely "accidental family" in which a wealthy white man raised two black kids from Harlem in his Park Avenue apartment, without any serious clash of cultures. This trend almost never extended from the ghetto to the barrio. The one great exception was "Chico and the Man," a generation-gap sitcom that paired an ebullient young Mexican American with an aging Bunkerish Anglo garage owner. This odd couple clicked with audiences, but the show's success was cut short by the suicide of comedian Freddy Prinze (Chico) in 1977.

Like the black sitcoms, "Chico" used minority culture as a spark to enliven a middle class white world that seemed bland or enervated by comparison. Minority characters of the early 1970s prided themselves not on their similarity to mainstream culture, but on their differences from it. Assimilated characters like Alexander Scott, Barney Collier, and Julia Baker gave way to the racial pride of George Jefferson, Fred of "Sanford and Son," and Rooster on "Starsky and Hutch." Where would Fred Sanford or George Jefferson be without their jive talk and street slang? Language was just one way of stressing the differences between racial and ethnic groups.

Minority characters also picked up flaws as they took on more complete roles. Fred Sanford was domineering and could appear foolish. George Jefferson could be as stubborn and narrow-minded as his one-time next-door neighbor. By badgering the interracial couple living upstairs and labelling their daughter a "zebra," he left no doubt about his views. But the thrust of the ethnic sitcom was not to ridicule minority cultures. Instead, racial and ethnic backgrounds were used as an educational tool. The religious, cultural, and other traditions that differentiate minorities from the mainstream were now treated as beneficial rather than problematic. Removed from the confines of the melting pot, these groups offered new approaches to old problems. Television charged them with the task of teaching new ways to the often obstinate world around them. Blacks and Hispanics participated in this era of racial and cultural re-education. It was Chico Rodriguez who taught Ed Brown to relax and be more tolerant on "Chico and the Man." Benson, the sharp-tongued butler, tried to maintain order amidst the chaos of "Soap," while steering his employers onto the right track. In one episode he even saved young Billy from the clutches of a religious cult.

The most spectacularly successful effort to combine education with entertainment was a hybrid of the miniseries and "big event" genres. Indeed, "Roots" became the biggest event in television history. This adaptation of Alex Haley's best-selling novel traced the history of four generations of a black family in America, beginning with Kunta Kinte, an African tribesman sold into slavery. It ran for eight consecutive nights in January 1977. When it was over, 130 million Americans had tuned in, including 80 million who viewed the final episode. Seven of the eight episodes ranked among the all-time top ten at that point in television's history. "Roots" created a kind of national town meeting comparable to the televised moon landing or the aftermath of President Kennedy's assassination. It was blamed for several racial disturbances but credited for stimulating a productive national debate on the history of American race relations.

While blacks could look to the high-profile presentation of African American history presented by "Roots," there was no similar presentation of Hispanic history. If Anglos relied exclusively on Hollywood for information on Latino contributions to American history, their knowledge would extend little further than John Wayne's defense of "The Alamo" against the Mexican "invaders." Illustrations of Latino culture were equally rare. In fact, the only high-profile Hispanic character during this period was Chico Rodriguez. Despite its popularity, "Chico and the Man" was not known as a series that explored Latino culture or Hispanic contributions to American history and culture.

Despite occasional failures, ethnic comedies became the hottest new programming trend of the 1970s. "All in the Family" was the top-rated show for an unprecedented five straight seasons, surpassing previous megahits "I Love Lucy" and "Gunsmoke." Other top twenty regulars included "Sanford and Son," "The Jeffersons," black comic Flip Wilson's variety show, and "Chico and the Man." The ethnic wave crested during the 1974–75 season, when a remarkable six of the seven top-rated shows were ethnic sitcoms—"All in the Family," "Sanford," "Chico," "Jeffersons," "Rhoda," and "Good Times."

If the new decade offered an unaccustomed array of new roles for minorities, it contained some traps as well. Ethnic characters gained more prominent and desirable roles, but also more unflattering ones. Bumblers, buffoons, and bimbos took their place alongside heroes and sages. For example, Vinnie Barbarino and Juan Epstein were two of the uneducated underachievers on "Welcome Back Kotter." Barbarino's Italian heritage added ethnic color to his machismo image, while Epstein's ethnic background was contrived for comic effect. He was presented as Buchanan High School's only Puerto Rican Jew. "Good Times" created some negative black characters, such as insensitive building supervisors and abusive politicians. In "What's Happening," the Thomas family made do without their con man father after he walked out on them. His occasional visits home were usually in search of money for some new scheme. A steady stream of minority characters began to show up as criminals in cop shows like "Kojak," "Baretta," and "Barney Miller."

"Barney Miller" also deserves note as one of the most multicultural shows of the time. In the 1975–76 season the squad room contained Polish detective Wojohowicz, Asian American Nick Yemana, African American Harris, and Puerto Rican Chano Amenguale. While Chano was far from perfect he appeared to be a capable officer and no more eccentric than his colleagues on the squad. In the next season Chano was replaced by Detective Baptista, who was a fiery Latina, but not as significant in the squad as Chano. These characters at least served to offset the Hispanic criminals they often arrested.

The late 1970s retained a mix of ethnic heroes and fools in some of the most popular shows of the day. But ethnic characters were beginning to lose their novelty. For instance, "CHiPs" ran from 1977 through 1983 and one of the starring characters was Officer Frank Poncherello. Even though Poncherello was played by the well-known Eric Estrada, Poncherello's Hispanic heritage was all but invisible. It no longer mattered in this series that one of the leads was a Latino. During the 1979 season, three dramatic series were launched with black leads, but none came close to the ratings necessary for renewal. "Paris" starred James Earl Jones as a supercop who ran the station house during the day and taught criminology at night. "The Lazarus Syndrome" featured Louis Gossett as the chief of cardiology in a large hospital. "Harris and Company" focused on the problems of a single parent raising a family. The

twist was that this black family was held together not by a matriarch but a middle-aged widower. Thus, Hollywood was at least trying to create some positive role models for black males. But no such efforts extended to Latinos. There were no network series built around a Latino family, Hispanic high school kids, or any of the other patterns found in sitcoms featuring blacks. It would be several years before the short-lived ABC series "Condo" would prominently cast Latinos as middle class characters.

Overall, the 1980s offered little that was new to racial or ethnic minority portrayals in the wake of TV's ethnic revival. These groups continued to be presented more or less as they were in the late 1970s. Despite the continuing presence of racial and ethnic diversity, however, racial themes were no longer in vogue. Integration was assumed as a backdrop, as the prime time world became less polarized. The age of pluralism had arrived, but the thrill was gone. The riots were over, the battles won, and characters got back to their other plot functions. Among these were crime and other wrongdoing. Comedies like "Taxi," "White Shadow," and "WKRP in Cincinnati" continued to present integrated casts, but ethnic characters in dramatic series were often on the dark side of the law.

Ironically, television's multicultural world of the 1980s provided an updated version of the stereotypical Hispanic banditos who populated the westerns thirty years earlier. In the fall of 1980, ABC's controversial sitcom "Soap" introduced a remake of Frito Bandito. Carlos "El Puerco" Valdez was a South American revolutionary playing a love interest of Jessica Tate. They had met when his band kidnapped her for ransom. This plan failed, but after things took a passionate turn, she became a benefactor of his revolution. "El Puerco" led a bumbling, low-budget revolution and he was not above taking time out to romance his new gringo benefactor. "El Puerco" was both Latin lover and bandito with a measure of Jerry Lewis buffoonishness thrown in. Thus, it was down this line that the Frito Bandito's sombrero had been passed—to a fatigue-wearing ne'er-do-well.

There were also more sinister turns in Latino portrayals. Crime shows like "Miami Vice," "Hill Street Blues," and "Hunter" presented Hispanic drug lords as a major nemesis. Trafficking in human misery made these characters rich enough to own cities and sometimes even small countries. They were among the nastiest criminals on TV in the 1980s. There were also petty Hispanic criminals in the slums of "Hill Street Blues" and "Cagney & Lacey." These small-time hoods, drug addicts, and pimps were less flamboyant than their big-league counterparts, but no less unsavory. Altogether, TV's latest crop of Hispanics included a cruel and vicious group of criminals.

"Miami Vice" was not only a source of criminal Hispanics—after all the squad was led by the enigmatic Lieutenant Martin Castillo and on the distaff side of the unit was detective Gina Navarro. However inconsistently, the show did attempt to show successful law-abiding Latinos mixed in with the criminal crop. For all of its flaws "Miami Vice" at least attempted to reflect the presence of Latinos in Miami. Contrast this attempt with more contemporary shows like "Baywatch," "Acapulco H.E.A.T.," and others that rarely if ever reference the Hispanic populations in their host cities.

There were occasional attempts to base shows on Hispanic casts, but all proved unsuccessful. In 1983 the Lear-wannabee sitcom "Condo" briefly pitted a bigoted WASP against his Latino next-door neighbors. The following season, the equally short-lived "A.K.A. Pablo" dealt somewhat more seriously with ethnic questions. Focusing on struggling young comic Pablo Rivera and his extended family, the series wrestled with questions about ethnic humor and the preservation of Hispanic culture. Pablo made many jokes about his family and his Mexican American heritage in his nightclub act. This frequently offended his traditionalist parents, who expected him to treat his heritage more respectfully. Despite its brief run, this series was one of the few to deal explicitly with aspects of Latino culture.

A more mixed portrayal appeared in the 1987 series "I Married Dora." In this fractured fairy tale, Dora Calderon was the housekeeper for widower Peter Farrell and his family. When faced with deportation, Dora and Peter joined in a marriage of convenience. Like many television housekeepers before her, Dora was the voice of wisdom and compassion in the household, but her own illegal status gave her role an ambiguous twist. In 1988, a series called "Trial and Error" was based on Latino characters from the barrio in East Los Angeles. The show revolved around a free-wheeling entrepreneur who ran a souvenir T-shirt company and his upwardly mobile roommate, who was a newly minted lawyer. This series had a lighter touch with less attention to Hispanic culture, but it met with the same quick demise as its predecessors.

Both "A.K.A. Pablo" and "Trial and Error" sprang from the efforts of comedian Paul Rodriguez. It is not uncommon for bankable stars to get their own television series. This is particularly true for stand-up comics, who have taken their nightclub acts into successful series like "Roseanne," "Home Improvement," "Grace Under Fire," and "Seinfeld." This approach has proven to be a very important avenue onto the screen for blacks. Several exclusively black shows currently on the air are the result of the work of a bankable star. Among those who have followed in the footsteps of Bill Cosby are Keenan Ivory Wayans of "In Living Color," Martin Lawrence of "Martin," Mark Curry of

"Hangin' with Mr. Cooper," and Charles Dutton of "Roc." Unfortunately, this approach has so far been a dead end for Latinos.

Blacks fared better in the 1980s, largely escaping the criminal portrayals of other minorities. When black characters did turn to crime, they were usually small-time criminals driven by desperation. There were even times when their criminal acts were presented as social commentary. For instance, in an episode of "Hill Street Blues," a black militant occupies a housing project and takes hostages. He threatens to kill them unless the city agrees to keep the project open and fix it up. The man is frustrated and angry that weeks of negotiating led to nothing. The city simply set a new closing date and moved on. Rage and desperation drive him to act and a tense standoff ensues. In the end, he is mistakenly shot by a police sniper. Everyone is shocked by his desperate act and his tragic death.

Meanwhile, TV turned out numerous positive black role models as diverse as "The Cosby Show's" Heathcliff Huxtable, Mary Jenkins of "227," Rico Tubbs on "Miami Vice," and Bobby Hill of "Hill Street Blues." These shows suggest the diversity of major roles that were at last becoming available to blacks. "227" and "Amen" continued the sharp-tongued tradition of 1970s sitcoms, without the abrasive or objectionable images that had brought criticism. Tubbs and Hill both carried on the tradition of "salt and pepper" law enforcement teams. Hill also represented the educative function of minorities by helping to wean his partner Renko, a southerner, away from residual racist tendencies.

Of course, "Cosby" was the biggest hit of all. This series further developed the low-key humanistic colorblind approach that Bill Cosby has popularized over two decades as "I Spy's" Alexander Scott, high school teacher Chet Kincaid on "The Bill Cosby Show," and finally in a black version of "Father Knows Best." The enormous success of this venture led some critics to snipe at Cosby for playing black characters in whiteface to maximize audience appeal. Black psychiatrist Alvin Pouissant, retained by the show to review scripts for racial authenticity, notes that the criticisms come from white reporters more often than black viewers: "Sometimes it seems they want the show to be 'culturally black' . . . and sometimes it seems they would be happier to see them cussing out white people, a sort of protest sitcom. Some seem to feel that because the family is middle class with no obvious racial problems, that constitutes a denial or dismissal of the black person."[6]

Compared to the plight of TV's Hispanics, debates over whether the Huxtables are divorced from the black experience may seem a luxury, a sign that a one-time outgroup has reached a mature phase in its relationship with the Hollywood community. In 1979 organized opposition even persuaded Norman Lear to withdraw a new comedy series at the last minute. "Mister Dugan," a sitcom about a black congressman, was scheduled to premier on CBS a week after Lear arranged a special screening for the Congressional Black Caucus. The screening was a disaster, with Congressman Mickey Leland calling the lead character "a reversion to the Steppin' Fetchit syndrome."

Lear promptly pulled the show from the schedule. He remarked at the time, "We have a high social conscience, and we want to get the story right. We do not favor the short-term gain over the long-term public interest. Dropping the show was an exercise in that commitment."[7] This was an extraordinary episode in a business often excoriated for caring only about the bottom line. When the medium's most successful producer is willing to withdraw a series on the eve of its broadcast, writing off a $700,000 investment, it shows the power of social commitment in television. The only question is the strength and direction of that commitment.

Moreover, such criticism is belied by the top ten ratings obtained by such diverse families as the Sanfords, Jeffersons, and Evans, not to mention Kunta Kinte and his kin. The success of upper and lower class, matriarchal and patriarchal black family series suggests that television has gone beyond using black characters as a sign of racial diversity. It has begun to show diversity within the black community as well, at last recognizing both the cultural distinctiveness and the universal humanity of this group of Americans. Unfortunately, Hispanics have never played a significant role in television's debate over race relations. When television has explored discrimination, prejudice, or the appropriateness of inter-racial relationships, it has almost always staged them as a black versus white issue. Whatever racial tensions exist between Latinos and other groups in American society, they have very rarely made it to the small screen.

A Tale of Two Minorities

Black representation continued to increase during the 1990s, as the number of shows with all-black or mostly black casts jumped. Driven largely by the Fox network's quest for new audiences and trademark shows, these new series drew heavily on the struttin' and jivin' characters of the 1970s. Both the 1992 and 1993 seasons featured ten such series, including hits like "Hangin' with Mr. Cooper," "Family Matters," "Martin," and "Fresh Prince of Bel Air." Intense debate has ensued over the quality of these roles and portrayals, which critics disparage as latter-day minstrel show stereotypes. However,

such complaints have not diminished the popularity of these shows, particularly among black audiences.

Despite continuing controversy, television's portrayal of blacks is in many ways more diverse and substantive than ever before. For instance, on Monday nights viewers could contrast the wealthy Banks family on "Fresh Prince of Bel Air" with the working class Cumberbatches in "704 Hauser Street." On Tuesday, they could see the struggles of a single mother in "South Central," followed by the stable two-parent extended family in "Roc." Then there were the Winslows, a comfortably middle class black family that was a cornerstone of Friday night viewing for years. In addition there were numerous black characters in integrated series such as "L.A. Law," "Law & Order," "Evening Shade," "Love & War," "NYPD Blue," "In the Heat of the Night," and "seaQuest DSV." African Americans were seen as lawyers, judges, police captains, and a host of other roles in these shows.

While shows that were exclusively or mainly about blacks comprised about one eighth of the prime time schedule in 1992–93, only one series in the previous three seasons was based on a Latino family or character. Moreover, that series—the short-lived "Frannie's Turn"—mainly used Hispanic traditions as a comic foil for feminist putdowns. This series revolved around the marriage of a Cuban emigré named Joseph Escobar and his wife, Frannie, an Anglo of unclear ethnic origins. Whatever ethnic and cultural differences may have existed between them were rarely played upon, since most of the plots dealt with Frannie's quest for equality. However, when aspects of heritage did come up, they frequently reflected poorly on Latinos. For instance, the first episode dealt with Frannie's discovery that Joseph has been sending money to a Cuban liberation movement while telling her to cut the household budget. At one point in the ensuing argument, she suggests sarcastically, "Who knows, maybe they'll send you the Bay of Pigs decoder ring." In the few episodes that aired, the couple's children seemed oblivious to their heritage, and no effort was made to teach them about their father's culture. Overall, this series made no greater use of ethnicity than "I Love Lucy" did almost forty years earlier.

Otherwise, Latino characters remained largely supporting players or background figures in the prime time schedule. The highest profile in 1992–93 was enjoyed by Daniel Morales, who replaced Victor Sifuentes on "L.A. Law." Most other recent Latino roles involved lower status jobs or far less airtime in low-rated series. Examples include Chuy Castillo, the cook at the "Golden Palace"; Jennifer Clemente, a very junior attorney in the U.S. Justice Department on "The Round Table"; and detective Rafael Martinez on the "Hat Squad." There was also Mahalia Sanchez, a bus station cashier in the "John Larroquette Show," rookie detective James Martinez in "NYPD Blue," and Paco Ortiz in "Nurses," none of them starring roles.

The cultural diversity within the Latino community was almost completely absent from prime time. Most Hispanic characters on television came from a "generic" background without reference to national origin or past. Television has rarely pointed out the cultural, historical, or economic differences among different groups within the Latino community. The few shows to make such distinctions, from "Miami Vice" to "Frannie's Turn," usually did so to place a particular nationality in a negative light. In "Miami Vice," differing national origins were connected with different types of illegal activities, while in "Frannie's Turn" a Cuban heritage was not a badge of honor. Sadly, the highest-profile Latino characters

of the season were Eric and Lyle Menendez, whose murder trial was featured in two made-for-television movies.

An Update

As we have seen, before 1965, prime time was a nearly all-white world populated mainly by generic northern Europeans, save for the occasional black servant or Mexican bandito. Soon thereafter, the spectrum widened to embrace an array of ethnic and cultural traditions. But various minority groups shared unequally in television's new search for ethnic roots.

Some of these disparities are summarized in Table 1. As the table makes clear, between 1955 and 1986, proportionately fewer Hispanic characters were professionals or executives and more were unskilled laborers. Fewer Hispanics had starring roles, were positively portrayed, or succeeded in attaining their goals. Indeed, according to our 1994 study,[8] the more villainous the character, the sharper the group differences that emerged. Hispanic characters were twice as likely as whites and three times as likely as blacks to commit a crime. Once TV's roster of Hispanic stereotypes solely included the grinning bandito criss-crossed with ammunition belts. More recently, as scriptwriter Ben Stein has observed, "Any time a Cuban or Colombian crosses the tube, he leaves a good thick trail of cocaine behind."[9]

In addition, because of their negative and criminal roles, Latinos stood apart from other characters in the methods they adopted to attain their goals. They were more likely than either whites or blacks to use violence and deceit. If Latinos were distinctive in the means they used to pursue their goals, they also differed in their motivations. Hispanic characters were much more likely to be driven by greed than other characters. More broadly, black characters

TABLE 1   Traits of TV Characters, 1955–1986

	White	Black	Latino
All characters	89%	6%	2%
*Social background**			
Attended college	72	44	**
Lacked high school diploma	25	49	**
Low economic status	22	47	40
Professional or executive	22	17	10
Unskilled laborer	13	16	22
Plot functions			
Starring role	17	15	8
Character succeeded	65	72	54
Character failed	23	16	34
Positive portrayal	40	44	32
Negative portrayal	31	24	41
Committed crime	11	7	22

*Characters were coded only if their backgrounds were clearly indicated by the script.
**Two few characters were coded for meaningful comparisons.
Source: Based on a content analysis of 7,639 prime time characters that appeared in 620 entertainment programs between 1955 and 1986.

managed to attain whatever they strove for more often than either whites or Hispanics. In fact, the failure rate among Hispanics was more than double that of blacks. Perusing these figures, it is difficult to resist the conclusion that Hollywood has cracked open the door to black concerns while letting Hispanics serve as window dressing.

Examining character portrayals in 1992, we found that compared to both Anglos and African Americans, television's Hispanics were low in number, low in social status, and lowdown in personal character, frequently portraying violent criminals. The worst offenders were "reality" shows, whose version of reality often consisted of white cops chasing black and Hispanic robbers. Utilizing the same scientific content analysis approach, we examined the more recent 1994–95 season. We focused on a composite month of prime time entertainment programs broadcast on the four major broadcast networks and in first-run syndication. We found some welcome progress in television's portrayal of Hispanics, combined with some lingering sins of both omission and commis-

sion. (These results reflect our analysis of 5,767 characters who appeared on 528 different episodes of 139 prime time series.)

The proportion of Hispanic characters was up but still far below the proportion of Hispanic Americans in the real world. Latinos were "ghettoized" in a handful of series, few of which are still on the air, and few portrayed prosperous, well-educated, authoritative characters. The most striking and hopeful result, however, was a dramatic decline in the portrayal of Hispanics as criminals. Among the major findings:

- *Visibility.* TV's Hispanic presence doubled from 1992 levels. And these characters were more likely to play major roles when they appeared. But the rise was from only 1 to 2 percent of all characters, far below the 10 percent of Americans with Hispanic ancestry in real life. And a majority appeared in only two series, one of which has been canceled.

- *Criminality.* Hispanic characters were less likely to play villains than they were in the 1992 network prime time schedules. The drop in criminal portrayals was down 63 percent (from 16 percent of all Hispanic characters in 1992 and 6 percent in 1994). But even this level of criminality was higher than the 4 percent we found among whites and 2 percent among blacks.

- *New "Realities."* The most striking changes appeared in the cops-and-robbers "reality" shows, such as "COPS" and "America's Most Wanted." In 1992, a staggering 45 percent of all Hispanics and 50 percent of African Americans who appeared in these shows committed crimes. In 1994–95, the "crime rate" for both minorities plummeted to less than half the previous levels—down from 45 to 16 percent of Latinos and from 50 to 20 percent of blacks portrayed.

NOTES

1. Harry Castleman and Walter Podrazik, *Watching TV: Four Decades of American Television* (New York: McGraw-Hill, 1982), 208.
2. Ibid., 226.
3. Laura Z. Hobson, quoted in Christopher Lasch, "Archie Bunker and the Liberal Mind," *Channels,* October/November 1981, 34.
4. Quoted in Castleman and Podrazik, *Watching TV,* 227.
5. See Richard Adler, ed., *All in the Family: A Critical Appraisal* (New York: Praeger, 1979).
6. Quoted in William Raspberry, "Cosby Show: Black or White?" *Washington Post,* 5 November 1984.
7. Quoted in *Time,* 19 March 1979, 85.
8. S. Robert Lichter and Daniel R. Amundson, *Distorted Reality: Hispanic Characters in TV Entertainment* (Washington, DC: Center for Media and Public Affairs, 1994).
9. Quoted in *Time,* 19 March 1979, 85.

33

THE NEW RACIAL STEREOTYPES

Richard E. Lapchick

Questions to Consider

Richard Lapchick asks why athletes are subject to such an intense level of scrutiny by the press. What argument does he make that links race, stereotypes, and celebrity culture to the attitudes most Americans have about student and professional athletes?

Athletes and Crime

The beginning of the twenty-first century brought the hope that many social injustices would be rectified. However, surveys taken throughout the 1990s indicated that many inaccurate perceptions persisted such as the majority of whites surveyed continuing to believe that most African-Americans are less intelligent, more prone to drug use, more violent, and more inclined towards violence against women than whites are.

Sport culture, as it is currently interpreted, now provides whites with the chance to talk about athletes in a way that reinforces these stereotypes of African-Americans. Because African-Americans dominate the most popular sports, whites tend to "think black" when they think about the major sports.

Each time any athlete gets into trouble, I receive many calls from writers and television producers seeking comments. After a fight involving a basketball or football player, the interrogation invariably includes, "What makes football or basketball players more inclined to get into fights?" I have never been asked this question of a hockey or baseball player, despite the fact that there are as many game fights in those sports.

After a reported incident of domestic violence involving a basketball or football player, the inevitable question is, "What makes football or basketball players more inclined to abuse women?" Equal numbers of hockey and baseball players are accused of domestic violence, yet I have never been asked this question about them.

Each year during the professional drafts in each sport I am asked, "What do you think about colleges and even high school football and basketball players jumping to the pros and missing their chance for an education?" I have never been asked that question about baseball or hockey, tennis or golf players who put higher education on hold to pursue athletic careers.

Shawn Fanning left Northeastern University early to turn pro and earn millions; he was called a genius for founding Napster.

The Dean of Northeastern University's School of Engineering told me that one of his biggest problems comes from companies attempting to lure away his top students each year. They leave for the money.

I believe that at least part of the systematic coupling of athletes and crime revolves around racial stereotyping. The media has persistently and consistently suggested that basketball and football players, who happen to be overwhelmingly African-American, are more violent than athletes in other sports and people in society in general. The result is that nearly everyone, including the police, women, fans, the media, sports administrators, and athletes themselves, believes that certain athletes, especially basketball or football players, are more inclined to be violent in general and violent against women in particular.

Rosalyn Dunlap, an African-American who was a five-time All American sprinter who now works on social issues involving athletes, including gender violence prevention, said, "perpetrators are not limited to any category or occupation. The difference is that athletes who rape or batter will end up on television or in the newspapers. Such images of athletes in trouble create a false and dangerous mindset with heavy racial overtones. Most other perpetrators will be known only to the victims, their families, the police, and the courts."

Once, while speaking to a group of distinguished international fellows at an elite academic institution, I asked members of the audience to write down five words that they would use to describe American athletes. In addition to listing positive adjectives, not one missed including one of the following words: dumb, violent, rapist or drug-user. I regularly meet with NBA and NFL players, as well as with college student-athletes on dozens of campuses. There are a lot of angry athletes who are convinced the public is stereotyping them because of the criminal acts of a few.

Many American men have grown to dislike athletes. A typical man might crave the money and the fame that a pro athlete enjoys, but he recognizes that such athletic success is unattainable for him. After reading all the negative press about athletes, he doesn't want to read that Mike Tyson felt he was treated unfairly by the justice system, knowing full well that Tyson made a reported hundred million dollars in his post-release rehabilitation program. He has little sympathy for the large number of pro athletes signing contracts worth more than ten million dollars a year. He is a micro-thought away from making egregious stereotypes about the "other groups" perceived as stealing his part of the American pie.

Big-time athletes fit the "other groups" category. Whether it is an African-American athlete or coach, or a white coach of African-American athletes, when something goes wrong with a player, a national reaction is likely to be immediate. Tom "Satch" Sanders, who helped the Boston Celtics win eight world championships, is now vice president for player programs for the NBA. His office encourages and guides players to finish their education, prepare for careers after basketball, and adjust to all the attention that NBA stars attract. Sanders presents a view complementary to Dunlap's. He proposes that the public has made a link between the stereotypes for athletes and African-Americans: "Everyone feels that athletes have to take the good with the bad, the glory with the negative publicity. However, no one appreciates the broad-brush application that is applied in so many instances. Of the few thousand that play sports on the highest level, if four or five individuals in each sport—particularly if they are black—have problems with the law, people won't have long to wait before some media people are talking about all those athletes."

APBnews.com released two revealing studies in 2000. The first was a study of NFL players on two teams that made it to the 2000 Super Bowl. The second was a study of the sixteen NBA teams in the 2000 playoffs. In the NFL study, 11 percent of the players had a criminal history. That stood in dramatic contrast to the 35 to 46 percent lifetime arrest rate (taken from extensive studies in California and New York) for adult males under thirty, the same age group as most NFL players. Most NFL players are between 18 and 30 years old although most of those are between the ages of 21 and 30. In the study of NBA players, the arrest rate of those on the sixteen playoff teams was 18 percent, again a fraction of the national figures for their comparable age group of males.

Jeff Benedict's book *Pros and Cons* created a sensation in 1998 by saying that 21 percent of NFL players had arrest records. In an article he coauthored in 1999 for the statistics journal *Chance,* he said that the lifetime arrest rates for the NFL players he documented in *Pros and Cons* was less than half the arrest rate in the general population.

Fans build stereotypes of athletes from media coverage of the athletes and the games. Fans, who are mostly white, observe sport through a media filter that is created by an overwhelming number of white men. There are 1,600 daily newspapers in America employing only nineteen African-American sports columnists. There are only two African-American sports editors who work on newspapers in a city that has professional sports franchises. The fact that the number of sports columnists, as reported in the 2000 conference of the National Association of Black Journalists, has almost doubled from 11 since 1998 is a positive sign. However, there are no African-American sports writers on 90 percent of the 1,600 daily newspapers.

I am not suggesting, nor would I ever suggest, that most or even many of the white news writers are racist. However, they were raised in a culture in which many white people have strong beliefs about what it means to be African-American. The obvious result is that their reporting provides reinforcement of white stereotypes of African-American athletes. According to the National Opinion Research Center Survey, sponsored by the National Science Foundation for the University of Chicago, whites surveyed share the following attitudes:

- Fifty-six percent of whites think African-Americans are more violent.
- Sixty-two percent of whites think African-Americans do not work as hard as whites.
- Seventy-seven percent of whites think most African-Americans live off welfare.
- Fifty-three percent think African-Americans are less intelligent.

Some white writers may have picked up these stereotypes in their own upbringing. When they write about an individual African-American athlete or several African-American athletes who have a problem, it becomes easy to unconsciously leap to the conclusion that fits the stereotype. Sanders said, "Blacks in general have been stereotyped for having drugs in the community as well as for being more prone to violence, However, now more than ever before, young black athletes are more individualistic and they resist the 'broad brush.' They insist on being judged as individuals for everything." But even that resistance can't be misinterpreted by the public and by the writers as off-the-court trash talking.

The athletes of the twenty-first century come from a generation of despairing youth cut adrift from the American dream. When the Center for the Study of Sport in Society started in 1984, one of its primary missions was to help young people balance academics and athletics. Since 1990, its mission has been extended to help young people lead healthy and safe lives.

Today our colleges are recruiting athletes:

- who have witnessed violent death. If an American child under the age of sixteen is killed every two hours with a handgun, then there is a good chance that young athletes will have a fallen family member or friend.
- who are mothers and fathers when they arrive at our schools. There are boys who helped 900,000 teenage girls get pregnant each year. Some student-athletes will leave after four years of college with one or more children who are four or five years old.
- who have seen friends or family members devastated by drugs.
- who have seen battering in their homes. An estimated 3 percent of American men are batterers and an estimated 3 million women are battered each year.
- who were victims of racism in school. Seventy-five percent of all students surveyed by Lou Harris reported seeing or hearing about racially or religiously motivated confrontations with overtones of violence very or somewhat often.
- who grew up as latchkey kids. Either a single parent or two working parents head 57 percent of American families, black and white alike.

Not enough campuses or athletic departments have the right people to help guide these young men and women into their adult lives. College campuses desperately need professionals that can deal with these nightmarish factors.

Academic Issues in College Sport

The amount of media coverage devoted to student-athlete literacy problems seem unique to athletes. The media rarely reports that 30 percent of *all* entering freshmen must take remedial English or mathematics. The same holds true for the media's portrayal of student-athlete graduation rates. Although college athletic departments should strive to increase the number of student-athletes who graduate, graduation rates for the student body as a whole have changed. Only 14 percent of entering freshmen graduated in four years. If an athlete does not graduate in four years, some call him dumb; others say the school failed him. Few note that he may be typical of college students.

Don McPherson nearly led Syracuse University to a national championship when he was their quarterback in the 1980s. After seven years in the NFL and CFL, McPherson worked until 1999 directing the Mentors in Violence Prevention (MVP) Program, the nation's largest program using athletes as leaders to address the issue of men's violence against women.

McPherson reflected on the image that associates athletes with a lack of intelligence: "When whites meet an uneducated black athlete who blew opportunities in college or high school, they think he is dumb. They don't question what kind of school he may have had to attend if he was poor, or how time pressures from sport may have affected him. If they don't make it as a pro athlete, they're through without a miracle. I met lots of 'Trust Fund Babies' at Syracuse. They blew opportunities. No one called them dumb, just rich. We knew they would not need a miracle to get a second chance. I played at Syracuse at a time when being a black quarterback had become more acceptable. But the stereotypes still remained. As a player, people still remember me as a great runner and scrambler. I had not dented their image of the physical vs. intelligent black athlete."

McPherson led the nation in passing efficiency over Troy Aikman and won many awards, including the Maxwell Award, but he was most proud of being the quarterback with the highest passing efficiency rating in the nation. "I should have shattered the image of the athletic and mobile black quarterback and replaced it with the intelligent black quarterback. Unfortunately, stereotypes of football players, mostly black, still prevail. They make me as angry as all the stereotypes of black people in general when I was growing up."

McPherson wore a suit to class and carried the *New York Times* under his arm. But McPherson said that those whites that recognize his style were "surprised and said I was 'a good black man,' as if I were different fom other black men. Most students assumed I was poor and that football was going to make me rich. Like many other blacks on campus, I was middle class. My father was a detective and my mother was a nurse."

Irrespective of color or gender, student-athletes graduate at higher rate than non student-athletes, yet it is difficult to get accurate reporting of this in the press. According to the NCAA's 1999 report:

- Fifty-eight percent of white male Division I student-athletes graduated vs. 57 percent of white male nonathletes. Forty-two percent of African American male Division I student-athletes graduated vs. 33 percent of African American male nonathletes.

- Seventy-one percent of white female Division I student-athletes graduated compared to 61 percent of white female nonathletes. Fifty-seven percent of African American female Division I student-athletes graduated vs. only 43 percent of African American female nonathletes.

Some disparities do appear when we compare white student-athletes to African American student-athletes:

- Fifty-three percent of white male Division I basketball student-athletes graduated versus 37 percent of African American male Division I basketball student athletes.

• Seventy percent of white female Division I basketball student-athletes graduated compared to only 56 percent of African American female Division I basketball student-athletes.

College sport does not own problems of illiteracy and low graduation rates. They belong to higher education in general and its inheritance of the near bankruptcy of secondary education in some communities.

The publication of graduation rates, long feared by athletic administrators, reveals scandalous rates, but it also shows poor graduation rates specifically for students of color. The predominantly white campuses of most colleges and universities are not welcoming environments for people of color. African American student-athletes arrive on most campuses and see that only 10 percent of the student body, 3 percent of the faculty, and less than 5 percent of top athletics administrators and coaches look like them. Unless there is a Martin Luther King Center or Boulevard, all of the buildings and streets are named after white people.

In many ways, the publication of graduation rates for student-athletes helped push the issue of diversity to the forefront of campus-wide discussions of issues of race, ethnicity, and gender. Educators finally recognized how they were failing students of color by not creating a conducive, welcoming educational environment.

Drugs and Alcohol Use Among Athletes

A common stereotype depicts athletes as abusing drugs and alcohol. Some athletes do use drugs. CNN Headline news broadcasts stories about famous athletes caught with drugs. Repeated exposure to such reports inflates the size of the problem, but the facts do not reveal widespread abuse among athletes at the professional, college or even high school level.

According to an extensive 1995 *Los Angeles Times* survey of athletes and the crimes they committed, a total of twenty-two professional and college athletes and three coaches were accused of drug use or a drug-related crime that year. On average, the media reported a story about a new sports figure with a drug problem every two weeks. Center estimates now put the number of sports figures accused of drug-related crimes at fifty per year or one media story per week on average.

Stories about athletes accused of drug use or drug-related crime are and should be disturbing. But those stories are rarely, if ever, put in the context of the 1.9 million Americans who use cocaine each month or the 12.1 million who use heroin throughout their lives. A total of 13 million individuals (6 percent of the American population) use some illicit drug each month, and 17 percent of men in the eighteen-to-twenty-five age group are drug users. Whether it is twenty-two or fifty, athletes who use drugs make up a small fraction of a single percent of the more than 400,000 athletes who play college and professional sports in America.

The NBA's drug policy, which leaves open the possibility of a lifetime ban for any athlete who is caught using drugs, is generally recognized as a model for the sports world. The policy may have stopped a substance abuse problem that predated its inception. According to an APBnews.com report, *Crime in the NBA*, released in June 2000, forty-one players were charged, booked, or arrested in eighty-two instances of crimes more serious than traffic tickets over the course of their time on the rosters of the sixteen NBA playoff teams. The story noted that "it is perhaps a credit to the NBA's antidrug policy that none of the eighty-two incidents noted in the APB-news.com study were related to hard drugs." (Marijuana was cited in six cases.) The forty-one players put the NBA's arrest rate at 18 percent. APBNews.com reported that,"By way of comparison, the lifetime arrest rate of the general population as measured in four different studies ranges from 31 to 50 percent."

On the subject of alcohol abuse, the same 1995 *Los Angeles Times* survey of athletes and the crimes they committed, reported that twenty-eight college and professional athletes and four coaches were charged with alcohol-related infractions. None of these thirty-two cases were put in the context of the 13 million Americans who engage in binge drinking at least five times per month. Yet we read about a new athlete with an alcohol problem every eleven days. Such images can fuel an exaggerated sense of crisis in athletics when they are not viewed in full social context.

McPherson remembered being "shocked" when he arrived on Syracuse's campus at how much drinking went on each night among the student body. He felt compelled to call football players he knew on other campuses. "It was the same everywhere. Now when I go to speak on college campuses I always ask. It is worse today. Athletes are part of that culture, but insist that practice and academics crowd their schedules too much to be in bars as often as other students." Student personnel administrators on college campuses acknowledge that abusive drinking is the number one issue on college campuses today.

Athletes and Violence

Media coverage of professional, college, and even high school athletes consistently implies that the violence of sport makes its participants more violent in society.

Are sports any more violent today than they were twenty years ago when no one would have made such an assertion? I don't think so. But the streets and schools across America surely are more violent than they were twenty years ago—there are 2,000 assaults in schools across the nation every hour of every day. The number of American children killed by guns in the 1900s has exceeded the total number of soldiers who died in the Vietnam War. Gun violence obeys no boundaries of race, class, or geography. School shootings occurred in Pearl (Mississippi), Paduka (Kentucky), Jonesboro (Arkansas), and Littleton (Colorado). Violence seems part of the school day.

If one were to put together a lowlights tape of the fights in sports that the public best remembers, I guarantee that most people would list Kermit Washington hitting Rudy Tomjanovich, Latrell Sprewell choking P. J. Carlesimo, and Roberto Alomar spitting at umpire John Hirschbeck. Fear of men of color attacking whites in our society is part of the culture. There is no doubt that the treatment afforded to Washington, Sprewell and Alomar was measurably different than that given Denver Bronco Bill Romanowski, who is white, after he spit in the face of a black player in 1999.

Most of the stories written about specific athletes who are violent or gender violent are about African American athletes. Stories about them that appear without appropriate filters of what is going on in society reinforce racial stereotyping.

Athletes and Gender Violence

In the wake of the O. J. Simpson case, any incident involving an athlete assaulting a woman has received extraordinary publicity. The individual cases add up to another stereotype of the new millennium: athletes, especially basketball and football players, are more inclined to be violent towards women than nonathletes are.

Joyce Williams-Mitchell has worked extensively in this field, most recently as the executive director of the Massachusetts Coalition of Battered Women's Service Groups. As an African American woman, she abhors the image of athletes being more prone to violence against women. "It is a myth. The facts do not bear this out. All the studies of patterns of batterers defined by occupation point to men who control women through their profession. We hear about police, clergy, dentists, and judges. I only hear about athletes as batterers when I read the paper. They are in the public's eye. Men from every profession have the potential to be batterers."

There have been, of course, too many cases of athletes committing assaults on girls and women. As I wrote this section, I received a voice mail message from a reporter: "Have you heard that Corey Dillion is the latest case of an athlete hitting a woman? I guess that depends on when you pick up the message. There may have already been another case!" His message implied that attacks on women by athletes took place hourly.

However, there has never been a thorough, scientific study conclusively showing that athletes are more inclined to violence. Jeffrey Benedict, Todd Crossett, and Mark McDonald wrote the only study that comes close. It was based on sixty-five cases of assault against women that took place on ten Division I campuses over a three year period. Thirteen of the cases involved athletes; seven of the athletes were basketball or football players.

Despite the authors' acknowledgment of both the small number of cases revealed and the fact that the survey did not control for alcohol and tobacco use or the man's attitude toward women (then three main predictors of a male's inclination to gender violence), the press regularly quoted their study without qualification. Media reports never stated that the study came up with only thirteen abusive athletes over three years. They simply said that the study concluded that student-athletes, in particular basketball or football players, committed nearly 20 percent of all campus assaults. Rosalyn Dunlap pointed out that, "This is a racially loaded conclusion. When I was a student-athlete at the University of Missouri, I never thought of keeping myself safe from a 260-pound football player any more than any other man on the street. In fact, male athletes on campus protected me."

The following is a list of data usually missing in the debate about athletes and violence against women.

- In 1994, 1,400 men killed their significant others. In that year, O. J. Simpson was the only athlete accused of murder.
- In 1998, an estimated 3 million women were battered and close to one million were raped. According to various reports in the press in the five years between 1995 and 2000, between seventy and one hundred athletes and coaches were accused of assault against a woman each year.
- The 1999 *Chronicle of Higher Education*'s annual campus crime survey showed that there were a total of 1,053 forcible sex offenses reported in 1997. Fewer than thirty-five student-athletes were arrested in conjunction with these crimes.

Gender violence is a serious problem among American men. The cost of crime to America is pegged at $500 billion per year, according to a National Institute for Justice research report for the Justice Department released in March 1996. Gender assault and child abuse accounted for $165 billion—more than one third of that total.

Rosalyn Dunlap, who worked with The National Consortium for Academics and Sport to create more awareness about the issue, said, "There are no men who should be exempted from being educated about the issue of gender violence although many believe they are. It is a problem for naval commanders, daycare providers, fraternities, guys in a bar, in corporations, in halls of higher education and, yes, on athletic teams. But no more so on athletic teams."

There have been numerous cases in which women brought suits against corporations from harassment and/or assault. The *Boston Globe* gave extensive coverage in the late 1990s to the case against Astra USA, Inc., a chemical company, where women lodged sixteen formal complaints for incidents ranging from sexual harassment to rape. Twenty-nine women brought suit against Mitsubishi for the same reasons. None of the press about Astra suggested that working in a chemical company produced a climate of sexual aggression. At Mitsubishi, no one suggested any relationship between the manufacturing process and gender assault. So why do stories about athletes imply such a linkage to athletics? Does it fit white America's racial imagery?

McPherson believes it does: "Football and basketball mean black. When the public talks about gender violence and athletes, it talks black. No one discusses the problems of golfer John Dailey or Braves manager Bobby Cox. Warren Moon was another story altogether. Problems about athletes hit the papers and people think they detect a pattern because of the seeming frequency. But no one else's problems get in the papers. How do we make legitimate comparisons? With Astra and Mitsubishi, we look at the corporate climate and don't generalize about individuals. But with athletes, especially black athletes, we look at players and look for patterns to add up."

Some observers say athletes are trained to be violent and that we can expect that training to carry over into their homes. If this is true, then what about the training in lethal force we give the police, the Army, the Air Force, the Navy, and the Marines? Will these men also come home and kill? McPherson adds, "There is no logic to connect these cases, but we do fit our stereotypes of African-Americans with such images when we carry through the implication for athletes."

With all the recent publicity about the horrors of gender violence, it would be easy to forget that it was America's big, dirty secret until the O. J. Simpson case made it a notorious subject. Before that trial, few Americans were willing to talk about gender violence. The same unwillingness to confront racism diminishes society's ability to eradicate it. But the situation will never change if it remains unconfronted.

Athletes should take a leadership role on this issue, just as they have on drug abuse and educational opportunity. The MVP Program, organized in 1992 by Northeastern University's Center for the Study of Sport in Society and now headed by Jeff O'Brien, a former football player, has worked on more than sixty-five campuses training male and female athletes to be spokespeople on the issue of gender violence. Each of those schools has become proactive on an issue that has hurt so many women and their families.

Don McPherson insists that "we have to do more to help our youth survive by including our athletes rather than excluding them in helping our youth. The stereotyping of our athletes does not help. We need to be ready with facts to dispute the easy labels."

McPherson and Tom Sanders both argue vigorously that America's athletes not only don't fit the emerging stereotypes about athletes and crime, but the vast majority of professional athletes are extremely positive role models. Sanders said, "when I look at the many NBA players who have their own foundations and who are very involved with giving back to the communities where they play and where they came from, I know they are hurt by the stereotypes." McPherson asserts that "most of the players in the NFL are deeply religious, family-centered men who are constantly giving back to their communities with time and money."

Rosalyn Dunlap wonders when the public and the media will stop being cynical about athletes. "I hear so many people say that if athletes do something in the community that they do it for publicity. Why can't we accept that athletes want to help? Sport and those who play it can help educate us and sensitize us. While we can't ignore the bad news, we should also focus on the overwhelming good news of what athletes do to make this a better world."

I do not believe the stereotypes. However, I do believe the high profile of all professional sports makes it incumbent on those involved to call on sports institutions to demand a higher standard for athletes. Athletes, once challenged, have played a leading role in the battle to educate our children; in the life and death fight against alcohol and drug abuse; and in the attempt to resolve conflicts with reason and not with fists or weapons. Now it is time to challenge them to fight the long overdue battle against gender violence.

The challenge to athletes involved a starting point of confronting the behavior of an individual athlete. Some universities had to make star athletes academically ineligible or expel them from school to convince others that they were serious about education and would not tolerate either poor academic records or athletes violating social norms.

After the tragic death of Len Bias, the nation was forced to recognize that cocaine was not "recreational," but lethal. Schools began random drug testing; the NBA promised to uphold a lifetime ban for players who ignored league drug policies. This ban was necessary to show players as well as their young fans that there could be no tolerance for the use of life-threatening drugs.

The ban will always seem unfair to the player caught with drugs. I am sure Michael Ray Richardson, who was the first NBA player banned for life, still looks in the mirror and asks, "Why me? There were other guys." But the discipline had to start somewhere. What was unfortunate for Richardson was fortunate for the NBA and for society. Action, no matter how symbolic, was critical.

Likewise, when street violence began to invade our rinks, courts, and fields, sport had to take a stand with automatic and serious sanctions that cost players money and cost teams their playing services. No commissioner or director of a players association wanted their entire league and all of its athletes branded as thugs because of those who acted out during the game.

The New England Patriots bit the bullet for all professional sports and decided not to sign draftee Christian Peter, the University of Nebraska's highly acclaimed football player, who carried numerous criminal charges on his record. It was a milestone decision. Patriot owner Robert Kraft felt compelled to take a strong stand immediately after they drafted Peter, despite the fact that he would lose dollars in the draft and could have faced lawsuits from Peter's representatives. The importance of his decision was not only that players would see clear consequences for their actions, but also that children who idolize those players would also see such consequences as relevant to their own choices in life.

Sports figures are in a unique position to effect change. Keith Lee, a six-year NFL

veteran who is now the chief operating officer of the National Consortium for Academics and Sport, works to improve race
relations among young people. He states,

"We need positive role models who can help
young people to believe in what they cannot
yet see. We need then now more than ever."

PART IV
Color-Blind or Color Bind: Thinking Through the American Dilemma

A nationally distributed, full-page magazine advertisement placed by IBM depicts nine of their employees at a business meeting. The employees, presumably managers, are focusing on a white-haired man who is pointing to a chart. The activity depicted is rather mundane—meetings of this type take place thousands of times every business day. What makes this ad exceptional is what it is selling. In large letters across the top of the page, the text of the ad announces "Diversity Works." The employees shown in the hand-drawn advertisement consist of an older white woman, a black woman, an Asian woman, a white man, an older black man with white hair, two men of ambiguous racial identity, and a white woman in a wheelchair. The racial and ethnic makeup of the cartoon characters in this ad is intended to convey to readers that IBM, as the supporting text tells us, "values individual differences." What is particularly interesting is the ratio of white males to others in this rendering of the inner workings of a large corporation.

IBM may indeed value diversity, but the reality is that the upper ranks of corporate management are still the domain of white men. The bipartisan Glass Ceiling Commission found that white men "hold about 95 of every 100 senior management positions, defined as vice president or above." How corporate America presents its work force to the public and how diverse the organization actually is, especially as one moves up the occupational ranks, is a contradiction. Perhaps there is a reason this advertisement was a drawing and not an actual photograph of a diverse work environment. What occupations or organizations can you name in which high-status positions reflect the racial, ethnic, and gender composition of the United States? Think about the racial and ethnic composition of members of Congress, or the CEOs of the *Fortune* 500 companies, or the fifty state governors, or tenured college professors. What is the race and gender of your university or college president? What about the racial or ethnic background of sports or entertainment celebrities? What patterns emerge, and what do they mean?

We are an incredibly diverse nation. We are reminded of this by the advertisements promoting diversity from corporations like IBM, McDonald's, Texaco, Denny's, and Du Pont. We are reminded of this when we are repeatedly told that by the year 2050, about half of U.S. residents will be white and the other half will be black, Asian, and Latino. We are reminded of this when we debate the relative merits of affirmative action, bilingual education, or immigration quotas.

In the public imagination, the idea of ethnic and racial diversity seems to be simultaneously celebrated, feared, and reviled. The United States is promoted as the land of opportunity, but some groups have had more opportunity than others. Why? The United States is defined as a country of immigrants, yet many citizens are fearful that the "new wave" of immigrants will radically change American culture. Why? The United States is proclaimed a color-blind nation, yet inequities based on race and ethnicity are still the norm for a sizable part of the population. If we are a color-blind nation, why is it very likely you will marry some-one from the same racial background?

The readings in Part IV examine these contradictions. The six readings in the first section of Part IV focus on the changing complexion of the United States. Min Zhou maps how immigration flows to the United States have changed over the last thirty years and the sociological implications of immigrants coming mostly from Asia and Central and South America. Stephen Steinberg examines how social and economic mobility are often reflections of the opportunity structure immigrants experience when they arrive in the United States. Michael Suleiman examines a community that until very recently received very little attention from the mainstream media. Suleiman describes the ebb and flow of Arab immigrants to the United States and their socioeconomic success relative to other immigrant groups. Mary Waters examines mobility and racial identity construction to explore how race, ethnicity, and opportunity shape the experiences of Afro-Caribbeans in New York City. The last reading in this section, by Albert Camarillo and Frank Bonilla, addresses the challenges poor Hispanics face in breaking out of the ranks of the impoverished in the United States.

The section "Race and Romance" explores the historical and contemporary trends in interracial marriage. Heather Dalmage explains how and why "racial borders" are patrolled in order to promote racial endogamy. Frank Wu discusses the cultural contradictions of interracial marriages among Asians and Asian Americans and provides a critique of the "mixed race movement." Based on her extensive research of mixed race couples around the country, Maria Root outlines what she calls "ten truths" about interracial marriage.

The next four readings focus on how different social conditions can exacerbate racial and ethnic relations and what might be done at both the macro- and micro-levels to ameliorate racial inequality. In reading 42, Charles A. Gallagher notes that current trends in popular culture have blurred the color line by linking the consumption of products across racial groups to racial harmony. Gallagher asks if racial equality has been achieved when groups from various races now share and consume the same products (for example, hip-hop music, McDonald hamburgers, and reality TV programs). In the next reading, Herbert Gans argues that a "beige-ing" of America is taking place that will incorporate some parts of the Latino and Asian populations but not blacks. Each of these readings points to some of the barriers to racial equality. The final two readings suggest what might be done to address racial inequities. Speaking from a public policy perspective, Melvin Oliver and Thomas Shapiro discuss what social issues need to be addressed if economic and social justice is to be realized. Finally, Charles A. Gallagher suggests ten things you can do to change the world as you go about your day.

The Changing Complexion of the United States: Race, Ethnicity, and Immigration

34

THE CHANGING FACE OF AMERICA
Immigration, Race/Ethnicity, and Social Mobility

Min Zhou

Questions to Consider

A century ago, immigrants were overwhelmingly white and from Europe. Since the 1980s, most immigrants have been coming to the United States from Asia and the Americas (excluding Canada). How have these new waves of immigrants shaped U.S. culture? How have these newcomers transformed urban areas? Which models discussed earlier—assimilation, ethnic pluralism, and melting pot—might best describe the current and future experiences of recent arrivals to the United States? Why do some groups in the United States feel threatened about current trends in immigration?

Contemporary immigration refers to the period of large-scale, non-European immigration to the United States that has begun to accelerate since the late 1960s after a long hiatus of restricted immigration (Massey 1995). Between 1971 and 1995, the United States admitted approximately 17.1 million immigrants, including 1.6 million formerly unauthorized aliens and 1.1 million "special agricultural workers" (SAWs) who were granted permanent resident status under the provisions of the Immigration Reform and Control Act of 1986 (IRCA). The scale of contemporary immigration almost matched that during the first quarter of the century (17.2 million admissions between 1901 and 1925), when immigration to the United States was at its peak. Although similar in numbers, the annual admission trends in these two peak periods looked quite different. During the first twenty-five years of the century, annual admission numbers fluctuated drastically with several noticeable ebbs and flows. In contrast, during the twenty-five years near the end of the millennium, the inflows were fairly steady, which had been kept under the half-million mark until 1978 and then gradually increased from 1978 to 1988. The year 1989 witnessed a sudden surge beyond the one-million mark that lasted for the next three consecutive years. This surge was almost entirely represented by the legalization of the formerly undocumented population permitted by IRCA. Clearly, had it not been for IRCA, immigration trends would have been stable, though heading in a gradual, upward direction.[1]

Just as the turn-of-the-century immigration dramatically transformed America, contemporary immigration has repeated history, changing the face of America in ways that are unique and challenging the traditional views of immigrant incorporation. In this chapter, I specifically examine the following issues: 1) the historical trends of immigration to the United States, 2) the settlement patterns of contemporary immigrants in America's largest metropolitan regions, 3) the nature of racial and ethnic relations in areas of high immigration, and 4) the key determinants of social mobility for new immigrants and their offspring. The chapter aims at understanding how contemporary immigration differs from turn-of-the-century immigration and how such differences may affect our approach to the issues and concerns over the changing face of America in the new millennium.

Distinctive Features of Contemporary Immigration

Trends

Several distinctive features of contemporary immigration are noteworthy in historical perspective. First, despite a similarity in the absolute numbers, the rate of contemporary immigration relative to the total U.S. population is much lower than that of the earlier period since the U.S. population has more than tripled during the course of the twentieth century (3.9 vs. 11.7 per thousand) (Smith and Edmonston 1997). The comparatively low rate of contemporary immigration implies a more modest overall impact on the U.S. population today than in the past. However, such an impact is disproportionately localized in areas of high immigration, not only in historic gateway cities but also in smaller urban or suburban areas in which few immigrants had settled in the past. Second, the rate of contemporary emigration is considerably lower today than in the past. It was estimated that, for every one hundred immigrants during the first two decades of high immigration, thirty-six had returned to their homelands. In contrast, between 1971 and 1990, less than a quarter had returned (U.S. Immigration and Naturalization Service 1997; Warren and Kraly 1985). This trend suggests a more steady growth today than in the past, indicating that contemporary immigrants are more likely than their earlier counterparts to stay in the United States permanently. Third, unlike immigration then, contemporary immigration is accompanied by a much larger number of undocumented immigrants because of historical patterns of reliance on Mexican labor migration, especially in agriculture, as well as the operation of migration networks that has facilitated undocumented immigration through back-door channels (Massey 1995; Massey et al. 1987). Fourth, compared to immigration then, today's inflows are made up of a much more visible proportion of refugees and asylees.[2] During past thirty-five years (1961–1995), annual admission of refugees averaged 68,150, compared to the average annual admission of 47,000 over the fifteen-year span immediately after World War II. The admission of refugees today implies a much enlarged base for later immigration through family reunification.

Last but not least, the all-time high presence of nonimmigrants arriving in the United States temporarily each year also bears a broad implication for potential immigration, both legal and illegal. Statistics from the Immigration and Naturalization Service (INS) showed that 22.6 million nonimmigrant visas were issued in 1995: 17.6 million (78 percent) were tourists who came for short visits for business or pleasure; the rest were on long-term nonimmigrant visas, including 395,000 foreign students (along with their spouses and children), 243,000 temporary workers or trainees (along with their immediate relatives), and a smaller number of traders and investors. These latter groups of nonimmigrants contain a significant pool of potential immigrants. The majority of those who initially entered as students can freely seek employment in the United States after the completion of their studies, which in turn increases the probability of later adjusting to permanent resident status. Among those who entered as tourists, the great majority will depart on time. However, a relatively small proportion, but a quantitatively large number, of those who might qualify for family-sponsored immigration may overstay their visas and wait in the United States to have their status adjusted. In 1995, almost half the legal immigrants admitted had their nonimmigrant visas adjusted in the United States.

About 40 percent of the total undocumented immigrant population was "nonimmigrant overstays" (U.S. Immigration and Naturalization Service 1997).

In sum, a lower rate of emigration, greater numbers of undocumented immigrants and refugees or asylees, and the larger pool of potential immigrants among nonimmigrants imply the complexity of contemporary immigration. Another significant implication for immigrant America is that it is a more challenging task than ever before to accurately measure the scale and impact of immigration and to manage or control the inflows.

Diversity

Compared with the turn-of-the-century immigrants, contemporary immigrants are markedly different in national origins, types of admission, spatial distribution, and socioeconomic characteristics. The newcomers are predominantly from non-European countries. Since the 1980s, more than 85 percent of the immigrants admitted to the United States come from Asia and the Americas (excluding Canada) and only 10 percent from Europe compared to more than 90 percent at the earlier peak. In particular, the share of immigrants from the Americas as a proportion of total legal immigrant admissions has risen substantially from 25 percent in the 1950s, moving to 39 percent in the 1960s, and jumping up to 50 percent since the 1980s. Similarly, the share of immigrants from Asia as a proportion of the total admissions grew from a tiny 5 percent in the 1950s, to 11 percent in the 1960s and 33 percent in the 1970s, and stayed at 35 percent since 1980, except for 1991, when the Asian share dropped to 18 percent because of the sudden increase in the legalizees under IRCA, most of whom were of Latin origins (U.S. Immigration and Naturalization Service

1997). The top five sending countries during the period between 1981 and 1995 were Mexico, the Philippines, China/Taiwan, the Dominican Republic, and India, compared to Italy, Austria–Hungary, the Soviet Union, Canada, and the United Kingdom during the first two decades of the century. Mexico alone accounted for more than one-fifth of the total legal admissions since the 1980s. In fact, Mexico was on the INS list of the top five countries of last residence between 1921 and 1960 and was number one after 1960 (U.S. Immigration and Naturalization Service 1997).

The composition of contemporary immigration has a lasting effect on the growth and composition of the general U.S. population. During the past thirty years, immigration accounted for more than a third of the total population growth. Asian- and Latin-origin populations grew particularly fast in both absolute and relative sizes. Some groups— Salvadorans, Guatemalans, Dominicans, Haitians, Jamaicans, Asian Indians, Koreans, Vietnamese, Cambodians, and Laotians— grew at spectacular rates, mainly as a result of immigration. It is estimated that, at the current levels of net immigration, intermarriage, and ethnic affiliation, the size of the Asian population will grow from nine million in 1995 to thirty-four million in 2050 (growing from 3 to 8 percent of the total U.S. population) and that the Hispanic population will grow from twenty-seven million in 1995 (about 9 percent of the population) to ninety-five million (or 25 percent of the population) in 2050 (Smith and Edmonston 1997).

Spatially, the turn-of-the-century immigrants were highly concentrated along the northeastern seaboard and the Midwest. For them, the top five most-preferred state destinations were New York, Pennsylvania, Illinois, Massachusetts, and New Jersey, and the top most-preferred immigrant urban destinations were New York, Chicago, Phila-

delphia, St. Louis, and Boston (Waldinger and Bozorgmehr 1996). In contrast, today's newcomers are highly concentrated, not simply in states or urban areas traditionally attracting most immigrants, but also in states or urban areas that had few immigrants in the past. Since 1971, the top five states of immigrant-intended residence have been California, New York, Florida, Texas, and New Jersey, accounting for almost two out of every three newly admitted immigrants. California was the leading state of immigrant destination since 1976. In 1995, the five leading urban areas of high immigrant concentration were New York, Los Angeles–Long Beach, Chicago, Miami–Hialeah, and Orange County (U.S. Immigration and Naturalization Service 1997).

The new immigrants also differ from the turn-of-the-century inflows in their diverse socioeconomic backgrounds. The image of the poor, uneducated, and unskilled "huddled masses," used to depict the turn-of-the-century European immigrants, no longer applies to today's newcomers. The 1990 U.S. census attests to the vast differences in levels of education, occupation, and income by national origins. For example, more than 60 percent of foreign-born persons (aged twenty-five years or older) from India reported having attained college degrees, three times the proportion of average Americans, but less than 5 percent of those from El Salvador and Mexico so reported. Among employed workers (aged sixteen years or older), more than 45 percent of the foreign-born persons from India held managerial or professional occupations, more than twice the proportion of average American workers, but less than 7 percent of those from El Salvador, Guatemala, and Mexico so reported. Moreover, immigrants from India reported a median household income of $48,000, compared to $30,000 for average American households; those from the Dominican Republic and the Soviet Union reported a median household income below $20,000. Poverty rates varied, ranging from a low of 5 percent for Indians and Filipinos to a high of 33 percent for Dominicans and an extreme high of more than 40 percent for Cambodians and 60 percent for Hmongs, compared to about 10 percent for average American families.

The New Second Generation

Spatial concentration, diverse origins, and socioeconomic status of new immigrants hinge not only on the fate of immigrants but also on their children. Because of the recency of contemporary immigration, a new generation of immigrant children and children of immigrant parentage is just coming of age. This new second generation is not only disproportionately young but also ethnically diverse. The Current Population Survey (CPS) for the period 1994–1998 shows that almost 40 percent of the second generation are under eighteen years of age, in contrast to 28 percent of the U.S. population. In the second generation, more than a third are of Latin American ancestry and 7 percent of Asian ancestry, compared with 12 and 4 percent, respectively, in the total U.S. population reported in the 2000 census. If it were distributed randomly across America's urban landscape, the new second generation would not be of great interest since it is relatively small in absolute numbers. However, historical and contemporary patterns of immigrant settlement suggest that immigrants and their children are highly concentrated in just a handful of metropolitan regions. For example, California alone accounted for some 45 percent of the nation's immigrant student population, more than one out of ten school-aged children in the state were foreign born, and more than a third of the state's school-aged children

spoke a language other than English at home (Cornelius 1995). In Los Angeles County, two-thirds of the public schools have a numerical majority of nonwhite students, and 39 percent are represented by more than three-quarters of U.S.- or foreign-born minority students. In major immigrant-receiving cities, such as Los Angeles, San Francisco, New York, and Miami, more than a third of the students in the entire school system speak a language other than English at home.

These changes, impacted by a massive immigration during the past three decades, along with the changes in local cultures, economies, and neighborhoods, have created diverse receiving contexts quite different from the ones in which European immigrants entered a century ago. The challenge for the adaptation of immigrant offspring into postindustrial America is profound. Differing from their immigrant parents, immigrant children lack meaningful connections to their "old" world. Thus, they are unlikely to consider a foreign country as a place to return to or as a point of reference. Instead, they are prone to evaluate themselves or to be evaluated by others by the standards of their new country (Gans 1992; Portes 1995; Portes and Zhou 1993). Nonetheless, the encounter in any metropolitan context is likely to invoke one of two, if not more, scenarios: The child either succeeds in school and moves ahead or falls behind (or remains the same as) the modest, often low status of the parents' generation. The latter scenario is labeled by the sociologist Herbert Gans (1992) as "second-generation decline." Thus, a more pressing issue is whether the new second generation will be able to incorporate into middle-class America, following the path taken by the "old" second generation arriving at the turn of the century, and to advance beyond their parents' generation.

Transforming Urban America: Old and New Immigrant Metropolises

Like earlier waves of European immigrants, contemporary immigrants are overwhelmingly urban bound, but they differ from their earlier counterparts in geographic distribution. While about 94 percent of immigrants from Asia and close to 90 percent of Latin American immigrants live in urban areas (compared to just over 70 percent of the native-born U.S. population), they are concentrated not only in metropolitan areas in the West and Northeast but also in the Southeast and the Southwest. New immigrants, like their fellow Americans, are spatially distributed not only by social class and race but also by social networks and family or kinship ties. The settlement patterns of contemporary immigrants are characteristic of dispersion and concentration. New immigrants are more spread out than ever before, yet they continue to be highly concentrated within the metropolitan region of settlement. Next, I focus on describing the particular patterns of spatial concentrations in selected metropolitan areas—New York, Los Angeles, Miami, San Francisco, and Chicago[3]—and examine how different national origin groups converge on particular urban centers and how these urban centers are in turn impacted by the arrival of newcomers.

The Old and New "Ellis Islands"

Ellis Island, where the Statue of Liberty stands, has been the historic gateway to immigrant America. Seeking a better life or an alternative means of livelihood in a new land, millions of European immigrants entered the United States through this gateway in the late nineteenth and early twentieth centuries. Many made New York City their new home, even though thousands returned to their homelands after a lengthy period of sojourning (Moch 1992; Morawska

1990). Since the 1970s, immigration has transformed the "old" Ellis Island and given rise to new ones. While New York remains the most popular immigrant-receiving center, Los Angeles has surpassed it as the largest immigrant metropolis in absolute and relative terms. In absolute numbers, Los Angeles metropolitan region had 600,000 more foreign-born persons than New York as of 1990. Relatively, a third of Los Angeles' residents are immigrants, compared to 27 percent in New York, whose immigrant share was as high as 40 percent at the turn of the century (Waldinger and Bozorgmehr 1996). Miami and San Francisco, though much smaller in size, have become more densely populated by new immigrants than any other U.S. metropolitan area, with a share of 34 and 27 percent, respectively. In contrast, Chicago, the second-largest immigrant metropolis in 1910, dropped a few places down the list in 1990 when measured by the immigrant share of the total population (13 percent).

Compared to the old urban centers, new immigrant-receiving centers take a much larger share of the country's foreign-born population. In 1910, the foreign-born shared 15 percent of the U.S. total population. About a quarter of them lived in the top five largest metropolises—New York, Chicago, Philadelphia, St. Louis, and Boston (Waldinger and Bozorgmehr 1996). The foreign stock's (immigrants and their children's) share of the total population in 1990 was much smaller, less than 9 percent. However, a much higher proportion (37 percent) of the immigrants were concentrated in the top five largest metropolitan areas—Los Angeles, New York, San Francisco, Miami, and Chicago. In addition, the majority of urban immigrants lived in the central city.

Preferred Destinations

Different immigrant urban centers today attract immigrants from different countries.

Table 1 displays the top ten national origin groups in each of the selected metropolitan areas. As shown, immigrants of different national origins are not evenly distributed across the urban landscape. New York, an urban center that received primarily European immigrants across the Atlantic Ocean at the turn of the century, has become the center for Caribbean immigrants. The three main Caribbean groups comprise almost a fifth of the area immigrant population. What is more striking is that none of these groups outnumbered others by an overwhelming margin and that none, except for the Chinese, appeared on the national top ten list, an indicator of extremely high concentration in just one area. In fact, 66 percent of Dominican immigrants, 36 percent of Haitian immigrants, and 39 percent of Jamaican immigrants in the United States lived in New York alone.

The picture in Los Angeles is drastically different. Mexican immigrants are the largest national origin group, comprising 40 percent of the area's foreign stock, 5.5 times larger than the second-largest group on the metropolis' top ten list and on the national top ten list. Also noticeable are immigrants from El Salvador and Guatemala, making up 11 percent of the area's immigrant population. Although these two Central American groups are not on the national top list, they are disproportionately concentrated in Los Angeles, which is home to 48 percent of Guatemalan immigrants and 46 percent of Salvadoran immigrants in the United States. Compared to immigrant New York, Los Angeles appears to be less diverse ethnically, though it may have as many national origins groups as one can count. It is also less diverse in class status because of the strong correlation between national origins and the skill levels of the newcomers.

The dominance of Cubans in Miami is a different story. Though Miami is a much smaller metropolitan area, not only does it have the highest proportion of immigrants, but it is also a metropolis with the largest presence of Cuban Americans. More than half of Miami's foreign stock is of Cuban origin, and the group is 6.5 times larger than the second-largest group on the metropolitan top ten list. Unlike Mexicans in Los Angeles, Cubans in Miami are not simply the largest group in size, but also socioeconomically diverse with a significantly large middle class and strong influence in the areas' political and economic matters.

Like Miami, San Francisco is also a much smaller metropolis. Though no single national origin group is dominant, the Asian presence is impressive, making up more than 40 percent of the foreign stock. In contrast, Chicago is a much larger metropolis, but its foreign-born stock is only 13 percent. Interestingly, Mexican immigrants form the largest national origin group, three times larger than the second group on the metropolitan top ten list. However, their visibility is blurred by the area's relatively large native-born population.

Demographic Transformation in Immigrant-Receiving Urban Centers

The diversity of contemporary immigrants and their geographic concentration, combined with recent trends of deindustrialization and suburbanization, have reshaped the demographic profiles of both old and new immigrant-receiving centers. Figure 1 illustrates the racial composition of the three largest metropolitan areas between 1980 and 2000. During the last two decades of the twentieth century, demographic transformation is drastic: The proportions of the "colored" components other than "black" in the general population increased corresponding to the decreasing dominance of the "white" component. In both New York and Los Angeles, non-Hispanic white populations

TABLE 1 Top-Ten Foreign-Born, National Origin Groups by Selected PMSAs, 1990 (in 1,000s)

Number	United States	N	New York	N	Los Angeles	N	Miami	N	San Francisco	N	Chicago	N
1	Mexico	4,298	Dominican Republic	232	Mexico	1,167	Cuba	429	China[1]	95	Mexico	238
2	Philippines	913	China[1]	166	El Salvador	213	Nicaragua	67	Philippines	60	Poland	76
3	China[1]	774	Jamaica	129	Philippines	161	Haiti	45	Mexico	48	Philippines	43
4	Canada	745	Italy	122	China[1]	136	Columbia	43	El Salvador	26	India	34
5	Cuba	737	Soviet Union	84	Korea	114	Jamaica	31	Vietnam	17	Italy	28
6	Germany	712	Haiti	80	Guatemala	108	Dominican Republic	16	Nicaragua	14	Germany	28
7	United Kingdom	640	Guyana	77	Vietnam	76	Honduras	16	United Kingdom	11	Korea	25
8	Italy	580	Columbia	71	Iran	67	Peru	15	Germany	11	China[1]	24
9	Korea	568	Poland	66	Soviet Union	51	Mexico	10	Soviet Union	9	Greece	18
10	Vietnam	543	Ecuador	64	Japan	40	Spain	10	Canada	9	Yugoslavia	18
Top Ten		10,510		1,092		2,102		682		300		532
Total		19,767		2,286		2,895		875		441		797

[1]Includes Hong Kong and Taiwan.
Source: U.S. Census Bureau (1993).

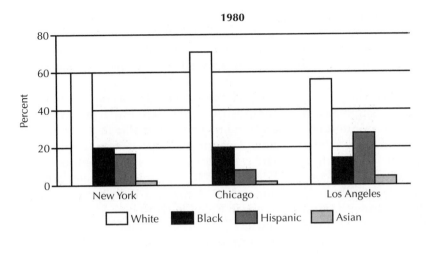

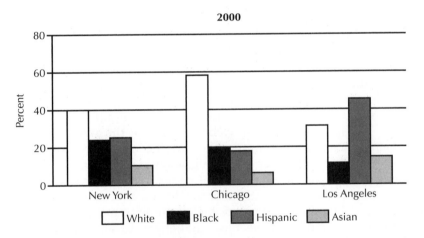

FIGURE 1 Population Growth by Race/Ethnicity, Selected Metropolitan Areas, 1980–2000 (PMSAS) *Source:* U.S. Census of Population (2000).

had become a numerical minority by the year 2000. Even in Chicago, the diminishing dominance of the white population is significant. What have altered the racial composition in these metropolises are the obvious influxes of Asians and Latinos. Past research on internal migration patterns in the United States has also shown consistent findings that, in high-immigration metropolitan areas, there is a significantly large out-migration and that out-migrants are predominantly

non-Hispanic whites (Frey 1995). At the metropolitan level, therefore, the demographic impact of immigrant influx is singularly on whites. But whether whites are pushed out by new immigrants or by other economic forces is debatable and may be a topic for yet another chapter.

Just thirty years ago, America's urban landscape, including the areas with high immigrant density, was predominantly white. The racial hierarchy was dictated by a black–white dichotomy with an unquestionable, all-encompassing white dominance. Although there were various immigrant groups coexisting within the urban social structure, these immigrants were expected to eventually become assimilated into the dominant white Anglo-Saxon Protestant (WASP) culture. Immigrant enclaves or ghettos did exist, mostly in the central city, but they did not constitute a permanent problem because they were considered transitional stops or springboards and would eventually die down with time. Indeed, with the span of only two or three generations and a long hiatus of low immigration, the white ethnics, such as the Irish, Jews, and Italians, who were once designated as inferior "races," have now become indistinguishably "white" (Alba and Nee 1997). Meanwhile, the majority of second- and third-generation Asian and Latin Americans also quietly dispersed into the white middle class without much public notice because they represented only a tiny fraction of the population.

In the first generation, the racial composition in major immigrant-receiving centers reflects the patterns of contemporary immigrant settlement I have just discussed: American cities have now become less "white" (but no less "black") and more "colored" than ever before. Los Angeles and Miami have turned into "Latin-dominant" cities. The middle chart displays racial/ethnic composition of the children of immigrants. Only Los Angeles contains a "Latin-dominant" second generation, with the same shift in Miami slowed down by its large concentration of white second-generation retirees, making Miami's second-generation population an ethnically diverse group. New York and Chicago contain a second-generation population that can only be described as "white dominant," a reflection of the impact of these regions' earlier immigration histories. San Francisco, the singularly "Asian-dominant" region, stands out as different, boasting the greatest variety in the ethnic composition of its second generation as well as the most pronounced Asian tilt.

It should be noted that changes in racial composition that were impacted by immigration have occurred also in areas historically receiving relatively few immigrants. The U.S. census data shows that, between 1990 and 2000, Hispanic and Asian populations grew at 631 and 172 percent, respectively, in Raleigh–Durham–Chapel Hill; 388 and 197 percent in Atlanta; and 189 and 111 percent in Minneapolis–St. Paul. These recent demographic trends suggest that new immigrants are more dispersed across America than earlier waves.

The Changing Dynamics of Race and Ethnicity

What is more striking about these demographic changes is that the arrival of new immigrants and the concurrent trend of rapid out-migration of non-Hispanic whites in immigrant metropolitan areas significantly alter the dynamics of race and ethnicity. They make ethnicity more salient and pose new challenges to all Americans—native-born whites, blacks, Asian and Latin Americans alike, as well as the newcomers themselves.

Non-Hispanic Whites

The non-Hispanic white population comprises primarily of the grandchildren or great-grandchildren of European immigrants. Decreasing numbers notwithstanding, non-Hispanic whites still hold dominant political and economic power in immigrant-receiving centers, and the shift of the black–white paradigm does not change this dominance. How, then, have non-Hispanic whites been affected by immigration? Perhaps the most significant impact has involved the notion of American identity, as many fear that newcomers would overtake America and that Americans would be un-Americanized by them. The hotly contested issues of multiculturalism, bilingualism, and immigration reform in the political arena reflect some of these deeply rooted fears. In areas of immigrant concentration, many whites are confronted with a new dilemma of becoming a minority with a majority mentality in a multiethnic society (Horton 1995). In affluent suburban communities with a large and sudden influx of middle-class newcomers, such fears are more pronounced. For example, in Monterey Park, California, whites used to be able to drop their hyphens as unqualified Americans. But in the wave of a large influx of affluent Asian immigrants, they find themselves on the defensive without an ethnic culture of resistance and empowerment to express their fears (Horton 1995). However, nativist fears manifest themselves differently in different metropolitan settings. For example, in Mexican Los Angeles, the Spanish language is stigmatized and is being banned from instruction in schools, whereas in Cuban Miami, the same language is considered an important marketable skill, and bilingualism is celebrated as the American way.

Non-Hispanic Blacks

The foreign-born component of non-Hispanic blacks is relatively small, though migration from the Afro-Caribbean region has been on the rise, and Afro-Caribbean immigrants tend to concentrate in New York and Miami. As essentially a native-born population and the most American of the Americans, non-Hispanic blacks have been socially affected by the influx of other "colored" immigrants in different ways. In the wake of immigration's surge, non-Hispanic

blacks have experienced increasing differentiation in socioeconomic characteristics at the individual level and bifurcation between the middle class and the poor (Grant et al. 1996; Oliver and Shapiro 1995). These patterns of differentiation and bifurcation are caused primarily by the drastic economic restructuring of America's urban labor markets that is simultaneous with rapid growth in immigration. Uneducated and poor blacks have been trapped in the inner city, where ladders of social mobility have disappeared and where the entry to low-skilled jobs is barred by employer discrimination and immigrant employment networks (Waldinger 1996; Wilson 1996). Middle-class blacks have experienced unprecedented social mobility, yet many have continued to face racial discrimination, especially in the housing market that constrains their residential mobility (Clark 1996; Massey and Denton 1987).

The arrival of large numbers of non-white immigrants has significantly changed the racial composition of the urban population, rendering the black–white paradigm outdated. However, such a change has not moved blacks up the racial hierarchy. Instead, blacks' racial caste status has been pushed down further by the internalization of other colored immigrants into, unfortunately, the "moral problem in the hearts and minds of Americans" (Myrdal 1962). For example, the widely publicized black–Korean conflicts in America's inner cities and the 1992 Los Angeles civil unrest were not caused by economic competition but rather by the realignment of race relations, manifested in the tension over "turf," which has continued to constrain blacks in virtually every aspect of their lives (Min 1996; Morrison and Lowry 1994). In their struggle for racial equality, many native-born blacks are confronted with a daunting dilemma: how to deal with being a minority competing with other new minorities whose members have come from different backgrounds and headed for many directions.

Native Americans of Asian and Latin Origin

The children and grandchildren of Asian and Latin immigrants have also felt the powerful social impact of contemporary immigration. Almost overnight, native-born Americans of Asian and Latin origin, especially those already "assimilated" or "melted" into white middle-class suburban communities, are confronted with the renewed image of "foreigners." Their American identity is constantly questioned because they look like the newcomers who do not fit the old characterization of an American as "either an European or the descendant of an European" (De Crevecoeur 1904) or as an "immaculate, well-dressed, accent-free Anglo" (Zangwill 1914). These phenotypical definitions of "American," widely and often unconsciously held, make it harder for some native-born people to feel fully American if they happen to be Native Americans or Mexican Americans, whose ancestors settled on this land long before the *Mayflower* reached shore.

Stereotyping images of an "American" create special problems for native-born Americans of non-European ancestry whose national origin groups contain a disproportionately large number of recent arrivals. Incidents of harassing a native-born Mexican American suspected of being an undocumented immigrant or comments about a third-generation Japanese American's "good English" are frequently heard. The children, U.S.-born and similar to other American children, have found to suffer from persistent disadvantages merely because they look "foreign" (U.S. Commission on Civil Rights 1988, 1992).

While they are infuriated by the unfair treatment as foreigners, native-born Hispanic and Asian Americans are also caught in a dilemma of inclusion versus exclusion in their struggle for racial equality. Similar to other Americans in speech, thought, and behavior, native-born Hispanic and Asian Americans and their foreign-born counterparts often hold contradictory values and standards over labor rights, individualism, civil liberty, and ultimately the ideology of assimilation. These differences, intertwined with the acculturation gap between immigrant and native-born generations, have impeded ethnic coalition and ideological consensus. For example, the picketing of restaurants in New York's Chinatown in 1994 and Los Angeles' Koreatown in 1998 was a conscious effort mostly by second-generation Asian Americans fighting for immigrant rights. But it was perceived by the ethnic community as a group of "whitened" kids trying to "destroy their parents' businesses" and the ethnic community. Ironically, the parent generation consciously struggles to push children to become "white" by moving their families into white neighborhoods, sending their children to white schools, and discouraging their children to play basketball and mimic hip-hop culture. For Afro-Caribbean immigrants, the parents even push their children to adopt certain strategies, such as invoking their accents or other references to French or British colonial culture to differentiate themselves from native-born blacks and to avoid the stigma of "blackness" (Portes and Stepick 1993; Waters 1994, 1996). But becoming "white" is politically incorrect and thus unacceptable for the native-born generation.

The Newcomers

The social impact of contemporary immigration is perhaps most intense on the newcomers themselves. Earlier labor migrants of Asian or Latin American origin were mostly sojourners with an intention of eventually returning to their homelands. In contrast, most new immigrants are permanent settlers, even though there is a significantly visible presence of transnationals who have maintained their homes or led their regular lives simultaneously in their countries of origin and destination. Most permanent settlers have made concerted efforts to assimilate first economically and then culturally. No matter how much they want to be like other Americans, however, the newcomers often find themselves facing an ambivalent public that questions their willingness to assimilate and doubts their assimilability. They also face the unrealistically high expectation that they should assimilate quickly. It took earlier European immigrants two or three generations to assimilate into the middle class, and such a pace was facilitated by economic expansion, industrialization, and a long hiatus of restricted immigration (Alba 1985; Alba and Nee 1997; Perlmann and Waldinger 1997). Today, the second generation of contemporary immigrants is just coming of age, and predictions about their future outcome of assimilation are only estimates.

Today's immigrants also encounter various structural constraints that limit their chances of integration. On the one hand, the continuous high volume of immigration has affected new arrivals in ways similar to their native-born coethnics. However assimilated they may have become, they are still likely to be viewed as foreigners "fresh off the boat." On the other hand, many newcomers, especially the low-skilled poor, lack contact with and exposure to the segment of American society into which they aspire to assimilate. In this case, they may either allow themselves and their children to assimilate into the inner city or build ethnic communities to help shield coethnic members from being trapped in the inner city (Portes and Zhou 1993). Either way, the process is viewed as a rejection to assimilation.

In real life, immigrants must first deal with the issue of economic survival. New immigrants arrived in cities where economic restructuring and globalization have created bifurcated labor markets with numerous labor-intensive and low-paying jobs on the one end and a growing sector of knowledge-intensive and well-paying jobs on the other. This bifurcated labor market renders many immigrants underemployed with substandard wages or occupational overqualification (Zhou 1997a). The 1990 census data reveal that immigrant men of all groups displayed fairly low rates of labor force nonparticipation (below 8 percent), except for Southeast Asians (16 percent) (Rumbaut 1995; Zhou and Bankston 1998).[4] In particular, Mexican men, who were most handicapped of all immigrant groups by the lack of skills and English proficiency, showed the lowest labor force nonparticipation rate, probably because of the fact that most of Mexican immigrant workers arrived through extensive employment and migrant networks (Massey 1996). Among those who were in the labor force, all male immigrants, except for the Europeans, were more likely than native white workers to be underemployed, with over half the immigrants—more than 60 percent of the Asians among them—experiencing underemployment measured by partial employment, low-wage employment, and overqualified employment. Mexicans were almost twice as likely as other groups to be underemployed by low wages. By contrast, Africans, Asians, and Europeans were more likely to be underemployed by being educationally overqualified for the jobs they held. It is clear that disadvantages in labor market status do not necessarily affect immigrant groups in the same manner. For those who are not able to obtain adequate employment, Mexican immigrants are more likely to be absorbed in partial or low-wage employment, while African and Asian immigrants are more likely to be occupationally overqualified in occupations.

The underemployment patterns among employed men were similar to those among employed women. Overall, however, gender expectations about employment are different. For example, male workers who are discouraged to seek work may be viewed as being forced to detach themselves from the labor market. But the same view may not be applicable to unemployed women because they may voluntarily withdraw from the labor force because of marriage or childbearing. By the same token, partial employment among men may be viewed as an imposed disadvantage, but partial employment among women may be voluntary or a strategy for supplementing husbands' underpaid family wages. Whether all forms of underemployment accrue to economic disadvantages remains a matter of debate. I would argue that unemployment is an absolute disadvantage. Partial employment or low-wage employment does not help much because their jobs are usually inadequate for sustaining a decent living, much less for moving up the socioeconomic ladder. This disadvantage affects Mexican immigrants disproportionately. Although Mexican immigrants have relatively easy access to the U.S. labor market, their employment stability is heavily affected by the uncertain demands of the highly competitive, volatile industries in which they work. These conditions in turn constrain Mexican immigrants' ability to achieve economic success commensurate with their high rate of labor force participation.

While many immigrant workers start out as low-wage workers and gradually move up in the labor market, others may be "stuck" in dead-end jobs. Of course, whether one can successfully move out of their underemployment depends not simply on individual human capital or incentive because the effects of human capital may be in-

tervened by factors beyond the control of individual group members. Immigration selectivity is one such factor. Immigrants who have arrived with strong human capital may be able to overcome labor market disadvantages by overqualification. Those who have arrived with little human capital are likely to be employed in low-wage and "bad" jobs. They usually have few economic resources and cannot afford the time for the kind of reeducation and retraining that can possibly move them up in the labor market. However, it would be premature to conclude that those who initially hold entry-level, low-wage jobs are necessarily "trapped" at the bottom of the labor market. In fact, as immigrants gain labor market experience, many are able to advance within and across industries to better-paying positions and even to self-employment (Portes and Zhou 1992, 1996; Zhou 1992). Thus, the long-term outcomes of underemployment as an alternative means to upward social mobility or as a dead-end street trapping immigrants in their starting point or pushing them further down toward the bottom are speculative but not mutually exclusive scenarios.

The Impact of Race/Ethnicity on Immigrant Incorporation

Classical sociological theories about immigrant adaptation predict a linear trajectory in which immigrants, starting their American life at disadvantaged positions, eventually converge toward the mean and become indistinguishable Americans (Alba 1985; Gordon 1964; Park 1928; Warner and Srole 1945). This conclusion is based on two assumptions. One is that there is a natural process by which diverse and initially disadvantaged ethnic groups come to share a common culture and to gradually gain equal access to the opportunity structure of the host society. The other is that this process consists of gradually deserting old cultural and behavioral patterns in favor of new ones and that, once set in motion, this process moves inevitably and irreversibly toward assimilation (Warner and Srole 1945).

Immigrants' intergenerational mobility has been empirically measured by the extent to which immigrant groups achieve parity with the society's dominant group in education, occupation, income and wealth, and political power, which is, in Gordon's (1964) term, "secondary structural assimilation." Looking back in history from the present standpoint, the experiences of the children and grandchildren of earlier European immigrants appear to confirm the assimilationist prediction about structural assimilation. Between the 1920s and the 1950s, when America experienced a long hiatus of restricted immigration, the host country seemed to have absorbed the great waves of immigrants who had experienced significant upward mobility across immigrant generations, as determined by the length of stay since immigration, the mastery of the English language, the acquisition of human capital, and increasing exposure to American culture (Alba 1985; Chiswick 1977; Greeley 1976; Sandberg 1974; Wytrwal 1961).

However, it remains an open question whether new immigrants and their offspring will follow the path of their European predecessors. In terms of the direction of intergeneration mobility, the distinctions between yesterday's European immigrants and today's newcomers may not be as sharp as they appear to be. However, with regard to the rate of structural assimilation—the degree to which immigrant groups achieve parity with the dominant group—the classical assimilationist paradigm shows its constraints. The historiography of the turn-of-the-century European immigrants reveals divergent rather than convergent outcomes among different national origin groups (Perlmann 1988). Past studies on intergenerational mobility have found persistent interethnic differences in the rate of progress even after controlling for measurable human capital characteristics and contextual factors. In a study of the Irish, Italian, Jewish, and African Americans in Providence, Rhode Island, Perlmann (1988) found that, with family background factors held constant, ethnic differences in levels of schooling and economic attainment persisted in the second and later generations. He also found that schooling did not equally commensurate with occupational advancement for African Americans as for other European Americans across generations. Recent studies have also indicated that the distance between immigrant offspring and the native-born population in key socioeconomic measures varies among different national origin groups and that for some it continues to remain substantial (Model 1991; Tang 1993; Tienda and Lii 1987; Zhou and Kamo 1994). Even the direction of intergenerational mobility does not appear to be linear, and research has found both general and group-specific trends of second- or third-generation decline (Gans 1992; Landale and Oropesa 1995). These findings about past and present immigrant experiences have suggested that the direction and the rate of social mobility are two distinct dimensions of the adaptational outcomes and that what determines the direction may not necessarily be what determines the rate. Next, I highlight the ways in which race and ethnicity impact the prospects of immigrant incorporation.

Ethnicity and Class

Ethnicity, which is intrinsically linked to national origin, has been found to be one of the most salient factors influencing social mobility of new immigrants. Classical assimilationist theories often treat ethnicity as a measure of old-country ways and consider it an impediment to structural assimilation, but acknowledge that ethnicity does more in predicting the rate than in predicting the direction of mobility (Park 1928; Warner and Srole 1945). Yet empirical research indicates significant differences in the magnitude of progress across different ethnic or national origin groups. Steinberg (1996) revealed a surprisingly prominent and strong role that ethnicity played in structuring the lives of adolescents, both in and outside of school. He found that students of Asian origin outperformed non-Hispanic white students, who in turn outperformed black and Hispanic students by significantly large margins. He also found that the ethnic differences remained marked and consistent across nine different high schools under study after controlling for social class, family structure, and place of birth of parents. He also found similar ethnic effects on other important predictors of school success, such as the belief in the payoff of schooling, attribution styles, and peer groups. A study reported in *Ethnic Los Angeles*, conducted by a research team at the University of California, Los Angeles, and headed by Roger Waldinger and Mehdi Bozorgmehr, showed significant intergroup differences in the rate of intergenerational progress while revealing trends of upward mobility for all immigrant groups. This study found that native-born Mexicans and Central Americans experienced greater earnings and educational disparities with non-Hispanic whites relative to their Asian and Middle Eastern counterparts (Bozorgmehr et al. 1996; Cheng and Yang 1996; Lopez et al. 1996; Ortiz 1996). Portes and Rumbaut (1996) attributed these differences to the interplay of premigration conditions, individual characteristics, host reception, and group adaptational patterns. They argue that the diverse socioeconomic characteristics on arrival among new immi-

grants give rise to varied modes of incorporation that in turn affect the rate as well as the direction of progress among second and later generations.

Ethnicity and the Ethnic Hierarchy

While ethnicity is intrinsically intertwined with national origin, it is deeply rooted in America's ethnic stratification system, exerting positive as well as negative effects on adaptational outcomes. What makes ethnicity favor some groups while penalizing others? One way to interpret the varied effects of ethnicity is to examine its interaction with class. Socioeconomic status has an independent effect on mobility outcomes because it influences where people live, where they go to school, with whom they are in close contact, and what kind of family and community resources are available. Wealthier and skilled immigrants are able to integrate into better sectors of the host economy with relative ease and settle directly in suburban middle-class communities, albeit with temporary downward mobility. Poorer and unskilled immigrants have few options but take up low-wage jobs and settle in declining urban areas, starting their American life either in poverty or on welfare. Becker (1963) found that early and insignificant differentials in class status can result in substantial differences in educational and occupational mobility in later years. The strong correlation between national origins and skill levels of contemporary immigrants also has a significant bearing on the varied effects of ethnicity. For example, the children of Mexican immigrants lag far behind their peers of Asian origins in academic performance and educational attainment, partly because of socioeconomic differences (Perlmann and Waldinger 1997) and partly because of differential resources generated in the family and the ethnic community

(Caplan et al. 1989; Gibson 1989; Rumbaut and Ima 1988).

However, controlling for the interactive effect between class and national origin does not seem to reduce the significance of ethnicity. Recent studies on the new second generation are a case in point. Using language proficiency as a proxy for the nativity or immigration status in a large-scale study in the San Diego School District during the 1986–1987 and 1989–1990 school years, Rumbaut found that first-generation Chinese, Korean, Japanese, Vietnamese, and Filipino students had the highest grade-point averages of all students in the district. More remarkable, even the Hmong, who came from preliterate peasant background, and the more recently arrived Cambodians outperformed all native-born English-only American students (Rumbaut 1995). Given the drastic differences in socioeconomic backgrounds of these Asian national origin groups, this finding complicates the effect of class. Portes and his associates reported findings from the Children of Immigrants Longitudinal Survey (CILS) showing that parents' socioeconomic status, length of U.S. residence, and homework hours significantly affected academic performance but that controlling for these factors did not eliminate the effect of ethnicity. More systematic analyses of the educational progress of children of immigrants using the CILS data generally confirmed these findings (Rumbaut and Portes 2001).

The fact that ethnicity continues to shape the American experience of immigrant groups implies that ethnicity also interacts with broader structural factors that produce and reinforce specific advantages or disadvantages in ethnic group membership and that the outcomes of adaptation may be segmented with potential and real risks of downward mobility (Portes and Zhou 1993). Portes and MacLeod (1996), using the National Educational Longitudinal Survey, reported that the negative effect of disadvantaged group memberships among immigrant children was reinforced rather than reduced in suburban schools but that the positive effect of advantaged group memberships remained significant even in inner-city schools. Using the same data set but employing a two-stage least-squares method, Hao and Bonstead-Bruns (1998) found that immigrant status increases educational expectations for Chinese, Koreans, and Filipino families more than for Mexican families. They also found that Chinese background consistently exerted positive effects on educational achievement, while Mexican background showed significantly negative effects, and that the ethnic effects persisted after controlling for important individual and contextual factors.

Why is it that ethnicity exerts opposite effects on the same outcome measures for different national origin groups? Existing literature has suggested that the advantages and disadvantages of ethnic group membership lie not merely in the class status and the corresponding modes of incorporation from which the first generation start life in America, but also in different levels of the social structures in which individuals and groups participate. At the macro level, the system of ethnic stratification functions to provide different ethnic groups with unequal access to economic resources and political power. At the micro level, the networks of social ties, which are often ethnically based, prescribe different strategies to cope with structural disadvantages and mobilize different types of social capital to provide support for group members. Either the members of disadvantaged ethnic groups accept an inferior status and a sense of basic inferiority as part of their collective self-definition or they create a positive view of their heritage on the basis of cultural and ethnic distinction, thereby establishing a sense of collective dignity (Ogbu 1974). If a socially defined ethnic group wishes to assimilate but finds that normal paths of integration are blocked on the basis of ethnicity, the group may be forced to take alternative survival strategies that enable its members to cope psychologically with structural barriers but that do not necessarily encourage structural assimilation. The group may also react to structural disadvantages by constructing resistance to assimilation (Fordham 1996; Kohl 1994). In this case, symbolic expressions of ethnicity and ethnic empowerment hinder rather than facilitate social mobility among group members.

As immigrants and their children are absorbed into different segments of American society, becoming American may not always be an advantage. When immigrants enter middle-class communities directly or after a short transition, they may find it advantageous to acculturate and assimilate. If the social environment surrounding immigrant children is rich in resources and if its goals are consistent with those of the immigrant family, then ethnic resources may be relatively less important, but those ethnic resources may still count. For example, many middle-class immigrant parents move into affluent white neighborhoods and send their children to schools attended mainly by white students from similar or more affluent socioeconomic backgrounds. But they still insist on enrolling their children in ethnic institutions during after-school hours and weekends or involving them in religious or cultural activities. The children then benefit both from privileged socioeconomic contacts with members of the dominant group in mainstream American society and from the group-specific expectations of and opportunities for intellectual development.

Thus, when immigrant children enter the bottom of the ethnic hierarchy, where the forces of assimilation come mainly from the underprivileged, acculturation and assimilation are likely to result in distinct disadvantages, viewed as maladjustment by both mainstream society and the ethnic community. Immigrant children from less fortunate socioeconomic backgrounds have a much harder time than middle-class children succeeding in school. A significant number of the children of poor, especially dark-skinned, immigrants can be trapped in permanent poverty in the era of stagnant economic growth, for in the process of Americanization, these immigrant children "will either not be asked, or will be reluctant, to work at immigrant wages and hours as their parents did but will lack job opportunities, skills and connections to do better" (Gans 1992: 173–174). The prospects facing children of the less fortunate may be high rates of unemployment, crime, alcoholism, drug use, and other pathologies associated with poverty and the frustration of rising expectation.

This new reality defines the world that confronts the children of new immigrants. Children growing up in households headed by poor, low-skilled immigrants face uncertain prospects for moving ahead through school success. The parents, of course, have few of the economic resources that can help children do well in school. The environment does not help when neighborhoods are poor and beset by violence and drugs and local schools do not function well. To add to this difficulty, immigrant children receive conflicting signals, hearing at home that they should achieve at school while learning a different lesson on the street—that of rebellion against authority and rejection of goals of achievement. At the same time, both real life and television expose children to the wage and consumption standards of U.S. society, and children come to expect more than their parents ever had. As a result, children of the foreign born are unwilling to work the low-paying, low-status jobs of their parents, but they do not have the education, skills, or opportunities to do better (Gans 1992). This mismatch between rising aspirations and shrinking opportunities will either lead to second-generation decline or provoke "second-generation revolt" (Perlmann and Waldinger 1997). However, young immigrants or children of immigrants may benefit from cultivating social ties within ethnic communities to develop forms of behavior likely to break the cycle of disadvantage and to lead to upward mobility. The extent to which young people are integrated into this community also becomes a major determinant of school adaptation, especially when the social environment otherwise places children at risk (Zhou and Bankston 1998).

Conclusion

The significant differences between contemporary and turn-of-the-century European immigration necessitate a reconceptualization of the phenomenon and the development of alternative theories. Because of the diverse socioeconomic backgrounds of new immigrants, the pathways toward integration into American society may be as rugged as they are segmented. Many new immigrants continue to follow the traditional rugged route, starting from the bottom rungs of the socioeconomic ladder and gradually working their way up. A visible proportion of them, however, manage to bypass the bottom starting line, incorporating directly into mainstream professional occupations and dispersing into suburban middle-class communities. Still, a significant number may be permanently "trapped" at the bottom, either unable to find work or working at "dead-end" jobs with little hope for social mobility.

Increasing diversity also poses challenges for Americans as they experience the drastic changes in the dynamics of race and ethnicity in an era of rapid social and economic transformations. Again, the old framework of assimilation has become outmoded. In multiethnic metropolises today, all native-born racial/ethnic groups are facing the challenge of adjustment to the new reality. Growing tensions are arising from an urgent need to negotiate the culture of diversity and to redefine oneself in the new racial/ethnic stratification system.

Finally, the future of new immigrants and their children is intrinsically linked to the diversity of immigration and to the current social stratification system into which today's immigrant children are assimilating. The American public still seems to allude to the idea that all immigrant children should move up and melt into the middle class. Because there are poor whites who have never assimilated into the white middle class, it is natural that some immigrant children may not make it, either, as immigrants are incorporating into a highly stratified society that accords individuals with varied life chances. Gans (1992) questions the American faith that mystifies an eventual immigrant success, particularly in regards to the new second generation. While children of the middle class have a better chance for success, the poor, especially the darker skinned, may not fare equally well. Consequently, assimilation as a widespread outcome for contemporary immigrant groups is possible for some but questionable for others. Indeed, for most Europeans, assimilation did not take place until the third or even the fourth generation. Thus, while the new second-generation immigrants may not assimilate, their children or grandchildren may. But with scenarios of second-generation decline still a matter of speculation, it seems clear that assimilation no longer means that everyone will eventually succeed.

NOTES

The original version of this chapter was presented at the Research Conference on Racial Trends in the United States, National Research Council, Washington, DC, October 15–16, 1998. Some of the main ideas were drawn from my previously published work (Zhou 1997b, 2001). I thank Roger Waldinger and Mary Waters for their helpful comments and Vincent Fu and Diana Lee for their research assistance.

1. In theory, all the IRCA legalizees should have been residing in the country for a considerable period of time prior to 1989, though a substantial portion of those legalized under the SAW program turned out to be relatively recent arrivals.

2. Refugees and asylees can be anyone with a well-founded fear of prosecution on the basis of race, religion, membership in a social group, political opinion, or national origin. Refugees are those seeking protection outside the United States, while asylees are those seeking protection once already in the United States.

3. These are Census Bureau–designated principal metropolitan statistical areas rather than cities proper.

4. African immigrants also include a significant component of refugees from Ethiopia who had a higher labor force participation rate than Southeast Asian refugees. African refugees, as well as European refugees, tend to have higher educational attainment, more fluent English proficiency, and better access to community-based employment networks than Southeast Asian refugees.

REFERENCES

ALBA, RICHARD D. 1985. *Italian Americans: Into the Twilight of Ethnicity.* Englewood Cliffs, NJ: Prentice Hall.

ALBA, RICHARD D., and VICTOR NEE. 1997. "Rethinking Assimilation Theory for a New Era of Immigration." *International Migration Review* 31 (4): 826–874.

BECKER, HOWARD S. 1963. *Outsiders: Studies in the Sociology of Deviance.* New York: The Free Press.

BOZORGMEHR, MEHDI, CLAUDIA DER-MARTIROSIAN, and GEORGES SABAGH. 1996. "Middle Easterners: A New Kind of Immigrant." In *Ethnic Los Angeles,* edited by Roger Waldinger and Mehdi Bozorgmehr. New York: Russell Sage Foundation.

CAPLAN, NATHAN, MARCELLA H. CHOY, and JOHN K. WHITMORE. 1989. *The Boat People and Achievement in America: A Study of Family Life, Hard Work, and Cultural Values.* Ann Arbor: University of Michigan Press.

CHENG, LUCIE, and PHILIP Q. YANG. 1996. "Asian: The 'Model Minority' Deconstructed." In *Ethnic Los Angeles,* edited by Roger Waldinger and Mehdi Bozorgmehr. New York: Russell Sage Foundation.

CHISWICK, BARRY R. 1977. "Sons of Immigrants: Are They at an Earnings Disadvantage?" *American Economic Review* 67 (February): 376–380.

CLARK, WILLIAM A. V. 1996. "Residential Patterns: Avoidance, Assimilation, and Succession." In *Ethnic Los Angeles,* edited by Roger Waldinger and Mehdi Bozorgmehr. New York: Russell Sage Foundation.

CORNELIUS, WAYNE A. 1995. "Educating California's Immigrant Children: Introduction and Overview." In *California's Immigrant Children: Theory, Research, and Implications for Educational Policy,* edited by Rubén Rumbaut and Wayne A. Cornelius. La Jolla, CA: Center for U.S.-Mexican Studies, University of California, San Diego.

DE CREVECOEUR, J. HECTOR ST. JOHN. 1904 [1782]. *Letters from an American Farmer.* New York: Fox, Duffield.

FORDHAM, SIGNITHIA. 1996. *Blacked Out: Dilemmas of Race, Identity, and Success at Capital High.* Chicago: University of Chicago Press.

FREY, WILLIAM H. 1995. "Immigration and Internal Migration 'Flight' from U.S. Metropolitan Areas: Toward a New Demographic Balkanization." *Urban Studies* 32 (4–5): 733–757.

GANS, HERBERT J. 1992. "Second-Generation Decline: Scenarios for the Economic and Ethnic Futures of the Post-1965 American Immigrants." *Ethnic and Racial Studies* 15 (2): 173–192.

GIBSON, MARGARET A. 1989. *Accommodation without Assimilation: Sikh Immigrants in an American High School.* Ithaca, NY: Cornell University Press.

GORDON, MILTON M. 1964. *Assimilation in American Life: The Role of Race, Religion, and National Origins.* New York: Oxford University Press.

GRANT, DAVID M., MELVIN L. OLIVER, and ANGELA D. JAMES. 1996. "African Americans: Social and Economic Bifurcation." In *Ethnic Los Angeles,* edited by Roger Waldinger and Mehdi Bozorgmehr. New York: Russell Sage Foundation.

GREELEY, ANDREW M. 1976. "The Ethnic Miracle." *The Public Interest* 45: 20–36.

HAO, LINGXIN, AND MELISSA BONSTEAD-BRUNS. 1998. "Parent-Child Differences in Educational Expectations and the Academic Achievement of Immigrant and Native Students." *Sociology of Education* 71: 175–198.

HORTON, JOHN. 1995. *The Politics of Diversity: Immigration, Resistance, and Change in Monterey Park, California.* Philadelphia: Temple University Press.

KOHL, HERBERT. 1994. *"I Won't Learn from You" and Other Thoughts on Creative Maladjustment.* New York: The New Press.

LANDALE, NANCY S., and R. S. OROPESA. 1995. "Immigrant Children and the Children of Immigrants: Inter- and Intra-Group Differences in the United States." Research Paper. Population Research Group, Michigan State University.

LOPEZ, DAVID E., ERIC POPKIN, and EDWARD TELLS. 1996. "Central Americans: At the Bottom, Struggling to Get Ahead." In *Ethnic Los Angeles,* edited by Roger Waldinger and Mehdi Bozorgmehr. New York: Russell Sage Foundation.

MASSEY, DOUGLAS S. 1995. "The New Immigration and Ethnicity in the United States." *Population and Development Review* 21 (3): 631–652.

———. 1996. "The Age of Extremes: Concentrated Affluence and Poverty in the Twenty-First Century." *Demography* 33 (4): 395–412.

MASSEY, DOUGLAS S., RAFAEL ALARCON, JORGE DURAND, and HUMBERTO GONZALEZ. 1987. *Return to Aztlan: The Social Process of International Migration from Western Mexico.* Berkeley and Los Angeles: University of California Press.

MASSEY, DOUGLAS S., and NANCY A. DENTON. 1987. "Trends in Residential Segregation of Black, Hispanics, and Asians: 1970–1980." *American Sociological Review* 52: 802–825.

MIN, PYONG GAP. 1996. *Caught in the Middle: Korean Communities in New York and Los Angeles.* Berkeley and Los Angeles: University of California Press.

MOCH, LESLIE PAGE. 1992. *Moving Europeans.* Bloomington: Indiana University Press.

MODEL, SUZANNE. 1991. "Caribbean Immigrants: A Black Success Story?" *International Migration Review* 25: 248–276.

MORAWSKA, EWA T. 1990. "The Sociology and Historiography of Immigration." In *Immigration Reconsidered: History, Sociology, and Politics,* edited by Virginia Yans-McLaughlin. New York: Oxford University Press.

MORRISON, PETER A., and IRA S. LOWRY. 1994. "A Riot of Color: The Demographic Setting." In *The Los Angeles Riot,* edited by Mark Baldassare. Boulder, CO: Westview Press.

MYRDAL, GUNNAR. 1962 [1944]. *An American Dilemma: The Negro Problem and Modern Democracy.* New York: Harper & Row.

OGBU, JOHN U. 1974. *The Next Generation: An Ethnography of Education in an Urban Neighborhood.* New York: Academic Press.

OLIVER, MELVIN L., and THOMAS M. SHAPIRO. 1995. *Black Wealth/White Wealth: A New Perspective on Racial Inequality.* New York: Routledge.

ORTIZ, VILMA. 1996. "The Mexican-Origin Population: Permanent Working Class or Emerging Middle Class?" In *Ethnic Los Angeles,* edited by Roger Waldinger and Mehdi Bozorgmehr. New York: Russell Sage Foundation.

PARK, ROBERT E. 1928. "Human Migration and the Marginal Man." *American Journal of Sociology* 33: 881–893.

PERLMANN, JOEL. 1988. *Ethnic Differences: Schooling and Social Structure among the Irish, Jews, and Blacks in an American City, 1988–1935.* New York: Cambridge University Press.

PERLMANN, JOEL, and ROGER WALDINGER. 1997. "Second Generation Decline? Immigrant Children Past and Present—A Reconsideration." *International Migration Review* 31 (4): 893–922.

PORTES, ALEJANDRO. 1995. "Economic Sociology and the Sociology of Immigration: A Conceptual Overview." In *The Economic Sociology of Immigration: Essays on Networks, Ethnicity, and Entrepreneurship,* edited by Alejandro Portes. New York: Russell Sage Foundation.

PORTES, ALEJANDRO, and DAG MACLEOD. 1996. "The Educational Progress of Children of Immigrants: The Roles of Class, Ethnicity, and School Context." *Sociology of Education* 69 (4): 255–275.

PORTES, ALEJANDRO, and RUBÉN G. RUMBAUT. 1996. *Immigrant America: A Portrait.* 2nd ed. Berkeley and Los Angeles: University of California Press.

PORTES, ALEJANDRO, and ALEX STEPICK. 1993. *City on the Edge: The Transformation of Miami.* Berkeley and Los Angeles: University of California Press.

PORTES, ALEJANDRO, and MIN ZHOU. 1992. "Gaining the Upper Hand: Economic Mobility among Immigrant and Domestic Minorities." *Ethnic and Racial Studies* 15: 491–522.

———. 1993. "The New Second Generation: Segmented Assimilation and Its Variants among Post-1965 Immigrant Youth." *Annals of the American Academy of Political and Social Science* 530 (November): 74–98.

———. 1996. "Self-Employment and the Earnings of Immigrants." *American Sociological Review* 61: 219–230.

RUMBAUT, RUBÉN G. 1995. "Vietnamese, Laotian, and Cambodian Americans." In *Asian Americans: Contemporary Trends and Issues,* edited by Pyong Gap Min. Thousand Oaks, CA: Sage Publications.

RUMBAUT, RUBÉN G., and KENJI IMA. 1988. *The Adaptation of Southeast Asian Refugee Youth: A Comparative Study.* Washington, DC: U.S. Office of Refugee Resettlement.

RUMBAUT, RUBÉN G., and ALEJANDRO PORTES, eds. 2001. *Ethnicities: Coming of Age in Immigrant America.* Berkeley and Los Angeles and New York: University of California Press and Russell Sage Foundation.

SANDBERG, N. C. 1974. *Ethnic Identity and Assimilation: The Polish-American Community.* New York: Praeger.

SMITH, JAMES P., and BARRY EDMONSTON, eds. 1997. *The New Americans: Economic, Demographic and Fiscal Effects of Immigration.* Washington, DC: National Academy Press.

STEINBERG, LAURENCE. 1996. *Beyond the Classroom.* New York: Simon & Schuster.

TANG, JOYCE. 1993. "The Career Attainment of Caucasian and Asian Engineers." *Sociological Quarterly* 34: 467–496.

TIENDA, MARTA, and D. T. LII. 1987. "Minority Concentration and Earnings Inequality: Blacks, Hispanics and Asians Compared." *American Journal of Sociology* 2: 141–165.

U.S. Census Bureau. 1993. *1990 Census of the Population: The Foreign Born Population in the United States.* Washington, DC: U.S. Government Printing Office.

U.S. Commission on Civil Rights. 1988. *The Economic Status of Americans of Asian Descent: An Exploratory Investigation.* Washington, DC: Clearinghouse Publications.

———. 1992. *Civil Rights Issues Facing Asian Americans in the 1990s: A Report.* Washington, DC: U.S. Government Printing Office.

U.S. Immigration and Naturalization Service. 1997. *Statistical Yearbook of the Immigration and Naturalization Service, 1995.* Washington, DC: U.S. Government Printing Office.

WALDINGER, ROGER. 1996. *Still the Promised City? African-Americans and New Immigrants in Postindustrial New York.* Cambridge, MA: Harvard University Press.

WALDINGER, ROGER, and MEHDI BOZORGMEHR. 1996. "The Making of a Multicultural Metropolis." In *Ethnic Los Angeles.* New York: Russell Sage Foundation.

WARNER, W. LLOYD, and LEO SROLE. 1945. *The Social Systems of American Ethnic Groups.* New Haven, CT: Yale University Press.

WARREN, ROBERT, and ELLEN PERCY KRALY. 1985. "The Elusive Exodus: Emigration from the United States." Population Trends and Public Policy Occasional Paper No. 8 (March). Washington, DC: Population Reference Bureau.

WATERS, MARY C. 1994. "Ethnic and Racial Identities of Second-Generation Black Immigrants in New York City." *International Migration Review* 28 (4): 795–820.

———. 1996. "Immigrant Families at Risk: Factors That Undermine Chances of Success." In *Immigration and the Family: Research and Policy on U.S. Immigrants,* edited by Alan Booth, Ann C. Crouter, and Nancy Landale. Hillsdale, NJ: Lawrence Erlbaum Associates.

WILSON, WILLIAM J. 1996. *When Work Disappears: The World of the New Urban Poor.* New York: Knopf.

WYTRWAL, J. A. 1961. *America's Polish Heritage: A Social History of Poles in America.* Detroit: Endurance Press.

ZANGWILL, ISRAEL. 1914. *The Melting Pot: Drama in Four Acts.* New York: Macmillan.

ZHOU, MIN. 1992. *Chinatown: The Socioeconomic Potential of an Urban Enclave.* Philadelphia: Temple University Press.

———. 1997a. "Employment Patterns of Immigrants in the U.S. Economy." Paper presented at the Conference on International Migration at Century's End: Trends and Issues, International Union for Scientific Study of the Population, Barcelona, Spain, May 7–10.

———. 1997b. "Growing up American: The Challenge Confronting Immigrant Children and Children of Immigrants." *Annual Review of Sociology* 23: 63–95.

———. 2001. "Contemporary Immigration and the Dynamics of Race and Ethnicity." In *America Becoming: Racial Trends and Their Consequences,* edited by Neil Smelser, William Julius Wilson, and Faith Mitchell. Washington, DC: National Academy Press.

ZHOU, MIN, and CARL L. BANKSTON III. 1998. *Growing up American: The Adaptation of Vietnamese Adolescents in the United States.* New York: Russell Sage Foundation.

ZHOU, MIN, and YOSHINORI KAMO. 1994. "An Analysis of Earnings Patterns for Chinese, Japanese and Non-Hispanic Whites in the United States." *Sociological Quarterly* 35 (4): 581–602.

35

WHY IRISH BECAME DOMESTICS AND ITALIANS AND JEWS DID NOT

Stephen Steinberg

Questions to Consider

In this reading, Steven Steinberg reminds us to think about three central questions when we examine the dynamics of immigration: (1) What transferable skills do individuals (or groups) bring with them? (2) How are these groups treated by the dominant group? (3) What employment opportunities are available when these groups arrive? Also, what specific historic experiences pushed Irish, but not Jewish or Italian, women into work as domestics? What allowed the children of Irish domestics to avoid this line of work?

"I hate the very words 'service' and 'servant.' We came to this country to better ourselves, and it's not bettering to have anybody ordering you around."

The Daughter of an Irish Domestic,
quoted in HELEN CAMPBELL,
Prisoners of Poverty, 1889

The familiar plaint that "it's hard to find good help these days" dates back to the earliest days of this country, when American-born women refused to work as domestics. According to one writer in 1904, "the servant class was never native American; even in Colonial days domestics came as indentured servants who ultimately moved up to higher-status jobs once their service was over."[1] In the South, of course, domestic work was a "negro job," but even in the North, as one writer commented in 1860, "domestic service certainly is held to be so

[1]Frances A. Kellor, "Immigration and Household Labor," *Charities* XII (1904). Reprinted in Lydio F. Tomasi, ed., *The Italian in America* (New York: Center for Migration Studies, 1972), 39.

degrading . . . that no natives will do it."[2] Those native women who did enter the labor market could usually find more attractive employment as teachers, bookkeepers, saleswomen, clerks, secretaries, and nurses.

While native-born Americans were loath to work as domestics, immigrants sometimes viewed domestic work more favorably. As a Norwegian wrote to a newspaper back home in 1868:

> America is an excellent country for capable and moral servant girls, because usually young American women show a decided unwillingness to submit to the kind of restraint connected with the position of a servant. . . . People are constantly looking for Norwegian and Swedish servant girls; and as they are treated very well, especially in Yankee families, there is no one whom I can so safely advise to emigrate as diligent, moral, and well-mannered young girls.[3]

As can be inferred from this passage, "the service" was not regarded with the opprobrium in Europe as in America. This can be traced to a number of demographic and economic factors.

As industrialization advanced in England, France, and other European countries, the hiring of servants became an integral part of the life-style of the new middle classes. At the same time, conditions of poverty and overpopulation in the countryside induced marginal peasants to apprentice their excess children to work as domestics in adjacent cities.[4] As one British historian notes, domestic service became "the major setting for female urban labour force participation during the transitional stages of industrialization."[5] It was often viewed as a respectable path for single young women, one that would indoctrinate them into the values and manners of the middle class, provide them with domestic skills, and in both these respects, prepare them for marriage. Thus, the prevailing cultural attitude sanctioned what was at bottom a matter of economic necessity. For poor country girls, domestic service functioned as a channel of social and economic mobility, and especially before there was a demand for female labor in the nascent textile industries, it provided rural women with an important stimulus for migrating to cities. It provided others with their only opportunity to emigrate to the United States.

From the vantage point of their employers, immigrants made ideal servants. In the first place, they could be paid little, since they had few alternative sources of employment. Perhaps for the same reason, or perhaps because they came from societies where rank was taken for granted, foreigners also tended to make more pliable and less disgruntled servants. As one observer wrote in 1904: "Although the immigrant so frequently lacks training, she is strong, asks few privileges, is content with lower wages and long hours, and has no consciousness of a social stigma attaching to her work."[6] The pariah status of immigrants also meant that their employers ran little risk that compromising details of their lives might be revealed to anyone in their own milieu.

While it is easy to see why immigrant women were in demand as servants, it might seem curious that immigrants in pursuit of the American Dream would accept such low-status employment. Actually, at

---

[2] Thomas Kettel, *Southern Wealth and Northern Profits* (New York: G. W. & J. A. Wood, 1860), 102.
[3] Theodore C. Blegen, ed., *Land of Their Choice* (St. Paul: University of Minnesota Press, 1955), 435–36.
[4] Theresa M. McBride, *The Domestic Revolution* (New York: Holmes & Meier, 1976), 38.

[5] Ibid., 14.
[6] Kellor, "Immigration and Household Labor," 39.

the end of the nineteenth century there was only one other major avenue of employment open to immigrant women. That was in the needle trades, an industry that includes dressmakers, milliners, seamstresses, and tailoresses, and could be stretched to include workers in textile mills. Both domestic labor and the needle trades were extensions of traditional female roles, in that they involved work that was similar to household tasks. Domestics, of course, were employed to do the household work of other women. In the case of the needle trades, women were engaged in clothing production that once had been carried out in the home, but by the end of the nineteenth century had been mechanized and transferred to small shops and factories. Among immigrant women in the labor force in 1900, a solid majority worked in these two occupations.[7]

However, women of different ethnic backgrounds differed greatly in their propensity to work as domestics or as workers in the needle trades. Though some Irish women were employed in mills scattered across small industrial towns in the Northeast, the vast majority worked as domestics. The proportion varied, depending on time and place, but its high point occurred during the famine migration of the 1850s. Of the 29,470 domestics that show up in the 1855 census of New York City, 23,386 were Irish.[8] Though Irish were about one-quarter of New York's population, they were over three-quarters of the domestic labor force. Germans were the other major immigrant group during this period, but the German proportion in the domestic labor force was exactly the same as in the city's population—15 percent. Not only were most domestics Irish, but it was also the case that virtually all Irish women who worked did so as domestics.

Of course, the peak of Irish immigration preceded by several decades the burgeoning of the garment industry. However, even after the waves of Jewish and Italian immigration at the end of the century, it was still the Irish who dominated the ranks of domestic workers. According to figures collected by the United States Immigration Commission in 1900, 71 percent of immigrant Irish women in the labor force were classified as "domestic and personal" workers; 54 percent were specifically classified as "servants and waitresses." In contrast, only 9 percent of Italian female workers and 14 percent of Jewish female workers were classified as "servants and waitresses." And whereas 38 percent of Italian women and 41 percent of Jewish women were in the needle trades, the figure for Irish was only 8 percent.[9]

How is this ethnic division to be explained? Why were Italian and Jewish women generally able to avoid working at one of the most menial and low-status jobs in the labor force, and why should so many Irish flock to it? As with occupations connoting success, social scientists have stressed the operation of cultural factors in explaining why some groups were more likely than others to become domestics.

For example, in *Blood of My Blood,* Richard Gambino implies that Italian women never deigned to work as domestics. As he writes:

> No matter how poor, the Italian-American woman to this day does not work as a domestic. For to work in the house of another family (sometimes an

[7]*Report of the United States Immigration Commission,* Vol. I (Washington, DC: Government Printing Office, 1911), 830–38.

[8]Robert Ernst, *Immigrant Life in New York City, 1825–1863* (Port Washington, NY: Ira J. Friedman, 1949), 219.

[9]*Report of the United States Immigration Commission,* 834–36.

absolute economic necessity in the old land) is seen as a usurpation of family loyalty by her family *and by her*. And if one loses one's place in *la via vecchia*, there is no self-respect. In American history, there is no Italian counterpart of Irish, German, black, Spanish-speaking, English, Scandinavian, and French maids.[10]

How is it that Italians were able to escape a fate that befell all these other groups? Gambino implies that a stubborn ethnic pride, buttressed by a strong family system, protected Italian women from the indignities of domestic labor. Would he then suggest that other groups were lacking in these traits? And if domestic labor was "an absolute economic necessity" in Italy, as Gambino says, why was this not so in America?

In her recent history of Italians in Buffalo, New York, Virginia Yans-McLaughlin also suggests that family pride, reinforced by a strong patriarchal tradition, protected Italian women from having to work as domestics:

> Truly enterprising women seeking year-round wages could become domestics; but the Italian women were more likely to take in boarders because the men rarely permitted their wives to work as maids, cleaning women, or factory hands. The Italian ideal was to keep women at home.[11]

For Yans-McLaughlin, the "decision" not to work as domestics constituted an "occupational choice," one that was governed by "cultural tradition." As she put it: "Culture, then, acted as an interface between family and economy, dictating which options were acceptable and which were not."[12]

Acting on the same assumptions, other writers have suggested that the Irish lacked the cultural repugnance that supposedly deterred Italians and Jews from working as domestics. As one historian comments: "The Irish community viewed domestic service favorably and no ethnic taboos or language barriers prevented Irish women from working in other people's homes."[13]

Are these writers correct in positing ethnic and cultural factors as the explanation of why some ethnic women became domestics and others did not? On reflection, it makes little sense to take the Irish "tolerance" of domestic work at face value. This is hardly a calling that any group would define as an ideal worth striving for, and, for better or worse, the idea that woman's place is in the home is no less characteristic of Irish than of Italians and Jews. As will be seen, it was not a different cultural norm but a different set of historical circumstances that explains why Irish became domestics and Italians and Jews did not.

Though both domestics and needle-trade workers were engaged in traditionally female occupations, there was one fundamental difference between them: needle-trade workers returned to their homes when the workday was finished, whereas domestics typically lived in with a family, usually occupying a single small room in the rear of the residence specifically designed for this purpose. Although some domestics worked in households where there were other servants and a clear-cut division of labor, most households employed a single domestic. Her daily regimen consisted of preparing and serving three meals, doing household cleaning according to a prescribed weekly schedule, and being "on call" for whatever demands might be made outside of her routine duties. The

---

[10]Richard Gambino, *Blood of My Blood* (Garden City, NY: Anchor, 1975), 14.
[11]Virginia Yans-McLaughlin, *Family and Community* (Ithaca, NY: Cornell University Press, 1977), 53.
[12]Ibid.

[13]Barbara Klaczynska, "Why Women Work: A Comparison of Various Groups—Philadelphia, 1910–1930," *Labor History* 17 (Winter 1976):81.

average day began at six in the morning and lasted until late into the evening. Most domestics worked seven days a week, though a generous employer might give servants Sunday and perhaps one evening off.[14]

By comparison, needle-trade workers clearly labored under more adverse physical conditions. Indeed, Marx and Engels singled out textile factories as typifying the most inhumane and brutalizing aspects of capitalism. Sweatshops and factories were notoriously dirty, crowded, and often dangerous, and the work itself had a relentless tedium. For meager wages, workers were reduced to repeating a single minute task under the watchful eye of a boss or foreman, and the average workweek lasted between fifty and sixty hours. In her 1919 study of *Italian Women in Industry*, Louise Odencrantz reported that a typical workday began at eight and went until six; Saturday was sometimes, though not always, a short day.[15]

Yet factory workers had decided advantages over domestics. The fact that they returned to their own homes necessarily limited the authority of their bosses to the workplace, and even there, once unions were organized, workers could place restraints on their employers and strike for better wages. Degraded as they were by the conditions that prevailed in textile factories, they still belonged to a class of free labor, and as the early garment-trade unions demonstrated, could realistically hope to achieve a measure of dignity.

Domestic work, in contrast, had the earmarks of feudalism. Lacking a separation between work and home, the domestic was, in effect, bonded to her employer, and scarcely an aspect of her life escaped scrutiny and regulation. The domestic had virtually no time, and except for the limited privacy of her maid's room, no space that she could claim as her own. Isolated from other workers, she was powerless to change the conditions of her employment. To be sure, she was nominally free to quit, but lacking a home of her own, she could hardly risk the perils of being unemployed.

Furthermore, the nature of her work involved an exploitation of the whole person. Motivated solely by profit, the factory owner took little interest in the personal lives of his workers so long as they executed their assigned tasks. Though the textile worker might be reduced to a commodity, paradoxically, her inner self was left intact. But the employers of a domestic need to be sure that the person with whom they share the intimacies of their lives, and to whom they entrust their children, is decent, kind, affable, well mannered, and so on. In this sense, it is not just labor that is purchased, but the laborer as well.[16]

Domestic servants implicitly understood the feudalistic aspects of their employment, as was revealed by a survey of over 5,000 domestics conducted in 1889 by an enterprising professor from Vassar College, Lucy Maynard Salmon.[17] Though only 1,000 responded to Salmon's survey, they provide valuable insight into the private sentiments of domestic laborers during this period.

---

[14] Daniel Katzman, *Seven Days a Week* (New York: Oxford University Press, 1978), 110–12.

[15] Louise C. Odencrantz, *Italian Women in Industry* (New York: Russell Sage Foundation, 1919), 317.

[16] Lewis Coser has suggested that the servant is engulfed by a "greedy institution" that demands total allegiance. As he writes: "The master's family operates as a 'greedy organization' in relation to the servant. It does not rest content with claiming a segment of the time, commitment, and energy of the servant, as is the case with other occupational arrangements in the modern world, but demands—though it does not always receive—full-time allegiance. Moreover, while in other occupational roles the incumbent's duties are largely independent of personal relationships with this or that client or employer, particularistic elements loom very large in the master-servant relationship." *Greedy Institutions* (New York: Free Press, 1974), 69.

[17] Lucy Maynard Salmon, *Domestic Service* (New York: Macmillan, 1901).

A common complaint among Salmon's respondents was that they felt lonely. This may seem curious since domestics lived in such close quarters to others and often developed personal ties with the families they served. However, one of Salmon's respondents eloquently describes the loneliness of the household domestic:

> Ladies wonder how their girls can complain of loneliness in a house full of people, but oh! it is the worst kind of loneliness—their share is but the work of the house, they do not share in the pleasures and delights of a home. One must remember that there is a difference between a *house,* a place of shelter, and a *home,* a place where all your affections are centered. Real love exists between my employer and myself, yet at times I grow almost desperate from the sense of being cut off from those pleasures to which I had always been accustomed.[18]

Another complaint among Salmon's respondents was that they had little time of their own; several said bluntly that they felt like prisoners. This feeling was articulated by an Irish woman in another 1889 survey who explained why she chose to work in a paper box factory instead of "the service":

> It's freedom that we want when the day's work is done. I know some nice girls . . . that make more money and dress better and everything for being in service. They're waitresses, and have Thursday afternoon out and part of every other Sunday. But they're never sure of one minute that's their own when they're in the house. Our day is ten hours long, but when it's done it's done, and we can do what we like with the evenings. That's what I've heard

from every nice girl that ever tried service. You're never sure that your soul's your own except when you are out of the house, and I couldn't stand that a day. Women care just as much for freedom as men do. Of course they don't get so much, but I know I'd fight for mine.[19]

When Salmon asked her respondents why more women do not choose housework as regular employment, the most common answer alluded to a loss of pride. Above all else, they bristled at being called "servants," a term that has a spasmodic history.

During Colonial times "servant" referred to indentured servants, but fell into disuse after the Revolution, apparently reflecting the democratic spirit of that period. Instead the term "help" was used, though "servant" was still applied to blacks in the South. With the influx of Irish and other foreigners in the second half of the nineteenth century, however, "servant" again came into vogue. Salmon herself acknowledged that it was "a mark of social degradation" that discouraged women from entering this occupation. There were efforts to substitute the term "maid" or "working housekeeper," but according to Salmon, this "excited little more than ridicule."[20]

A less offensive nomenclature, however, could hardly disguise the stigma of servitude that was inescapably associated with domestic work. It is endemic to a master-servant relationship that even friendly gestures on the part of employers inevitably assume a patronizing cast, and unwittingly frustrate the servant's need to maintain a modicum of social distance. For example, Salmon's respondents complained that their employers took the liberty of addressing them by their Christian names. "It may

---

[18]Ibid., 151.

[19]Helen Campbell, *Prisoners of Poverty* (Boston: Roberts Brothers, 1889), 224.
[20]Salmon, *Domestic Service,* 156.

seem a trifling matter," Salmon commented, "yet the fact remains that domestic employees are the only class of workers, except day laborers, who are thus addressed."[21] Domestics also objected to the cap and apron as still another badge of social inferiority.

What kinds of women, then, were willing to submit to the indignities of a cap and apron, and what kinds opted instead for the drudgery of the sweatshop? And why should Irish go one way, and Italians and Jews another?

The answer, in a nutshell, has to do with the fact that comparatively large numbers of Irish female immigrants were unmarried and unattached to families. Italian and Jewish women rarely immigrated unless they were accompanied or preceded by husbands or fathers, but it was common for Irish women to migrate on their own. For an unattached woman in an alien country—impoverished, uprooted, and often isolated from friends and family—domestic work had practical appeal. At least, it provided them with a roof over their head and a degree of personal security until they were able to forge a more desirable set of circumstances.

The reasons why Irish women were far more likely than either Italians or Jews to be single has to do with conditions in their respective countries of origin. In the case of Italians, an economic crisis in agriculture induced men to emigrate in pursuit of industrial labor and higher wages, and there was an overwhelming preponderance of males in the immigration pool. Between 1899 and 1910, nearly two million Italian men, but fewer than half a million Italian women entered the United States.[22] In some cases the men planned to send for their families once they had accumulated some savings; more often, they planned to return to Italy. An excerpt from a 1903 study on the Italian colonies in New York City describes this immigration pattern:

> The Italian population in this country is predominantly male. The reason for this is plainly seen. In nine cases out of ten, the father of a family decides to emigrate to America; he would like to take with him his wife and children, but since the least cost of a steerage ticket is something over $30, it becomes an impossibility for the entire family to come at once. The result is the wife and children are left behind and the father comes. On the other hand, few women indeed come here of their own accord—they are brought or sent for by husband or prospective husband.[23]

Thus, few Italian women immigrated as independent breadwinners. Invariably, a husband or family member preceded them, sometimes by many years, and by the time the women arrived, they were already part of families that had established at least a tenuous economic foothold. Married women generally stayed out of the job market altogether, though some took in lodgers or homework. Those women who did enter the job market generally found employment in the manufacturing sectors, especially in the expanding needle trades. In other words, neither economic necessity nor circumstances forced Italian women into domestic labor.

In Italy the situation was different. According to a study of women's employment in Milan in 1881, 23,000 women, or 20 percent of all female workers, were employed as domestics.[24] If few Italian women

---

[21] Ibid.
[22] *Report of the United States Immigration Commission*, 97.

[23] Antonio Mangano, "The Italian Colonies of New York City," in *Italians in the City* (New York: Arno Press, 1975), 13.
[24] Louise A. Tilly, "Urban Growth, Industrialization, and Women's Employment in Milan, Italy, 1881–1911," *Journal of Urban History* 3 (August 1977):476–78.

worked as domestics in America, this can hardly be attributed to a distinctively Italian attitude toward women and the home.

Immigrant Jewish women, like their Italian counterparts, rarely immigrated alone, though for very different reasons. Eastern European Jews were refugees from religious persecution and political violence, and unlike Italians, those who left harbored no thoughts of returning. As a consequence, Jews typically immigrated as families. Whereas there were nearly four Italian men for every woman among those who immigrated between 1899 and 1910, Jews had a much more even sexual balance—608,000 men and 467,000 women.[25] That Jews tended to immigrate as families is also indicated by the fact that a quarter of all Jewish immigrants during this period were children under fourteen years of age. Thus, most Jewish women came to America with husbands or fathers. Few were independent breadwinners, and when they did work, they usually found employment in the burgeoning garment industry. Often they worked in small shops with other family members.

The demographic character of Irish immigration was different from that of either Italians or Jews in that it included large numbers of single women. Unfortunately, no data exist on the marital status of immigrants, and consequently there is no exact measure of how many were unmarried. However, a rough estimate can be gleaned from examining the sex ratios of the various immigrant pools. In contrast to the situation among Italians and Jews, there were actually more women than men among Irish immigrants around the turn of the century. Specifically, among Irish arriving between 1899 and 1910, there were 109 women for every 100 men. Among Jews,

there were 77 women for every 100 men; among Italians, only 27 women for every 100 men.[26] Not only were Irish women far less likely to be married when they immigrated, but the sex ratio did not favor their finding Irish husbands after they arrived.

A similar situation existed earlier in the century as well. For example, according to the 1860 census, New York's Irish-born population consisted of 87,000 males, but 117,000 females. Not surprisingly, the marriage rates of Irish in American cities were generally lower than those for other groups throughout the nineteenth century. Hence, from a demographic standpoint, Irish women were an ideal source of live-in domestics. That they also spoke English made them all the more desirable.

Further impetus was given to the immigration of Irish domestics by agencies that sprang up on both sides of the Atlantic. Beginning in the 1850s, a number of British emigration societies were organized to encourage and assist the emigration of surplus population, especially single women of childbearing age who were unlikely to emigrate on their own. They bore imposing names like the London Female Emigration Society, the British Ladies Emigration Society, the Girls' Friendly Society, and the Travelers' Aid Society for Girls and Women. With philanthropic pretense, these societies recruited indigent women, paid for their steerage, escorted them to the port of embarkation, and dispatched them to the New World where they were commonly placed in private households as domestic servants.[27] Not all the recipients of this dubious largess were Irish, and many were sent to Canada and other British colonies. Nevertheless, the very existence of these societies

---

[25] *Report of the United States Immigration Commission*, 97.

[26] Ibid.

[27] Stanley C. Johnson, *A History of Emigration from the United Kingdom to North America, 1763–1812* (London: Frank Case, 1966 [1913]), chap. 11, 264.

testifies to the popular currency given to the idea of sending poor young girls across the Atlantic to work as domestic servants.

There were also employment agencies in the United States that recruited and transported young foreign girls to work as domestics in New York. According to one account, in 1904 there were as many as 300 "intelligence offices" in New York City alone.[28] To some extent, then, "Bridget" was the creation of employment agencies that engaged in this human commerce and collected fees for supplying households with Irish domestics.

There is still other evidence that many Irish women emigrated with the express purpose of finding work as domestics. Among immigrants arriving between 1899 and 1910, 40 percent of the Irish were classified as servants; in contrast, the figure for both Italians and Jews was only 6 percent.[29] Only 14 percent of Irish immigrants were classified as having "no occupation," a category that consisted mostly of children and women who considered themselves homemakers. The comparable figure for Southern Italians was 23 percent; for Jews it was 45 percent. From this it is reasonable to assume that most Irish women who immigrated around the turn of the century planned to enter the labor force, presumably in the servant occupation that they named when asked their occupation at the port of entry.

The reasons why so many young women left Ireland just to become servants in America must be traced to a series of economic crises in the nineteenth century, and the social and cultural changes that ensued. The infamous potato famine of the late 1840s was only one such crisis. Almost as important was a process of land consolidation that, between 1849 and 1851 alone,

involved the dispossession of some million people from the land and the physical destruction of their homes.[30] To make matters worse, English colonial policy had reduced Ireland to a producer of wool and food, and the island had no industrial base that might have absorbed its surplus rural population. Irish emigration reached its peak during the potato famine, but it was already gaining momentum before the famine and it continued at substantial levels long after. Incredibly, Ireland's population in 1900 was almost half of what it had been in 1850.[31]

Ireland's prolonged economic depression played havoc with the family system. Traditionally, marriage was bound up with the inheritance of land, and as land became more scarce, there was a tendency to postpone marriage. For nearly a century after the famine, as one recent study has shown, "the average age at marriage increased, the marriage rate decreased, and the percentage who remained permanently celibate increased."[32] In 1891, for example, two-thirds of men and half the women between the ages of 25 and 34 were single. Even among those between 35 and 44, a third of the men and a quarter of the women were single. One out of six of each sex never married.

The impact of these trends was especially harsh on women, since they were forced onto a labor market that was hardly favorable to them. Against this background it is easy to understand why young women, even more often than men, decided to emigrate. And given their vulnerability as single women in an alien country, as well as the limited alternatives that existed, it is

---

[28] Kellor, "Immigration and Household Labor," 39.

[29] *Report of the United States Immigration Commission,* 173.

[30] Oscar Handlin, *Boston's Immigrants* (New York: Atheneum, 1968), 46.

[31] Walter F. Willcox, ed., *International Migrations,* Vol. II (New York: National Bureau of Economic Research, 1931), 274.

[32] Richard Stivers, *A Hair of the Dog* (University Park: Pennsylvania State University Press, 1976), 56.

TABLE 1   Occupations of First- and Second-Generation Irish, Italian, and Jewish Female Breadwinners, 1900

Ethnic Group	Irish		Italian		Jews	
Generation	*First*	*Second*	*First*	*Second*	*First*	*Second*
Occupation*						
Domestic & personal service (includes waitresses)	71%	25%	21%	15%	18%	21%
Needle trades & textiles	16	29	48	33	44	26
Other manufacturing	6	17	20	28	23	17
Saleswomen, bookkeepers, clerks, etc.	5	19	10	20	14	31
Professional	2	10	1	4	1	5
	100%	100%	100%	100%	100%	100%
Number of cases	(245,792)	(388,108)	(20,307)	(5,751)	(35,030)	(5,781)

*The small number of cases whose occupations could not be classified are excluded from the percentages.

Source: Adapted from the *Reports of the United States Immigration Commission,* Vol. 1 (Washington, DC: Government Printing Office, 1911), 834–36.

also easy to understand why "the service" provided at least a temporary solution to their dilemma. It made emigration possible, provided them with food and lodging, and carried them over until such time as they could find either husbands or more desirable employment.

If historical circumstances and economic necessity forced immigrant Irish women to accept work as domestics, this was not a trend that continued into the second generation. Table 1 reports the occupations in 1900 of first- and second-generation Irish, Italian, and Jewish women. The most striking observation is that whereas 71 percent of immigrant Irish women were classified as working in "domestic and personal service," only 25 percent of their children were so classified. Thus, by the second generation, Irish were not much more likely than other groups to work as domestics.

What the female children of Irish immigrants did was to follow in the footsteps of Italian and Jewish immigrants. As can also be seen in Table 1, by 1900 they were entering the needle trades and other branches of manufacturing, precisely at the point

when second-generation Italian and Jewish women were abandoning these occupations in favor of work as saleswomen, bookkeepers, clerks, and the like. In a sense, Irish women started out on a lower occupational threshold than either Italians or Jews, and remained one generational step behind. But as far as domestic service is concerned, by the second generation few women in any of these groups were so employed.

Culture and family morality have little or nothing to do with explaining why Irish became domestics and Italians and Jews did not. It was not that Irish husbands were less protective of their wives, but rather that immigrant Irish women were less likely to have husbands in the first place. It was not that as a group Irish had less aversion to working in other people's homes, but that their choices were far more limited. For these courageous women who migrated alone to the New World, domestic work was merely a temporary expedient to allow them to forge new lives. That the Irish had no cultural tolerance for domestic work is pointed up by the fact that they fled "the service" just as quickly as they could establish families of their own or gain access to more desirable employment. If other groups were spared the indignities of domestic labor, it is

not that they had better cultural defenses or a superior moral code, but because their circumstances did not compel them to place economic survival ahead of their pride.

36

THE ARAB IMMIGRANT EXPERIENCE

Michael W. Suleiman

Questions to Consider

Since 9/11, the media seem to have newly discovered the Arab-American population in the United States, even though this group has been a significant presence in this country for almost one hundred and fifty years. This article maps Arab migration to the United States and the process of "Americanization" that this group, like almost all immigrant groups to this country, has experienced. In this article, Michael Suleiman suggests that an ambiguous racial status and racism were used to deny Arab immigrants of citizenship. How and why did this happen?

Introduction

In 1977, William E. Leuchtenburg, the prominent American historian, remarked, "From the perspective of the American historian, the most striking aspect of the relationship between Arab and American cultures is that, to Americans, the Arabs are

a people who have lived outside of history."[1] Professor Leuchtenburg could have just as accurately made the same observation about Arabs in America.

Ignorance about Arab Americans among North Americans at large means that, before looking at more detailed accounts of the Arab-American experience, we may benefit from a quick overview of Arab immigration to North America and what the Arab-American communities here have been like.

There have been two major waves of Arab immigration to North America. The first lasted from the 1870s to World War II and the second from World War II to the present. Members of the two waves of immigrants had somewhat different characteristics and faced different challenges in the social and political arena. Any examination of the immigrant communities must take into account these differences. As we shall see, the two communities began to come together in the 1960s, especially after the 1967 Arab-Israeli war,[2] and this rapprochement must also be taken into account.

The term "Arab Americans" refers to the immigrants to North America from the Arabic-speaking countries of the Middle East and their descendants. The Arabic-speaking countries today include Algeria, Bahrain, Egypt, Iraq, Jordan, Kuwait, Lebanon, Libya, Mauritania, Morocco, Oman, pre-1948 Palestine and the Palestinians, Qatar, Saudi Arabia, Sudan, Syria, Tunisia, United Arab Emirates, and Yemen. Somalia and Djibouti are also members of The League of Arab States and have some Arabic-speaking populations. Most Arab immigrants of the first wave came from the Greater Syria region, especially present-day Lebanon, and were overwhelmingly Christian; later immigrants came from all parts of the Arab world, but especially from Palestine, Lebanon, Syria, Egypt, Iraq, and Yemen, and had large numbers of Muslims among them. Although most Muslim Arab immigrants have been Sunni (reflecting the population in the region), there is a substantial Shi'a minority. Druze started immigrating in small numbers late in the nineteenth century.

Immigrants from the Arabic-speaking countries have been referred to and have referred to themselves by different names at different times, including Arabs or Arabians, but until World War II the designation Syrian or Syrian-Lebanese was used most often. The changeability of the name may indicate the absence of a definite and enduring identity, an issue that is discussed later. For the purposes of this chapter, the various names are used interchangeably, but the community primarily is referred to as Arab or Arab American.[3]

It is impossible to determine the exact number of Arab immigrants to North America, because U.S. and Canadian immigration officials have at different times used different classification schemes. Until 1899 in the United States, for instance, immigration statistics lumped the Arabs with Greeks, Armenians, and Turks. For this and other reasons, only estimates can be provided.

According to U.S. immigration figures, which generally are considered to be low, about 130,000 Arabs had immigrated to the United States by the late 1930s.[4] Estimates of the size of the Arab-American community by scholars and community leaders vary widely. A conservative estimate is that there were approximately 350,000 persons of Arab background in the United States on the eve of World War II.[5] In the 1990s, the size of the Arab community in the United States has been estimated at less than one million to the most frequently cited figure of two and one-half to three million.[6]

Numerous reasons have been given for the first wave of Arab immigration to America, which began in large numbers in the 1880s, but the reasons usually fall into two categories: push and pull factors, with the push factors accorded greater weight.

Most scholars argue that the most important reasons for emigration were economic necessity and personal advancement.[7] According to this view, although the economy in geographic or Greater Syria (a term encompassing the present-day countries and peoples of Syria, Lebanon, the Palestinians, Israel, Jordan, and possibly Iraq) registered some clear gains in the late nineteenth and early twentieth centuries, this progress was uneven in its impact and did not manifest itself in a sustained manner until "after emigration to the New World began to gather momentum."[8] The economy of Mount Lebanon suffered two major crippling blows in the mid-1800s. The first was the opening of the Suez Canal, which sidetracked world traffic from Syria to Egypt and made the trip to the Far East so easy and fast that Japanese silk became a major competitor for the Lebanese silk industry. The second blow came in the 1890s, when Lebanese vineyards were invaded by phylloxera and practically ruined.[9]

Also contributing to the economic stress in the Syrian hinterland was a rapid increase in population without a commensurate increase in agricultural or industrial productivity. Many families found that the subsistence economy could support only one child, who eventually inherited the farm or household. Other male children had to fend for themselves, and emigration to a New World of great wealth became an irresistible option.[10]

Many Lebanese Christians, who constituted most of the early Arab arrivals in North America, emphasize religious persecution and the lack of political and civil freedom as the main causes of their emigration from lands ruled by an oppressive Ottoman regime.[11] Under Ottoman rule, Christians in the Syrian province were not accorded equal status with their Muslim neighbors. They were subjected to many restrictions on their behavior and often suffered persecution. These oppressive conditions worsened and discriminatory actions occurred more often as the Ottoman rulers became weaker and their empire earned the title of the "Sick Man of Europe." As the power of the sultan declined, the local rulers began to assert greater authority and power, which they at times used to suppress and oppress further their subjects, particularly Christians. In part, this persecution took place in response to the increased power and prestige of "Christian" Europe and the encroachment of its rulers on Ottoman sovereignty. This effect, combined with the Christian population's desire for greater equality, threatened the Muslim public's sense of security. Like the "poor white trash" of the American South at the time of the Civil War and the Civil Rights Movement, the Muslim population in the Syrian province was poor and oppressed—but it still enjoyed a social status that was superior to that of the non-Muslims, particularly the Christians. The threat of losing that "high" status made many Muslims susceptible to suggestions from local Ottoman rulers that their Christian neighbors were the cause of rather than companions in their troubles. The worsened social and economic conditions in Syria in the mid-1800s and the beginning of the disintegration of feudalism, especially among the Druze, produced social turmoil that erupted in sectarian riots in which thousands of Christians perished.[12] Many Christian Lebanese, especially Maronites, cite the 1860 disturbances and massacres as the main factor contributing to the exodus from their homeland.

In addition to the economic, political, and social causes of the early Arab immigration to North America, some incidental factors should be cited. Among these are improved transportation and communication facilities worldwide, development of steam navigation that made the sea voyage safer and shorter, and aggressiveness of agents of the steamship companies in recruiting new immigrant passengers. Although American missionaries often actively discouraged Syrians or Arabs from migrating to the United States, their very presence as model Americans, their educational activities, and their reports about American life ignited a desire, especially among the graduates of American schools and colleges in Syria, to emigrate to America.

After the feasibility and profitability of immigration to the United States and to "America" in general were well established, chain migration became the norm, with immigrants making it possible for the ambitious and the disgruntled in the old homeland to seek newer horizons. Those wanting to escape military service in the Ottoman army and those craving freedom from oppression and the liberty to speak and publish without censorship or reprisal left their homeland quickly and stealthily and sought what they thought would be a temporary refuge in America.

The Early Arab Community in America

Before World War II, most Arabs in America were Christians who came from the Mount Lebanon region of geographic Syria. Especially until the turn of the century, these travelers were mainly poor, uneducated, and illiterate in any language. They were not trained for a particular profession. As unskilled workers, after they learned the rudiments of the English language, they could work in factories and mines. However, such jobs were taxing and monotonous and, most importantly, did not offer opportunities for the fast accumulation of wealth, which was the primary objective of these early Arab arrivals. Farming presented them with the added hardships of isolation, loneliness, and severe weather conditions. Peddling therefore was an attractive alternative. It did not require much training, capital, or knowledge of English. With a few words of English learned on the run, a suitcase (*Kashshi*) full of notions (e.g., needles, thread, lace) provided by a better-established fellow Lebanese or other Arab supplier, probably a relative who helped bring them to the New World, many new arrivals often were on the road hawking their wares only a day or so after they landed in America. Success in peddling required thrift, hard work, very long hours, the stamina to endure harsh travel conditions (mostly walking the countryside on

unpaved roads), and not infrequently, the taunting and insults from children or disgruntled customers. These conditions were made tolerable for most early Arab arrivals by their vision of a brighter economic future and the concomitant prestige they and their families would eventually acquire in the old country. When they could afford to do so, they switched to the "luxury" of a horse and buggy and later to a dry-goods store.[13]

Before World War I, Arabs in North America thought of themselves as sojourners, as people who were in, but not part of, American society. Their politics reflected and emulated the politics of their original homeland in substance and style, because they were only *temporarily* away from home. In New York, *Kawkab America* (*Kawkab Amirka*), the first Arabic-language newspaper established in North America, declared in its very first issue its unequivocal support for the Ottoman sultan, whose exemplary virtues it detailed at length.[14] All other newspapers had to define in one way or another their attitude toward and their relationship with the Ottoman authorities. Although *Kawkab America* was pro-Ottoman, at least initially, *Al-Ayam* (*al-Ayyam*) was the most vehement opponent of the Ottoman authorities, a role it later shared with *Al-Musheer* (*al-Mushir*).[15] It excoriated the cruelty and corruption of Ottoman rulers, especially in the Mount Lebanon region. It also called for rebellion against the Turkish tyrants and urged its readers to exercise their freedom in America to call for freedom back home. Other newspapers, including *Al-Hoda* (*al-Huda*) and *Meraat-ul-Gharb* (*Mir'at al-gharb*), fell between these two extremes of total support or clear rejection of Ottoman authority.

The orientation of early Arab Americans toward their homeland meant that their political activities were also focused on issues that were important in their country or village of origin. There was communal solidarity, but the community was a collective of several communities. The sectarian and regional disputes that separated the Arabs back home were also salient in this "temporary" residence. The newspapers they established were in the main socializing agencies conveying the messages of their sectarian leadership. Because the Orthodox already had their *Kawkab America, Al-Hoda* was set up to represent and speak for the Maronites. Later, *Al-Bayan (al-Bayan)* proclaimed itself the newspaper of the Druze.[16] Within each community there were rivalries and competing newspapers, each claiming to be the best defender or representative of its sect.

World War I was a watershed event for Arabs in North America, cutting them off from their people back home. This separation from the homeland became almost complete with the introduction of very restrictive quota systems in the United States and Canada after World War I, which practically cut off emigration from Arab regions. These developments intensified the community's sense of isolation and separation, simultaneously enhancing its sense of solidarity. One consequence was a strengthening of the assimilationist trend—a trend already reinforced by the American-born children of these Arab immigrants.

The substance and style of the Arab community's politics changed after the war, with a clear realization that they had become part of American society. Intersectarian conflicts became less intense and fewer in number. Calls for unity were heeded more often. For instance, Syrian-Lebanese clubs formed regional federations that joined together to form a national federation.[17] A process of socialization into American politics resulted in greater participation in voting and party membership and in public and political service at local or state levels. "Syrian" Republican and Democratic Clubs were formed in the United States, and

the arena for political competition changed as the Arab community became part of the American body politic. There also emerged a clear change in matters of style—generally for the better. By the 1930s and 1940s, conflicts became fewer and somewhat less personal, and the language of discourse became much less offensive.

Whereas first-generation Arabs in America managed as best they could in an alien environment, their children were thoroughly immersed in American society and culture—and their first or only language was English. Consequently, English-language newspapers and journals were established to cater to young Americans of Arab heritage.[18] Eastern churches began to translate some of the liturgy and conduct part of the services in English to prevent the loss of members,[19] although many members left the church nonetheless. Some intellectuals, including some of the most celebrated Arab-American writers and poets, took advantage of the blessings of freedom and democracy in North America to attack the tyranny and corruption of the clergy, especially in the old homeland but also in America. Some also expressed atheistic or agnostic views, and others left their old churches and joined new ones.[20]

As Arabs assimilated in American society, they also worked harder for a better image of themselves and their people in the old homeland. More effort was spent on campaigns to inform Americans about the rich Arab heritage. In the political arena, especially in the United States, there were many, serious efforts to get the government to support foreign policy positions favored by the Arab community, especially in regard to Palestine. During World War I and its aftermath, the main political preoccupation of the Arabic-speaking groups in North America was to achieve the liberation of their homelands from Ottoman rule and to provide economic assistance to their starving relatives, especially in the Mount Lebanon region. To accomplish these objectives, their leaders set up relief committees, raised funds, and sent money and supplies whenever it was possible to do so. They also urged Arab young men in the United States to join the American armed forces to help their new country and to liberate their old homeland.[21] Leaders organized campaigns to have their people buy American Liberty bonds to help with the war effort.[22]

After the war, the Arabs in America were divided over the destiny of the regions liberated from Ottoman rule. In general, there was a strong sentiment among the Maronites to support French control over Syria and Lebanon under the League of Nations' Mandate.[23] Others argued for complete independence, viewing France as a new occupying power.[24] On the question of Palestine, there was general agreement in support of the Palestinian-Arab population and for eventual, if not immediate, independence. There was widespread opposition to Zionism as a movement bent on establishing a Jewish state there.[25] Arabs in America showed their support for the Palestinians through lectures, publications, fund raising, and political lobbying, especially with U.S. government officials.[26]

Until World War I, Arabs in North America may be considered sojourners exhibiting many traits of a middleman minority—a community whose members primarily engage in one particular specialized activity such as migrant farm work or peddling. Substantial numbers of Arabs in America engaged in commerce, most often beginning as peddlers commissioned by their own countrymen. Their objective was to make the greatest amount of money in the shortest possible time to help their families in the old country and eventually to retire in comfort in their village or neighborhood. In the meantime, they spent as little as possible of their income in America, often living in

crowded tenements and, while on the road, in barns or shacks to avoid expensive hotel costs. They did not live rounded lives, allowing themselves no luxuries and finding contentment and solace in family life. Because they could pull up stakes anytime, they sought liquidity in their economic enterprises. Long-term investments were avoided. For that reason, in addition to other advantages, they preferred peddling, dry goods stores, restaurants, the professions, and a cottage industry in lace and needlework. In all of these activities, their primary contacts were with other Arab Americans, especially relatives or people from the same town, religious sect, or geographic region.[27] They developed few lasting relationships with "Americans." *Al-Nizala*, the term the Arab-American community used to refer to itself, is a name that clearly describes its status and purpose. It means a temporary settlement, and it was used in contrast to "the Americans" to indicate the alien or stranger status of Arabs in America. At first, Arabs in America formed their own residential colonies, especially in New York and Boston. Even when they did not, they encouraged within-group marriage, frequently praising its virtues and especially pointing out the disadvantages of marrying "American" girls. In other words, they resisted assimilation, even after their intellectuals began to urge acculturation to life in America.[28]

Arabs in America, sharing an attitude common to other middleman or sojourner communities, were charged with being "clannish, alien, and unassimilable."[29] Such attitudes were fairly common among influential American journalists and public officials, who also viewed Arabs as inferior to whites. In the economic field, Arabs were sometimes seen as parasites, because they allegedly did not engage in any productive industry, merely being engaged in trade. They were sometimes attacked as a drain on the American economy, because they sent part of their income back home.[30]

The Process of Americanization

Arab immigrants soon found out that the land of opportunity was also strewn with hardship and an "unwelcome" mat. In response to insults and charges of inferiority, they did occasionally defend themselves.[31] However, to add injury to insult, the U.S. and Canadian authorities began to claim that Arabs had no right to naturalization and citizenship because they allegedly were Asian and did not belong to the white race.[32] This problem of racial identification and citizenship traumatized the Arabic-speaking community. In their attempt to resolve this crisis, the "Syrians" searched for their roots and found them in their *Arab* background, which ensured them Caucasian racial status and therefore eligibility for U.S. citizenship—or so they argued.[33] Beginning in 1909, Arabic-speaking individuals from geographic Syria began to be challenged in their citizenship petitions. It was not until 1914, however, that George Dow was denied a petition to become a U.S. citizen because, as a "Syrian of Asiatic birth," he was not a free white person within the meaning of the 1790 U.S. statute.[34] In 1915, the Dow decision was reversed based on the argument that the pertinent binding legislation was not that of 1790 but the laws of 1873 and 1875, and in accordance with these, Syrians "were so closely related to Europeans that they could be considered 'white persons.'"[35] Despite this precise and authoritative language, "Syrians" in the United States continued to be challenged and to feel insecure about their naturalization status until the period of 1923 to 1924.[36]

Even during World War II, the status of Arabs remained unclear. In 1942, a Muslim Arab from Yemen was denied U.S. citizenship because "Arabs as a class are not white and therefore not eligible for citizenship," especially because of their dark skin and the fact that they are "part of the Mohammedan world," separated from Christian Europe by a wide gulf.[37] On the other hand, in 1944, an "Arabian" Muslim was granted citizenship status under the 1940 Nationality Act, because "as every schoolboy knows, the Arabs have at various times inhabited parts of Europe, lived along the Mediterranean, been contiguous to European nations and been assimilated culturally and otherwise by them."[38]

Apart from the legal battles to ensure they were allowed to reside in their new homelands, especially in the United States, Arabic-speaking persons had to figure out what identity best fit their indeterminate status. They knew who they were and had a very strong sense of personal identity centered first and foremost in the family. There were, however, other lesser but still important identities related to clan, village, or sect. Because these identities were strong, a "national" identity could remain amorphous or at least indeterminate, shifting from one orientation to another with relative ease and without much psychological dislocation. In practical terms, the Arabic-speaking people in North America functioned as a collective of communities whose bonds of solidarity beyond the family were mainly related to sect or country, such as Maronite, Orthodox, Muslim, Druze, and Palestinian affiliations. Before World War II, the primary or most acceptable designation for the group was "Syrian." However, when Lebanon emerged as a country in the 1920s, some Maronites, especially N. Mokarzel, the editor and publisher of *Al-Hoda*, spearheaded a campaign to get the community to change its name to Lebanese, because Lebanon was where most of its members originally came from.[39] The campaign was not a big success, although, many of the clubs did change their name to Syrian-Lebanese.[40]

Another and more important identity crisis occurred when these peripatetic sojourners realized that they had to decide whether to become "settlers" or return to the old homeland. It had become increasingly difficult for them to function as temporary aliens. After World War I, it became clear to large numbers of Arabs in North America that it was not possible to go "home" again and that the United States and Canada were their homes.[41] This change from sojourner to permanent settler necessitated and was accompanied by other changes in the way Arabs in America thought and in the way they behaved. The substantial investments they had made in homes, property, and real estate in the old country lost their original purpose, and much more attention was paid to material improvements and investments in their new countries. In the United States, one manifestation was the migration by substantial numbers of the New York Arab community from the run-down and extremely crowded tenements of Manhattan to the nicer environment of South Ferry in Brooklyn and beyond.[42]

Arabs in America saw that they had to become full-fledged Americans. Assimilation became strongly and widely advocated, and citizenship training and naturalization were greatly encouraged. Although out-marriage was still not favored, some now claimed that success in such situations was possible if the American partner (usually female) was a "good" person who behaved in a conservative or traditional manner.[43] Along the same lines, Arab women were told to retain the modesty code of the old homeland.[44]

Although Arab women in America constituted a major asset to their kinfolk, they also presented the community with many difficulties, primarily related to issues of honor and modesty. This problem was most acute among the Druze, some of whom asked to restrict or totally ban the immigration of Druze women to America. Among Christians, women peddlers were a big concern. The complaints and areas targeted for reform included the act of peddling itself, the personal appearance and dress of the woman peddler, the distance she covered and whether she had to stay away from home overnight, and her demeanor or behavior. These problems were viewed as especially serious because large numbers had decided to stay in America and wanted to become "acceptable" to the host society. The preference was for Arab women to help their kinfolk by crocheting or sewing at home or by minding their family's store. Work in factories was also acceptable, although not favored, especially among the rising middle-class Arab Americans.[45]

The decision to settle in America meant setting a higher priority on children's education for boys and girls. This was viewed as more important than any contribution the children might make to the family's economic welfare. The result was a marked improvement in women's education and an increase in the number of male and female graduates from universities and professional institutions.

Another consequence of the decision to stay in America was that parents and children had to learn to be good Americans, and they flocked to citizenship classes. Parents attended English-language classes and studied the American governmental system in preparation for their new role as American citizens. Americanization was seen as a process of shedding old loyalties, the traditional culture, and the Arabic language. The children therefore grew up barely aware of their Arabic heritage.

Although the assimilationist approach began to gain favor and was encouraged by the leadership, it was not presented in ideological terms. Often, it took the form of a suggestion that Arabs should no longer feel like strangers in their new country and that they should make a positive contribution to American society.[46] Nevertheless, in the heyday of the melting pot approach to assimilation, the Arabs in America strove to remove any differences, except perhaps food and music, that separated them from the general American population. They also neglected or chose not to teach their children Arabic or to instill into them much pride of heritage.[47] The result was that, by World War II, Arabs in North America were, for all practical purposes, an indistinguishable group from the host society. It took a second wave of immigration and other developments to rekindle interest in their Arab heritage and to revive them as an ethnic community.

Post–World War II Immigration

The second wave of Arab immigration brought to North America a much more diverse population, one that differed greatly from the early pioneering group. Whereas the first-wave immigrants came almost exclusively from the area of Greater Syria and were overwhelmingly Lebanese, the new immigrants came from all parts of the Arab world, including North Africa. Unlike early arrivals, who were predominantly Christian, the new immigrants were Christians and Muslims.

The two groups' reasons for immigration were also somewhat different. In addition to economic need and the attraction of a major industrial society, new immigrants often were driven out of their homes as a result of regional conflicts (e.g., Palestine-Israel, Arab-Israeli, Iraq-Iran, Iraq-Kuwait) or civil wars (e.g., Lebanon, Yemen) or as a consequence of major social and political changes in the homeland that made life difficult, especially for the wealthy or the middle class in Egypt, Iraq, Syria, and other countries. The search for a democratic haven, where it is possible to live in freedom without political or economic harassment and suppression by the government was a strong motivation, even more so than during the earlier period, that affected much larger numbers of individuals. To these political and economic motivations can be added a psychological one. The great improvements in transportation and communication facilitated the process of immigration, and by making the world seem smaller, they made it much easier for people to accept the notion of migration to other parts of the world, especially to the United States and Canada.

Whereas the early Arab immigrants were mainly uneducated and relatively poor, the new arrivals included large numbers of relatively well-off, highly educated professionals: lawyers, professors, teachers, engineers, and doctors. Many of the new immigrants began as students at American universities who decided to stay, often as a result of lack of employment opportunities back home or because of the unstable political conditions in the homeland—conditions that often threatened imprisonment or death for returnees.[48] Besides these comparatively affluent immigrants, especially in the 1990s, relatively large numbers of semi-educated Arabs, primarily engaged in commerce, came to North America as political refugees or as temporary residents to escape the wars and violence of the Middle East region.

An important difference between members of the two immigration waves is the way each group thought of itself in terms of American society and politics. First-wave immigrants were viewed and thought of themselves as mere sojourners staying in the United States on a temporary basis with the primary or sole purpose of making a fortune they could enjoy back home. This orientation remained dominant at least until World War I and probably well into the 1920s. Such a stance meant that they avoided participation in American society beyond taking care of basic needs such as commerce. They were "Syrians" or "Arabians" and sought to establish their own churches, clubs, or newspapers. They sought (and preached to their people) not to "meddle" in the affairs of the host society. They were anxious not to offend their hosts, not to break the law, and not to behave in a manner offensive to Americans, but they also tried not to imitate American social customs (i.e., Americanize), not to mix socially with Americans, and not to intermarry. Although most did not participate in politics much beyond voting, they nevertheless expressed pride in the occasional Arab who was able to make it as a city alderman, political party functionary, or a candidate for local political office.

The change from these conditions came slowly and as a result of changes in the world around them, especially World War I, the Ottomans' oppressive treatment of their subjects in the Syria-Lebanon region, and the success of Zionism in securing Western, especially British and American, support for its objective of establishing a Jewish homeland in Palestine.

Immigrants who arrived after World War II came with a well-defined view of democracy and the role of citizens in it— ideas they had learned in their homeland but that had originally been imported from Europe and America. Their higher level of education and social status gave them greater confidence about participating in American politics almost as soon as they arrived in their new country. Even when they thought about returning to their Arab homeland, they were anxious to live full and productive lives in the United States or Canada for themselves and their children. The Arab-American community today constitutes a combination of the diversities of the early and more recent immigrants. In addition to the sectarian and mainly social clubs that

the early immigrants formed, new political organizations were gradually established. In the United States, Syrian Democratic and Syrian Republican clubs were formed in the 1920s and 1930s. These were, as the Arab Democratic and Arab Republican clubs are today, adjuncts to the main two major parties designed to encourage political participation and to integrate Arabs into the American body politic. What was new and significant was the establishment of bona fide Arab-American pressure groups and voluntary associations whose main function has been to protect themselves against harassment from private groups or public agencies and to influence policy in the United States and Canada concerning different parts of the Arab World or Middle East.

As World War I had marked a watershed for the early Arab immigrants, the 1967 Arab-Israeli war did for the entire community. The older and newer Arab-American communities were shocked and traumatized by the 1967 war. In particular, they were dismayed and extremely disappointed to see how greatly one-sided and pro-Israeli the American communications media were in reporting on the Middle East.[49] The war itself also produced soul-searching on the part of many Arab Americans, old and new, and often reinforced or strengthened their Arab identity. This group included many members already active in various Palestinian, Syrian, and Lebanese clubs, which were mainly social in nature.

By 1967, members of the third generation of the early Arab immigrants had started to awaken to their own identity and to see that identity as Arab, not "Syrian." Elements of this third generation combined with politically sophisticated immigrants to work for their ethnic community and the causes of their people in the old homelands. The result was establishment of the Association of Arab-American University Graduates (AAUG) in late 1967, which was the first post–World War II national, credible, nonsectarian organization seeking to represent diverse elements of the Arab-American community and to advance an Arab rather than regional or country orientation.

To the AAUG, however, American hostility to "Arabs" and the concept of Arabism was so extreme and so widespread among policy makers and the general public that influencing the political process or public policy, especially in the United States, seemed futile. The Republican and Democratic parties were almost completely and solidly one sided in their support of Israel and in their hostility to Arab causes, even though the United States had huge economic and military assets in the region and was on the friendliest terms with most leaders and countries of the Arab world. The AAUG sought support from or identified with other individuals and groups. Among these were a few politicians such as Senator William Fulbright and others who were courageous enough to voice criticism of U.S. policy in the Middle East, other minority or disenfranchised groups in American society, and some intellectuals who began to criticize the administration and its policies.

The AAUG's first priority was the need to provide accurate information about the Arab world and Arabs in North America and to distribute this literature to the public at large, wherever access was possible. It sought to educate the Arab countries and people about the true nature of the problems facing the region and to educate Arab intellectuals and political leaders about U.S. and Canadian policies and the American political process. While the AAUG sought mainly to inform and educate, it also performed other tasks, because no other organizations existed to perform them. Among the tasks to which the AAUG devoted some time and effort were political lobbying, attacks against defamation of and discrimination against Arabs and Arab Americans, and ac-

tivism among Arab Americans to get them to participate in politics.

These ancillary tasks were later championed and performed by newer organizations. The National Association of Arab Americans (NAAA) was formed in 1972 in the United States to act as a political lobby to defend and advance Arab-American interests and causes. In 1980, in response to the continuing slanders and attacks against Arabs and Arab Americans, the American-Arab Anti-Discrimination Committee (ADC) was established and quickly drew widespread support from the varied elements of the Arab community. In 1985, the Arab American Institute (AAI) was formed, primarily to encourage Arab Americans to become active in the American political arena.[50]

Building a New Future

To get a feel for how the Arab community has fared in America, it is useful to review some of the challenges and concerns that Arabs have faced in their new homeland and how they have coped with building a new future. Among the most important issues with which Arabs in America have had to wrestle is the definition of who they are, their sense of identity as a people, especially as they encountered and continue to encounter bias and discrimination in their new homeland.

Although Arabs in the United States and Canada constitute an ethnic group, they were not an ethnic minority in their old homeland. Their new identity has been shaped by many factors but especially by continuing interactions between conditions in the old and new homelands and by the interplay between their perceptions of themselves and how others see them. The early immigrants spoke Arabic and came from a predominantly Arabic culture and heritage, but they did not think of themselves as "Arabs." The main bond of solidarity among them at that time was based on familial, sectarian, and village- or region-oriented factors. The plethora of names by which they were known in the New World reflects their lack of "national" identity and ignorance or confusion on the part of the host society. Another factor in this process was the American, especially U.S., obsession with the idea of race and the various attempts early in this century to classify every immigrant group, no matter how small, by its racial composition.[51] The early Arabic-speaking groups were called Asians, "other Asians," Turks from Asia, Caucasian, white, black, or "colored."

Although immigration officials and the general press looked down on Arabic-speaking peoples, they nevertheless viewed them as part of the "white race," at least for the first thirty years or so of their presence in North America. These authorities then decided those immigrants were not white. With their very identity questioned and maligned, the reaction of the early Arab Americans was to try to refute what they saw as demeaning and untrue charges. They argued that they were very much part of the white race.[52] Stung by accusations of inferiority in terms of scientific and technological accomplishments, Syrian-Arab Americans developed a two-cultures thesis long before C. P. Snow discussed it.[53] Their argument, which became popular in the community, especially among Arab literati, was that, although America was the most advanced country in the world in science, technology, and industrialization, the East was spiritually superior.[54] Coming from the Holy Land, they offered themselves as guides and instructors to Americans in their search for and desire to experience the life and times of Jesus—where he was born, preached, was crucified, and rose from the dead.[55] Arab Americans spoke and wrote about the "spir-

itual" East in terms that suggested perpetuity: it was always so and would always be so. By accident or not, these writers in essence condemned the East to an absence of material progress and desire to produce such for all time.

The emphasis on Eastern spirituality, although useful in making Arabs feel good about themselves compared with "materialist" Americans, still left Arabs in America with little cultural heritage to offer their American-born children. The result often was to ignore their Arab heritage and, especially beginning in the 1920s, to emphasize almost full assimilation in American society. As the children grew up immersed in American society and culture while simultaneously exposed to a smattering of Arabic words at home and some Arabic food and music, they often found themselves experiencing an identity crisis of some kind, mainly resulting in rootlessness, ambiguity, and a fractionalized personality.[56] These were the reactions of some of the Arab-American literati of the post–World War II period. The very culture of their own country denied them the privilege of being openly proud of their heritage. They sometimes dealt with this awkward situation by complaining about American prejudice and discrimination against Arabs and by simultaneously denigrating their own people and heritage—if only to ingratiate themselves with their readers, their fellow Americans.[57]

The 1967 war changed the situation radically. Israel, in the short period of seven days, defeated the Arab armies. The Arab people generally felt let down and humiliated. Arabs in America, both newcomers and third-generation descendants of the early pioneers, deeply resented the extreme partisanship America and Americans (especially the U.S. government and people) showed toward Israel and the occasional hostility toward Arabs. The consequence was for Arab Americans to shake off their malaise and to organize. Their first goal was to fight against the negative stereotyping of Arabs. Their second was to help modify American policy toward the Middle East and make it more balanced. In the process, sectors of the well-established older community de-assimilated. They began openly to call themselves Arab and to join political groupings set up to defend Arab and Arab-American causes.[58] Arab Americans also began to organize conferences and publish journals and books in defense of their cause. They wrote fiction, poetry, and memoirs declaring pride in and solidarity with Arabs and the Arab community in America.

Open Arab-American pride in their heritage and activism on behalf of their cause does not, however, mean that prejudice against them ceased. On the contrary, many in the community feel that prejudice and discrimination have increased. Different reasons have been advanced to explain the prejudice and discrimination that Arabs encounter in North America, and different individuals and groups have emphasized what they believe to be the main cause or the one most pertinent to their situation.

The most popular explanation for the negative stereotypes Americans hold about Arabs is that they are ignorant of the truth because they have not read or have read inaccurate and false reports about Arabs and have not come into contact with Arabs. According to this view, the stereotypes are mainly the result of propaganda by and on behalf of Zionist and pro-Israeli supporters. The primary objective of this propaganda has been to deprive Arabs, especially Palestinians, from presenting their case to the American public and the American political leadership.[59]

In this view, the attempt to deny Arabs and Arab Americans a public voice also extends to the political arena. In this way, it becomes a "politics of exclusion" in an attempt to prevent debate on any issues that reflect poorly on Zionists or Israel. It also smears and defames Arab candidates for political office to defeat them and exclude them from effective participation in political decision making. This "political racism" is presumed to be ideological in nature and not necessarily directed against Arabs or Arab Americans as a people or as an ethnic community.[60]

Another view sees hostility and violence against Arabs and Arab Americans as anti-Arab racism. This hostility is seen as part of the native racist attitudes and is believed to be present in all sectors of American society, not just among fringe groups. Somewhat related to this view is "jingoistic racism," which is directed at whatever foreign enemy is perceived to be out there.[61] Because of the many recent conflicts in the Middle East in which the United States directly or indirectly became involved and where incidents of hijacking and hostage taking occurred, many Americans reacted negatively against a vaguely perceived enemy next door, often not distinguishing between Arabs and Muslims or between Arabs and any foreigner who "looks" Arab.[62]

Still another view of negative Arab stereotypes, at least in the United States, argues that these ideas are "rooted in a core of hostile archetypes that our culture applies to those with whom it clashes."[63] According to this argument, most of the elements that constitute the Arab image in America are not unique to Arabs but also have been applied to other ethnic groups, especially blacks and Jews in the form of racism and anti-Semitism. These negative stereotypes have been transferred to a new group, the Arabs or Arab Americans.

Part of the negative stereotyping and hostility many Americans harbor toward Arabs is based on the latter's alleged mistreatment of their women. It is rather ironic, therefore, that Arab-American women find themselves the subject of prejudice, discrimination, and hostility at the hands of American men and women. This is often the result of hostility based on race, color, or religion.[64]

Arab-American women have had more problems than their male counterparts in defining an acceptable or comfortable identity. The problem is multifaceted and affects different sectors differently. Women who have come from the most traditional countries of the Arab world have experienced a greater restriction of their freedom in the United States. This is primarily the result of an inability on the part of traditional husbands, fathers, and brothers to deal with the nearly complete freedom accorded to women in American society. Just as important is the inability of the women to participate fully in the United States because they do not know the language, lack the necessary education, and are unfamiliar with American customs. They are not psychologically ready to countenance, let alone internalize, certain mores pertaining to the public display of affection and male-female interaction. Because many cannot drive and probably do not have a car, they find themselves much more isolated than they were back home, where they often had a vibrant and full life, albeit within the confines of the family and female friends.[65]

Among middle-class, first-generation Arab-American women, there is perhaps not much adjustment necessary. They usually follow the somewhat liberal mores they brought with them from the old homeland. On the other hand, Arab girls reaching their adolescence in the United States are likely to experience more problems as a result of the potential clash between traditional child-rearing practices and the freer atmosphere found in North America.[66]

Among better-educated, young Arab-American women, the issue of identity is both more subtle and more openly discussed. Like their male Arab-American coun-terparts, these women suffer from and are offended by the hostility against Arabs and Arab Americans. They also find American views of how women are allegedly treated in the Arab world to be inaccurate and grotesque. Nevertheless, they would like to expand the rights of Arab women and to improve the quality of their lives. They resent and reject any attempt on the part of Arab-American men to define what their role should be in maintaining Arab culture and mores in North America. In particular, they want to reject the notion that family honor resides in women and that the way a woman behaves, especially concerning her modesty and sexuality, can bring honor or dishonor to the family. They do not wish to be the conveyors or transmitters of tradition and culture—at least not as these are defined by men or as they prevail in the old homeland.[67]

Women and men in the Arab-American community of the 1990s find that the "white" racial classification that the early Syrian-Arab community worked so hard to attain is flawed. In practical daily interactions, Arabs in America are often treated as "honorary whites" or "white but not quite."[68] In reaction to this situation, at least four different orientations have been advocated. For the majority, especially among the older and well-established Christian community, there is some disgruntlement but general passivity about the discrimination and the prejudice that accompany their "white but not quite" status, and they work to remove these negative attitudes. Others, especially the Arab American Institute, have argued for a special designation of Arabs in the United States as a minority (e.g., the Hispanics) or as a specific census category encompassing all peoples of the Middle East.[69] Still others, especially some young, educated Arab-American women, have expressed a preference for the designation "people of color."[70] This would place them as part of a larger category that includes most of the federally recognized minorities in the United States. There are also those who resent being boxed into one category. Their sense of identity is multifaceted; they are men or women; Arab, American, Muslim or Christian; white or dark skinned; and so on. They think of themselves in different ways at different times or in different contexts, and they argue for getting rid of such categories or for the use of more descriptive categories that recognize different aspects of their background, culture, or physical appearance.[71]

The search for an adequate or comfortable identity for Arabs in America has been guided and perhaps complicated by the need to feel pride in their heritage and simultaneously avoid prejudice and discrimination in their new homeland. For most, the search is neither successful nor final. They continue to experience marginality in American society and politics, and they try to overcome this in various ways. Some resort to ethnic denial; they de-emphasize their Arab or Islamic background by claiming a connection with what they believe is a more acceptable appearance in America. Instead of proclaiming their Arabism, for instance, they claim that they are Lebanese or Egyptian. Some may even deny their heritage altogether, claiming to be Greek or Italian. Some new arrivals instead choose ethnic isolation. They are unwilling to change themselves and do not believe they can change the host society.

Among those who want full integration or assimilation into American society, especially middle-class Arab Americans, many emphasize the strong cultural link between Arabs and Americans. They refuse to give up and continue to work hard to show where the dominant American view is wrong. For most, accommodation is the easiest and most comfortable stance. These men and women consciously or subconsciously act in ways that reduce their difference from the American dominant group. They attempt "to pass."[72] Others, especially those who seek material success, especially those who are in public professions (e.g., television, radio, movies), often give in and convert to the prevailing view. Not infrequently, the very individuals who are looked down on by the Arab-American community are selected to speak for and represent the Arabs in America.[73]

The Arab-American Community in the 1990s

After more than a century of immigration, it is clear that the basic reasons Arabs came are no different from those that drove or attracted other groups to come here. They came because of the promise of a quick fortune and a sense of adventure; the threat of war or economic disaster; education, training, technology; and the thrill of living in a free democratic system. Whatever their reasons, true integration and full assimilation have eluded them. In part, this is the result of the many developments leading to the debunking of the notion of a melting pot and the greater tolerance of a multicultural society. The more important reason, however, has been the hostility the host society has shown toward Arab immigrants.[74]

Nevertheless, Arabs in America have done very well. Since the 1960s, there has always been at least one representative of Arab background in the U.S. Congress (e.g., James Abourezk, Mary Rose Oakar, Mark Joe [Nick] Rahall II). Others have served as state governors (e.g., Victor Atiyeh, OR) or on the White House staff (e.g., John H. Sununu). Similarly, individuals of Arab descent have been elected to the Canadian parliament (e.g., Mac Harb, Mark Assad) and to provincial legislatures. Many of these individuals have faced difficulties in attaining their positions because they were of

Arab background. Some have found it useful to de-emphasize or deny that background to get or maintain their positions. Most also have not been strong or vocal supporters of Arab or Arab nationalist causes. Nonetheless, ethnic pride is more openly displayed by an increasing number of political candidates at local, state, and national levels.[75]

Arab Americans have done well and fared better economically than the general population average in many areas. The 1980 and 1990 U.S. census data show that Arab Americans reach a higher educational level than the American population as a whole. According to the 1990 census, 15.2 percent of Arab Americans have "graduate degrees or higher"—more than twice the national average of 7.2 percent. Household income among Arab Americans also tends to be higher than the average. Arab Americans have also done well in professional, management, and sales professions.[76]

Although many Arabs in America have reached the highest level of their profession in almost all professions,[77] the American media primarily highlight the negative achievements of Arabs and Muslims. Quite often, the media announce the Arab or Islamic origin or affiliation of anyone accused of a terrorist act—even before they know whether the perpetrator is Arab or Muslim. In the case of positive role models such as Michael DeBakey or Ralph Nader, the media often never mention their Arab background. One reason is that "some [too many] have found it necessary to hide their origins because of racism."[78] Lists of prominent Arab Americans occasionally are published in the press to inform the public about the community's accomplishments, but the fact that such lists are compiled indicates that Arab Americans feel the sting of negative stereotyping and try to correct the bad publicity. Despite the fact that Arabs have lived in America for more than a century and de-

spite their major successes, they are still struggling to be accepted in American society. Full integration and assimilation will not be achieved until that happens.[79]

NOTES

1. See William E. Leuchtenburg, "The American Perception of the Arab World." In George N. Atiyeh, ed., *Arab and American Cultures* (Washington, DC: American Enterprise Institute for Public Policy Research, 1977), p. 15.
2. Although it is possible to speak of several waves of Arab immigration to North America (e.g., 1880s to World War I, World War I to World War II, 1945 to 1967, 1968 to the present), there have been two main waves: from the 1880s to World War II and from World War II to the present. The major differences in the character and composition of the immigrant populations can be detected primarily between these two groups.
3. Unless otherwise indicated, references to the Arab community include the Arabs in Canada and those in the United States. Because of the much smaller numbers of Arabs in Canada, leadership on major issues usually has come from the Arab community in the United States.
4. See appendixes 1 and 2 in Gregory Orfalea, *Before the Flames: Quest for the History of Arab Americans* (Austin, TX: University of Texas Press, 1988), pp. 314–15. There were about 11,000 Arabs in Canada in 1931. For more on the subject of Arab immigration to Canada, see Baha Abu-Laban, *An Olive Branch on the Family Tree: The Arabs in Canada* (Toronto: McClelland and Stewart, 1980).
5. This is the official U.S. government figure cited in Philip Hitti's "The Emigrants," published in the 1963 edition of the *Encyclopedia of Islam* and reproduced in *Al-Hoda, 1898–1968* (New York: Al-Hoda Press, 1968), p. 133. A much larger estimate of 800,000 (Lebanese) was given by Ashad G. Hawie, *The Rainbow Ends* (New York: Theo. Gaus' Sons, 1942), pp. 149, 151.
6. This figure does not include the Arab community in Canada, which has fewer than 400,000 persons today. For estimates of Arab immigration to Canada, see Baha Abu-Laban, *An Olive Branch on the Family Tree: The Arabs in Canada* (Toronto: McClelland and Stewart, 1980) and Ibrahim Hayani's chapter

in this book. Philip M. Kayal gave the low estimate in 1974 for Arabs in the United States but provided a revised estimate much closer to the generally accepted figure in 1987. See his "Estimating Arab-American Population," *Migration Today* 2, no. 5 (1974): 3, 9, and "Report: Counting the 'Arabs' Among Us," *Arab Studies Quarterly* 9, no. 1 (1987): 98–104.

7. See Philip K. Hitti, *The Syrians in America* (New York: George H. Doran, 1924), p. 48; Alixa Naff, *Becoming American: The Early Arab Immigrant Experience* (Carbondale, IL: Southern Illinois University Press, 1985), p. 83; Samir Khalaf, "The Background and Causes of Lebanese/Syrian Immigration to the United States before World War I." In Eric J. Hooglund, ed., *Crossing the Waters: Arabic-Speaking Immigrants to the United States before 1940* (Washington, DC: Smithsonian Institution Press, 1987), pp. 17–35; and Charles Issawi, "The Historical Background of Lebanese Emigration: 1800–1914." In Albert Hourani and Nadim Shehadi, eds., *The Lebanese in the World: A Century of Emigration* (London: I.B. Tauris, 1992), pp. 13–31. See also Baha Abu-Laban, "The Lebanese in Montreal." In Albert Hourani and Nadim Shehadi, eds., *The Lebanese in the World: A Century of Emigration* (London: I.B. Tauris, 1992), pp. 227–42.

8. Charles Issawi, "The Historical Background of Lebanese Emigration: 1800–1914." In Albert Hourani and Nadim Shehadi, eds., *The Lebanese in the World: A Century of Emigration* (London: I.B. Tauris, 1992), p. 22.

9. Philip K. Hitti, *The Syrians in America* (New York: George H. Doran, 1924), pp. 49–50. See also Akram Fouad Khater, "'House' to 'Goddess of the House': Gender, Class, and Silk in 19th-Century Mount Lebanon," *International Journal of Middle East Studies* 28, no. 3 (1996): 325–48.

10. For an informed and intelligent discussion on this and related issues, see Louise Seymour Houghton's series of articles entitled "Syrians in the United States," *The Survey* 26 (1 July, 5 August, 2 September, 7 October, 1911), pp. 480–95, 647–65, 786–803, 957–68.

11. For an early account of Arab immigration to the United States and to North America in general, which cites religious persecution as the reason for migration, see Basil M. Kherbawi, "History of the Syrian Emigration," which is part seven of Kherbawi's

tarikh al-Wilayat al-Muttahida (*History of the United States*) (New York: al Dalil Press, 1913), pp. 726–96, published in Arabic.

12. See Leila Tarazi Fawaz, *An Occasion for War: Civil Conflict in Lebanon and Damascus in 1860* (Berkeley, CA: University of California Press, 1995). See also, Mikha'il Mishaqa, *Murder, Mayhem, Pillage and Pluder: The History of Lebanon in the 18th and 19th Centuries.* Translated by Wheeler M. Thackston, Jr. (Albany, NY: State University of New York Press, 1988).

13. See Louise Seymour Houghton's series of articles entitled "Syrians in the United States," *The Survey,* 26 (1911), pp. 480–95; and Alixa Naff, *Becoming American: The Early Arab Immigrant Experience* (Carbondale, IL: Southern Illinois University Press, 1985), pp. 128–200. For Canadian statistics, see Baha Abu-Laban, *An Olive Branch on the Family Tree: The Arabs in Canada* (Toronto: McClelland and Stewart, 1980).

14. *Kawkab America* (15 April 1892): 1, English section. The English titles of Arabic newspapers cited here are provided as originally used. The titles in parentheses are the transliterations used by the Library of Congress.

15. Even though *Kawkab America* was published for about seventeen years, only copies of the first four years are available, the others have been lost.

16. See Motaz Abdullah Alhourani, "The Arab-American Press and the Arab World: News Coverage in Al-Bayan and Al-Dalil" (master's thesis, Kansas State University, Manhattan, KS, 1993).

17. For a history of the organizational and political activities of Arabic-speaking groups in the United States during this period, see James Ansara, "The Immigration and Settlement of the Syrians" (master's thesis, Harvard University, Cambridge, MA, 1931).

18. Among these, the most important journal was *The Syrian World,* published and edited by Salloum Mokarzel. A useful publication is the *Annotated Index to the Syrian World, 1926–1932* by John G. Moses and Eugene Paul Nassar (Saint Paul, MN: Immigration History Research Center, University of Minnesota, 1994).

19. See Philip M. and Joseph M. Kayal, *The Syrian-Lebanese in America: A Study in Religion and Assimilation* (Boston, MA: Twayne Publishers, 1975).

20. A good account of the most prominent of these writers is provided by Nadira Jamil

Sarraj, *Shu'ara' al-Rabitah al-Qalamiyah* (Poets of the Pen League) (Cairo, Egypt: Dar al-Ma'arif, 1964), published in Arabic.

21. See, for instance, Ameen Rihani, "To Syrians in the [American] Armed Forces," *As-Sayeh (al-Sa'ih)* (16 September 1918): 2, published in Arabic.

22. Advertisements and editorials in support of American Liberty bonds were found in most Arabic publications of that period, including *Al-Hoda* and *Meraat-ul-Gharb*.

23. See, in particular, *Syria Before the Peace Conference* (New York: Syrian-Lebanese League of North America, 1919).

24. This was the view often voiced after French entrenchment in Syria and Lebanon in the late 1920s and the 1930s.

25. For a summary of these views, see "Editors and Arabian Newspapers Give Opinions on Zionism," *The Jewish Criterion* (5 July 1918): 16–17.

26. Among the more active participants in public lectures and writings on this issue were Ameen Rihani and F. I. Shatara. The Arab National League was established in 1936, and members spoke out on Palestine and other issues. For coverage of these and other activities related to the Palestine issue, see *Palestine & Transjordan* for that period. See also "A Communique from the Arab National League," *As-Sayeh* (6 August 1936): 9.

27. On the occupations of emigrant Arabs, especially in North America and specifically about those engaged in commerce, see Salloum Mokarzel, *Tarikh al-tijara al-Suriyya fi al-mahajir al-Amrikiyya* (The History of Trade of Syrian Immigrants in the Americas) (New York: Syrian-American Press, 1920), published in Arabic. On peddling activity, see Alixa Naff, *Becoming American: The Early Arab Immigrant Experience* (Carbondale, IL: Southern Illinois University Press, 1985), pp. 128–200.

28. The Arabic press of the period was replete with such advice.

29. Edna Bonacich, "A Theory of Middleman Minorities," *American Sociological Review* 38 (1973): 591.

30. Prejudice against Arabs in America was widespread, and there was also some discrimination, especially in the southern United States. See, for instance, Nancy Faires Conklin and Nora Faires, "'Colored' and Catholic: The Lebanese in Birmingham, Alabama." In Eric J. Hooglund, ed., *Crossing the Waters: Arabic-Speaking Immigrants to the United States before 1940* (Washington, DC: Smithsonian Institution Press, 1987), pp. 69–84.

31. See, for instance, H. A. El-Kourie, "Dr. El-Kourie Defends Syrian Immigrants," *Birmingham Ledger* (20 September 1907) and "El-Kourie Takes Burnett to Task," *Age-Herald* (Birmingham, AL) (20 October 1907): 6.

32. In 1908, Canada issued the Order-in-Council, P.C. 926, which severely restricted Asiatic immigration. Negative attitudes about "Syrians," mistaking them for "Turks," also were a factor in reducing the level of Arab immigration to Canada. See Baha Abu-Laban, "The Lebanese in Montreal." In Albert Hourani and Nadim Shehadi, eds., *The Lebanese in the World: A Century of Emigration* (London: I.B. Tauris, 1992), p. 229.

33. See Kalil A. Bishara, *The Origins of the Modern Syrian* (New York: Al-Hoda Publishing House, 1914), published in English and Arabic.

34. See *Ex Parte Dow*, 211 F. 486 (E.D. South Carolina 1914) and *In Re Dow*, 213 F. 355 (E.D. South Carolina 1914).

35. *Dow v. United States et al*, 26 F. 145 (4th Cir. 1915).

36. See Joseph W. Ferris, "Syrian Naturalization Question in the United States: Certain Legal Aspects of Our Naturalization Laws," Part II, *The Syrian World* 2, no. 9 (1928): 18–24.

37. *In Re Ahmed Hassan*, 48 F. Supp. 843 (E.D. Michigan 1942).

38. *Ex Parte Mohriez*, 54 F. Supp. 941 (D. Massachusetts 1944).

39. See the Arabic edition of *Al-Hoda, 1898–1968* (New York: Al-Hoda Press, 1968).

40. *The Syrian Voice* changed its name to *The Syrian and Lebanonite Voice* in the late 1930s.

41. See M[ichael A.] Shadid, "Syria for the Syrians," *Syrian World* 1, no. 8 (1927): 21–24, and see "'Syria for the Syrians' Again: An Explanation and a Retraction," *Syrian World* 3, no. 4 (1928): 24–28.

42. For an excellent early study of New York Arabs, see Lucius Hopkins Miller, "A Study of the Syrian Communities of Greater New York," *Federation* 3 (1903): 11–58.

43. This was the message often presented in *Al-Akhlaq (al-Akhlaq)* (Character) in the 1920s.

44. See the various articles in the Arabic press by Afifa Karam and Victoria Tannous.

45. This issue occupied the Arab community for a long time and was almost a weekly subject in the main newspapers until peddling activity dwindled in the late 1920s. See, for instance, Afifa Karam's (untitled) article about women peddlers and the *Kashshi* in *Al-Hoda* (14 July, 1903): 2.

46. See, for instance, Habib I. Katibah, "What Is Americanism?" *The Syrian World* 1, no. 3 (1926): 16–20; W. A. Mansur, "The Future of Syrian Americans," *The Syrian World* 2, no. 3 (1927): 11–17, and see "Modern Syrians' Contributions to Civilization," *The Syrian World* 4, no. 5 (1930): 7–14.

47. The question about whether to teach Arabic to their children was a controversial issue in the 1920s and hotly debated in two main journals, *The Syrian World* and *Al-Akhlaq*.

48. See Michael W. Suleiman, "A Community Profile of Arab-Americans: Major Challenges and Concerns," *Arab Perspectives* (September 1983): pp. 6–13.

49. See Ibrahim Abu-Lughod, ed., *The Arab-Israeli Confrontation of June, 1967: An Arab Perspective* (Evanston, IL: Northwestern University Press, 1970).

50. Michael W. Suleiman, "Arab-Americans and the Political Process." In Ernest McCarus, ed., *The Development of Arab-American Identity* (Ann Arbor, MI: University of Michigan Press, 1994), pp. 37–60.

51. See "Dictionary of Races or Peoples." In *United States Reports of the Immigration Commission* (Washington, DC: Government Printing Office, 1911).

52. The details of these appeals are discussed in Michael W. Suleiman, "Early Arab-Americans: The Search for Identity." In Eric J. Hooglund, ed., *Crossing the Waters: Arabic-Speaking Immigrants to the United States before 1940* (Washington, DC: Smithsonian Institution Press, 1987), pp. 37–54.

53. C. P. Snow, *The Two Cultures and the Scientific Revolution* (Cambridge, England: Cambridge University Press, 1961).

54. This became a popular theme among many Arab-American writers. See, for instance, Abraham Mitry Rihbany, *A Far Journey* (Boston, MA: Houghton-Mifflin, 1914).

55. Abraham Mitrie Rihbany, *The Syrian Christ* (Boston, MA: Houghton-Mifflin, 1916).

56. See Evelyn Shakir, "Pretending to Be Arab: Role-Playing in Vance Bourjaily's 'The Fractional Man,'" MELUS 9, no. 1 (1982): 7–21.

See also Vance Bourjaily, *Confessions of a Spent Youth* (New York: Bantam Books, 1961).

57. See, for instance, William Peter Blatty, *Which Way to Mecca, Jack?* (New York: Bernard Geis Associates, 1960).

58. See Ali Shteiwi Zaghel, "Changing Patterns of Identification among Arab Americans: The Palestine Ramallites and the Christian Syrian-Lebanese" (Ph.D. diss., Northwestern University, 1977).

59. Much has been written in this vein. For a lengthy bibliography, see Michael W. Suleiman, *The Arabs in the Mind of America* (Brattleboro, VT: Amana Books, 1988). For a Canadian-Arab activist's view, see Sheikh Muhammad Said Massoud, *I Fought as I Believed* (Montreal: Sheikh Muhammad Said Massoud, 1976).

60. Helen Hatab Samhan, "Politics and Exclusion: The Arab American Experience," *Journal of Palestine Studies* 16, no. 2 (1987): 11–28.

61. Nabeel Abraham, "Anti-Arab Racism and Violence in the United States." In Ernest McCarus, ed., *The Development of Arab-American Identity* (Ann Arbor, MI: University of Michigan Press, 1994), pp. 155–214.

62. For documentation, see, for instance, *1990 ADC Annual Report on Political and Hate Violence* (Washington, DC: American-Arab Anti-Discrimination Committee, 1991). For Canadian statistics, see Zuhair Kashmeri, *The Gulf Within: Canadian Arabs, Racism and the Gulf War* (Toronto: James Lorimer & Co., 1991).

63. Ronald Stockton, "Ethnic Archetypes and the Arab Image." In Ernest McCarus, ed., *The Development of Arab-American Identity* (Ann Arbor, MI: University of Michigan Press, 1994), p. 120.

64. See the various essays and poems in Joanna Kadi, ed., *Food for Our Grandmothers: Writings by Arab-American and Arab-Canadian Feminists* (Boston, MA: South End Press, 1994).

65. See Louise Cainkar, "Palestinian Women in the United States: Coping with Tradition, Change, and Alienation" (Ph.D. diss., Northwestern University, 1988).

66. See Charlene Joyce Eisenlohr, "The Dilemma of Adolescent Arab Girls in an American High School" (Ph.D. diss., University of Michigan, 1988).

67. For an excellent study on Arab-American women, see Evelyn Shakir, *Bint Arab: Arab and Arab American Women in the United States* (Westport, CT: Praeger, 1997).

68. Joseph Massad, "Palestinians and the Limits of Racialized Discourse," *Social Text* 11, no. 1 (1993): 108.

69. The attempt has failed, at least so far. See the 16 September 1997 letter to Katherine K. Wellman of the Office of Management and Budget sent on Arab American Institute (AAI) stationery and signed by Helen Hatab Samhan (AAI), Samia El Badry (Census 2000 Advisory Committee), and Hala Maksoud, American-Arab Anti-Discrimination Committee.

70. Lisa Suhair Majaj, "Two Worlds: Arab-American Writing," *Forkroads* 1, no. 3 (1996): 64–80. See also different entries in Joanna Kadi, ed., *Food for Our Grandmothers: Writings by Arab-American and Arab-Canadian Feminists* (Boston, MA: South End Press, 1994).

71. See, for instance, Pauline Kaldas, "Exotic." In Joanna Kadi, ed., *Food for Our Grandmothers: Writings by Arab-American and Arab-Canadian Feminists* (Boston, MA: South End Press, 1994), pp. 168–69.

72. See Nabeel Abraham, "Arab-American Marginality: Mythos and Praxis." In Baha Abu-Laban and Michael W. Suleiman, eds., *Arab Americans: Continuity and Change* (Belmont, MA: AAUG Press, 1989), pp. 17–43.

73. See Michael W. Suleiman, "American Views of Arabs and the Impact of These Views on Arab Americans," *Al-Mustaqbal Al-Arabi* 16 (1993): 93–107, published in Arabic.

74. Milton Gordon states that the absence of a hostile attitude on the part of the host society is a key factor in the integration and assimilation of immigrants. See his *Assimilation in American Life: The Role of Race, Religion, and National Origins* (New York: Oxford University Press, 1964).

75. These attitudes were evident in a 1998 survey of Arabs active in U.S. politics, an analysis of which I plan to publish.

76. For analyses of some of the 1980 and 1990 U.S. census data, see John Zogby, *Arab America Today: A Demographic Profile of Arab Americans* (Washington, DC: Arab American Institute, 1990), and Samia El-Badry, "The Arab-American Market," *American Demographics* (January 1994): 22–27, 30. See also "CPH-L-149 Selected Characteristics for Persons of Arab Ancestry: 1990," U.S. Bureau of the Census, 1990 Census of Population and Housing, C-P-3-2, Ancestry of the Population in the United States: 1990.

77. Examples include Michael DeBakey in medicine (heart surgery); Elias Corey in chemistry (1990 Nobel Prize winner); Casey Kasem, Danny Thomas, and Paula Abdul in entertainment; Helen Thomas in journalism; Doug Flutie in sports (1984 Heisman Trophy winner); and Ralph Nader in consumer advocacy.

78. Casey Kasem, "We're Proud of Our Heritage," *Parade* (*Kansas City Star*) (16 January 1994): 1.

79. See Lisa Suhair Majaj, "Boundaries: Arab/American." In Joanna Kadi, ed., *Food for Our Grandmothers: Writings by Arab-American and Arab-Canadian Feminists* (Boston, MA: South End Press, 1994), pp. 65–84.

37

ETHNIC AND RACIAL IDENTITIES OF SECOND-GENERATION BLACK IMMIGRANTS IN NEW YORK CITY

Mary C. Waters

Questions to Consider

Based on her research of West Indians and Haitian Americans in New York City, Mary Waters found that first generation black immigrants "tended to distance themselves from American blacks." Why? What does this "distancing" strategy say about the way American blacks are perceived by new immigrant groups? How is racism within a racial group possible?

The growth of nonwhite voluntary immigrants to the United States since 1965 challenges the dichotomy that once explained different patterns of American inclusion and assimilation—the ethnic pattern of assimilation of European immigrants and the racial pattern of exclusion of America's nonwhite peoples. The new wave of immigrants includes people who are still defined racially in the United States but who migrate voluntarily and often under an immigrant preference system that selects for people with jobs and education that puts them well above their coethnics in the economy. Do the processes of immigration and assimilation for nonwhite immigrants resemble the processes for earlier white immigrants? Or do these immigrants and their children face very different choices and con-straints because they are defined racially by other Americans?

This [reading] examines a small piece of this puzzle—the question of the development of an ethnic identity among the second generation of black immigrants from the Caribbean. While there has been a substantial amount of interest in the identities and affiliations of these immigrants, very little research has been conducted on the identities of their children. The children of black immigrants in the United States face a choice about whether to identify as black American or whether to maintain an ethnic identity reflecting their parents' national origins. First-generation black immigrants to the United States have tended to distance themselves from American blacks, stressing their national origins and ethnic identities as Jamaican or Haitian or Trinidadian, but they also face overwhelming pressures in the United States to identify only as blacks (Foner 1987; Kasinitz 1992; Stafford 1987; Sutton and Makiesky 1975; Woldemikael 1989). In fact, they have been described as "invisible immigrants", because rather than being contrasted with other immigrants (for example, contrasting how Jamaicans are doing relative to Chinese), they are compared with black Americans. The children of black immigrants, because they lack their parents' distinctive accents, can choose to be even more invisible as ethnics than their parents. Second-generation West Indians in the United States most often will be seen by others as merely "American"—and must actively work to assert their ethnic identities.

The types of racial and ethnic identities adopted by a sample of second-generation West Indians[1] and Haitian Americans in New York City are explored here, along with subjective understandings these youngsters have of being American, being black American, and being their ethnic identity. After a short discussion of current theoretical approaches to understanding assimilation among the second generation, three types of identities adopted by the second generation are described and the different experiences of race relations associated with these identities are traced. Finally this [reading] suggests some implications for future patterns of identity development. . . .

Interviews with first-generation immigrants and their American coworkers reveal a great deal of tension between foreign-born and American-born blacks in both the working-class and the middle-class work sites. Long-standing tensions between newly arrived West Indians and American blacks have left a legacy of mutual stereotyping. (See Kasinitz 1992.) The immigrants see themselves as hardworking, ambitious, militant about their racial identities but not oversensitive or obsessed with race, and committed to education and family. They see black Americans as lazy, disorganized, obsessed with racial slights and barriers, with a disorganized and laissez-faire attitude toward family life and child raising.

American blacks describe the immigrants as arrogant, selfish, exploited in the workplace, oblivious to racial tensions and politics in the United States, and unfriendly and unwilling to have relations with black Americans. The first generation believes that their status as foreign-born blacks is higher than American blacks, and they tend to accentuate their identities as immigrants. Their accent is usually a clear and unambiguous signal to other Americans that they are foreign born.

The dilemma facing the second generation is that they grow up exposed to the negative opinions voiced by their parents about American blacks and to the belief that whites respond more favorably to foreign-born blacks. But they also realize that because they lack their parents' accents and other identifying characteristics, other people, including their peers, are likely to identify them as American blacks. How does the second generation handle this dilemma? Do they follow their parents' lead and identify with their ethnic identities such as Jamaican or Haitian or West Indian? Or do they try to become "American" and reject their parents' ethnic immigrant identities? . . .

Theoretical Approaches to Assimilation

Theories derived from the experiences of European immigrants and their children in the early twentieth century predicted that the more time spent in the United States, the more likely second-generation youths were to adopt an "American identity" and to reduce ties to the ethnic identities and culture of their parents. This "straight-line" assimilation model assumes that with each succeeding generation, the groups become more similar to mainstream Americans and more economically successful. For instance,

Warner and Srole's (1945) study of ethnic groups in Yankee City (Newburyport, Massachusetts) in the early 1930s describes the generational march from initial residential and occupational segregation and poverty to residential, occupational, and identificational integration and Americanization.

However, the situation faced by immigrant blacks in the 1990s differs in many of the background assumptions of the straight-line model. The immigrants do not enter a society that assumes an undifferentiated monolithic American culture but rather a consciously pluralistic society in which a variety of subcultures and racial and ethnic identities coexist. In fact, if these immigrants assimilate, they become not just Americans but black Americans. The immigrants generally believe that it is higher social status to be an immigrant black than to be an American black. Second, the economic opportunity structure is very different now from what it was at the beginning of the twentieth century. The unskilled jobs in manufacturing that enhanced job mobility for immigrants' children at the turn of the century have been lost as economic restructuring in the United States has shifted to a service economy (Gans 1992). The immigrants also are quite varied in the skills they bring with them. Some arrive with advanced educations and professional qualifications to take relatively well-paying jobs, which put them ahead of native American blacks (for example, Jamaican nurses). Others are less skilled and face difficulties finding work in the United States. Finally, the degree of residential segregation faced by blacks in the United States, whether foreign born or American born, has always been, and continues to be, of a much higher order than the segregation faced by foreign-born white immigrants (Lieberson 1980; Massey 1990). Thus, even with occupational mobility, it is not clear that blacks would be able to move into higher-status

neighborhoods in the orderly progression that Warner and Srole (1945) describe in their Yankee City study of European ethnic succession. A further complication for the black second generation is that part of being a black American involves dealing with American racism. Because immigrants and black Americans report a large difference in the perception and expectation of racism in American society, part of becoming American for the second generation involves developing a knowledge and perception of racism and its subtle nuances. . . .

Patterns in the Second Generation

The interviews suggest that while the individuals in this study vary a great deal in their identities, perceptions, and opinions, they can be sorted into three general types: identifying as Americans, identifying as ethnic Americans with some distancing from black Americans, or identifying as an immigrant in a way that does not reckon with American racial and ethnic categories.

A black American identity characterized the responses of approximately 42 percent of the eighty-three second-generation respondents interviewed. These youngsters identified with other black Americans. They did not see their "ethnic" identities as important to their self-image. When their parents or friends criticized American blacks or described what they perceived as fundamental differences between Caribbean-origin people and American blacks, these youngsters disagreed. They tended to downplay a national-origin identity and described themselves as American.

Another 30 percent of the respondents adopted a very strong ethnic identity that involved a considerable amount of distancing from American blacks. It was important for these respondents to stress their ethnic identities and for other people to recognize that they were not American blacks. These respondents tended to agree with parental judgments that there were strong differences between Americans and West Indians. This often involved a stance that West Indians were superior to American blacks in their behaviors and attitudes.

A final 28 percent of respondents had an immigrant attitude toward their identities, as opposed to American-identified youth or ethnic-identified youth. Most, but not all, of these respondents were more recent immigrants themselves. A crucial factor for these youngsters is that their accents and styles of clothing and behavior clearly signaled to others that they were foreign born. In a sense, their identity as an immigrant people precluded having to make a "choice" about what kind of American they were. These respondents had a strong identity, such as Jamaican or Trinidadian, but did not evidence much distancing from American blacks. Rather their identities were strongly linked to their experiences on the islands, and they did not worry much about how they were seen by other Americans, white or black.

A number of factors influence the type of identity the youngsters develop. They include the class background of the parents, the social networks in which the parents are involved, the type of school the child attends, and the family structure. All of these factors affect the ability of parents and other family members to shield children from neighborhood peer groups that espouse antischool values.

The type of identity and outlook on American race and ethnic relations that the youngsters developed was strongly related to their social class and its trajectory. The ethnic-identified youngsters were most likely to come from a middle-class background. Of the eighty-three second-generation teens and young adults interviewed, 57 percent of the middle-class teens identified ethnically, whereas only 17 percent of the working-class and poor teens identified ethnically.[2] The poorest students were the most likely to be immigrant or American identified. Only one out of the twelve teens whose parents were on public assistance identified ethnically. The American identified, perhaps not surprisingly, were also more likely to be born in the United States—67 percent of the American identified were born in the United States, as opposed to only 13 percent of the immigrant identified and 42 percent of the ethnically identified.

Parents with more education and income were able to provide better schools for their offspring. Among the respondents, some of the middle class had moved from the inner-city neighborhoods they had originally settled in to middle-class neighborhoods in the borough of Queens or to suburban areas where the schools were of higher academic quality and more likely to be racially integrated. Other middle-class parents sent their children to Catholic parochial schools or to citywide magnet schools such as Brooklyn Tech or Stuyvesant. Thus, the children were far more likely to attend schools with other immigrant children and with other middle-class whites and blacks, although some of the Catholic high schools were all black in enrollment.

The children of middle-class parents who did attend the local high schools were likely to be recent immigrants who had an immigrant identity. Because of their superior education in the West Indies, these students were the best in the local high schools, attended honors classes, and were bound for college. The children of middle-class parents who identified as American and were pessimistic about their own future opportunities and adopted antischool ideologies were likely to have arrived early in their lives and to have attended New York City public schools in inner-city areas from an early age.

The social networks of parents also influenced the type of identity the children developed. Regardless of social class, parents who were involved in ethnic voluntary organizations or heavily involved in their churches seemed to instill a strong sense of ethnic identity in their children. Parents whose social networks transcended neighborhood boundaries seemed to have more ability to provide guidance and social contacts for their children.

The two neighborhood schools where we interviewed the teenagers were among the five most dangerous schools in New York City—they were inadequate facilities with crumbling physical buildings, high dropout rates, and serious problems with violence. Both schools were all minority, with over 90 percent of the student body composed of black students, both American and foreign born. The students who attended these schools and were not in the separate honors tract (which was overwhelmingly filled with newly arrived immigrants) faced very limited future options, even if they managed to graduate.

Finally, the family structure and the experience of migration itself have a profound effect on the degree of control parents have over teenage children. Many families are composed of single working mothers and children. These mothers have not been able to supervise their children as much as they would like, and many do not have any extended family or close friends available to help with discipline and control. Even families with two spouses present often have been apart for long periods because one spouse preceded the family in migration. Often children have been left in the islands or sent ahead with relatives to New York,

with the parents often struggling to reassert authority after the family reunites. The generational conflict that ensues tends to create greater pressure for students to want to be "American" to differentiate themselves from parents.

Ethnic Response

All of the teenage respondents reported comments by their parents about American blacks that were very similar to those recorded in our interviews with the first generation. The differences were in how the teens interpreted what their parents were saying. In general, the ethnic-identified teens agreed with their parents and reported seeing a strong difference between themselves and black Americans, stressing that being black is not synonymous with being black American. They accept their parents' and the wider society's negative portrayals of poor blacks and wanted to avoid any chance that they will be identified with them. They described the culture and values of lower-class black Americans as lacking discipline, a work ethic, good child-rearing practices, and respect for education. They contrast these failures with the values of their parents' ethnic groups, which include an emphasis on education, strict discipline for children, a strong work ethic, and social mobility. They try to impress that they are Jamaican or Haitian and most definitely not black American. This allows them less dissonance with their parents' negative views of American blacks. They do not reject their parents' culture and identities but rather reject the American social system that would identify them as black American and strongly reject the African American peer group culture to which they would be assigned by whites and others if they did not consciously transmit their ethnic identities.

Although society may define the second generation on the basis of skin color, the second-generation ethnic teens believed that being black American involves more than merely having black skin. One young woman criticized American blacks in this way:

Some of them [black Americans] think that their heritage includes not being able to speak correctly or walk correctly, or act loud and obnoxious to make a point. I don't think they have to do that. Just when I see black Americans, it depends on how I see you on the street. Walking down the street with that walk that moves a little bit too much. I would say, I'd think you dropped out of high school.

These teens also differentiated themselves from black Americans in terms of their sensitivity to racism, real or imagined. Some of the ethnic-identified second generation echo the feelings we heard from the first generation that American blacks are too quick to use race as an explanation or excuse for not doing well:

There was a time back in the '40s and '50s and '60s or whenever when people was actually trying to keep down black people and stuff like that. But, you know, some black people now, it's like they not actually trying to make it better, you know? Some are just like, people are like, oh, this place is trying to keep me down, and they sulk and they cry about it, and they're not really doing that much to help themselves. . . . It's just like hyping the problem if they keep [saying] everything is racial, everything is racial.

The second-generation teens who are doing well try to understand how it is that they are so successful when black Americans are not—and often they chalk it up to

family values. They say that their immigrant families have close-knit family values that stress education. Aware of, and sometimes sharing, the negative images of black Americans that the whites they encounter believe, the second generation also perceives that whites treat them better when they realize they are not "just" black Americans. When asked if they benefited ever from their ethnicity, they responded "yes": "It seems white Americans don't tend to put you in the same category as black Americans." Another respondent said:

The West Indians tend to go that extra step because they, whites, don't usually consider them really black Americans, which would be working class. They don't consider them, I guess, as black. They see them as a person.

The dilemma for the second generation is that while they have a strong sense of their own identities as very different from black Americans, this was not clear to other people. Often both whites and blacks saw them as just black Americans and did not notice that they were ethnically different. When people did comment on their ethnic difference it was often because of the way they talked and the way they walked. These two characteristics were cited as reasons that whites and other blacks gave for thinking those of the second generation were not "really black." Whites tend to let these children know that they think of them as exceptions to the rule, with the rule being that most blacks are not good people. However, these young people also know that unless they tell people of their ethnicity, most whites have no idea they are not black Americans.

Many of these teens coped with this dilemma by devising ways to telegraph their identities as second-generation West Indians or Haitians. One girl carried a Guyanese map as part of her key chain so that when people looked at her keys they would ask her about it and she could tell them that her parents were from Guyana. One young woman described having her mother teach her an accent so that she could use it when she applied for a job or a place to live. Others just try to work it into conversation when they meet someone. This means that their self-identification is almost always at odds with the identifications others make of them in impersonal encounters in American society and that, as a result, they must consciously try to accentuate their ethnic identity:

Q: When a form or survey asks for your race what do you put down?

A: Oh boy, that is a tough one. It's funny because, you know, when we fill applications I never know what to check off, you know. I'm serious. 'Cause they have Afro-American, but they never have like Caribbean. They do have white, Chinese. To tell the truth, I would like to be called Caribbean, West Indian. Black West Indian.

The teens who were around many black Americans felt pressure from their peers to be part of the group and identify as black American. These teens would consciously talk about passing for American at some points and passing for Haitian or Jamaican at others by changing the way they talked or acted:

When I'm at school and I sit with my black friends and, sometimes I'm ashamed to say this, but my accent changes. I learn all the words. I switch. Well, when I'm with my friends, my black friends, I say I'm black, black American. When I'm with my Haitian-American friends, I say I'm Haitian. Well, my being black, I guess that puts me when I'm with black Americans, it makes people think that I'm lower class. . . . Then, if I'm talking like this

[regular voice] with my friends at school, they call me white.

American-Identified Second Generation

The American-identified second-generation teenagers differed in how little they stressed their immigrant or ethnic identities to the interviewers. They follow a path that is more similar to the model posed in the straight-line theory. They stress that they are American because they were born here, and they are disdainful of their parents' lack of understanding of the American social system. Instead of rejecting black American culture, it becomes their peer culture, and they embrace many aspects of it. This brings them in conflict with their parents' generation, most especially with their parents' understandings of American blacks. They most definitely assimilate to black America; they speak black English with their peers, they listen to rap music, and they accept the peer culture of their black American friends. They are aware of the fact that they are considered black American by others and that they can be accused of "acting white" if they don't speak black English and behave in particular ways. Most included their ethnic identities as background, but none of them adopted the stance that they were not, in a major sense, black American. When asked about ethnic background and how other people think of it, one respondent replied:

Q: What is your ethnic background?

A: I put down American because I was born up here. I feel that is what I should put down. . . .

Q: What do other people think you are?

A: Black American because if I don't say. . . . Like if they hear my parents talk or something they always think they are from Jamaica. . . . But they just think I am black American because I was born up here.

Many of these teens discuss how they do not control how others see them:

> Some people just think I am American because I have no accent. So I talk like American people. I don't talk Brooklynese. They think I am from down south or something. . . . A lot of people say you don't look Haitian. I think I look Haitian enough. I don't know, maybe they are expecting us to look fresh off the boat. I was born here and I grew up here, so I guess I look American and I have an American accent.

Q: If people think you are black American do you ever do anything about it?
A: No, I don't. If they ask me if I am American, I say yes. If they ask me where my parents are from, I tell them Haiti.

In fact, they imply that being a black American is more stylish and "with it" than being from the islands:

> I consider myself a black American. When I think of a black American I don't think of them as coming from the West Indies.

Q: Any characteristics that come to mind?
A: I would not think of someone in a suit. I would think of a regular teenager. I would think of a regular person. I think of someone that is in style.
Q: What about someone from the islands?
A: Jamaicans. They dress with neon colors. Most of the girls wear gold and stuff like that.

Some of the young people told us that they saw little if any difference between the ethnic blacks and the American blacks. Many stressed the Caribbeanization of black New York and described how all the Americans were interested in being Caribbean now:

> It use to be Jamaicans and American blacks did not get along because everyone was afraid of Jamaicans. But now I guess we are closer now. You tell an American that you are Jamaican and it is no big deal. Americans are acting more like Jamaicans. Jamaicans are acting like Americans.

Q: What do you mean by acting like each other?
A: Sure there are a lot of Americans out there speaking patois. And then all the Jamaicans are coming over here and they are like "Yo, what's up" and they are like that. Pretty soon you can't really tell who is Jamaican and who is American.

However, the parents of the American-identified teens have expressed to their children the same negative impressions of American blacks that the ethnic-identified teens reported. These teenagers report many negative appraisals of American blacks by their parents:

> They always say Haiti is better in this way or in that way. They say the kids here have no respect. The kids here are brought up without any supervision. My father is always talking about they [American blacks] be hanging out on the corner. And he says you won't find Haitians doing that. My mom always says you will marry a Haitian. Why are you talking to those American boys?

This young Haitian American teen tries to disagree with her mother and to temper her mother's interpretations of American blacks:

Q: Are there any characteristics or traits that come to mind about Haitian Americans?

A: Not really. I don't really—cause most people are Haitian American if they are born here. . . . Like me, I don't know if I act like a Haitian or do I have Haitian characteristics, but I'm mostly—like everything I do or like is American. My parents, they do not like American blacks, but they feel that they are lazy. They don't want to work and stuff like that from what they see. And I feel that, um, I feel that way too, but sometimes it won't be that person's fault, so I try to stick up for them. And my mother is like, yeah, you're just too American.

In marked contrast to the ethnic-identified teens, though, the American-identified teens disagreed with their parents' statements about American blacks, reluctantly agreed with some of it but provided qualifications, or perhaps, most disturbingly, accepted the appraisals as true of American blacks in general and themselves as American blacks. This young Trinidadian American swallows her parents' stereotypes and applies them directly to herself:

Q: How close do you feel in your ideas about things to West Indians?
A: Not very close. My feelings are more like blacks than theirs. I am lazy. I am really lazy and my parents are always making comments and things about how I am lazy. They are always like, in Trinidad you could not be this lazy. In Trinidad you would have to keep on working.

The fact that the teens are identifying as American and that their parents have such negative opinions of Americans causes some conflict. The teens either adopt a negative opinion of themselves or disagree with their parents' assessments of American blacks. But it is not just their parents who criticize black Americans. These youngsters are very aware of the generalized negative view of blacks in the wider culture. In answer to the question, "Do whites have an image of blacks?" all of them responded that whites have a negative view of blacks, seeing them as criminal, lazy, violent, and uncaring about family. Many of the teenagers prefaced their remarks by saying that they did not know any whites but that they knew this is what whites thought through the mass media and through the behaviors of whites they encountered in buses, trains, and stores. This mostly involved incidents such as whites protecting their handbags when the teenagers arrived or store clerks following them and expecting them to shoplift. This knowledge that the society in which they live devalues them because of their skin color and their identity affected these teens deeply.

Immigrant-Identified Teens

The more recently arrived young people who still identify as immigrant differed from both the ethnic- and the American-identified youth. They did not feel as much pressure to "choose" between identifying with or distancing from black Americans as did either the American or the ethnic teens. Strong in their national-origin identities, they were neutral toward American distinctions between ethnics and black Americans. They tended to stress their nationality or their birthplace as defining their identity. They also pointed to their experiences growing up and attending school in a different country. This young man had dreadlocks and a strong Jamaican accent. He stresses his African roots and lets his Jamaican origin speak for itself:

Q: What is your ethnicity? For example, when forms or surveys ask what your ethnic group or ancestry is what do you put?
A: African.

Q: Do you ever put Jamaican or anything?

A: No, not really. Only where Jamaican comes up is if someone asks where you're from. I'll say I am from Jamaica.

Q: What do people usually think you are?

A: They say I am Jamaican.

Q: They know that immediately?

A: Yeah.

Q: How do they know?

A: I change my voice. I don't have to tell them. I think it's also because of my locks sometimes and the way I carry myself, the way I dress.

While an ethnic-identified Jamaican American is aware that she might be seen by others as American and thus actively chooses to present herself as Jamaican, an immigrant-identified Jamaican could not conceive of herself as having a choice, nor could she conceive of being perceived by others as American. While an ethnic-identified teen might describe herself as Jamaican American, for the immigrant teen Jamaican would be all the label needed. Most teens in this category were recent immigrants. The few U.S.-born teens classified as immigrant identified had strong family roots on the islands, were frequent visitors to the islands, and had plans to return to live there as adults. A crucial factor that allows these youngsters to maintain this identity is that their accents and styles of clothing and behavior clearly signaled to others that they were foreign born.

Q: How important is it to you that your friends think of you in terms of your ethnicity?

A: Oh, very important. You know, I try hard not to lose my roots, you know, when I come to the United States. A lot of people who come here try to lose their accent, you know. Even in the workplace, you know, because they fear what other people might think of them. Even in the workplace. Me, I never try to change, you know, the way I am. I always try to,

you know, stay with them, the way of my culture.

Q: So it's something you want people to recognize?

A: Yeah, definitely, definitely, absolutely.

Q: Why?

A: Why? I'm proud of who I am, you know. I'm proud of where I'm from and I'm not going to change because somebody might not like the way I walk, talk or dress, you know.

The importance of birthplace was stressed repeatedly by the immigrant identified as they stressed their difference from American-born coethnics:

Q: What would you put on a form or survey that asked about your ethnicity?

A: I'll say I'm Jamaican. You gotta say where you come from.

Q: And do you think of yourself more as a Jamaican or more as an American?

A: I think of more of a Jamaican 'cause it's, I wasn't born here. I was born in Jamaica and was there for fourteen years.

Q: And what about kids who are born in America, but their parents were born in Jamaica?

A: Well, you see that is the problem. You see, kids whose parents are Jamaican, they think that, well, they are Jamaican. They need to recheck that they're Americans 'cause they was born in the country and they wasn't born outside the country. So I think they should, you know, know more about American than Jamaican.

Some who adopt this strong identity with the immigrant country were born in the United States, but the combination of strong family roots on the island, frequent visits, and plans to go live there when they are older allows them to think of themselves as not really American at all. This is especially easy to do in the public high schools where there are large numbers of freshly arrived youngsters from the islands.

Q: What do you think your race is?

A: Well, I'm black. I consider myself black. I don't consider myself black American, Afro-American and stuff like that because it's hard to determine, you know, for a person as an individual to determine himself to be Afro-American. . . . I'll be more a Guyanese person because certain things and traditions that I am accustomed to back home, it's still within the roots of me. And those things have not changed for a long period of time, even though you have to adapt to the system over here in order to get ahead and cope with what is going on around you.

While the ethnics tended to describe people as treating them better when they described their ethnic origins, and the Americans tended to stress the antiblack experiences they have had and the lack of difference between the foreign born and the American, the immigrant teens spoke about anti-immigrant feelings and discrimination and responded with pride in their national origins.

Contrasting Identities

In some sense one can see each of these identities as an embrace of one identity and an opposition to another. The American-identified youth are assimilating, in fact, to the American black subculture in the neighborhood. They are adapting to American black cultural forms, and they do so in distinction to their parents' ethnic identities and the wider mainstream white identities. These students adopt some of the "oppositional" poses that American black teenagers show toward academic achievement: the idea of America, the idea of opportunity, and the wider society (Fordham 1988; Ogbu 1990; Portes and Zhou 1993). They also are opposed to their parents' outlooks and ideas, stressing that what worked as a life strategy

and a child-raising technique in the islands does not work in the United States. These teens tend to adopt a peer culture of racial solidarity and opposition to school authorities. What is clear from the interviews is that this stance is in part a socialized response to a peer culture, but the vast majority of it comes about as a reaction to their life experiences. Most specifically, the teens respond to their experiences with racial discrimination and their perceptions of blocked social mobility. The lives of these youngsters basically lead them to reject their parents' immigrant dream of individual social mobility and to accept their peers' analysis of the United States as a place with blocked social mobility where they will not move far.

The American-identified teens do not seem aware of the scholarly literature and the perceptions among ethnic- and immigrant-identified youngsters that the foreign born are of higher social status than the American born. In the peer culture of the neighborhood and the school, these teenagers describe a situation in which being American offers higher social status than being ethnic. For instance, several youngsters described "passing" as black American in order not to be ridiculed or picked on in school:

> I used to be scared to tell people that I was Haitian. Like when I was in eighth grade there were lots of Haitians in the ESL classes, and people used to beat them up. They used to pick on them. I said to myself I am going to quiet down, say I am American.

When asked about the images others held of being from the islands, most of the teens described neutral attributes, such as styles of dress. However, many who identified as Americans also described negative associations with the immigrants' identities. The Jamaicans said most people thought of drug dealers when they thought of Jamaicans. A few of the teens also intimated that people from the islands were backward in not knowing how to live in a big city, both in appreciating the wonders of the city and being street smart to avoid crime and hassles with other people. In terms of the former attribute, the teens described people from the islands who were not accustomed to shopping in big malls or having access to a wide variety of consumer goods.

Not one of the American-identified teens voiced the opinion of the overwhelming majority of the ethnic teens that whites were more likely to like the foreign born. In part, this reflected the differences the groups had in their contact with whites. Most of the inner-city ethnic-identified teens had almost no contact with whites, except for teachers. They also are in schools where the vast majority of the students are foreign born or second generation. The larger number of middle-class teens who were ethnic-identified were more likely to have white classmates in citywide magnet high schools, in parochial schools, or in suburban schools or workplaces.

The inner-city American-identified teens also voiced more positive appraisals of black Americans than did the immigrant- or the ethnic-identified teens. Their descriptions reflect the reality of living in neighborhoods where there is crime and violence. A majority of the American-identified teens said that a good trait of black Americans is that they work hard and they struggle. These are the very same children whose parents describe black Americans primarily as lazy and unwilling to take advantage of the opportunities available to them. The children seem to be perceiving a reality that the parents cannot or will not.

Many of these teens live in neighborhoods that are all black and also attend schools that are all black. So, aside from teachers, these young people have almost no contact with white Americans. This does not stop them from absorbing the fact that whites have negative stereotypic views of blacks. But unlike the middle-class blacks who come in contact with whites who tell them that they are "good blacks," these youths live in the urban areas associated with crime, they dress like the typical black urban youth, and they talk with Brooklyn accents and black American slang. When they do encounter whites in public places, the whites do not ask about their parents' backgrounds.

Q: Have you ever experienced any discrimination or hostility in New York?
A: From being Trinidadian no. But because of being black, you know, everybody stereotypes. And they say "blacks, they tend to steal, and stuff like that." So, like, if I am walking down the street and a white lady go by and they smile and I smile. They put their bag on the other side.

The parents of these teens grew up in situations where blacks were the majority. The parents do not want their children to be "racial" in the United States. They define "being racial" as being overly concerned with race and with using race as an excuse or explanation for lack of success at school or on the job. The first generation tends to believe that, while racism exists in the United States, it can be overcome or circumvented through hard work, perseverance, and the right values and attitudes. The second generation experiences racism and discrimination constantly and develops perceptions of the overwhelming influence of race on their lives. These teens experience being hassled by police and store owners, not being given jobs, even being attacked on the streets if they venture into white neighborhoods. The boys adopt black American culture in their schools, wearing flattops, baggy pants, and certain types of jewelry. This contributes to the projection of the "cool pose," which in turn causes whites to be afraid of them. This makes them angry and resentful. The media also tells these youngsters that blacks are disvalued by American society. While parents tell their children to strive for upward mobility and to work harder in the face of discrimination, the American-identified teens think the rewards for doing so will be very slim.

This causes a wide gulf between the parents and their children. These parents are absolutely terrified of their children becoming Americans. For the children, to be American is to have freedom from the strict parental controls of the immigrant parents. This is an old story in the immigrant saga, one visible in novels and movies about conflicts between Jewish and Italian immigrants and their children. But the added dimension here is that these parents are afraid of the downward social mobility that becoming an American black represents to them. And this idea is reinforced constantly to these parents by whites who tell them that they are better than American blacks.

One question about how things had changed since the civil rights movement shows the different perceptions of the teens about race in American society. The ethnically identified gave answers I suspect most white Americans would give. They said that things are much better for blacks now. They state that blacks now can ride at the front of the bus and go to school with whites. The irony, of course, is that I was sitting in an all-black school when they told this story. The vast majority of the American-identified teens state that things are not better since the civil rights movement; the change is that discrimination now is "on the down low," covered up, more crafty. Some pointed out that we were in an all-black school. The result of these different world views is that the parents' view of an opportunity structure that is open to hard work is systematically undermined by their children's peer culture and, more important, by the actual experience of these teens.

On the other hand, the ethnic-identified teens, whose parents are more likely to be middle class and doing well or who attend parochial or magnet schools, see clearer opportunities and rewards ahead, despite the existence of racism and discrimination. Their parents' message that hard work and perseverance can circumvent racial barriers does not fall on unreceptive ears. The ethnic-identified youngsters embrace an identity derived directly from their parents' immigrant identity. Such an identity is in opposition to their peers' identities and in solidarity with their parents' identities. These youngsters stress that they are Jamaican Americans and that, while they may be proud of their racial identity as black, they see strong differences between themselves and black Americans. They specifically see their ethnic identities as keys to upward social mobility, stressing, for instance, that their parents' values of hard work and strict discipline help them to succeed in the United States when black Americans fail. This ethnic identity is very much an American-based identity—it is in the context of American social life that these youngsters base their assumptions of what it means to be Jamaican or Trinidadian. In fact, the pan-ethnic identities of Caribbean or West Indian often are the most salient label for these youngsters, as they see little differences among the groups and it is more important to differentiate themselves as second-generation Americans. The distancing that these teens show from black Americans often leads them to accept many negative stereotypes of black Americans. These youngsters tend to have ethnic friends from a West Indian background, white American friends, and very few, if any, black American friends.

The immigrant-identified teens are different from either of the other two, because of how they think about who they are not as well as how they think about who they are.

These teens have a strong identity as Jamaican or Trinidadian, but this identity tends to be related to their interactions with other Jamaicans or Trinidadians rather than their interactions with black or white Americans. These youngsters identify with their homelands or their parents' homelands, but not in opposition to black Americans or in opposition to white Americans. They tend to be immersed in the immigrant community, to have friends who are all the same ethnicity or from other islands. They tend to be more recent arrivals. Unlike the ethnically identified, however, they do not distance themselves from American blacks, and they have neutral or positive attitudes and relations with them. At the same time, they see themselves as different from, but not opposed to, black Americans.

These identities are fluid and change over time and in different social contexts. We found cases of people who describe identifying very strongly as black American when they were younger and who became more immigrant identified when they reached high school and found a large immigrant community. Most new arrivals to the United States start out as immigrant identified, and the longer they stay in the United States, the more they begin to think of themselves in terms of American categories. The kind of social milieu the child faces, especially the school environment, has a strong influence on the outcome. A school with many black Americans creates pressure to identify racially; likewise a neighborhood and school with many immigrants makes it possible to avoid thinking much about American categories. In the face of much pressure not to follow the rules and not to succeed academically, youngsters who are doing well in school and do value education increasingly come to stress their ethnic backgrounds as an explanation for their ambition and success.

The American racial classification system that pushes toward an either/or—

"black or white"—designation of people makes the immigrant option harder to hold onto. When others constantly identify the individual as black and refuse to make distinctions based on black ethnicity, pressure builds for the individual to adapt his or her identity to that outside identification— either to say "Yes, I am black," and to accept categorization with black Americans or to resent the characterization and strongly make an ethnic identification as Trinidadian American. The American myopia about ethnic differences within the black community makes the middle-ground immigrant identity unstable. Because every young person is aware of the negative images held by whites and the wider society of black Americans, the acceptance of an American black identity also means the acceptance of the oppositional character of that identity. Oppositional identities, as Ogbu (1990) clearly argues, are self- and group-affirming identities for stigmatized groups—defining as good and worthy those traits and characteristics that are the opposite of those valued by the majority group. This tends to draw the aspirations of the teens downward.

Implications of the Patterns

Some of the distancing shown by the ethnic-identified teens vis-à-vis underclass black identity is the same as that exhibited by middle-class black Americans. Elijah Anderson (1990) has noted that middle-class blacks in a gentrifying neighborhood in Philadelphia use various verbal and nonverbal strategies to convey to others that they are not from the ghetto and that they disapprove of the ghetto-specific behaviors of the blacks who live there. Being an ethnic black in interactions with whites seems to be a shorthand way of conveying distance from the ghetto blacks. Thus, the second generation reserves their ethnic status for use as an identity device to stress their distance from poor blacks and to stress their cultural values, which are consistent with American middle-class values. This same use of an ethnic identity is present among first-generation immigrants of all social classes, even those in racially segregated poor neighborhoods in New York.

The second generation in the segregated neighborhoods, with little chance for social mobility, seems to be unaware that status as a black ethnic conveys higher social status among whites, in part because they have not had much contact with whites. The mass media conveys to them the negative image of American blacks held by whites but does not convey to them the image among intellectuals, middle-class whites, and conservative scholars, such as Thomas Sowell, that they have cultural capital by virtue of their immigrant status. They do get the message that blacks are stereotyped by whites in negative ways, that the all-black neighborhoods they live in are violent and dangerous, and that the neighborhoods of whites are relatively safe. They also encounter a peer culture that values black American cultural forms. The immigrant culture of struggle, hard work, and educational success that their parents try to enforce is experienced in negative ways by these youngsters. They see their parents denying them privileges that their American peers enjoy and, unlike the middle-class youth, they do not automatically associate hard work, lack of dating and partying, and stress on scholastic achievement with social mobility. In the peer culture of the school, immigrant- and ethnic-identified teens tend to be the best students. In the neighborhood inner-city schools, newly arrived immigrants who have attended better schools in the islands tend to outperform the students who have spent their lives in substandard New York City public schools. This tends to reinforce the association

between ethnicity and school success—and the more American-identified teens adopt an adversarial stance toward school.

Warner and Srole (1945), in their study of Yankee City in the 1930s, report that it is the socially mobile white ethnics whose ties to the ethnic group and the ethnic identity decline. In their work, those individuals stuck in the lower classes turned to their ethnic identities and groups as a sort of consolation prize:

> Our class system functions for a large proportion of ethnics to destroy the ethnic subsystems and to increase assimilation. The mobile ethnic is much more likely to be assimilated than the nonmobile one. The latter retains many of the social characteristics of his homeland. . . . Some of the unsuccessfully mobile turn hostile to the host culture, develop increasing feelings of loyalty to their ethnic traditions, become active in maintaining their ethnic subsystems, and prevent others from becoming assimilated. But, generally speaking, our class order disunites ethnic groups and accelerates their assimilation. (p. 284)

It could be that the process will be exactly the opposite for black immigrants and black ethnics. In this case, the more socially mobile cling to ethnic identity as a hedge against their racial identity. The less mobile blacks see little advantage to stressing an ethnic identity in the social worlds in which they travel, which are shared mostly with black Americans. Stressing an ethnic identity in that context risks being described as "acting white," being seen as rejecting the race and accepting the white stereotypes, which they know through their everyday lives are not true.

The changes in race relations in the United States since the 1960s are very complicated and most surely involve a mixing of class and race. Some white Americans are trying to see the difference between ghetto inner-city blacks, whom they fear and do not like, and middle-class blacks, whom they do not fear and with whom they would like to have contact, if only to prove to themselves that they are not racist or, in a more formal sense, to meet their affirmative goals.

Middle-class blacks realize this and try to convey their class status in subtle and not so subtle ways (Feagin 1991). The immigrants also utilize the fact that New Yorkers tend to use foreign-born status as a proxy for the class information they are seeking. The white New Yorkers we interviewed do notice differences among blacks, and they use ethnic differences as clues for class differences. If the association found here between social class and ethnic identity is widespread, this perception could become a self-fulfilling prophesy. It could be that the children of poor parents will not keep an ethnic identity and the children whose parents achieve social mobility will keep the ethnic identity. This will reinforce the image in the minds of whites that the "island people" are "good blacks," thus giving the edge in employment decisions and the like to ethnic blacks over American blacks.

On the other hand, it remains to be seen how long the ethnic-identified second generation will continue to identify with their ethnic backgrounds. This also is related to the fact that whites tend to make racial judgments about identity when it comes to blacks. The second generation does not have an accent or other clues that immediately telegraph their ethnic status to others. They are aware that, unless they are active in conveying their identities, they are seen as black Americans, and that often in encounters with whites, the status of their black race is all that matters. It could be that by the time they have children, they will have decided that the quest not to be seen as a black American will be a futile one.

NOTES

1. The families of the teens were from twelve different countries including Jamaica (31 percent); Trinidad (21 percent); Guyana (16 percent); Barbados (10 percent); Haiti (10 percent); Grenada (5 percent); and a few each from the smaller islands of Montserrat, Saint Thomas, Anguilla, Saint Lucia, Dominica, and Nevis.
2. Middle class was defined as having at least one parent with a college degree or a professional or business position. Working class was defined as a parent with a low-skill job; poor were students whose parents were not currently employed.

REFERENCES

Anderson, E. 1990. *Streetwise: Race, Class, and Change in an Urban Community.* Chicago: University of Chicago Press.

Feagin, J. R. 1991. "The Continuing Significance of Race—Antiblack Discrimination in Public Places." *American Sociological Review* 56(1): 101–116.

Foner, N. 1987. "The Jamaicans: Race and Ethnicity Among Migrants in New York City." In *New Immigrants in New York,* edited by N. Foner. New York: Columbia University Press.

Fordham, S. 1988. "Racelessness as a Factor in Black Students' School Success: Pragmatic Strategy or Pyrrhic Victory?" *Harvard Education Review* 58(1) (February).

Gans, H. J. 1992. "Second-Generation Decline: Scenarios for the Economic and Ethnic Futures of Post-1965 American Immigrants." *Ethnic and Racial Studies* 15 (April):173–192.

Kasinitz, P. 1992. *Caribbean New York: Black Immigrants and the Politics of Race.* Ithaca, NY: Cornell University Press.

Lieberson, A. 1980. *A Piece of the Pie: Blacks and White Immigrants Since 1980.* Berkeley: University of California Press.

Massey, D. 1990. "American Apartheid: Segregation and the Making of the Underclass." *American Journal of Sociology* 96(2) (September): 329–357.

Ogbu, J. U. 1990. "Minority Status and Literacy in Comparative Perspective." *Daedalus* 119(2) (Spring):141–168.

Portes, A., and M. Zhou. 1993. "The New Second Generation: Segmented Assimilation and Its Variants." *Annals of the American Academy of*

Political and Social Sciences 530 (November):74–96.

STAFFORD, S.B. 1987. "Language and Identity: Haitians in New York City." In *Caribbean Life in New York City: Sociocultural Dimensions,* edited by C.R. Sutton and E.M. Chaney. New York: Center for Migration Studies.

SUTTON, C.R., and S.P. MAKIESKY. 1975. "Migration and West Indian Racial and Ethnic Consciousness." In *Migration and Development:* *Implications for Ethnic Identity and Political Conflict,* edited by H.I. Safa and B.M. Du Toit. Paris: Mouton.

WARNER, W.L., and L. SROLE. 1945. *The Social Systems of American Ethnic Groups.* New Haven, CT: Yale University Press.

WOLDEMIKAEL, T.M. 1989. *Becoming Black American: Haitian and American Institutions in Evanston, Illinois.* New York: AMS Press.

38

HISPANICS IN A MULTICULTURAL SOCIETY
A New American Dilemma?

Albert M. Camarillo and Frank Bonilla

Questions to Consider

Latinos now make up a larger portion of the U.S. population than blacks. However, it would be a mistake to categorize Latinos as constituting one homogenous culture. Puerto Rican Americans in New York are culturally different from Cuban Americans in Miami, and these two groups are quite different from Mexican Americans in San Antonio. In this reading, we are given a quick historical and socioeconomic overview of the various populations that make up the category Latino *and the various social, economic, and political issues these culturally disparate groups currently face. How will the rapid growth of the Latino population challenge the black–white dichotomy that has historically defined U.S. race relations?*

As the twenty-first century dawns, and as the U.S. Bureau of the Census (USBC) prepares for another decen-

nial snapshot of demographic change in American society, the population enumeration for the year 2000 is certain to reveal the continuation of dramatic shifts in U.S. ethnic and racial group makeup. The multiethnic and multiracial character of the nation is accelerating at a pace even more rapid than many demographers had projected. The most recent projections from USBC confirm the population increases of American minority groups, in particular that of Hispanics. Indeed, the term "minority," as a useful population classification, will become increasingly outmoded with each passing decade.

Much is being made of the projection that Hispanics will constitute the nation's largest minority population by 2050. High birth rates and continual immigration from Mexico, Central and South America, and the Caribbean are pushing Hispanics' numbers higher than those of Blacks. But what will it mean for this highly diverse group to become the largest minority in the United States? In the early twenty-first century, will patterns of residential, occupational, educational, and other measures of mobility resemble those of the great waves of immigrants from Europe and their offspring in the early twentieth century? Or will large numbers of Hispanics, midway through the next century, be described as a "new American dilemma," members of the nation's largest ethnic group and economically isolated from mainstream American society? In 1944, in *An American Dilemma: The Negro Problem and Modern Democracy* (1944), Gunnar Myrdal identified a central tension. In this landmark study, he outlined the moral dilemma between the "American Creed . . . [a value system] . . . where the American thinks, talks, and acts under the influence of high national and Christian precepts"—and the discriminatory treatment of Blacks. Will a new American dilemma characterize growing sectors of the Hispanic and Black populations, cut off from economic opportunity and meaningful participation in the civic life of the nation in the twenty-first century (Bonilla, 1988)?

The status of Hispanics is a mixed bag, with signs of group progress matched by signs of decline and stagnation. Some Hispanics are achieving impressive upward socioeconomic gains, having successfully climbed the ladder of occupational and geographic mobility to better jobs and better homes in safer neighborhoods. Others languish in deepening chasms of poverty and despair, seemingly trapped in urban *barrios* increasingly isolated geographically from opportunities in the larger society. The changing dynamics of U.S. and global economies are altering labor markets in fundamental ways that will have important consequences for Hispanic workers. Will the legions of today's Hispanic youngsters be incorporated fully into the body politic and institutional life of the nation in the next century, or will too many of them remain outside a "gated" American community? Will fears about the "Balkanization" of American society and identity politics result in a "Quebec-type" situation for Hispanics?

Historical Legacies and Hispanic America

Any starting point for discussion of the contemporary status or future prospects of Hispanics must begin with consideration of critical historical legacies—developments of the past that continue to indelibly stamp the contemporary reality of Hispanic subgroups. Among the many benchmarks that have influenced the course of history for Hispanics in the United States, two stand out as being particularly important—the Mexican-American War in 1848 and the Spanish-American War in 1898. These events set the stage for the incorporation of Spanish-speaking peoples from Mexico, Puerto Rico, and Cuba into the United States, and, at the same time, established economic, political, and international diplomatic relations that later played a great role in the migration and immigration of millions of Spanish-surnamed people to the United States.

The Treaty of Guadalupe Hidalgo, between the United States and Mexico, resulted in the annexation of nearly half of Mexico's territory and the incorporation of a new regional minority—Mexican Americans of the Southwest (Camarillo, 1993; Griswold del Castillo, 1990). During the early twentieth century, growing instability in the Republic of Mexico, and a heavy-handed dictatorship, gave rise to the first modern revolution—a civil war that unleashed the first great wave of Mexican immigrants to venture north to the United States. Throughout the past 100 years, U.S. dependence on workers from south of U.S. borders, coupled with Mexico's economic instability and inability to absorb its expanding workforce, resulted in many millions of Mexican immigrants settling in the United States. With the exception of the Great Depression years, immigration from Mexico was continuous throughout the twentieth century, swelled the ranks of existing Mexican American communities, and spawned the development of newer communities in the Southwest and elsewhere (Gutiérrez, 1995).

Although the manner of incorporation into the United States was different for both Puerto Ricans and Cubans, a war—the Spanish-American War—also set in motion forces that later propelled millions of people from those islands to U.S. shores. The United States acquired Puerto Rico from Spain in 1898 and established a colonial relationship with the island. Puerto Ricans were not accorded the status of U.S. citizenship, however, until 1917, just in time to make them eligible for military service in World War I. In 1947, Puerto Rico was accorded commonwealth status, a development that did not appreciably change the status of the island and its people as possessions of the United States. Numerous factors—interdependency, U.S. domination of the island's economy, unemployment, poverty, and lack of opportunity, combined with cheap transportation costs to the

United States—resulted in Puerto Ricans migrating to the U.S. mainland; and the movement gained momentum in the decades after World War II. Steady migration streams of Puerto Ricans arrived in mainland cities, especially New York City, where a highly segregated urban experience unfolded (Sánchez-Korrol, 1983).

The Cubans' experience was quite different. A few years after military occupation of the island in 1898, the United States turned over control to the Cubans. Though a small Cuban immigrant community had developed in Florida, especially in Miami, mass migration did not occur until after Castro's socialist revolution in 1959 (Portes and Bach, 1985). Successive migrations followed.

With the exception of the first wave of immigrants from Cuba, the historical legacies of the wars in 1848 and 1898—conquest, racial and class subordination, colonialism, and economic interdependency—created political, economic, and social patterns for Mexicans and Puerto Ricans that persisted into the late twentieth century. As racialized minorities in American society, most Hispanics share a dubious distinction with other U.S. citizens of color. Generalizations of this type, however, must be considered in light of significant differences between each Hispanic subgroup. Because of the enormous diversity within this broadly defined group, any demographic profile of Hispanics must consider the particulars of each nationality.

Contemporary Trends

Demographic Profile

The increasing national attention on, and concern about, Hispanics in U.S. society has been driven, in large part, by the spectacular growth of this population, especially since the 1960s. That Hispanics will soon become the nation's largest minority—a demographic shift frequently noted in the media, and one that causes consternation for many Americans—is testimony to the dramatic growth of this diverse group. The expansion of Hispanic America must be considered one of the fundamental demographic trends that is sure to continue in the future. Thus, when one considers projections for the future, the question of whether this group will constitute an essential component of a "new" American dilemma turns basically on the issue of numbers.

Though the specific numbers may be imprecise (because of such factors as census undercounting, different ways used by USBC to identify Hispanics over time, and undocumented immigration), the general patterns are clear. Between 1960 and 1996, the total population of Hispanics soared from about 6.9 million to more than 25.3 million (Table 1); and the Hispanic percentage of the total U.S. population more than doubled, increasing from less than 4 percent to 11 percent. There is no end in sight for this population growth. USBC projections estimate a total of 31.4 million Hispanics in 2000, increasing to 95.5 million by 2050. Nearly a quarter of the entire U.S. population in 2050 is projected to be of Hispanic origin. The driving force of this population expansion is the high fertility rate among Hispanic women (with the exception of Cuban women), but nearly as important is the constant stream of both documented and undocumented immigrants from Latin American nations (especially Mexico) and the ongoing circulation of Puerto Ricans from the island to the mainland (del Pinal and Singer, 1997; Torre, 1992).

Among the different Hispanic subgroups, Mexicans have always constituted the largest contingent. In 1970, the Mexican-origin population comprised about half of the Hispanic people enumerated in the census. The percentage increased to 64 percent by the mid-1990s. Puerto Ricans made up the second largest Hispanic subgroup, between 15 and 11 percent of the total Hispanic population between 1970 and 1996. Cubans have accounted for 4 percent to 6 percent of the Hispanic population since 1970, and Central and South Americans, and a category labeled by USBC as "Other Hispanic" (including immigrants from Spain and people of mixed Hispanic heritage from other countries), constitute sizable proportions of the total Hispanic population (Figure 1) (Bean and Tienda, 1987; del Pinal and Singer, 1997).

The historical legacy of regionally concentrated Hispanic subgroups is still plainly visible today (Table 2). Mexican-origin people continue to be overwhelmingly concentrated in the five states of the American Southwest, especially California and Texas, whereas most Puerto Ricans are located in New York and other Northeastern states, and Cubans are clustered primarily in Florida.

TABLE 1 Hispanic Population in the United States 1960 to 1996 with Projections for 2000 to 2050 (millions)

	1960	1970	1980	1996	2000	2030	2050
Total Hispanic population	6.9	9.1	14.6	25.3	31.4	65.6	95.5
Hispanics as percent of total U.S. population	3.9	4.5	6.4	10.7	11.4	18.9	24.5

Sources: Adapted from Bean and Tienda (1987:59, Table 3.1); U.S. Bureau of the Census (1996:12, Table 1); del Pinal and Singer (1997:6, Table 1).

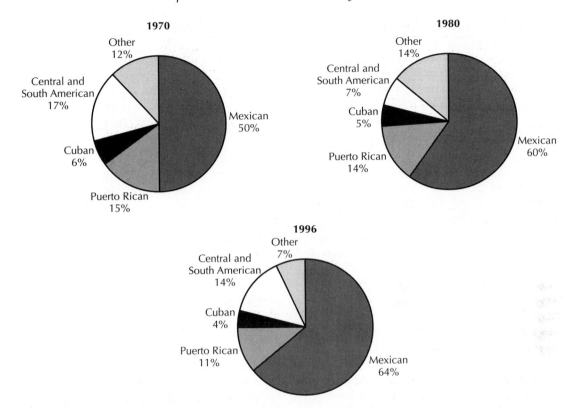

FIGURE 1　Hispanic population in the United States, by national origin, 1970 to 1996. The decrease in the number and percentage of people of Central and South American origin between 1970 and 1980 is likely due to changes in self-reporting for Mexicans made by the U.S. Bureau of the Census during the 1970s. *Source:* Adapted from the U.S. Bureau of the Census (1974:2, 9:Tables 1-1 and 1-3); del Pinal and Singer (1997:7:Figure 1); Bean and Tienda (1987:60).

Since the 1970s, Central and South American immigrants have gravitated to particular cities, especially port-of-entry cities, such as New York, Los Angeles, San Francisco, and Miami. Central Americans also form substantial communities in Chicago, Washington, D.C., and New Orleans; and Spanish-speaking Caribbean people are concentrated in New York City and other Atlantic seaboard cities (Ueda, 1994). With few exceptions, all Hispanic subgroups are highly urbanized (more than 80 percent lived in cities in 1980), one of the defining demographic patterns of Hispanic America since before World War II (Bean and Tienda, 1987).

City life for Hispanics since the 1950s has gone hand in hand with residential segregation, both in long-established *barrios* and in newer urban localities. Only since 1960 have scholars attempted to assess the levels of residential isolation of various Hispanic subgroups from Whites, and the picture that has emerged fits somewhere between the extremely high levels of residential segregation experienced by Blacks and the patterns of neighborhood formation and dispersal experienced by many European groups.

The analysis of the spatial characteristics of Hispanics, conducted by Frank Bean

TABLE 2   Hispanic Population in Selected States, 1970 to 1990 with Projections to 2020 (millions)

State	1970		1980		1990		2020	
	n	*% of State Population*	*n*	*% of State Population*	*n*	*% of State Population*	*n*	*% of State Population*
California	2.0	12	4.5	19	7.7	26	17.5	36.5
Texas	1.8	16	3.0	21	4.3	25	10.3	40.3
New York	1.2	7	1.7	9	2.2	12	3.0	15.9
Florida	0.4	6	0.6	6	1.6	12	4.2	21.5
Illinois	0.5	4	0.6	6	0.9	8	2.1	15.7
Arizona	0.3	15	0.4	16	0.7	18	1.8	31.7
New Jersey	0.3	5	0.5	7	0.7	10	1.5	17.0
New Mexico	0.3	30	0.5	37	0.6	38	1.3	55.4
Colorado	0.2	10	0.3	12	0.4	13	1.0	20.0

Sources: Adapted from Bean and Tienda (1987:77–81); U.S. Bureau of the Census (1996); Horner (1997:12–15, 17–18).

and Marta Tienda (1987), using 1980 Census data, also revealed that substantial variety exists among Hispanics regarding residential segregation. Hispanics concentrated in the largest metropolitan areas—i.e., Los Angeles, New York, and Chicago—had the highest levels of residential segregation from Whites, while only moderate levels of segregation characterized the smaller metropolitan areas in which Hispanics reside. Among the various Hispanic subgroups, Puerto Ricans had much higher levels of residential segregation from Whites—an historical pattern that continues to define the group's urban experiences—than both Mexicans and Cubans. Ongoing immigration has increased levels of residential isolation, especially for Mexicans in the largest metropolitan areas where they reside in great numbers. If this trend continues through the 21st century, we may see sprawling urban *barrios* that look increasingly like the inner-city ghettos inhabited by Blacks.

Economic, Occupational, and Educational Status

However one chooses to characterize the socioeconomic restructuring of the United States since the mid-1970s, the impact of these changes on Hispanics has been felt most directly through major labor-market shifts. These changes have contributed to increasing the segmentation of Hispanic workers at the lower end of the occupational ladder. General trends of growing inequality and absolute poverty have weighed heavily on substantial Hispanic working sectors, especially Hispanics born outside the United States. A large body of research now tracks the main forces, domestic and transnational, defining the magnitude, composition, and circuits of labor-force movement and the distinctive patterns shaping the incorporation of Hispanics in the regions and principal cities to which they have gravitated.

Because they are the largest and fastest growing sector of the Hispanic population, and because of their particular modes of entry and accommodation within the United States, both U.S.-born and foreign-born Mexicans dramatically illustrate some of the most fundamental changes taking place in the United States. In addition, their large numbers make possible a more refined analysis of the dynamics of these processes and their impacts on youth and women, and on particular occupations and sectors of the economy. Nevertheless, this summary account can only point to general characteristics of the present labor force and its ethnic and racial composition.

Unemployment rates in 1996 for Hispanics, put at 10 percent for both men and women, hovered at double the rates for Whites. Rates for Hispanics had been between those for Whites and Blacks for decades; but the gap between Hispanics and Blacks seemed to be closing, with "Other Hispanics" apparently adding to the ranks of Hispanic unemployed and pushing the joblessness rates closer to those for Black males. Puerto Ricans and most other Hispanics, except Cubans (whose unemployment rates tended to be closer to those for Whites than for other Hispanics), were all clustered around the 10 percent rate, though other analyses suggest that patterns of labor-market participation and exclusion for the larger subgroups vary considerably. Mexicans generally remain longer in low-wage jobs; Puerto Ricans are more likely to step out of, or lose connection to, low-end job markets; and Cubans, constituting a special case, are moving, in the present generation, toward patterns long shared by other disadvantaged groups.

Occupational patterns from 1996 Census data point to the sustained segmentation of job-market access, with White males about evenly divided between professional, administrative, and sales positions, as opposed to jobs in the service, skilled, and unskilled labor market (Table 3). By contrast, two-thirds of Blacks were in service and low-skilled jobs, and almost three-fourths of all Hispanic males held these types of jobs. Slightly more than one-half of Cuban males were also employed in these job categories. Fully four-fifths of Hispanics born outside the United States remain at the bottom of the occupational hierarchy. It is interesting to note, however, that Hispanic women manifest a markedly superior capacity to break through into the professional and managerial sectors, especially the U.S.-born.

Poverty rates and family incomes closely match labor-force participation and placement (Table 4). About 25 percent of Black and Hispanic families are estimated to be living below poverty levels, whereas only 6 percent of White families are in that income group. Among Hispanics, 36 percent of Puerto Rican families and 30 percent of those born outside the United States stand out as the most deprived; the rate of poverty for Cubans (16 percent) is closest to the figure for all American families. Cubans and U.S.-born Hispanics, as a group, stand out among Hispanic families with annual incomes of $25,000 or more, an indication of the modest inroads that some have made into the ranks of middle- and higher income classes. Median family income by race and ethnicity since the 1970s reveals that great disparities still characterize annual income levels between Whites and Asians at the higher end and Blacks and Hispanics at the lower end (Figure 2). Hispanic and Black family income, relative to that of White families, has decreased since the mid-1970s. Hispanic median family income has actually dropped substantially, in fact; but much of this decrease is attributed to large-scale immigration of people who are relatively unskilled and who do not possess much formal education. In a report prepared by the Council of Economic Advisers (1998a), which President Clinton transmitted to Congress in February 1998, important explanations were offered regarding the growth of income inequality among ethnic and racial minorities.

> Thirty-four years ago the signing of the Civil Rights Act of 1964 set the Nation on a course toward racial equality. As the economy surged, income differences narrowed for a full decade. The sharp recessions of the mid-1970s and early 1980s hit Black and Hispanic Americans particularly hard, however. And in the expansion of the 1980s, economic

TABLE 3 Percentages of Unemployed and Employed Persons (16 years and older) and Employment Categories by Race and Ethnicity, 1996

| | % Unemployed[a] | | Employed Workers | | | |
| | | | Men | | Women | |
Race/Ethnic Group	Men	Women	Professional, Administrative, Sales	Service, Skilled/Unskilled Labor	Professional, Administrative, Sales	Service, Skilled/Unskilled Labor
Total	7	5	48	52	72	28
Non-Hispanic	6	5	50	50	74	26
White	5	4	51	49	76	24
Black	14	9	34	66	61	39
Other Non-Hispanic[b]	7	5	58	42	67	33
Hispanic	10	10	27	73	56	44
Mexican	10	10	23	77	55	45
Puerto Rican	10	11	37	63	64	36
Cuban	6	6	44	56	72	28
Central/South American	8	10	29	71	48	52
Other Hispanic	16	7	45	55	60	40
Born in U.S.	10	9	41	59	72	40
Born outside United States[c]	9	11	18	82	40	60

[a]Persons age 16 or older in the labor force.
[b]Includes Asians, Pacific Islanders, American Indians, Eskimos, Aleuts, and other non-Hispanics.
[c]Includes Puerto Ricans born outside the contiguous states.
Source: del Pinal and Singer (1997:38, Table 8). Reprinted with permission from the Population Reference Bureau, Washington, D.C.

TABLE 4 Family Income and Poverty Rates, by Race and Ethnicity, 1995

Race/Ethnic Group	Number of Families (1000s)	Family Income (%)			Percent Below Poverty		
		Under $10,000	$10,000–24,999	$25,000 or more	All Families	Female-headed	Elderly[a]
Total	69,597	7	21	72	11	32	6
Non-Hispanic	63,311	7	20	74	9	30	5
White	52,861	5	18	77	6	22	4
Black	7,871	19	29	51	26	45	17
Other Non-Hispanic[b]	2,579	10	20	70	15	33	10
Hispanic	6,287	16	35	49	27	49	18
Mexican	3,815	15	37	47	28	50	18
Puerto Rican	742	26	29	45	36	64	19
Cuban	312	10	28	62	16	29	12
Central/South American	929	11	35	54	22	35	19
Other Hispanic	489	20	26	54	25	50	20
Born in U.S.	2,466	15	29	56	22	47	16
Born outside United States[c]	3,821	17	38	45	30	51	20

[a] Householders age 65 or older.

[b] Non-Hispanic American Indian, Eskimo, Aleuts, Asian, and Pacific Islander.

[c] Includes Puerto Rican householders born outside the 50 contiguous states.

Note: Percentages may not add to 100 because of rounding.

Source: del Pinal and Singer (1997:40, Table 9). Reprinted with permission from the Population Reference Bureau, Washington, D.C.

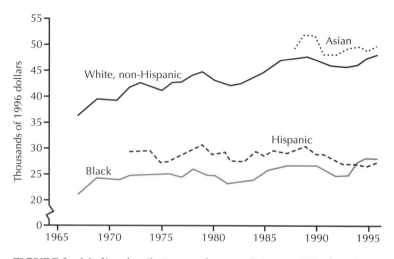

FIGURE 2 Median family income by race. Prior to 1972, data for Whites include Hispanic Whites. *Source:* Council of Economic Advisers (1998b).

growth was accompanied by sharp increases in overall income inequality. As a result, despite the economic growth of this period, income differences between Black and Hispanic families on the one hand, and non-Hispanic White families on the other, did not diminish. The recession of the early 1990s brought further economic hardship, as the poverty rate climbed to a new 30-year high (p. 119).

Educational attainment is, of course, an essential key to job access and improved incomes. Among the many factors that promote success, adequate schooling remains a serious obstacle to Hispanic progress. Hispanics' educational attainment rates are significantly lower than those for both Whites and Blacks, although, again, U.S.-born Hispanics of every national origin have made some gains in the number of years of high school education completed. For example, the median number of years of schooling attained by native born Mexicans (age 25 and over) went from a low of 6.4 years in 1960 to 9.1 years in 1980. For other Hispanic groups, between 1960 and 1980, the median number

of school years increased from 7.5 to 10.0 years for Puerto Ricans and from 8.0 to 11.7 years for Cuban-Americans. By contrast, the median school years attained by Blacks during these years increased markedly from 8.0 in 1960 to 12.0 years in 1980 (Bean and Tienda, 1987), a figure that matched those of non-Hispanic Whites (11.0 years attained in 1960 and 12.0 years in 1980). Comparing high school completion rates also reveals a similar pattern of educational disadvantage among Hispanics. Figure 3 illustrates how the gap between Hispanics, Whites, and Blacks, with regard to high school completion (and equivalency), has actually increased since the 1980s; only about 60 percent of Hispanics completed four years of high school in 1997.

The relatively low rates of high school completion for Hispanics is, to a substantial degree, attributable to the large percentage of immigrants who generally have lower levels of educational attainment. Indeed, the rather dismal educational profile of Hispanics brightens when one compares the rates between U.S. born and foreign born. Figure 4 compares the educational attainment rates

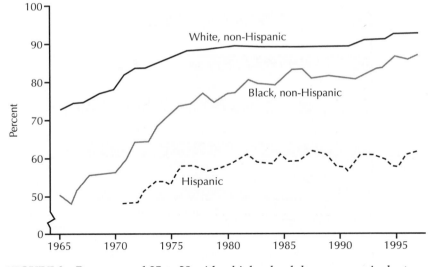

FIGURE 3 Persons aged 25 to 29 with a high school degree or equivalent.
Source: Council of Economic Advisers (1998b).

among the various Hispanic groups by nativity. In 1996, about 70 percent of all U.S.-born Hispanics had completed high school or some higher education level; Cubans and Central and South Americans achieved the highest levels of educational attainment (86 percent and 84 percent, respectively); Mexican-Americans had the lowest rate (67 percent). Across the board, foreign-born Hispanics were less educated, especially immigrants from Mexico. Although second-generation Hispanics have narrowed the educational gap, compared with Whites and Blacks, large numbers of them are still disadvantaged educationally—a fact that continues to have great influence on individual and group socioeconomic status.

A pattern of under-education for Hispanics is also illustrated when one considers institutions of higher learning. Since the 1960s, the percentage of Americans aged 25 to 29 who completed a four-year college education has steadily increased. The percentage of Hispanic and non-Hispanic Blacks who completed four years of higher education also increased, but at a disproportion-

ately lower rate than that for non-Hispanic Whites. In 1997, about 33 percent of Whites had completed college, compared with about 11 percent for Hispanics and 14 percent for Blacks. As is indicated in Figure 5, Hispanics and Blacks continue to fall significantly behind Whites in attaining four or more years of college (Council of Economic Advisors, 1998b), and this higher-education gap actually widened rather than narrowed in the 1990s.

The identification of groups by race and ethnicity reported here with respect to jobs, incomes, and formal schooling, though drawn from "official" sources, provides only a broad overview of a volatile and complex process that can elude observation or obscure the actual dynamics shaping outcomes (del Pinal and Singer, 1997). Unemployment rates, for example, generally reported in recent years as close to a "full-employment" standard, omit millions of part-time workers who would like full-time jobs, and millions of additional "discouraged workers" who need jobs but no longer actively pursue opportunities. School

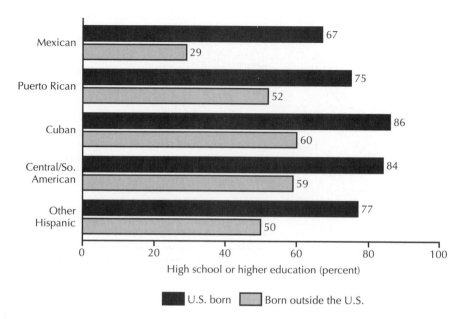

FIGURE 4   Educational attainment of Hispanics by national origin and by nativity, 1996. Sample includes persons ages 25 or older. Puerto Ricans born in Puerto Rico or outside the 50 states and the District of Columbia. *Source:* del Pinal and Singer (1997:p. 33, Figure 11). Reprinted with permission from the Population Reference Bureau, Washington, D.C.

drop-out rates similarly reflect a multifaceted dynamic of school readiness among pupils, family conditions, and institutional readiness, especially in public schools confronted with unprecedented levels of ethnic and racial diversity.

Political Participation and Group Identity

Looking back to the 1950s, at the participation of Hispanics in American political institutions at the local, state, or national levels, one cannot help but be impressed by gains that have occurred. Fifty years ago, with the exception of New Mexico, the number of Hispanic elected officials at the state or federal level could be counted on one hand. Though Hispanics were able to help elect a few of their own kind to local public offices, for the most part discriminatory practices

such as poll taxes, gerrymandering, and English language-literacy provisions excluded Hispanics from the political process. These historical legacies, when combined with high poverty and low naturalization rates, effectively disenfranchised huge numbers of Hispanics.

By the 1970s and 1980s, however, more and more political commentators and prospective candidates—including those attached to the national political parties— began to take notice of the growing Hispanic influence. Significantly, the Voting Rights Act of 1965, intended to help unlock the ballot box for Blacks, also helped to make the political process more open to Hispanics (Moore and Pachon, 1985). Characterizations of a "sleeping brown giant" beginning to show political awakening in the late 1960s and 1970s were reinforced by signs that, indeed, Hispanics were emerging as a politi-

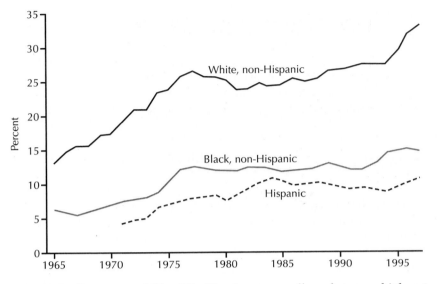

FIGURE 5   Persons aged 25 to 29 with a four-year college degree or higher. *Source:* Council of Economic Advisers (1998b:22).

cal force to be reckoned with in the 1980s, the so-called "Decade of the Hispanic."

Clearly, Hispanics have come a long way in the past generation with regard to flexing their growing political muscle. Hispanic elected officials at all levels now number more than 5,000; and there are hundreds of Spanish-surnamed persons who have been elected to state and federal positions. But although these gains are impressive, Hispanics are still grossly underrepresented, based on their percentage of the U.S. population (DeSipio, 1996). Greater political participation of Hispanics in electoral politics may take a long time, and may be difficult to achieve. One must raise the question of whether Hispanics will follow the political paths of other ethnic and racial minorities— Eastern and Southern European immigrants and their children in the earlier decades of the twentieth century and Blacks since the Civil Rights era—toward ever-increasing inclusion in the American political system.

Some political pundits and politicians point to the low voter registration and vot-

ing rates of Hispanics as indications of less interest in things political. In the 1992 and 1994 elections, Hispanic voter turnout ranged between 20 percent and 28 percent of registered voters, whereas the rate for Whites hovered around 64 to 65 percent, and that for Blacks ranged from 37 to 54 percent (DeSipio, 1996; del Pinal and Singer, 1997). In rebuttal, Hispanic advocacy organizations and ethnic political leaders argue that ongoing voter registration and education drives will result in more and more Hispanics who will exercise the franchise, ensuring greater and greater Hispanic political influence at all levels of government, especially at the local levels where they are currently more concentrated (Hero, 1992).

Several factors will help determine the eventual outcome of Hispanics as a powerful political force in the United States. First, it is commonly understood that low socioeconomic and educational status have a huge bearing on political participation rates; on this count, Hispanics have a long way to go. This factor is particularly important for the

Mexican-American and Puerto Rican populations, which are disproportionately represented among the ranks of the poorer working classes and who continue to have lower rates of higher education attainment. Second, the Hispanic population is one of the youngest in the nation; one-third of all Hispanics are younger than 18 years old, and more than one-fifth of all Hispanics of voting age are between the ages of 18 and 24. It is a fact that younger voters simply do not participate as actively in the political process as older voters. Third, immigrants and their children comprise about two-thirds of all Hispanics; and naturalization rates among them, especially among Mexican immigrants, is one of the lowest of any group in U.S. history. In 1996, for example, more than 40 percent of Hispanics older than age 18 were not naturalized citizens of the United States and, therefore, were ineligible to register to vote (del Pinal and Singer, 1997; Young, 1991). Finally, Hispanics do not constitute an ethnic voting bloc; they are composed of diverse constituencies with different political attitudes and are unlikely to combine their political power in the near future.

Scholars who analyzed data from the Latino National Political Survey of 1990 concluded that the various Hispanic subgroups do not view themselves in common. There are, however, issues of importance—such as increased government action to support education, especially bilingual education, to fight crime, and to provide child care services—that cut across national-origin group interests. It would, nevertheless, be misleading to describe an "Hispanic partisanship," because the political differences between Mexicans, Puerto Ricans, and Cubans are too great to lend themselves to a vision of a united Hispanic electorate (de la Garza et al., 1992). In some specific locales, however, historical circumstances have converged, bringing together different Hispanic sub-

groups for concerted political action. Chicago is a case in point (Padilla, 1985).

To no one's surprise, the Latino National Political Survey also revealed that Hispanics overwhelmingly prefer to use national-origin terms as primary ethnic identifiers—i.e., Mexican, Puerto Rican, Cuban, etc.—although U.S.-born Hispanics use these terms less than the foreign born, as one would expect (de la Garza et al., 1992). The pan-ethnic labels, Hispanic or Latino, are used as secondary terms of identification; and here, again, the U.S. born are more likely to use the pan-ethnic terms than the foreign born. Among those who use the pan-ethnic labels, a 1996 USBC survey found, a majority—58 percent—use the term Hispanic rather than Latino, the term used by only 12 percent (Pinal and Singer, 1997).

Ethnic or national-origin identity for Hispanics raises some interesting questions about race and ethnicity in America, not only about how the different subgroups view themselves, but also how the larger society views Hispanics. The U.S. government classifies Hispanics as an ethnic group; yet, Hispanics can be of any race (most classify as White, a minority as Black, and a growing percentage as "Other"). In the minds of the majority population, and in the minds of many Hispanics, there is ambiguity about racial or ethnic categories—an ambiguity that has indeed characterized Americans' preoccupation with skin color, national origin, and other sociocultural/religious differences that have separated Americans from other Americans for hundreds of years. This ambiguity is aptly reflected in the many confusing ways USBC has categorized Hispanics over the past century. For example, with the exception of the 1930 Census, when Mexicans were classified as a separate "race," Hispanics have been identified by foreign parentage, birthplace, "Spanish mother tongue," "Spanish surname,"

"Spanish origin," and, beginning in 1980, Spanish/Hispanic origin (Bean and Tienda, 1987). Given the diverse makeup of the nation's Hispanic populations—in terms of immigrant cohorts, national origins, cultural roots, distinct local and regional concentrations, and socioeconomic status—it is clear that any attempt to categorize them as a distinct, homogeneous group is counterproductive. Consequently, the catch-all term "Hispanic," as the preferred label of the federal government, includes the foreign born with the native born of many generations in the United States, political refugees, undocumented and legal immigrants, and people from many national origins. Yes, they derive from common Spanish-language origins and Roman Catholic religious traditions, and can trace their heritage to Spain's colonial legacies in the New World, but Hispanics in the United States at the dawn of the twenty-first century defy generalizations as a single group. The diversity that distinguishes Hispanics will surely continue to be one of the main characteristics of the group, a diversity that exists not only across but within each national-origin group.

Problems and Prospects

It may seem ironic to many that one of the thorniest intellectual and social-policy challenges presented by the surging number of Hispanics on the U.S. mainland today is identifying and counting them. The problem is far from new but is now at the center of heated controversy with respect to the 2000 Census and the related prescriptions for federal data-keeping mandated by the Office of Management and Budget (1997). There has been a growing furor about where and how the color line will be drawn in the twenty-first century, which has clearly displaced the complacency on this issue reflected in a 1983 report to the U.S. Department of Health and Human Services. That report (Davis et al., 1983) stated:

> Prior to the 1970 census, the concept of Hispanics as a group barely existed. Information on some components of the population, such as Mexicans, could be obtained from the usual census questions on a person's country of birth or that of parents, use of a language other than English at home, and ancestry. . . . But none of the identifiers used prior to 1970 could satisfy the need for a definition which could be applied nationwide and with reasonable consistency over time (p. 5).

Beyond the problem of accuracy in population counts, until recently seen as safely anchored in mutually exclusive racial categories and thorough enumeration, lies a dawning awareness of the multiracial character of Hispanic peoples and the potential significance of the growing pace of interethnic and interracial marriages, which adds yet more ambiguity to existing racial classifications. In fact the catalytic power of Hispanics in stimulating racial mixing in the rigidly divided United States of the 1940s was noted at the time by Myrdal (1944) in his study of more than 400 industrial plants. He noted:

> The most frequently encountered policy was one based on the belief that 'Negro and White workers will not mix.' They did "mix", however, in over 50 of the plants studied. In certain plants where Mexicans were regarded as White, Negroes were not allowed to "mix" with them; where Mexicans were classed as colored, Negroes not only worked with them but were given positions over them. In certain plants Mexicans and Whites worked together; in some others White workers accepted Mexicans and objected to Japanese.

Mexicans and Negroes worked under a White foreman; Italians and Mexicans under a Negro foreman (p. 393).

It is worth noting that at about that same time, Puerto Ricans in New York were configured together with Blacks in the first "minority/majority" senatorial district for the state legislature in what are today parts of Harlem and "el barrio." A 1935 pamphlet (The Tragedy of the Puerto Ricans and Colored Americans) delineated the obstacles in that setting to effective transracial/ethnic coalition-building in terms that have considerable resonance today (Martinez, 1935). Clearly, efforts to link the resources and capabilities of Hispanics with other marginalized communities to contest subordination are hardly new; there is, however, much to be done to pin down key elements of the present conjuncture in this regard as well as to critically revisit key historical experiences.

As discussed regarding Hispanics' demographic profile, despite the acknowledged constraints on the range and precision of public data gathering on Hispanics since the 1960s, a fairly consensual depiction of the dramatic shifts in the size, composition, location, and basic conditions of that population has been assembled by both official bodies and independent scholars, much of it by Hispanics themselves. On this front, public discourse on these questions has been decisively transformed. Still, in recent years, USBC's insistence on the qualifying proviso in every tabulation that "Hispanics may be of any race" has hammered home the idea of Hispanic communities as multiracial social formations, without seriously addressing the challenges and enigmas for research methods.

Present quandaries, and the need for pertinent inquiry, thus cluster on both of these fronts. The decision to combine data on ethnicity with race, and perhaps to allow more than one self-designation in both cate-gories, generates complexities in the collection and manipulation of these identifiers as well as their linkages to other variables. The alternatives in data collection now under discussion all confront difficulties, especially when coupled with the added dimension of adjustments being considered to remedy a troubling growth in census undercounts that disproportionately affect minorities. Expert opinions range from those who consider any such assignations unnecessary, and, perhaps, absurd and wasteful, to others bent on fully charting the rich mosaic of U.S. society, even if it means radically enlarging the number of racial categories and allowing multiple options per respondent. Some of the latter voices are, of course, psychometricians and geneticists determined to track "race" links to "capacities" and behaviors, though the task of unraveling these from developmental and environmental conditions, and deciding which genes are at work in any instance, may be effectively moot in present circumstances. At least one member of the citizens' board advising USBC insisted that with 95 percent of Americans still checking only one race, the essential racial order remains firmly in place and all the brouhaha is pointless (Holmes, 1998).

Significant population growth is sure to increase the role of Hispanics in the American political system; and more-or-less "official" readings of the most recent data confirm protracted demographic growth, continued diversification, and potential assimilation (notably via intermarriage with non-Hispanic Whites). Recent economic slippage for most Hispanics and barriers to increased political participation likely reflect the limiting constraints of newness to the society, noncitizenship, language barriers, education lags, and class factors, rather than racial discrimination. Hispanic newcomers are said to bring positive work, gender, family, and community values (social capital) into the troubled milieus to which they gravitate. Thus, whatever the evolving dynamics in the immediate future, Hispanics are expected to play an important role in transforming the United States. Ensuring their well-being is manifestly in the national interest (Davis et al., 1983).

But the emergence of Hispanics as strategic actors in major processes of social change within the United States has even more far-reaching implications. In the context of expanding transnational interdependence and international migration, Hispanic communities in the United States are integral to the economic and political restructurings that are redefining identities, citizenship, democracy, and human rights. As millions of individuals are obliged to maintain viable lives simultaneously in more than one society, and as formal legal structures to accommodate these realities— e.g., dual citizenship—begin to be brought into place, every arena of policy formulation and implementation is impacted. It is into this essentially uncharted terrain that Hispanics are now called on to play an important role (Bonilla et al., 1998).

Contemporary Policies, Issues, and Challenges

The Problem of Inequality and Exclusion

Since the 1960s, a number of key public policies have helped to open doors of opportunity for Hispanics and other minorities who were historically cut off from avenues of educational, occupational, and political mobility. Affirmative action-oriented admissions policies and new financial-aid opportunities facilitated access to institutions of higher learning that had been out of reach of the great majority of Hispanics. In addition, employment policies that provided protections against discriminatory practices in the workplace (e.g., those overseen by the Equal Employment Opportunity Commission) and policies that promoted the growth of minority-owned businesses (e.g., those overseen by the Office of Federal Contract Compliance Programs) helped to establish a beachhead for economic progress in Hispanic communities.

Similarly, fair-housing statutes, voting-rights laws, and bilingual-education programs were efforts orchestrated by the federal government to combat discrimination as well as attempts to create new paths for individual and group advancement. These laws and policies, and others, were important for three principal reasons. (1) They acknowledged the contemporary effects of historical discrimination that were embedded in the institutions of society. (2) They represented proactive federal-government intervention and allocation of resources required to turn American society in a direction where all citizens of the nation—regardless of race, ethnicity, national origin, sex, age, or disabilities—could have a fair chance to pursue opportunities as far as their individual capabilities would permit. (3) These policies contributed to the burgeoning Hispanic middle class and served as proof that new policies made a difference in the life chances of hundreds of thousands of Mexican-Americans, Puerto Ricans, and other Hispanic Americans.

Just as important, many of the policies of the past generation were evidence that the American "creed of opportunity"— sewn into the fabric of democratic society and culture—though narrowly conceived originally, could expand and change over time. During the course of U.S. history, citizens have sacrificed and struggled to reconceive this creed so that women, racial and ethnic minorities, disabled people, the poor, and others historically outside the gates of opportunity could enter. For those Americans who, over many generations, were denied opportunity, the legacies of exclusion and inequality are still painfully visible at the dawn of the twenty-first century. For many Hispanics and other minorities, history weighs heavily on their contemporary reality. To be sure, socioeconomic and educational group progress was achieved in the last quarter of the 1900s, in ways unimaginable to previous generations of Hispanics; but the modest gains made must be sustained and accelerated if members of the nation's soon-to-be largest ethnic group have a chance to become full shareholders in American society.

The current public-policy discourse and acerbic debates about programs such as affirmative action in employment and education (admission to colleges and universities), bilingualism and educational reform (English-only state laws, bilingual education curricula, and voucher programs), immigration (services to documented and undocumented immigrants), and welfare reform (consequences for the poor as a result of the welfare reform policies of 1996) tend to exacerbate the racial and ethnic divides in society. A more productive policy discourse about these and other existing policies—most of which were developed by lawmakers to promote opportunity—should center on a fundamental question critical to the well-being of all Americans: As U.S. and global economies move toward ever increasing interdependence, and as the nature of the American economic system shifts in the postindustrial era, which existing policies should be amended and which new policies should be envisioned that will sustain and improve opportunities for all Americans?

Any consideration of future public policies that does not take into account the human and economic costs of large sectors of society who are undereducated, underemployed, impoverished, and in ill health will surely undermine the foundations of American civilization. If the demographic projections are correct, and if the disturbing trends that characterize so many Hispanics today continue into the mid-twenty-first century, when Hispanics will constitute a quarter of the entire population, it may well be impossible to change the course of history for such a huge sector of the citizenry. For the well-being of American society in general, improving the life chances and opportunities for disadvantaged Hispanics and other poor Americans may indeed be one of the challenges that will determine the course of American democracy in the present century.

Hispanics in the Postindustrial Order

The Hispanic condition, as we look ahead, reflects, in stark ways, an overarching contraposition of social promise and denial in the contemporary relations of nation-state and market, both within the most advanced postindustrial U.S. setting and in the countries of origin of Hispanic peoples. As a major living link in the playing out of economic restructuring in the hemisphere, Hispanics confront massive shortfalls in the capacity of market and state to provide employment at a living wage or adequate social infrastructures for all. As the global rush to embrace free markets surges ahead, along with the ascendancy of the need to privilege capital and its freedom of movement, two key questions emerge: (1) When and how will some new forms of state control or legal norms be brought into place in response to the deepening social crises generated by the untrammeled movement of transnational capital? (2) What voice can workers, themselves trying to balance attachments to multiple national and cultural identities, have in shaping whatever social pact will undergird the emergent transnational global order, and protect their rights to work and decent living standards (Morales and Bonilla, 1993)?

Having become an overwhelmingly urban population, Hispanics now also stand at the epicenter of social transformations that dramatize the social pathologies of big-city decline. For these communities, the bad news continues. Inner-city Hispanics are now reported to be the most discriminated-against group in housing markets across the country. Their neighborhoods are awash with environmental perils, just as their workplaces are exposed to the severest job hazards (Yinger, 1995; Goldman, 1991). Yet, we begin to hear, as well, that newness to the society and social isolation may temporarily shield some Hispanics, especially those freshly arrived, from the perverse effects of urban poverty. For example, despite more modest human-capital endowments, Mexican immigrants are perceived by some employers as more willing and disciplined low-wage workers than Blacks. New immigrants have been hailed not only for their willingness to fill the demand for low-wage service workers, but also for their entrepreneurial energies in the informal economy and small enterprise. Thus, recent immigrants, in contrast to long-time resident Blacks and Puerto Ricans, are now credited with producing for New York City a "low cost equivalent of gentrification" (Sassen, 1991).

Cultural Citizenship

Historically, both indigenous groups and immigrant populations, including Hispanics, were expected to shed their cultural and ethnic baggage and conform to Anglo-Saxon norms as a condition for inclusion into mainstream American society. A host of social, institutional, political, and cultural forces together weighed heavily on efforts by groups to maintain some semblance of their ethnic or cultural identity. Indeed, society's expectation for assimilation was pervasive for any group identified as culturally or ethnically different. For many groups, this expectation was internalized, thus hastening the processes of assimilation and acculturation. But despite the so-called "Anglo conformity" or "one-way" model of group assimilation, certain racial and immigrant minorities remained outside the gates of the American community. This has been the experience for large numbers of Hispanics.

In the second half of the twentieth century, recognition that many groups had maintained distinctive elements of their ethnic and cultural heritage, and others had insisted on preserving the integrity of their social and cultural differences, gave rise to ideas about the United States as an ethnically diverse democracy that did not have to force assimilation on all its citizens. These ideas are best reflected in the pluralism and multiculturalism models of group relations in a diverse society. In contrast to the dominant paradigm of assimilation, these two approaches help explain how different groups are able to maintain their cultural distinctiveness and how society benefits from an understanding and appreciation of the many cultures that constitute the larger society. Though pluralistic and multicultural models promote cultural democracy in the United States and encourage celebration of contributions to society from many different groups, neither explains satisfactorily how groups can change society—its social, cultural, and political norms.

The idea of "cultural citizenship" has been developed by a team of Hispanic scholars (Flores and Benmayor, 1997) exploring ways to understand how Hispanics and other groups not only make cultural contributions to a plural society, but also alter society. By the sheer size of the Hispanic population and the myriad ways they are influencing society, this idea of cultural citizenship provides some valuable insights into how Hispanics, now and in the future, are bound up in dynamic interaction in

American society, a dialectical process in which both the group and the society at large are constantly changing one another. "In our opinion," the authors state, "what makes cultural citizenship so exciting is that it offers us an alternative perspective to better comprehend cultural processes that result in community building and in political claims raised by marginalized groups in the broader society" (Flores and Benmayor, 1997:15). Using the idea of citizenship as a concept that extends universal rights to members of a society, cultural citizenship broadens the concept to include groups historically positioned, in the legal sense, as "second class" or "noncitizens." This concept helps account for how these and other groups build communities and develop identities, how they lay claim to cultural "spaces," and how they claim rights in society. These spaces and claims have the potential not only to reform society—e.g., the Civil Rights era reforms and reaffirmation of Black identity—but also to elevate various subcultures to a level where no one culture dominates. Thus, the idea of cultural citizenship, by logical extension, may form the basis on which Americans see themselves not in contentious ways, but as cultural citizens of a nation with connected and interdependent cultural communities that constitute the whole.

As the Hispanic population continues to grow, and thus leaves American society with no "majority" population, the idea of cultural citizenship in a heterogeneous society may serve as a useful way to envision society and cultural change as a key component of American democracy in the twenty-first century.

Country of Origin Linkages

To complicate matters, the growing importance given to Hispanics in the United States by governments in their countries of origin

has not escaped worried observers. In 1987, for example, the Mexican government established an outreach program for its citizens, and their offspring, in the United States. Components of this program proliferated and took on new dimensions as the North American Free Trade Agreement between the United States, Mexico, and Canada took shape. Components now include several newspapers geared to community interests; sponsorship of cultural and sports events and organizations; academic exchanges; networking among labor, feminist, environmental, and religious entities; and so on. In 1997, the Mexican legislature, with unanimous support from all major parties, legalized dual citizenship, permitting immigrants who chose to become naturalized U.S. citizens to also retain their full rights as Mexican citizens. Parallel developments, especially with respect to absentee voting in presidential elections, are being pursued by numerous other countries—e.g., Peru, Colombia, the Dominican Republic, and some Central American nations. In every instance, a major consideration stimulating this outreach to the millions in the diaspora is, of course, the millions in dollars and other remittances channeled homeward by immigrant communities.

In the late 1980s, Puerto Rico's Commonwealth government similarly moved to establish a cabinet-level Department of Community Affairs for Puerto Ricans in the United States. This agency soon mounted major voter mobilization campaigns in several states, thus raising major questions about "cross-state" political interference—i.e., using public monies from one state for political action in another. The repeated calls for binding referendums on the island's political status also highlight concerns about the rights of Puerto Rican mainland dwellers to a formal voice in such crucial matters. The intensifying debate about the island's status brings sharply into focus the fluidity and paradoxes of the waning powers of nation-states, of whatever order, to sustain the economic and social rights of their citizens within the emergent hemispheric and global context.

An official "dialogue" between the Cuban government and its nationals in exile in the United States was also mounted in 1987, and consultations involving the United States and other governments and international bodies along with Cuban-American organizations continue apace. Even the Spanish government has forthrightly declared its interest in U.S. "Hispanics" as a function of their "increasing political, social, and economic weight" (Cortina and Moncada, 1988). In brief, new kinds of transnational political relations are being pieced together, strengthened by the historic, existential ties of family, locality, culture, and other networks that have maintained immigrants' connections to their countries of origin over generations. Parallel efforts by federal agencies to engage Hispanic interests and political energies in support of U.S. foreign policy objectives further enhance the opportunities for Hispanic communities to assert independent perspectives in this terrain, rather than passively bowing to home-country or U.S. objectives.

Coalition Building

The record of misfires, divisive contention, and deliberate interventions by established power wielders to disrupt coalitions of Hispanics, especially with Blacks, goes back a long way. Mainstream apprehensions in this connection have peaked recently as part of the broad backlash against "big" government and social spending. Lance Liebman, a Harvard law professor, put the matter as succinctly and coldly as anyone in the early 1980s (Liebman, 1982):

> . . . we should hope for a Supreme Court wise enough and ingenious

enough to uphold legislative decisions that assist Blacks but refuse to uphold, because the justifications are weaker and the costs to the social fabric so great, extensions of those arrangements to other groups (p. 173).

"Other groups" here means, of course, chiefly Hispanics and especially new arrivals among them, whatever their immigrant status. As a matter of fact, despite these intimations of hardening resistance to any moves to unify racial and ethnic interests, the 1990s opened on a very positive note in this connection with a major conference at the Lyndon B. Johnson School of Public Affairs (University of Texas at Austin), bringing together notables from local communities and from outside the communities—politicians, academics, policy analysts, and community organizers. Present at the forum, launched by the Inter-University Program for Latino Research (IUPLR) and the Joint Center for Policy Studies, were such figures as David Dinkins, Barbara Jordan, Henry Cisneros, Nicholas Katzenbach, and Robert Reischauer. A landmark volume, *Hispanics and Blacks in the Cities: Policies for the 1990s* (Romo, 1990) provided a solid grounding for continued initiatives that are stretching into the present.

Taking stock of progress during the 1990s, there was the positioning of a critical mass of information, organizational capacity, and leadership resources backing minority coalitions that nevertheless confront serious reversals, determined opposition, shallow supports, and systemic challenges (Betancurt and Gills, 2000). For example, what early in the 1990s appeared as major electoral breakthroughs for Blacks and Hispanics in major cities—New York, Chicago, Los Angeles, San Francisco—soon gave way to conservative counterattacks and a crumbling disarray under the pressures of deepening inequality and poverty, budget deficits, and waning federal social infrastructure supports. Locally, there was contention at municipal and state levels over minimal resources. Competition for jobs, especially in the public sector, also surfaced as a divisive issue. Growing political apathy and withdrawal from partisan and electoral activity have also put a chill on efforts to mobilize coalitions within and across ethnic and racial lines. Still, newly articulated visions of comprehensive social development, with enhanced democratic participation and recognition of the social value of diversity, continue to propel scattered initiatives and "model" programs around the country (Hartman, 1997; Pacific Coast Council on International Policy, 1998). Many of these must manage to overcome entrenched obstacles to effective action—individualism, elitism, and the challenges to giving a genuine voice in decisions to marginalized participants. An encouraging development is the increasing recognition and practical implementation of transnational perspectives and organizational strategies in many of these undertakings (Brecher and Castello, 1994).

Responses to Public-Policy Initiatives

Shared empowerment pursued through coalition-building may remain elusive. Nevertheless, a critical advantage is gained through intensified communication and collaboration across groups, however limited. The amplification of horizons and synergizing impact of the give and take about policy perspectives on common issues enhances and strengthens communication and mutual empowerment. In this connection, IUPLR, mentioned earlier, has been a driving force among Hispanic academics and has fostered collaboration for scholarly research, policy formulation, and commu-

nity mobilization around matters crucial to all disadvantaged Hispanics and the nation at large. The more pertinent point is the virtual explosion of parallel endeavors validating and implementing, in new venues, IUPLR's approach to overcoming the barriers between the academic world, public-policy arenas, and communities in need. Numerous such entities come to mind; one in particular, the National Jobs for All Coalition (NJFAC), can serve as exemplar here.

NJFAC, in operation since the mid-1990s, joined forces with an IUPLR working group on "Hispanics in a Changing U.S. Economy" to create a model advocacy forum in New York City to prepare a diverse group of Hispanic and other agencies to have a voice in municipal and state policies bearing on jobs and welfare rights. The nature of their contribution is well conveyed in their statement of task (Hernandez and Torres-Saillant, 1998):

> We will develop and disseminate economic and political analyses in formats appropriate for reaching the target audiences. These include new issues of our "Uncommon Sense" publications, written by experts on specific dimensions of the employment-unemployment area. The coalition has published more than 20 in this series; they are used by a wide range of organizations. The Coalition will also develop materials suitable for dissemination on the web, and in the form of video cassettes appropriate to school, university, and general audiences. We will expand our speakers' bureau for talks and appearances in universities and schools, on public forums, radio and television interviews and commentary, community and religious groups and other appropriate occasions (pp. 20–21).

NJFAC has a score of distinguished individuals on its executive committee and nearly 80 specialists, advocates, and important organizations on its national advisory board. Thus, as Hispanics move into the policy arena, they will have opportunities to draw on exceptional resources in bringing informed and responsible perspectives into this discourse. Parallel groups exist or are being formed to address many other issue areas—immigration, language, education, health, environmental conditions, youth, the roles and needs of women, community revitalization, and so on. The full inclusion of well-articulated minority perspectives and voices continues to be an aspiration rather than an accomplished fact; but the stage is set for a transformation of the coordination of research, explorations of policy alternatives, and community-driven political initiatives in which Hispanics may make creative contributions.

Conclusion

In many ways, Hispanics at the beginning of the twenty-first century stand at a crossroads in American society. On one level of analysis—especially if one examines the growing ranks of the emergent middle class—Hispanic families seem to be doing just fine. They have, in ever-increasing numbers, accessed opportunities in education and employment and have carved out a niche of American prosperity for themselves and their children. They tend to live in integrated neighborhoods and appear in so many ways to have achieved the "American dream," if one measures that aspiration by a standard of material possessions and economic stability. To the casual observer, tens of thousands of second- and third-generation Mexican Americans (predominantly a people with immigrant roots in the twentieth century) as well as Puerto Ricans

and Cubans (who have lived on the mainland for dozens of years) seem to be following a stair-step rise in status, as each successive wave of migrants and immigrants settles in the United States.

If one looks deeper and more critically, however, at the diverse Hispanic population, there is cause for real concern—in some cases, cause for alarm. Below the thin ranks of the Hispanic middle class lies a much larger group. They are not thriving. They are increasingly falling into the new categories of the "working poor" or, worse, are seemingly trapped as a class of severely impoverished people living in urban *barrios.* They are the Hispanic underclass. Given the current size of the Hispanic population, the great diversity that characterizes the group, and the sustained projected growth, Hispanics themselves and the society and its institutions must search for explanations for why some are faring well and others are faring so poorly. It is this latter group of Hispanics, particularly the great numbers of young people, who stand at a crossroads in American society. If the path can lead to educational achievement that ends with good jobs that pay a decent wage and provide hope, Hispanics in the twenty-first century will be productive citizens who will contribute in significant ways to society. But if these disturbing trends persist or increase, the potential for a "new" American dilemma seems frighteningly real.

The challenge is for Hispanics to muster a unified response, drawing on all their resources and capabilities, and become an integral part of the movement to uncover the complex forces intensifying inequality, poverty, political passivity, exploitation, and social isolation, not only within their own ranks but in the United States as a whole. This means reaching out and grasping every opportunity to share in the scholarly debate, policy assessment, and organized movement to restore priority to human rights objectives, despite the limitations under which all such initiatives now operate. These limitations, and their accompanying enigmas, have thrown disciplines, institutions, and even social philosophy into disarray. We must remember that the societal transformations affecting the dynamics of race, ethnicity, class, and gender demand patience and commitment and unconditional resistance to any tendencies toward withdrawal or self-isolation.

REFERENCES

BEAN, F., AND M. TIENDA. 1987. *The Hispanic Population of the United States.* New York: Russell Sage Foundation.

BETANCURT, J., AND D. GILLS. 2000. *The Collaborative City: Opportunities and Challenges for Blacks and Latinos.* New York: Garland Publishing.

BONILLA, F. 1988. *From Racial Justice to Economic Rights: The New American Dilemma.* Washington, D.C.: Smithsonian Institution.

BONILLA, F., E. MELENDEZ, R. MORALES, AND M. DE LOS ANGELES TORRES. 1998. *Borderless Borders: U.S. Latinos, Latin Americans, and the Paradox of Interdependence.* Philadelphia: Temple University Press.

BRECHER, J., AND T. CASTELLO. 1994. *Global Village or Global Pillage: Economic Reconstruction from the Bottom Up.* Boston: South End Press.

CAMARILLO, A. 1993. Latin Americans. In *Encyclopedia of American Social History*, Vol. 1, M. Kupiec Cayton, E. Gorn, and P. Williams, eds. New York: Charles Scribner's Sons.

CORTINA, R., AND A. MONCADA. 1988. *Hispanos en los Estados Unidos.* Madrid: Ediciones de la Cultura Hispanica.

Council of Economic Advisers. 1998a. *Economic Report of the President.* Washington, D.C.: U.S. Government Printing Office. 1998b. *Changing America: Indicators of Social and Economic Well-Being by Race and Hispanic Origin.* Washington, D.C.: U.S. Government Printing Office.

DAVIS, C., C. HAUB, and J. WILLETTE. 1983. U.S. Hispanics: Changing the face of America. *Population Bulletin* (38)3. Washington, D.C.: Population Reference Bureau.

DE LA GARZA, R., L. DESIPIO, F. GARCIA, J. GARCIA, and A. FALCON. 1992. *Latino Voices: Mexican, Puerto Rican and Cuban Perspectives on American Politics.* Boulder, Colo.: Westview Press.

DEL PINAL, J., and A. SINGER. 1997. Generations of diversity: Latinos in the United States. *Population Bulletin* (52):3. Washington, D.C.: Population Reference Bureau.

DESIPIO, L. 1996. *Counting on the Latino Vote: Latinos as a New Electorate.* Charlottesville, Va.: University of Virginia Press.

FLORES, W., and R. BENMAYOR, eds. 1997. *Latino Cultural Citizenship: Claiming Identity, Space, and Rights.* Boston: Beacon Press.

GOLDMAN, B. 1991. *The Truth About Where You Live.* New York: Random House.

GRISWOLD DEL CASTILLO, R. 1990. *The Treaty of Guadalupe Hidalgo: A Legacy of Conflict.* Norman: University of Oklahoma Press.

GUTIÉRREZ, D. 1995. *Walls and Mirrors: Mexican Americans, Mexican Immigrants, and the Politics of Ethnicity.* Berkeley: University of California Press.

HARTMAN, C., ed. 1997. *Double Exposure: Poverty and Race in America.* Armonk, N.Y.: M.E. Sharpe.

HERNANDEZ, R., and S. TORRES-SAILLANT. 1998. An advocacy forum for Latino empowerment. Unpublished paper. New York: City College of New York, CUNY Dominican Studies Institute.

HERO, R. 1992. *Latinos and the U.S. Political System: Two-Tiered Pluralism.* Philadelphia: Temple University Press.

HOLMES, S. 1998. U.S. officials are struggling to measure multiracial marriages. *New York Times* June 13.

HORNER, L., ed. 1997. *Hispanic Americans: A Statistical Sourcebook.* Palo Alto, Calif.: Information Publications.

LIEBMAN, L., ed. 1982. *Ethnic Relations in America.* Englewood Cliffs, N.J.: Prentice-Hall.

MARTINEZ, F. 1935. The Tragedy of the Puerto Ricans and the Colored Americans. New York: n.p.

MOORE, J., and H. PACHON. 1985. *Hispanics in the United States.* Englewood Cliffs, N.J.: Prentice-Hall.

MORALES, R., and F. BONILLA. 1993. *Latinos in a Changing U.S. Economy: Comparative Perspectives on Growing Inequality.* Newbury Park, Calif.: Sage Publications.

MYRDAL, G. 1944. *An American Dilemma: The Negro Problem and Modern Democracy*, Vol. 1. New York: Harper and Row.

Office of Management and Budget. 1997. Revisions to the standards for the classification of federal data on race and ethnicity, Part II. *Federal Register* (62):210.

Pacific Coast Council on International Policy. 1998. *Advancing the International Interests of African-Americans, Asian-Americans and Latinos.* Los Angeles: Pacific Coast Council.

PADILLA, F. 1985. *Latino Ethnic Consciousness: The Case of Mexican Americans and Puerto Ricans in Chicago.* Notre Dame: University of Notre Dame Press.

PORTES, A., and R. BACH. 1985. *Latin Journey: Cuban and Mexican Immigrants in the United States.* Berkeley: University of California Press.

ROMO, H., ed. 1990. *Latinos and Blacks in the Cities: Policies for the 1990s.* Austin: University of Texas Press.

SÁNCHEZ-KORROL, V. 1983. *From Colonia to Community.* Westport, Conn.: Greenwood Press.

SASSEN, S. 1991. *The Global City: New York, London, Tokyo.* Princeton: Princeton University Press.

TORRE, C., ed. 1992. *The Commuter Nation: Perspectives on Puerto Rican Migration.* Rio Piedras, Puerto Rico: Editorial Universitaria.

UEDA, R. 1994. *Postwar Immigrant America: A Social History.* Boston: St. Martin's Press.

U.S. Bureau of the Census. 1974. Americans of Spanish Origin. *A Study of Selected Socio-Economic Characteristics of Ethnic Minorities Based on the 1970 Census,* Vol. I. Washington, D.C.: U.S. Department of Health, Education, and Welfare. 1973. *1970 Census of the Population, Subject Reports: Persons of Spanish Origin.* PC-92-1C. Washington, D.C.: U.S. Bureau of the Census.. 1996. Current Population Reports. *Population Projections of the United States by Age, Sex, Race, and Hispanic Origin: 1995–2050.* P25-1130 (February). Washington, D.C.: U.S. Bureau of the Census.

YINGER, J. 1995. *Closed Doors, Opportunities Lost: The Continuing Costs of Housing Discrimination.* New York: Russell Sage Foundation.

YOUNG, W. 1991. *Unlocking the Golden Door: Hispanics and the Citizenship Process.* Washington, D.C.: National Council of La Raza.

Race and Romance: Blurring Boundaries

39

DISCOVERING RACIAL BORDERS

Heather M. Dalmage

Questions to Consider

Heather Dalmage explains how racial borders are "policed" to discourage individuals from falling in love across the color line. How and in what ways, if any, were racial borders enforced in your own life so that dating across the color line was not very likely to happen? How would your family react if your new romantic partner was from a racial category different from your own? Given that such unions are often stigmatized, what strategies do interracial couples employ, according to Dalmage, to dismiss such views and normalize their relationship?

Border Patrolling

The belief that people ought to stick with their own is the driving force behind efforts to force individuals to follow prescribed racial rules. Border patrollers often think (without much critical analysis) that they can easily differentiate between insiders and outsiders. Once the patroller has determined a person's appropriate category, he or she will attempt to coerce that person into following the category's racial scripts. In *Race, Nation, Class: Ambiguous Identities,* Etienne Balibar and Immanuel Wallerstein observe that "people shoot each other every day over the question of labels. And yet, the very people who do so tend to deny that the issue is complex or puzzling or indeed anything but self-evident."[1] Border patrollers tend to take race and racial categories for granted. Whether grounding themselves in essentialist thinking or hoping to strengthen socially constructed racial categories, they believe they have the right and the need to patrol. Some people, especially whites, do not recognize the centrality and problems of the color line, as evinced in color-blind claims that "there is only one race: the human race" or "race doesn't really matter any more." Such thinking dismisses the terror and power of race in society. These individuals may patrol without being aware of doing so. In contrast, blacks generally see patrolling the border as both problematic and necessary.

While border patrolling from either side may be scary, hurtful, or annoying, we must recognize that blacks and whites are situated differently. The color line was imposed by whites, who now have institutional means for maintaining their power; in contrast, blacks must consciously and actively struggle for liberation. Repeatedly, people in multiracial families have told me, "The one thing that David Duke and Louis Farrakhan agree on is that we should not exist." What is not analyzed are the different historical legacies that bring both men to the same conclusion. The only form of borderism in which blacks engage is border patrolling, although they can act on prejudicial feelings and discriminate. After centuries of systemic control, only whites can be racist. As Joe Feagin and Hernán Vera explain, "black racism would require not only a widely accepted racist ideology directed at whites, but also the power to systematically exclude whites from opportunities and rewards in major economic, cultural, and political institutions."[2] White and black border patrollers may both dislike interracial couples and multiracial families, but their dislike comes from different historical and social perspectives. Moreover, border patrolling tends to take place intraracially: whites patrol whites, and blacks patrol black and multiracial people.

White Border Patrolling

Despite the institutional mechanisms in place to safeguard whiteness, many whites feel both the right and the obligation to act out against interracial couples. If a white person wants to maintain a sense of racial superiority, then he or she must attempt to locate motives and explain the actions of the white partner in the interracial couple. A white person who crosses the color line threatens the assumption that racial superiority is essential to whites. The interracially involved white person is thus often recategorized as inherently flawed—as "polluted."[3] In this way, racist and essentialist thinking remains unchallenged.

Frequently white families disown a relative who marries a person of color, but several people have told me that their families accepted them again once their children were born. The need to disown demonstrates the desire to maintain the facade of a pure white family.[4] By the time children are born, however, extended family members have had time to shift their racial thinking. Some grant acceptance by making an exception to the "rule," others by claiming to be color blind. Neither form of racial thinking, however, challenges the color line or white supremacy. In fact, both can be painful for the multiracial family members, who may face unending racist compliments such as "I'll always think of you as white."

The myth of purity is maintained by controlling white women's wombs. Thus, white women are patrolled more harshly than white men are. The regulations women face have not always been overtly displayed but have developed within the culture's conception of the *family ethic,* an ideal extant since the arrival of the early settlers that has influenced perceptions of proper work and home roles for white, middle-class family members.[5] The proper family should have a male breadwinner and patriarch and a female who makes her husband and obedient children her life's central work. According to Mimi Abramowitz, the family ethic "has made [women] the guardians of family and community morality, expected them to remain pious and chaste and to tame male sexuality, and defined them as weak and in need of male protection and control."[6] Ultimately, the family ethic has kept white women under the control of white men. In *Whiteness Visible: The Meaning of Whiteness in American Literature and Culture,* Valerie Babb notes that images depicting white women as helpless and in need of white men's protection grew against a backdrop of a developing patriarchy. White women faced particularly harsh regulations because the "loss of sexual purity through intercourse with other races endangers visible race difference, a key driving force behind an ideology of whiteness that gives political, economic, and social advantage to those with 'appropriate' race lineage."[7] The myth of white racial purity required white women to give birth to the offspring of white men— and only white men. Unfortunately, many white women have played active roles in maintaining this myth of purity. For instance, in 1897 one wrote: "If it takes lynching to protect women's dearest possession from drunken, ravening beasts, then I say lynch a thousand a week if it becomes necessary."[8] Today many white women who give birth to children of color give them up for adoption, fearing that as mothers of children of color they will become pariahs in their families and society at large.[9] Such complicity has worked to strengthen the color line and white-supremacist abuses.

It has been argued that white women should be protected because they are the gatekeepers of racial purity.[10] Any white woman who would trade in her white privilege and connections to white male power must be dismissed as unnaturally bad and bizarre. Julie, a white mother recently divorced from her black husband, has contended with white border patrolling and its underlying images. One incident (although not the only one) occurred while she was on a date with a white physician:

> He asked to see a picture of my daughter. I handed it to him. He was very clever; he asked, "Is her dad from the U.S.?"
>
> I think he was praying her dad was Spanish, and he could deal with that, anything but black. I could tell it bothered him, so I said, "Listen, I can see by the look on your face that there is obviously a problem here, so why don't we just talk about it right now."

He said, "You want to know the truth? Well, I have a real problem with the fact that you slept with a black man." Then he went on with the whole, "You're such a pretty and intelligent woman; why would you marry a black man?"

Her date was drawing on the interlocking imagery of race and sex and what it means to be a good white woman. In his attempt to explain away Julie's behavior, he searched for motives, implying that only unattractive, unintelligent white women sleep with and marry black men. Further, the fact that she slept with a black man removed her eligibility as a white woman. She is assumed to be fundamentally and essentially changed. Perhaps he feared that his white purity would be contaminated with blackness through this bad white woman. Perhaps he felt threatened because he could not immediately detect her racial flaw. He may have begun to discover the mutability of race, which could undermine his own sense of racial superiority. While all people of color face some form of racist imagery in a white racist society, Julie notes the centrality and power given to racist images directed specifically against black people and interracially involved whites and blacks: "I think he was praying her dad was Spanish, and he could deal with that, anything but black."

Black men are seen "as a constant threat" to patriarchal whiteness.[11] Abby Ferber writes: "A photograph of a white woman with an Asian American man, for example, does not have the same symbolic power. The image of interracial sexuality between a white woman and a black man is pregnant with meaning in the American imagery. Powerful enough to serve as a symbol of all interracial sexuality."[12] White women who enter into interracial relationships with black men are often treated as aberrant, misguided white trash who are in this relationship solely for sex or rebellion. Barbara gained forty pounds because she "got tired of being mistaken for a prostitute." She explains, "It's assumed that the only reason you're involved in the relationship is because you're sexually depraved . . . that you've got to be the dregs of society to get involved or you want to hurt somebody." Women may be explained away as money or status seekers.[13] Often when we are out, people will ask Philip what he does for work. After learning he's an attorney, they don't bother to ask me what I do. This could be a gender issue; in a patriarchal world men are seen as the subjects, women the objects. But I often wonder how much it has do with assumptions about uncovering the motive behind our relationship—that I have traded my white status for his occupational and class status.[14]

The strength of racist images is manifested in the comments directed at women who are assumed to be good, upstanding white women. June, a businesswoman who is raising two biracial sons in suburban New Jersey, commented, "I think America still hates [white] women who sleep with black men. And when they see you with these children, they want to believe you adopted them, which is usually the first question people will ask: 'Did you adopt them?' I always just say, 'No, I slept with a black man.'"

June's comments highlight a few issues. First, she does not specify who constitutes "America." Whites may hate these women because they threaten the color line that maintains white privilege and power. At the same time, blacks may hate them because they threaten the unity of African Americans. Second, several white women talked to me about the frequency of the adoption question—one more attempt to explain their behavior. If women who appear to be good turn out to be polluted, white border patrollers become nervous. Their inability to tell "us" from "them" calls into question their own racial identity. The more the border patroller clings to an identity of racial superiority, the more he or she looks for ways to explain away these aberrant white women. Third, like June, many interracially married white women resist allowing whites to recategorize them in an attempt to regain or maintain a sense of superiority. "No, I used the good-old fashioned method" is a common retort to such questioners.

Not all white women resist border patrollers. Many succumb to the hostility and end their relationships with black men. Several white women told me they had temporarily ended their interracial relationship, each citing border patrolling as the reason. For instance, Barbara, the woman who gained forty pounds to avoid being seen as a prostitute, said:

> When I met my husband, he was the sweetest, kindest—he was a wonderful human being, everything I was looking for except for the color and at one point I was really apprehensive about it. The race thing really bothered me 'cause I didn't like being stared at and I didn't like people hating me. I didn't like how black women viewed me, and to white men I was a possession. It's like, "you crossed the line." You know the feeling, like you have to be the lowest of the low to be with an African American. "Who are you trying to hurt?" It was just really sick. So I went away for a while.

Although she did eventually marry this "wonderful human being," she needed time away to think about race on a more sophisticated level—time to question her internalization of racist images and the color line.

The stereotype of black male sexuality converges with the myth of the chaste and virtuous good white woman, making white female–black male relationships the ones most patrolled by whites.[15] White men contend with a different type of border patrolling in a society that privileges both whiteness and maleness. Historically, white men who interracially marry were reported to come from lower economic classes and were at times designated as crazy.[16] Today the more common image that white interracially married men face is of being in the relationship solely for sex. These men may be seen as committing an individual transgression but are not held responsible for protecting whiteness. In her study of white supremacist publications, Abby Ferber found that "while relationships between white women and black men are condemned, and described as repulsive, relationships between white men and black women were common and remain beyond condemnation."[17] The lack of imagery about white male–black female relations reflects a history of silence among whites concerning their complicity in the rape of black women. Moreover, in a society in which whiteness (and maleness) represents power, privilege, and unearned advantage, many white men view their privilege in the world as normal. They risk "outing" these taken-for-granted privileges when they talk about race.[18]

The white men with whom I spoke were split about the importance of—even the existence of—border patrolling. Unlike black men, black women, and white women, they did not consistently talk about the effects of racialized images. When I asked, "As an interracially married white man, how do you think others view you?" responses were split: half the men spoke of border patrollers; the other half denied the importance of race in their lives and society. The first few times I heard white men deny or disregard the importance of racism and border patrolling, I was surprised. It took me some time and several more interviews to make sense of this.

Joe, the first interracially married white man I interviewed, lived in a predominantly white, upper-class community about an hour from New York City. With his infant daughter on his lap and a tape recorder on the table, he began to unfold the details of his life. I asked how he thinks others view him. He responded, "I can't worry about what other people think. For a long time my wife worried, but once she got over that, we had a big wedding. . . . It took a lot to convince her that's how we should think about it, and I think she's more comfortable with that." He said that they do not have problems as an interracial couple, that everything is smooth. We were chatting after the interview when his wife walked into the room. She began to cite several problems they had faced because of their interracial relationship. When she referred to each incident, he nodded in agreement.

Several months later I interviewed Raymond, a white interracially married man living on Chicago's north side. Drinking coffee in a local café, he discussed the meaning of race in his life. When I asked him about how others view him, he replied staunchly, "I don't know, and I don't care. I never thought about it. I don't think about it. What do they think when they see my wife and me together? Pardon my language, but I don't give a shit what they think; I just don't give a shit. I go for months, and that never occupies my mind."

These men may be proving masculinity through a show of strength, rugged individualism, and disinterest and thus verbally disregard border patrolling and racial images. Each, however, repeatedly claimed that race does not matter. Instead, they believed the focus "should be on ethnic backgrounds" or on the fact that "we are all Americans." Men who did not want to recognize racial images tended not to recognize the privilege associated with whiteness, drawing instead on notions of meritocracy. Whether or not they recognized differences, they did not recognize power. Nevertheless,

they used their power as white males to create a racial discussion with which they felt comfortable. For instance, Joe's comfort came from not having to hear any racially derogatory comments: "If somebody would make a derogatory comment, I would just say, 'My wife is black.' Usually I wouldn't even have to say, 'I don't want to hear comments like that'—they would just stop." Whiteness is about privilege and power. It is a privilege to be able to set the parameters of racial discussions and expect that others will comply. Moreover, the power of these professional white men overrides the power that white border patrollers may have to influence them.

In addition to proving masculinity, these men may be attempting to downplay the prevalent stereotype that interracial couples are together for sexual reasons only. For instance, Raymond repeatedly stated that his relationship was not about "jungle fever," a phrase that filmmaker Spike Lee popularized to suggest that interracial couples are attracted only because of sexual curiosity. At the end of our interview I asked Raymond if there was anything else he wanted to say. He answered, "Let people know that this is not about jungle fever. Race does not matter. I love my wife." His repeated references to jungle fever reflected his awareness of border patrolling despite his claim of colorblindness. Rather than critically thinking about race and the origins of such stereotypes, he defensively dismisses the significance of race.

Some white men did recognize and address the importance of racial images, border patrollers, and the relationship between race and power. The common thread for these men was that they had friendships and networks with black males before meeting their spouse. Through these male friends they began to recognize the privileges that remain invisible to so many other white men. The importance of friendships with black males cannot be understated. White men sit in a position of power because of both their race and sex. When sex differences are removed as a factor in their relationships, they can understand more clearly the ways in which race mediates power relations. This is not as obvious to white men who are introduced to blackness (and thus whiteness) through intimate relations with a woman.

Clancy, a fifty-year-old white man who grew up outside Chicago, had black roommates and friends in college. By the time he met his wife he understood from his buddies the effects of racism in society. He spoke in detail about the border patrolling he faced from the white teachers at the Chicago elementary school where he taught after getting married: "My wife and I walked into a meeting with the white teachers and the people from the neighborhood, and it sent those people into conniptions. I won't forget that. It was my first year teaching there, and from then on it was like, 'God have mercy on my soul,' I was a dead person in that school and that stayed with me for seventeen years— the whole time I was there." In this case, Clancy's teaching position was continually threatened by white border patrollers.

Peter, a white minister living on Chicago's South Side, had graduated from a black seminary in the southern United States. As the only white in many situations, he was immersed in black culture. The privileges and power bestowed to whites in a system of whiteness and the richness of black culture became visible to him. Like Clancy, he recognized and addressed the border patrolling he encountered from whites. In the following case, Peter had just been named the pastor of a white church in a white working-class neighborhood in Cleveland: "I had gotten moved to a white church. That turned out to be two years

from hell. The church did not want me to be appointed there. They actually had a special meeting after they got wind of who was coming; 95 percent of the church did not want me there because I was interracially married. The first church meeting I was at, the chair asked for further motions. One person said, 'I make a motion that the reverend resign from this church.'" Peter laughed about the absurdity of the situation and then continued: "The first sermon, attendance was over one hundred; everyone came out to see the show. From then on, attendance never got above sixty, so basically about forty people boycotted the whole time I was there. I had people who still attended but resigned all their offices." In addition, church members began a letter-writing campaign to the bishop accusing Peter of various wrongdoings—for example, claiming he had taken all the Bibles out of the church. Peter and his family eventually moved to a black church in Chicago. The Ohio church members who had resigned their offices returned to them after he left.

Privileges granted to people with white skin have been institutionalized and made largely invisible to the beneficiaries. With overwhelming power in society, why do individual whites insist on border patrolling? As economic insecurity heightens and demographics show that whites are losing numerical majority status, the desire to scapegoat people of color, especially the poor, also heightens. As whites lose their economic footing, they claim white skin as a liability. Far from recognizing whiteness as privilege, they become conscious of whiteness only when defining themselves as innocent victims of "unjust" laws, including affirmative action.[19] In their insecurity they cling to images that promote feelings of superiority. This, of course, requires a racial hierarchy and a firm essentialist color line. Border patrolling helps to maintain the myth of purity and thus a color line created to ensure that whites maintain privileges and power.

Black Border Patrolling

Some blacks in interracial relationships discover, for the first time, a lack of acceptance from black communities. Others experienced border patrolling before their marriage, perhaps because of hobbies and interests, class, politics, educational goals, skin tone, vernacular, or friendship networks. Patrolling takes on new proportions, however, when they go the "other way" and marry a white person. While all relationships with individuals not seen as black are looked down on, relationships with whites represent the gravest transgression. Interracially married black women and men often believe they are viewed as having lost their identity and culture—that they risk being seen as "no longer really black." Before their interracial marriage, most called black communities their home, the place from which they gained a sense of humanity, where they gained cultural and personal affirmation. During their interracial relationship many discovered black border patrolling. Cathy Cohen suggests that "those failing to meet indigenous standards of blackness find their life chances threatened not only by dominant institutions or groups, but also by their lack of access to indigenous resources and support."[20] Interracially involved blacks needed to carefully weigh their decision to cross the color line.

George, a black man, lives with his wife, Dorothy, a white woman, and their two young children in Montclair, New Jersey, a racially mixed suburb of New York City. I drove along the town's big, clean, tree-lined streets one Sunday morning to meet with George in his home. During our interview he explained that he had dated a white girl in high school and was aware of how blacks and whites respond to such a relationship. Nonetheless, a recent event at his Manhattan workplace troubled him. Bill, a black male co-worker, told him:

"I couldn't marry a white woman. How about you?"

I said, "I am married to a white woman."

"You joking me, George! Big strong handsome brother like you!"

I said, "Yo, man, I don't know what all that handsome stuff you comin' with."

He said, "All jokes aside, George, you telling me you went the other way?"

I said, "There's nothing wrong with that."

And he's like "Oh, George, I don't believe it."

He was just solemn after that and looked down, so I said, " Bill, does that mean we're not going to be friends anymore?"

He goes, "No, man, you still my man."

He gave me the ole handshake; I said, "Bill, no, man, you frontin' now."

He said, "I'm just surprised, you know. You never told me about your wife."

The implication here is that a "strong brother" would not sell out his community like this; only weak men would do that. Before this confrontation George had been an integral part of many conversations at work about race, racism, and black culture. After it he found "they'll be talking about something totally in the black culture. I come into the room and be listening; and when I would put my opinion in, the conversation would end—just like that. The room goes empty. . . . because I'm married to a white woman, blacks figure my culture is gone; it's shot." He is accused of having lost connectedness to African Americans, being weak, and marrying a white woman to escape his blackness.

Blacks in interracial relationships defend themselves against accusations of weakness, neurosis, and betrayal. In *Black Skin, White Masks,* Frantz Fanon writes about black men in interracial relationships: "I marry white culture, white beauty, white whiteness. When my restless hands caress those white breasts, they grasp white civilization and dignity and make them mine."[21] In his psychoanalytic interpretation of the effects of colonization and racism, Fanon suggests that many black men who intermarry suffer from neurosis created in a world in which black men are not valued and thus do not value themselves. They think that a relationship with a white woman will validate them—that is, whiten them. Of black women, Fanon writes, "It is because the Negress feels inferior that she aspires to win admittance into the white world."[22] Without acknowledging the pain caused by border patrolling and the desire many interracially married blacks have to maintain strong ties with other blacks, Fanon labels black men and black women in interracial relationships as pathological and neurotic.

More recently, Paul Rosenblatt and his colleagues conducted a study of forty-two multiracial couples in the Minneapolis–St. Paul area. They conclude that many African Americans feel that "it is inappropriate to choose as a partner somebody from the group that has been oppressing African Americans."[23] Many black border patrollers have an overriding concern about loyalty to the race. If an individual is not being loyal, then he or she is explained away as weak, acting in ways that are complicit with the oppression of other black Americans. In "Essentialism and the Complexities of Racial Identity," Michael Eric Dyson suggests, "Loyalty to race has been historically construed as primary and unquestioning allegiance to the racial quest for freedom and

the refusal to betray that quest to personal benefit or the diverting pursuit of lesser goals. Those who detour from the prescribed path are labeled 'sellouts,' 'weak,' 'traitors,' or 'Uncle Toms.'"[24] Thus, black men and women face differing social realities and forms of patrolling.

An overwhelming percentage of black-white couples involve a black male and a white female at a time when there are "more single women in the black community than single men."[25] Many black men are hindered by a racist educational system and job market that make them less desirable for marriage. Many others are scooped into the prison industrial complex. High-profile athletes and entertainers who marry white women confirm for many that black men who are educated and earn a good living sell out, attempting to buy white status through their interracial relationship.[26] Beyond issues of money and status, many black women see black male-white female interracial relationships "as a rejection of black women's beauty, [and] as a failure to acknowledge and reward the support that black women give black men."[27] In *Rooted against the Wind,* Gloria Wade-Gayles writes about the pain and feeling of rejection that black women experience when they see black men with white women:

> We see them, and we feel abandoned. We feel abandoned because we have been abandoned in so many ways, by so many people, and for so many centuries. We are the group of women furthest removed from the concept of beauty and femininity which invades almost every spot of the planet, and as a result, we are taught not to like ourselves, or, as my student said, not to believe that we can ever do enough or be enough to be loved or desired.[28]

Black women and men may both feel a sense of rejection when they see an interracial couple, but for each that sense of rejection comes from a different place. In a society in which women's worth is judged largely by beauty—more specifically, Eurocentric standards of beauty—black women are presumed to be the farthest removed from such a standard. Men's worth is judged largely by their educational and occupational status, two primary areas in which black men are undermined in a racist system. Black men with few educational and job opportunities lack status in the marriage market. Thus, when black men see a black woman with a white man, they may be reminded of the numerous ways in which the white-supremacist system has denied them opportunities. The privilege and power granted to whites, particularly to white males, is paraded in front of them; and they see the black women in these relationships as complicit with the oppressor.

I met Parsia, a successful businesswoman and a black interracially married mother living in Connecticut, through a family friend. Having grown up in a close-knit African American community, she was uncertain if she wanted to marry interracially and risk losing the support of that community. Now happily married and the mother of a beautiful little girl, she is still very aware of border patrolling. For this reason she prefers not to bring her husband to some areas in Harlem and to black-centered events:

> African Americans do view blacks in
> interracial relationships as turncoats.
> There is a pervasive belief in the
> African American community that it is
> much more difficult to maintain your
> identity in an interracial relationship.
> I believe that once blacks see me as part
> of an interracial couple, it changes their
> perception of me right away. They dis-
> respect me as another black person,
> and then they just disregard my belong-

> ing to the community, and suddenly
> I become the outsider—an outsider
> because I am with him.

Her fears are not unfounded. One day she and her husband were walking in Philadelphia when a young black man accosted them:

> If I had been alone and this young
> brother was hassling me in any way, I
> would have stopped, turned around,
> and said, "Look, why are you bothering
> me? What's the deal here?" But I didn't
> feel at all that I could have this conver-
> sation with this young man. He was so
> hostile, and the source of his hostility
> was totally his perception of black-white
> relationships, and there was nothing I
> could say to change that perception.

This young border patroller may be responding to a belief that Parsia is a race traitor. She is no longer an insider worthy of respect but an outsider who signifies neurosis in the form of self-hate and community betrayal—perhaps the highest form of betrayal. The prospect of rejection by other African Americans is enough for many blacks to deny, hide, or avoid interracial relationships. Border patrolling from other blacks, racism from whites, and the prospect of struggling alone in a racist society seem too high a price; so many who enter interracial relationships end them in short time.

Today there are no longer legal sanctions against interracial marriage, but de facto sanctions remain. At times, family and friends exert pressure to end the interracial relationship; at other times, pressure may come from the border patrolling of strangers. Even if the relationship is clandestine, thoughts of how friends, family members, co-workers, employers, and the general public might respond can deter people from moving forward in a relationship. In each of the following cases the couples did get back together eventually, but all the black women took some time away from the relationship to make this choice.

Lisa met her white husband when she was a college student at a historically black college in the South.

> [I was] the only female in the jazz orchestra, [so] there were all these [black] guys saying, "Why are you with this white guy?" And one band member would make racial comments about "Don't marry whitey, don't trust whitey, don't do this for whitey." This guy in the band tried to talk me out of marrying Peter. I had some apprehension, so I broke up with him and told him I did not want to develop a relationship.

Parsia explains why she temporarily ended her relationship before finally deciding to marry her white husband, Joe:

> When I met Joe, I was really resistant to dating across racial lines. No way would I do that. It took me a very long time to get over that and deal with those feelings, biases, and expectations. I expected friends would feel very uncomfortable socializing with us. I still do believe that there is a certain language that blacks have when we are apart from other races, when we are alone socially. That's a very important part of my life, and I expected that I might lose that, and that was a very fearful thing for me. The more I felt him getting closer, the more I started seeing the possibility of longevity in the relationship, the more afraid I got. I was terrified that I would be in an interracial relationship for the rest of my life, so I pulled back in a big way and we

broke up. There was definitely a shame and a guilt I had to get over because I felt that by dating interracially I was betraying black men.

Her fear reflects her reliance on other African Americans for mutual support in a white-supremacist system. Moreover, her observation that "there is a certain language that blacks have when we are apart from other races" indicates a shared cultural identity that creates and demands the enforcement of borders.

In some cases parents and family reinforce reservations about crossing over. Quisha, like Parsia, broke up with her white boyfriend, Raymond, because she needed time to think about what life would be like in an interracial relationship. "I was really excited about him and told my mom, and she just had a heart attack because he was white. I totally did not expect this from her. She would call everyday and was just hammering it into me to just forget this—and so I really badly and abruptly broke it off with Raymond. He was a real gentleman; he kept calling to find out what happened, and I totally blew him off." She explained her underlying fears as she discussed how she handles people staring at her: "I can feel my grandmother and my mother and my aunts disapproving in those stares, so that's intimidating." Lisa, Parsia, and Quisha all married the men they had left, but they needed time to think about risks, their own understandings of race and community, and what it means to be a black woman in the United States.

They are three of the many black women in interracial relationships who challenge the idea that white men are responsible for the low number of black female–white male interracial marriages. Theorists attempting to explain motives behind interracial marriages have often pointed to the low number of these marriages as evidence that white men are choosing not to marry black women.[29] These theorists suggest that white men are least likely to intermarry with black women because they would gain nothing in these marriages: no money, no status. My research, however, demonstrates the power of black women. The stories they share directly challenge longheld motive myths that imply that black women would marry white men if only white men would choose them. On the contrary, in each of the relationships just discussed, the black woman instigated a breakup. Perhaps their understanding of what it means to be strong, dedicated, and connected to black communities is responsible for the lower numbers of black female—white male marriages.

Border patrolling plays a central role in life decisions and the reproduction of the color line. As decisions are made to enter and remain in an interracial relationship, the color line is challenged and racial identities shift. Many blacks spoke of the growth they experienced because of their interracial relationship and border patrolling. Parsia explains, "I used to be real concerned about how I would be perceived and that as an interracially married female I would be taken less seriously in terms of my dedication to African American causes. I'm not nearly as concerned anymore. I would hold my record up to most of those in single-race relationships, and I would say, 'Okay, let's go toe to toe, and you tell me who's making the biggest difference,' and so I don't worry about it anymore." Identities, once grounded in the presumed acceptance of other black Americans, have become more reflective. Acceptance can no longer be assumed. Definitions of what it means to be black are reworked. Likewise, because of border patrolling, many whites in interracial relationships began to acknowledge that race matters. Whiteness becomes visible in their claims to racial identity.

Conclusion

Unlike transracially adopted and multiracial people who are raised across the color line, people in interracial relationships discover borderism when they decide to cross the line. This unique form of discrimination, grounded in a racist and segregated society, is always at work even when multiracial family members are not present. Yet by examining the experiences of multiracial family members, we can see the myriad ways in which the color line is both reproduced and resisted. Because interracially married people are often raised in single-race worlds, they have internalized borderism. Thus, part of the decision to become involved interracially includes the need to overcome internalized borderist thoughts. Most of them begin questioning color-blind and essentialist perspectives and learn to understand race as more fluid and complex. Skin color and physical features become just one set of criteria used to think about community and belonging. Many of the people I interviewed referred to this growth process (although not all interracially married people accept the invitation to rethink race).

In a society that often rejects people who cross the color line, individuals involved in such relationships have much to consider before making a permanent commitment. Given the significance of race in our society, a basic choice that all couples contend with is whether or not to stay together in the face of borderism. A few individuals claimed that there was no decision; they fell in love, and that was it. For most others, however, a life across the color line and facing borderism did not look all that inviting and in fact was enough to cause some to terminate their relationships.[30] While the number of people involved in interracial relationships is not known, we do know that in 1995 the census bureau estimated that there were only 246,000 black-white interracial marriages in the United States.[31] This is quite a small percentage considering that in the same year there were more than 50 million total marriages.[32] Borderism and its various components are strong and painful enough to keep black-white interracial marriages the least common marriage pattern for both blacks and whites.

NOTES

1. Etienne Balibar and Immanuel Wallerstein, *Race, Nation, Class: Ambiguous Identities* (New York: Verso, 1991), 71.
2. Joe Feagin and Hernán Vera, *White Racism* (New York: Routledge, 1995), ix–x.
3. Ferber, *White Man Falling*, 100.
4. Naomi Zack, *Race and Mixed Race* (Philadelphia: Temple University Press, 1994).
5. Mimi Abramowitz, *Regulating the Lives of Women: Social Welfare Policy from Colonial Times to the Present* (Boston: South End Press, 1996).
6. Ibid., 3.
7. Valerie Babb, *Whiteness Visible: The Meaning of Whiteness in American Literature and Culture* (New York: New York University Press, 1998), 76.
8. Hale, *Making Whiteness*, 109.
9. See, for instance, Gail Folaron and McCartt Hess, "Placement Considerations for Children of Mixed African American and Caucasian Parentage," *Child Welfare League of America* 72, 3 (1993): 113–135.
10. See for instance, Ferber, *White Man Falling*.
11. Ibid.
12. Ibid., 104.
13. Robert Merton, "Intermarriage and the Social Structure: Fact and Theory," *Psychiatry* 4 (1941): 361–374; see also Matthijs Kalmijn, "Trends in Black/White Intermarriage," *Social Forces* 72, 1 (1996): 119–146.
14. Merton, "Intermarriage"; Kingsley Davis, "Intermarriage in Caste Societies," *American Anthropologist* (September 1941): 388–395.
15. Ferber, *White Man Falling*.
16. Zack, *Race and Mixed Race*; Joel Williamson, *New People: Miscegenation and Mulattoes in the United States* (New York: New York University Press, 1984); Spikard, *Mixed Blood*.
17. Ferber, *White Man Falling*, 103.
18. Kate Davy, "Outing Whiteness." *Theatre* 47, 2 (1995): 189–205.
19. Charles Gallagher, "White Reconstruction in the University," *Socialist Review* 24, 1 and 2 (1995): 165–188.
20. Cathy J. Cohen, "Contested Membership: Black Gay Identities and the Politics of AIDS," in *Queer Theory/Sociology*, ed. Steven Seidman (Cambridge, Mass.: Blackwell, 1996), 365.
21. Frantz Fanon, *Black Skins, White Masks* (New York: Grove), 83.
22. Ibid., 60.
23. Paul C. Rosenblatt, Terri A. Karis, and Richard D. Powell, *Multiracial Couples: Black and White Voices* (Thousand Oaks, Calif.: Sage, 1995), 155.
24. Dyson, "Essentialism," 222.
25. Rosenblatt et al., *Multiracial Couples*, 150.
26. Ibid., 151.
27. Ibid.
28. Gloria Wade-Gayles, *Rooted against the Wind* (Boston: Beacon, 1996), 110.
29. David Heer, "Negro-White Marriages in the United States," *Journal of Marriage and the Family* 28 (1966): 262–273; Kalmijn, "Trends"; Merton, "Intermarriage"; Davis, "Intermarriage in Caste Societies."
30. Although many people break up permanently, I interviewed individuals who eventually made the decision to commit to an interracial marriage.
31. Claudette Bennett, "Interracial Children: Implications for a Multiracial Category" (paper presented at the annual meeting of the American Sociological Association, Washington, D.C., 1995).
32. Rosenblatt et al., *Multiracial Couples*, 5.

40

THE CHANGING FACE OF AMERICA
Intermarriage and the Mixed Race Movement

Frank Wu

Questions to Consider

Frank Wu examines the interracial marriage rates for Asians and Asian Americans. Who are Asian Americans most likely to marry when they marry across the color line, and what do these trends suggest about racial group perceptions? What is the author referring to when he discusses the "passing of Asian Americans"?

I am a white American female. My husband is Chinese, born in Vietnam. He has a permanent resident visa. My question: What nationality does that make our children? Someone told me that they are white American, but to me that means that they are ignoring their Oriental heritage. My daughter says she is half-Chinese and half-American. Please straighten this out, as we never know how to fill out the forms when this question is asked.

—Letter to "DEAR ABBY" advice
column, *Chicago Tribune*,
June 24, 1991

The Chinese Girl in the Sixth Grade

When I was a boy, I once asked my mother if she would love me if I married an American girl. She answered that she would love me if I married a foreigner. But she added

that she would love me more if I married a Chinese girl.

I'm not sure how I would have avoided marrying somebody white, if I wanted to be married at all. In elementary school, there was only one grade in which an Asian American girl was in the same class as me. Everyone teased us that we were supposed to be married someday, but she avoided me. Without her, I was left with nobody. I had not learned it, but as much as boys and girls didn't play together as children, whites and non-whites didn't marry one another as adults.

When I was much older, I dated a woman who was white but spoke Chinese fluently. Her father was a Scottish immigrant; her mother was from the impeccable WASP milieu of mainline Philadelphia. She had studied Mandarin in college and Japanese in graduate school; lived in China, Taiwan, and Japan for extended periods of time; and earned advanced degrees with a concentration in Asian studies. Her accent was perfect; her vocabulary was extensive. She was literate. She could pass the "telephone test," meaning that a listener who could not see her would be fooled into believing that she was Chinese. She even had a job once as a radio broadcaster in Japan, using her similarly impressive Japanese. Her expertise with all matters Asian surpassed that of most Asian Americans, and she was better able than I to chat with my parents. She is an "egg": white outside, yellow inside.

I enjoyed more than she did surprising people at restaurants or overseas, who made assumptions about race and gender and expected me to communicate with them in Chinese only to find that she was in charge. There are enough whites who are fluent in Asian languages that in major cities abroad they are no longer even commended for having learned the native tongue, even though they are novel even now here at home.

Eventually, I married a Japanese American woman. On her paternal side, she is second generation (*nisei*); on her maternal side, she is third generation (*sansei*). As we started dating, I traveled with her to meet her mother in St. Louis. After we were introduced, my girlfriend's mother said to her, "He's good looking. . . . He looks Japanese."

By the time we were engaged, my parents had realized I would follow my own course in life. From their perspective, their prospective daughter-in-law might as well have been white. But they were relieved I would not end up an eccentric bachelor, never mind that the woman I had found was not Chinese.

Both my nieces by marriage have husbands who are white. Anybody familiar with Japanese Americans would find the family photographs shown off atop the mantelpiece to be quite ordinary. Japanese Americans can be distinguished from white Americans who lead otherwise similar lives, albeit only barely. My brother-in-law and sister-in-law have memories of the internment camp, but their children are as integrated as can be. The whiteness of their

daughters' spouses is insignificant, in a good sense. The *hakujin* husbands have included themselves in the Asian American community, such as it is.

I remember a white friend I had in elementary school. (I only had white friends in elementary school, because there were no other Asian Americans or any people of color for that matter in any of my classes, other than that one girl.) Like many of my white friends whom I made and lost, a few of whose parents did not want them playing with me, he asked me what my nationality was. I can still recall it, because, although I had developed my vocabulary from almost no English when I'd enrolled in kindergarten, I did not know the word "nationality." Once I figured it out, I gave myself too much credit for being clever in returning the favor with the question, "Well, what nationality are you?" I was puzzled by his answer, which used a metaphor that was restricted to white mixtures, "I'm Heinz 57. . . . Like the ketchup, 57 varieties."

In just my lifetime, intermarriage has become the taboo that binds. Mixed race individuals are accustomed to hearing "what are you?" rather than "Who are you?" and being fixed in an unwelcome gaze, but the mixed race movement is informing others that the "What are you?" inquiry is inappropriate even if it cannot ensure that it becomes irrelevant.

The future of race relations is mixed, literally as well as figuratively. Gradually, interracial relationships have become normal rather than forbidden, and the progeny of such relationships are accepted for their varied ancestries rather than rejected as abominations whose very existence violates natural laws. Although Asian Americans as a group may challenge the prevailing black-white racial paradigm, mixed race persons as individuals confound the concept of such straightforward racial opposites. For better or worse, they personify ambiguities because they demonstrate that race is not always hereditary.

Because the families of America are changing, the self-conception of America itself is changing. The 1960 Census, taken at a time when intermarriage was criminal conduct in more than a dozen states, showed only 149,000 interracial marriages within a total population of 179 million. The 1990 Census, taken when the number of multiracial babies being born was growing at a higher rate than the number of monoracial babies being born, showed more than 1.46 million interracial marriages within a total population of 281 million. Mixed marriages constituted about 3 percent of all marriages in 1980 nationwide and an estimated 5 percent in 1990. In California, which leads the mainland United States, about one out of six marriages now brings together couples of different racial or ethnic backgrounds. Among Asian Americans under the age of thirty-five who are married, half have found a spouse of a non-Asian background. Experts forecast that more than 20 percent of all marriages will be mixed by 2050. By 1990, more than 60 percent of Hawaiian babies were mixed race; by 2000, more than 20 percent of the Hawaiian population was mixed race. The 2000 Census counted about 6.8 million people of mixed race background, making up 2.4 percent of the population.

The transformation is recent. It was only in 1967 that the Supreme Court struck down legal bans on intermarriage in a case involving the aptly named Loving couple.[1] Since then, states have slowly repealed the bars that they had on the books. Alabama did not revise its statutes until 1999.[2] Local authorities reportedly were enforcing the rules in violation of the mandate from the highest court in the land. They did so by referring to the nullification doctrine of the antebellum era by which their predecessors had tried to ignore federal legislation against slavery by appealing to states' rights.

In the less than two generations since the *Loving* case, what social scientists have called "exogamy" or "outmarriage" has proliferated by an order of magnitude. Because of the personal nature of the relationships, the unions symbolize much more. Yet as with other demographic patterns, as a society we are only beginning to comprehend the complexities that they bequeath us. However sanguine we are about intermarriage and mixed race children, the success of all marriages and the future of any child depend on many factors. Intermarriage and the mixed race movement are positive, but they are no panacea. Both can reflect the effects of racial discrimination in the most intimate manner. Jeanne Wakatsuki Houston, author of a popular memoir about the internment, *Farewell to Manzanar*, writes that she saw her white husband as her "Anglo Samurai" who by "wielding his sword of integrity" would "slay the dragons that prevented my acceptance as an equal human being in his world."[3]

In this chapter, I begin by considering white opposition to interracial marriage and white attraction to people of color. I then turn to the ambivalence toward mixed marriages expressed by minority communities, both racial and religious. Finally, I consider the mixed race movement and its implications specifically for Asian Americans.

The Core of the Heart of the Race Problem

Both proponents and opponents of racial justice grasped that intermarriage was the culmination of racial equality. James Weldon Johnson, composer of the hymn "Lift Every Voice and Sing" (sometimes referred to as the black national anthem) and author of the novel *The Autobiography of an Ex-Colored Man*,[4] once wrote, "in the core of the heart of the race problem the sex factor is rooted."[5]

Gunnar Myrdal ranked "intermarriage" and in particular "sexual contacts with white women" as the area of greatest racial discrimination.[6]

When Abraham Lincoln signed the Emancipation Proclamation, his adversaries were fixated on the probability of legal equality leading to social equality.[7] When he ran for reelection in 1864, two pro-slavery writers sought to associate him with a fake Republican pamphlet purporting to endorse miscegenation, to inspire backlash. They coined the term "miscegenation" from Latin roots for mixture and race. Earlier, abolitionist Wendell Phillips actually had issued a similar call in earnest.[8] He preached "amalgamation" as the best means of uniting a divided nation.

A century later, as integration actually began in earnest, the paranoid fear that whites articulated again was the possibility that race mixing would proceed apace from the classroom to the bedroom. Foreseeing the impending upheaval of the old South, Theodore G. Bilbo, twice the governor of Mississippi and a three-term U.S. Senator, penned a book, *Take Your Choice: Separation or Mongrelization*,[9] in which he argued for "repatriation" of blacks to Africa specifically to avoid intermarriage. "The incontrovertible truths of this book and its sincere warnings," he wrote, "are respectfully inscribed to every white man and woman, regardless of nationality, who is a bona fide citizen of the United States of America."[10] He inveighed against what he believes to be false interpretations of democracy and Christianity, which would require recognizing African Americans as equal persons. He stated that intermarriage is "totally destructive to the white race" because "the Negro race is physically, mentally, and morally inferior."[11] Even if the mulatto might be the equal of the white man, "amalgamation must be condemned" because "it cannot be said to be a matter of trial and error . . . corrupted blood cannot be redeemed."[12] He concluded his book with his own bill for "voluntary resettlement" of African Americans on the African continent.[13]

The official end of racial segregation in public education, decreed by the Supreme Court decision in *Brown v. Board of Education,* was thought to be the harbinger of a sexual calamity. Congressman Jon Bell Williams of Mississippi called the issuance of the *Brown* decision "black Monday," and Judge Thomas Brady of the same state borrowed the phrase for the title of his pamphlet, issued by the white supremacist Citizens' Councils of Mississippi, in which he asserted that the Supreme Court is tending toward Communism and proposes either that a new state be created and blacks transported there for their own benefit or that all public schools be closed and African Americans left to their own devices. Insisting that he would like harmony between races, Brady predicted that white Southern men would fight to the death to preserve racial purity, defined as whiteness and the honor of their women. "We say to the Supreme Court and to the entire world," he wrote, "'you shall not make us drink from this cup.'"[14] He warned, "those who do not believe this may try through force of arms to accomplish it. If this happens, then it will take an army of one hundred million men to compel it." He concluded, "You shall not mongrelize our children and grandchildren!"[15]

The defining occasion of desegregation came in 1957, as federal troops had to be ordered out to enable blacks to attend Little Rock Central High School.[16] State officials were heading the campaign of massive resistance to school integration. A list of seven questions circulated by white leaders in Little Rock at the time began with, "Would the Negro boys be permitted to solicit the white girls for dances at school-soirees?" It ended with, "When the script calls for the enactment of tender love scenes, will these parts be assigned to negro boys and white girls without respect to race and color in drama classes?"

Such segregationist propaganda, like the hoax perpetrated against Lincoln, was based on the premise that whites who backed racial integration would blanch at sexual contact between their white daughters and black men. A popular line of reasoning was that segregationists were willing to abide integration, but integrationists would have to understand that their morality would necessitate Southern belles bedding black men indiscriminately. The presumption was that once such an abhorrent result became apparent, even self-proclaimed liberals would come to their senses. Novelist Norman Mailer explained that, "The white man fears the sexual potency of the Negro. . . . The white loathes the idea of the Negro attaining equality in the classroom because the white feels that the Negro already enjoys sensual superiority."[17]

In reply, African American men were reduced to pledging that, even as they sought to be admitted to all spheres of public life on equal terms, they would not aspire to the hands of white women, and to assuring whites that not all black men were superstuds. They did not wish to appear like Bigger Thomas, the African American male in Richard Wright's 1940 novel, *Native Son.* Thomas accidentally kills the wealthy young white woman for whom he works, and toward whom he is attracted, but Thomas also brutally kills his black girlfriend, the latter crime being both the more intentional and insignificant in the context of his wretched life.[18] They knew the strategic advantage of stopping short of intermarriage. Michael Lind, in *The Next American Nation: The New Nationalism and the Fourth American Revolution,*[19] argues that intermarriage is crucial to the future of a diverse democracy. He observes that "even Martin Luther King Jr. dared dream, at least in public, only of black and white children playing together in the red hills of Birmingham, Alabama, instead of dreaming of weddings of mixed-race couples in the churches of Birmingham." In 1971, Robert E. Kuttner (a leading racialist not to be confused with the liberal economist of the same name) published in the now-defunct *American Mercury* magazine a think piece entitled, "Race Mixing: Suicide or Salvation?" Kuttner left no doubt that he considered it the former: "Legalized pornography teaches that the height of sexual pleasure can be attained only with Negro partners. . . . Who has not seen teenage girls with pale blond hair carrying Negro babies in Hippie settlements or in the drug communes around our elite universities?" He concluded, "Racial instincts in man deserve objective investigation by the methods of modern psychology" because white men prefer white women and "cannot be dismissed merely because womanless soldiers, explorers and colonizers mated with native women." In sum, "Race mixing between advanced and lower stocks is of no benefit to the higher type."[20]

Whites could be as upset by Asian Americans joining the family as they were by African Americans doing so. In the Western states, their dread of an Asian California was exceeded only by their horror at an Asian and Caucasian Pacific Coast. A white minister named Ralph Newman, living in Sacramento, said in 1931:

> Near my home is an eighty-acre tract of as fine land as there is in California. On that tract lives a Japanese. With that Japanese lives a white woman. In that woman's arms is a baby. What is that baby? It isn't white. It isn't Japanese. It is a germ of the mightiest problem that ever faced this state; a problem that will make the black problem of the South look white.[21]

Newman could have been confident that whites would back up his sentiments virtually unanimously. Whites from ardent segregationists to moderate integrationists opposed intermarriage. President Harry S Truman replied frankly to a reporter who asked whether intermarriage would become common, "I hope not; I don't believe in it."[22] Truman, who had taken incremental steps to dismantle segregation, was known to ask "Would you want your daughter to marry a Negro?"[23] In 1958, the Gallup organization reported that 96 percent of whites were against intermarriage.

With the civil rights movement, approval and disapproval of intermarriage have switched places in the polls, but the figures still show discrepancies by racial group. When the Gallup poll broke out separate figures for whites and blacks on this issue for the first time in 1972, the results were mirror images: 27 percent of whites approved of intermarriage and 73 percent disapproved of it; 76 percent of blacks approved of intermarriage and 24 percent disapproved of it. Since then, the attitudes of whites and blacks have converged, as have the attitudes in the North and the South and of the college educated and the non-college educated. By 1997, the last year for which data are available, a majority of respondents approved of intermarriage: 67 percent of whites approved of intermarriage and 33 percent disapproved of it; 83 percent of blacks approved of intermarriage and 17 percent disapproved of it. According to a survey published in 2001 by *The Washington Post*, Harvard University, and the Kaiser Foundation, approval of intermarriage is rising, but "nearly half of all whites—more than any other group—still believe it is better for people to marry someone of their own race."[24]

Among Asian Americans, intermarriage is as pervasive as resistance to it. A 1998 study by the Organization of Chinese Americans found that 69 percent of Chinese American parents strongly agreed or agreed with the statement "I prefer that my children marry someone in the same ethnic group."[25] Among children, only 50 percent agreed with that sentiment.

As salutary as the overall statistics may appear, they are likely to be inflated.[26] Social science data are often distorted by preference falsification. Interviewees give answers they suppose will be acceptable to society or pleasing to the interviewer, tending not to disclose their true outlook. In any event, attitudes and behavior are not the same. Intermarriage rates are well below what they would be if people acted on their stated willingness to intermarry, and progress has come slower than appearances would suggest.

Yellow Fever and Trophy Boyfriends

Inequality runs as a theme through the literature of mixed race liaisons. Poet Langston Hughes wrote a poem, entitled "Cross," about mixed parentage, ending with the stanza:

> My old man died in a fine big house.
> My ma died in a shack.
> I wonder where I'm gonna die,
> Being neither white nor black?[27]

The most famous such relationship in American history involved a white man and a black woman; he was as powerful as she was not.[28] As was rumored in the press in his time and verified by genetic testing in ours, founding father Thomas Jefferson carried on a long-term affair with his slave Sally Hemings.[29] Until the genetic testing resolved the matter, as Mount Holyoke College historian Joseph Ellis has noted, the Jefferson-Hemings relationship was rejected as a scurrilous rumor by the mostly white academic community as much as it was repeated as common knowledge in the black oral tradition.[30] The relationship between the future president and the woman who was his late wife's half-sister probably began when she was an adolescent serving as a nanny in his household. They may have been passionate and devoted. It is inspirational to imagine that they worked out a semblance of parity through mutual commitment. The truth may be disheartening.

Whatever their private personas, their public roles were grossly unequal. When Jefferson demanded that Hemings return from France, where he was serving as ambassador, to Virginia and his Monticello estate, both of them knew that she was free overseas but would be held in bondage once back home. Jefferson owned her. The children born to them were his chattel property, too.

Intermarriage still occurs in distinct configurations, and not all individuals have the same ability to engage in it. Races come together asymmetrically. Intermarriage may reinforce rather than break down the color line that separates whites from blacks, because intermarriage has risen primarily due to alliances among whites, Asian Americans, and Latinos, not African Americans. White-black intermarriage lags behind as the least frequent. Whites are much more likely to marry Asian Americans than African Americans. The Asian American intermarriage rate is triple the African American rate.

Asian Americans generally marry up. Just as the idea of "marrying up" is an admission of socioeconomic hierarchy, so is "marrying up" interracially an acknowledgment of racial hierarchy. For most Asian Americans, a white spouse ranks higher than a black spouse. Whites and blacks may both be "foreign devils," but whites are the more sought-after foreign devils. Halford Fairchild, a noted psychologist who is of African American and Hawaiian Japanese descent, has said that "the black community, in general, has been a lot more accepting of racial differences than other communities."[31]

His Japanese American mother's family disowned her for marrying a black man, cautioning her that when they returned to his home in California, she would find "he has nothing."

In 1990, thirty times as many intermarried Asian Americans had white spouses as had black spouses, even though years ago intermarriage between Chinese Americans and African Americans in Harlem was not unheard of. The 1992 independent movie *Mississippi Masala* by director Mira Nair, about a South Asian woman from Uganda who falls in love with an African American man who owns a carpet-cleaning business (essayed by Denzel Washington, whom women of all races have pursued to the box office), is abnormal even within the atypicality of interracial romances. The 1997 Disney remake of Rodgers and Hammerstein's *Cinderella,* starring African American television actress Brandy in the title role and Asian American stage actor Paolo Montalban as Prince Charming, is anomalous in the opposite direction.

White Americans also rank above other Asian Americans. Although Asian Americans are marrying across Asian ethnicities more often than before—as my wife and I did—they are more likely to intermarry with white Americans than with Asian Americans of a different ethnicity. Few fail to grasp that it is the white look, not the Asian look, that is in demand. In John Updike's short story, "Metamorphosis," the white male protagonist is naïve in his infatuation with his Asian American female doctor. Fantasizing that he can capture her attention, he asks for reverse eyelid surgery to give himself almond eyes. In the O. Henry-style surprise ending, however, once he has undergone the painful operation, he spies on her desk her family photograph showing her husband "not old, exactly, probably younger than [him] by some years, but craggy, Caucasian, grinning, big-nosed, rather monstrously bumpy and creased." As he leaves the office, he ponders "how foolish he must look!" and he is grateful that he still has his right tear duct.[32]

The various pairings also exhibit the mutual influence of race and gender. Among African American-white married couples, an African American husband with a white wife remains more widespread than a white husband with an African American wife. According to the 1990 Census, 72 percent of African American-white couples consist of an African American male and a white female. It appears that the African American man who marries a white woman is exchanging his higher economic status for her higher social status. He is augmenting his material success with a woman who is regarded as belonging to a superior class; she is acquiring access to his affluence.

Terry McMillan's best-selling novel *Waiting to Exhale*[33] chronicled the love lives of a quartet of African American women. Among them was Bernadine Harris, whose trauma of being left by her African American husband was aggravated by the identity of the "other woman." Bernadine and her friends list the problems with black men: "with white women" comes second in the litany, after "scared to make a damned commitment," before "gay," and well ahead of ugly, stupid, and in prison.[34] After Bernadine had supported him as he struggled through his career, her husband left her for a younger white woman once his business became profitable. In the book, Bernadine reviews her mistake of trusting him: "Kathleen the bookkeeper, who was fresh out of some two-year college and California pretty" was "not at all a threat because, number one, she was white and you knew [he] would never look at a white girl and number two, he loved you and the kids."[35] In the movie, Angela Bassett in the role of Bernadine was cheered by audiences as she acted on her anger: she visited her husband's office, slapped her rival, and confronted her husband, before returning home, clearing out the contents of his closet, dumping his fancy shirts and expensive suits into his luxury car, and setting it all ablaze.

The modern white-black intermarriage that prompted record outcry, from whites and blacks alike, was the 1949 marriage of Walter White and Poppy Cannon.[36] White, the long-time secretary of the NAACP, divorced his African American wife to take up with Cannon, a white businesswoman. Many whites found in the two of them proof of the conspiracy of black men to steal their women. Some black women deplored the dumping of a black woman for a white woman, treating the divorce and remarriage as an exercise in crass racial upward mobility. What White and Cannon should have made apparent was the fabrication of race. When they traveled, they were regarded as an interracial couple, but people made assumptions that reversed their racial roles.[37] White fit his name: He was light-skinned, blonde, and blue-eyed; both of his parents could have passed as white and his daughter was so light she had problems pursuing an acting career because she could not credibly play a black person but could not be cast as a white person.[38] Cannon was darker all-around, blacker in a physical sense.

Shortly thereafter, the widower Thurgood Marshall wed Cecile "Cissy" Suyatt. Known as Mr. Civil Rights for his courtroom victories against racial segregation, Marshall served for many years as the general counsel for the NAACP Legal Defense Fund prior to his historic appointment to the U.S. Supreme Court. Suyatt was a Filipina secretary at his office. She initially turned down his proposal for fear of the likely reactions. She reported whispers against her that she was a "foreigner," and she worried about what her family would say about an African American husband. Like White's marriage, Marshall's met the censure of some Southern whites. In response to the newspaper editorial that called him a racist for marrying a white woman, Marshall said, "I just think you ought to be accurate. . . . I've had two wives and both of 'em are colored."[39] In 1995, *Ebony* magazine listed the Marshall-Suyat wedding among its fifty "best" of the past half-century.[40]

In a reversal of the black-white interaction, 72 percent of Asian American-white couples consist of an Asian American wife and a white husband. Writing in *American Demographics* magazine, journalist Robert Suro reported that Asian women are intermarrying at twice the rate of Asian men.[41] In a 2000 California survey of Asian-white intermarriages, Filipina-white intermarriages were the most common. In the Golden State throughout the 1990s, there were 16,503 births of children to Filipina mothers and white fathers and only 5,556 births to white mothers and Filipino fathers. The former occurred almost three times as often as the latter.

The data produce a puzzle, however: Unless there are many more Asian American women than there are Asian American men, there must be enormous numbers of single Asian American men compared to single Asian American women. The solution to the conundrum of uneven rates of outmarriage is immigration. It appears to be foreign-born Asian women who are intermarrying as much as it is Asian American women.

Tiger, Keanu, and the Passing of Asian Americans

Support for the mixed race movement can be blended with caution about its implications. As compelling as the desire to define oneself may be, the mixed race movement poses the risk of increasing rather than decreasing the invidious forms of color consciousness. A range of color categories expands the reach of prejudice. By a Creole or mestizo sensibility, half-white may come to look better than all-black. Just as African Americans straighten their hair, Asian Americans perm theirs; just as African Americans have cosmetic surgery for a "classical" nose and Asian Americans do so for round eyes, the mixed race movement may promote, even if inadvertently, the practices of whitening.

University of North Carolina professor Jon Michael Spencer, who happens to be mixed race himself, argues against the ambitions of the mixed race movement in his 1997 book, *The New Colored People: The Mixed-Race Movement in America.*[42] Spencer believes that race can bring together oppressed peoples. He notes that historically and even at present, in areas with large numbers of individuals who are both black and white, such as nineteenth-century New Orleans, apartheid South Africa, or contemporary Hawaii and Brazil, the gradations among hues can be much finer in distinction than black and white but no less odious as discrimination against the darker skinned. None of the places whose populations have multiplied creatively have become racial nirvanas. The various methods of classifying people according to pedigree—for example, by the moons of fingernails—have in common the placement of whites at the top and the ordering of everyone else from swarthy to tawny in descending order. The expressions for every ancestral assortment are no better for being archaic. In addition to the official terms allocating with false precision the admixture of heredity, from "mulatto" to "quadroon" to "octoroon," were slang terms that could be decidedly uncomplimentary, such as "Sambo," which originally meant three-quarters black, and "high yellow" or "yella."

As much as some of us might proclaim enthusiastically, "There is only one race, the human race," few of us live up to the belief through our actions. Among African Americans, the colorism of "lighter is righter" has copied white prejudice.[43] Under slavery, white owners might choose lighter-skinned slaves for household duties instead of the toil of field work, and white men might take the lighter women as mistresses. Light-skinned mulattos, many of whom were freed through the wills of their white fathers, could have contempt for their darker brethren. Some of them even became slaveholders themselves, occupying a middle position between black and white. One of the most scathing attacks on black culture, *The American Negro,* was written a century ago by William Hannibal Thomas about his darker fellows. His vitriolic comments were scarcely distinguishable from those of white supremacists.[44] Even up to the civil rights era, an emphasis by some "blue veined" mixed race individuals on their white derivation can harken back to the "paper bag" test. A few "bougie"—"bougie" is a vernacular derivation of "bourgeois"—social clubs within African American communities, such as the Bon Ton Society of Washington, D.C., were said to employ a "paper bag" test for membership: Successful applicants had to be as light as the pallid brown of a paper bag.

The practice of passing, or "crossing over," bears out the pecking order. People of color who have the requisite skin tone and facial features are able to pretend that they are exclusively white so that they can enjoy the tangible advantages. They may even become white permanently, leaving behind their family, friends, and community, as they follow the excruciating path of forsaking their identity for their livelihood.

Passing usually occurs in only one direction. People who are white rarely try to disguise themselves as people of color and would have few reasons to do so. There are only a handful of people who became what was dubbed a "voluntary Negro": More-

house College founder William Jefferson White, who had black ancestors and was raised within the black community; turn-of-the-century novelist Charles W. Chesnutt, who used the honorific "FMC," an antebellum term for "free man of color"; Adam Clayton Powell, who was virtually blonde and blue-eyed, but as a minister and Congressman was an advocate of black power; and jazz musician Mezz Mezzrow, nee Milton Mesirow, the Russian Jewish author of an autobiography, *Really the Blues.*[45]

The opposite is much more common. Whites even sued to avoid being classified as black. Until recently, it was considered libel of the worst form to call a white person black. It was an offense because it offended; black was decidedly inferior. In 1982, a well-to-do woman named Susie Guillory Phipps filed suit as an anonymous "Jane Doe" to challenge a Louisiana statute that made anyone with black ancestry automatically black.[46] She wanted to be white, not black or multiracial. Snubbing some of her relatives, she maintained she had had no idea she was even remotely black. Recalling her devastation at the revelation, she said she took sick for three days. "I was brought up white, I married white twice," she said. She lost. But publicity about her case prompted the state to amend its laws so that parents were allowed to list the race of newborns and an individual could adjust her birth certificate upon a showing that she was white by a preponderance of the evidence.

In the nineteenth and early twentieth centuries, the Asian population would have been driven out of existence by a combination of the rules on immigration and those on intermarriage. Immigration laws made it difficult for Asian women to come to the country. The ratio of Chinese men to Chinese women exceeded one hundred to one. Anti-miscegenation laws passed by states prevented Asian men from marrying white women. The Cable Act passed by Congress stripped non-Asian women of their citizenship if they married Asian men. Asian-black children were black. The government argued against granting of birthright citizenship to the few native-born children of Asian parents. If the mutually reinforcing public policies had been fully effective, Asian Americans could not have reproduced themselves.

Nowadays, Asian Americans are melting away voluntarily. Even as Asian Americans are continuing to appear through immigration, we are constantly disappearing through intermarriage. Japanese Americans, who have outmarried in the highest proportions, are joined by very few new arrivals from Japan. The Yasui family of Hood River, Oregon, is typical. The subject of Lauren Kessler's *Stubborn Twig: Three Generations in the Life of a Japanese-American Family*,[47] only one of eighteen third-generation cousins of the clan married another Japanese American (and then only in a second marriage). As go the Yasuis's children, so go Japanese Americans. They are likely to vanish as a distinctive ethnic group within another generation unless large numbers of mixed race individuals in the fourth and fifth generations choose an Asian American identity rather than a white identity. Some have said that Japanese American integration was hastened by the internment, but other Asian American ethnic groups also are intermarrying at high rates.

So for Asian Americans, passing presents a dilemma. Few are as unique as sculptor Isamu Noguchi, whose father was Yone Noguchi, a Japanese (not Japanese American) poet, and whose mother was Leonie Gilmour, a white American. Noguchi grew up in Japan and the United States; lived in Paris, where he was an apprentice to sculptor Constantin Brancusi; worked with choreographer Martha Graham while also designing the lamps for which he is best known; and became an internationally renowned artist representing the United States at the Venice Biennial and being recognized as a national treasure by Japan. Many Asian Americans are forced toward whiteness or blackness as two extremes along a spectrum with a preferred pole. Tiger Woods and Keanu Reeves show the effects of such dispersion.

Golf sensation Tiger Woods has become a reluctant poster child for the mixed race movement. (The unsuccessful legislation that would have required the Census to include a multiracial category was dubbed the "Tiger Woods bill.") As an athlete who has revitalized his sport as no other single competitor has ever done for any game, Woods can hardly be considered average in any terms. Just as it is inappropriate to make an individual the representative of everyone else of his specific racial background, it is unseemly to turn a single person into a symbol for everyone of mixed race background. He may be the product of the fusion of diverse cultures, but it would be absurd to give him the mixed man's burden of leading us to racial reconciliation.

Indeed, Woods reveals the contradictions of the mixed race movement. Even for international celebrities whose lives are known in every detail by total strangers, private and public racial identities do not align neatly.

In 1997, the twenty-one-year-old Woods became the youngest player ever to win the Masters Tournament as he began his ascent toward legendary status. Having left Stanford University as the top-rated amateur golfer, he defeated the professional field with a seemingly invincible superiority. Again and again, he defeated all comers while drawing a swelling crowd of spectators, many of whom would not have idolized Arnold Palmer or Jack Nicklaus as they putted on the links of exclusive country clubs. Shoal Creek in Birmingham, Alabama, was excluding blacks as late as 1990.

Its rules prompted the PGA to adopt an anti-discrimination policy. In response, some clubs decided to give up their affiliation with the PGA.

Woods was different from his seniors. Poised and telegenic, he thrilled spectators by coming back to win even if he had had a poor start well over par. He graded himself after he played his rounds, to the irritation of his peers. His "C" game beat everybody else's "A" game. He was extraordinary even when he wasn't bothering to try too much. His most spectacular television advertisement used footage that was filmed accidentally. Before he was about to shoot the scripted material, he was goofing off by bouncing a ball on his club head two dozen times in a row without dropping it, before hitting it into the air and sending it flying several hundred yards.

Immediately, the story of his life introduced his fans to the mixed race movement. The son of Earl Woods, an African American Green Beret lieutenant colonel, and Kultida Punsawad, a well-to-do Thai secretary who was raised as a devout Buddhist near the bridge on the River Kwai (as in the movie of that title), Eldrick Woods was nicknamed Tiger in honor of Phong Nguyen, a Vietnamese officer who had saved his father's life more than once.

Woods was imitating his father's golf swing before he was a year old. By the time he was three, he had won against a club professional and appeared on television with Bob Hope. He shot his first hole in one when he was six. Because his mother wanted him to develop academically as well, she allowed him to play golf only if he had finished his homework.

From time to time, Woods has returned to his mother's homeland as a conquering hero. There he is said to be Asian "from the eyes up." He has even led a Thai national golf team in Asian regional contests. He also believes in most of the principles of Buddhism. But Woods is not simply African American some of the time and Asian American the rest of the time. His background is more complicated, and societal reactions to it more problematic, than that.

Appearing on Oprah Winfrey's television program just after his record victory at the Masters, Woods talked about his lineage at length. He told a nationwide viewership that he had invented a term for himself, "Cablinasian," to unify verbally his Caucasian, Black, Indian, and Asian heritage. To be precise, if it is possible to be precise in these matters, his father is half black, one-quarter Native American, and one-quarter Chinese; his mother is half Thai, one-quarter Dutch, and one-quarter Chinese. Woods said, "I just am who I am." Asked whether it bothered him to be labeled as an African American, he said, "It does." He checked off the official boxes on forms for both African American and Asian American, because, "Those are the two I was raised under, and the only two I know."

Winfrey christened him "America's son." But the episode proved controversial. As soon as Tiger became a precious commodity, Asian Americans and African Americans began an unbecoming dispute over who would claim him as one of their own. Asian Americans noted that technically, as half Thai and one-quarter Chinese, Woods was three-quarters Asian, and that was the largest portion of his makeup. African Americans were dismayed that someone who paid homage to black golfers of the past and alluded to continuing racial segregation seemed to be disowning his blackness when presented with the chance and selecting a paler self.

The tension between Asian Americans and African Americans was made superfluous, even if it was not quite resolved, thanks to the intervention of a white observer. Notwithstanding the intense publicity over Woods's compound bloodlines, in most people's eyes, Woods turned out to be effectively black.

The pivotal incident came when Fuzzy Zoeller, a veteran of the PGA tour who happens to be white, made remarks about Woods to a television crew. Referring to the winner's prerogative of setting the dinner menu for the festivities at the Masters, Zoeller referred to Woods's race in a nonchalant remark. Calling Woods "that little boy," Zoeller said he should be told not to serve fried chicken or collard greens "or whatever it is they serve."[48] Even aside from the use of "that little boy," Zoeller was undoubtedly talking about race by referring to stereotypical Southern black cuisine.

Released by his major sponsor, K-Mart, as a spokesperson, Zoeller then delivered a tearful explanation about his penchant for being "a jokester"; he added, "I just didn't deliver the line well."[49] He even withdrew temporarily from the professional tour.

Woods accepted Zoeller's apology. But giving Zoeller the benefit of the doubt and treating him as a decent man acting in good faith only makes the mistake of his perception worse. It is as if he cannot help himself: When he looks at Woods he sees race; he sees blackness. He is cued to talk about soul food. He does not bring up curry chicken or lemongrass soup. That would have been equally (in)apt.

Woods may be one of the most well-known people on the face of the earth. He may even be renowned for his mixed race status and acquainted personally with the observer who is engrossed with race. Whatever Woods declared for himself and however Asian Americans and African Americans calculated their fractions, the real test of his race is how he is treated by strangers on the street who don't recognize his celebrity status. Woods himself has said, "I am 90 percent Oriental, more Thai than anything." But he also has said that while he was in college, "What I realized is that even

though I'm mathematically Asian—if anything—if you have one drop of black blood in the United States, you're black."[50]

The one drop rule to which Woods referred was a legal rule. On the theory that a single drop of black blood would contaminate white virtue, any person whose ancestry could be traced back to a black person was deemed to be black no matter how distant the relationship. The one drop rule, which has no basis in biology, has been abolished legally but not culturally. Somebody who is like Woods but who is not instantly identifiable from shoe advertisements is for practical purposes black. In a recent anthology of essays on being "half and half," one writer said of Woods, "'When the black truck comes around, they're going to haul his ass on it.'"[51]

Movie actor Keanu Reeves provides a contrasting example. He played the epitome of a clueless Californian in the teen favorite *Bill and Ted's Excellent Adventure*. He has been the Buddha and the son of the Devil in other films. He earned raves for his Hamlet on stage and he turned in an admirable Don Juan in Kenneth Branagh's cinematic version of Shakespeare's *Much Ado About Nothing* (with Denzel Washington as his better brother). He emerged as an action superstar with the thriller *Speed*, one of the highest-grossing movies of the 1990s.

Billed by *Vanity Fair* as "Hollywood's hottest heartthrob," Reeves was born in 1964 in Beirut. His father was a wealthy geologist of Hawaiian-Chinese extraction. His mother was a British showgirl who became a costume designer for rock musicians. Readers of sensational accounts of his life know that his father was estranged from the family and imprisoned for drug possession and that his mother raised him in Toronto with a series of stepfathers. His first name is based on a Hawaiian term for the wind over the mountains. He was a high school hockey player of some talent. A serious motorcyclist, he rides a vintage Norton Commando even after two accidents. He has opted to tour with his band, Dogstar, in obscure venues instead of taking on lucrative but unsatisfying acting roles.

Reeves is a closeted Asian American. He has become a Caucasian Asian. To most moviegoers, he is an average white guy. He is an archetypal dude. He can easily be accepted as white. There is no reason for him to publicize that he is anything else. Only a fanatical devotee of tabloid news would even know his paternity. Neither his facial features nor his family name are obviously Asian. His father, however, can be readily identified as Asian from the few published photographs. He peers out from the shadows as an enigmatic figure.

There would be no reason other than excessive ethnic pride for Reeves to out himself as Asian. But the ease with which he has adopted whiteness is fascinating. To the extent that he has chosen to be white and has consciously selected his whiteness, he confirms that whiteness is beneficial. Other than Reeves, whose martial arts exploits were enhanced by "bullet time" special effects in the science fiction blockbuster *The Matrix*, Asian men are leading men and heroes only in the kung fu chop socky genre; unless Reeves is regarded as Asian American, the highest-grossing movie ever made without a white male lead is the Jackie Chan-Chris Tucker buddy flick *Rush Hour*. To the extent that Reeves has not selected whiteness but has stumbled into it, he indicates how whiteness is the default mode. Unless he deviates blatantly from the norm, he is assumed to be white.

Even though Reeves is essentially white, the uniformly negative commentary of film critics on his work unwittingly echoes the classic line about Asians. To many reviewers, ironically, he is inscrutable. Reeves himself once said about his skills as thespian, "I don't know anything, man."

It should give us pause that Woods is black and Reeves is white and neither is Asian. They are not even Eurasian or Amerasian. The terms have become antiquated exactly as they were on the cusp of becoming commonly applicable.

In the Mississippi Delta, where a few thousand Chinese laborers were brought during Reconstruction, many of their descendants intermarried long ago.[52] Families with Chinese roots came to have both white branches and black branches. With successive intermarriage, the Chinese roots have been forgotten, and the white branches and the black branches have grown apart. The same has happened to the little-known community of Punjabi Mexican Americans in California.[53]

Mixed race individuals do not leave race behind. A study conducted using 1980 Census data showed wide divergences in the racial identity of mixed race children. Among children with white mothers, only 35 percent of those with Chinese fathers were identified by their parents as white, but 74 percent of those with Asian Indian fathers were; conversely, among children with white fathers, about 62 percent of those with Chinese mothers were identified by their parents as white but 93 percent of those with Asian Indian mothers were.

Although the research on these topics is just beginning, the only summary that can be made thus far is that matters seem to be complicated and dynamic. The point should not be some sort of futile effort to make Woods and Reeves, along with the groups in Mississippi and California, into Asians through the dubious transmogrification of racial alchemy. In truth, they are no more Asian than they are black or white. They cannot be reduced to race with any coherence. Darby Li Po Price, a comedian with a doctorate in ethnic studies, tells the following opening joke: "I am of Chinese descent from my mother, and Scots-Irish, Welsh, and

Cherokee descent from my father, so in the United States that means I'm Latino."[54] Yet as mixed race people take on their own identities, their cumulative choices create a new identity, such as Japanese, white, and Jewish combined.

As mixed race status becomes hip, however, individuals start to make superficial claims to be part this or part that, without any actual appreciation of the minority culture or acceptance of the consequences of affinity with it. The Native American population is growing much faster than its birthrate (and, needless to say, it has no immigration), thanks to people who are outsiders to Indian culture suddenly discovering their Indianness. When Disney released its animated movie *Pocahantas,* it inspired many such superficial Indians to fantasize about identity.[55]

Many Native Americans have contempt for ersatz Native Americans who are not enrolled in a tribe who casually say that they had a great-grandparent who was an Indian brave or an Indian maiden, some of whom seem to be doing nothing more than trolling for government benefits or speculating that they can cash in on the exaggerated riches of casino gambling. Most Native Americans grant that it is possible to be a bona fide Indian without being a pureblood, but they have had more than enough experience, largely catastrophic, with outsiders defining who is an Indian and what it means to be an Indian.[56]

The wannabees who announce that they are Native Americans but who have no actual experience as a Native American have not grappled with the alcoholism, poverty, and suicide of reservations.[57] They know nothing of the difficulty of enforcing treaty rights or the humiliation of seeing skeletons of their ancestors displayed in museums and caricatures of themselves as sports mascots. (They are not like the "black Seminoles," African Americans who more than a

century ago took on the customs of neighboring Native Americans, part of the largely neglected integration of African Americans and Native Americans.)

Among Asian immigrants, the poignant case of children fathered by U.S. military personnel in Vietnam shows how the standing of mixed race individuals depends on the situation.[58] From their birth, they were snubbed as *bui doi,* the dust of life. Their mothers were considered prostitutes. With passage of the Homecoming Act by Congress in 1987, allowing them and their families to come here, they became *con van,* golden children. They could be the ticket to the United States for the relatives who rushed to claim them.

Our expectations of the mixed race movement should not be naïve. The mixed race movement can conceal a pessimistic message, namely that American society is most likely to flourish if it is monoracial rather than if it is multiracial. Few of its current adherents state their belief this way, but earlier enthusiasts of intermarriage candidly doubted that any culture could be sustained with numerous races. For them, intermarriage was the only hope and not the best hope. Cultural critic (then on the left, now on the right) Norman Podhoretz wrote that the "Negro problem" would not be solved unless we "let the brutal word come out—miscegenation."[59] Podhoretz would have been mortified if "a daughter of mine" were "'to marry one',," and he "would rail and rave and rant and tear my hair." However, he would hope to "have the courage to curse myself for raving and ranting, and to give her my blessing."[60] Political philosopher Hannah Arendt once made the same recommendation. Even though Arendt's argument was implicit rather than explicit, according to Harvard professor Werner Sollors, "she had a hard time getting her views published and generated a venomous debate." Even *Dissent* magazine, where the essay originally appeared, published a disclaimer and two separate rebuttals.[61] Intermarriage was the means of achieving a single racial identity. Native Americans, for example, could be rescued only if their cultures were destroyed and they were absorbed into white society. The Reverend Jedidiah Morse, an orthodox Calvinist, could try to save Indian souls by ensuring that they become "literally of one blood with us."[62]

The mixed race movement could bring about an unfortunate rediscovery: The most bitter enemies are your kin. Cousins can hate one another with an intensity not summoned against the unfamiliar. The great tragedies are family tragedies. Blood is the proper metaphor for race, even if it does not comport with biological fact.[63] Whites and blacks of the old South, masters and slaves, were often ill-fated relations. The world has witnessed, in the vengeful repetitiveness of divisive ethnic conflicts that emerge repeatedly, that people who know history can be damned to repeat it, as groups who seem to be the same to outsiders become all the more fierce for their similarity in their avowal that they are special and each is better than the other. It was their fellow Greeks, the Spartans, and not their foreign enemies, the Persians, who demolished the Athenian democracy; the hubris of the Athenians themselves hastened their downfall in the Peloponnesian War. Veteran political consultant Kevin Phillips argued in *The Cousin's Wars: Religion, Politics, and the Triumph of Anglo-America* that it was fratricide of the English Civil War, the American Revolution and the Civil War, that formed our national spirit.[64] The latest research has turned up intriguing hints that the Japanese and the Korean royal families may once have been the same; their enmity becomes a feud like that of the British and the French.[65]

Our familiarity with other races also should not lead us to premature self-congratulation.[66] The clichéd rejoinder "many of my friends are black" is not persuasive, because that very friendship may mislead a person into treating those who are close to them as exceptions who prove the rules of race. Marrying someone of a different race provides no immunity from prejudice, as exposed by the ongoing case involving serial rapes of Asian American women in the Chicago area, the suspect in which was arrested in the Philippines when he visited his Filipina wife. Dating someone of a different race does not even grant a license to take liberties, as actor Ted Danson found out when he was dating comedian Whoopi Goldberg and he performed an embarrassing skit in blackface at the 1993 Friars Club roast in her honor. Having children who were of mixed racial background did not much move most of the white masters of slaves, other than to perform the gesture of manumitting them in a will.

At its best, the mixed race movement makes us think. Race may be fictional, but racism is real.[67] Although most of us may be reluctant to blame people who yearn for the benefits of passing, seeking privileges that many whites are not even aware of, we also may be hesitant to receive them as people of color, if they can conceal their identities when it is convenient.

The mixed race movement and passing give to some individuals who were assumed to be members of a stigmatized group the wherewithal to disassociate themselves from the group. It would be better if society recognized their right to belong to the groups of their choosing rather than coercing them into groups with whom they may have nothing in common. But it would be best if we stopped subjugating whole groups to the point where those who can would rather leave them. We will know we have achieved genuine racial equality when people who could claim to be white if they wanted to would rather stand up to say that they are proud to be black and they will lead lives within black communities. If everyone makes the same choice—white—then it is clear that there is no meaningful choice.

Perhaps the mixed race movement can be of lasting importance not by elevating some individuals out of the darker boxes but by persuading us that racial classifications in general are pernicious. If intermarriage and the mixed race movement are to live up to the optimistic claims that they are the future of race relations, they must hold out a greater promise than that some individuals can make a good match and a few individuals are able by themselves to ascend to whiteness. We will have accepted the mixed race movement as another form of our manifest diversity only when we know in our bones that "they" are "us."

NOTES

1. *Loving v. Virginia,* 388 U.S. 1 (1967).
2. David Greenberg, "White Weddings," *Slate,* June 14, 1999.
3. Jeanne Wakatsuki Houston, *Beyond Manzanar: Views of Asian American Womanhood* (Santa Barbara, Calif.: Capra Press, 1985), 20. This essay is reprinted in Russell Endo et al., *Asian Americans: Social Psychological Perspectives,* vol. 2 (Palo Alto, Calif.: Science and Behavior Books, 1980), 17–25.
4. James Weldon Johnson, *Along This Way* (New York: Viking, 1934).
5. Ibid., 170.
6. Gunnar Myrdal, *An American Dilemma: The Negro Problem and Modern Democracy* (New York: Harper & Row, 1944), 60–61.
7. Sidney Kaplan, "The Miscegenation Issues in the Election of 1864)" in Werner Sollors, ed., *Interracialism: Black-White Intermarriage in American History, Literature, and the Law* (Oxford: Oxford University Press, 2000), 219.
8. Michae Lind, *The Next American Nation: The New Nationalism and the Fourth American Revolution* (New York, Free Press, 1995), 291.
9. Theodore G. Bilbo, *Take Your Choice: Separation or Mongrelization* (Poplarville, Miss.: Dream House Publishing Co., 1947).
10. Ibid., frontispiece.
11. Ibid., 198.
12. Ibid., 201.
13. Ibid., appendix A.
14. Tom Brady, *Black Monday* (Winona, Miss.: Association of Citizens' Councils, 1954), 88.
15. Ibid., 89.
16. Charles Herbert Stember, *Sexual Racism: The Emotional Barrier to an Integrated Society* (New York: Elsevier, 1976), 24–25.
17. Norman Mailer, *Advertisements for Myself* (New York: G.P. Putnam's Sons, 1959), 332. Mailer also says in his famous "White Negro" essay that "the deeper issue is not desegregation but miscegenation." Ibid., 356.
18. Richard Wright, *Native Son* (New York: Literary Classics of America, 1991), 525–26, 667–68.
19. Lind, *Next American Nation,* 290.
20. Robert E. Kuttner, "Race Mixing: Suicide or Salvation," *American Mercury* (Winter 1971): 45–48.
21. Paul R. Spickard, *Mixed Blood: Intermarriage and Ethnic Identity in Twentieth-Century America* (Madison, Wis.: University of Wisconsin Press, 1989), 25.
22. William D. Zabel, "Interracial Marriage and the Law," in Sollors, *Interracialism,* 54.
23. Sollors, *Interracialism,* 13.
24. Darryl Fears and Claudia Deane, "Biracial Couples Report Tolerance; Survey Finds Most Are Accepted by Families," *Washington Post,* July 5, 2001, A1.
25. Flavia Tam et al., *Inter-Generational Paper on Asian American Attitudes Towards Family Values, Interracial Dating and Marriage* (Washington, D.C.: Organization of Chinese Americans, 1998). *See also* Betty Lee Sung, *Chinese American Intermarriage* (New York: Center for Migration Studies, 1990).
26. Timur Kuran, *Private Truths, Public Lies: The Social Consequences of Preference Falsification* (Cambridge, Mass.: Harvard University Press, 1995).
27. Arnold Rampersad, ed., *The Collected Poems of Langston Hughes* (New York: Alfred A. Knopf, 1995), 305. The "tragic mulatto" was a recurring theme of Hughes's; he later turned "Cross" into a play.
28. Fawn M. Brodie, *Thomas Jefferson: An Intimate History* (New York: W.W. Norton, 1974); Annette Gordon-Reed, *Thomas Jefferson and Sally Hemings: An American Controversy* (Charlottesville: University Press of Virginia, 1997).
29. Leef Smith, "Tests Link Jefferson, Slave's Son; DNA Suggests a Monticello Liaison," *Wash-*

ington Post, November 1, 1998, A1. The scientific data were reported in Eugene A. Foster et al., "Jefferson Fathered Slave's Last Child." *Nature* 396 (November 5, 1998): 27–28 and Eric S. Lander and Joseph J. Ellis, "Founding Father," *Nature* 396 (November 5, 1998): 13–14.

30. Joseph J. Ellis, *American Sphinx: The Character of Thomas Jefferson* (New York: Knopf, 1997), 20. For an example of the pre-genetic testing debate, *see* Edwin McDowell, "Jefferson Liaison Is Disputed Again," *New York Times,* June 2, 1981, C7.

31. Itabari Njeri, "The Challenge of Diversity in an L.A. Cultural Crucible; In Crenshaw Neighborhood, Japanese-American, Blacks Have Forged a History of Complex Relationships," *Los Angeles Times,* May 2, 1990, E1.

32. John Updike, "Metamorphosis," *New Yorker,* August 9, 1999, 66–70. The title alludes to Franz Kafka's short story of the same name in which Gregor Samsa awakes to find himself transformed into a giant cockroach.

33. Terry McMillan, *Waiting to Exhale* (New York: Viking Productions, 1992).

34. Ibid., 329.

35. Ibid., 29–30.

36. Poppy Cannon, *A Gentle Knight: My Husband, Walter White* (New York: Rhinehart & Co., 1956), 12–13. The O.J. Simpson murder trial, in which he was acquitted of the murders of his ex-wife Nicole and her friend Ronald Goldman, also focused attention on the complexities of interracial marriages. *See* Jacqueline Adams, "The White Wife," *New York Times Magazine,* September 18, 1994, 36–38.

37. Cannon, *Gentle Knight,* 14.

38. Walter White, *A Man Called White: The Autobiography of Walter White* (New York: Viking Press, 1948), 338.

39. Juan Williams, *Thurgood Marshall: American Revolutionary* (New York: Times Books, 1998), 244.

40. Lynn Norment, "The Best Weddings of the Last 50 Years," *Ebony* (June 1995): 82.

41. Robert Suro, "Mixed Doubles," *American Demographics* (November 1999): 58.

42. Jon Michael Spencer, *The New Colored People: The Mixed-Race Movement in America* (New York: New York University Press, 1997).

43. Kathy Russell, Midge Wilson and Ronald Hall, *The Color Complex: The Politics of Skin Color Among African Americans* (New York: Doubleday, Anchor Books, 1992).

44. William Hannibal Thomas, *The American Negro: What He Was, What He Is, and What He May Become: A Critical and Practical Discussion* (New York: Macmillan, 1901). *See also* John David Smith, *Black Judas: William Hannibal Thomas and the American Negro* (Athens: University of Georgia Press, 2000).

45. Mezz Mezzrow, *Really the Blues: An Autobiography* (New York: Random House, 1946).

46. Associated Press, "Slave Descendant Fights Race Listing," *New York Times,* September 15, 1982, A1; Calvin Trillin, "American Chronicles: Black or White," *New Yorker,* April 14, 1986, 62–78.

47. Lauren Kessler, *Stubborn Twig: Three Generations in the Life of a Japanese-American Family* (New York: Random House, 1993).

48. Woods ultimately decided on cheeseburgers and French Fries, an historic first. Thomas Bonk, "It's Food That's Fit for This Golf King; The Masters: Wood's Choice for the Traditional Tournament Dinner Includes Cheeseburgers and Fries," *Los Angeles Times,* April 7, 1998, C1.

49. Hal Bock, "The Inside Track; Say What You Mean, Mean What You Say," *Los Angeles Times,* April 27, 1997, C2.

50. Gary Smith, "The Chosen; Tiger Woods Was Raised to Believe That His Destiny Is Not Only to Be the Greatest Golfer Ever, But Also to Change the World. Will the Pressures of Celebrity Grind Him Down First?" *Sports Illustrated,* December 23, 1996, 28.

51. Claudine Chiawei O'Hearn, *Half and Half: Writers on Growing Up Biracial and Bicultural* (New York: Pantheon Books, 1998), xxxiv.

52. Lucy M. Cohen, *Chinese in the Post Civil-War South: A People Without A History* (Baton Rouge. La.: University of Louisiana Press, 1984); James Loewen, *The Mississippi Chinese: Between Black and White* (Cambridge, Mass.: Harvard University Press, 1971).

53. Karen Isaksen Leonard, *Making Ethnic Choices: California's Punjabi Mexican Americans* (Philadelphia: Temple University Press, 1992).

54. Darby Li Po Price, "Mixed Laughter," in Paul Spickard and W. Jeffrey Burroughs, eds., *We Are a People: Narrative and Multiplicity in Constructing Ethnic Identity* (Philadelphia: Temple University Press, 2000), 179.

55. Leef Smith, "A Powhatan Princess in Their Past; Disney's 'Pocahontas' Inspires Virginians to Shake the Family Tree," *Washington Post,* July 3, 1995, B1. Regarding Indian iden-

tity, *see generally* Joane Nagel, *American Indian Ethnic Renewal: Red Power and the Resurgence of Identity and Culture* (New York: Oxford University Press, 1986).

56. For a discussion of these issues, *see* William S. Penn, *As We Are Now: Mixblood Essays on Race and Identity* (Berkeley: University of California Press, 1997).

57. For a contemporary account of Indian life, *see* Ian Frazier, *On the Rez* (New York: Farrar, Straus & Giroux, 2000).

58. Kieu-Linh Caroline Valverde, "From Dust to Gold: The Vietnamese Amerasian Experience," in Maria P.P. Root, ed., *Racially Mixed People in America* (Newbury Park, Calif.: Sage, 1992), 144–61.

59. Norman Podhoretz, "My Negro Problem—And Ours," *Commentary* (February 1963): 93–101. He wrote a postscript to this famous essay thirty years later. *See* Mark Gerson, ed., *The Essential Neoconservative Reader* (Reading, Mass.: Addison-Wesley, 1996), 18–22.

60. Ibid., 101

61. Hannah Arendt, "Reflections on Little Rock," in Sollors, *Interracialism,* 492–502. Sollors's account of the reaction to Arendt's article is in Werner Sollors, *Neither Black Nor White Yet Both: Thematic Explorations of Interracial Literature* (Cambridge: Harvard University Press, 1997), 316.

62. Robert William Fogel, *The Fourth Great Awakening and the Future of Egalitarianism* (Chicago: University of Chicago Press, 2000), 96.

63. Michael Ignatieff, *Blood and Belonging: Journeys into the New Nationalism* (New York: Farrar, Straus & Giroux, 1993).

64. Kevin Phillips, *The Cousins' Wars: Religion, Politics, and the Triumph of Anglo-America* (New York: Basic, 1999).

65. Alissa Quart, "The Lost Emperors: Japanese Scholars Struggle to Unearth the Past," *Lingua Franca* (December 2000/January 2001): 55–59.

66. Benjamin DeMott, *The Trouble with Friendship: Why Americans Can't Think Straight About Race* (New York: Atlantic Monthly Press, 1995).

67. Race has been dead for some time as a serious concept in the hard sciences. For a recent survey of the literature, I have relied on Joseph L. Graves Jr., *The Emperor's New Clothes: Biological Theories of Race at the Millennium* (New Brunswick, N.J.: Rutgers University Press, 2001).

41

TEN TRUTHS OF INTERRACIAL MARRIAGE

Maria Root

Questions to Consider

In her extensive research on interracial dating and marriage patterns in the United States, Maria Root was moved to ask "what distinguished families who could take in a racially different family member from those who could not." How does she answer this question? How did her list "Ten Truths About Interracial Marriage" challenge your own beliefs about love across the color line?

In 1944 the Swedish sociologist Gunnar Myrdal published his classic study of race relations, *An American Dilemma: The Negro Problem and Modern Democracy.* In identifying race as the American dilemma, Myrdal echoed W.E.B. Du Bois's observation half a century earlier that the color line would be the problem of the twentieth century. At the dawn of the twenty-first century, with Jim Crow laws and other legal barriers gone but not forgotten, we still struggle with the problem of race in America. And while race is no longer an issue only for black and white Americans, it remains defined by a long history that constructed black and white relations. This explains why even though only one-quarter of interracial marriages take place between black and white partners, intermarriage still predominantly conjures up images of black and white. Iron-

ically, some of the younger participants in my study, who had not learned all the old, harmful rules of race, did not see their relationship as interracial because it was not black and white.

One of the obstacles to progress may be that racism and sexism, and the power struggles within each sphere, have been regarded as separate. Psychologist Aida Hurtado observes that the difficulties of feminist theory in analyzing gender subordination are similar to the difficulties of race theorists analyzing race. Whereas both are analyzed as evidence of institutionalized imbalances in structural power, they are not constructed simultaneously.[1] Sociologist Abby Ferber[2] and philosopher Naomi Zack[3] also observe how imperative it is to understand the simultaneous influences and intersections of race and gender. My study demonstrates that when we see race and gender as master statuses connected by sex and fear of interracial sexuality, we gain a better understanding of the ways in which race and gender are constructed. This finding helps us understand why interracial marriage is not more common and why we seem to be moving toward increased possibilities of interracial intimacy, dissolving centuries of racial apartheid in intimate relationships and kinship networks.

Interracial relationships, and particularly interracial marriage, leave a permanent record of a transgression against what has been considered normal, "sticking with your own kind." They challenge the privilege and property of whiteness and any other rigid category of race—or gender. Some people fear that opening the way to interracial marriage might open the door to same-sex marriage and violate other cultural norms. Thus interracial marriage is a vehicle for examining race and gender relations as well as the structures that shape them. Anthropologist Roger Sanjek notes that "Race, sex and power remain the essential ingredients of the continuing 'American dilemma' of the United States . . . the power of race has long been expressed and mediated through sex. Rape, forced disruption of black conjugal ties and kinship networks, sexual mythology and fear, and legal bars to interracial marriage, and the overriding of kinship by race are historic features of the race-sex-power equation."[4]

Although the "colors of race" have expanded through imported labor and immigration, we see that race has achieved a more rapid transformation from a fictional category based on real or imagined physical features, essence of character, and capabilities to ethnicity for virtually all groups except blacks. And with this transformation from a racial caste category to an ethnic class category, objections based on "essences" recede. Thus, although there are objections to all forms of intermarriage, the strongest objections still pertain to black-white marriage.

Participants in my study repeatedly illustrated the point that race is a social and cultural invention, a make-believe tale that is hard to stop believing. Americans even

today have countless devices that we use to convince ourselves that race is more than a fiction, that it is a real division between people that must be observed and respected. Afro-American Studies Professor Henry Louis Gates lists these devices that proclaim race to be real: birth certificates, biographical sketches, treatises, certificates, pamphlets, and so on.[5] The result is that race becomes very confusing, its boundaries simultaneously real and unreal. The meaning placed on interracial marriage, biracial children, or multiple and simultaneous racial alliances is part of the struggle to come to terms with the race fiction Europeans and Americans invented. President Clinton's Race Advisory Board chairman John Hope Franklin wrote, "stereotypes remain because Americans cling to the idea that it is best to try to ignore race. That, in turn, forces people to bury—and therefore harbor—beliefs they form from stereotypes heard at school, in the media and from family members."[6] In the public discussions hosted by this advisory board, comments on interracial marriage and the classification of multiracial children were conspicuous for their absence. The board contained no representatives of the various multiracial groups in this country. Even in a progressive attempt to discuss race, race was bounded and bordered, creating a fiction that race mixing is inconsequential to the American landscape of race, gender, and politics despite a history of legislative struggle for civil rights against a backdrop of fear.[7] Bigotry, fear, and denial are still formidable forces in this country's racial culture. Lynnette, a white woman, reflected on how racial boundaries were reinforced by her black husband, even in her own interracial family:

> I think it is the way we view ourselves as interracial. My husband, though, is not very accepting of white people. He doesn't view me as white, he never

really kinda has. I don't know what kind of perception he has. So in some ways that has been a split in providing some more unity to the family. He's very color conscious. He says a lot of things at home that could be divisive and the kids don't feel comfortable with . . . my daughter will go around and tease him with things like, "I'm going to marry somebody white, and know the color of this family."

This husband probably had no intention of creating an interracial family. But, ironically, by in effect using the one-drop rule invented to serve white male privilege, his family becomes a black family and he remains authentically black. He has also applied male privilege in denying his wife's racial identity, knowing that his racial identity will dominate hers, rather than the other way around. The experience of the younger generation, raised in the aftermath of civil rights reforms, confirms that race is socially constructed by the majority.

Families are the initial socializing agent, in questions of race as in everything else. As a psychologist, my prime interest in developing this study was to understand the process of political, social, and spiritual transformation that interracial marriages instigate in families. It seems that the theories of the past were limited by the attitudes of the era in which they evolved. Female gender roles in this American drama were either passive roles or victim roles, pawns rather than agents. Women have always been central to the creation and maintenance of families, and my research strongly suggests that current theories must make the role of women central in race relations, racial construction, and interracial marriage. A year after her daughter's wedding to a black man, Ann, a white woman from Seattle, had gained new respect for her daughter's ability to make independent decisions and saw her as an embodiment of the changing roles of women.

Probably extended family members would have more concern than her own parents, since we know her well. In a sense, we were more surprised than upset about the dating going on. But she has also, for two summers, gone fishing on a commercial fishing boat, so what I am saying is she's probably broken ground in other areas by being the first. . . . My sisters and I would never have been on a commercial fishing boat with four or five men. But a new generation. I guess she is more of a risk taker than perhaps myself. . . . We had visiting students in our home where we raised our kids. So I think that added to her feeling she could come to us and share this. Our home was open. So I was surprised, but I wasn't offended. I didn't go home or cry or stew or anything. I think probably behind doors some of our extended family did. For example, we had a grandpa who was in his eighties, and so there may have been some rolling of the eyes, so to speak. But my husband and I were anxious to meet him . . . [and] he is wonderful. They were married about a year ago. He enhances our family, and if the others don't see it, that's their problem. But they came to the wedding, and grandpa came.

One of the main questions I sought to answer was what distinguished families who could take in a racially different family member from those who could not. As T. W. Adorno and his colleagues showed, the definition of who can belong to a family and who cannot is a way of asserting and maintaining authority and privilege. But in order to do this, tremendous self-deception must be practiced, for it involves the rewriting of the character and contributions of whole groups of people.[8] It became clear in thinking about families as variations of closed or open systems that the key element in distinguishing these families was the degree to which racial reproduction was considered a significant product of the family. This led me to realize that even in modern America, families are about business: mergers, franchises, and acquisitions. And when one becomes a liability to the business of family, the pain and rejection that follow can cause deep and lasting wounds. Regardless of what happens to a marriage, whether it is a lifelong success or a short-lived fiasco, one cannot go home the same person who was banished from the original corporation.

The dynamics that prevailed in closed, pseudo-closed, and even pseudo-open families had the elements of psychologist Gordon Allport's ten sociocultural laws of prejudice.[9] Allport noted that at the root of discrimination, ten conditions fed and sustained prejudice. The more conditions that were present in any particular place or time, the more likely we would be to see prejudiced personalities. Allport defined these conditions as follows:

> Where the social structure is marked by heterogeneity;
>
> Where vertical mobility is permitted;
>
> Where rapid social change is in progress;
>
> Where there are ignorance and barriers to communication;
>
> Where the size of a minority group is large or increasing;
>
> Where direct competition and realistic threats exist;
>
> Where exploitation sustains important interests in the community;
>
> Where customs regulating aggression are favorable to bigotry;

> Where traditional justifications for ethnocentrism are available; and
>
> Where neither assimilation nor cultural pluralism is favored.[10]

Allport's conclusions are important to this study. We live in a period of rapidly changing gender roles, technological development and expansion, and increased global and cultural exchange—in an increasingly competitive world. Many of Allport's conditions prevail now. Simultaneously, we have a young generation of people operating under some changing principles of competition, discrimination, and gender role expansion.

Discussions of interracial marriage through the past century have replicated the very dynamics that are central to it; that is, they usually take place intraracially rather than interracially. The black feminist scholar bell hooks notes that racial reality looks quite different when constructed from a white perspective than it does from a black perspective.[11] Historian Paul Spickard's research on intermarriage documented the significant protest in communities of color against aspects of integration and miscegenation.[12] In the course of his work as an attorney for the NAACP before his appointment to the U.S. Supreme Court, Thurgood Marshall noted that the difficulty with repealing Jim Crow laws and reversing *Plessy v. Ferguson* was the opposition from black communities.[13] The audible voice of protest, whether white or non-white, has been male. The voices of people of color and women have been muffled and marginalized, though they are so central to the phenomenon.[14]

Racial intermarriage looks quite different from a male perspective than from a female perspective. Women's primary responsibility for childbearing and child rearing makes them central to any discussion of interracial mixing. In these discussions, women and their bodies have historically been seen as the property of men. Rod, a black man in his thirties, provided a glimpse of this double standard in black families and communities when I asked him how his family was likely to react if his sisters married interracially. Rod was married to a white woman.

> Well, you know, honestly, they would probably not be accepted. We're all educated and cordial, but then again, when our family gets together, there's no telling who's going to say what or who's going to do what and if there's something like this introduced that's upsetting, anything can happen. You know, a person might, he might be called a white boy or he might be caught in a deep conversation that you're not normally exposed to black perception—real black perception. And it's oftentimes difficult for someone of a different race to socialize with the family because those real realities come and so that's uncomfortable. So for the men, most of the men, we have had relationships, have brought the women to a family gathering, but not for my sisters. Too much negative response from the family. I believe that a lot of that has to do with how the women's role is perceived by the men in our family and that the rules [for] women [with] regard to interracial relationships is generally not something the men in our family saw. The history of white men using black women. We're suspicious.

My research has led me to conclude that women will become central gatekeepers of race and racial construction, reconstruction, and deconstruction. Women, rather than being pawns, are central figures in the growth of interracial marriage. Increased female financial independence, access and options for birth control—even abortion—as well as geographic mobility and relocation, provide more control over a woman's choice of partners. Already intermarriage rates for Asian American women, Hispanic women, and American Indian women are substantial, and often higher than for their male counterparts. With the sex-ratio imbalances in the African American communities across the country, with more women of marriageable age than available men; with the advanced education of a growing number of African American women; with the inscription of blackness on mixed-race children regardless of the sex of the parent who is black; and with the assignment of child cultural socialization to women, African American women will become significant to the discussion on interracial marriage as their rates of intermarriage increase. This will be a direct contrast to their forced interracial experiences in previous eras.[15] I believe that the current reconstruction of black femininity will be related to continued examinations of race and gender and their intersection through sex and interracial relationships and marriage. White women will continue to make choices across color lines; when both gender and race are taken into account, white women's power in its totality is not that different from that of men of color. Thus, the potential outcome of such transformations may be that discussions of race will increasingly have a female voice.

Sanjek suggests that the transformation of race to ethnicity will likewise allow some people of color to assume privileges that were previously reserved for whiteness. Recall that Roberta, the white grandmother introduced earlier, has a biracial Asian-white grandson. When I asked if she now saw her family as an interracial or mixed family, she replied, "Oh, yes. . . . We're all white." By defining race in black and white terms—

even though her Japanese son-in-law is not considered white by U.S. racial classifications, and her grandson is not considered "really" white by those who patrol the borders of whiteness—Roberta makes her daughter's marriage less objectionable. Her answer, ironically, can be seen as a way of reconstructing race by broadening the boundaries of whiteness. But can these boundaries be broadened to include mixing with the black population? Without this expansion, we will not accomplish true racial deconstruction but only the reconstruction of whiteness. Attempts to retain a white ethnic identity—for example, Polish American, Irish American, Italian American—do not have to feed white supremacist notions or reinforce the fiction of race. Unfortunately, whiteness as race in the U.S. seems to tolerate only symbolic ethnicity, particularly for newer immigrant groups.[16] Perhaps this is also part of the explanation for the distance between black and white—that many if not most blacks will not willingly give up their African American identity.

Though they make strange bedfellows, love and prejudice can coexist between partners, as I saw again and again in my research. Sometimes this was manifested in acts of collusion in which partners left their spouses standing alone to take their family's racial prejudice and abuse. I doubt that intermarriage is the solution to all of America's race problems in America. But it does provide one avenue for the challenging of stereotypes, particularly when it involves an extended kinship network of different-race and mixed-race kin. It is an opportunity to move into a different dialogue about race, a dialogue in which the voices of multiracial adult children and women and people of color can also be heard. Intermarriage will soon affect a substantial portion of Americans of all colors.

Individual and family identities may be transformed through these marriages. In her recent work, bell hooks has emphasized love as action and attitude that can inspire us to end oppressive practices. Whereas Martin Luther King, Jr. and others stressed the political uses and meanings of love, we hear love discussed less frequently in these terms as a powerful and transcendent force.[17] Joseph Campbell spoke to the transformation that marriage heralds when he wrote, "Marriage is not a simple love affair, it's an ordeal, and the ordeal is the sacrifice of ego to a relationship in which two have become one."[18] Campbell's statement is reflected in Martin Luther King, Jr.'s observation that "all men [and women] are caught in an inescapable network of mutuality, tied in a single garment of destiny. Whatever affects one directly affects all indirectly."[19] At its most intense, love provides a reminder that two people have merged their lives and that they are having to negotiate some new boundaries and definitions of self. In the case of interracial love, some fictions around race must be challenged. People are resilient when they are deeply in love. They are open to new ideas and experiences because their love can override fear. Thus they promise hope of transformation in attitudes. The partnership between individualism, so highly prized by American culture, and romantic love makes interracial marriage an increasing possibility for most families now that legal barriers have been removed.

The psychologist Robert Sternberg found that three components form romantic love, the major motivating force in the marriage decisions of almost all of the participants in my study. The degree of their presence determines the quality or definition of love in a relationship.[20] First, he notes that there is an intimacy component from which connectedness arises. The intimacy involved in a lasting love relationship has several dimensions that are neither defined nor limited by race. Prager observes that intimacy can occur at different levels: (1) the frequency of personal sharing; (2) the depth and risk involved in the sharing; and (3) the amount of sharing that takes place and continues over time.[21] Conversations about racial experiences, culture, gender, and class were part of the experiences that provided a depth to the intimacy many participants had with their partners.

Second, there is a passion component that drives the initial physical attraction and sexual desire. In stereotypes of interracial relationships, the first component—intimacy—is often dismissed and only sexual desire and attraction are given credence as motivating forces. The third component is commitment, which requires a person to distinguish between liking and loving, infatuation and love, and lust and love.

When an interracial marriage or engagement is met with hostility, its opponents assume that the individuals involved lack the capacity to make the commitment that is Sternberg's third component of romantic love. Instead, interracial love is constructed as an immature form of attachment motivated by anger, rebellion, and pathology, rather than as an engulfing, embracing form of love that John Welwood describes as a soul connection. Two people come together to realize their deepest potential—to be the best people *they* can be.[22] When motivations and individuals are stereotyped in a dismissive way, all individuals who love across color lines are seen as more similar than dissimilar. But research offers little data to support the notion that there is a consistent profile or type that is more inclined than others to intermarriage.[23]

In one of the few empirical studies designed to examine profiles of persons who intermarry, a longitudinal family study in Hawaii, Johnson and colleagues found few differences between groups. Among women who intermarried and women who did not, Asian American women who married interracially tended to be more independent than Asian American women who did not. Men who intermarried were less domineering than men who did not.[24] Even though this study was conducted almost twenty years ago, it captured an important aspect of flexibility in gender roles that I think contributes to the possibility of intermarriage. Many of the white men married to women of color in the study seemed willing to give up some aspects of white male privilege. Many were willing to be minorities in racial or ethnic communities. While I do not suggest that a white man in a black or Asian or Hispanic community suffers the same discrimination that a black or Asian or Hispanic or Indian man does in a white community, Johnson's findings suggest that these white men had less investment in maintaining a special sense of self through their whiteness.

With flexibility to redefine masculine and feminine roles in relationships, the heart of what might be exchanged between people may be more difficult to pinpoint. Such changes may also redefine standards of physical attractiveness. For example, an attractive man does not have to be tall; an attractive woman does not have to be small or thin. If standards of attractiveness can extend beyond European standards of beauty, so, perhaps, can our motivation to know persons who would otherwise not be of interest. If our culture ever reaches the point where height is not associated with power, we might also see more frequent exceptions to one of the rules of heterosexual coupling, that is, that the male is supposed to be taller than the female. The ability to break this rule would reflect an expansion of the definitions of masculinity and femininity. Just as we have invented fictions about race and gender, we maintain many fictions about physical attractiveness as well. Race, ethnicity, and class influence what we consider acceptable and desirable gender roles. Living in a more pluralistic way could make physical attraction that much more mysterious, because we would become that much more aware of how socially and culturally conditioned attraction is.

It is no wonder that love is difficult to study. Although it can be a psychological state of mind, a judgment, an action, or an orientation, the meaning of love can be so individualistic as to make its study frustratingly complicated. Seldom is the love that binds people together the subject of studies of interracial marriage. Yet I observed that despite cultural, class, gender, religious, and racial differences, people satisfied essential needs through their partners that seemed to transcend these categories.

Despite the human drama that accompanies every search for love, companionship, and understanding, interracial marriage is most often depicted as foolhardy and irrational rather than heroic. At some level it seems easy for many people to dismiss interracial love as irrationality, infatuation, curiosity, or immaturity—a stage that will pass. Or else it is simply fetishized—she has a thing for black men, he has a thing for Asian women.

The irrationality of love has been associated with "addiction" or "fatal attraction"—and interracial love has certainly been depicted as irrational, addictive, even fetishistic. Fortunately, Peele and Brodsky untangle these issues in their book *Love and Addiction*.[25] They offer eight ways that infatuation and sustained love can be distinguished. In contrast to addiction, love is

1. an expansive experience rather than total focus on another person;
2. a helping relationship rather than idealization of another person;
3. an opportunity for enhanced growth rather than retreat to a private world;
4. the intensification of pleasure in life rather than intensification of pain;

5. a productive and beneficial experience rather than an incapacitating one;
6. a natural outcome of one's self and life rather than purely accidental and tentative;
7. an experience that continues and intensifies friendship and affection rather than an all-or-nothing experience; and
8. a responsibility that has an attendant heightened awareness rather than an uncontrollable urge or unconscious motivation.

The participants in my study all spoke of love as a motivating force for their choices. Although some divorced and some married persons reflected on their naïveté or youthful optimism at the time of their marriage, these marriages were about love. Participants referred to the psychological needs they thought their relationships provided. When both partners had the ability to work, emotional and relational needs took precedence over instrumental needs.

The hundreds of hours of interviews and background research I conducted can be distilled into what I call "Ten Truths About Interracial Marriage."

1. The civil rights movement and subsequent patterns of racial desegregation created opportunities for people to interact in meaningful ways, which has resulted in an increased rate of interracial marriage.
2. In the past twenty-five years, women's decreased financial dependence on their families has given them freedom to choose mates regardless of family approval.
3. Love, shared vision, and common values compel an interracial couple to marry, just as they do other couples.
4. The motives behind interracial marriage seldom include the desire to rebel or to make a political or social statement.

5. Families that reject an interracial marriage value the reproduction of their race over love, integrity, and commitment.

6. In order to live in an affirming emotional climate, an interracial couple may have to replace estranged blood kin with a fictive family of friends.

7. Conflicts within interracial marriages are more likely to arise from cultural, gender, class, social, and personal differences than from racial ones.

8. Irreconcilable differences within interracial marriages are similar to those within same-race marriages: loss of respect, unwillingness to compromise, hurtful actions, lack of responsibility, dishonesty, and conflicting values.

9. The rate of divorce for interracial marriages is only slightly higher than for same-race couples in the continental United States; the gap is quickly closing as divorce rates rise for all marriages.

10. Interracial couples can and do produce healthy, well-adjusted children.

In Puccini's last opera, *Turandot,* set in legendary Peking, the Chinese princess Turandot declares that she will accept the hand of the suitor who can answer three riddles. Those who try and fail will be executed, allowing Turandot to avenge an ancestor who was raped and murdered by a Tartar prince. Unbeknownst to her, one of the suitors, Prince Calaf, is the son of the exiled king of Tartary. Turandot lives in the past and Calaf in the future, as she reminds him that failure to solve the three riddles results in death and he reminds her of the possibility of life. "Turandot poses the first enigma: what rises at night, invoked by all the world, only to die at dawn reborn in the heart? Calaf rightly answers: hope. The second riddle is: what darts like a flame but is not a flame, that grows cold with death yet blazes with dreams of conquest? Turandot is furious

when Calaf solves it with the answer: blood. Thirdly she demands what inflames you, white yet dark, that enslaves if it wants you free, but in taking you captive makes you king. Calaf, after hesitation, answers: Turandot."[26] Seeing her fear and fury at losing her superior position, he offers her his head nonetheless if she can discover his identity by dawn. No one in the kingdom sleeps that night as his identity is sought. Just before dawn, his father and his attendant, Liù, are brought before her. Liù, protective of the exiled king and pressed by Turandot to explain why she would endure torture or even death for him, answers "love." The concept is foreign to Turandot, but she is nevertheless moved momentarily. She soon recovers herself, however, and has Liù's tongue cut out. Calaf appears and reveals his identity as the son of the exiled king. Turandot believes she has turned the tables and has restored her power over him. Fearless in the face of death, he kisses her as a challenge to experience his love. With his identity in her possession, Turandot surprises all. She opens her heart after years of lovelessness and reveals Calaf's name to the court as Love, thus sparing his life and starting hers anew, freed from her fear and hatred of Tartars.

Whereas the riddles are solved with the answers hope, blood, and love, these are indeed real-life enigmas when it comes to discussions of interracial marriage. Interracial marriage gives us hope that love can transcend some of the barriers that legislation has not. Its power to transform us, one at a time, cannot be underestimated, allowing us to release the hate, fear, and guilt of the past and move into the future with love as a political device. Despite some almost universal propensities for stratification, competition, and ethnocentrism, I believe that with stealth and persistence the people in my study demonstrated that love has the capacity to erode the fear and hate that have blemished many a participant's family landscape.

Interracial marriage and its children provide an opportunity for a different discussion of race relations within the power matrices formed by race, gender, and ethnicity. Today's children are tomorrow's adults. I hope we teach them well.

NOTES

1. A. Hurtado, *The Color of Privilege: Three Blasphemies on Race and Feminism* (Ann Arbor: The University of Michigan Press, 1996), p. 33.
2. Ferber, *White Man Falling.*
3. N. Zack, *Race/Sex" Their Sameness, Difference, and Interplay* (New York: Routledge, 1997).
4. Sanjek, "Intermarriage," p. 103.
5. H. L. Gates, Jr., *Thirteen Ways of Looking at a Black Man* (New York: Vintage Books, 1997), pp. 207–8.
6. *Seattle Post-Intelligencer,* "Race Advisory Board."
7. H. Ball, *A Defiant Life: Thurgood Marshall and the Persistence of Racism in America* (New York, Crown Publishers, 1998); I. Bernstein, *Guns or Butter: The Presidency of Lyndon Johnson* (New York: Oxford University Press, 1996).
8. Adorno et al., *The Authoritarian Personality.*
9. G. W. Allport, *The Nature of Prejudice* (Reading, Mass.: Addison-Wesley, 1954; 1979).
10. Ibid., p. 221.
11. hooks, "Representing Whiteness."
12. Spickard, *Mixed Blood.*
13. Ball, *A Defiant Life.*
14. Frankenburg, *White Women, Race Matters.*
15. Spickard, *Mixed Blood;* Wyatt, *Stolen Women.*
16. Waters, *Ethnic Options.*
17. b. hooks, *All about Love: New Visions* (New York, William Morrow, 2000).
18. Quoted in Erlich and de Bruhl, eds., *Thesaurus of Quotations,* p. 411.
19. Ibid., p. 143.
20. R. J. Sternberg, "A Triangular Theory of Love," *Psychological Review* 93: 119–35.
21. K. Prager, *The Psychology of Intimacy* (New York: Guilford Press, 1995), pp. 259–66.
22. Welwood, *Love and Awakening.*
23. Tucker and Mitchell-Kernan, "New Trends in Black American Interracial Marriage."
24. Nagoshi et al., "Assortative Mating"; see also Ahern et al., "Personality Attributes."
25. S. Peele, "Fools for Love: The Romantic Ideal, Psychological Theory, and Addictive Love," in *The Psychology of Love,* ed. R. J. Sternberg and M. L. Barnes (New Haven: Yale University Press, 1988), pp. 179–82, a review of some of the earlier work of Peele and Brodsky.
26. Earl of Harewood and Antony Peattie, eds., *The New Kobbe's Opera Book* (New York, Putnam, 1997), p. 610.

Constructing a Nonracist World: Obstacles to Racial Justice . . .

42

COLOR-BLIND PRIVILEGE
The Social and Political Functions of Erasing the Color Line in Post-Race America

Charles A. Gallagher

Questions to Consider

The dominant view in the United States is that we are now a color-blind nation. Rap and hip-hop are thoroughly mainstream commodities available for sale in every mall across the country. Celebrities, CEOs, high-level politicians, and opinion makers are drawn from every racial and ethnic group, as if race no longer mattered. Charles A. Gallagher argues that the story of color-blindness promoted in the mass media disguises a more troubling reality: continued racial inequality. How does presenting the United States as a color-blind nation serve various political, ideological, and social functions?

Introduction

An adolescent white male at a bar mitzvah wears a FUBU[1] shirt while his white friend preens his tightly set, perfectly braided corn rows. A black model dressed in yachting attire peddles a New England yuppie boating look in Nautica advertisements. It is

quite unremarkable to observe whites, Asians, or African Americans with dyed purple, blond, or red hair. White, black, and Asian students decorate their bodies with tattoos of Chinese characters and symbols. In cities and suburbs, young adults across the color line wear hip-hop clothing and listen to white rapper Eminem and black rapper Jay-Z. A north Georgia branch of the NAACP installs a white biology professor as its president. The music of Jimi Hendrix is used to sell Apple Computers. Du-Rag kits, complete with bandana headscarf and elastic headband, are on sale for $2.95 at

Charles A. Gallagher, "Color Blind Privilege: The Social and Political Functions of Erasing the Color Line in Post-Race America" from the *RGC Journal Special Edition on Privilege*, Abby L. Ferber and Dena R. Samuels, co-editors, Vol. 10, No. 4, 2003.

hip-hop clothing stores and family-centered theme parks like Six Flags. Salsa has replaced ketchup as the best-selling condiment in the United States. Companies as diverse as Polo, McDonald's, Tommy Hilfiger, Walt Disney World, Master Card, Skechers sneakers, IBM, Giorgio Armani, and Neosporin antibiotic ointment have each crafted advertisements that show a balanced, multiracial cast of characters interacting and consuming their products in a post-race, color-blind world.[2]

Americans are constantly bombarded by depictions of race relations in the media which suggest that discriminatory racial barriers have been dismantled. Social and cultural indicators suggest that America is on the verge, or has already become, a truly color-blind nation. National polling data indicate that a majority of whites now believe discrimination against racial minorities no longer exists. A majority of whites believe that blacks have as good a chance as whites in procuring housing and employment or achieving middle-class status while a 1995 survey of white adults found that a majority of whites (58%) believed that African Americans were better off finding jobs than whites.[3] Much of white America now sees a level playing field, while a majority of black Americans see a field which is still quite uneven. Best-selling books like The *End of Racism*[4] and *Color-Blind: Seeing Beyond Race in a Race-Obsessed World* suggest the United States is not very far from making color blindness a social and political reality.[5] The color-blind or race neutral perspective holds that in an environment where institutional racism and discrimination have been replaced by equal opportunity, one's qualifications, not one's color or ethnicity, should be the mechanism by which upward mobility is achieved. Whites and blacks differ significantly, however, on their support for affirmative action, the perceived fairness of the criminal justice system, the ability to ac-

quire the "American Dream," and the extent to which whites have benefited from past discrimination.[6]

This article examines the social and political functions color blindness serves for whites in the United States. Drawing on information compiled from interviews and focus groups with whites around the country, I argue that color blindness maintains white privilege by negating racial inequality. Embracing a post-race, color-blind perspective provides whites with a degree of psychological comfort by allowing them to imagine that being white or black or brown has no bearing on an individual's or a group's relative place in the socioeconomic hierarchy. My research included interviews with seventeen focus groups and thirty individual whites around the country. While my sample is not representative of the total white population, I used personal contacts and snowball sampling to purposively locate respondents raised in urban, suburban, and rural environments. Twelve of the seventeen focus groups were conducted in a university setting, one in a liberal arts college in the Rocky Mountains and the other at a large urban university in the Northeast. Respondents in these focus groups were selected randomly from the student population. The occupational range for my individual interviews was quite eclectic and included a butcher, construction worker, hair stylist, partner in a prestigious corporate law firm, executive secretary, high school principal, bank president from a small town, retail workers, country lawyer, and custodial workers. Twelve of the thirty individual interviews were with respondents who were raised in rural and/or agrarian settings. The remaining respondents lived in suburbs of large cities or in urban areas.

What linked this rather disparate group of white individuals together was their belief that race-based privilege had ended. As a majority of my respondents saw it, color blindness was now the norm in the United States. The illusion of racial equality implicit in the myth of color blindness was, for many whites, a form of comfort. This aspect of pleasure took the form of political empowerment ("what about whites' rights") and moral gratification from being liberated from "oppressor" charges ("we are not responsible for the past"). The rosy picture that color blindness presumes about race relations and the satisfying sense that one is part of a period in American history that is morally superior to the racist days of the past is, quite simply, a less stressful and more pleasurable social place for whites to inhabit.

The Norm of Color Blindness

The perception among a majority of white Americans that the socioeconomic playing field is now level, along with whites' belief that they have purged themselves of overt racist attitudes and behaviors, has made color blindness the dominant lens through which whites understand contemporary race relations. Color blindness allows whites to believe that segregation and discrimination are no longer an issue because it is now illegal for individuals to be denied access to housing, public accommodations, or jobs because of their race. Indeed, lawsuits alleging institutional racism against companies like Texaco, Denny's, Coca Cola, and Cracker Barrel validate what many whites know at a visceral level is true; firms which deviate from the color-blind norms embedded in classic liberalism will be punished. As a political ideology, the commodification and mass marketing of products that signify color but are intended for consumption across the color line further legitimate color blindness. Almost every household in the United States has a television that, accord-

ing to the U.S. Census, is on for seven hours every day.[7] Individuals from any racial background can wear hip-hop clothing, listen to rap music (both purchased at Wal-Mart) and root for their favorite, majority black, professional sports team. Within the context of racial symbols that are bought and sold in the market, color blindness means that one's race has no bearing on who can purchase an SUV, live in an exclusive neighborhood, attend private schools, or own a Rolex.

The passive interaction whites have with people of color through the media creates the impression that little, if any, socioeconomic difference exists between the races. Research has found that whites who are exposed to images of upper-middle class African Americans, like the Huxtable family in *The Cosby Show,* believe that blacks have the same socioeconomic opportunities as whites.[8] Highly visible and successful racial minorities like Secretary of State Colin Powell and National Security Advisor Condoleezza Rice are further proof to white America that the nation's efforts to enforce and promote racial equality have been accomplished. Reflecting on the extent to which discrimination is an obstacle to socioeconomic advancement and the perception of seeing African Americans in leadership roles, Tom explained:

> If you look at some prominent black people in society today, and I don't really see [racial discrimination], I don't understand how they can keep bringing this problem onto themselves. If they did what society would want them to, I don't see that society is making problems for them. I don't see it.

The achievement ideology implicit in the color-blind perspective is also given legitimacy and stripped of any racist implications by black neoconservatives like anti-affirmative action advocate Ward Connerly,

Shelby Steele, and Clarence Thomas, and Asian American Secretary of Labor Elaine Chou.[9] Each espouses a color-blind, race-neutral doctrine that treats race-based government programs as a violation of the sacrosanct belief that American society only recognizes the rights of individuals. These individuals also serve as an important public example that in a post-race, color-blind society climbing the occupational ladder is now a matter of individual choice.

The new color-blind ideology does not, however, ignore race; it acknowledges race while ignoring racial hierarchy by taking racially coded styles and products and reducing these symbols to commodities or experiences which whites and racial minorities can purchase and share. It is through such acts of shared consumption that race becomes nothing more than an innocuous cultural signifier. Large corporations have made American culture more homogenous through the ubiquity of fast food, television, and shopping malls but this trend has also created the illusion that we are all the same through consumption. Most adults eat at national fast-food chains like McDonald's, shop at mall anchor stores like Sears and J.C. Penney's, and watch major league sports, situation comedies, or television dramas. Defining race only as cultural symbols that are for sale allows whites to experience and view race as nothing more than a benign cultural marker that has been stripped of all forms of institutional, discriminatory or coercive power. The post-race, color-blind perspective allows whites to imagine that depictions of racial minorities working in high status jobs and consuming the same products, or at least appearing in commercials for products whites desire or consume, is the same as living in a society where color is no longer used to allocate resources or shape group outcomes. By constructing a picture of society where racial harmony is the norm, the color-blind perspective func-

tions to make white privilege invisible while removing from public discussion the need to maintain any social programs that are race-based.

How then is color blindness linked to privilege? Starting with the deeply held belief that America is now a meritocracy, whites are able to imagine that the socioeconomic success they enjoy relative to racial minorities is a function of individual hard work, determination, thrift, and investments in education. The color-blind perspective removes from personal thought and public discussion any taint or suggestion of white supremacy or white guilt while legitimating the existing social, political, and economic arrangements that whites are privileged to receive. This perspective insinuates that class and culture, and not institutional racism, are responsible for social inequality. Color blindness allows whites to define themselves as politically progressive and racially tolerant as they proclaim their adherence to a belief system that does not see or judge individuals by the "color of their skin." This perspective ignores, as Ruth Frankenberg puts it, how whiteness is a "location of structural advantage societies structured in racial dominance."[10] Frankenberg uses the term "color and power evasiveness" rather than color blindness to convey how the ability to ignore race by members of the dominant group reflects a position of power and privilege. Color blindness hides white privilege behind a mask of assumed meritocracy while rendering invisible the institutional arrangements that perpetuate racial inequality. The veneer of equality implied in color blindness allows whites to present their place in the racialized social structure as one that was earned.

Given the pervasiveness of color blindness, it was not surprising that respondents in this study believed that using race to promote group interests was a form of racism.

Joe, a student in his early twenties from a working class background, was quite adamant that the opportunity structure in the United States did not favor one racial group over another.

> I mean, I think that the black person of our age has as much opportunity as me, maybe he didn't have the same guidance and that might hurt him. But I mean, he's got the same opportunities that I do to go to school, maybe even more, to get more money. I can't get any aid. . . . I think that blacks have the same opportunities as whites nowadays and I think it's old hat.

Not only does Joe believe that young blacks and whites have similar educational experiences and opportunity but it is his contention that blacks are more likely or able to receive money for higher education. The idea that race matters in any way, according to Joe, is anachronistic; it is "old hat" in a color-blind society to blame one's shortcomings on something as irrelevant as race.

Believing and acting as if America is now color blind allows whites to imagine a society where institutional racism no longer exists and racial barriers to upward mobility have been removed. The use of group identity to challenge the existing racial order by making demands for the amelioration of racial inequities is viewed as racist because such claims violate the belief that we are a nation that recognizes the rights of individuals, not rights demanded by groups. Sam, an upper-middle-class respondent in his twenties, draws on a pre– and post–civil rights framework to explain racial opportunity among his peers:

> I guess I can understand my parents' generation. My parents are older, my dad is almost sixty and my mother is in her mid-fifties, ok? But the kids I'm going to school with, the minorities I'm going to school with, I don't think they should use racism as an excuse for not getting a job. Maybe their parents, sure, I mean they were discriminated against. But these kids have *every* opportunity that I do to do well.

In one generation, as Sam sees it, the color line has been erased. Like Sam's view that there are opportunities for all, there is, according to Tara, a reason to celebrate the current state of race relations.

> I mean, like you are not the only people that have been persecuted—I mean, yeah, you have been, but so has every group. I mean, if there's any time to be black in America, it's now.

Seeing society as race-neutral serves to decouple past historical practices and social conditions from present-day racial inequality. A number of respondents viewed society this way and pointed out that job discrimination had ended. Michelle was quite direct in her perception that the labor market is now free of discrimination, stating that "don't think people hire and fire because someone is black and white now." Ken also believed that discrimination in hiring did not occur since racial minorities now have legal recourse if discrimination occurs.

> I think that pretty much we got past that point as far as jobs. I think people realize that you really can't discriminate that way because you will end up losing . . . because you will have a lawsuit against you.

Critical race theorist David Theo Goldberg sees this narrative as part of the "continued insistence on implementing an ideal of color-blindness [that] either denies historical reality and its abiding contemporary legacies, or serves to cut off any claims to contemporary entitlements."[11] It also means that whites can picture themselves as victims of reverse discrimination and racism, as Anne, a woman in a focus group explained:

> Why is it so important to forget about, you know, white people's rights? I mean, not that, not being racist or anything, but why is it such a big deal that they have to have it their way or no way when it should be a compromise between the two, and the whites should be able to voice their opinions as much as the blacks do.

There is the belief that whites have been silenced by race politics and as Jodie explains, "The tables have turned where they're getting more rights than we have. Like it never balanced out."

The logic inherent in the color-blind approach is circular; since race no longer shapes life opportunities in a color-blind world, there is no need to take race into account when discussing differences in outcomes between racial groups. This approach erases America's racial hierarchy by implying that social, economic, and political power and mobility are equally shared among all racial groups. Ignoring the extent or ways in which race shapes life opportunities validates whites' social location in the existing racial hierarchy while legitimating the political and economic arrangements that perpetuate and reproduce racial inequality and privilege.

Color Is Now a Matter of Choice

Leslie Carr suggests "the roots of color-blind ideology are found in classic liberal doctrines of freedom—the freedom of the individual created by the free capitalist marketplace."[12] Within the context of a free-market model, color blindness has come to mean that ignoring or attending to one's racial identity is a matter of individual choice, much like the ways in which whites can choose whether or not to emphasize part of their ethnic background. Many whites, for example, claim to be Irish on St. Patty's Day. Some Italian Americans feel purchasing a meal at the Olive Garden Restaurant is an ethnic dining experience that reconnects them to their immigrant past or fictive ethnic family tree. Some whites don kilts at Highlander Fairs or dress as medieval artisans or knights at Renaissance Festivals. These individuals experience their ethnicity as an option. There is no social cost to "being ethnic" for a day, nor does this voluntary behavior circumscribe opportunities in life. The color-blind narrative holds that affirming racial identity is, like whites who have the luxury of an optional ethnicity, an individual, voluntary decision.[13] If pride in one's ethnicity and by extension one's color is a matter of choice, then race no longer matters as an independent force which organizes social life, allocates resources, or creates obstacles to upward mobility.[14] In post-race, color-blind America, one can now consume images and products for, from, and about any racial or ethnic group. Racial styles, like clothing fashion, food choices, or musical preferences are like interchangeable, mix-and-match commodities for sale at the mall.

The color-blind narrative allows racial identity to be acknowledged in individual and superficial ways but using race to assert group demands violates the cherished notion that as a nation we recognize the rights of individuals rather than group rights. Within the color-blind perspective, it is understood that one does not choose one's race, but one should be conscious, or at least cautious, not to make race more than background cultural information. In a post-race, color-blind world, race can be seen, but pointing out race-based inequities should not be heard. The idea of identity, race, and the fluidity of individual choices was part of Jeff's explanation of race relations:

> It just seems like a gap's been bridged, where people don't have like separate things. You know, like in past generations there were things that each group had to itself, but now it's like there are plenty of things you can find in, like, black people that white people do. You know, there's music; rap music is no longer, . . . it's not a black thing anymore. . . . When it first came out, it was black music, but now it's just music. It's another choice, just like country music can be considered like white hick music or whatever. You know, it's just a choice.

Tom makes the point that race categories exist, but assimilation allows any individual to become an American, if they so choose:

> Blacks don't seem, poor blacks seem like they're more immigrant than we are.
>
> Interviewer: In what way?
>
> Because they try to keep pushing the differences. You know, like I said, the Asians just meld in a little bit better than the blacks. . . . Why do they have to be caught up in being African American? They've been in America all their lives. They were born here. They're not African Americans. That's just separate.

There was the perception that Asians did not embrace identity politics or use their racial identity to promote group rights. As Mike, a young white man in a focus group told me:

> It's just becoming like really, really popular for black students to be black and proud and racist. But with Asians, it's not that way. I mean there is a magazine *Ebony* for strictly black people— I've never really read it. I mean there is

no magazine for just Asian people. There's nothing saying, like, "Asian power."

Comedian Chris Rock points to how erasing the color line and color blindness are linked when he asked rhetorically "What does it say about America when the greatest golfer in the world [Tiger Woods] is black and the greatest rapper [Eminem] is white." Rock's message is clear: No role or occupation (at least in sports and music) is now determined by skin color. By allowing anyone to claim ownership of racial styles, color-blind narratives negate the ways in which race continues to circumscribe opportunities in life. The color-blind approach requires that these preferences, while racially bracketed, be available to all for purchase or consumption. At its core, the color-blind philosophy holds that racial minorities can succeed if they rid themselves of any notion that their race entitles them to special treatment. Racial identity can still be expressed or acknowledged, but one's race should mean nothing more than a tendency towards individualistic expressions, like music, foods, or clothes.

Within the color-blind perspective, it is not race per se which determines upward mobility, but how much an individual *chooses* to pay attention to race that determines one's fate. According to this perspective, race is only as important as you allow it to be, as Kevin, a 33-year-old white male custodial worker in Colorado told me:

> I never really look at anyone as a color, you know. Your skin's a color, but that doesn't mean, . . . I don't know, I never look at someone being black or Chinese. Yeah, you're Chinese because of the way your eyes are slanted, but you talk just like me. You're just like me. I don't look at you any different than you being me. You know, that's how I've always looked at it. You know.

Implicit in this expression of color-blindness is that color does not matter as long as blacks and Chinese assimilate to the point where they are "just like" Kevin. As a member of the dominant group, Kevin has the privilege of defining color blindness as the expectation that racial minorities will mirror his own cultural and social experiences while denying how racism shapes the experiences of racial minorities.[15]

When racial identity shifts from being an individual expression to one that is used to organize politically or make group-based grievances, whites view it as racist. Mary believes that race is used to force whites to think about color and inequality:

> I think that they are making it worse for themselves. I think that anybody can see in this country—I think it's you [blacks]. It doesn't matter what color you are. I mean, sure there are black things but why put it on a T-shirt? Why not just have a plain black T-shirt? Why would you have to make such a big statement that pushes people away, that threatens people. I would never want to threaten anybody.

As Mary's comments make clear, embracing racial symbols that serve to socially isolate and challenge the racial status quo is a "threat." Implicit in this exchange is that it is not very pleasurable for Mary to interact with those who would use race to promote a political agenda.

The respondents below were bothered by what they saw as a double standard concerning beauty pageants; blacks could have their own pageant but whites could not. Their anger is, at least based in part, on an understanding that the norm of color blindness has been violated. Jodie lamented that:

> You know, it's amazing. Like, even, like even, like the Miss America pageants.

There's a black Miss America pageant. But there's also black contestants in the Miss America pageant and then there's a separate pageant for blacks only. And if we had a separate pageant for whites only I just think that things would be . . . more hell would be raised.

Michelle was also bothered by her perception that the idea of race was taken too seriously by blacks:

> You know, it just seems, even for silly things, even the fact that you have to have black women in the Miss America pageant but then they have their own Miss Black America pageant. You know, like that type of thing, and it's like, come on. . . .

John, a 22-year-old male from New Jersey, also felt that whites were held to a different set of social expectations than blacks:

> I watch Miss America and we've had what, a black Miss America three out of the last five years, yet they do have a black Miss America (contest). They don't have white contestants, they only have black contestants. Now, I'm not saying that a black person can't enter the white contest, but it's just kind of ironic that here a black woman enters a predominately white contest and, you know, usually a Miss America's supposed to be representative of the whole population, yet only 12% of the population is black. . . . It just kind of seems strange that if a white person tried to enter a black contest, forget it, you'd have mayhem.

Viewed within the color-blind perspective, the Miss Black America pageant is a form of institutional racism because it denies all racial groups full access to participation. The Miss Black America pageant is, as suggested above, racist for excluding whites because of the color of their skin. The long history of racial minorities being excluded from white organizations and institutions as the reason behind why black, Latino, and Asian organizations were formed in the first place is now only viewed as irrelevant.

Like the anger expressed over what was perceived as a racial double standard concerning the Miss America pageant, Malcolm X also came to represent challenges to the color-blind perspective, which were viewed as illegitimate because they advocate group solutions to race-based inequities. As one respondent told me about Malcolm X:

> He got into Buddha [sic] and changed his violence. When he was younger, I think that's when he was violent but in the years before he was killed I think he definitely went towards peace, like Martin Luther King. I don't know why they can't wear Martin Luther King hats [instead of Malcolm X hats].

Color blindness has emerged as America's newest racial mythology because it provides a level-playing-field narrative that allows whites to inhabit a psychological space that is free of racial tension. This new era of color blindness is a respite from the racial identity movements which often result in white guilt, defensiveness, or the avoidance of racially charged issues. Color blindness provides whites with the belief that they live in an era that is free of racism. Convinced that these racist attitudes and practices are over, whites today are able to define themselves as racially progressive and tolerant. Within this universe where racial differences are almost meaningless, whites are able to claim that their privileged social position relative to racial minorities reflects individual achievement rather than the fruits of white supremacy. The constant

barrage of color-blind messages and messengers reinforce and confirm that the egalitarian and meritocractic norms that undergird American culture are intact. Embracing color blindness allows whites to be blind to or ignore the fact that racial and ethnic minorities lag behind whites on almost every measure of quality of life. Color-blind pleasure means whites are able to think about contemporary race relations as a clean slate where the crimes of slavery, Jim Crow, institutional racism, and white privilege have been ended and the racist sins of their grandparents have been erased.

Our Survey Says— "Color-Blind Nation"

National survey data suggest that a majority of whites view race relations through the lens of color blindness. A 1997 Gallup poll found that a majority of whites believe that blacks have "as good a chance as whites" in their community in procuring employment (79%).[16] A Kaiser Family Poll (1997) found that a majority of whites believe that blacks are doing at least as well or better than whites in income and educational attainment. The poll found that "almost two-thirds (64%) of whites do NOT believe that whites have benefited from past and present discrimination against African Americans."[17] In their study on racial attitudes, Schuman and associates found that when white Americans are asked to account for black disadvantage, the most popular explanation is that of black people's lack of motivation or will power to get ahead.[18] These surveys suggest a majority of whites view the opportunity structure as being open to all, regardless of color. Not only do whites see parity compared to blacks in access to housing, employment, education, and achieving a middle-class life style, but where differences do exist, whites attribute racial inequities to the individual shortcomings of blacks.

Reflecting on affirmative action, Monica articulates an all-is-now-equal argument as to why color should no longer matter in hiring decisions or school admissions:

> I think all the backgrounds have come a long way to where they don't need it any more. Basically everyone has equal opportunity to get a certain job, to get into a certain school, and now it should be based on your performance and not for what you are.

Drawing on an ideology of egalitarianism and meritocracy, Monica believes, as most white Americans do, that color is no longer a factor in obtaining employment or a quality education. Given the premise that racial equality has now been achieved, Monica is able to argue that achievement and not skin color should shape the allocation of resources. In other words, since the playing field is now level, any group claims to address real or imagined inequities are illegitimate. Joan voiced the anger that whites should in some way be held accountable for past or present racial inequities.

> That's what bothers me. They say "we" have been oppressed. They have not. The students here at the university right now have not been oppressed. They did not experience the Watts riot, they didn't experience physically being hosed down by police. Granted, the white population was responsible for that, but we are not. We are not responsible. Therefore, we should not be put out because of that. We didn't do it. We're not doing it now, therefore they have no right to say, well, we've been oppressed.

Neither Joan, nor the white race, should be "put out" for past racist practices. The color-blind perspective is a historical rendering of the actions of the near and distant past as events which are disconnected from contemporary racial inequality.

James expresses a number of the trends found in the surveys cited earlier. After stating that "hey, everybody's got the same opportunity" when asked about what his views were on the idea of white privilege, James countered that:

> They say that I have white privileges. Uh, and if they say it's like because where I live, I live in a big house or something like that, they're wrong, because that's not a privilege. That's something my parents worked for. And if they don't live in a big fancy houses that's something that their parents didn't work for. And if they want to change that . . . I've got black people living across from me. Uh, they're no different than me. They're different from the black people down here because they worked for what they wanted. These people [blacks in a poor segregated part of the city], they don't have to live here. There's no one holding them back. They can get into school as well as everybody else can. I was lucky my parents could pay for school and I didn't need financial aid. . . . You know, the opportunity is there. You've just got to take hold of it.

James suggests that when class background is taken into account whites and blacks are the same. The blacks who are unable to leave poor, segregated neighborhoods reflect individual shortcomings on the part of blacks, not structural obstacles. Rob implies that it is hard work and individual merit, not one's skin color that matters. Examining his own mobility, Rob remarks, "I don't know if their situation is any different than mine. I mean, I can only gauge on the fact that I've been busting my ass for the last ten years to get to where I want to be."

How Color Blind a Nation?

The beliefs voiced by whites in national survey data and my own interviews raise an empirical question; to what extent are we now a color-blind nation? If educational opportunity, occupational advancement, health, upward mobility, and equal treatment in the public sphere can be used as indicators of how color-blind we are as a nation, then we have failed. U.S. census figures present a picture of America that is far from color-blind. In 1999, over 73% of white households owned their own homes compared to 46% for blacks, 45% for Hispanics, 53% for Asians, and 56% for American Indians.[19] In 1993, whites had about ten times more in assets than blacks or Latinos.[20] Median family income in 1998 was $42,439 for whites, $25,351 for blacks, $27,330 for Latinos, and $46,637 for Asians. In 1997, almost 25% of whites over the age of 25 had four years of college or more compared to less than 14% for blacks and Latinos. In 1997, 8.6% of whites compared to 26.5% blacks, 27% of Latinos, and 14% of Asians lived at or below the poverty line.[21] A national study found that even after controlling for individual credit history, blacks in 33 states were charged more for car loans than whites.[22] Health statistics tell a similar tale. Whites have lower rates of diabetes, tuberculosis, pregnancy-related mortality, and sudden infant death syndrome (SIDS), and are more likely to have prenatal care in the first trimester than blacks, Latinos, or Asians. In 1997, 15% of whites did not have public or private health care coverage compared to 21.5% for blacks, 34% for Latinos, and 20.7% for Asians.[23]

In 1998, blacks and Latinos were also underrepresented as lawyers, physicians, professors, dentists, engineers, and registered nurses. A Glass Ceiling study commissioned by the federal government found that when one reaches the level of vice president and above at *Fortune* 1000 industrial companies and *Fortune* 500 service industries, 96.6% of the executives are white males. Nationally, white men comprise 90% of the newspaper editors and 77% of television news directors.[24] In 1999, the Department of Justice found that blacks and Latinos were twice as likely as whites to be subject to force when they encounter a police officer, were more likely to be subjected to car searches during a traffic stop, and were more likely to be ticketed than whites. Although blacks and whites are just as likely to use drugs, almost two-thirds of those convicted on drug charges are black.[25] Congress does not represent the racial and ethnic diversity of this country. In 2000, blacks were 13% of the population, Asians and Pacific Islanders 4%, and Latinos 12%. Yet the House of Representatives was only 9% black, 4% Latino, and 0.9% Asian. The U.S. Senate is 97% white and only 2% Asian and 1% American Indian, and therefore has no black or Latino members.[26] In early 2003, there were no black or Latino governors. According to another report, if you were black and living in Florida, you were four times as likely as whites to have your ballot invalidated in the 2000 presidential election.[27] We are not now, nor have we ever been, a color-blind nation.

The Cost of Racialized Pleasures

Being able to ignore or being oblivious to the ways in which almost all whites are privileged in a society cleaved on race has a number of implications. Whites derive pleasure in being told that the current system for allocating resources is fair and equitable. Creating and internalizing a color-blind view of race relations reflects how the dominant group is able to use the mass media, immigration stories of upward mobility, rags-to-riches narratives, and achievement ideology to make white privilege invisible.

Frankenberg argues that whiteness can be "displaced," as is the case with whiteness hiding behind the veil of color blindness. It can also be made "normative" rather than specifically "racial," as is the case when being white is defined by white respondents as being no different than being black or Asian.[28] Lawrence Bobo and associates have advanced a theory of laissez-faire racism that draws on the color-blind perspective. As whites embrace the equality of opportunity narrative they suggest that

> laissez-faire racism encompasses an ideology that blames blacks themselves for their poorer relative economic standing, seeing it as a function of perceived cultural inferiority. The analysis of the bases of laissez-faire racism underscores two central components: contemporary stereotypes of blacks held by whites, and the denial of societal (structural) responsibility for the conditions in black communities.[29]

As many of my respondents make clear, if the opportunity structure is open ("It doesn't matter what color you are"), there must be something inherently wrong with racial minorities or their culture that explains group-level differences.

Leslie Carr argues a "that color blindness is not the opposite of racism; it is another form of racism. . . ."[30] I would add that the form color blindness takes as the nation's hegemonic political discourse is a variant of laissez-faire racism. Historian David Roediger contends that in order for the Irish to have been absorbed into the white race in the mid-nineteenth century "the imperative to define themselves as whites came from the particular "public and psychological wages whiteness offered" these new immigrants.[31] There is still a "wage" to whiteness, that element of ascribed status whites automatically receive because of their membership in the dominant group. But within the framework of color blindness the imperative has switched from whites overtly defining themselves or their interests as white, to one where they claim that color is irrelevant; being white is the same as being black, yellow, brown, or red. Some time ago, Ralph Ellison asked this important question about race relations that continues to go unanswered:

> What, by the way, is one to make of a white youngster who, with a transistor radio glued to his ear, screaming a Stevie Wonder tune, shouts racial epithets at black youngsters trying to swim at a public beach. . . . ?[32]

My interviews with whites around the country suggest that in this post-race era of color-blind ideology Ellison's keen observations about race relations need modification. The question now is what are we to make of a young white man from the suburbs who listens to hip-hop, wears baggy hip-hop pants, a baseball cap turned sideways, unlaced sneakers, and an oversized shirt emblazoned with a famous NBA player who, far from shouting racial epithets, lists a number of racial minorities as his heroes? It is now possible to define oneself as not being racist because of the clothes you wear, the celebrities you like, or the music you listen to while believing that blacks or Latinos are disproportionately poor or overrepresented in low-pay, dead-end jobs because these they are part of a debased, culturally deficient group. Having a narrative that smooths over the cognitive dissonance and oft time schizophrenic dance that whites must do when they navigate race relations is likely an invaluable source of pleasure.

REFERENCES

1. FUBU (For Us By Us) is a black-owned manufacturer of urban, hip-hop style clothing.
2. For an excellent overview of how the media construct a view of race relations that is

overly optimistic, see Benjamin DeMott, *The Trouble with Friendship: Why Americans Can't Think Straight About Race* (New York: The Atlantic Monthly Press, 1995).

3. The Gallup Organization, "Black/White Relations in the U.S." (June 10, 1997):1–5; David Shipler, *A Country of Strangers: Blacks and Whites in America* (New York: Vintage Books, 1998).

4. For an insightful discussion of how neoconservative writers like Dinesh D'Souza distort history and contemporary race relations, see David Theo Goldberg, "The New Segregation," *Race and Society* 1, no. 1 (1998).

5. Dinesh D'Souza, *The End of Racism: Principles for a Multiracial Society* (New York: Free Press, 1995); Ellis Cose, *Color-Blind: Seeing Beyond Race in a Race-Obsessed World* (New York: Harper Collins, 1997).

6. David Moore, "Americans Most Important Sources of Information: Local News," *The Gallup Poll Monthly,* 2–5 September 1995; David Moore and Lydia Saad, "No Immediate Signs That Simpson Trial Intensified Racial Animosity," *The Gallup Poll Monthly,* 2–5 October 1995; Kaiser Foundation, *The Four Americas: Government and Social Policy Through the Eyes of America's Multi-Racial and Multi-Ethnic Society* (Menlo Park, CA: Kaiser Family Foundation, 1995).

7. A. C. Nielsen, *Information Please Almanac* (Boston: Houghton Mifflin, 1997).

8. John Lewis and Sut Jhally, "Affirming Inaction: Television and the New Politics of Race," in *Marxism in the Postmodern Age: Confronting the New World Order,* edited by A. Callari, S. Cullenberg, and C. Biewener (New York: Guilford Press).

9. For an outstanding discussion of how color blindness is used politically by neoconservatives, see Amy Ansell, *New Right, New Racism: Race and Reaction in the United States* (New York: New York University Press, 1997); Howard Winant, *Racial Conditions: Politics, Theory, Comparisons* (Minneapolis: University of Minneapolis Press, 1994); Stephen Steinberg, *Turning Back: The Retreat from Racial Justice in American Thought and Policy* (New York: Beacon Press, 1995); Eduardo Bonilla-Silva, *White Supremacy and Racism in the Post-Civil Rights Era* (Boulder: Lynne Rienner Publishers); and Michael Omi, "Racism," in *The Making and Unmaking of Whiteness,* edited by Birget Brander Rasmussen, Eric Klineberg, Irene J. Nexica, and Matt Wray (Durham: Duke University Press, 2001).

10. Ruth Frankenberg, "The Mirage of an Unmarked Whiteness," in *The Making and Unmaking of Whiteness,* edited by Birget Brander Rasmussen, Eric Klineberg, Irene J. Nexica, and Matt Wray (Durham: Duke University Press, 2001).

11. David Theo Goldberg, *Racial Subjects: Writing on Race in America* (Thousand Oaks: Routledge, 1997), 55; see also Charles Jaret, *Contemporary Racial and Ethnic Relations* (New York: Harper Collins, 1995), 265–270.

12. Leslie G. Carr, *Color-Blind Racism* (Thousand Oaks: Sage Publications), 108; see also David Carroll Cochran, *The Color of Freedom: Race and Contemporary American Liberalism* (New York: State University of New York Press).

13. Mary Waters, *Ethnic Options: Choosing Identities in America* (Berkeley: University of California Press); Charles A. Gallagher, "Playing the Ethnic Card: Using Ethnic Identity to Negate Contemporary Racism," in *Deconstructing Whiteness, Deconstructing White Supremacy,* edited by Ashley Doane and Eduardo Bonilla-Silva (Lynne Rienner Publishers, forthcoming 2002).

14. Ashley W. Doane Jr., "Dominant Group Identity in the United States: The Role of "Hidden" Ethnicity in Intergroup Relations," *The Sociological Quarterly* 38, no. 3: 378.

15. Joe Feagin and Melvin Sikes, *Living With Racism: The Black Middle Class Experience* (Boston: Beacon Press, 1994).

16. The Gallup Organization, "Black/White Relations in the U.S.," 10 June 1997, 1–5.

17. Kaiser Foundation, *The Four Americas: Government and Social Policy Through the Eyes of America's Multi-Racial and Multi-Ethnic Society* (Menlo Park, CA: Kaiser Family Foundation, 1995).

18. Howard Schuman et al (1997), 193.

19. U.S. Bureau of the Census, *Housing Vacancies and Home Ownership Annual Statistics* (Washington D.C.: U.S. Government Printing Office, 1999).

20. U.S. Bureau of the Census, *Asset Ownership of Households* (Washington D.C.: U.S. Government Printing Office, 1993); see also *Black Wealth/White Wealth: A New Perspective on Racial Inequality* (New York: Routledge, 1995).

21. John J. Macionis, *Sociology,* 7th ed. (Saddle River, NJ: Prentice Hall, 1999).

22. Diana B. Henriques, *New York Times* 4 July, 2001, p. A1.

23. U.S. Department of Health and Human Services, *National Center for Chronic Disease Prevention and Health Promotion,* 1998; Centers for Disease Control and Prevention, National Center for Health Statistics, *Monthly Vital Statistics Report* 46.

24. Feagin, 2000.

25. Karen Gullo, *The Atlanta Journal and Constitution,* 12 March 2001, p. A7.

26. Jim Abrams, *The Atlanta Journal and Constitution,* 2 December 2000, p. A9.

27. Laura Parker and Peter Eisler, *USA Today,* 6–8 April 2001, p. A1.

28. Frankenberg (2001), p. 76.

29. Lawrence Bobo and James R. Kluegel, "Status, Ideology, and Dimensions of Whites' Racial Beliefs and Attitudes: Progress and Stagnation," in *Racial Attitudes in the 1990s: Continuity and Change,* edited by Steven A. Tuch and Jack K. Martin (Westport, CN: Praeger 1997), p. 95.

30. Carr, p. x.

31. David Roediger, *The Wages of Whiteness: Race and the Making of the American Working Class* (New York: Verso Press 1991), p. 137.

32. Cited in David Roediger, "The White Question," *Race Traitor* (Winter 1993): 104.

43

THE POSSIBILITY OF A NEW RACIAL HIERARCHY IN THE TWENTY-FIRST-CENTURY UNITED STATES

Herbert J. Gans

Questions to Consider

In a timely and provocative article, Herbert Gans suggests that racial categories, as currently understood, are undergoing fundamental changes. He argues that the current racial hierarchy will collapse into two categories: black and nonblack. How will this happen? Which groups will be placed in which of these two categories and why?

Over the last decade, a number of social scientists writing on race and ethnicity have suggested that the

country may be moving toward a new racial structure (Alba 1990; Sanjek 1994; Gitlin 1995). If current trends persist, today's multiracial hierarchy could be replaced by what I think of as a dual or bimodal one consisting of "nonblack" and "black" population categories, with a third, "residual," category for the groups that do not, or do not yet, fit into the basic dualism.[1]

More important, this hierarchy may be based not just on color or other visible bodily features, but also on a distinction between undeserving and deserving, or stigmatized and respectable, races.[2] The hierarchy is new only insofar as the old white-nonwhite dichotomy may be replaced by a nonblack-black one, but it is hardly new for blacks, who are likely to remain at the bottom once again. I fear this hierarchy could develop even if more blacks achieve educational mobility, obtain professional and managerial jobs, and gain access to middle-class incomes, wealth, and other "perks." Still, the hierarchy could also end, particularly if the black distribution of income and wealth resembles that of the then-dominant races, and if interracial marriage eliminates many of the visible bodily features by which Americans now define race.

Since no one can even guess much less model the many causal factors that will influence the future, the observations that follow are not intended to be read as a prediction but as an exercise in speculative analysis. The weakness of such an analysis is its empirical reliance on the extrapolation of too many current trends and the assumed persistence of too many current phenomena. The analysis becomes a justifiable exercise, however, because it aims only to speculate about what future "scenarios" are possible, and what variables might shape these.

Obviously, the observations about such a hierarchy are not meant to suggest that it is desirable. Indeed, I wrote the paper with the hope that if such a future threatens to become real, it can be prevented.

The remainder of this paper elaborates the basic scenario, adds a set of qualifications, and considers the variables and alternative scenarios now most likely to be significant for the future. The paper concludes with observations about the contemporary construction of race in the United States raised by my analysis about a possible future.

The Dual Racial Hierarchy

Before what is now described, somewhat incorrectly, as the post-1965 immigration, the United States was structured as a predominantly Caucasian, or white, society, with a limited number of numerically and otherwise inferior races, who were typically called Negroes, Orientals, and American Indians—or blacks, yellows, and reds to go with the pinkish-skinned people called whites. There was also a smattering of groups involving a huge number of people who were still described by their national or geographic origins rather than language, including Filipinos, Mexicans and Puerto Ricans, Cubans, etc.[3]

After 1965, when many other Central and Latin American countries began to send migrants, the Spanish-speaking groups were all recategorized by language and called Hispanics. Newcomers from Southeast Asia were classified by continental origin and called Asians, which meant that the later Indian, Pakistani, and Sri Lankan newcomers had to be distinguished regionally, and called South Asians.

At the end of the twentieth century, the country continues to be dominated by whites. Nevertheless, both the immigrants who started to arrive after the end of World War II and the political, cultural, and racial changes that took place in the wake of their arrival have further invalidated many old racial divisions and labels. They have also set into motion what may turn out to be significant transformations in at least part of the basic racial hierarchy.

These transformations are still in an early phase but one of the first has been the elevation of a significant, and mostly affluent, part of the Asian and Asian-American population into a "model minority" that also bids to eradicate many of the boundaries between it and whites. Upward socioeconomic mobility and increasing intermarriage with whites may even end up in eliminating the boundary that now constructs them as a separate race. Thus, one possible future trend may lead to all but poor Asians and Asian-Americans being perceived and even treated so much like whites that currently visible bodily differences will no longer be judged negatively or even noticed, except when and where Asians or Asian-Americans threaten white interests (e.g., Newman 1993). The same treatment as quasi whites may spread to other successfully mobile and intermarrying immigrants and their descendants, for example Filipinos and white Hispanics.[4]

What these minorities have in common now with Asians, and might have in common even more in the future, is that they are all nonblack, although not as many are currently as affluent as Asians. Nonetheless, by the middle of the twenty-first century, as whites could perhaps become, or will worry about becoming, a numerical minority in the country, they might cast about for political and cultural allies.[5] Their search for allies, which may not even be conscious or deliberate, could hasten the emergence of a new, nonblack racial category, whatever it is named, in which skin color, or in the case of "Hispanics," racially constructed ethnic differences, will be ignored, even if whites would probably remain the dominant subcategory.

The lower part of the emerging dual hierarchy will likely consist of people classified as blacks, including African-Americans, as well as Caribbean and other blacks, dark-skinned or black Hispanics, Native Americans, and anyone else who is dark skinned enough and/or possessed of visible bodily features and behavior patterns, actual or imagined, that remind nonblacks of blacks. Many of these people will also be poor, and if whites and other nonblacks continue to blame America's troubles on a low-status scapegoat, the new black category will be characterized as an undeserving race.

In effect, class will presumably play nearly as much of a role in the boundary changes as race, but with some important exceptions. For example, if a significant number of very poor whites remain as the twenty-first-century equivalent of today's "white trash," they will probably be viewed as less undeserving than equally poor blacks simply because they are whites.[6]

Furthermore, the limits of class are indicated, at least for today, by the continued stigmatization of affluent and otherwise high-status blacks, who suffer some of the same indignities as poor blacks (Feagin and Sykes 1994).[7] So, of course, do moderate- and middle-income members of the working class, who constitute the majority of blacks in America even if whites do not know it. The high visibility of "black" or Negroid physical features renders class position invisible to whites, so that even affluent blacks are suspected of criminal or pathological behavior that is actually found only among a minority of very poor blacks.

Despite continuing white hatreds and fears of blacks that continue almost 150 years after the Civil War, racial classification systems involving others have been more flexible. When the first Irish immigrants came to New York, they were so poor that they were perceived by Anglo-Saxon whites as the black Irish and often treated like blacks. Even so, it did not take the Irish long to separate themselves from blacks, and more important, to be so separated by the city's Anglo-Saxons. A generation later, the Irish were whites (Roediger 1991; Ignatiev 1995).

Perhaps their new whiteness was reinforced by the arrival of the next set of newcomers: people from Eastern and Southern Europe who were often described as members of "swarthy races." Even though the word *race* was used the way we today use *ethnicity*, the newcomers were clearly not white in the Anglo-Saxon sense, and Southern Italians were sometimes called "guineas" because of their dark skin. Nonetheless, over time, they too became white, thanks in part to their acculturation, their integration into the mainstream economy, and after World War II, their entry into the middle class. Perhaps the disappearance of their swarthiness was also reinforced by the arrival in the cities of a new wave of Southern blacks during and after World War II.

A less typical racial transformation occurred about that time in Mississippi, where whites began to treat the Chinese merchants who provided stores for poor blacks as near whites. As Loewen (1988) tells the story, increased affluence and acculturation were again relevant factors. Although whites neither socialized nor intermarried with the Chinese, they accorded them greater social deference and political respect than when they had first arrived. They turned the Chinese into what I previously called a residual category, and in the process created an early version of the nonblack-black duality that may appear in the United States in the next century.

As the Mississippi example suggests, changes in racial classification schemes need not require racial or class equality, for as long as scarce resources or positions remain, justifications for discrimination also remain and physical features that are invisible in some social settings can still become visible in others. Glass ceilings supply the best example, because they seem to change more slowly than some other hierarchical boundaries. Even ceilings for Jews, non-Irish Catholics, and others long classified as whites are still lower than those for WASPs in the upper reaches of the class and prestige structures.

I should note that the racial hierarchy I have sketched here, together with the qualifications that follow, are described both from the perspective of the (overtly) de-

tached social scientist, and also from the perspective of the populations that end up as dominant in the structure. A longer paper would analyze how very differently the people who are fitted into the lower or residual parts of the hierarchy see it.[8]

Qualifications to the Dual Hierarchy

Even if the country would someday replace its current set of racial classifications, the result would not be a simple dual structure, and this model needs to be qualified in at least three ways.

Residuals

The first qualification is the near certainty of a residual or middle category that includes groups placed in a waiting position by the dominant population until it becomes clear whether they will be allowed to become nonblack, face the seemingly permanent inferiority that goes with being black, or become long-term residuals.

If such a structure were to develop in the near future, those likely to be placed in a residual category would include the less affluent members of today's Asian, Hispanic and Filipino, Central and South American Indian, and mixed Indian-Latino populations. The future of the dark-skinned members of the South Asian newcomers is harder to predict. Indeed, their treatment will become an important test of how whites deal with the race-class nexus when the people involved are very dark skinned but are not Negroid—and when their class position is so high that in 1990 it outranked that of all other immigrants (Rumbaut 1997, table 1.4).[9]

Who is classified as residual will, like all other categorizations, be shaped by both class and race. To borrow Milton Gordon's (1964) useful but too rarely used notion of "ethclass," what may be developing are "race-classes," with lower-class members of otherwise racially acceptable groups and higher-class members of racially inferior ones being placed in the residual category.

It is also possible for two or more residual categories to emerge, one for nonwhite and Hispanic populations of lower- and working-class position, and another for nonwhites and Hispanics of higher-class position, with the latter more likely to be eligible eventually to join whites in the nonblack portion of a dual hierarchy. Yet other variations are conceivable, however, for white America has not yet given any clues about how it will treat middle-class Latinos of various skin colors and other bodily features. Perhaps today's ad hoc solution, to treat nonblack Hispanics as a quasi-racial ethnic group that is neither white nor black, may survive for another generation or more, particularly if enough Hispanics remain poor or are falsely accused of rejecting linguistic Americanization.

Being placed in a residual classification means more than location in a middle analytic category; it is also a socially enforced, even if covert, category, and it will be accompanied by all the social, political, and emotional uncertainties that go with being placed in a holding pattern and all the pains these create (Marris 1996). True, residuals may not know they are waiting, but then the second-generation white ethnic "marginal men" identified by Stonequist (1937) did not know they were waiting for eventual acculturation and assimilation.

Multiracials

A second qualification to the dual model is created by the emergence of biracials or multiracials that result from the rising intermarriage rates among Asian, Hispanic, and black and white immigrants as well as black and white native-born Americans.[10] Interra-cial marriages increased from 1 percent of all marriages in 1960 to 3 percent in 1990 (Harrison and Bennett 1995, 165).[11] They are expected to increase much faster in the future, particularly Asian-white ones, since even now, about a third of all Asian marriages, and more than half of all Japanese ones, are intermarriages.[12] If Hispanic-white marriages were also counted, they would exceed all the rest in current number and expected growth, but these are usually treated as ethnic rather than racial intermarriages.

Another set of recruits for a residual position includes the light-skinned blacks, once called mulattos, who today dominate the African-American upper class, some of whom may be sufficiently elite and light-skinned to be viewed as nonblack. Even now, the most prominent among the light-skinned black-white biracials, including business and civic leaders, celebrities and entertainers, are already treated as honorary whites, although many refuse this option and take special pride in their blackness and become "race leaders."[13]

Meanwhile, "multiracial" is in the process of slowly becoming a public racial category, and someday it could become an official one codified by the U.S. Census.[14] At this writing, however, many people of mixed race are not ready to define themselves publicly as such, and those who can choose which racial origin to use are sometimes flexible on instrumental grounds, or may choose different racial origins on different occasions.[15] How people of various racial mixtures construct themselves in the longer run is impossible to tell, since issues of their identification and treatment by others, their own identity, and the social, occupational, financial, and political benefits and costs involved cannot be predicted either.

As far as the country's long-term future racial structure is concerned, however, what matters most is how whites will eventually view and treat multiracial people. This will be affected by the variations in class and visible physical features among multiracial people—for example, how closely they resemble whites or other deserving races. Another question is the future of the traditional identification of race with "blood," which counts all nonwhites in halves, quarters, or even eighths, depending on how many and which ancestors intermarried with whom.[16] If the late twentieth-century belief in the power of genes continues, blood might simply be replaced by genes someday.

Mixed race is a particularly complex category, for several reasons. In any racial intermarriage with more than one offspring, each sibling is likely to look somewhat different racially from the others, ranging from darker to lighter or more and less nonwhite. Thus, one black-white sibling could be viewed as black and another as nonblack—even before they decide how they view themselves. What happens in subsequent generations is virtually unimaginable, since even if mixed-race individuals marry others of the same mixture, their children will not resemble their grandparents and some may barely resemble their parents. Eventually, a rising number will be treated as, and will think of themselves as, white or nonblack, but this is possible only when people of multiracial origin can no longer bear children who resemble a black ancestor.

Empirical evidence about the effects of racial intermarriage from countries where it has taken place for a long time is unfortunately not very relevant. The closest case, the Caribbean islands, are for the most part, tiny. They are also former plantation societies, with a small number of white and light-skinned elites, and a large number of nonwhites—and a differential conception of white and nonwhite from island to island.[17] Caribbean nonwhites appear to intermarry fairly freely but skin color does count and the darkest-skinned peoples are invariably

lowest in socioeconomic class and status (Mintz 1989; Rodriguez 1989).

The only large country, Brazil, also began as a plantation society, and it differs from the United States particularly in that the Brazilian state eschewed racial legislation. As a result, Brazil never passed Jim Crow laws, but as of this writing (January 1998) it has not passed civil rights legislation either. Racial stratification, as well as discrimination and segregation, has persisted nonetheless, but it has been maintained through the class system. Drastic class inequalities, including a high rate of illiteracy among the poor, have enabled whites to virtually monopolize the higher class and status positions.

The absence of state involvement has given Brazil an undeserved reputation as a society that encourages intermarriage but ignores racial differences, a reputation the state has publicized as "racial democracy." The reality is not very different from that of the United States, however, for while there has been more intermarriage, it appears to have taken place mainly among blacks and black-white biracials, who together make up about half the country's population. Moreover, biracials gain little socioeconomic advantage from their lighter skins, even as the darkest-skinned blacks are kept at the bottom, forced into slums and prisons as in the United States.[18]

In effect, the Brazilian experience would suggest an empirical precedent for my hypothesis that blacks will remain a separate, and discriminated-against, population in the United States of the future. Indeed, in just about every society in which blacks first arrived as slaves, they are still at the bottom, and the political, socioeconomic, and cultural mechanisms to keep them there remain in place. Although blacks obtain higher incomes and prestige than Asians or white Hispanics in a number of American communities, the descendants of nonblack immigrants are, with some notable exceptions, still able to overtake most blacks in the long run.

Since parts of the United States were also a plantation society in which the slaves were black, the leftovers of the racial stratification pattern will likely continue here as well. Thus, children of black-white intermarriages who turn out to be dark skinned are classified as blacks, even if the United States is on the whole kinder to light-skinned biracials than Brazil.

The future of Asian-white biracials remains more unpredictable, in part because no empirical data exist that can be used to shore up guesses about them. The same observation applies to the endless number of other multiracial combinations that will be created when the children of multiracial parents intermarry with yet other multiracials. There will be few limits to new variations in bodily features, though which will be visible or noticed, and which of the latter will be stigmatized or celebrated as exotic cannot be guessed now.[19] Most likely, however, the larger the number of multiracials and of multiracial variations, the more difficult it will be for nonblacks to define and enforce racial boundaries, or to figure out which of the many darker-skinned varieties of multiracials had black ancestors. In that case, an eventual end to racial discrimination is possible.

If future racial self-identification patterns will also resemble today's ethnic ones, the racial equivalent of today's voluntary white ethnicity and its associated lack of ethnic loyalty may mean that many future triracial, quadriracial, and other multiracial people may eventually know little, and care even less, about the various racial mixtures they have inherited. It is even conceivable that this change will extend to black multiracials, and should race become voluntary for them as well, the possibility of an end to racial discrimination will be increased. Un-

fortunately, at the moment such extrapolations are far closer to utopian thinking than to sociological speculation.

Regional Variations

A third qualification to the dual model is that the portrait I have drawn is national, but given the regional variations in old racial groups and new immigrant populations, it fits no single U.S. region. Moreover, some parts of the country are now still so devoid of new immigrants, with the exception of the handful who come to establish "ethnic" restaurants, that the present racial hierarchies, categories, and attitudes, many of them based on stereotypes imported from elsewhere, could survive unchanged for quite a while in such areas. Furthermore, some areas that have experienced heavy immigration from Asia and Latin America are currently seeing an outmigration of whites, especially lower-income ones (Frey 1996). Thus, even current patterns in the racial makeup of U.S. regions could change fairly quickly.

In addition, regional differences remain in the demography of the lowest strata. The racial hierarchy of the Deep South will probably continue to bear many direct marks of slavery, although the de facto black experience elsewhere in the country has so far not been totally different. Moreover, in some regions, Latin American and other poor nonblack immigrants have already been able to jump over the poor black population economically and socially, partly because whites, including institutions such as banks, are less hostile—or less necessary—to them than they are to blacks.

In the Southwest, Mexicans and other Hispanics remain at the socioeconomic bottom, although in California, they may be joined by the Hmong, Laotians, and other very poor Asians. And Native Americans still occupy the lowest socioeconomic stratum in the handful of mostly rural parts of the country where they now live, although tribes with gambling casinos may be able to effect some changes in that pattern.

Even though some of the new immigrants can by now be found just about everywhere in America, the Los Angeles and New York City areas not only remain the major immigrant arrival centers but also contain the most diverse populations. As a result, a number of the issues discussed in this paper will be played out there, even as they are barely noticeable in the many smaller American cities that may have attracted only a handful of the newcomers. Since these two cities are also the country's prime creators of popular culture, however, their distinctive racial and ethnic characteristics will probably be diffused in subtle ways through the country as a whole.

Alternative Scenarios

Speculating about the future also requires some explicit consideration of the variables that could affect the guesses I have made here, which in turn could lead to alternative scenarios. Generally speaking these variables are macrosociological—major changes in the economy, demographic patterns including internal migration and immigration, as well as political realignments and racial divisions of labor, among others. These in turn can result in changes in racial and ethnic relations as well as in classification systems.

As noted earlier, dominant groups can alter racial categories and constructions. Model minorities are "chosen" by the dominant population precisely because they appear to share, and thereby to uphold, that population's behavior or values. If new behavior or values need to be upheld, new model minorities may be recruited. Scapegoats are populations that can be blamed for

social problems, although the dominant populations choose, or even create, the social problems for which scapegoats will be blamed. Scapegoats, or targets for blame, generally come in two varieties: *higher* scapegoats, usually recruited from higher-status minority groups that can be blamed for obtaining too much economic or cultural power; and *lower* ones, typically the undeserving poor, who can be accused of deviant behavior or values said to hold back economic growth, require public expenditures that could bankrupt governmental budgets, threaten familial and sexual norms, or impair the moral fabric of the rest of society. Blaming both types of scapegoats is a politically easy way of responding to a crisis, particularly one for which immediate and feasible solutions are lacking.

During the long Cold War, the Soviets and other foreign scapegoats could be blamed for American problems, but now, domestic scapegoats have again become the primary target. While illegal and even legal American immigrants are once again joining poor blacks as the country's principal lower scapegoats, only a few states have sufficient immigrants to serve as targets for blame, which may help to explain why conservative politicians, particularly Republicans, have more often demonized poor blacks.

The most likely candidates for change in current racial categories, other than of model minorities, are the people whites now call Hispanics, as well as descendants of some now officially nonwhite populations in the new immigration. They will have to be allowed into the higher-status occupations in larger number if and when the supply of whites runs out, and in that case, today's forms of racial and ethnic discrimination against them, particularly those shaped by class considerations, would have to give way. In fact, by the middle of the twenty-first century, demographers and journalists may be amazed that fifty years earlier, whites expected to be swamped in 2050 by an aggregate of diverse peoples then all called Hispanics.

Two macrosocial factors are probably most important in thinking about alternative scenarios. One is the set of geopolitical and economic demographics that can be produced by cross-national population movements, including the one that has fueled the immigration from Central and Latin America, as well as Russia, Asia, and now Africa, during the last half century. These movements were controlled at least in part by U.S. government legislation, but world catastrophes could take place that could force even the United States to open its borders to much larger numbers of people who might alter the racial distribution significantly.

National demographics can also be changed by domestic political considerations, however, which could lead to a new search for white—and non-Hispanic—immigrants. The United States found its late-nineteenth-century industrial workforce in white Europe rather than among the newly freed slaves in the South. Likewise, Australia has recently looked for European immigrants to discourage the arrival of further Asians.

The second major factor is the state of the domestic economy. If late-twentieth-century trends in the world economy and on Wall Street continue in their present forms, the further disappearance of American firms, jobs, and high wages, as well as related changes in the country's economy, would persist too.

Suppose, for example, that unemployment, or the decline of real income, or both, worsened in the first quarter of the twenty-first century, and Americans in large numbers conclude that the country's economy can never again supply full-time jobs paying a living wage for everyone. While the

descendants of the poorer immigrants would be the first to experience what I once called "second generation decline" (Gans 1992), other immigrants can also be dispatched into persistent poverty when not enough jobs are available, with the appropriate racial stereotypes invented or reinvented to justify their downward mobility. Even some middle-class descendants of Asian, Russian, and other newcomers could be transformed into lower scapegoats. Then, the dual racial hierarchy I have described would look very different or might not come to pass at all.

Should economic crises result in political crises as well, or raise religious and culture "wars" to more feverish pitches, the current movement toward a dual racial structure could also end quickly. Then, a modern version of the nineteenth-century American monoracial pattern might reappear, with the children of white newcomers joining older white ethnics and WASPs as the only acceptable race. Some members of the newly scapegoated races would probably react in turn, inaugurating political protest, intensifying identity politics and slowing down on intermarriage and other forms of acculturation and assimilation. Some descendants of today's newcomers might return to the old country.

What if a very different economic scenario were assumed, involving a return of old-style economic growth accompanied by a stronger U.S. position in the global economy, a shortage of domestic workers, and an upward trend in real income? In that case, the trend toward a dual structure might be hastened, and the erosion of perceived racial differences speeded up as well.

At that point, the now still visible bodily differences of Asian-Americans and their descendants might no longer be noticed, and these groups would repeat the post-World War II pattern by which Southern and Eastern European "races" were redefined as "ethnic groups." The reclassification of Hispanics, including the treatment of third-generation Central and Latin Americans, would probably move in the same direction.

The fate of blacks is more difficult to imagine. If the economy created a seller's market for people with job skills at all levels from blue collar to professional and managerial, all poverty would decline sharply, including that of blacks. Moreover, blacks would be able to enter the upper middle and middle classes in such numbers as to disturb white America's long association of poverty with blackness. Indeed, in an economy with enough decent jobs for all, private and public affirmative action policies to assure the spread of blacks at all levels of the occupational and socioeconomic structure would be likely as well.

Under such conditions, those aspects of white racism due to fear of and anger at black poverty would begin to decline, and if the federal government was committed to fight racial discrimination and segregation, so would the construction of blacks as an undeserving race. Black-white intermarriage rates might also rise more quickly.

If the prosperity were long term, and it as well as other events in the society and the world reduced the country's resort to domestic scapegoats, a dual racial hierarchy might be replaced by the beginnings of a multiracial structure in which the boundaries of all races would become fuzzier and weaker. Since now-stigmatized visible bodily differences would then lose their negative connotations, they might not only be ignored but even come to be celebrated as positive contributions to American diversity, just as current ethnic differences among Europeans provide the country with non-threatening cultural diversities.

Prosperity alone does not necessarily solve a society's other problems, however, and political, cultural, and religious conflicts could remain, encouraging dominant groups to choose and stigmatize an undeserving race, even if it is not a poor one. Anti-Semitic activities, for example, have occurred in prosperous times and societies, and in nations with minuscule Jewish populations.

Likewise, more economic prosperity and other positive economic tendencies alone do not necessarily produce more acculturation and assimilation of immigrants. Even the acculturation of large numbers of immigrants and their descendants does not automatically preclude identity politics, for today's college and university campuses are rife with rapidly acculturating newcomers who nevertheless feel strongly enough about their racial identity to become active in identity politics.

It is even possible that in a multiracial America, some latter-day descendants of WASPs and white ethnics will resort to identity politics as an attempt to retain or restore their political and cultural dominance.[20] And if a global economy also produced pressures toward global cultural and political homogeneities, nation-states or their successors might develop now unimagined forms of national identity politics or cultural revivals to maintain some kind of national distinctiveness. Immigrants and their descendants might be victimized by such developments more than blacks, however.

Three Tendencies in the Contemporary Construction of Race

Biological Constructions

The first tendency is the continuing construction of race from biological as well as social building blocks. Most scientific experts agree that there are no biologically definable races, and that race is therefore not a useful biological concept. The lay public, however, which is not ready to accept expert opinion, sees differences in visible bodily features, mostly facial, between people and treats them as racial differences caused by differences in "blood." People also racialize differences in personality traits such as "soul"—and national character in the case of immigrants.

The visible bodily differences are not imaginary, for people do differ by skin color, and the shapes or other characteristics of various body parts, including heads, eyelids, noses, hair, and others. To cite just a few examples, even in third-generation white ethnic America, one can find Irish and Welsh (or "Celtic") faces, southern Italian and Sicilian ones, and Slavic as well as Scandinavian ones.

What people notice are not scientifically defined races or subraces, but the descendants of once-isolated peoples who had been inbreeding for centuries.[21] Since most have now stopped doing so as a result of rural to urban and other migrations, their distinctiveness is disappearing with each new generation, but it has by no means disappeared.

Some of the variations in personality and social characteristics that laypeople correlate with race or "blood" can undoubtedly be traced in part to the societies and economies, as well as the racial hierarchies, in which these once-isolated peoples lived. The occupational and other social roles that immigrants play in their new societies also play a part, one reason why immigrant shopkeepers in "middlemen" roles are often seen as "clannish" by the populations they serve, for example.

Some visible bodily features that distinguish people are noticed and judged; some are noticed but not judged one way or another; and yet others are not even noticed, seeming to be virtually invisible. Although how features are judged can be traced in part to the popular Darwinisms of the last two centuries, in general, the bodily features of the most prestigious peoples are usually adopted as ideals of physical perfection, while features found among the lower social classes are judged pejoratively.[22]

Variations in skin color, as well as in head shapes, noses, eyes, lips, and hair, have been noticed in many societies, but differences in some bodily parts have been ignored, for example, the size of fingers and the shapes of ears and earlobes.[23] Yet other bodily features are not noticed because they are hidden by clothes; while a few are not noticed because people wear clothes to hide them. These often spur fantasies, for example about black penis size and other imagined racial differences in reproductive and other organs.[24]

A major ingredient of the social construction of race is the determination of which visible bodily features are noticed and used to delineate race and which remain unnoticed. In the process shaping that construction, various social constructors, including laypersons, experts, and, when relevant, commercial and political decision makers, take part. Unless explicit ideological, commercial, or political reasons are involved, the constructors may not be aware of the process in which they are involved, or the causes that shape the final determination. Usually, whites are the major constructors, but increasingly, representatives of the racial minorities to be constructed participate when they can politicize the process, or can frighten manufacturers or advertisers of national consumer goods.[25]

Strictly speaking, a biological construction should make racial characteristics and classifications relatively fixed, but lay biological construction is almost as flexible as social construction. The reason for the lack of fixity is not hard to find, for the choice of which visible bodily features are to be noticed has almost nothing to do with race and everything to do with stratification.

As the Brazilian and United States experiences indicate, the race of the lowest class became the lowest race because slaves were almost by definition the lowest class and race. That captured blacks were the only population economically and otherwise powerless to prevent their becoming enslaved in recent centuries led whites to use their distinguishable skin color and facial features to translate their class inferiority into a racial one (Fields 1990). Similarly, the stigmatization of "yellow" skin resulted from the serflike status of Chinese "coolies" on railroad construction gangs; the stigmatization of "swarthiness" followed from the low status of the Southern and Eastern European newcomers; and a century later, white Hispanic immigrants are sometimes called a race because of their low class position.[26] That the ancestors of now-respected Americans were once damned for their swarthy skins has been quietly forgotten, both among their descendants and among the peoples who "invented" the original stigma.

Ethnicity as Racial

The second, and related, tendency is the continuing lay practice of identifying ethnic and national differences as racial, particularly in private self-naming. Census analysts have discovered that in the 1990 census, respondents to open-ended questions claimed membership in nearly three hundred races or ethnic groups, including seventy Hispanic categories (Morganthau 1995, 64). In many instances, they equated their race with their nationality—or with their tribes in the case of Native Americans.[27] As Eleanor Gerber and Manuel de la Puente pointed out in reporting on a study of test questions for the 2000 census: "Most respondents recognized the term 'ethnic group' but . . . would indicate it was 'the same thing' as race . . . [and] often coined the term 'ethnic race' during our discussions" (Gerber and de la Puente 1996, 21).

The two Bureau of Census researchers suggest lack of education as the causal factor in this conflation, indicating that only the college educated could distinguish ethnic group from race. However, as long as Americans notice visible bodily differences among people of the same official race, they will hold on to *private* constructions of race that differ from the official definitions.[28] Even among the third- and fourth-generation white multiethnics whose "ethnic options" Mary Waters (1990) studied, some chose their ethnicities on the basis of racial conceptions of national origin.[29] In effect, ethnicity continues to be a matter of "blood."[30]

Racial Tolerance

The third and perhaps most important tendency is the apparently increasing white tolerance for racial differences, except with respect to blacks. At the same time, whites seem to use race less often as an indicator of class, except when they are considering poor blacks. This trend may become more widespread as racial intermarriage among people of similar class increases further. Today, class homogamy is apparently outranking racial homogamy among college-educated young people (Kalmijn 1991).

If this pattern spreads to other Americans of the same age and if it becomes permanent, and if whites were willing and able to see that their hatreds and fears of blacks and other very poor nonwhites are so often reactions to their extreme and persistent poverty rather than their race, class could become more important and more overt as a boundary and a principle of stratification in the future. If Americans could also realize that class is more than a matter of "lifestyle" differences among near equals, class stratification might someday become a matter of general public discussion. In that case, the myth of a classless America might eventually be laid to rest.[31]

Even a more modest increase in awareness of class would be desirable, because class is after all an achieved status, while race is not, even in its reasonably flexible lay construction. However, the shift from race to class would also require Americans to develop a more fundamental understanding of the United States and to invent a new conception of the American dream and its underlying myth to replace that of the classless society. So far, there is no indication of this happening.

In fact, it would probably not happen until events in the political economy make it possible to achieve a drastic reduction of joblessness and poverty, so that the correlation of poverty with blackness is significantly lowered. If and when blacks become roughly equal economically to nonblacks, blacks can no longer be treated as an undeserving race.

If poverty and inequality are not lessened, however, and if more poor blacks are condemned to work for nothing but their welfare benefits, they could be treated as an ever more undeserving race, and other populations who cannot enter, or stay in, the middle class, including poor Hispanics and Asians, might join them. In that case, the racial hierarchy of the next century's United States would look very different from the one I have sketched here.

Conclusion

A society's reconstruction of racial categories appears to require at least the following conditions: (1) an influx of immigrants who do not fit the existing racial categories and their associated class backgrounds; (2) a healthy economy with sufficient opportunity for upward mobility even for poorer immigrants; (3) a lack of demand for new lower (and higher) racial scapegoats; and (4) an at least temporary demand for model minorities.

If these conditions are met, existing racial definitions and categories will be altered, sometimes even quickly if there is a proliferation of interracial marriages. However, in a society with a history of slavery, one possible effect is a dual racial hierarchy, in which one part consists mostly of ex-slaves. However, since even the effects of slavery should eventually be eliminated, at least in theory, the United States could become a predominantly interracial or multiracial society someday.

Even then, the more prestigious racial mixtures are apt to remain somewhat whiter for a while than the rest, and the less prestigious ones darker. But if the country's racial mixing ever became so thorough that skin color and other currently used bodily features were sufficiently unrecognizable or no longer of sufficient interest to be noticed, race would no longer be associated with social ranking. If Americans then still needed to rank each other, new criteria would have to be found.

NOTES

I am grateful for comments on earlier drafts of this paper from Margaret Chin, Jennifer Lee, an anonymous reviewer—and from my fellow authors in this volume.

1. These categories are constructions, but they also contain populations experiencing all the pleasures and pains of being located in a hierarchy. And although I am often discussing constructions, I will forgo the practice of putting all racial, national, and related names and labels between quotes, except for unusual racial stereotypes.
2. The two races may not be called that openly, but ambiguous pejoratives have long been part of the American vocabulary, for example *underclass* now, and *pauper* a century earlier (Gans 1995). Since races are social constructions, their names will depend in large part on who does the naming—and

whose names become dominant in the public vocabulary.

3. Puerto Ricans are still often described as immigrants, even though they have been American citizens for a long time and their move from the island to the mainland is a form of interstate mobility. Racial, class, and linguistic considerations have undoubtedly influenced this labeling.

The same dominant-race thinking led Irving Kristol and other neoconservatives to argue in the 1960s that blacks were similar enough to the white European immigrants to be able to adopt and act on immigrant values. They also assumed that blacks would then assimilate like immigrants, ignoring such facts as that blacks had originally come as slaves, not immigrants; had been here several centuries; and had not yet been allowed by whites to assimilate. Thirty years later, many whites ignore the same facts to propose the newest immigrants as role models for blacks.

4. Much less is said about black Hispanics, including Puerto Ricans, who suffer virtually all of the discriminatory and other injustices imposed on African-Americans.

5. Some highly placed whites are already worrying, for example in a *Time* cover story by William Henry III (1990), but then similar whites worried a century earlier what the then arriving Catholic and Jewish newcomers would do to *their* country. The current worries are as meaningless as the old ones, since they are based on extrapolations of current patterns of immigration, not to mention current constructions of (nonwhite) race and (Hispanic) ethnicity.

6. Hacker (1996) notes, for example, that the term "white trash" is no longer in common use. Indeed, for reasons worth studying, the more popular term of the moment is "trailer trash," which nonetheless seems to be applied solely to poor whites.

7. In this respect, the United States differs from many other countries in the Western hemisphere, where blacks who have managed to become affluent are treated, within limits, as whites.

8. Not only might they perceive it more angrily than I am here doing, but they might be angrier about it than about the present hierarchy, simply because it is new but no great improvement. One result could be their constructions of new racial identities for themselves that depart drastically from the ones future nonblacks consider reasonable.

9. Being far fewer than Asians in number, South Asians are nationally not very visible now. Moreover, for religious and other reasons, South Asian immigrants have so far often been able to discourage their children from intermarrying.

10. My observations on multiracial constructions and people have benefited from many conversations with Valli Rajah.

11. Between 1970 and 1994, the number of people in interracial marriages grew from 676,000 to more than three million (Fletcher 1997). In 1990, biracial children made up 4 percent of all children, increasing from half a million in 1970 to about two million that year. The largest number were Asian-white children, followed by Native American-white and African American-white ones (Harrison and Bennett 1995).

12. Some observers currently estimate that 70 percent of all Japanese and Japanese-Americans are intermarried, mostly with whites. Since they came to the United States as families long before 1965, this estimate may supply a clue about what will happen to second-, third-, and later-generation descendants of other Asian-American populations.

13. Presumably class position will affect how other descendants of old Southern mulatto and creole populations (Dominguez 1986) will be classified.

14. In the political debates over the racial categories to be used in the Year 2000 Census, vocal multiracials preferred to be counted as and with various people of color. African-Americans and other officially recognized racial groups also indicated their opposition to a multiracial category, being reluctant to reduce the power of their numbers or the federal benefits that now go to racial minorities (e.g., Holmes 1996).

15. Kohne (1996) reports that light-skinned biracial Columbia University students who identify as whites also apply for scholarships as blacks. But then, four decades earlier, I met Italian-Americans in Boston's West End who took Irish names in order to obtain jobs in Irish-dominated city hall.

16. The practice of quantifying racial bloods has a long history in Europe and the United States, thanks to both eugenics and slavery. Perhaps it will disappear when enough peo-

ple have to start counting three or more races. However, people also still use blood fractions when they marry across religions, so that the notion of racial, ethnic, or religious "blood" is by no means obsolete.

17. They are also different, for "one and the same person may be considered white in the Dominican Republic or Puerto Rico . . . 'colored' in Jamaica, Martinique, or Curacao . . . [and] a 'Negro' in Georgia" (Hoetink 1967, xii).

18. This account is based mainly on the data summarized in Fiola 1990 and Skidmore 1992, the classic analysis of the Brazilian racial system in Skidmore 1993, Adamo's 1983 case study of race and class in Rio de Janeiro, and the sociopolitical analyses by Marx (1995, 1996). I am indebted to Anthony Marx for guiding me into the literature on Brazil, although there is still precious little social research, especially with current data, in English.

19. No one has so far paid much attention to who is constructed as exotic and why, except the multiracial people, mostly women, to whom it is applied. Some of them benefit because they are sought by industries that hire workers with exotic facial features; but women without these occupational interests resent such labeling because it turns them into sexual objects.

Industries that employ workers with exotic features, facial and otherwise, such as the fashion and entertainment industries, play an interesting, and probably unduly influential, role in the country's public racial construction.

20. Even now, at the close of the twentieth century, whites who argue that America is a "Christian" nation are pursuing a politics of identity as much as of religious dominance.

21. I am indebted to my Columbia University colleague, biologist Robert Pollack, for my understanding of this phenomenon.

22. Originally, people drew on nineteenth-century and earlier comparisons of apes and humans, with those determined to be closer to apes in facial appearance being thought inferior. Brain size was also used, at least until scientific research debunked its relevance, and the researchers also discovered that it did not correlate with status. The final blow was the discovery that the much maligned Neanderthalers had larger brains than *Homo sapiens*.

23. Ears have served mainly as anchors for adornment, although protruding ones have sometimes been brought surgically closer to the head.

24. Now that some young women show their navels or wear bathing suits with uncovered buttocks, these could become eligible for racial typing.

25. Constructionists in the social sciences and the humanities have so far mainly emphasized that races, like other human notions, are socially constructed, but social scientists have paid little attention to the actual construction process and its participants. What we know about that process comes mostly from scholars who analyze racial images over time, in literature or the popular culture, and have collected process information as part of their work.

26. Forced Chinese labor was also recruited for the cotton plantations, but the Chinese workers turned out to be inefficient cotton pickers and thus managed to avoid becoming slaves.

27. I am indebted to Roderick Harrison and especially Manuel de la Puente of the U.S. Bureau of the Census for materials that clarified this set of responses.

28. Social scientists on the staff of the Census Bureau and the Bureau of Labor Statistics spend part of their time analyzing the large number of private races that people supply in answer to open-ended questions to produce the small number of public ones reported by the federal government.

29. For some similar practices by Jews in post-Holocaust Germany, see Rapaport 1997, 166–67.

30. For example, one of Waters's respondents explained that she traced her bad moods to "the Irish in me," while "all of the good things" were Italian (Waters 1990, 25). Embryo clinics are asked by some of their customers to supply sperm and egg donors of similar ethnic origin, in one case to obtain an "Irish background, or at least light hair and light eyes" (Kolata 1997, 34). As a result, ethnicity may be so racialized that it is not very voluntary, although voluntary ethnicity may also be used to achieve voluntarily chosen racial features.

31. Needless to say, traumatic and long-lasting economic decline is a more likely cause for a public recognition of class in America.

REFERENCES

ADAMO, SAMUEL C. 1983. "The Broken Promise: Race, Health and Justice in Rio de Janeiro, 1890–1940." Ph.D. diss., University of New Mexico.

ALBA, RICHARD D. 1990. *Ethnic Identity.* New Haven: Yale University Press.

DOMINGUEZ, VIRGINIA R. 1986. *White by Definition.* New Brunswick: Rutgers University Press.

FEAGIN, JOE R., and MICHAEL P. SYKES. 1994. *Living with Racism.* Boston: Beacon.

FIELDS, BARBARA J. 1990. "Slavery, Race and Ideology in the United States of America." *New Left Review* 15:95–108.

Fiola, Jan. 1990. "Race Relations in Brazil: A Reassessment of the 'Racial Democracy' Thesis." Occasional Papers Series no. 34. University of Massachusetts Latin American Studies Program, Amherst.

FLETCHER, MICHAEL A. 1997. "More Than a Black-White Issue." *Washington Post National Weekly Edition,* May 26, 34.

FREY, WILLIAM H. 1996. "Immigration, Domestic Migration and Demographic Balkanization in America." *Population and Development Review* 22:741–63.

GANS, HERBERT J. 1992. "Second Generation Decline: Scenarios for the Economic and Ethnic Futures of the post-1965 American Immigrants." *Ethnic and Racial Studies* 15:173–92.

———. 1995. *The War against the Poor.* New York: Basic.

GERBER, ELEANOR, and MANUEL DE LA PUENTE. 1996. "The Development of and Cognitive Testing of Race and Ethnic Origin Questions for the Year 2000 Census." In Bureau of the Census, *1996 Annual Research Conference.* Washington: Government Printing Office.

GITLIN, TODD. 1995. *The Twilight of Common Dreams.* New York: Metropolitan.

GORDON, MILTON M. 1964. *Assimilation in American Life.* New York: Oxford University Press.

HACKER, ANDREW. 1996. Foreword to *The Coming Race War?* by Richard Delgado. New York: New York University Press.

HARRISON, RODERICK J., and CLAUDETTE BENNETT. 1995. "Racial and Ethnic Diversity." In *State of the Union: America in the 1990s,* vol. 2, *Social Trends,* edited by Reynolds Farley. New York: Russell Sage Foundation.

HENRY, WILLIAM, III. 1990. "Beyond the Melting Pot." *Time,* April 9, 29–32.

HOETINK, HARRY. 1967. *The Two Variants in Caribbean Race Relations.* London: Oxford University Press.

HOLMES, STEVEN. 1996. "Census Tests New Category to Identify Racial Groups." *New York Times,* December 4, A25.

IGNATIEV, NOEL. 1995. *How the Irish Became White.* New York: Routledge.

KALMIJN, MATTHIJS. 1991. "Status Homogamy in the United States." *American Journal of Sociology* 93:496–523.

KOHNE, NATASHA G. 1996. "The Experience of Mixed-Race Women: Challenging Racial Boundaries." Unpublished senior thesis, department of sociology, Columbia University, New York.

KOLATA, GINA. 1997. "Clinics Selling Embryos Made for 'Adoption.'" *New York Times,* November 23, 1, 34.

LOEWEN, JAMES W. 1988. *The Mississippi Chinese.* 2d ed. Prospect Heights, Ill.: Waveland

MARRIS, PETER. 1996. *The Politics of Uncertainty.* New York: Routledge.

MARX, ANTHONY W. 1995. "Contested Citizenship: The Dynamics of Racial Identity and Social Movements." *International Review of History* 40, supplement 3: 159–83.

———. 1996 "Race-Making and the Nation-State." *World Politics,* January, 180–208.

MINTZ, SIDNEY W. 1989. *Caribbean Transformations.* New York: Columbia University Press.

MORGANTHAU, TOM. 1995. "What Color Is Black?" *Newsweek,* February 12, 63–67.

NEWMAN, KATHERINE. 1993. *Declining Fortunes.* New York: Basic.

RAPAPORT, LYNN. 1997. *Jews in Germany after the Holocaust.* Cambridge: Cambridge University Press.

RODRIGUEZ, CLARA E. 1989. *Puerto Ricans: Born in the U.S.A.* Boston: Unwin Hyman.

ROEDIGER, DAVID R. 1991. *Wages of Whiteness.* London: Verso.

RUMBAUT, RUBEN G. 1997. "Ties That Bind: Immigration and Immigrant Families in the United States." In *Immigration and the Family,* edited by Alan Booth, Ann C. Crouter, and Nancy Landale. Mahwah, N.J.: Erlbaum.

SANJEK, ROGER. 1994. "Intermarriage and the Future of the Races in the United States." In *Race,* edited by Steven Gregory and Roger Sanjek. New Brunswick: Rutgers University Press.

SKIDMORE, THOMAS L. 1992. "Fact and Myth: Discovering a Racial Problem in Brazil." Working paper 173. Helen Kellogg Institute for International Studies, University of Notre Dame.

———. 1993. *Black into White.* Durham: Duke University Press.

STONEQUIST, EVERETT V. 1937. *The Marginal Man.* New York: Scribner's.

WATERS, MARY. 1990. *Ethnic Options: Choosing Identities in America.* Berkeley: University of California Press.

. . . and Opportunities

44

GETTING ALONG
Renewing America's Commitment to Racial Justice

Melvin L. Oliver • Thomas M. Shapiro

Questions to Consider

Melvin Oliver and Thomas Shapiro discuss how and why the accumulation of wealth is an under-examined facet of racial inequality. Why is examining the accumulation of wealth rather than just examining income data so important? What public policy solutions do these authors suggest we embrace to create greater opportunity for racial and ethnic groups who have not been able to pass on socioeconomic opportunity to their children? Do you believe such policy prescriptions are possible given the current political and economic climate in the United States?

In America, though, life seems to move faster than anywhere else on the globe and each generation is promised more than it will get; which creates, in each generation, a furious, bewildered rage, the rage of people who cannot find solid ground beneath their feet.

> —JAMES BALDWIN,
> "The Harlem Ghetto"

Can we all just get along?

> —RODNEY KING, Los Angeles, 1992

Introduction: The Meaning of Money

Wealth is money that is not typically used to purchase milk, shoes, or other necessities. Sometimes it bails families out of financial and personal crises, but more often it is used to create opportunities, secure a desired stature and standard of living, or pass along a class status already obtained to a new generation. We have seen how funds transferred by parents to their children both before and after death are often treated as very special money. Such funds are used for down payments on houses, closing costs on a mortgage, start-up money for a business, maternal and early childhood expenses, private education, and college costs. Parental endowments, for those fortunate enough to receive them, are enormously consequential in shaping their recipients' opportunities, life chances, and outlooks on life.

A common literary theme shows how money debases character, love, and relationships. In *A Room of One's Own* Virginia Woolf reminds us that the absence of money also deeply corrupts. As a woman, Virginia Woolf thought that her financial inheritance would be more important in her life than even gaining the right to vote. Suppose a black person inherited a good deal of money (let's not inquire about the source) at about the time the slaves were emancipated in 1863. Of the two events—the acquisition of wealth and the attainment of freedom—which would be more important in shaping the life of this person and his or her family? John Rock, the abolitionist, pre–Civil War orator, and first African American attorney to argue before the Supreme Court, lectured that "you will find no prejudice in the Yankee whatsoever," when the avenues of wealth are opened to the formerly enslaved.[1]

Over a century and a third later Ellis Cose disagrees with this assessment in *The Rage of a Privileged Class.* His book illustrates the daily discriminations, presumptions, and reproaches to which even very successful upper-middle-class blacks are subject. Cose reminds us that the color of the hand holding the money matters. The former mayor of New York, David Dinkins, stated pointedly:

From *Black Wealth/White Wealth* by Melvin L. Oliver and Thomas M. Shapiro. Copyright © 1995. Reproduced by permission of Routledge, Inc., part of The Taylor & Francis Group.

"a white man with a million dollars is a millionaire, and a black man with a million dollars is a nigger with a million dollars."[2] Even highly accomplished and prosperous black professionals bitterly lament that their personal success does not translate into status, at least not outside the black community.

This notion is further elaborated in *Living with Racism* by Joe Feagin and Melvin Sikes, a book based on the life experiences of two hundred black middle-class individuals. Feagin and Sikes found that no amount of hard work and achievement, or money and resources, provides immunity for black people from the persistent, commonplace injury of white racism. Modern racism must be understood as lived experience, as middle-class blacks "tell of mistreatment encountered as they traverse traditionally white places."[3] Occasions of serious discrimination are immediately painful and stressful, and they have a cumulative impact on individuals, their psyches, families, and communities. The repeated experience of racism affects a person's understanding of and outlook on life. It is from the well of institutionalized racism that daily incidents of racial hostility are drawn.

One's sense of autonomy and security about the future is not merely or necessarily characterological; it is also a reflection of one's personal position and status. "The secret point of money and power in America is neither the things that money can buy nor power for power's sake . . . but absolute personal freedom, mobility, privacy," according to the writer Joan Didion. Money allows one "to be a free agent, live by one's own rules."[4]

Mary Ellen comes from an upper-middle-class business- and property-owning black family and is well on the road to building her own wealth portfolio. She talks about how her background helped shape her attitudes toward economic security and risk-taking.

I think that growing up as I did, I think my mindset is a little different because I don't feel like I'm going to fall back. I don't feel that. A lot of people I talk to feel that. They don't see options that I see. They don't take as many risks. You know, I could always run home to my parents if something drastic happened. A lot of people don't have those alternatives.

As the twentieth century draws to a close the mixed legacy of racial progress and persistent racial disadvantage continues to confront America and shape our political landscape. Our focus in this book on assets has yielded a fuller comprehension of the extent and the sources of continued racial inequality. But how can we use this understanding to begin to close the racial gap?

This [reading] steps back from the detailed examination of wealth to place our major substantive findings into the larger picture. Our exploration of racial wealth differences began with theoretical speculations about how wealth differences might force us to revise previous thinking about racial inequality. The unreflective use of income as the standard way to measure inequality has contributed to a serious underestimation of the magnitude and scope of the racial disadvantage, revealing only one of its causes. If income disparities are not the crux of the problem, then policies that seek to redress inequality by creating equal opportunities and narrowing racial differences are doomed to fail, even when such programs succeed in putting blacks in good jobs. The more one learns about patterns of racial wealth differences, the more misguided current policies appear. One of our greatest hopes is [bringing] to widespread attention the urgent need for new thinking on the part of those in the world of policymaking. Given the role played by racial wealth dif-

ferences in reproducing inequality anew, we are more convinced than ever that well-intended current policies fail not simply because they are inadequately funded and prematurely curtailed but, perhaps more important, because they are exclusively focused on income. In some key respects our analysis of racial wealth differences forms an agenda for the future.

Why Racial Wealth Inequality Persists

The contemporary effects of race are vividly depicted in the racial pattern of wealth accumulation that our analysis has exposed. We have compiled a careful, factual account of how contemporary discrimination along demographic, social, and economic lines results in unequal wealth reservoirs for whites and blacks. Our examination has proven insightful in two respects. It shows that unequal background and social conditions result in unequal resources. Whether it be a matter of education, occupation, family status, or other characteristics positively correlated with income and wealth, blacks are most likely to come out on the short end of the stick. This is no surprise.

Our examination of contemporary conditions also found, more surprisingly, that equally positioned whites and blacks have highly unequal amounts of wealth. Matching whites and blacks on key individual factors correlated with asset acquisition, demonstrated the gnawing persistence of large magnitudes of wealth difference. Because it allows us to look at several factors at once, regression analysis was then called into play. Even when whites and blacks were matched on all the identifiably important factors, we could still not account for about three-quarters of the racial wealth difference. If white and black households shared all the wealth-associated characteristics we examined, blacks would still confront a $43,000 net worth handicap!

We argue, furthermore, that the racialization of the welfare state and institutional discrimination are fundamental reasons for the persistent wealth disparities we observed. Government policies that have paved the way for whites to amass wealth have simultaneously discriminated against blacks in their quest for economic security. From the era of slavery on through the failure of the freedman to gain land and the Jim Crow laws that restricted black entrepreneurs, opportunity structures for asset accumulation rewarded whites and penalized blacks. FHA policies then thwarted black attempts to get in on the ground floor of home ownership, and segregation limited their ability to take advantage of the massive equity build-up that whites have benefited from in the housing market. As we have also seen, the formal rules of government programs like Social Security and AFDC have had discriminatory impacts on black Americans. And finally, the U.S. tax code has systematically privileged whites and those with assets over and against asset-poor black Americans.

These policies are not the result of the workings of the free market or the demands of modern industrial society; they are, rather, a function of the political power of elites. The powerful protect and extend their interests by way of discriminatory laws and social policies, while minorities unite to contest them. Black political mobilization has removed barriers to black economic security, but the process is uneven. As blacks take one step forward, new and more intransigent legislative or judicial decisions push them back two steps. Nowhere has this trend been more evident than in the quest for housing. While the Supreme Court barred state courts from enforcing restrictive covenants, they did not prevent property owners from adhering to these covenants voluntarily, thereby denying black homeowners any legal recourse against racist whites. Similarly, while the Fair Housing Act banned discrimination by race in the housing market, it provided compensation only for "individual victims of discrimination," a fact that blunts the act's effectiveness as an antidiscrimination tool. These pyrrhic victories have in no way put an end to residential segregation, and black fortunes continue to stagnate.[5]

Our empirical investigation of housing and mortgage markets demonstrates the way in which racialized state policies interact with other forms of institutional discrimination to prevent blacks from accumulating wealth in the form of residential equity. At each stage of the process blacks are thwarted. It is harder for blacks to get approved for a mortgage—and thus to buy a home—than for whites, even when applicants are equally qualified. More insidious still, African Americans who do get mortgages pay higher interest rates than whites. Finally, given the persistence of residential segregation, houses located in black communities do not rise in value nearly as much as those in white neighborhoods. The average racial difference in home equity amounts to over $20,000 among those who currently hold mortgages.

The inheritance of accumulated disadvantages over generations has, in many ways, shortchanged African Americans of the rather dramatic mobility gains they have achieved. While blacks have made stunning educational strides, entered middle-class occupations at an impressive rate, and moved into political positions in numbers unheard of a quarter of a century ago, they have been unable to surmount the historical obstacles that inhibit their accumulation of wealth. Still today, they bear the brunt of the sedimentation of racial inequality.

The Substantive Implications of Our Findings

What are the implications of our findings? First, our research underscores the need to include in any analysis of economic well-being not only income but private wealth. In American society, a stable economic foundation must include a command over assets as well as an adequate income flow. Nowhere is this observation better illustrated than by the case of black Americans. Too much of the current celebration of black success is related to the emergence of a professional and middle-class black population that has access to a steady income. Even the most visibly successful numbers of the black community—movie and TV stars, athletes, and other performers—are on salary. But, income streams do not necessarily translate into wealth pools. Furthermore, when one is black, one's current status is not easily passed on to the next generation. The presence of assets can pave the way for an extension and consolidation of status for a family over several generations.

This is not, however, an analysis that emphasizes large levels of wealth. The wealth that can make a difference in the lives of families and children need not be in the million-dollar or six-figure range. Nonetheless, it is increasingly clear that a significant amount of assets will be needed in order to provide the requisites for success in our increasingly technologically minded society. Technological change and the new organization of jobs have challenged our traditional conception of how to prepare for a career and what to expect from it. Education in the future will be lifelong, as technological jobs change at a rapid pace. Assets will play an important role in allowing people to take advantage of training and retraining opportunities. In the economy of the twenty-first century children will require a solid educational foundation, and

parents will most likely need to develop new skills on a regular basis. The presence or absence of assets will have much to say about the mobility patterns of the future.

Second, our investigation of wealth has revealed deeper, historically rooted economic cleavages between the races than were previously believed to exist. The interaction of race and class in the wealth accumulation process is clear. Historical practices racist in their essence have produced class hierarchies that, on the contemporary scene, reproduce wealth inequality. As important, contemporary racial disadvantages deprive those in the black middle class from building on their wealth assets at the same pace as similarly situated white Americans. The shadow of race falls most darkly, however, on the black underclass, whose members find themselves at the bottom of the economic hierarchy. Their inability to accumulate assets is thus grounded primarily in their low-class backgrounds. The wealth deficit of the black middle class, by contrast, is affected more by the racial character of certain policies deriving in part from the fears and anxieties that whites harbor regarding lower-class blacks than by the actual class background of middle-class blacks. As Raymond Franklin suggests in his *Shadows of Race and Class:*

> The overcrowding of blacks in the lower class . . . casts a shadow on middle-class members of the black population that have credentials but are excluded and discriminated against on racial grounds.

Given the mutually reinforcing and historically accumulated race and class barriers that blacks encounter in attempting to achieve a measure of economic security, we argue that a focus on job opportunity is not sufficient to the task of eradicating racial disadvantage in America. Equal opportunity, even in the best of circumstances, does not lead to equality. This is a double-edged statement. First, we believe that equal opportunity policies and programs, when given a chance, do succeed in lowering some of the more blatant barriers to black advancement. But given the historically sedimented nature of racial wealth disparities, a focus on equal opportunity will only yield partial results. Blacks will make some gains, but so will whites, with initial inequalities persisting at another level. As blacks get better jobs and higher incomes, whites also advance. Thus, as Edwin Dorn points out in *Rules and Racial Equality:*

> To say that current inequality is the result of discrimination against blacks is to state only half the problem. The other half—is discrimination in favor of whites. It follows that merely eliminating discrimination is insufficient. The very direction of bias must be reversed, at least temporarily. If we wish to eliminate substantive inequality we waste effort when we debate whether some form of special treatment for the disadvantaged group is necessary. What we must debate is how it can be accomplished.

How do we link the opportunity structure to policies that promote asset formation and begin to close the wealth gap? In our view we must take a three-pronged approach. First, we must directly address the historically generated as well as current institutional disadvantages that limit the ability of blacks, as a group, to accumulate wealth resources. Second, we must resolutely promote asset acquisition among those at the bottom of the social structure who have been locked out of the wealth accumulation process, be they black or white. Third, we must take aim at the massive concentration of wealth that is held by the richest Americans. Without redistributing America's wealth, we will not succeed at creating a more just society. Even as we advance this agenda, policies that safeguard equal opportunity must be defended. In short, we must make racial justice a national priority.

Toward a More Equal Equality

Our recommendations are designed to move the discourse on race in America beyond "equality of opportunity" and toward the more controversial notion of "equality of achievement." The traditional debate in this area is between fair shakes and fair shares. The thrust of our examination allows us to break into this debate with a different perspective. We have demonstrated that equal achievement does not return equal wealth rewards—indeed, our results have shown vast inequality. Of course, this may simply be another way of saying that wealth is not only a function of achievement; rather, it can rise or fall in accordance with racially differential state policies and in the presence or absence of an intergenerational bequest.

We are not left, however, with a pessimistic, nothing-can-be-done message. Instead, the evidence we have presented clearly suggests the need for new approaches to the goal of equality. We have many ideas related to this topic and several concrete suggestions for change that can lead to increased wealth for black and poor families. On the individual and family level, proposals are already on the table concerning the development of asset-based policies for welfare, housing, education, business, and retirement. On the institutional level we have a whole series of recommendations on how to tighten up the enforcement of existing laws that supposedly prohibit racial discrimination on the part of banks and saving and loans. After presenting those recommendations we shall broach the sensitive, yet wholly defensible strategy of racial reparations. Then we will reflect on the leadership role that the black community must play in closing the wealth gap.

Promoting Asset Foundation for Individuals and Families[6]

In the United States, as in advanced welfare states the world over, social policies for the poor primarily focus on ways to maintain an essential supply of consumptive services like housing, food, heat, clothing, health care, and education. Welfare is premised on the notion that families from time to time or on a more permanent basis lack adequate income sources to furnish these goods and services, in which case the government steps in to fill the breach. Questions about how well, adequately, or even if government should perform this function fuel public policy concerns.

In *Assets and the Poor* Michael Sherraden challenges conventional wisdom regarding the efficacy of welfare measures designed to reduce poverty and offers a fresh and imaginative approach to a persistent problem. He argues that the welfare state in its current and historical guise has not fundamentally reduced poverty or class or racial divisions and that it has not stimulated economic growth. He identifies a focus on income as the theoretically unquestioned and deficient basis of an imperfect welfare policy. Welfare as we know it provides income maintenance for the poor; welfare policies for the non-poor, by contrast, emphasize tax and fiscal measures that facilitate the acquisition of wealth. Sherraden suggests that "asset accumulation and investment, rather than income and consumption, are the keys to leaving poverty," concluding that "welfare policy should promote asset accumulation—stakeholding—by the poor."[7] Welfare for the poor should be designed to provide the same capacity for asset accumulation that tax expenditures now offer the nonpoor. By giving individuals a "stake" in their society,

Sherraden believes that this type of policy will channel them along more stable and productive paths. Sherraden's asset-based welfare policy combines maintenance of the consumptive goods and services with economic development. While the claim that stakeholding would provide a wide range of psychological and behavioral benefits is probably overly optimistic, and too deterministic in our view, Sherraden is clearly onto something.

Our analysis of assets and Sherraden's bold challenge to existing welfare policies spring from similar concerns, namely, that a family's life chances and opportunities emanate from the resources, or lack thereof, at its command. Sherraden's critique of the income-maintaining and consumptive welfare state leads him to advocate asset-based welfare policies. Our work points to how the welfare state has developed along racial lines, grafting new layers of accumulated disadvantage onto inequalities inherited from the past. It corroborates Sherraden's findings on the subject of asset accumulation among members of the middle class and the exclusion of the poor from the asset game. But it also shows how a racialized welfare state, both historically and in modern times, has either systematically excluded African Americans or made it very difficult for them to accumulate assets. Furthermore, our examination of assets reveals that assets, or the lack thereof, is a paramount issue: one in three American families possesses no assets whatsoever, and only 45 percent possess enough to live above the poverty line for three months in times of no income.

A number of policy implications follow from our focus on resources, economic well-being, and the racialization of the welfare state. Existing programs such as AFDC must be reexamined. In particular, the amount of assets an AFDC recipient may hold and remain eligible for benefits must be increased. Poor people should not be forced to draw down existing assets in order to meet draconian eligibility requirements any more than seniors should have to pass an asset-means test to receive social security. Personal and business assets should be separated so that recipients can engage in self-employment activities. The work-search requirement should be redefined to make it possible for the part-time self-employed individual to qualify for benefits as well.

Mechanisms to Promote Asset Formation

Welfare does not help young people prepare for the future, nor is it designed to. At best it allows young people and their families to survive at the subsistence level. Sherraden's *Assets and the Poor* is the most fruitful work in this area, and since its analysis of asset poverty and its effects is similar to ours, we believe that some of Sherraden's key policy ideas merit serious consideration. Sherraden suggests that maintenance income and services should be supplemented by broad-based asset accounts. In many situations, where accumulation is desirable and feasible, asset-based policies are preferable to those based on income. Some of the most promising areas include education, home ownership, start-up capital for businesses, self-employment, and funds for retirement. Each year a given sum of money could be invested in an asset account restricted to a specific purpose, and the accounts would have monetary limits. These accounts could be established at different points over the life course. Standard initial deposits could be matched by federal grants on the basis of a sliding scale for poor individuals who also meet asset criteria.

Education and Youth Asset Accounts

The global economy stresses job flexibility, training in multiple areas, and technologi-cal and computer literacy. Education, training, continual skill enhancement, lifelong learning, and the ability to shift fields are the new hallmarks of modern employability. Formal schooling is a minimum requirement, with college education best preparing people for opportunities in the global marketplace. Blacks and the poor, we fear, are falling further behind in their quest to secure credentials necessary to qualify for the kinds of jobs and careers that lead to economic well-being. Since 1976 black college enrollment and completion rates have declined sharply, threatening to wipe out the gains of the civil rights era. The growing racial discrepancy in higher education is caused by blacks' increasing inability to afford the ever-soaring cost of college tuition, government's flagging fiscal commitment to higher education, and poverty rates that are more than twice as high for blacks as for whites. Without assets to fall back on, the average black family simply has no way to finance college.

Instead of asking students to assume heavy debts to foot the bill for college, Sherraden suggests establishing universal nontaxable educational asset accounts. Deposits would be linked to benchmark events: say, a one-thousand-dollar deposit at birth, a five-hundred-dollar deposit for completing each grade, and twenty-five hundred dollars for high school graduation. Student fundraising projects and businesses could underwrite other contributions to these accounts. A year of military or civilian national service might earn a five-thousand-dollar deposit. While anyone could establish such an account, the government would subsidize these accounts for poor people on a sliding scale. For example, a poor child's family might deposit $250 with the government matching that amount. With the interest that they earn and their nontaxed status, educational asset accounts would be a wise investment in any child's future. The primary purpose of the accounts would be to provide resources upon high school graduation, after which funds would be available only for postsecondary education and training of the recipient's choosing. Such accounts would not only allow children from poor families to obtain a college education or other, equivalent training but also go a considerable distance toward closing the-quality-of-education gap. After a certain age individuals could transfer the funds in their account to their children or grandchildren. Or they could cash out their account withdrawing only their original deposits and earnings, not the government's matched share, less a 10 percent penalty. They would pay income taxes on the full amount withdrawn.

Housing Asset Accounts

We have continually stressed how essential homeownership is to the American Dream: owning a home is not only a source of residential security, stability, and pride, but also a potential means of increasing one's wealth. We suggest here several ways to close the racial home owning and housing-appreciation gap. Homeownership rates declined significantly during the late 1980s and early 1990s. First-time buyers are edged out of the market when the rise in housing prices exceeds the rise in wages for most Americans. Down payments and closing costs are the most critical barriers to homeownership, and thus housing asset accounts should focus on accumulating funds for these purposes. We have taken Michael Sherraden's suggestions as a model of how a housing asset program might work.

Beginning at age eighteen individuals who are first-time homebuyers or who have not owned a home for longer than three years may open a housing asset account. These nontaxable interest-earning accounts would be open to everyone on the sole basis of housing status. There would be an annual deposit limit of two thousand dollars per individual account, with an overall family limit not exceeding 20 or 25 percent of the price of a region's median home. Individuals who fall below specified income and asset levels would be eligible for matching grants from the federal government, for up to 90 percent of their annual deposit. The government would thus match or supplement the deposits made by poor individuals, on a sliding scale, but would not match the deposits of those not in need. Funds accumulated in housing asset accounts would be available only for down payments and other costs associated with buying or owning a home. After ten years unused funds could be transferred to educational or housing accounts for children or grandchildren or else cashed in on the same terms we outlined in the case of educational asset accounts.

Self-Employment and Business Accounts

Self-employment is one of the most celebrated paths to economic self-sufficiency in American society. Even though self-employment is enshrouded in Horatio Alger–like cultural myths, and even though most small ventures fail within the first five years, the rewards of success, financial independence, and autonomy have been many. Severe economic restrictions have historically prevented many African Americans from establishing successful businesses. These include segregation, legal prohibition, acts of violence, discrimination, and general access only to so-called black markets. We want to emphasize the very risky nature and often low returns of self-employment. Yet, given a progressively less-favorable labor market, high unemployment rates in the black community, and the often entrepreneurial essence of the American Dream, we believe that for certain individuals self-employment represents an important path to economic well-being. Successful black businesses also contribute to community development. The absence of start-up capital is, among the asset-poor, one of the most formidable barriers to self-employment. Credit is needed to seed most businesses and the banking record on this score leaves much to be desired. Self-employment accounts would provide another option.

We have already discussed proposals to restructure AFDC criteria and payments that would remove some of the disincentives to self-employment or the establishment of small business by poor people. Michael Sherraden's work proposes a more expansive program to encourage self-employment and business ventures. Self-employment asset trusts would be open to anyone eighteen or older to be used only for start-up money for business ventures. Annual deposits of $500 would be permitted, with an overall limit of $15,000. These accounts would be nontaxable as long as they were used for starting a new business or for family expenses associated with running the business, such as child care. Income-poor individuals who meet certain asset criteria would be eligible for 50 percent matching contributions from the federal government. These funds could be used without penalty, according to Sherraden, "only after a business plan is developed and approved by a voluntary local review board made up of businesspeople."[8] Individuals could pool their accounts with others in order to launch a joint venture. Funds not used as seed capital after ten years could be disbursed, the fundholder receiving only his or her original contributions and earnings, less a 10 percent penalty; income tax would be paid on the full amount.

Removing Institutional Barriers to Asset Formation

The Homeowner Deduction

Our explication of the racialization of the welfare state draws attention to the ways in which a host of government programs and policies have historically assisted the white middle class to acquire, secure, and expand assets. One case in point is the nation's largest annual housing subsidy, a subsidy that goes not to the poor or to stimulate low-cost housing but to often well-heeled homeowners in the form of $54 billion in tax deductions for mortgage interest and property taxes. While the homeowner deduction primarily benefits the affluent, fewer than one in five low-income Americans receive federal housing assistance. Those with the highest incomes and the most expensive homes get the lion's share of federal subsidies. The Congressional Joint Taxation Committee analysis of taxation data shows that more than one-third (38.5 percent) of the $54 billion government subsidy goes to the 5 percent of taxpayers who have incomes above $100,000.[9]

The homeowner deduction has come under increasing scrutiny, however, and several reforms have been suggested. Recognizing that through the tax code the state has assisted home ownership and asset formation among certain groups, notably the middle class, that this aid has increasingly benefited the affluent, and that whites are far more likely than blacks to profit from current tax policy, many have suggested that a corrective is clearly in order. The goal of helping families purchase homes could be maintained and expanded in order to apply to more moderate income families, and thereby proportionately more minorities. Simultaneously, tax reform could place benefits to affluent Americans within a progressive context. Current home mortgage interest and property tax deductions should be scrapped and replaced by a simple homeowner tax credit available to all taxpayers, not just those who itemize deductions. The credit would apply to one's primary residence and could be capped at a specific amount or tied progressively to income, thus limiting subsidies for the wealthy while preserving them for the middle class and extending the goal of homeownership to moderate-income Americans. A homeowner tax credit could make the difference between renting and owning for millions of working families now shut out of the American Dream. Such a policy would enable more blacks to buy homes than can do so under the current tax law and thereby represent a step in the direction of greater racial equity.

Capital Gains Tax

All sources of earnings are not treated equally under America's tax laws. Most notably, net proceeds from financial assets are privileged over paycheck earnings. In 1993 the top tax bracket for wages, tips, and salaries was fixed at 39.6 percent on earnings over $250,000. Capital gains, by contrast—the profits from selling something for an amount more than it cost, whether it be stocks, bonds, homes, property, or works of art—are taxed at the more favorable top rate of 28 percent, a rate that can go down as low as 14 percent in some situations. Barlett and Steele in *America; Who Really Pays the Taxes?* refers to "different dollar bills; different rates.[10] They report that one twenty-fifth of one percent of Americans filing taxes collects one-third of all capital gains incomes. Conversely, 93 percent of all persons filing tax returns have no need to fill out a Schedule D form because they have no capital gains. We doubt if more than a relative handful of blacks are among the small affluent group advantaged by this favored child of free marketers and conservatives.

Reform of the capital gains tax would help simplify the tax forms and end an unfair subsidy designed for the rich. Income from playing the stock market should be treated just like income from work, and capital gains should be taxed at the same rates as earnings. Changes would affect only those

in the highest income brackets, leaving people with modest investment unaffected.

Inheritance Tax

Donald Barlett and James Steele write in *America: Who Really Pays the Taxes?* that one of the most cherished tax privileges of the very rich resides in the ability of that group to pass along its accumulated wealth in stocks, bonds, and other financial instruments to heirs free of capital gains tax. Taxpayers who sell financial assets to fund a child's education, make a down payment on a house, or weather a financial crisis pay a capital gains tax on the increased value of their investment. But under current tax law, stocks, bonds, and other capital assets can be passed along at death and escape all capital gains. "Better still," according to Barlett and Steele, "when you inherit the stock it gets a new 'original' value—the price at which it was selling on the day you received it." Thus, one can sell the stock immediately and pocket the entire proceeds without paying any capital gains tax. In large part, Barlett and Steele go on to say, "this is how the rich stay rich—by passing on from generation to generation assets that have appreciated greatly in value but on which they never pay capital gains taxes."[11]

The wealth of many families has thus escaped taxes since the establishment of the income tax in 1924. The time has come to seriously challenge this capital gains tax exemption. Just how large is the inheritance tax break for the very rich? *America: Who Really Pays the Taxes?* cites a Treasury Department and Office of Management and Budget calculation that the very rich escaped paying $24 billion in 1991 alone because of this exemption. While Americans do not begrudge their fellow citizens the opportunity of becoming rich, they might not be so willing to accept the extent to which the very wealthy and powerful rig the rules to hold onto their wealth at everybody else's expense.

Antidiscrimination Laws

In the 1960s and 1970s Congress passed important legislation and strengthened the banking regulatory structure so that all groups would have access to credit and communities would not be written off by unscrupulous financial institutions. The Reagan administration weakened this regulatory system, and some banks read its change as an opportunity to revert to past practices and ignore or prey upon minority and low-income neighborhoods. We estimate that discriminatory mortgage practices, higher interest-rate charges, and biased housing inflation cost the black community approximately $83 billion. Both the private and public sectors have a lot of work ahead of them if they are to redress this history of institutional discrimination.

Bankers do not sit down with a map and census tract data and draw red lines around low-income and minority neighborhoods. As we have seen, however, some have policies and practices that effectively do the same thing. Banks that set minimum loan amounts effectively exclude whole neighborhoods from the conventional mortgage market. Lenders must discontinue this practice.[12]

We have also seen that the tiering of interest rates for mortgages has a disparate impact on minority and female applicants, and on minority, integrated, and ethnic neighborhoods. Because of tiered interest rates, minorities and low-income home buyers pay more to borrow less. This policy, too, must be changed.

Every good business designs a marketing strategy to capture the market it wants to serve. Lenders need to review the media they use to reach minority and low-income consumers as well as the messages they

send. A bank becomes known, or fails to do so, not only by its advertising efforts but also by the services it offers to a community. A bank must be conveniently located and accessible to the consumers it wants to attract. The services it offers should be tailored to meet the needs and interests of its customers. To respond to their needs, some banks offer investment seminars free of charge to their high-income customers. They should also be offering free seminars on how to buy a home or start a small business to their low-income depositors. These ideas are not new, and they have had a public hearing. Their implementation is long overdue.

Closing the Gap is the name of a brochure put together in 1993 by the Federal Reserve Bank of Boston for lending institutions. It starts, "Fair lending is good business. Access to credit, free from considerations of race or national origin, is essential to the economic health of both lenders and borrowers." The brochure proposes a series of practices and standards designed to constitute "good banking" and to close the mortgage loan gap. Its recommendations include reviewing minimum loan amounts because they negatively affect low-income applicants and giving special consideration to applicants who have demonstrated an ability to cover high housing expenses (relative to income) in the past. Lenders should allow down payment and closing costs to be paid by gifts, grants, and loans from relatives or agencies. Credit history criteria should be reviewed and made more sensitive to the needs of those with no credit history, problem histories, or low incomes. *Closing the Gap* also points out that subjective aspects of property and neighborhood appraisal using terms like "desirable area," "pride of ownership," "homogeneous neighborhood," and "remaining economic life" allow room for racial bias and bias against urban areas. It advocates the elimination of such concepts from the process of property appraisal. The brochure further advises lenders to distinguish between length of employment and employment stability in reviewing an applicant's work history, pointing out that many low-income people work in sectors of the economy where job changes are frequent. Lenders should focus on an applicant's ability to maintain or increase income levels, not on the number of jobs he or she has held.

"Good-Neighbor Mortgages" and Banking Restitution

"Good-Neighbor Mortgages" are new mortgage products featuring little or no down payment and minimal or no closing costs, often below-market interest rates, expanded debt-to-income ratios, no costly private mortgage insurance, and an open option to refinance at 100 percent of a home's appraised value. These mortgages can be used for purchase and rehabilitation, so homes in distressed communities can be revitalized. Credit for small business, on comparable terms, can also be obtained as part of a comprehensive community revitalization effort. The key to the success of Good-Neighbor programs is not only their generous terms but commitment on the part of the bank. Such programs should not be viewed as a penalty paid by a bank to redress past discriminatory practices; instead, they must be seen as establishing a new partnership designed to meet the needs of a once prejudicially underserviced community.

In 1994 Fleet Financial Group, a corporation that has drawn a lot of fire because of its biased community-lending policies, announced a stunning settlement with one of its most severe critics. The bank had been in trouble with community activists in Boston and Atlanta and with the Federal Reserve Bank because of its practice of redlining large sections of central cities and then quietly backing small second-mortgage companies that loaned money at pawnbroker rates. It set aside an $8 billion loan pool aimed at inner-city, low-income, and small-business borrowers. One Fleet insider ominously told the *Wall Street Journal* that "Fleet did nothing that wasn't common practice in the consumer-finance business. But we took the heat."[13]

An alternative and supplement to private-sector banks could come in the form of community development banks. These federally sponsored banks would give creative people in inner-city areas the tools with which to rebuild strong supportive communities and help poor people to develop assets for the future. They would hark back to the strong financial institutions that once helped American communities save their own money, invest, borrow, and grow. Modeled after Chicago's famous South Shorebank, enabling legislation sponsored by Senator Bill Bradley of New Jersey envisions developing a range of community-based financial institutions, all of which will respond to the capital and savings needs in their service areas.

The Racial Reparations Movement

A growing social movement within the black community for racial reparations attempts to address the historical origins of what House Resolution 40 in 1993 called the "lingering negative effects of the institution of slavery and discrimination" in the United States. With a host of community-based organizations agitating and educating with respect to the issue, this movement has taken off since the passage of the legislation approving reparations for Japanese Americans interned during World War II. For the torment and humiliation suffered at that time each family was awarded $20,000.

Since 1989 black Representative John Conyers of Michigan has introduced into the House Judiciary Committee each year a bill to set up a commission to study whether "any form of compensation to the descendants of African slaves is warranted." While the bill has yet to reach the floor of Congress, it has opened up this issue to public debate and discussion.

Given the historical nature of wealth, monetary reparations are, in our view, an appropriate way of addressing the issue of racial inequity. The fruits of their labor and the ability to accumulate wealth was denied African Americans by law and social custom during two hundred fifty years of slavery. This initial inequality has been aggravated during each new generation, as the artificial head start accorded to practically all whites has been reinforced by racialized state policy and economic disadvantages to which only blacks have been subject. We can trace the sedimented material inequality that now confronts us directly to this opprobrious past. Reparations would represent both a practical and a moral approach to the issue of racial injustice. As the philosopher Bernard Boxill argues:

> One of the reasons for which blacks claim the right to compensation for slavery is that since the property rights of slaves to "keep what they produce" were violated by the system of slavery to the general advantage of the white population, and, since the slaves would presumably have exercised their libertarian-right to bequeath their property to their descendants, their descendants, the present black population, have rights to that part of the wealth of the present white population derived from violating black property rights during slavery . . . [Whites] also wronged [the slaves] by depriving them of their inheritance—of what

Kunta Kinte would have provided them with, and passed on to them, had *he* been compensated—a stable home, education, income, and traditions.

While reparations based on similar logic have occurred in both the United States and other societies, it may be a testament to the persistence of antiblack racial attitudes in America that the prospects for such compensation are minimal. The objections are many: Are present-day whites to blame for the past? Who among blacks should receive such reparations? Would reparations of this sort really improve the economic situation of blacks today? We are not sure that racial reparations are the choice—political or economic—that America should make at this historical juncture. They may inflame more racial antagonism than they extinguish. But the reparations debate does open up the issue of how the past affects the present; it can focus attention on the historical structuring of racial inequality and, in particular, wealth. What we fear most is the prospect of reparations becoming a settlement, a payoff for silence, the terms of which go something like this: "Okay. You have been wronged. My family didn't do it, but some amends are in order. Let's pay it. But in return, we will hear no more about racial inequality and racism. Everything is now colorblind and fair. The social programs that were supposed to help you because you were disadvantaged are now over. No more!" Instead, racial reparations should be the first step in a collective journey to racial equality.

Any set of policy recommendations that requires new revenues and implies a redistribution of benefits toward the disadvantaged faces formidable political and ideological obstacles. In an era of stagnant incomes for the working and middle classes, race has become even more of an ideological hot button in the arena of national politics. The conservative cast of American political discourse in the 1990s is in large measure rooted in white opposition to the liberal policies of the sixties. According to Thomas and Mary Edsall's *Chain Reaction,* a pernicious ideology that joins opposition to opportunities for blacks and a distrust of government has "functioned to force the attention of the public on the costs of federal policies and programs."[14]

We believe that the program we have outlined could be put into place within the fiscal confines of present budget realities. For example, the tax structure reforms we discussed would help defray the expenses associated with asset development accounts and other increased social welfare benefits. But when it comes to race and social policy, ideology tends to reign. Despite the cost effectiveness of our program it is likely that it would be opposed mostly on ideological grounds. As Martin Carnoy in *Faded Dreams* resignedly notes:

> The negative intertwining of race with "tax and spend," "welfare state" economic policy remains a potentially highly successful conservative political card . . . There is absolutely no doubt that the card will be played and played repeatedly.[15]

To move beyond the present impasse we must embark on a national conversation that realistically interprets our present dilemmas as a legacy of the past that if not addressed will forever distort the American Dream.

The African American Community's Role in Wealth Creation

Our interviews with African Americans revealed the importance of barriers to wealth creation that our policy proposals are designed to address. However, many interviewees also placed significant responsibil-

ity for the lack of assets in the black community on blacks themselves. Implicit in these criticisms was a feeling that blacks can do much to help themselves in creating greater wealth and using it more productively. The desire to increase wealth in the black community is seen in many ways as the civil rights theme of the twenty-first century. "The black community will not be free until we control the wealth in it," said one respondent. Three ideas continued to come up in our interviews regarding what the black community could do to increase wealth: entrepreneurship and business development, better education and information on the subject of financial planning, and networking to develop capital and economic opportunity.

The lack of business development was one of the key factors cited by one respondent as a barrier to black wealth accumulation: "I do believe that we really need to get into our own businesses." A lack of capital was cited as the most important barrier to business creation. As Mary Ellen, who left the corporate world to join her father's family business, noted, problems "in the banking system" stopped many people that she knew from being able to make their dream of self-employment a reality. Many of those who did start businesses had the age-old problem of being "undercapitalized." As Mary Ellen summarized, "You know you just can't succeed in a business without having capital. And we just don't have it."

While the lack of material resources was seen as important, our respondents were just as concerned about the dearth of social capital, particularly information and ways to communicate it, in the black community. Many worry that the kind of education that prepares one to take advantage of investment and business opportunities is not as available in the black community as it is elsewhere. Some of the information blacks are less apt to have access to is formal in nature: "People are not taught about entrepreneurship . . . in the universities . . . to go into business for themselves. . . . In school we learn how to add and subtract and divide and all that, but you really aren't taught . . . about finances." Much crucial information is transmitted informally, however. Interviewees often spoke of a separate "dialogue that goes on in the white community," generating investment information that is inaccessible to those in the black community. African Americans as a group are seen as "isolated" from basic knowledge pertaining to investment instruments, business opportunities, and financial markets. On a subtler level one respondent suggested that the real rules of the game are unknown to African Americans. As a consequence

> the playing field is not level—we do everything as we're supposed to do— we go through all the right channels. We don't know the back doors.

Our interviewees looked to the self-organization and self-activity of the black community for solutions to these problems. While supporting policies to force mainstream financial institutions to be more responsive to blacks, these respondents were quite pessimistic that any other aid would come from the wider society. They looked instead to actions that could be taken within, for, and by the black community. Pointing out significant increases in assets and financial knowledge in certain sectors of the black community (e.g., successful African American entrepreneurs), they argued that these resources had to be socially shared in order to help the less fortunate lay claim to a wealth stake. Over and over again respondents spoke of the way in which the well-off had to give back to the community. Our most affluent black respondent, the owner of several businesses, spoke of how she is

> attempting to help as many young people as I can now. I have a program now

that is doing exactly that with a female organization. Business Opportunities Unlimited [a pseudonym] is helping young minorities open businesses. And I mentor young people that want to do that. The funding is there. The grants are there. It's knowing how to go in there and fill them out. Instead of training our children as my parents trained us, you know, work for the County, City, or State. Those are good stable jobs [laughter]. You gotta tell them, look, you're gonna take some risks. You know, you're young. What do you have to lose? You got the education. If you fall down, you pick yourself up again.

Another person in business talked about creating "rotating credit associations" that would help generate capital for new businesses and other financial opportunities.

> If banks are not going to give us money, we're going to get an investment pool together to help each other . . . Basically what they [immigrants] do is everybody puts in ten thousand dollars into a pot, and let's say there are ten people in the pool. So there's a hundred thousand dollars. We give this hundred thousand to Johnny. He starts a business and gets it growing. Then it goes to the next person and they can start a business. Or they can borrow against this pool, so they have their own internal banking system.

Blacks need to "network" with each other in order to socialize people in the culture of business and finances, as well as to circulate the crucial information one needs to be successful. As an example Camille spoke of how her success is owed in part to the advice and business counsel that she has received from a successful black real estate entrepreneur. He informs her of "easy-ins without huge sums of money. Someone's losing something. Dell will say, Camille, I have five thousand dollars. Do you have five thousand dollars? Let's pick this up. You know, that kind of thing."

Despite the concerns of our respondents, more and more blacks are taking advantage of financial self-employment opportunities—both formal and informal. Entrepreneurship programs are erupting everywhere. Schools and community-based organizations are teaching youth about the essentials of self-employment. In Los Angeles, the African American community's dominant response to the civil disorders that rocked the city in 1992 has been to "promote entrepreneurship among community residents as a primary job creation and wealth accumulation strategy."[16] Traditional black self-help organizations like the First African Methodist Episcopal Church (FAME) have launched entrepreneurial development programs that help fund and provide counseling and business services to budding businesspeople. Likewise, a recent spate of self-help books have begun to celebrate the power of networking for blacks.[17] One of the most successful black magazines is *Black Enterprise,* which, under the leadership of its editor, Earl Graves, has served as a clearinghouse for information about black business and investment opportunities. National organizations like the NAACP and the Nation of Islam have also joined this effort.

We applaud these initiatives. They will help energize African Americans to seek ownership and control of their community. They will in time increase by some as yet unknown factor the wealth of some members of that community. The limits of unilateral community-based self-help measures also need to be recognized, however. Two interrelated concerns are paramount. First, the emphasis on owning and controlling business in the black community re-creates many of the negative features of the segregated market that characterized the economic detour described earlier. The purchase of small retail and service establishments within the black community places black entrepreneurs in unnecessarily restrictive economic markets. The key to growth is to break out of segregated markets and into the wider economic mainstream. Second, a primary focus on traditional retail and service outlets may very well leave blacks out of the most dynamic parts of the economy. Each period of economic growth in America has been ushered in by new industrial and technological breakthroughs. The winners have increasingly been those who have been able to master these technologies and to market them rapidly and economically. In order to succeed African American business in the twenty-first century needs to set its sights on the next great frontier of economic growth: information processing. An emphasis on retail and service will divert the energies of able black businesspeople away from the most fertile area of economic growth.

Any viable strategy for enhancing black wealth must include both the development of local community-based entrepreneurs and their penetration into the newest and most profitable sectors of the wider economy. Neither goal can be accomplished without the kinds of redistributive and wealth accumulation policies that we have outlined.

Conclusion

Racial inequality is still the unsolved American dilemma. The nation's character has been forged on the contradiction of the promise of equality and its systematic denial. For most of our nation's history we have allowed racial inequality to fester. But there are other choices. These choices represent a commitment to equality and to closing the gap as much as possible, and in so doing redefine the values, preferences, interests, and ideals that define us. Fundamental change must be addressed before we can begin to affirmatively answer Rodney King's poignant plea: "Can we all just get along?"

To address these fundamental issues, to rejuvenate America's commitment to racial justice, we must first acknowledge the real nature of racial inequality in this country. We must turn away from explanations of black disadvantage that focus exclusively on the supposed moral failings of the black community and attempt to create the kinds of structural supports that will allow blacks to live full and socially productive lives. The effort will require an avowedly egalitarian antiracist stance that transcends our racist past and brings blacks from the margin to the mainstream.

In her novel *Beloved* Toni Morrison tells the tale of forty-seven men on a chain gang in Alfred, Georgia. They all want to be free, but because they are chained together, no individual escape is possible. If "one lost, all lost," Morrison says, "the chain that held them would save all or none." The men learn to work together, to converse, because they have to. When the opportunity presents itself, they converse quietly with one another and slip out of prison together. Like the convicts in Morrison's story, we need to realize a future undivided by race because we have to. No individual solution is possible. The chain that holds us all will save all or none.

NOTES

1. Quote on no prejudice in the Yankee, see Rock 1858.

2. The quote is from Cose 1993, 28.
3. The quote is from Feagin and Sikes 1994, 15.
4. The quote is from Didion's 1967 essay "7000 Romaine, Los Angeles."
5. On restrictive covenants see Zarembka 1990, 101–102. On the Fair Housing Act see ibid., 106.
6. Our emphasis on asset acquisition is not meant to discount the need for income and employment policy. On the contrary, we believe that it is imperative to institute policies that encourage full employment at wages consistent with a decent standard of living. In fact, many of our proposals assume that people have some kind of income. However, to dwell on the intricacies of this area would divert our attention from the unique implications of our argument. There are several important proposals already under discussion that merit serious consideration (see Carnoy 1994).
7. The quote is from Sherraden 1991, 294.
8. The quote is from Sherraden 1991, 256–57.
9. See Dreier and Atlas 1994.
10. The quote is from Barlett and Steele 1994, 29.
11. The quotes are from Barlett and Steele 1994, 335.
12. Our focus is on the role of financial institutions in providing mortgages. However, an equally important aspect of the low wealth accumulation of black households has been persistent residential segregation. Massey and Denton (1993, 186–216) have provided a blueprint for policy in this area that we need not rehash here. Their proposals, if implemented, would be an important complement to the ones we suggest regarding lending discrimination.
13. The quote is from Ryan and Wilke 1994, A5.
14. The quote is from Edsall and Edsall 1991, 11.
15. The quote is from Carnoy 1994, 225–26.
16. On efforts to "promote entrepreneurship among [black] community residents" in Los Angeles see Jackson, Johnson, and Farrell 1994.
17. On self-help books see Anderson 1994 and Fraser 1994.

REFERENCES

ANDERSON, CLAUD. 1994. *Black Labor, White Wealth: The Search for Power and Economic Justice.* Edgewood, MD: Duncan & Duncan.

BARLETT, DONALD L., and JAMES B. STEELE. 1994. *America: Who Really Pays the Taxes?* New York: Touchstone.

BOXILL, BERNARD. 1984. *Blacks and Social Justice.* Totowa, NJ: Rowman & Allanheld.

CARNOY, MARTIN. 1994. *Faded Dreams: The Politics and Economics of Race in America.* Cambridge: Cambridge University Press.

COSE, ELLIS. 1993. *The Rage of a Privileged Class.* New York: HarperCollins.

DORN, EDWIN. 1979. *Rules and Racial Equality.* New Haven, CT: Yale University Press.

DREIER, PETER, and JOHN ATLAS. 1994. "Tax Break for the Rich: Reforming the Mansion Subsidy." *The Nation* 258(17), pp. 592–95.

EDSALL, THOMAS BYRNE, and MARY EDSALL. 1991. *Chain Reaction.* New York: Norton.

FEAGIN, JOE R., and MELVIN P. SIKES. 1994. *Living with Racism: The Black Middle-Class Experience.* Boston: Beacon Press.

FRANKLIN, RAYMOND S. 1991. *Shadows of Race and Class.* Minneapolis: University of Minnesota Press.

FRASER, GEORGE C. 1994. *Success Runs in Our Race: The Complete Guide to Networking in the African-American Community.* New York: Morrow.

JACKSON, MARIA-ROSARIO, JAMES H. JOHNSON, JR., and WALTER C. FARRELL, JR. 1994. "After the Smoke Has Cleared: An Analysis of Selected Responses to the Los Angeles Civil Unrest of 1992." *Contention* 3(3) (Spring):3–22.

MASSEY, DOUGLAS S., and NANCY A. DENTON. 1993. *American Apartheid: Segregation and the Making of the Underclass.* Cambridge, MA: Harvard University Press.

ROCK, JOHN S. 1858. "Address to Boston Antislavery Society, March 5." *Antislavery Collection.* Rare Book Division, Boston Public Library.

RYAN, SUZANNE ALEXANDER, and JOHN R. WILKE. 1994. "Banking on Publicity, Mr. Marks Got Fleet to Lend Billions." *Wall Street Journal,* February 11, pp. A1, A5.

SHERRADEN, MICHAEL. 1991. *Assets and the Poor: A New American Welfare Policy.* New York: Sharpe.

WOOLF, VIRGINIA. 1929. *A Room of One's Own.* New York: Harcourt.

ZAREMBKA, ARLENE. 1989. *The Urban Housing Crisis.* New York: Greenwood Press.

45

TEN SIMPLE THINGS YOU CAN DO TO IMPROVE RACE RELATIONS

Charles A. Gallagher

Questions to Consider

Photocopy and pass along the reading "Ten Simple Things You Can Do to Improve Race Relations" to family, friends, teachers, and spiritual leaders. Please contact me with any additions you might have for my list. I can be reached at cgallagher@gsu.edu.

The study of race and ethnic relations in the United States can be a rather depressing and disempowering undertaking. Ongoing institutional racism in education, employment, housing, lending, and law enforcement; continued wealth and income disparities between racial groups; and the persistence of racial prejudice and discrimination in most spheres of social life may leave one with the impression that nothing can be done to improve race relations. The modern civil rights movement was three hundred years in the making, and while movement toward racial equality has been substantial, racism and racial inequality still infect our nation and poison civic life. Such prejudice and inequality persist in part because changing the institutional barriers that allocate occupational and educational opportunity is a slow and difficult task. Upward mobility for different racial and ethnic groups is typically measured in generations rather than decades or years.

One is tempted to throw one's hands in the air and yell, "There is nothing I can do!!!" But there is. You have the power to influence your family, friends, and peers by discussing the topics raised in this class. At the individual, interpersonal, and community level you can engage in activities to promote equal opportunity while building bridges between people from different racial backgrounds. Understanding the root causes of ethnic and racial inequality in the United States and examining in this class the facts, theories, evidence, and examples that pertain to such inequality will allow you to explain to others why racism and racial and ethnic inequality remain so stubbornly part of our culture. You now have the sociological tools to calmly, intelligently, and rationally engage in conversations with other adults about racism in America and what individuals, institutions, and the government *could* and *should* do to fashion a society where equal opportunity exists for all groups. Following are ten simple things you can do as you go about your day to raise your own and other people's consciousness about race relations and racial justice in America.

1. Talk to Your Family

Respectfully engage your friends and family in what you learned in this class. If you have family members that are racist or use stereotypes, ask them politely and nonjudgmentally why they harbor such animosity towards a whole group of people. Did they have a bad experience with someone from that group? Ask them if they have ever been the target of animosity or hatred because of their race, ethnic background, religion, or nationality. How did such an encounter make them feel? Were their parents or grandparents ever subject to such prejudice or discrimination? Why? Ask them if they think their prejudice or racism violates the American creed of equal treatment and opportunity for all regardless of group membership. If they believe in the American creed, how do they reconcile their racism or prejudice? Ask them if they believe in the golden rule that states "do unto others as you would have them do unto you."

2. Avoid Sterotypical Language

Be mindful that certain words or phrases typically mean the person is about to use stereotypes to describe a group. When you hear someone say "All black people do this . . . ," or "Latinos always like to . . . ," or "I never met a white person who could . . . ," a red flag should go up that stereotypes are in use. Politely ask if they are referring to an individual encounter with someone from another group or if they mean to speak for thirty-eight million blacks, forty million Latinos, ten million Asians, two hundred million whites or 2.5 million American Indians in this country. Ask the person if they really believe *all people* in that group actually share the same behaviors and attitudes. Is it possible that certain behaviors or

beliefs only appear in one racial or ethnic group and not another?

3. Racism Isn't Funny

Don't tolerate racist jokes. If you hear a joke being told that disparages someone because of his or her group membership, stop the person from telling the joke. If they insist on finishing, ask them why they don't like black people or white people or Asians or Catholics or whomever they are ridiculing in their attempt at humor. You have many retorts to such simplistic and retrograde behavior. You might say; "Hey, I don't think putting down other people is funny," or "I have gay friends, I don't want to hear you trashing them," or "My brother-in-law is black (or white or Asian or Catholic or Jewish, etc.) and I think he's great." Be willing to "take the stand" about what is appropriate public discourse. If you do not speak up and let the person know that such remarks are socially inappropriate, you are condoning their beliefs and behavior. Inaction is a form of action.

4. Be Introspective

Think back to reading 11, in which Robert Merton discussed the unprejudiced nondiscriminator. This person was not prejudiced, nor did she discriminate against anyone in any way. How can we live our lives so social or peer pressure do not push us toward racist, prejudiced, or bigoted beliefs or actions? If you find yourself being a prejudiced nondiscriminator (fair-weather illiberal) or an unprejudiced discriminator (fair-weather liberal), ask yourself how you got there. Be introspective and honest about why you acted or behaved a certain way toward someone from a different ethnic or racial group. What scared you about the situation that made you deviate from your core beliefs or values? Did you overreact? Were you defensive? If you could relive that experience, what would you do differently? Is it possible you were socialized or taught to react the way you did? What role did peer pressure play in your actions? The most important thing you can do is to think critically about the root causes of your anxieties, attitudes, and actions. Be introspective and be willing to change how you think about groups different from your own.

5. Be a Good Citizen—Vote

Vote in every election. Take the time to find out candidates' positions on policies that have implications for race relations. Do not support a politician whose campaign rhetoric is racially divisive or attempts to win votes by manipulating racial (or class) fears. Knowing what the issues are (and are not) requires reading a newspaper everyday.

6. TV, Rap, Rock: Appeals to the Lowest Common Denominator

When you watch television, realize that you are under constant bombardment by the most simplistic and stereotypical images of ethnic and racial groups. Ask yourself which racial and ethnic groups are on prime time and how those groups are represented. Are whites, blacks, Asians, Latinos, or American Indians in a wide range of roles, or are some groups more likely to be maids, gangbangers, exotics, or lawyers? Why? What you watch on television is not just entertainment. The mass media provide the images, symbols, and narratives that shape the way we understand society. The media cement existing stereotypes and construct expectations about where groups should be placed in America's racial hierarchy. The television industry uses stereotypes to make racial inequality look like the "normal" order of society. How are you are being manipulated by the programs you watch?

7. Learn Your Family's History

Take time to talk to the elderly people in your life. Ask your parents, aunts and uncles, neighbors, and spiritual leaders in your community about how race relations have changed since they were children. Ask your parents, grandparents, and other relatives about the *Brown* decision, the Civil Rights movement, Martin Luther King, Jr.'s assassination, the American Indian Movement (AIM), La Raza, and the L.A. riots. How do they explain these events? What were they doing as these monumental events unfolded? Your elders are resources. Talk to them about the past and the present.

8. Teach through Example

Be a positive role model to all the younger people in your life. If you are of college age or older, you probably have a number of children and young adults who look up to you for moral guidance. If they hear you use foul language, then in all likelihood they will too. If you speak and act in a racist manner, they will learn your racism. Explain to those who view you as a role model what it means to live in a multiracial, multi-ethnic society. Explain to them what the American creed and the "golden rule" mean.

9. Step Out of Your Comfort Zone

Involve yourself in activities that place you in an environment where you will be exposed to people from different racial and ethnic backgrounds. Think about attending museums, music events, ethnic festivals, restaurants, supermarkets, shops, or any other public place where you will share space with people different from yourself.

10. Know Thyself

Did you grow up in a community that was racially homogenous? Was your house of worship pretty much composed of people who looked like you? Are your best friends all of the same race? Was your elementary school segregated? How about your high school? What did it look like in terms of racial composition? Do you think being raised in a segregated environment shapes racial attitudes? How? How do you think being the only racial minority in most social settings might shape a person's views of race relations? Have your ideas about race changed since you were fifteen years old? How and why? Reflect on these questions and write your answers as an essay. Circulate what you write to your friends and family. Set up a meeting to have a discussion on what you wrote and what their views on race relations in the United States are.

"If You're Not Part of the Solution, You're Part of the Problem."